The Complete Chinese Cookbook

The Complete Chinese Cookbook

Over 500 Authentic Recipes from China

Jacki Passmore and Daniel P. Reid
Photographs in China taken by Nik Wheeler

WH SMITH
EXCLUSIVE
· BOOKS ·

Editorial and production co-ordinator: Allan Amsel

Editors: Betsy Gurlatz and Lesley Hargreaves

Recipes edited and tested by Jacki Passmore

Photography in China: Nik Wheeler

Food preparation for photography: Annie Wong

Food photography: John Leung Studio

Art Direction: Hon Bing-wah

Acknowledgements: The reproduction from 'Going Down the River at the Ch'ing Ming Festival', p.10-11, is by kind permission of Nigel Cameron.
Settings for photography kindly loaned by Amazing Grace Elephant Company; Nic Nac; and Cynthia Ambrose.

Editor's Note:
The recently introduced Pin Yin system of romanisation of Chinese characters is shown, where appropriate, in parentheses after the Wade Giles romanisation, which is still more commonly used in reference to regions and food.

A Kevin Weldon Production
Published by Weldon Publishing
a division of Kevin Weldon & Associates
Pty Limited
372 Eastern Valley Way, Willoughby,
NSW 2068, Australia
First published by Lansdowne Press 1982
Reprinted 1983, 1984
Reprinted by Weldon Publishing 1990
This U.K. edition produced exclusively for
W.H. Smith Ltd
Greenbridge Road
Swindon
SN3 3LD

© Copyright design: Kevin Weldon & Associates Pty Limited 1982

ISBN 1 86302 077 2

Contents

MONGOLIA

SINKIANG
(XINJIANG)

KANSU
(GANSU)

TSING HAI
(QINGHAI)

TIBET
(XIZANG)

SZECHUAN
(SICHUAN)

Chengtu ●
(Chengdu)

YUNNAN

Introduction

HEILUNGKIANG
(HEILONGJIANG)

INNER MONGOLIA
(NEI MONGGOL)

LIAONING

KIRIN
(JILIN)

Hwang Ho (Yellow River)

Peking
(Beijing)

Tientsin
(Tianjin)

SHANSI
(SHANXI)

HOPEH
(HEBEI)

SHANTUNG
(SHANDONG)

YELLOW SEA

NINGSIA
(NINGXIA)

NORTHERN REGION

KIANGSU
(JIANGSU)

SHENSI
(SHAANXI)

HONAN
(HENAN)

Nanking
(Nanjing)

Soochow
(Suzhou)

Shanghai

ANHWEI
(ANHUI)

Hangchow
(Hongzhou)

HUPEH
(HUBEI)

Ningpo
(Ningbo)

EAST CHINA SEA

Yangtze River   Wuhan

Chungking
(Chongqing)

KIANGSI
(JIANGXI)

CHEKIANG
(ZHEJIANG)

WESTERN REGION

EASTERN REGION

HUNAN

Foochow
(Fuzhou)

KWEICHOW
(GUIZHOU)

FUKIEN
(FUJIAN)

Taipei
(Taibei)

KWANGSI
(GUANGXI)

TAIWAN

KWANGTUNG
(GUANGDONG)

SOUTHERN REGION

Canton
(Guangzhou)

Nanning

Si Kiang (Xijiang) (West River)

Hong Kong

SOUTH CHINA SEA

HAINAN

'Have you eaten yet?'

This common Chinese greeting is roughly equivalent to the English, 'Hi, how are you?' It carries the implicit cultural assumption that if you've eaten recently, you must be feeling fine. And if you haven't, whoever asked you is obliged to offer you something to eat before proceeding with the business at hand. First things first.

Food is the most central concern of the Chinese people in their day-to-day

lives, and both its quality and quantity are the most direct measures by which the Chinese judge their standard. So important is food in Chinese culture that even the spirits of the dead must be regularly offered the tastiest delica-

The pictures here and opposite correspond to those introducing Chapters III, IV, V and VI (Northern, Eastern, Western and Southern cuisine). The Chinese character in the box on each chapter introduction represents North, East, West and South.

cies which the living family can afford. After the spirits have devoured the 'essence' of the tempting offerings set before them on the alter, the family consumes the 'gross' remains. In this world or the next, the Chinese eat better and more often than any other people in the world.

The reason the Chinese eat so well lies in the past: food has periodically been very scarce in China, and the people know the gnawing pangs of hunger all too well. To the Chinese, it is no mere cliché that food is 'the staff of life.' Over the centuries they have hewn and fashioned that staff from a wider range of materials than anyone else. In times of famine, the discovery of a new food, or a new way to preserve food, or a better way to utilise food was literally a matter of life and death. The Chinese have been so inventive in their cuisine simply because they had to be in order to survive.

The infinite variety of Chinese cuisine is based upon this broad foundation of necessity. But the sophisticated refinement and high aesthetic standards associated with Chinese culinary culture go far beyond mere necessity. Chinese cuisine is a direct reflection of Chinese civilization as a whole. To the style-conscious Chinese, *how* one does something is at least as important as *what* one does. Historically, the average Chinese could not afford to be fussy about *what* was available or how *much* he could purchase, but he could be particular about

how it was prepared, *how* it tasted, and *how* it looked on the table. The key to Chinese cooking is not in the materials, but in the methods.

Chinese cuisine evolved from the distinctive regional styles of the far-flung provinces. In ancient times, when means of preserving and transporting foods were still insufficient for regional exchange of ingredients, regional styles of cooking were relatively restricted to their places of origin. Each unique style was based on the prevailing geographic conditions, climate, available ingredients, and local customs.

Chinese regional cooking styles began to coalesce and form a national cuisine during the Sung Dynasty (960 1279 A.D.), when methods of growing, preserving, storing and distributing food progressed rapidly. Many foreign culinary influences were also absorbed, for so important was good food to the Chinese that they readily dropped their usual air of cultural superiority in order to absorb and adapt foods and cooking methods from barbarians. During the Sung era, Chinese writers also began to expound the principles and practices of Chinese cuisine, which established it as one of the most respected and well-defined arts of traditional China. Food and eating became an extension of Chinese philosophy and was intimately connected with other aspects of Chinese civilization such as art and medicine.

Like *Yin* and *Yang*, complementary opposing forces, food and culture were distinct yet inseparable elements of life in ancient China.

This book is written to serve the general reader as a comprehensive guide to Chinese culinary culture. Food, cooking and culture are inseparable in Chinese cuisine; ingredients, methods of preparation, and eating customs are all equally important. Chapter I describes Chinese culinary history — the various historical, geographical, and social factors which have contributed to Chinese cuisine — and delineates the most important principles which underlie and govern it. Chapter II introduces the basic utensils, condiments, and methods commonly used and offers some advice regarding the best ways to successfully put this information into practice.

The next four chapters are brief introductions to Chinese regional cuisine. Debate continues to rage among Chinese gourmets and scholars over the classification of regional styles of Chinese food. Many factors are involved, so these divisions are somewhat arbitrary. Nine major regional styles are officially recognised by chefs in China today: Peking (Beijing), Anhui, Shantung (Shandong), Chekiang (Zhejiang), Fukien (Fujian), Kiangsu (Jiangsu), Hunan, Szechuan (Sichuan), and Canton (Guangdong).

Our regional classification of Chinese cuisine is based on commonly shared historical, geographical, and cultural factors; and have divided China into four broad culinary regions. They are Northern Style, Eastern/ Coastal Style, Western/Central Style, and Southern Style. These divisions are based upon real geographic, historical, and hence culinary boundaries. The nine styles recognised in contemporary China fall into our culinary categories as follows: Northern — Peking (Beijing), Shantung (Shandong), Anhui; Eastern/Coastal — Chekiang (Zhejiang), Fukien (Fujian), Kiangsu (Jiangsu); Western/Central — Hunan, Szechuan (Sichuan); Southern — Canton (Guangdong). Each regional chapter describes the food of the area in terms of prevailing geographic conditions, climate, major ingredients and condiments used, favoured cooking methods, and overall cultural style.

Chapter VII, 'A Word on Wines and Spirits', offers an overview of the roles of liquor and drinking in Chinese culinary culture. The various types of Chinese and Western beverages suitable for consumption with Chinese food are discussed, as well as various Chinese drinking customs.

The recipe section, which follows the text, presents 518 Chinese recipes garnered from original sources. To collect recipes and other vital information, we interviewed renowned chefs in Peking (Beijing), Nanking (Nanjing), Soochow (Suzhou), Hangchow (Hang-

zhou), Chengtu (Chengdu), Canton (Guangzhou), Taipei (Taibei), and Hong Kong. Other recipes were translated from such authoritative sources as the *Peking Hotel Cookbook*, a collection of 1,000 recipes written by top-ranked chefs from all over China. Original recipes, or new versions of old favourites, were also developed by the author, editors, and other cooks of gourmet Chinese food. The recipes are presented in the clear-cut format used

in most Chinese-language cookbooks.

The text will have served its purpose if it kindles in the reader a strong enough interest in Chinese cuisine to try a few of the recipes. From there, the food will take over and speak for itself.

The reproduction on the following page, part of an early 17th century handscroll more than eight metres (27 feet) long, shows country folk going to town for special food and other things for the Ch'ing Ming festival.

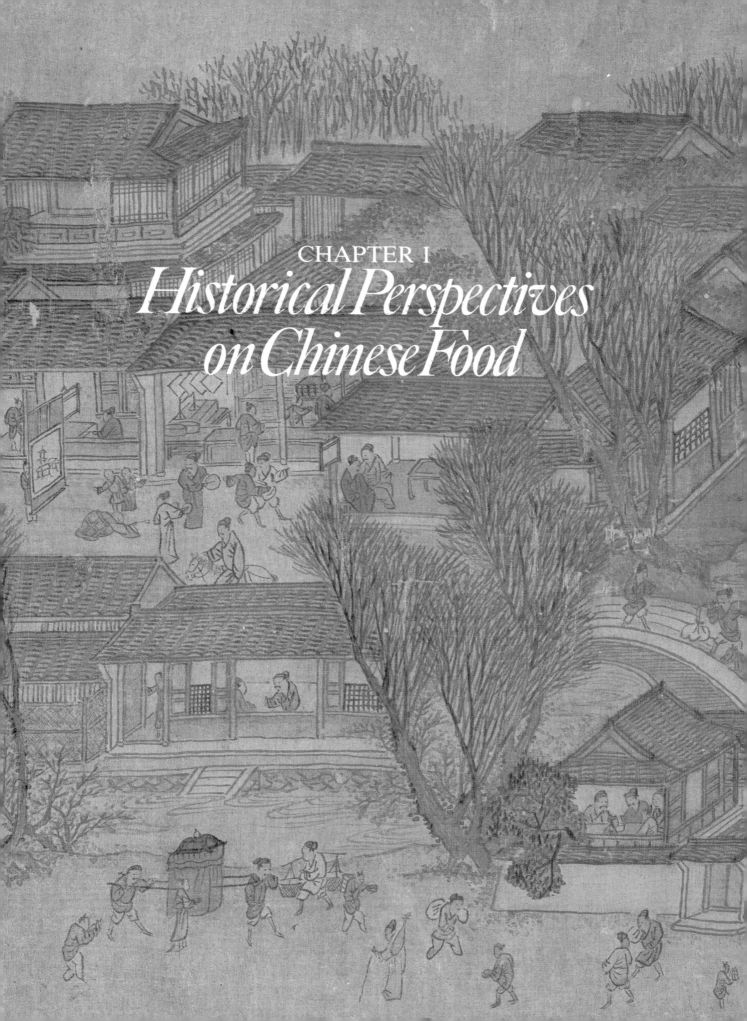

CHAPTER I
Historical Perspectives on Chinese Food

Food has never been regarded as a mere necessity in China. Since earliest antiquity, Chinese eating habits have been intimately bound to and reflective of other aspects of Chinese culture. What and how the Chinese eat is highly symbolic of their general view of the world and their overall philosophy of life. Chinese food and eating habits have always been, and still remain, dominated by two major considerations: the pleasure principle, reflected in China's sophisticated gourmet traditions, and — equally important — the health principle, based on traditional Chinese medical theories. Nowhere else in the world has food been so exhaustively researched and categorised and the culinary arts so highly developed as in China. And no people in the world maintain such a high degree of culinary consciousness as the Chinese. They are, quite literally, a nation of gourmets.

The principles and practices which define Chinese cuisine as we know it today evolved gradually over a period of 5,000 years. To fully understand why the Chinese cook and eat as they do, and to appreciate the subtle sophistications of their cuisine, it is necessary first to review China's long culinary history, tracing those developments and conditions which have had a decisive influence on its evolution. Our historical review begins with the earliest recorded dynasty, the Shang, and takes us down through 3,500 years to the present-day People's Republic of China.

Early Antiquity: Shang (1766-1123 B.C.) — Han (206 B.C.-220 A.D.)

The earliest archeological artifacts discovered in China are ornate bronze eating and drinking vessels dating from the Shang dynasty, which flourished 3,500 years ago in the region of the Yellow River. This fact alone proves that eating and drinking had already become formalised activities in Chinese culture as early as the 18th century B.C. Eating and drinking were ritualised affairs governed by a codified etiquette. Indeed, it seems that the ruling house of Shang did little else but eat and drink, for gluttony and drunkenness are usually cited as major reasons for its downfall. In 1123 B.C., the house of Shang fell in an orgy of wretched excess and was replaced by the virtuous house of Chou, thus beginning China's longest historical era (1122-249 B.C.) and its classical age of philosophy.

It was during the Chou era that food first became associated with native Chinese philosophy, cosmic theories, and medical practices. The theories of Yin and Yang and the Five Elements, China's oldest cosmological concepts, were broadly applied to food and drink. For example, drinking was viewed as a Yang activity (hot, stimulating, depleting) and eating as Yin (cool, calming, nourishing). Grain was associated with the element Earth and therefore always served in earthenware clay vessels. Meat, on the other hand, was identified with the element Fire and served in bronze vessels because the elements Fire and Metal were considered to be harmonious rather than antagonistic. These early associations with cosmic theory were very basic compared to the colourful elaborations which would appear in succeeding eras, but they laid the philosophical foundations of Chinese food culture for all time to come. The many rules and regulations stipulated by the Chou classics to govern ritualistic and ceremonial uses of food, for example, continued to be followed in the imperial palaces and private homes of China right through to the 20th century.

Two words sum up all the intricate principles and cosmic premises of Chinese cuisine: balance and harmony. The cosmic significance of food lay in the effects it had on the body after ingestion: if the food is balanced and harmoniously blended, then the body and spirit will naturally become so too after eating it. The *Tso Chuan*, a classical text about Chou life and philosophy dating from 521 B.C., contains an excellent statement of this concept:

> Harmony may be illustrated by soup. You have water and fire, vinegar, pickle, salt, and plums with which to cook fish and meat. It is made to boil by firewood, and then the cook mixes the ingredients, harmoniously equalising the several flavours, so as to supply whatever is deficient and carry off whatever is in excess. Then the master eats it, and his mind is made equable.

Another important aspect of traditional China's eating habits which dates back to the Chou and earlier times is the sensual appreciation of food. Kaotze, a 5th century B.C. philosopher, summed it all up with his famous equation, 'Food plus sex equals nature.' Throughout China's long epicurean history, gourmet food has been intimately associated with gourmet sex, and both pleasures were commonly enjoyed together in the restaurants, winehouses, and tea-shops of ancient China.

The oldest, most fundamental principle of Chinese cuisine was formulated so long ago that it had already marked

Chinese eating habits long before the dawn of recorded history. The *tsai/fan* principle is the universally recognised mark of Chinese cuisine the world over. *Tsai* means any cooked dish of meat, fish, vegetables, and so forth, and *fan* literally means 'cooked rice,' although it refers to any staple grain food such as rice, noodles, buns, cakes, bread-rolls, gruel, etc. The idea is quite simple: no meal is complete unless it is built around a basic staple food derived from rice, wheat, millet, barley, sorghum, or other grain. So ingrained is this habit that the average Chinese misses the rice or noodles at a meal much more than any *tsai*. Regardless of how costly and tasty the *tsai*, without *fan* it does not qualify as a Chinese meal. In fact, many Chinese refuse to eat at all without some form of *fan* before them. The central role of grains in the Chinese diet and the indispensability of grain-derived staples at any Chinese meal is the oldest definitive aspect of Chinese cuisine and stems from pre-historic times.

By the time Confucious appeared on the scene towards the end of the Chou era, cultured Chinese gentlemen were already quite fussy about what and how they ate. This passage from the *Analects* describes the eating habits of the Sage himself and is quite revealing:

He liked to have his rice cleaned, and to have his meat cut quite small. He did not eat rice which had been injured by heat or damp and turned sour, nor fish or flesh which was gone. He did not eat what was discoloured, or what was of a bad flavour, nor anything which was ill-cooked, or was not in season. He did not eat meat which was not cut properly, nor what was served without its proper sauce...He did not partake of wine and dried meat bought in the market. He was never without ginger when he ate. He did not eat much.

The importance of fresh foods, foods in season, proper preparation, appropriate condiments, correct proportions, Chinese medicine (ginger), home cooking, and general avoidance of excess are all reflected in this 2,300-year-old passage.

After a prolonged period of disunity and political turmoil, the Han dynasty finally established itself in the wake of the Chou and the short-lived Chin. The Han dynasty (220 B.C. — 206 A.D.) was so decisive in the development of Chinese culture and society that ever since ethnic Chinese have called themselves 'People of Han.' From the Han come the first written recipes and detailed descriptions of food, and fully prepared, recognisable *tsai* have been unearthed recently in China in tombs dating from the Han era.

The most common form of Han food was *keng*, a rich, slow-cooked stew consisting of grains, vegetables, fish, and meats. The latter two were generally omitted among poorer families. *Keng* is cooked in large cauldrons over slow fires and usually contains a wide variety of ingredients. Roasted and broiled wild game comprised the other major element in the Han diet.

The expansion of China's borders to the west and south by the Han emperors was an important factor in the development of Chinese cuisine. Formerly restricted to the relatively arid, cold regions of the north, the Chinese empire now embraced the lush, temperate zones of the south and the rugged, mountainous regions to the west. The southern regions, in those days called Ling-nan (present-day Kuangchou, or Guangzhou province), produced litchis, longans, and many other Oriental fruits which we today identify with the Chinese diet, as well as a whole new range of vegetables and wild game. From the western regions came grapes, both for eating and as wine, sesame, walnuts, peas, coriander, and much more. Prior to the Han, the range of ingredients used in the Chinese diet was relatively narrow, but after China's expansion to the west and south, the endless variety and infinite combinations of foods which we today associate with Chinese cuisine began to appear.

So delicious and renowned had Chinese food become by the dawn of the Han era that food was an effective strategic weapon in China's perennial confrontations with barbaric tribes on its borders. Chia I, a Han strategist of the 2nd century B.C., left this advice regarding the best way to deal with the Hsiung-nu, a fierce and troublesome tribe that had plagued civilised China for centuries:

When the Hsiung-nu have developed a craving for our cooked rice, keng *stew, roasted meats, and wine, this will have become their fatal weakness.*

He suggested to the emperor that a string of Chinese restaurants be established along the frontiers to entice the fierce barbarians to eat and drink with rather than fight the Chinese. Chinese food and wine have always ranked high among the items demanded as tribute from China by victorious barbaric tribes. This and a similar strategy involving the betrothal of beautiful Chinese princesses to powerful tribal chiefs have been remarkably successful in taming the ferocious barbarians who have troubled China throughout its history.

The two most important culinary innovations of the Han era were the creation of a fermented bean paste condiment and the development of various wheat-based foods. Fermented bean paste rapidly became the primary condiment in the kitchens and on the tables of rich and poor alike, and today it still plays a vital role in Chinese cooking. Even more significant was the appearance of various wheat-derived foods, such as noodles, breads, buns, baked cakes, fried pancakes, dumplings, and others. This development made a whole new range of nutritious yet inexpensive foods available to the common people of China. Rice was still considered a southern luxury product in those days, and the only other choice of grain was millet or sorghum, which are not nearly as versatile or nourishing as wheat. The writer Shu Hsi (ca. 300 A.D.) makes this significant observation about the origins of wheat foods in China:

The various kinds of noodles and cakes were mainly the invention of the common people, while some of the cooking methods came from foreign lands.

Both the technique of grinding wheat to flour for cooking and the art of baking breads came to China from its western frontiers, perhaps originating in Persia. But the infinite variety of dishes based on these techniques which appeared in China after their introduction grew directly from the culinary inventiveness of the Chinese people.

T'ang (618-906 A.D.)

The T'ang dynasty is known as China's 'Golden Age,' when the 'good life' as the Chinese define it flourished in the fabulous T'ang capital of Chang-an (contemporary Sian). In its heyday, Chang-an was the world's greatest, most civilised city.

Chinese cuisine developed by leaps and bounds during the T'ang, and the variety of form and content in food continued to multiply. Many new foreign foods were borrowed and adopted by the Chinese during this open-minded, adventurous period of Chinese history. However, it would not be until the studious Sung dynasty which followed that the many disparate styles of cooking in use throughout the empire would coalesce into a consciously cultivated national style which could be distinctively defined as 'Chinese.'

The most important culinary development of T'ang lies in the intimate association which grew between

the principles and practices of food and medicine. During the T'ang, Chinese herbal pharmacologists rather than cooks or gourmets determined what foods could and could not be eaten, when, how, in what quantities and which combinations. This close identification of food and medicine became, and still remains, one of the most distinctive features of Chinese cuisine.

Many renowned Chinese herbal physicians flourished during the T'ang era, the most famous of whom were Meng Shen and Sun Ssu-mo. Both lived during the 7th century A.D. and wrote important treatises on food. Sun Ssu-mo, who lived to the ripe old age of 101 and attended to emperors and peasants alike, is well remembered in China for his famous statement about food's role as medicine:

A truly good physician first finds out the cause of the illness, and having found out that, he tries first to cure it by food. Only when food fails does he prescribe medication.

T'ang physicians and pharmacologists had much to say about food, most of which made a lot of sense, and their advice was seriously heeded by the people of China. A few examples will suffice to illustrate the subtlety of their insights. T'ang doctors recommended eating whole rather than milled barley in order to provide balance between the heating (Yang) effects of the meal and the cooling (Yin) effects of the bran. Some 1,200 years later, modern Western nutritional science has come to the same conclusion about the nutritional value of whole grains, though the specific terminology differs. Sun Ssu-mo prescribed a diet rich in seaweed for persons suffering from goiter, an iodine-deficiency disease of the thyroid glands common in land-locked areas far from the sea. This is probably the earliest recorded case of nutritional therapy in the world. He also prescribed a rich porridge of wheat-germ for similar vitamin-deficiency diseases such as scurvy and beri-beri. Though the medical terminology and concepts of ancient China differ from those of the modern West, the conclusions reached have much in common.

The culinary advice offered by the doctors of T'ang is endless. Meng Shen warned sternly against eating leeks in combination with honey or beef. Peo-

ple with sluggish digestion were advised to include plenty of *ta-huang* (rhubarb) in their diets. Onions, leeks, and garlic were all highly recommended in winter for their warming properties but generally avoided on hot summer days.

Interestingly, T'ang doctors were unanimous in their condemnation of the flesh of domestic animals as food for man: pork, beef, and mutton were considered highly deleterious to health, unless consumed very sparingly. The only exception to this rule was dog, the flesh of which was regarded by all pharmacologists as highly beneficial to man's health, dog's liver being especially recommended for weak kidneys. Such advice runs throughout traditional Chinese treatises on both food and medicine.

The T'ang emperors also significantly expanded China's borders, opening up vast new sources of food. The lush southern regions provided new fruits such as limes, oranges, tangerines, and pomelos, in addition to the beloved litchis and longans. History claims that the emperor T'ang Ming-huang's favourite concubine Yang kui-fei ('Precious Concubine') was so enamoured of litchis that she established a special pony express between their source in the far southeast corner of China and the T'ang capital of Chang-an in the northwest in order to provide fresh litchis for her table. Crab-apples were discovered in the south and appealed greatly to the Chinese palate: one common method of eating them was to steep them in honey and cinnabar and take them as a stimulating

elixir after dinner. The cinnabar and its aphrodisiac properties reflect both the influence of Chinese medicine and the connection of food to sex.

The sugar palm (Arenga saccharifera) provided sago meal, jaggery sugar, and a fermented beverage called toddy. This useful plant probably came to China from India as a result of the proliferous cultural exchanges between the two countries during the T'ang era. Wheat and millet remained the primary staple grains of China, although consumption of rice increased steadily as agricultural technology improved. When available, rice was always preferred. Grains were often supplemented in the north with 'Job's Tears' (Coix lacryma-job), a wild grain. Three new fruits were considered by the medical community to have 'magical' curative properties: they were emblic (Phyllanthus emblica), belleric (Terminalia bellerica), and chebullic (Terminalia chebula).

Since the flesh of domestic animals other than dog was considered bad for health, the people of T'ang relied on wild game for their meats. In the north, venison had always been an important part of the Chinese diet, and it continued to be so throughout the T'ang. The 'racoon-dog' or li (Nyctereutes procyonoides) was a popular food all over China, as it still is today, and was listed by Sun Ssu-mo as an excellent tonic food. The marmot or to-pa (Marmota himalayana robusta) was highly prized as food among both Han Chinese and minorities along the western frontier regions. In addition,

the T'ang diet included all sorts of deer, wild boar, bear, otter, bamboo rat, and many other varieties of wild game.

Naturally the natives of Ling-nan (forebears of the Cantonese) led the culinary field in exotica when it came to game. A favourite dish was stewed elephant's trunk, preferably from a black variety with pink ivory. Dog was consumed all over China, but in Ling-nan cats of all kinds comprised a favourite source of meat as well. Another banquet specialty was newborn baby rats stuffed with honey and placed live on the table, where they crawled blindly around waiting to be picked up at will by a diner's roving chopsticks, popped into his mouth, and eaten alive. Yet another artfully contrived dish was produced by dumping live frogs into a boiling urn of soup with bamboo shoots in it: when they hit the scalding water, the poor creatures clutch at the bamboo shoots so that when picked up with chopsticks they 'carry' a bamboo shoot along into the diner's mouth. The variety of culinary exotica in this region of China is endless, and some of the reasons for this will be discussed in the chapter on Southern Style Cuisine.

For fowl, T'ang Chinese used both domestic and wild varieties. Of the latter, chicken (especially black chickens), duck (especially white ducks), and goose were most common. All sorts of songbirds were eaten in China all year round, including sparrows, swallows, thrushes, and, in the south, parrots and parakeets as well. Songbirds were considered especially beneficial to male sexual potency during winter. Wild birds such as pheasant, quail, partridge, dove, and others were hunted with birds of prey such as falcons, peregrines, and goshawks, each of which was used for a specific type of prey.

All sorts of wild and cultivated fish appeared on the T'ang menu. Carp was, and still remains, the great favourite. Many varieties of carp have been cultivated in China for millenia, the most popular being Black Carp. Pomfret, mullet, bass, trout, perch, white-bait, yellowfish, and all sorts of shrimps and shellfish also comprised important parts of the T'ang diet. Strangely, the favourite T'ang method of preparing and eating fish seems to have all but disappeared from China. There are many references in T'ang literature to fresh fish finely sliced into extremely delicate, paper-thin leaves,

variously described as 'snow flakes,' 'silver threads,' 'butterfly wings,' and other poetic metaphors. Chefs skilled in this dainty art of flaking fish were in great demand at the court and in the kitchens of wealthy families.

Contrary to the popular misconception that the Chinese have never used or liked dairy products, milk and milk products formed important and well-liked elements of the Chinese diet during T'ang times. The Chinese and most other Asian peoples stop producing the enzyme required to break down the lactose in raw milk soon after the age of six. After boiling, fermenting, and otherwise processing the raw milk, however, it becomes a perfectly acceptable part of Asian diets, as attested to by its central role in the diet of India. The Chinese probably learned the use of dairy products from the northern nomads with whom they mingled on the frontiers. Though many Chinese writers have claimed that the Chinese deliberately refrained from using dairy products in order not to be identified too closely with milk-consuming barbarians, this theory hardly seems plausible in light of the facts. For example, the famous T'ang poet Pai Chu-yi records in his journal that he preferred Rehmannia (a Chinese herbal medicine) mixed with milk first thing in the morning. Milk was modified in three stages and valued as food accordingly. Lo or kumiss was prepared by heating milk and letting it ferment naturally. Su or kaymak was skimmed from the top of the kumiss and is the equivalent of 'Devonshire' cream. Ti-hu or clarified butter was made by reducing kaymak over heat and is the same as the ghee of India. Clarified butter was highly valued as food: Sun Ssu-mo wrote that it tones the bones and marrow and promotes longevity. Clarified butter also played an important ceremonial role as a food offering in Buddhist religious rituals.

Sweets became more popular than ever during the T'ang and led to the invention of many new dishes. Ever since antiquity honey had been the most common sweetener in China and was highly valued as food, both wild and cultivated varieties being used. Even more precious than honey was the so-called 'thorn honey,' the sweet exudate of a leafless desert plant called Camel Thorn (Alhagi camelorum). During the T'ang, however, the technique of refining sugar from cane was introduced to China from the western regions, and gradually it replaced honey as the primary sweetener. Sugar was a less expensive and far more versatile ingredient than honey and was used in a wide variety of pastries and beverages. More significantly, sugar also became a common seasoning in the kitchen and was used along with salt, soy, sesame, vinegar, and other condiments to balance the flavours of foods while cooking them.

The spices used in T'ang China were drawn mostly from Chinese herbal pharmocopeias. Their purpose was as much to balance the physiological effects of various ingredients in a dish as it was to balance the flavours for the palate. An excessively 'hot' food could be somewhat neutralised by adding some 'cool' spices, and vice versa. Peppers of the fagara family, indigenous to China, had been used since antiquity to spice up dishes, but during the T'ang the more pungent black peppers were introduced from Indonesia and quickly became the favourite type. Salt was used generously, for it too was highly recommended by T'ang physicians. Nutmeg, cinnamon, ginger, and ginseng were other commonly used spices. Perhaps the most popular spice was licorice, which pharmacologists said could counteract any and all toxins which might appear in other ingredients used in a dish.

Pickling and preserving, common food processing methods since antiquity, remained important during the T'ang as well. Vegetables, meats, fish, and fowl of every type were pickled with vinegar, salt, or wine or preserved by wind-drying and smoking. This type of food became especially important during times of scarcity and during the long cold winters in the north.

The relatively new technique of baking, first introduced during the Han, became even more widespread in T'ang times, and many new varieties of baked cakes and breads, both sweet and salty, appeared on the culinary scene. Wheatcakes were baked in the north and ricecakes in the south.

There were important new developments in the realm of beverages as well. Grape wine imported from the western frontiers became so popular at the T'ang court that it was demanded as tribute from subjugated tribes there. The technology of fermenting wine from grapes was gradually absorbed in the north, and grapes were cultivated there as well. Today in the P.R.C., the best grape

wines still come from Shensi (Shaanxi) province, where Chang-an was located, and from Chi-lin in Manchuria. Kumiss retained its popularity as a drink throughout the T'ang and following Sung eras. Most important, that quintessential Chinese beverage, tea, finally became the national drink of China. Formerly it had been available only to the wealthy and privileged, but during the T'ang it became everyman's drink. The *Cha-Ching* or *Classic of Tea*, China's bible of tea lore and etiquette, was written by Lu Yu during the late 8th century A.D.

As for eating and cooking utensils, metal became increasingly important, gradually displacing wood, stone, and clay implements. Precious metals such as gold and silver were used to fashion the chopsticks, wine goblets, and dishes of the imperial court and wealthy families of China: the type and quantity of metal used became an important indicator of one's social status.

T'ang China had taverns, inns, and wine-shops which offered drinks, girls, and entertainment, but there were still no restaurants as such, which specialised mainly in food service. Food in these T'ang establishments was provided by sending servants out to nearby open-air food stalls, which sprouted up like mushrooms in the streets of Chinese cities every evening. Permanent facilities for the preparation, sale, and enjoyment of food, i.e. restaurants as we know them, did not appear until the Sung era.

Sung: Northern (960-1126 A.D.) and Southern (1127-1279 A.D.)

The Sung era was the greatest single period of development in the history of Chinese food culture. The distinctive features which we identify with Chinese cuisine and eating habits today grew directly from the historical and cultural conditions which prevailed during the Sung. The appearance of the restaurant industry, the commercialisation of agriculture and food distribution, the move from cushions on the floor to tables and chairs, the emergence of rice as the primary staple, the codification of culinary principles, and the conscious cultivation of regional style cuisines can all be traced back to the culturally rich and active Sung period.

Three main reasons may be cited for the rapid development of culinary culture and agriculture in Sung China. The first is urbanisation: during the

Sung period there was a large-scale movement of people into the cities, which became great centres of culture and commerce. Concurrently with urbanisation came the rise of sophisticated urban culture and cosmopolitan tastes. The second watershed development was the conquest of the north by the Jurchen Mongols in 1126 A.D., a traumatic event which forced the Sung court to flee south of the Yangtze, where it established a new southern capital at Hangchou (Hangzhou). The transfer of the seat of empire to the south strongly influenced Chinese eating habits. Finally, the introduction of Champa and other high-yield, fast-growing strains of rice made China a primarily rice-eating nation for the first time and permitted a major expansion of the population. The pre-eminence of rice, a southern grain, coupled with the emperor's flight to the south shifted the overall culinary emphasis in China from northern to southern styles.

The shift to rice as the staple foundation of the Chinese diet was highly significant. Rice can support a greater number of people per acre at a lower cost than any other food in the world. It also contains the most concentrated source of nutritionally balanced calories per acre of any food. The introduction of Champa rice south of the Yangtze created for the first time a sufficient surplus of the grain to feed other regions of China as well. Gradually wheat and millet, staple grains of the Chinese diet since earliest antiquity, became less important sources of food energy. This process was completed when the Jurchens conquered the north, China's major wheat and millet producing region. So salient became the role of rice in agriculture and other aspects of the food industry that its price and availability became general barometers for the state of the entire food industry. This remains true today.

Commercialisation of agriculture and food distribution during the Sung stemmed from both increased production and rapid urbanisation. The rise of cities led the way to the emergence of vast, centralised markets where everything edible in the empire was available. Consequently, the variety and supply of food items in the cities increased significantly, permitting ever greater culinary diversification and supporting the burgeoning restaurant industry. These huge open-air urban markets still comprise the primary daily source of food for households and restaurants alike in China, Hong Kong, and Taiwan. They also gave rise to another important agricultural industry: cash crops. With the appearance of city markets where large quantities of food could be sold out in less than a day, nearby farm communities began to cultivate fast-growing, high-profit specialty items, especially vegetables and fresh-water fish. The cash crop industry contributed much to the great leap forward in food variety during the Sung. To support all these new developments, the food distribution system in China also underwent great improvement: the Grand Canal and other inland waterways formed intricate commercial networks which brought food from and supplied food to every part of the empire, not just the capital. Storage depots and wholesalers made distribution more efficient. Rice, tea, and sugar became the most important and heavily traded items in the food distribution networks.

The needs of city dwellers and their urban life-styles gave birth to the restaurant industry in China. Urbanisation produced a broad new range of gourmets with refined culinary tastes and plenty of money to indulge those tastes. Formerly, haute cuisine was enjoyed exclusively by the imperial court and by wealthy, noble families. But in the cities of Sung China entire new classes of gourmets appeared: merchants, bureaucrats, artisans, professionals of all types, and city dwellers in general all required places to eat out and to entertain their friends and associates. Restaurants of all types arose to serve them: multi-storied gourmet palaces, simple and inexpensive specialty restaurants, private catering establishments, floating restaurants on Hangchou's (Hangzhou's) West Lake and other waterways, and wine-houses and tea-shops which prepared food. During this time, the transition from sitting on cushions on the floor to using tables and chairs was completed, an important development in Chinese food service. To top it all off, a class of professional chefs appeared to operate the great commercial kitchens of Sung China. It was finally possible not only to eat out every night but also to choose from a wide variety of food styles and accompanying entertainment whenever doing so.

The restaurant industry in Sung China was intimately bound with the lives of courtesans and prostitutes, for food and sex continued to be enjoyed together as they had for millenia. Girls (or boys) of all types and ages were available to customers who wanted them. Eating also continued to be strongly associated with drinking, and famous wines from all over the empire were stocked by restaurants. The motto in a Sung restaurant seemed to be *chr, he, wan, lle*, 'eat, drink, and be merry,' and — with the sole exception of sexual services — this remains generally true today in the restaurants of modern China. In effect, food, drink, and sex were a package deal in many of the restaurants of old China.

The best restaurants and wine-houses were located in the Northern Sung capital of Kaifeng and later in the Southern Sung capital of Hangchou (Hangzhou). These were places where 'wind and rain, cold and heat do not occur, and day mingles with night.' Guests often stayed ensconced in these pleasure palaces for several days. Paintings and calligraphy by famous poets and painters decorated the walls, and utensils of sterling silver and gold were common. The apex of Sung culinary life occurred in the southern capital of Hanchou, which Marco Polo described as 'the greatest city which may be found in the world, where so many pleasures may be found that one fancies himself in Paradise.' It is a significant point that Marco Polo rarely distinguished among the pleasures of food, drink and sex in his descriptions of China, for all three were part and parcel of the good life in Hangchou (hangzhou). The 'Lou-Wai'Lou' restaurant, one of the original Chinese restaurants in Hangchou located directly on the banks of West Lake, still operates at the same location under the same name in the Peoples' Republic 800 years later.

There was progress in the realm of beverages as well. The art of distilling spirits from grains entered China during the Sung, resulting in the creation of a variety of potent new liquors. Most of these were distilled from sorghum or *kaoliang*. Fermented alcoholic beverages, such as grape wine and kumiss of mare's milk, continued to enjoy great popularity as well.

The links between food and medicine remained just as important during the Sung as they had been previously and were further elaborated. This aspect of Chinese cuisine is well illustrated by the fact that the Chinese written character used for 'prescription' (*fang*) is the same one used for 'recipe,' a semantic usage established by Sung scholars.

The Sung was the most studious, intellectually oriented period of Chinese history. Sung scholars liked to philosophise about everything and food was certainly no exception. Under the direction of Sung scholar-gourmets, the traditional principles germane to Chinese cuisine were discussed, elaborated, and explicitly analysed in writing. The importance of naturalness (*dze-ran*) in food received great emphasis: the primary ingredients in a dish must be absolutely fresh that day, in season, and locally produced to fully meet the requirements of naturalness. The intrinsic natures and pharmodynamics of foods were meticulously analysed based on both medical and philosophical considerations: the con-

clusions reached determined what one should eat, in what quantities and combinations, at what time of year, and which methods of preparation should be used. The cosmological concepts of balance and harmony, the theories of Yin/Yang, 'hot/cold', and the Five Elements were extended to cover increasing varieties of foods and other relevant culinary factors. Wretched excess, a perennial problem among the ruling classes of old China, was viewed as the ultimate infraction of the laws of balance and harmony.

An important yet subtle aspect of Chinese food philosophy, and a theme which has run throughout Chinese literature on food ever since the Sung era, is the cardinal contradiction between rustic simplicity and gourmet extravagance. This dichotomy was created by Sung scholars, who, on the one hand, preached the philosophical and pharmacological superiority of simple foods simply prepared and, on the other, regularly indulged in gourmet extravaganzas featuring the most exotic, complex culinary creations which their cooks could muster. The very scholars who praised the rustic purity of country life did so from the cosmopolitan comfort of the city. These two opposite culinary options have never been compromised in China. And since it is impossible to mix simplicity and extravagance in the same dish, they appear side by side in different dishes on the same table instead. Authentic Shark's Fin Soup, for example, which requires over a dozen chickens just for the broth alone and at least three days for proper preparation, might well appear on the same banquet menu alongside a simple but equally delicious country dish like 'Pock-marked Mama's Bean-curd,' a famous Szechuan (Sichuan) specialty. Since the Chinese have never been able to choose decisively between the rustic, earthy tendencies of their philosophy and the extravagant, highly aesthetic preferences of their senses, they have preserved both. This dichotomy appears over and over again in culinary references of the succeeding Yuan, Ming, and Ch'ing dynasties and constitutes one of the most singular aspects of Chinese cuisine.

To the Sung flight south we owe both the emergence of a Chinese cuisine *per se* and the conscious cultivation of distinctive regional styles. When the imperial court moved south across the Yangtze to Hangchou (Hangzhou), an inevitable blending of typical northern and southern cooking styles resulted in the new capital city. It was this new hybrid which finally bridged the culinary gap between north and south and gave birth to a distinctive national cuisine with universally recognised principles. At the same time, however, this new hybrid awakened a renewed awareness and appreciation of the special regional styles from which it grew. Hard-core connoisseurs of northern style food demanded places where their favourite dishes could be found, as did southern purists. Consequently, a hybrid 'all-China' cuisine developed side by side with thoroughbred regional styles in the southern cities of Sung China. Urbanisation and commercialisation accelerated this process, for thousands of merchants and bureaucrats from all over China constantly travelled among the cities on business and pleasure, and they usually demanded food from their own native provinces wherever they went. To accommodate these influential travellers, regional specialty restaurants sprang up all over the empire.

The irony of Sung culinary literature is that all of it was written by cultured intellectuals with gourmet interests, not by professional chefs and restaurateurs, who remained by and large illiterate in those days. This fact explains the subtlety and sophistication of these writings, as well as their tendency to emphasise the subjective and theoretical while overlooking the technical details of cooking. This situation remained true down through the early decades of the 20th century, when professional chefs began for the first time to leave their own written culinary records.

By the end of the Sung era, China's population had leapt to 150 million people, a development directly attributable to food factors. Increased production, improved rice strains, better use of land, faster and more efficient food distribution, and the rise of great cities, where everything was available in abundance and sophisticated urban culture flourished, all contributed to the boom in population and the flowering of culinary culture during the Sung.

Yuan (1260-1368) and Ming (1368-1644)

The Mongol invasion and occupation of China devastated the sophisticated society and flourishing economy which had developed under the Sung. By the end of the Mongol Yuan dynasty, the population of China had dropped from 150 million back down to 100 million — a loss of 40% in only 100 years!

Genghis Khan's grandson Kublai Khan declared himself the founding emperor of the Yuan in 1260 and built the city of Peking (Beijing) as his capital. Both Chinese and foreign observers alike have recorded that drunkenness, gluttony, and riotous behaviour prevailed at the Yuan court. The Mongols never quite succeeded in absorbing the niceties of Chinese civilisation. They enjoyed Chinese food and women but rejected the cultural context which was so vital for a true appreciation of them. They remained barbarians in Mandarin clothing throughout their occupation of China.

While the Mongol interlopers often enjoyed Chinese food as daily fare, Yuan imperial banquets and other formal occasions clove closely to traditional Mongol eating habits. Their favourite dish was lamb boiled whole in huge cauldrons and brought out whole to the dining room. There a servant hacked the carcasses into big joints and placed one before each diner, who tore into it with the small, sharp daggers carried by all Mongols and ate the meat barehanded. They washed down the mutton with copious quantities of kumiss, the Mongols' favourite drink, the best of which was made from 'the milk of young mares which have not conceived.' Imagine the consternation of refined Chinese court officials as they stood by and witnessed the emperor of China and his imperial entourage carrying on with such barbaric customs and uncivilised behaviour!

The Mongol interlude in China was brief: no barbarian power could hold the Dragon Throne for long unless it fully absorbed Chinese culture and customs and became, in effect, Chinese. After driving the Mongols back to the northern steppes and restoring Chinese rule, the founder of the Ming took strong and effective measures to revive traditional Chinese culture and promote orthodox Chinese life-styles. Traditional culture and cuisine developed rapidly under this policy. The only culinary legacy which might be attributed to the Mongols was an increased appetite for mutton in the north.

Since Chinese orthodoxy was central to Ming society, the ritualistic and ceremonial uses of food, so important in previous eras, were revived and strongly emphasised. In one year alone, the myriad shrines and altars of the Forbidden City, the fabulous home of Ming emperors in Peking (Beijing), required thousands of sheep, pigs, and oxen for slaughter and tens of thousands of chickens, ducks, and geese. Sacrificial animals slaughtered before a shrine were cooked whole in large bronze cauldrons according to the rules and regulations stipulated in the ancient Chou classics. Ritualistic use of food became an important factor in the lives of the common people as well. On the first and fifteenth days of the lunar calendar, special food offerings were made to ancestral spirits at the family altars kept in all Chinese homes. The offerings were as elaborate as the fami-

18

ly could afford. After proper ceremonial observances and a long enough interval for the spirits to descend and glean the 'essence' of the food before the shrine, the living family itself would feast on the gross remains of the offerings. This custom is still very much alive in Hong Kong, Singapore, Taiwan, and other Chinese communities around the world.

The kitchens of the Forbidden City employed a staff of over 5,000 persons to attend to the meals of the emperor, his concubines, and their entourage. To mention just one item, 250 head of sheep per day were required to provide mutton for the imperial tables of the palace. Entire ministries were occupied solely with the various functions of procuring, transporting, storing, allocating, cooking, and serving food within the confines of the Forbidden City. The sheer quantities of food prepared in the kitchens of the Forbidden City alone combined with the Ming demand for orthodox Chinese cuisine gave great impetus to the further development and subtle refinement of Chinese food.

The abundance and variety of foods available in the markets of Peking (Beijing) during the Ming era were even greater than in Chang-an during the T'ang or Hangchou (Hangzhou) under the Southern Sung. By the Ming period, refrigerated transport and storage of food was systematised and in common use, permitting fresh fruits and vegetables, fish, and other perishable delicacies from every corner of the empire to be shipped fresh to the capital all year round. Huge blocks of ice were carved from frozen rivers and lakes during the winter, wrapped in clean straw, and stored in deep mountain caves for use during the warmer seasons. These ice-blocks kept perishables fresh on the long journeys to Peking (Beijing) and were also used for cold storage underground. Strawberries, plums, fresh fish from far-away regions, and many other items formerly unavailable in the far north could now be enjoyed daily in the Forbidden City and were on sale in Peking's (Beijing's) markets.

The theoretical and practical connections between Chinese cuisine and Chinese medicine continued to grow significantly under the Ming, who were interested in anything traditionally Chinese. The identification of food as medicine was one of the most orthodox and ancient aspects of Chinese food. It

has always been a basic tenet of traditional Chinese medicine that 'many diseases can be cured by food alone.' Joseph Needham quotes a Chinese physician of the 11th century:

> Old people are generally averse to taking medicine but are fond of food. It is therefore better to treat their complaint with proper food than with drugs. Nutritional therapy should be resorted to first, and drugs only after proper feeding has failed.

This statement bears remarkable resemblance to that of Sun Ssu-mo, the great T'ang physician quoted earlier.

Two important books dealing with the pharmacology of food appeared during the Ming. The first, *Essential Knowledge for Eating and Drinking*, was presented to the Ming founder in 1368, the year he declared his new dynasty, by the author Chia Ming, who had just celebrated his 100th birthday that year. When the emperor asked him for his secret to health and longevity, Chia Ming simply replied, 'It is essential to be most cautious about what one eats and drinks.' After presenting his book to the throne, Chia Ming returned to his native home in Chekiang (Zhejiang), where he died at the ripe old age of 106.

Chia Ming's book describes hundreds of varieties of food items and their deleterious affects on health when improperly prepared or taken in combination with the wrong items. He lists their intrinsic pharmacological properties and presents other relevant medical information about food. In the foreword to his book, he states his purpose clearly:

> Drink and food are relied upon to nourish life, yet if one does not know that the natures of substances may be opposed to each other and even incompatible with each other, and one consumes them all together indiscriminately, at the least, the five viscera will be thrown out of harmony, and at the most, disastrous consequences will immediately arise. Thus it is that persons nourishing their lives have always avoided doing such damage to life. I have examined all the commentaries and subcommentaries in all the various authorities' herbals and have found that, for each substance discussed, both good and bad properties are noted, so that the reader is left not knowing what to do. I have made a point of selecting those facts relating to opposition and incompatibility in compiling the present work, as a contribution to those who in practicing reverence for life will find it convenient to investigate matters here.

In other words, those interested in living long, healthy lives must acquire a working knowledge of the pharmoadynamics of food. Otherwise, they risk 'doing such damage to life' through indiscriminate eating habits that their vital organs will not function properly and their lives will be considerably shortened.

The other great Ming treatise which discussed food pharmacology was Li Shih-chen's massive tome, *General Outlines and Divisions of Herbology (Pen Tsao Kang Mu)*, which today still remains the bible of Chinese herbalists. Dr. Li spent 27 years of his life researching and compiling this definitive book on Chinese herbal medicine, and much of it deals with the medicinal properties and therapeutic uses of food.

Food culture permeated every aspect of life in Ming society. Appropriate foods were designated for every conceivable occasion, formal or informal. The journals and diaries left by Ming scholars are full of references to food etiquette, cooking, regional specialties, famous recipes, and other food lore. Gourmet interests comprised the great common denominator among the literati of the Ming. Educated gentlemen were expected to be gourmets.

The *Golden Lotus (Ching Ping Mei)*, China's great novel of sensuality, captures in perfect, vivid details the central role of food in Ming social life. Not a single one of the book's 100 long chapters fails to mention and describe food and eating in colourful, elaborate details. Every visitor to the hero's household, regardless of his station in life or the occasion of his visit, is greeted with a dazzling array of delicacies provided by the host's kitchen. If a casual guest drops by unexpectedly to gossip with one of the hero's six wives, the hostess first orders her servants to set up a table and serve tea immediately. Within a few minutes a tray of food is brought out, typically consisting of such tasty treats as Flaked Ice-fish, Pickled Duck's Feet, Sweet Lotus Seeds, Fresh Walnut Meats, Goose in Aspic, Pork Knuckle in Vinegar, and fruits and pastries of all kinds. Wine is heated and served. Only after the guest has drunk a few cups of wine and tasted a few bites of food does the gossip get under way and the plot continue. As an erotic novel, *The Golden Lotus* also elaborates in great detail the link between enjoyment of food and sex, and one rarely appears

19

without the other close behind.

The restaurant industry grew rapidly during the Ming, especially those specialising in regional cuisines. One reason for this was the development and immense popularity of tourism in China at this time. City life was well established, and the number of wealthy merchants, officials, scholars, and writers grew steadily as China prospered. These cultured, wealthy urbanites loved to travel to famous scenic spots throughout the empire. Being cultured and wealthy, they were by definition also gourmets. While always open to experimentation with local cuisines, these wealthy gourmet travellers also demanded the availability of their own native provincial foods wherever they went. Thus, regional specialty restaurants catering to the tourist trade sprang up all over China, not just in the capital and other major cities. And since these travellers also required a place to sleep at night as well as someone to sleep with, the extent of sensual indulgence in the restaurants/inns of Ming China exceeded even that of Hangchou (Hangzhou) 500 years earlier, where the restaurant industry was born. Food, drink, sex, music, and poetry all mixed together in a heady but harmonious blend of refined sensuality

in these places. And while only the wealthy could afford the more extravagant dishes and pleasures, Ming restaurants catered to every taste and budget, and people from all walks of life used them frequently. The Sung gave birth to restaurants in China, but the Ming institutionalised and popularised them.

Ch'ing (1644-1911)

The Ch'ing dynasty was a period of both continuity and change in the patterns of Chinese eating habits. The momentum of 5,000 years of steady culinary development provided the continuity. The changes were brought about by population pressures and by contacts with the West.

During the Ch'ing era, China underwent the greatest population growth in its history, from 150 million in the early 18th to 450 million by the mid-19th century, a leap of 300 percent in less than 150 years. This phenomenal growth was made possible not so much by improvements in native crops or agricultural technology as it was by the introduction of vital new crops from the New World. Maize, sweet potatoes, Irish potatoes, and peanuts came to China during the Ch'ing era and soon became the staple diets of significant portions of the population. These new foods did not much affect eating habits in the agricultural and demographic heartland of China, but they did make life possible in corners of China which were formerly considered uninhabitable. Where rice, wheat, millet, barley, and other common crops could not

grow, New World crops such as maize and sweet potatoes thrived. The sweet potato became especially important as a source of vital nutrients, particularly in the north, during times of food shortages. The humble peanut provided a valuable new source of oil-seed to produce the voluminous quantities of cooking oil required for Chinese cuisine. Tobacco, incidentally, was also introduced to China at this time. The ultimate importance of these new crops cannot be underestimated.

By the time of the Ch'ing, the principles and techniques which defined Chinese cuisine were already fully developed. During the Ch'ing, they spread to every segment of China's population until they were in universal use throughout the empire. China had become, in effect, a nation of gourmet cooks and eaters. Robert Fortune, an Englishman travelling in China during the 1850's, noted in his journal that even 'the poorest classes in China seem to understand the art of preparing their food much better than the same classes at home.' Basically, the only difference in the eating habits of the rich and the poor was the cost and variety of ingredients each could afford to use.

Due to the Maltheusian pressures of a booming population and limited food supplies, wide disparities between the fares of the rich and the poor became a marked aspect of Chinese society for the first time during the Ch'ing. This very disparity, however, made wealthy gourmets all the more conscious of

their calling, and the cuisine they enjoyed accordingly became all the more refined and elaborate. The 'Great Manchu Banquets' and 'Great Chinese Banquets' which evolved at the Ch'ing court in Peking are perfect examples of the extravagance and self-indulgence of Ch'ing gourmets.

As for the common people, their culinary disparity with the rich made them all the more appreciative of whatever food they could get and provided fuel to fire their creative imaginations. The poor in China were, and still are, heirs to the great Chinese gourmet traditions every bit as much as the rich. Thus, they excelled in inventing new dishes from simple, inexpensive ingredients, dishes which nourished the body and pleased the palate just as well as the fare of the wealthy. The poor pioneered the fuel-saving cooking methods and cost-efficient recipes for which Chinese cooking is so renowned today. The one cooking method universally identified with Chinese cuisine today is *chao*, variously translated as 'stir-fry,' 'sauté,' or 'fast-fry.' This

method was not commonly used before the Ch'ing era, but its efficiency and economy made it the most popular technique of all by the turn of the 20th century. Not only does the *chao* method save precious fuel and cooking oil, it also turns out to be the superior method from gourmet and nutritional points of view: it beautifully and quickly blends the flavours of the various main ingredients and condiments without sacrificing their texture, colour, fragrance, or nutritional potency. Flavour and nutrients are sealed in rather than cooked out. Many of China's most beloved recipes come not from the kitchens of wealthy, jaded gourmets, but rather from the in-

genious inventions and clever improvisations of the common people. Many such recipes are included in this book.

The Ch'ing dynasty produced a wealth of gourmet literature, the most famous of which is the poet Yuan Mei's cookbook, *The Menu*. *The Menu* provides both an important summary of all previous principles, practices, and lore connected with food in China as well as significant elaborations and practical explanations of gourmet cooking and eating habits. Again, the three principles most often alluded to are pristine naturalness, food pharmacology, and harmonious balance. One of Yuan Mei's most salient themes is that correct preparation is far more important than costly ingredients in food. He states his case with amusing examples:

A good cook cannot with the utmost application produce more than four successful dishes in one day, and even then it is hard for him to give proper attention to every detail; and he certainly won't get through unless everything is in its right place and he is on his feet the whole time. It is no use to give him a lot of assistants; each of them will have his own ideas, and there will be no proper discipline. The more help he gets, the worse the results will be.

I once dined with a merchant. There were three successive sets of dishes and sixteen different sweets. Altogether, more than 40 kinds of food were served. My host regarded the dinner as an enormous success. But when I got home I was so hungry that I ordered a bowl of plain rice-gruel. From this it may be imagined how little there was, despite this profusion of dishes, that was at all fit to eat.

I always say that chicken, pork, fish, and duck are the original geniuses of the board, each with a flavour of its own, each with its distinctive style; whereas sea-slug and swallows-nest (despite their costliness) are commonplace fellows, with no character — in fact, mere hangers-on. I was once asked to a party given by a certain Governor, who gave us a plain boiled swallows-nest, served in enormous vases, like flower-pots. It had no taste at all. The other guests were obsequious in their praise of it. But I said, 'We are here to eat swallows-nest, not to take delivery of it wholesale.' If our host's object was simply to impress, it would have been better to put a hundred pearls into each bowl. Then we should have known that the meal had cost him tens of thousands, without the unpleasantness of being expected to eat what was uneatable.

Yuan Mei had strong opinions about the correct way to prepare and enjoy food, and the above passages reflect his willingness to state his views frankly. This was a common characteristic of Ch'ing gourmet writers.

The dichotomy between the rustic and the extravagant, between the requirements of frugality and the demands of refinement, became even more pronounced in Ch'ing culinary culture due to the disparities between the rich and poor. This theme runs throughout Yuan Mei's lively discussion of food in *The Menu*. He roundly criticizes many famous Ch'ing gourmets for tasteless extravagance, pompous pretension, and wretched excess. Similarly, he has nothing but praise for many . rustic, inexpensive dishes which are prepared simply and reflect perfectly the cardinal principle of balance and harmony in food. *The Menu* is both a practical cookbook containing famous recipes from throughout the empire as well as a rich storehouse of Chinese food lcre, gourmet opinion, and amusing anecdotes.

The aesthetic link between the enjoyment of food and sex continued to thrive among gourmet circles in Ch'ing China. Ch'ing literature is full of food terminology applied to sex, such as a virgin girl described as 'a sweet, ripe melon ready to cut,' hands as white and slender as 'freshly peeled Spring onions,' a mouth like a 'fresh cherry,' cheeks as white and fresh as the 'flesh of the litchi,' and many more. *The Dream of the Red Chamber*, *The Scholars*, and other Ch'ing novels offer colourful and insightful descriptions of food, food lore, and the sensual enjoyment of food and sex together.

A significant economic development of the Ch'ing era was the emergence of large, commercial corporate associations to handle the logistics of food supply, transport, distribution, and other aspects of the food industry. These associations were usually based on provincial and professional affiliations, such as the fishermen of Chekiang (Zhejiang), the wheat-millers of Shantung (Shandong), the rice-dealers of Kuangtung (Guangdong), the tea producers of Kiangsu (Jiangsu), and so forth. The associations gained enormous economic power, often monopoly, in their respective fields. These were highly organised, large-scale enterprises which greatly promoted the commercialisation of the food industry and helped spread Chinese culinary culture to every corner of the empire.

The restaurant industry continued to flourish during the Ch'ing, and courtesans, singers, and musicians continued to be associated with and provided by restaurants. The centre of the restaurant world during the Ch'ing was the famous commercial and pleasure city of Yangchou (Yangzhou), located where the Grand Canal meets the Yangtze River in Kiangsu (Jiangsu). Elaborate floating restaurant boats, with full banquet and entertainment services, became the rage of the day in Yangchou (Yangzhou), Hangchou (Hangzhou), and Canton (Guangzhou). By the mid-19th century, most gourmet restaurants offered another new diversion as well — opium-smoking.

The grand Chinese tradition of itinerant vendors of prepared foods thrived throughout the Ch'ing era, as it still does today in China, Taiwan, Hong Kong, and Singapore. Even the Son of Heaven, ensconced in the Forbidden City, occasionally tired of the fancy fare in his palace and sent a runner out to the local night market to get a bowl of 'Old Man Wang's Spicy Beef Noodles,' 'Pock-marked Mama's Bean-curd,' or other such rustically named, simply prepared, and incomparably delicious snacks. The kitchens of fancy restaurants and palaces simply could not duplicate these marvellous folk dishes.

The Ch'ing was the last imperial dynasty of China, during which time classical Chinese cuisine developed to its highest stage, traditional culinary principles were universally recognised throughout the empire, and sophisticated gourmet literature flourished. Such original, subtle gourmets as Yuan Mei cut through the fancy facades of costliness and exotica with which so many self-styled epicures surrounded themselves and got down to the real heart of the matter — correct preparation, originality, and creative improvisation. Yuan once said to his cook, 'What astonishes me is that, out of a couple of eggs, you can make a dish that no one else could have made.' His clever cook replied,

The cook who can work only on a large scale must lack daintiness, just as one who can handle common ingredients but fails with rare and costly ones can only be reckoned as a feeble practitioner. Good cooking, however, does not de-

pend on whether the dish is large or small, expensive or economical. If one has the art, then a piece of celery or salted cabbage can be made into a marvellous delicacy; whereas if one has not the art, not all the greatest delicacies and rarities of land, sea, or sky are of any avail.

20th Century China and the People's Republic

The 20th century has seen some of China's worst and best times for food. During the final decade of the Ch'ing dynasty and the early years of the Republic, political upheavals disrupted agriculture and destroyed the delicate local trade networks so vital to equitable distribution of food supplies; most Chinese lived a very marginal existence at this time. Central authority was weak and ineffectual, and all effective power fell to the hands of rapacious warlords. Dams and dikes, roads and canals, and other vital facilities for producing and distributing food were left in hopeless states of disrepair.

There was another reason for the paucity of the Chinese diet during the opening decades of this century: opium. Widely used among rich and poor alike, opium had become the bane of Chinese society by the time the Republic was established in 1912. Money normally spent on food went for opium instead. Land normally used to raise food crops was converted to cultivation of opium poppies. And one of the most basic physiological effects of opium on the body is to kill the appetite: addicts gradually waste away from malnutrition and indifference, regardless of how much food might be available to them.

In 1937, the Japanese invaded China with one of the most vicious, destructive military campaigns ever launched by one country against another. Burning, pillaging, and raping their way across the land, they deliberately ruined China's economic infrastructure. Rich and poor alike suffered from hunger and starvation in the wake of the Japanese onslaught.

No sooner had the Japanese been defeated by America than the Chinese Civil War broke out again, further prolonging the misery of the people and the stagnation of China's food production. Finally, in 1949, halfway through the 20th century, the Communist victory brought peace and stability to China again for the first time in a cen-

tury. The gradual recovery of agriculture and food distribution networks resulted in the restoration of nutritional balance and sufficiency in the Chinese diet. The early years were lean, but at least people stopped starving. Today, it is a well-known fact that as many people suffer from malnutrition and other dietary problems in certain parts of America as anywhere in China.

Looking at the Chinese diet today, we see that the traditional reliance on *fan*, grains, is more evident than ever. When rice or wheat are in short supply in contemporary China, millet, sorghum, *kaoliang*, soybeans, and even sweet potatoes are routinely substituted. An interesting survey of the dietary habits of typical rural households in central and coastal China was done during the 1920's. The households surveyed were in relatively peaceful and prosperous areas of China and representative of typical Chinese culinary habits. This survey revealed that 90 percent of food energy was derived from grains and grain products, only 1 percent from animal products, and the balance from vegetables, fruits, and sweets. The average American household of the same period derived only 39 percent of food energy from grains, a whopping 38 per cent from animal products, and the balance from other sources, mostly sugar. The successful reliance on grain foods in China is instructive, for it may well be the wave of the future as population explosions make animal products less and less viable as major sources of food energy.

It is interesting to note that the centrality of grain in the Chinese diet is built directly into the language. For example, one of the highest compliments you can give a *tsai* is that it really *hsia fan*, or 'helps the rice go down,' the implicit assumption being that the proper role of good *tsai* is to help the all-important grain staples go down pleasantly. Only at major festivals or other important occasions do the *tsai* receive major emphasis, and less *fan* is consumed. When asking someone in Chinese whether he has eaten yet or not, the correct phrase translates literally as, 'Have you eaten rice yet?' And just as children in the West were once told by their mothers to eat everything on their plates because 'there are children starving in China,' so Chinese mothers have always admonished their children to eat up every last grain of

rice in their bowls because 'each and every grain is bitter toil' in the fields.

Next to rice, the main items which comprise the daily diet of the common people in contemporary China are soy beans, cabbages, several varieties of mustard greens and turnips, and the various onions, scallions, and garlics of the Allium family. These items form the bulk of the food consumed on a daily basis, though there are regional differences in the mix, the diet being somewhat richer and more varied south of the Yangtze. In semi-arid and inclement regions, where the above won't grow, New World food staples form the basis of the diet: Maize, sweet potatoes, Irish potatoes, peanuts, tomatoes, and red chilies. Though these foods have been common in China for less than a century, they have already been fully integrated into the Chinese diet. Red chillies are an especially valuable import from the New World, for they contain among the richest and most available sources of Vitamins A and C of any food in the world.

The greatest legacy inherited by modern China from its imperial past is a diet which is naturally balanced. Due to its intrinsic diversity and its long-standing concurrent role as medicine, Chinese food needs no artificial supplements such as vitamin pills, protein powders, fiber supplements, and other nutritional boosters commonly used to bring contemporary Western diets up to nutritional par. Moreover, the nutritional balance is built into every dish and has nothing to do with the cost of ingredients. Despite the disparity in cost and content of a 12-course gourmet banquet and a simple bowl of noodles with beef, vegetables, and stock taken with a few side-orders such as dried beancurd and salt-fish, the actual nutritional balance of the two is about the same, and the supply of vital nutrients provided by the latter is perfectly sufficient for health and vitality. Indeed, the most concentrated and complete sources of proteins in the world are soy bean products and dried salt-fish, both of which comprise major portions of the Chinese diet and are among the least expensive of all foods. In China, the lack of money is no object to getting a nutritious — and delicious — meal.

Not only has modern science verified that the Chinese diet is the most nutritionally well balanced in the world, it has also proven that it is the most efficient and economical in terms of utilisation of land and other natural resources. The Chinese style of growing, preparing, cooking, and eating food can adequately support more people on less land at lower per capita cost than any other diet in the world. Coastal and southern China, with its intense agriculture and dense population, is living proof of this fact. Whether one uses the modern scientific jargon of the West (vitamins, proteins, minerals, etc.) or the more colourful terminology of traditional Chinese medicine (Yin/Yang, hot/cold, Five Elements, etc.), the singular conclusion remains the same: the Chinese have developed the world's most well balanced and economical cuisine, one that can equally satisfy the refined demands of the wealthiest gourmet and the frugal requirements of the poorest peasant. In this modern day and age, when poor nations are starving due to inadequate food supplies and rich nations are starving from serious nutritional imbalances and deficiencies, despite their gluttonous eating habits, it would seem that the entire world stands to benefit by adopting some of the ancient, time-tested principles and practices of Chinese cuisine.

Every food item that has evolved to a position of prominence in the Chinese diet turns out to be the most nutritious item of its kind. Modern nutritional science verifies this fact as well. Red chillies, for example, which are so popular in all styles of Chinese cooking, are one of the very best sources of Vitamins A and C. Pork, the favourite and most widely consumed meat in China past and present, is the most nutritious of domestic meats: it contains the highest deposits of riboflavin and other vitamins and minerals of all flesh foods, and pork liver contains double the amount of iron of any other liver. Soybeans have already been mentioned as the world's greatest source of complete proteins, especially when processed into bean-curd, a staple food almost as common as rice in China today. Sweet potatoes, the best source of carotene (from which Vitamin A is derived), have supported millions of Chinese during times of scarcity ever since their introduction. And the traditional Chinese love of fish as food goes far beyond its gourmet value: fish is the best, and in many places the only, source of certain vital amino acids such as methione, which are missing both in flesh and fowl. The point is that today, after 5,000 years of continuous culinary

and medical evolution, you can implicitly trust each Chinese recipe to be nutritionally well balanced and the Chinese diet in general to give you everything your body needs on a daily basis.

The diet in the P.R.C. today provides balanced nutrition without sacrificing the traditional Chinese demand for good taste. The gourmet inclinations of the Chinese people are very much alive and well: restaurants which fail to satisfy them are not patronised, and their managers soon find themselves called upon the carpet before some stern cadre to explain why they have failed to properly 'Serve the People,' modern China's great motto. Nor has home-cooking in China lost its traditional flair: gourmet cuisine aside, a typical meal prepared in the kitchen of a typical rural commune in China today is better balanced and better tasting than a typical meal prepared in a typical household in the West. And in China, it is prepared at a mere fraction of the cost of its Western equivalent.

Ironically, the traditional balance and nutrition of the Chinese diet is today being somewhat eroded by incursions of the three 'whites' from the West: low-extraction white flour, highly polished white rice, and refined white sugar. Western methods of milling and polishing wheat and rice are more convenient, especially for shipping and storage, and have been largely adopted in China, Taiwan, and elsewhere in the Orient. But these Western methods rob wheat and rice of virtually all of their vital nutrients, leaving nothing but 'empty calories.' As for white sugar, its evils are well known: It erodes both the teeth and the appetite for better foods. In former times, adults and children alike in China snacked on such things as dried bean-curd, pickled vegetables, preserved meats, dried salt-fish, watermelon and pumpkin seeds, and other nutritionally valuable items. Today, sugary soft-drinks, factory-made candies and cookies, cakes of white flour, white sugar, and cheap oil, chewing gum, and other banes of good nutrition are slowly but surely replacing the traditional snacks of China. The power of mass advertising and the automatic identification with the 'progressive, modern West' which these 'foods' impart are partly to blame for this unfortunate state of affairs. Perhaps only when the West begins to appreciate and adopt certain traditional Chinese eating habits

will the Chinese themselves once again realise the superiority of their own native culinary system.

It is at best difficult and arbitrary to conclude that one cuisine is 'superior' to another, especially in light of the many subjective factors involved. Yet in a comparative analysis of different cuisines, China's comes out on top in so many respects that it is equally difficult not to conclude that it is the overall superior diet from both nutritional and gourmet standpoints. On this ever more crowded planet of ours, it is certainly the most viable diet in the world. Its superiority in terms of variety, nutrition, taste, and economy have already been discussed. However, the actual style of eating food is also a crucial aspect of any cuisine, and here again the Chinese way seems to be far ahead of the rest of the field.

Eating *a la Chinoise* provides each diner with automatic portion control, something lacking in Western-style food service. Each diner may select as much or little as he wishes from the various dishes on the table without insulting his host or the chef. In Western cuisine, each person receives a set portion of one type of food on his plate: If the portion is insufficient to satisfy his appetite, it is awkward and usually socially impermissible to order a second entrée from the kitchen. If the portion is too large and he fails to finish it, he risks insulting the host or chef.

Chinese eating style also permits each diner to exercise automatic flavour control and to mix the tastes of the dishes and condiments creatively. Diners select more from the dishes that please their palates and less from those that don't, again without insulting the host or chef. Morsels may be dipped in a variety of sauces provided on the table to alter or enhance their flavours. Best of all, bites of food from various different dishes may be mixed together in the mouth to produce infinite different combinations of taste sensations. This is impossible in Western cuisine, in which you are often tantalised by the aroma and appearance of the food on your neighbour's plate but prevented from tasting it by social etiquette and the constrictions of Western food service.

Finally, in the Chinese style of eating, with a wide assortment of nutritionally and pharmacologically different dishes on the table before you, your body automatically guides your chopsticks to those dishes richest in the elements your body needs most at the moment. This is a chemical response, triggered perhaps by the aromas of the foods. Again, this is impossible in Western cuisine, in which set meals are placed before each diner, and it becomes a matter of pure luck whether the food on your plate happens to be what your body needs most that day.

A discussion of food in the P.R.C. would be incomplete without mentioning the social functions of food as distinct from its nutritional and gourmet aspects. Food has always been an important form of social communication in China, and this still holds true today. With the relative abundance, availability, and equitable distribution of food in China, a far greater proportion of the populace can now afford to eat out in restaurants than at any other time in Chinese history. Everywhere you travel in the P.R.C. you notice that restaurants are jammed with people eating, drinking, and socialising. While the fare is generally simple and inexpensive, it is still highly nutritious and very delicious. Simple, rustic foods have always formed an important part of Chinese cuisine and are actually preferred on a regular basis to complex and fancy dishes, even by those who can afford the latter.

Those who can afford it, however, can still find the very best of China's traditional *haute cuisine* in the best restaurants of contemporary China. Such excellent establishments as the 'Pine Crane' in Soochou (Suzhou) — now in its fourth century of operation, the 'Lou-Wai-Lou' (800 years old) and the 'Hangchou Wine-House' in Hangchou (Hangzhou), the 'North Garden' and the 'South Garden' in Canton (Giangzhou), and many others still serve the famous gourmet dishes of China with traditional flair and original style. In the 'V.I.P. Rooms' of these restaurants, where the best dishes are available and all foreign visitors are entertained, you will invariably notice that most of the tables are occupied by important comrades and cadres entertaining or being entertained by their colleagues. Eating out is the one traditional pleasure which the new state has not eliminated from the Chinese scene, simply because its social functions are far too important and the habit too well ingrained in Chinese society.

Going out to eat in China, Hong Kong, Taiwan, Singapore, or other Chinese communities is different from going out to eat Western style. First of all, a special occasion of some kind is usually involved: should one be missing, one is invented. The criteria for selecting a restaurant are also quite different. As long as the food is famously good, Chinese will climb the highest mountains, ford the widest rivers, and endure all manner of inconvenience to get to a simple open-air food stall in some remote village just to sample a famous specialty unrivalled anywhere else. In Hong Kong and Taiwan, people sometimes drive for hours through unbearable traffic to get to a 'famous restaurant,' which, to the novice Western eye, would appear little better than a hovel, with bare walls, spartan furnishings, peeling ceilings, and no 'atmosphere' whatsoever. Yet Chinese gourmets, rich and poor alike, flock to such places to sample some unique dish produced only by the proprietor.

In the West, the measure of a meal's worth when dining out is often gauged by factors unrelated to the food itself: fancy decor, soft music, and candlelight, sterling silver tableware and crystal goblets, liveried waiters hovering in attendance, and plush furnishing are the important requirements. After all, how much can be done with a grilled steak, baked potato, boiled vegetables, and a salad? In effect, eating out in expensive gourmet restaurants in the West is often more a matter of renting sumptuous premises and elegant ambiance in which to eat a mediocre meal than it is of purchasing creatively original and unusually good food. In China, the main criterion for eating out has always been, and still remains, the quality and nature of the food itself. Chinese restaurants are notorious among sensitive Western diners for their complete indifference to ambiance and the cacophonous din which prevails in them. But the Chinese don't even notice these things: to them the quality of the food and the company with which it is enjoyed are the all-important and overriding factors. You can't eat atmosphere, and in a country where money and resources are limited but everyone has gourmet tastes, you cannot afford to waste money and materials on it either.

Hosting a banquet for one's friends and associates has always been the most quintessentially Chinese way of celebrating an important event in one's life or a major public festival. Even in spartan, egalitarian China today, this still remains true. The degree of formality and the lavishness which mark the banquet are still accurate indicators of the host's social position, his relationship to his guests, and the importance of the occasion itself. None of these factors are ever explicitly stated: They are all implicitly implied by the dishes which appear on the table under the host's directions. The dishes he selects reflect not only his economic status (how much he can afford to spend), and his social status (how much he owes his guests and the occasion), but also his culinary cultural status (whether he has gourmet or plebeian tastes). Communism has rid China of the wretched excess of the rich as well as the abject dearth of the poor, but the gourmet tastes which have always been shared by both remain intact, and the foods available now fall somewhere in between the former extremes. Numerically, more people than ever can afford to eat out in China today and indulge their native craving for good food. By 'breaking bread together,' social bonds are re-affirmed, and one of life's most natural and gratifying pleasures, one that can be renewed and enjoyed each and every day, is shared with one's chosen companions. While the camaraderie of eating together is shared to some extent all over the world, it lies at the very heart of the Chinese concept of eating. Rarely does a Chinese eat alone at home or in a restaurant.

The foregoing culinary tour of Chinese history is meant to give the reader some fundamental feelings and facts about Chinese cuisine. It is always easier to understand and accept foreign ways if you first glimpse the historical context in which they evolved and grasp the underlying principles through which they developed. For a complete, detailed account of Chinese food history, the reader is referred to *Food in Chinese Culture*, edited by K.C. Chang (Yale, 1977). Much of the information presented in this chapter is derived from this comprehensive and scholarly book, a pioneer in the field of food history.

The authors hope that this chapter whets your intellectual appetite for Chinese cuisine and encourages you to pursue the art of Chinese cooking and eating in your own home. Should you do so, you will surely derive the same nutritional, aesthetic, and economic advantages enjoyed today by one quarter of the world's population.

CHAPTER II
Chinese Cooking Utensils, Condiments and Methods

Of all the world's great cuisines, Chinese cooking is probably the easiest to learn and practise. All the utensils and cooking methods commonly used to produce even the most complex dishes are very simple. With only four of the most ancient and rudimentary implements (cleaver, board, wok, and spatula), plus any source of intense heat, (charcoal or wood are fine), at least 75 percent of a typical Chinese menu is easily prepared. Recipes are never rigid in application, there is always plenty of room for substitution and creative improvisation.

Yet many people regard Chinese cooking as an inscrutable art, supremely difficult, if not impossible, to master. Ironically, the perceived difficulties lie precisely in its very simplicity: in Chinese cooking, one need not follow complex recipes by rote, and many of the modern technological conveniences of the Western kitchen prove of no use. Instead, one simply needs to develop the proper 'touch' or 'feel' for Chinese cooking. But since such vague, non-rational concepts are foreign to the Western mind, most Westerners view Chinese cuisine as a highly contrived and basically unapproachable Oriental art. Nothing could be further from the truth.

The utensils, methods, and most of the condiments employed today in Chinese cooking have been in continuous use in China for several thousand years. After such a long evolution, only the simplest, most flexible tools and techniques have survived. The utensils, condiments, and methods introduced below are commonly used by millions of Chinese cooks — from gourmet chefs to simple peasants — and there is absolutely no reason why the average Westerner with an interest in cooking should not be able to acquire these skills as well.

It is the concept of 'feel' or 'touch' in Chinese cooking that troubles most aspiring Western adepts of the art: they would prefer to have everything laid out in recipes, especially seasoning proportions and exact cooking times, rather than have to rely on their own senses and intuition. In Chinese cuisine, however, written recipes should only serve as guidelines, especially for pre-cooking preparations in the kitchen. As for the exact proportions of cooking condiments and the correct cooking times, these decisions are ultimately in the hands of the cook, and they usually must be made instantly, without thought, while cooking. Many Western cooks are needlessly cowed by this requirement, but it is no different than developing a 'touch' for tennis or a 'feel' for driving sports cars. More than any other style of cooking, practice makes perfect in Chinese cuisine.

There are four basic goals in cooking Chinese food, and these are also the basic indicators which tell you how much to add when, how hot the fire should be, and how long the dish should be cooked. All these indicators are directly related to the senses.

The four cardinal conditions by which every Chinese dish must be judged are flavour, fragrance, colour, and texture. The primary purpose of all the different ways of cutting meats and vegetables, marinating various ingredients, pre-cooking some while leaving others raw, and all the elaborate preparations prior to cooking, is to ensure that these four classical requirements are properly met. Successful Chinese cooking is simply a matter of learning how to use your basic senses rather than your head while in the kitchen.

The foremost factor is flavour. The goal is to capture and preserve the innate, natural fresh flavours of the main ingredients. Seasonings are used to enhance these 'fresh-natural'(*xian*) flavours while suppressing any foul or rank (*xing*) flavours. Excessive use of strong seasonings not only masks the natural (*xian*) flavours of foods, but is also employed by unskilled chefs to mask their culinary shortcomings. Properly prepared foods should leave a pleasant aftertaste on the palate, vaguely reminiscent of the main ingredients' original flavours, rather than the flavours of the condiments.

Closely related to flavour is fragrance. It is perhaps even more vital to the full enjoyment of gourmet foods, for many subtle flavours come through only through the fragrance. Note how food tastes absolutely flavourless when you have a cold. Fragrance passes not only through the nostrils but up from the mouth and into the sinuses while chewing. Fragrance is easily diluted or lost in cooking, and proper prior preparation protects the innate fragrance of foods before they hit the fire. Treatment with appropriate seasonings, application of proper cooking methods, and, most important, proper timing for each different kind of food are the methods employed to preserve and enhance natural fragrances.

Colour is the visual indicator used in Chinese cooking. It is also important for the full appreciation of gourmet foods, for we all eat with our eyes first and then with our mouths as we sit down to a beautifully arranged banquet table. Various ingredients with contrasting colours are combined in the same dish for visual effect, such as green and red peppers, black mushrooms and yellow bamboo shoots, orange carrots and white turnips, etc. Colour also indicates when many foods are done in sauté cooking, such as string beans turning from light to dark green, meat turning from red to brown and translucent fish meat turning opaque white. Chinese food preparation and cooking methods aim at preserving beautiful colours and altering drab ones in food.

Finally, there is texture, which is perhaps the most unique requirement of classical Chinese cuisine. Nowhere

else is so much emphasis placed on texture. This opens up an entirely new realm of sensual enjoyment of food: the feel and consistency on the tongue, palate, throat, and especially between the teeth. The number of different textures distinguished by Chinese cooks and gourmets is incredible. There are crunchy, crispy, tender, slippery, melting, smooth, soft, hard, creamy, spongy, dry, juicy, rubbery, chewy, fluffy, and fibrous textures, plus infinite combinations thereof. This is by far the most sophisticated and subtle aspect of gourmet Chinese cuisine and one that is purely aesthetic in nature. Ingredients are selected for similar or contrasting textures within the same dish and in the meal as a whole. A classical example is fresh bamboo shoots (crunchy) cooked with black mushrooms (soft and chewy); this particular dish also offers a similar contrast in colours. Deep-fried foods are favoured for their crispy, dry texture outside and tender, juicy texture inside. Eel has a slippery texture, steamed pastries are creamy, squid is rubbery, and so forth.

Texture is also the most difficult aspect of foods to control while cooking. Once the texture 'sets,' it is impossible to alter it. Unlike flavour and fragrance, textures cannot be influenced by condiments. Texture is where the 'magic touch' in Chinese cooking is most vital. Certain pre-cooking methods such as parboiling, steaming, deep-frying, and light sautéing are sometimes employed to properly set the textures of certain ingredients. Some ingredients used to prepare a dish are there purely to lend textural qualities to it: 'wood ears' (tree fungus), jellyfish,

peanuts, beancurd, and other texture foods often appear in supporting rather than primary roles in a dish to provide contrasting textures. Fortunately, if the conditions of flavour, fragrance, and colour are all properly met in cooking, texture usually comes out correctly as well. The main trick to texture is to select the appropriate ingredients in the first place, making sure that they are absolutely fresh. If not, substitute something else or leave it out altogether. Different textures are enjoyed with different parts of the mouth, including lips, tongue, palate, and throat, but most of them are best appreciated between the molars.

Below, various vital aspects of Chinese cooking are briefly introduced, beginning with common cooking utensils, then proceeding to pre-cooking kitchen preparations, followed by common cooking condiments, and ending with the most common cooking methods. The chapter concludes with a brief word on creative improvisation in Chinese cooking.

CHINESE COOKING UTENSILS

Chinese cooking utensils are the simplest, most practical, and easiest to maintain cooking implements in the world. Of ancient design, they are made of basic, sturdy, and inexpensive materials, primarily iron, wood, and bamboo. The overwhelming majority of Chinese dishes can be prepared with only four basic implements: a Chinese cleaver, a sturdy cutting board, a round-bottomed pan or 'wok', and a spatula.

Chinese Cleaver: A good Chinese cleaver is the most versatile implement

in the kitchen. It can cut, chop, slice, shred, mince (grind), pound, peel, scrape, flatten, and otherwise process every type of ingredient used in Chinese cooking. When charcoal and wood are used for stoves, the cleaver is used to cut kindling. It can also be used to ward off unwanted intruders from the kitchen.

The most important skills to develop for using the cleaver are rhythm and relaxation. Start out slowly with a cutting rhythm you can handle and gradually increase the tempo. Wrist and arm should be loose and relaxed, a short burst of strength applied only at the actual moment of cutting. A properly used and cared-for cleaver will last a lifetime; indiscriminate hacking and careless cutting will ruin it in less than a year. The great taoist philosopher and humourist Zhuang-Zi (4th century B.C.) relates the words of a bullock butcher in one of his anecdotes:

A good cook changes his chopper once a year — because he cuts, an ordinary cook once a month — because he hacks. But I have had this chopper for 19 years, and although I have cut up many thousands of bullocks, its edge is as if fresh from the whetstone.

It is best to have two types of cleavers: a light one for fine cuts such as shredding and mincing (grinding) and a heavy one for chopping through meat with bones. When chopping up spareribs, whole chickens, or ducks and so forth, you should aim for the joints, ligaments, and relatively soft spots. Cleavers come in steel and iron; steel is best for heavy choppers, but iron is infinitely superior for lighter cleavers used in most cutting. Iron holds a better edge and can be easily honed on a whetstone. The stainless steel cleavers available now in many home-product stores tend to lose their edge quickly and are also less suited to the heavy tasks an iron or steel cleaver manages so capably. See also page 396 for specific techniques with the Chinese cleaver.

Chopping Board: A good hardwood board is indispensable for proper cutting and other preparations. The type most favoured by Chinese cooks is a round cross-section of a hardwood tree. Western-style standing butcher blocks are ideal for use in the Chinese kitchen. After use, cutting boards may be scraped clean with the back edge of the cleaver, rinsed with warm water, and hung to dry.

An efficient Chinese kitchen will have several chopping boards reserved for different tasks. An older board for use when chopping through bones, one reserved for preparing such strong-smelling ingredients as onions, garlic, and ginger and another for preparing fruit.

The Wok: Today the round-bottomed wok (Cantonese pronunciation; Mandarin is guo) is the most universally recognised utensil of the Chinese kitchen. It is highly versatile and may be substituted for all other Chinese cooking vessels whenever necessary.

Woks come in many sizes, shapes, and materials; there are flat-bottomed, teflon-coated woks for use on electric hotplates, and even electric woks, but these are a poor substitute for the simple, traditional Chinese iron wok, particularly if used with a gas wok cooker, see also below. The best type of wok is one with a single, sturdy wooden handle rather than the double 'ear' type of handles which can be difficult to manipulate.

Iron has the advantage of distributing heat very quickly and uniformly throughout the surface of the pan. Iron seasons well, and an iron wok improves with age. With the high

heat and constant rapid stirring used in most wok cookery, nutritionally significant amounts of natural iron are also imparted to foods during the cooking process, an important consideration in restricted diets. A single, wooden handle permits you to manipulate the pan with one hand while wielding a spatula with the other, and makes pouring from the wok considerably easier as well.

Due to the round shape of this original Chinese cooking vessel, minimum amounts of cooking oil and cooking fuel are used, an important consideration for everyone in this energy-conscious age. The wok's versatility is legend; you can fry a single egg or saute a kilo of chopped cabbage, sauté a few slivers of meat or stew a whole chicken, fry, steam, stew, boil, or braise just about anything.

New woks tend to stick. A new iron wok should first be heated dry over an intense flame to burn off any surface impurities or coatings. However, this same process should not be undertaken with a stainless steel or aluminium wok as the result may be a 'burn' spot which will affect its performance later. The wok should then be well oiled and heated again, then the oil poured off and the inside of the wok rubbed vigorously with a piece of crumbled kit-

chen paper. Rinse the wok well and hang to dry, or wipe out with a cloth and store upside down. After each use, clean the wok by rinsing it under hot water while scrubbing well with a bamboo or hair wok brush. Do not use detergents unless absolutely necessary. Woks should be treated like the old iron skillets common to many Western kitchens; the older and more seasoned they become, the better they cook.

When using the wok for sautéing, first heat it dry, then add the oil, swirling it around the sides just below the rim and allowing it to run to the bottom, thus coating the entire interior of the wok. Heat again until it smokes, after which the ingredients can be thrown in and stir-fried. This way the pan always remains slightly hotter than the oil, which helps prevent sticking. This is called 'hot pan/warm oil' in Chinese. When cooking fish or other delicate items that stick easily, it is helpful to rub the entire interior surface of the wok well with a piece of peeled fresh ginger before heating and adding the oil

Wok Spatula ('Charn'): The indispensable long-handled, shovel-like implement used for lifting and stirring foods in the wok. Steel is the best material, and the scraping edge should be slightly rounded to fit the wok. The spatula should have a wooden or plastic grip to insulate the heat. An egg slice (egg lifter) or wooden spatula will handle the task fairly well.

In addition to the basic four implements described above, there are a variety of other traditional Chinese cooking utensils which are useful to have on hand in the kitchen.

Wok Lid: The wok usually comes equipped with a large dome-shaped lid which fits inside the lip of the wok, giving an excellent seal. It is used when braising, slow-cooking, and poaching and sometimes also in the final stages of cooking stir-fried vegetables, and when the wok is used as a steamer or smoking pan. There is plenty of space beneath the wok lid for a rack (see below) and the ingredients to be steamed or smoked.

Wok Rack: A collapsible bamboo (see illustration, page 32) or fixed-in-place wire or aluminium stand for use inside the wok to hold dishes or ingredients above the surface of the wok when steaming or smoking. The open construction of the rack allows free and even distribution of the steam or smoke. A makeshift rack can be made using two wooden (bamboo) chopsticks. Place them across the wok, with a reasonable space between them and balance the plate or dish on top. Another makeshift rack can be produced using a wide, empty food can, such as that used to pack processed fish. Puncture the can in several places around the sides and across the bottom; the top should be removed completely. Place upside-down in the bottom of the wok and support the dish on top. This is ideal when using an old saucepan as a steamer.

Wok Stand: A metal ring which fits over a gas or electric element to provide a firm base for a round-bottomed wok.

Ladle: Ladles of various sizes and shapes are useful in preparing, tasting, and serving soups and stews. unlike the deep soup ladles used in the Western kitchen, the Chinese ladle is shallower, more saucer-shaped. An experienced cook needs only his ladle for measuring even the smallest quantities of ingredients and seasonings.

Strainer/Slotted Spoon: Two basic types of strainers are used in Chinese cooking. A flat, woven wire strainer retrives food from deep-frying oil or hot stock and is used for supporting items in a deep-fryer. The larger smooth metal strainer with round perforations and flat saucer-shape is best used for retrieving fried foods from hot oil and for draining these same foods over a basin. Many come complete with a fitted drip dish.

A slotted spoon, a metal colander, and a frying basket can replace the Chinese strainers. The wire strainers used in several recipes for shaping noodle or potato 'nests' are standard round, deep, wire mesh strainers with handles.

Frying Basket: A wire basket with one long handle, or two hooped handles, is invaluable in deep-frying, particularly for cooking smaller ingredients or shredded meats. The larger metal Chinese strainer can be used for this purpose also.

Cooking Chopsticks: These are a jumbo version of the smaller type used for eating. They are long enough to reach into a wok or stew-pot without getting the hands burned or splattered. They

are useful for plucking, arranging, stirring, turning, testing, and otherwise manipulating various types of food in the kitchen.

Steamer/Bamboo Steaming Basket: One of the most ancient of Chinese cooking vessels, the steamer (illustrated on page 33) is used to steam foods to final perfection, to pre-cook ingredients, warm up leftovers, and keep foods waiting to be served hot and moist. Steamers preserve the pristine flavours of foods, seal in nutrients, keep food moist, and require no fats or oils for cooking. Bamboo steaming baskets are used for the many kinds of steamed buns, pastries, and breads in the Chinese diet. The baskets can be placed inside the wok and a piece of clean cheesecloth or perforated greaseproof paper placed over the slats before putting in the food, to prevent

sticking. Or the slats may be well oiled with lard or vegetable oil before use. When a single steaming basket is used, it should be covered with its own lid and placed inside the wok or steamer and the pan lid set firmly in place. However, the baskets are designed to be stacked, and fit tightly one on top of the other, with a single lid on top. Stacked baskets can be set in a wok or over a saucepan of boiling water and, if well enough sealed around the lower edge, will not require a lid covering the lot. Certain recipes require that the lid be removed for a few seconds at several intervals during cooking. This is to prevent the food from bursting open due to the intense cooking heat. Snack foods such as dim sum are taken straight from straight from steamer to table in the attractive bamboo baskets. These are now readily available from Chinese products and rattanware retailers.

Aluminium multi-tiered steamers are useful for cooking the many types of steamed dishes and whole fish, poultry, or large cuts of meat. There is ample space in the Chinese steamer for cooking several dishes at once. Most have at least two tiers over a lower water dish and have a domed lid. Each tier has a series of large round holes in its base to allow the steam to circulate freely. Meats may be placed directly onto the well-oiled surface of the steamer, but usually foods are placed in a dish to prevent sticking and to collect the cooking liquids. Foods can be effectively steamed in a wok, see above, or in a saucepan with a rack, see above, Wok Rack.

Casserole/'Sand Pot': For braising, stewing, soup making, and a multitude of other cooking processes, the Chinese lightweight clay 'sand pot' has few rivals (two types are illustrated here). Its base is usually reinforced with a wire bracket making it strong enough for cooking over a gas flame or directly over high charcoal heat. They have, however, been known to stick to flat electric hot plates, and it is not advisable to use them directly on these. An asbestos mat placed underneath will protect the base. A wok or heavy metal pot may be used instead, but earthenware stew pots have certain advantages: they diffuse heat slowly and evenly: excess moisture is released through the surface while excess grease is absorbed by it; and the thick surface protects simmering foods from intense exposure to the heat. The pots come in varying sizes and shapes and each has a well-fitted heavy clay lid. Additional useful cooking vessels and implements include:

'Fire-Pot': A table-top cooking device with a tray in the base to contain char-

coal, and a funnel-shaped chimney surrounded with a moat in which stock is heated for cooking at the table. Small woven wire baskets on long handles come with the fire-pot, but wooden chopsticks may be used instead to add and retrieve food from the hot stock. A substitute fire-pot can be made with a table-top gas ring or electric hot plate and an attractive saucepan or stew pan. Or use a fondue pot with a strong spirit or gas flame underneath.

Electric Rice Cookers: These are rapidly replacing conventional saucepan cooking in Chinese households. They cook rice perfectly and keep it warm throughout a meal. They are also used for rice-pot dishes and other simple cooking. A thick aluminium saucepan

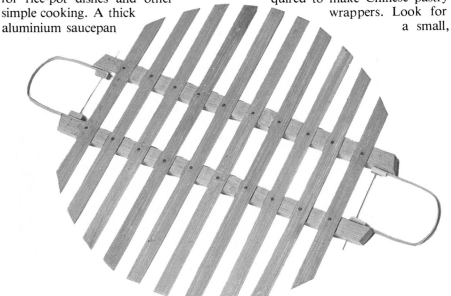

with a tight-fitting lid also produces excellent results, see more on rice cooking, Chapter VIII, Noodles and Rice-Accompaniments

Bamboo Wok Brush: This ancient implement has two uses. Immediately after use, the wok should be held under hot running water and scrubbed with the bamboo brush. The brush cleans the surface without requiring detergents and therefore without sacrificing the seasoning of the wok. They are sometimes also used instead of a spatula when stir-frying very finely shredded meats which must be cooked as quickly as possible. The bamboo brush-ends turn and stir such finely cut meats faster than a spatula. Separate brushes should be kept for each type of use. The brush is made from hair-thin slivers of bamboo and bound together at one end with strips of bamboo. They

should be well rinsed in hot water after use and hung to drip-dry.

Bamboo Tongs: A simple but useful tool to have on hand, bamboo tongs may be used to pluck unwanted items from a dish while cooking, pull out a tender morsel for tasting, transfer hot foods from oil to plate, and other similar uses. Tongs are a handy tool for those who have not yet mastered the art of using cooking chopsticks.

Dough Roller: Rollers are used to prepare dumpling skins, dough for buns and breads, and other pastry preparations. The heavy rollers common to Western kitchens are too big and unwieldy for the precision work required to make Chinese pastry wrappers. Look for a small, thin, short roller for this task.

Pastry Cleaver: A type of blunt-edged cleaver is used to make the crystal-clear pastries for such dim sum as 'shrimp dumplings.' These are sold at Chinese specialist stores, but a large metal cake spatula will perform the function just as well. It should be of the rigid-bladed type rather than one with a thin flexible blade.

Cookers: An important point to remember when cooking Chinese food, especially when using the ever-popular stir-frying method, is that the intensity of the heat must be sufficient, or else all of your careful kitchen preparations will have gone to nought. Electric ranges are unsuited to Chinese cooking; the heat being too highly concentrated at the bottom of the dish and changes in temperature too slow. The various

rings and stands sold with woks in the West to 'adapt' them to electric ranges do not overcome these drawbacks. The most ideal source of heat for Chinese cooking is an intense charcoal fire flamed by a fan, or gas heating. As charcoal is impractical in the home kitchen, we turn to gas and the gas cooker. Provided that at least one burner produces a flame big enough for stir-frying, the ordinary gas cooker will do. Unfortunately, most gas ranges manufactured in the West for household use do not produce such a flame. This problem may be overcome by having one burner in the range adjusted to produce the required flame, or by having a separate single burner for stir-frying. There are several types of portable gas wok-cookers available. All have a curved stand to accommodate the round-bottomed wok and produce the necessary high heat. The correct flame is one that is intense and large enough to lick up over the entire exterior surface of the wok when turned on full blast. A sufficient source of intense heat is one element in Chinese cooking for which there is no substitute. Single-burner gas cookers, of the kind using bottled gas are additionally practical in their portability. They can be used in the kitchen and stored away when not needed, they can be taken to the dining room for table-top cooking, and they can be used outdoors. Another type of simple portable cooker much used in traditional Chinese households is a small, clay, charcoal-and wood-burning cooker which supports just one wok or a 'sand pot.' These can be found in some specialist Chinese goods stores.

KITCHEN PREPARATIONS

The purpose of the various methods described in this section is to enhance the desirable aspects of flavour, fragrance, colour, and texture in foods, while suppressing the undesirable qualities. In Chinese cuisine, much more time and effort go into initial preparation of ingredients prior to cooking than into the actual cooking itself; the opposite is true in Western cuisine. Pre-cooking preparations are aimed at fine tuning the factors of flavour, fragrance, colour, and texture so that in the final product an optimum balance and harmony is achieved. Each ingredient must preserve its own unique identity while blending harmoniously with all the other ingredients used in the dish. To achieve this, each ingredient must be treated in specific ways prior to cooking everything together.

Cutting is the first step in preparing ingredients for Chinese cooking. All cutting is done in the kitchen, not at the table: all foods are prepared so that they can be eaten with chopsticks. Different cutting methods are used for different ingredients and purposes. When preparing meat, fish, and fowl, first scrape and cut away tendons, ligaments, and other extraneous membranes to ensure evenness of texture. When nothing but the meat is desired, skin and bones should also be removed.

The most common cut is called *si* or 'silk-cut' which involves finely shredding the meat across the grain to produce long, slender slivers. Beef, pork, and mutton are commonly cut this way for sautés. Meats are finely minced (*sui*) when they play supporting roles in dishes dominated by vegetables or for dumpling stuffings. Silk and mince cuts expose the maximum surface area to the hot oil and the condiments, permitting quick cooking and facilitating the blending of juices and condiments. Dicing into small cubes is used for boned chicken and lean meats for sautés, while large cubes are cut for simmered stews. Chopping into rough chunks complete with bone is used for spareribs, chicken, and duck, usually for 'red-stew' cooking. All of these cuts are done with cleaver and cutting board. See also page 392 for detailed instructions on preparation of ingredients and the use of the Chinese cleaver.

After cutting, marinating is the most common method used to prepare foods for cooking. Marinades are used for pre-cut meat, fish, and fowl to enhance their natural flavours, balance and impart others, and eliminate any rank tastes. Salt and wine are used to marinate kidneys: the salt extracts undesirable juices while the wine suppresses *xing* (rank) flavours. Salt is used alone to extract excess water from foods prior to cooking. Marination in water alone adds water to the ingredient; it is often used for prawns, fish, chicken, and certain vegetables. Water should never be added to cut beef or pork. The most common marinade for shredded or diced meats and chicken consists of soy sauce and wine with sugar and cornflour (cornstarch). Cornflour (Cornstarch) tenderises meats and imparts the 'slippery' texture. Wine counteracts rankness, while soy

sauce and sugar bring out the proper balance of salty and sweet flavours. An unusual marinade called *zao* consists of the fermented grain-mash dregs left over from distilling spirits. This method is used for meat, fish, and fowl and gives a very rich, aromatic flavour while tenderising at the same time.

Pre-cooking is a common preparatory technique in the Chinese kitchen, especially when various ingredients used in a dish have widely differing cooking times. Blanching is achieved by dumping the cut ingredients into boiling water: this sets the texture, tenderises, and removes any undesirable slime or scum from the tissues of meat, fish, and fowl. Hard vegetables to be used for stir-fried dishes with meat are often prepared this way.

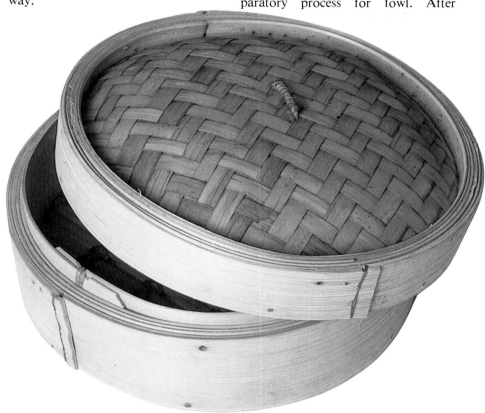

Poaching is also a common way of preparing foods for the final cooking process. Similar to the Western method, it requires that the temperature of the water be kept below the boiling point, while the food remains in the hot water anywhere from 5 minutes to an hour or more. When preparing water for poaching fish or fowl, add sliced ginger root and spring onions (scallions) to help suppress rankness. Poultry and seafoods are the most commonly poached foods.

Steaming is often used to soften or

pre-cook such items as shark's fin, lotus root, whole chickens, and ducks. Stir-frying is also used to pre-cook certain ingredients prior to mixing with others in the final cooking process. Sometimes minced ginger, garlic, spring onions (scallions), and chillies are pre-sautéed to release their flavours into the oil before the oil is used to cook other items.

Pre-soaking in hot water softens certain ingredients prior to cooking. Dried tree fungus ('wood ears'), dried salted shrimps, and dried black mushrooms are commonly treated this way. The remaining water is often used as a seasoning during the subsequent cooking process. See also page 392 for specific preparation of dried ingredients.

Air-drying is an important preparatory process for fowl. After marination and pre-steaming, chicken and duck are hung to air-dry. This method dries out the skin thoroughly and ensures the proper crispy texture when the subsequent deep-frying method is applied.

Bone-breaking with the dull edge of a cleaver is applied to bones before boiling them for stock. This exposes the marrow, which gives the best flavour to stocks. When whole joints of chicken are marinated for deep-frying or broiling, the bones should be cracked first by hitting the joint hard with the dull edge of a cleaver, making sure not to break the flesh open. This way the cooking time is reduced because heat is more evenly distributed inside; it also releases the flavour and fragrance of the marrow into the meat during cooking.

COMMON CHINESE COOKING CONDIMENTS

The Chinese style of cooking has often been called 'a marriage of flavours.' While the oil or fat used in cooking brings the partners together, the condiments enhance and harmonise their relationship. The oil or fat used to cook a dish is often an important condiment as well.

Most Chinese cooking is done with some type of vegetable oil, usually peanut oil. This gives a slightly nutty flavour and fragrance to foods. Soybean oil, corn oil, and mixed vegetable oils are also used. For fat, the most common choice is lard: it has a rich aromatic flavour of its own and is commonly used to sauté bland ingredients or pre-fry foods prior to further cooking. Rendered chicken fat is also an excellent shortening, especially for sautéing green, leafy vegetables such as spinach. Duck fat may also be used.

Among the vast array of Chinese condiments available, the five 'S's' are the most important items: soy sauce, sherry, salt, sugar, and sesame oil. It is impossible to cook Chinese food properly without these, but other condiments may be improvised when they are unavailable. Below, a dozen common Chinese cooking condiments are briefly introduced, starting with the indispensable five 'S's':

Soy sauce (jiang-you): Fermented from soybeans, wheat, salt, and water, soy sauce is the cardinal condiment of Chinese cuisine. It is used in marinades, cooking, and table sauces. Few meat dishes are prepared without it. Soy sauce has a salty, smoky flavour, rich fragrance, and reddish-brown colour. The best, most consistently reliable brand on the market is Japan's excellent 'Kikkoman.'

Sherry or rice wine (mi-jiu): The Chinese generally use rice wine or *Shao-xing* wine in cooking. The closest Western equivalent is dry sherry, which many experienced connoisseurs of Chinese cooking deem to be superior. Japanese *sake* is also quite good for

Chinese cooking. Sherry or rice wine is used in marinades and in cooking, mostly for meat, fish, and fowl. Its foremost purpose is to eliminate rank flavours and unpleasant odours in animal foods, and secondly to tenderise the texture and facilitate the blending of flavours in the sauce.

Salt (yan): Salt is used in marinades to extract excess water or unwanted juices from fish, chicken, and vegetables. In cooking, it lends the basic salty flavour to foods, while balancing sweet flavours. Salt should be used sparingly in Chinese cooking, especially when large quantities of soy sauce, which is quite salty, are called for in the recipe.

Sugar (tang): The Chinese use sugar in the kitchen, but rarely on the dining table. White refined, raw, and rock crystal varieties are used. White refined sugar is used in most marinades and as a flavouring agent during cooking. It brings out the natural sweet flavours of all foods, including vegetables. Raw sugar is used for stews, sweet soups, and pastries. Rock crystal sugar appears in 'red-stews,' especially with pork knuckle spareribs and fish. Besides adding sweetness to the flavour, rock crystal sugar imparts a slightly viscous texture to the sauce and a bright sheen to the colour.

Sesame oil (ma-you): This is a highly aromatic condiment with a strong, smoky flavour. It should always be used sparingly. It is generally added to dishes at the last moment, and its purpose is both to add its smoky flavour and to suppress strong or rank tastes in certain foods, especially fish and fowl. It is a common ingredient in cold-plate dressings and table sauces used for dipping. A few drops dribbled onto prawns and fish while steaming eliminate the 'fishy' taste.

Garlic (suan), *ginger* (jiang), *spring onion* (cong), *and red chilli* (hong-la-jiao): In various proportions and combinations, these four items are the most common fresh seasonings in Chinese cooking. Hardly a dish in the vast repertoire of Chinese cuisine is prepared without at least one of these condiments. For sauces, dips, and sautés, they are finely minced; for stews they are roughly cut or bruised and removed after cooking. They intensify the 'fresh-natural' (xian) flavours and give pungency and piquance to the sauce. In larger quantities, they have a

tingling effect on the palate and improve the appetite. All are prominently listed in traditional Chinese herbal pharmacopeias and have important 'food-as-medicine' therapeutic uses. They also subdue rank flavours and offensive odours.

Vinegar (cu): Vinegar imparts the basic sour (*suan*) flavour to foods and sauces. It should be used sparingly at the last minute so that its piquant flavour is not lost in the heat of cooking. It is generally used with an equivalent amount of sugar, producing the renowned Chinese 'sweet-and-sour' flavour. Vinegar is used in most cold-plate dressings and table sauces, as well as in sautés and stews. The dark, smoky variety is most commonly used.

Below and right: *Prepared condiments in a Chinese grocery.*

Cornflour (chien-fen): Cornflour (Cornstarch) is used to control texture, not flavour. Added to marinades, it tenderises meat, fish, and fowl prior to cooking. A teaspoon or two dissolved in some cold water is added at the last minute to sautés, stews, or soups to thicken the sauce, bind the juices of meats to the condiments and oils, and lend a smooth and slippery texture to foods. Cornflour (Cornstarch) also makes the colours of foods shine. For tender, boned chicken and fish, cornflour (cornstarch) and egg white are used to marinate the diced meat before applying the bao-style sauté method: this forms a protective coating between the delicate meat and the scalding hot oil, ensuring a maximum tenderness and flavour inside and a golden-brown colour and slightly crisp texture outside.

A selection of Chinese condiments: Centre garlic, spring onion and red chilli. Clockwise from top *soy sauce; shrimp paste; Chinese pepper-salt and brown vinegar; mustard and chilli sauce; fermented beancurd.*

Fermented Bean Paste (dou-ban-jiang): This is a very commonly used cooking condiment in western/central-style cuisine. It consists of fermented beans and chilli sauce, at once pungent, piquant, and slightly sour. It is used in meat, fish, and fowl sautés and is added directly to the hot oil with the ingredients and other condiments.

Fermented Salted Black Beans (dou-shi): This is the classical Chinese condiment developed during the Han dynasty and popular in China ever since. It is fermented black beans packed in salt. The flavour is very salty, highly piquant, but not pungent. It is used to spice up sautés, and to add flavour and remove rankness from steamed fish.

Oyster Sauce (hao-you): Oyster sauce imparts a very rich taste to sautéd meats and vegetables. It enhances the 'fresh-natural' (*xian*) flavours of foods as well. It is most commonly used with beef and green, leafy vegetables.

Sesame Paste (zhi-ma-jiang): Chinese sesame paste is made from roasted rather than raw sesame seeds; it is dark in colour and smoky in flavour. Western-style blond sesame *tahini* may be substituted but is not as good. It is most commonly employed to make dressings for cold-plates and table sauces for dipping. It has a pleasant, nutty taste and is highly aromatic. You can make your own sesame powder by roasting plain sesame seeds in a dry wok with some salt until they turn golden-brown, then grinding them up with mortar and pestle or a food processor. This makes an excellent table condiment all by itself.

All of the condiments described above are generally available in Chinese and Japanese grocery stores the world over. China, Hong Kong, and Taiwan produce all of them for export to world markets.

A few practical words on the use of Chinese condiments are in order here. First of all, have everything conveniently arranged on a shelf or counter near the stove. Most condiments must be added at just the right time, a splash here and a dash there, and there is no time to rummage through your pantry or refrigerator while cooking. Second, original Chinese recipes never indicate

measures for seasonings, and it is important for the aspiring cook to develop the habit of 'free-pouring' from the very start. There are no correct or incorrect proportions for condiments in Chinese cooking, just the general goal of harmony and balance in the final product. How much of this or that seasoning you use depends entirely on the quantity of food being cooked and the type of flavour balance which appeals to you and your guests. Change the proportions and experiment with different combinations from time to time until you achieve an instinctive 'feel' for using Chinese condiments. It's easier than you think. The only prerequisites are a sufficient measure of self-confidence and the willingness to exercise one's creative culinary imagination.

Detailed information on all Chinese ingredients used in this book, their uses, how to store them and suggested substitutes can be found in the Glossary page 406.

CHINESE COOKING METHODS

Other than fresh fruits, the Chinese eat very little raw food. Almost everything in the Chinese diet is subjected to some degree of cooking, from a few seconds up to a full day. Over a dozen cooking techniques are distinguished by Chinese chefs, and many of them are used in sequence to prepare the final product for the table. The techniques chosen depend upon the nature of the foods to be cooked, the heat and time required for the cooking, considerations of flavour, fragrance, colour, and texture and the type of utensils available.

Three broad categories of cooking are used in the Chinese kitchen: cooking with oil, cooking with water, and cooking with neither oil nor water. Including the preparation of rice, stews, and soups as well as parboiling, par-steaming, and poaching techniques, cooking with water remains the single most commonly used category of cooking. Cooking with oil includes deep-frying, shallow-frying, sautéing, 'explode-frying,' and other oil-based methods. Cooking with neither oil nor water, which includes baking, roasting, and grilling/broiling, is far less common in Chinese cuisine, for applying fire directly to foods has always been considered a custom of the nomadic barbarians. Chinese chefs usually prefer to have an 'honourable intermediary' of oil or water between the food and the fire.

Chao, 'stir-fry,' 'sauté': This is the most popular method of cooking cai (food). Chao cooking is done in a wok with a very little oil over high heat with constant turning and turning. It seals in flavours and nutrients and preserves original textures. Since chao-cai (stir-fried dishes) cook quickly, they should be cooked last so they may be served fresh and piping hot.

Zheng, 'steam': Foods are placed on a rack in a closed container over boiling water and cooked by intense, concentrated, moist heat. Multi-tiered bamboo or metal steamers are the right tool. Cooking times range anywhere from 15 minutes to 5 hours or more. Steaming is often used to cook seafood and poultry as well as a wide variety of snacks and pastries.

Hong-shao, 'red-stew,' 'red-braise': This is a uniquely Chinese cooking method which derives its name from the characteristically reddish-brown colour a stew gets from soy sauce and sugar, the primary condiments. Either water or stock is used as a base and Hong-shai-cai (red-stewed foods) have a rich, sweet-and-salty flavour, reddish-brown colour, and smooth, slippery texture. Meat, fish, and fowl are the major ingredients, followed by hard vegetables such as carrots or potatoes. Cooking times range from 1 to 6 hours, depending on the type of ingredient used. Like spaghetti sauce and other Western stews, red-stews many connoisseurs claim, taste even better after a night or two in the refrigerator.

Zhu, 'boil': Other than cooking rice and soups, boiling is primarily a preparatory method applied to foods prior to the final cooking process. This parboiling (blanching) is often applied to vegetables and is followed by cold rinsing to set the colours and textures. Intense but brief boiling in a covered vessel is used to cook prawns, squid, and other types of seafood when they are to be served plain with a variety of table sauces for dipping.

Zha, 'deep-fry': Cooking in a large quantity of hot vegetable oil or sometimes lard. The zha method is often the last step in cooking, after pre-steaming or simmering. Such dishes are called ziang-su, 'fragrant-crispy.' Zha-

cai (deep-fried foods) should be crispy and dry on the outside and tender and juicy on the inside. Cooking times vary; the general indicators are a golden-brown colour and a puffy appearance.

Jian, 'shallow-fry': This method is done in a flat pan; the ordinary Western cast-iron frying pan (skillet) is best, with a thin layer of oil on the bottom. Medium heat is used and ingredients are spread evenly across the surface and turned occasionally. 'Potsticker' dumplings are also made this way, with a splash of water and a tight lid added at the last moment to produce a steam.

Men, 'simmer': This method is similar to hong-shao, but it does not necessarily use soy sauce or sugar. It is applied to foods which require long cooking times, such as tendon, ligament, pork knuckle, whole joints of meat, etc. It is important to keep the pot tightly covered with the flame very low. This ensures that the cooking liquid remains perfectly clear. 'Sand pot' casseroles are best for this kind of cooking.

Kao, 'roast,' 'bake,' 'grill/broil': In China, kao-cai (roasted foods) are usually prepared in specialty shops or restaurants since most household kitchens are not equipped with the necessary ovens and grills. Roasting and baking are done in brick and clay ovens of the Indian 'tandoor' kind over open charcoal or wood fires. Roasted meats are hung inside on metal hooks, baked breads stuck to the inside of the oven. Grilled/broiled foods are cooked on iron grills over charcoal fires. Happily, most Western kitchens are ideally equipped for cooking all sorts of roasted, baked, and grilled/broiled Chinese foods with excellent results. Besides, as the Chinese themselves admit, barbarians are best at roasting and grilling/broiling meats. Foods are usually marinated first and then basted with the remaining marinade throughout the cooking process.

Xun, 'smoke': Smoke is applied to meat, fish, and fowl. Smokehouses are ideal for large quantities of meat, but single cuts or smaller fish and fowl may be smoked in the kitchen in an old iron wok or cooking pot, or even in the oven. Tea leaves, fragrant wood shavings, sugar, and orange peel provide the smoke-fuel which imparts its fragrant

essences to the food. Smoked foods are usually submitted to additional cooking processes before or after the smoking.

Liang-ban 'cold-mix': This is the Chinese version of the mixed salad or cold-cut plate, except that Chinese liang-ban are far more complex, varied, and spicy than their Western equivalents. The main ingredients are usually blanched, poached, or steamed and then chilled prior to mixing. Rich and piquant dressings of soy sauce, sesame oil, vinegar, garlic, ginger, sugar, and other condiments are added and stirred in just before serving. Chicken, kidneys, seafoods, cold meats, and all sorts of vegetables readily lend themselves to this form of cai (dish).

Speed and a hot wok are the keys to stir-frying above. Below, *left deep frying, and* right *a specialty shop displays its succulent roasted ducks.*

Detailed information on Chinese cooking processes and techniques is included in Chapter XI, Preparation and Cooking Techniques.

CREATIVE IMPROVISATION IN CHINESE COOKING

The foregoing information on utensils, preparations, condiments, and methods should serve as a general guide to Chinese cooking techniques. Exact proportions of condiments and combinations of methods actually used, however, must ultimately be determined by the cook and may well vary each

time a dish is prepared. The possibilities are infinite. The key to learning Chinese cooking is not to memorise individual recipes but rather to master the underlying concepts and the common techniques. The opposite case is true in Western cooking, in which exact recipe proportions and cooking times must be followed, but cooking concepts and methods are relatively easy and require little attention. To acquire the 'magic touch' and precision timing, you must exercise your imagination and constantly practise your skills. Chinese cooking brings out the creative cook in all of us and is never boring.

One of the best opportunities for creativity in Chinese cooking is substitution. Many common condiments may be used as replacements: in the West, sherry is a common, if not superior, substitute for rice wine; if you run out of soy sauce, try a bit of Worcestershire sauce instead; substitute some of the many spicy vinegars available in the West for Chinese vinegar in various dishes. The wok may be used as a steamer, stewer, deep-fryer, boiler, or smoker in the absence of specialised vessels. Main ingredients are as flexible as condiments and utensils: apply your favourite recipes to a wide range of ingredients, not just the ones specified in the recipes. For example, if you try a pork recipe but really prefer the taste of beef, use beef the next time. If carp is offensive to your palate or unavailable in your town, try the same recipe with trout instead. The opportunities for exercising creative imagination in Chinese cooking are endless. One of the drawbacks of Western-style cooking is that it is too rigid and repetitive to sustain interest and thus becomes boring after a while. In Chinese-style cooking, each and every trip to the kitchen is an opportunity to try something new, to exercise your culinary imagination, and to create better and different versions of your favourite dishes.

We recommend that newcomers to Chinese cooking begin with the most basic methods and recipes and gradually work into the more complex. To aid in the selection of dishes for menus from simple through more complex to quite intricate and exotic, we have grouped these recipes into three sections of varying complexity, see page 413, Guide to Recipes. When self-confidence and familiarity with techniques develop, try a few of the more complex recipes, using costly ingredients and multiple-cooking methods.

Meanwhile, continue to experiment with, improvise, and improve the basic recipes you've already mastered.

Don't over-extend yourself when cooking a Chinese meal. As Yuan Mei stated in *The Menu*, even a great cook is hard-pressed to successfully produce more than four dishes for a single meal. Should you wish to prepare a 12-course Chinese banquet for your friends, recruit two more cooks and assign each person four specific dishes. Do not help each other, for too many cooks spoil the broth, especially when the broth is Chinese. The best way is for each cook to prepare the few dishes at which he or she excels.

Create your own original menus, always bearing in mind the basic principles of balance and harmony. You might select a chicken, a fish, a beef, and a vegetable dish. Based on cooking methods and textures, your menu might include a crispy, deep-fried dish, a fluffy steamed dish, a smooth stew, and a tender, slippery sautéd dish. Creative flavour balancing might result in a menu of pungent, sour, salty, and sweet dishes. Colour considerations could lead to a menu of green, leafy vegetables, a steamed white fish, a red-stew, and a multi-coloured sauté. Once again, the combinations are endless, the senses play vital roles, and creative improvisation is the key.

While the ingredients, condiments, utensils, and methods used in Chinese cooking are highly flexible, the basic principles are inviolate and must always be followed faithfully. Naturalness must never be sacrificed: select fresh ingredients in season as much as possible, and apply cooking methods and condiments which are naturally suited to them. One of the fundamentals of Chinese cuisine is the medical aspect, the basic principles of which have long influenced cooking in China. The ingredients and procedures which comprise each recipe have undergone centuries of evolution based on medical principles. For those interested in further pursuing this subject, a fascinating new area of creative improvisation in Chinese cooking awaits you: ingredients and dishes may be selected for their pharmacodynamics and suited to the season, the weather, and your own health. Above all, always bear in mind the key words to Chinese cuisine: balance and harmony.

CHAPTER III
Northern Style Cuisine

Northern Chinese winters are long and cold, reducing the variety of available culinary ingredients. The lake of the Summer Palace previous page *outside Peking freezes over in winter, but still provides fresh-water fish to nearby restaurants.*

The Great Wall of China above *historically separated the civilized Middle Kingdom from nomadic barbarian tribes such as the Mongols, who nevertheless taught the Chinese to eat mutton and to barbecue meats.*

Northern-style cuisine embraces the geographical areas of China which lie north of the Yangtze River and includes three of the nine distinct regional styles recognised in China today: Peking (Beijing), Shantung (Shandong), and Anhwei (Anhui). The cooking of Honan also falls into this regional category. The entire northern region is relatively dry and arid compared to the rest of China, and this has severely limited the variety of ingredients available for cooking. Dusty, biting winds from Mongolia pervade the northernmost parts of the area, especially around Peking (Beijing), and the winters are long and cold.

Peking (Beijing) has been the capital of China since the Mongols established it as such in the 13th century. Therefore, despite the paucity of food produced locally, Peking (Beijing) has generally had abundant supplies of the best food products from every province of China, and this remains true today. Excellent regional restaurants have been in operation in Peking (Beijing) for centuries. In this section, however, we deal only with the nature of the foods indigenous to the region.

Shantung (Shandong) and Anhwei (Anhui) are among China's oldest provinces. Shantung (Shandong) was the birthplace of Confucius, and Anhui gave birth to several founding emperors of Chinese dynasties. Despite their rich cultural and historical heritages, however, these two provinces have remained relatively poor in terms of agriculture. The climate and topography are not suitable for the cultivation of the wide range of food crops required to support an elaborate gourmet cuisine. Northern gourmet cuisine relies heavily on foods brought in from other provinces.

The most distinctive feature native to northern cuisine is the fan: wheat and millet, not rice, are the staple foundations of the northern diet. It is too cold and dry to grow rice, which must be brought in from the warm, lush southern regions. Millet is perhaps the oldest of all foods in China, pre-dating both rice and wheat. The most common preparation is millet-gruel, a hearty, warming dish most suitable for winter consumption. Taken with a few side-dishes such as dried beancurd, salt-fish, beans, and pickled vegetables, millet-gruel makes a complete and satisfying winter meal.

Wheat has been popular in the north ever since the Han dynasty, when the arts of milling flour and baking breads were first introduced to China. Steamed and baked buns, noodles of every type, dumplings, rolls, and other wheat-derived foods are common fare in the north, while rice has generally been regarded as a luxury there. Two wheat-based foods which are original innovations of the Peking (Beijing) kitchen are *jiao-zi* (stuffed dumplings) and *chun-juan* (spring rolls), both of which may be stuffed with a wide variety of different fillings, depending on what's available.

As for *cai*, the northern menu is the briefest, simply because locally produced ingredients are limited. The classic dish associated with the capital city is Peking (Beijing) Duck, a truly original and delicious northern innovation. This is served with three very typical northern items: wheat crepes in which to wrap the tender meat and crispy skin; sliced spring onions, a favourite northern condiment; and fermented sweet flour paste, also native to the north. The preparation of Peking (Beijing) Duck is a long, involved process and is usually handled by specialty restaurants. However, with a good oven, this dish may also be prepared at home.

Mongolian Barbecue and Mongolian Fire-Pot are two other world-famous foods of northern China, and their origins provide an excellent example of how the Chinese have managed to adapt barbarian innovations to suit their own refined culinary requirements. The Mongols were a primitive people with simple customs, but they just happened to be neighbours of the world's most cultured, civilised society. After a hard day of fighting or hunting on the steppes, Mongol horsemen would gather in camps at night to eat. Animals hunted or slaughtered that day were cleaned and the raw meat cut up. Wild onions, garlic, and other edible herbs and vegetables gathered on the steppes were also chopped up. The only remaining problem was how to cook them, and here the Mongols must be credited with an original idea: they placed their sturdy iron shields, which protected them from enemy arrows and lances by day, over hot coal fires until they became smoking hot. Then the meat and vegetables were dumped onto the hot metal surface, stirred around until cooked, and removed. Mongolian Fire-Pot has similar origins, except instead of using shields, the diners used their

From the fields to the markets, timeless traditional ways still mark China's agricultural life, and manpower remains the primary source of energy.

metal helmets. Water was brought to boil in the helmets, and each diner could cook his own meat and wild vegetables in the boiling liquid. When everyone was finished, the rich broth in the helmet was drunk as a final course.

The Chinese were familiar with this barbaric manner of eating, and after the Mongol occupation of China in the 13th century, Chinese chefs embellished it, civilised it, and renamed it Peking (Beijing) Barbecue. Custom-designed iron griddles and brass cooking pots replaced the shields and helmets of the steppes, and the variety of meats and vegetables used increased many-fold. More important, a wide range of fragrant, flavourful condiments was added to the meal, so that each diner could create his own blend of ingredients to suit his own palate. Today, Mongolian or Peking (Beijing) Barbecue and Hot-Pot are among the most popular of all Chinese specialty foods throughout the Far East. Both are quint-essentially northern contributions to the Chinese menu and are readily adaptable to Western kitchens and ingredients. Ingredients and condiments for these meals are highly flexible, and the host has ample opportunity to exercise his culinary imagination in preparing them. These meals are invariably a big hit at parties because they permit each individual guest to vary the blend of flavours and control the cooking times himself. Recipes for Mongolian Barbecue and Hot-Pot are included in the recipe section.

41

Other *cai* commonly consumed in the north are made from mutton, freshwater fish, and chicken. Mutton is very popular due to the influence of northern nomads as well as large Moslem minorities living there. Moslem restaurants specialising in mutton dishes are still among the most popular in Peking (Beijing) today. Various breeds of fish from rivers and lakes are highly favoured when available: Mandarin fish is particularly popular. Chicken and ducks are raised for food on farms. From the vegetable world, the selection in the north is quite limited due to climatic and geographical conditions. The most common vegetables are those of the cabbage, turnip, and onion families.

The most popular condiments in the north are garlic, spring onions, and ginger. Chillies are not so highly favoured as elsewhere in China. Northerners like their food to have *xien* ('fresh-natural') flavours but shy away from excessively pungent tastes. Soy sauce, wine, sesame oil, sesame paste, and fermented sweet flour paste are other commonly employed cooking condiments in the northern kitchen.

Steaming (*zheng*), baking (*kao*), and 'explode-frying' (*bao*) are the most popular cooking methods in the north. Steaming is applied primarily to the many varieties of wheat-derived foods, such as buns and dumplings. It has already been noted that *kao*, which includes the techniques of baking, grilling, and roasting, is the least commonly employed method in Chinese cooking because of its historical associations with the barbarians. It is more common in the north because contact with barbarian tribes has been most frequent there. These methods are used to bake breads, roast ducks and meats, and grill all sorts of meat and poultry.

Most northern *cai*, however, are cooked in the *bao* style. One reason for this is the scarcity of cooking fuel in the north: *bao* is by far the fastest cooking method in the Chinese repertoire, usually requiring only 30 — 90 seconds. Though *bao* cooking consumes more oil (5 — 6 oz.) than other sautés, the north has had sufficient supplies of oil-seed to support *bao* cooking ever since the introduction from the New World of the humble peanut, which thrives in the harsh northern environment. There are many varieties of *bao*-style cooking, including oil-*bao*, onion-*bao*, sauce-*bao*, and salt-*bao*. The main differences between them are the seasonings added and the order of preparatory and cooking processes.

Opposite page: *Panoramic view of the Summer Palace near Peking in winter. The 'Listening to Orioles Pavilion' there has been converted to an excellent northern Chinese restaurant.*

A reluctant chicken top *flies the coop in a public market in Peking.* Centre left: *Peking residents line up to purchase daily ration of meat; foreign guests* lower middle *dig into hearty winter lunch at 'Listening to Orioles Pavilion' at Summer Palace.* Middle right: *Typical 'masses restaurant' in Peking serves excellent northern food in no-frills atmosphere.*

Some use marinated raw ingredients, some require pre-cooking, but either way, the final cooking process involves dumping all the prepared ingredients into a bowl together with the condiments, then turning the entire contents into a wok with 5 — 6 oz of oil. The oil must be heated until it smokes over the highest possible flame before the ingredients are added. When they hit the scalding oil, it sounds like an explosion, hence the name 'explode-fry.' *Bao*-cooking locks original flavours inside of foods and keeps condiments coated on their outside surfaces, so that both fresh-natural and contrived flavours achieve a harmonious balance.

For Westerners, the most appealing features of northern-style Chinese cuisine are the relatively conventional ingredients and condiments and the relatively bland flavours. Of all Chinese foods, northern food strikes the most familiar note on the Western palate and is usually preferred by newcomers to China. The Chinese, on the other hand, generally regard northern-style food as simple and unsophisticated compared to the fancier southern styles. While northern food may be less fancy than southern styles, it is far more filling: you are unlikely to feel hungry again an hour later. From a nutritional standpoint, northern cooking styles are perhaps superior because they rely heavily on steam and *bao* techniques, both of which seal in nutrients. However, due to the relatively narrow range of ingredients, northern dishes probably do not provide as broad a balance of vital nutrients as the more diverse southern styles.

BRAISED SHARK'S FIN WITH PORK KNUCKLE AND CHICKEN

500 g (1 lb)	prepared shark's fin (see page 393), about 125 g (4 oz) dry weight
315 g (10 oz)	pork knuckle (hock/shank)
½ 1¼ kg (2½ lb)	chicken
4	dried scallops (about 30 g / 1 oz), soaked for 1 hour
2 cups (16 fl oz)	enriched stock
45 g (1½ oz)	Chinese or cured (Smithfield) ham
1 tablespoon	rendered chicken fat (chicken grease)
1 tablespoon	softened lard
1 tablespoon	frying or sesame oil
3 tablespoons	cornflour (cornstarch)
¼ cup (2 fl oz)	cold water

Seasoning:

1½ teaspoons	salt
1¼ teaspoons	m.s.g. (optional)
2 tablespoons	rice wine or dry sherry
2	spring onions (scallions), trimmed and sliced
4 thick slices	fresh ginger

Prepare the shark's fins according to the directions on page 393, allowing at least 4 hours. Drain well.

Blanch the pork knuckle and chicken in boiling water for 5 ·minutes. Drain well. Add the drained scallops to the water, simmer for 10 minutes, then drain.

Place the pork knuckle and chicken in a casserole and add the shark's fin, scallops, enriched stock, the ham and seasonings. Add water to cover and bring to the boil. Reduce the heat to simmer for about 2½ hours, skimming occasionally.

Remove the pork and chicken and debone. Shred the meat and place in a serving dish. Add the drained shark's fin. Thinly slice the ham and place on top of the fin. Discard the ginger and onion.

Bring the stock to the boil and add the fat, lard, and oil, then check the seasonings and thicken the sauce with a mixture of the cornflour and water. Simmer for 2 minutes, then pour over the shark's fin and serve.

SEA CUCUMBER IN BROWN SAUCE

3	prepared dried sea cucumbers (about 375 g / 12 oz, dry weight) (see page 392)
3	spring onions (scallions), trimmed and sliced
3 thick slices	fresh ginger
2½ tablespoons	softened lard or frying oil
2 cups (16 fl oz)	chicken stock
1 tablespoon	rendered chicken fat (chicken grease), optional
½ teaspoon	sesame oil
1½ tablespoons	cornflour (cornstarch)

Seasoning/Sauce:

¼ cup (2 fl oz)	dark soy sauce
1 tablespoon	rice wine or dry sherry
1 teaspoon	m.s.g. (optional)
1 teaspoon	sugar

Prepare the sea cucumber according to the directions on page 392 Drain and cut into pieces about 5 × 2 cm (2 × ¾ in).

Fry the spring onions and ginger in the lard or oil for 45 seconds. Remove. Add the sea cucumber and stir-fry for about 2 minutes on moderate heat, then add the seasoning/sauce ingredients and stir-fry on high heat for 30 seconds. Pour in the chicken stock, return the onions and ginger and bring to the boil.

Reduce the heat and simmer for 15 minutes, then add the rendered chicken fat, if used, and the sesame oil. Thicken with a thin paste of the cornflour and cold water and simmer until the sauce thickens.

Pour into a serving dish and serve hot.

Drunken Chicken (recipe page 48).

SMOKED CHICKEN

Serve hot or cold as an appetiser or main dish.

1 1¼ kg (2½ lb)	chicken
2 tablespoons	brown peppercorns
2 teaspoons	salt
1	spring onion (scallion), trimmed and halved
3 slices	fresh ginger
2	star anise
1	cinnamon stick
1 cup (8 fl oz)	light soy sauce
1 tablespoon	sesame oil, softened rendered chicken fat or lard

For smoking:

½ cup	sugar
⅓ cup	flour
½ cup	black tea leaves

Clean the chicken, wash in cold water and wipe dry. Dry-fry the peppercorns in a wok until fragrant, remove and grind to a fine powder, then reheat with the salt, taking care not to burn. Rub the spiced salt thoroughly over the chicken and pour the remainder into the cavity.

Bring a large saucepan of water to the boil and add the spring onion, ginger, star anise, cinnamon stick, and soy sauce. Put in the chicken and simmer on low heat for 10 minutes, turning once. Remove from the heat, cover the pan with a thick towel, and leave the chicken to gently poach in the hot liquid for a further 30 minutes.

Place the smoking ingredients in a large old iron wok or saucepan and set a rack over them. Lift out the chicken and drain well. Set on the rack. Heat until the ingredients begin to smoke, then cover tightly and smoke on moderate heat for about 7 minutes. Turn the chicken, decrease the heat and smoke for a further 6 minutes.

Remove, brush with sesame oil and cut into bite-sized pieces. Serve hot or prepare in advance and chill thoroughly before serving.

Use also for dishes requiring smoked chicken, see following (Crisp-Fried Shredded Smoked Chicken).

JELLIED CHICKEN

Serve as an appetiser or main dish.

1 kg (2 lb)	chicken pieces
185 g (6 oz)	pork rind (skin)*
2	spring onions (scallions), trimmed and cut in halves
3 slices	fresh ginger
1	star anise
5 cups (1¼ litres)	water
1 tablespoon	chopped fresh coriander (optional)
1 tablespoon	chopped cooked ham (optional)

Seasoning:

⅓ cup	light soy sauce
1 teaspoon	dark soy sauce
1 tablespoon	rice wine or dry sherry
1 teaspoon	salt
2 teaspoons	sugar

Debone the chicken and cut into cubes. Cut the pork rind into several pieces. Place the chicken and pork rind in a saucepan and cover with boiling water. Leave for 2 minutes, then drain well. Scrape any fat from the pork skin and return to the saucepan with the chicken.

Add the spring onions, ginger, star anise, and water, then stir in the seasoning ingredients and bring to the boil. Simmer on low heat until the liquid is reduced to about 1½ cups (12 fl oz). Remove the chicken and pork skin. Cut the pork skin into very small squares and return to the saucepan. Simmer for a further 30 minutes.

Return the chicken and simmer together for about 10 minutes, then transfer the lot to a greased baking tin and add the fresh coriander and ham, if used. Stir in lightly and leave to set, then refrigerate until firm.

Slice to serve.

* If preferred, use unflavoured gelatine in place of the pork rind. Cook chicken as outlined above and reduce the liquid, then add 1 package of unflavoured gelatine, dissolved in ½ cup of boiling water. Cook for 10 minutes, then leave to cool and set.

CRISP-FRIED SHREDDED SMOKED CHICKEN

½	smoked chicken (see previous recipe, Smoked Chicken)
2½ tablespoons	sweet bean paste
1¼ teaspoons	spiced salt
1½ teaspoons	caster sugar
2 tablespoons	cornflour (cornstarch)
4 cups (1 litre)	deep-frying oil

Debone the chicken and tear the meat into slivers along the grain. Mix with the sweet bean paste, spiced salt, and sugar and leave for 20 minutes. Add the cornflour and mix well.

Heat the deep-frying oil to smoking point. Reduce the heat slightly and deep-fry the chicken in a frying basket until crisp and golden. Drain well.

Pile onto a serving plate and surround with sprigs of fresh coriander. Serve with extra spiced salt (see page 384) and light soy sauce as dips.

CHICKEN IN SWEET WINE

1 1¼ kg (2½ lb)	chicken
2/3 cup	ginger wine, see page 387
185 g (6 oz)	lean pork
20 g (¾ oz)	dried 'wood ear' fungus, soaked for 25 minutes
4 5cm (2 in) pieces	fresh ginger, peeled
3 cloves	garlic
2	spring onions (scallions), trimmed and sliced
2½ tablespoons	softened lard or frying oil

Seasoning A:

1 teaspoon	light soy sauce
1 teaspoon	rice wine or dry sherry
1 teaspoon	cornflour (cornstarch)

Seasoning B:

3 cups (24 fl oz)	sweet rice wine or Japanese mirin*
1 cup (8 fl oz)	rice wine or dry sherry
1½ teaspoons	salt
1½ teaspoons	sugar

Clean and dress the chicken. Cut into large pieces. Place in a dish and pour on the ginger wine. Leave for 30 minutes, turning occasionally. Drain, reserving the wine.

Cut the pork into thin slices and place in a dish with the seasoning A ingredients. Leave for 25 minutes. Cut the 'wood ears' into bite-sized pieces. Cut the ginger into smaller pieces and bruise with the handle of a cleaver.

Heat the wok and sauté the ginger, garlic, and spring onions in the lard or oil over moderate heat. Add the chicken pieces and sauté until lightly coloured, about 5 minutes. Pour in the pre-mixed seasoning B ingredients and the reserved ginger wine and bring to the boil. Cover, reduce heat and simmer for 15 minutes, then add the 'wood ears' and pork and simmer until tender.

Transfer to a deep serving dish and serve in the sauce.

* Or use sweet or cream sherry.

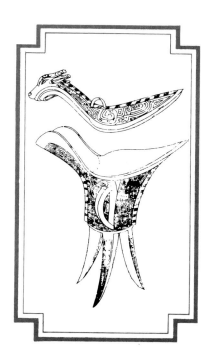

DRUNKEN CHICKEN

Serve cold as an appetiser or main dish.

½ 1¼ kg (2½ lb)   chicken
1 teaspoon   salt
2½ teaspoons   sugar
½ teaspoon   m.s.g. (optional)
1¼ cups (10 fl
oz)   rice wine*
2 tablespoons   frying oil
                   fresh coriander

Wash the chicken and place in a saucepan. Cover with boiling water and bring to the boil. Reduce the heat and simmer, tightly covered, for about 20 minutes.

Drain the chicken and place in a dish. Mix the remaining ingredients, except the coriander and pour over the chicken. Cover with plastic wrap and leave overnight to marinate. Garnish with fresh coriander and serve cold.

* The yellow *Shao Hsing* wine is usually used. The dish has a strong flavour of wine and therefore a good quality wine should be used. Japanese *mirin,* not unlike a sweet sherry, is ideal. If using this, use less sugar.

CHICKEN *'TEH-CHOW'* STYLE

1 1¼ kg (2½ lb)   chicken
2 tablespoons   malt sugar
¼ cup (2 fl oz)   boiling water
8 cups (2 litres) deep-frying oil
1 tablespoon   sesame oil

Seasoning/Sauce:
5 cups (1¼
litres)   chicken stock
¾ cup (6 fl oz)   light soy sauce
¾ cup (6 fl oz)   rice wine or dry sherry
1½ teaspoons   salt
¾ teaspoon   m.s.g. (optional)
½ cup   sugar
2   spice bags

Clean and dress the chicken. Rinse and dry with kitchen paper. Mix the malt sugar and boiling water and pour evenly over the chicken. Tie a string under the wings and across the back and suspend the chicken in a well-ventilated place until the skin dries, about 6 hours.

Heat the deep-frying oil to moderately hot. Fry the chicken completely immersed until golden all over. Lift out and drain well. Leave to cool slightly.

Bring the seasoning/sauce ingredients to the boil and reduce to a simmer. Add the chicken, cover and simmer until cooked through and completely tender, about 1¾ hours. Remove, drain, and brush with sesame oil.

Cut into bite-sized pieces and arrange on a serving plate. Serve with dips of spiced salt (see page 384) and light soy sauce.

FRIED DICED CHICKED WITH SWEET BEAN PASTE

500 g (1 lb)   chicken pieces
2   eggs, well beaten
                   cornflour (cornstarch)
5 cups (1¼
litres)   deep-frying oil
2 tablespoons   sweet bean paste*
½ teaspoon   m.s.g. (optional)
1   large spring onion (scallion), trimmed and thinly sliced

Cut the chicken into bite-sized pieces through the bones. Dip into beaten egg, then coat thickly with cornflour.

Heat the deep-frying oil to smoking point and deep-fry the chicken pieces for about 2 minutes. Lift out and drain well. Pour off all but 2 tablespoons of the oil. Or if the wok is floury, pour off all the oil, wipe out the wok and return about 2 tablespoons of the oil.

Heat the oil and stir-fry the chicken briefly, then add the sweet bean paste, m.s.g., if used, and spring onion and stir-fry together on moderate heat until the chicken is cooked through and well glazed with the sauce and the spring onion is tender.

* Oyster sauce, hot bean paste, salted yellow beans, or hot black bean sauce can be used in place of the sweet bean paste, adding a little sugar to taste. Add diced drained water chestnuts for variety.

Three Courses of Peking Duck (recipe page 51).

CHICKEN WITH CRISP HOT PEPPERS AND ORANGE PEEL

375 g (12 oz)	boneless chicken
2	dried red chilli peppers
3 pieces	dried orange peel
3 cups (24 fl oz)	deep-frying oil
1 slice	fresh ginger
2	spring onions (scallions), trimmed and sliced

Seasoning A:

¼ teaspoon	salt
½ teaspoon	m.s.g. (optional)
½ teaspoon	rice wine or dry sherry
2 teaspoons	cornflour (cornstarch)

Seasoning B:

¼ teaspoon	salt
½ teaspoon	m.s.g. (optional)
1½ teaspoons	sugar
1 tablespoon	light soy sauce
½ teaspoon	white vinegar
½ teaspoon	sesame oil
1 tablespoon	water
½ teaspoon	cornflour (cornstarch)

Cut the chicken into small cubes and mix with the seasoning A ingredients. Marinate for 15 minutes. Cut the chillies into 3 — 4 pieces and the orange peel into 2 — 3 pieces.

Heat the deep-frying oil to moderately hot and fry the chillies and orange peel until both are dark brown. Remove and set aside. Add the chicken and fry until white and firm, about 1½ minutes. Remove. Pour off all but 2½ tablespoons of the oil and add the ginger and spring onions. Stir-fry briefly, then return the chillies, orange peel, and chicken and stir-fry together for 1 minute. Add the pre-mixed seasoning B ingredients and simmer until the chicken is well glazed with the sauce, then serve.

CHICKEN BRAISED WITH CHESTNUTS

625 g (1¼ lb)	chicken pieces
¼ cup (2 fl oz)	light soy sauce
5 cups (1¼ litres)	deep-frying oil
90 g (3 oz)	fresh chestnuts, blanched and peeled*
1½ tablespoons	finely chopped spring onion (Scallion)
1½ teaspoons	finely chopped fresh ginger
1 tablespoon	rice wine or dry sherry
1 teaspoon	rendered chicken fat (chicken grease) optional

Seasoning/Sauce:

1¼ cups (10 fl oz)	chicken stock
⅓ teaspoon	salt
⅓ teaspoon	m.s.g. (optional)
¼ teaspoon	ground black pepper
2 teaspoons	sugar

Cut the chicken into bite-sized pieces, cutting through the bones. Place in a dish with the soy sauce and leave for 10 minutes, then drain reserving the sauce. Heat the deep-frying oil to smoking point and deep-fry the drained chicken for 2 minutes. Drain well. Add the chestnuts and deep-fry for 2 minutes and drain.

Pour off all but 2 tablespoons of the oil and sauté the spring onion and ginger. Add the chicken and chestnuts and sizzle the wine onto the sides of the pan. Add the seasoning/sauce ingredients and bring to the boil. Simmer until the chicken and chestnuts are both tender, about 15 minutes. Add the chicken fat, if used, and serve.

* Chestnuts can also be purchased in dried or canned form. Dried chestnuts need to be soaked for about 20 minutes. Canned chestnuts should be drained and rinsed before using. Deep-fry, then add to the dish.

THREE COURSES OF PEKING DUCK

Dish 1:

1	*Peking duck, freshly roasted (see recipe, page 329)*
12	*steamed flower-shaped buns or 'Mandarin' pancakes (see recipes, page 372 and 373)*
1	*young leek or 6 spring onions (scallions), trimmed and sliced*
½ cup	*'duck' sauce (see page 385)*

Dish 2:

2 tablespoons	*softened lard or frying oil*
1 — 2	*fresh red chilli peppers, shredded*
125 g (4 oz)	*fresh bean sprouts**
1	*spring onion (scallion), trimmed and shredded*
¼ teaspoon	*grated fresh ginger*
½ teaspoon	*finely chopped garlic*
1 tablespoon	*rice wine or dry sherry*
½ teaspoon	*salt*
½ teaspoon	*m.s.g. (optional)*

Dish 3:

6 cups (1¼ litres)	*chicken stock*
2 tablespoons	*evaporated milk*
1	*spring onion (scallion), trimmed and sliced*
1 slice	*fresh ginger*
155 g (5 oz)	*young Chinese green vegetables, trimmed*
1¼ teaspoons	*salt*
½ teaspoon	*m.s.g. (optional)*
2 — 3 teaspoons	*rice wine or dry sherry*

First slice the crisp skin of the roasted duck into in bite-sized pieces and serve with the pancakes or buns, sauce and sliced leek or spring onion.

Slice off the meat and place the carcass in a soup pot with the dish 3 ingredients. Simmer for 15 minutes.

In the meantime, stir-fry the chilli, bean sprouts, or other vegetables, onion, ginger and garlic in the lard or oil for 1½ — 2 minutes. Add the sliced meat and stir-fry a further 1½ minutes, then sizzle the wine onto the sides of the pan and add the salt and m.s.g, if used. Serve with steamed white rice.

Check the seasoning of the soup, lift out the carcass, and scrape the meat into the soup. Pour into a tureen and serve as the last course.

DUCK FAT IN STEAMED EGG CUSTARD

185 g (6 oz)	*fresh duck fat, minced (ground)*
3	*whole eggs, well beaten*
1 cup (8 fl oz)	*chicken stock*
1¼ teaspoons	*salt*
½ teaspoon	*m.s.g. (optional)*
1¼ tablespoons	*cornflour (cornstarch)*
2 tablespoons	*finely chopped spring onion (scallion)*

Mix all the ingredients except the spring onion and pour into a dish. Set on a rack in a steamer and steam over rapidly boiling water for 5 minutes. Remove the lid of the steamer for a few seconds to release the steam which will cause the custard to puff up unevenly. Re-cover and steam for a further 10 minutes or until the mixture is softly set.

Lift out and garnish the dish with the spring onion. Serve at once. If preferred, pour off any fat which has accumulated on top of the dish.

Fresh chicken fat can be used, but the flavour will be much less interesting.

CRISPY HOME-STYLE DUCK

1 2 kg (4 lb)	duck
2 tablespoons	Chinese brown peppercorns
2 tablespoons	table salt
2 tablespoons	finely chopped spring onion (scallion)
1 tablespoon	finely chopped fresh ginger
1 tablespoon	rice wine or dry sherry
1 tablespoon	dark soy sauce
	flour
8 cups (2 litres)	deep-frying oil
12	steamed flower-shaped buns or 'Mandarin' pancakes (see recipes page 372 and 373)

Clean and dress the duck. Fry the peppercorns in a dry wok for 2 minutes over moderate heat, then pour into a mortar and grind to a fine powder. Return to the wok and add the salt. Dry-fry together on moderate to low heat, stirring constantly to avoid burning, for 2 minutes.

Mix the spiced salt with the spring onion, ginger and wine and rub thoroughly over the duck, pour the remainder inside and leave for 2 hours.

Place the duck breast up in a large dish and set on a rack in a steamer. Steam over high heat until the duck is completely tender, about 3 hours. Remove and leave to cool, then brush with the soy sauce and coat lightly with flour.

Heat the deep-frying oil to smoking point and then reduce the heat slightly. Deep-fry the duck, completely immersed in the oil if possible, for 3 minutes. Lift out and reheat the oil, then deep-fry a further 3 minutes until the duck is very crisp and deeply coloured on the surface.

Serve with the buns or pancakes and with additional spiced salt (see page 384) as a dip. For a sweeter flavour, serve 'duck' sauce (see recipe, page 385) or plum sauce as an additional dip.

WHOLE BAKED FISH SERVED ON A HOT PLATE

1 1 kg (2 lb)	Hilsa herring (sea bass or snapper)
75 g (2½ oz)	'five flowered' pork (belly/fresh bacon)
5 cm (2 in) piece	fresh young leek, shredded
1	fresh red chilli pepper, shredded
4 thick slices	fresh ginger, shredded
6 sprigs	fresh coriander
2 tablespoons	frying oil

Seasoning A:

¾ teaspoon	salt
½ teaspoon	m.s.g. (optional)
1 tablespoon	rice wine or dry sherry
2 teaspoons	sesame oil
1 tablespoon	frying oil
1¾ teaspoons	five spice powder

Seasoning B/Sauce:

¼ cup (2 fl oz)	chicken stock
1½ tablespoons	rice wine or dry sherry
¼ cup (2 fl oz)	light soy sauce
2 teaspoons	dark soy sauce
1 tablespoon	sugar
½ teaspoon	salt
2 tablespoons	frying oil

Cut the fish in halves lengthways, cutting right through the head, but do not sever along the top of the back, so the fish can be pressed out flat in one piece. Trim away the backbone. Leave the skin and scales intact. Place the fish in a large dish and cover with boiling water. Leave for 2 minutes, then drain well. Rub on both sides with the seasoning A ingredients and leave for 25 minutes.

Heat a baking pan or large ovenproof dish and add the frying oil. Spread the fish, scales upwards, on the tray and arrange the shredded ingredients on top. Bake in a preheated moderately hot oven at 220°C (425°F) for about 30 minutes. Put a metal serving tray, preferably one with a sturdy wooden detachable base, in the oven while the fish is cooking so it heats through thoroughly.

Drain the pan juices into a wok and return the fish to the oven. Heat the wok and add the seasoning B/sauce ingredients. Bring to the boil and check the seasoning.

Remove the fish and the heated tray from the oven. Use two large spatulas or egg lifters to transfer the fish to the hot serving tray. Pour on the piping hot sauce and carry sizzling to the table.

Whole Baked Fish Served on a Hot Plate (recipe this page).

STEAMED GOLDEN CARP

1 750 g (1½ lb)	golden carp (or fresh water trout)
30 g (1 oz)	Chinese or cured (Smithfield) ham
4	dried black mushrooms, soaked for 25 minutes
30 g (1 oz)	canned bamboo shoots, drained
1	spring onion (scallion), trimmed and shredded
3 slices	fresh ginger, shredded
90 g (3 oz)	pork omentum, or use 3 slices streaky bacon
¼ cup (2 fl oz)	chicken stock
¼ cup (2 fl oz)	frying oil

Seasoning:

1¼ teaspoons	salt
½ teaspoon	m.s.g. (optional)
½ teaspoon	sugar
2 teaspoons	rice wine or dry sherry
1 tablespoon	softened lard

Clean the carp and score diagonally on one side at 2 cm (¾ in) intervals. Cut the ham into slices. Drain the mushrooms and remove the stems. Cut the caps in halves. Thinly slice the bamboo shoots.

Place the fish on an oiled plate, score side upwards. Insert the slices of ham, mushroom halves, and bamboo shoot slices in alternate rows in the cuts. Arrange the spring onion and ginger on top of the fish and sprinkle the seasonings evenly over it.

Place the pork omentum, if used, on top or arrange the streaky bacon so that it covers as much of the fish as possible. Pour on the chicken stock, then set the plate on a rack in a steamer and steam over high heat for about 20 minutes.

Test if the fish is done by pushing a fork into the thickest part. If the meat lifts cleanly from the bones it is ready. Lift out the plate. Remove the bacon or pork fat and discard.

Strain the liquid into a wok and bring to the boil. Adjust seasoning to taste and thicken slightly, if preferred, with a thin solution of cornflour (cornstarch) and cold water. Pour over the fish.

Heat the frying oil to smoking point and pour quickly over the fish. Serve at once.

FRIED YELLOW FISH WITH GARLIC CHIVES

1 750 g (1½ lb)	yellow fish (trout or grouper)
1 teaspoon	salt
	flour
2	eggs, beaten
8 cups (2 litres)	deep-frying oil
5 cm (2 in) piece	fresh ginger, peeled
10	garlic chives, shredded (or use 4 — 5 spring onions/scallions)
1 tablespoon	sesame oil
1 teaspoon	salt
2 teaspoons	rice wine or dry sherry
	vinegar and ginger dip

Clean the fish and score diagonally on both sides, cutting almost to the bones. Rub with the salt, then coat lightly with flour and brush with beaten egg. Coat with the flour again and set aside.

Heat a large wok and rub vigorously with the piece of ginger to prevent the fish from sticking. Add the deep-frying oil and heat to smoking point. Carefully slide in the fish, holding it by its tail. Cook for 1 minute, then turn and cook the other side for 1 minute. Turn again and cook for 4 minutes on one side, then 4 minutes on the other side. Decrease the heat after the first side has cooked for about 2 minutes.

Lift out the fish on two spatulas and place it on a serving dish. Drain off the oil and wipe out the wok. Return about 3 tablespoons of the oil and fry the shredded garlic chives or spring onion until softened. Add the sesame oil, salt, and wine and stir in.

Pour over the fish and serve at once with small dishes of vinegar and ginger dip (see page 384).

'BULLFROG' SILVER CARP

1 1 kg (2 lb)	silver carp (trout, bream, or snapper)
8 cups (2 litres)	deep-frying oil
	cornflour (cornstarch)
2	spring onions (scallions), trimmed and shredded
2 thick slices	fresh ginger, shredded
	extra shredded spring onion (scallion) and ginger

Seasoning:

1	egg white, beaten
½ teaspoon	salt
¼ teaspoon	m.s.g. (optional)
1 tablespoon	rice wine or dry sherry
¼ teaspoon	white pepper
1 tablespoon	cornflour (cornstarch)

Sauce:

½ cup (4 fl oz)	chicken stock
⅓ teaspoon	salt
½ teaspoon	m.s.g. (optional)
¼ teaspoon	white pepper
1 teaspoon	rice wine or dry sherry
1 teaspoon	cornflour (cornstarch)

Clean and scale the fish and cut in halves along the backbone. Remove the backbone entirely, but keep the tail fin attached to the fillets. Cut off the head and cut open from the underside so it can be pressed out flat. Separate the fillets by cutting the tail in halves in the centre, then trim each part 'vandyke' style into two points to resemble the original tail.

Turn the fillets meat side up on a board and use a sharp paring knife to score right to the skin without piercing it, in a criss-cross pattern. Run the fingers from tail to top several times to make the points created by the scoring stand up. Mix the seasoning ingredients and pour over the fish. Leave for 10 minutes.

Heat the deep-frying oil to fairly hot. Coat the fillets with cornflour and deep-fry until cooked through and golden on the surface, about 3 minutes. Remove and drain well. Crisp-fry the head in the deep-frying oil and set on a plate to resemble a bullfrog head. Place the fillets with the points upwards on the plate so that the centre parts of the fillets curve outward giving the appearance of a jumping frog.

Pour off the oil from the wok, wipe out and return 2 tablespoons. Stir-fry the spring onion and ginger for 45 seconds, then add the pre-mixed sauce ingredients and simmer until thickened. Pour over the fish and garnish the dish with the extra shredded spring onion and ginger.

YELLOW CROAKER WITH PINE SEEDS

1 750 g (1½ lb)	yellow croaker (or fresh trout or perch)
45 g (1½ oz)	pine seeds*
3 cups (24 fl oz)	frying oil
3	dried black mushrooms, soaked for 25 minutes
30 g (1 oz)	canned bamboo shoots, drained
2	spring onions (scallions), trimmed

Seasoning A:

½ teaspoon	salt
2 teaspoons	rice wine or dry sherry
1 tablespoon	cornflour (cornstarch)

Seasoning B/Sauce:

2 tablespoons	cold water
1 tablespoon	light soy sauce
2 tablespoons	white vinegar
1 teaspoon	rice wine or dry sherry
¼ teaspoon	salt
¼ teaspoon	white pepper
1 teaspoon	cornflour (cornstarch)

Clean the fish and remove the head. Cut the fish from the underside to the back without cutting in halves. Remove the backbone by trimming the meat away all around, then press the two sides out flat. Turn the fish meat upwards on a board and score in a close criss-cross pattern, cutting down to the skin but not through it. Rub with the seasoning A ingredients and leave for 20 minutes.

Heat the frying oil and fry the pine seeds or other nuts until golden. Drain and set aside. Keep the oil warm. Squeeze the water from the mushrooms and cut the mushrooms, bamboo shoots and spring onions into small dice.

Reheat the oil to fairly hot and fry the fish, meat downwards, until crisp and golden, about 4 minutes. Remove and drain well. Place on a serving plate with the spikes facing upwards. Pour off all but 2 tablespoons of the oil and stir-fry the diced ingredients for 1 minute. Add the seasoning B/sauce ingredients, pre-mixed, and simmer until the sauce has thickened.

Pour over the fish and garnish with the fried pine seeds or nuts. Serve at once.
* Or use almonds, raw cashew nuts or walnuts, chopped.

FISH IN WINE SAUCE WITH 'WOOD EAR' FUNGUS

500 g (1 lb)	meaty white fish fillets
1	spring onion (scallion), trimmed and sliced
20 g (¾ oz)	dried 'wood ear' fungus, soaked for 25 minutes
3 cups (24 fl oz)	frying oil

Seasoning A:

1	egg white, beaten
½ teaspoon	salt
½ teaspoon	m.s.g. (optional)
2 teaspoons	ginger wine
1 tablespoon	cornflour (cornstarch)

Seasoning B/Sauce:

¾ cup (6 fl oz)	fish or chicken stock
2 tablespoons	sweet rice wine, Japanese mirin or sweet sherry
½ teaspoon	salt
¼ teaspoon	m.s.g. (optional)
¾ teaspoon	sugar
2 teaspoons	cornflour (cornstarch)

Cut the fish into thin slices and place in a dish with the seasoning A ingredients. Leave for 20 minutes, turning occasionally.

Heat about 2 tablespoons of the frying oil and stir-fry the spring onion briefly. Cut the 'wood ears' into bite-sized squares and add to the pan. Stir-fry for 45 seconds. Remove and set aside.

Wipe out the wok and add the frying oil. Heat to moderate, then add the fish in a frying basket and deep-fry until white and firm, 45 seconds to 1 minute. Remove and drain off all but 2 tablespoons of the oil.

Add the pre-mixed seasoning B/sauce ingredients and return the spring onions and 'wood ears.' Simmer for 1 minute, then add the sliced fish and heat through. Serve at once.

CURLED PRAWNS STEAMED WITH FIVE SHREDS

500 g (1 lb)	large green prawns (shrimps), in the shell
1	egg, well beaten
3	dried black mushrooms, soaked for 25 minutes
45 g (1½ oz)	canned bamboo shoots, drained and shredded
30 g (1 oz)	cooked ham, shredded
2	spring onions (scallions), trimmed and shredded

Seasoning:

⅓ teaspoon	salt
1 teaspoon	rice wine or dry sherry
1 teaspoon	cornflour (cornstarch)

Sauce:

½ cup (4 fl oz)	enriched or chicken stock
2 teaspoons	rice wine or dry sherry
1 teaspoon	sesame oil
½ teaspoon	salt
¼ teaspoon	m.s.g. (optional)
1 teaspoon	cornflour (cornstarch)

Peel the prawns leaving the tail section intact. Place the prawns in a dish with the seasoning ingredients and leave for 15 minutes. Reserve the heads.

Wipe out an omelette pan with an oiled cloth and heat to moderate. Pour in the beaten egg and tilt the pan to give a thin even coating. Cook until firm but not coloured underneath, turn and cook the other side. Remove and spread on a board to cool. Roll up and cut into narrow shreds.

Squeeze the water from the mushrooms and remove the stems. Shred the caps.

Cut down the centre backs of the prawns, cutting deep enough to allow the prawns to be pressed out flat. Remove the dark veins. Make a central slit and pass the tails through this so that the prawns are curled up.

Arrange the prawns with their heads in a dish and arrange the shredded ingredients on top. Set the dish on a rack in a steamer and steam over high heat for 5 minutes.

Remove from the steamer and drain any liquid into a wok. Add the pre-mixed sauce ingredients and bring to the boil. Simmer until the sauce thickens, then pour over the prawns and serve at once.

Curled Prawns Steamed with Five Shreds (recipe this page).

FISH MASQUERADING AS CRAB

An imaginative dish employing less expensive ingredients to give the appearance and taste of stir-fried fresh crabmeat.

125 g (4 oz)	white fish fillets, coarsely minced (ground)
2	dried scallops or 1 tablespoon dried shrimps, soaked for 1½ hours
6	egg whites, well beaten
1 teaspoon	finely chopped fresh ginger
1½ teaspoons	finely chopped spring onion (scallion)
30 g (1 oz)	cooked crabmeat (optional)
2 tablespoons	softened lard or frying oil
½ teaspoon	Chinese red vinegar
1	egg yolk (optional)

Seasoning A:

½ teaspoon	salt
½ teaspoon	m.s.g. (optional)
2 teaspoons	rice wine or dry sherry
½ teaspoon	white vinegar
1¼ tablespoons	cold water
2 teaspoons	cornflour (cornstarch)

Seasoning B:

2 tablespoons	liquid from soaked scallops or shrimps
1 teaspoon	rice wine or dry sherry
1 teaspoon	light soy sauce
¼ teaspoon	salt
¼ teaspoon	sugar
¾ teaspoon	cornflour (cornstarch)

Mix the fish with the seasoning A ingredients and leave for 20 minutes. Steam the dried scallops or shrimps in 2 tablespoons of water until soft, then drain, reserving the liquid. Flake the scallops by rubbing between forefinger and thumb or finely chop the shrimps.

Mix the fish, shrimps or scallops, beaten egg, ginger, onion, and crabmeat, if used. Heat the lard or oil to warm and add the mixture. Cook, stirring slowly, until just set, then pour in the pre-mixed seasoning B ingredients and continue to cook until the mixture is firm and a small amount of liquid remains in the pan.

Transfer the mock crabmeat to a serving dish, or serve in a well-washed crab or clam shell. Make a small depression in the centre. Drizzle in the red vinegar and add the egg yolk, if used. Stir lightly into the crabmeat to give the appearance of roe. Serve at once.

BRAISED PRAWNS

500 g (1 lb)	large green prawns (shrimps) in the shell
⅓ cup	melted lard or frying oil
2 tablespoons	finely chopped spring onion (scallion)
2 teaspoons	finely chopped fresh ginger
2 teaspoons	cornflour (cornstarch)

Seasoning/Sauce:

2/3 cup	chicken stock
1 tablespoon	rice wine or dry sherry
¼ teaspoon	salt
¼ teaspoon	m.s.g. (optional)
1½ teaspoons	sugar

Wash the prawns and cut open on the underside to allow the sauce to penetrate. Remove the legs. Heat the lard or oil to moderately hot and fry the prawns until red, about 1¾ minutes. Remove and keep warm.

Add the onions and ginger and stir-fry briefly, then add the seasoning/sauce ingredients and bring to the boil. Return the prawns, cover and simmer for 5 — 6 minutes until the prawns are cooked through. Mix the cornflour with a little cold water and stir into the sauce. Simmer until thickened then transfer to a serving plate.

For extra flavour, add 2 tablespoons of tomato sauce (ketchup) or sweet bean paste, or 1 tablespoon of hot bean paste.

PRAWNS PEKING STYLE

6	green prawn cutlets* (about 280 g/9 oz)
3	egg whites
2 tablespoons	cornflour (cornstarch)
2 teaspoons	flour
¼ teaspoon	salt
1 cup	dry breadcrumbs
	extra cornflour (cornstarch)
7 cups (1¾ litres)	deep-frying oil
	Chinese pepper-salt

Seasoning:

1 tablespoon	finely chopped spring onion
1 teaspoon	grated fresh ginger
1 teaspoon	rice wine or dry sherry
¼ teaspoon	salt

Rinse the prawn cutlets and wipe dry. Rub on the seasoning ingredients and leave for 15 minutes.

Beat the eggs to soft peaks and stir in the cornflour, flour, and salt lightly. Heat the deep-frying oil to moderately hot. Coat the cutlets lightly with cornflour, shaking off excess. Dip into the batter, then into breadcrumbs.

Cook 3 at a time in the oil until golden and cooked through, about 1¾ minutes. Drain well. Arrange on a paper napkin in a serving dish or basket and serve with dips of Chinese pepper-salt (see recipe, page 384).

* Prawns with heads and shells removed, with the tail section left intact and cut deeply down the back so they can be pressed out flat, 'butterfly' style.

PRAWNS IN SWEET WINE SAUCE WITH CHILLIES AND GARLIC

500 g (1 lb)	fresh green prawns (shrimps) in the shell
5 cups (1¼ litres)	deep-frying oil
5 cloves	garlic, sliced
1 slice	fresh ginger, shredded
1 — 2	fresh red chilli peppers, shredded
2	spring onions (scallions), trimmed and shredded

Batter:

1	whole egg, well beaten
⅓ cup	cornflour (cornstarch)
1 tablespoon	flour
¼ teaspoon	salt

Sauce:

¾ cup (6 fl oz)	chicken stock
2¾ tablespoons	sweet rice wine or Japanese mirin*
¾ teaspoon	salt
1½ teaspoons	sugar
2¼ teaspoons	cornflour (cornstarch)

Peel the prawns and cut in halves lengthways, devein and rinse in cold water. Dry on kitchen paper, then coat very lightly with cornflour.

Mix the batter ingredients together adding enough water to make a creamy batter.

Heat the deep-frying oil to moderate. Dip the prawns into the batter and deep-fry about 8 pieces at a time until cooked through, crisp and golden, about 1¼ minutes. Remove and drain well, then keep warm.

Pour off the oil and wipe out the wok. Return about 2½ tablespoons of the oil and add the garlic, ginger, chillies, and spring onions. Stir-fry for 45 seconds, then pour in the premixed sauce ingredients. Bring to the boil and simmer for 1½ minutes, or until the sauce has thickened.

Arrange the drained prawns on a serving plate and pour on the sauce. Serve at once. To make the prawns crisper, fry a second time in hot oil immediately before adding the sauce.

* Or use sweet or cream sherry.

CRISP-FRIED SHRIMPS WITH GARLIC AND CHILLI

625 g (1¼ lb)	raw shrimps, in the shell
6 cups (1½ litres)	deep-frying oil
2	spring onions (scallions), trimmed and diced
5 — 6 cloves	garlic, thinly sliced
1 — 2	fresh red chilli peppers, seeded and sliced
1 tablespoon	rice wine or dry sherry

Seasoning:

1 teaspoon	salt or Chinese pepper-salt
½ teaspoon	m.s.g. (optional)
¼ teaspoon	ground black pepper (omit if using pepper-salt)

Thoroughly wash the shrimps and wipe dry. Do not peel. Heat the deep-frying oil to fairly hot and fry the whole shrimps until they turn bright pink, about 35 seconds. Remove and drain.

Pour off all but 2½ tablespoons of the oil and stir-fry the spring onions, garlic, and chilli for 1 minute on moderate heat. Return the shrimps and stir-fry briefly, then sizzle the wine onto the sides of the pan and stir in.

Add the seasoning ingredients and mix well. Transfer to a serving plate.

The shrimps should be served in their shells, the intention being to first nibble the whole thing to extract the flavour and saltiness on the shell, then to remove the shell and eat the tender shrimps. They may, however, be cooked without the shells. In this instance, do not deep-fry but quickly sauté in shallow oil with the other ingredients and serve at once.

SHRIMPS, PORK, AND VEGETABLES IN TOMATO SAUCE ON CRISP RICE

185 g (6 oz)	small peeled raw shrimps
125 g (4 oz)	pork fillet (tenderloin)
90 g (3 oz)	canned water chestnuts or bamboo shoots, drained
6	dried black mushrooms, soaked for 25 minutes
3 tablespoons	cooked green peas
2 tablespoons	finely chopped spring onion (scallion)
¾ teaspoon	finely chopped fresh ginger
½ teaspoon	finely chopped garlic (optional)
10 pieces	crisp rice cakes (see page 417)
4 cups (1 litre)	deep-frying oil

Seasoning A:

½ teaspoon	salt
2 teaspoons	ginger wine, see page 387
2 teaspoons	cornflour (cornstarch)

Seasoning B:

1 tablespoon	light soy sauce
2 teaspoons	cornflour (cornstarch)

Sauce:

3 cups (24 fl oz)	chicken stock
½ cup (4 fl oz)	tomato sauce (ketchup)
2 tablespoons	frying oil
1 tablespoon	light soy sauce
1 tablespoon	white vinegar
1 teaspoon	sesame oil (optional)
1½ teaspoons	salt
2 teaspoons	sugar
½ teaspoon	m.s.g. (optional)
3 tablespoons	cornflour (cornstarch)

Wash the shrimps and dry well. Devein with a toothpick (see page 394), and place in a dish with the seasoning A ingredients. Leave for 10 minutes. Cut the pork into narrow shreds and mix with the seasoning B ingredients.

Cut the water chestnuts or bamboo shoots and the mushrooms into small dice and stir-fry in 2½ tablespoons of the deep-frying oil for 1 minute. Push to one side of the pan and add the spring onion, ginger, and garlic, if, used and stir-fry a further 30 seconds. Remove.

Add the shrimps and pork and stir-fry together in the remaining oil, adding a little more if needed. When lightly coloured, return the other fried ingredients and the sauce ingredients and bring to the boil.

In the meantime, heat the deep-frying oil to smoking hot. Place the rice cakes in a frying basket or strainer and dip into the hot oil. Fry until golden and crisp, then remove and drain well. Transfer to a deep serving dish.

When the sauce has thickened, check seasonings and pour over the rice cakes. Serve immediately, or if preferred take the rice cakes and sauce separately to the table. When the sauce is poured over the cakes, it should snap and crackle, so it is necessary to ensure that the rice cakes have been freshly fried and are still piping hot when served.

Pearls Hiding in a Crab (recipe page 63).

SAUTÉD SHRIMPS, SCALLOPS, AND ABALONE

125 g (4 oz)	raw peeled shrimps
125 g (4 oz)	fresh sea scallops, without shells
90 g (3 oz)	canned abalone, drained
1	small carrot, thinly sliced
30 g (1 oz)	canned bamboo shoots, drained and sliced
15 g (½ oz)	dried 'wood ear' fungus, soaked for 25 minutes*
2½ tablespoons	softened lard or frying oil

Seasoning A:

1	large egg white, beaten
¾ teaspoon	salt
2 teaspoons	rice wine or dry sherry
2 teaspoons	cornflour (cornstarch)

Seasoning B/Sauce:

2½ tablespoons	chicken stock
⅓ teaspoon	salt
¼ teaspoon	m.s.g. (optional)
2 teaspoons	rice wine or dry sherry
¼ teaspoon	sesame oil (optional)
⅓ teaspoon	cornflour (cornstarch)

Rinse the shrimps, devein with a toothpick (see page 394), and place in a dish with the scallops and the seasoning A ingredients. Leave for 15 minutes to marinate.

Thinly slice the abalone and soak in cold water.

Heat the frying oil in a wok and sauté the carrot, bamboo shoots, and 'wood ears' for 1½ minutes. Push to one side of the pan and add the shrimps and scallops. Sauté until the scallops turn white and firm and the shrimps pink, about 1¾ minutes. Add the seasoning B/sauce ingredients, pre-mixed, and the sliced abalone and stir in the vegetables.

Sauté together for a further 30 seconds, then serve.

* Or use canned straw mushrooms, sliced.

SALTED JELLYFISH AND SHRIMP SALAD

Serve cold as an appetiser or main dish.

310 g (10 oz)	prepared salted jellyfish
90 g (3 oz)	raw peeled shrimps*
1	small cucumber
4	garlic chives or 1 spring onion (scallion)

Seasoning:

1 cup (8 fl oz)	chicken stock
½ teaspoon	salt
¾ teaspoon	rice wine or dry sherry

Sauce:

2 tablespoons	sesame oil
2¼ tablespoons	white vinegar
2 teaspoons	rice wine or dry sherry
1½ teaspoons	salt
½ teaspoon	m.s.g. (optional)
1¼ teaspoons	sugar

Prepare the jellyfish according to the directions on page 392 and pile on a serving plate. Devein the shrimps with a toothpick (see page 394) and poach with the seasoning ingredients until pink and firm. Drain well. Peel the cucumber and cut into matchstick pieces, discarding the seeds. Shred the garlic chives or spring onion.

Mix the sauce ingredients together, beating until thoroughly amalgamated. Pile the shrimps, cucumber, and chives or onion onto the jellyfish and pour on the sauce. Stir in lightly with chopsticks and serve.

* Or substitute fresh squid cut into matchstick strips, or cooked chicken.

SHRIMP TOAST

Serve as an appetiser. Makes 12.

250 g (8 oz)	shrimp meat, finely minced (ground)
60 g (2 oz)	pork fat, finely minced (ground)
6 slices	fresh white bread
2	beaten eggs
1 teaspoon	black or white sesame seeds
1 tablespoon	finely chopped cooked ham (optional)
3 cups (24 fl oz)	deep-frying oil

Seasoning:

1	egg white, beaten
1 teaspoon	ginger wine, (see page 387)
¾ teaspoon	salt
1 tablespoon	cornflour (cornstarch)

Mince the shrimp and pork with a cleaver or food processor (see page 395). Mix with the seasoning ingredients and work until smooth and sticky, then cover with plastic wrap and refrigerate for 1 hour.

Remove crusts from the bread and cut each slice in halves. Brush one side with beaten egg and cover with a thick layer of the shrimp paste, smoothing around the edges. Brush with more beaten egg and decorate with sesame seeds and ham, if used.

Heat the deep-frying oil to moderately hot and fry the toasts, topping downwards, until golden and crisp. Drain well and serve with dips of Chinese pepper-salt or spiced salt (see page 384) and light soy sauce, or with sweet and sour sauce (see page 385).

PEARLS HIDING IN A CRAB

1 625 g (1¼ lb)	fresh crab
6	canned quail or pigeon eggs, drained
½ cup (4 fl oz)	chicken stock
1	egg white

Seasoning:

¾ teaspoon	salt
¼ teaspoon	m.s.g. (optional)
¼ teaspoon	white pepper
1 teaspoon	rice wine or dry sherry
2 teaspoons	cold water
2 teaspoons	cornflour (cornstarch)

Place the crab in a dish and steam over rapidly boiling water for 12 — 15 minutes. Lift out and leave until cool enough to handle, then remove the top shell and discard the inedible parts. Lift out the meat and flake finely. Clean the shell thoroughly, rubbing with salt. Rinse well.

Break open the legs and extract the meat, or leave intact to decorate the dish.

Place the quail eggs in a small saucepan with the stock and bring to the boil. Add the seasoning ingredients and simmer briefly, then add the flaked crabmeat and heat until the sauce thickens.

Place the lower part of the crab shell on a bed of shredded lettuce on a serving plate and arrange the legs in place around it. Pile the crab and egg mixture into the shell and set the top shell in place.

Beat the egg white until it forms soft peaks. Heat a small saucepan of slightly salted water to a rolling boil and add the beaten egg. Cook until set and firm, then place in front of the crab to resemble bubbles exuding from its mouth. Serve at once.

CLAMS IN EGG CUSTARD

500 g (1 lb)	fresh clams, in the shell
2	spring onions (scallions), trimmed and sliced
2 slices	fresh ginger, shredded
2 tablespoons	frying oil
6	egg whites, well beaten
3	whole eggs, beaten
1¾ cups (14 fl oz)	chicken stock
2 tablespoons	cornflour (cornstarch)

Seasoning:

1¾ teaspoons	salt
½ teaspoon	m.s.g. (optional)
1 tablespoon	rice wine or dry sherry
¼ teaspoon	ground black pepper

Thoroughly wash the clams, brushing the shells with a soft brush. Rinse well in cold water and place in a wok with the spring onions, ginger, and frying oil. Cover and cook on moderate heat, shaking the pan occasionally to encourage the shells to open. When most of the shells have opened, discard those which are still closed. Transfer to a large dish.

Mix the egg whites, whole eggs, and chicken stock with the cornflour and seasoning ingredients and pour into the dish. Set the dish on a rack in a steamer and steam over rapidly boiling water for about 20 minutes.

Serve hot in the same dish.

SQUID STIR-FRIED WITH GARLIC AND PICKLED CUCUMBER

625 g (1¼ lb)	fresh squid
2	spring onions (scallions), trimmed and chopped
2 teaspoons	finely chopped garlic
2 tablespoons	finely chopped sweet pickled cucumber or Chinese mixed pickles
⅓ cup	frying oil

Seasoning/Sauce:

¼ cup (2 fl oz)	chicken stock
½ teaspoon	salt
¼ teaspoon	m.s.g. (optional)
¾ teaspoon	rice wine or dry sherry
½ teaspoon	white vinegar
1 tablespoon	liquid from pickled cucumbers
½ teaspoon	cornflour (cornstarch)

Clean the squid by removing the heads and stomach, pulling away the pink skin with fins attached and washing thoroughly. Cut along the length and press open. Scrape away any remaining gelatinous tissue and score on the inside in a close criss-cross pattern, cutting at a slight angle (see page 397). Cut the squid into 4 cm (1 2/3 in) squares, then drop into a saucepan of boiling water to blanch for 30 seconds. Remove and drain well.

Stir-fry the spring onions and garlic in the frying oil for 1 minute, then add the chopped cucumber or pickles and stir-fry briefly. Add the squid and stir-fry for 30 seconds, then add the pre-mixed seasoning/sauce ingredients and simmer until heated through and the sauce slightly thickened. Transfer to a serving plate and serve at once.

ABALONE SOUP WITH CHICKEN AND EGG

½ 315 g (10 oz) can	abalone, drained
2 tablespoons	softened lard
1	spring onion (scallion), shredded
4 cups (1 litre)	enriched stock *
1½ teaspoons	salt
2 teaspoons	rice wine or dry sherry
90 g (3 oz)	boneless chicken, coarsely minced (ground)
3	egg whites, well beaten
1 tablespoon	finely shredded cooked ham
1 tablespoon	rendered chicken fat (chicken grease)

Thinly slice the abalone and set aside. Heat the lard and briefly fry the spring onion, then add the abalone and fry lightly. Remove.

Bring the stock to the boil, add the salt (to taste), wine, and the chicken and simmer until the chicken turns white. Remove from the heat, slowly drizzle in the beaten egg whites and do not stir for at least 45 seconds while the egg sets into white strands in the soup. Return the abalone and onion and heat through.

Transfer to a soup tureen and garnish with the shredded ham. Stir in the chicken fat and serve at once.

* Or use chicken stock with ½ stock cube crumbled into it. Adjust salt to taste.

Shredded Pork in Sesame Pouches (recipe page 67).

HOT POT OF FISH, SHRIMPS, PORK, AND CHICKEN

155 g (5 oz)	white fish fillets
90 g (3 oz)	boneless chicken breast
90 g (3 oz)	pork fillet (tenderloin)
125 g (4 oz)	raw peeled shrimps
1 teaspoon	salt
2 teaspoons	cornflour (cornstarch)
155 g (5 oz)	fresh young Chinese green vegetables or spinach (collard greens)
45 g (1½ oz)	bean thread vermicelli
4	dried black mushrooms, soaked for 25 minutes
6 cups (1½ litres)	chicken stock
1¼ teaspoons	salt
½ teaspoon	m.s.g. (optional)
45 g (1½ oz)	canned bamboo shoots, drained and sliced

Special Equipment: A table-top chafing dish, fondue pot, or table-top gas or electric ring and a large saucepan.

Very thinly slice the fish, chicken, and pork and arrange on separate plates. Devein the shrimps with a toothpick (see page 394) and rub with the salt and cornflour. Rinse well with cold water and dry on kitchen paper. Place on another plate.

Thoroughly wash the vegetables and arrange on a plate. Soak the vermicelli in warm water until softened, cut into 10 cm (4 in) lengths, drain well and place in a dish. Squeeze the water from the mushrooms and remove the stems. Cut the caps into quarters.

Bring the chicken stock to the boil in the chafing dish, fondue pot, or saucepan and add the mushrooms, salt, m.s.g., and bamboo shoots.

Add the remaining ingredients at the table all together, or separately, and simmer until just done. The meat and seafood should be rare, the vegetables still crisp.

Serve some vegetables and the noodles in the stock as a soup after the meat and most of the vegetables have been eaten.

Soft beancurd, fish balls, and water chestnuts can be added to the hot pot, or substituted for any of the above ingredients.

COLD SPICY PEKING-STYLE PORK

Serve cold as an appetiser.

700 g (1⅓ lb)	pork leg (fresh ham)*
6 cups (1½ litres)	chicken stock

Seasoning:

2 teaspoons	salt
1 tablespoon	sugar
1 teaspoon	Chinese brown peppercorns
2	star anise
2 tablespoons	light soy sauce
1 tablespoon	rice wine or dry sherry
3	spring onions (scallions), trimmed and diced
3 slices	fresh ginger, shredded

Remove the rind and boil for about 8 minutes in lightly salted water. Remove and scrape off any fat. Cut the rind into small pieces. Dice the pork and place rind and pork in a saucepan with the chicken stock and seasoning ingredients.

Cover and bring to the boil, then reduce to a simmer and cook for 2 hours on very low heat. Skim once or twice during cooking. Discard the spices, onion, and ginger, transfer the meat to a dish and pack tightly.

Reduce the liquid, if necessary, until just enough to cover the meat. Pour over and leave to set, then refrigerate until firm. Slice and serve cold as an appetiser or use with other cold meat cuts.

* Select a cut with a large covering of rind (skin).

SAUTÉD PORK WITH PINE SEEDS

375 g (12 oz)	pork fillet (tenderloin)
1 cup	pine seeds*
2 cups (16 fl oz)	frying oil
½ teaspoon	salt
1¼ teaspoons	sugar
3	spring onions (scallions), trimmed and sliced

Seasoning:

1 tablespoon	light soy sauce
2 tablespoons	rice wine or dry sherry
2 teaspoons	cornflour (cornstarch)

Cut the pork into thin slices across the grain and mix with the seasoning ingredients. Leave for 20 minutes, turning several times.

Heat the deep-frying oil to moderate and fry the pine seeds in a basket until golden, about 30 seconds. Drain and pour off all but 3 tablespoons of the oil. Add the salt, sugar, and spring onions and sauté briefly, then push to one side of the pan and add the pork slices. Sauté until cooked through, stirring continually.

Add the fried pine seeds and serve at once.

* Sometimes called 'olive seeds' in Chinese stores. Use cashews or walnuts, if unobtainable. Often stocked by Middle Eastern food suppliers.

'MU HSU' PORK

250 g (8 oz)	pork fillet (tenderloin)
15 g (½ oz)	dried 'wood ear' fungus, soaked for 25 minutes
30 g (1 oz)	canned champignons or straw mushrooms, drained
4	dried black mushrooms, soaked for 25 minutes
3	eggs, well beaten
½ teaspoon	salt
2	spring onions (scallions), trimmed and sliced
2 slices	fresh ginger, shredded
45 g (1½ oz)	canned bamboo shoots, drained and sliced
½ cup (4 fl oz)	frying oil

Seasoning A:

¼ teaspoon	sugar
¼ teaspoon	m.s.g. (optional)
2 teaspoons	light soy sauce
1 teaspoon	rice wine or dry sherry
2 teaspoons	cornflour (cornstarch)

Seasoning B/Sauce:

⅓ cup	chicken stock
1½ tablespoons	light soy sauce
1 teaspoon	rice wine or dry sherry
½ teaspoon	salt
¼ teaspoon	m.s.g. (optional)
½ teaspoon	sesame oil (optional)
¾ teaspoon	cornflour (cornstarch)

Cut the pork into thin slices, then cut each in halves. Place in a dish with the seasoning A ingredients, mix well and leave for 20 minutes.

Drain the 'wood ears' and chop into small pieces. Slice the champignons or straw mushrooms into two or three pieces each. Squeeze the water from the mushrooms, remove stems and cut the caps into quarters.

Mix the egg with salt. Add about 1 tablespoon of the oil to the wok and heat to moderate. Pour in the beaten egg and cook until firm underneath. Lift a corner to allow the uncooked egg to run underneath. Continue cooking until firm enough to turn, then carefully turn and cook the underside until lightly coloured. Remove and break into several large pieces with a fork. Leave to cool.

Add the remaining oil and stir-fry the pork on fairly high heat until lightly coloured. Add the ginger and fry briefly, then add the spring onion and stir-fry until beginning to soften. Add the 'wood ear', mushrooms, and bamboo shoots and fry on moderate heat for about 2 minutes.

Pour off any excess oil, then add the pre-mixed seasoning B/sauce ingredients and bring to the boil. Return the egg and simmer in the sauce until thickened.

This dish is often served with *Mandarin* pancakes or sesame pocket bread in the West (see recipes, page 373 and 372), though this custom is not necessarily one adopted directly from China where this dish is usually served with plain rice.

SHREDDED PORK IN SESAME POUCHES

375 g (12 oz)	pork leg (fresh ham)
1 tablespoon	dark soy sauce
60 g (2 oz)	Szechuan preserved vegetable or salted mustard root*
¼ cup (2 fl oz)	frying oil
6 pieces	sesame pocket bread (see recipes, page 372)

Seasoning:

2 teaspoons	sugar (or to taste)
½ teaspoon	m.s.g. (optional)
1 tablespoon	rice wine or dry sherry

Thinly slice the pork across the grain, then cut into very fine short shreds. Place in a dish and add the soy sauce. Mix well and leave for 20 minutes. Soak the preserved vegetables in cold water for 20 minutes, then drain and squeeze out as much water as possible. Cut into fine shreds.

Heat the frying oil and stir-fry the pork until it changes colour, about 1 minute. Add the preserved vegetables and fry for 1 minute, then stir in the seasoning ingredients and mix well. Cook for about 4 minutes on fairly high heat, stirring continually.

Warm the breads in the oven if cooked in advance. Cut in halves and arrange on a plate. Serve with the shredded pork. To eat, a portion of the meat is stuffed into the 'pocket' of the bread and eaten like a sandwich.

* Finely shredded dry beancurd is often added to this dish and may be substituted for the preserved or salted vegetable.

FIVE SPICE AND GARLIC SPARE RIBS

18	American-style spare ribs (about 700 g / 1⅓ lb)
8 cups (2 litres)	deep-frying oil
	Chinese pepper-salt

Seasoning A:

½ teaspoon	salt
2 teaspoons	sugar
¾ teaspoon	five spice powder
2 teaspoons	light soy sauce
1 teaspoon	white vinegar
2 teaspoons	rice wine or dry sherry
3 tablespoons	cornflour (cornstarch)

Seasoning B:

1 tablespoon	chopped garlic
2 tablespoons	light soy sauce
1 tablespoon	white vinegar
1 tablespoon	sugar

Cut the ribs into 7.5 cm (3 in) pieces or leave whole as preferred. Place in a dish and add the pre-mixed seasoning A ingredients, rubbing thoroughly over each piece. Leave for 1 hour.

Heat the deep-frying oil to fairly hot and deep-fry the ribs until crisped on the surface and cooked through, about 3 minutes. Remove and retain the oil.

Transfer about 2 tablespoons of the oil to another wok and add the seasoning B ingredients. Cook, stirring on high heat for 1 minute, then remove from the heat. Reheat the deep-frying oil and fry the ribs again briefly, until very crisp. Remove and drain, then add to the sauce and simmer briefly.

Transfer to a serving plate and serve with a Chinese pepper-salt (see page 384).

PORK LIVERS IN SWEET FERMENTED RICE SAUCE

315 g (10 oz)	pork liver
2 slices	fresh ginger
2 tablespoons	frying oil
1 cup	sweet fermented rice (see page 387)*
2	spring onions (scallions), trimmed and chopped
½ teaspoon	salt
½ teaspoon	m.s.g. (optional)

Seasoning:

1 tablespoon	light soy sauce
½ teaspoon	sugar
2 teaspoons	cornflour (cornstarch)

Remove the skin from the liver and slice thinly. Soak in cold water for 10 minutes, drain and place in a dish with the seasoning ingredients. Leave for 10 minutes.

Heat the frying oil in a wok and sauté the ginger briefly, then add the sliced liver and sauté until lightly coloured. Add the fermented rice or substitute ingredients and the spring onions. Bring just to the boil and reduce heat to a simmer. Cook until the liver is cooked through but is still slightly pink inside, then add the salt and m.s.g., if used, and serve.

* Or mix 1¾ tablespoons Japanese light miso paste with 1 tablespoon sugar, 2 tablespoons rice wine or dry sherry, and ½ cup (4 fl oz) water.

Five Spice and Garlic Spare Ribs (recipe this page).

SAUTÉD PORK KIDNEYS WITH BAMBOO SHOOTS, CARROTS AND 'WOOD EARS'

310 g (10 oz)	pork kidneys
60 g (2 oz)	canned bamboo shoots, drained
20 g (2/3 oz)	dried 'wood ear' fungus, soaked for 25 minutes
1	small carrot, thinly sliced
4	garlic chives, sliced
1 cup (8 fl oz)	frying oil
1 teaspoon	rice wine or dry sherry
2 teaspoons	light soy sauce

Seasoning/Sauce:

2½ tablespoons	water
½ teaspoon	white vinegar
½ teaspoon	sesame oil
1 teaspoon	salt
½ teaspoon	m.s.g. (optional)
½ teaspoon	sugar
¼ teaspoon	ground black pepper
1 teaspoon	cornflour (cornstarch)

Cut the kidneys in halves diagonally and trim away the white fatty tissue. Remove the skin and soak in cold water for 10 minutes. Drain well. Score on the skin side in a close criss-cross pattern (see page 397), then cut into thin slices. This gives slices with one fluted edge. Blanch in boiling water for 1 minute and drain well.

Thinly slice the bamboo shoots. Drain the fungus and cut into small squares. Heat the frying oil and sauté the kidneys until lightly coloured, then add the prepared vegetables and chives and sauté for 30 seconds. Sizzle the wine and soy sauce onto the sides of the wok and stir in, then add the pre-mixed seasoning/sauce ingredients.

Simmer until the kidneys are cooked through and the sauce thickened, about 1¼ minutes. Do not overcook or the kidneys will toughen.

PORK FILLET SAUTÉD WITH BAMBOO SHOOTS AND MUSHROOMS

280 g (9 oz)	pork fillet (tenderloin)
60 g (2 oz)	canned champignons or straw mushrooms, drained
1 cup (8 fl oz)	frying oil
2	spring onions (scallions), trimmed and sliced
2 slices	fresh ginger, shredded
30 g (1 oz)	canned bamboo shoots, drained and sliced
1 teaspoon	sesame oil (optional)

Seasoning A:

1	egg white, beaten
½ teaspoon	salt
½ teaspoon	m.s.g. (optional)
2 teaspoons	cornflour (cornstarch)

Seasoning B/Sauce:

¼ cup (2 fl oz)	chicken stock
1 tablespoon	light soy sauce
2 teaspoons	rice wine or dry sherry
½ teaspoon	salt
½ teaspoon	cornflour (cornstarch)

Cut the pork into thin slices across the grain and place in a dish with the seasoning A ingredients. Leave for 20 minutes, turning several times.

Thinly slice the mushrooms. Heat a frying pan and sauté the onion and ginger briefly, then add the sliced pork and sauté on moderate heat until it changes colour. Remove and add the mushrooms and bamboo shoots. Sauté briefly, then pour off as much oil as possible and add the pre-mixed seasoning B/sauce ingredients. Return the pork and bring to the boil. Simmer until the sauce thickens, stir in the sesame oil, if used, and serve.

RED-BRAISED FIVE SPICE BEEF

Serve hot or cold as an appetiser or main dish.

1 kg (2 lb)	braising beef (shank, round, topside)
3	spring onions (scallions), trimmed and sliced
5 thick slices	fresh ginger, bruised
2	spice bags
3 pieces	dried orange peel

Seasonings:

¼ cup (2 fl oz)	rice wine or dry sherry
¾ cup (6 fl oz)	light soy sauce
2 tablespoons	dark soy sauce (optional)
⅓ cup	sugar

Cut the beef into three large pieces and blanch in boiling water for 2 minutes. Drain and place in a stew pan with the onions, ginger, spice bags, and orange peel. Add the seasoning ingredients with water to just cover. Place a plate on top of the meat and weight with a heavy heatproof and waterproof object. Cover the pan and bring to the boil. Cook for about 8 minutes on high heat, then turn the heat to the lowest point and simmer until the meat is completely tender, about 1 hour. Remove the weight when the heat is decreased.

Place the beef in a dish and weight again. When cool, chill thoroughly before cutting very thinly to serve as an appetiser by itself or with other cold cuts.

The sliced cooked meat may also be crisp-fried (see the following recipe).

CRISP-FRIED BEEF WITH SESAME SEEDS

280 g (9 oz)	Red-Braised Five Spice Beef (see previous recipe)
1¼ tablespoons	white sesame seeds
4 cups (1 litre)	deep-frying oil

Seasoning:

¼ teaspoon	salt
½ teaspoon	m.s.g. (optional)
1¼ tablespoons	sugar
1 teaspoon	light soy sauce
1 tablespoon	sweet rice wine, Japanese mirin or sweet sherry
1½ tablespoons	chicken stock or cold water

Very thinly slice the beef and cut into 4 cm (1 2/3 in) squares. Place in a frying basket. Wipe out a wok with an oiled cloth and dry-fry the sesame seeds until lightly toasted. Set aside.

Wipe out the wok again and add the deep-frying oil. Heat to smoking point. Deep-fry the beef for 1 minute, then remove and reheat the oil. Fry the meat again and remove. Continue frying and reheating the oil until the meat is very dark and crisp, then remove and drain well. Pour off the oil.

Return the meat to the wok and add the pre-mixed seasoning ingredients. Stir on moderate heat until the liquid has been completely absorbed. Add the sesame seeds, stir well, and transfer to a warmed serving plate.

STEWED BEEF NORTHERN STYLE

750 g (1½ lb)	silverside or shin (brisket or shank)
3	spring onions (scallions), trimmed and halved
5 thick slices	fresh ginger, bruised
¼ cup (2 fl oz)	softened lard or frying oil

Seasoning:

3	star anise
2 tablespoons	sugar
2/3 cup	light soy sauce
2 tablespoons	dark soy sauce
¼ cup (2 fl oz)	rice wine or dry sherry

Cut the beef into cubes and blanch in boiling water to cover for 2 minutes. Remove the beef and drain well. Skim the stock and add the seasonings, return to the boil.

Stir-fry the cubed beef, spring onions, and ginger in the lard or oil until lightly coloured. Transfer to the stock and cover the pan. Simmer on low heat for at least 2 hours until the meat is completely tender and the sauce well reduced. Thicken the remaining sauce if necessary with a thin solution of cornflour (cornstarch) and cold water.

SLICED BEEF WITH ORANGE PEEL AND CHILLI PEPPERS

315 g (10 oz)	lean beef steak (rump or fillet/tenderloin)
2	dried red chilli peppers, cut into quarters
3 pieces	dried orange peel
1 teaspoon	Chinese brown peppercorns (optional)
¼ cup (2 fl oz)	frying oil

Seasoning A:

¼ teaspoon	salt
¼ teaspoon	m.s.g. (optional)
1 tablespoon	dark soy sauce
1 tablespoon	finely chopped spring onion (scallion)
1 teaspoon	grated fresh ginger
2 teaspoons	cornflour (cornstarch)
1 tablespoon	frying oil

Seasoning B:

1 tablespoon	light soy sauce
2 teaspoons	dark soy sauce
2 teaspoons	sesame oil

Partially freeze the beef to cut into paper-thin slices across the grain, then cut into strips about 4 × 2.5 cm (1 2/3 × 1 in). Place in a dish and rub on the seasoning A ingredients. Leave for 20 minutes.

Heat the frying oil and fry the peppers, orange peel, and peppercorns for about 3 minutes, until dark brown. Remove and set aside. Reheat the wok and add the beef. Stir-fry on high heat until the meat is crisp on the edges, then return the fried ingredients and add the seasoning B ingredients. Stir briefly on high heat, then transfer to a warmed serving plate.

If preferred, the beef may be deep-fried in fairly hot oil until quite crisp, then stir-fried with the seasoning B and other fried ingredients.

BEEF BRAISED WITH DRY BEANCURD AND VEGETABLES

625 g (1¼ lb)	braising beef (round, topside/chuck)
2 squares	dry beancurd
2 cups (16 fl oz)	frying oil
3	small sweet white turnips
5	small carrots
60 g (2 oz)	fresh or frozen peas
3	spring onions (scallions), trimmed and sliced
3 thick slices	fresh ginger, braised
5 cloves	garlic, sliced
1 — 2	fresh red chilli peppers, sliced (optional)

Seasoning A:

1 tablespoon	finely chopped spring onion (scallion)
½ teaspoon	grated fresh ginger
1 tablespoon	light soy sauce
2 teaspoons	rice wine or dry sherry
2 teaspoons	cornflour (cornstarch)

Seasoning B:

¼ cup (2 fl oz)	light soy sauce
2 teaspoons	rice wine or dry sherry
1½ teaspoons	sugar
½ teaspoon	m.s.g. (optional)

Cut the beef into cubes and place in a dish with the seasoning A ingredients, mix well and leave for 20 minutes.

Cut the beancurd into small cubes. Heat the frying oil and fry the beancurd until crisp on the surface, about 2 minutes. Remove and drain well.

Peel and cube the turnips and carrots. Pour off all but 2½ tablespoons of the oil and sauté the vegetables, spring onions, ginger, garlic, and chillies, if used, for 2 minutes. Add the meat and sauté until evenly coloured.

Transfer meat and vegetables to a casserole and add the beancurd. Add boiling water or beef stock to cover and the seasoning B ingredients. Simmer until the beef is tender, about 1 hour. Add salt to taste and a dash of sesame oil. Serve hot in the casserole.

Sliced Beef with Orange Peel and Chilli Peppers (recipe this page).

BEEF IN BUDDHIST ROBES

Serve as an appetiser.

This is a classic Northern dish, named after the bright yellow coloured egg pancake pastry which resembles a Buddhist monk's saffron robes.

Batter:

5	eggs, well beaten
1 tablespoon	cornflour (cornstarch)
1 tablespoon	water
1 teaspoon	vegetable oil
¾ teaspoon	salt
¼ teaspoon	m.s.g. (optional)
	few drops of orange-red food colouring

Filling:

375 g (12 oz)	lean beef, finely minced (ground)
1½ tablespoons	finely chopped spring onion (scallion)
1 teaspoon	grated fresh ginger

Seasoning:

1 tablespoon	Chinese pepper-salt*
1 tablespoon	light soy sauce
2 tablespoons	water
1 tablespoon	cornflour (cornstarch)

Sealing Paste:

1	egg, well beaten
1 tablespoon	cornflour (cornstarch)
2 teaspoons	water

Beat the batter ingredients together thoroughly, then set aside for 25 minutes. Mix the beef, spring onion, and ginger with the seasoning ingredients and leave for 20 minutes, then refrigerate for 1 hour.

Wipe out an omelette pan with a 22 cm (9 in) diameter and rub with an oiled cloth. Pour in one-sixth of the batter and cook on moderate heat until small bubbles appear on the surface and the underside is specked with brown. Lift one corner and carefully turn. Cook the other side until firm and very lightly coloured. Cook the remaining batter in this way, giving 6 pancakes.

Mix the sealing paste ingredients together and spread on one side of each pancake when cool. Cover half of the pancakes with a thick layer of the beef mixture and press the remaining pancakes on top, pasted sides down.

Cut each into wide slices, then into diamond shaped pieces by cutting diagonally to the first cuts.

Heat shallow oil to moderately hot and fry the pancake slices until golden brown, turning once. Lift out and drain well. Arrange on a bed of shredded lettuce or a paper napkin on a serving plate and serve with dips of Chinese pepper-salt (see page 384) and light soy sauce.

* Made with 1 tablespoon of Chinese brown peppercorns and 1¼ teaspoons of salt (see directions on page 384).

MONGOLIAN BEEF FIRE-POT

Serve as a complete main course.

1 kg (2 lb)	beef sirloin steak (loin, striploin)
2 squares	soft beancurd
500 g (1 lb)	young Chinese green vegetables
90 g (3 oz)	bean thread vermicelli, soaked to soften
8	large spring onions (scallions), trimmed and sliced
6	whole eggs
8 cups (2 litres)	water
1½ teaspoons	salt
½ teaspoon	m.s.g. (optional)
2 teaspoons	rice wine or dry sherry

Sauce Dips:

1 small jar	sha chia jiang or commercial satay sauce
½ cup	Hoisin sauce
	light soy sauce
	chillies sauce
	hot mustard

Special Equipment: A charcoal heated 'fire-pot' or table-top chafing dish.

Partially freeze the beef so that it can be cut into wafer-thin slices across the grain. Arrange on several plates. Cut the beancurd into small cubes. Soak in cold water for 10 minutes, then drain and place on a serving plate. Thoroughly wash the vegetables, cut into pieces and place in a dish. Drain the vermicelli and transfer to a serving dish. Serve the spring onions on another plate and place one egg in each of six rice bowls. Place one in front of each diner.

Serve the various sauce dips in small plates so they are all within reach of each diner.

Take the plates of meat and other ingredients to the table. Heat the fire-pot and add the water, salt, m.s.g., if used, and wine. Bring to the boil, then reduce to a simmer.

Use wooden chopsticks to place slices of meat and vegetables in the simmering stock. Retrieve when the meat is still quite rare and the vegetables crisp and lightly cooked. Dip into one or several of the sauces before eating.

The eggs should be broken into the rice bowls, beaten lightly and used as an additional tasty dip. Omit, if preferred.

The noodles may be eaten with the soup when the meat, vegetables, and beancurd are finished.

SAUTÉD LAMB WITH GARLIC

280 g (9 oz)	lean lamb
2	spring onions (scallions), trimmed and sliced
10 cloves	garlic, sliced
¼ cup (2 fl oz)	frying oil

Seasoning A:

¼ teaspoon	salt
1½ teaspoons	ground Chinese brown peppercorns
2 tablespoons	light soy sauce
2 teaspoons	rice wine or dry sherry
1 tablespoon	frying oil
1 teaspoon	sesame oil
1 teaspoon	cornflour (cornstarch)

Seasoning B:

1 tablespoon	light soy sauce
1 teaspoon	rice wine or dry sherry
2 teaspoons	sesame oil

Slice the lamb thinly across the grain, then cut into fine shreds. Place in a dish with the seasoning A ingredients, mix well and leave for 20 minutes.

Heat the oil in a wok and fry the spring onions for 30 seconds. Remove, add the garlic and fry until lightly coloured. Remove.

Reheat the pan to fairly hot and fry the shredded lamb until lightly coloured, about 2 minutes. Return the onions and garlic and add the seasoning B ingredients, sizzling them separately onto the sides of the pan. Stir in and cook for a few seconds more until the lamb is just done.

Transfer to a warmed serving plate.

MONGOLIAN LAMB

280 g (9 oz)	lean lamb*
¼ cup (2 fl oz)	frying oil
1	small leek, shredded
1	small carrot, parboiled and thinly sliced
2 teaspoons	toasted white sesame seeds

Seasoning A:

½ teaspoon	m.s.g. (optional)
2 teaspoons	sugar
1 teaspoon	crushed garlic
2 tablespoons	dark soy sauce
2 tablespoons	rice wine or dry sherry
1 tablespoon	sesame oil
2 teaspoons	cornflour (cornstarch)

Seasoning B/Sauce:

¼ cup (2 fl oz)	cold water
1 tablespoon	light soy sauce
1 tablespoon	rice wine or dry sherry
1 tablespoon	sesame oil
¼ teaspoon	salt
½ teaspoon	m.s.g. (optional)
1 teaspoon	sugar
1¼ teaspoons	cornflour (cornstarch)

Special Equipment: An iron frying pan or steak pan with a wooden stand.

Partially freeze the meat, cut into wafer-thin slices across the grain, then into pieces about 5 cm (2 in) square. Mix with the seasoning A ingredients and leave for about 45 minutes.

Heat the oil in a wok and stir-fry the shredded leek until lightly coloured. Push to one side of the pan and add the sliced carrot. Stir-fry briefly, then push aside. Heat the pan to very high and stir-fry the lamb (or beef) until lightly coloured.

Place the frying pan or steak pan on another heat source to thoroughly heat through. Pour the pre-mixed seasoning B/sauce ingredients onto the meat and stir in the vegetables. Heat to boiling point, then pour into the prepared hot pan and garnish with the sesame seeds. Carry sizzling to the table.

* Or use fillet (tenderloin) of beef.

VENISON SAUTÉD WITH LEEKS

315 g (10 oz)	fresh venison fillet (tenderloin), or rump
2	fresh young leeks
¼ cup (2 fl oz)	frying oil
1 teaspoon	sesame oil
½ teaspoon	white vinegar

Seasoning A:

¼ teaspoon	salt
1 teaspoon	sugar
2 tablespoons	light soy sauce
1 tablespoon	rice wine or dry sherry
2 teaspoons	sesame oil
1 tablespoon	finely chopped spring onion (scallion)
1½ teaspoons	grated fresh ginger
1½ teaspoons	cornflour (cornstarch)
1 tablespoon	frying oil

Seasoning B:

½ teaspoon	salt
¾ teaspoon	sugar
2 tablespoons	light soy sauce
1 tablespoon	rice wine or dry sherry

Cut the meat across the grain into thin slices, then into shreds, and place in a dish with the seasoning A ingredients. Mix well and leave for 1 hour.

Thoroughly wash the leeks and cut into 5 cm (2 in) pieces, then shred finely lengthwise. Heat the oil in a wok and fry the leeks until softened. Push to one side of the pan and add the meat. Sauté until it changes colour, then cook for a further 1 minute. Stir in the sesame oil and add the seasoning B ingredients, sizzling the soy and wine separately onto the sides of the pan.

Mix in the leeks and cook, stirring, until the meat is just done. Transfer to a warmed serving plate. Sprinkle on the vinegar and stir in lightly.

SLOW-SIMMERED PIGEONS

3	young pigeons (about 700 g / 1⅓ lb dressed weight)
2	spice bags
1½ cups (12 fl oz)	light soy sauce
¼ cup (2 fl oz)	dark soy sauce
¼ cup (2 fl oz)	rice wine or dry sherry
1 cup	sugar
2 teaspoons	sesame oil

Blanch the pigeons in boiling water for 1 minute. Remove and drain well. Pour out the water and return the pigeons to the saucepan. Add the remaining ingredients, except the sesame oil and add water to cover. Bring just to the boil, then reduce heat and simmer until the pigeons are completely tender, about 1¼ hours. Remove and drain well. Brush with sesame oil, cut in halves or quarters and serve on a bed of shredded or fresh whole lettuce leaves.

Beef in Buddhist Robes (recipe page 74).

SAUTÉD PIGEON MEAT WITH LIVERS AND EGGS IN NOODLE NEST

250 g (8 oz)	sliced pigeon meat
60 g (2 oz)	pigeons' livers
6	pigeon eggs
6 cups (1½ litres)	deep-frying oil
45 g (1½ oz)	rice vermicelli or bean thread vermicelli
1	spring onion (scallion), trimmed and diced
2 slices	fresh ginger, shredded
45 g (1½ oz)	canned straw mushrooms, drained and thinly sliced
45 g (1½ oz)	canned bamboo shoots, drained and thinly sliced
2 teaspoons	rice wine or dry sherry
1 teaspoon	sesame oil

Seasoning A:

1 teaspoon	dark soy sauce
1 teaspoon	ginger wine
1½ teaspoons	cornflour (cornstarch)

Seasoning B/Sauce:

⅓ cup	chicken stock
1 teaspoon	light soy sauce
½ teaspoon	salt
¼ teaspoon	m.s.g. (optional)
½ teaspon	sugar
¼ teaspoon	ground black pepper
1 teaspoon	cornflour (cornstarch)

Special Equipment: Two wire strainers, one slightly larger than the other.

Blanch the pigeon meat in biling water for a few seconds, then drain well and place in a dish with the diced livers and the seasoning A ingredients. Leave for 20 minutes.

Hard boil (hard cook) the eggs and drain, then cool under running cold water and remove the shells. Heat the deep-frying oil to smoking point and decrease the heat slightly. Break the rice vermicelli (or cut the bean threads) into short lengths and use to line the inside of the larger strainer. Press the smaller strainer inside to compress the noodles into a nest shape. Lower into the hot oil, holding the two handles firmly together. Deep-fry until the nest is crisp and a light golden colour. Remove and upturn onto absorbent paper.

Place the pigeon meat and livers in one of the strainers and deep-fry for about 45 seconds. Remove and drain well. Deep-fry the eggs until golden and drain well.

Pour off all but 2 tablespoons of the oil and stir-fry the spring onion, ginger, mushrooms, and bamboo shoots for 1½ minutes. Push to one side of the pan and add the pigeon meat and livers and stir-fry briefly, then mix in with the vegetables and sizzle the wine onto the sides of the pan and add the sesame oil. Add the seasoning B/sauce ingredients, pre-mixed. Simmer for about 1 minute, then add the eggs and heat through thoroughly.

Place the nest on a bed of shredded lettuce or fresh coriander and spoon the cooked dish into the centre. Serve at once.

SPICED PIGEON EGGS

Serve hot or cold as an appetiser.

12	fresh pigeon eggs, or use canned quail eggs, drained

Seasoning:

½ teaspoon	salt
¼ teaspoon	m.s.g. (optional)
1 teaspoon	Chinese brown peppercorns
2 tablespoons	light soy sauce
1 cup (8 fl oz)	chicken stock
1	spring onion (scallion), trimmed and sliced
2 slices	fresh ginger

Boil the eggs in gently bubbling water until firm, about 4 minutes. Lift out and cool under running cold water. Remove the shells and set aside.

Bring the seasoning ingredients to the boil in another saucepan and add the eggs. Simmer for 8 minutes, then remove and leave to cool. Cut in halves and arrange on a bed of shredded lettuce. Serve hot or cold.

EGG DUMPLINGS

Makes 18

Batter:

4	eggs
2 teaspoons	cornflour (cornstarch)
1 teaspoon	water
1/3 teaspoon	salt

Filling:

90 g (3 oz)	lean pork, finely minced (ground)
3 — 4	water chestnuts, finely chopped
1 1/2 teaspoons	finely chopped spring onion (scallion)
1/2 teaspoon	grated fresh ginger

Seasoning:

1/2 teaspoon	salt
1/4 teaspoon	m.s.g. (optional)
1/2 teaspoon	sugar
	pinch of white pepper
1/4 teaspoon	sesame oil
1 teaspoon	cornflour (cornstarch)

Sauce:

3/4 cup (6 fl oz)	chicken stock
1 tablespoon	light soy sauce
1/2 teaspoon	rice wine or dry sherry
1/4 teaspoon	salt
1/2 teaspoon	sugar
1/4 teaspoon	m.s.g. (optional)
1/4 teaspoon	ground black pepper

Beat the batter ingredients together thoroughly, then leave for 25 minutes.

Mix the filling ingredients with the seasoning ingredients and knead until smooth and evenly mixed, then cover with plastic wrap and refrigerate.

Wipe out a small omelette pan with an oiled cloth and heat to moderate. Pour in about 1 tablespoon of the mixture and tilt the pan to spread the batter as evenly as possible in a round shape about 6.5 cm (2 1/2 in) in diameter. Cook until very lightly coloured underneath and still soft and sticky on top. Do not overcook.

Place a small spoonful of the filling in the centre of the pancake and fold in halves. Gently press the edges together with the back of a spoon to stick down firmly. Proceed with the remaining dumplings.

Bring the sauce ingredients to a slow simmer in a larger frying pan or wok and add the dumplings. Simmer for about 5 minutes, then invert the pan onto a serving plate and serve the dumplings with any remaining sauce while piping hot.

FRIED FRESH MILK WITH CRABMEAT ON RICE NOODLES

1 1/2 tablespoons	chopped cooked ham or bacon
1 tablespoon	frying oil
1 cup (8 fl oz)	fresh milk
6	egg whites
1/2 cup (4 fl oz)	softened lard
90 g (3 oz)	cooked crabmeat, flaked
1 tablespoon	finely chopped canned champignons (optional)
1 1/2 tablespoons	canned sweet corn kernels, well drained (optional)
45 g (1 1/2 oz)	rice vermicelli, broken
4 cups (1 litre)	deep-frying oil

Seasoning:

1 1/2 teaspoons	salt
1/2 teaspoon	m.s.g. (optional)
2 tablespoons	cornflour (cornstarch)

Fry the chopped ham or bacon in the oil until crisp. Remove and set aside. Wipe out the wok. Pour the milk into a basin and add the seasoning ingredients. Beat the egg whites to soft peaks and mix with the milk. Add the flaked crabmeat and stir in lightly, adding the chopped champignons and sweet corn, if used.

Heat the lard in the wok until warm, pour in the mixture and cook, stirring slowly until the mixture begins to set.

In another pan, heat the deep-frying oil to smoking point. Place the broken rice vermicelli in a frying basket and lower into the hot oil to fry until it expands into a cloud of crisp white noodles. Remove, drain well and place on a serving dish. Pour the softly cooked milk and crabmeat mixture on top and garnish with the cooked ham. Serve at once.

OMELETTE IN SPICY SAUCE

6	whole eggs, well beaten
½ teaspoon	salt
2½ tablespoons	softened lard
30 g (1 oz)	lean pork, minced (ground)
4	canned water chestnuts, drained and finely chopped
15 g (½ oz)	dried 'wood ear' fungus, soaked for 25 minutes, then finely chopped
1 tablespoon	finely chopped spring onion (scallion)
1 teaspoon	finely chopped fresh ginger
¾ teaspoon	finely chopped garlic (or to taste)

Sauce:

½ cup (4 fl oz)	chicken stock
1 tablespoon	hot bean paste
1 tablespoon	light soy sauce
½ teaspoon	white vinegar
2 teaspoons	sugar
½ teaspoon	sesame oil (optional)
1½ teaspoons	cornflour (cornstarch)

Mix the eggs with the salt. Heat a wok and add 1 tablespoon of the lard. Pour in the egg mixture when the oil is quite warm and cook on moderate heat until firm underneath, then turn and cook the underside until firm. Lift onto a serving plate and cut into 6 pieces. Keep warm.

Wipe out the wok and add the remaining lard. Heat to moderate and add the remaining prepared ingredients. Stir-fry for 2 minutes, then add the sauce ingredients and simmer until the sauce is thickened. Check the seasoning and simmer a further 1 minute.

Pour over the omelette and serve at once.

PEKING STYLE FRIED DUMPLINGS

Makes 24

Pastry:

1½ cups	flour
½ cup	warm water

Filling:

125 g (4 oz)	lean pork, finely minced (ground)
1	medium white onion, finely chopped
1 tablespoon	finely chopped spring onion (scallion)
½ teaspoon	finely chopped fresh ginger

Seasoning:

1	egg, beaten
½ teaspoon	salt
½ teaspoon	m.s.g. (optional)
2 teaspoons	light soy sauce
2 teaspoons	sesame oil
2 teaspoons	cornflour (cornstarch)

Sift the flour into a bowl and make a well in the centre. Pour in the warm water and work until well mixed, then knead to a smooth soft dough, about 5 minutes. Cover with a damp cloth and leave for 30 minutes.

Mix the pork, onion, spring onion, and ginger with the seasoning ingredients. Knead to produce a smooth paste, then chill until needed.

Roll the dough into a long sausage shape and cut into 24 pieces. Roll each out on a lightly oiled board with a dry rolling pin, making sure that the upper side remains free of oil. Place a spoonful of the mixture in the centre of each wrapper and fold in halves. Press the edges firmly together. Slightly flatten the dumplings at the fold so they can be stood up, with the joined edges upwards.

Wipe out a large flat frying pan, preferably a heavy iron type, with an oiled cloth and add about 1½ tablespoons of clean vegetable or frying oil. Heat to moderate, then arrange the dumplings in a circle in the pan. Cook over moderate heat until the dumplings are golden underneath, then pour in ⅓ cup of chicken stock or water and cover the pan tightly. Cook on moderate heat until the liquid has been absorbed, about 6 minutes.

Invert the pan onto a serving plate and serve at once with accompanying sauce dips of hot mustard, chilli sauce, and light soy sauce.

Venison Sautéd with Leeks (recipe page 76).

SMOKED VEGETARIAN 'DUCK'

Serve as an appetiser or main dish.

10 sheets	dried beancurd skin
1	medium carrot
4	dried black mushrooms, soaked for 25 minutes
¼ cup (2 fl oz)	frying oil
1 cup	sugar

Seasoning:

1 cup (8 fl oz)	light soy sauce
1 tablespoon	dark soy sauce
1 tablespoon	sesame oil
1½ tablespoons	sugar
¼ teaspoon	salt
½ teaspoon	m.s.g. (optional)

Wipe the beancurd skins with a damp cloth to clean and soften. Set two aside and roll the others up. Shred coarsely. Peel and dice the carrot and parboil. Drain well. Squeeze the water from the mushrooms, remove the stems and dice the caps.

Heat the frying oil and stir-fry the carrot and mushrooms for 1 minute. Add the shredded beancurd skins and stir-fry for 2 minutes on moderate heat. Add half the pre-mixed seasoning ingredients and cook a further 1 minute.

Place the two remaining sheets of beancurd skin on a board and brush with some of the remaining seasoning ingredients. Divide the stir-fried vegetables and beancurd skin between the two sheets, arranging in a 5 cm (2 in) strip across the centre of each piece. Pour on some of the remaining sauce, then fold in the sides and then the two larger flaps to produce two long flat sausage shapes. Press in the sides to form into square-sided, rectangular shape. Place the two rolls in a dish and pour on the remaining sauce.

Leave for 1 hour to absorb the sauce, then set the dish on a rack in a steamer and steam for 10 minutes. Drain any water or sauce from the dish and discard. Wipe out the wok and add the sugar. Heat until the sugar begins to smoke, then place the dish on a rack over the sugar, cover the pan tightly and smoke for 5 minutes.

Remove and cut diagonally into thick slices. Serve hot or cold.

The rolls, smoked or unsmoked, can be used in vegetarian dishes as a meat substitute, or can be thinly sliced to serve with other cold cuts.

BEANCURD SKIN 'NOODLES' WITH YOUNG SOYBEANS

2 sheets	dried beancurd skin, about 30 cm (12 in) square
250 g (8 oz)	fresh or frozen young soy or lima beans
⅓ cup	frying oil or softened lard

Seasoning:

¾ teaspoon	salt
½ teaspoon	sugar
1 tablespoon	light soy sauce
1 teaspoon	rice wine or dry sherry

Cover the beancurd skins with a wet cloth until softened, then cut into noodle-like shreds. Boil the soy or lima beans in lightly salted water until beginning to soften, about 5 minutes. Drain. Rub off the outer skin of lima beans, if used.

Heat the oil in a wok and stir-fry the beans for 2½ minutes on moderate heat. Add the noodles and stir-fry for 1½ minutes, then add the seasoning ingredients, sizzling the soy sauce and wine separately onto the sides of the pan. Stir in and transfer to a warmed serving plate.

SWEET AND SOUR CABBAGE

1 kg (2 lb)	Chinese (celery) cabbage
1 tablespoon	salt
3	fresh red chilli peppers, shredded
2.5 cm (1 in) piece	fresh ginger, shredded

Seasoning:

½ cup (4 fl oz)	sesame oil
2 teaspoons	Chinese brown peppercorns
½ cup	sugar
½ cup (4 fl oz)	white vinegar
½ teaspoon	m.s.g. (optional)

Thoroughly wash the cabbage and cut into bite-sized pieces. Drain very well and place in a large glass dish. Add the salt and toss lightly. Cover with plastic wrap and leave for 4 hours. Add the chilli and ginger and toss again lightly.

Heat the sesame oil to smoking point and add the peppercorns. Remove immediately from the heat and leave to cool, then add the remaining seasoning ingredients, stirring until the sugar dissolves.

Pour over the salad and toss lightly. Re-cover and leave for a further 4 hours, tossing occasionally. Serve as a side dish with appetisers and main courses.

To store the cabbage, first blanch in boiling water until softened, then proceed as above. Keeps for up to a week in the refrigerator.

SOUR AND HOT CUCUMBER

Serve as an appetiser or side dish.

3	small cucumbers
2.5 cm (1 in) piece	fresh ginger
2	fresh red chilli peppers
¼ cup (2 fl oz)	white vinegar
⅓ cup	sugar

Slice the cucumbers thickly lengthways, scrape out the seeds, then cut into sticks about 6 cm (2½ in) long. Shred the ginger and chilli, removing the chilli seeds for a milder taste.

Mix the cucumber, ginger, and chilli in a dish. Pour on the pre-mixed vinegar and sugar and leave for about 5 hours, turning occasionally. Serve cold.

COLD MARINATED CORIANDER

500 g (1 lb)	fresh coriander
½ cup	shelled roasted peanuts

Dressing:

½ teaspoon	salt
1 tablespoon	sugar
1¼ tablespoons	white vinegar
¼ cup (2 fl oz)	light soy sauce
1 tablespoon	sesame oil
1 tablespoon	frying or vegetable oil
1 teaspoon	crushed garlic

Thoroughly wash the coriander and remove the stalks. Drop into a saucepan of boiling water and poach for 1¼ minutes. Remove and drain well. When cool, squeeze out as much water as possible. Chop coarsely and place in a salad bowl.

Coarsely chop the peanuts or leave whole as preferred. Add to the coriander. Mix the dressing ingredients, stirring until the sugar dissolves. Pour over the salad, stir and toss lightly, and chill before serving. Serve as a side dish to appetisers or main courses.

CELERY WITH DRIED SHRIMPS

250 g (8 oz)	fresh young celery
45 g (1½ oz)	dried shrimps
2 tablespoons	Shao Hsing or other yellow wine*

Seasoning:

1½ tablespoons	sesame oil
1½ teaspoons	Chinese brown peppercorns
¾ teaspoon	salt
¼ teaspoon	m.s.g. (optional)

Cut the celery into 5 cm (2 in) pieces, then cut each piece into two or three strips, lengthways. Blanch in boiling water until just softened, about 2½ minutes. Drain thoroughly and leave to cool.

Soak the dried shrimps in the wine until softened. Drain, reserving the wine. Heat the sesame oil to smoking point, add the peppercorns and remove from the heat. Let stand until cool, then strain off the oil and discard the peppercorns. Add the salt, m.s.g., and a little of the wine and pour over the celery, add the shrimps and toss lightly.

Serve cold as a vegetable or side dish.

* Or use brandy or Japanese sake.

STIR-FRIED BEAN SPROUTS WITH CHICKEN

280 g (9 oz)	fresh bean sprouts
185 g (6 oz)	boneless chicken
2 tablespoons	frying oil

Seasoning A:

1	egg white, beaten
½ teaspoon	salt
1 teaspoon	rice wine or dry sherry
2 teaspoons	cornflour (cornstarch)

Seasoning B:

½ teaspoon	salt
¼ teaspoon	m.s.g. (optional)
½ teaspoon	sugar
¼ teaspoon	ground black pepper
½ teaspoon	rice wine or dry sherry
½ teaspoon	sesame oil
1 tablespoon	cold water
½ teaspoon	cornflour (cornstarch)

Remove the roots and pods from the sprouts and wash well. Dry thoroughly in a kitchen towel.

Thinly slice the chicken, then cut into fine shreds. Place in a dish with the seasoning A ingredients, mix well and leave for 15 minutes.

Heat the oil in a wok and stir-fry the bean sprouts for 1 minute. Push to one side of the pan and add the chicken shreds. Stir-fry until white, about 1½ minutes, then mix in the bean sprouts and add the pre-mixed seasoning B ingredients.

Stir on high heat until thoroughly mixed, then serve.

*Beancurd Skin 'Noodles' with Young Soybeans (recipe page 82)
and Mandarin Fish with Vinegar and Pepper in Rich Soup (recipe page 88).*

'FOUR JEWELS' IN CHICKEN OIL SAUCE

½ 315 g (10 oz) can	asparagus spears, drained
¾ 280g (9 oz) can	quail eggs, drained
½ 315 g (10 oz) can	straw mushrooms or champignons
250 g (8 oz)	Chinese green vegetable hearts (young bok choy, kale, or mustard)
2 tablespoons	softened lard or frying oil
2½ tablespoons	rendered chicken fat (chicken grease)

Seasoning:

1 tablespoon	finely chopped spring onion (scallion)
¾ teaspoon	grated fresh ginger
1 cup (8 fl oz)	chicken stock
1½ teaspoons	salt
½ teaspoon	m.s.g. (optional)
¾ teaspoon	sugar
2 teaspoons	rice wine or dry sherry

Cut the asparagus in halves. Simmer the quail eggs in chicken stock or water for 5 minutes, then remove with a slotted spoon. Add the mushrooms and simmer for 5 minutes, then remove. Thoroughly wash the vegetables and cut in halves lengthways. Simmer in slightly salted water until softened. Drain well.

Heat the lard or frying oil in a wok and fry the spring onion and ginger briefly. Add the stock and remaining seasoning ingredients and then add the vegetables, asparagus, mushrooms, and quail eggs keeping them in separate groups. Cover and simmer for 5 minutes.

Drain off and reserve the liquid, then slide the contents of the wok carefully onto a serving plate without disturbing the arrangement of the ingredients. Return the stock and bring to the boil. Thicken with a solution of cornflour (cornstarch) and cold water and stir in the chicken fat. Heat to boiling and pour over the vegetables. Serve at once.

'EIGHT TREASURE' WINTER MELON POND

Serves 8 — 10.

1 3½ — 4 kg (7 — 8 lb)	winter melon
60 g (2 oz)	dried lotus seeds, soaked for 1 hour
2	dried scallops, soaked for 1 hour
4	dried black mushrooms, soaked for 25 minutes
150 g (5 oz)	duck gizzards
30 g (1 oz)	canned champignons, drained and sliced
60 g (2 oz)	canned bamboo shoots, drained and diced
90 g (3 oz)	lean pork, diced
30 g (1 oz)	Chinese or cured (Smithfield) ham, diced
6 — 8 cups (1½ — 2 litres)	chicken stock, boiling
2 teaspoons	salt, or to taste
1 teaspoon	m.s.g. (optional)
6 slices	fresh ginger, bruised
1 tablespoon	rendered chicken fat (chicken grease), optional or use lard
½ teaspoon	white pepper (optional)

Wash the melon and cut a large slice from the top. Scoop out the seeds and decorate the rim in a zig-zag or scalloped design. Carve a pattern in the skin around the sides, if desired. Fill the melon with boiling, lightly salted water, stand in a bowl and steam for 10 minutes.

Drain the lotus seeds, cover with cold water and bring to the boil. Simmer for 25 minutes. Simmer the scallops in water or chicken stock until tender, about 25 minutes, then shred between forefinger and thumb. Squeeze the water from the black mushrooms, remove stems and dice. Cut open the gizzards, clean well and trim away the thick inner skin. Cut into dice and blanch in boiling water for 2 minutes. Drain well.

Drain the winter melon and return to the bowl. Add all the ingredients except chicken fat and white pepper and return to the steamer. Cover and steam over rapidly boiling water for 35 — 40 minutes until the ingredients are cooked through and the melon tender but retaining its shape.

Stir in the chicken fat and white pepper, if used, and serve the melon still in its bowl or transfer to a decorative bowl or rack before taking to the table.

CRISP-FRIED BAMBOO SHOOTS AND SCALLOPS

1 500 g (1 lb) can	bamboo shoots, drained
4	dried scallops (about 30 g / 1 oz), soaked for 1 hour
1 large bunch	fresh coriander or parsley
5 cups (1¼ litres)	deep-frying oil

Seasoning:

¼ cup (2 fl oz)	light soy sauce
1½ tablespoons	sugar
1 tablespoon	sesame oil

Cut the bamboo shoots into 4 cm (1 2/3 in) cubes. Place in a plastic bag and add the seasoning ingredients. Leave for 40 minutes, shaking the bag occasionally.

Drain the scallops, cover with water or chicken stock and simmer until softened, about 35 minutes. Drain and shred by rubbing between forefinger and thumb.

Heat the deep-frying oil to smoking point, then decrease the heat slightly. Drain the bamboo shoots and place in a frying basket. Deep-fry until crisp on the surface and thoroughly cooked, about 4 minutes. Remove and drain well.

Reheat the oil. Remove the stems from the coriander or parsley. Place in the frying basket and deep-fry for about 30 seconds. Drain well and arrange around the rim of a serving plate. Return the bamboo shoots to the oil to briefly fry for a second time. Drain and place on the serving plate. Add the shredded scallops to the oil, in a wire strainer, and fry until crisp. Scatter over the bamboo shoots and serve at once.

ASSORTED MEAT AND SHARK'S FIN SOUP

90 g (3 oz)	prepared shark's fin (see page 393)
90 g (3 oz)	prepared shark's skin (see page 393)*
2 tablespoons	softened lard
2	spring onions (scallions), trimmed and finely shredded
2 thick slices	fresh ginger, finely shredded
3 cups (24 fl oz)	chicken stock
60 g (2 oz)	lean pork, shredded
60 g (2 oz)	boneless chicken, shredded
45 g (1½ oz)	canned bamboo shoots, drained and shredded
3	large dried black mushrooms, soaked and shredded
2 tablespoons	finely shredded cooked ham
2 tablespoons	chopped fresh coriander
1 tablespoon	white vinegar
1 teaspoon	ground black pepper

Seasoning:

¾ teaspoon	salt
½ teaspoon	m.s.g. (optional)
2 tablespoons	light soy sauce
½ teaspoon	dark soy sauce
2 teaspoons	rice wine or dry sherry
2 tablespoons	cold water
2 tablespoons	cornflour (cornstarch)

Prepare the shark's fin and shark's skin according to the directions on page 393. Shred the shark's skin finely. Drain well.

Lightly fry the onion and ginger in the lard then add the shark's fin and shark's skin and fry briefly.

Bring the chicken stock to the boil in a large saucepan. Add the shark's fin and skin, the onions, ginger, pork, chicken, bamboo shoots, and ginger.

Return to the boil and skim, then add the pre-mixed seasoning ingredients. Simmer for 20 minutes, then transfer to a soup tureen and add the ham coriander, vinegar, and pepper. Stir well and serve.

* Or use fish maw or fish lips.

HOT AND SOUR SOUP

60 g (2 oz)	lean pork, finely shredded
30 g (1 oz)	Chinese or cured (Smithfield) ham, shredded
45 g (1½ oz)	cleaned fresh squid or prepared sea cucumber, finely shredded*
30 g (1 oz)	dried 'wood ear' fungus, soaked and shredded
2	dried black mushrooms, soaked and shredded
30 g (1 oz)	bean thread vermicelli, soaked
1 square	dry beancurd, finely shredded
30 g (1 oz)	canned bamboo shoots, drained and shredded
1	small carrot, peeled and shredded
2	spring onions (scallions), trimmed and shredded
2	eggs, well beaten
4 cups (1 litre)	chicken stock
2 tablespoons	cornflour (cornstarch)

Seasoning:

1½ teaspoons	salt
1 teaspoon	m.s.g. (optional)
½ teaspoon	sugar
1½ tablespoons	light soy sauce
2 tablespoons	white vinegar
1½ teaspoons	sesame oil (optional)
½ teaspoon	ground black pepper

Blanch the pork and ham in boiling water and drain. Bring the stock to the boil and add the salt, m.s.g., if used, and sugar. Add the shredded meat and vegetables and the noodles and return to the boil. Reduce to a simmer and cook for 2 minutes. Slowly drizzle in the beaten eggs and do not stir for at least 45 seconds while the egg sets into fine strands in the soup. Add the remaining seasoning and stir in.

Thicken with a thin paste of the cornflour and cold water and simmer until the soup thickens. Transfer to a soup tureen and garnish with generous amounts of chopped fresh coriander or flat leaf parsley, shredded fresh ginger, and shredded spring onions (scallions).

* Or use shredded congealed chicken blood.

MANDARIN FISH WITH VINEGAR AND PEPPER IN RICH SOUP

1 750 g (1½ lb)	Mandarin fish (perch, trout, or grouper)
5 cm (2 in) piece	fresh ginger
4 cups (1 litre)	deep-frying oil
4 slices	fresh ginger, shredded
4 cups (1 litre)	enriched stock*

Seasoning A:

1¼ teaspoons	salt
¾ teaspoon	m.s.g. (optional)
¼ teaspoon	white pepper
1 tablespoon	rice wine or dry sherry

Seasoning B:

10	garlic chives, shredded
8 — 10 sprigs	fresh coriander
⅓ cup	white vinegar
1½ teaspoons	sesame oil
¾ teaspoon	ground black pepper

Clean the fish, remove fins and gills and place in boiling water for 20 seconds. Lift out and carefully scrape off the skin. Heat a large wok and rub vigorously with the ginger to prevent the fish sticking.

Add the deep-frying oil and heat to smoking point, then reduce the heat slightly. Slide in the fish and deep-fry for 3 minutes on each side. Remove and reheat the oil to smoking point. Fry the fish for a further 2 minutes on each side.

Carefully lift out the fish and set aside. Pour off all but 2½ tablespoons of the oil and fry the shredded ginger briefly on moderate heat. Add the stock and seasoning A ingredients and bring to the boil. Add the fish, reduce the heat and simmer for 20 minutes.

Use two spatulas to lift the fish carefully into a soup tureen and strain the stock onto it. Add the seasoning B ingredients, stir in lightly and serve at once.

*See recipe page 388, or use chicken stock and additional stock powder or crumbled stock cube. Adjust salt to taste.

Candied Apples (recipe page 90) and Lotus Seeds in Sugar Syrup (recipe page 91).

CANDIED APPLES

3	cooking apples
6 cups (1½ litres)	clean deep-frying oil
1 cup	sesame oil
½ cup	sugar
	flour
2 teaspoons	toasted white sesame seeds
	iced water

Batter:

2	eggs, beaten
⅓ cup	flour
⅓ cup	cornflour (cornstarch)
	cold water

Peel and core the apples and cut into thick slices. Heat the deep-frying oil to moderate. Brush a serving plate with sesame oil, then add the remainder to the frying oil.

Beat the batter ingredients, adding enough water to make a smooth, fairly thick batter. Lightly coat the apple slices with flour and dip into the batter. Deep-fry the slices, several at a time, until golden on the surface and softening inside, about 1 minute. Drain and set aside.

Reheat the oil to hot and fry the apple pieces for a second time until crisp, about 45 seconds. Drain and set aside. Pour off all but 2 tablespoons of the oil and add the sugar. Stir constantly on high heat until the sugar caramelises and turns golden. Quickly return the apple pieces and add the sesame seeds. Turn the apple slices to coat evenly with the sugar syrup. Transfer to the oiled plate and serve at once with a dish of iced water.

Dip the apple into the water before eating to set the hot syrup into crisp toffee.

Sliced firm bananas, pineapple, sweet potato, or taro may all be used for this recipe, varying the deep-frying times accordingly.

ALMOND CREAM

1½ cups	blanched sweet almonds*
½ cup	sugar
5 cups (1¼ litres)	water
½ cup (4 fl oz)	evaporated milk or cream
2 tablespoons	cornflour (cornstarch)
2 tablespoons	cold water

Place the almonds in a low oven to cook until completely dried out, but without taking on any colour. Grind in a food processor, coffee grinder, or heavy duty blender (adding a little water to prevent the machine clogging).

Bring the water to the boil and add the sugar and powdered almonds. Stir until boiling again, then add the evaporated milk, if used, and the cornflour mixed to a paste with the cold water. Boil, stirring for 4 minutes. If using cream, add at this point.

Pour into a deep dish and serve hot or cold.

* Most Chinese food suppliers have both sweet and bitter almonds, the latter being smaller and more rounded in shape.

SWEET FERMENTED RICE WITH DICED FRESH FRUIT

1 cup	sweet fermented rice (see page 387)
½ cup	sugar
6 cups (1½ litres)	water
1 tablespoon	cornflour (cornstarch)
1	small red apple
6	maraschino cherries
½	orange
2 slices	canned or fresh pineapple
1	canned or fresh pear

Pour the rice and its liquid into a saucepan and add the sugar, water, and cornflour. Stir until the cornflour is well mixed, then bring to the boil and simmer for 2 minutes.

Peel and finely dice the apple, cut the cherries in halves, discarding the stones, if any, peel and dice the orange and dice the pineapple and pear. Stir the fruit into the rice liquid and simmer briefly.

Serve hot or allow to cool, then chill thoroughly and serve cold. Use additional fresh fruit to garnish.

EGG PUFFS WITH RED BEAN FILLING

5	egg whites
2 tablespoons	cornflour (cornstarch)
250 g (8 oz)	red bean paste (see page 386)
3 cups (24 fl oz)	vegetable oil
1 cup (8 fl oz)	sesame oil
2 tablespoons	castor sugar

Beat the egg whites to stiff peaks, then carefully fold in the cornflour.

Heat the vegetable oil and sesame oil together until warm. Dip each ball of red bean paste into the egg whites, coating thickly. Place in the oil, about 6 at a time and cook gently until golden, turning once.

Arrange on a warmed serving plate and sprinkle on the sugar to garnish. As the egg puffs deflate quickly after cooking, for best results serve as soon as they leave the pan.

In place of red bean filling, sweet lotus seed paste, a mixture of crunchy peanut paste (butter) and sugar or sweetened mashed taro or sweet potato could be substituted. Or use thoroughly drained canned fruit coated lightly with cornflour (cornstarch) so the batter will adhere.

'SNOW' FUNGUS IN SWEET SOUP

60 g (2 oz)	dried lotus seeds, soaked for 2 hours
6	dried lung an fruit, soaked for 1 hour (optional)*
15 g (½ oz)	'snow' fungus (white wood ears), soaked for 1 hour
60 g (2 oz)	Chinese red dates
¾ cup	sugar
12	canned quail eggs, drained

Drain the lotus seeds and place in a small saucepan with plenty of hot water. Bring to the boil and simmer gently until softened, about 30 minutes. Drain well. Separately simmer the lung an and 'snow' fungus for 10 minutes and drain well.

Place the dates and sugar in a saucepan and add 7 cups (1¾ litres) cold water. Bring to the boil and simmer for 10 minutes, then add the 'lung an' and snow fungus and simmer for a further 30 minutes.

Add the drained lotus seeds and the quail eggs and simmer gently for about 3 minutes. Serve hot.
* A dried fruit similar to loquat. Use sliced pear, papaya or apple as a substitute, or omit.

LOTUS SEEDS IN SUGAR SYRUP

250 g (8 oz) dried lotus seeds	
6 cups (1½ litres) boiling water	
2/3 cup sugar, or to taste	

Soak the lotus seeds in cold water for 20 minutes, then drain. Cover with cold water and simmer briefly, then drain again. Use a needle to pick out the bitter central core and then place the lotus seeds in a dish with half of the boiling water and set in a rack in a steamer.

Steam until tender, about 30 minutes over rapidly boiling water. Dissolve the sugar in the remaining water and pour into a serving bowl. Add the cooked lotus seeds and the liquid. Serve hot, or refrigerate until well chilled and serve as a refreshing cold dessert.

CHAPTER IV
Eastern Coastal Style Cuisine

東

Previous page: *Grain ripens along canal in scenic Soochow (Suzhou), one of China's great culinary centres.*

Ancient sailing sampans above *still ply the canals of Soochow (Suzhou) as they have for over 2,000 years.*

The eastern/coastal culinary region centres around the lower Yangtze River basin and extends south along the coast as far as the borders of Kuangtung (Guangdong) province. It includes the provinces and culinary styles of Kiangsu (Jiangsu), Chekiang (Zhejiang), and Fukien (Fujian). The native cuisine of Taiwan is an offshoot of Fukien (Fujian) style and is included in that category. The main gastronomic centres of this region are Nanking (Nanjing), Shanghai, Hangchow (Hangzhou), Soochow (Suzhou), and Taipei (Taibei).

The climate of the eastern/coastal region is the mildest in China, rainfall is abundant, and the soil is fertile. The four seasons are distinct and well balanced in this area, and major gastronomic festivals mark the changing of the seasons. The region is dominated by the lower Yangtze River and its intricate network of mini-rivers and lakes, which are further interconnected by countless man-made canals. These multi-purpose waterways provide water for irrigation, produce fresh-water fish and molluscs, and form extensive transportation networks for harvested foods. Gentle rolling hills and verdant foliage mark this pleasant, temperate region.

Historically, this part of China has been the favourite destination of Chinese tourists and gastronomes ever since the T'ang dynasty. Hangchow (Hangzhou) was the city which Marco Polo praised with such rapture as a 'Heavenly Paradise.' Soochow (Suzhou) has been renowned since ancient times as the city which produces the most beautiful women in China, and many writers have attributed this to the benefits of the excellent food, for which the city is equally famous. An ancient Chinese adage says, 'Above there is heaven; below there are Soochow (Suzhou) and Hangchow (Hangzhou).' Food is one of the main reasons that these cities acquired their 'celestial' reputation. Poets have praised the culinary arts of this region for centuries, as illustrated by this ode to the kitchens of Soochow (Suzhou), written by the Shing dynasty poet Gu Die-Jing:

Soochow (Suzhou), the good place.
At dawn
The bamboo is cut as smooth as jade,
Fresh and tender on a crockery plate.

Soochow (Suzhou), the good place.
Fresh arbutus,
Sweet as heavenly dew,
Fills my cheeks with juice.

Soochow (Suzhou), the good place.
Big beans
Picked when the flowers bend low
And munched at tea-time.

Soochow (Suzhou), the good place.
Where the shad
Are found, and globefish from the river
Are cooked in spring with ginger and chives.

Soochow (Suzhou), the good place.
In summer
Plump fish dart about the river
Avoiding the fisherman's boat.

Purple crabs in red-wine dregs
Make the autumn pass,
And when at last the sturgeon appear,
Carp and bream leap into the pot.

Seafood and fresh-water fish form the mainstays of the eastern/coastal menu. China's favourite fish are found here in abundance: carp, river eel, shad, Mandarin fish, whitebait, mullet, bream, perch, and many varieties of molluscs. Crab, prawn, and other seafoods are caught off the eastern seaboard. The fish recipes from this area are among the best in China. Abundant supplies of every type of vegetable are available as well, adding much colour and variety to the menu. Meat and poultry are also popular, the favourite choices being pork and chicken.

Eastern/coastal cooking involves

Manual labour still prevails on China's farms. Here and opposite page, greening fields of grain are carefully tended by hand for maximum output. Harvested and winnowed with ancient implements, the grain then travels by canal to town for distribution.

heavy use of vegetable oils, and the dishes appear somewhat oily as a result. This does not detract from the taste, however, since most of the oil remains on the platter. Sugar is used in cooking more than elsewhere, while soy sauce is employed sparingly: consequently, sauces are slightly on the sweet side and light in colour. Spring onions and ginger are the favoured fresh seasonings. For flavour, the people of this region prefer distinct, fresh tastes in the main ingredients and sweet, rich flavours in the sauces. For fragrance, the *xian* (fresh-natural) aromas are emphasized, especially in fish and seafoods. For colour, chefs aim for bright colours with a shiny sheen, the latter effect produced with cornflour (cornstarch). The region is famous for its cold hors-d'oeuvre plates contrived

in elaborate floral and animal designs with multi-coloured, multi-textured ingredients. In texture, the dishes tend towards the soft and tender, smooth and slippery types, though crispy textures are also provided in deep-fried foods.

The eastern/coastal region is home of the *hong-shao* or 'red-stew,' and this technique is applied to a wide range of ingredients. The other three most commonly employed cooking methods in Soochow (Suzhou), Hangchow (Hangzhou), and other culinary centres of the region are *bao, zhao,* and *zha.*

The eastern/coastal region is one of the most diverse culinary areas of China, and each of the three provincial cuisines which comprise it has its own distinct features. Fukien (Fujian) is most famous for its rich stews, soups,

and stocks, as well as *congee* or rice-gruel. Coagulated pig's and chicken's blood are also used extensively in Fukien (Fujian) cuisine. The most distinctive aspect of this cooking is the rich stock which is always kept on hand in the kitchen for use in practically every dish. To produce this stock, the bones and leftover meat of beef, pork, ham, and mutton are thrown together and boiled for a long time, after which the stock is filtered. Then, splintered chicken bones (to expose the marrow) are added, and the stock is boiled again, reduced, and filtered once more. The rich broth which remains is used as a general, multi-purpose cooking condiment and lends rich flavour to all dishes. Fukien (Fujian) is also home of the *zao* method of marination: meat, fish, and fowl are marinated in the fermented dregs of grain-mash left over from distilling spirits.

Kiangsu's (Jiangsu's) culinary capital is the charming city of Soochow (Suzhou), where the 'red-stew' was developed to perfection. Soochow's (Suzhou's) red-stews employ rock crystal sugar to achieve the light sweetness, the shiny colours, and the smooth textures which characterize this type of dish. This city boasts China's best river eel, Mandarin fish, and fresh-water crab, which are supplied by beautiful Lake Tai and other water-ways in the vicinity. Even today, Chinese gourmets from Shanghai flock to Soochow (Suzhou) in droves several times a year to participate in seasonal food festivals and sample the famous specialties. The great Ching emperor Chian-lung was converted to eastern/coastal cuisine when he paid a visit to Soochow (Suzhou) during one of his pleasure excursions to the south. He ate at the Pine-Crane restaurant, which still operates at the same address and serves some of the best food in all China.

Hangchow (Hangzhou), provincial capital of Chekiang (Zhejiang), has been one of China's greatest culinary centres since its heyday as the capital of the Southern Sung. The restaurant industry was born there, and today the city still boasts some of China's top eating establishments. Elaborate kitchen preparations, especially very fine, even cutting into slender slivers, are involved in Hangchow's (Hangzhou's) style of cooking. To protect the fresh-natural flavours and produce the light colours favoured in Hangzhou, soy sauce is used sparingly. West Lake, China's most famous scenic spot, provides much of the fish favoured in Hangzhou cuisine, especially the much-loved and highly prized Silver Carp. Silver Carp is used to make the city's most renowned dish, 'West Lake Sour Fish,' an unforgettable taste treat in which the whole fish is split in half lengthwise, lightly poached, covered with minced fresh ginger, and smothered with a rich, viscous sweet/sour sauce. The recipe, which is included in the recipe section, may be applied to other types of fresh-water fish as well. West Lake also provides *shun-chai*, a highly nutritious aquatic weed used to make soup. *Shun-chai* is as rich in flavour as it is in nutrition and has a unique slippery texture.

Other famous dishes of Hangchow (Hangzhou) are Onion-and-Oil Fish,

Typical open-air noodle stand in Shanghai, serving China's traditional version of fast-food. Menus in such stalls haven't changed for millennia.

Eel Fried in Batter, Boned Chicken with Green Chillies, Fried Beancurd Skin, Beggar's Chicken, and One Fish/Two Flavours, in which a fresh carp is split in half lengthwise, one half poached and the other half braised.

Taiwanese cuisine is an elaboration of Fukien (Fujian) style, with strong emphasis on fresh seafoods and rich, piquant sauces. The island produces an incredible variety of fresh garden vegetables, most of which are available year round and comprise important elements of the diet. *Geng* stew, one of the most ancient of Chinese dishes, is still very popular in Taiwan and is sold everywhere from little itinerant food stalls. Taipei's (Taibei's) restaurants offer not only the best of Taiwanese (Fukien (Fujian)) cuisine, but also excellent versions of all the other great regional cuisines of China.

Eastern/coastal China is one of the most pleasant regions in the country, and the food there reflects its natural blessings. Textures tend towards the soft and tender, smooth and slippery, while flavours and fragrances lean towards the sweet and the *xian* (fresh-natural). The heavy reliance on fresh fish and fresh vegetables makes the eastern/coastal diet one of the healthiest and best balanced in the world, as attested to by the dense population it supports. Connoisseurs of fresh-water fish and seafood will prefer the recipes from this region.

While southern-style cuisine, specifically Cantonese, has generally been, and still is, regarded as China's most highly developed, elaborate gourmet style, many experienced connoisseurs of Chinese food still prefer the eastern/coastal style above all else. If northern food is viewed as relatively austere and rustic while southern food is seen as highly exotic and complex, then eastern/coastal cuisine strikes a harmonious balance somewhere in between.

Hungry youngsters above *wait for woman vendor to finish frying 'Chinese doughnuts' in Shanghai alley. Bucolic West Lake* left *is the source of Hangchow's (Hangzhou's) Silver Carp, main ingredient of the city's famous 'West Lake Vinegar Fish.' Right: Foreign guests tuck into big bountiful winter banquet, including traditional 'hot-pot,' in Nanking (Nanjing) restaurant.*

CHICKEN STUFFED WITH SHARK'S FIN

750 g (1½ lb)	prepared shark's fin (see page 393) (about 185 g/6 oz dry weight)
1 — 1¾ kg (3½ lb)	chicken, deboned *
3	spring onions (scallions) cut in halves
4 thick slices	fresh ginger, bruised
1 tablespoon	rice wine or dry sherry
6 cups (1½ litres)	enriched stock
125 g (4 oz)	lean pork, thinly sliced (optional), or use 3 slices cooked ham or 1 ham bone
1½ teaspoons	salt
	m.s.g. (optional)

Drain the shark's fin and stuff into the chicken. Secure the opening with poultry pins and place in a casserole on the onions and ginger. Add the wine and stock and spread the pork or ham (or place the ham bone) on top. Add the salt and cover tightly.

Bring to the boil, then reduce heat to the very lowest point and simmer for about 4 hours. Discard the ham bone, if used, or serve the ham or pork separately (or reserve for another use). Remove the onion and ginger. Check the seasoning, adding a dash of m.s.g., if used. Serve in the pot.

* A deboned duck may be used instead of the chicken. If so, use ham or a ham bone in preference to pork.

STEAMED CHICKEN STUFFED WITH EIGHT PRECIOUS INGREDIENTS

1 — 1¾ (3½ lb)	chicken
1 teaspoon	salt
1 tablespoon	rice wine or dry sherry
60 g (2 oz)	glutinous rice, soaked for 1 hour
45 g (1½ oz)	dried lotus seeds, soaked for 1 hour
6	dried black mushrooms, soaked for 25 minutes
2 sets	chicken gizzards, blanched and drained
15 g (½ oz)	dried shrimps, soaked for 1 hour
30 g (1 oz)	frozen or fresh peas, parboiled
30 g (1 oz)	canned bamboo shoots, drained and diced
30 g (1 oz)	Chinese or cured (Smithfield) ham, finely diced
¼ cup (2 fl oz)	frying oil or softened lard
7 cups (1¾ litres)	chicken stock
1 tablespoon	dark soy sauce
8 cups (2 litres)	deep frying oil
	Chinese pepper-salt or spiced salt

Seasoning A:

½ teaspoon	salt
½ teaspoon	m.s.g. (optional)
1 teaspoon	rice wine or dry sherry
¼ cup (2 fl oz)	chicken stock

Seasoning B:

1 tablespoon	rice wine or dry sherry
1 teaspoon	Chinese brown peppercorns
2	spring onions (scallions), trimmed and diced
2 slices	fresh ginger
1½ teaspoons	salt

Debone the chicken, leaving the leg and wing bones intact. Rub inside with the salt and wine.

Place the rice and lotus seeds in a dish with ¾ cup (6 fl oz) water and steam until tender. Remove mushroom stems, squeeze out water and cut into small dice. Trim off the thick inner skin from the gizzards and cut into small dice. Drain the shrimp and peas.

Heat the frying oil in wok and stir-fry the diced gizzards for 3 minutes, then add the mushrooms, bamboo shoots, ham, and shrimps and stir-fry for 2 minutes. Add the seasoning A ingredients, the peas, rice, and lotus seeds and mix thoroughly.

Stuff the 'eight precious' ingredients mixture into the chicken, taking care not to tear the skin. Sew up the opening or secure with poultry pins.

Place the chicken bones in a casserole and set the chicken, breast upwards, on top. Cover with chicken stock and add the seasoning B ingredients. Cover and place on a rack in a steamer over rapidly boiling water. Steam for 1¾ hours until tender. Lift out carefully and wipe dry. Brush with the dark soy sauce while still hot and leave to dry for ½ hour.

Heat the deep-frying oil to smoking point, then reduce the heat slightly. Fry the chicken, completely immersed if possible, until brown. Drain well. Make several cuts across the body to expose the filling and serve whole, with Chinese pepper-salt or spiced salt dips.

STEWED SHARK'S FIN WITH CHICKEN, DUCK, AND PORK

Serves 6 as the main course.

250 g (8 oz)	prepared shark's fin, see page 393 (about 60 g/2 oz dry weight)
1 kg (2 lb)	chicken
500 g (1 lb)	duck meat
500 g (1 lb)	boneless pork (leg or shoulder)
2	spring onions (scallions), trimmed
4 thick slices	fresh ginger, bruised
2 tablespoons	rice wine or dry sherry
8 cups (2 litres)	enriched stock
6 pieces	dried scallops (about 45 g/1½ oz), soaked for 2 hours
125 g (4 oz)	Chinese cabbage or bok choy (celery cabbage)
¼ cup (2 fl oz)	frying oil
30 g (1 oz)	Chinese or cured (Smithfield) ham, shredded
60 g (2 oz)	canned bamboo shoots, drained and sliced
	white pepper
	extra frying oil
2 tablespoons	rendered chicken fat (chicken grease), optional

Seasoning:

	salt to taste
1 teaspoon	m.s.g. (optional)
1 teaspoon	sugar
1 tablespoon	rice wine or dry sherry
¼ cup (2 fl oz)	light soy sauce
3 tablespoons	cornflour (cornstarch)
¼ cup (2 fl oz)	chicken stock or cold water

Prepare dried shark's fin according to the instructions on page 393, allowing at least 3 hours advance preparation.

Cut the chicken, duck, and pork into 2.5 cm (1 in) cubes and blanch in boiling water.

Arrange the drained shark's fin in a bamboo basket which fits into a casserole or slow cooker and place the cubed meats on top with the onions and ginger slices. Add the wine and enriched stock and bring to the boil. Cover tightly and simmer on low heat for 3 hours, until the meat and fins are tender.

In the meantime, steam the drained scallops in ¾ cup (6 fl oz) water with a dash of rice wine or dry sherry and salt added, until tender

Wash the vegetables and cut into 5 cm (2 in) pieces. Shake out excess water. Heat the wok, add the oil and fry the vegetables on moderately high heat for 2 minutes. Add the ham and fry for 1 minute, then add the sliced bamboo shoots and the drained scallops and fry together a further 1 minute. Add a dash of rice wine or dry sherry, salt and sugar to taste. Set aside.

Remove the meat from the casserole and cut into small dice, discarding all bones. Wipe out the wok and heat about 3 tablespoons frying oil to very hot. Add the meat and fry for 2 minutes.

Remove the shark's fin to a serving dish. Strain the juices into the wok and bring to the boil. Add the pre-mixed seasoning ingredients and bring to the boil. Return the vegetables, ham, and scallops and simmer for about 3 minutes. Adjust seasoning as necessary, adding plenty of white pepper. Stir in the chicken fat, if used, and pour over the shark's fin. Serve.

STEAMED SHARK'S FIN WITH CRABMEAT

250 g (8 oz)	prepared shark's fin (see page 393), about 60 g/2 oz dry weight
4 cups (1 litre)	enriched stock
2	spring onions (scallions), trimmed
4 thick slices	fresh ginger
315 g (10 oz)	Chinese cabbage hearts or young bok choy
⅓ cup	frying oil or softened lard
1 tablespoon	rice wine or dry sherry
250 g (8 oz)	fresh, frozen, or canned crabmeat, flaked
60 g (2 oz)	crab roe (optional)

Seasoning:

	salt to taste
1 teaspoon	m.s.g.(optional)
2 tablespoons	cornflour (cornstarch)
¼ cup (2 fl oz)	cold water

Prepare dried shark's fins according to the instructions on page 393, allowing at least 3 hours advance preparation. Arrange the drained fins in a covered dish and add the enriched stock, spring onions and ginger. Cover and set on a rack in a steamer or large saucepan of rapidly boiling water. Cover the steamer tightly and steam in high heat for 2½ hours.

Wash the vegetables and cut any larger pieces in halves. Shake out the excess water. Heat the wok and add the oil or lard. Fry the vegetables on moderately high heat for 3 minutes. Remove. Splash in the wine and add the crabmeat and roe, if used. Saute for 1 minute and add the pre-mixed seasoning ingredients with the liquid from the shark's fins. Bring to the boil. Simmer until thickened. Arrange the drained fins in a serving dish and pour on the sauce.

Arrange the vegetables around the edge of the dish and serve.

SLICED ABALONE WITH MINCED CHICKEN

1 310 g (10 oz) can	abalone
185 g (6 oz)	boneless chicken, finely minced (ground)
90 g (3 oz)	pork fat, finely minced (ground)
2 tablespoons	finely chopped spring onion (scallion)
½ teaspoon	grated fresh ginger
2 tablespoons	frying oil or softened lard
2 teaspoons	rendered chicken fat, (chicken grease), optional
2 tablespoons	finely chopped cooked ham

Seasoning:

2	large egg whites, beaten
½ teaspoon	salt
¾ teaspoon	m.s.g. (optional)
½ teaspoon	white pepper
⅓ cup	cold water or chicken stock

Drain the abalone and place on a cutting board. Trim the ruffled edges, then slice thinly, following directions on page 392

Mix the chicken, pork fat, onion, and ginger with the seasoning ingredients, stirring thoroughly.

Heat the wok and add lard. Fry the creamed chicken on moderate heat until white, about 2 minutes, then add the sliced abalone and stir gently on low heat until well warmed through. Add a little chicken stock or water if the mixture begins to stick. Stir in chicken fat, if used.

Transfer to a warmed serving plate and garnish with the ham.

STEAMED SEA CUCUMBER AND HAM

700 g (1⅓ lb)	prepared sea cucumber (see page 392), about 4 large dried sea cucumbers
90 g (3 oz)	Chinese or cured (Smithfield) ham, sliced
6	spring onions (scallions), cut in halves
6 thick slices	fresh ginger, bruised
1 tablespoon	rice wine or dry sherry cornflour (cornstarch) white pepper
1 tablespoon	rendered chicken fat (chicken grease), optional
3 cups (24 fl oz)	hot chicken stock

Drain the sea cucumbers, cut open and score in a criss-cross pattern on the inside. Cut into 4 cm (1 2/3 in) squares. Place the cucumber and sliced ham in separate dishes and divide the spring onions, ginger, and wine between them. Add the salt to the sea cucumbers and cover each with the chicken stock. Place on a rack in a steaming pot, cover tightly and steam over rapidly boiling water for 25 minutes.

Strain the liquid from the ham over the sea cucumbers and thicken the sauce with a thin solution of cornflour mixed with cold water. Add white pepper to taste and the rendered chicken fat, if used, and arrange the sliced ham on top. Serve in the same dish.

Stewed Shark's Fin with Chicken, Duck and Pork (recipe page 99).

FISH MAW SALAD WITH SESAME SAUCE

Serve hot as a main dish, or cold as an appetiser.

125 g (4 oz)	dried fish maw
3 cups (24 fl oz)	chicken stock
2	spring onions (scallions), trimmed and sliced
3 slices	fresh ginger
	fresh coriander

Seasoning:

1½ teaspoons	salt
¾ teaspoon	m.s.g. (optional)
1 tablespoon	rice wine or dry sherry

Sauce:

½ cup (4 fl oz)	chicken stock
2 tablespoons	sesame paste
1 tablespoon	sesame oil
½ teaspoon	salt
½ teaspoon	m.s.g. (optional)
	chilli oil (optional)

Prepare the fish maw according to the directions on page 392, cutting it into bite-sized pieces.

Place in a saucepan with the spring onions and ginger and add the chicken stock. Bring to the boil and simmer for 15 minutes, then add the seasoning ingredients and simmer until the liquid has been completely absorbed and the fish maw is tender. Increase the heat to high to evaporate any remaining liquid, if necessary.

If serving cold, remove from the heat and transfer to a serving plate. Leave to cool. Mix the sauce ingredients and pour over the dish. Stir in lightly and garnish with fresh coriander. Serve.

To serve hot, add the sauce to the fish maw immediately after it is removed from the heat. Stir in and transfer to a serving plate. Serve at once.

BRAISED FISH MAW WITH ASSORTED MEATS

90 g (3 oz)	dried fish maw
2 cups (16 fl oz)	chicken stock
1	spring onion (scallion), trimmed and sliced
2 slices	fresh ginger, shredded
90 g (3 oz)	raw peeled shrimps
90 g (3 oz)	boneless chicken breast
45 g (1½ oz)	cooked ham
90 g (3 oz)	Chinese cabbage or bok choy (celery cabbage)
1½ cups (12 fl oz)	softened lard or frying oil
	cornflour (cornstarch)
1 tablespoon	rendered chicken fat (chicken grease), optional

Seasoning A and B: (Prepare two)

1	egg white
⅓ teaspoon	salt
2 teaspoons	cornflour (cornstarch)

Seasoning C:

2 tablespoons	chicken stock
2 teaspoons	rice wine or dry sherry
¾ teaspoon	salt
½ teaspoon	m.s.g. (optional)

Prepare the fish maw according to the directions on page 392, cutting into short strips. Drain well and place in a saucepan with the chicken stock, spring onion, and ginger. Bring to the boil and simmer on low heat until most of the liquid has been absorbed and the fish maw is tender.

Devein the shrimps with a toothpick (see page 394). Wash and pat dry, then place in a dish with the seasoning A ingredients. Cut the chicken into narrow strips, mix with the seasoning B ingredients and leave for 10 minutes. Shred the ham and cut the cabbage into bite-sized pieces.

Heat the lard and quickly fry the shrimps and chicken until almost cooked, about 45 seconds. Remove and drain off most of the oil. Thicken the remaining fish maw sauce with a thin solution of cornflour and cold water and transfer to a serving dish.

Reheat the wok and add the ham and cabbage. Briefly stir-fry, then return the shrimps and chicken and add the seasoning C ingredients. Stir-fry briefly, then pour over the fish maw and serve at once.

STEWED STUFFED CHICKEN

1 1¾ kg (3½ lb)	chicken
250 g (8 oz)	slightly fat pork, finely minced (ground)
75 g (8 oz)	pine seeds or walnuts, blanched and drained
4 cups (1 litre)	deep frying oil
155 g (5 oz)	Chinese cabbage hearts, young bok choy or kale
¼ cup (2 fl oz)	frying oil or softened lard
2 teaspoons	rendered chicken fat (chicken grease), optional

Batter:

1	egg white, beaten
¼ teaspoon	salt
	pinch of white pepper
2 tablespoons	cornflour (cornstarch)

Seasoning:

1 tablespoon	finely chopped spring onion (scallion)
½ teaspoon	grated fresh ginger
½ teaspoon	m.s.g. (optional)
½ teaspoon	sugar
½ teaspoon	rice wine or dry sherry
1½ tablespoons	light soy sauce

Sauce:

¾ cup (6 fl oz)	chicken stock
½ cup (4 fl oz)	sugar colouring (see page 388)
2 teaspoons	rice wine
1 tablespoon	light soy sauce

Remove legs and wings from the chicken and set aside. Cut the body into four even-sized pieces and place, skin downwards, on a cutting board. Use a sharp paring knife to score the meat closely in a criss-cross pattern, cutting almost through but taking care not to pierce the skin. Sprinkle on a little salt. Mix the batter ingredients and add a little water to make a creamy paste. Spread over the chicken where scored.

Mix the pork with the seasoning ingredients and divide between the chicken pieces, moulding it on smoothly. Lightly toast the nuts and chop coarsely. Spread thickly over the pork filling, pressing on lightly with the fingertips. Heat the deep oil to fairly hot and fry the stuffed chicken pieces, stuffing downwards, until brown, Drain well.

Arrange the legs and wings in a saucepan and place the stuffed chicken pieces on top, filling upwards. Carefully pour in the sauce ingredients, cover tightly and braise on moderate to low heat for 45 minutes.

Wash the vegetables, cutting any larger ones in halves. Shake out excess water and sauté in the frying oil or lard on moderate heat for 4 minutes. Season with a splash of wine and a dash of sugar, salt, and white pepper. Arrange in a ring around the edge of a serving plate.

Drain the chicken pieces, discarding legs and wings or serving these separately. Cut the stuffed chicken into thin slices and arrange on the plate. Strain the cooking liquid into the wok and bring to the boil. Adjust seasoning and thicken with a thin solution of cornflour (cornstarch) mixed with cold water. Stir in the chicken fat, if used, and pour over the chicken.

CHICKEN SHREDS SAUTÉD WITH TUBERROSE PETALS

250 g (8 oz)	boneless chicken breasts
50	tuberrose petals (or use white chrysanthemum petals)
2 tablespoons	frying oil or softened lard
1 teaspoon	rendered chicken fat (chicken grease), optional

Seasoning:

1	egg white, beaten
¼ teaspoon	salt
½ teaspoon	m.s.g. (optional)
1 teaspoon	cornflour (cornstarch)

Sauce:

½ cup (4 fl oz)	chicken stock
½ teaspoon	rice wine or dry sherry
¼ teaspoon	salt
½ teaspoon	m.s.g. (optional)
1 teaspoon	cornflour (cornstarch)

Skin the chicken breasts and slice thinly, then cut into shreds and mix with the seasoning ingredients. Leave to marinate for 15 minutes.

Rinse the rose (or chrysanthemim) petals in warn water and drain well.

Heat the wok and add the oil or lard. Sauté the chicken shreds on moderate heat until white, about 1½ minutes. Remove to a serving plate. Sauté the petals with a little more oil, if needed, for 30 seconds then pour in the pre-mixed sauce ingredients and bring to the boil.

Stir in the chicken fat, if used, just before serving.

CHICKEN WALNUT ROLLS

250 g (8 oz)	boneless chicken breast
45 g (1½ oz)	walnuts, blanched and drained
4 cups (1 litre)	deep frying oil
155 g (5 oz)	young bok choy or broccoli broken into florets
½ teaspoon	white vinegar
1 teaspoon	sesame oil (optional)

Seasoning A:

1	egg white, beaten
¼ teaspoon	salt
½ teaspoon	m.s.g. (optional)
1 tablespoon	cornflour (cornstarch)
1 tablespoon	water

Seasoning B:

2 tablespoons	softened lard
¼ teaspoon	grated fresh ginger
1 tablespoon	finely chopped spring onion (scallion)
¼ teaspoon	crushed garlic

Sauce:

½ cup (4 fl oz)	chicken stock
1 tablespoon	light soy sauce
¼ teaspoon	salt
¼ teaspoon	m.s.g. (optional)
½ teaspoon	sugar
¼ teaspoon	white pepper
½ teaspoon	cornflour (cornstarch)

Skin the chicken breasts and cut the meat across the grain into reasonably thin slices. Bat gently with the side of a cleaver to flatten a little more. Mix with the seasoning A ingredients and set aside to marinate for 15 minutes. Dry the walnuts and deep-fry in fairly hot oil until lightly coloured. Lift out and drain well. Leave to cool. Place a walnut in the centre of each chicken slice, roll up and squeeze gently to hold. Toothpicks may be necessary to secure some of the rolls, but most should stay in place unaided.

Reheat the deep-frying oil to moderate and fry the chicken walnut rolls until the meat whitens, about 1 minute. Lift out and drain well. Pour off all but 2 tablespoons of the oil and sauté the vegetables for 4 minutes. Add a dash of wine, salt and sugar and 2 tablespoons of cold water or chicken stock and cook, covered, for a further 1 minute.

Fry the seasoning B ingredients together in another pan, then add the pre-mixed sauce ingredients and bring to the boil. Add the chicken rolls and warm through in the sauce. Season with vinegar and sesame oil, if used. Transfer to a warmed serving dish.

OYSTER SAUCE CHICKEN IN PARCELS

Serve as an appetiser or main course.

250 g (8 oz)	boneless chicken breast
	several sheets of edible rice paper, cellophane or greaseproof paper
	sesame oil
3 cups (24 fl oz)	deep-frying oil
	small bunch of fresh coriander, broken into sprigs with stems removed

Seasoning:

½ teaspoon	m.s.g. (optional)
1¼ teaspoons	sugar
	pinch of white pepper
1 tablespoon	oyster sauce
2 teaspoons	sesame oil
¼ teaspoon	grated fresh ginger
1 tablespoon	finely chopped spring onion (scallion)

Skin the chicken breasts and cut across the grain into thin slices, about 5 × 2.5 cm (2 × 1 in). Mix with the seasoning ingredients and leave to marinate for 20 minutes.

Cut the paper into 12 cm (5 in) squares and brush one side with sesame oil. Place a slice of chicken on each paper, towards one corner. Add a sprig of coriander and top with another chicken slice. Fold the closest corner over the chicken, then fold in the two sides and lastly the end flap, tucking it securely inside the other folds.

Heat the deep oil to moderate and fry the chicken parcels, turning once or twice, until they float to the surface, about 3 minutes.

Drain well, arrange on a serving plate and surround with fresh coriander. Serve piping hot. If using cellophane or greaseproof paper, use scissors to cut an opening in the tops to facilitate removal of the chicken.

Chicken Walnut Rolls (recipe this page).

DEEP-FRIED MOCK-CHICKEN DRUMSTICKS

Serve as an appetiser or main course.

12	small chicken feet, about 375 g (12 oz), optional, or use short wooden sticks or bamboo skewers
185 g (6 oz)	boneless chicken, minced (ground)
60 g (2 oz)	canned water chestnuts, drained and finely chopped
2	large eggs, beaten
	cornflour (cornstarch)
4 cups (1 litre)	deep-frying oil

Seasoning A:

1 teaspoon	salt
1 teaspoon	m.s.g. (optional)
2	spring onions (scallions), trimmed
3 thick slices	fresh ginger

Seasoning B:

1	egg white, beaten
¼ teaspoon	salt
½ teaspoon	m.s.g. (optional)
	pinch of white pepper
½ teaspoon	sugar
1 tablespoon	onion and ginger infusion (see page 386)
1 tablespoon	cornflour (cornstarch)

Place the chicken feet in a saucepan with water to cover. Add the seasoning A ingredients and bring to the boil. Simmer for 1 hour or until tender, then drain well and remove the claws. If the chicken feet have the skin on, remove by blanching in boiling water for 2 minutes, draining and pulling the skin away before cooking.

Mix the chicken, pork, and water chestnuts with the seasoning B ingredients, kneading to a smooth sticky paste. Divide into 12 portions and form each into a ball shape around the leg-end of each foot to resemble drumsticks. Dip into beaten egg and coat thickly with cornflour.

Heat deep-frying oil to moderately hot and fry the drumsticks until golden brown and cooked through, about 4 minutes. Lift out and drain well. Arrange on a bed of shredded lettuce and serve with a chilli pepper and soy sauce dip (see page 407)

CHICKEN WINGS SIMMERED IN WINE

('Wings of the Magnificent Concubine')

12	chicken wings
6	large dried black mushrooms, soaked for 25 minutes
½ cup (4 fl oz)	frying oil or softened lard
2 tablespoons	finely chopped spring onion (scallion)
1 teaspoon	grated fresh ginger
1	large brown onion, thinly sliced
2 tablespoons	red grape wine

Seasoning A:

2 tablespoons	light soy sauce
½ teaspoon	m.s.g. (optional)
1 teaspoon	sugar

Seasoning B/Sauce:

2¼ cups (18 fl oz)	chicken stock
1 tablespoon	light soy sauce
2 teaspoons	dark soy sauce
1¼ teaspoons	sugar
¼ teaspoon	salt
2 tablespoons	red grape wine

Cut off the wing tips and divide each wing into two at the joints. Drain the mushrooms and remove the stems.

Heat half the oil or lard and fry the spring onions and ginger on moderately high heat for 1 minute. Add the wings with the seasoning A ingredients and stir-fry on high heat until the seasoning is absorbed into the wings and they turn a red-brown colour.

Transfer to a casserole or slow cooker and add the seasoning B/sauce ingredients. Cover and braise for 20 minutes, or the equivalent in a slow cooker.

Fry the sliced onion in the remaining oil or lard until well browned. Add the mushrooms and fry briefly, then add to the casserole. Re-cover and braise a further 15 minutes. Stir in the remaining red wine just before serving.

SPRING CHICKEN SHOWERED WITH HOT OIL

1 1¼ kg (2 lb)	spring chicken
8 cups (2 litres)	deep frying oil

Seasoning:

¼ teaspoon	salt
½ teaspoon	m.s.g. (optional)
2 teaspoons	sugar
¼ teaspoon	white pepper
¼ teaspoon	ground Chinese brown pepper
2 tablespoons	light soy sauce
1 tablespoon	rice wine or dry sherry
1 teaspoon	white vinegar (optional)
1 tablespoon	spring onion (scallion), finely chopped
1¼ teaspoon	grated fresh ginger

Sauce:

2 tablespoons	enriched or chicken stock
¼ cup	light soy sauce
1½ tablespoons	white vinegar
¼ cup	sesame oil
1½ tablespoons	sugar
1½ tablespoons	spring onion (scallion), finely chopped
1½ tablespoons	grated fresh ginger

Cut the chicken in halves through back and breast bones, rub with the pre-mixed seasoning ingredients and set aside for 1 hour.

Bring the sauce ingredients to a rolling boil. Remove from the heat and leave to cool, then pour into several small dishes.

Heat the deep oil to moderate. Place the chicken, skin upwards, in a large frying basket and suspend over the oil. Ladle the hot oil over the chicken continually until cooked through, about 45 minutes.

As this process is somewhat tedious, acceptable results can be obtained by gently poaching the chicken in warm oil until cooked through. To avoid greasiness, remove the chicken every 6-7 minutes and reheat the oil to moderate. Cooking time is approximately 25 minutes.

Drain well and slice. Serve with the prepared sauce dips.

PRESERVED CUCUMBER, AND GINGER STEWED CHICKEN WITH BEANS

750 g (1½ lb)	chicken pieces
125 g (4 oz)	fresh or frozen lima (fava) beans (or fresh soybeans, shelled, if available)
30 g (1 oz)	soy-preserved cucumber (see page 389)
30 g (1 oz)	soy-preserved ginger (see page 389)
¼ cup (2 fl oz)	frying oil or softened lard
2	spring onions (scallions), trimmed and diced salt to taste sesame oil (optional)

Seasoning A:

¼ teaspoon	salt
½ teaspoon	sugar
1 tablespoon	light soy sauce
1 tablespoon	rice wine or dry sherry

Seasoning B/Sauce:

⅓ cup	chicken stock or cold water
1 tablespoon	light soy sauce
½ teaspoon	rice wine or dry sherry
2 teaspoons	sugar

Wash the chicken and cut into bite-sized pieces through the bones. Mix with the seasoning A ingredients and set aside for 20 minutes. Boil the lima or soybeans until just tender in slightly salted water. Drain, refresh in cold water and drain again. Wash the cucumber and ginger in warm water, drain well and cut into small shreds.

Heat the lard in a wok and stir-fry the chicken until almost cooked through, about 6 minutes on moderate heat. Add the cucumber, ginger, and onion and stir-fry a further 1 minute. Stir in the seasoning B/sauce ingredients, pre-mixed, and cover. Reduce heat when boiling and simmer for 4 minutes. Add the beans and heat through. Adjust seasoning with salt and stir in sesame oil, if used.

Transfer to a serving dish.

CREAMED CHICKEN WITH MUSHROOMS, HAM AND PEA SPROUTS

185 g (6 oz)	boneless chicken, finely minced (ground)
60 g (2 oz)	sweet pea sprouts, snow peas, bean sprouts, or fresh spinach (collard greens)
60 g (2 oz)	canned straw mushrooms or champignons, drained and sliced
30 g (1 oz)	fresh ham, sliced the size of the champignons
1½ cups (12 fl oz)	frying oil
1½ teaspoons	rendered chicken fat (chicken grease), optional

Seasoning A:

2	egg whites, beaten
¼ teaspoon	salt
½ teaspoon	m.s.g. (optional)
¼ teaspoon	sugar
½ teaspoon	rice wine or dry sherry
1 tablespoon	onion and ginger infusion (see page 386)
1 tablespoon	cornflour (cornstarch)
2 tablespoons	cold water

Seasoning B/Sauce:

⅓ cup	chicken stock
¼ teaspoon	salt
½ teaspoon	m.s.g. (optional)
¼ teaspoon	sugar
½ teaspoon	rice wine or dry sherry
½ teaspoon	cornflour (cornstarch)

Mix the minced chicken with the seasoning A ingredients, stirring in one direction for about 5 minutes to make a smooth creamy paste. Wash the vegetables and chop the spinach finely, if used. Heat the oil to moderate in a wok and pour in the chicken paste. Stir gently in the oil until it turns white, about 1¾ minutes. Transfer to a plastic strainer to drain.

Pour off all but 2 tablespoons of the oil and sauté the vegetables, mushrooms, and ham on moderate to high heat for 2 minutes. Add the seasoning B/sauce ingredients, pre-mixed, and bring to the boil.

Reduce heat and simmer for about 2 minutes, then return the chicken paste and heat through, stirring continually. Add the chicken fat, if used, and transfer to a warmed serving plate.

STEAMED CHICKEN AND MUSHROOM POT

750 g (1½ lb)	chicken pieces
8 — 10	dried black mushrooms, soaked for 25 minutes
3	spring onions (scallions), trimmed and sliced
1 thick slice	fresh ginger, shredded finely
1 teaspoon	cornflour (cornstarch)
1 tablespoon	cold water

Seasoning:

1 tablespoon	light soy sauce
2 teaspoons	rice wine or dry sherry
½ teaspoon	salt
¼ teaspoon	m.s.g. (optional)
	pinch of white pepper
½ teaspoon	sugar
½ cup (4 fl oz)	chicken stock or cold water

Wash the chicken and cut through the bones into bite-sized pieces. Drain the mushrooms and remove the stems.

Arrange the chicken, mushrooms, onion, and ginger in a covered dish and add the pre-mixed seasoning ingredients. Set on a rack in a steamer over gently boiling water. Cover the pan and steam for 1¼ hours on moderate heat. Thicken the sauce with the mixed cornflour and cold water and serve the chicken and mushrooms in the dish in which they were cooked.

Chicken Wings Simmered in Wine (recipe page 106).

DEEP-FRIED CHICKEN LIVERS WITH SPICY DRESSING

375 g (12 oz)	fresh chicken livers
6 cups (1½ litres)	deep-frying oil
1 tablespoon	sesame oil
3 tablespoons	finely chopped spring onion scallion)
2 teaspoons	finely chopped fresh ginger
1½-2 teaspoons	Chinese pepper-salt

Seasoning:

1½ teaspoons	rice wine or dry sherry
¼ teaspoon	white pepper
½ teaspoon	m.s.g. (optional)
2 teaspoons	sugar
2 teaspoons	grated fresh ginger

Batter:

2	eggs, well beaten
3 tablespoons	cornflour (cornstarch)
3 tablespoons	flour

Wash the livers and cut into bite-sized pieces. Mix with the seasoning ingredients, and leave to marinate for 20 minutes. Make a thick batter with the eggs, cornflour, and flour, adding a little water. Beat well.

Heat the deep-frying oil to smoking. Drain the chicken and dip into the batter, coating thickly. Deep-fry until well browned. Drain well.

Pour off the oil and wipe out the pan. Add the sesame oil and heat through, then return the chicken livers and add the spring onion, ginger, and pepper-salt. Stir on moderate heat until the chicken livers are cooked through, about 3 minutes. Serve.

SLICED ROAST DUCK WITH BROCCOLI

½	cold roast duck (see recipe page 111, Charcoal Roast Duck)
500 g (1 lb)	fresh broccoli, broken into florets
2	spring onions (scallions), trimmed and sliced
⅓ cup	frying oil or softened lard
2 slices	fresh ginger, shredded
½ teaspoon	white vinegar (optional)
½ teaspoon	sesame oil (optional)

Seasoning:

½ teaspoon	salt
¾ teaspoon	m.s.g. (optional)
¾ teaspoon	sugar
1 tablespoon	light soy sauce
2 teaspoons	rice wine or dry sherry
⅓ cup	chicken stock
¾ teaspoon	cornflour (cornstarch)

Debone the duck and cut into bite-sized pieces. Fry in a wok with the oil or lard until lightly browned, then add the broccoli and spring onions and fry a further 3 minutes, stirring constantly.

Add the ginger and seasoning ingredients and bring to the boil. Stir until thickened. Add sesame oil and vinegar, if used, and transfer to a serving plate.

CHARCOAL-ROASTED DUCK STUFFED WITH LOTUS LEAVES

1 2½ kg (5 lb)	fairly fat duck
1 teaspoon	salt
1 tablespoon	rice wine or dry sherry
6	dried or fresh lotus leaves
12	large spring onions (scallions), trimmed
	sweet bean paste or hoisin sauce
	sesame oil (optional)
	sugar
24	mandarin pancakes (see recipe, page 373)

Glaze:

3 tablespoons	malt sugar (or golden syrup, clear honey, or light corn syrup)
½ cup (4 fl oz)	boiling water

If possible, have the duck drawn through an incision beneath one wing. Rub the salt and wine inside the cavity and prop the body open with a short stick placed inside the breast cavity between the shoulders.

soak dried lotus leaves, if used, in boiling water until softened. If using fresh leaves, blanch in boiling water for 10 seconds. Drain and roll the leaves up together, then shred coarsely. Place the lotus leaves and two spring onions into the cavity and tie a string around the neck, then under the wings. Hang in a well-ventilated area over a drip tray. Pour on several lots of boiling water to tighten the skin, then mix the malt sugar, or substitute, with the ½ cup boiling water and pour slowly and evenly over the duck. Leave for at least 6 hours until the skin is dry to the touch

Charcoal roast the duck, turning frequently until cooked through, with skin crisp and dark, about 1½ hours, oven roast on a rotisserie at 200°C (400°F).

Using a sharp carving knife, pare off the crisp skin in pieces about 4 cm (1 2/3 in) square and arrange on a plate. Cut the meat into bite-sized pieces and serve on another plate. Save the carcass for soup or stock. Discard the lotus leaves.

Have the pancakes warm and ready. (They keep well if wrapped in aluminium foil.) Heat the sweet bean paste with sugar and sesame oil to taste, or use pre-made duck sauce (hoisin or plum). Cut the trimmed spring onions into 5 cm (2 in) lengths and cut in halves lengthwise.

To eat the duck, place a slice of spring onion in the centre of a pancake. Dip a piece of crisp skin into the sauce, followed by a piece of meat. Place on the pancake, add more onion if desired and roll up, tucking in the ends.

ROAST DUCK WITH SPICY SAUCE

1	hot roast duck (see recipe, on this page) Charcoal-Roasted Duck)

Sauce:

⅓ cup	chicken stock
1 tablespoon	light soy sauce
1 teaspoon	white vinegar
1½ tablespoons	soybean paste or dark soy sauce
1 tablespoon	sesame oil
¼ teaspoon	m.s.g. (optional)
1 tablespoon	sugar
½ teaspoon	ground black pepper
1 tablespoon	finely chopped spring onion (scallion)
¾ teaspoon	grated fresh ginger
1 teaspoon	crushed garlic
½ teaspoon	cornflour (cornstarch)

Slice the duck, debone if preferred, and arrange on a plate. Mix the sauce ingredients in a saucepan and bring to the boil, pour over the duck and serve.

DEEP-FRIED AND SIMMERED DUCK STUFFED WITH EIGHT PRECIOUS INGREDIENTS

1 2¼ kg (4½ lb)	duck with giblets
1½ teaspoons	salt
1 tablespoon	rice wine or dry sherry
30 g (1 oz)	pearl barley, washed
45 g (1½ oz)	dried lotus seeds, soaked for 1 hour
60 g (2 oz)	glutinous rice, soaked for 1 hour
5	dried black mushrooms, soaked for 25 minutes
45 g (1½ oz)	Chinese or cured (Smithfield) ham, diced
60 g (2 oz	canned bamboo shoots, drained and diced
30 g (1 oz)	dried shrimps, soaked for 1 hour
2	spring onions (scallions), trimmed and diced
2 slices	fresh ginger finely chopped
1 tablespoon	dark soy sauce
8 cups (2 litres)	deep-frying oil
¼ cup (2 fl oz)	frying oil

Seasoning A:

¾ teaspoon	salt
1 teaspoon	m.s.g. (optional)
1½ teaspoon	sugar
½ teaspoon	ground black pepper
1 tablespoon	light soy sauce
1 teaspoon	rice wine or dry sherry
¼ cup (2 fl oz)	chicken stock

Seasoning B/Sauce:

2½ cups (20 fl oz)	chicken stock or water
¾ cup (6 fl oz)	sugar colouring (see page 388)
2 tablespoons	light soy sauce
1 tablespoon	rice wine or dry sherry
1 teaspoon	sugar
2	spring onions (scallions), trimmed and sliced
4 slices	fresh ginger

Debone the duck, leaving the legs and wings intact. Turn inside out and scald with boiling water. Pat dry and rub with the salt and wine, then turn right side out again.

Drain the barley, lotus seeds, and rice and steam together with 1 cup (8 fl oz) chicken stock or water until tender. Drain the mushrooms, remove stems and dice. Blanch the duck giblets in boiling water. Skin the gizzard, trim the heart, and cut all into small dice.

Fry the giblets in the frying oil for 3 minutes on moderate heat. Add the onions, ginger, mushrooms, and ham and stir-fry for 1 minute, then add the bamboo shoots, drained shrimp, rice, barley, and lotus seeds. Fry together, mixing well, for 2 minutes, then add the seasoning A ingredients, mix well and remove from the heat. Leave to cool for 10 minutes, then stuff into the duck and sew up the opening or secure carefully with poultry pins.

Rub the skin wth the dark soy sauce. Heat the deep-frying oil to smoking point and deep-fry the duck on high heat until the skin is a rich red-brown. Drain and place, breast downwards, in a casserole. Add the seasoning B/sauce ingredients and cover the pot. Bring to the boil, then reduce heat and simmer for about 2 hours until completely tender.

Carefully lift the duck onto a serving plate and make several cuts across the breast to expose the filling. Strain the cooking liquid into a wok, bring to the boil and simmer until wellreduced. Thicken if necessary with a thin solution of cornflour (cornstarch) and cold water and check the seasoning. Pour over the duck.

Deep-Fried and Simmered Duck Stuffed with Eight Precious Ingredients (recipe this page).

STEAMED STUFFED DUCK WITH PINE SEED CRUST

1 2 kg (4 lb)	duck
1 teaspoon	salt
1 tablespoon	rice wine or dry sherry
315 g (10 oz)	slightly fat pork, finely minced (ground)
2	small egg whites, beaten
2 tablespoons	cornflour (cornstarch)
75 g (2½ oz)	pine seed or walnuts, blanched and drained
6 cups (1½ litres)	deep frying oil

Seasoning:

1½ tablespoons	finely chopped spring onion (scallion)
¾ teaspoon	grated fresh ginger
1	egg, beaten
¾ teaspoon	salt
½ teaspoon	m.s.g. (optional)
½ teaspoon	sugar
1 teaspoon	rice wine or dry sherry

Sauce:

1 cup (8 fl oz)	chicken stock or water
½ cup (4 fl oz)	sugar colouring (see page 388)
2 tablespoons	light soy sauce
1 tablespoon	rice wine or dry sherry
¼ teaspoon	salt
1 teaspoon	m.s.g. (optional)
3	spring onions (scallions), trimmed and sliced
4 slices	fresh ginger

Wash the duck and cut open along the backbone. Debone, leaving the drumsticks in place but removing the wings. Keep the bones.

Slice off any thick parts of the meat and chop finely. Use a sharp knife to score quite deeply in a criss-cross pattern across the meat, taking care not to pierce the skin. Season with the salt and wine or sherry.

Mix the chopped duck meat with the pork and seasoning ingredients. Make a paste of the egg whites and cornflour, adding a little water. Brush over the duck where scored, and cover with a thick layer of the pork paste, smoothing the edges. Brush with any remaining batter. Toast the pine seeds or walnuts and chop coarsley. Press onto the pork stuffing, coating thickly. Place the duck in a large frying basket.

Heat the deep oil to smoking hot and fry the duck until browned. Lift out and drain well. Arrange the wings and reserve bones in a casserole and set the duck, stuffing upwards, on top. Add the sauce ingredients, cover and set on a rack in a steamer. Steam over rapidly boiling water until tender, about 1½ hours.

Strain the juices into a pan, bring to the boil and adjust the seasoning. Thicken if necessary with a thin solution of cornflour and water. Pour over the duck and serve.

STEAMED DUCK IN LOTUS LEAF PACKAGES

1½ 2 kg (4 lb)	duck
4	dried or fresh lotus leaves
1 cup	spiced rice powder (see page 386)

Seasoning:

2 tablespoons	finely chopped spring onion (scallion)
1 tablespoon	finely chopped fresh ginger
1 teaspoon	finely chopped fresh red chilli pepper (optional)
2 tablespoons	light soy sauce
1 tablespoon	dark soy sauce or soybean paste
1 tablespoon	vegetable oil
2 teaspoons	sesame oil
1 tablespoon	rice wine or dry sherry
1 tablespoon	sugar

Cut the duck into bite-sized pieces, deboning if preferred. Place in a dish with the pre-mixed seasoning ingredients. Mix thoroughly, then leave for 1 hour.

Soak dried lotus leaves in warm water to soften, then cut into squares. Blanch fresh leaves, if used, in boiling water until softened.

Brush off most of the onion, ginger, and chilli pepper and dip the duck pieces into the rice powder, coating generously. Divide between the lotus leaf squares and fold each into a parcel shape.

Place the parcels in a dish with the open side upwards. Put a plate over them to hold in place and set the dish on a rack in a steamer. Steam over rapidly boiling water for about 1 hour.

Invert the dish onto a serving plate so the smooth sides of the parcels are upmost. Serve at once. Remove the leaves before eating.

*The lotus leaves should be large enough to cut each into 3 pieces, about 15 cm (6 in) square. If lotus leaves are unobtainable, use pieces of greased aluminium foil and remove before serving.

RED-SIMMERED DUCK

1 2¼ kg (4½ lb)	duck
1½ teaspons	salt
4 tablespoons	red fermented rice (or use 2½ tablespoons Japanese dark miso paste)

Seasoning:

3 pieces	rock candy (or 1½ tablespoons sugar)
1 teaspoon	salt
2	spice bags (see page 386)
1 tablespoon	rice wine or dry sherry

Wash the duck and dry well. Rub inside and out with the salt and leave for 1 hour, then rinse and drain again.

Mix the miso, if used, with enough water to make a smooth paste and rub this or the red rice over the duck. Place, breast downwards, on a bamboo rack in a casserole and add the seasoning. Pour in water to just cover the duck, adding it slowly down the side of the pan. Cover and bring to the boil, then reduce the heat and simmer until the duck is completely tender, about 2½ hours. In the last 20 minutes of cooking, uncover the pan to reduce the sauce.

Lift out the duck and cut into bite-sized pieces. Serve with the sauce.

GARLIC CATFISH

An excellent dish which is at its best if a live catfish is used, in which case the method involves 'drowning' the fish in rice wine before cooking.

1 1½ kg (3 lb)	live catfish (jewfish, monkfish, halibut)
3 cups (24 fl oz)	rice wine or dry sherry
5 cm (2 in) piece	fresh ginger
6 cups (1½ litres)	deep frying oil

Seasoning A:

½ cup (4 fl oz)	light soy sauce
½ cup (4 fl oz)	rice wine or dry sherry
1 tablespoon	soybean paste or dark soy sauce
1 tablespoon	grated fresh ginger
3 tablespoons	crushed garlic
1	fresh red chilli pepper, seeds removed and chopped
1 teaspoon	salt
2 teaspoons	sugar
½ ccp (4 fl oz)	fish stock or water

Seasoning B/Sauce:

¼ cup (2 fl oz)	cold water
2 teaspoons	white vinegar
1 teaspoon	sesame oil
2 teaspoons	cornflour (cornstarch)

Place the fish in a pot with a tight-fitting lid, add the wine or sherry, cover and leave for at least 20 minutes. Drain.

Rub the peeled ginger over the wok vigorously. This prevents the fish from sticking during cooking. The ginger may be trimmed and used again. Pour in the oil and heat to smoking point, then reduce heat slightly. Deep-fry the fish for 6 minutes on each side. Carefully lift out and pour off all but 3 tablespoons oil. Set the fish aside, keeping warm.

Add the pre-mixed seasoning A ingredients to the pan and bring to the boil. Return the fish, cover and cook on moderately high heat for 2 minutes, then add the pre-mixed seasoning B/sauce ingredients, and bring to the boil again. Stir carefully around the fish until the sauce thickens.

Serve with a garnish of shredded spring onions and fresh chilli pepper or coriander.

FISH IN BROWN SAUCE

1 1 kg (2 lb)	fresh carp (or 2 mackerel or red snapper)
1 tablespoon	cornflour (cornstarch)
1 tablespoon	flour
2 cups (16 fl oz)	frying oil
5 cm (2 in) piece	fresh ginger, peeled
6 cloves	garlic, thinly sliced
3 thick slices	fresh ginger, shredded
2 — 3	fresh red chilli peppers, seeds removed and shredded
1	star anise (optional)
¾ teaspoon	salt
1¼ cups (10 fl oz)	fish stock or water
2	spring onions (scallions), trimmed and shredded
½ teaspoon	sesame oil (optional)
½ teaspoon	white vinegar

Seasoning A:

½ teaspoon	salt
2 tablespoons	light soy sauce
1½ tablespoons	rice wine or dry sherry
1 teaspoon	grated fresh ginger

Seasoning B:

½ teaspoon	sugar
2 tablespoons	dark soy sauce
2 teaspoons	rice wine and dry sherry
½ cup (4 fl oz)	sugar colouring (see page 388) (optional)

Clean, scale and thoroughly wash the fish. Score several times diagonally acorss each side, cutting almost through to the bone. Rub with the seasoning A ingredients and leave for 10 minutes, then coat lightly with a mixture of the cornflour and flour.

Heat a large wok and rub vigorously with the peeled ginger to prevent the fish from sticking during cooking. Heat the oil to hot and fry the fish for about 5 minutes on each side. Remove and keep warm. Drain the oil.

Rinse out the wok and return ⅓ cup of the drained oil. Heat to moderate and fry the garlic, chillies and the star anise, if used, for 2 minutes. Add the seasoning B ingredients, salt, and fish stock and bring to the boil. Return the fish and simmer, covered, for 10 minutes. Remove the lid and cook a further 5 minutes or until the fish is completely tender, with the meat easily lifting from the bones.

Transfer the fish carefully to a serving plate and place the garlic, ginger, and chilli pepper on top with the shredded spring onions over them. Keep warm. Bring the sauce to the boil, add the sesame oil, if used, and the vinegar. Check the seasonings and thicken if preferred with a thin solution of cornflour mixed with cold water. Pour over the fish and serve at once.

RED-BRAISED MACKEREL TAILS

2 kg (4 lb)	mackerel (fresh trout or grass carp), use the tail halves only
½ teaspoon	salt
2 teaspoons	rice wine or dry sherry
⅓ cup	frying oil or softened lard
2	spring onions (scallions), trimmed and sliced
2 teaspoons	grated fresh ginger
60 g (2 oz)	canned bamboo shoots, drained and diced
30 g (1 oz)	canned straw mushrooms or champignons drained and diced
½ teaspoon	m.s.g. (optional)
1 teaspoon	white vinegar
½ teaspoon	sesame oil (optional)

Seasoning/Sauce:

¼ cup (2 fl oz)	light soy sauce
1½ cups (12 fl oz)	chicken stock or cold water
1 tablespoon	rice wine or dry sherry
1 tablespoon	sugar

Scale and wash the fish tails. The heads may be reserved for other dishes (see Index). Rub with the salt and wine and leave for 20 minutes.

Heat the oil or lard in a wok and fry the tails on moderate heat until beginning to colour, about 3 minutes. Add the onion and ginger and cook a further 2 minutes, then add the diced vegetables and the seasoning/sauce ingredients and bring to the boil.

Cover, reduce heat and braise for 10 minutes. Increase the heat and stir in 1 tablespoon vegetable oil, the m.s.g. and sesame oil, if used, and the vinegar. The sauce may be thickened, if preferred, with a thin solution of cornflour and cold water.

'Squirrel' Fish (recipe page 120).

'WESTLAKE STYLE' BRAISED CARP

1 1½ kg (3 lb)	fresh silver or grass carp (or fresh water trout)
5 cm (2 in) piece	fresh ginger, peeled
8 cups (2 litres)	deep-frying oil
	cornflour (cornstarch)
	flour

Seasoning:

½ teaspoon	salt
½ teaspoon	m.s.g. (optional)
1 tablespoon	rice wine or dry sherry

Sauce A:

1½ teaspoons	grated fresh ginger
2 teaspoons	crushed garlic
1½ cups (12 fl oz)	fish stock or water
½ cup (4 fl oz)	light soy sauce
1 tablespoon	rice wine or dry sherry
½ teaspoon	salt
2 tablespoons	sugar
1 teaspoon	m.s.g. (optional)
½ teaspoon	ground black pepper

Sauce B:

½ cup (4 fl oz)	fish stock or cold water
1 — 2	fresh red chilli peppers, seeds removed and shredded
3 slices	fresh ginger, shredded
2	spring onions (scallions), trimmed and shredded
1½ tablespoons	sesame oil
2 teaspoons	white vinegar
¾ teaspoon	cornflour (cornstarch)

Clean, scale, and thoroughly wash the fish. Trim the fins and remove gills. Slit open from the underside without cutting right through, open flat and rub with the seasoning ingredients.

Heat a large wok, rub vigorously with the peeled ginger to prevent the fish from sticking during cooking, and heat the deep-frying oil to smoking point. Reduce heat slightly with a mixture of cornflour and flour and deep-fry for 6 minutes on one side, turn and fry the other side for 3 minutes. Lift out and drain well.

Pour off the oil, rinse the pan and return only ¼ cup (2 fl oz) of the oil. Fry the ginger and garlic for 30 seconds and add the remaining sauce A ingredients. Bring to the boil, return the fish skin side upwards, and when the sauce boils again, cover and braise over lowered heat for 4 minutes. Turn the fish and cook, covered, for a further 10 minutes. Lift onto a serving plate, skin upwards, and keep warm.

Add the sauce B ingredients to the pan. Bring to the boil and simmer until reduced to about 1½ cups (12 fl oz). Pour over the fish and serve.

BRAISED GOLDEN CARP WITH ONIONS

2 375 g (12 oz)	golden carp (snapper or perch)
¾ teaspoon	salt
2 teaspoons	rice wine or dry sherry
2	large brown onions
75 g (2½ oz)	slightly fat pork, diced
3 cups (24 fl oz)	frying oil
1 tablespoon	light soy sauce
1 teaspoon	dark soy sauce
	m.s.g. (optional)
	white vinegar (optional)

Seasoning:

2 teaspoons	rice wine or dry sherry
⅓ teaspoon	salt
¾ teaspoon	sugar
2 teaspoons	softened lard
3 slices	fresh ginger, shredded

Clean and scale the fish and score diagonally across each side. Rub with the salt and wine and leave for 20 minutes. Peel the onions and slice narrowly from stem to root.

Heat the frying oil to moderately hot and fry the diced pork until lightly coloured. Remove and fry the onions for 30 seconds. Remove and set aside with the pork. Wipe the fish, rub with the light and dark soy sauce and deep-fry until half-cooked, about 7 minutes cooking, turning once. Lift out and drain well.

Pour off the oil, wipe out the wok and return about 2 tablespoons of the oil. Return the onions and pork and fry briefly, then add the fish and the seasoning ingredients with water to cover. Bring to the boil, cover the wok and reduce the heat. Simmer until the fish are cooked through and the sauce well reduced, about 40 minutes. Add a dash of m.s.g. and white vinegar, if used, and transfer to a serving plate. Serve at once.

GOLDEN CARP STUFFED WITH PORK AND BAMBOO SHOOTS

1 1 kg (2 lb)	golden carp (or red snapper)
155 g (5 oz)	slightly fat pork
45 g (1½ oz)	canned bamboo shoots, drained
3	dried black mushrooms, soaked for 25 minutes
1 tablespoon	finely chopped spring onion (scallion)
1 teaspoon	finely chopped fresh ginger
5 cups (1¼ litres)	deep-frying oil
5	spring onions (scallions), trimmed and sliced
5 thick slices	fresh ginger, shredded
2 teaspoons	softened lard
⅓ teaspoon	m.s.g. (optional)

Seasoning A:

1 tablespoon	rice wine or dry sherry
1½ teaspoons	salt
1 tablespoon	light soy sauce

Seasoning B:

½ teaspoon	salt
¼ teaspoon	m.s.g. (optional)
¼ teaspoon	white pepper
1 teaspoon	sugar
2 teaspoons	light soy sauce
2 teaspoons	rice wine or dry sherry
1 tablespoon	cornflour (cornstarch)

Seasoning C/Sauce:

2 cups (16 fl oz)	chicken stock
1½ tablespoons	light soy sauce
1 tablespoon	rice wine or dry sherry
1 teaspoon	salt
½ teaspoon	sugar

Clean the fish through an opening made near the gills. Scale and wash thoroughly. Make several diagonal scores across each side, cutting almost to the bone. Rub on both sides with the seasoning A ingredients and pour the remainder inside. Set the fish aside.

Finely dice the pork, bamboo shoots, and mushroom caps, and mix with the chopped spring onion and ginger and the seasoning B ingredients. Stuff into the fish and secure the opening with toothpicks or a poultry pin.

Heat the deep-frying oil in a wok and deep-fry the fish until lightly coloured, about 1½ minutes on each side. Remove and drain off the oil.

Arrange the shredded spring onions and ginger in the wok and place the fish on top. Pour in the seasoning C/sauce ingredients and bring to the boil. Cover and simmer until the fish is tender and the filling cooked through, about 45 minutes. Stir in the lard and m.s.g., if used.

Thicken the sauce, if preferred, with a thin solution of cornflour and cold water. Transfer the fish to a serving plate and pour on the sauce.

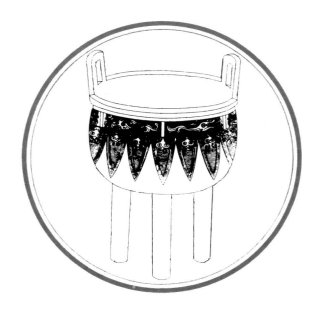

'SQUIRREL' FISH

So named by the imaginative chef who created it centuries ago. The fish is turned inside out and the meat scored so that it stands in spikes when cooked, thereby resembling the furry creature after which it was named.

1 1 kg (2 lb)	yellow fish or sea bass
1 teaspoon	salt
1 tablespoon	rice wine or dry sherry cornflour (cornstarch)
8 cups (2 litres)	deep-frying oil
155 g (5 oz)	canned straw mushrooms or champignon, drained and diced
30 g (1 oz)	canned bamboo shoots, drained and diced
1	small carrot, diced and parboiled
2 tablespoons	frozen or fresh peas, parboiled
1 tablespoon	finely chopped spring onion (scallion)
1½ teaspoons	grated fresh ginger
¾ teaspoon	crushed garlic
¼ cup (2 fl oz)	frying oil

Sauce:

¼ cup (2 fl oz)	chicken stock
1 tablespoon	light soy sauce
¼ cup (2 fl oz)	white vinegar
½ cup (2 fl oz)	tomato sauce (ketchup)
2 teaspoons	rice wine or dry sherry
⅓ teaspoon	salt
½ cup	sugar
1 teaspoon	cornflour (cornstarch)

Clean the fish, scale and trim the fins. Cut open from the underside and remove the backbone and gills. Lay the fish flat, meat upwards and use a sharp paring knife to score the meat closely in a criss-cross pattern, taking care not to pierce through the skin. Sprinkle on the salt and wine and leave for 15 minutes, then coat thickly with cornflour and rub with fingers from tail to head until the meat stands up in spikes.

Heat the deep oil to moderate and deep-fry the fish until crisp and golden on the surface with the meat tender inside, about 7 minutes, turning once. Drain and keep warm.

In another pan, stir-fry the diced vegetables and ham with the onion, ginger, and garlic for 3 minutes, add the sauce ingredients and bring to the boil. Stir unitl thickened and pour over the fish.

SLICED FISH IN WALNUT CRUMB BATTER

Serve as an appetiser or main course.

315 g (10 oz)	meaty white fish fillets
155 g (5 oz)	walnuts, blanched, skinned and dried
3	egg whites, beaten
2 tablespoons	flour
3 tablespoons	cornflour (cornstarch)
6 cups (1½ litres)	deep-frying oil

Seasoning:

½ teaspoon	salt
½ teaspoon	m.s.g. (optional) pinch of white pepper
½ teaspoon	rice wine or dry sherry
1 tablespoon	finely chopped spring onion (scallion)
1½ teaspoons	grated fresh ginger

Cut the fish into pieces about 4 × 2 cm (1 2/3 × ¾ in) and mix with the seasoning ingredients. Leave for 15 minutes.

Toast the walnuts and chop finely. Make a thick batter with the egg whites, flour, and cornflour, adding just a little water.

Heat the deep oil to moderate. Dip the fish into the batter, coat thickly with the chopped walnuts and deep-fry until golden brown, about 2½ minutes. Drain well.

STEAMED GRASS CARP DRESSED WITH SHREDDED VEGETABLES

1 1¼ kg (2½ lb)	grass carp (fresh water trout or sea bass)
1 tablespoon	rice wine or dry sherry
¾ teaspoon	salt
3	spring onions (scallions), trimmed and shredded
3 slices	fresh ginger, shredded
2 tablespoons	frying oil or softened lard
30 g (1 oz)	canned bamboo shoots, drained and shredded
15 g (½ oz)	canned champignons, drained and shredded
1	small green capsicum (bell pepper), trimmed and shredded

Seasoning A:

1½ tablespoons	rendered chicken fat (chicken grease), warmed
1 teaspoon	m.s.g. (optional)
	pinch of white pepper
¼ cup (2 fl oz)	chicken stock

Seasoning B:

1 teaspoon	rice wine or dry sherry
½ teaspoon	m.s.g. (optional)
1 teaspoon	sugar
2 tablespoons	light soy sauce
½ teaspoon	white vinegar

Clean, scale, and thoroughly wash the fish and trim the fins. Remove the gills, cut open on the underside and remove the backbone entirely. Blanch the fish in boiling water for 1 minute and drain well. Rub with the wine and salt and place in an oiled large oval dish with the shredded spring onions and ginger arranged op top. Add the seasoning A ingredients and set on a rack in a steamer. Steam over high heat, tightly covered, for 20 to 25 minutes.

Heat the oil or lard in a wok and sauté the shredded vegetables for 2 minutes. Add the seasoning B ingredients and cook a further 1 minute. Lift the fish onto a serving plate and strain any liquid from the oval dish into the wok. Bring to the boil and thicken, if preferred, with a thin solution of cornflour and cold water. Pour the sauce and vegetables over the fish and garnish with shredded spring onion or fresh coriander. Serve at once.

MANDARIN FISH IN POT-STICKER STYLE

Serve as an appetiser or main dish.

250 g (8 oz)	mandarin fish (pearl perch, sea bass, or grouper)
185 g (6 oz)	pork fat
5 pieces	preserved mustard green leaves (omit if unavailable)
2	egg whites, beaten
2 tablespoons	cornflour (cornstarch)
2 tablespoons	onion-pepper-salt (see page 384)
2 tablespoons	frying oil or softened lard
1 tablespoon	rice wine or dry sherry
2 tablespoons	chicken stock

Seasoning:

¼ teaspoon	salt
½ teaspoon	m.s.g. (optional)
	pinch of white pepper
½ teaspoon	rice wine or dry sherry
½ teaspoon	sugar
1	egg white, beaten
1 tablespoon	onion and ginger infusion (see page 386)

Cut the fish into thin slices about 5 × 2.5 cm (2 × 1 in) and mix with the seasoning ingredients. Leave for 15 minutes.

Cut the pork fat into very thin slices the same size as the fish. Wash the mustard leaves, dry and cut to fit the pork fat and fish. Make a smooth, creamy batter with the egg whites and cornflour and brush over the pork fat. Sprinkle on a generous amount of the onion-pepper-salt and top each piece with a slice of fish and a portion of the mustard leaf. Brush on the remaining batter after thinning with a dash of water.

Heat a shallow flat pan to moderate and add the oil or lard. Arrange the pot-stickers in the pan, fat downwards, and cook on moderate to low heat for 3 minutes. Cover the pan and cook gently until the fish is tender and the fat crisp and almost transparent. Remove the lid, increase the heat and splash in the wine, followed by the chicken stock a few seconds later. Cook briefly and serve.

DEEP-FRIED CARP WITH SWEET AND SOUR SAUCE

1 1¼ kg (2½ lb)	grass carp (sea bass or fresh water trout)
¾ teaspoon	salt
2 teaspoon	rice wine or dry sherry
5 cm (2 in) piece	fresh ginger, peeled
8 cups (2 litres)	deep-frying oil
Batter:	
2	egg whites, well beaten
2 tablespoons	cornflour (cornstarch)
	extra cornflour (cornstarch)
Sauce:	
¼ cup (2 fl oz)	frying oil
2 tablespoons	finely chopped spring onion
1 tablespoon	finely shredded fresh ginger
1½ — 2 teaspoons	chopped garlic
⅓ cup	chicken stock
1 tablespoon	light soy sauce
2 teaspoons	rice wine or dry sherry
¼ cup (2 fl oz)	white vinegar
⅓ cup	sugar
2 teaspoons	sesame oil (optional)
	pinch of salt
	pinch of ground black pepper
1½ teaspoons	cornflour (cornstarch)

Clean and scale the fish and trim the fins. Remove the gills, wash well and wipe dry. Score diagonally on both sides and rub with the salt and wine. Leave for 10 minutes.

Mix the egg whites and cornflour with a very little cold water to make a thick batter. Brush over the fish, then coat lightly with extra cornflour. Shake off excess. Heat the wok and rub vigorously with the peeled ginger to prevent the fish from sticking during cooking. Add the oil and heat to smoking. Fry the fish until golden and crisp on both sides, about 12 minutes total cooking time, reducing the heat after the first 3 minutes. The fish should be cooked through. Test by inserting a fork into the thickest part. It should lift easily from the bones. Remove the fish and place in a strainer or on absorbent paper to drain.

In another pan, heat the frying oil and fry the onions, ginger, and garlic for 2 minutes on moderate heat. Increase the heat and add the remaining sauce ingredients, pre-mixed, and boil until thickened. Keep hot.

Reheat the deep oil and fry the fish a further 2 minutes, then lift out and drain well. Place on a heated metal serving tray. Transfer the hot sauce to a jug, and pour over the fish at the table.

CUBED MANDARIN FISH AND PINEAPPLE IN TOMATO SAUCE

315 g (10 oz)	mandarin fish fillets (or pearl perch)
¼ teaspoon	salt
1½ teaspoons	rice wine or dry sherry
1 cup	cornflour (cornstarch)
4 cups (1 litre)	deep-frying oil
2	spring onions (scallions), trimmed and diced
3 slices	fresh ginger, shredded
1 teaspoon	crushed garlic (or to taste)
90 g (3 oz)	fresh or canned pineapple, drained and diced
45 g (1½ oz)	cooked green peas
Sauce:	
2½ tablespoons	white vinegar
¼ cup (2 fl oz)	tomato sauce (ketchup)
2 teaspoons	rice wine or dry sherry
¼ cup (2 oz)	sugar
½ teaspoon	salt
¼ teaspoon	m.s.g. (optional)
1 teaspoon	cornflour (cornstarch)
1 tablespoon	cold water

Cut the fish into bite-sized pieces and season with the salt and wine. Pour the cornflour into a plastic or paper bag and add the fish. Close the bag and shake vigorously to thickly coat the fish. Empty into a collandar and shake well to remove excess flour.

Heat the deep oil to fairly hot and deep fry the fish, 10 pieces at a time, until golden and crisp. Drain well and keep the oil warm.

In another wok or pan, add about ½ cup (4 fl oz) of the fish frying oil and heat to smoking. Sauté the onion, ginger, and garlic for 1 minute, then add the sauce ingredients and bring to the boil. Stir in the pineapple and peas and keep warm.

Reheat the deep-frying oil and re-fry the fish for a further 1 minute, drain and transfer to the sauce. Heat through, turning with a wok spatula until evenly coated with the sauce. Arrange on a warmed serving plate.

MANDARIN FISH BALLS WITH VEGETABLES IN CHICKEN STOCK

500 g (1 lb)	mandarin fish fillets (or pearl perch)
6 cups (1½ litres)	deep-frying oil
¼ cup (2 fl oz)	frying oil or softened lard
30 g (1 oz)	canned champignons, sliced
30 g (1 oz)	cooked ham, shredded
155 g (5 oz)	fresh sweet pea sprouts, snow peas, or chopped spinach
1 tablespoon	finely chopped spring onion (scallion)
1 teaspoon	grated fresh ginger

Seasoning:

2	egg whites, beaten
2 tablespoons	onion and ginger infusion (see page 386)
½ teaspoon	salt
1 teaspoon	m.s.g. (optional)
¼ teaspoon	white pepper
1 tablespoon	cornflour (cornstarch)

Sauce:

2 cups (16 fl oz)	chicken stock
¾ teaspoon	salt
½ teaspoon	m.s.g. (optional)
¾ teaspoon	rice wine or dry sherry
2 teaspoons	cornflour (cornstarch)

Pulverise the fish in a food processor or by using two cleavers simultaneously (see page 396). Mix thoroughly with the seasoning ingredients, working in one direction only until the mixture is smooth, thick and creamy.

Heat the deep oil to moderate. Squeeze the fish mixture through the right hand to form small balls (see page 395), and scoop into the oil with a spoon. Cook until they rise to he surface and colour lightly, then remove and drain well.

In another pan, heat the frying oil and sauté the mushrooms, ham, and washed vegetables, adding the onion and ginger. When softened, pour in the pre-mixed sauce ingredients and bring to the boil. Add the fish balls and heat through before transferring to a serving dish.

FRIED FISH SLICES WITH GINGER AND SWEET PICKLES

375 g (12 oz)	meaty white fish fillets
1½ cups (12 fl oz)	frying oil
2	spring onions (scallions), trimmed and shredded
6-8 thin slices	fresh young ginger, shredded
60 g (2 oz)	canned bamboo shoots, drained and shredded
30 g (1 oz)	sweet Chinese pickles, shredded
1 tablespoon	Chinese pickle liquid
1 teaspoon	sesame oil (optional)

Seasoning:

1	egg white, beaten
½ teaspoon	salt
½ teaspoon	sugar
2 teaspoons	cornflour (cornstarch)

Sauce:

⅓ cup	chicken stock
½ teaspoon	salt
½ teaspoon	sugar
½ teaspoon	rice wine or dry sherry
½ teaspoon	cornflour (cornstarch)

Cut the fish into 1 cm (⅓ in) slices, cutting across the fillets at an angle. Mix with the seasoning ingredients and leave to marinate for 20 minutes.

Heat the oil in a wok and fry the fish for 2 minutes, until cooked through. Remove and drain. Pour off all but 2 tablespoons of the oil and sauté the spring onions briefly, then add the ginger, bamboo shoots, and pickles and sauté for 1 minute. Add the pickle liquid and the pre-mixed sauce ingredients and bring to the boil. Simmer until thickened, then return the fish and heat through.

ONE FISH SERVED IN TWO WAYS

1 1 kg (2 lb)	sea bass or fresh trout
2½ tablespoons	softened lard or rendered chicken fat (chicken grease)
1	large white onion, thickly sliced
2 slices	fresh ginger, chopped
60 g (2 oz)	canned bamboo shoots, drained and shredded
20 g (¾ oz)	dried 'wood ear' fungus, soaked for 25 minutes and shredded
2	spring onions (scallions), trimmed and shredded
2 slices	fresh ginger, shredded
¼ cup (2 fl oz)	frying oil

Seasoning A:

2	egg whites, well beaten
¾ teaspoon	salt
1 tablespoon	cornflour (cornstarch)

Seasoning B:

1 tablespoon	rice wine or dry sherry
1¼ teaspoons	salt
¼ teaspoon	m.s.g. (optional)
	pinch of white pepper

Seasoning C/Sauce:

½ cup (4 fl oz)	reserved fish stock*
2 teaspoons	rice wine or dry sherry
½ teaspoon	salt
¼ teaspoon	m.s.g. (optional)
¾ teaspoon	sugar
¾ teaspoon	cornflour (cornstarch)

Clean and scale the fish and remove the two fillets. Skin the fillets and cut across them into thin slices. Place in a dish and add the seasoning A ingredients, rub in lightly and leave for 20 minutes.

Wash the head and backbone and cut into several pieces. Heat half the lard in a wok and sauté the onion and chopped ginger for 1 minute. Add the head and bone pieces and sauté until lightly coloured. Sizzle in the wine, then add the remaining seasoning B ingredients and pour in about 3 cups (24 fl oz) cold water. Bring to the boil, cover tightly and simmer for 25 minutes.

Bring a saucepan of water to a rolling boil and add the sliced fish. Poach for about 1½ minutes, until the fish is firm and white, then drain, reserving ½ cup of the stock for the sauce.

Heat another wok, and stir-fry the bamboo shoots and shredded 'wood ears,' spring onions, and ginger in the frying oil until softened and lightly colored. Add the pre-mixed seasoning C/sauce ingredients and bring to the boil. Add the fish and simmer until cooked through. Transfer to a serving plate.

Stir the remaining lard into the fish soup and adjust the seasoning to taste. Transfer to a soup tureen and serve at the same time as the stir-fried fish. Serve with small dishes of Vinegar and Ginger Dip (see page 384).

* Reserved from poaching the sliced fish.

SILVER CARP'S HEAD SIMMERED IN AN EARTHEN CROCK

1	1¼ kg (2½lb) silver carp's head, or several fish heads of the same weight
2 cups (16 fl oz)	frying oil
2 tablespoons	dark soy sauce
2	bean sheets, or 30 g bean thread vermicelli, soaked
8	garlic chives, sliced
15 cm (½ oz)	dried 'wood ear' fungus, soaked for 25 minutes and diced
30 g (1 oz)	canned bamboo shoots, drained and diced
60 g (2 oz)	lean pork
6 cups (1½ litres)	water or fish stock
1½	pickled or fresh red chilli peppers, sliced

Seasoning:

¼ cup (2 fl oz)	light soy sauce
1 tablespoon	rice wine or dry sherry
1½ teaspoons	salt
½ teaspoon	white pepper
1 teaspoon	sugar

Thoroughly wash the fish head(s) and cut in halves. Rub with the dark soy sauce. Heat the deep-frying oil to smoking point and add the fish heads. Fry until lightly coloured, then remove and drain well.

Place the fish heads in a casserole and add the shredded bean sheets or soaked vermicelli, the garlic chives and diced 'wood ears.' Fry the bamboo shoots briefly and add to the casserole, then fry the pork until lightly coloured. Drain and add to the casserole with the water or fish stock. Add pickled or fresh red chilli peppers.

Add the seasoning ingredients and bring to the boil. Simmer until the fish heads are completely cooked, then scrape the meat from the bones. Discard as many bones as possible before serving.

JUMBO PRAWNS SERVED IN TWO STYLES

Serves 8

16	large raw prawns (shrimps), in the shell, about 1¼ kg (2½ lb)
¾ teaspoon	salt
2 teaspoons	rice wine or dry sherry
1 tablespoon	onion and ginger infusion (see page 386)
4 slices	white bread
2	egg whites, beaten cornflour (cornstarch)
4	spring onions (scallions), trimmed and shredded
3 slices	fresh ginger, shredded
¼ cup (2 fl oz)	frying oil or softened lard
4 cups (1 litre)	deep-frying oil

Sauce:

⅓ cup	chicken stock
2 teaspoons	rice wine or dry sherry
2 teaspoons	white vinegar
¼ cup (2 fl oz)	tomato sauce (ketchup)
1½ tablespoons	sugar
½ teaspoon	salt
¼ teaspoon	m.s.g. (optional)
1½ teaspoons	cornflour (cornstarch)

Cut the prawns in halves across the widest part of the body. Shell the lower half and cut deeply down the back, removing the dark vein. Spread flat and season with ½ teaspoon salt and the rice wine. Leave for 10 minutes. Wash the heads and season with the remaining ¼ teaspoon salt and the onion and ginger infusion. Leave for 15 minutes.

Remove crusts from the bread and cut each slice into quarters. Dip the prawn tails into beaten egg, coat lightly with cornflour, then dip into the beaten egg again. Press one onto each piece of bread and coat lightly all over with cornflour. Heat the deep-frying oil.

Heat the oil or lard and fry the onion and ginger for 1 minute on moderate heat. Increase the heat slightly and fry the heads, stirring frequently until red, about 2½ minutes. Pour in the pre-mixed sauce ingredients and bring to the boil. Reduce the heat slightly and simmer until the prawns are cooked through.

At the same time, fry the prawn and bread slices, prawn-side downwards, in the moderately hot oil to a rich golden brown. Turn once during cooking. Drain well.

Arrange the prawn toast on one serving plate and the sautéd prawns on another and serve together.

PHOENIX TAIL PRAWNS

500 g (1 lb)	fresh green prawns (shrimps), in the shell
1	large brown onion, sliced
4 cups (1 litre)	deep-frying oil
60 g (2 oz)	canned bamboo shoots, drained and sliced
3	dried black mushrooms, soaked for 25 minutes
1/4 teaspoon	white vinegar (optional)
1/2 teaspoon	sesame oil

Seasoning:

1	egg white, beaten
1/2 teaspoon	salt
2 teaspoons	cornflour (cornstarch)

Sauce:

1/4 cup (2 fl oz)	chicken stock
2 teaspoons	light soy sauce
1 teaspoon	rice wine or dry sherry
1/2 teaspoon	salt
1/4 teaspoon	m.s.g. (optional)
1/2 teaspoon	sugar

Shell the prawns leaving the tail sections intact. Remove the dark veins with a toothpick (see page 394), and mix with the seasoning ingredients. Leave for 15 minutes.

Heat the deep-frying oil to moderate and fry the prawns until they turn white with the tails bright red, about 1 1/2 minutes. Lift out and drain well.

Squeeze the water from the mushrooms, remove the stems and slice thinly. Pour off all but 1 1/2 tablespoons of the oil and fry the sliced onion until beginning to colour, then add the bamboo shoots and sliced mushrooms and stir-fry on high heat for 1/2 minute. Return the prawns and pour in the pre-mixed sauce ingredients. Bring to the boil, season with white vinegar, if used, and the sesame oil. Serve.

DEEP-FRIED PRAWN PUFFS

Serve as an appetiser or main dish.

375 g (12 oz)	fresh green prawns, in the shell (shrimps)
6	egg whites
1 1/4 tablespoons	flour
2 tablespoons	cornflour (cornstarch)
1 tablespoon	finely chopped cooked ham
1 tablespoon	finely chopped spring onion (scallion)

cornflour (cornstarch)

4 cups (1 litre)	deep-frying oil

Chinese pepper-salt

Seasoning:

2 tablespoons	onion and ginger infusion (see page 386)
1/2 teaspoon	salt
1/4 teaspoon	m.s.g. (optional)
	pinch of white pepper
1/2 teaspoon	rice wine or dry sherry

Shell the prawns and cut in halves lengthwise, discarding the dark veins. Cut any larger prawns in halves again. Mix with the seasoning ingredients and leave for 10 minutes.

Beat the egg whites to stiff peaks and carefully fold in the flour, cornflour, chopped ham, and onion.

Heat the deep-frying oil to moderate. Drain the prawns, pat dry, and coat lightly with cornflour, shaking off excess. Dip into the egg white batter, coating thickly. Deep-fry several pieces at a time until golden, about 1 1/4 minutes. Remove from oil, drain for a minute and lower prawn puffs into hot oil again. Deep-fry for 30 seconds. Drain and arrange on a serving plate. Sprinkle on pepper-salt or serve in separate dishes for dipping. Serve at once.

CRYSTAL SHRIMP BALLS GLAZED WITH SWEET AND SOUR SAUCE

Serve as an appetiser or main course.

375 g (12 oz)	shrimp meat
45 g (1½ oz)	pork fat
45 g (1½ oz)	canned water chestnuts, drained
6 cups (1½ litres)	deep-frying oil

Seasoning:

1	egg white, beaten
¼ teaspoon	salt
½ teaspoon	m.s.g. (optional)
½ teaspoon	sugar
1 teaspoon	ginger wine
2 tablespoons	cornflour (cornstarch)

Sauce:

⅓ cup	chicken stock
2 tablespoons	white vinegar
2 tablespoons	sugar
2 teaspoons	finely chopped spring onion (scallion)
½ teaspoon	grated fresh ginger
¼ teaspoon	crushed garlic
½ teaspoon	cornflour (cornstarch)

Pulverise the shrimp meat and pork fat in a food processor or by using two cleavers (see page 396). Add finely chopped water chestnuts and the seasoning ingredients and beat in one direction until the paste is smooth.

Heat deep-frying oil to moderately hot. Form the mixture into balls in the left hand as explained on page 395 and scoop into the oil with a spoon. Cook gently until they rise to the surface. Lift out in a perforated spoon and drain.

In a wok, heat about 2 tablespoons of the deep-frying oil and add the sauce ingredients. Bring to the boil, stirring. Add the shrimp balls and gently move the pan to keep the balls slowly turning in the sauce until evenly glazed. Transfer to a serving plate.

DRUNKEN CRABS

6	small fresh Shanghai hairy crabs*
2 pieces	dried orange peel, chopped
1 tablespoon	finely chopped fresh ginger
2 teaspoons	finely chopped spring onion (scallion)
2 teaspoons	sugar
2 tablespoons	salt
3 cups (24 fl oz)	yellow rice wine
½ teaspoon	m.s.g. (optional)

* Available from specialist food suppliers in late November. They are distinguishable by their small hair-covered pincers and coveted by Chinese gourmets around the world.

Thoroughly wash the crabs, cleaning with a soft brush to ensure all muddy particles are removed. Rinse in cold water and place, live in a large preserving jar. Add the remaining ingredients, place a piece of greaseproof paper over the top of the jar and press the lid firmly into place over it. Leave for 1 week in a cool place, though do not refrigerate unless the weather is particularly hot.

To serve, lift off the top shell and discard the inedible parts. Cut the crabs, with legs attached, into quarters and rearrange in their original shapes on a serving plate. Return the top shells.

Serve with ginger tea made by infusing fresh sliced ginger in boiling water. This counteracts the excessive richness of the crab. The yellow creamy roe is eaten along with the tender white meat.

Silver Carp's Head Simmered in an Earthen Crock (recipe page 126).

SAUTÉD CRABMEAT ON CRISP NOODLES

60 g (2 oz)	rice vermicelli, broken
4 cups (1 litre)	deep-frying oil
2	spring onions (scallions), trimmed and shredded
2 slices	fresh ginger, shredded
3 tablespoons	softened lard or vegetable oil
1 tablespoon	rice wine or dry sherry
185 g (6 oz)	fresh, frozen, or canned crabmeat, flaked
1½ cups (12 fl oz)	chicken stock
3	egg whites, well beaten

Seasoning:

¾ teaspoon	salt
¾ teaspoon	sugar
½ teaspoon	m.s.g. (optional)
1 tablespoon	light soy sauce
2 teaspoons	cornflour (cornstarch)
1 tablespoon	cold water

Heat the deep oil and fry the broken rice vermicelli in a frying basket until it expands into a mass of crisp white noodles, about 15 seconds. Drain and transfer to a serving plate.

Fry the shredded spring onions and ginger in the lard or vegetable oil in another pan for 1 minute. Add the wine and stir for a few seconds, then add the crabmeat and sauté briefly. Pour in the chicken stock, add the seasoning ingredients and bring to the boil. Slowly drizzle in the beaten egg and cook without stirring for 1 minute, then stir into the sauce and pour over the noodles. Serve at once.

DEEP-FRIED CRABMEAT BALLS

Serve as an appetiser or main dish.

315 g (10 oz)	fresh crabmeat
60 g (2 oz)	prawn meat (shrimp meat)
45 g (1½ oz)	pork fat
2	egg whites, beaten
1 tablespoon	finely chopped spring onion (scallion)
1½ teaspoons	grated fresh ginger
6 cups (1½ litres)	deep-frying oil
	Chinese pepper-salt
	sweet soy sauce (see page 385)

Seasoning:

½ teaspoon	salt
½ teaspoon	sugar
1 teaspoon	rice wine or dry sherry
1 tablespoon	cornflour (cornstarch)

Pulverise the crabmeat, prawn meat, and pork fat in the food processor or by using two cleavers (see page 396). Add the egg whites, onion, ginger, and seasonings and mix in one direction only, adding ½ — 1 tablespoon of water to make a smooth paste.

Heat the deep-frying oil to moderate. Form the mixture into balls in the left hand as explained on page 395 and scoop the balls into the oil with a spoon. Cook gently until they rise to the surface and colour lightly. Lift out with a perforated spoon and drain well.

Serve on a bed of shredded lettuce with accompaniments of pepper-salt and sweet soy sauce.

CLAMS IN YELLOW BEAN SAUCE

1 kg (2 lb)	fresh clams, in the shell
2	spring onions (scallions), trimmed and sliced
2 teaspoons	chopped garlic
¼ cup (2 fl oz)	frying oil

Seasoning/Sauce:

½ cup (4 fl oz)	chicken stock
1½ tablespoons	salted yellow bean sauce
2 teaspoons	rice wine or dry sherry
¼ teaspoon	m.s.g. (optional)
2 teaspoons	sugar
1 teaspoon	cornflour (cornstarch)
1 — 2 teaspoons	finely chopped fresh red chilli pepper (optional)

Thoroughly wash the clams, brushing the shells with a soft brush. Rinse well in cold water and place in a large wok. Add the spring onions, garlic, and oil and cover the pan. Cook on moderate heat, shaking the pan occasionally to encourage the shells to open.

When the shells are open, add the seasoning/sauce ingredients and bring to the boil. Simmer for about 1½ minutes. Discard those shells which have not opened, then transfer the clams and sauce to a serving dish.

OYSTERS WITH BARBECUED PORK AND VEGETABLES IN SAUCE

155 g (5 oz)	dried oysters, soaked overnight (or use 250 g / 8 oz fresh oysters)
125 g (4 oz)	Chinese barbecue or roast pork, diced
30 g (1 oz)	canned bamboo shoots, drained and diced
30 g (1 oz)	canned champignons, drained and diced
30 g (1 oz)	canned water chestnuts, drained and diced
2 tablespoons	finely chopped salted mustard greens, rinsed
3	spring onions (scallions), trimmed and diced
2 slices	fresh ginger, finely chopped
2 tablespoons	frying oil
1 tablespoon	vegetable oil, smoking hot

Seasoning A:

½ teaspoon	rice wine or dry sherry
1 tablespoon	frying oil
1	spring onion (scallion), trimmed and cut in halves
2 slices	fresh ginger
¼ cup (2 fl oz)	chicken stock

Seasoning B/Sauce:

2/3 teaspoon	salt
½ teaspoon	sugar
1 teaspoon	rice wine or dry sherry
2 teaspoons	oyster sauce, or dark soy sauce
2 teaspoons	light soy sauce
¼ teaspoon	white pepper
½ teaspoon	sesame oil
¼ cup (2 fl oz)	chicken stock or cold water
1 teaspoon	cornflour (cornstarch)

Drain the oysters and place in a dish with the seasoning A ingredients. Set on a rack in a steamer and steam for 1 hour, then discard the onion and ginger and dice the oysters. Set aside.*

Heat the 2 tablespoons oil and sauté the onion and ginger for 1 minute. Add the diced ingredients (except oysters) and sauté for 2 minutes, then add the pre-mixed seasoning B/sauce ingredients and bring to the boil. Reduce heat, add the oysters and simmer on moderate heat for 3 minutes. Transfer to a serving plate and pour on the piping hot oil just before serving.

*If using fresh oysters, omit the steaming and use whole.

SQUID IN SOUR AND HOT SAUCE ON CRISP RICE CAKES

2 cups	cooked white rice
750 g (1½ lb)	fresh squid
45 g (1½ oz)	canned bamboo shoots, drained and sliced
15 g (½ oz)	canned champignons, drained and thinly sliced
90 g (3 oz)	boneless chicken, shredded
2	spring onions (scallions), trimmed and diced
1 teaspoon	grated fresh ginger
1½ teaspoons	crushed garlic (or to taste)
6 cups (1½ litres)	deep-frying oil

Sauce:

4 cups (1 litre)	chicken stock
2 teaspoons	rice wine or dry sherry
1 tablespoon	white vinegar
½ cup (4 fl oz)	tomato sauce (ketchup)
½ teaspoon	chilli oil
1 teaspoon	sesame oil (optional)
¾ teaspoon	salt
¼ teaspoon	m.s.g. (optional)
½ teaspoon	white pepper
1 teaspoon	sugar
1 tablespoon	cornflour (cornstarch)

To make the rice cakes, press the cooked rice into a greased baking tray and bake in a low oven for 1 hour, then increase the heat to hot and roast until golden. Break into pieces about 5 cm (2 in) square.

Clean the squid, removing the heads, stomachs, skin, tentacles, and fins. Wash well and cut open. Score the inside in a close criss-cross pattern then cut into 5 cm (2 in) squares.

Bring the sauce ingredients to the boil and add the bamboo shoots, champignons, chicken, onions, ginger, and garlic and simmer for 2 minutes. Add the squid and cook for just 2 minutes.

In the meantime, heat the deep-frying oil to fairly hot and fry the rice cakes until deep gold and crisp. Drain and place in a deep serving dish. Transfer the squid and sauce to a large jug and pour over the rice cakes at the table.

It is important to prepare both elements of this dish simultaneously. The rice cakes will lose their crispness if done in advance, and the squid becomes tough and chewy with overcooking.

POACHED SQUID WITH SESAME SAUCE

Serve warm or cold.

500 g (1 lb)	large fresh squid
2	spring onions (scallions), trimmed
3 thick slices	fresh ginger, bruised

Sauce:

⅓ cup	chicken stock or water
1 tablespoon	light soy sauce
½ teaspoon	white vinegar
2 tablespoons	sesame paste
1 teaspoon	sesame oil
¾ teaspoon	chilli oil (or to taste)
1 teaspoon	sugar
1 tablespoon	finely chopped spring onion (scallion)
1 teaspoon	grated fresh ginger

Clean the squid, removing skin, head and tentacles, stomach, and fins. Cut the tubular bodies open and wash well. Pat dry and score on the inside with a closely worked criss-cross pattern, taking care not to pierce the skin (see page 397) Cut into pieces of 5 × 2.5 cm (2 × 1 in).

Bring a saucepan of water to the boil, add the spring onions and ginger and boil for 2 minutes, then add the squid and poach for 1½ minutes. Drain and set aside. Discard the onion and ginger.

Mix the sauce ingredients together. Pour into a small bowl and place in the centre of a large serving plate. Arrange the poached squid around the bowl of sauce, garnish with shredded spring onion, ginger, or fresh coriander and serve. Dip the squid into the sauce before eating.

Clams in Yellow Bean Sauce (recipe page 131).

STEAMED FRESH-WATER EEL WITH SPICY AND HOT SAUCE

750 g (1½ lb)	small fresh-water eels
2	spring onions (scallions), trimmed and shredded
3 thick slices	fresh ginger, finely shredded
1 tablespoon	sesame oil, heated to smoking point
¼ — ½ teaspoon	white pepper
	fresh coriander or shredded spring onion (scallion)

Seasoning:

¼ teaspoon	salt
1 teaspoon	Chinese brown peppercorns
1½ tablespoons	rice wine or dry sherry
1 cup (8 fl oz)	chicken stock

Sauce:

¼ cup (2 fl oz)	light soy sauce
2 teaspoons	white vinegar
1 teaspoon	sesame oil
1½ teaspoons	sugar
1 tablespoon	finely chopped garlic, or to taste
1 — 2 teaspoons	finely chopped fresh red chilli pepper
1 tablespoon	finely chopped spring onion

Remove the heads and the lower tail sections of the eels, split open, remove stomachs and wash well. Drop into boiling water for 1 minute, lift out, and rub with salt, then rinse well with cold water. They may be skinned, if preferred, by securing the heads firmly to a work top and cutting through the skin around the heads. Take a firm grip with a pair of pincers and strip off the entire skin in one clean action. The meat, however, will become much drier after skinning.

Cut the eels into 5 cm (2 in) pieces and place in a dish with the onion, ginger, and seasoning ingredients. Set on a rack in a steaming pot, cover and steam over rapidly boiling water until tender, about 15 minutes. Remove the onion and ginger and strain off the cooking liquid.

Mix the sauce ingredients together. Pour the piping hot sesame oil over the eel and then pour on the sauce. Add the white pepper, if used, and garnish with fresh coriander or spring onion. Serve at once.

FRESH WATER EEL AND HAM STEAMED IN A POT

750 g (1½ lb)	large fresh-water eel
1 tablespoon	rice wine or dry sherry
1 tablespoon	salt
125 g (4 oz)	Chinese or cured (Smithfield) ham, cubed
2	spring onions (scallions), trimmed and sliced
3 slices	fresh ginger
1 cup (8 fl oz)	chicken stock

Seasoning:

1½ teaspoons	salt
1 teaspoon	sugar
½ teaspoon	m.s.g. (optional)
½ teaspoon	white pepper

Remove the eel head, slit open the stomach, clean and wash well. Cut into 2.5 cm (1 in) pieces and rub with the salt and wine. Leave for 10 minutes, then rinse again and place in a greased casserole with the cubed ham and the onions and ginger. Add the chicken stock and seasonings and place a piece of wet greaseproof paper across the top of the casserole. Press the lid firmly in place over the paper and stand the pot on a rack in a steamer. Steam over gently boiling water for 1½ — 1¾ hours until the eel is tender. Remove the onion and ginger and taste for seasoning before serving in the casserole.

Garnish, if desired, with white pepper and chopped fresh coriander.

STIR-FRIED FRESH-WATER EEL

500 g (1 lb)	small fresh-water eels
2 teaspoons	salt
¼ cup (2 fl oz)	softened lard or frying oil
2 teaspoons	rice wine or dry sherry
2 tablespoons	light soy sauce
6	spring onions (scallions), trimmed and shredded
2 tablespoons	finely shredded fresh ginger
2 tablespoons	chopped garlic, or to taste

Seasoning/Sauce:

¼ teaspoon	salt
½ teaspoon	m.s.g. (optional)
2 teaspoons	sugar
½ teaspoon	ground black pepper
¾ cup (6 fl oz)	chicken stock
2 teaspoons	cornflour (cornstarch)

Cut off the heads, slit the eels open, remove the stomachs and rinse well. Drop into boiling water to blanch for 1 minute, drain and rub with salt, then rinse again. Cut into three lengthwise strips, and cut these into 5 cm (2 in) pieces.

Heat the lard or frying oil in a wok and fry the eels on high heat until almost cooked through, about 3 minutes. Drizzle the wine into the sides of the wok, then do the same with the soy sauce. Pour in the pre-mixed seasoning/sauce ingredients and bring to the boil. Reduce the heat slightly and simmer for 5 minutes.

Transfer to a serving plate and make a hollow in the centre. Add the spring onions, ginger and garlic. Reheat the wok and add 2½ — 3 tablespoons frying oil. Heat to smoking and quickly pour over the onion, ginger, and garlic. Stir lightly into the eels and serve.

RED-BRAISED TURTLE

1 1 kg (2 lb)	turtle, preferably alive
1 tablespoon	rice wine or dry sherry
2 tablespoons	dark soy sauce
⅓ cup	frying oil
8 — 10 cloves	garlic, bruised
4	spring onions (scallions), trimmed and cut into 5 cm (2 in) pieces
4 thick slices	fresh ginger, bruised
125 g (4 oz)	'five flowered' pork (belly/fresh bacon)
1½ cups (12 fl oz)	chicken stock or water
75 g (2½ oz)	canned bamboo shoots, drained and cubed (or use fresh chestnuts and omit the garlic)
2 teaspoons	cornflour (cornstarch)
1 tablespoon	cold water
½ teaspoon	white vinegar

Seasoning:

¼ cup (2 fl oz)	light soy sauce
1 tablespoon	rice wine or dry sherry
1 tablespoon	sugar
½ teaspoon	m.s.g. (optional)
¼ teaspoon	ground black pepper

See page 395 for the preparation of live turtle. Cut the meat into 4 cm (1 2/3 in) cubes and rub with the wine and soy sauce. Heat the wok, add oil and when smoking, fry the turtle until evenly coloured. Remove and keep warm. Add the garlic and fry until lightly browned, and set aside.

If using chestnuts, they should be blanched to loosen the skin, the skin removed, and the nuts dried before frying to a light golden colour. Remove and set aside.

Add the onion, ginger, and pork and sauté until the pork is lightly coloured. Pour in the chicken stock or water. Add the bamboo shoots (or chestnuts) and garlic, the turtle meat and seasoning ingredients and mix well. Bring to the boil, then transfer to a casserole and cover tightly. Simmer or steam until the turtle is tender, about 20 minutes if simmered, 45 minutes if steamed.

Transfer the turtle meat, bamboo shoots and garlic, or the chestnuts, to a serving dish. Discard the pork, onion, and ginger and return the cooking liquid to the boil.

Thicken with the cornflour mixed with the cold water and check the seasoning. Pour over the turtle and garnish with shredded spring onion or ham.

SLOW-COOKED CORNED PORK

Serve hot or cold, as an appetiser or main dish.

1¼ kg (2½ lb)	pork shoulder (butt)
1 tablespoon	saltpetre

Seasoning:

1 tablespoon	rice wine or dry sherry
3	spring onions (scallions), trimmed
1½ teaspoons	grated fresh ginger
1½ teaspoons	salt
2	star anise
2 teaspoons	Chinese brown peppercorns
5 cm (2 in) piece	cinnamon stick

Blanch the pork in boiling water, then place in a pan with water to cover and add the saltpetre. Leave, covered, for 2 hours. Blanch again in boiling water and rinse in cold water. Drain well. This process gives a rosy colour to the meat and helps to preserve and tenderise.

Place the pork with seasoning ingredients in a heavy saucepan and add water to cover. Bring to the boil, reduce heat to low and simmer for 2½ hours, turning often. Remove from the heat and leave to cool in the pot.

Remove the meat when cool, slice thinly and arrange on a serving plate. Pour a little of the sauce on top. Serve with a dip of shredded ginger and garlic in vinegar (see page 384).

Pork leg (fresh ham) can also be prepared in this way. The skin may be left on and pricked thoroughly all over to allow the seasonings to penetrate. The resultant cooking liquid will have a gelatinous quality which will keep the sliced meat moist if brushed over before serving.

PORK AND CRABMEAT 'LION'S HEAD' MEATBALLS

750 g (1½ lb)	lean pork, minced (ground)
185 g (6 oz)	crabmeat
2 tablespoons	finely chopped spring onion (scallion)
1 teaspoon	grated fresh ginger
750 g (1½ lb)	Chinese cabbage, bok choy (celery cabbage)
¼ cup (2 fl oz)	frying oil
1 teaspoon	salt
	hot chicken stock

Seasoning:

1½ teaspoons	salt
½ teaspoon	m.s.g. (optional)
¼ teaspoon	white pepper
1 tablespoon	rice wine or dry sherry
2 tablespoons	cornflour (cornstarch)

Mix the pork with half the crabmeat, the onion and ginger, and the seasoning ingredients. Knead to a smooth paste and form into five large meatballs. Press a thumb into the centre of each to form a cavity and fill with the remaining crabmeat. Re-form the balls.

Wash the cabbage and cut into 7.5 cm (3 in) pieces. Sauté in the oil for 2-3 minutes until beginning to change colour, add the salt, stir well and transfer half to a casserole. Place the meatballs on the vegetables and arrange the remaining vegetables on top. Pour hot chicken stock into the casserole until the meatballs are just covered. Cover the pan and simmer on low heat for 1½ hours, adding more stock during cooking if needed, though this is usually unnecessary as the vegetables provide substantial extra liquid.

Remove the vegetables and place around the edge of a serving dish. Place the meatballs in the centre and pour on some of the sauce, which may be thickened slightly with a cornflour (cornstarch) solution if preferred. Or remove the top layer of vegetables to a separate plate and serve the meatballs in the casserole.

SLOW-COOKED LEG OF PORK WITH FERMENTED BEANCURD AND GARLIC

750 g (1½ lb)	pork leg (fresh ham)
4 cubes	fermented beancurd, with the liquid
8 — 10 cloves	garlic, bruised
¼ cup (2 fl oz)	frying oil or softened lard
3	spring onions (scallions), trimmed and cut in halves
3 thick slices	fresh ginger, bruised
1 teaspoon	m.s.g. (optional)

Seasoning:

⅓ cup	light soy sauce
2 tablespoons	rice wine or dry sherry
1 cup (8 fl oz)	sugar colouring (see page 388) chicken stock
1 tablespoon	sugar

Cut the pork into 4 cm (1 2/3 in) cubes and blanch in boiling water. Drain. Mash the beancurd with a fork, adding the liquid and sauté with the garlic cloves in the oil or lard for 2 minutes. Add the pork and fry until well coloured.

Add the onions and ginger, fry briefly, then pour in the premixed seasoning ingredients with enough chicken stock to barely cover the meat. Bring to the boil and transfer to a casserole.

Simmer for 1½ — 1¾ hours until the pork is completely tender, add the m.s.g., if used, and serve.

SHREDDED BEEF AND BEAN SPROUTS ON CRISP NOODLES

250 g (8 oz)	frying steak (rump, fillet/tenderloin)
30 g (1 oz)	bean thread vermicelli
3 cups (24 fl oz)	deep-frying oil
185 g (6 oz)	fresh bean sprouts
1	large spring onion (scallion), shredded

Seasoning A:

1	egg white, beaten
¼ teaspoon	salt
½ teaspoon	sugar
2 teaspoons	light soy sauce
2 teaspoons	sesame oil
2 teaspoons	cornflour (cornstarch)
2 tablespoons	cold water

Seasoning B/Sauce:

½ cup (4 fl oz)	beef or chicken stock
¾ teaspoon	light soy sauce
½ teaspoon	rice wine or dry sherry
¼ teaspoon	salt
½ teaspoon	m.s.g. (optional) pinch of white pepper
½ teaspoon	cornflour (cornstarch)

Partially freeze the beef to facilitate slicing and cut across the grain into very thin slices, then cut these into shreds. Place in a dish and add the seasoning A ingredients. Mix well and leave to marinate for 15 minutes.

Break the vermicelli into short pieces and place in a frying basket. Heat the deep-frying oil in a wok until smoking and fry the noodles for a few seconds until they expand into a cloud of crisp white noodles. Do not allow to colour. Remove quickly, drain well, and pile on a serving plate.

Transfer the beef to the frying basket and lower into the hot oil for 10 seconds only. Lift out and shake the basket to remove excess oil. Set aside.

Drain off all but 2 tablespoons oil and fry the bean sprouts with the shredded onion until softened. Return the beef to fry briefly, stirring continually, then pour in the pre-mixed seasoning B/sauce ingredients and bring to the boil. Cook, stirring, for 1 minute then pour over the noodles and serve at once.

'SU TUNG PO' PORK

825 g (1¾ lb)	'five flowered' pork (belly/fresh bacon)
1 tablespoon	salt
8 pieces	rock candy (or ½ cup crystal sugar)
⅓ cup	light soy sauce
¼ cup (2 fl oz)	rice wine or dry sherry
2	spring onions (scallions), trimmed and cut in halves
4 thick slices	fresh ginger, bruised
90 g (3 oz)	canned champignons, drained and sliced
8	dried black mushrooms, soaked for 25 minutes

Rub the salt over the pork and leave for 1 hour, then blanch in boiling water for 2 minutes and rinse thoroughly in cold water. Drain well. Sear in a very hot dry pan until the surface is coloured and beginning to crisp. Cut into slices about 1 cm (⅓ in) thick, then into strips 5 cm (2 in) wide. Arrange in a covered pot and add the remaining ingredients. (First squeeze excess water from the black mushrooms and remove the stems.) Simmer for 2½ — 3 hours until the pork is completely tender.

Transfer the meat and mushrooms to a serving dish and discard the onion and ginger. Bring the sauce to the boil, check the seasoning and strain over the meat. Serve at once.

SIMMERED BELL PEPPERS STUFFED WITH PORK

Serve as an appetiser or main dish.

6	small green capsicums (bell peppers)
125 g (4 oz)	lean pork, finely minced (ground)
45 g (1½ oz)	fresh shrimp meat, minced (ground)
30 g (1 oz)	canned water chestnuts, drained and finely chopped
1 tablespoon	finely chopped spring onion (scallion)
½ teaspoon	grated fresh ginger
1 cup (8 fl oz)	frying oil
	cornflour (cornstarch)

Seasoning A:

1	egg white, beaten
¼ teaspoon	salt
½ teaspoon	m.s.g. (optional)
1 tablespoon	onion and ginger infusion (see page 386)
1 teaspoon	rice wine or dry sherry
1 tablespoon	cornflour (cornstarch)

Seasoning B/Sauce:

¾ cup (6 fl oz)	chicken stock
1 tablespoon	light soy sauce
1 teaspoon	rice wine or dry sherry
½ teaspoon	salt
½ teaspoon	m.s.g. (optional)
¼ teaspoon	sugar
1	spring onion (scallion), trimmed and shredded
1 slice	fresh ginger, shredded

Wash the peppers, cut in halves and remove the stem and seed core and the inner white ribs. Mix the minced pork, shrimp, water chestnuts, onion, and ginger with the seasoning A ingredients, stirring thoroughly.

Heat the shallow oil to moderate. Dust the inside of the peppers lightly with cornflour and fill each with a portion of the stuffing mixture, smoothing the edges. Squeeze each gently and coat lightly with cornflour.

Fry for about 8 minutes, turning occasionally. Remove and drain well. Bring the seasoning B/sauce ingredients to the boil in another pan and add the stuffed peppers. Simmer, uncovered, for a further 5 minutes. Serve with the sauce which may be thickened slightly with a thin solution of cornflour (cornstarch) and cold water, if preferred.

ROASTED PORK 'COINS'

Serve as an appetiser or main dish.

500 g (1 lb)	pork fillet (tenderloin)
500 g (1 lb)	pork fat
125 g (4 oz)	Chinese or cured (Smithfield) ham
2 tablespoons	softened lard or frying oil

Seasoning:

1 tablespoon	oyster sauce
1 tablespoon	soy bean paste (or dark soy sauce)
1 tablespoon	rice wine or dry sherry
1 tablespoon	sugar
¼ teaspoon	white pepper
1 teaspoon	m.s.g. (optional)
2 teaspoons	finely chopped spring onion (scallion)
¾ teaspoon	grated fresh ginger

Cut the pork into slices across the grain and bat lightly with the side of a cleaver to produce thin escalopes. Thinly slice the pork fat and ham and cut into pieces the same size as the pork. Mix the three meats with the seasoning ingredients and leave to marinate for 25 minutes.

Thread pork, pork fat, and ham pieces alternately onto small bamboo skewers previously soaked in oil, and arrange on an oiled baking sheet (cookie tray).

Roast in a preheated hot oven at 230°C(450°F) for about 25 minutes, turning frequently.

Remove from the skewers and arrange on a warmed plate to serve.

MINCED PORK IN CLAMS SERVED IN A CROCK

24	fresh clams (about 750 1½ g lb)
185 g (6 oz)	fatty pork, finely minced (ground)
45 g (1½ oz)	canned water chestnuts, drained and chopped
1 tablespoon	finely chopped spring onion (scallion)
1 teaspoon	grated fresh ginger cornflour (cornstarch)
5 cups (1¼ litres)	deep-frying oil

Seasoning A:

½ teaspoon	salt
½ teaspoon	m.s.g. (optional)
2 teaspoons	rice wine or dry sherry
½ teaspoon	sesame oil
1 tablespoon	cornflour (cornstarch)

Seasoning B/Sauce:

2 tablespoons	finely chopped spring onion (scallion)
1 tablespoon	finely chopped fresh ginger
½ cup (4 fl oz)	sugar colouring (see page 388)
1½ tablespoons	rice wine or dry sherry
2 teaspoons	dark soy sauce
1 teaspoon	salt
½ teaspoon	m.s.g. (optional)
½ teaspoon	sugar
¼ teaspoon	ground black pepper
1 teaspoon	sesame oil (optional)

Mix the pork with the seasoning A ingredients and set aside. Thoroughly wash the clams and place in a saucepan with water to cover. Bring to the boil and simmer until the clams open. Shake the pan occasionally as this helps them open. Drain, reserving the liquid.

Remove the clams and chop finely. Wipe out the shells, separating the two pieces. Mix the chopped clam with the pork, water chestnuts, spring onion, and ginger. Stuff into the clam shells, smooth the edges and coat lightly with cornflour.

Heat the deep-frying oil to smoking point and deep-fry the clams in several lots until well coloured. Remove to an earthenware crock. Bring the reserved stock to the boil and pour over the clams. Add the seasoning B/sauce ingredients and simmer for 12 minutes.

Thicken the sauce with a thin solution of cornflour and cold water and serve in the pot.

PORK KIDNEYS, TURNIP, AND DRIED SCALLOPS STEAMED IN A BOWL

Serve as an appetiser or main dish.

280 g (9 oz)	pork kidneys
5	dried scallops (about 40 g (1⅓ oz)), soaked for 25 minutes
280 g (9 oz)	sweet white turnips or giant white (icicle) radish, peeled
2 cups (16 fl oz)	deep-frying oil
2	spring onions (scallions), trimmed and shredded
2 slices	fresh ginger, shredded
125 g (4 oz)	ham skin (or use 2 streaky bacon rashers)

Seasoning A:

⅓ cup	chicken stock
1½ teaspoons	rice wine or dry sherry

Seasoning B:

½ teaspoon	salt
1 tablespoon	finely diced fresh chicken fat (chicken grease)

Sauce:

⅓ cup	reserved stock*
½ teaspoon	m.s.g. (optional)
¾ teaspoon	cornflour (cornstarch)
	pinch of white pepper
1 tablespoon	vegetable oil

Cut the pork kidneys in halves and remove the white fatty tissue. Peel off the skin. Place cut sides down on a cutting board and score to the depth of ⅓ cm (1/8 in) in a criss-cross pattern across each piece of kidney. Cut into thin slices, to give pieces with one fluted edge. Soak in boiling water for 30 seconds, then drain and place in a dish of cold water.

Drain the scallops and place in a dish with the seasoning A ingredients. Steam for 30 minutes, then drain, reserving the stock for the sauce. Shred the scallops by rubbing between forefinger and thumb. Arrange in the bottom of a bowl.

Cut the turnip or radish into small cubes and deep-fry until lightly coloured on the surface, or cook in shallow oil. Drain and transfer to a small saucepan of boiling water. Simmer until tender. Drain and arrange over the shredded scallops. Place the sliced kidneys on top and add the seasoning B ingredients and the shredded spring onions and ginger.

Cover the lot with the ham skin or bacon and set the bowl in a steamer to steam over rapidly boiling water for 20 minutes. Remove and discard the ham skin or bacon and chicken fat residue.

Heat a wok and strain in the liquid from the bowl, then add the sauce ingredients and bring to the boil. Simmer until thickened, then pour into the bowl and serve.

* Liquid from steamed scallops.

SAUTÉD LIVER AND ONIONS IN HOT SAUCE

280 g (9 oz)	fresh pork or calves liver
1	large white onion
1 cup (8 fl oz)	frying oil

Seasoning A:

2	egg whites, well beaten
½ teaspoon	salt
½ teaspoon	m.s.g. (optional)
¼ teaspoon	white pepper
2 teaspoons	rice wine or dry sherry
2 slices	fresh ginger, shredded
1 tablespoon	cornflour (cornstarch)

Seasoning B/Sauce:

1 tablespoon	hot bean paste
1½ tablespoons	light soy sauce
1 tablespoon	rice wine or dry sherry
1½ teaspoons	sugar
¼ teaspoon	m.s.g. (optional)
¼ teaspoon	white pepper

Very thinly slice the liver and place in a dish with the seasoning A ingredients, except the cornflour. Mix well and leave for 15 minutes, then add the cornflour and stir in lightly.

Peel the onion and cut from stem to root into thin slices. Heat the frying oil to smoking point and add the liver. Separate with chopsticks and fry until it changes colour, then remove the liver and drain off all but 2 tablespoons of the oil. Return the liver and fry on both sides until lightly coloured. Remove. Add the onions and fry until softened. Add the seasoning B/sauce ingredients and sauté briefly, then return the liver and splash in a very little water. Sauté together until the liver is just cooked through, about 45 seconds. Serve.

Red-Braised Turtle (recipe page 135).

BONELESS RACK OF LAMB FLAVOURED WITH WHITE RICE WINE

Serve as an appetiser or main dish.

1½ kg (3 lb)	boned rack of lamb
185 g (6 oz)	giant white (icicle) radish, small red radishes or sweet white turnips
	sesame oil

Seasoning A:

½ teaspoon	salt
¼ teaspoon	white pepper
1 tablespoon	sugar
1 tablespoon	light soy sauce
2 tablespoons	white rice wine (Mao Tai or similar, or use malt whisky or brandy)
1½ tablespoons	finely chopped spring onion
1 teaspoon	grated fresh ginger

Seasoning B:

1 teaspoon	salt
1 tablespoon	sugar
¼ cup (2 fl oz)	white vinegar

Trim away excess fat from the rack, score the skin side with a criss-cross pattern and rub the pre-mixed seasoning A ingredients on both sides of the rack. Leave covered for 2 hours, preferably in a sealed plastic bag.

Preheat the oven to moderate, 200°C (375°F). Place the rack on an oiled baking tray, brush with sesame oil and roast for 30 minutes, then turn and roast for a further 25 — 30 minutes until cooked through, but remaining tender and slightly pink inside.

In the meantime, peel and thinly slice the radish or turnip, and marinate with the seasoning B ingredients with water to cover.

To serve, cut the lamb into pieces about 5 × 2 cm (2 × ¾ in) and arrange on a plate surrounded with the drained pickled radish or turnip.

SAUTÉD SHREDDED LAMB AND SPRING ONIONS

375 g (12 oz)	boneless lamb (leg or loin)
10	large spring onions (scallions), (or use 2 brown onions),* thinly sliced
¼ cup (2 fl oz)	frying oil
2 teaspoons	sesame oil (optional)

Seasoning A:

½ teaspoon	sugar
½ teaspoon	m.s.g. (optional)
1 tablespoon	light soy sauce
½ teaspoon	rice wine or dry sherry

Seasoning B:

½ teaspoon	sugar
¼ teaspoon	white pepper
¼ teaspoon	m.s.g. (optional)
1 tablespoon	light soy sauce
½ teaspoon	rice wine or dry sherry
2 teaspoons	sesame oil

Partially freeze the lamb, cut into very thin slices across the grain, then cut into shreds. Mix with the seasoning A ingredients and leave to marinate for 20 minutes.

Trim away most of the green parts of the spring onions, cut into 4 cm (1 2/3 in) pieces and shred finely.

Heat the oil with sesame oil, if used, in a wok and when smoking sauté the shredded lamb on fairly high heat until the colour changes, about 1½ minutes. Add the spring onions and fry a further ½ minute, then stir in the pre-mixed seasoning B ingredients and cook on high heat until well mixed and bubbling. Transfer to a serving plate.

* If using sliced brown onions, brown in the oil before cooking the meat.

BRAISED LAMB AND HOT SPICES

750 g (1½ lb)	boneless lamb (leg or shoulder)
125 g (4 oz)	canned bamboo shoots or water chestnuts, drained
90 g (3 oz)	small carrots
¼ cup (2 fl oz)	frying oil or softened lard
2	spring onions (scallions), trimmed and shredded
2 thick slices	fresh ginger, shredded
2 tablespoons	hot bean paste, hot black bean sauce (or 2 teaspoons chilli sauce and 2 tablespoons soy sauce)
1 small bunch	garlic chives or 1 fresh young leek, shredded
2 teaspoons	sesame oil (optional)

Seasoning:

¾ teaspoon	salt
1 teaspoon	sugar
1 tablespoon	light soy sauce
1 teaspoon	rice wine or dry sherry

Trim the lamb and cut into 2.5 cm (1 in) cubes. Cut bamboo shoots into 2 cm (¾ in) cubes, or cut water chestnuts in halves horizontally, if used. Peel and cube the carrots.

Heat the oil or lard in a wok and sauté the lamb on moderately high heat for 1½ — 2 minutes, until lightly coloured. Add the spring onion and ginger, fry briefly, then add the hot bean paste, the bean sauce or chilli and soy sauce mixed together and fry for 1 minute.

Add the seasoning ingredients and water to just cover the meat. Stir well and bring to the boil. Cover the pan, reduce heat to low and simmer for 1½ hours until the lamb is tender. Remove the cover for the last stages of cooking to reduce the sauce. Thicken if needed with a thin solution of cornflour (cornstarch) and cold water.

Stir in the shredded garlic chives or leek and the sesame oil, if used, and transfer to a warmed plate to serve.

BRAISED AND STEAMED WILD DUCK

Serves 10

2 1 kg (2 lb)	wild ducks (or use domestic ducks)
15 large	spring onions (scallions)
155 g (5 oz)	lean pork
125 g (4 oz)	canned bamboo shoots, drained
4 thick slices	fresh ginger, bruised
1 cup (8 fl oz)	frying oil
	cornflour (cornstarch)

Seasoning/Sauce:

4 cups (1 litre)	chicken stock
1 cup (8 fl oz)	sugar colouring (see page 388)
⅓ cup	light soy sauce
1½ tablespoons	rice wine or dry sherry
1½ teaspoons	sugar

Clean and dress the ducks. Prick the thighs with a skewer to release any blood and blanch in boiling water for 2 minutes. Drain well, then rinse in cold water and set aside.

Trim the green ends from the onions. Cut each in halves lengthwise, then into 4 cm (1 2/3 in) pieces.

Slice the pork and cut into short strips. Cube the bamboo shoots.

Arrange half the pork with several pieces of onion in a casserole or heavy-based cooking pot and place the ducks, breasts down, on top. Cover with the remaining pork and add several more pieces of onion and the ginger slices. Pour the pre-mixed seasoning/sauce ingredients into the pan and cover. Bring to the boil over high heat, then reduce to low and simmer for 1¾ hours.

Remove the ducks, leave to cool and cut into bite-sized pieces, discarding the bones if preferred.

Fry the remaining onions in the oil until lightly browned. Remove and fry the bamboo shoots until lightly coloured. Place the onions and bamboo shoots in a large dish and arrange the duck meat and pork on top. Pour in ¾ cup (6 fl oz) of the braising liquid and set the dish on a rack in a steaming pot. Cover tightly and steam over high heat for 20 minutes.

Strain the liquid into a wok and bring to the boil. Check seasoning and thicken with a thin solution of cornflour and cold water. Pour over the dish and serve.

WILD DUCK WITH MASHED TARO STUFFING AND OYSTER SAUCE

½ 2 kg (4 lb)	wild duck (or use domestic duck)
2 tablespoons	dark soy sauce
8 cups (2 litres)	deep-frying oil
2	spring onions (scallions), trimmed and shredded
4 slices	fresh ginger, shredded
1½	star anise, broken
1½ teaspoons	Chinese brown peppercorns cornflour (cornstarch)

Stuffing:

500 g (1 lb)	taro, sweet potato or potato, peeled
¾ cup	taro flour (potato flour or cornflour)
½ cup	boiling water
¼ cup (2 fl oz)	softened lard or pastry shortening
1½ teaspoons	salt
½ teaspoon	ground black pepper
2	dried black mushrooms, soaked and finely diced
2 tablespoons	cooked ham, finely diced

Sauce:

1½ tablespoons	oyster sauce
1½ tablespoons	light soy sauce
½ cup (4 fl oz)	chicken stock
1 teaspoon	sugar
	pinch of salt
	pinch of ground black pepper
2 teaspoons	cornflour (cornstarch)
2 tablespoons	finely chopped spring onion (scallion)

Wash the duck and blanch in boiling water. Drain well. Rub with the soy sauce and leave for 15 minutes, then deep-fry in smoking hot deep-frying oil until well coloured, about 3 minutes. Remove and drain well.

Place the duck on a plate, cut side upwards, and sprinkle on the shredded spring onion, ginger, the star anise, and the peppercorns. Set the plate on a rack in a steamer and steam over rapidly boiling water for 1¾ hours.

Boil the taro or potato until soft enough to mash smoothly. Mix the taro flour with the boiling water and add to the mashed taro. Work in the lard, salt pepper, and the diced ingredients and knead to a smooth paste.

Remove the duck and wipe dry. Carefully debone, keeping it in its original shape. Discard the spices, onion, and ginger, and sprinkle with cornflour. Spread the stuffing over the inside of the duck in a thick layer, smoothing the top and edges. Coat lightly with cornflour.

Reheat the deep-frying oil and slide the stuffed duck carefully into the oil. Deep-fry until golden brown and the stuffings crisp. Carefully lift onto a cutting board and cut into bite-sized pieces. Arrange on a plate of shredded lettuce.

Bring the sauce ingredients, except the spring onions, to the boil and simmer until thickened, then add the onions. Pour over the duck or serve as a dip.

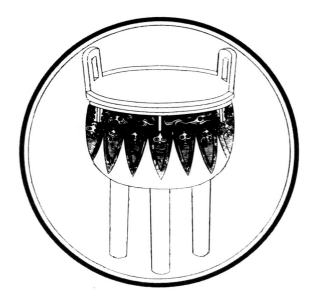

Pork and Crabmeat 'Lion's Head' Meatballs (recipe page 136).

WILD DUCK, VEGETABLES, AND ASSORTED MEATS SIMMERED WITH RICE

Serves 6 as a main course

½ — 1½ kg (3 lb)	wild duck (or use domestic duck)
2	spring onions (scallions), trimmed and diced
3 thick slices	fresh ginger, bruised
125 g (4 oz)	lean pork, diced
125 g (4 oz)	boneless chicken, diced
6	dried black mushrooms, soaked for 25 minutes
60 g (2 oz)	Chinese or cured (Smithfield) ham, diced
2 cups (13 oz)	short grain white rice, soaked for 10 minutes
250 g (½ lb)	fresh green vegetables (Chinese cabbage, mustard, broccoli)
1 thin slice	fresh ginger, shredded
1½ tablespoons	frying oil or softened lard

Seasoning A:

½ teaspoon	salt
2 teaspoons	rice wine or dry sherry
	pinch of white pepper

Seasoning B:

2 tablespoons	dried shrimps, soaked (optional)
2 teaspoons	salt
1 teaspoon	m.s.g. (optional)
½ teaspoon	ground black pepper
2 teaspoons	rice wine or dry sherry
1 tablespoon	lard or rendered chicken fat (chicken grease), warmed

Clean and dress the wild duck and place in a saucepan with the diced onions and ginger slices. Cover with water, bring to the boil and simmer, covered, until tender. Remove, drain well and reserve the stock. Debone the duck and cut into small dice.

In another saucepan, simmer the pork and chicken with just enough water to cover, and the seasoning A ingredients. When tender, drain and reserve this stock also.

Squeeze the water from the mushrooms, trim off stems and shred the caps finely.

Mix the duck, pork, chicken, mushrooms, ham, and drained rice thoroughly in a heavy-based saucepan. Stir in the seasoning B ingredients and add equal amounts of the two reserved stocks. The liquid should be 2 cm (¾ in) above the level of the rice and meats. Cover the pan tightly, bring to the boil, then reduce the heat to very low and simmer for 15 minutes.

In the meantime, wash and dry the vegetables, cutting larger stems into pieces about 7.5 cm (3 in) long.

Sauté in the oil or lard for 3 minutes, adding a dash of rice wine, the shredded ginger and seasoning with salt, sugar, and white pepper to taste.

Arrange the vegetables on the rice, re-cover and continue to simmer for a further 6 — 8 minutes until the rice is tender and fluffy.

Transfer the vegetables to a serving plate, making a border around the edge. Stir the rice lightly with a chopstick or the handle of a wooden spoon, pile onto the serving plate.

FROGS' LEGS BRAISED WITH GARLIC

625 g (1¼ lb)	skinned frogs' legs
2 teaspoons	light soy sauce
1 teaspoon	rice wine or dry sherry
12 cloves	garlic, peeled and bruised
¼ cup (2 fl oz)	frying oil or softened lard
2	spring onions (scallions), trimmed and cut into 2.5 cm (1 in) pieces
1 thin slice	fresh ginger, shredded sesame oil

Seasoning/Sauce:

½ cup (4 fl oz)	chicken stock or water
2 teaspoons	light soy sauce
¼ teaspoon	salt
½ teaspoon	sugar
	pinch of ground black pepper
½ teaspoon	cornflour (cornstarch)

Divide the frogs' legs at the central joint, rinse in cold water, pat dry and rub with the soy sauce and wine. Set aside for 15 minutes.

Heat the oil or lard in a wok and fry the garlic until lightly coloured. Remove. Increase the heat to high and stir-fry the frogs' legs for 2 minutes and add the onion and ginger. Fry briefly, then pour in the pre-mixed seasoning/sauce ingredients and bring to the boil. Return the garlic, reduce heat and braise for 10 — 12 minutes, covered. Stir in sesame oil to taste and transfer to a serving plate.

Add shredded fresh chilli pepper for extra piquancy, or stir in 1 — 2 teaspoons hot black bean sauce or hot bean paste, adding a little more sugar to taste.

SLICED PHEASANT SAUTÉD WITH BAMBOO SHOOTS AND MUSTARD GREENS

250 g (8 oz)	boneless breast of pheasant (or use wild duck, domestic duck or pigeon)
90 g (3 oz)	canned winter bamboo shoots, drained
45 g (1½ oz)	salted mustard root, soaked for 20 minutes
¼ cup (2 fl oz)	frying oil or softened lard
2	spring onions (scallions), trimmed and diced
2 slices	fresh ginger, shredded
1 teaspoon	sesame oil (optional)
½ teaspoon	white vinegar (optional)

Seasoning A:

1	egg white, beaten
¼ teaspoon	salt
1½ teaspoons	sesame oil (optional)
½ teaspoon	cornflour (cornstarch)

Seasoning B/Sauce:

½ cup (4 fl oz)	chicken stock
1 tablespoon	light soy sauce
½ teaspoon	rice wine or dry sherry
¼ teaspoon	salt
½ teaspoon	m.s.g. (optional)
	pinch of white pepper
¼ teaspoon	sugar
½ teaspoon	cornflour (cornstarch)

Blanch the pheasant breasts in boiling water for 1 minute, drain and slice thinly, then cut into narrow shreds. Mix the meat with the seasoning A ingredients and leave to marinate for 20 minutes. Shred the bamboo shoots and the drained mustard root.

Heat the oil or lard in a wok until smoking and sauté the pheasant on high heat for 1½ minutes. Remove and sauté the bamboo shoots for 1 minute, then add the onions and ginger and sauté briefly before returning the meat.

Add the shredded mustard root and fry for a few seconds, then pour in the pre-mixed seasoning B/sauce ingredients and cook, stirring, until the sauce thickens.

Season with vinegar and sesame oil, if used, and transfer to a warmed serving plate.

DEEP-FRIED BEANCURD, SHRIMP, AND CHICKEN FRITTERS

Serve as an appetiser or main dish.

4 squares	soft beancurd (or 16 pieces canned beancurd, drained)
75 g (2½ oz)	shrimp meat, minced (ground)
60 g (2 oz)	boneless chicken, minced (ground)
60 g (2 oz)	pork fat, minced (ground)
60 g (2 oz)	pine seeds or toasted peanuts cornflour (cornstarch)
4 cups (1 litre)	deep-frying oil

Seasoning:

2	egg whites, beaten
1 teaspoon	salt
1 tablespoon	onion and ginger infusion (see page 386)
1½ tablespoons	cornflour (cornstarch)

Mash the beancurd with a fork and mix with the shrimp, chicken, and pork fat. Add the seasoning ingredients and mix thoroughly. Blanch the pine seeds, if used, in boiling water for 1 minute. Drain then dry and deep-fry until golden. Drain and chop finely. Stir half into the beancurd mixture.

Press the mixture into an oiled square baking tin and decorate with the remaining chopped nuts, pressing on lightly. Set the tin on a rack in a steaming pot and steam over rapidly boiling water for 15 — 20 minutes until firm.

Remove the tin from the steamer and invert onto a board. Cut the beancurd into pieces about 4 × 2 cm (1 2/3 × ¾ in) and coat lightly with cornflour.

Heat the deep-frying oil to moderately hot and fry the fritters until golden brown. Drain and season generously with pepper-salt. Serve hot.

RED-BRAISED PIGEONS WITH FIVE SPICES

6	small pigeons, about 825 g / 1¾ lb dressed weight
125 g (4 oz)	lean pork, thinly sliced (optional)
2	spring onions (scallions), cut into 2.5 cm (1 in) pieces
3 thick slices	fresh ginger, bruised
2	spice bags (see page 386) sesame oil

Seasoning/Sauce:

1 cup (8 fl oz)	sugar colouring (see page 388)
1 cup (8 fl oz)	light soy sauce
¼ cup (2 fl oz)	rice wine or dry sherry
1 teaspoon	salt
1 teaspoon	m.s.g. (optional)
2/3 cup (5 oz)	sugar

Blanch the pigeons in boiling water for 1 minute, then rinse well in cold water. Place a bamboo rack in a casserole and arrange the pigeons, breasts up, on the rack with the sliced pork on top, if used.

Push the onions, ginger slices, and the two spice bags down the inside of the casserole, taking care not to disturb the pigeons or pork slices. Add the pre-mixed seasoning/sauce ingredients with water to cover.

Bring to the boil, tightly cover the casserole and reduce the heat to low. Simmer for 40 minutes until the pigeons are completely tender. Lift out, brush lightly with sesame oil and arrange the whole birds on a serving plate, breasts up. Keep warm.

Strain the cooking liquid into a wok, bring to the boil and reduce to about 1 cup (8 fl oz). Thicken with a thin solution of cornflour mixed with cold water, if desired, and pour over the pigeons. Serve.

SAUTÉD MINCED PIGEON WITH VEGETABLES AND HOT PEPPERS

185 g (6 oz)	boneless breast of pigeon (or use duck)
¼ cup (2 fl oz)	frying oil or softened lard
125 g (4 oz)	canned water chestnuts, drained and diced
2	spring onions (scallions), trimmed and diced
¾ teaspoon	grated fresh ginger
¾ teaspoon	crushed garlic (or to taste)
1 stalk	fresh celery, diced
1 — 2	fresh red chilli peppers, seeds removed and chopped
1 piece	dried orange peel (see page 416) sesame oil white vinegar toasted white sesame seeds prawn crackers (see page 416), optional deep-frying oil, optional

Seasoning A:

1	egg white, beaten
½ teaspoon	salt
2 teaspoons	sesame oil
¾ teaspoon	cornflour (cornstarch)

Seasoning B:

¼ teaspoon	salt
¼ teaspoon	m.s.g. (optional)
1 teaspoon	sugar
¼ teaspoon	ground black pepper
1 tablespoon	light soy sauce
½ teaspoon	rice wine or dry sherry

Blanch the pigeon breasts in boiling water, rinse in cold water and wipe dry. Cut into small dice and mix with the seasoning A ingredients, leaving to marinate for 20 minutes.

Heat the oil or lard in a wok until smoking and sauté the diced pigeon over high heat for 2 minutes. Add the water chestnuts, onion, ginger, and garlic and fry briefly, then add the celery, chilli pepper, and orange peel and continue to sauté on slightly reduced heat for a further 2 minutes.

Increase the heat, add the seasoning B ingredients and fry for 30 seconds. Season with a dash each of sesame oil and vinegar and transfer to a serving plate. Garnish with toasted sesame seeds.

If the prawn crackers are used, they should be quickly fried in very hot deep-frying oil until they expand and become crisp. Drain well and arrange around the dish.

'Su Tung Po' Pork (recipe page 138).

148

WINTER BAMBOO SHOOTS IN CHICKEN OIL SAUCE

1 315 (10 g oz) can	winter bamboo shoots, drained
1 cup (8 fl oz)	frying oil
60 g (2 oz)	fresh spinach, mustard or watercress, finely chopped
2 tablespoons	rendered chicken fat (chicken grease)
30 g (1 oz)	Chinese or cured (Smithfield) ham, finely shredded

Seasoning/Sauce:

¾ cup (6 fl oz)	chicken stock
½ teaspoon	rice wine
½ teaspoon	salt
¼ teaspoon	m.s.g. (optional)
½ teaspoon	sugar
¾ teaspoon	cornflour (cornstarch)

Thinly slice the bamboo shoots. Warm the frying oil in a wok and gently cook the bamboo shoots for 2 minutes. Remove and drain.

Thoroughly wash the green vegetables and squeeze out as much water as possible. Drain off all but 2 tablespoons oil from the wok, reheat to moderate and fry the chopped vegetables for 1 minute. Return the bamboo shoots and add the pre-mixed seasoning/sauce ingredients. Bring to the boil and cook, stirring, until the sauce thickens.

Stir in the chicken fat and heat through. Transfer to a serving plate and garnish with the shredded ham.

STEAMED BLACK MUSHROOMS WITH SHRIMP STUFFING

Serve as an appetiser or main dish.

12	large black mushrooms, soaked for 25 minutes
155 g (5 oz)	fresh prawn meat (shrimp meat) minced (ground)
60 g (2 oz)	fatty pork, finely minced (ground) cornflour (cornstarch)
1	hard-boiled (hard cooked) egg yolk large bunch of fresh coriander leaves (optional)

Seasoning A:

2 cups (16 fl oz)	chicken stock
¾ teaspoon	salt
½ teaspoon	m.s.g. (optional)
1	spring onion (scallion), trimmed and sliced
2 slices	fresh ginger, bruised

Seasoning B:

1	egg white, beaten
½ teaspoon	ginger wine (see page 387)
⅓ teaspoon	salt
½ teaspoon	m.s.g. (optional) pinch of white pepper
2 teaspoons	cornflour (cornstarch)

Sauce:

1 tablespoon	frying oil
½ cup (4 fl oz)	chicken stock
¼ teaspoon	salt
¾ teaspoon	cornflour (cornstarch)

Drain the mushrooms and squeeze out excess water. Remove the stems and simmer the caps in a saucepan with the seasoning A ingredients for 40 minutes.

Mix the minced prawn and pork meat with the seasoning B ingredients, kneading to a smooth paste.

Drain the mushrooms and squeeze dry again. Coat the undersides lightly with cornflour and press in a generous amount of the filling, smoothing the edges.

Garnish with the egg yolk, finely chopped, and set on an oiled plate to steam.

Bring the stock used to simmer the mushrooms (or use water) to boil in a steaming pot and add the washed coriander. Set a rack on top and place the mushrooms on their plate on this. Cover tightly and steam over high heat for 10 minutes.

Heat the wok and add the frying oil. When it is smoking, pour in the remaining pre-mixed sauce ingredients and bring to the boil, stirring. Drain any liquid from the mushroom plate into the wok and mix well, then pour the sauce over the mushrooms and serve.

CAULIFLOWER WITH CREAMED CHICKEN SAUCE

625 g (1¼ lb)	fresh cauliflower, divided into florets
2 teaspoons	salt
125 g (4 oz)	boneless chicken, finely minced (ground)
30 g (1 oz)	pork fat, finely minced (ground)
⅓ cup	frying oil
1 tablespoon	finely chopped cooked ham or spring onion

Seasoning:

½ teaspoon	salt
½ teaspoon	m.s.g. (optional)
1 teaspoon	ginger wine (see page 387)
1	egg white, beaten
1½ tablespoons	cornflour (cornstarch)
½ cup (4 fl oz)	chicken stock

Sauce:

1 cup (8 fl oz)	chicken stock
¾ teaspoon	salt
½ teaspoon	m.s.g. (optional)
	pinch of white pepper

Wash the cauliflower, drain, then boil in water to cover with the salt added for 2 minutes. Drain well and leave to cool.

Mix the minced chicken and pork fat with the seasoning ingredients, stirring to a smooth creamy paste.

Heat half the oil to warm and fry the chicken cream until it turns white, about 2 minutes. Remove and rinse the pan. Add the remaining oil and stir-fry the cauliflower on fairly high heat for 2 minutes, then add the pre-mixed sauce ingredients and bring to the boil.

Cook on moderately high heat until the liquid has evaporated and the cauliflower is tender but retaining crispness.

Pour in the creamed chicken and mix in carefully. Warm through, then transfer to a warmed serving plate and garnish with the ham or onion.

LIMA BEANS SAUTÉD WITH MUSHROOMS, HAM, AND SHRIMPS

250 g (8 oz)	shelled fresh or frozen lima (fava)beans
60 g (2 oz)	raw shrimps, peeled
2 tablespoons	frying oil or softened lard
30 g (1 oz)	canned champignons, thinly sliced
2 — 3 teaspoons	rendered chicken fat (chicken grease)
1 tablespoon	finely diced cooked ham

Seasoning A:

½	egg white, beaten
¼ teaspoon	salt
¼ teaspoon	cornflour (cornstarch)

Seasoning B/Sauce:

½ cup (4 fl oz)	chicken stock
¼ teaspoon	salt
½ teaspoon	m.s.g. (optional)
½ teaspoon	sugar
½ teaspoon	rice wine or dry sherry
½ teaspoon	cornflour (cornstarch)

Rinse or thaw the beans and dry thoroughly. Mix the shrimps with the seasoning A ingredients and leave to marinate for 15 minutes. Heat the wok and add the oil or lard. Fry the lima beans on moderate heat until they turn bright green, about 2 minutes, then add the shrimps and sliced mushrooms and fry together, stirring frequently, for 1 minute.

Pour in the pre-mixed seasoning B/sauce ingredients and bring to the boil. Reduce the heat and simmer for 2 minutes, then stir in the diced ham and chicken fat and warm through.

CRISP-FRIED SALTED MUSTARD GREENS WITH BAMBOO SHOOTS

1 500g (1 lb) can	bamboo shoots, drained
75 g (2½ oz)	dried salted mustard leaves, soaked for 20 minutes
4 cups (1 litre)	deep-frying oil
2	spring onions (scallions), shredded
2 teaspoons	sesame oil (optional)

Seasoning/Sauce:

½ cup (4 fl oz)	chicken stock
1 tablespoon	light soy sauce
½ teaspoon	rice wine or dry sherry
½ teaspoon	m.s.g. (optional)
½ teaspoon	sugar

Cut the bamboo shoots into 2.5 cm (1 in) cubes. Drain the mustard leaves and squeeze out the excess water, cut into pieces about 5 cm (2 in) square.

Heat the deep-frying oil to smoking point and deep-fry the mustard greens until crisp. Remove and drain well. Add the bamboo shoots and fry until crisped on the surface and well coloured. Remove.

Drain off all but 1 tablespoon oil and pour in the pre-mixed seasoning/sauce ingredients and bring to the boil. Return the bamboo shoots and cook on high heat until the sauce is well reduced. Stir occasionally. Add the onions, cook briefly and transfer with the bamboo shoots and sauce to a warmed serving plate. Surround with the crisp mustard leaves and sprinkle on sesame oil, if used.

FRESH MUSTARD GREENS WITH SCALLOPS IN CREAM SAUCE

750 g (1½ lb)	fresh mustard greens or Chinese spinach
6 pieces	dried scallops (about 1½ oz), soaked for 2 hours

Seasoning A:

1 tablespoon	rice wine or dry sherry
1	spring onion (scallion), trimmed
1 slice	fresh ginger, bruised
1 cup (8 fl oz)	chicken stock

Seasoning B:

¾ teaspoon	salt
½ teaspoon	m.s.g. (optional)
¾ teaspoon	sugar
1 teaspoon	rice wine or dry sherry
¼ cup (2 fl oz)	chicken stock

Sauce:

¾ cup (6 fl oz)	chicken stock
2 teaspoons	rendered chicken fat (chicken grease)
2 tablespoons	evaporated or fresh milk
1 teaspoon	cornflour (cornstarch)

Thoroughly wash the vegetables and cut into 10 cm (4 in) pieces. Steam the dried scallops with the seasoning A ingredients for 1 hour, then drain and shred, using fingers.

Simmer the vegetables with the seasoning B ingredients, tightly covered, for 10 minutes. Add the shredded scallops and simmer a further 5 minutes. Drain and remove to a serving plate. Bring the sauce to the boil and simmer until thickened. Pour over the vegetables and scallops and serve.

Wild Duck, Vegetables, and Assorted Meats Simmered with Rice (recipe page 146).

CHOPPED PEA SPROUTS WITH CREAMED CHICKEN

500 g (1 lb)	sweet pea sprouts (spinach or watercress)
155 g (5 oz)	boneless chicken, minced (ground)
60 g (2 oz)	pork fat, minced (ground)
1/3 cup	frying oil or softened lard

Seasoning A:

1	egg white, beaten
1/2 teaspoon	salt
1/2 teaspoon	m.s.g. (optional)
1 tablespoon	onion and ginger infusion (see page 386)
2 teaspoons	rice wine or dry sherry
1 tablespoon	cornflour (cornstarch)
3/4 cup (6 fl oz)	chicken stock

Seasoning B:

3/4 teaspoon	salt
1/4 teaspoon	m.s.g. (optional)
1/2 teaspoon	sugar
1/3 cup	chicken stock
3/4 teaspoon	cornflour (cornstarch)

Wash the pea sprouts or other vegetables and chop finely. Mix the chicken and pork fat with the seasoning A ingredients and stir until smooth and creamy.

Heat half the oil or lard in a wok and gently fry the chicken mixture until it turns white. Remove to one side of a warmed serving plate. Keep warm. Add the remaining oil and gently fry the vegetables for 5 minutes, adding the seasoning B ingredients after the first 2 minutes. Pour onto the other side of the plate and serve.

ASSORTED SAUTÉD VEGETABLES IN CREAM SAUCE

2	small cucumbers
6	dried black mushrooms, soaked for 25 minutes
2	medium carrots, sliced
60 g (2 oz)	sweet white turnips, peeled and cubed
4 cups (1 litre)	chicken stock
1/3 cup	frying oil
45 g (1 1/2 oz)	canned bamboo shoots, drained and sliced
6 cubes	deep-fried beancurd, soaked for 10 minutes (optional)
1 tablespoon	rendered chicken fat (chicken grease), optional

Seasoning/Sauce:

3/4 cup (6 fl oz)	chicken stock
1 tablespoon	light soy sauce
3/4 teaspoon	salt
1/2 teaspoon	m.s.g. (optional)
1/2 teaspoon	sugar
1 teaspoon	cornflour (cornstarch)

Cut the cucumber into sticks about 5 cm (2 in) long and discard the seeds but do not peel. Drain the mushrooms and remove stems. Parboil the cucumbers, mushrooms, carrots, and turnips in the chicken stock for 5 minutes and drain well.

Heat the oil in a wok and sauté all the vegetables together for 2 minutes. Add the beancurd, if used, after squeezing out excess water. Fry for 2 minutes, then pour in the pre-mixed seasoning/sauce ingredients and bring to the boil. Simmer for 1 minute, stir in the chicken fat, if used, and transfer to a serving plate.

CHINESE CABBAGE WITH CRABMEAT AND CRAB ROE SAUCE

625 g (1¼ lb)	Chinese cabbage (celery cabbage)
1½ teaspoons	salt
½ cup (4 fl oz)	frying oil or softened lard
1 tablespoon	finely chopped spring onion (scallion)
¼ teaspoon	grated fresh ginger
75 g (2½ oz)	fresh frozen or canned crabmeat
15 g (½ oz)	crab roe (optional)

Seasoning A:

¾ cup (6 fl oz)	chicken stock
1 teaspoon	salt
¾ teaspoon	sugar
¼ teaspoon	white pepper

Seasoning B/Sauce:

1¼ cups (10 fl oz)	chicken stock
¾ teaspoon	salt
½ teaspoon	rice wine or dry sherry
1 tablespoon	cornflour (cornstarch)
2	egg whites, well beaten

Thoroughly wash the cabbage and cut into 10 cm (4 in) pieces. Parboil in water to cover with the salt added, or in chicken stock, for 2 minutes. Drain well. Heat half the oil in a wok and sauté the cabbage for 3 minutes. Add the seasoning A ingredients and bring to the boil. Simmer for 2 minutes. Drain and arrange on a serving plate.

Heat the remaining oil and fry onion and ginger for 45 seconds. Add the crabmeat and sauté for 2 minutes, then add the pre-mixed seasoning B/sauce ingredients and bring to the boil. Stir in the crab roe and slowly drizzle in the beaten eggs which will set into white strings in the sauce. Heat for 1 minute, then pour over the cabbage and serve.

Florets of broccoli or cauliflower are also excellent with this sauce.

BAMBOO SHOOTS WITH CHICKEN, HAM, AND SPINACH BALLS IN SOUP

90 g (3 oz)	boneless chicken, minced (ground)
1½ tablespoons	finely chopped cooked ham
90 g (3 oz)	fresh young spinach leaves (collard greens), washed
125 g (3 oz)	canned bamboo shoots, drained and thinly sliced
6 cups (1½ litres)	chicken stock
2	spring onions (scallions), cut in halves
3 thick slices	fresh ginger, bruised
1 tablespoon	rice wine or dry sherry (optional)
1½ teaspoons	salt, or to taste

Seasoning:

1	egg white, beaten
1 teaspoon	ginger wine (see page 387)
¼ teaspoon	salt
¼ teaspoon	m.s.g. (optional)
2 teaspoons	cornflour (cornstarch)

Mix the chicken and ham with the seasoning ingredients, knead well, then form into small balls. Wrap a spinach leaf around each ball, squeezing to hold in shape.

Bring the chicken stock to the boil, then reduce heat to a gentle simmer. Add the bamboo shoots, spring onions, and ginger, the rice wine, if used, and salt. Simmer for 2 — 3 minutes, then add the chicken balls and simmer in the soup until cooked through, about 5 minutes. Transfer to a soup tureen and serve.

RADISH BALLS WITH SCALLOPS IN CREAM SAUCE

375 g (12 oz)	peeled giant white (icicle) radishes, sweet white turnips or about 24 small red radishes, peeled
1½ teaspoons	salt
4 pieces (30 g / 1 oz)	dried scallops, soaked for 2 hours
2 cups (16 fl oz)	chicken stock
1 thick slice	fresh ginger, bruised
2 slices	fresh ginger, shredded
⅓ cup	frying oil or softened lard
1 tablespoon	rendered chicken fat (chicken grease)

Seasoning/Sauce:

¾ teaspoon	salt
½ teaspoon	m.s.g. (optional)
½ teaspoon	sugar
1 teaspoon	rice wine or dry sherry

Wash the radishes or turnips and use a melon scoop to form into balls. Boil for 10 minutes in water to cover with the salt added. Drain well. Simmer the drained scallops in the chicken stock with the slice of ginger for 1 hour, until completely tender. Drain and reserve the liquid. Shred the scallops by rubbing gently between forefinger and thumb.

Heat the frying oil or lard in a wok and fry the vegetable balls with shredded ginger for 1½ minutes. Add the shredded scallop and fry briefly, then pour in the reserved stock mixed with the seasoning/sauce ingredients and bring to the boil.

Thicken with a paste of 1 tablespoon cornflour mixed with 1 tablespoon cold water and stir in the chicken fat. Transfer to a serving dish.

TOMATOES IN CREAM SAUCE

500 g (1 lb)	firm ripe tomatoes
1 tablespoon	cornflour (cornstarch)
¼ cup (2 fl oz)	fresh milk
2 teaspoons	rendered chicken fat (chicken grease) (optional)

Seasoning:

¾ teaspoon	salt
½ teaspoon	m.s.g. (optional)
2 teaspoons	rice wine or dry sherry
¾ teaspoon	sugar
½ cup (4 fl oz)	chicken stock

Scald the tomatoes in boiling water for 8 seconds, drain and peel. Cut into quarters. Simmer in a wok with the seasoning ingredients until softened, about 4 minutes, then thicken the sauce with the cornflour mixed with milk. Add the chicken fat, if used, and serve.

SPINACH EGG PUFFS

Serve as an appetiser or accompanying a main course.

500 g (1 lb)	fresh spinach (collard greens)
8	egg whites
½ teaspoon	salt
2 tablespoons	flour
1 tablespoon	cornflour (cornstarch)
6 cups (1½ litres)	deep-frying oil
	Chinese pepper-salt

Thoroughly wash the spinach and squeeze out as much water as possible. Spread on kitchen towels and leave to dry, then cut into pieces about 5 cm (2 in) long.

Beat the egg whites to stiff peaks and gently fold in the salt, flour, and cornflour. Heat the deep-frying oil to moderate. Dip small bundles of the spinach into the egg batter, coating thickly. Deep-fry until golden and cooked through, about 2½ minutes.

Drain well and sprinkle generously with pepper-salt before serving.

Radish Balls with Scallops in Cream Sauce (recipe this page).

STEAMED ASPARAGUS ON EGG CUSTARD

1 315 g (10 oz) can	asparagus spears, drained
8	eggs
1 tablespoon	shredded cooked ham

Seasoning:

¾ teaspoon	salt
½ teaspoon	m.s.g. (optional)
2 tablespoons	chicken stock

Sauce:

¾ cup (6 fl oz)	chicken stock
½ teaspoon	rice wine or dry sherry
¼ teaspoon	salt
¼ teaspoon	m.s.g. (optional)
½ teaspoon	cornflour (cornstarch)

Soak the asparagus in cold water for 10 minutes. Drain well. Discard three egg yolks and beat the remaining eggs and whites together, adding the seasoning ingredients.

Pour into an oiled dish and set on a rack in a steamer. Steam over rapidly boiling water for 10 minutes. Arrange the well-drained asparagus on top and steam for a few more minutes until set.

In a wok or saucepan, boil the sauce ingredients together until thickened. Pour over the egg and garnish with the ham.

EGGPLANT BRAISED WITH SOYBEAN PASTE

375 g (¾ lb)	eggplant (aubergine)
2 teaspoons	salt
2 cups (16 fl oz)	deep-frying oil
2 tablespoons	finely chopped spring onion (scallion)
1¼ teaspoons	grated fresh ginger
1½ teaspoons	crushed garlic
1¼ tablespoons	soybean paste (or hot bean paste, if preferred)
	sesame oil

Seasoning/Sauce:

½ cup (4 fl oz)	chicken stock
1 tablespoon	light soy sauce
1 teaspoon	rice wine or dry sherry
½ teaspoon	m.s.g. (optional)
1 tablespoon	sugar

Wash the eggplants, remove skin if preferred, and cut into 2.5 cm (1 in) cubes. Sprinkle on the salt, cover with a plate and leave, weighted lightly, for 45 minutes. Rinse in cold water and pat dry.

Deep-fry the eggplant in moderately hot oil until brown. Drain and pour off all but 2 tablespoons oil.

Sauté the onion, ginger, and garlic for 1 minute, add the bean paste and cook a further 1 minute, stirring constantly.

Pour in the pre-mixed seasoning/sauce ingredients and bring to the boil. Return the eggplant, reduce heat and cook, covered, until the eggplant is tender and the sauce absorbed. Stir in a dash of sesame oil.

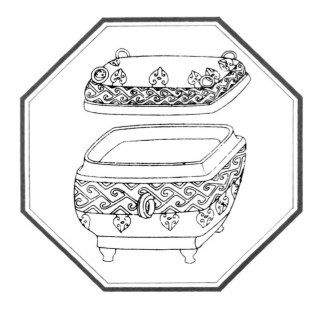

SLICED CUCUMBER STUFFED WITH SHRIMP AND PORK

2	large cucumbers
60 g (2 oz)	fresh shrimp meat, minced (ground)
185 g (6 oz)	fatty pork, finely minced (ground)
1 tablespoon	finely chopped spring onion (scallion)
1 teaspoon	grated fresh ginger
	cornflour (cornstarch)
2 cups (16 fl oz)	frying oil

Seasoning A:

1	egg white, beaten
2 teaspoons	light soy sauce
1 teaspoon	rice wine or dry sherry
¼ teaspoon	salt
¼ teaspoon	m.s.g. (optional)
¾ teaspoon	sugar

Seasoning B/Sauce:

¾ cup (6 fl oz)	chicken stock
1 tablespoon	light soy sauce
½ teaspoon	rice wine or dry sherry
1 teaspoon	salt
¾ teaspoon	sugar

Cut the cucumbers into 4 cm (1 2/3 in) pieces without peeling and use a sharp paring knife to trim away the seed cores. Mix the shrimp, pork, onion, and ginger with the seasoning A ingredients, kneading to a smooth paste. Dust the cucumber rings with cornflour and fill with the prepared stuffing. Smooth the edges and coat lightly all over with cornflour.

Heat the shallow oil to moderate and fry the cucumbers on both sides until golden brown, about 3 minutes. Drain well.

Bring the seasoning B/sauce ingredients to the boil in another pan. Add the stuffed cucumbers and simmer, covered, for 20 minutes. Remove the lid and continue to cook until the cucumber is tender and the sauce well reduced.

Transfer cucumbers to a serving plate. Reheat the sauce and adjust seasonings. Thicken, if preferred, with a thin solution of cornflour (cornstarch) and cold water. Pour over the cucumbers and serve.

PORK AND CABBAGE DUMPLINGS

Makes 24

Pastry:

2 cups	flour
1	whole egg, well beaten
¾ cup	water
1 teaspoon	baking powder
¾ teaspoon	salt

Filling:

185 g (6 oz)	lean pork, finely minced (ground)
3	cabbage leaves, finely chopped
1 tablespoon	finely chopped spring onion (scallion)
½ teaspoon	crushed garlic
1½ tablespoons	frying oil

Seasoning:

1 tablespoon	light soy sauce
2 teaspoons	rice wine or dry sherry
2 teaspoons	sesame oil
2 teaspoons	sugar
¼ teaspoon	ground black pepper
2 tablespoons	water
2½ teaspoons	cornflour (cornstarch)
3 — 4	fresh cabbage leaves, blanched

Sift the flour into a mixing bowl and make a well in the centre. Add the beaten egg and half the water. Mix lightly into the flour, then add the baking powder and salt and slowly add the remaining water to make a soft batter. Knead for 4 — 5 minutes, then cover with a damp cloth and set aside.

Mix the filling ingredients together and fry in the oil for 2 minutes. Add the seasoning ingredients (excluding the whole cabbage leaves) and sauté until the mixture thickens. Transfer to a plate to cool.

Roll the dough into a long sausage shape and divide into 24 parts.

Roll each into a ball and roll out flat on a lightly greased board, using a dry rolling pin and ensuring the top side does not become greasy. Place a spoonful of the filling in the centre of each wrapper and pull up the edges to meet at the top. Pleat into a central point and twist the point to seal in the filling. Hold by the points and press the dumplings, one by one, to flatten the bases.

Use the cabbage leaves to line large bamboo steaming baskets and set the dumplings on top. Steam over high heat for about 15 minutes, then serve hot in the baskets.

DUCK IN ORANGE-FLAVOURED SOUP

1½ — 2 kg (4 lb)	duck
1½ teaspoons	salt
2 tablespoons	rice wine or dry sherry
6 cups (1½ litres)	deep-frying oil
5 cups (1¼ litres)	water
6 pieces	dried orange peel
3 pieces	fresh ginger
15 g (1 oz)	dried 'wood ear' or 'snow' fungus, soaked for 25 minutes
	white pepper

Wash the duck and rub with the salt and wine. Leave for 30 minutes, then wipe the skin. Heat the deep-frying oil to smoking point and deep-fry the duck until lightly coloured. Remove and drain well, then wipe off excess oil.

Bring the water to the boil and add the orange peel and ginger. Transfer to a casserole, place the duck in the stock, cover and simmer on very low heat until the duck is completely tender, about 1½ hours.

Drain the fungus and cut into bite-sized pieces. Add to the pot in the last 25 minutes of cooking. Check the seasonings and add a dash of white pepper. Serve in the casserole.

ASPARAGUS AND PIGEON EGG SOUP

½ 315 g (10 oz) can	asparagus spears or cuts
1 280 g (9 oz) can	quail or pigeon eggs
5 cups (1¼ litres)	chicken stock
1½ teaspoons	salt
½ teaspoon	m.s.g. (optional)
¼ teaspoon	ground black pepper
2 teaspoons	rice wine or dry sherry
2 teaspoons	softened lard

Drain the asparagus and eggs. If using asparagus spears, cut in halves. Divide among individual soup bowls.

Bring the chicken stock to the boil and add the remaining ingredients. Simmer for 2 minutes, then pour over the asparagus and eggs and serve at once.

WHITE FUNGUS, PIGEON EGGS, AND DICED HAM SOUP

45 g (1½ oz)	dried white (snow) fungus, soaked for 1 hour
12	pigeon eggs*
2 teaspoons	finely chopped cooked ham
2 teaspoons	finely chopped fresh coriander
5 cups (1¼ litres)	chicken stock
2 teaspoons	rice wine or dry sherry
1½ teaspoons	salt
½ teaspoon	m.s.g. (optional)
¼ teaspoon	ground black pepper

Prepare the white fungus according to the directions on page 393 Lightly grease 12 small soy sauce dishes and break an egg into each. Garnish with the ham and coriander and set on a rack in a steamer to steam until set, about 5 minutes. Remove the eggs from the dishes and soak in cold water for 10 minutes.

Bring the chicken stock to the boil and add the wine, salt, m.s.g., if used, and pepper. Simmer for 1 minute, then add the white fungus and simmer for 2 — 3 minutes. Drain the eggs and pour on a cupful of the boiling stock to heat through, then drain, returning the stock to the saucepan to reheat and divide the eggs among 6 individual soup bowls.

Pour the stock and the fungus over the eggs and serve.
* If fresh pigeon eggs are unobtainable, used canned quail or pigeon eggs. As these are hard boiled (hard cooked), the diced ham and coriander may be omitted or added to the soup as a garnish.

YOUNG PIGEONS AND HAM STEAMED IN SOUP

3	*young pigeons, plucked and cleaned (about 625 g (1¼ lb)*
60 g (2 oz)	*Chinese or cured (Smithfield) ham, sliced*
6 cups (1½ litres)	*hot chicken stock*
1 tablepoon	*rice wine or dry sherry*
¾ teaspoon	*salt*
¼ teaspoon	*ground black pepper*
1	*spring onion (scallion), trimmed and sliced*
3 slices	*fresh ginger*
½ teaspoon	*m.s.g. (optional)*

Cut the pigeons in halves and boil gently in just enough water to cover for 20 minutes. Drain and rinse in cold water. Arrange the pigeons in a casserole with the sliced ham on top. Add the hot chicken stock, wine, salt and pepper, the spring onion and ginger. Cover and set on a rack in a steamer to steam over gently boiling water for 2½ — 3 hours until the pigeons are completely tender.

Remove from the heat, adjust the seasonings, and add m.s.g., if used. Discard the ginger and onion and serve in the casserole.

Avoid stirring the dish during cooking to maintain optimum clarity of the stock.

CHICKEN SLIVERS AND JASMINE IN CLEAR BROTH

90 g (3 oz)	*boneless chicken breast*
12	*jasmine flowers*
6 cups (1½ litres)	*chicken stock*
2	*spring onions (scallions), trimmed and diced*
3 slices	*fresh ginger, shredded*
	cornflour (cornstarch)

Seasoning A:

1	*egg white, beaten*
¼ teaspoon	*salt*
½ teaspoon	*m.s.g. (optional)*
½ teaspoon	*sugar*
	pinch of white pepper
2 teaspoons	*cornflour (cornstarch)*

Seasoning B:

1 tablespoon	*rice wine or dry sherry*
1¼ teaspoons	*salt*
¼ teaspoon	*m.s.g. (optional)*
¼ teaspoon	*ground black pepper*

Cut the chicken into small cubes. Mix with the seasoning A ingredients and leave for 5 minutes. Trim the stems from the jasmine flowers and rinse in cold water. Bring the chicken stock to the boil, add the onions, ginger, and the seasoning B ingredients and simmer on low heat.

Spread cornflour thickly over a board. Roll the chicken cubes in the cornflour, then bat with the side of a cleaver, alternating with a further coating of cornflour, until the chicken is reduced to thin, near transparent slivers.

Bring a saucepan of water to the boil, then turn heat to the lowest point and leave until it stops bubbling. Add the chicken and cook until white, about 1½ minutes. Drain and rinse in cold water.

Place two jasmine flowers into each of six individual soup bowls.

Add the chicken slivers to the simmering soup, cook briefly, then pour over the jasmine. Serve immediately. The jasmine flavour may be enhanced by simmering them in hot stock for 1 — 2 minutes before adding the chicken, if preferred.

CREAMY FISH SOUP WITH SOUR AND HOT FLAVOURS

1 750 g (1½ lb)	yellow fish (herring, sea bass, or flounder)
90 g (3 oz)	prepared sea cucumber (optional), or use 2 squares soft beancurd, diced, or 90 g (3 oz) diced fresh squid
30 g (1 oz)	canned bamboo shoot, drained and diced
2	spring onions (scallions), trimmed and diced
2 slices	fresh ginger, shredded
⅓ cup	frying oil or softened lard
1½ cups (12 fl oz)	chicken stock
2	egg whites, well beaten
2 tablespoons	white vinegar
1	spring onion (scallion), trimmed and finely shredded
2 slices	fresh ginger, finely shredded

Seasoning:

2 teaspoons	salt
¼ teaspoon	sugar
¼ teaspoon	ground white pepper
2 teaspoons	rice wine or dry sherry
1 tablespoon	cornflour (cornstarch)
1 tablespoon	cold water

Clean and scale the fish and wash well. Place in a saucepan with water to cover and bring to the boil. Simmer until the meat is tender enough to flake from the bones. Strain the liquid into a jug and set aside. Flake the meat and discard the head and bones.

Fry the spring onions and ginger in the oil or lard for about 1 minute until lightly coloured and beginning to soften. Add the sea cucumber and the bamboo shoots and fry lightly. Pour in the strained stock and bring to the boil, adding the chicken stock and seasoning ingredients. Simmer for 3 minutes, then add the flaked fish.

If beancurd or squid are being used instead of sea cucumber, add at this point. Simmer for 2 minutes, then slowly drizzle in the beaten egg and add the vinegar. Cook without stirring for 1 minute, then transfer to a soup tureen and garnish with the shredded spring onion and ginger.

SILVER CARP'S HEAD IN RICH SOUP

1 1 kg (2 lb)	silver carp's head or several fish heads of the same weight
2 slices	fresh ginger
45 g (1½ oz)	straw mushrooms, or 3 dried black mushrooms soaked to soften
45 g (1½ oz)	Chinese or cured (Smithfield) ham
30 g (1 oz)	chicken breast or leg meat
6	young Chinese green vegetables
6 cups (1½ litres)	chicken or enriched stock
2 tablespoons	softened lard
2	spring onions (scallions), trimmed and shredded
4 slices	fresh ginger, shredded
1 tablespoon	rendered chicken fat (chicken grease)
	salt
	m.s.g. (optional)

Wash the fish head(s) and cut in halves. Place in a saucepan with water to cover and bring to the boil. Add the sliced ginger and simmer the fish heads until completely tender. Drain and scrape all the meat from the bones, then discard the bones and ginger.

Finely shred the mushrooms, ham, and chicken and thoroughly wash the vegetables. Bring the chicken or enriched stock to the boil and add the fish meat. Simmer gently. Heat the lard and sauté the spring onions and ginger briefly, then add the mushrooms, ham, and chicken and sauté for 1 minute. Transfer to the soup and simmer for 2 minutes, then add the vegetables and simmer until tender. Add the chicken fat, salt to taste, and the m.s.g., if used, and transfer to a soup tureen.

ASSORTED MEAT AND CHRYSANTHEMUM FIRE-POT

Serves 6 — 8 as the main course.

125 g (4 oz)	*boneless fish fillet*
125 g (4 oz)	*fillet of beef (tenderloin)*
125 g (4 oz)	*boneless chicken breast*
125 g (4 oz)	*lean pork*
125 g (4 oz)	*pork kidney, trimmed and blanched*
125 g (4 oz)	*peeled raw prawns (shrimps)*
60 g (2 oz)	*frozen wonton wrappers, thawed and sliced*
30 g (1 oz)	*bean thread vermicelli, broken into short pieces and deep-fried until crisp (about 15 seconds)*
90 g (3 oz)	*fresh spinach leaves (collard greens), well washed*
30 g (1 oz)	*white chrysanthemum petals, well washed (or use sliced champignons or bamboo shoots)*
90 g (3 oz)	*young bok choy or other green vegetable leaves*
60 g (2 oz)	*young cabbage hearts, halved and well washed small bunch of fresh coriander*
8 cups (2 litres)	*chicken stock*

Seasoning:

2	*spring onions (scallions), cut in halves*
3 thick slices	*fresh ginger, bruised*
1 tablespoon	*rice wine or dry sherry*

Sauce Dip:

3 tablespoons	*finely chopped spring onion (scallion)*
3 tablespoons	*finely shredded fresh ginger*
3 tablespoons	*finely chopped fresh coriander*
2 tablespoons	*sesame paste (mixed with 2 tablespoons cold water)*
¼ cup (2 fl oz)	*rice wine or dry sherry*
¾ cup (6 fl oz)	*light soy sauce*
¼ cup (2 fl oz)	*peanut or vegetable oil*
2 tablespoons	*sesame oil (optional)*
¼ cup (2 fl oz)	*white vinegar*
1 tablespoon	*chilli oil, or to taste*
	salt
	m.s.g. (optional)
	ground black pepper

Special Equipment: A charcoal 'fire-pot,' or a table-top gas or electric cooker, wooden chopsticks.

To prepare the sauce dip, place the spring onion, ginger, and coriander on small individual plates. Mix the remaining ingredients, adding more or less of each according to taste. Divide among 6 — 8 small bowls and place on the table with a pair of wooden chopsticks for each diner.

Partially freeze the meat to make it easier to cut into wafer-thin slices. Arrange on individual plates. Cut the prawns in halves, lengthwise, or slice any large ones. Serve all the remaining ingredients except the chicken stock and seasonings, on separate plates.

Heat the fire-pot or a large stewpan and bring the chicken stock to the boil. Add the seasoning ingredients.

Cook the meats first, holding them in the bubbling stock with the wooden chopsticks. When the stock has been enriched by the meats, add the vegetables and other ingredients. Both meat and vegetables should be cooked rare to retain maximum flavour and texture.

Mix chopped spring onion, ginger, and coriander into the sauce dip to taste and dunk each mouthful before eating.

The soup may be served at the end of the meal, with a splash of the sauce dip for extra flavour.

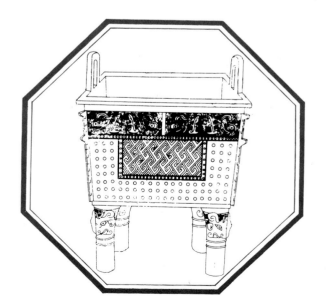

SALTED AND FRESH PORK IN SOUP

250 g (8 oz)	salt-cooked pork (see page 136. Slow Cooked Corned Pork)
250 g (8 oz)	'five flowered' pork (belly/fresh bacon)
5 cups (1¼ litres)	chicken stock
60 g (2 oz)	canned bamboo shoots, drained and diced
1 tablespoon	finely chopped spring onion (scallion)
¾ teaspoon	finely shredded fresh ginger
1 tablespoon	rice wine or dry sherry
½ teaspoon	m.s.g. (optional)
	salt to taste

Cut the salt-cooked pork and the fresh pork into small cubes. Parboil the fresh pork only in water to cover for 3 minutes. Drain and rinse with cold water.

Bring the chicken stock to the boil and add the meats, bamboo shoots, onion, ginger, and the wine. Bring to the boil. Skim, then reduce heat to very low, cover tightly and simmer until the meat is completely tender. Skim once or twice during cooking, if necessary. Very slow cooking will ensure that the soup remains clear, with flavours well blended and the meat tender rather than stringy.

Add the m.s.g., if used, and salt to taste just before serving.

ASSORTED MEAT AND VEGETABLES IN WINTER MELON

8 pieces	dry scallops, soaked for 1 hour (about 60 g (2 oz))
1 3½ — 4 kg (7 — 8 lb)	winter melon
1 set	duck gizzards, trimmed and diced
4	dried black mushrooms, soaked for 25 minutes
125 g (4 oz)	cooked duck meat, diced
20 g (1 oz)	Chinese or cured (Smithfield) ham, diced
60 g (2 oz)	peeled raw shrimps, well washed
60 g (2 oz)	canned champignons, drained and sliced
6 slices	fresh ginger, bruised
5 — 6 cups (1¼ — 1½ litres)	chicken stock, heated
1 tablespoon	rice wine or dry sherry (optional)
1½ teaspoons	salt, or to taste
1 teaspoon	m.s.g. (optional)
1 tablespoon	rendered chicken fat (chicken grease) (optional)

Cover the dry scallops with ½ cup chicken stock and steam for 1 hour until tender, then drain and flake between forefinger and thumb. Wash the winter melon and remove the top section with a sharp knife. Carve a scalloped or zig-zag pattern around the rim. Scoop out the seeds and discard. Rinse with plenty of cold water, then fill with lightly salted boiling water and set in a close-fitting bowl or in a heatproof stand and place in a steamer. Cover and steam over high heat for 25 minutes. Pour off the stock and set the melon back into the bowl or stand.

Blanch the diced gizzards in boiling water and drain well. Squeeze water from the soaked mushrooms, remove the stems and dice.

Place all the ingredients, except the m.s.g. and chicken fat, in the melon and return to the steamer. Steam for 35 minutes or until the ingredients are tender and the flesh of the melon can be easily scraped from the skin. Add the m.s.g. and chicken fat, if used, and serve the melon in the bowl or stand, or transfer to an ornamental stand to take to the table.

To serve, scoop out the mixed ingredients with a portion of the stock, then carefully remove the soft melon with the ladle.

Sliced Cucumber Stuffed with Shrimp and Pork (recipe page 159).

'EMBROIDERED' SOUP

Serves 12

60 g (2 oz)	*prepared fish maws (see page 392), diced*
60 g (2 oz)	*prepared sea cucumber (see page 393), diced*
60 g (2 oz)	*boneless fish fillet, sliced*
125 g (4 oz)	*lean pork, finely minced (ground)*
60 g (2 oz)	*pork kidney, trimmed, blanched and sliced*
45 g (1½ oz)	*peeled raw shrimps*
375 g (12 oz)	bok choy, *spinach or kale leaves*
90 g (3 oz)	*rice vermicelli, soaked in cold water*
60 g (2 oz)	*cooked chicken, diced .*
60 g (2 oz)	*cooked beef tongue, diced*
45 g (1½ oz)	*cooked ham, shredded*
45 g (1½ oz)	*canned bamboo shoots, drained and sliced*
3	*spring onions (scallions), cut in halves*
4 thick slices	*fresh ginger, bruised*
8 cups (2 litres)	*chicken stock*

Seasoning A:

¼ teaspoon	*salt*
½ teaspoon	*m.s.g. (optional)*

Seasoning B:

1 tablespoon	*rice wine or dry sherry*
2 teaspoons	*salt (or to taste)*
½ teaspoon	*ground black pepper*
¾ teaspoon	*m.s.g. (optional)*
1 tablespoon	*rendered chicken fat (chicken grease), or use lard*

Rinse the prepared fish maw and sea cucumber with cold water, then leave to soak until needed. Rub a dash of salt and rice wine into the fish. Mix the pork with the seasoning A ingredients, kneading until smooth, then form into small meatballs and soak in cold water until needed. Rinse the kidney and shrimps in cold water and drain well.

Line a large earthenware pot or heavy-based saucepan with the washed *bok choy* or other green vegetables and arrange the drained rice vermicelli on top. Layer the other ingredients into the pot, beginning with the fish maw and sea cucumber.

Mix the seasoning B ingredients with the stock in a separate saucepan. Bring to the boil and pour into the pot. Simmer on low heat until all the ingredients are cooked through and the flavours well blended, about 30 minutes. Serve in the pot using a table-top hot plate or a portable gas or electric cooker to keep it piping hot.

DRIED OYSTERS AND CHICKEN IN SOUP

500 g (1 lb)	*chicken pieces*
125 g (4 oz)	*dried oysters, soaked overnight**
1 tablespoon	*salt*
1 slice	*Chinese or cured (Smithfield) ham, shredded*
2	*spring onions (scallions), trimmed and sliced*
3 slices	*fresh ginger*
6 cups (1½ litres)	*chicken stock*
1 tablespoon	*rice wine or dry sherry*
1¼ teaspoons	*salt*
1 teaspoon	*m.s.g. (optional)*

Cut the chicken into 2.5 cm (1 in) pieces through the bones and blanch in boiling water for 2 minutes. Drain and rinse in cold water. Drain the soaked oysters, rub with 1 tablespoon of salt, then rinse thoroughly in cold water. Steam until tender about 40 minutes, then dice.

Arrange the chicken, ham, ginger, and onions in a saucepan and add the chicken stock, wine, and salt. Bring to the boil and simmer on very low heat for 3 hours. Add the oysters and season with the m.s.g., if used. Remove the onion and ginger before serving.

* Fresh oysters may be used instead of dried. Use about 250 g (8 oz) whole fresh oysters, removed from the shell and rinsed thoroughly in salted water, then in cold water.

SLICED KIDNEYS AND BEANCURD SKIN IN SOUP

2	pork kidneys (about 315 g / 10 oz)
3 strips	dried beancurd skin, soaked for 25 minutes
12	dried black mushrooms, soaked for 25 minutes
30 g (1 oz)	canned bamboo shoots, drained and thinly sliced
5 cups (1¼ litres)	chicken stock
1 teaspoon	salt
½ teaspoon	m.s.g. (optional)
¼ teaspoon	ground black pepper
2 teaspoons	light soy sauce
2	spring onions (scallions), trimmed and sliced
2 slices	fresh ginger

Skin the kidneys and cut in halves. Remove the white fatty membrane and turn over. Score in a close criss-cross pattern, cutting to about ½ cm (1/6 in) deep. Cut into thin slices and blanch in boiling water, then drain and soak in cold water for 10 minutes. Drain the beancurd skin and cut into 5 cm (2 in) squares. Drain mushrooms and remove stems, then slice thinly.

Bring the chicken stock to the boil. Add the salt, m.s.g., if used, pepper, soy sauce, the spring onions, and ginger and boil for 2 minutes. Add the sliced kidney and simmer for 1 minute, then remove to individual soup bowls with enough soup to cover. Return the soup to the boil, skim if necessary and add the beancurd skin, mushrooms, and bamboo shoots. Simmer for 5 minutes, then pour over the kidneys and serve.

BEANCURD, MUSHROOMS AND VEGETABLES SIMMERED IN AN EARTHENWARE CROCK

3 squares	soft beancurd
45 g (1½ oz)	golden mushrooms*
6	dried black mushrooms, soaked for 25 minutes
30 g (1 oz)	canned bamboo shoots, drained and shredded
½ cup (4 fl oz)	frying oil or softened lard
30 g (1 oz)	cooked chicken breast, shredded
30 g (1 oz)	cooked ham, shredded
7 cups (1¾ litres)	chicken stock
6	Chinese cabbage hearts, young bok choy or kale
1 tablespoon	rendered chicken fat (chicken grease) (optional)

Seasoning:

1 tablespoon	rice wine
1¾ teaspoons	salt
¼ teaspoon	m.s.g. (optional)
½ teaspoon	ground black pepper

Cut the beancurd into small diamond-shaped pieces and soak in hot water for 10 minutes. Drain the golden mushrooms and rinse in cold water. Squeeze the water from soaked mushrooms, remove the stems and slice finely.

Heat half the lard or frying oil in a wok and fry the golden mushrooms, black mushrooms, and bamboo shoots for 1 minute. Add the ham and chicken and fry briefly, then add the chicken stock and the seasoning ingredients and bring to the boil. Simmer for 1 minute and transfer to an earthenware casserole. Add the beancurd and cover tightly. Simmer for 15 minutes on very low heat.

Fry the washed vegetable hearts in the remaining oil or lard for 2 minutes, then add to the crock and simmer a few more minutes. Check the seasoning, adding the chicken fat, if used. Serve in the crock.

* Golden mushrooms have minute golden caps on long, thin golden stems. They are sold in cans or jars where Chinese or Japanese foods are available. If unobtainable, substitute thinly sliced champignons.

SWALLOWS' NESTS IN CLEAR BROTH

30 g (1 oz)	dried birds' nests
6 cups (1½ litres)	chicken or enriched stock
2 teaspoons	rice wine or dry sherry
2 teaspoons	salt
1 teaspoon	m.s.g. (optional)
¼ teaspoon	white pepper

Soak the birds' nests in boiling water, covered, until the water cools. Drain, cover again with boiling water and leave until this lot of water cools also, then add 1 tablespoon clean vegetable oil. This will collect any fragments of feather or grit trapped in the nests. Drain off and rinse with cold water.

Place the drained birds' nests in a casserole and add the remaining ingredients. Set on a rack in a steamer and steam, tightly covered, over rapidly boiling water for 30 minutes. Serve.

APPLE FRITTERS STUFFED WITH RED BEAN PASTE

3	large cooking apples
155 g (5 oz)	sweet red bean paste (see page 00)
5	egg whites
1½ tablespoons	flour
1½ tablespoons	cornflour (cornstarch)
6 cups (1½ litres)	deep-frying oil
2 tablespoons	sesame oil (optional)

Glaze:

1 cup	sugar
¾ cup (6 fl oz)	water
	few drops of red food colouring

Peel the apples and cut out the cores. Cut each apple into 6 even-sized wedges. Make a slit on the rounded side of each apple wedge and fill with red bean paste. Sprinkle lightly with cornflour.

Beat the egg whites until they form soft peaks, then carefully fold in the flour and cornflour. Heat the deep-frying oil to moderate and add the sesame oil, if used.

Bring the sugar and water to a slow boil and colour a bright red. Reduce heat and simmer slowly while the apple is cooking.

Coat the apple pieces with the batter and deep-fry several at a time until the batter is golden and crisp and the apple beginning to soften, about 2½ minutes. Drain and set aside while the remainder is cooked.

Reheat the oil and quickly deep-fry the apple pieces a second time until deep golden in colour. Drain and arrange on an oiled serving plate. Drizzle the hot toffee over the fritters and serve at once.

TARO CUBES WITH CINNAMON FLAVOUR

1 kg (2 lb)	fresh taro or yam
¾ teaspoon	bicarbonate of soda
210 g (7 oz)	rock candy (sugar)
¼ cup	sugar
1 stick	cinnamon
	cornflour (cornstarch)

Peel the taro, wash thoroughly and cut into 4 cm (1 2/3 in) cubes, then trim the edges to give oval shapes. Place in a saucepan of boiling water, add the soda and return to the boil. Cook for 5 minutes, then drain and rinse with cold water. Spread on a plate to cool. The taro will turn a reddish colour.

Dissolve the lightly crushed rock candy and the sugar in several cups of boiling water. Transfer the taro to a large dish and pour on the sugar syrup, adding enough water to just cover the taro. Break the cinnamon stick into several pieces and place on the taro.

Set the dish on a rack in a steamer and steam over rapidly boiling water until the taro is completely tender. Strain the syrup into a saucepan and bring to the boil. Thicken with a paste of cornflour and cold water and continue to simmer until the sauce is thick and clear.

Transfer the taro to a serving dish and discard the cinnamon. Pour on the hot syrup and serve at once.

Beancurd, Mushrooms and Vegetables Simmered in an Earthenware Crock (recipe page 167).

SWEET WALNUT AND RED DATE SOUP

210 g (7 oz)	*fresh walnuts, shelled*
45 g (1½ oz)	*Chinese dried red dates*
½ cup	*glutinous rice, soaked for 2 hours*
1 cup	*sugar*

Soak the walnuts in boiling water until the skins loosen. Drain and cool slightly, then peel away the skins and chop the walnuts coarsely.

Steam the red dates with water to cover until tender. Drain and mash to a smooth paste, discarding the skin and stones.

Drain the rice and place it and walnuts in a blender with enough water to blend to a smooth paste.

Bring about 3½ cups (28 fl oz) water to the boil and add the sugar. Stir until dissolved, then add the walnut and rice paste and bring to the boil. Reduce to a simmer and add the mashed red dates. Stir in thoroughly and cook until the soup is sweet and thick. Serve hot.

STEAMED LOTUS SEED AND RED BEAN PASTE PUDDING

250 g (8 oz)	*dried lotus seeds, soaked for 15 minutes*
155 g (5 oz)	*long grain glutinous rice*
90 g (3 oz)	*sweet red bean paste (see page 389)*
155 g (5 oz)	*rock candy (sugar)*
⅓ cup	*softened lard*
2 tablespoons	*sugar*
¾ teaspoon	*powdered cinnamon*

Drain the lotus seeds, place in a saucepan with water to cover and a pinch of bicarbonate of soda and bring to the boil. Remove and rinse well in cold water. Use a needle to pick out the bitter tasting central core. Place the seeds in a dish, crumble on a little rock sugar and cover with water. Set the dish in a steamer and steam until the seeds are beginning to soften. Remove, drain and leave to cool.

Wash the rice well and pour into a saucepan of boiling water. Cook for 10 minutes, then drain and pour into a dish lined with a piece of clean cheesecloth. Steam over rapidly boiling water until cooked.

Thickly grease a pudding basin with the lard, and arrange the lotus seeds in a formation in the bottom and as far up the sides as they will go. Crush the remaining rock sugar and sprinkle over the lotus seeds.

Add the remaining lard and sugar to the rice and add the cinnamon. Work in evenly, then spread a thick layer of rice over the lotus seeds, reserving about one-third. Leave a depression in the centre of the bowl. Put the sweet red bean paste in the depression and cover with the remaining rice. Smooth the top and cover with a piece of perforated and greased greaseproof paper.

Set the dish in a steamer and steam over rapidly boiling water for 1 hour. Turn out the pudding onto a serving plate. The rock sugar will have melted into a sweet clear syrup. Serve hot.

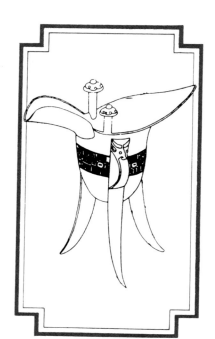

BIRDS' NEST DESSERT

30 g (1 oz)	dried birds' nests, soaked for 1 hour
210 g (7 oz)	rock candy (sugar)
¾ teaspoon	bicarbonate of soda

Drain and thoroughly wash the birds' nests, picking out any bits of feather or grit with tweezers. Pour on boiling water and soak until tender, then drain.

Sprinkle on the bicarbonate of soda and cover again with boiling water. Leave for 5 minutes to soften and expand, then drain and cover with more boiling water. Drain and rinse thoroughly.

Crumble the rock sugar and place in a saucepan with about 5 cups (1½ litres) of cold water. Bring to the boil and simmer very slowly until the sugar has completely dissolved. Strain into a bowl. Add the prepared birds' nests and steam for 10 minutes over rapidly boiling water.

Serve hot, or chill thoroughly and serve cold.

FRIED THREE-TREASURE PURÉE

700 g (1⅓ lb)	yam or sweet potato
75 g (2½ oz)	Chinese dried red dates
280 g (9 oz)	fresh or frozen peas
1 stick	cinnamon
2/3 cup	softened lard
1¼ cups	sugar

Thoroughly wash the yam and place in a saucepan of boiling water. Simmer until completely softened, then drain and leave to cool. Peel off the skin and mash the yam to a smooth paste.

Steam the dates until softened, then mash to a smooth paste, discarding the skin and stones. Boil the peas until softened, mash and remove as much skin as possible.

Steam the cinnamon stick in ½ cup water until softened and the water well flavoured. Discard the stick.

Heat one-third of the lard in a wok and add the yam paste, one-third of the sugar and half the cinnamon water. Stir on moderate heat until the mixture is dry and smooth. Remove to one end of an oval serving plate.

Wash the wok, reheat with half the remaining lard, add the dates and one-third of the sugar and stir on moderate heat until the paste is smooth and dry. Place at the other end of the serving plate.

Wash the wok again, heat the remaining lard with the remaining sugar and cinnamon water and the pea paste. Stir on moderate heat until smooth and dry, then pour into the remaining section of the serving plate. Serve hot.

SWEET YAM SOUP

625 g (1¼ lb)	peeled fresh yams (taro or sweet potato)
5 cups (1¼ litres)	water
2/3 cup	sugar
⅓ cup	softened lard
2½ tablespoons	cornflour (cornstarch)
¼ cup (2 fl oz)	cold water

Cut the yam into cubes and place in a saucepan with the water and sugar. Bring to the boil and simmer until softened, then transfer to a blender and blend until smooth and creamy. Return to the heat and add the lard. Stir for 2 — 3 minutes, then thicken with the cornflour and cold water and serve hot.

For extra flavour, add diced candied winter melon, gourd, or peel.

CHAPTER V
Western Central Style Cuisine

Previous page: *Field workers pause to pose for camera on agricultual commune near Chengtu (Chengdu) in Szechuan (Sichuan). Electricity is about the only modern covenience such communes enjoy.*

Above from left to right: *Western cuisine features river fish, pork, and a variety of vegetables, as well as fresh herbs from the mountains. Opposite from left to right: fisherman and his faithful cormorant fishing-bird pause for rest on a sampan near Kweilin (Guilin); typical farmhouse near Chengtu (Chengdu), captial of Szechuan (Sichuan); herbal medicine shop in Chengtu (Chengdu) displays fresh-picked herbs from the mountains, commonly used in Szechuanese cooking; farmers tend their greening fields outside of Chengtu (Chengdu); farmers sell their products on the free market in Chengtu (Chengdu), which has recently seen a remarkable boom in production due to private enterprise; a pig enroute to market by bicycle in suburb of Chengtu (Chengdu).*

The western/central culinary region of China includes the provinces and cuisines of Szechuan (Sichuan) and Hunan, two of China's most ancient provinces. Sichuan, today the largest and most populous province of China, thrived for many centuries as the Kingdom of Shu prior to the unification of China in 221 B.C. Hunan is centrally located, grographically as well as historically, and today is best known as the birthplace of Mao Tse-tung (Mao Zedong), who continued to demand the fiery flavours of his native province throughout his life. The cuisine of the western/central region is the most distinctive in all of China in terms of flavour.

While the climates of Szechuan (Sichuan) and Hunan are quite similar, their geographical conditions differ significantly, and these differences are reflected in the food. Both provinces are dominated by hot, humid weather. Hunan is a verdant province of fertile soil, abundant rainfall, and gentle topography, where most ingredients for the Chinese kitchen thrive. Meat, fish, and fowl play prominent roles on the Hunan menu, and the entire spectrum of the vegetable kingdom is represented as well. Sichuan, however, is a land of craggy mountains, abrupt, deep valleys, and steep, jagged cliffs. The bulk of the province's crops are grown in the broad plains surrounding the capital city of Chengtu (Chengdu): this entire area is supplied by a vast, highly efficient irrigation system first built to harness the Min River over 2,000 years ago. Szechuan (Sichuan) cuisine offers less variety of cultivated ingredients than Hunan, but the mountain recesses

provide a wide range of medicinal cooking herbs as well as wild game.

Red chillies of the *capsicum* family are the king of condiments in the western/central style of cooking. Due to their pharmacological effects — they tend to dry out the body and thus balance excess dampness — chillies have been extremely popular in this intensely humid region ever since their introduction from the New World. The native *fagara* pepper is also extensively used, as well as garlic, ginger, and spring onions. Fermented bean paste and chilli sauce play prominent roles too. The flavours of western/central style dishes tend toward the pungent.

Lush Hunan province produces plenty of meat, fish, and fowl for its tables, and these rich items are central in the Hunan diet. However, they are rarely, if ever, cooked in the raw state: instead, they are usually cured, marinated, pickled, or otherwise processed prior to use in cooking. A classic Hunan specialty is Honey-glazed Ham, served with thinly sliced bread to form dainty, fragrant, little 'Chinese sandwiches.' Vagabond Ham, Beggar's Chicken, and Squirrel Fish are other rich, flavourful specials of Hunan made with meat, fish, or fowl.

Szechuan (Sichuan) has a more limited selection of ingredients for cooking. Most prominent in the Szechuan (Sichuan) kitchen are pork, poultry, legumes, soybean products, nuts of various sorts, and wild mountain products, including medicinal herbs and wild game. Szechuan (Sichuan) produces the world's most potent Chinese medicinal herbs in its deep valleys and high mountains. Many are used to prepare potent, highly nourishing dishes: Chinese Wolfberry (*Lycium chinensis*), medlar, ginseng, aconite, Shepherd's Purse, jujubes, licorice root, and many others appear in Szechuan (Sichuan) dishes. Medicinal herbs are usually applied to wild game, which, according to tradi-

tional Chinese medical theories, is the most potent source of energy. For more conventional dishes, pork and poultry are utilised in an incredible variety of ways. Some popular dishes from the Szechuan (Sichuan) menu include Pine-and-Tea-Smoked Duck, Exotic Flavoured Chicken, Chicken and Chillies, Fragrant Spicy Shredded Pork, Pock-marked Mama's Bean-curd, Braised Eggplant, Braised String Beans, and Hot-and-Sour Soup.

A few brief remarks about red chillies and their uses are in order here. Used extensively throughout the western/central region, red chillies serve a variety of functions. They provide the pungent flavour in cooking, but such dishes need not be so 'hot' that they scorch the palate and throat. Since most dishes in which chillies appear are *chao* or *bao* cooked, their pungent flavour enters the oil and sauces but has no time to cook deeply into the main ingredients, such as in the slowly simmered curries of India and Southeast Asia. The pungency of red chillies is all contained in the seeds and white fibres which cling to the interior. The red, fleshy exterior has a very fragrant, fresh, delectable flavour. Therefore, in order to tame chillies for more tender palates, all you need to do is cut them open lengthwise and scrape away some, or all, of the seeds and fibres.

The primary reason for the prominence of chillies in this region, however, is medical, not culinary: they stave off excess dampness by providing a pharmacological drying factor to balance it. The evils of excessive external humidity are thus negated by the introduction of an internal 'de-humidifier': chillies induce perspiration and literally 'squeeze' the excess moisture out of your system like a sponge. This is also why chillies are not so popular in the excessively dry climates of the north. In addition, chillies are antiseptic (kill germs) and anthelmintic (kill worms), important

considerations in hot, humid climates with no refrigeration facilities to keep foods absolutely fresh. The concentrated pungency of the seeds and fibres stimulates the palate and greatly facilitates *xia-fan* ('getting the rice down'), also important in a region such as Szechuan (Sichuan), where the selection and quantity of *cai* are often severely limited. Red chillies also serve the function of 'opening up' the palate with a strong, frontal assault so that the many other flavours which follow in the aftertastes can be more fully appreciated.

The most distinctive features of this region's cuisine reside in the flavour: flavour and freshness are emphasised far more than colour and appearance. This feature reflects the earthy, practical, 'no-nonsense' nature of the region's inhabitants. The distinctive flavours of the region go far beyond the pungent frontal assault referred to above. After chillies have opened up the palate and paved the way for subtle appreciation of other flavours experienced during chewing, swallowing, and aftertasting, the true uniqueness of western/central flavours comes out. As soon as the palate cools down, the other flavours suddenly burst upon the taste buds in a harmonious medley. This second wave of sensations on the palate and olfactory buds reveals the 'manifold' flavour and fragrance of the region's food, which comprise its most unique feature. The 'five flavours' of traditional Chinese medical theory — sweet, sour, salty, pungent, bitter — all appear together in subtle combinations and harmonious balance. Manifold flavour is no doubt the

source of this cuisine's enduring popularity.

As noted above, colour and appearance are not strongly emphasised, and therefore western/central-style dishes are not as pretty to look at as those of the eastern/coastal and southern regions. In texture, the dishes tend towards the dry (another medical balance to excess humidity) and the chewy. Many of the dishes are highly potent and stimulating to the system and are not recommended for people with weak digestive systems or gastrointestinal ailments. They are best suited for energetic, naturally active people, and for consumption in damp climates.

Another distinctive feature of Szechuan (Sichuan) cuisine is its rustic, 'down-home' style. *Jia-chang-cai*, literally 'dishes often eaten at home,' appear prominently on the Szechuan (Sichuan) menu, even in the fanciest restaurants. This is another reflection of the earthy, informal personality of Suzchuan's (Sichuan's) people, who want their guests to 'make themselves at home' even in the most formal settings. While *jia-chang-cai* are neither fancy in appearance nor expensive to make, they are among the tastiest and most nourishing dishes in China, which accounts for their everlasting popularity. The classic example of this type of dish is 'Pock-marked Mama's Bean-curd,' which was invented by, and carries the name of, an old pock-marked woman who operated a small beancurd stall on some obscure street corner in Chengdu countless centuries ago. Employing only a few cakes of bean-curd, a little ground pork, and some spices, this is one of the least expensive and easiest to produce of all Chinese dishes. Yet it is also one of the most nourishing and well balanced (bean-curd and pork provide complete protein), medically potent (ginger, garlic, chillies, and spring onions are all used), and delicious dishes in the entire Chinese culinary repertoire.

Today, Szechuan (Sichuan) cuisine is the overall most popular Chinese (regional) style in the world, and Hunan is not far behind. One of the reasons for the contemporary popularity of Szechuan (Sichuan) food among Chinese and foreigners alike lies in recent history, for prior to World War II Szechuan (Sichuan) food was virtually unknown outside its provincial borders. However, to escape the Japanese onslaught in 1937, the Nationalist government of China moved its headquarters to the city of Chungking (Chongqing), deep within the rugged recesses of Szechuan (Sichuan) province. Here, for eight long years, everyone from top government ministers and military officers down to simple clerks and foot-soldiers ate Szechuan (Sichuan)-style food exclusively. For one thing, nothing else was available; for another, the newcomers quickly discovered that the chillies, garlic, ginger, and onions used so extensively in Szechuan (Sichuan) dishes effectively helped to ward off the oppressive dampness of summer and the penetrating damp chills of winter. When the government and army returned to Shanghai and Nanking (Nanjing) after the Japanese surrender, they brought along thousands of skilled Szechuan (Sichuan) chefs, to whose culinary style their palates and systems had become addicted. In the subsequent Nationalist move to Taiwan, most of these chefs followed, and there they set up their own Szechuan (Sichuan) restaurants. Many soon moved on to the west to ply their trade. In Taipei (Taibei), an affluent city of sophisticated, highly fussy gourmets who have thousands of the best regional Chinese restaurants to choose from, Szechuan (Sichuan) cuisine remains the most popular, frequent choice for eating out. The same is increasingly true in San Francisco, New York, Paris, and London.

The other reason for the immense contemporary popularity of Szechuan (Sichuan) food has already been mentioned: manifold flavour. Both the initial pungency and the subsequent aftertastes are highly stimulating to the senses and make eating more exciting and interesting. In this crowded, busy, sensation-oriented world, the fiery flavours and stimulating sensations of Szechuan (Sichuan) food stand out as highly appealing. The jaded palates of jet-setters and trend-makers, their threshholds of stimulation driven sky-high by their lavish life-styles, were the first to discover the sensory delights of Szechuan's (Sichuan's) manifold flavours and appreciate the physical stimulation imparted by the dishes to the system. As usual, the rest of the world has begun to follow their lead. The strong flavours and stimulating after-effects of Szechuan (Sichuan) and Hunan dishes are perhaps best suited to the fast pace and excitement of modern urban life-styles.

BRAISED SHARK'S FINS IN BROWN SAUCE

750 g (1½ lb)	prepared whole shark's fins (see page 393) , (about 185 g / 6 oz dry weight)
250 g (8 oz)	fresh chicken fat
375 g (12 oz)	lean pork
2	spring onions (scallions), trimmed and sliced
3 slices	fresh ginger
1½ tablespoons	rice wine or dry sherry
4 cups (1 litre)	water
60 g (2 oz)	Chinese or cured (Smithfield) ham
30 g (1 oz)	dried scallops, soaked for 1 hour

Seasoning:

2½ tablespoons	dark soy sauce or oyster sauce
½ teaspoon	m.s.g. (optional)
2 teaspoons	sugar
¼ teaspoon	white pepper
3 tablespoons	cornflour (cornstarch)
¼ cup (2 fl oz)	cold water
1 tablespoon	finely chopped fresh coriander (optional)

Drain the prepared shark's fins and set aside. Cut the chicken fat and pork into dice and stir-fry with the spring onions and ginger on fairly high heat for 1½ minutes. Sizzle the wine onto the side of the pan and then add the water and the drained shark's fins and bring to the boil. Reduce to simmer and cook for 1½ hours.

Strain the stock into another saucepan and add the ham, cut into small cubes, and the drained scallops. Simmer for about 45 minutes, then add the seasoning ingredients and simmer, stirring, until the sauce is thick. Add the shark's fins and pork, discarding the chicken fat and simmer until thoroughly heated, then transfer to a serving dish and serve at once.

'LUNGCHING' TEA-FLAVOURED ABALONE

2/3 500 g (1 lb) can	abalone*
1½ tablespoons	Lungching tea (or use oolong tea)
¾ cup (6 fl oz)	chicken stock
90 g (3 oz)	fresh pea sprouts or young spinach

Seasoning:

½ teaspoon	salt
⅓ teaspoon	m.s.g. (optional)
2 teaspoons	rice wine or dry sherry

Drain the abalone, reserving the liquid. Trim the ruffled edges and cut the abalone into thick slices, then return to the liquid to soak until needed.

Brew the tea with 1 cup (8 fl oz) of water and leave to infuse for 30 seconds, then drain away the water and brew with a second lot of freshly boiled water.

Bring the chicken stock to the boil and add the seasoning ingredients, the sliced abalone and pea sprouts or spinach. Simmer briefly.

Strain the tea liquid (about ½ cup) into a cup and discard the remaining tea, reserving the leaves. Transfer the leaves to a small porcelain teacup and upturn in the centre of a serving dish. Leave the cup in place. Pour in the reserved half cup of tea and add the heated abalone and its suace. Stir very lightly without disturbing the teacup.

Carry to the table and remove the teacup to expose the tea leaves immediately before serving.

* Unused abalone can be frozen for later use.

BRAISED FISH MAW WITH HAM AND MUSHROOMS

250 g (8 oz)	dried fish maw, precooked (see page 392)
125 g (4 oz)	Chinese or cured (Smithfield) ham
8	dried black mushrooms, soaked for 25 minutes
2½ tablespoons	frying oil
2	spring onions (scallions), trimmed and sliced
4 slices	fresh ginger
1 tablespoon	rendered chicken fat (chicken grease), (optional)
3 cups (24 fl oz)	chicken stock
1 teaspoon	salt
¼ teaspoon	m.s.g. (optional)
1 tablespoon	rice wine or dry sherry
375 g (12 oz)	fresh spinach (collard greens)
2 tablespoons	softened lard or frying oil cornflour (cornstarch)

Seasoning:

½ teaspoon	salt
⅓ cup	chicken stock
¼ teaspoon	m.s.g. (optional)
½ teaspoon	sugar

Prepare the fish maw following the directions on page 392. Cut into bite-sized pieces and soak in cold water until needed. Cut the ham into dice. Squeeze the water from the mushrooms, remove the stems and cut the caps into quarters.

Heat the frying oil and stir-fry the spring onions and ginger briefly. Add the chicken fat, if used, and the chicken stock and bring to the boil. Add the salt, m.s.g., and wine and add the well-drained fish maw, ham, and mushrooms. Cover and simmer or steam for about 1 hour until the fish maw is completely tender.

Wash the spinach and discard any stems. Sauté in the lard or frying oil for a few seconds, then add the seasoning ingredients, cover and simmer until tender.

Thicken the sauce on the fish maw with a paste of cornflour and cold water and cook until the sauce turns clear. Transfer to a serving dish and surround with the spinach. Serve.

FISH LIPS WITH VEGETABLES ON CRISP RICE

155 g (5 oz)	dried fish lips, precooked (see page 392)
¼ cup (2 fl oz)	frying oil
2	spring onions (scallions), trimmed and diced
1½ teaspoons	finely chopped fresh ginger
60 g (2 oz)	canned bamboo shoots, drained and sliced
60 g (2 oz)	canned straw mushrooms, drained and sliced
90 g (3 oz)	bok choy or choy sum stems, parboiled
1 tablespoon	cornflour (cornstarch)
1 teaspoon	sesame oil
12 pieces	rice cakes (see page 417)
5 cups (1¼ litres)	deep-frying oil

Seasoning/Sauce:

3 cups (24 fl oz)	chicken stock
¾ teaspoon	salt
½ teaspoon	m.s.g. (optional)
1 tablespoon	dark soy sauce or oyster sauce
2 teaspoons	rice wine or dry sherry
½ teaspoon	Chinese brown vinegar

Prepare the fish lips according to the directions on page 392. Soak until needed. Stir-fry the spring onions, ginger, bamboo shoots, straw mushrooms, and sliced vegetable stems in the frying oil for 1½ minutes. Add the pre-mixed seasoning/sauce ingredients and bring to the boil.

Drain the fish lips and cut into bite-sized pieces. Add to the pan and simmer for 4 — 5 minutes. Heat the deep-frying oil to smoking point and deep-fry the rice cakes in a frying basket until crisp and golden. Drain and transfer to a serving dish.

Thicken the sauce with the cornflour mixed with an equal amount of cold water and stir in the sesame oil. Pour immediately over the rice cakes and serve.

'PRECIOUS CONCUBINE' CHICKEN

Serve as an appetiser or main dish.

1 1¼ kg (2½ lb)	chicken
2	spring onions (scallions), trimmed and halved
3 thin slices	fresh ginger
1 tablespoon	rice wine or dry sherry
1	medium carrot, peeled and shredded
1	medium cucumber, shredded
½	giant white (icicle) radish, shredded
1 tablespoon	salt

Seasoning:

1 teaspoon	salt
½ teaspoon	m.s.g. (optional)
1 tablespoon	sesame oil
¼ cup (2 fl oz)	warm chicken stock

Sauce 1:

2 tablespoons	finely chopped spring onion (scallion)
¼ cup (2 fl oz)	light soy sauce
2 tablespoons	water
2 tablespoons	sesame oil
¾ teaspoon	chilli sauce or chilli oil
2 teaspoons	dark soy sauce
2 teaspoons	sugar
½ teaspoon	m.s.g. (optional)

Sauce 2:

2 tablespoons	finely shredded fresh ginger
2 tablespoons	Chinese red vinegar
1 teaspoon	salt
¼ teaspoon	m.s.g. (optional)
1½ teaspoons	sugar
1 tablespoon	water
2 teaspoons	sesame oil

Clean and dress the chicken and place in a saucepan with the spring onions, ginger, and wine. Cover with water and bring to the boil. Simmer on very low heat until just cooked, about 50 minutes. Drain, debone (see page 394), and slice.

Sprinkle the salt onto the carrot and radish and stir in lightly. Leave for about 25 minutes, then rinse with cold water and drain thoroughly. Pile each of the shredded vegetables onto separate serving dishes, or into separate groups on a large serving platter.

Arrange the sliced chicken breast on the cucumber, the sliced thigh meat on the carrots, and the remaining meat, torn into shreds, on the radish.

Garnish the dish with parsley or fresh coriander. Mix the seasoning ingredients together and pour over the chicken.

Mix the two sauces in separate jugs and serve with the chicken, to be poured over or transferred to small dip dishes at the table.

Chicken Steamed in a Pumpkin (recipe page 187).

'BON BON' CHICKEN

Serve hot or cold as an appetiser or main dish.

1 1½ kg (3 lb)	chicken
1	cucumber, peeled and shredded
5 — 6	fresh lettuce leaves
1 tablespoon	toasted white sesame seeds (optional)

Sauce:

2½ tablespoons	sesame paste
2 tablespoons	chicken stock
1 tablespoon	sesame oil
2 tablespoons	light soy sauce
1 tablespoon	Chinese brown vinegar
1 tablespoon	grated fresh ginger
2 — 3 teaspoons	finely chopped garlic
½ teaspoon	salt
½ teaspoon	m.s.g. (optional)
1 tablespoon	sugar

Clean and dress the chicken, place in a saucepan with water to cover and bring to the boil. Cover tightly and cook on very low heat for 10 minutes. Remove from the heat and leave to stand in the hot stock for a further 30 minutes. Return to the boil and remove again from the heat. Leave for 5 — 6 minutes.

Remove the chicken. The meat should be white and moist with a hint of pink around the bones. Drain well and rub a little of the sesame oil over the skin. Debone and tear the meat into strips.

Line a serving plate with the lettuce and pile the cucumber and chicken on top. Sprinkle on the sesame seeds, if used.

Mix the sauce ingredients together, stirring until thoroughly amalgamated. Serve separately as a dip or pour over the chicken at the table.

ROAST STUFFED CHICKEN

1 1½ kg (3 lb)	chicken
90 g (3 oz)	fresh bean sprouts
125 g (4 oz)	fat pork
3 slices	fresh ginger
4	spring onions (scallions)
¼ cup (2 fl oz)	softened lard or frying oil
500 g (1 lb)	pork omentum (caul fat)
1 tablespoon	sesame oil

Batter:

3	egg whites, well beaten
3 tablespoons	cornflour (cornstarch)

Seasoning A:

1 tablespoon	finely chopped spring onion (scallion)
1 teaspoon	grated fresh ginger
1 teaspoon	salt
2 teaspoons	light soy sauce
1 tablespoon	rice wine or dry sherry
¼ teaspoon	m.s.g. (optional)

Seasoning B:

¼ teaspoon	m.s.g. (optional)
2 teaspoons	light soy sauce
1 teaspoon	rice wine or dry sherry
1 teaspoon	chilli oil or chilli flakes

Wash the chicken and wipe dry. Rub thoroughly with the pre-mixed seasoning A ingredients and set aside. Wash and drain the bean sprouts, then chop finely. Finely dice the pork and mix with the seasoning B ingredients. Chop 1 slice of ginger and 2 spring onions into small dice and sauté in the lard or oil for 30 seconds. Add the pork and sauté until lightly coloured, then add the bean sprouts and cook very briefly.

Stuff the mixture into the chicken with the remaining ginger and spring onions. Close the opening with poultry pins. Mix the batter ingredients together and spread thickly over the chicken, then cut the pork net in halves and wrap one piece around the chicken. Brush with the remaining batter and cover with the other piece of pork net.

Roast over an open charcoal fire, securely fastened to a spit, or cook in a moderate oven 190°C (375°F), preferably on a rotisserie, until the chicken is golden brown and cooked through, about 1 hour. Increase the heat and cook for a further 6 — 7 minutes until the pork net coating is very crisp and quite dark. Brush with the sesame oil.

Remove from the oven and open the first piece of pork net. Cut into diamond-shaped pieces and place on one side of a serving plate. Discard the inner piece of net and cut the chicken into serving slices. Arrange on the plate with the stuffing on the other side. Discard the ginger and onion. Serve at once.

CHICKEN STEAMED IN A YUNNAN STEAMPOT

The Yunnan Steam-Pot is an unglazed ceramic cooking pot which has a central funnel inside. This allows a small but continuous flow of steam to enter the pot, thus gently cooking the ingredients and adding liquid to the dish by way of condensation. These pots are available at most leading suppliers of Chinese food and kitchen products. No other cooking pot can produce the same results.

1 1/2 kg (3 lb)	chicken
90 g (3 oz)	Chinese or cured (Smithfield) ham
90 g (3 oz)	canned bamboo shoots, drained
1	spring onion (scallion), trimmed and sliced
2 slices	fresh ginger
	salt
	m.s.g. (optional)

Seasoning:

3/4 teaspoon	salt
1 teaspoon	sugar
2 1/2 tablespoons	rice wine or dry sherry
1/2 teaspoon	chilli oil (optional)

Clean the chicken and cut into 5 cm (2 in) squares. Place in a dish with the seasoning ingredients and leave for 30 minutes, turning occasionally.

Transfer to the steam-pot. Cut the ham and bamboo shoots into small cubes and add to the pot with the spring onion and ginger. Mix the ingredients together using chopsticks.

Place the pot in a steamer without using a rack and pour in water until it reaches a level half way up the sides of the steam-pot. Cover the steam-pot with its lid, then cover the steamer and bring the water to the boil. Reduce to a simmer and cook for 1 — 1 1/4 hours until the chicken is completely tender. Add salt and m.s.g. to taste and serve in the steam-pot.

HOT SPICED CHICKEN WITH GREEN ONIONS

625 g (1 1/4 lb)	chicken pieces
8	large spring onions (scallions)
1/3 cup	frying oil
1 teaspoon	Chinese brown peppercorns
1 — 2	dried red chilli peppers, cut into 3 pieces each
1 tablespoon	soybean paste
4 slices	fresh ginger
1/2 teaspoon	m.s.g. (optional)
3/4 teaspoon	Chinese brown vinegar (optional)

Seasoning/Sauce:

3/4 cup (6 fl oz)	chicken stock
2 teaspoons	light soy sauce
2 teaspoons	dark soy sauce
1 tablespoon	rice wine or dry sherry
1 tablespoon	sugar

Cut the chicken into bite-sized pieces through the bones. Cut the spring onions into 2 cm (3/4 in) pieces after trimming the roots and tops.

Heat the frying oil and fry the peppercorns and sliced chilli peppers until the chillies are dark brown and crisp. Remove and set aside. Add the bean paste and stir on moderate heat for 20 seconds, then add the chicken pieces and ginger and stir-fry until almost cooked, about 3 minutes.

Add the spring onions and return the chillies and peppercorns. Stir-fry on lowered heat for 1 minute, then stir in the pre-mixed seasoning/sauce ingredients and simmer until the chicken is tender and the sauce well reduced.

Thicken the sauce lightly, if preferred, with a solution of cornflour and cold water, and add the m.s.g. and vinegar, if used.

'KUNG PAO' CHICKEN

440 g (14 oz)	boneless chicken breasts, or use slightly more chicken on the bone
5	fresh red chilli peppers
90 g (3 oz)	raw peanuts (ground nuts)
¾ cup (6 fl oz)	frying oil
3	spring onions (scallions), trimmed and sliced
5 — 6 cloves	garlic, sliced
¾ teaspoon	Chinese brown vinegar

Seasoning A:

2 tablespoons	light soy sauce
2 tablespoons	rice wine or dry sherry
1 teaspoon	sugar
1½ teaspoons	cornflour (cornstarch)
1 tablespoon	finely chopped spring onion (scallion)
1½ teaspoons	grated fresh ginger

Seasoning B/Sauce:

2/3 cup	chicken stock
2 tablespoons	light soy sauce
1 tablespoon	rice wine or dry sherry
1 teaspoon	salt
1½ teaspoons	sugar
1½ teaspoons	cornflour (cornstarch)

Cut the chicken into bite-sized pieces. Place in a dish with the seasoning A ingredients, mix well and leave for 20 minutes. Drop the peanuts into a pot of boiling water and leave for 2 minutes, then drain and remove the skins. Cut the chillies into about 4 pieces each and discard the seeds for a milder taste.

Heat the frying oil and fry the chillies until they turn dark brown. Remove and set aside. Add the peanuts and fry until golden. Remove and drain well.

Pour off all but 2½ tablespoons of the oil and stir-fry the chicken for 2 minutes. Add the sliced spring onions and garlic and stir-fry a further 30 seconds, then add the chilli peppers and the pre-mixed seasoning B/sauce ingredients. Cover and simmer until the chicken is tender, about 2 minutes. Cooking will take longer for chicken on the bone, so leave out the cornflour until the chicken is done, then mix to a paste with cold water and use to thicken the sauce.

Stir in the vinegar and the peanuts and transfer to a serving plate. Serve at once.

FRIED CHICKEN PATTIES WITH MARINATED CABBAGE

210 g (7 oz)	boneless chicken
90 g (3 oz)	pork fat
3	egg whites, well beaten
155 g (5 oz)	white cabbage
	cornflour (cornstarch)
5 cups (1¼ litres)	deep-frying oil

Seasoning A:

½ teaspoon	salt
½ teaspoon	m.s.g. (optional)
¼ teaspoon	white pepper
2 teaspoons	rice wine
1½ tablespoons	onion and ginger infusion (see page 386)
2 tablespoons	cornflour (cornstarch)

Seasoning B:

¼ cup (2 fl oz)	boiling water
¼ cup (2 fl oz)	white vinegar
1½ teaspoons	salt
1½ tablespoons	sugar
2 teaspoons	finely chopped fresh ginger

Pulverise the chicken and pork fat in a food processor or by using two cleavers (see page 396). Add egg whites and the seasoning A ingredients and mix in one direction only until the mixture is smooth and fairly thick. Wipe out a dish with an oiled cloth and pour in the chicken paste. Set on a rack in a steamer and steam over rapidly boiling water until firm, about 15 minutes.

Wash the cabbage and shred finely. Squeeze out excess water and place the cabbage in a dish. Add the seasoning B ingredients and toss lightly. Cover with plastic wrap and leave for about 30 minutes.

Remove the chicken from the steamer and turn out onto an oiled plate or board. Leave to cool, then cut into bite-sized pieces and coat lightly with cornflour. Heat the deep-frying oil to fairly hot and deep-fry the chicken patties, several at a time, until crisp and golden. Remove and drain well.

Thoroughly drain the marinated cabbage and arrange around the edge of a serving plate. Place the fried chicken patties in the centre and serve at once.

Crisp-skin Fish with Hot and Sour Sauce (recipe page 195).

SPICED CHICKEN WITH PEANUTS AND BAMBOO SHOOTS

310 g (10 oz)	boneless chicken breast
90 g (3 oz)	canned bamboo shoots or water chestnuts, drained
60 g (2 oz)	raw peanuts (groundnuts)
¼ cup (2 fl oz)	softened lard or frying oil
1 — 2	pickled red chilli peppers, shredded
4	garlic chives, sliced
2	spring onions (scallions), trimmed and diced
2 thick slices	fresh ginger, diced
1¼ tablespoons	hot bean paste

Seasoning A:

1	egg white, beaten
½ teaspoon	salt
2 teaspoons	light soy sauce
1 teaspoon	rice wine or dry sherry
½ teaspoon	cornflour (cornstarch)

Seasoning B/Sauce:

⅓ cup	chicken stock
1 tablespoon	light soy sauce
2 teaspoons	dark soy sauce
2 teaspoons	rice wine or dry sherry
1¾ teaspoons	sugar
1¼ teaspoons	cornflour (cornstarch)

Cut the chicken into 2 cm (¾ in) cubes and place in a dish with the seasoning A ingredients. Mix well and leave for 45 minutes, turning occasionally.

Cut the bamboo shoots or water chestnuts into small cubes. Drop the peanuts into a saucepan of boiling water and cook for 1 minute, then drain and remove the skins. Drain thoroughly.

Heat the lard or frying oil in a wok and stir-fry the chicken for 1 minute. Remove and keep warm. Add the bamboo shoots or water chestnuts and the peanuts and stir-fry for 1 minute, then push to one side of the pan and add the chilli peppers, garlic chives, spring onions, and ginger and stir-fry for 30 seconds. Add the hot bean paste and fry briefly, then return the chicken and stir in the vegetables and peanuts.

Add the pre-mixed seasoning B/sauce ingredients and simmer on moderate heat until the sauce thickens, then transfer to a serving plate.

For a crunchier texture, deep-fry the peanuts separately and add to the dish just before serving.

'HIBISCUS' CHICKEN

155 g (5 oz)	boneless chicken breast
2 tablespoons	onion and ginger infusion (see page 386)
¼ cup (2 fl oz)	chicken stock
3	egg whites, well beaten
1½—2 tablespoons	cornflour (cornstarch)
3 cups (24 fl oz)	deep-frying oil
60 g (2 oz)	canned bamboo shoots, drained
60 g (2 oz)	'silver' sprouts

Seasoning A:

½ teaspoon	salt
¼ teaspoon	m.s.g. (optional)
½ teaspoon	sugar
1 teaspoon	rice wine or dry sherry

Seasoning B/Sauce:

½ cup (4 fl oz)	chicken stock
¾ teaspoon	salt
¼ teaspoon	m.s.g. (optional)
1 teaspoon	rice wine or dry sherry
1 teaspoon	cornflour (cornstarch)

Pulverise the chicken in a food processor using the chopping blade, or use two cleavers (see page 396). Mix with the onion and ginger infusion, chicken stock, egg whites, cornflour, and the seasoning A ingredients and beat in one direction only until the mixture is smooth and thick.

Heat the deep-frying oil to moderate and slide in spoonfuls of the mixture to cook until white and firm, remove and drain on absorbent paper. Cut the bamboo shoots into thin slices and rinse the 'silver' sprouts.

Pour off all but 2½ tablespoons of the oil and stir-fry the bamboo shoots and 'silver' sprouts for 1½ minutes, then add the pre-mixed seasoning B/sauce ingredients and simmer for 1 minute. Return the chicken and simmer until the sauce has thickened. Adjust the seasoning if necessary and serve.

'FIRECRACKER' CHICKEN

185 g (6 oz)	boneless chicken breast
4	Chinese sausages*
6 cups (1½ litres)	deep-frying oil
60 g (2 oz)	canned bamboo shoots, drained
60 g (2 oz)	fresh young spinach leaves (collard greens)

Seasoning A:

1	egg white, beaten
½ teaspoon	salt
½ teaspoon	m.s.g. (optional)
1 teaspoon	sugar
1 teaspoon	rice wine or dry sherry
2 teaspoons	cornflour (cornstarch)

Seasoning B/Sauce:

¾ cup (6 fl oz)	chicken stock
¾ teaspoon	salt
¼ teaspoon	ground black pepper
½ teaspoon	m.s.g. (optional)
½ teaspoon	sugar
1 teaspoon	rice wine or dry sherry
1 tablespoon	finely chopped spring onion (scallion)
¾ teaspoon	grated fresh ginger
2 teaspoons	cornflour (cornstarch)

Cut the chicken into thin slices and dust lightly with cornflour. Gently bat with the end of the cleaver handle until spread into thin escalopes. Place in a dish with the seasoning A ingredients, mix well and leave for 20 minutes.

Steam the Chinese sausage for 10 minutes, then cut each piece into three. Wrap a piece of chicken around each piece of sausage and squeeze firmly to hold in place. If the sausage feels too moist, coat very lightly with cornflour before covering with the chicken.

Cut the bamboo shoots into thin slices and rinse the spinach leaves. Set aside. Heat the deep-frying oil to moderate and deep-fry the chicken and sausage rolls for about 1 minute, then drain and set aside. Pour off all but 2½ tablespoons of the oil and stir-fry the bamboo shoots for 30 seconds, then add the spinach leaves and stir-fry briefly.

Add the pre-mixed seasoning B/sauce ingredients and bring to the boil. Reduce heat and simmer briefly, then return the chicken rolls and simmer until the sauce thickens enough to glaze the rolls. Transfer to a warmed serving plate.

* Dried pork and liver sausage. If unobtainable use sticks of steamed Chinese ham.

CHICKEN STEAMED IN A PUMPKIN

1 2 kg (4 lb)	fresh pumpkin
1¼ kg (2½ lb)	chicken pieces
2	spring onions (scallions), trimmed and sliced
2 slices	fresh ginger, shredded
1 cup	spiced rice powder*

Seasoning:

½ teaspoon	salt
¼ teaspoon	m.s.g. (optional)
1 tablespoon	sugar
2 teaspoons	dark soy sauce
2 cubes	fermented beancurd, mashed with the liquid
1 tablespoon	rice wine or brandy

Wash the pumpkin and wipe with kitchen paper. Cut off the top and scrape away the seeds. Trim the stem to form a handle and scrape the inside and edges so it forms a lid for the pumpkin. Rinse the pumpkin and lid with salted water and upturn to drain.

Cut the chicken into bite-sized pieces, cutting through the bones. Place in a dish and mix with the seasoning ingredients. Leave for 20 minutes, then roll the chicken in the spiced rice and place inside the pumpkin, distributing the spring onions and ginger evenly between the chicken pieces.

Set the lid in position and place the pumpkin on a rack in a steamer to steam over rapidly boiling water for about 55 minutes, or until the chicken and pumpkin are both tender. Serve straight from the steamer and eat the pumpkin with the chicken.

* Use Chinese brown peppercorns in preference to star anise when preparing the spiced rice powder (see page 386).

COUNTRY-STYLE CHICKEN

210 g (7 oz)	boneless chicken
60 g (2 oz)	canned bamboo shoots, drained
1	small carrot, peeled
⅓ stalk	celery*
4 thin slices	fresh ginger
1 — 2	fresh red chilli peppers
6	garlic chives
1½ cups (12 fl oz)	frying oil
1 tablespoon	soybean paste

Seasoning A:

2	egg whites, well beaten
½ teaspoon	salt
½ teaspoon	m.s.g. (optional)
½ teaspoon	sugar
2 teaspoons	rice wine or dry sherry
1 tablespoon	cornflour (cornstarch)

Seasong B/Sauce

1 tablespoon	light soy sauce
1 tablespoon	rice wine or dry sherry
¼ cup (2 fl oz)	chicken stock
1 teaspoon	Chinese brown vinegar
½ teaspoon	m.s.g. (optional)
1¼ teaspoons	sugar
1½ teaspoons	cornflour (cornstarch)

Cut the chicken into thin slices, then into narrow shreds and place in a dish with the seasoning A ingredients. Mix well and leave for 15 minutes. Cut the bamboo shoots, carrot, celery, ginger, chillies, and chives into narrow shreds.

Heat the frying oil to moderate and fry the shredded chicken in a frying basket for about 45 seconds, remove and drain well. Pour off all but 2½ tablespoons of the oil and stir-fry the shredded ingredients for about 1½ minutes, then push to one side of the pan and add the soybean paste. Fry briefly, then sizzle the soy sauce and wine onto the sides of the pan and add the remaining seasoning B/sauce ingredients, pre-mixed. Bring to the boil, return the chicken and stir all ingredients together.

Simmer until the sauce thickens, then serve.

* Or use shredded green capsicum (bell pepper).

'TWICE EATEN' CHICKEN

1¼ kg (2½ lb)	chicken pieces
¼ cup (2 fl oz)	softened lard or frying oil
2	spring onions (scallions), trimmed and sliced
3 slices	fresh ginger
1 tablespoon	rice wine or dry sherry
⅓ teaspoon	ground black pepper
4 cups (1 litre)	water
20 g (¾ oz)	dried 'wood ear' fungus, soaked for 25 minutes
1 tablespoon	rendered chicken fat (chicken grease)
	salt
	m.s.g. (optional)

Wash the chicken and cut through the bones into 2.5 cm (1 in) pieces. Heat the lard and stir-fry the chicken until lightly coloured, about 2½ minutes. Push to one side of the pan and add the spring onions and ginger and stir-fry briefly.

Sizzle the wine onto the sides of the pan and add the black pepper, stir in, then pour in the water and bring to the boil. Simmer on low heat until the chicken is completely tender, about 35 minutes.

Strain the liquid into a saucepan and simmer slowly, adjusting the seasoning with salt and m.s.g., if used, to taste.

Drain the 'wood ears' well and cut into small squares. Stir-fry the well-drained chicken pieces with the 'wood ears' in the chicken fat for about 1 minute. Add a dash of salt and m.s.g., to taste.

Serve the soup in a deep dish and arrange the chicken and 'wood ears' on another dish to serve at the same time. For extra flavour, add sliced young green vegetables to the soup.

Szechuan (Sichuan) Prawns in Chilli Oil Sauce (recipe page 204).

SPICED DEEP-FRIED CHICKEN LEGS

Sever as an appetiser or main dish.

12	small chicken drumsticks
2	eggs, well beaten
	cornflour (cornstarch)
	dry breadcrumbs (optional)
7 cups (1¾ litres)	deep-frying oil
	Chinese pepper-salt

Seasoning:

½ teaspoon	salt
¾ teaspoon	five spice powder
1 tablespoon	light soy sauce
2 teaspoons	dark soy sauce
2 teaspoons	rice wine or dry sherry
½ teaspoon	sesame oil
1 tablespoon	finely chopped spring onion (scallion)
2 teaspoons	finely chopped fresh ginger

Prick the drumsticks all over with a sharp skewer and place in a dish. Add the pre-mixed seasoning ingredients and rub the drumsticks thoroughly. Leave for 1 hour to marinate, turning occasionally.

Heat the deep-frying oil to moderate. Wipe the drumsticks with kitchen paper and brush with beaten eggs, then coat with the cornflour or dry breadcrumbs. Deep-fry several at a time until well coloured and cooked through, about 3½ minutes.

Drain and arrange on a serving plate on crisp fresh lettuce. Sprinkle on a generous amount of Chinese pepper-salt (see page 384) or serve separately as a dip.

DUCK SMOKED OVER CAMPHOR WOOD AND TEA LEAVES

1 2¼ kg (4½ lb)	fat duck
2½ tablespoons	Chinese pepper-salt (see page 384)
1½ tablespoons	saltpetre (optional)
8 cups (2 litres)	deep-frying oil

For Smoking:

2 cups	camphor wood chips
½ cup	Chinese black tea leaves
2 pieces	dried orange peel

Clean and dress the duck. Wash well and dry with kitchen paper, then rub thoroughly inside and out with a mixture of the pepper-salt and saltpetre, if used. Place in a dish and leave for at least 5 hours to absorb the flavours. Wrap with plastic wrap to prevent the skin drying out while marinating.

Place the wood chips, tea leaves, and orange peel in a large old iron wok or cooking pot and set a rack over it. Place the duck, breast down, on the rack. Cover with a wok lid or another old cooking pan and smoke over moderate heat for about 10 minutes. Reduce the heat once the wood starts smoking well. Turn the duck and smoke the other side for about 6 minutes, then remove.

Transfer to a dish and set in a steamer to steam for 1¾ hours. Remove, drain well and wipe the moisture from the skin. Heat the deep-frying oil to smoking point and deep-fry the duck until the skin is dark brown and very crisp, about 2 minutes.

Cut into serving portions and arrange on a plate, or debone and tear the meat into slivers. Serve with accompaniments of sliced spring onion or leek, hoisin, plum, or 'duck' sauce (see page 385) and steamed bread or 'Mandarin' pancakes (see page 373).

Another method of preparing a smoked duck involves marinating in the same way, then steaming for about 45 minutes before smoking over a mixture of jasmine tea leaves and pine needles, then deep-frying until the skin is crisp and red-gold.

Either method produces moist meat permeated with a delicate smoky flavour.

CRISP OIL-BASTED DUCK COOKED TWICE

1 1¾ kg (3½ lb)	duck
375 g (12 oz)	salted turnip or mustard leaves*
¼ cup (2 fl oz)	rice wine or dry sherry
⅓ cup	sugar
2 tablespoons	boiling water
8 cups (2 litres)	deep-frying oil

Dish 1:

12	flower-shaped steamed buns (see recipe, page 372)
4 tablespoons	'duck', hoisin, or plum sauce (see page 385)
6	spring onions (scallions), or 1 shredded leek

Dish 2:

2 tablespoons	softened lard or frying oil
½	small leek, shredded
1	small green or red capsicum (bell pepper), shredded
1	fresh red chilli pepper, shredded
45 g (1½ oz)	'silver' or bean sprouts, blanched
2 slices	fresh ginger, shredded
2 cloves	garlic, sliced (optional)

Seasoning:

¼ teaspoon	salt
¼ teaspoon	m.s.g. (optional)
¾ teaspoon	sugar
2 teaspoons	rice wine or dry sherry
1 tablespoon	hot black bean sauce or sweet bean paste

Clean and dress the duck and rinse well. Wipe dry and stuff the salted vegetables into the cavity, or put in the pepper-salt and shake the bird to evenly distribute around the inside. Tie a string around the neck and hang in a well-ventilated place over a drip tray. Leave for 2 hours. Heat the wine, sugar, and water together until the sugar has completely dissolved, then pour slowly and evenly over the duck and leave until the skin is completely dry, about 6 hours.

Prepare the steamed buns and other accompaniments for dish 1, and the ingredients for dish 2.

Heat the deep-frying oil to smoking point. Place the duck in a large strainer or frying basket and hold over the oil. Ladle the hot oil continuously over the duck until completely cooked through, about 45 minutes. Or lower the duck into slightly cooler oil to deep-fry for 10 minutes, then remove and leave to cool. Re-fry again in warm oil until cooked through, about 25 minutes more, removing several times to cool.

To serve, take the accompaniments for dish 1 to the table. Slice off the crisp skin and arrange on a serving plate with a little of the meat, preferably the breast cuts. Return the duck to the kitchen.

The duck skin, together with a few shreds of spring onion, or leek, should be dipped into the sauce and eaten with the buns. Or the buns may be opened at the fold and the skin and onion inserted, sandwich fashion.

Slice off the remaining meat and cut any of the larger pieces into bite-sized chunks. Heat the lard or oil and stir-fry the duck until the edges are crisp and lightly coloured. Remove and keep warm. Add the shredded ingredients and the garlic, if used, and stir-fry together for about 2 minutes, then add the seasoning ingredients and stir-fry briefly. Return the duck pieces and reduce the heat slightly. Stir-fry together until evenly mixed and heated through.

Serve with any remaining steamed buns or with white rice. As an additional course, the duck carcass can be simmered in water with spring onion, ginger, and seasonings added to be served as a soup at the end of the meal.

*Or use 1 tablespoon of Chinese pepper-salt (see page 384)

SMOKED DUCK SAUTÉD WITH YOUNG GINGER

½	smoked duck (see previous page)
2½ tablespoons	softened lard or frying oil
5 cm (2 in) piece	fresh young ginger, peeled and thinly sliced*
2	fresh red chilli peppers, shred
1 tablespoon	hot bean paste**
5	garlic chives, sliced
½ teaspoon	Chinese brown vinegar

Seasoning:

2 tablespoons	light soy sauce
1 tablespoon	rice wine or dry sherry
1 tablespoon	sugar

Debone the duck and cut the meat into bite-sized pieces. Heat the lard or frying oil in a wok and sauté the duck until lightly coloured and crisp on the edges, about 2 minutes. Remove and drain.

Reheat the pan and add the ginger and chilli peppers. Sauté briefly on moderate heat and add the hot bean paste, or sweet bean paste, if used. Sauté for 20 seconds, then return the duck and add the garlic chives and stir-fry briefly.

Add the seasoning ingredients and sauté together for 1 minute, then stir in the vinegar and transfer to a serving plate.
* Choose a piece with smooth pale cream skin and pink buds.
** If preferred, omit the hot bean paste, substitute sweet bean paste and use less sugar.

ROAST DUCK STUFFED WITH PORK AND BEAN SPROUTS

1 1½ kg (3 lb)	duck
90 g (3 oz)	fresh bean sprouts
90 g (3 oz)	lean pork
2	spring onions (scallions), trimmed and shredded
3 slices	fresh ginger, shredded
2 tablespoons	frying oil
185 g (6 oz)	Chinese (celery) cabbage

Glaze:

2 tablespoons	rice wine or dry sherry
2½ tablespoons	malt sugar
¾ teaspoon	salt

Seasoning:

¾ teaspoon	salt
1 tablespoon	light soy sauce
2 teaspoons	rice wine or dry sherry

Sauce:

2 teaspoons	sugar
1 tablespoon	light soy sauce
1 tablespoon	white vinegar
1 tablespoon	sesame oil
¼ teaspoon	m.s.g. (optional)
½ teaspoon	chilli oil

Clean and dress the duck and pour several lots of boiling water over the skin. Mix the glaze ingredients in a small saucepan and heat until the sugar has completely dissolved, then pour slowly and evenly over the duck. Tie a string around the neck and hang in a well-ventilated place to dry, about 7 hours.

Wash the bean sprouts, drain well, and chop coarsely. Cut the pork into small dice. Stir-fry the spring onions and ginger in the frying oil for 30 seconds, then add the pork and stir-fry until the colour changes. Add the seasoning ingredients and stir-fry briefly, then remove from the heat and mix in the chopped bean sprouts.

Stuff into the duck and close the openings with poultry pins. Roast the duck slowly on a spit over a glowing charcoal fire or on a rotisserie in a moderate oven (190°C/375°F) for 1 hour, then increase the heat to fairly hot and continue to cook until the skin is crisp and deep gold in colour. Remove from the heat and cut into serving pieces.

Wash and shred the cabbage and mix with the sauce ingredients. Arrange around the edge of a large serving plate. Place the duck in the centre with the stuffing underneath the meat. Serve.

HUNAN CRISPY DUCK

1 2kg (4 lb)	duck
8 cups (2 litres)	deep-frying oil
	Chinese pepper-salt (see page 384)
	'duck', hoisin, or plum sauce (see page 385)
	steam flower-shaped buns (see page 372)

Seasoning:

4	star anise, crushed
1 tablespoon	Chinese brown peppercorns, crushed
1 tablespoon	fennel seeds, crushed
2 teaspoons	salt
1 tablespoon	rice wine or dry sherry
2 tablespoons	fine chopped spring onion (scallion)
2 tablespoons	fine chopped fresh ginger

Clean and dress the duck and rub inside and out with the pre-mixed seasoning ingredients. Set in a large dish and place on a rack in a steamer. Cover and steam over rapidly boiling water for 2½ hours. Remove duck and wipe off the seasonings, scraping away those that are inside.

Heat the deep-frying oil to fairly hot and place the duck in a frying basket. Lower into the oil to deep-fry until the duck is completely crisp. Serve whole to be torn into strips and served with the accompaniments of pepper-salt, sauce, and steamed buns.

The duck will be so tender after the long steaming and deep-frying that the bones can be eaten with the meat. Top up the level of the water in the steamer frequently during cooking to prevent it from boiling dry.

Honey-Glazed Ham (recipe page 210).

STEAMED DUCK MARINATED WITH PRESERVED EGG AND WINE

1 1½ kg (3 lb)	duck
2	spring onions (scallions), trimmed and sliced
5 slices	fresh ginger

Seasoning:

2	preserved duck eggs*
¼ cup (2 fl oz)	rice wine or dry sherry
2 tablespoons	sweet rice wine or Japanese mirin (optional)
1½ teaspoons	salt
2 teaspoons	sugar
¾ teaspoon	m.s.g. (optional)

Clean and dress the duck, wash well and dry with kitchen paper. Tie a string around the neck and hang the duck in a well-ventilated place for about 4 hours to dry the skin. Place the spring onions and ginger in the cavity.

Mix the seasoning ingredients together, mashing to a smooth paste. Smear thickly over the duck and leave for 30 minutes. Place the duck in a casserole, breast up, and cover with a sheet of greaseproof paper, then press the lid firmly into place over it. Set on a rack in a steamer and steam over high heat until the duck is tender, about 1½ hours.

Serve whole to be sliced at the table.

* 'Thousand Year' eggs. If unobtainable, use salted duck eggs (see page 363) or mash two hard-boiled (hard cooked) duck or chicken egg yolks with 2 cubes of fermented beancurd.

DEEP-FRIED DUCK WITH LAVER

1 1¾ kg (3½ lb)	duck
45 g (1½ oz)	dried laver or Japanese nori*
8 cups (2 litres)	deep-frying oil
¾ teaspoon	salt
2 teaspoons	rice wine or dry sherry
2 tablespoons	duck stock**
1 tablespoon	rendered chicken fat (chicken grease) (optional)

Seasoning A:

¾ teaspoon	salt
1 tablespoon	rice wine or dry sherry
2 tablespoons	finely chopped spring onion (scallion)
2 teaspoons	grated fresh ginger

Seasoning B/Sauce:

2 tablespoons	finely chopped spring onion (scallion)
2 teaspoons	finely chopped fresh ginger
1 — 2 tablespoons	finely chopped fresh red chilli peppers
2 tablespoons	light soy sauce
2 teaspoons	dark soy sauce
¼ cup (2 fl oz)	duck stock**
1½ teaspoons	rice wine or dry sherry
1 tablespoon	sugar
2 teaspoons	white vinegar
1½ teaspoons	cornflour (cornstarch)

Clean and dress the duck and place in a dish. Rub with the seasoning A ingredients and leave for 20 minutes, then set the dish on a rack in a steamer and add ½ cup water. Steam over high heat until the duck is tender, about 1¼ hours.

Remove the duck and wipe off the moisture, reserving the liquid for later use. Soak the laver or *nori* in cold water to soften. Heat the deep-frying oil to smoking point and deep-fry the duck until golden. Remove, drain, and place, breast up, on a serving plate.

Pour off all but 2½ tablespoons of the oil and sauté the well-drained laver for 45 seconds. Add the salt, wine, 2 tablespoons of the duck stock, and the chicken fat, if used, and sauté a further 1 minute, then arrange around the duck.

Wipe out the wok and add another 2½ tablespoons of oil. Sauté the spring onion, ginger, and chilli peppers for about 45 seconds, then add the remaining ingredients, pre-mixed. Bring to the boil and simmer until thickened, then pour over the duck.

If using broccoli or cauliflower, sauté with the same ingredients until softened.

* Use fresh broccoli or cauliflower broken into florets as a substitute.

** Reserve after steaming the duck.

'LANTERN' CHICKEN

1 1/4 kg (2 1/2 lb)	chicken
750 g (1 1/2 lb)	pork omentum (caul fat)
1 teaspoon	chilli oil
3	eggs, beaten
	cornflour (cornstarch)
8 cups (2 litres)	deep-frying oil
1 cup	canned sweet pickled garlic*
	(optional)

Seasoning:

3/4 teaspoon	salt
1/2 teaspoon	m.s.g. (optional)
1 1/2 tablespoons	rice wine or dry sherry
2 tablespoons	chopped spring onion (scallion)
1 tablespoon	chopped fresh ginger
1 1/2 teaspoons	five spice powder

Clean and dress the chicken and wipe with kitchen paper. Mix the salt, m.s.g., if used, and wine and rub over the skin, then pour the remainder into the cavity. Place the remaining seasoning ingredients inside the bird and place in a dish. Cover with plastic wrap and leave for 2 1/2 hours.

Place the chicken, breast up, in a heatproof dish and cover with a sheet of greaseproof paper. Stick the paper onto the bowl with a thick paste of flour and water, then set the dish on a rack in a steamer and steam over high heat until cooked, about 50 minutes.

Remove, drain, and cut off the leg and wing bones, leaving just the body section. Spread the caul fat on a board and wipe carefully with a wet cloth to clean. Rub the chilli oil over the chicken. Cut the caul fat into three even-sized pieces, each large enough to wrap the chicken. Wrap one piece around the chicken, then brush thickly with beaten egg and wrap another piece of fat around. Coat with more beaten egg and the final piece of fat, then coat with cornflour.

Heat the deep-frying oil to moderately hot. Place the chicken in a large strainer and lower into the hot oil to deep-fry until the surface is crisp and golden. Drain well.

Cut open the uppermost layer of crisp fat and remove. Cut into cubes and arrange on one side of a serving plate. Remove and discard the other layers of fat, unless very crisp. Cut the chicken into serving portions and arrange in the centre of the plate, then arrange the drained sweet pickled garlic on the other side.

* If sweet pickled garlic is unobtainable, substitute pickled shallots or ginger, or prepare home-made sweet pickled cucumber and carrot by marinating sliced cucumber and carrot in a mixture of white vinegar, salt, and sugar.

CRISP-SKIN FISH WITH HOT AND SOUR SAUCE

1 1 kg (2 lb)	whole fresh fish
2	egg whites, beaten
2 tablespoons	cornflour (cornstarch)
	extra cornflour (cornstarch)
8 cups (2 litres)	deep-frying oil
2	pickled red chilli peppers, shredded
2	spring onions (scallions), trimmed and shredded
5 thick slices	fresh ginger, shredded

Seasoning:

1/2 teaspoon	salt
1 tablespoon	light soy sauce
1 tablespoon	rice wine or dry sherry

Sauce:

1/3 cup	chicken stock
2 tablespoons	light soy sauce
1 teaspoon	dark soy sauce
1/4 cup (2 fl oz)	Chinese brown vinegar
1/4 cup	sugar
2 teaspoons	rice wine or dry sherry
2 1/2 teaspoons	cornflour (cornstarch)
1 1/2 teaspoons	chilli oil

Clean and scale the fish and score diagonally across each side. Mix the seasoning A ingredients together and rub over the fish. Leave for 20 minutes, turning once. Mix the cornflour and egg whites together and brush thickly over the fish. Coat lightly with extra cornflour.

Heat the deep-frying oil to fairly hot and slide in the fish. Fry for 3 minutes on one side, then turn and fry for about 4 minutes on the other side. Turn again and cook for about 2 minutes, then lift out, drain well and place on a serving plate. Keep warm.

Pour off the oil, wipe out the wok and return about 2 tablespoons of the oil, or use softened lard. Stir-fry the chilli peppers, spring onions, and ginger for 1 minute, then add the pre-mixed sauce ingredients and bring to the boil. Simmer for 2 minutes, then pour over the fish.

GOLDEN CARP WITH A PHOENIX TAIL

2 625 g (1 ¼ lb)	golden carp (sea bass or red snapper)
1 440 g (14 oz) can	asparagus spears*
45 g (1 ½ fl oz)	canned small champignons, drained
3 cups (24 fl oz)	frying oil
1 ½ tablespoons	finely chopped spring onion
2 teaspoons	finely chopped fresh ginger

Seasoning A:

1 tablespoon	ginger wine (see page 387)
1 ½ teaspoons	salt
1 tablespoon	cornflour (cornstarch)

Seasoning B/Sauce:

1 ¾ cups (14 fl oz)	chicken stock
1 ½ tablespoons	evaporated milk (optional)
1 tablespoon	light soy sauce
2 teaspoons	rice wine or dry sherry
¾ teaspoon	salt
¼ teaspoon	white pepper

Clean and scale the fish and score in a criss-cross pattern across each side. Place in a dish with the seasoning A ingredients and leave for 25 minutes, turning occasionally. Drain the asparagus and cut each spear in halves lengthwise. Return to the canning liquid. Cut the mushrooms in halves horizontally.

Heat the frying oil in a wok to fairly hot and fry the fish on both sides until lightly coloured. Remove and drain well. Pour off all but 3 tablespoons of the oil and add the spring onion and ginger. Sauté briefly, then return the fish, placing them head to tail. Add the seasoning B ingredients, then arrange the asparagus on one side of the fish and the mushrooms on the other side.

Cover and simmer for about 20 minutes until the fish are tender, then carefully slide the fish onto a serving plate, keeping the two heads at opposite ends of the plate. Arrange half of the asparagus over each fish tail in an elaborate phoenix-tail shape and decorate with the sliced mushrooms. Bring the sauce to the boil, check the seasoning and thicken with a paste of cornflour and cold water. Pour over the fish and serve.
* Choose the dark green type.

WHOLE STUFFED FISH DEEP-FRIED IN A CRISP PORK FAT COATING

1 750 g (1 ½ lb)	whole fish (sea bass, fresh trout, snapper)
90 g (3 oz)	fatty pork, coarsely minced (ground)
60 g (2 oz)	Szechuan (Sichuan) preserved vegetables, soaked
8 cups (2 litres)	deep-frying oil
625 g (1 ¼ lb)	pork omentum (caul fat)
3	egg whites, well beaten
¼ cup	cornflour (cornstarch)
	Chinese pepper-salt
	chilli oil

Seasoning A:

1 teaspoon	salt
½ teaspoon	m.s.g. (optional)
1 tablespoon	rice wine or dry sherry

Seasoning B:

2 tablespoons	finely chopped spring onion (scallion)
1 ½ teaspoons	finely chopped fresh ginger
1 tablespoon	rice wine or dry sherry
1 tablespoon	light soy sauce

Scale the fish, then remove the backbone and entrails by cutting down through the back. Score in a criss-cross pattern across each side, cutting just through the skin. Rub with the seasoning A ingredients and leave for 15 minutes.

Mix the pork with the seasoning B ingredients and stir-fry in 2 tablespoons of the deep-frying oil until the pork changes colour. Drain the preserved vegetable and squeeze out as much water as possible. Cut into fine dice and add to the pork, frying briefly. Remove and spread on a plate to cool.

Wipe the pork net with a wet cloth and cut into two pieces, each large enough to completely wrap the fish. Stuff the pork and vegetable mixture into the fish. Make a paste with the egg whites and cornflour and brush thickly over the fish. Wrap in one piece of the pork net, then brush the whole wrapped fish from one end to the other with the remaining egg batter.

Wrap with the other piece of pork net and coat thickly with cornflour. Heat the deep-frying oil to smoking point, then lower the heat slightly. Slide the fish in carefully and deep-fry, completely immersed, until the coating has turned crisp and golden and the fish is cooked through, about 7 minutes. Decrease the heat if the surface colours too quickly.

Remove the fish and carefully remove the outer layer. Cut into diamond-shaped pieces and arrange around the edge of a serving plate. Remove the second layer of net and discard, then scrape the skin off the fish and place the whole fish in the centre of the plate. Garnish and serve with dips of Chinese pepper-salt and chilli oil (see pages 384 and 385).

196

'Pearl' Balls (recipe page 216).

STEAMED FRESH FISH WITH SZECHUAN (SICHUAN) PICKLED VEGETABLES AND 'WOOD EARS'

1 825 g (1¾ lb)	whole fresh fish (snapper, sea bass, etc.)
30 g (1 oz)	fat pork
20 g (¾ oz)	Szechuan (Sichuan) preserved vegetables, soaked
10 g (⅓ oz)	dried 'wood ear' fungus, soaked for 25 minutes
2	spring onions (scallions), trimmed and shredded
4 slices	fresh ginger, shredded
1	fresh red chilli pepper, shredded
2 cloves	garlic, cut into slivers
2 tablespoons	frying oil
1 teaspoon	sesame oil
	white pepper

Seasoning:

1 teaspoon	salt
½ teaspoon	m.s.g. (optional)
¼ teaspoon	white pepper
1 tablespoon	light soy sauce
1 tablespoon	rice wine or dry sherry
1 tablespoon	vegetable oil
1 teaspoon	sesame oil
½ teaspoon	cornflour (cornstarch)

Wash the fish and scale. Make several diagonal scores across each side. Place on a large oval plate. Cut the pork, drained vegetables and 'wood ears' into fine shreds and arrange with the spring onions, ginger, chilli peppers, and garlic over the fish. Pour on the pre-mixed seasoning ingredients and set the plate on a rack in a steamer.

Steam over high heat for 17 — 20 minutes, then test by inserting a fork into the thickest part of the meat. It should easily lift away from the bones. Remove from the heat and strain the pan juices into a wok. Bring to the boil and adjust the seasoning to taste.

In a separate pan, heat the frying oil and sesame oil together to smoking point. Pour over the fish, then pour on the sauce and season generously with white pepper. Serve at once.

WHOLE FISH WITH GARLIC IN HOT SAUCE

1 1 kg (2 lb)	reef fish (sea bass, snapper, perch)
¾ teaspoon	salt
1 tablespoon	rice wine or dry sherry
2 cups (16 fl oz)	frying oil
2 whole heads	fresh garlic, peeled
1½ tablespoons	hot bean paste
2	spring onions (scallions), trimmed and sliced
2 teaspoons	finely chopped fresh ginger
½ teaspoon	m.s.g. (optional)

Seasoning/Sauce:

1¾ cups (14 fl oz)	chicken or fish stock
2 tablespoons	light soy sauce
2 teaspoons	Chinese brown vinegar
2 teaspoons	sugar
2 teaspoons	rice wine or dry sherry

Clean and scale the fish and score diagonally across both sides, cutting almost to the bone. Rub with the salt and wine and set aside.

Heat the oil to moderate and fry the garlic until softened, about 2 minutes. Remove and set aside. Add the fish to the oil and fry on both sides until golden, then carefully lift out. Pour off all but 2 tablespoons of the oil and fry the bean paste briefly, then add the spring onions and ginger and fry for a few seconds.

Pour in the pre-mixed seasoning/sauce ingredients and return the fish. Bring to the boil, add the garlic, cover the pan and simmer until the fish is tender and the sauce well reduced, about 25 minutes.

Thicken the sauce, if necessary, with a thin solution of cornflour (cornstarch) and cold water. Stir in the m.s.g., if used, and serve.

HERRING IN BLACK BEAN SAUCE

1 1 kg (2 lb)	Hilsa herring (sea bass or perch)
1	small red capsicum (bell pepper)
1	small green capsicum (bell pepper)
1½ tablespoons	fermented black beans
6 cups (1½ litres)	deep-frying oil
3	spring onions (scallions), trimmed and diced
3 slices	fresh ginger, chopped
1 teaspoon	Chinese brown vinegar

Seasoning A:

1	egg white, beaten
¾ teaspoon	salt
1 tablespoon	light soy sauce
1 tablespoon	rice wine or dry sherry
2 tablespoons	cornflour (cornstarch)

Seasoning B/Sauce:

1¼ cups (10 fl oz)	fish stock or water
2 tablespoons	light soy sauce
2 teaspoons	dark soy sauce
2 teaspoons	rice wine or dry sherry
2¼ teaspoons	sugar

Clean and scale the fish and place in a dish with the seasoning A ingredients. Leave for 20 minutes, turning once. Cut the peppers in halves and trim away the stems, seed cores, and inner white ribs and cut into narrow shreds. Wash the black beans, dry and chop finely.

Heat the deep-frying oil to smoking point, then reduce the heat slightly. Slide in the fish to fry for about 2 minutes on each side. Lift out and set aside. Pour off all but 2 tablespoons of the oil and add the peppers, black beans, spring onions, and ginger. Stir-fry together for 1½ minutes, then add the seasoning B/sauce ingredients and bring to the boil. Return the fish, cover and simmer for about 20 minutes until the fish is tender and the sauce reduced.

Transfer the fish to a serving plate with the shredded pepper on top. Bring the sauce to the boil and thicken with a thin solution of cornflour and cold water. Check the seasonings and add the vinegar. Pour over the fish and serve.

POACHED FISH IN EGG FLOWER SAUCE

1 750 g (1½ lb)	fresh-water fish
2 tablespoons	rice wine or dry sherry
2	spring onions (scallions), trimmed and halved
3 slices	fresh ginger, shredded
2/3 teaspoon	salt
¼ teaspoon	m.s.g. (optional)
1 tablespoon	frying oil
3	whole eggs, well beaten

Clean and scale the fish and place in a large oval-shaped fish kettle. Add the remaining ingredients, except the eggs, and cover with warm water. Allow the water to come almost to the boil, then reduce the heat to low and gently poach until the fish is tender, about 15 minutes.

Lift out the fish, using two large spatulas, and place in a serving dish. Bring the stock to a rapid boil and discard the onion and ginger. Remove from the heat and slowly drizzle in the beaten egg, then leave to set without stirring. Check the seasoning and pour over the fish.

If preferred, thicken the sauce slightly with a thin solution of cornflour (cornstarch) and cold water. Add finely chopped fresh coriander or spring onion for extra flavour and colour.

SZECHUAN (SICHUAN) SMOKED FISH

1 750 g (1½ lb)	fresh fish (perch, snapper, sea bass)
6 cups (1½ litres)	deep-frying oil
1½ cups	wood chips
1 cup	chopped dry straw (or use black tea leaves)
	sesame oil

Seasoning A:

2 tablespoons	finely chopped spring onion (scallion)
1 tablespoon	finely chopped fresh ginger
1 tablespoon	rice wine or dry sherry
1¼ teaspoons	salt

Seasoning B:

2 tablespoons	frying oil
1½ tablespoons	finely chopped spring onion (scallion)
2 teaspoons	finely chopped fresh ginger
1 — 2	fresh red chilli peppers, chopped
¼ cup (2 fl oz)	light soy sauce
1 tablespoon	Chinese brown vinegar
2 teaspoons	rice wine or dry sherry
1 tablespoon	sugar
¼ teaspoon	m.s.g. (optional)
1½ cups (12 fl oz)	chicken stock

Clean the fish and remove the gills and fins. Score in a criss-cross pattern over both sides. Place in a dish with the seasoning A ingredients and leave for 20 minutes, turning occasionally. Heat the deep-frying oil to fairly hot and deep-fry the fish until golden, about 2 minutes. Remove and drain well.

Heat the frying oil and stir-fry the spring onion, ginger, and chilli peppers briefly, then add the remaining seasoning B ingredients and bring to the boil. Add the fish and simmer on low heat until the fish is tender, about 15 minutes, then carefully lift out the fish and place on a wire rack. Retain the sauce.

Heat the smoking ingredients (wood chips and straw or tea) in a large old iron wok or saucepan until they begin to smoke. Place the fish on the rack in the wok or pan and cover. Smoke for about 6 minutes on one side, then carefully turn and smoke the other side for 4 — 5 minutes.

Return the fish to the sauce and simmer briefly. Add sesame oil to taste and transfer to a serving plate with the sauce. Serve hot.

SLICED FISH AND CELERY IN HOT AND SOUR SAUCE

250 g (8 oz)	white fish fillets
1 stalk	young celery
3	egg whites, well beaten
	cornflour (cornstarch)
4 cups (1 litre)	deep-frying oil
1 tablespoon	softened lard (optional)
1	spring onion (scallion), trimmed and shredded
3 thick slices	fresh ginger, shredded
1 — 2	pickled red chilli peppers, shredded
	sesame oil (optional)

Seasoning A:

½ teaspoon	salt
½ teaspoon	m.s.g. (optional)
2 teaspoons	rice wine or dry sherry

Seasoning B/Sauce:

2/3 cup	fish or chicken stock
¾ teaspoon	salt
½ teaspoon	m.s.g. (optional)
2 teaspoons	sugar
1 tablespoon	Chinese brown vinegar
1½ teaspoons	cornflour (cornstarch)

Skin the fillets and cut into thin slices, then rub with the seasoning A ingredients and leave for 15 minutes. Cut the celery into matchstick pieces. Coat the fish first in beaten egg white, then thickly with cornflour, shaking off the excess.

Heat the deep-frying oil to fairly hot and deep-fry the fish slices, about 6 at a time, until crisp and lightly coloured, about 1½ minutes. Remove and drain well.

Pour off the oil and add the lard, or retain 2 tablespoons of the oil. Stir-fry the celery and carrot until softened on moderate heat, then add the spring onions, ginger and chilli and stir-fry briefly. Pour in the pre-mixed seasoning B/sauce ingredients and bring to the boil. Reduce the heat slightly and return the fish slices. Simmer until the sauce thickens, then stir in a dash of sesame oil and serve.

Shredded Beef with Bamboo Shoots (recipe page 219).

SLICED FISH BRAISED IN SPICY SAUCE

375 g (12 oz)	meaty white fish fillets
3 cups (24 fl oz)	deep-frying oil
1½	spring onions (scallions), trimmed and diced
3 thick slices	fresh ginger, shredded
2	pickled red chilli peppers, shredded
¾ teaspoon	crushed garlic
2 tablespoons	soy bean paste
2 teaspoons	Chinese brown vinegar

Seasoning A:

½ teaspoon	salt
½ teaspoon	sugar
1 tablespoon	rice wine or dry sherry

Seasoning B/Sauce:

1½ cups (10 fl oz)	fish stock or water
2 tablespoons	light soysauce
2¼ teaspoons	sugar
1 tablespoon	rice wine or dry sherry

Cut the fish into thick slices across the fillets, cutting at a slight angle. Place in a dish with the seasoning A ingredients and leave for 15 minutes, turning occasionally.

Heat the deep-frying oil to moderately hot and fry the fish for about 20 seconds, then remove and drain well. Pour off all but 2½ tablespoons of the oil and stir-fry the spring onions, ginger, chillies, and garlic for 1 minute, then add the soybean paste and stir-fry a further 30 seconds. Add the pre-mixed seasoning B/sauce ingredients and simmer briefly, return the fish and cover the pan. Simmer on moderate to low heat until the fish is completely tender and the sauce well reduced. Stir in the vinegar and thicken the sauce with a thin solution of cornflour (cornstarch) and cold water. Transfer to a serving plate.

TWO-TONED STEAMED FISH CAKE

250 g (8 oz)	white fish fillets
75 g (2½ oz)	pork fat
90 g (3 oz)	young spinach leaves (collard greens)
⅓ cup	boiling chicken stock or water
¼ cup (2 fl oz)	onion and ginger infusion (see page 386)
4	egg whites, well beaten
3 tablespoons	cornflour (cornstarch)

Seasoning A:

¾ teaspoon	salt
½ teaspoon	m.s.g. (optional)
¼ teaspoon	ground black pepper
2 teaspoons	rice wine or dry sherry

Seasoning B:

½ cup (4 fl oz)	chicken stock
½ teaspoon	salt
¼ teaspoon	ground black pepper
1 teaspoon	rice wine or dry sherry
2 tablespoons	rendered chicken fat (chicken grease) (optional)
1 teaspoon	cornflour (cornstarch)

Pulverise the fish and pork fat using two cleavers (see page 396) or in a food processor with the chopping blade. Mix with the seasoning A ingredients. Blend the spinach leaves and hot stock or water until well puréed, then transfer to a dish lined with a piece of clean muslin and squeeze out as much green liquid as possible.

Divide the fish paste into two equal parts and add the spinach liquid to one and the onion and ginger infusion to the other. Add half of the beaten egg whites and cornflour to each portion and stir in one direction only until both mixtures are smooth and thick.

Grease a dish and pour in the white mixture. Place on a rack in a steamer and steam for 6 minutes, then carefully wipe the moisture from the top and pour on the green-coloured paste. Return to the steamer and steam until the fish cake is firm.

Invert onto a serving plate. Bring the seasoning B ingredients to the boil in a wok, adding 2 tablespoons of softened lard or oil if the chicken fat is not being used. Add the squeezed spinach and simmer in the sauce until thickened. Pour over the cake and serve at once.

FISH HEADS AND BEANCURD SIMMERED IN A POT

750 g (1½ lb)	fresh fish heads*
⅓ cup	frying oil
1 tablespoon	softened lard (optional)
2 tablespoons	finely chopped spring onion (scallion)
1½ teaspoons	finely chopped fresh ginger
1 tablespoon	rice wine or dry sherry
6	dried black mushrooms, soaked for 25 minutes
30 g (1 oz)	dried shrimps, soaked for 1 hour (optional)
60 g (2 oz)	canned bamboo shoots, drained
3 squares	soft beancurd
¾ teaspoon	m.s.g. (optional)
4	garlic chives, shredded

Seasoning/Sauce:

5 cups (1¼ litres)	fish stock
1¼ teaspoons	salt
¼ teaspoon	white pepper
1 tablespoon	rice wine or dry sherry

Wash the fish heads and cut in halves. Heat the oil and fry the heads until lightly coloured, then transfer to a casserole. Pour off the oil and add the lard, if used, or retain 1½ tablespoons of the oil. Stir-fry the spring onion and ginger for 30 seconds, then sizzle in the rice wine and stir in. Add to the casserole.

Drain the mushrooms and squeeze out the water, remove the stems and cut the caps into dice. Drain the shrimps, if used. Cube the bamboo shoots. Stir-fry for 1 minute, then add to the casserole. Pour in the seasoning/sauce ingredients and bring to the boil. Reduce heat to low and simmer for 35 minutes.

Soak the beancurd in cold water after cutting into small cubes. When the fish heads are done, remove the smaller bones and add the beancurd. Simmer for 3 minutes, add the m.s.g., if used, and garlic chives and simmer briefly, then serve in the casserole.

* Choose large meaty heads of oily fish such as reef fish, mullet, or herring.

SLICED PRAWNS IN SOUR SAUCE

6	large raw prawns (shrimps), in the shell (about 500 g / 1 lb) cornflour (cornstarch)
15 g (½ oz)	dried 'snow' fungus, soaked for 25 minutes
45 g (1½ oz)	fresh or frozen green peas, parboiled
1	small carrot, thinly sliced and parboiled
4 cups (1 litre)	deep-frying oil
⅓ teaspoon	sesame oil

Seasoning A:

2	egg whites, well beaten
½ teaspoon	salt
1 teaspoon	ginger wine
1 tablespoon	cornflour (cornstarch)

Seasoning B/Sauce:

⅓ cup	chicken stock
⅓ cup	sugar
¼ cup (2 fl oz)	Chinese brown vinegar
½ teaspoon	salt
½ teaspoon	m.s.g. (optional)
1 teaspoon	cornflour (cornstarch)

Shell the prawns leaving the tail sections intact. Slit in halves down the centre back and remove the dark vein. Cut the prawn halves crosswise to give 24 pieces. Place in a dish with the seasoning A ingredients, mix well and leave for 10 minutes, then coat lightly with cornflour. Squeeze the water from the fungus and trim off the hard root sections, then cut into small squares. Prepare the peas and carrot and set aside.

Heat the frying oil to moderate and deep-fry the prawns for 45 seconds, then remove and drain well. Leave to cool for 10 minutes, then reheat the oil and deep-fry the prawns for a second time until the surface is crisp and golden. Drain and transfer to a plate. Keep warm.

Pour off all but 2½ tablespoons of the oil and stir-fry the fungus, peas, and carrot for 45 seconds, then add the pre-mixed seasoning B/sauce ingredients and simmer until thickened. Return the prawns and turn carefully in the sauce until thoroughly glazed, then transfer to a warmed serving plate and pour on the sauce. In another pan, heat 1 tablespoon of frying oil to smoking point and add the sesame oil. Pour over the dish and serve at once.

SZECHUAN (SICHUAN) PRAWNS IN CHILLI OIL SAUCE

500 g (1 lb)	medium-sized raw peeled prawns (shrimps)
4 cups (1 litre)	deep-frying oil
2 tablespoons	chopped leeks
1 tablespoon	finely chopped ginger
1 teaspoon	sesame oil
1 tablespoon	chilli oil

Seasoning A:

1	egg white, beaten
1 teaspoon	salt
¼ teaspoon	m.s.g. (optional)
1½ teaspoons	ginger wine
1½ tablespoons	cornflour (cornstarch)

Seasoning B/Sauce:

2 tablespoons	tomato sauce (ketchup)
½ teaspoon	salt
1 teaspoon	sugar
¼ cup (2 fl oz)	chicken stock
1 teaspoon	cornflour (cornstarch)

Wash the prawns and cut in halves lengthwise. Place in a dish with the seasoning A ingredients, mix well and leave for 20 minutes. Heat the deep-frying oil to moderately hot and deep-fry the prawns in a basket for about 45 seconds. Remove and drain well.

Pour off all but 2 tablespoons of the oil and fry the leeks and ginger for 30 seconds. Add the sesame and chilli oil and stir-fry for 1 — 2 seconds, then add the pre-mixed seasoning B/sauce ingredients and bring to the boil. Return the prawns and stir in the sauce until warmed through.

Transfer to a serving plate and garnish with chopped fresh coriander or spring onions.

SHRIMP ROLLS SERVED ON MARINATED CARROT AND RADISH

Serve as an appetiser or main dish.

Makes 12.

2	medium carrots, peeled
½	giant white (icicle) radish, peeled
185 g (6 oz)	raw peeled shrimps
90 g (3 oz)	pork fat
6	canned water chestnuts, drained
1	large round beancurd skin*
1	egg white, beaten
1 tablespoon	cornflour (cornstarch)
2 teaspoons	flour
5 cups (1¼ litres)	deep-frying oil

Seasoning A:

⅓ cup	white vinegar
¼ cup (2 fl oz)	cold water
2½ teaspoons	salt
1 tablespoon	sugar
¼ cup (2 fl oz)	sesame oil

Seasoning B:

¼ teaspoon	salt
½ teaspoon	m.s.g. (optional)
¼ teaspoon	white pepper
1 teaspoon	sugar
1 teaspoon	light soy sauce
1 teaspoon	finely chopped spring onion (scallion)
¼ teaspoon	grated fresh ginger
1	egg white, beaten
2 teaspoons	cornflour (cornstarch)

Cut the vegetables into short sticks or thin slices and place in a dish with the seasoning A ingredients. Leave for at least 1 hour.

Pulverise the shrimps and pork fat in a food processor with the chopping blade, or use two cleavers (see page 396). Finely chop the water chestnuts and stir into the pork, adding the seasoning B ingredients. Mix thoroughly, then chill.

Wipe the beancurd skin with a damp cloth and cut into 12 squares of even size. Mix the egg white, cornflour, and flour into a paste. Brush over the beancurd skins, reserving a little. Place a portion of the filling in one corner of each beancurd wrapper and fold over the closest corner, then fold in the two sides, sticking down with the egg paste, and roll up. Use more egg paste to stick down the final flaps.

Heat the deep-frying oil to moderate and deep-fry the shrimp rolls, about 4 at a time, until crisp and cooked through, 3 — 4 minutes. Drain well. Drain the vegetables thoroughly and arrange on a serving plate. Place the shrimp rolls on top. Serve with Chinese pepper-salt (see page 384) and red or brown Chinese vinegar as dips.
* Or use dried beancurd skin pieces soaked until soft.

Szechuan Beef Stew (recipe page 220).

SHRIMPS IN HOT SAUCE ON CRISP RICE CAKES

375 g (12 oz)	raw peeled shrimps
1 stalk	celery
3 cups (24 fl oz)	chicken stock
2 teaspoons	salt
2 teaspoons	sesame oil
10 pieces	rice cakes (see page 386)
4 cups (1 litre)	deep-frying oil

Seasoning A:

½ teaspoon	salt
½ teaspoon	sugar
1½ teaspoons	cornflour (cornstarch)
2 teaspoons	rice wine or dry sherry

Seasoning B:

1 tablespoon	finely chopped fresh ginger
1 teaspoon	finely chopped garlic
⅓ cup	tomato sauce (ketchup)
1 tablespoon	chilli oil
1 tablespoon	light soy sauce
1 tablespoon	Chinese brown vinegar
1 tablespoon	sugar
3 tablespoons	cornflour (cornstarch)
¼ cup (2 fl oz)	cold water

Wash and devein the shrimps and place in a dish with the seasoning A ingredients. Cut the celery into fine dice and set aside. Use a little of the deep-frying oil to stir-fry the shrimps until pink. Remove and set aside. Add the celery and stir-fry until softened, about 1½ minutes. Remove and set aside.

Stir-fry the ginger and garlic, then add the stock and remaining seasoning B ingredients. Bring to the boil and simmer until thickened. Add the salt and sesame oil and the shrimps and celery. Simmer briefly.

Heat the deep-frying oil to smoking point and deep-fry the rice cakes in a frying basket until golden and crisp. Drain and place in a large, well-warmed serving dish. Heat the shrimp sauce to boiling and pour over the rice cakes. Serve at once.

SEA CUCUMBER WITH VEGETABLES AND CRISP PRETZELS

700 g (1⅓ lb)	prepared sea cucumbers (about 4 pieces) (see page 392)
2	spring onions (scallions), trimmed and sliced
6 slices	fresh ginger
45 g (1½ oz)	canned bamboo shoots, drained and sliced
45 g (1½ oz)	canned straw mushrooms or champignons, drained and sliced
60 g (2 oz)	fresh bok choy, cut into 2.5 cm (1 in) pieces
⅓ cup	frying oil
12	wonton wrappers (see page 376)
3 cups (24 fl oz)	deep-frying oil

Seasoning/Sauce:

2 tablespoons	light soy sauce
2 teaspoons	rice wine or dry sherry
¼ teaspoon	m.s.g. (optional)
½ teaspoon	sugar
½ teaspoon	sesame oil
¾ cup (6 fl oz)	chicken stock
1 tablespoon	cornflour (cornstarch)

Soak the prepared sea cucumbers in cold water until needed. Sauté the spring onions, ginger, bamboo shoots, mushrooms, and vegetables in the frying oil for 2 minutes. Drain the sea cucumber and cut into bite-sized pieces. Add to the oil and stir-fry for 1 minute. Add the seasoning/sauce ingredients and bring to the boil.

Simmer until the sauce thickens and the ingredients are cooked. In the meantime, heat the deep-frying oil to smoking point. Cut the wonton wrappers into strips and deep-fry in a frying basket until crisp and golden. Remove and drain well.

Place the fried wonton strips in a serving dish and pour on the sea cucumber mixture. Serve at once.

BRAISED FRESH-WATER EELS

1 625 g (1¼ lb)	*fresh-water eel*
2	*young leeks, trimmed and shredded*
4 cloves	*garlic, slivered*
5 slices	*fresh ginger, shredded*
⅓ cup	*frying oil*
1 tablespoon	*rice wine or dry sherry*
2 teaspoons	*soybean paste*
1½ tablespoons	*cornflour (cornstarch)*
2 tablespoons	*cold water*
	sesame oil
	Chinese brown vinegar

Seasoning:

¼ cup (2 fl oz)	*light soy sauce*
1 tablespoon	*sugar*
¼ teaspoon	*ground black pepper*

Clean and gut the eel and remove the head. Drop into a large pot of boiling water and blanch for 1 minute, then remove and rub with salt to remove the slimy residue on the skin. Rinse thoroughly in cold water. Cut into 4 cm (1 2/3 in) pieces.

Stir-fry the leeks, garlic, and ginger in the frying oil for 30 seconds. Push to one side of the pan and add the eel. Stir-fry on high heat for about 2 minutes, then sizzle the wine onto the sides of the pan and add the soybean paste. Stir in thoroughly.

Add the pre-mixed seasoning ingredients and water to cover and simmer, stirring occasionally, until the eel is tender, about 10 minutes. Add the cornflour mixed with cold water and cook until the sauce thickens. Season with a dash of sesame oil and brown vinegar and serve.

STIR-FRIED SEA SCALLOPS WITH PORK KIDNEYS

280 g (9 oz)	*fresh or frozen sea scallops with coral removed*
250 g (8 oz)	*pork kidneys*
¼ cup (2 fl oz)	*softened lard or frying oil*
1½ tablespoons	*finely chopped spring onion (scallion)*
1½ teaspoon	*finely chopped fresh ginger*
45 g (1½ oz)	*canned champignons, drained*
2 teaspoons	*rice wine or dry sherry*

Seasoning A:

¼ teaspoon	*salt*
¼ teaspoon	*m.s.g. (optional)*
2 teaspoons	*ginger wine*

Seasoning B:

⅓ teaspoon	*salt*
½ teaspoon	*m.s.g. (optional)*
1 teaspoon	*rice wine or dry sherry*
1 teaspoon	*cornflour (cornstarch)*

Seasoning C/Sauce:

⅓ cup	*chicken stock*
⅓ teaspoon	*salt*
¼ teaspoon	*m.s.g. (optional)*
½ teaspoon	*sugar*
1 tablespoon	*light soy sauce*
¼ teaspoon	*sesame oil (optional)*
1 teaspoon	*cornflour (cornstarch)*

Defrost the frozen scallops, if used, and drain thoroughly. Rinse in cold water and dry on kitchen paper, then place in a dish with the seasoning A ingredients and leave for 10 minutes. Cut the kidneys in halves, horizontally and trim away the white fatty tissue. Pull off the skin and then score the outside in a close criss-cross design (see page 397), cutting about 0.5 cm (1/5 in) deep. Cut across into thin slices and place in a saucepan of boiling water to blanch for 30 seconds, then drain and transfer to a dish of cold water. Leave for 5 minutes, then drain again and add the seasoning B ingredients.

Heat the lard or oil and stir-fry the scallops until white and beginning to firm up, about 45 seconds. Remove and set aside. Add the spring onion and ginger and stir-fry for 30 seconds, then add the champignons and stir-fry for a further 30 seconds. Remove and drain well.

Add a very little more oil or lard if needed and reheat the wok to fairly hot. Stir-fry the kidney for 2 minutes until cooked, then return the scallops and stir-fry briefly. Sizzle the wine onto the sides of the pan and stir in. Add the other cooked ingredients and the pre-mixed seasoning C/sauce ingredients and simmer until the sauce thickens. Serve.

SQUID WITH GARLIC AND GINGER SAUCE

Serve as an appetiser or main dish.

625 g (1¼ lb)	fresh large squid
5 cm (2 in) piece	fresh ginger

Sauce:

2 teaspoons	finely chopped garlic
¼ cup (2 fl oz)	tomato sauce (ketchup)
2 tablespoons	Chinese brown vinegar
1½ teaspoons	sesame oil
2 teaspoons	light soy sauce
1 tablespoon	sugar
½ teaspoon	m.s.g. (optional)

Clean the squid, discarding the heads and stomachs. Peel off the skins with the fins attached. Cut open the tubular bodies and scrape the white membranes from the inside. Score across the inside in a close criss-cross pattern, cutting fairly deeply and at a slight angle.

Cut into 1.25 cm (1 in) squares and rinse in cold water. Drain well. Drop into a saucepan of lightly salted boiling water to poach for about 30 seconds, then drain well and transfer to a serving dish.

Peel and finely shred the ginger and scatter over the squid. Mix the sauce ingredients together and pour over the squid. Serve at once.

Serve hot or cold. If serving hot, prepare the squid, ginger, and sauce before poaching the squid. The sauce may be heated in a small saucepan.

SZECHUAN (SICHUAN)-STYLE SQUID

700 g (1⅓ lb)	fresh squid
90 g (3 oz)	fat pork
½ stalk	fresh celery
1	small leek
2½ tablespoons	softened lard or frying oil
1 tablespoon	hot bean paste

Seasoning/Sauce:

1 cup (8 fl oz)	chicken stock
1 tablespoon	light soy sauce
1 tablespoon	rice wine or dry sherry
¼ teaspoon	salt
¼ teaspoon	m.s.g. (optional)
¼ teaspoon	sugar
2 teaspoons	cornflour (cornstarch)

Clean the squid, discarding the heads, tentacles and stomachs. Pull off the pink skin with the fins attached. Cut the squid open and score in a close criss-cross pattern on the inside, cutting at an angle (see page 397). Cut the squid into 4 cm (1 2/3 in) pieces and blanch in boiling water for 30 seconds. Drain and cover with warm water.

Finely chop the pork, celery, and leeks and stir-fry in the lard or oil for 1½ minutes. Add the bean paste and stir-fry for 30 seconds, then add the pre-mixed seasoning/sauce ingredients and bring to the boil. Simmer for 3 minutes, then add the drained squid and heat through briefly. Transfer to a warmed serving plate.

Braised Spiced Lamb Shanks (recipe page 220).

SPICED JELLIED PORK

Serve as an appetiser or main dish.

1½ kg (3 lb)	pork leg (fresh ham), with a large section of rind (skin)
1 tablespoon	Chinese brown peppercorns
¼ cup	salt
2 teaspoons	saltpetre (optional)
2	spring onions (scallions), trimmed and halved
4 thin slices	fresh ginger
2	spice bags

Wash the pork and cut into large pieces, discarding the bone. Dry-fry the peppercorns in a wok until fragrant and beginning to smoke, then grind to a fine powder and return to the wok with the salt. Fry on low heat until well mixed and warmed through, but take care that the salt does not begin to colour.

Leave to cool, then mix with the saltpetre, if used, and rub thoroughly over the pork. Place in a dish and cover tightly with plastic wrap. Refrigerate for 3 days, turning daily. The meat will acquire a rosy pink colour and slight saltiness. Blanch for 3 minutes in hot water and drain.

Place in a saucepan with the spring onions, ginger, and spice bags and add water to cover. Simmer for about 2½ hours, topping up the level of the water to keep the pork completely under water. Drain well and discard the onion, ginger, and spice bags.

Cut the pork into small cubes after removing the skin. Place the pork in a greased dish and set aside. Return the skin to the liquid and boil until the liquid is well reduced. Drain the skin and cut into small pieces. Mix with the pork. Pour the liquid over the meat and weight with a heavy object to compress. Refrigerate for 24 hours. Cut the jellied pork into bite-sized pieces and serve with a vinegar and garlic dip (see page 384) or with light soy sauce and chilli oil.

HONEY-GLAZED HAM

750 g (1½ lb)	Chinese or cured (Smithfield) ham
2	spring onions (scallions), trimmed and sliced
8 slices	fresh ginger or 125 g (4 oz) Chinese red dates
1 cup	rock candy (sugar), crushed to a powder
¼ cup (2 fl oz)	sweet rice wine or Japanese mirin*
2 tablespoons	softened lard
1 teaspoon	guei hwa sauce (optional)
1½ teaspoons	cornflour (cornstarch)

Cut off the ham skin and wash the ham well. Place in a saucepan and cover with cold water. Add the spring onions. Bring to the boil and then reduce heat and simmer for about 35 minutes. Remove and drain well. Cut the ham into thin slices, then into pieces about 7.25 cm (2½ in) wide.

Boil the red dates, if used, in 2 cups of water for 10 minutes, then drain. Arrange the ham slices, overlapping, in a dish. Place the ginger or dates on top and add one-third of the sugar. Place in a dish and steam for about 20 minutes, then add the remaining sugar and wine and steam for a further 1½ hours. Strain the liquid into a wok and bring to the boil. Top up with water to make at least 1 cupful and thicken with the cornflour mixed with a little cold water. Stir in the guei hwa, if used, and simmer briefly. Pour over the ham.

Honey-glazed ham is traditionally served with large-sized steamed buns (see Steamed Flower-Shaped Buns, page 372). The buns are opened at the fold and the sweet ham inserted, sandwich fashion, with the sauce being mopped up with the remains of the bread. Thinly sliced white bread can be substituted.
* Or use sweet or cream sherry.

STEAMED YUNNAN HAM

1½ kg (3 lb)	middle-cut Yunnan or cured (Smithfield) ham
3	spring onions (scallions), trimmed and sliced
5 slices	fresh ginger
¼ cup (2 fl oz)	rice wine or dry sherry
2 cups (16 fl oz)	chicken stock
3 tablespoons	finely chopped spring onion (scallion)
2 tablespoons	finely chopped fresh ginger
2 teaspoons	Chinese brown peppercorns
500 g (1 lb)	Chinese (celery) cabbage

Seasoning:

1 cup (8 fl oz)	chicken stock
½ teaspoon	salt
1 teaspoon	sugar
2 teaspoons	rice wine or dry sherry

Hold the piece of ham over a flame until bubbles appear on the skin, then soak the whole ham in hot water until soft and scrape off the blackened parts. Scrub with a soft brush and rinse well. Place the ham in a pot and add the sliced onions and ginger and the wine. Add water to cover and steam or gently simmer for about 1½ hours until the ham is soft, but not completely cooked. Drain and discard the onions and ginger.

Bone and trim the ham and score deeply on the upper side in a criss-cross pattern. Place in a large dish and add the chicken stock, chopped onion, ginger, and the peppercorns. Place on a rack in a steamer and steam over rapidly boiling water until cooked, about 1½ hours.

Trim and wash the cabbage and cut into 5 cm (2 in) pieces. Blanch in boiling water for 2 minutes, then drain and add the seasoning ingredients. Simmer until tender, then drain.

Place the ham, scored side upwards, on a serving plate and surround with the vegetables. Retain ¾ cup (6 fl oz) the stock in which the ham was steamed and strain into a wok. Adjust the seasoning and thicken with a thin solution of cornflour (cornstarch) and cold water. Pour over the ham and serve.

HOT AND SPICY SLICED PORK WITH 'WOOD EAR' FUNGUS

250 g (8 oz)	pork fillet (tenderloin)
45 g (1½ oz)	dried 'wood ear' brown fungus, soaked for 25 minutes
45 g (1½ oz)	young spinach leaves (optional)
2	spring onions (scallions), trimmed and diced
3 thick slices	fresh ginger, diced
1¼ teaspoons	finely chopped garlic
1 — 3	fresh or pickled red chilli peppers, chopped
2 tablespoons	softened lard
2 tablespoons	frying oil

Seasoning A:

¼ teaspoon	salt
1 tablespoon	light soy sauce
1 tablespoon	rice wine or dry sherry
2 teaspoons	cornflour (cornstarch)
1 tablespoon	vegetable oil

Seasoning B/Sauce:

½ cup (4 fl oz)	chicken stock
2 tablespoons	light soy sauce
2 teaspoons	Chinese brown vinegar (or to taste)
1 teaspoon	rice wine or dry sherry
½ teaspoon	m.s.g. (optional)
1¼ teaspoons	sugar
1 teaspoon	cornflour (cornstarch)

Slice the pork across the grain into very thin slices and cut into bite-sized pieces. Place in a dish with the seasoning A ingredients, mix well and leave for 20 minutes.

Drain the 'wood ears' and chop finely. Wash and dry the spinach leaves, if used, and chop coarsely. Heat the wok and add the lard and frying oil. Stir-fry the spring onion, garlic, and chilli peppers together for 1 minute, then add the 'wood ears' and spinach and stir-fry briefly. Push to one side of the pan and add the sliced pork. Fry on both sides until lightly coloured, then stir in the other ingredients and continue to stir-fry until the pork is almost cooked, about 1¼ minutes.

Pour in the pre-mixed seasoning B/sauce ingredients and simmer until the sauce has thickened. Add a dash of salt to taste and serve.

SHREDDED HOT PORK AND MUSHROOMS ON CRISP RICE CAKES

375 g (12 oz)	lean pork
6	dried black mushrooms, soaked for 25 minutes
3 slices	fresh ginger, shredded
1 teaspoon	finely chopped garlic
1	fresh red chilli pepper, chopped
45 g (1½ oz)	canned bamboo shoots, drained and diced
5 cups (1¼ litres)	deep-frying oil
10 pieces	rice cakes (see page 386)
2	spring onions (scallions), trimmed and shredded

Seasoning A:

½ teaspoon	salt
2 teaspoons	rice wine or dry sherry
1 teaspoon	cornflour (cornstarch)

Seasoning B/Sauce:

¾ cup (6 fl oz)	chicken stock
1 tablespoon	light soy sauce
2 teaspoons	hot bean paste
1 teaspoon	Chinese brown vinegar
1½ teaspoons	sugar
¼ teaspoon	m.s.g. (optional)
¼ teaspoon	ground black pepper

Cut the pork into thin slices, then into shreds, and place in a dish with the seasoning A ingredients. Mix well and leave for 10 minutes. Drain the mushrooms, squeeze out the excess water and remove the stems, then cut the caps into fine dice. Stir-fry the mushrooms, ginger, garlic, chilli peppers and bamboo shoots in ¼ cup (2 fl oz) of the deep-frying oil for 1 minute. Push to one side of the pan and add the pork. Stir-fry until it changes colour, then mix with the other fried ingredients and add the pre-mixed seasoning B/sauce ingredients. Bring to the boil, then reduce the heat to simmer for 2 — 3 minutes.

In the meantime, heat the remaining deep-frying oil to smoking point and deep-fry the rice cakes in a frying basket until crisp and golden. Drain well and transfer to a well-warmed serving dish. Arrange the shredded spring onions on top and pour on the hot pork and sauce. Serve at once.

It is essential to time the cooking of the pork and rice cakes accurately so they are both piping hot when brought together. The rice cakes will snap and pop when served.

PORK TRIPE IN HOT PEPPER SAUCE WITH PEANUTS

625 g (1¼ lb)	pork tripe
4	spring onions (scallions), trimmed
6 slices	fresh ginger
1 tablespoon	white vinegar
1 teaspoon	salt
75 g (2½ oz)	raw peanuts (groundnuts)
2 cups (16 fl oz)	frying oil

Sauce:

1 tablespoon	sesame oil
1 tablespoon	chilli oil
2 teaspoons	light soy sauce
2 teaspoons	Chinese brown vinegar
½ teaspoon	salt
½ teaspoon	m.s.g. (optional)
1 teaspoon	sugar
1 teaspoon	Chinese brown peppercorn powder

Wash the tripe well and cut into pieces about 1 cm (¾ in) square. Place in a saucepan with half the spring onions and ginger, the vinegar, and salt and add water to cover. Bring to the boil and simmer until the tripe is tender, then drain well.

Drop the peanuts into boiling water and cook briefly, then drain and when cool enough to handle, remove the skins. Dry thoroughly, then deep-fry in the oil until golden. Drain again.

Mix the sauce ingredients together. Arrange the cooked tripe in a dish and add the remaining spring onions and ginger, finely shredded. Pour on the sauce and garnish with the peanuts. Stir up lightly and serve.

Pigeon Pâté with Chinese Herbs Steamed in Soup Ramekins (recipe page 222).

'GOLD AND SILVER' PORK

500 g (1 lb)	lean pork
3	egg whites, well beaten
½ cup	cornflour (cornstarch)
2	whole eggs, well beaten
	dash of yellow
	food colouring
4 cups (1 litre)	deep-frying oil
60 g (2 oz)	canned bamboo shoots, drained and shredded
2	dried black mushrooms, soaked for 25 minutes and shredded
45 g (1½ oz)	young spinach leaves, coarsely chopped

Seasoning A:

¾ teaspoon	salt
1 tablespoon	rice wine or dry sherry
½ teaspoon	m.s.g. (optional)
2 tablespoons	finely chopped spring onion (scallion)
2 teaspoons	finely chopped fresh ginger

Seasoning B/Sauce:

¾ cup (6 fl oz)	chicken stock
⅓ teaspoon	salt
½ teaspoon	m.s.g. (optional)
½ teaspoon	rice wine or dry sherry
2 teaspoons	cornflour (cornstarch)

Cut the pork into thin slices across the grain, then into strips about 2.5 cm (1 in) wide. Place in a dish with the seasoning A ingredients, mix well and leave for 20 minutes. Mix the egg whites with half of the cornflour and the whole eggs with the remaining cornflour, adding enough food colouring to colour a bright yellow.

Heat the deep-frying oil to moderately hot and on another heat source heat a saucepan of lightly salted water until slowly simmering. Dip half the pork slices into the egg white batter and drop into the simmering water to poach until just cooked through, firm and white, then drain well. Dip the remaining pork into the yellow batter and deep-fry until crisp and golden. Drain.

Arrange the 'silver' and 'gold' pork slices at either side of an oval serving plate. Pour off the oil, retaining about 2 tablespoons, and stir-fry the bamboo shoots and mushrooms for 45 seconds, then add the spinach and stir-fry briefly. Pour in the pre-mixed seasoning B/sauce ingredients and simmer until the sauce thickens and the spinach is tender. Pour over the pork and serve at once.

PORK STEAMED WITH SALTED CABBAGE

750 g (1½ lb)	leg pork (fresh ham), boneless
1 tablespoon	dark soy sauce
8 cups (2 litres)	deep-frying oil
155 g (5 oz)	Szechuan (Sichuan) pickled cabbage, soaked
3	spring onions (scallions), trimmed and diced
3 thick slices	fresh ginger, coarsely chopped
2	pickled red chilli peppers, coarsely chopped

Seasoning:

1½ tablespoons	fermented black beans, washed and chopped
⅓ cup	light soy sauce
¼ cup (2 fl oz)	rice wine or dry sherry
1½ tablespoons	sugar

Wash the pork in boiling water, scrape the skin to remove any tiny hairs and place in a saucepan with boiling water to cover. Simmer for 2 hours, then drain and reserve ¾ cup of the liquid. Wipe the pork and rub with the dark soy sauce, then deep-fry in fairly hot oil until the skin is dark brown. Keep arms covered with a cloth when turning the pork, as the moisture trapped beneath the skin often causes small explosions in the hot oil.

Remove the pork and cut into thick slices and place in a dish. Shred the cabbage and arrange with the spring onions, ginger, and chillies over the pork. Add the seasoning ingredients evenly and pour the reserved stock down the inside of the dish without disturbing the contents.

Set on a rack in a steamer and steam over high heat for a further 1 hour or until the pork is completely tender. Invert the dish onto a serving plate after straining the liquid into a wok. Check the seasonings of the sauce, thicken slightly with a thin cornflour and cold water solution and pour over the pork.

A whole duck can also be cooked in this way, reducing the simmering time to about 1¼ hours and the steaming time to about 30 minutes.

SZECHUAN (SICHUAN) STEWED PORK

1 kg (2 lb)	pork hand (picnic shoulder), deboned*
10	spring onions (scallions), trimmed
2	star anise
1 cup (8 fl oz)	light soy sauce
½ cup (4 fl oz)	rice wine or dry sherry
2/3 cup	sugar

Cut the pork into large cubes and the skin into 4 cm (1 2/3 in) squares. Place the trimmed onions in the bottom of a casserole with the pork and skin on top. Add the remaining ingredients and water to cover. Cover the casserole and bring to the boil, then reduce heat and simmer for at least 1 hour until the pork is completely tender and the sauce well reduced and thick.

Do not remove the cover during cooking, but occasionally shake the pan to turn the contents. To serve, invert the contents of the casserole onto a serving plate and arrange the spring onions around the pork.

* The meat should have a large covering of skin (rind). If not, buy an extra piece of skin.

'TWICE-COOKED' PORK

375 g (12 oz)	'five flowered' pork (belly/fresh bacon)
1	green capsicum (bell pepper)
3	garlic chives, sliced
2 cloves	garlic, sliced
1	fresh red chilli pepper, shredded (optional)
¼ cup (2 fl oz)	frying oil

Seasoning:

1 teaspoon	sugar
2 teaspoons	hot bean paste
1 tablespoon	sweet bean paste
1 tablespoon	light soy sauce
1 teaspoon	dark soy sauce
2 teaspoons	rice wine or dry sherry
2 tablespoons	water

Wash the pork and place the whole piece in a saucepan with water to cover. Bring slowly to the boil, then simmer for 25 minutes. Drain and cut across the grain into wafer-thin slices. Cut the pepper in halves, remove the seed core, stem, and inner white ribs and cut into 2.5 cm (1 in) squares.

Heat the frying oil in a wok and stir-fry the chives, garlic, and chilli peppers for 30 seconds. Remove. Add the capsicum and stir-fry for 45 seconds, then add the pork and stir-fry on fairly high heat until the pork is crisped on the edges. Remove.

Add the seasoning ingredients to the pan, with a little more oil if needed, and stir-fry briefly, then return the fried ingredients and mix well together, stirring until thoroughly coated with the sauce.

Transfer to a serving plate and serve at once. Young leek, finely shredded, can be used in place of the garlic chives, and for extra colour use both red and green capsicum.

SHREDDED PORK WITH SWEET BEAN PASTE

440 g (14 oz)	'five flowered' pork (belly/fresh bacon) or lean pork
10	spring onions (scallions), trimmed and shredded
¼ cup (2 fl oz)	softened lard or frying oil
1 tablespoon	rice wine or dry sherry
2 tablespoons	sweet bean paste
1½ tablespoons	light soy sauce
½ teaspoon	sugar

Seasoning:

½ teaspoon	salt
¾ teaspoon	sugar
2 teaspoons	light soy sauce
2 teaspoons	rice wine or dry sherry

Cut the pork into thin slices across the grain, then into narrow shreds. Place in a dish with the seasoning ingredients, mix well and leave for 15 minutes.

Arrange the spring onions on a serving plate. Heat the lard or oil in a wok and add the shredded pork. Stir-fry on moderate heat until the pork changes colour, then sizzle the wine onto the sides of the pan and stir in. Add the sweet bean paste, soy sauce, and sugar separately, cooking each briefly.

Spoon the meat over the onions and serve at once.

'PEARL' BALLS

250 g (8 oz)	lean pork, finely minced (ground)
6	canned water chestnuts, chopped
15 g (½ oz)	dried shrimp, soaked for 1 hour and chopped (optional)
1 tablespoon	finely chopped spring onion (scallion)
1 teaspoon	finely chopped fresh ginger
1 cup	long grain raw glutinous rice, soaked for 2 hours

Seasoning:

1 tablespoon	light soy sauce
2 teaspoons	rice wine or dry sherry
¼ teaspoon	salt
¼ teaspoon	m.s.g. (optional)
½ teaspoon	sugar
¼ teaspoon	ground black pepper
1¼ tablespoons	cornflour (cornstarch)

Mix the pork and water chestnuts with the seasoning ingredients. Drain and finely chop the dried shrimps, if used, and mix into the pork with the spring onion and ginger. Knead to a smooth paste, squeezing continually through the fingers until thoroughly mixed and sticky.

Use wet hands to roll the mixture into 24 balls. Drain the rice thoroughly and spread on a plate. Roll each ball in the rice until thickly coated with rice grains. Arrange on a lightly oiled plate and set on a rack in a steamer. Leave a little space between each ball to allow the rice to expand.

Steam over rapidly boiling water for about 30 minutes until the rice is transparent and tender and the pork cooked through. Serve on the same plate with a garnish of fresh coriander and dips of light soy and chilli sauces.

CHILLI PORK SPARE-RIBS

750 g (1½ lb)	meaty pork spare ribs or 'five flowered' pork
6 cups (1½ litres)	deep-frying oil
3	spring onions (scallions), trimmed and sliced
3 thick slices	fresh ginger, chopped
1	fresh red chilli pepper, shredded (optional)
1 teaspoon	finely chopped garlic (optional)

Seasoning A:

1	egg white, beaten
1 tablespoon	finely chopped spring onion (scallion)
2 teaspoons	finely chopped fresh ginger
1 teaspoon	salt
½ teaspoon	m.s.g. (optional)
¼ teaspoon	white pepper
1 tablespoon	rice wine or dry sherry
1 tablespoon	frying oil
2 tablespoons	cornflour (cornstarch)

Seasoning B/Sauce:

2 tablespoons	hot bean paste
3½ cups (28 fl oz)	chicken stock
2 tablespoons	light soy sauce
1 tablespoon	rice wine or dry sherry
½ teaspoon	salt
1 tablespoon	sugar

Cut the ribs or pork into bite-sized chunks and place in a dish with the seasoning A ingredients. Mix well and leave for 30 minutes.

Heat the deep-frying oil to fairly hot and deep-fry the pork until golden, cooking in several lots to keep the oil hot. Drain and transfer to a casserole. Pour off all but 2 tablespoons of the oil and add the spring onions, ginger, chilli pepper, and garlic, if used. Stir-fry briefly, then add the soybean paste and stir-fry for several seconds. Add the chicken stock and remaining seasoning B/sauce ingredients and bring to the boil.

Pour over the pork and cover. Simmer until the pork is completely tender, about 1¼ hours. Transfer the pork to a serving plate with a slotted spoon and thicken the sauce, if necessary, with a thin solution of cornflour and cold water. Check the seasonings and pour over the pork.

For a more substantial dish, surround the pork with braised fresh green vegetables and serve with boiled thick egg noodles.

'Ma Pwo' Beancurd (Pork-marked Mama's Beancurd) (recipe page 227).

'DRAGON'S EYE' BONE MARROW WITH CHICKEN

625 g (1¼ lb)	fresh pork bone marrow
1½ teaspoons	white vinegar
250 g (8 oz)	boneless chicken breast
155 g (5 oz)	pork fat
2 slices	cooked ham
280 g (9 oz)	fresh mustard greens
¼ cup (2 fl oz)	frying oil

Seasoning A:

2 tablespoons	finely chopped spring onion (scallion)
1½ teaspoons	finely chopped fresh ginger
3	egg whites, well beaten
2 tablespoons	chicken stock
½ teaspoon	salt
¼ teaspoon	m.s.g. (optional)
¼ teaspoon	white pepper
2 teaspoons	rice wine or dry sherry
1 tablespoon	cornflour (cornstarch)

Seasoning B:

¾ cup (6 fl oz)	chicken stock
½ teaspoon	salt
¼ teaspoon	m.s.g. (optional)
1½ teaspoons	rice wine or dry sherry
	pinch of white pepper
1½ teaspoons	cornflour (cornstarch)

Seasoning C:

⅓ teaspoon	salt
¼ teaspoon	m.s.g. (optional)
2 teaspoons	rice wine or dry sherry
¼ teaspoon	sugar

Wash the pork bone marrow thoroughly and simmer in water to cover with the vinegar for 6 minutes. Remove, drain well and soak in cold water.

Mince (grind) the chicken and pork fat finely and mix with the seasoning A ingredients, stirring continually in one direction until the mixture is thick and smooth. Divide the pork marrow into 18 pieces and place one piece in the bottom of 12 lightly oiled wide-necked wine glasses. Stamp out 12 small discs from the ham and place on top of the marrow, then divide the chicken mixture among the glasses, using a wet finger to smooth the top of the chicken paste.

Set the glasses on a rack in a steamer and steam over rapidly boiling water until the chicken paste is firm. Simmer the remaining bone marrow with the seasoning B ingredients until tender and the sauce thickened. Sauté the mustard greens in the frying oil after cutting into bite-sized pieces. Add the seasoning C ingredients and cover. Cook until the vegetables are tender, but retaining crispness.

Invert the glasses onto a serving plate and remove the 'dragon's eyes.' Arrange the vegetables and simmered bone marrow around them and pour on the sauce from the marrow. Serve.

KIDNEYS IN SOUR AND HOT SAUCE

Serve cold as an appetiser.

250 g (8 oz)	pork kidneys
3	bean sheets, soaked to soften
¾ teaspoon	salt
2 teaspoons	sesame oil

Sauce:

2 tablespoons	finely chopped spring onion (scallion)
1½ tablespoons	finely chopped fresh ginger
¼ cup (2 fl oz)	light soy sauce
1 tablespoon	sesame oil
1 tablespoon	white vinegar
2 teaspoons	chilli oil (or to taste)
1½ tablespoons	Chinese brown peppercorns, crushed
¼ teaspoon	salt
¼ teaspoon	m.s.g. (optional)
1 teaspoon	sugar

Cut the kidneys in halves and remove the inner white fatty section and the skin. Score in a close criss-cross pattern across the outside, then cut through into thin slices. Blanch in boiling water for about 30 seconds, remove and drain well, then soak in cold water.

Drain the bean sheets and cut into shreds. Mix with the salt and sesame oil and arrange on a serving plate. Drain the kidney slices and arrange over the bean sheets. Mix the sauce ingredients together and pour over the kidneys. Serve.

SHREDDED BEEF WITH BAMBOO SHOOTS

250 g (8 oz)	beef fillet (tenderloin)
45 g (1½ oz)	canned bamboo shoots, drained
1	medium carrot, peeled*
3	garlic chives
1 — 2	fresh red chilli peppers
3 slices	fresh ginger
1½ cups (12 fl oz)	deep-frying oil
½ teaspoon	ground black pepper
¾ teaspoon	sesame oil

Seasoning A:

½ teaspoon	salt
1 tablespoon	light soy sauce
2 teaspoons	dark soy sauce
2 teaspoons	rice wine or dry sherry
2 teaspoons	sesame oil
2 teaspoons	ginger wine or ginger juice

Seasoning B/Sauce:

2 tablespoons	light soy sauce
1 teaspoon	white vinegar
½ teaspoon	rice wine or dry sherry
1½ teaspoons	sugar
½ teaspoon	m.s.g. (optional)
½ teaspoon	cornflour (cornstarch)

Cut the beef into paper-thin slices across the grain, then into long narrow shreds and place in a dish with the seasoning A ingredients. Mix well and leave for 20 minutes.

Cut the bamboo shoots, carrot, chives, chilli peppers, and ginger into long narrow shreds and set aside.

Heat the oil in a wok and fry the beef shreds in a frying basket for 45 seconds. Remove and drain well. Pour off all but 2½ tablespoons of the oil and stir-fry the shredded ingredients for about 1½ minutes, then return the beef. Sizzle the soy sauce onto the sides of the pan and add the remaining seasoning B/sauce ingredients. Stir on high heat until the liquid has been almost completely absorbed, then transfer to a serving plate and season with the pepper and sesame oil, stirring in lightly.

* Or use shredded green or red capsicum (bell pepper).

SPICY SHREDDED BEEF WITH 'WOOD EAR' FUNGUS AND WATER CHESTNUTS

375 g (12 oz)	beef fillet (tenderloin)*
15 g (½ oz)	dried 'wood ear' fungus, soaked for 25 minutes
90 g (3 oz)	canned water chestnuts, drained
2	fresh red chilli peppers
2 teaspoons	grated fresh ginger
⅓ cup	frying oil

Seasoning A:

1 teaspoon	sugar
1 tablespoon	light soy sauce
1 tablespoon	rice wine or dry sherry
1½ teaspoons	cornflour (cornstarch)
2 teaspoons	frying oil

Seasoning B/Sauce:

1 tablespoon	light soy sauce
2 teaspoons	rice wine or dry sherry
½ teaspoon	chilli oil
½ teaspoon	sesame oil
1 teaspoon	salt
1 teaspoon	sugar
½ teaspoon	Chinese brown vinegar

Very thinly slice the beef across the grain, then cut into fine shreds. Place in a dish with the seasoning A ingredients, mix well and leave for 20 minutes. Drain the 'wood ears' and shred finely. Cut the water chestnuts into thin slices. Shred the chillies discarding the seeds.

Heat the frying oil in a wok to moderate and stir-fry the shredded beef until it changes colour. Remove and drain well. Add the shredded 'wood ear,' the water chestnuts, chillies, and ginger and stir-fry for 1½ minutes, then return the beef and stir-fry briefly with the vegetables.

Add the pre-mixed seasoning B/sauce ingredients and simmer until the liquid is partially absorbed and the beef tender, about 1 minute. Serve with steamed bread or sesame pocket bread (see page 372).

* This recipe is also excellent with pork.

SZECHUAN (SICHUAN) BEEF STEW

1 kg (2 lb)	flank or silverside (brisket)
4	spring onions (scallions), trimmed and halved
2.5 cm (1 in) piece	fresh ginger, sliced and bruised
3	star anise
3 pieces	dried orange peel
¼ cup (2 fl oz)	softened lard or frying oil

Seasoning:

2 teaspoons	finely chopped garlic
1 tablespoon	Chinese brown peppercorns
½ cup (4 fl oz)	light soy sauce
2 tablespoons	dark soy sauce
⅓ cup	rice wine or dry sherry
2 tablespoons	sweet bean paste
1 tablespoon	hot bean paste
2 teaspoons	sugar

Cut the meat into 5 cm (2 in) cubes and place in a deep pot with the spring onions, ginger, star anise, and orange peel. Cover with water and bring to the boil, skim, then simmer for 2 hours tightly covered over low heat.

Heat the lard or frying oil and fry the seasoning ingredients for 1 minute, then pour into the pot and re-cover. Simmer a further 1 hour or until the meat is very tender. Transfer meat to a serving dish and thicken the sauce with a paste of cornflour (cornstarch) and cold water. Pour over the meat after discarding the onion, ginger, star anise, and orange peel.

BRAISED SPICED LAMB SHANKS

625 g (1¼ lb)	boneless shoulder-shank-end (shank) of lamb
6	spring onions (scallions)
8 slices	fresh ginger
⅓ cup	frying oil
3 tablespoons	soybean paste
3 cubes	fermented beancurd, mashed with the liquid
1	large carrot or turnip, peeled and cubed
½ teaspoon	m.s.g. (optional) cornflour (cornstarch)

Seasoning/Sauce:

3 cups (24 fl oz)	chicken stock
2 tablespoons	light soy sauce
2 tablespoons	rice wine or dry sherry
1 tablespoon	sugar
1 teaspoon	Chinese brown peppercorns

Chop the lamb into 4 cm (1 2/3 in) cubes and place in a saucepan with water to cover. Add half the spring onions and ginger and bring to the boil. Reduce the heat to low and simmer for 35 minutes, then drain. Cut the remaining spring onions into slices and shred the remaining ginger.

Heat the frying oil in a wok and stir-fry the onions and ginger for 30 seconds, then add the cubed lamb and stir-fry until well coloured. Add the soy bean paste and the mashed beancurd and stir-fry for 30 seconds, splashing in a little cold water to prevent the seasonings from sticking to the pan. Add the cubed carrot or turnip and the pre-mixed seasoning/sauce ingredients and bring to the boil.

Reduce to low and simmer until the lamb is completely tender, about 1½ hours. Add the m.s.g., if used, and thicken the sauce with a solution of cornflour and cold water. Transfer to a deep serving dish and garnish with fresh coriander. Serve a dipping sauce of mashed fermented beancurd diluted with a little rice wine or dry sherry.

For an original and interesting flavour, use finely shredded lemon leaves in place of the fresh coriander to garnish.

'Twice Cooked' Pork (recipe page 215) and Fish-Flavoured Eggplant (recipe page 234).

LAMB KIDNEYS STIR-FRIED WITH CELERY AND BAMBOO SHOOTS

310 g (10 oz)	lamb kidneys
45 g (1½ oz)	canned bamboo shoots, drained and sliced
45 g (1½ oz)	young celery, thinly sliced diagonally*
⅓ cup	frying oil

Seasoning A:

1	egg white, beaten
½ teaspoon	salt
¼ teaspoon	m.s.g. (optional)
2 teaspoons	rice wine or dry sherry
1 teaspoon	cornflour (cornstarch)

Seasoning B:

2 tablespoons	finely chopped spring onion (scallion)
2 teaspoons	finely chopped fresh ginger
1 — 2	fresh red chilli peppers, finely chopped
⅓ teaspoon	finely chopped garlic (optional)
¼ teaspoon	ground black pepper
½ teaspoon	salt
2 teaspoons	rice wine or dry sherry
½ cup (4 fl oz)	chicken stock
1½ teaspoons	cornflour (cornstarch)

Cut the kidneys in halves horizontally and trim away the white fatty section inside. Peel off the skin, then cut each piece in halves.

Blanch in boiling water, then rinse with cold water and drain thoroughly. Place in a dish with the seasoning A ingredients and leave for 15 minutes.

Heat the frying oil in a wok and stir-fry the kidneys on moderately high heat until almost cooked through, about 2 minutes. Remove and keep warm. Add the bamboo shoots and celery and stir-fry together for 1 minute, then add the spring onion, ginger, chilli peppers, and garlic, if used, and stir-fry for a further 1 minute, adding a little more oil if needed to prevent sticking.

Add the pre-mixed remaining seasoning B ingredients and bring to the boil, return the kidneys and simmer until the sauce thickens. Serve.

* Or use green capsicum (bell pepper) cut into 2.5 cm (1 in) squares.

PIGEON PÂTÉ WITH CHINESE HERBS STEAMED IN SOUP RAMEKINS

625 g (1¼ lb)	pigeon breast meat
1½	spring onions (scallions), trimmed and diced
3 slices	fresh ginger, shredded
1¾ tablespoons	rice wine or dry sherry
6 slices	dan guei*

Seasoning:

2	egg whites, well beaten
¾ teaspoon	salt
¼ teaspoon	ground black pepper
½ teaspoon	sugar
1 teaspoon	rice wine or dry sherry
1 tablespoon	frying oil
2 teaspoons	cornflour (cornstarch)

Special Equipment: Six bamboo containers or soup ramekins.

Pulverise the pigeon meat in a food processor or by using two cleavers (see page 396). Add the seasoning ingredients and mix thoroughly. Divide among the bamboo containers, pushing the paste to the bottom of the cup. Divide the spring onions, ginger, wine, and *dan guei* among the cups and fill each with water.

Set on a rack in a steamer and steam over high heat until the pigeon pâté is cooked, about 30 minutes. Serve in the bamboo cups.

* *Dan guei* is a dried pungent herb said to have beneficial and highly nutritional qualities. It is often used in poultry dishes and gives a mildly medicinal taste. Available in specialist Chinese food or drug stores.

DEEP-FRIED SQUAB WITH SALTED VEGETABLE STUFFING

6	squab (about 825 g / 1¾ lb dressed weight)
¾ teaspoon	salt
1½ tablespoons	rice wine or dry sherry
8 cups (2 litres)	deep-frying oil
	Chinese pepper-salt

Stuffing:

2 tablespoons	finely chopped spring onion (scallion)
2 teaspoons	finely chopped fresh ginger
90 g (3 oz)	salt preserved vegetables,* soaked
1½ teaspoons	five spice powder
¼ teaspoon	salt
1½ teaspoons	sugar

Rinse the squab in boiling water and drain thoroughly. Wipe dry and rub with the salt and wine. Tie a string around each neck and hang in a well-ventilated place for about 3 hours to dry the skin.

Mix the stuffing ingredients together after draining the preserved vegetables, squeezing out as much water as possible and shredding finely. Stuff into the birds and close the openings with toothpicks or poultry pins. Place in a wide dish and steam over rapidly boiling water for about 40 minutes. Remove and wipe the skin.

Heat the deep-frying oil to smoking point and deep-fry the squab in a frying basket, two or three at a time until dark and crisp on the surface. Arrange, breasts upwards, on a bed of fresh lettuce and serve with the Chinese pepper-salt as a dip (see page 384).

* Canned pickled cabbage, salted mustard leaves or roots, or Szechuan (Sichuan) preserved vegetables.

SAUTÉD FROGS' LEGS WITH CHILLI PEPPERS AND CASHEW NUTS

500 g (1 lb)	large frogs' legs
	cornflour (cornstarch)
2 cups (16 fl oz)	frying oil
3	dried red chilli peppers, halved
4 pieces	dried orange peel
75 g (2½ oz)	raw cashew nuts or peanuts (groundnuts)
2	spring onions (scallions), trimmed and sliced
3 slices	fresh ginger

Seasoning/Sauce:

¼ cup (2 fl oz)	chicken stock
1¾ tablespoons	light soy sauce
2 teaspoons	rice wine or dry sherry
2 teaspoons	sesame oil
¼ teaspoon	salt
¼ teaspoon	m.s.g. (optional)
¾ teaspoon	sugar
¼ teaspoon	white vinegar
½ teaspoon	cornflour (cornstarch)

Skin the frogs' legs and divide at the central joint. Coat lightly with cornflour and fry in the fairly hot oil until lightly coloured, about 1½ minutes. Remove and drain.

Reheat the oil and fry the chilli peppers, orange peel, and cashews until the chillies and peel are a deep brown and the nuts golden. Remove and drain. Pour off all but 2 tablespoons of the oil and sauté the spring onions and ginger briefly, then return the frogs' legs and sauté for about 1 minute. Pour in the pre-mixed seasoning/sauce ingredients and bring to the boil. Simmer for 30 seconds, then return the chillies and orange peel and continue to simmer until the sauce thickens.

Transfer to a serving plate, stir in the crisp cashews and serve.

BEAR'S PAW SIMMERED WITH DUCK, CHICKEN, SCALLOPS, AND HAM

Bear's paw has a gamey flavour and a smooth, almost gelatinous texture similar to beef or pork tendon. It is still served today as a feature at banquets, though the practice of cooking exotic animals and birds has become somewhat restricted in recent years. A passable facsimile of bear's paw is beef tongue, and this, being more readily available and less expensive, is often substituted.

1 1½ kg (3 lb)	beef tongue
500 g (1 lb)	chicken pieces
290 g (9 oz)	duck breast or thigh
3	dried scallops, soaked for 1 hour, (or use 1 tablespoon soaked dried shrimps)
30 g (1 oz)	Chinese or cured (Smithfield) ham, diced
3	spring onions (scallions), trimmed and sliced
3 thick slices	fresh ginger
⅓ cup	softened lard or frying oil

Seasoning/Sauce:

¼ cup (2 fl oz)	light soy sauce
¼ cup (2 fl oz)	rice wine or dry sherry
2	spring onions (scallions), trimmed and sliced
3 thin slices	fresh ginger
1½ teaspoons	sugar
½ teaspoon	m.s.g. (optional)
⅓ teaspoon	ground black pepper

Wash the tongue and place in a saucepan with water to cover. Bring to the boil, then reduce heat and simmer for 3 hours. Wash the chicken, duck, scallops or shrimps, and diced ham and place on top of the tongue with the spring onions and ginger. Add enough additional hot water to cover the contents of the pan, re-cover the pan and simmer a further 1 hour.

Remove the tongue and other ingredients from the pan and strain 4 cups (1 litre) of the liquid into another saucepan. Scrape the skin from the tongue, return to the stock and add the seasoning/sauce ingredients and return the scallops or shrimps and ham.

The chicken and duck meat should be cut into small cubes, fried in the lard or oil until lightly coloured, then added to the pan. Bring to the boil, skim if necessary, and simmer a further 2 hours. Remove the tongue and cut into thick slices. Arrange on a bed of shredded letuce on serving plate. Reduce the sauce to about 1½ cups, then thicken with a paste of cornflour (cornstarch) and cold water and pour over the tongue or serve separately.

'CROSSING THE BRIDGE' NOODLES

7 cups (1¾ litres)	chicken stock
3 slices	fresh ginger
1½ teaspoons	salt
1 teaspoon	sugar
2 teaspoons	Chinese brown or white vinegar
185 g (6 oz)	pork fillet (tenderloin)
185 g (6 oz)	white fish fillets
185 g (6 oz)	raw peeled prawns
185 g (6 oz)	fresh cleaned squid or chicken breast
1 kg (2 lb)	fresh thick egg noodles, blanched and drained

Sauces:

	light soy sauce
	chilli sauce
	vinegar and chilli dip (see opposite)

Special Equipment: A fire-pot or table top gas or electric cooking ring and a large stewpan.

Bring the chicken stock to the boil and add the ginger and salt, sugar and vinegar. Pour into the stewpan and keep hot.

Very thinly slice the pork, fish, prawns, and squid or chicken and arrange on separate plates with the noodles in a deep dish. Prepare several small dishes of soy and chilli sauce and prepare the vinegar and chilli dip by mixing 2 — 3 thinly sliced fresh red chillies with white vinegar, a little vegetable oil, and sugar and salt to taste. Pour into several small dishes.

Return the stock to the boil at the table. Use wooden or bamboo chopsticks to add the meat and noodles to the stock and simmer for several minutes. Serve into large soup bowls and add a mixture of the sauces to taste.

Eight-Treasure Rice (recipe page 241).

BOILED WONTONS SERVED WITH FOUR SAUCES

Serve as an appetiser.

Makes 24.

Wonton Wrappers:

2 cups	flour
2 teaspoons	frying oil
½ teaspoon	salt
7/8 cup (7 fl oz)	warm water

Wonton Filling:

185 g (6 oz)	lean pork, finely minced (ground)
3	cabbage leaves, finely chopped
1	spring onion (scallion), trimmed and diced
½ teaspoon	finely chopped fresh ginger
¼ teaspoon	salt
2 teaspoons	light soy sauce
1 teaspoon	rice wine or dry sherry
½ teaspoon	ground black pepper
½ teaspoon	sesame oil

Sauce 1:

¼ cup (2 fl oz)	frying oil
1 tablespoon	paprika powder
1 teaspoon	chilli powder
¼ teaspoon	salt

Sauce 2:

¼ cup (2 fl oz)	light soy sauce
1 piece	cinnamon stick
1	star anise
2½ tablespoons	soft brown sugar

Sauce 3:

¼ cup (2 fl oz)	Chinese red vinegar
1 teaspoon	sesame oil
1 teaspoon	sugar
2 teaspoons	finely chopped spring onion (scallion)

Sauce 4:

1 tablespoon	crushed garlic
2 tablespoons	frying oil
1 teaspoon	sesame oil
1 teaspoon	white vinegar

Sift the flour into a mixing bowl and add the oil, salt, and warm water. Mix well, then knead gently until the dough is smooth and elastic. Cover with plastic wrap and leave for 30 minutes. Mix the filling ingredients together and work until thoroughly mixed, then chill until needed.

Heat the frying oil for sauce 1 to warm and then remove from the heat and add the paprika, chilli powder, and salt. Leave for 20 minutes, then stir thoroughly.

Heat the soy sauce for sauce 2 to warm and add the remaining ingredients, stirring until the sugar dissolves. Leave to cool. Mix the ingredients for sauces 3 and 4 in separate dishes, adding a little salt to sauce 4.

Roll the dough into a long sausage shape and cut into 24 pieces. Roll each out on a lightly floured board into a disc about 7.5 cm (3 in) in diameter. Place a portion of the filling in the centre and fold in halves. Pinch the edges firmly together.

When all the wontons are prepared, bring a large saucepan of water to the boil and reduce heat until gently simmering. Add the wontons and poach for about 5 minutes. Add 1 tablespoon of oil to the water to prevent the wontons from sticking together during cooking.

Remove from the water, drain well and arrange on fresh lettuce leaves or finely shredded cabbage on a serving plate. Pour the four sauces into dip dishes and serve with the wontons.

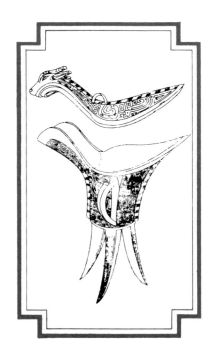

'MA PWO' BEANCURD
(POCK-MARKED MAMA'S BEANCURD)

4 squares	soft beancurd
210 g (7 oz)	lean beef, finely minced (ground)
1	small leek
1/3 cup	frying oil
1 tablespoon	fermented black beans, finely chopped
2 teaspoons	hot bean paste
2 teaspoons	crushed garlic
2 teaspoons	finely chopped fresh ginger
1 teaspoon	finely chopped fresh red chilli pepper or chilli sauce
1 teaspoon	Chinese brown peppercorn powder

Seasoning:

1½ tablespoons	light soy sauce
1 tablespoon	rice wine or dry sherry
½ teaspoon	salt
1½ teaspoons	sugar
1 cup (8 fl oz)	chicken stock or water
1 tablespoon	cornflour (cornstarch)

Cut the beancurd into 1.25 cm (½ in) cubes and soak in hot water until needed. Trim and shred the leeks. Heat the frying oil and stir-fry the beef until lightly coloured, then add the leeks and stir-fry a further 30 seconds. Add the chopped black beans, the bean paste, garlic, ginger, and chilli pepper or chilli sauce and stir-fry for a further 30 seconds, then add the pre-mixed seasoning ingredients and bring to the boil. Simmer for 1 minute.

Drain the beancurd and add to the sauce, reduce the heat and simmer until the sauce is well reduced and the flavour thoroughly permeating the beancurd. Transfer to a serving dish and season with the pepper.

PHOENIX MOUNTAIN BEANCURD

3 squares	soft beancurd
1/3 cup	softened lard or frying oil
210 g (7 oz)	lean pork or beef, finely minced (ground)
2½ teaspoons	finely chopped garlic
1 — 3	fresh red chilli peppers, finely chopped
2 teaspoons	fermented black beans, finely chopped
2	whole eggs
2 tablespoons	finely chopped spring onion (scallion)
	Chinese pepper-salt

Seasoning A:

½ teaspoon	salt
¼ teaspoon	m.s.g. (optional)
¾ teaspoon	sugar
1½ teaspoons	rice wine or dry sherry
1 teaspoon	cornflour (cornstarch)

Seasoning B/Sauce:

1¼ cups (10 fl oz)	chicken stock
2 teaspoons	light soy sauce
2 teaspoons	rice wine or dry sherry
2 teaspoons	sweet bean paste
1 — 1½ teaspoons	chilli oil
½ teaspoon	sesame oil (optional)
½ teaspoon	salt
1 teaspoon	sugar

Soak the beancurd in cold water for 10 minutes, then drain and cut in halves horizontally. Score the top of each piece in a criss-cross pattern, cutting quite deeply. Mix the minced (ground) meat with the seasoning A ingredients and stir-fry in the lard or oil until the colour changes. Add the garlic, chilli pepper, and black beans and stir-fry for 1 minute.

Pour in the seasoning B/sauce ingredients and bring to the boil, then reduce heat to low and carefully add the beancurd. Simmer, covered, for about 8 minutes, basting frequently with the meat sauce.

Transfer the contents of the saucepan to a large dish and pour the beaten eggs over the beancurd. Garnish with half the chopped spring onion and set the dish on a rack in a steamer. Steam over rapidly boiling water for 5 minutes, or until the eggs are set, then remove and garnish with the remaining chopped spring onion and a generous sprinkling of Chinese pepper-salt. Serve at once.

HOME-STYLE BEANCURD

90 g (3 oz)	lean pork or beef
1	medium green capsicum (bell pepper)
1	small carrot
45 g (1½ oz)	canned bamboo shoots, drained
3	dried black mushrooms, soaked for 25 minutes, or use 90 g (3 oz) canned champignons, drained
2	spring onions (scallions), trimmed and diced
3 slices	fresh ginger, chopped
1 — 2	fresh red chilli peppers, chopped
12 cubes	fried beancurd*
2 cups (16 fl oz)	frying oil

Seasoning A:

¼ teaspoon	salt
¼ teaspoon	m.s.g. (optional)
1 teaspoon	sugar
1 teaspoon	light soy sauce
1 teaspoon	rice wine or dry sherry
2 teaspoons	cornflour (cornstarch)
2 teaspoons	frying oil

Seasoning B/Sauce:

1 cup (8 fl oz)	water or chicken stock
1 tablespoon	dark soy sauce
2 tablespoons	oyster sauce
1 teaspoon	Chinese vinegar
2 teaspoons	sugar
1 teaspoon	sesame oil (optional)
2 teaspoons	cornflour (cornstarch)

Very thinly slice the pork or beef and cut into bite-sized pieces. Place in a dish with the seasoning A ingredients, mix well and leave for 15 minutes. Trim the capsicum, removing the stem, seed core, and the inner white ribs. Cut into small dice. Thinly slice the carrot and bamboo shoots. Squeeze the water from the mushrooms and remove the stems, cut the caps into quarters. If using the champignons, cut the caps in halves horizontally. Prepare the spring onions, ginger and chilli and set aside.

Heat the frying oil to fairly hot and deep-fry the fried beancurd for 1 minute, remove and drain well. Add the pork or beef and deep-fry for about 45 seconds, then remove and drain thoroughly. Pour off all but ¼ cup of the oil and stir-fry the capsicum and carrots for about 1 minute, then add the bamboo shoots and remaining vegetables and the ginger and chilli peppers and stir-fry together for 1¼ minutes. Return the fried beancurd and add the seasoning B/sauce ingredients.

Bring to the boil and simmer for 5 minutes, then return the meat and continue to simmer until the beancurd and meat are tender. Serve.

* Dried beancurd cut into cubes and deep-fried until crisp on the surface and almost dried out inside (see glossary page 406).

BEANCURD SIMMERED WITH MUSHROOMS

3 squares	soft beancurd
8	dried black mushrooms, soaked for 25 minutes
2 tablespoons	softened lard or frying oil
2	spring onions (scallions), trimmed and diced
2 slices	fresh ginger, shredded
1 tablespoon	rendered chicken fat (chicken grease) (optional)

Seasoning/Sauce:

1 cup (8 fl oz)	chicken stock
¾ teaspoon	salt
½ teaspoon	m.s.g. (optional)
2 teaspoons	rice wine or dry sherry
2½ teaspoons	cornflour (cornstarch)

Steam the beancurd for about 10 minutes, then cover with cold water and soak for about 10 minutes. Squeeze the water from the mushrooms and remove the stems. Cut the caps into three or four pieces each. Steam for 10 minutes.

Heat the lard or oil in a wok and stir-fry the onions and ginger on fairly high heat for 1 minute, add the chicken stock and bring just to the boil, then add the remaining seasoning ingredients and the drained mushrooms and beancurd and simmer until the sauce has thickened. Stir in the chicken fat, if used, and transfer to a warmed serving plate.

Steamed Date Cake (recipe page 240).

MINCED BEANCURD CAKE WITH SPINACH

4 squares	soft beancurd
1½ tablespoons	finely chopped cooked ham
90 g (3 oz)	fresh young spinach leaves (collard greens)
	chicken stock

Seasoning A:

¾ teaspoon	salt
½ teaspoon	m.s.g. (optional)
¼ teaspoon	white pepper
5	egg whites, well beaten
⅓ cup	cornflour (cornstarch)

Seasoning B/Sauce:

1 cup (8 fl oz)	chicken stock
2 teaspoons	rice wine or dry sherry
⅓ teaspoon	salt
¼ teaspoon	m.s.g. (optional)
¼ teaspoon	ground black pepper

Mash the beancurd with a fork and mix in the seasoning A ingredients. Grease a round baking tin with lard or frying oil and pour in the beancurd mixture. Sprinkle the chopped ham on top and set on a rack in a steamer to steam over high heat for 6 — 8 minutes or until set. Slide the beancurd cake from the tin into a dish of cold chicken stock.

Heat the wok and add the seasoning B ingredients and the spinach, coarsely chopped. Simmer for 1 minute, then add the beancurd cake and simmer gently until the beancurd and spinach are both tender, about 5 minutes on low heat. Transfer the spinach to a serving plate and thicken the sauce around the beancurd cake with a paste of cornflour (cornstarch) and cold water. Simmer until thickened and then slide the cake with its sauce onto the spinach. Serve at once.

The beancurd cake may crumble at the edges but should remain intact as a soft textured mound.

SPICED CABBAGE

500 g (1 lb)	Chinese (celery) cabbage
1 tablespoon	salt
4 cm (1 2/3 in) piece	fresh ginger
2½ tablespoons	frying oil
¼ cup (2 fl oz)	Chinese brown vinegar
1 tablespoon	sugar
1 teaspoon	chilli oil, or chilli flakes soaked in oil

Wash the cabbage thoroughly and separate the leaves. Cut into 5 cm (2 in) squares and place in a glass dish. Add the salt and toss lightly then cover with plastic wrap and leave for 4 hours. Peel and finely shred the ginger and add to the cabbage.

Heat the frying oil until warm and add the remaining ingredients. Pour over the cabbage, toss thoroughly and leave for a further 4 hours.

Spiced Cabbage can be served as a side dish with most dishes from this region. Keeps for up to a week in the refrigerator, tightly covered with plastic wrap.

PICKLED ASSORTED VEGETABLES

500 g (1 lb)	Chinese (celery) or white cabbage
500 g (1 lb)	peeled carrots
500 g (1 lb)	peeled turnips or giant white (icicle) radishes

Pickling Liquid:

10 cups (2½ litres)	water
¾ cup	salt
¼ cup (2 fl oz)	rice wine or dry sherry
1 tablespoon	Chinese brown peppercorns
¼ cup	finely chopped fresh ginger
¼ cup	finely chopped fresh red chilli peppers

Cut the cabbage into 2.5 cm (1 in) squares and wash thoroughly. Cut the carrots and turnips or radishes into 1.25 cm (½ in) cubes and wash thoroughly.

Mix the pickling liquid in a large glass dish and add the well-drained vegetables. Place a plate on top and weight lightly so that the vegetables remain completely covered by the liquid. Leave for 3 — 4 days.

The pickling liquid can be re-used, adding more salt with each use. Pickled vegetables can be kept for up to two weeks in the refrigerator, covered with plastic wrap.

CUCUMBER SAUTÉD IN SESAME OIL WITH HOT SPICES

2	medium-sized cucumbers
2	spring onions (scallions), trimmed and shredded
6 slices	fresh ginger, shredded
2 cloves	garlic, sliced (optional)

Seasoning:

⅓ cup	sesame oil
1 teaspoon	Chinese brown peppercorns
1½ teaspoons	dried chilli flakes or chopped fresh red chilli pepper
1 tablespoon	sugar
¼ cup (2 fl oz)	white vinegar
2 tablespoons	light soy sauce
2 tablespoons	cold water
1 teaspoon	cornflour (cornstarch)

Peel the cucumber and rub with salt to eliminate the bitter taste, then rinse with cold water and wipe dry. Cut into sticks about 5 cm (2 in) long, discarding the seed cores.

Heat the sesame oil to moderate, add the peppercorns and fry briefly, then add the chilli flakes and stir for a few seconds. Add the remaining seasoning ingredients and bring to the boil. Add the cucumber, spring onions, ginger, and garlic, if used, and cover the pan. Simmer until the sauce thickens and the cucumber is slightly softened, but retaining its crunchiness.

Serve as an accompaniment to any Szechuan (Sichuan) meal, particularly crisp-fried or roasted meats.

SPINACH WITH SHREDDED FISH

625 g (1¼ lb)	fresh spinach (collard greens)
75 g (2½ oz)	white fish fillets
2½ tablespoons	softened lard or frying oil
1½ tablespoons	softened chopped spring onion (scallion)
½ teaspoon	grated fresh ginger
¾ cup (6 fl oz)	chicken stock

Seasoning A:

1	egg white, beaten
¼ teaspoon	salt
¼ teaspoon	m.s.g. (optional)
1 tablespoon	cornflour (cornstarch)

Seasoning B:

2/3 teaspoon	salt
¼ teaspoon	m.s.g. (optional)
¼ teaspoon	ground black pepper
1½ teaspoons	rice wine or dry sherry
2 tablespoons	evaporated milk
1 tablespoon	cornflour (cornstarch)

Wash the spinach thoroughly, remove the stems and roughly chop the leaves. Cut the fish into narrow shreds and mix with the seasoning A ingredients. Leave for 5 minutes, then simmer in a saucepan of gently boiling water until firm and white, about 45 seconds. Drain and soak in cold water.

Heat the lard or frying oil and sauté the spring onions and ginger for 30 seconds. Add the chicken stock and the seasoning B ingredients and bring to the boil. Add the chopped spinach and simmer until tender, about 5 minutes. Add the drained fish and heat through.

Transfer to a warmed serving plate and serve at once. For variety, use raw peeled shrimps or diced chicken in place of the fish.

YOUNG LETTUCE SAUTÉD WITH CRABMEAT AND ROE

2	fresh young cos lettuce
1½ tablespoons	frying oil
2 tablespoons	softened lard
75 g (2½ oz)	fresh crabmeat with roe*
1 tablespoon	finely chopped spring onion (scallion)
¼ teaspoon	grated fresh ginger
	cornflour (cornstarch)
1 tablespoon	rendered chicken fat (chicken grease) (optional)

Seasoning/Sauce:

¾ teaspoon	salt
¼ teaspoon	m.s.g. (optional)
¼ teaspoon	ground black pepper
2 teaspoons	rice wine or dry sherry
¾ cup (6 fl oz)	chicken stock

Thoroughly wash the lettuce and cut each into three parts, cutting from the root section to the top of the leaves so that the leaves remain connected to a part of the stem. Blanch in boiling water with the frying oil added for 1½ minutes, then drain and arrange on a serving plate.

Heat the lard in a wok and sauté the crabmeat and roe for 30 seconds, then add the spring onion and ginger and sauté briefly. Add the seasoning/sauce ingredients and bring to the boil. Simmer for 1 minute, then add a paste of the cornflour and cold water and stir until thickened.

Pour the sauce over the lettuce and add the chicken fat, if used. Serve at once.

* As an alternative to the crabmeat and roe, substitute the same amount of finely chopped raw peeled shrimps and add 1½ teaspoons of dried shrimp roe.

STRING BEANS WITH DICED BEEF AND PEANUTS

310 g (10 oz)	fresh green beans (string beans)*
5 — 6 cloves	garlic, finely chopped
125 g (4 oz)	beef fillet (tenderloin)
1½ teaspoons	finely chopped fresh ginger
1 — 2	fresh red chilli peppers, shredded
1	spring onion (scallion), trimmed and diced
¼ cup (2 fl oz)	frying oil
½ cup	shelled roasted peanuts (groundnuts)
1½ teaspoons	hot bean paste (optional)

Seasoning A:

1 teaspoon	sugar
1 tablespoon	rice wine or dry sherry
½ teaspoon	cornflour (cornstarch)

Seasoning B:

2 teaspoons	sugar
2 tablespoons	light soy sauce
1 tablespoon	rice wine or dry sherry

String the beans, if necessary, and cut into 5 cm (2 in) lengths. Mix with the garlic and set aside. Cut the beef into narrow shreds and mix with the seasoning A ingredients. Sprinkle the chopped ginger, shredded chilli peppers, and diced spring onion on top and set aside.

Heat the frying oil and stir-fry the peanuts for 45 seconds. Remove and drain well. Add the beans and stir-fry over fairly high heat until they turn a darker green and are wrinkled in appearance, about 4 minutes. Remove and set aside. Add the beef, and a little extra oil if needed, and stir-fry for 1½ minutes, then add the bean paste, if used, and stir-fry briefly.

Add the seasoning B ingredients and return the beans. Stir-fry together for 30 seconds, then add the peanuts, mix well and transfer to a serving plate. Serve at once.

* Or use Chinese long beans.

BAMBOO SHOOTS WITH DRIED SHRIMPS AND SZECHUAN (SICHUAN) CABBAGE

375 g (12 oz)	canned bamboo shoots, drained
1 tablespoon	dried shrimps, soaked for 25 minutes*
30 g (1 oz)	Szechuan (Sichuan) pickled cabbage
2½ cups (20 fl oz)	deep-frying oil
2	spring onions (scallions), trimmed and shredded
1 tablespoon	sesame oil

Seasoning/Sauce:

½ cups (4 fl oz)	water
2 teaspoons	light soy sauce
2 teaspoons	rice wine or dry sherry
¼ teaspoon	salt
¼ teaspoon	m.s.g. (optional)
2 teaspoons	sugar

Cut the bamboo shoots into thin slices, then bat with the end of the cleaver handle to crush the fibres. Coarsely chop the drained shrimps and the pickled cabbage.

Heat the deep-frying oil to fairly hot and deep-fry the bamboo shoots until crisp and dry. Remove and drain thoroughly. Pour off all but 2½ tablespoons of the oil and stir-fry the shrimps and cabbage briefly, then return the bamboo shoots and add the pre-mixed seasoning/sauce ingredients. Simmer over slightly reduced heat until the liquid is partially absorbed, then add the spring onions and sesame oil and stir in lightly. Transfer to a serving plate and serve at once.

* Or use 1½ teaspoons dried shrimp roe, soaked for 20 minutes and drained.

WINTER BAMBOO SHOOTS WITH PORK AND SZECHUAN (SICHUAN) VEGETABLES

1 500 g (1 lb) can	winter bamboo shoots, drained
4 cups (1 litre)	deep-frying oil
2 tablespoons	sesame oil
60 g (2 oz)	lean pork, coarsely minced (ground)
2 tablespoons	finely chopped spring onion (scallion)
1 teaspoon	finely chopped fresh ginger
½ teaspoon	crushed garlic (optional)
20 g (2/3 oz)	Szechuan (Sichuan) preserved vegetables, finely diced

Seasoning:

½ teaspoon	salt
1 tablespoon	light soy sauce
2 teaspoons	rice wine or dry sherry
1¼ teaspoons	sugar

Roll-cut the bamboo shoots into 2 cm (¾ in) pieces. Heat the deep-frying oil to moderately hot and deep-fry the bamboo shoots until golden. Drain well. Pour off the oil, retaining 1 tablespoon, and add the sesame oil. Heat to smoking point and quickly stir-fry the minced pork until it changes colour. Decrease the heat and add the spring onion, ginger, and garlic, if used, and stir-fry for 45 seconds.

Add the diced vegetables and the seasoning ingredients and stir-fry for a further 45 seconds, then return the bamboo shoots and heat through. Transfer to a serving plate and serve.

FISH-FLAVOURED EGGPLANT

375 g (12 oz)	eggplant (aubergine)
3 cups (24 fl oz)	deep-frying oil
90 g (3 oz)	coarsely minced (ground) pork
1½ tablespoons	finely chopped spring onion (scallion)
2 teaspoons	finely chopped fresh ginger
1 tablespoon	finely chopped garlic (or to taste)
2 teaspoons	hot bean paste

Seasoning:

1 teaspoon	light soy sauce
1 teaspoon	rice wine or dry sherry
1 teaspoon	sugar
¼ teaspoon	m.s.g. (optional)
¼ teaspoon	ground black pepper
½ teaspoon	Chinese brown vinegar

Cut the eggplants in halves lengthwise, remove the stems and cut each piece into 3 — 4 slices. Heat the deep-frying oil and deep-fry the eggplant on fairly high heat until coloured. Remove and drain well.

Pour off all but ¼ cup (2 fl oz) of the oil and stir-fry the pork, onion, ginger, and garlic until the pork changes colour. Add the hot bean paste and stir-fry briefly, then add the seasoning ingredients and stir-fry for 30 seconds. Add salt to taste.

Return the eggplant, cover and cook on low heat, splashing in a little water to prevent sticking, until the eggplant is tender. Serve.

BRAISED EGGPLANT

250 g (8 oz)	eggplant (aubergine)
1 teaspoon	salt
310 g (10 oz)	lean pork or beef
2 cups (16 fl oz)	frying oil
4 slices	fresh ginger, shredded
2	spring onions (scallions), trimmed and diced
1 — 2	fresh red chilli peppers, shredded
1½ teaspoons	crushed garlic
1 tablespoon	soybean paste
2 teaspoons	sesame oil
¾ teaspoon	Chinese brown vinegar
½ teaspoon	ground black pepper

Seasoning A:

¼ teaspoon	salt
½ teaspoon	m.s.g. (optional)
1 tablespoon	rice wine or dry sherry
1 teaspoon	sesame oil
2 teaspoons	frying oil
2 teaspoons	cornflour (cornstarch)

Seasoning B/Sauce:

2 tablespoons	water
2 teaspoons	light soy sauce
1 tablespoon	rice wine or dry sherry
2 teaspoons	sugar
1 teaspoon	chilli oil (optional)
¼ teaspoon	salt
1 teaspoon	cornflour (cornstarch)

Wash the eggplants and remove the stems. Cut into 2.5 cm (1 in) cubes and sprinkle on the salt. Leave in a colander for 1 hour to draw off the bitter juices, then rinse well in cold water. Drain thoroughly.

Mince (grind) the beef or pork and mix with the seasoning A ingredients, leave for 20 minutes. Heat the frying oil in a wok to moderate and fry the eggplant until beginning to soften and colour. Remove and drain thoroughly. Pour off all but 2½ tablespoons of the oil and stir-fry the ginger, onions, chilli peppers, and garlic for 30 seconds. Add the soybean paste and stir-fry a further 30 seconds.

Add the meat and a little more oil if needed, and stir-fry until the meat changes colour, then add the seasoning B/sauce ingredients and return the eggplant. Cover and cook on moderate heat, turning occasionally, until the eggplant is tender and the seasonings well absorbed.

Stir in the sesame oil, vinegar, and pepper and transfer to a serving plate.

SAUTÉD VEGETABLES AND WHITE FUNGUS

280 g (9 oz)	Chinese (celery) cabbage
280 g (9 oz)	fresh broccoli
125 g (4 oz)	canned bamboo shoots
125 g (4 oz)	snow peas
30 g (1 oz)	dried 'snow' fungus, soaked for 25 minutes
3 slices	fresh ginger, shredded
¼ cup (2 fl oz)	softened lard or frying oil
3 cups (24 fl oz)	chicken stock

Seasoning:

¾ teaspoon	salt
½ teaspoon	m.s.g. (optional)
1 teaspoon	sugar
2 teaspoons	rice wine or dry sherry

Thoroughly wash the cabbage, separate the leaves and cut into 5 cm (2 in) lengths. Cut larger pieces in halves lengthwise. Cut the broccoli into florets and wash thoroughly, drain well. Thinly slice the bamboo shoots. String the snow peas and trim the root sections from the 'snow' fungus, then cut into squares.

Bring 1 cup of the stock to the boil in a wok and add the cabbage and 1 tablespoon of the lard or frying oil. Simmer for about 5 minutes until tender, then remove the cabbage, drain well and set aside. Pour off the liquid, add another 1 cup of the stock and add the broccoli. Simmer until tender, but retaining crispness. Drain and set aside. Add the 'snow' fungus to the stock and simmer for 5 — 6 minutes.

Heat the remaining lard or oil and sauté the bamboo shoots and snow peas together for 1 minute. Add the fungus and ginger and sauté for a further 1 minute, then add the seasoning ingredients and the remaining stock and return the broccoli.

Simmer together until the vegetables are tender. Push to one side of the pan and return the cabbage. Heat thoroughly then remove the cabbage to a serving plate. Transfer the other vegetables to the plate using a slotted spoon and arrange over the cabbage.

Reheat the sauce, check the seasonings and thicken with a thin solution of cornflour (cornstarch) and cold water. Pour over the vegetables and serve.

HAM AND WINTER MELON SANDWICHES IN SOUP

625 g (1¼ lb)	winter melon
45 g (1½ oz)	Chinese or cured (Smithfield) ham
½ cup (4 fl oz)	chicken stock

Seasoning:

¾ teaspoon	salt
½ teaspoon	m.s.g. (optional)
¼ teaspoon	ground black pepper
1 tablespoon	frying oil
1 teaspoon	rice wine or dry sherry

Soup:

2½ cups (20 fl oz)	chicken stock
⅓ teaspoon	salt
2 teaspoons	rice wine or dry sherry
¼ teaspoon	sesame oil (optional)
4 slices	fresh ginger, finely shredded

Cut the melon into 24 pieces after removing the peel and seeds. Make a slit in the rounded side of each piece. Cut the ham into 24 pieces. Blanch the melon in boiling water for 1½ minutes, then drain and insert a piece of ham into each slit. Arrange the melon in a large bowl and add the chicken stock and seasoning ingredients.

Set on a rack in a steamer and steam over rapidly boiling water until the melon is tender, about 12 minutes. Transfer to a soup tureen. Bring the soup ingredients to the boil and simmer briefly, then pour over the melon sandwiches and serve.

TRANSLUCENT SLICED CHICKEN AND BAMBOO SHOOT SOUP

155 g (5 oz)	boneless chicken breast
75 g (2½ oz)	canned bamboo shoots, drained
	cornflour (cornstarch)
5 cups (1¼ litres)	chicken stock
12	fresh spinach leaves (collard greens)
1 tablespoon	finely shredded cooked ham
Seasoning:	
1¼ teaspoons	salt
½ teaspoon	m.s.g. (optional)
¼ teaspoon	white pepper
2 teaspoons	rice wine or dry sherry

Cut the chicken into small cubes and place on a board. Cut the bamboo shoots into very thin slices and soak in a little of the chicken stock.

Cover the chicken pieces with a thick layer of cornflour and roll to coat evenly. Use a rolling pin or the side of the cleaver to bat the pieces into transparent escalopes. Continually coat with more cornflour to keep the pieces completely dry. Shake off any excess flour, then drop the chicken slices into a saucepan of simmering water to cook until firm and white, about 45 seconds. Drain and transfer to a dish of cold water.

Bring the stock to the boil and add the bamboo shoots and the seasoning ingredients. Simmer for 1 minute, then add the washed spinach leaves and simmer briefly. Add the chicken slices and the ham and heat through, then transfer to a soup tureen.

DUCK SOUP IN YUNNAN STEAM-POT

½ 2 kg (4 lb)	duck
60 g (2 oz)	Chinese or cured (Smithfield) ham
8 slices	fresh ginger
2 tablespoons	rice wine or dry sherry
2 teaspoons	salt

Cut the duck through the bones into bite-sized pieces. Blanch in boiling water for 1 minute, drain and rinse in cold water. Drain well. Place in a Yunnan steam-pot. Cut the ham into large dice and add to the pot with the wine and salt.

Add boiling water to just cover the duck, then place the pot in a large saucepan with the lid firmly in place. Pour cold water into the pan until it comes half-way up the sides of the steam-pot, then cover the pan and boil gently for 2½ — 3 hours, adding more boiling water as the level drops.

Serve the duck soup in the casserole.

WATERCRESS SOUP

375 g (12 oz)	fresh watercress
4	Chinese red dates
5 cups (1¼ litres)	chicken stock
3 slices	fresh ginger
2 teaspoons	light soy sauce
2 teaspoons	rice wine or dry sherry
1 teaspoon	sugar
1¼ teaspoons	salt

Pick off the stems and thoroughly wash the watercress removing any discoloured or wilted leaves. Drain well. Bring the chicken stock to the boil and add the dates and ginger. Simmer for about 15 minutes until the dates are soft and tender, then add the watercress and the remaining ingredients and simmer for 5 — 6 minutes until the watercress is tender. Transfer to a soup tureen and serve.

Peaches in Honey Syrup (recipe page 241).

DUMPLINGS OF SHRIMP, PORK, AND WHITE FUNGUS IN CHICKEN SOUP

30	wonton wrappers (see recipe, page 376)
30 g (1 oz)	dried white (snow) fungus, soaked for 25 minutes
125 g (4 oz)	fat pork, finely minced (ground)
125 g (4 oz)	raw peeled shrimps, minced (ground)
1	egg, beaten
5 cups (1¼ litres)	chicken stock

Seasoning A:

1¼ tablespoons	frying oil
½ teaspoon	salt
1 teaspoon	sugar
½ teaspoon	m.s.g. (optional)
2 teaspoons	ginger wine
2 teaspoons	cornflour (cornstarch)

Seasoning B:

1¼ teaspoons	salt
¼ teaspoon	m.s.g. (optional)
¼ teaspoon	ground black pepper
2	spring onions (scallions), trimmed and diced
2 slices	fresh ginger, chopped or shredded

Prepare the wonton wrappers following the instructions on page 376, or use frozen wrappers and thaw under a lightly dampened cloth until soft enough to separate.

Drain and finely chop the fungus, discarding the hard root section. Mix with the pork and shrimps and the seasoning A ingredients. Chill for about 20 minutes, then place a portion in one corner of each wonton wrapper. Brush all around the edge with beaten egg, then fold the lower point up to the top point and press the edges together all around to give a triangular shape. Pull the two bottom corners gently downwards, then brush one with a little beaten egg and pinch the two corners together forcing the filling into a circular shape with the top corner flaring away in the centre.

Bring a large saucepan of water to a gentle boil and add the dumplings. Simmer for about 5 minutes, then drain and transfer to the well-heated chicken stock. Add the seasoning B ingredients and simmer briefly, then serve.

For extra colour, add shredded spinach or watercress to the soup.

SLICED FISH AND PICKLED MUSTARD GREENS IN SOUP

185 g (6 oz)	white fish fillets
185 g (6 oz)	pickled mustard root or leaves
4½ cups (1 1/8 litres)	fish stock
2 thin slices	fresh ginger, shredded

Seasoning A:

2 tablespoons	onion and ginger infusion (see page 386)
¾ teaspoon	salt
1	egg white, beaten
1 tablespoon	cornflour (cornstarch)

Seasoning B:

1 teaspoon	salt
1 teaspoon	m.s.g. (optional)
¼ teaspoon	ground black pepper
2 teaspoons	rice wine or dry sherry
½ teaspoon	sesame oil

Cut the fish into very thin slices and place in a dish with the onion and ginger infusion. Leave for 6 — 7 minutes, then add the remaining seasoning A ingredients, mix well and leave a further 6 — 7 minutes.

Wash the mustard and cut into very thin slices. Bring the fish stock to the boil and add the ginger, mustard, and seasoning B ingredients. Simmer for 2 — 3 minutes. Heat a separate saucepan of water until gently simmering. Add the fish slices and poach until firm, then drain and transfer to the soup.

Simmer briefly, then pour into a soup tureen and serve at once.

BEANCURD SKIN AND CLAMS IN SOUP

90 g (3 oz)	dried beancurd skins
185 g (6 oz)	canned clams, drained
2½ tablespoons	softened lard or frying oil
2 tablespoons	finely chopped spring onion (scallion)
2 teaspoons	finely chopped fresh ginger
5 cups (1¼ litres)	chicken stock
2 tablespoons	rendered chicken fat (chicken grease) (optional)

Seasoning:

1¼ teaspoons	salt
½ teaspoon	m.s.g. (optional)
¼ teaspoon	ground black pepper
2 teaspoons	rice wine or dry sherry
1½ tablespoons	cornflour (cornstarch)

Wash the beancurd skins and place in a dish with water to cover. Add 1 teaspoon of bicarbonate of soda and soak for about 1½ hours, then drain and rinse in cold water. Cut into small squares and place in a saucepan. Cover with boiling water or chicken stock and simmer for about 20 minutes until softened.

Heat the lard or oil in a wok and stir-fry the clams for 30 seconds. Push to one side of the pan and add the spring onions and ginger and stir-fry briefly, then add the seasoning ingredients and the beancurd skin and bring to the boil. Simmer for 2 — 3 minutes, then stir in the chicken fat, if used, and heat through. Transfer to a soup tureen and serve.

Use coarsely minced (ground) pork or beef in place of clams, or use diced fresh squid or sea cucumber.

ABALONE AND LILY BUD SOUP

1 500 g (1 lb) can	abalone
4	eggs
1½	spring onions (scallions), trimmed and sliced
3 slices	fresh ginger
1½ tablespoons	frying oil
5 cups (1¼ litres)	chicken stock
1¼ tablespoons	cornflour (cornstarch)

Seasoning:

1½ teaspoons	salt
¼ teaspoon	white pepper
1 tablespoon	rice wine or dry sherry
1 tablespoon	rendered chicken fat (chicken grease)

Drain the abalone reserving the juice. Trim the ruffled edges and cut horizontally into thin slices. Return to the liquid and set aside. Hard boil (hard cook) the eggs and cool under running cold water, then shell and cut lengthwise into four wedges. Discard the yolks or reserve for another use and trim the pointed ends of the whites to give an oval-shaped petal effect. Cover with cold water and set aside.

Sauté the spring onion and ginger in the oil for about 30 seconds, then add the chicken stock and bring to the boil. Simmer briefly, then add the seasoning ingredients and discard the onion and ginger. Add the sliced abalone and cooked egg whites, well drained, and simmer for 2 — 3 minutes.

Thicken the stock with the cornflour mixed with an equal amount of cold water and simmer briefly, then transfer to a soup tureen and serve.

SHREDDED TURNIP AND GOLDEN CARP IN SOUP

250 g (½ lb)	peeled turnips (or giant white/icicle radishes)
1 315 g (10 oz)	golden carp, or use half a larger fish
1	spring onion (scallion), trimmed and sliced
3 thin slices	fresh ginger
1½ tablespoons	softened lard
5 cups (1¼ litres)	water
1¼ teaspoons	salt
½ teaspoon	m.s.g. (optional)
1 tablespoon	rendered chicken fat (chicken grease)

Cut the turnips into matchstick strips, or grate coarsely. Scale and clean the fish and wash well. Stir-fry the spring onion and ginger in the lard for 30 seconds. Add the turnip and stir-fry for a further 30 seconds, splashing in a little of the water if it begins to stick to the pan. Add the remaining water and bring to the boil.

Put in the fish and add the salt. Simmer on low heat for about 20 minutes until the fish is tender, then stir in the m.s.g., if used, and add the chicken fat. Transfer to a soup tureen.

The fish may be removed from the soup and served separately on a bed of finely shredded spring onion, ginger, chilli pepper, and chopped garlic with dips of light soy sauce and Chinese red vinegar.

STEAMED DATE CAKE

125 g (4 oz)	Chinese red dates
125 g (4 oz)	candied winter melon*
1½ tablespoons	candied orange or mixed peel
1½ tablespoons	toasted white sesame seeds
10	canned water chestnuts, drained and diced
125 g (4 oz)	plain (pound) cake
2 tablespoon	water
4	eggs, well beaten
¾ cup	sugar
2 large pieces	pork fat

Steam the dates with a little water until soft, then remove the skins and seeds and mash. Dice the winter melon and orange or mixed peel.

Prepare the sesame seeds and water chestnuts and sprinkle the water over the cake, then cut into 1 cm (¾ in) cubes.

Mix all the ingredients, except the pork fat, together and add about ⅓ cup water. Place one piece of pork fat in the bottom of a pudding basin and add the mixed ingredients. Top with the remaining fat and weight lightly.

Set the basin on a rack in a steamer and steam over rapidly boiling water for about 35 minutes. Remove from the steamer and discard the top piece of pork fat, then invert the pudding onto a serving plate and remove the other piece of pork fat. Serve the pudding hot.

If preferred, substitute parboiled glutinous rice for the cake and proceed in the same way.

* Or use candied papaya (pawpaw) or pineapple.

SWEET BLACK SESAME SOUP

155 g (5 oz)	black sesame seeds
7 cups (1¾ litres)	water
1 cup	white sugar
⅓ cup	cornflour (cornstarch)
⅓ cup	cold water
1 teaspoon	salt

Toast the sesame seeds in a dry pan until they begin to pop, then transfer to a mortar, coffee, or spice grinder and grind to a fairly fine powder.

Bring half the water to the boil in one saucepan and add the sesame seeds. Bring the remaining water to the boil in another pan and add the sugar. Simmer, stirring both pans, for 10 minutes. Remove from the heat. Pour the sesame paste into a blender and blend at high speed until smooth, adding some of the sugar syrup if the mixture becomes too thick.

Remove from the blender and combine with the remaining sugar syrup, then add the salt. Mix the cornflour and cold water together, pour into the soup and simmer until thickened. Serve hot.

WALNUT PUDDING UNDER 'SNOW COVERED MOUNTAINS'

90 g (3 oz)	walnut pieces
2 cups (16 fl oz)	vegetable oil
75 g (2½ oz)	arrowroot powder
1 cup	sugar
5	egg whites

Blanch the walnuts in boiling water for 1 minute, then remove the skins. Dry well. Heat the oil to fairly hot and deep-fry the walnuts until golden. Remove and drain well, then chop finely.

Place the arrowroot powder in a dish. Pour all but 2½ tablespoons of the sugar into a saucepan and add 3 cups (24 fl oz) water. Bring to the boil and simmer until it turns into a syrup, about 15 minutes on moderate heat. Pour 1 cup of the hot syrup into the arrowroot powder and stir quickly until thoroughly mixed. The hot syrup will cook the arrowroot, turning it into a semi-transparent paste. Add the chopped walnuts, mixing well.

Pour the remaining sugar syrup into a heatproof serving dish and place the arrowroot walnut mixture in the centre of the dish, submerged in the syrup.

Mix the reserved sugar with the egg whites and beat to stiff peaks. Heat a saucepan of water to a gentle boil and put in the beaten egg whites. Cook until the egg whites are firm, then transfer to the serving dish, floating on the syrup and serve.

PEACHES IN HONEY SYRUP

6	large fresh peaches
1 tablespoon	dried peppermint leaves
2 tablespoons	clear honey
⅓ cup	sugar
1 teaspoon	rose water (optional)

Drop the peaches into boiling water, leave for 6 — 7 seconds, then remove and peel. Cut in halves and discard the seeds. Place in a dish, cut sides downwards, and sprinkle on the peppermint leaves. Steam over rapidly boiling water until the peaches are tender.

Mix the honey and sugar in a small saucepan with ½ cup water and bring to the boil. Simmer until the syrup turns thick and sticky, then add the rose water, if used.

Remove the peaches from the steamer, scrape off the peppermint leaves and discard. Arrange the peaches on a serving plate and cover with the honey syrup. Serve hot.

EIGHT-TREASURE RICE

60 g (2 oz)	dried lotus seeds
1½ cups	short grain raw glutinous rice
30 g (1 oz)	dried Chinese red dates
30 g (1 oz)	black dates
45 g (1½ oz)	candied papaya (pawpaw) shreds*
30 g (1 oz)	sweet preserved orange or kumquat**
45 g (1½ oz)	pearl barley
90 g (3 oz)	fresh pork fat
1 cup	soft brown sugar
¼ cup	white or castor sugar

* Use candied winter melon or pineapple as an alternative.
** Or use mixed peel.

Steam the lotus seeds with a little water until softened, then drain and use a needle to pick out the bitter cores. Wash the rice thoroughly and place in a dish. Steam until softened, but not cooked through.

Wash the dates, papaya, orange, and barley and place in separate groups in a dish to steam until softened. Drain and remove the date skins and pips. Cut any larger pieces into dice. Cut the pork fat into small dice.

Grease a pudding basin with lard and place the diced pork fat in the bottom, then arrange the dates, papaya, orange, and lotus seeds in a design over the fat. Add the pearl barley and lastly the rice, which has been thoroughly mixed with the brown sugar. Press down gently and smooth the top. Set the basin on a rack in a steamer and steam over rapidly boiling water for 1 hour.

Invert the basin over a serving dish and remove the pudding, sprinkle the white sugar over the top and serve hot.

If preferred, use white sugar in the pudding for a lighter colour, and make a thick sugar syrup or use clear honey to pour over the pudding.

CHAPTER VI
Southern Style Cuisine

Previous page: The lush green mountains and valleys of southern China produce ingredients for China's most varied and exotic cuisine. Water buffalo ramain the single most important piece of farm equipment throughout the country.

Farmer above *relaxes in bamboo chair while casting for fish with a bamboo pole on Li River near Kweilin (Guilin).*

Southern-style Chinese cuisine is the type with which the Western world is most familiar. Overseas Chinese communities hail primarily from the province of Kuangtung (Guangdong), and these hardy immigrants brought with them their southern cooking styles, establishing Chinese restaurants in every corner of the globe. The southern culinary style includes the cooking of Kuangtung (Guangdong) province and surrounding areas, collectively known as Ling-nan in ancient times. The culinary capital of this region, and indeed of all China, is the city of Canton (Guangzhou), which boasts more restaurants and more original culinary creations than any other city of China. Lively debate continues among Chinese gourmets as to whether Yunnan, Kweichow (Guizhou), Chiewchow (Chaozhou), and other sub-sets of this cuisine should be regarded as independent culinary styles. However, since the entire Ling-nan region shares a common historical and culinary heritage, dominated by its geographical conditions and centred around the city of Canton (Guangzhou), we feel that the entire region falls into the same broad culinary category.

Historically and geographically, Ling-nan has been China's rice-bowl. Its warm, moist climate and lush, fertile conditions have permitted rice to be cultivated there in abundance, and it has been the staple of the southern diet ever since the Chinese first entered the region during the Han dynasty. Rice remained an exclusive southern luxury up until the Sung dynasty, when new, faster growing strains permitted cultivation further north. The ever-popular Mixed Fried Rice is a Cantonese innovation. It is traditionally served as the last course at Cantonese banquets, in case anyone at the table did not get his or her fill from the preceding *cai*.

The southern region is geographically blessed with optimum conditions for supporting a gourmet cuisine. Rich soil, abundant rainfall, and dense vegetation produce a broad range of exotic plants and animals unavailable elsewhere in China. Its location on the coast also gives this region access to abundant sources of fresh seafoods from the South China Sea. Almost every living thing in the region has been somehow adapted to the diet, and there are few, if any, culinary taboos. An old Chinese adage tells us that 'if it moves on four legs, the Cantonese will eat it.'

Among the main ingredients which commonly appear on the southern menu, fish and crustaceans from the ocean and from ponds and paddies play prominent roles. Poultry is also central to the southern cuisine: southern chefs work wonders with every part of chicken and ducks. From the vegetable kingdom come an incredible variety of fresh vegetables: the green, leafy varieties with crispy textures are especially favoured. Wild game provides yet another source of primary ingredients: civet, racoon, bear, elephant, snake, parrots, monkeys, and many other odd creatures appear regularly in the Cantonese kitchen. Restaurants which specialise in these exotic dishes usually keep the animals live in cages near the entrance, where discriminating diners muse over the selection and choose appropriate beasts for their banquets. Cantonese cuisine is further renowned for its great variety of snack foods, collectively called *dim-sum* in Cantonese or *dian-xin* in Mandarin. *Dim-sum* are usually eaten for lunch or as mid-afternoon snacks and are taken with pots of strong, fragrant tea. They include stuffed dumplings of every shape and flavour, delicate pastries (salty and sweet), cakes, puddings, and cold-plates of roasted meats and poultry.

The popular Western stereotype of Cantonese food is that it is all sweet, or sweet-and-sour. This misconception has been perpetrated, above all, by one culprit: Chinese/American-style sweet-and-sour pork. Cantonese chefs in America discovered long ago that by adding extra sugar and plenty of tomato ketchup to their sauces, their restaurants attracted extra Western customers. *Real* Cantonese food appears in the West usually only on menus handwritten in Chinese, which are presented just to Chinese patrons.

The fact is that southern-style cuisine employs less sugar, and less of the other common Chinese cooking condiments, than any other regional style. Cooking condiments are used sparingly only to bring out and enhance the fresh-natural flavours of the main ingredients, which themselves serve as the primary flavouring agents for each dish. If any condiment is particularly favoured, it is good vinegar, with its characteristic piquant, sour flavour. Garlic and chillies are used less than elsewhere in China, but ginger and spring onions retain important roles. Vegetable oils are preferred over lard for deep-frying and sauté-

Farmer draws water from the limpid Li River near Kweilin (Guilin) to irrigate his greening crops. Above right: *Typical rural scenes in the countryside near Yangshuo, south of Kweilin (Guilin). The pace of rural life is still very slow and easy in China.*

ing. Cantonese chefs are masters of fragrant table sauces and spicy dips, a custom which permits each diner to dip each bite as deeply or superficially as he pleases, thereby controlling the flavours himself. Sauce, for example, is commonly served with steamed or poached prawns, good vinegar is used to dip steamed crab, soy sauce and sesame oil are popular dips for *dim-sum*, and Chinese pepper-salt powder often appears with deep-fried foods.

Southern chefs prefer the *chao* method of cooking above all others. *Chao* cooking is fuel - and oil-efficient, an important consideration everywhere in China; it preserves the *xien* (fresh-natural) flavours better than any other method; and it is the best technique for blending different flavours together quickly into harmonious combinations. Due to the prevalence of sautéing, ingredients in the Cantonese kitchen must be cut very finely and evenly prior to cooking. This permits maximum blending of their natural flavours in minimum cooking times. Rare and expensive ingredients are 'stretched' by using minimum quantities, cutting them super-fine, and blending them with other less expensive items: the

costly foods thereby impart their exquisite flavours and distinctive bouquets to the entire dish. In Cantonese cooking, fresh primary ingredients always provide the main flavours, not concentrated cooking condiments, and these flavours are blended to complement one another.

The second most important southern cooking technique is steaming. Many *dim-sum* are steamed, as are many fish and seafoods. Steaming preserves original flavours and locks in vital nutrients, as sautéing does. The combination of steam and sauté methods is very convenient in the kitchen: while the steamed dishes cook, the sautéd dishes are prepared, and everything is ready about the same time.

Southern cooking places greater emphasis on the colour and overall appearance of dishes than any other culinary region of China. In the south, appearances are always important measures of a dish's success, and few dishes appear on the table without elaborate embellishments and colourful garnishes. Ingredients are selected for contrasting colours which please the eye, as well as for flavours which please the palate. Kitchen preparation em-

phasises preservation and intensification of pretty colours and alteration of drab ones. Cold-platters are artfully contrived to look like dragons, phoenixes, and other mythological animals. And the Cantonese savour the rich, deep-green colours of their leafy vegetables as much as they enjoy their fresh flavours and crispy textures.

The importance of appearances in southern-style cuisine reflects the sensual, aesthetic orientation of the south and the total immersion of all the senses in eating. This tendency appears not only in the food itself, but also in the setting in which food is enjoyed. Nowhere else in China are the restaurants as beautifully designed as in Canton (Guangzhou). Rambling gardens and rustling bamboo groves, hidden private terraces and pavilions, exquisitely carved hardwood furniture, paintings and calligraphy by renowned artists, carved screens with cut-glass panels, and a general ambiance of the highest aesthetic standards have always been, and still are, common features of such well-known restaurants in Canton (Guangzhou) as the North Garden, the South Garden, the Canton (Guangzhou) Wine-House, the Da-

tong, and others.

The qualities of texture in food are also more strongly emphasised in the sensual south than elsewhere around the country. Southern gourmets are particularly partial to the crispy textures of certain fresh vegetables and the tender, juicy textures of meat, fish, and fowl. Such textures often appear in contrast within the same dish. Crispy textures are well preserved by the *chao* method, while steaming ensures optimum tenderness, softness, and juiciness in fish, fowl, and *dim-sum*. Meats are kept tender and juicy by appropriate marination prior to cooking.

The inhabitants of the Ling-nan region have always been known in China for their exotic, complex culinary tastes. In northern China and around the world, southern Chinese eating habits are the butt of many culinary jokes and a source of endless wonder and amusement. Nevertheless, such culinary prejudice against certain southern dishes only reflects the culinary conservatism of the north and of the rest of the world, not any failing of southern cuisine, for even the most exotic four-legged creatures are prepared for the table with consummate skill and care. The novice would be hard-pressed to taste the difference between dog and lamb, racoon and pork, monkey and beef. Furthermore, these dishes are exotic only by the *choice* of ingredients, not by their flavours. Indeed, the natural flavour of a Cantonese simmered-stew of young dog, for example, is at least as good, if not better, than the taste of beef, lamb, or pork. People who adamantly refuse to sample such dishes as dog, cat, civet, racoon, snake, and other Cantonese delicacies simply display their own acquired cultural prejudices rather than any sound culinary judgment. Such people would be surprised how quickly revulsion can change to fascination with just one bold bite.

Yet, one still wonders why the

Selecting only the most tender leaves, girls above *pick tea on large plantation in sunny southern China. The various blends are dried, mixed, and stored in old chests* top right *on the plantations, where they await shipment to the cities and abroad.*

southern Chinese have adapted all the strange flora and fauna of their environment into their diet, when they have such abundant sources of more conventional foods at their disposal. One reason is simply because 'it's there': the entire region teems with exotic plant and animal life, and it is only natural that a people as curious about nature and as concerned about eating as the Chinese should investigate and adapt anything edible into their diet. Another reason for the exotic diversity of the southern diet lies in traditional Chinese medical theories, which state that wild life provides the most potent source of food-energy and the most stimulating pharmacological effects. Proximity to wild aborigine tribes has also had significant influence on the exotic side of the southern menu. Ling-

nan aborigines were responsible for teaching Han settlers about the culinary value of rats (both adult and newborn), reptiles, monkeys, and many other unconventional items. An extreme example of aboriginal culinary exotica was their custom of cooking and eating the half-digested contents from the stomachs of freshly butchered cows. Fortunately, this dish has not survived on the Chinese menu, although it was reputed to be highly nutritious and tasty.

Perhaps the most important reason for the exotic and complex overtones of southern cuisine is that the south developed the most highly sophisticated and aesthetically refined culinary culture in all of China. Southerners submerged themselves totally in food culture and constantly hungered for new culinary creations drawn from the

rich treasure-trove of ingredients which filled their environment. Appearance and texture have always been so important in southern food due to this aesthetic, sensual orientation. The very abundance and dazzling array of available ingredients meant that Cantonese chefs had to come up with increasingly ingenious and complex creations in order to satisfy the jaded palates of their patrons. Resident gourmets of Canton (Guangzhou), living far from the political pressures of the capital and surrounded with natural abundance, enjoyed far more leisure time in which to indulge their appetites and refine their culinary standards than their northern cousins. The provident combination of abundant food resources, advanced culinary culture, and ample leisure time led logically to the evolution of China's most refined and diverse cuisine.

The demand for fresh-natural flavours rather than the strong tastes of concentrated condiments make complexity a necessary element in southern cooking. Since condiments are only used to enhance inherant flavours, southern chefs use meat, fish, fowl, and vegetables to complement and flavour one another. To achieve a harmonious balance by this method, many different ingredients and multiple cooking processes are required.

Southern-style cuisine is generally considered to be the most highly developed form of Chinese cooking. It is certainly the most diverse. Southern

flavours are the least contrived, relying almost entirely on the fresh-natural flavours of the main ingredients and the consummate skill required to bring them out without resorting to heavy use of condiments. Colour and texture are greatly appreciated in the south and add extrasensory dimensions to southern dishes. It is without a doubt the fanciest of Chinese regional cuisines, and the menu includes very few of the rustic 'foods eaten often at home,' which are so popular in northern and western/central styles. Cantonese cuisine is an excellent choice for dining out, but it is more difficult to prepare a complete southern banquet at home than other styles. Kitchen preparations are often long and involved, and many of the rare or exotic ingredients commonly called for in Cantonese recipes are difficult to obtain in the West. When planning a Chinese banquet at home, it is advisable to include only one or two southern-style dishes on the menu and select the balance from the other three regional styles.

Above: *In Canton (Guangzhou), China's acknowledged culinary capital, the meals are more elaborate and the restaurants more aesthetically pleasing than anywhere else in China.* Left: *Entire families still live and work on their boats on the major waterways of southern China. Here a typical boating family on Canton's Pearl River pauses for a pleasant alfresco lunch of local delicacies.*

SHARK'S FIN SAUTÉD WITH SILVER SPROUTS, AND LEEKS

250 g (8 oz)	prepared shark's fin (see page 393)
90 g (3 oz)	'silver' sprouts, well washed
2	young leeks, well washed
8	whole eggs, beaten
1	spring onion (scallion), trimmed and finely chopped
1/3 cup	frying oil
1 1/2 teaspoons	rice wine or dry sherry
1 tablespoon	finely chopped cooked ham

Seasoning A:

1/3 teaspoon	salt
1/2 teaspoon	m.s.g. (optional)

Seasoning B:

3/4 teaspoon	salt
1/4 teaspoon	sugar
1/4 teaspoon	m.s.g. (optional)
	pinch of white pepper
1/4 teaspoon	sesame oil (optional)
2 tablespoons	chicken stock or water
2 teaspoons	cornflour (cornstarch)

Prepare the shark's fin according to the instructions on page 393, allowing at least 3 hours advance preparation. Drain well. Drain the 'silver' sprouts and sauté in 1 tablespoon of the frying oil until beginning to soften, add the wine, then remove from the pan and set aside. Finely shred the leek and mex with the shark's fin, chopped spring onion, and the seasoning A ingredients. Mix well, then stir in the 'silver' sprouts.

Heat the remaining oil in a wok and pour in the shark's fin and egg mixture. Cook on moderate heat, moving the pan slowly in a circular motion to prevent the egg from burning in the centre. Stir in the pre-mixed seasoning B ingredients just before the egg sets, and continue to cook gently until firm. Lift into a serving plate and garnish with the chopped ham. Serve at once.

CRISP SKIN CHICKEN

1 1 1/2 kg (3 lb)	plump chicken
2	spice bags (see page 386)
2	spring onions (scallions), trimmed and cut in halves
3 thick slices	fresh ginger, bruised
8 cups (2 litres)	deep-frying oil
	fresh coriander (optional)
	shredded spring onion (scallion)

Glaze:

2 1/2 tablespoons	malt sugar (golden syrup, clear honey or light corn syrup)
1 1/2 tablespoons	white vinegar
1 teaspoon	Chinese pepper-salt
2 tablespoons	boiling water

Clean and dress the chicken and place breast down in a saucepan with the spice bags, spring onions, and ginger. Cover with water, add a pinch of salt and bring to the boil. Reduce the heat to simmer for 5 minutes, then remove from the heat and leave in the water to gently poach for 15 — 20 minutes. Drain and transfer to a colander to cool and dry.

Mix the glaze ingredients together, heating slightly if the malt sugar is slow to dissolve. Tie a strong string around the neck of the chicken and suspend it in a breezy place over a drip tray. Pour the glaze slowly and evenly over the chicken, making sure that some of it goes into the cavity. Leave to dry for about 5 hours. The skin should feel quite dry and firm.

Heat the deep-frying oil to moderately hot and immerse the chicken completely. Cook for at least 10 minutes, turning once or twice, until the skin is a rich red brown and the meat is cooked through, but remaining moist and a slightly pink colour. Lift out carefully and drain well. Use cooking chopsticks or the handles of two wooden spoons when moving the chicken as metal utensils may tear the skin.

Cut the chicken in halves, then divide into bite-sized pieces, cutting through the bones. Or debone the chicken completely before cutting into bite-sized pieces. Assemble on the serving plate in the shape of a chicken (see page 394). Garnish with the fresh coriander and shredded spring onion and serve with a Chinese pepper-salt dip (see page 384)

SPECIAL SOY SAUCE CHICKEN

1 1¼ kg (2½ lb)	*chicken*
2	*spring onions (scallions), trimmed and cut in halves*
2 slices	*fresh ginger*
	sesame oil

Seasoning/Sauce:

1½ cups (12 fl oz)	*chicken stock*
1 cup (8 fl oz)	*light soy sauce*
½ cup (4 fl oz)	*dark soy sauce*
1 tablespoon	*rice wine or dry sherry*
½ cup	*sugar*
2	*star anise*
2	*spring onions (scallions), trimmed and sliced*
3 slices	*fresh ginger, bruised*

Clean and dress the chicken and dry with kitchen paper. Place the spring onions and ginger in the cavity.

Bring the seasoning/sauce ingredients to the boil in a saucepan or casserole and add the chicken. Simmer for 30 — 35 minutes, then turn and cook a further 10 minutes.

Remove to a colander to drain. Brush the skin with sesame oil and cut into bite-sized pieces. Serve hot.

Hard-boiled eggs can be added to this dish in the last 15 minutes of cooking. To serve, cut lengthwise into quarters and arrange around the chicken.

SALT-BAKED CHICKEN

1 1¼ kg (2½ lb)	*plump chicken*
4 kg (8 lb)	*rock or coarse salt*
2	*dried or fresh lotus leaves**
3	*spring onions (scallions), trimmed and cut in halves*
4 thick slices	*fresh ginger*
155 g (5 oz)	*fresh broccoli, cut into florets*

Seasoning A:

½ teaspoon	*m.s.g. (optional)*
½ teaspoon	*white pepper*
1¼ teaspoons	*sugar*
1 tablespoon	*rice wine*
1 tablespoon	*finely chopped spring onion (scallion)*
½ teaspoon	*grated fresh ginger*

Seasoning B:

⅓ teaspoon	*salt*
¼ teaspoon	*m.s.g. (optional)*
½ teaspoon	*sugar*
1 teaspoon	*rice wine or dry sherry*
2 tablespoons	*chicken stock or water*
1 teaspoon	*cornflour (cornstarch)*

Clean and dress the chicken and rub the skin with the seasoning A ingredients. Leave for 1 hour to marinate. Soak the dried lotus leaves, if used, in boiling water until softened, or blanch fresh leaves in boiling water for 1 minute and drain well. If using greaseproof paper, brush one side generously with vegetable oil. Stuff the spring onions and ginger into the cavity and wrap the chicken in the drained leaves or paper. Heat the salt in a large saucepan or wok taking care not to let it smoke. Make a cavity in the centre and place the chicken in this. Cover with salt, then cover the saucepan or wok and cook over moderate heat for 20 — 25 minutes. Scrape away the salt, then turn the chicken, re-cover with salt and bake a further 20-25 minutes. Remove the chicken and discard the leaves or paper.

Cut the chicken into bite-sized pieces, cutting through the bones. Simmer the broccoli in boiling water for 2 minutes. Drain and sauté in a wok with a little oil and the seasoning B ingredients for a further 2 minutes, then arrange around the chicken on a serving plate. Serve at once.

* Or use greaseproof paper.

WHOLE CHICKEN STUFFED WITH GLUTINOUS RICE

1 1/4 kg (2 1/2 lb)	chicken
125 g (4 oz)	glutinous rice, soaked for 1 hour
4	dried black mushrooms, soaked for 25 minutes
3	spring onions (scallions), trimmed and diced
3 slices	fresh ginger, chopped
45 g (1 1/2 oz)	Chinese or cured (Smithfield) ham, diced
2 tablespoons	rendered chicken fat (chicken grease), or lard
1 tablespoon	dark soy sauce cornflour (cornstarch)
8 cups (2 litres)	deep-frying oil

Seasoning:

3/4 teaspoon	salt
1/2 teaspoon	m.s.g. (optional)
1/2 teaspoon	sugar
1 tablespoon	light soy sauce
1/2 teaspoon	rice wine or dry sherry

Clean and debone the chicken. Rinse out with boiling water and turn inside out. Trim off some of the thicker parts of the meat and cut into small dice. Place the rice, with water to cover, in a dish and set on a rack in a steamer. Steam until almost cooked through, about 35 minutes. Squeeze the water from the mushrooms and remove stems, dice the caps.

Heat the chicken fat in a wok and stir-fry the onion and ginger for 1 minute. Add the diced chicken and stir-fry until it changes colour, then add the mushrooms and ham and fry for 1 minute. Mix in the seasoning ingredients and the rice and stir-fry for a further 1 minute. Remove to a plate to cool.

Stuff the rice mixture into the chicken and sew up the opening or secure with poultry pins. Rub with the dark soy sauce and place in a deep dish. Set on a rack in the steamer and steam over high heat for about 50 minutes. Remove, wipe the skin and coat lightly with cornflour.

Heat the deep-frying oil to smoking point and quickly deep-fry the chicken, completely immersed if possible, until crisp and golden brown on the surface. Remove and drain. Place breast up on a serving dish and slash across the breast in two places to expose the filling.

CHICKEN DINNER HAINAN STYLE

Serves 4 — 6 as a complete meal.

1 1/3 kg (2 2/3 lb)	chicken
2 teaspoons	sesame oil
1 1/2 - 2 cups	short grain white rice
2 tablespoons	rendered chicken fat (chicken grease) (optional)
500 g (1 lb)	young green vegetables* ginger and spring onion sauce

Seasoning A:

1 1/2 teaspoons	salt
1/2 teaspoon	m.s.g. (optional)
1	spring onion (scallion), trimmed and sliced
3 slices	fresh ginger

Seasoning B:

1/2 teaspoon	salt
1/2 teaspoon	m.s.g. (optional)
1 teaspoon	rice wine or dry sherry

Clean and dress the chicken and place in a saucepan with water to cover. Add the seasoning A ingredients and bring to the boil, cover and reduce heat to simmer. Cook for 45 minutes, then drain and brush with sesame oil. Reserve the stock.

In the meantime, cook the rice by the absorption method (see page 354), adding the chicken fat, if used, before cooking.

Reheat the stock to boiling and add the vegetables and the seasoning B ingredients. Simmer until tender but retaining some crispness. Cooking time will depend on the kind of vegetables used. Drain and arrange on a serving plate.

Slice the chicken through the bones into bite-sized pieces and assemble on a serving plate in the shape of a chicken (see page 394). Or debone and shred the meat into slivers with the fingers.

Check the cooking stock for seasoning and pour into 4 — 6 soup bowls.

Serve the chicken, vegetables, rice, and soup at the same time plus several small dishes of ginger and spring onion sauce (see page 384) as a dip for the chicken.

*Use Chinese vegetables, spinach, broccoli, or small lettuce.

SLICED CHICKEN WITH CHRYSANTHEMUM PETALS

280 g (9 oz)	boneless chicken breast
30 g (1 oz)	white chrysanthemum petals
4 cups (1 litre)	deep-frying oil
1 tablespoon	softened lard
1	spring onion (scallion), trimmed and shredded
1 slice	fresh ginger, shredded
¾ teaspoon	rice wine or dry sherry

Seasoning A:

1	egg white, beaten
½ teaspoon	salt
½ teaspoon	m.s.g. (optional)
	pinch of white pepper
½ teaspoon	rice wine or dry sherry
½ teaspoon	cornflour (cornstarch)

Seasoning B/Sauce:

¼ cup (2 fl oz)	chicken stock
½ teaspoon	salt
¼ teaspoon	m.s.g. (optional)
¾ teaspoon	sugar
½ teaspoon	cornflour (cornstarch)

Slice the chicken across the grain fairly thinly and place in a dish with the Seasoning A ingredients. Mix well and leave to marinate for 15 minutes.

Wash the chrysanthemum petals and spread on a kitchen towel to dry.

Heat the deep-frying oil to moderately hot and deep-fry the chicken until it turns white, about 45 seconds. Remove and set aside. Pour off the oil. Add the lard to the pan and stir-fry the spring onion and ginger briefly. Sizzle the wine onto the sides of the pan and return the chicken. Stir-fry for 1 minute, then add the pre-mixed seasoning B/sauce ingredients and bring to the boil, stirring. Add the chrysanthemum petals and stir for a few seconds, then transfer to a serving plate.

DICED CHICKEN AND CASHEW NUTS

250 g (8 oz)	boneless chicken
45 g (1½ oz)	raw cashew nuts or peanuts (groundnuts)
2 cups (16 fl oz)	frying oil
12	snow peas
12	canned champignons, drained
4	canned water chestnuts, drained
45 g (1½ oz)	canned bamboo shoots, drained and sliced
280 g (9 oz)	young bok choy or choy sum

Seasoning A:

½ teaspoon	salt
¼ teaspoon	m.s.g. (optional)
¾ teaspoon	sugar
1 teaspoon	light soy sauce
1 teaspoon	rice wine or dry sherry
½ teaspoon	cornflour (cornstarch)

Seasoning B/Sauce:

¼ cup (2 fl oz)	chicken stock or water
½ teaspoon	dark soy sauce
½ teaspoon	salt
¼ teaspoon	m.s.g. (optional)
¼ teaspoon	sugar
	pinch of ground black pepper
½ teaspoon	cornflour (cornstarch)

Cut the chicken into small cubes and place in a dish with the Seasoning A ingredients. Mix well and leave for 20 minutes. Heat the deep-frying oil to fairly hot and deep-fry the cashew nuts for about 2 minutes, until light gold in colour. Remove and drain well. Leave to cool. String the snow peas. Cut the champignons in halves horizontally, cut the water chestnuts into three pieces each, horizontally. Rinse the vegetables well and cut the stems into 5 cm (2 in) lengths.

Heat a wok and add 2 tablespoons of the frying oil. When smoking hot add the chicken and stir-fry for 2 minutes. Remove from the pan and add the bok choy or choy sum. Splash in a little water, cover the pan and cook on fairly high heat, shaking the pan to keep the vegetables turning, for 1½ — 2 minutes. Add the remaining vegetables and stir-fry for 30 — 45 seconds. Add the pre-mixed seasoning B/sauce ingredients and simmer briefly, then return the chicken and continue to cook until the sauce thickens. Stir in the cashews and transfer to a serving plate.

STEAMED CHICKEN DRESSED WITH SPRING ONIONS AND GINGER

1 1⅓ kg (2 2/3 lb)	chicken
5	spring onions (scallions), trimmed and shredded
6 slices	fresh ginger, shredded
¼ cup (2 fl oz)	frying oil

Seasoning:

2 teaspoons	salt
1 teaspoon	m.s.g. (optional)
½ teaspoon	sugar
1 tablespoon	rice wine or dry sherry
2 tablespoons	finely chopped spring onion (scallion)
1 tablespoon	grated fresh ginger

Clean and dress the chicken and rub all over with the pre-mixed seasoning ingredients. Leave to marinate for 1 hour, then place breast up in a dish and set on a rack in a steamer.

Steam over rapidly boiling water for 45 — 50 minutes, then drain and remove to a cutting board. Cut into bite-sized pieces and assemble on a serving plate in the shape of a chicken (see page 394).

Garnish the chicken with the shredded spring onion and ginger. Heat the frying oil to smoking point and pour over the chicken. Serve at once.

PAN-FRIED CHICKEN WITH YOUNG GINGER AND PINEAPPLE

250 g (8 oz)	boneless chicken breast
5 cm (2 in) piece	fresh young ginger, peeled*
3 thin slices	fresh or canned or pineapple
2	medium green capsicums (bell peppers)
2	spring onions (scallions), trimmed and sliced
¼ cup (2 fl oz)	frying oil

Seasoning A:

1	egg white, beaten
½ teaspoon	salt
¼ teaspoon	m.s.g. (optional)
¼ teaspoon	white pepper
½ teaspoon	rice wine or dry sherry
1 tablespoon	water
1 tablespoon	cornflour (cornstarch)

Seasoning B/Sauce:

2/3 cup	chicken stock
1 tablespoon	tomato sauce (ketchup), or use light soy sauce
½ teaspoon	white vinegar
¼ teaspoon	chilli oil (optional)
½ teaspoon	salt
1 teaspoon	sugar
¼ teaspoon	m.s.g. (optional)
¼ teaspoon	white pepper
¾ teaspoon	crushed garlic
1 teaspoon	cornflour (cornstarch)

Marinade for Ginger:

2 tablespoons	cold water
1 tablespoon	white vinegar
½ teaspoon	salt
1½ teaspoons	sugar

Skin and debone the chicken and cut across the grain into thin strips. Mix with the seasoning A ingredients and leave for 20 minutes to marinate.

Peel the ginger and cut into thin slices. Mix the marinade ingredients together, pour over the ginger and leave until needed.

Cut the pineapple in halves horizontally, then cut each slice into about 12 pieces. Remove the stem and seed cores from the peppers, cut in halves and remove the inner white ribs, then cut into 2 cm (¾ in) squares.

Heat the frying oil in a wok and gently fry the chicken until it turns white. Remove. Add the peppers and onion, cover for the first 1 minute of cooking, and fry until beginning to soften, about 2 minutes. Add the pineapple, increase the heat to fairly high and return the chicken. Pour in the pre-mixed seasoning B/sauce ingredients and cook until the sauce thickens. Add drained ginger, heat through, then transfer to a serving plate.

* Select ginger with pale cream-coloured skin and pink buds. Older ginger with darker, slightly wrinkled skin is much stronger in taste and would be unsuitable for this dish. If unobtainable, use sweet pickled ginger and omit the marination.

Chicken Dinner Hainan Style (recipe page 250).

QUICK-FRIED CHICKEN SHREDS WITH ONION

375 g (12 oz)	boneless chicken breast
1	large brown onion
¼ cup (2 fl oz)	frying oil

Seasoning A:

1	egg white
½ teaspoon	salt
¼	m.s.g. (optional)
	pinch of white pepper
1 teaspoon	rice wine or dry sherry
½ teaspoon	cornflour (cornstarch)

Seasoning B/Sauce:

¼ cup (2 fl oz)	chicken stock
2 tablespoons	tomato sauce (ketchup) or 1 tablespoon light soy sauce
½ — ¾ teaspoon	chilli oil
¾ teaspoon	sesame oil
1 teaspoon	cornflour (cornstarch)

Slice the chicken, then cut into narrow shreds. Mix with the seasoning A ingredients and leave to marinate for 15 minutes.

Peel the onion and cut in halves from stem to root. Trim away the root section and cut into thin slices, then separate the layers.

Heat the frying oil in a wok and fry the chicken on moderately high heat until white, about 1¼ minutes. Remove and keep warm. Add the onion to the pan and stir-fry for 1½ minutes on high heat, then pour in the pre-mixed seasoning B sauce ingredients and bring to the boil. Return the chicken and stir on high heat until the sauce thickens. Transfer to a warmed serving plate and serve at once.

Bean spouts may be added in place of the onion, substituting soy sauce for the tomato sauce.

FRIED STUFFED CHICKEN ROLLS

Serve as an appetiser or main dish.

250 g (8 oz)	boneless chicken breast
155 g (5 oz)	raw peeled prawns (shrimps)
30 g (1 oz)	pork fat
1½ tablespoons	finely chopped cooked ham
1 tablespoon	finely chopped fresh coriander
5 cups (1¼ litres)	deep-frying oil

Seasoning A:

1	egg white, beaten
¼ teaspoon	salt
¼ teaspoon	m.s.g. (optional)
	pinch of white pepper
½ teaspoon	bicarbonate of soda (optional)
½ teaspoon	rice wine or dry sherry
1 tablespoon	water

Seasoning B:

¼ teaspoon	salt
	pinch of m.s.g. (optional)
	pinch of white pepper
1 teaspoon	finely chopped spring onion (scallion)
⅓ teaspoon	grated fresh ginger

Sauce:

½ cup (4 fl oz)	chicken stock
2 teaspoons	light soy sauce
⅓ teaspoon	salt
¾ teaspoon	cornflour (cornstarch)

Cut the chicken into slices and bat each slice gently with the side of a cleaver or a rolling pin until flattened into thin escalopes. Dust both sides with cornflour before working to prevent sticking. Place in a dish and rub on the seasoning A ingredients. Leave for 10 minutes, then turn and leave a further 10 minutes.

Mince (grind) the prawns and pork fat together and add the seasoning B ingredients. Lay the chicken pieces out on a floured board and spread prawn filling over each. Garnish with a sprinkling of ham and coriander and roll into cylindrical shapes. Secure the rolls with toothpicks or squeeze gently to hold in shape.

Heat the deep-frying oil to moderate and fry several rolls at a time until lightly coloured, about 2½ minutes, then return all together and fry for an additional 30 seconds. Drain and arrange on a serving plate.

Pour off all but 2 tablespoons of the oil and reheat. Add the pre-mixed sauce ingredients and bring to the boil. Simmer for 1 minute, then pour over the chicken rolls and serve.

CHICKEN SOUTH CHINA STYLE

1 1¼ kg (2½ lb)	chicken (only the skin is required for this dish)
625 g (1¼ lb)	raw peeled prawns, finely minced (ground)
75 g (2½ oz)	pork fat, finely minced (ground)
45 g (1½ oz)	cooked ham, finely shredded
1 tablespoon	finely chopped fresh coriander
2 tablespoons	frying oil
280 g (9 oz)	fresh spinach leaves

Seasoning A:

¾ teaspoon	salt
½ teaspoon	m.s.g. (optional)
⅓ teaspoon	ground black pepper
1 teaspoon	ginger wine (see page 387)

Seasoning B:

¼ teaspoon	salt
	pinch of m.s.g. (optional)
½ teaspoon	rice wine or dry sherry
¼ cup (2 fl oz)	chicken stock

Sauce:

1 tablespoon	rendered chicken fat (chicken grease) (optional)
⅓ cup	chicken stock
¼ teaspoon	salt
	pinch of ground black pepper
½ teaspoon	cornflour (cornstarch)

Skin the chicken, reserving the meat for another use. Wash the chicken skin and wipe dry. Cut into four even-sized pieces. Mix the prawn meat and pork fat together and add the seasoning A ingredients. Mix well and leave for 15 minutes. Spread over the chicken skin leaving a wide border all around and garnish with the shredded ham and chopped coriander. Roll up and squeeze into sausage shapes, then sew up or secure the ends with toothpicks or poultry pins.

Set the rolls in an oiled dish and place on a rack in a steamer. Steam over rapidly boiling water for 20 minutes, then lift out and cut into thick slices. Arrange on a serving plate.

Sauté the spinach in the frying oil for 2 minutes, then add the seasoning B ingredients and cover. Simmer until tender, then arrange around the chicken.

Wipe out the wok and add the chicken fat, if used, or 1 tablespoon of frying oil and the remaining sauce ingredients, premixed. Bring to the boil and simmer until thickened, then pour over the chicken rolls and serve.

STEAMED CHOPPED CHICKEN AND STRAW MUSHROOMS

375 g (12 oz)	chicken*
½ 315 g (10 oz) can	straw mushrooms, drained
2	spring onions (scallions), trimmed and sliced
3 slices	fresh ginger
1 tablespoon	cornflour (cornstarch)
1 tablespoon	cold water

Seasoning:

½ teaspoon	salt
½ teaspoon	m.s.g. (optional)
½ teaspoon	sugar
1 tablespoon	light soy sauce
¾ teaspoon	rice wine or dry sherry
2 teaspoons	rendered chicken fat (chicken grease)

Cut the chicken into 2 cm (¾ in) cubes and place in a dish with the mushrooms, spring onions, and ginger on top. Add the seasoning ingredients and cold water or chicken stock to just cover the contents of the dish.

Set on a rack in a steamer and steam over rapidly boiling water until the chicken is tender, about 35 minutes. Discard the ginger and onion and strain the liquid into a wok. Add the cornflour mixed with cold water and stir until thickened. Check the seasonings and pour over the chicken and mushrooms. Stir in and serve.

This is an excellent base for a rice hot-pot. Add 1¼ cups of soaked short grain white rice, uncooked, to the pot and place the chicken and mushrooms on top. Add chicken stock or water to just cover the chicken and steam, tightly covered until the contents are tender.

Lightly sautéd fresh green vegetables can be added to either dish 10 minutes before the end of cooking time.
*With bone or boneless, as preferred.

STEAMED STUFFED CHICKEN WINGS

Serve as an appetiser or main dish.

12	chicken wings, lower joints only
3 cups (24 fl oz)	deep-frying oil
45 g (1½ oz)	Chinese or cooked ham
3	dried black mushrooms, soaked for 25 minutes
45 g (1½ oz)	canned bamboo shoots, drained
6 stems	young bok choy or fresh mustard greens
	cornflour (cornstarch)

Seasoning A:

1 tablespoon	dark soy sauce
1 teaspoon	rice wine or dry sherry

Seasoning B:

¼ teaspoon	salt
⅓ teaspoon	sugar
	pinch of m.s.g. (optional)
	pinch of white pepper

Using a sharp small-bladed knife, remove the two thin bones from the wings. Rub with the seasoning A ingredients and leave for 10 minutes. Heat the deep-frying oil to smoking point and deep-fry the wings for 20 seconds. Remove and drain well.

Cut the ham, mushrooms, and bamboo shoots into matchstick-sized pieces, after removing the mushroom stems and squeezing out excess water. Place several pieces into each wing where the bones have been removed. Arrange the stuffed wings on an oiled plate and set on a rack in a steamer. Cover tightly and steam over gently boiling water for 40 minutes.

Stir-fry the bok choy or mustard in 2 tablespoons of frying oil, adding the seasoning A ingredients and the liquid that has accumulated in the dish containing the wings. Simmer until the vegetables are tender, but retaining crispness.

Arrange the chicken wings on a plate and surround with the vegetables. Thicken the sauce with a thin solution of cornflour and cold water, if necessary, and pour over the wings. Serve at once.

CASSEROLE WITH THREE KINDS OF POULTRY

Serves 6 — 8 as the main course.

½ 1¼ kg (2½ lb)	chicken
½ 1¾ kg (3½ lb)	duck
1	pigeon
3	spring onions (scallions), trimmed and cut in halves
4 thick slices	fresh ginger, bruised
1 tablespoon	rice wine
45 g (1½ oz)	Chinese or cured (Smithfield) ham (optional)
250 g (8 oz)	young Chinese green vegetables
	salt

Cut the chicken and duck into even-sized pieces about 4 cm (1 2/3 in) square. Cut the pigeon into 6 — 8 pieces. Arrange the poultry in a dish and place the ginger and onion on top. Sprinkle on the wine and add boiling water to cover. Cover the dish and place on a rack in a steamer to steam over high heat for 1½ — 1¾ hours.

Discard the ginger and onion and arrange the thinly sliced ham, if using, in the centre of the dish and the washed vegetables around the edge. Re-cover and steam for a further 15 minutes or until the vegetables are tender. Add salt to taste.

Serve in the casserole. If preferred, the liquid can be strained into a wok, the seasonings adjusted to taste, and the sauce thickened with a paste of cornflour (cornstarch) and cold water.

Diced Chicken and Cashew Nuts (recipe page 251) and *Watercress and Liver Soup (recipe page 319).*

CHICKEN STIR-FRIED WITH OYSTER SAUCE

440 g (14 oz)	chicken pieces
2 tablespoons	frying oil
1½	spring onions (scallions), trimmed and sliced
½ slices	fresh ginger, shredded
½ teaspoon	finely chopped garlic
2½ teaspoons	rice wine or dry sherry

Seasoning A:

⅓ teaspoon	salt
¼ teaspoon	m.s.g. (optional)
2 teaspoons	light soy sauce
1 teaspoon	cornflour (cornstarch)

Seasoning B:

1 tablespoon	light soy sauce
2 tablespoons	oyster sauce
¾ teaspoon	sugar
½ teaspoon	sesame oil (optional)
¼ teaspoon	ground black pepper (optional)

Cut the chicken through the bones into bite-sized cubes and place in a dish with the seasoning A ingredients. Leave for 20 minutes, then stir-fry in the oil until just cooked through, about 3 minutes. Push to one side of the pan and add the spring onions, ginger, and garlic and sauté for 1 minute, then mix in the chicken pieces and sizzle the chicken onto the sides of the pan.

Drain off the excess oil and add the seasoning B ingredients, stirring to thoroughly coat the chicken pieces. Transfer to a warmed serving plate and serve.

CANTONESE ROAST DUCK

1 1½ kg (3 lb)	duck

Glaze:

2½ tablespoons	malt sugar
¼ cup (2 fl oz)	white vinegar
1½ tablespoons	boiling water

Seasoning:

2 tablespoons	soybean paste
1 tablespoon	rice wine or dry sherry
1 teaspoon	salt
1 teaspoon	m.s.g. (optional)
1 tablespoon	sugar
½ teaspoon	powdered licorice root, or 1 small piece licorice root (optional), or use 1 star anise
3 tablespoons	finely chopped spring onion
1 tablespoon	finely chopped fresh ginger
1¼ teaspoons	crushed garlic

Clean and dress the duck and blanch in boiling water for 2 minutes. Remove and drain well. Tie a strong string around its neck, passing it beneath the wings to hold them away from the body. Hang in a well-ventilated place over a drip tray.

Mix the seasoning ingredients together and smear thickly over the inside of the duck. Secure the lower opening with poultry pins, or sew up.

Mix the glaze ingredients, stirring over a pan of boiling water if the malt sugar is slow to dissolve. Slowly pour over the duck's skin to coat evenly. Catch the drips and brush these onto the skin until thickly coated. Leave to dry for 1 hour.

Place the duck, breast down, on a rack in a baking tin and bake in a preheated hot oven at 200°C/400°F for 20 minutes, then reduce the heat to 170°C/325°F and roast a further 55 minutes, turning the duck once. If preferred, secure the duck on the rotisserie pin and cool on high heat for 25 minutes, then reduce to low for the remainder of the cooking.

Drain the pan juices into a wok and bring to the boil. Supplement with a little chicken stock or water if the amount is small. Check the seasonings and keep hot.

Cut the duck into serving portions or bite-sized pieces, as preferred, and arrange on a serving plate. Pour on the sauce and serve at once.

HONEY-BASTED ROAST DUCK

1 1½ kg (3 lb)	duck
⅓ cup	clear honey
1½ tablespoons	boiling water

Seasoning:

3 cubes	fermented beancurd with the liquid, mashed
1 teaspoon	salt
½ teaspoon	m.s.g. (optional)
1 tablespoon	sugar
¼ teaspoon	ground black pepper

Sauce:

⅓ cup	chicken stock
¼ cup (2 fl oz)	light soy sauce
1½ teaspoons	rice wine or dry sherry
⅓ teaspoon	salt
⅓ teaspoon	m.s.g. (optional)
1 teaspoon	sugar
1½ teaspoons	cornflour (cornstarch)

Clean and dress the duck. Make a fairly large opening near the rear and work through this to rub the pre-mixed seasoning ingredients thoroughly over the insides. Leave for 2 hours.

Tie a string around the duck's neck and suspend above a drip tray. Pour boiling water over the skin, taking care not to allow any inside, as it will wash away the seasonings. When the skin has dried slightly, pour on the pre-mixed honey and boiling water, working slowly and thoroughly over the entire outside of the duck and allowing a little to run inside. Hang the duck in a well-ventilated place until the skin is dry.

Fix the duck onto a rotisserie bar set over a charcoal fire (or cook on the rotisserie in a preheated 200°C (400°F) for 25 minutes, then reduce the oven to low, 120°C (250°F) and roast for a further 55 minutes). Cook, turning constantly, until the duck is just cooked through and the skin crisp and a deep golden colour. Remove to a cutting board and cut in halves, then slice through the bones into bite-sized pieces and arrange on a plate.

Bring the sauce ingredients to the boil and simmer until thickened. Pour over the duck just before serving. Serve with additional condiments of hot mustard and plum sauce.

STEWED WHOLE DUCK WITH CHINESE CABBAGE

1 2 kg (4 lb)	duck
2 teaspoons	dark soy sauce
2 teaspoons	rice wine or dry sherry
8 cups (2 litres)	deep-frying oil
5 cups (1¼ litres)	chicken stock
500 g (1 lb)	Chinese (celery) cabbage
2 tablespoons	softened lard (optional)

Seasoning A:

1¾ tablespoons	light soy sauce
1 tablespoon	rice wine or dry sherry
1 teaspoon	salt
1½ teaspoons	sugar
½ teaspoon	m.s.g. (optional)
4	spring onions (scallions), trimmed and cut in halves
4 thick slices	fresh ginger, bruised

Seasoning B:

¼ teaspoon	salt
½ teaspoon	sugar
	pinch of ground black pepper
1 teaspoon	cornflour (cornstarch)

Clean and dress the duck and rub thoroughly with the soy sauce and wine. Heat the deep-frying oil to smoking point and deep-fry the duck until well coloured. Lift out and drain well. Cut along the breast and flatten out. Place in a casserole and add the chicken stock and the seasoning A ingredients. Bring to the boil, cover and reduce the heat. Simmer until tender, 1½ — 1¾ hours. Drain and carefully remove the bones, keeping the duck as close as possible to its original shape.

Cut the cabbage into long strips about 2.5 cm (1 in) wide. Sauté in the softened lard or 2 tablespoons of the deep-frying oil for 2 minutes, then add the seasoning B ingredients and ¼ cup of the liquid in which the duck was cooked. Cover and cook on moderate heat until tender.

Arrange the cabbage on a serving plate and place the duck on top. Reduce the liquid in the casserole to about ¾ cup, or transfer ¾ cup of the liquid to a wok and bring to the boil. Check the seasoning and thicken with a thin solution of cornflour and cold water. Pour over the duck and serve at once.

DUCK SIMMERED IN YELLOW RICE WINE

1 1½ kg (3 lb)	duck
¼ cup (2 fl oz)	light soy sauce
2/3 cup	yellow rice wine (Shao Hsing)
6 cups (1½ litres)	deep-frying oil
7 cups (1¾ litres)	chicken stock or water
	cornflour (cornstarch)

Seasoning:

2 tablespoons	light soy sauce
2	spring onions (scallions), trimmed and sliced
3 thick slices	fresh ginger, bruised
1½ teaspoons	salt
2 teaspoons	sugar
¾ teaspoon	m.s.g. (optional)

Clean and thoroughly wash the duck and wipe dry. Pour the soy sauce and wine over the duck, rubbing inside and out and leave for 1 hour, then drain the liquid into a dish and add the remaining seasoning ingredients.

Heat the deep-frying oil to smoking point and deep-fry the duck until well coloured. Lift out and drain well. Place the duck, breast downwards, on a bamboo rack in a casserole and add the stock and seasoning ingredients. Bring to the boil, then cook on low heat for at least 1½ hours until the duck is completely tender.

Carefully lift out and cut into serving portions. Reduce the sauce to about 1 cup. Check the seasonings and thicken with a paste of cornflour and cold water. Pour over the duck and serve.

HOME STYLE SIMMER-STEWED DUCK

1 1¾ kg (3½ lb)	duck
500 g (1 lb)	fatty pork or 'five flowered' belly pork (fresh bacon)
8 cups (2 litres)	deep-frying oil
30 g (1 oz)	Chinese red dates, or use black dates or Japanese salted plums (umeboshi)
45 g (1½ oz)	salted mustard root, washed and diced*
2	spring onions (scallions), trimmed and sliced
5 slices	fresh ginger
6	young bok choy or lettuce
	cornflour (cornstarch)

Seasoning A:

¼ cup (2 fl oz)	light soy sauce
2 tablespoons	rice wine or dry sherry

Seasoning B:

¼ cup (2 fl oz)	soybean paste
3 cups (24 fl oz)	chicken stock
1 tablespoon	sugar
¾ teaspoon	m.s.g. (optional)
½ teaspoon	ground black pepper

Clean and dress the duck and blanch in boiling water for 2 minutes. Drain and rub with some of the seasoning A ingredients, reserving that which is not used. Blanch the pork and drain well. Wipe dry and also rub with the seasoning A ingredients. Mix any remaining seasoning A with the seasoning B ingredients, except the soybean paste, and set aside.

Heat the deep-frying oil to fairly hot. Deep-fry the duck and pork separately until well coloured. Drain well. Cut the pork into cubes and stuff into the cavity of the duck, then place the duck, breast down, in a casserole.

Transfer 2 tablespoons of the deep-frying oil to another pan and sauté the soybean paste for 1 minute. Add the seasoning B ingredients and bring to the boil. Pour over the duck. Add the dates, diced mustard root, spring onions, and ginger and add water to just cover. Bring to the boil and simmer, tightly covered, until the duck is completely tender, about 2 hours. Lift out the duck, cut open and remove the pork. Reserve the stock.

Shred the duck meat by hand, discarding the bones. Pile the duck in the centre of a dish and surround with the pork. Set on a rack in a steamer and steam over gently boiling water for 15 minutes. In the meantime, strain the reserved stock into a wok and reduce to about ¾ cup.

In another pan, sauté the vegetables in 2 tablespoons of the deep-frying oil, adding a pinch of salt and sugar and a dash of rice wine or sherry. Arrange on top of the meat and steam a further 5 minutes. Thicken the sauce with a thin solution of cornflour and cold water and pour over the dish.

* Or use pickled cabbage or Szechuan (Sichuan) pickled vegetables

Steamed Stuffed Chicken Wings (recipe page 256).

CHOPPED DUCK WITH LOTUS ROOT AND VEGETABLES

1 1¾ kg (3½ lb)	duck
90 g (3 oz)	canned lotus root, drained
45 g (1½ oz)	Chinese or cured (Smithfield) ham (optional)
90 g (3 oz)	squash or winter melon
60 g (2 oz)	canned champignons, drained*
2 tablespoons	softened lard or frying oil

Seasoning A:

1	egg white, beaten
¼ teaspoon	salt
¼ teaspoon	m.s.g. (optional)
1 tablespoon	cold water
1 tablespoon	cornflour (cornstarch)

Seasoning B:

¼ cup (2 fl oz)	chicken stock
½ teaspoon	salt
2 tablespoons	light soy sauce
1 teaspoon	rice wine or dry sherry
2	spring onions (scallions), trimmed and sliced
2 slices	fresh ginger

Debone the duck and cut into 4 cm (1 2/3 in) squares. Place in a dish with the seasoning A ingredients and leave for 20 minutes to marinate.

Slice the lotus roots lengthwise and cut into 4 cm (1 2/3 in) squares. Cut the ham into the same sized pieces, if used. Peel and cube the squash or melon. Slice the champignons in halves horizontally, or squeeze the water from soaked mushrooms, remove the stems and cut the caps into quarters.

Arrange the duck, mushrooms, and ham, if used, in a large bowl and add the seasoning B ingredients. Cover and set on a rack in a steamer. Steam over rapidly boiling water for 35 minutes, discard the onion and ginger.

Blanch the lotus root in boiling water and drain well. Heat the lard or frying oil in a wok and stir-fry the lotus root for 1 minute. Add the drained duck, mushrooms, and ham, reserving the stock, and stir-fry together for 2 minutes. Add the melon and stir-fry for a further 2 minutes, then pour in the reserved stock and reduce the heat. Simmer together until the melon is tender, then thicken the sauce with a thin solution of cornflour and cold water and simmer until thickened. Check the seasonings and serve.

* Or use 6 — 8 dried black mushrooms, soaked for 25 minutes.

DUCK LIVERS WITH HOT PEPPER SAUCE

315 g (10 oz)	fresh duck livers
4 cups (1 litre)	deep-frying oil
3	spring onions (scallions), trimmed and diced
2 slices	fresh ginger, chopped
½ teaspoon	crushed garlic
1 tablespoon	sesame oil
½ teaspoon	ground black pepper (optional)

Seasoning A:

⅓ teaspoon	salt
¼ teaspoon	m.s.g. (optional)
¼ teaspoon	ground black pepper
1 tablespoon	rice wine or dry sherry

Seasoning B/Sauce:

½ cup (4 fl oz)	chicken stock
2 tablespoons	light soy sauce
1½ teaspoons	dark soy sauce
1 teaspoon	chilli oil (or less, to taste)
½ teaspoon	salt
¼ teaspoon	ground black pepper
¾ teaspoon	sugar
1 teaspoon	cornflour (cornstarch)

Blanch the livers in boiling water, drain and cut into bite-sized pieces. Place in a dish with the seasoning A ingredients and leave for 30 minutes.

Deep-fry the livers in smoking hot deep oil for 30 — 45 seconds. Drain and pour off all but 2½ tablespoons of the oil. Add the sesame oil and sauté the onions, ginger, and garlic for 1 minute. Add the livers and sauté briefly, then pour in the premixed seasoning B/sauce ingredients and bring to the boil.

Reduce the heat and simmer for about 5 minutes until the livers are tender and the sauce well reduced. Stir in the black pepper, if used, and serve.

DEEP-FRIED DUCK FEET WITH SHRIMP STUFFING

12	duck feet*
125 g (4 oz)	raw peeled shrimp, finely minced (ground)
30 g (1 oz)	pork fat, finely minced (ground)
	cornflour (cornstarch)
1½ tablespoons	finely chopped cooked ham
1½ teaspoons	finely chopped fresh coriander
8 cups (2 litres)	deep-frying oil

Seasoning A:

¼ teaspoon	salt
½ teaspoon	m.s.g. (optional)
1 tablespoon	rice wine or dry sherry
1	spring onion (scallion), trimmed and diced
2 slices	fresh ginger, shredded

Seasoning B:

¼ teaspoon	salt
¼ teaspoon	m.s.g. (optional)
	pinch of ground black pepper
1½ teaspoons	ginger wine

Sauce:

2/3 cup	chicken stock
⅓ teaspoon	salt
	pinch of ground black pepper
½ teaspoon	sugar
1½ teaspoons	cornflour (cornstarch)

Blanch the duck feet in boiling water for 1 minute, then lift out and scrape off the skin. Return to the water, add a small piece of fresh ginger and a dash of salt and simmer until softened, about 25 minutes. Drain and cut off the claws.

Place the duck feet and seasoning A ingredients in a saucepan, cover with boiling water and simmer for 2 — 3 minutes, then remove and drain. Wipe dry.

Mix the shrimp and pork fat with the seasoning B ingredients. Coat the web section lightly with cornflour and press a ball of the shrimp stuffing on the top of each, smoothing at the edges. Garnish with chopped ham and coriander, pressing on lightly.

Heat the deep-frying oil to moderate and deep-fry the stuffed feet, stuffing downwards, until golden. Lift out and increase the heat, then quickly fry in the hot oil until crisp on the surface. Drain and arrange on a serving plate. Bring the sauce ingredients to boil in another saucepan, adding 2 tablespoons of the deep-frying oil. Simmer for 1 minute then pour over the feet and serve.

* The duck's webs with leg to the middle joint. Available fresh or frozen from specialist Chinese food suppliers.

SALTED DUCK EGGS

12	duck eggs (or use large chicken eggs)
1 cup	salt
¼ cup (2 fl oz)	rice wine or dry sherry
1 tablespoon	Chinese brown peppercorns
6 cups (1½ litres)	lukewarm water

Wash the eggs, brushing the shells gently with a soft brush. Rinse in cold water and stack in a preserve jar with a tight-fitting lid.

Mix the remaining ingredients together, stirring until the salt is completely dissolved. Pour over the eggs, close the jar and leave for 1 month.

The salting process should solidify the egg. If still soft in the very centre, steam for a few minutes before using for recipes requiring chopped egg yolk.

Excellent served as an appetiser with thinly sliced fresh ginger marinated in sweetened vinegar. Use also with an assortment of cold appetisers (see page 381).

FRAGRANT CRISPY DUCK STUFFED WITH LOTUS SEEDS AND PORK

1 2 kg (4 lb)	duck
1½ teaspoons	salt
1 tablespoon	rice wine or dry sherry
125 g (4 oz)	dried lotus seeds, soaked for 1 hour*
125 g (4 oz)	fatty pork, diced
4	dried black mushrooms, soaked for 25 minutes
30 g (1 oz)	cooked ham, shredded
2	egg whites, beaten
2½ tablespoons	cornflour (cornstarch)
	extra cornflour (cornstarch)
8 cups (2 litres)	deep-frying oil

Seasoning A:

½ teaspoon	salt
¼ teaspoon	white pepper
1 teaspoon	sesame oil
1 teaspoon	cornflour (cornstarch)

Seasoning B:

¼ teaspoon	salt
¼ teaspoon	white pepper
½ teaspoon	rice wine or dry sherry
1 teaspoon	cornflour (cornstarch)

Seasoning C/Sauce:

1½ cups (12 fl oz)	chicken stock
¾ teaspoon	salt
¼ teaspoon	m.s.g. (optional)
¼ teaspoon	white pepper
2 teaspoons	rice wine or dry sherry
3	spring onions (scallions), trimmed and sliced
3 slices	fresh ginger

Clean the duck, debone and rinse with cold water. Turn inside out and rub with half of the salt and wine, then turn right side out again and rub with the remaining salt and wine. Set aside.

Place the washed lotus seeds in a dish with water to cover. Steam over rapidly boiling water until tender, drain if necessary. Mash the lotus seeds to a smooth paste and mix with the seasoning A ingredients.

Season the pork with the seasoning B ingredients and leave for 10 minutes. Dice. Remove the stems from the mushrooms, squeeze out excess water and dice the caps. Mix the lotus seeds, pork, ham, and mushrooms together.

Stuff the mixture into the duck and secure the openings with poultry pins. Place the duck, breast up, in a casserole and add the seasoning C/sauce ingredients. Cover the casserole and set on a rack in a steamer to steam over gently boiling water for 1¾ hours. Lift out the duck, wipe the skin and coat with a batter made by mixing the beaten egg whites and cornflour. Then coat lightly with extra cornflour.

Heat the deep-frying oil to smoking point and deep-fry the duck, completely immersed in the oil if possible, until golden brown. Carefully lift out and drain well. Remove the wings and legs and cut the body straight through into thick slices. Arrange the wings and drumsticks around the stuffed sliced duck and serve.

A sauce can be made by reducing the cooking liquid to about ¾ cup and thickening with a thin solution of cornflour and cold water. Simmer until thickened, adjust seasonings and pour over the duck.

* If canned lotus seeds are available, use approximately 185 g and omit the steaming.

SLOW-SIMMERED GOOSE WITH VINEGAR AND GARLIC SAUCE

1 3 kg (6 lb)	goose with giblets
4	spring onions (scallions), trimmed and cut in halves
6 thick slices	fresh ginger, bruised
2	spice bags (see page 386)
1¼ cups (10 fl oz)	light soy sauce
½ cup (4 fl oz)	rice wine or dry sherry
1½ tablespoon	sugar
⅓ teaspoon	salt
	vinegar and garlic sauce

Clean and dress the goose. Clean the giblets and slice the heart and gizzard, but keep the liver in one piece. Place the goose and giblets in a large saucepan and arrange the onion, ginger, and spice bags around it. Add the soy sauce, wine, sugar and salt. Cover with cold water. Bring slowly to the boil and simmer, tightly covered for 3 hours. Replenish the liquid with boiling water when the level drops, and skim occasionally to remove surface froth.

Drain and transfer the goose to a cutting board. Cut into thin slices and serve the goose and the sliced liver, discarding the remaining giblets. Prepare a generous amount of vinegar and garlic sauce (see page 384) for dipping.

Serve hot or cold as an appetiser or main dish, and use cold as an ingredient for assorted cold meat appetisers (see page 381).

Cantonese roast duck (recipe page 258).

STEAMED MANDARIN FISH

1 1 kg (2 lb)	*Mandarin fish (pearl perch, fresh water trout or sea bass)*
3	*spring onions (scallions), trimmed and shredded*
5 slices	*fresh ginger, shredded*
30 g (1 oz)	*canned champignons, drained and sliced*
30 g (1 oz)	*canned bamboo shoots, drained and shredded*
30 g (1 oz)	*fatty pork, shredded*
1	*small carrot, peeled and shredded*
10 cm (4 in) piece	*fresh celery, shredded*
1 cup (8 fl oz)	*chicken stock, warmed*
	vinegar and ginger dip

Seasoning:

1½ teaspoons	*salt*
½ teaspoon	*m.s.g. (optional)*
¾ teaspoon	*sugar*
½ teaspoon	*white pepper*
1 tablespoon	*rice wine or dry sherry*
2 tablespoons	*rendered chicken fat (chicken grease), warmed*

Clean and scale the fish and remove the gills. Drop into boiling water and remove after 20 seconds. Carefully scrape off the skin. Place the fish in a large oval dish and sprinkle on the seasoning ingredients. Arrange the shredded vegetables and meat on top and pour the chicken stock into the dish. Set the dish on a rack in a steamer and cover tightly. Steam over rapidly boiling water until the fish is cooked through, about 25 minutes.

Strain the liquid from the dish into a wok and bring to the boil. Adjust the seasoning and thicken, if preferred, with a thin solution of cornflour and cold water.

Transfer the fish to a serving plate or serve in the same dish and pour on the sauce just before serving. Serve with small dishes of vinegar and ginger dip (see recipe, page 384)

POACHED FISH WITH GINGER, ONION, AND OIL DRESSING

1 1 kg (2 lb)	*fresh fish (sea bass or fresh trout)*
2	*spring onions (scallions), shredded*
4 thick slices	*fresh ginger, shredded*
¼ cup (2 fl oz)	*frying oil*
	fresh coriander
	white pepper

Seasoning A:

1½ teaspoons	*salt*
¼ cup (2 fl oz)	*vegetable oil*
1	*spring onion (scallion), trimmed and sliced*
2 slices	*fresh ginger*

Seasoning B:

¼ teaspoon	*salt*
1½ tablespoons	*light soy sauce*
	pinch of white pepper

Clean and scale the fish. Place it on an oiled plate and add the seasoning A ingredients. Set the plate in a large saucepan and add hot water to just cover. Cover the saucepan and bring the water almost to the boil, then simmer on very low heat for 20 minutes. Move from the heat and leave the fish in the stock for a further 5 minutes.

Lift out the plate with the fish on it and strain about ¾ cup of the stock into a wok, adding the seasoning B ingredients. Bring to the boil, then reduce heat slightly and simmer for 1 — 2 minutes.

Carefully transfer the fish to a serving plate and arrange the shredded onion and ginger on top. Heat the frying oil to smoking point and splash over the fish, then garnish with the coriander and season generously with white pepper. Pour on the sauce and serve.

DEEP-FRIED WHOLE FISH SEASONED WITH SPICED SALT

1 1 kg (2 lb)	whole pearl perch or red snapper
2	spring onions (scallions), trimmed and sliced
2 slices	fresh ginger, shredded
2 teaspoons	spiced salt or Chinese pepper-salt (see page 384)
7 cups (1¾ litres)	deep-frying oil

Seasoning:

1 teaspoon	sugar
½ teaspoon	m.s.g. (optional)
1 teaspoon	spiced salt
2 teaspoons	light soy sauce
1 tablespoon	rice wine or dry sherry

Clean and scale the fish and score diagonally across the body on both sides, cutting almost to the bone. Place in a dish and rub on the seasoning ingredients, then place the spring onions and ginger on top and leave for 10 minutes. Turn, transfer the onion and ginger to the other side and leave a further 10 minutes.

Heat the deep-frying oil to moderate. Wipe the fish and place in the oil to fry until cooked through, about 6 minutes. Remove from the oil and drain well. Place on a bed of shredded lettuce on a serving plate and sprinkle on the spiced salt or pepper-salt. Serve at once.

Additional spiced salt or pepper-salt and light soy sauce can be served as dips.

BAKED STUFFED MANDARIN FISH

1 750 g (1½ lb)	Mandarin fish (perch or trout)
75 g (2½ oz)	fatty pork, minced (ground)
30 g (1 oz)	blanched almonds, toasted and chopped
30 g (1 oz)	duck or chicken liver, diced
15 g (1 oz)	canned water chestnuts, drained and diced
1½	spring onions (scallions), trimmed and diced
3 thick slices	fresh ginger, shredded cornflour (cornstarch)

Seasoning A:

¼ teaspoon	white pepper
1 tablespoon	light soy sauce
2 teaspoons	rice wine or dry sherry
¾ teaspoon	sesame oil

Seasoning B:

⅓ teaspoon	salt
½ teaspoon	m.s.g. (optional)
¼ teaspoon	white pepper
1 teaspoon	rice wine or dry sherry
1 tablespoon	chicken stock
2 teaspoons	cornflour (cornstarch)

Sauce:

1 cup (8 fl oz)	chicken stock
2 tablespoons	light soy sauce
2 teaspoons	rice wine or dry sherry
1 teaspoon	sesame oil
½ teaspoon	salt
¼ teaspoon	m.s.g. (optional)
½ teaspoon	sugar

Scale and clean the fish and carefully cut away the backbone with a thick layer of meat attached to it. Rub the fish inside and out with the seasoning A ingredients and half the ginger. Leave for 10 minutes.

Scrape the fish from the bones and mix with the pork, almonds, livers, water chestnuts, diced spring onions, the remaining ginger, and the seasoning B ingredients. Wipe out the fish, dust lightly with cornflour and fill with prepared stuffing. Stand the fish on its stomach on a greased baking tray or sew up the opening and cook on its side, turning once.

Pour the pre-mixed sauce ingredients over the fish, add 2 tablespoons of frying oil and bake in a preheated low oven at 120°C (250°F) until golden and cooked through, about 40 minutes. Baste frequently with the sauce during cooking to prevent the fish drying out.

Carefully transfer to a serving plate and garnish with additional shredded onion and ginger. Serve at once.

WHOLE FISH WITH FIVE SHREDS IN HOT SAUCE

1 1 kg (2 lb)	fresh perch, bream, or red snapper
3	dried black mushrooms, soaked for 25 minutes
15 g (½ oz)	Chinese pickles
30 g (1 oz)	canned bamboo shoots, drained
1	small green capsicum (bell pepper)
3	spring onions (scallions), trimmed and shredded
3 thick slices	fresh ginger, shredded
¼ cup (2 fl oz)	frying oil
	white pepper

Seasoning:

½ teaspoon	salt
1	spring onion (scallion), trimmed and shredded
2 slices	fresh ginger, shredded
1 tablespoon	softened lard or frying oil

Sauce:

⅓ cup	chicken stock
¼ cup (2 fl oz)	white vinegar
¼ cup (2 fl oz)	tomato sauce (ketchup)
1½ teaspoons	salt
⅓ cup	sugar
½ teaspoon	finely chopped garlic
½ — 1 teaspoon	chilli oil
1½ teaspoons	cornflour (cornstarch)

Clean the fish and place in a large wok. Add the seasoning ingredients and water to cover. Cover the wok and bring just to the boil, reduce heat and poach on low heat for 15 minutes, or until just cooked through. Test by inserting a fork into the thickest part of the fish. It should almost lift cleanly from the bones. Drain and transfer to a serving plate.

Squeeze excess water from the mushrooms and remove the stems. Shred the caps. Cut the pickles, bamboo shoots, and pepper into matchstick strips.

Arrange the spring onions and ginger on the fish. Drain the liquid from the wok, wipe out and heat the frying oil to piping hot. Pour half over the fish. Fry the shredded ingredients in the remaining oil for 2 minutes, stirring constantly. Add the pre-mixed sauce ingredients and bring to the boil. Simmer for 2 minutes, then pour over the fish and season generously with white pepper. Serve.

SMOKED POMFRET

1 700 g (1 ⅓ lb)	pomfret or John Dory
½ cup	green tea leaves*
2 tablespoons	sugar

Seasoning:

¼ teaspoon	salt
1 tablespoon	sugar
¼ cup (2 fl oz)	light soy sauce
1 tablespoons	rice wine or dry sherry
4	spring onions (scallions), trimmed and sliced
4 slices	fresh ginger, shredded

Sauce:

¼ cup (2 fl oz)	chicken stock
2 teaspoons	light soy sauce
½ teaspoon	rice wine or dry sherry
½ teaspoon	m.s.g. (optional)
½ teaspoon	sugar
½ teaspoon	sesame oil
½ teaspoon	cornflour (cornstarch)

Clean the fish and cut in halves at an angle from in front of the top fin to behind the lower fin. Mix the seasoning ingredients and pour over the fish. Leave for one hour to marinate.

Brush a cake-cooling rack with oil and place the fish on this. Set in a baking tray containing the tea leaves or wood chips and sugar and place in a preheated hot over at 230°C(450°F). Bake for 25 Minutes, turning once. Wipe out the oven with a damp cloth after use.

Bring the sauce ingredients to the boil and pour over the fish just before serving. This fish is now frequently served with mayonnaise.

* Or use pine wood chips.

Whole Fish with Five Shreds in Hot Sauce (recipe this page).

SLICED FISH SAUTÉD WITH BLACK BEANS

315 g (10 oz)	boneless white fish fillets
1	large white onion
1	large green capsicum (bell pepper)
1 tablespoon	fermented black beans
1 teaspoon	finely chopped garlic
1 slice	fresh ginger, finely shredded
3 cups (24 fl oz)	deep-frying oil
2 teaspoons	rice wine or dry sherry

Seasoning A:

1	egg white, beaten
½ teaspoon	salt
½ teaspoon	m.s.g. (optional)
	pinch of white pepper
1 tablespoon	cornflour (cornstarch)
2 tablespoons	vegetable oil

Seasoning B/Sauce:

¼ cup (2 fl oz)	chicken stock
2 tablespoons	light soy sauce
⅓ teaspoon	salt
1½ teaspoons	sugar
½ teaspoon	m.s.g. (optional)

Slice the fish, cutting across the fillets at a sharp angle to produce slices of about 7.5 x 2.5 cm (3 x 1 in) and about 1 cm (⅓ in) thick. Place in a dish and add the seasoning A ingredients, mix well and leave for 15 minutes to marinate.

Peel the onion and trim away the root section, then cut into slices from stem to root and separate the pieces. Cut the pepper in halves, remove the stem and seed core and trim away the inner white ribs. Shred finely. Wash the black beans, dry on kitchen paper and chop lightly. Mix with the garlic.

Heat the deep-frying oil to fairly hot and fry the fish in a basket for 45 seconds to 1 minute, until crisped on the surface and just cooked through. Drain and set aside. Pour off all but 3 tablespoons of the oil and sauté the onion and ginger for 1 minute, then add the black bean mixture and sauté for 30 seconds. Sizzle the wine onto the sides of the pan and stir in.

Add the shredded pepper and sauté until just softened. Pour in the pre-mixed seasoning B/sauce ingredients and bring to the boil. Return the fish slices and heat thoroughly. Serve.

CUBED FISH IN PINEAPPLE SAUCE

1 750 g (1½ lb)	meaty white fish (pearl perch)
	cornflour (cornstarch)
6 cups (1½ litres)	deep-frying oil
½ — ¾ teaspoon	finely chopped garlic
¾ teaspoon	finely chopped fresh ginger
2 tablespoons	fresh or frozen peas, parboiled
1	small carrot, diced and parboiled
1 thick slice	canned pineapple, drained and diced

Seasoning A:

¾ teaspoon	salt
½ teaspoon	m.s.g. (optional)
¼ teaspoon	white pepper
2 teaspoons	rice wine or dry sherry
2 tablespoons	onion and ginger infusion (see page 386)
1 teaspoon	sesame oil (optional)

Seasoning B/Sauce:

½ cup (4 fl oz)	liquid from canned pineapple or mango
¼ cup (2 fl oz)	chicken stock
2 tablespoons	tomato sauce (ketchup)
¾ teaspoon	sesame oil (optional)
¼ — ½ teaspoon	chilli oil
¾ teaspoon	salt
¼ teaspoon	m.s.g. (optional)
1½ teaspoons	cornflour (cornstarch)

Clean and scale the fish and remove the fillets, leaving the head, backbone, and tail connected. Coat this thickly with cornflour and set aside. Cut the fillets into 2.5 cm (1 in) cubes and place in a dish with the seasoning A ingredients. Skin the fillets first, if preferred. Leave for 15 minutes to marinate.

Place about 1 cupful of cornflour in a paper or plastic bag and add the fish. Close the bag and shake vigorously to thickly coat the fish with the flour. Empty into a colander and shake off excess flour. Heat the deep-frying oil to smoking point. Deep-fry the carcass until crisp and golden. Remove, drain and place on a large serving plate. Deep-fry the fish pieces, about 10 at a time, until crisp and golden. Drain well. Keep the oil warm.

Transfer about 3 tablespoons of the oil to another wok and fry the garlic and ginger for 45 seconds. Add the carrot and peas and fry briefly, then add the pre-mixed seasoning B/sauce ingredients and bring to the boil. Simmer until thickened, then stir in the diced pineapple.

Reheat the oil to smoking point and briefly deep-fry the fish for the second time. Remove to the sauce and stir until evenly coated, then arrange on the carcass and pour on any remaining sauce. Serve at once.

SAUTÉD FIVE SHREDS WITH SLICED FISH

185 g (6 oz)	boneless white fish
1	medium carrot
1	medium green capsicum (bell pepper)
3	dried black mushrooms, soaked for 25 minutes
30 g (1 oz)	fresh bean sprouts
1	large white onion
3 cups (24 fl oz)	deep-frying oil
2 tablespoons	sesame oil
1½ teaspoons	rice wine or dry sherry

Seasoning A:

1	egg white, beaten
½ teaspoon	salt
½ teaspoon	m.s.g. (optional)
¼ teaspoon	white pepper
1½ teaspoons	rice wine or dry sherry
1 tablespoon	cornflour (cornstarch)

Seasoning B/Sauce:

⅓ cup	chicken stock
1 teaspoon	sesame oil (optional)
½ teaspoon	salt
½ teaspoon	m.s.g. (optional)
¼ teaspoon	ground black pepper
¾ teaspoon	cornflour (cornstarch)

Cut the fish into narrow strips, then into pieces about 5 cm (2 in) long. Place in a dish with the seasoning A ingredients, mix well and leave for 15 minutes.

Peel the carrot. Remove the seed core, stem, and inner white ribs of the pepper, squeeze water from the mushrooms and remove the stems. Shred the three vegetables and set aside with the bean sprouts. Remove roots and pods from the bean sprouts, if preferred. Cut the onion in halves from stem to root. Trim away the root section, then cut into thin slices and separate the pieces.

Heat the deep-frying oil to moderately hot and add the sesame oil. Fry the fish until it turns white, about 45 seconds. Drain well. Pour off all but 3 tablespoons of the oil and fry the shredded vegetables on moderate heat for 3 minutes, stirring continually. Add the fish and sizzle the wine onto the sides of the pan.

Pour in the pre-mixed seasoning B/sauce ingredients and stir until the sauce thickens. Transfer to a serving plate.

DEEP-FRIED FISH FILLETS WITH BLACK SESAME SEED DRESSING

315 g (10 oz)	boneless white fish
1 cup	flour
2	eggs, well beaten
60 g (2 oz)	black sesame seeds
4 cups (1 litre)	deep-frying oil
	Chinese pepper-salt

Seasoning:

½ teaspoon	salt
½ teaspoon	m.s.g. (optional)
¼ teaspoon	white pepper
1 tablespoon	rice wine or dry sherry
2 teaspoons	sesame oil
1 tablespoon	finely chopped spring onion (scallion)
1 tablespoon	grated fresh ginger

Cut the fish into slices across the fillets, cutting at a sharp angle so that the slices are about 2.5 cm (1 in) wide. Place in a dish with the seasoning ingredients and leave to marinate for 20 minutes. Drain and coat with flour, then dip into the beaten egg.

Heat the deep-frying oil to moderately hot. Dip the fish slices into the sesame seeds, coating thickly. Deep-fry until the fish is cooked through, about 2 minutes. Drain well.

Serve with dips of Chinese pepper-salt (see recipe, page 384).

FRIED STUFFED FISH ROLLS WITH SAUTÉD VEGETABLES

280 g (9 oz)	white fish fillets
2	dried black mushrooms, soaked for 25 minutes
60 g (2 oz)	canned bamboo shoots, drained
125 g (4 oz)	Chinese (celery) cabbage
60 g (2 oz)	canned champignons, drained
30 g (1 oz)	cooked ham (optional)
2	small egg whites
2½ tablespoons	cornflour (cornstarch)
2 teaspoons	onion-pepper-salt*
1	spring onion (scallion), trimmed and sliced
2 slices	fresh ginger, shredded
	extra cornflour (cornstarch)
4 cups (1 litre)	deep-frying oil

Seasoning A:

½ teaspoon	salt
¼ teaspoon	m.s.g. (optional)
¼ teaspoon	ground black pepper
1 teaspoon	ginger wine
1 teaspoon	sesame oil (optional)

Seasoning B/Sauce:

⅓ cup	chicken stock
½ teaspoon	sesame oil
⅓ teaspoon	salt
¼ teaspoon	ground black pepper
1 teaspoon	sugar
¾ teaspoon	cornflour (cornstarch)

Cut the fish into slices about 10 x 5 cm (4 x 2 in) and about 0.3 cm (1/8 in) thick, cutting across the fillets at a sharp angle. Place in a dish with the seasoning A ingredients and leave for 10 minutes.

Squeeze excess water from the mushrooms and remove the stems. Shred the caps and one-quarter of the bamboo shoots. Cut the remainder of the bamboo shoots into thin slices. Cut the leafy tops of the cabbage into small squares and the lower parts into larger pieces. Thinly slice the champignons and shred the ham.

Make a paste with the egg whites and cornflour. Spread over one side of the fish and sprinkle on onion-pepper-salt. Top with a few shreds of mushroom, bamboo shoot, champignon, and ham and add a piece of cabbage leaf. Roll each into a cylindrical shape and squeeze tightly. Coat the rolls lightly with cornflour.

Heat the deep-frying oil to moderate and deep-fry the fish rolls until golden and cooked through, about 2¼ minutes. Drain and set aside. Transfer 2½ tablespoons of the oil to another pan and stir-fry the remaining vegetables for 2 minutes. Add the pre-mixed seasoning B/sauce and simmer for 1½ minutes. Reheat the deep oil, briefly fry the rolls for a second time, then arrange on a serving plate with the vegetables and pour on the sauce. Serve at once.

* A mixture of chopped spring onions and Chinese pepper-salt (see page 384).

SHRIMPS COOKED IN THEIR SHELLS

Serve hot or cold.

375 g (12 oz)	raw shrimps, in their shells
5 cups (1¼ litres)	deep-frying oil
2	spring onions (scallions), shredded
3 slices	fresh ginger, shredded
1	fresh red chilli pepper, seeds removed and shredded (optional)

Seasoning:

1¼ teaspoons	salt
½ teaspoon	m.s.g. (optional)
1¼ teaspoons	sugar
1 teaspoon	sesame oil (optional)
¼ cup (2 fl oz)	chicken stock

Remove the legs and the undershells of the shrimps, but leave the heads, tails, and top of the shells intact. Heat the deep-frying oil to smoking point and fry the shrimps in a basket for 25 seconds. Remove and drain.

Pour off all but 2 tablespoons of the oil. Reduce the heat to moderate and fry the spring onions, ginger, and chilli, if used, for 1 minute, stirring frequently. Add the shrimps and fry for 30 seconds, then add the seasoning ingredients and simmer until the liquid has almost evaporated. Transfer to a serving plate.

Smoked Pomfret (recipe page 268).

SAUTÉD SHRIMPS WITH PEAS AND CASHEW NUTS

185 g (6 oz)	raw peeled shrimps
60 g (2 oz)	fresh or frozen peas
45 g (1½ oz)	raw cashew nuts
2 cups (16 fl oz)	frying oil
¼ cup (2 fl oz)	softened lard (optional)

Seasoning A:

1	egg white, beaten
½ teaspoon	salt
2 teaspoons	ginger wine
1½ teaspoons	cornflour (cornstarch)

Seasoning B/Sauce:

¼ cup (2 fl oz)	chicken stock
1 tablespoon	light soy sauce
2 teaspoons	rice wine or dry sherry
½ teaspoon	salt
¼ teaspoon	m.s.g. (optional)
½ teaspoon	sugar
¼ teaspoon	ground black pepper
½ teaspoon	cornflour (cornstarch)

Wash the shrimps, pat dry with kitchen paper and place in a bowl with the Seasoning A ingredients. Mix well and leave to marinate for 15 minutes.

Boil the peas in lightly salted water until cooked, but still firm. Drain and set aside. Heat the oil to moderately hot and fry the cashews until golden, about 2 minutes. Remove and drain well.

Pour off the oil and wipe out the wok. Add the lard and heat to smoking point, or retain 3 tablespoons of the frying oil. Add the shrimps and sauté until pink, turning frequently. Add the peas and seasoning B ingredients and bring to the boil. Simmer, stirring for 45 seconds, then stir in the cashews and transfer to a serving plate.

STIR-FRIED CRAB *FU YUNG*

2 375 g (12 oz)	crabs
1 tablespoon	ginger wine
5 cups (1¼ litres)	deep-frying oil
1	spring onion (scallion), trimmed and diced
3 slices	fresh ginger, shredded
2 teaspoons	rice wine or dry sherry
4	eggs, well beaten

Seasoning/Sauce:

¼ cup (2 fl oz)	chicken stock
1 teaspoon	salt
¼ teaspoon	m.s.g. (optional)
¼ teaspoon	ground black pepper
½ teaspoon	sesame oil (optional)
1 teaspoon	cornflour (cornstarch)

Wash the crabs well and break open. Remove all inedible parts, then chop the crabs through the shells into large pieces. Place in a dish and sprinkle on the ginger wine. Leave for 20 minutes.

Heat the deep-frying oil to smoking point and deep-fry the crab pieces for 1 minute. Remove and drain well. If preferred, the crab can be stir-fried in ⅓ cup frying oil for 2½ minutes.

Pour off all but 2½ tablespoons of the oil and stir-fry the spring onion and ginger for 30 seconds, then return the crab and add the pre-mixed seasoning/sauce ingredients. Simmer for 2 minutes, then pour in the well-beaten eggs and cook without stirring until the eggs are set. Stir lightly and transfer to a serving plate.

SHRIMP AND CHICKEN OMELETTE

75 g (2½ 0z)	boneless chicken breast
75 g (2½ oz)	raw peeled shrimps
2	whole eggs, beaten
4	egg whites, well beaten
½ teaspoon	salt
½ teaspoon	m.s.g. (optional)
2 tablespoons	frying oil
1	spring onion (scallion), trimmed and shredded

Seasoning A:

¼ teaspoon	salt
¼ teaspoon	sugar
½ teaspoon	finely chopped spring onion
½ teaspoon	grated fresh ginger

Seasoning B:

¼ teaspoon	salt
¼ teaspoon	m.s.g. (optional)
2 teaspoons	ginger wine (see page 387)

Sauce:

¼ cup (2 fl oz)	chicken stock
¼ teaspoon	salt
¼ teaspoon	m.s.g. (optional)
½ teaspoon	cornflour (cornstarch)

Cut the chicken into narrow shreds and mix with the seasoning A ingredients. Leave for 10 minutes. Wash the shrimps, devein with a toothpick (see page 394) and mix with the seasoning B ingredients. Leave for 10 minutes.

Beat the whole eggs and egg whites together, adding the salt and m.s.g., if used. Heat the oil in a wok and lightly sauté the spring onion, then push to one side of the pan and add the chicken and shrimps and sauté together for 1½ minutes. Pour in the egg batter and cook on moderate heat until just beginning to colour underneath. Carefully lift up and turn to cook the other side. Transfer to a serving plate.

Wipe out the wok and add the sauce ingredients, pre-mixed. Simmer until thickened and pour over the omelette. Garnish with fresh coriander or shredded spring onion and serve.

HIBISCUS SHRIMPS

155 g (5 oz)	raw peeled shrimps
30 g (1 oz)	Cantonese roast pork (see recipe, page 291)*
2	large dried black mushrooms, soaked for 25 minutes
3	garlic chives, cut into 4 cm (1 2/3 in) pieces
4	eggs, well beaten
⅓ cup	softened lard or frying oil

Seasoning:

1	egg white, beaten
½ teaspoon	salt
¼ teaspoon	m.s.g. (optional)
	pinch of white pepper
½ teaspoon	rice wine or dry sherry
2 teaspoons	cornflour (cornstarch)
1 tablespoon	frying oil

Sauce:

⅓ cup	chicken stock
1 tablespoon	oyster sauce
¼ teaspoon	m.s.g. (optional)
¼ teaspoon	white pepper
½ teaspoon	sugar
¾ teaspoon	cornflour (cornstarch)

Clean the shrimps and remove the dark veins with a toothpick (see page 394). Mix with the seasoning ingredients and leave for 15 minutes.

Slice the roast pork, then shred finely. Squeeze the water from the mushrooms, remove the stems and shred finely. Mix the pork, mushrooms and garlic chives with the beaten eggs and add a dash of salt.

Heat the wok and add 2 tablespoons of the lard or oil. Fry the shrimps on moderate heat until pink, about 1 minute. Remove and leave to cool. Add to the egg mixture and mix well.

Add the remaining lard or oil to the wok and heat thoroughly. Pour in the egg mixture and cook on moderate heat until browned underneath, then turn and cook the other side. The omelette may be cut into 4 or 6 pieces to make turning easier. When done, transfer to a warmed serving plate.

Wipe out the wok and add the pre-mixed sauce ingredients. Bring to the boil and simmer briefly, then pour over the omelette and serve at once.

*Or use cooked ham.

FRIED SHRIMP PATTIES IN FRUITY SAUCE

Serve as an appetiser or main dish. Makes 18.

375 g (12 oz)	raw peeled shrimps
200 g (6½ oz)	pork fat
1 tablespoon	finely chopped cooked ham
2 teaspoons	finely chopped fresh coriander
2 tablespoons	softened lard or frying oil

Seasoning:

1	egg white, beaten
¾ teaspoon	salt
¼ teaspoon	m.s.g. (optional)
¼ teaspoon	white pepper
2 teaspoons	ginger wine
1 tablespoon	cornflour (cornstarch)

Sauce:

2 tablespoons	chicken stock
½ cup (4 fl oz)	liquid from canned pineapple or mango
2 tablespoons	tomato sauce (ketchup)
½ teaspoon	chilli oil
½ teaspoon	salt
¼ teaspoon	m.s.g. (optional)
1½ teaspoons	sugar
2 teaspoons	cornflour (cornstarch)

Finely mince (grind) the shrimps and 45 g (1½ oz) of the pork fat, or pulverise in a food processor. Add the seasoning ingredients and form into walnut-sized balls, then flatten into patties.

Thinly slice the remaining pork fat and cut into circles to fit the shrimp patties. Garnish the patties with the chopped ham and coriander, pressing on lightly, then stand each pattie on a piece of pork fat.

Heat a flat-bottomed iron griddle or large frying pan to moderate and add the softened lard or frying oil. Place the patties in the pan fat downwards, and fry on moderate heat for 2 minutes, then cover and continue to cook until the fat is crisp and golden and the patties cooked through, about 6 minutes. Splash in a little water if they begin to stick or the fat is cooking too fast.

Bring the pre-mixed sauce ingredients to the boil in another pan and simmer for 1 minute. Transfer the patties to a serving plate and cover with the sauce just before serving.

SHRIMP SAUSAGE SAUTÉD WITH BEAN SPROUTS

185 g (6 oz)	raw peeled shrimps
2	spring onions (scallions), trimmed and shredded
4 slices	fresh ginger, shredded
185 g (6 oz)	fresh bean sprouts
¼ cup (2 fl oz)	softened lard or frying oil

Seasoning A:

1	egg white, beaten
¼ teaspoon	salt
½ teaspoon	m.s.g. (optional)
	pinch of white pepper
1 tablespoon	cornflour (cornstarch)
1 tablespoon	rendered chicken fat (chicken grease), or use lard

Seasoning B/Sauce:

⅓ cup	chicken stock
1 teaspoon	rice wine or dry sherry
1 teaspoon	sesame oil
⅓ teaspoon	salt
¼ teaspoon	m.s.g. (optional)
¼ teaspoon	white pepper
¼ teaspoon	sugar
1 teaspoon	cornflour (cornstarch)

Pulverise the shrimp in a food processor or by using 2 cleavers (see page 396). Add the seasoning A ingredients and mix thoroughly until the mixture is smooth. Heat a saucepan of lightly salted water to boiling, then reduce the heat until the water is gently simmering.

Transfer the shrimp paste to a piping bag fitted with a large plain nozzle and pipe a continuous stream of the paste in a circle into the simmering water. Cook for 1 minute, then lift out and rinse in cold water. Leave to cool, then cut into pieces about 5 cm (2 in) long.

Heat the wok and add the lard or oil. Sauté the spring onions and ginger for 45 seconds, then push to one side of the pan and add the bean sprouts and sauté until softened. Remove. Reheat the pan and sauté the shrimp sausage for 1½ minutes, until lightly coloured. Add the pre-mixed seasoning B/sauce ingredients and return the spring onions, ginger, and bean sprouts and mix well. Simmer until the sauce has thickened, then transfer to a warmed serving plate.

Shrimp Sausage Sautéd with Bean Sprouts (recipe this page) and Mushroom with Chicken Wings in Soup (recipe page 318).

PAPER-WRAPPED SHRIMPS

Serve as an appetiser or main dish.

315 g (10 oz)	raw peeled shrimps
45 g (1½ oz)	Chinese or cured (Smithfield) ham, or use cooked ham
30 g (1 oz)	canned champignons, drained
12 small sprigs	fresh coriander
12 sheets	edible rice paper (about 10 cm/4 in square)*
1	egg yolk, beaten
4 cups (1 litre)	deep-frying oil

Seasoning:

1	egg white, beaten
½ teaspoon	salt
½ teaspoon	m.s.g. (optional)
¼ teaspoon	white pepper
¼ teaspoon	bicarbonate of soda (optional)
1 teaspoon	cornflour (cornstarch)

Wash the shrimps and devein with a toothpick (see page 394). Place in a dish with the seasoning ingredients and leave for 10 minutes. Finely slice the ham and champignons.

Spread the rice papers on a board and arrange several shrimps diagonally across the centre of each. Add several pieces of ham, champignon, and a sprig of coriander to each parcel and fold up. Stick the flap down with egg yolk.

Heat the deep-frying oil to moderate and fry the shrimp parcels, several at a time, until cooked through, about 1½ minutes. Drain and place on a serving plate. Serve at once with Chinese pepper-salt (see page 384) and light soy sauce as dips.

* If unobtainable, use cellophane paper and cut the parcels open before serving.

STEAMED FRESH PRAWNS

750 g (1½ lb)	large green prawns (shrimps) in the shell
1 tablespoon	frying oil

Sauce Dip:

⅓ cup	dark soy sauce
2½ tablespoons	vegetable oil
1 teaspoon	sugar
2	fresh red chilli peppers

Prepare the sauce first. Thinly slice the chillies, discarding the seeds. Mix the soy sauce, oil, and sugar until amalgamated, then add the chillies and pour into several small dishes. Set aside. If preferred, chopped spring onion and/or fresh ginger can be used in place of the chilli peppers.

Wash the prawns in cold, lightly salted water and place in a large dish so that none overlaps. Sprinkle on the oil and set the dish on a rack in a steamer. Cover and steam over rapidly boiling water for about 8 minutes. The actual cooking time will depend on the size of the prawns. Test by opening one after 6 minutes.

Serve the prawns straight from the steamer with the sauce dips and damp napkins or finger bowls.

PRAWNS CLEAR AS CRYSTAL

625 g (1¼ lb)	green prawns (shrimps), in the shell
1 tablespoon	bicarbonate of soda
1 teaspoon	salt
1 tablespoon	cornflour (cornstarch)
6	spring onions (scallions), trimmed and finely shredded
5 cm (2 in) piece	fresh ginger, finely shredded
	small bunch of fresh coriander
	oyster sauce*
	Chinese shrimp sauce
3 cups (24 fl oz)	deep-frying oil

Seasoning/Sauce:

¼ cup (2 fl oz)	chicken stock
2 teaspoons	rice wine or dry sherry
½ teaspoon	sesame oil (optional)
¼ teaspoon	salt
½ teaspoon	m.s.g. (optional)
	pinch of white pepper

Shell the prawns and cut in halves lengthwise. Remove the veins and place in a dish with water to cover. Add the bicarbonate of soda, mix in and leave for 2 — 3 hours, then rinse well in cold water, gently rubbing on the salt and cornflour in the process. Drain and wipe dry with kitchen paper. This process whitens the prawns and eliminates the slight fishy odour.

Arrange the shredded onions and ginger on a serving plate. Wash the coriander thoroughly, remove the stems and set aside for garnish. Make up several dip dishes of oyster sauce and shrimp paste. If shrimp paste is unobtainable, use anchovy sauce or essence.

Bring a saucepan of water to the boil and in another pan heat the deep-frying oil to fairly hot. Place the prawns in a wire strainer and dip into the boiling water for 30 seconds. Lift out and drain well. Shake in a kitchen towel to absorb excess water, then transfer to a frying basket and dip into the hot oil for 10 seconds. Lift out and shake off the oil, then return to the hot oil for a further 10 seconds. Remove and drain well.

Pour off the water and wipe out the pan. Add the pre-mixed seasoning/sauce ingredients and bring to the boil. Simmer briefly, then add the prawns and turn quickly in the sauce until glazed. Arrange on the onions and ginger and garnish with the fresh coriander. Serve at once with the prepared dips.

* Some of the less expensive of the commercial brands of oyster sauce are not suitable for use as a dipping sauce. The better brands have the strong salty taste necessary when serving straight from the bottle.

STIR-FRIED PRAWNS AND CHOY SUM

250 g (8 oz)	peeled green prawns (shrimps)
375 g (12 oz)	fresh choy sum*
3 slices	fresh ginger
¼ cup (2 fl oz)	frying oil

Seasoning/Sauce:

¼ cup (2 fl oz)	chicken stock
2 teaspoons	light soy sauce
2 teaspoons	rice wine or dry sherry
¼ teaspoon	sesame oil
⅓ teaspoon	salt
½ teaspoon	sugar
	pinch of white pepper
¾ teaspoon	cornflour (cornstarch)

Wash and devein the prawns and wipe dry. Cut the choy sum into 4 cm (1 2/3 in) pieces and blanch in boiling water for 1½ minutes. Drain.

Heat the oil in a wok and add the ginger. Fry briefly, then stir-fry the prawns until they turn pink, about 1½ minutes. Remove and keep warm.

Add the vegetables and stir-fry for 2 minutes, then add the pre-mixed seasoning/sauce ingredients and bring to the boil. Simmer for 1 minute, return the prawns and heat through. Serve.

* Or use fresh broccoli, broken into florets.

STEAMED JUMBO PRAWNS SERVED IN CLEAR SAUCE

750 g (1½ lb)	large green prawns (shrimps), in the shell
¾ teaspoon	salt
¼ teaspoon	m.s.g. (optional)
½ teaspoon	sugar
¼ teaspoon	white pepper
2 teaspoons	rice wine or dry sherry
1½ teaspoons	sesame oil (optional)
2	spring onions (scallions), finely shredded
3 thick slices	fresh ginger, finely shredded

Use a sharp knife to cut down the backs of the prawns through the shells. Remove the dark veins but leave the shells in place.

Place the prawns in a dish and sprinkle on the remaining ingredients. Set on a rack in a steamer, cover tightly and steam over rapidly boiling water for 8 — 9 minutes.

The dish containing the prawns should not be covered inside the steamer. Condensation and the drawing out of the natural juices of the prawns during cooking will result in a quantity of clear liquid accumulating in the dish. Strain this into a separate bowl and adjust the seasoning.

Transfer the prawns to a serving dish and pour on the sauce. Serve at once.

DEEP-FRIED PRAWN BALLS

Serve as an appetiser or main dish.

375 g (12 oz)	peeled green prawns (shrimps)
45 g (1½ oz)	pork fat
30 g (1 oz)	canned water chestnuts, drained
4 cups (1 litre)	deep-frying oil

Seasoning:

1	egg white, beaten
¾ teaspoon	salt
¼ teaspoon	m.s.g. (optional)
¼ teaspoon	ground black pepper
¾ teaspoon	rice wine or dry sherry
½ teaspoon	sesame oil (optional)
1 tablespoon	cornflour (cornstarch)

Devein the prawns with a toothpick (see page 394), then pulverise with the pork fat in a food processor or by using 2 cleavers. Finely chop the water chestnuts and add to the prawn paste with the seasoning ingredients. Work into a smooth paste by gathering into a ball and throwing repeatedly against the side of the bowl (see page 395).

If possible, prepare the prawn mixture several hours beforehand and chilli thoroughly. This gives a better consistency to the mixture.

Heat the deep-frying oil to moderately hot. Form the mixture into small balls by squeezing a portion of the paste from the left hand (see page 395) and scooping into the oil with a spoon. Cook about 6 at a time for 2½ — 3 minutes, or until golden. Drain and keep warm until all are cooked. Quickly deep-fry all the balls together to reheat, then drain well and serve on a plate of shredded lettuce with hot mustard and light soy sauce as dips.

Deep-Fried Fish Fillets with Black Sesame Seed Dressing (recipe page 271).

BRAISED PRAWNS IN GRAVY

500 g (1 lb)	green prawns (shrimps) in the shell
1 cup (8 fl oz)	frying oil
4	spring onions (scallions), trimmed and sliced
4 slices	fresh ginger

Seasoning A:

⅓ teaspoon	salt
¼ teaspoon	m.s.g. (optional)
¼ teaspoon	white pepper
2 teaspoons	sesame oil

Seasoning B/Sauce:

1 cup (8 fl oz)	chicken stock
2 tablespoons	light soy sauce
¾ teaspoon	chilli oil*
1½ teaspoons	sesame oil
¼ teaspoon	salt
¾ teaspoon	sugar
¼ teaspoon	white pepper
1½ teaspoons	cornflour (cornstarch)

Peel the prawns, leaving the heads and tails intact. Devein with a toothpick (see page 394) and place in a dish. Add the seasoning A ingredients and leave for 15 minutes to marinate.

Heat the frying oil to fairly hot and stir-fry the prawns until the heads turn bright red, about 1 minute. Remove. Add the onions and ginger and stir-fry for 30 seconds, then pour in the pre-mixed seasoning B/sauce ingredients and bring to the boil. Return the prawns.

Reduce the heat to simmer until the prawns are tender and the sauce thickened. Transfer to a warmed serving dish.

*Or omit the chilli oil and use oyster sauce or hot black bean sauce. Add slightly less soy sauce, to taste.

WALNUT-STUFFED PRAWNS

Serve as an appetiser or main dish.

375 g (12 oz)	green prawn (shrimp) cutlets*
90 g (3 oz)	shelled walnuts
4 cups (1 litre)	deep-frying oil
6	dried black mushrooms, soaked for 25 minutes
2	egg whites, well beaten
3 tablespoons	cornflour (cornstarch) extra cornflour (cornstarch)
6	young Chinese (celery) cabbage hearts, young bok choy or kale
2	spring onions (scallions), trimmed and sliced
2 slices	fresh ginger, shredded

Seasoning/Sauce:

⅓ cup	chicken stock
½ teaspoon	rice wine or dry sherry
¾ teaspoon	sesame oil (optional)
½ teaspoon	salt
½ teaspoon	m.s.g. (optional)
¾ teaspoon	sugar
	pinch of white pepper
1 teaspoon	cornflour (cornstarch)

Rinse the prawn cutlets in cold water and dry well. Peel the walnuts by first dropping into boiling water for 20 seconds, draining and pulling away the dark skin while the nuts are still warm. Dry well and deep-fry in hot oil for 1½ — 1¾ minutes, until golden. Drain and leave to cool.

Squeeze the water from the mushrooms and remove the stems. Use a sharp paring knife to cut a cross shape in the top of each cap. Set aside.

Bat the prawn cutlets lightly with the side of a cleaver to flatten and tenderise. Place a walnut in the centre of each prawn, fold the prawn around it with the tail folded across the roll and squeeze firmly. The tails may be removed, if preferred.

Make a batter with the egg whites, cornflour, and a little water. Heat the deep-frying oil to fairly hot. Dip the prawn rolls into the batter, then dust lightly with cornflour. Deep-fry until golden, about 1½ minutes. Remove and drain well.

Pour off all but 3 tablespoons of the oil and sauté the vegetables until softened. Remove to a serving plate. Add the spring onions and ginger and sauté briefly, then add the pre-mixed seasoning/sauce ingredients and bring to the boil. Simmer until thickened, add the prawns and stir in the sauce, then arrange over the vegetables and pour on any remaining sauce. Serve.

*Reasonably large prawns, peeled, deveined, and cut open down the back so they can be pressed out flat, butterfly style.

STUFFED PRAWNS IN HOT SAUCE

500 g (1 lb)	large green prawns (shrimps), in the shell
1 teaspoon	salt
60 g (2 oz)	fatty pork, finely minced (ground)
2 teaspoons	finely chopped cooked ham
2 teaspoons	finely chopped softened dried mushrooms or champignons
1	large egg, beaten
	cornflour (cornstarch)
4 cups (1 litre)	deep-frying oil

Sauce:

¼ cup (2 fl oz)	chicken stock
2 tablespoons	light soy sauce
1 teaspoon	rice wine or dry sherry
½ — ¾ teaspoon	chilli oil*
¼ teaspoon	salt
½ teaspoon	m.s.g. (optional)
½ teaspoon	sugar
	pinch of white pepper
1 teaspoon	cornflour (cornstarch)

Remove heads from the prawns and sprinkle them with salt. Set aside. Cut off about 2.5 cm (1 in) of meat from the top end of each prawn, devein and chop finely. Mix with the minced pork and add a dash of salt, m.s.g., if used, and white pepper.

Cut the remaining parts of the prawns open along the back, cutting deep enough that they can be pressed out flat. Devein and coat lightly with cornflour. Press a portion of the prawn and pork mixture onto each, forming into a fanned shape. Garnish with the chopped ham and mushrooms and brush with beaten egg. Coat lightly with cornflour.

Heat the deep-frying oil to fairly hot and fry the stuffed prawns for 1½ minutes, until golden. Drain and set aside, keeping warm. Pour off all but 2 tablespoons of the oil and stir-fry the prawn heads for about 3 minutes until bright red and cooked through.

Line up the heads on a serving dish and arrange the tails near them. Wipe out the pan and add 1 tablespoon of the deep-frying oil. Pour in the pre-mixed sauce ingredients and bring to the boil. Stir until thickened, then pour over the prawn tails and serve at once.

*Or substitute 1½ tablespoons hot black bean sauce for the chilli oil and use only 1½ — 2 teaspoons of soy sauce.

STEAMED FEMALE CRABS WITH GINGER SAUCE

6	small female crabs
2	spring onions (scallions), trimmed and shredded
6 slices	fresh ginger, shredded
2 teaspoons	rice wine or dry sherry

Ginger Sauce:

5 cm (2 in) piece	fresh ginger peeled and minced
½ cup (4 fl oz)	white vinegar
1 tablespoon	sugar
2 teaspoons	sesame oil

Prepare the sauce first to allow time for the flavours to blend. Mix the four ingredients together, stirring until the sugar is completely dissolved. Pour into several small dishes and set aside.

Wash the crabs, cut open underneath and remove the inedible parts, then crack the claws. Reassemble the crabs and place in a large dish. Sprinkle on the wine and scatter the shredded onion and ginger over the crabs. Set on a rack in a steamer and steam over high heat for 15 minutes.

Serve with the sauce.

CRABMEAT OMELETTE

3	egg whites
2	whole eggs
2 tablespoons	chicken stock
¼ teaspoon	salt
2 tablespoons	softened lard
1	large spring onion (scallion), trimmed and shredded
1 slice	fresh ginger, shredded
60 g (2 oz)	fresh crabmeat
15 g (1 oz)	crab roe
1 teaspoon	rice wine or dry sherry

Sauce:

2 tablespoons	chicken stock
1 tablespoon	oyster sauce
½ teaspoon	rice wine or dry sherry
½ teaspoon	m.s.g. (optional)
½ teaspoon	sugar, or to taste
	pinch of ground black pepper
2/3 teaspoon	cornflour (cornstarch)

Beat the egg whites and whole eggs together and add the chicken stock and salt.

Heat half the lard in a wok and sauté the spring onion and ginger briefly. Add the crabmeat and cook until lightly coloured, then add the roe and sizzle the wine onto the sides of the pan and stir in. Remove and keep warm.

Reheat the wok and add the remaining lard. Pour in the egg mixture and cook on moderate heat until lightly coloured underneath, then spread the cooked crab over the egg and carefully turn the omelette. Cook the underside until just firm, lift onto a serving plate. It may be cut into quarters to make turning easier.

Wipe out the wok and add the pre-mixed sauce ingredients. Simmer, stirring until thickened, about 45 seconds. Pour over the omelette and serve at once.

STUFFED CRAB CLAWS

Serve as an appetiser.

12	large crab pincers, meat intact
375 g (12 oz)	raw peeled shrimps
1¼ cups	fresh breadcrumbs
2	eggs, well beaten
	cornflour (cornstarch)
⅓ cup	toasted white sesame seeds
6 cups (1½ litres)	deep-frying oil

Seasoning:

2	egg whites, beaten
¾ teaspoon	salt
¼ teaspoon	white pepper
⅓ teaspoon	hot mustard powder
1½ teaspoons	lemon juice

Break away the shell from the top of the pincer, leaving the meat attached to the central tendon and the claw. Pulverise the shrimps in a food processor, then add the breadcrumbs and seasoning ingredients and mix to a smooth paste. Add a very little water if the mixture is dry. Dust the crab meat with cornflour and press on a coating of the shrimp mixture, forming into a ball shape around the crabmeat and smoothing around so that only the tip of the claw shows. Dust very lightly with cornflour, then brush with beaten egg and dip the ends of the stuffed crab claws into the sesame seeds.

Heat the deep-frying oil to moderately hot and deep-fry the crab claws, several at a time, to a golden brown, 2½ — 3 minutes. Drain well.

. Arrange on a bed of shredded lettuce and serve with dips of light soy sauce and Chinese pepper-salt (see page 384).

RED-STEWED CAMEL'S PADS

A Chinese recipe in its original form rarely provides detailed information as to the exact amount of seasonings and spices. These are left open to interpretation by the chef undertaking the dish. We follow that example with this recipe.

1 catty (approximately 500 g/1 lb) | *water-soaked camel's pads*
30 g (1 oz) | *bamboo shoots*
6 | *dried black mushrooms, soaked to soften*
10 | *young vegetable hearts*
2 catties (approximately 4 cups) | *chicken stock*

Seasoning:

rice wine or dry sherry
light soy sauce
dark soy sauce
salt
m.s.g. (optional)
white sugar
rendered chicken fat
cornflour (cornstarch)
shredded spring onions (scallions)
shredded ginger

Cut the drained camel's pads into chunks. Slice the bamboo shoots, drain the mushrooms and remove the stems. Wash the vegetables.

Place the cubed pads in a saucepan, cover with cold water and bring to the boil. Drain and cover with water again. Bring back to the boil, add the spring onions, ginger and wine and simmer for 6 — 7 minutes. This process will remove the rather pungent smell. Drain well and rinse in cold water.

Bring the chicken stock to the boil. Add the cubed pads, mushrooms, bamboo shoots, and the seasoning ingredients. Simmer for 15 minutes, then thicken with the cornflour. Transfer to a serving plate.

Simmer the vegetables in slightly salted stock or water until tender. Arrange around the meat and serve.

DEEP-FRIED BOILED CAMEL'S HUMP

1 catty (approximately 500 g/1 lb) | *water-soaked camel's hump*
1½ catties (approximately 3 cups) | *chicken stock*
| *cooking oil*

Seasoning:

light soy sauce
salt
m.s.g. (optional)
Chinese pepper-salt
shredded spring onions (scallions)
shredded fresh ginger
cornflour (cornstarch)

Cut the hump into angled pieces. Place in a saucepan and cover with cold water. Bring to the boil, drain and cover with more cold water. Add the spring onions and ginger and bring to the boil. Drain again.

Bring the chicken stock to the boil, add the camel's hump pieces and the seasonings and simmer for 10 — 15 minutes, then drain and discard the soup.

Heat deep-frying oil to smoking point. Dust the hump pieces lightly with cornflour and deep-fry until crisp and golden on the surface. Drain well.

Serve hot with the pepper-salt as a dip

LOBSTER WITH BLACK BEANS AND CHILLIES

1 750 g (1½ lb)	fresh lobster
1 tablespoon	fermented black beans
¾ teaspoon	crushed garlic
1 teaspoon	sugar
¼ cup (2 fl oz)	frying oil
1	spring onion (scallion), trimmed and diced
1 — 2	fresh red chilli peppers, thinly sliced
4 slices	fresh ginger, shredded
¾ teaspoon	rice wine or dry sherry
1 tablespoon	light soy sauce

Seasoning/Sauce:

¼ cup (2 fl oz)	chicken stock
1 teaspoon	ginger wine
¼ teaspoon	salt
¼ teaspoon	ground black pepper
¾ teaspoon	cornflour (cornstarch)

Cut the lobster in halves and discard inedible parts. Scoop out the flesh and cut into cubes. Scrape out the shell and drop it, with the head, into a saucepan of boiling water. Cook until bright red, then drain, rinse with cold water and brush again to remove any residue. Rinse in cold, salted water and dry with kitchen towels. Place on a serving plate.

Wash the black beans, dry well and chop finely. Mix with the garlic and sugar and fry in a wok with the frying oil for 1 minute. Add the lobster pieces and stir-fry until white and firm, about 2 minutes, then remove. Reheat the wok and stir-fry the spring onion, chilli pepper and ginger together for 1 minute, sizzle the wine and soy sauce onto the sides of the wok and stir in, then add the pre-mixed seasoning/sauce ingredients and bring to the boil. Return the lobster and black beans and simmer until the sauce is thickened.

Spoon into the lobster shell and serve at once.

STIR-FRIED SQUID WITH VEGETABLES

625 g (1¼ lb)	fresh squid
30 g (1 oz)	canned bamboo shoots, drained and sliced
1	medium carrot, peeled and thinly sliced
12	snow peas, strings removed*
1½	spring onions (scallions), trimmed and sliced
6 thin slices	fresh ginger
½ teaspoon	crushed garlic
5 cups (1¼ litres)	deep-frying oil

Seasoning/Sauce:

¼ cup (2 fl oz)	chicken stock
½ teaspoon	sesame oil (optional)
1 teaspoon	salt
½ teaspoon	m.s.g. (optional)
½ teaspoon	sugar
¼ teaspoon	ground black pepper
1 teaspoon	cornflour (cornstarch)

Remove the heads and stomachs from the squid and discard. Pull away the pink skin with fins attached, leaving only the white tubular bodies. Cut open and press out flat. Rinse well, pulling away any white membrane. Score on the inside in a close diagonal criss-cross pattern, cutting at a slight angle (see page 395).

Cut into diamond-shaped bite-sized pieces and blanch for 10 seconds in boiling water, then drain well. Blanch the bamboo shoots, carrots, and snow peas or other vegetables and drain well.

Heat the deep-frying oil to moderate and fry the squid in a basket for 20 seconds only. Lift out and drain well. Pour off all but ⅓ cup of the oil and stir-fry the spring onions, ginger, and garlic on fairly high heat for 45 seconds. Add the vegetables and stir-fry together until beginning to soften, about 1 minute.

Pour in the pre-mixed seasoning/sauce ingredients and bring to the boil. Simmer briefly, return the squid and heat through. Transfer to a serving plate.

For convenience, stir-fry the squid also. Extend the blanching time to 25 seconds and stir-fry only briefly with the vegetables. Do not overcook or the squid will become tough and chewy.
*Or use 1 small green capsicum pepper, cut into small squares, 12 broccoli or cauliflower florets, or 6 soaked dried black mushrooms.

DEEP-FRIED OYSTERS

Serve as an appetiser or main dish.

12	very large oysters or 24 medium oysters
1 teaspoon	Chinese pepper-salt
6 cups (1½ litres)	deep-frying oil

Batter:

⅓ cup	flour
½ cup	cornflour (cornstarch)
2½ teaspoons	baking powder
1 teaspoon	salt
	pinch of white pepper
1½ tablespoons	vegetable oil

Wash the oysters in lightly salted water, then rub with the pepper-salt. Set aside.

Make a smooth, fairly thick batter by mixing the batter ingredients with cold water. Beat for 1½ — 2 minutes, then set aside for 10 minutes.

Heat the deep-frying oil to smoking point. Coat the oysters thickly with batter and deep-fry, several at a time, until golden and well puffed up. Drain on absorbent paper.

Arrange on a bed of shredded lettuce and serve with dips of Chinese pepper-salt and sweet and sour sauce (see page 384 and 385).

SCALLOPS WITH SHRIMPS AND MUSHROOMS

12	large fresh sea scallops
155 g (5 oz)	raw peeled shrimps
90 g (3 oz)	canned straw mushrooms, drained and cut in halves
¼ cup (2 fl oz)	frying oil
2	spring onions (scallions), trimmed and sliced
3 slices	fresh ginger
2	egg whites, well beaten cornflour (cornstarch)

Seasoning A:

½ teaspoon	salt
2 teaspoons	ginger wine (see page 387)

Seasoning B:

⅓ teaspoon	salt
¾ teaspoon	sugar
½ cup (4 fl oz)	chicken stock

Rinse the scallops in cold water and drain well. Place in a dish and add the seasoning A ingredients. Devein the shrimps, rinse with cold water and add to the scallops. Leave to marinate for 10 minutes.

Bring the seasoning B ingredients to the boil in a small saucepan. Add the mushrooms and simmer for 3 minutes. Remove from the heat and leave in the stock.

Heat the frying oil and sauté the spring onions and ginger until softened, then add the scallops and shrimps and sauté on moderately high heat until barely cooked through. The scallops should be white and just firm, the shrimps pink and firm.

Add the mushrooms and the stock and bring to the boil. Mix a little cornflour with cold water and pour into the sauce. Simmer until thickened, then slowly drizzle in the beaten egg whites and cook without stirring until the egg sets in white strands in the sauce. Serve at once.

CHARCOAL ROASTED EEL ON SKEWERS

Serve as an appetiser or main dish.

1 750 g (1½ lb)	fresh-water eel
2 tablespoons	frying oil
1½ teaspoons	sesame oil (optional)

Seasoning:

3 tablespoons	finely chopped spring onion (scallion)
1 tablespoon	grated fresh ginger
¼ cup (2 fl oz)	light soy sauce
1 tablespoon	dark soy sauce
2 tablespoons	rice wine or dry sherry
	juice of 1 lemon
2 tablespoons	vegetable oil
½ teaspoon	m.s.g. (optional)
2 tablespoons	sugar
⅓ teaspoon	ground black pepper

Clean the eel, cut off the head and tail section and discard. Cut the body into pieces about 4 cm (1 2/3 in) long and cut down to the backbone so the pieces can be pressed out flat.

Place on a tray and pour on the seasoning ingredients. Leave for 10 minutes, then turn and leave for a further 10 minutes. Thread each piece onto two metal skewers, passing across the pieces so they remain flat.

Place the eel on an oiled grid, skin side downwards over glowing charcoal, and grill (broil) for 3 minutes. Turn and cook the other side for 2 minutes. Brush with any remaining marinade and continue to cook and turn until evenly cooked with the outside crisp, dark, and glazed with the sauce, the meat inside, moist and white. Do not overcook.

Serve on a bed of shredded lettuce.

STEWED RIVER EEL WITH DICED PORK AND MUSHROOMS

1 750 g (1½ lb)	fresh-water eel
125 g (4 oz)	fatty or roast pork, diced
6 cups (1½ litres)	deep-frying oil
8 cloves	garlic
3 pieces	dried orange peel
4	spring onions (scallions), trimmed and cut in halves
5 slices	fresh ginger
6	dried black mushrooms, soaked for 25 minutes
3 cups (24 fl oz)	chicken stock
	cornflour (cornstarch)
	sesame oil
	white pepper

Seasoning A:

¾ teaspoon	salt
¼ cup (2 fl oz)	light soy sauce
1½ teaspoons	dark soy sauce
1½ tablespoons	rice wine or dry sherry

Seasoning B/Sauce:

2 tablespoons	light soy sauce
1 tablespoon	sugar
¾ teaspoon	m.s.g. (optional)
	pinch of white pepper

Wash the eels, rubbing with salt to remove the slime. Rinse in cold water and cut into 5 cm (2 in) pieces, discarding the head and tail. Blanch in boiling water for 1 minute, drain and place in a dish with the seasoning A ingredients. Leave for 20 minutes. Drain, reserving the marinade.

Heat the deep-frying oil and fry the pork until lightly coloured. Drain and set aside. Add the eel and deep-fry for 1 minute, drain and transfer to a casserole. Scatter the diced pork on top. Drain off all but ⅓ cup of the oil and fry the garlic and orange peel for 1 minute, place with the eel, then fry the spring onions, ginger and drained mushrooms briefly and transfer, with the oil, to a casserole.

Add the reserved marinade and seasoning B/sauce ingredients. Heat the stock to boiling and pour over the eel. Cover and simmer until the eel is tender, about 30 minutes. Strain the sauce into a wok and bring to the boil, simmer until well reduced, then thicken with cornflour mixed with a little cold water and check the seasoning. Pour over the eel and season with a dash of sesame oil and white pepper. Serve in the casserole.

Stuffed Crab Claws (recipe page 284).

THREE COURSES OF ROAST SUCKLING PIG

Serves 10 — 12.

Dishes 1 and 2:

1	*freshly roasted suckling pig (see recipe, page 328; Roast Suckling Pig)*
24	*'Mandarin' pancakes (see page 373)*
12	*spring onions (scallions)*
½ cup (4 fl oz)	*'duck' sauce (see page 385)*

Dish 3:

¼ cup (2 fl oz)	*frying oil*
375 g (12 oz)	*fresh broccoli, broken into florets*
1½	*spring onions (scallions), trimmed and sliced*
3 slices	*fresh ginger, shredded*
1 tablespoon	*rice wine or dry sherry*

Seasoning/Sauce:

2/3 cup	*chicken stock*
1¼ teaspoons	*salt*
¾ teaspoon	*m.s.g. (optional)*
½ teaspoon	*sugar*
1½ teaspoons	*cornflour (cornstarch)*

Dish 1:

Prepare the pancakes and arrange half on a serving plate. Remove the roots and leafy green tops from the spring onions and shred one end of each piece. Place on another serving plate. Fill several small dishes with the sauce.

Carve the crisp skin from the pork and cut into bite-sized pieces. Arrange back over the pig and surround with an attractive garnish of fresh vegetables and parsley. Take to the table with the accompaniments.

To eat, dip several pieces of skin into the sauce and place in the centre of a pancake, add a piece of spring onion and roll up.

Dish 2:

Return the pig to the kitchen and carve off the choicest pieces of the meat. Cut into bite-sized pieces and rearrange on the pig. Serve with the remaining pancakes and onions. Again, roll in the pancake after dipping in the sauce.

Dish 3:

Return the pig to the kitchen again and carve off the remaining meat. Cut into bite-sized pieces. Heat the frying oil in a wok and sauté the broccoli for 2 minutes, then push to one side of the pan and add the spring onions and ginger. Sauté briefly, then add the pork and fry on high heat, turning constantly. Mix in the broccoli and sizzle the wine onto the sides of the wok.

Pour in the pre-mixed seasoning/sauce ingredients and simmer until the sauce thickens. Transfer to a serving plate and serve.

PORK AND DUCK LIVER ROLL

Serve as an appetiser or main dish.

280 g (9 oz)	*lean pork, finely minced (ground)*
60 g (2 oz)	*canned water chestnuts, drained and finely chopped*
1	*duck (or chicken) liver, cubed*
1	*small onion, diced*
185 g (6 oz)	*pork omentum**
1	*egg white, beaten*
1 tablespoon	*cornflour (cornstarch)*
4 cups (1 litre)	*deep-frying oil*

Seasoning:

1	*egg white, beaten*
¾ teaspoon	*salt*
½ teaspoon	*m.s.g. (optional)*
1 tablespoon	*light soy sauce*
1 teaspoon	*rice wine or dry sherry*
2 teaspoons	*cornflour (cornstarch)*

Mix the pork and water chestnuts with the seasoning ingredients and set aside. Use a little of the deep-frying oil to sauté the liver and diced onion, then add to the pork mixture.

Wash the pork omentum and spread on a board. It may be easier to work if divided into several even-sized squares. If using the chicken skin, cut in halves for easier handling. Make a paste of the egg white and cornflour and spread over the pork fat or beancurd skin. Omit if using chicken skin. Spread on the pork mixture, leaving a wide border all round. Roll into a long sausage shape and stick down the ends and long edge with more of the egg white paste. The chicken skin rolls should be secured with toothpicks or sewn up with a needle and thread.

Heat the deep-frying oil to moderate and fry the roll(s) until cooked through, and crisp and golden, about 4 minutes. Remove from the oil and drain well. Cut diagonally across the rolls into thick slices and arrange on a serving plate. Serve with sweet and sour sauce or with spiced salt (see page 385 and 384).
*If pork omentum (caul net/fat) is unobtainable, use either a dampened sheet of beancurd skin or a chicken skin.

CANTONESE ROAST PORK

Serve hot or cold as an appetiser or main dish.

1 kg (2 lb)	*pork fillet (tenderloin)*
1 tablespoon	*five spice powder*
2 teaspoons	*finely ground Chinese brown peppercorns*
3 tablespoons	*finely chopped spring onion (scallion)*
1 tablespoon	*finely chopped fresh ginger*

Seasoning:

½ cup (4 fl oz)	*light soy sauce*
2½ tablespoons	*soybean paste, dark soy sauce or oyster sauce*
1 tablespoon	*sesame oil*
2 tablespoons	*rice wine or dry sherry*
⅓ cup	*sugar*
	red food colouring

Special Equipment: A rotisserie oven or metal hooks for hanging the meat in the oven.

Choose large fillets and cut lengthwise into two or three strips, about 15 cm (6 in) long and 5 cm (2 in) wide. Rub with the five spice powder and ground peppercorns and place in a dish. Arrange the chopped spring onion and ginger on top, then pour on the pre-mixed seasoning ingredients after stirring until the sugar dissolves. (Add red food colouring to give a fairly bright colour.) Cover the dish with plastic wrap and leave for about 4 hours to marinate.

If the oven has a rotisserie, thread the strips of meat through one end onto the spike so that they hang down in the oven. Place a drip tray underneath. Otherwise, secure each strip by one end on metal hooks. Position one rack on the highest setting in the oven and remove the other racks. Hang the hooks on this rack, separating each piece as much as possible.

Do not set the rotisserie in motion. Cook the pork on very high heat for the first 10 minutes, about 240°C (450°F) then reduce to around 170°C (325 — 350°F) to cook for a further 20 minutes. Brush frequently with the pan drippings to keep the meat moist and to glaze the surface.

When done, leave to cool slightly, then slice and serve with hot mustard and light soy sauce as dips. Use in recipes requiring barbecue or roast pork and in assortments of cold cuts as an appetiser (see recipe, page 381).

A popular way to serve this pork is to arrange it over crisp deep-fried peanuts, or over peanuts (groundnuts) or soybeans that have been boiled, then sauté in sweetened soy sauce.

DEEP-FRIED PORK CHOPS

6	*small pork loin chops (about 700 g/1⅓ lb)*
1½ cups	*dry breadcrumbs*
2	*eggs, well beaten*
	cornflour (cornstarch)
6 cups (1½ litres)	*deep-frying oil*
	spiced salt (see page 384)
	Worcestershire or light soy sauce

Seasoning:

½ teaspoon	*salt*
¾ teaspoon	*m.s.g. (optional)*
1 tablespoon·	*rice wine or dry sherry*
1 tablespoon	*finely chopped spring onion*
1½ teaspoons	*grated fresh ginger*

Bat the meaty centres of the chops with the side of a cleaver to flatten and tenderise. Rub on the seasoning ingredients and leave for 25 minutes to marinate.

Spread the breadcrumbs on a board. Dust the pork chops lightly with cornflour, then dip into beaten egg and place on the breadcrumbs. Press down on one side to coat thickly, then turn and coat the other side.

Heat the deep-frying oil to fairly hot and fry the pork chops for 1 minute. Lower the heat and continue to cook until the chops are well browned on the surface and cooked through, about 3 minutes longer.

Drain well and serve with dips of spiced salt and Worcestershire or soy sauce.

If preferred, the chops can be cut into bite-sized pieces, through the bones.

PORK FILLET ROLLS IN SWEET AND SOUR SAUCE

375 g (12 oz)	pork fillet (tenderloin)
	cornflour (cornstarch)
3 cups (24 fl oz)	deep-frying oil
1	small carrot, diced and par-boiled
1	small cucumber, diced
30 g (1 oz)	canned bamboo shoots, drained and diced
1	medium brown onion, diced

Seasoning A:

½ teaspoon	salt
¾ teaspoon	m.s.g. (optional)
¼ teaspoon	white pepper
2 teaspoons	rice wine or dry sherry
1 teaspoon	sesame oil (optional)

Seasoning B/Sauce:

2 tablespoons	finely chopped spring onion (scallion)
2 teaspoons	finely chopped fresh ginger
¼ cup (2 fl oz)	chicken stock or cold water
¼ cup (2 fl oz)	tomato sauce (ketchup)
2 tablespoons	white vinegar
2¾ tablespoons	sugar
½ teaspoon	salt
1 teaspoon	cornflour (cornstarch)

Thinly slice the pork, then score on one side in a criss-cross pattern and cut into 5 cm (2 in) squares. Mix with the seasoning A ingredients and leave for 20 minutes. Coat the pork lightly with cornflour, roll each piece into a cylindrical shape and deep-fry in the smoking hot oil for 1 minute. Remove and drain well. Turn the heat down to moderate and return the pork. Cook for about 2 minutes more, until cooked through and golden brown on the surface. Remove and keep warm.

Pour off the oil, wipe out the wok and return 3 tablespoons of the oil. Reheat to moderate and stir-fry the diced vegetables for 2 minutes, then add the chopped spring onion and ginger and stir-fry for 30 seconds. Pour in the remaining pre-mixed seasoning B/sauce ingredients and bring to the boil. Simmer for 2½ minutes, then add the pork and stir until the meat is evenly glazed with the sauce. Serve.

SWEET AND SOUR PORK RIBS

500 g (1 lb)	meaty pork ribs or chops
1	small green capsicum (bell pepper)
1	small red capsicum (bell pepper)
2 slices	canned pineapple, drained
1	small white onion
1	small carrot, sliced and par-boiled
	cornflour (cornstarch)
7 cups (1¾ litres)	deep-frying oil

Sauce:

⅓ cup	liquid from canned pineapple
⅓ cup	white vinegar
2 tablespoons	tomato sauce (ketchup)
1 tablespoon	vegetable oil
2½ tablespoons	sugar
½ teaspoon	salt
	pinch of ground black pepper
½ — ¾ teaspoon	finely chopped garlic
2 teaspoons	cornflour (cornstarch)

Cut the pork ribs or chops into 2.5 cm (1 in) cubes. Wash the peppers and cut in halves, remove the stems, seed cores, and inner white ribs. Cut into quarters. Cut the pineapple into pieces about the same size as the peppers. Peel the onion and cut into quarters, cutting from stem to root. Trim away the base to allow the pieces to separate.

Pour about 1½ cups of cornflour into a paper or plastic bag and add the meat. Close the bag and shake vigorously to thickly coat the meat with flour. Empty into a colander and shake off excess flour.

Heat the deep-frying oil to fairly hot. Fry the pork, about 10 pieces at a time, until well browned and crisp on the surface, about 3 minutes. Drain and keep the oil warm.

Transfer 2 — 3 tablespoons of the oil to another wok and fry the onion for 30 seconds. Add the peppers and fry a further 30 seconds, then add the carrots and stir-fry the vegetables together for a further 1 minute. Pour in the pre-mixed sauce ingredients and bring to the boil. Simmer for 2 minutes, then add the pineapple.

Reheat the deepfrying oil and fry the pork for a second time until crisp, about 1 minute. Drain and transfer to the sauce. Stir until evenly glazed with the sauce, then serve.

Lobster with Black Beans and Chillies (recipe page 286).

PORK RIBS WITH BLACK BEAN SAUCE

6	meaty pork ribs (about 625 g/1¼ lb)*
1½ tablespoons	fermented black beans
¾ teaspoon	crushed garlic
1½ teaspoons	sugar
2 tablespoons	light soy sauce
1 teaspoon	dark soy sauce
2 teaspoons	dry sherry
2 tablespoons	water
1 tablespoon	vegetable oil
1	fresh red chilli pepper (optional)

Trim the ribs and cut into 5 or 6 pieces each. Wash the black beans and dry well. Chop coarsely and mix with the remaining ingredients. Place the ribs in a dish and cover with the prepared seasonings. Leave for 1 — 2 hours to absorb the flavourings.

Set the dish on a rack in a steamer and steam over gently boiling water until the pork is completely tender, about 1 hour. Serve in the dish.

If using the chilli pepper, add before steaming.

* Or use pork chops.

SWEET AND SPICY SPARE RIBS

18	American-style pork spare ribs (about 700 g/1⅓ lb)*
Seasoning:	
¼ teaspoon	salt
1½ tablespoons	sugar
2 teaspoons	five spice powder
2 tablespoons	light soy sauce
2 tablespoons	rice wine or dry sherry
2 tablespoons	soy bean paste
2 cubes	fermented beancurd with the liquid, mashed
2 tablespoons	vegetables oil
1½ teaspoons	crushed garlic

Wash the spare ribs and dry on kitchen paper. Mix the seasoning ingredients together. Place the ribs in a dish and smear thickly on both sides with the seasoning paste. Leave for 1½ — 2 hours to absorb the flavourings, then arrange on an oiled oven tray and roast in a preheated moderately hot oven 220°C (425°F) or under a slow grill for about 25 minutes.

Turn the ribs occasionally during cooking and brush with any remaining seasoning paste and the pan drippings. Add also a little vegetable oil if they begin to dry.

Serve with spiced salt (see page 384) as a dip and with plum sauce.

*Pork rib bones with a sparce covering of meat. If unobtainable use small pork chops.

STIR-FRIED PORK WITH SPRING ONIONS IN SOY SAUCE

250 g (8 oz)	pork fillet (tenderloin)
2	large spring onions (scallions)
1 thick slice	fresh ginger, shredded
½ teaspoon	crushed garlic
¼ cup (2 fl oz)	frying oil
2 teaspoons	rice wine or dry sherry
2 tablespoons	light soy sauce
Seasoning A:	
2 teaspoons	sugar
1 tablespoon	light soy sauce
2 teaspoons	rice wine or dry sherry
2 teaspoons	cornflour (cornstarch)
Seasoning B:	
2 teaspoons	dark soy sauce
½ teaspoon	m.s.g. (optional)
¼ teaspoon.	ground black pepper
½ teaspoon	sugar

Very thinly slice the pork across the grain, then place in a dish with the seasoning A ingredients, mix well and leave for 30 minutes.

Cut the spring onions in halves lengthwise and cut into 4 cm (1 2/3 in) pieces. Heat the oil in a wok and stir-fry the spring onions, ginger and garlic for 1 minute. Add the pork and stir-fry on high heat until lightly coloured, 1½ — 2 minutes.

Sizzle the wine and soy sauce onto the sides of the pan and stir in, then add the seasoning B ingredients and mix thoroughly.

Transfer to a serving plate and serve at once

PORK SEASONED WITH SPICED RICE POWDER

750 g (1½ lb)	'five flowered' pork (belly/fresh bacon) on the rind*
¾ cup	spiced rice powder (see page 386).
2	dried or fresh lotus leaves (optional)

Seasoning A:

2½ tablespoons	soybean paste or dark soy sauce
1½ tablespoons	sesame oil
1 tablespoon	frying oil

Seasoning B:

1 teaspoon	salt
1¼ tablespoons	sugar
¾ teaspoon	m.s.g. (optional)
¼ cup (2 fl oz)	rice wine or dry sherry
2 tablespoons	dark soy sauce
3 tablespoons	finely chopped spring onion (scallion)
1½ teaspoons	grated fresh ginger
½ cup (4 fl oz)	cold water

Cut the pork into 1.5 cm (½ in) thick slices, then into strips about 2.5 cm (1 in) wide. Rub with the seasoning A ingredients, place in a dish and leave for 20 minutes, then add the pre-mixed seasoning B ingredients, mix well and leave for 1 hour.

Blanch the dried lotus leaves, if used, in boiling water then drain and place one in the bottom of a dish large enough to contain the pork. If using fresh lotus leaves, place in a saucepan, cover with cold water and bring to the boil, then drain well.

Dip the pork slices into the rice powder, coating generously. Arrange on the lotus leaf and top with the other leaf. Cover the dish and set it on a rack in a steamer. Steam over rapidly boiling water until the pork is completely tender, about 2½ hours.

Leftover spiced rice powder can be stored indefinitely in an airtight jar.

*Or use a less fatty cut, if preferred.

STEWED PORK WITH FERMENTED BEANCURD AND TARO

750 g (1½ lb)	'five flowered' pork (belly/fresh bacon)*
1 tablespoon	dark soy sauce
6 cups (1½ litres)	deep-frying oil
185 g (6 oz)	fresh taro, yam, or sweet potato
4 cups (1 litre)	chicken stock
	cornflour (cornstarch)

Seasoning A:

2 tablespoons	finely chopped spring onion (scallion)
2 teaspoons	finely chopped fresh ginger
1½ teaspoons	finely chopped garlic
4 cubes	fermented beancurd with the liquid, mashed

Seasoning B:

1½ teaspoons	salt
2 teaspoons	sugar
¼ cup (2 fl oz)	light soy sauce
2 teaspoons	dark soy sauce
1 tablespoon	rice wine or dry sherry

Wipe the pork and blanch in boiling water for 2 minutes, then remove and leave to dry. Rub with the dark soy sauce and deep-fry in hot oil until well coloured on the surface, about 5 minutes. Drain well.

Peel the taro and cut into cubes. Deep-fry until lightly coloured, about 2 minutes. Drain. Cut the pork into the same sized pieces.

Pour off most of the oil, retaining about 2 tablespoons. Fry the seasoning A ingredients for 2 minutes, adding a little of the chicken stock to prevent them from sticking to the pan. Add the seasoning B ingredients and cook briefly, then pour in the chicken stock and bring to the boil. Reduce the heat and add the pork. Simmer for about 30 minutes, then add the taro and cook until both pork and taro are tender.

Transfer the meat and vegetables to a serving plate. Return about 1 cupful of the sauce to the boil and thicken with a paste of cornflour and cold water. Pour over the dish and serve.

*Or use a less fatty cut, if preferred.

STEAMED PORK WITH CARROTS AND MUSHROOMS

500 g (1 lb)	lean pork, from the upper leg
1	medium to large carrot
90 g (3 oz)	canned champignons, drained
2	spring onions (scallions), trimmed and cut in halves
3 slices	fresh ginger
	chicken stock or cold water
	cornflour (cornstarch)

Seasoning:

¼ cup (2 fl oz)	light soy sauce
2 teaspoons	rice wine or dry sherry
½ teaspoon	salt
1 teaspoon	sugar
½ teaspoon	m.s.g. (optional)
¼ teaspoon	ground Chinese brown peppercorns

Trim any fat from the meat and cut into 2 cm (¾ in) cubes. Peel the carrot and cut into small cubes. Place half the pork in the bottom of a dish and add half the onion and a piece of ginger. Layer the carrot, champignons, and remaining pork on top and add the remaining onion and ginger.

Mix the sauce ingredients together and pour evenly over the dish, then add chicken stock or water to barely cover the top layer.

Set the dish on a rack in a steamer and steam over rapidly boiling water until tender, about 1¼ hours.

Strain the liquid into a wok and check the seasonings. Thicken with a thin solution of cornflour and cold water and stir well. Pour over the dish and serve.

Dried black mushrooms previously soaked to soften and stems removed, canned bamboo shoots, young Chinese green vegetables, turnip or white onions could replace either the carrots or champignons in this dish.

For dramatic presentation, arrange the ingredients alternately in a sunburst design in a large round dish.

FILLET OF BEEF WITH SALTED MUSTARD GREENS AND BLACK BEAN SAUCE

250 g (8 oz)	beef fillet (tenderloin)
30 g (1 oz)	salted mustard root*
1 tablespoon	fermented black beans
¾ teaspoon	finely chopped garlic
¾ teaspoon	sugar
3 cups (24 fl oz)	deep-frying oil, or use ⅓ cup frying oil
2 teaspoons	rice wine or dry sherry
1 tablespoon	light soy sauce

Seasoning A:

½ teaspoon	salt
¼ teaspoon	m.s.g. (optional)
¼ teaspoon	bicarbonate of soda (optional)
1¼ teaspoons	sugar
2 tablespoons	water
1½ tablespoons	vegetable oil
2 teaspoons	cornflour (cornstarch)

Seasoning B/Sauce:

2 tablespoons	chicken stock
¼ teaspoon	salt
½ teaspoon	sugar
½ teaspoon	m.s.g. (optional)
¼ teaspoon	ground black pepper (optional)
½ teaspoon	sesame oil (optional)
¾ teaspoon	cornflour (cornstarch)

Partially freeze the beef, cut into very thin slices across the grain and then cut each piece into three. Add the seasoning A ingredients, except the cornflour and leave for 15 minutes, then add the cornflour, mix in and leave a further 10 minutes.

Soak the mustard root or other pickled vegetables in cold water for 20 minutes, drain well and squeeze out the excess water. Cut into small dice. Wash the black beans and dry well, chop and mix with the garlic and sugar.

Heat the deep-frying oil in a wok to smoking point and fry the beef in a frying basket for 30 seconds. Or stir-fry in the frying oil on very high heat for 1 minute. Remove and drain well. Keep warm. Pour off all but 2 tablespoons oil and add the black bean mixture. Stir-fry for 30 seconds, then add the mustard or pickled vegetables and stir-fry for 30 seconds longer. Sizzle the wine and soy sauce onto the sides of the pan and stir in.

Add the pre-mixed seasoning B/sauce ingredients and bring to the boil. Return the beef and heat through, then serve.

*Or use pickled cabbage or Szechuan pickled vegetables.

BEEF IN OYSTER SAUCE

250 g (8 oz)	beef steak (fillet/tenderloin or rump)
280 g (9 oz)	Chinese (celery) cabbage
6	dried black mushrooms, soaked for 25 minutes
¼ cup (2 fl oz)	frying oil

Seasoning A:

½ teaspoon	salt
1½ teaspoons	sugar
½ teaspoon	m.s.g. (optional)
¼ teaspoon	white pepper
1 tablespoon	water
2 teaspoons	dark soy sauce
2 teaspoons	rice wine or dry sherry
1 tablespoon	vegetable oil
2 teaspoons	cornflour (cornstarch)

Seasoning B/Sauce:

2 tablespoons	chicken stock
1½ teaspoons	dark soy sauce
1 tablespoon	light soy sauce
1 tablespoon	rice wine or dry sherry
½ teaspoon	salt
1 teaspoon	sugar
½ teaspoon	cornflour (cornstarch)
2 tablespoons	oyster sauce

Partially freeze the beef and cut into very thin slices, then into narrow strips. Place in a dish with the seasoning A ingredients, mix well and leave for 45 minutes to marinate.

Wash the cabbage and cut into 5 cm (2 in) pieces. Simmer in lightly salted water for 3 minutes and drain well. Drain the mushrooms, remove the stems and simmer the mushroom caps in a little chicken stock or water for 10 minutes, adding a dash each of salt, sugar, and pepper. Remove from the heat and leave in the liquid until needed.

Heat the frying oil in a wok and stir-fry the beef on very high heat until it changes colour. Remove. Add the cabbage and stir-fry briefly, then add the drained mushrooms and the pre-mixed seasoning B/sauce ingredients except the oyster sauce. Simmer until thickened.

Return the beef and stir in the oyster sauce. Heat through and serve.

STIR-FRIED BEEF WITH YOUNG GINGER AND PINEAPPLE

250 g (8 oz)	beef fillet (tenderloin)
45 g (1½ oz)	canned pineapple pieces, drained
2 cm (¾ in) piece	fresh young ginger*
1	spring onion (scallion), trimmed and sliced
¼ cup (2 fl oz)	frying oil
2 teaspoons	rice wine or dry sherry

Seasoning A:

1	egg white, beaten
½ teaspoon	salt
2 teaspoons	vegetable oil
2 teaspoons	cornflour (cornstarch)

Seasoning B/Sauce:

2 tablespoons	chicken stock
1 tablespoon	light soy sauce
⅓ teaspoon	salt
½ teaspoon	sugar
½ teaspoon	cornflour (cornstarch)

Partially freeze the beef and cut across the grain into paper-thin slices, then cut into strips about 2.5 × 5 cm (1 × 2 in). Place in a dish with the seasoning A ingredients and leave to marinate for 20 minutes.

Cut each of the pineapple pieces in halves. Peel and very thinly slice the ginger. Heat the frying oil in a wok and stir-fry the spring onion and ginger for 1 minute, then push to one side of the pan and add the beef. Stir-fry until it changes colour, then sizzle in the wine and add the pre-mixed seasoning B/sauce ingredients. Simmer for 1 minute, then add the pineapple and heat through.

Transfer to a serving plate.

*For a milder taste, blanch the sliced ginger before use.

STIR-FRIED BEEF WITH GREEN AND RED PEPPERS

185 g (6 oz)	beef fillet (tenderloin)
1	medium green capsicum (bell pepper)
1 — 2	fresh red chilli peppers
1/3 cup	frying oil
1	large spring onion (scallion), trimmed and sliced
1½ teaspoons	finely chopped fresh ginger
1½ teaspoons	finely chopped garlic
1 tablespoon	fermented black beans, or use hot black bean sauce
1½ teaspoons	rice wine or dry sherry

Seasoning A:

¼ teaspoon	m.s.g. (optional)
1 tablespoon	light soy sauce
2 teaspoons	rice wine or dry sherry
1 tablespoon	frying oil
1 tablespoon	cold water
2 teaspoons	cornflour (cornstarch)

Seasoning B/Sauce:

¼ cup (2 fl oz)	chicken stock or water
½ teaspoon	sesame oil
½ teaspoon	salt
¼ teaspoon	m.s.g. (optional)
½ teaspoon	sugar
¼ teaspoon	ground black pepper
1 teaspoon	cornflour (cornstarch)

Partially freeze the beef then cut into paper-thin slices across the grain and into fine shreds. Place the beef shreds in a dish with the seasoning A ingredients, mix well and leave for 25 minutes. Cut open the green pepper and red chillies and remove the stems, seed-cores, and inner white ribs. Cut into shreds.

Heat the frying oil and stir-fry the beef until it changes colour, then remove from the oil and keep warm. Add the onion, ginger, and garlic to the pan and stir-fry for 45 seconds. Push to one side of the pan and add the capsicum and chilli peppers. Stir-fry until softened, splashing in about 1½ tablespoons of cold water to soften the peppers. When the liquid dries up, add the chopped black beans or black bean sauce and fry briefly, then return the meat and sizzle the wine onto the sides of the pan and stir in.

Add the pre-mixed seasoning B/sauce ingredients and stir on high heat until thickened. Transfer to a serving plate.

Any combination of vegetables could replace the capsicum and chilli peppers, such as shredded carrots and celery, diced water chestnuts, soaked 'wood ear' fungus, green peas, sliced Chinese green vegetables, or onions.

RAINBOW BEEF IN LETTUCE LEAVES

155 g (5 oz)	beef fillet (tenderloin)
60 g (2 oz)	canned bamboo shoots, drained
60 g (2 oz)	fresh celery
1	small carrot
1	small green capsicum (bell pepper)
1	fresh red chilli pepper
3	dried black mushrooms, soaked for 25 minutes
45 g (1½ oz)	rice vermicelli
6 cups (1½ litres)	deep-frying oil
12	fresh lettuce leaf cups

Seasoning:

¼ teaspoon	salt
½ teaspoon	sugar
1 teaspoon	light soy sauce
1 teaspoon	rice wine or dry sherry
1½ teaspoons	vegetable oil
1 tablespoon	cold water
1 teaspoon	cornflour (cornstarch)

Thinly slice the beef, then cut into fine shreds. Place in a dish with the seasoning ingredients, mix well and leave for 1 hour. Cut the vegetables into fine shreds.

Heat the deep-frying oil to smoking point. Break the rice vermicelli into small pieces and place in a frying basket. Deep-fry for about 20 seconds until it expands and turns crisp. Drain and place on a serving plate.

Pour off all but 2½ tablespoons of the oil and fry the meat until it changes colour, then push to one side of the wok and add the shredded vegetables. Stir-fry until softened but retaining crispness, about 2 minutes, then stir in the beef and spoon onto the rice vermicelli.

Wash the lettuce leaves and place on a serving plate. Serve with the beef. To eat, spoon a portion of the meat, vegetables, and noodles into the lettuce leaf and roll up. Hoisin or plum sauce can be served as a dip.

BEEF *FU YUNG*

90 g (3 oz)	beef fillet (tenderloin)
4	eggs, beaten
2	egg whites, well beaten
2 teaspoons	cornflour (cornstarch)
1 tablespoon	water
¼ teaspoon	salt
2	spring onions (scallions), trimmed and shredded
1 slice	fresh ginger, shredded
1 teaspoon	sesame oil
2 tablespoons	frying oil

Seasoning A:

⅓ teaspoon	salt
¼ teaspoon	m.s.g. (optional)
2 teaspoons	light soy sauce
1 teaspoon	rice wine or dry sherry
1½ teaspoons	cornflour (cornstarch)

Seasoning B/Sauce:

¼ cup (2 fl oz)	chicken stock
2 teaspoons	light soy sauce
1 tablespoon	oyster sauce
1 teaspoon	rice wine or dry sherry
⅓ teaspoon	sugar
1 tablespoon	frying oil
½ teaspoon	cornflour (cornstarch)

Partially freeze the beef, cut into very thin slices across the grain, then into long thin shreds. Mix with the seasoning A ingredients and leave for 15 minutes to marinate.

Mix the eggs, egg whites, cornflour, water, and salt together, beat for 1 minute, then set aside.

Heat the sesame oil and frying oil together in a wok and sauté the spring onions and ginger for 30 seconds. Push to one side of the pan and add the shredded beef. Sauté on high heat until the meat changes colour, then reduce the heat to moderate.

Pour in the egg mixture and cook until the underside is lightly coloured and firm. Cut into quarters and turn each piece. Cook until the omelette is just done right through. Do not allow to dry out. Transfer to a warmed serving plate and keep warm.

Wipe out the wok and add the pre-mixed seasoning B/sauce ingredients. Bring to the boil and simmer until thickened. Pour over the omelette and serve immediately.

STEAMED BEEF MEATBALLS AND SPINACH ON RICE

1¼ cups	raw short grain white rice
375 g (12 oz)	lean beef, finely minced (ground)
60 g (2 oz)	pork fat, coarsely minced (ground)
2 tablespoons	finely chopped spring onion (scallion)
1¼ teaspoons	finely chopped fresh ginger
60 g (2 oz)	canned water chestnuts or bamboo shoots, finely diced
250 g (8 oz)	fresh spinach leaves (collard greens)

Seasoning:

1¼ teaspoons	salt
½ teaspoon	sugar
1 tablespoon ·	light soy sauce
2 tablespoons	cold water
1 tablespoon	frying oil
2 teaspoons	cornflour (cornstarch)

Soak the rice in cold water. Mix the beef and pork fat together and add the seasoning ingredients. Knead into a smooth paste and leave for at least 1 hour, then add the remaining ingredients, except the spinach.

Drain the rice and pour into a saucepan. Add 1 teaspoon salt and water to cover by 2.5 cm (1 in). Cook, covered, until the water level recedes below the rice, then arrange well-washed spinach leaves on top.

Form the meat paste into large meatballs and place on the spinach leaves. Continue to cook on very low heat until the rice is tender and fluffy and the meatballs cooked through, about 12 minutes.

Transfer the meatballs and vegetables to one serving plate. Stir up the rice and serve into rice bowls or a separate serving plate and serve with the meatballs.

SAUTÉD SHREDDED LAMB ON RICE NOODLES

185 g (6 oz)	lean lamb*
5 cups (1¼ litres)	deep-frying oil
45 g (1½ oz)	rice vermicelli, broken
45 g (1½ oz)	canned champignons, drained and sliced
30 g (1 oz)	canned bamboo shoots, drained and shredded
1	medium green capsicum (bell pepper), trimmed and shredded

Seasoning A:

1	egg white, beaten
½ teaspoon	salt
½ teaspoon	bicarbonate of soda (optional)
1 tablespoon	light soy sauce
2 teaspoons	rice wine or dry sherry
1½ tablespoons	finely chopped spring onion (scallion)
1 teaspoon	grated fresh ginger
1 teaspoon	cornflour (cornstarch)

Seasoning B/Sauce:

½ cup (4 fl oz)	chicken stock
1 tablespoon	light soy sauce
1 teaspoon	rice wine or dry sherry
⅓ teaspoon	salt
	pinch of white pepper
¼ teaspoon	sugar
¾ teaspoon	cornflour (cornstarch)

Partially freeze the lamb and cut into thin slices, then into fine shreds. Place in a dish and add the seasoning A ingredients, mix well and leave to marinate for 20 minutes.

Heat the deep-frying oil to smoking point and fry the broken rice vermicelli in a frying basket until it expands into a cloud of crisp white noodles, about 20 seconds. Drain well and place on a serving plate. Pour off all but 3 tablespoons of the oil.

Reheat the wok and sauté the shredded lamb until it changes colour, push to one side of the pan and sauté the shredded vegetables for 2 minutes, then mix in the lamb and add the seasoning B/sauce ingredients, pre-mixed, and simmer until thickened. Pour over the noodles and serve at once.

*Lean pork, beef fillet (tenderloin), or chicken breast can replace the lamb in this dish.

LETTUCE WITH OYSTER SAUCE

1	large fresh lettuce
1½ tablespoons	frying oil
½ teaspoon	salt
2½ tablespoons	oyster sauce*

Thoroughly wash the lettuce and separate the leaves. Bring a large saucepan of water to the boil and add the oil and salt. Add the lettuce and simmer until tender, about 1½ minutes. Drain well and arrange on a serving plate.

Pour the oyster sauce evenly over the lettuce and serve at once.

* Use a good quality oyster sauce, as the less expensive brands do not have the same rich flavour.

Rainbow Beef in Lettuce Leaves (recipe page 298).

CANTONESE BEEF STEAKS

500 g (1 lb)	beef fillet (tenderloin)
2	spring onions (scallions), trimmed and shredded
2 slices	fresh ginger, shredded
2 — 3 cloves	garlic, thinly sliced
⅓ cup	frying oil

Seasoning A:

½ teaspoon	salt
½ teaspoon	m.s.g. (optional)
¼ teaspoon	bicarbonate of soda (optional)
½ teaspoon	sugar
1 teaspoon	dark soy sauce
2 teaspoons	rice wine or dry sherry
1 tablespoon	cold water
2 teaspoons	cornflour (cornstarch)

Seasoning B/Sauce:

⅓ cup	chicken stock
2 teaspoons	dark soy sauce
2 teaspoons	light soy sauce
2 teaspoons	Worcestershire sauce
1 tablespoon	barbecue sauce or soybean paste
1 tablespoon	tomato sauce (ketchup)
2 teaspoons	rice wine or dry sherry
2 teaspoons	sugar
1 teaspoon	cornflour (cornstarch)
¼ teaspoon	salt
¼ teaspoon	white pepper

Chill the meat, then cut into thin steaks across the grain. Place in a dish and add the pre-mixed Seasoning A ingredients. Rub into the meat and leave for 10 minutes, then turn and marinate for a further 10 minutes.

Heat the oil in a wok and sauté the spring onions, ginger, and garlic for 1½ minutes. Remove. Add the meat and fry on high heat until lightly coloured on both sides. Turn only once and do not overcook. Push to one side of the pan and return the onion, ginger, and garlic and add the pre-mixed seasoning B/sauce ingredients.

Bring to the boil, then simmer until thickened, stirring the beef into the sauce. Transfer to a warmed serving plate and garnish with fresh coriander. Serve at once

STIR-FRIED FROGS' LEGS

500 g (1 lb)	frogs' legs
	cornflour (cornstarch)
5 cups (1¼ litres)	deep-frying oil
1	spring onion (scallion), trimmed and sliced
2 slices	fresh ginger, shredded
2 cloves	garlic, thinly sliced
45 g (1½ oz)	canned bamboo shoots, drained and thinly sliced
1	small carrot, parboiled and thinly sliced
1	small green capsicum (bell pepper), cut into small squares
1 tablespoon	rice wine or dry sherry

Seasoning/Sauce:

1 tablespoon	light soy sauce
2 teaspoons	oyster sauce
½ teaspoon	salt
½ teaspoon	m.s.g. (optional)
¼ teaspoon	ground black pepper
½ teaspoon	sugar
1 teaspoon	sesame oil

Wash the frogs' legs and divide at the central joint. Coat thickly with cornflour and deep-fry in the smoking hot deep-frying oil for 30 seconds. Remove and drain well.

Pour off all but 2 tablespoons of the oil and stir-fry the spring onions, ginger, and garlic for 45 seconds. Push to one side of the pan and add the prepared vegetables. Stir-fry for 1½ minutes, then return the frogs' legs to the pan and stir-fry briefly. Sizzle the wine onto the sides of the pan and add the pre-mixed seasoning/sauce ingredients.

Simmer for 30 seconds, then transfer to a warmed serving plate.

LAMB WITH BEAN SPROUTS IN A CRISP POTATO BASKET

185 g (6 oz)	lean lamb
2	medium potatoes
8 cups (2 litres)	deep-frying oil
125 g (4 oz)	fresh bean sprouts
2	spring onions (scallions), trimmed shredded
2 slices	fresh ginger, shredded
1½ teaspoons	rice wine or dry sherry

Seasoning A:

1	egg white, beaten
½ teaspoon	salt
½ teaspoon	m.s.g. (optional)
¾ teaspoon	sugar
1 tablespoon	cornflour (cornstarch)
1½ tablespoons	sesame oil

Seasoning B/Sauce:

¼ cup (2 fl oz)	chicken stock
⅓ teaspoon	salt
¼ teaspoon	m.s.g. (optional)
½ teaspoon	sugar
¾ teaspoon	cornflour (cornstarch)

Special Equipment: Two wire strainers, one slightly larger than the other.

Partially freeze the lamb and cut into very thin slices, then into strips about 5 × 2.5 cm (2 × 1 in). Mix with the seasoning A ingredients, except the sesame oil, and leave for 10 minutes, then add the sesame oil, mix well and leave a further 15 minutes.

Peel the potatoes and cut into very fine strings. Soak in cold water for 10 minutes, drain and dry in a kitchen towel, then dust lightly with cornflour and spread in a layer inside the larger strainer.

Heat the deep-frying oil to smoking point and decrease the heat slightly. Press the smaller strainer inside the larger one, over the shredded potato to force into a nest shape. Hold the two handles firmly together, then lower the strainers into the hot oil. Fry until the potato basket is crisp and golden. Remove and drain well, then remove the smaller strainer and upturn the larger one onto a piece of absorbent paper. Tap the top until the basket dislodges and leave to drain, upside down.

Drain off all but 3 tablespoons of the oil and sauté the lamb on high heat for 1 minute. Remove. Reheat the pan and fry the bean sprouts until beginning to soften, push to one side of the pan and add the spring onions and ginger, frying until softened, then mix with the bean sprouts and return the lamb. Sizzle the wine onto the sides of the pan and stir in, then add the pre-mixed seasoning B/sauce ingredients and heat to boiling. Stir for a few seconds.

Upturn the basket onto a serving plate and surround with shredded lettuce, fresh parsley, or coriander sprigs and pour the lamb and sprouts into the basket. Serve at once. The basket can be eaten with the dish.

SAUTÉD SNAILS WITH GARLIC

280 g (9 oz)	fresh or canned snails
2 tablespoons	softened lard or frying oil
2	spring onions (scallions), trimmed and diced
2 slices	fresh ginger, shredded
8 cloves	garlic, sliced

Seasoning A:

½ teaspoon	salt
¼ teaspoon	white pepper
1 teaspoon	bicarbonate of soda (optional)
1 tablespoon	rice wine or dry sherry
2 tablespoons	frying oil
1 tablespoon	cold water

Seasoning B/Sauce:

½ cup (4 fl oz)	chicken stock
½ teaspoon	salt
¼ teaspoon	m.s.g. (optional)
¼ teaspoon	white pepper
½ teaspoon	sugar
1 teaspoon	cornflour (cornstarch)

Thoroughly wash fresh snails or drain the canned snails. Cut larger ones in halves. Place in a dish with the seasoning A ingredients, omitting the bicarbonate of soda if using canned snails. Leave for 2 hours. Rinse fresh snails lightly in cold water.

Heat the lard or oil and sauté the spring onions, ginger, and garlic until softened. Add the snails and sauté for 2 minutes, then pour in the pre-mixed seasoning B/sauce ingredients and simmer until thickened.

Transfer to a serving plate.

DICED RABBIT SAUTÉD WITH BELL PEPPERS

375 g (12 oz)	meaty rabbit pieces, preferably thighs
1	medium green capsicum (bell pepper)
2	spring onions (scallions), trimmed and diced
1 teaspoon	finely chopped fresh ginger
1½ teaspoons	chopped garlic
⅓ cup	frying oil

Seasoning A:

1	egg white, beaten
½ teaspoon	salt
½ teaspoon	m.s.g. (optional)
2 teaspoons	rice wine or dry sherry
1 teaspoon	cornflour (cornstarch)

Seasoning B/Sauce:

⅓ cup	chicken stock
2 tablespoons	light soy sauce
¼ teaspoon	salt
1 teaspoon	sugar
½ teaspoon	m.s.g. (optional)
½ teaspoon	cornflour (cornstarch)

Cube the rabbit meat, discarding the bones if preferred. Place in a dish, add the seasoning A ingredients and mix well. Leave for 25 minutes.

Cut the pepper in halves, remove the stem, seed-core, and inner white ribs, and cut into squares about the same size as the rabbit.

Heat the oil in a wok and sauté the spring onions, ginger, and garlic for 45 seconds, then push to one side of the pan and add the rabbit. Sauté on moderately high heat until it changes colour, about 3 minutes, then remove. Reheat the pan and add the peppers and splash in a very little water. Cook until softened, then return the rabbit and add the pre-mixed seasoning B/sauce ingredients and simmer until thickened and the rabbit is tender.

Transfer to a warmed serving plate.

SLICED QUAIL SAUTÉD WITH BAMBOO SHOOTS

155 g (5 oz)	quail meat*
60 g (2 oz)	canned bamboo shoots, drained and sliced
30 g (1 oz)	canned straw mushrooms, drained and sliced
2½ tablespoons	softened lard or frying oil
1	spring onion (scallion), trimmed and diced
1 slice	fresh ginger, shredded
2 teaspoons	rice wine or dry sherry

Seasoning A:

1	egg white, beaten
¼ teaspoon	salt
½ teaspoon	m.s.g. (optional)
1 teaspoon	cornflour (cornstarch)

Seasoning B/Sauce:

2 tablespoons	chicken stock or water
2 tablespoons	light soy sauce
¼ teaspoon	salt
¼ teaspoon	ground black pepper
½ teaspoon	m.s.g. (optional)
¾ teaspoon	cornflour (cornstarch)

Slice the quail meat and place in a dish with the seasoning A ingredients. Leave for 20 minutes. Blanch the bamboo shoots and mushrooms in boiling water for 30 seconds, then drain well.

Heat the lard or oil in a wok and sauté the quail meat until lightly coloured. Remove and keep warm. Add the spring onion and ginger and sauté for 30 seconds, then add the sliced bamboo shoots and mushrooms and sauté for a further 30 seconds. Sizzle the wine onto the sides of the pan, return the quail meat and stir-fry until tender.

Add the pre-mixed seasoning B/sauce ingredients and simmer until the sauce thickens. Serve.

*Use quail on the bone, if preferred, or sliced pheasant breast or pigeon as an alternative.

Steamed Broccoli with Crabmeat Sauce (recipe page 314).

DEEP-FRIED RICE BIRDS SERVED WITH QUAIL EGGS AND SLICED QUAIL IN A NOODLE NEST

6	rice birds*
125 g (4 oz)	quail meat**
6	canned quail eggs, drained
¾ cup (6 fl oz)	chicken stock
125 g (4 oz)	beancurd noodles, or use 45 g (1½ oz) rice vermicelli or bean thread vermicelli
6 cups (1½ litres)	deep-frying oil
30 g (1 oz)	canned bamboo shoots, drained and diced
3	dried black mushrooms, soaked to soften and diced
2 tablespoons	finely chopped spring onion (scallion)
½ teaspoon	finely chopped fresh ginger

Seasoning A:

½ teaspoon	salt
1 tablespoon	rice wine or dry sherry
1 teaspoon	sesame oil (optional)
1 tablespoon	finely chopped spring onion (scallion)
1 teaspoon	finely chopped fresh ginger
¼ teaspoon	crushed garlic

Seasoning B:

¼ teaspoon	salt
¼ teaspoon	m.s.g. (optional)
1 teaspoon	light soy sauce
1 teaspoon	rice wine or dry sherry
1 teaspoon	cornflour (cornstarch)

Seasoning C/Sauce:

¼ cup (2 fl oz)	chicken stock
1 tablespoon	light soy sauce
2 teaspoons	rice wine or dry sherry
½ teaspoon	sesame oil (optional)
⅓ — ½ teaspoon	chilli oil (optional)
¼ teaspoon	salt
¼ teaspoon	m.s.g. (optional)
¼ teaspoon	sugar
½ teaspoon	cornflour (cornstarch)

Special Equipment: Two wire strainers, one slightly larger than the other.

Wash the rice birds and place in a dish with the seasoning A ingredients. Leave to marinate for 30 minutes. Slice the quail meat and mix with the seasoning B ingredients and leave for 20 minutes.

Simmer the quail eggs in the chicken stock for 10 minutes, then remove from the heat and leave in the stock. Heat the deep-frying oil to fairly hot. Dust the beancurd noodles lightly with cornflour and spread around the inside of the larger strainer. Press the smaller one inside, forcing the noodles into a nest shape. Hold the two handles firmly together and lower into the hot oil. Deep-fry until the noodles are crisp and dry, about 3 minutes. Decrease the heat slightly after the first 30 seconds. Remove and upturn onto absorbent paper. Leave to dry.

Reheat the deep-frying oil and fry the rice birds until crisp and golden, about 3½ minutes. Place the drained nest on a serving plate on a bed of finely shredded lettuce. Set the fried rice birds around it.

Reheat the deep-frying oil and fry the drained eggs until golden. Remove. Pour off all but 2 tablespoons of the oil and stir-fry the bamboo shoots, mushrooms, spring onion and ginger on fairly high heat for 1½ minutes. Push to one side of the pan and add the sliced quail. Stir-fry until just cooked through, then mix with the diced ingredients and return the eggs.

Pour in the pre-mixed seasoning C/sauce ingredients and simmer until the sauce thickens. Spoon into the nest and serve at once.

*A type of sparrow. Substitute small chicken drumsticks.
**Use sliced pigeon or chicken breast meat as an alternative.

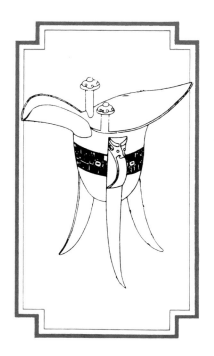

BEANCURD CAKES WITH FRESH CORIANDER AND SOY SAUCE

6 squares	soft beancurd
1 large bunch	fresh coriander

Sauce:

2 tablespoons	light soy sauce
1 tablespoon	dark soy sauce
1½ tablespoons	vegetable oil
1 tablespoon	water
1 — 2 teaspoons	sesame oil
¼ teaspoon	m.s.g. (optional)
1½ teaspoons	sugar

Separately wrap each square of beancurd in a piece of clean muslin or cheesecloth. Place in a dish and set on a rack in a steamer. Steam over rapidly boiling water for 15 minutes, then remove from the heat. Unwrap and place on a serving plate. Garnish with the well-washed fresh coriander.

Mix the sauce ingredients together in a wok and bring to the boil. Pour over the beancurd and serve at once.

CANTONESE STUFFED BEANCURD

3 squares	soft beancurd
1 teaspoon	salt
90 g (3 oz)	raw peeled shrimp or white fish
60 g (2 oz)	fatty pork
1 tablespoon	dried shrimp, soaked for 1 hour
1 cup (8 fl oz)	frying oil
	cornflour (cornstarch)
⅓ cup	chicken stock
¼ cup (2 fl oz)	oyster sauce

Seasoning:

1	egg white, beaten
1 tablespoon	very finely chopped spring onion (scallion)
⅓ teaspoon	grated fresh ginger (optional)
¾ teaspoon	salt
¾ teaspoon	sugar
¼ teaspoon	ground black pepper
½ teaspoon	sesame oil (optional)

Place the beancurd in a saucepan and add the salt. Cover with cold water and bring to the boil. Simmer for 1 minute, then drain. Leave for about 15 minutes to firm up, then cut each square into four triangular shaped pieces.

Pulverise the shrimp or fish and fatty pork in a food processor. Finely chop the drained, soaked shrimps and mix with the pork mixture, adding the seasoning ingredients. Make a slit in the widest side of each beancurd triangle, dust lightly with cornflour and stuff with a teaspoon of the mixture.

Heat the frying oil in a large frying pan and add the beancurd. Cook on moderate heat, carefully turning once or twice until evenly cooked and golden. Add the chicken stock and increase the heat. Simmer until the liquid is absorbed, then transfer to a serving plate and pour on the oyster sauce.

Fresh *bok choy* or *choy sum* quickly simmered in salted water are a good accompaniment to this dish and add colour when placed around the beancurd on the serving plate.

BEANCURD STIR-FRIED WITH CRABMEAT

4 squares	soft beancurd
185 g (6 oz)	fresh crabmeat
1	spring onion (scallion), trimmed and shredded
⅓ cup	frying oil
2	egg whites, well beaten

Seasoning A:

¼ teaspoon	salt
1 teaspoon	ginger wine (see page 387)
⅓ teaspoon	sugar

Seasoning B/Sauce:

⅓ cup	chicken stock
2 teaspoons	light soy sauce
¾ teaspoon	salt
¼ teaspoon	ground black pepper
¾ teaspoon	cornflour (cornstarch)

Soak the beancurd in cold water for 20 minutes, then drain and cut into cubes. Cut the crabmeat into small pieces and mix with the seasoning A ingredients. Heat the frying oil in a wok and sauté the spring onion briefly, then add the beancurd and stir-fry on high heat until lightly coloured. Remove and keep warm.

Reheat the wok and stir-fry the crabmeat for 1½ minutes, then add the pre-mixed seasoning B/sauce ingredients and simmer for a further 1½ minutes. Remove from the heat and slowly drizzle in the beaten egg. Leave to set into strands in the sauce, then return to the heat and add the beancurd.

Heat through, mixing together, then spoon onto a serving plate.

BRAISED BEANCURD WITH SHRIMPS

3 squares	soft beancurd
2	whole eggs, well beaten
	flour
1 cup (8 fl oz)	frying oil
2 tablespoons	finely chopped spring onion (scallion)
2 teaspoons	finely chopped fresh ginger
½ teaspoon	finely chopped garlic
90 g (3 oz)	raw peeled shrimps, deveined

Seasoning/Sauce:

½ cup (4 fl oz)	chicken stock
1 tablespoon	light soy sauce
2 teaspoons	rice wine or dry sherry
1½ teaspoons	sesame oil (optional)
1 teaspoon	salt
½ teaspoon	sugar
¼ teaspoon	ground black pepper
½ teaspoon	cornflour (cornstarch)

Cut the beancurd in halves horizontally, then cut each piece into quarters. Dip into beaten egg, then coat lightly with the flour. Heat the oil to smoking point and fry the beancurd until golden. Drain and keep warm.

Pour off all but 2½ tablespoons of the oil and sauté the onion, ginger and garlic for 45 seconds, then push to one side of the pan and add the shrimps. Stir-fry until pink, about 1 minute, then mix with the onion and return the beancurd. Prick each piece with a fork several times to allow the seasonings to penetrate.

Pour on the pre-mixed seasoning/sauce ingredients and bring to the boil. Reduce the heat and simmer for about 3 minutes until the sauce is almost completely absorbed. Serve at once.

Three Kinds of Mushrooms (recipe page 315).

MIXED VEGETABLE PLATTER

1	medium carrot
1	medium white onion
6	dried black mushrooms, soaked for 25 minutes
6	canned water chestnuts, drained
6	canned champignons, drained
6	canned baby corn cobs, drained
250 g (8 oz)	fresh lettuce or Chinese (celery) cabbage
1/3 cup	frying oil

Seasoning/Sauce:

2/3 cup	chicken stock
¾ teaspoon	salt
1/3 teaspoon	chicken stock powder (optional)
¾ teaspoon	sugar
1¼ teaspoons	cornflour (cornstarch)

Peel the carrot, thinly slice lengthwise, then cut into rectangular pieces. Peel the onion, cut in halves from stem to root, then cut into thick slices from stem to root and trim away the root section to allow the pieces to separate. Squeeze the water from the mushrooms and remove the stems. Slice the water chestnuts and champignons in halves horizontally. Cut the baby corn in halves. Thoroughly wash the lettuce or cabbage, separating the leaves.

Parboil the carrot and drain well. Blanch the onion for 20 seconds and drain well. Heat the frying oil in a wok and stir-fry the carrot and onions for 30 seconds. Push to one side of the pan and add the mushrooms, water chestnuts and champignons and stir-fry together for 1 minute, then add the corn and mix the vegetables together. Stir-fry on high heat for a further 30 seconds, then add the pre-mixed seasoning/sauce ingredients and simmer until the sauce thickens.

In the meantime, heat a saucepan of water to boiling and add 1 tablespoon of frying oil and a dash of salt. Add the lettuce or cabbage and simmer until tender. Lettuce needs only about 45 seconds, the cabbage a little longer. Drain well and arrange on a serving plate. Spoon the vegetables on top and serve at once.

SAUTÉD CHINESE SPINACH WITH SHRIMP SAUCE

500 g (1 lb)	fresh Chinese spinach*
1	spring onion (scallion), trimmed and shredded
2 cloves	garlic, chopped
½ cup (2 fl oz)	frying oil
2 teaspoons	Chinese shrimp sauce**
¼ cup (2 fl oz)	chicken stock
½ teaspoon	cornflour (cornstarch)

Thoroughly wash the vegetables and cut into 7.5 cm (3 in) lengths. Heat the frying oil and sauté the spring onion and garlic briefly, then add the spinach and sauté on moderate heat until tender. Stir in the shrimp sauce (use more or less, to taste) and sauté briefly, then add the chicken stock mixed with cornflour and simmer until the sauce thickens.

Transfer to a serving plate and serve at once.

* A green leafy vegetable with narrow white stems similar to *bok choy*, which can be used as a substitute.

** A pale pink pungent sauce made by grinding and salting fresh shrimps, sun-drying, then storing in vats until fermented. If unobtainable, use anchovy sauce or essence.

CHINESE CABBAGE WITH MINCED SHRIMP DRESSING

625 g (1¼ lb)	fresh Chinese (celery) cabbage
75 g (2½ oz)	raw peeled shrimps
2	egg whites, beaten
¼ cup (2 fl oz)	cold water
1 teaspoon	cornflour (cornstarch)
	pinch of salt
⅓ cup	softened lard or frying oil

Seasoning A:

¼ cup (2 fl oz)	chicken stock
¾ teaspoon	salt
½ teaspoon	m.s.g. (optional)
¼ teaspoon	sugar
	pinch of white pepper

Seasoning B/Sauce:

½ cup (4 fl oz)	chicken stock
1 teaspoon	salt
½ teaspoon	m.s.g. (optional)
¼ teaspoon	white pepper
½ teaspoon	cornflour (cornstarch)

Wash the cabbage well, discard the outer leaves and cut lengthwise into quarters, or into smaller pieces if the head is large. Blanch in boiling water for 1 minute, then drain well.

Pulverise the shrimps in a food processor or by batting with the side of a cleaver blade. Mix with the egg whites, cold water, cornflour, and salt.

Sauté the cabbage in half the lard or frying oil for 2 minutes on moderate heat, then add the seasoning A ingredients and simmer until the liquid has evaporated. Remove from the pan and arrange on a serving plate.

Add the remaining lard or oil to the pan and sauté the shrimp paste until it turns white, about 1 minute on moderate heat. Add the pre-mixed seasoning B/sauce ingredients and bring to the boil. Simmer until thickened, then pour over the cabbage and serve.

FRESH CELERY WITH CREAMY MUSTARD SAUCE

3 stalks	fresh celery
½ teaspoon	salt

Sauce:

½ cup (4 fl oz)	chicken stock or water
1 tablespoon	evaporated milk
2 tablespoons	vegetable oil
1—1½ teaspoons	hot mustard powder
½ teaspoon	salt
½ teaspoon	sugar
1¼ teaspoons	cornflour (cornstarch)

String the celery and cut into pieces about 4 cm (1 2/3 in) long, then cut each piece lengthwise into two or three sticks. Blanch in boiling water with the salt added, for 1 minute, then drain and refresh with cold water. Drain again and arrange on a serving plate.

Pour the pre-mixed sauce ingredients into a wok and bring to the boil. Simmer until thickened, then pour over the vegetables and serve at once.

SAUTÉD FRESH *CHOY SUM*

625 g (1¼ lb)	fresh young choy sum*
2 tablespoons	frying oil
2 tablespoons	rendered chicken fat (chicken grease) or lard
¾ teaspoon	salt
⅓ teaspoon	m.s.g. (optional)
½ teaspoon	sugar
1½ teaspoons	rice wine or dry sherry

Trim off any wilted leaves and cut the *choy sum* into 5 cm (2 in) pieces. Peel the thick skin from the lower section of the stems, if preferred. Simmer in boiling water for 2 minutes, then drain.

Heat the frying oil and chicken fat or lard in a wok and add the salt, m.s.g., and sugar. Sauté the vegetables on moderate heat for 2 minutes or until tender, then sizzle the wine onto the sides of the pan, stir in and serve.

* Or use any fresh seasonal green vegetables.

STEWED WINTER MELON BALLS WITH SCALLOP SAUCE

6	dried scallops (about 45 g / 1½ oz), soaked for 1 hour
½ cup (4 fl oz)	chicken stock
1 thick slice	fresh ginger
700 g (1 ⅓ lb)	fresh winter melon*
	cornflour (cornstarch)

Seasoning/Sauce:

1¼ cups (10 fl oz)	chicken stock
1 tablespoon	rendered chicken fat (chicken grease) or lard
2 teaspoons	rice wine or dry sherry
1¼ teaspoons	salt
1½ teaspoons	sugar
¾ teaspoon	m.s.g. (optional)

Place the drained scallops in a dish and add the chicken stock and ginger slice. Steam until tender, about 45 minutes, then remove scallops from the stock and shred by rubbing between forefinger and thumb. Return to the stock and set aside.

Peel the melon and remove the seeds. Cut into 2.5 cm (1 in) cubes or make into balls with a melon baller. Cover with boiling, slightly salted water and simmer for 20 minutes. Drain well.

Bring the seasoning/sauce ingredients to the boil and add the drained melon. Cover and simmer on low heat until the melon is completely tender, then transfer to a serving plate with a slotted spoon.

Bring the sauce back to the boil, add the drained scallops and simmer until reduced to about ¾ cup. Thicken with a thin paste of cornflour and cold water and simmer for 1 minute, then pour over the melon and serve.

Turnips can be cooked in exactly the same way as the melon. If using canned winter melon or cucumber, omit the initial simmering and simply braise in the sauce until tender.

* Or use about 625 g (1¼ lb) canned winter melon or fresh sweet white turnips or cucumbers.

STEAMED WINTER MELON FILLED WITH VEGETABLES

1 1¼ kg (2½ lb)	winter melon, or use a large pumpkin
60 g (2 oz)	canned bamboo shoots, drained and cubed
60 g (2 oz)	canned straw mushrooms, drained and sliced
60 g (2 oz)	canned lotus root, drained and cubed
1	medium carrot, parboiled and cubed
60 g (2 oz)	canned champignons, drained and halved
30 g (1 oz)	canned gingko or white nuts, drained (optional)
12	green vegetable hearts, trimmed and washed
2 tablespoons	chopped cooked ham
1 tablespoon	rendered chicken fat (chicken grease) or lard

Seasoning:

2 cups (16 fl oz)	chicken stock
2 tablespoons	oyster or light soy sauce
2 teaspoons	rice wine or dry sherry
1¼ teaspoons	salt
½ teaspoon	m.s.g. (optional)
¾ teaspoon	sugar

Wash the winter melon, peel off the skin very thinly so that the outside remains a bright green. Cut a section from the top and scoop out the seeds and pith. If using a pumpkin, do not peel until after it is cooked.

Fill with boiling lightly salted water and add 1 tablespoon of vegetable oil. Set in a dish and place on a rack in a steamer. Cover and steam over rapidly boiling water for 20 minutes. Drain and fill with the prepared vegetables, except the green vegetables. Add the seasoning ingredients and return to the steamer.

Steam again over rapidly boiling water for 25 minutes or until the melon or pumpkin is tender, but not softening too much to lose its shape. In the final 10 minutes of cooking, place the green vegetables on top of the other ingredients in the melon.

To serve, place the melon in the centre of a serving dish and surround with the green vegetables. Garnish with the chopped ham and add the chicken fat. Thicken the sauce, if preferred, by straining into a wok, bring to the boil and adding a thin paste of cornflour and cold water.

Alternatively, serve as 'Winter Melon Surprise.' Strain the liquid from the melon into a wok. Remove the green vegetables. Invert the filled melon onto a serving plate and surround with the greens. Thicken the sauce and pour over the melon. If pumpkin is served in this way, carefully peel off the skin before serving. Slice right through the top of the melon, serving a portion of the melon with the vegetables underneath.

Assorted Vegetables with Beancurd Skin (recipe page 316).

STEAMED BROCCOLI WITH CRABMEAT SAUCE

500 g (1 lb)	fresh broccoli, trimmed and cut into florets
¼ cup (2 fl oz)	frying oil
60 g (2 oz)	fresh crabmeat
1½ tablespoons	chopped spring onion
⅓ teaspoon	grated fresh ginger
2 teaspoons	rice wine or dry sherry
2	egg whites, well beaten
	chopped cooked ham (optional)

Seasoning A:

1 teaspoon	salt
½ teaspoon	m.s.g. (optional)
	pinch of white pepper
½ teaspoon	sugar
1 teaspoon	rice wine or dry sherry
¾ cup (6 fl oz)	chicken stock

Seasoning B/Sauce:

¾ cup (6 fl oz)	chicken stock
½ teaspoon	salt
½ teaspoon	m.s.g. (optional)
	pinch of white pepper
½ teaspoon	sugar
1 teaspoon	cornflour (cornstarch)

Wash the broccoli and drain well. Heat the oil in a wok and sauté the broccoli on moderate heat for 2 minutes, then remove and drain well. Transfer to a dish and add the seasoning A ingredients and steam over rapidly boiling water for 10 minutes. Remove, drain and arrange on a serving plate.

Reheat the wok and sauté the crabmeat with spring onion and ginger for 1 minute. Sizzle the wine onto the sides of the pan, then add the pre-mixed seasoning B/sauce ingredients and bring to the boil.

Remove from the heat and drizzle in the beaten egg whites, allowing to set in the sauce before stirring. Check the seasonings and pour over the broccoli. Garnish with the chopped ham, if used, and serve.

BAMBOO SHOOTS WITH MUSHROOMS AND QUAIL EGGS

6	dried black mushrooms, soaked for 25 minutes
125 g (4 oz)	canned bamboo shoots, drained and thinly sliced
½ cup (4 fl oz)	chicken stock
60 g (2 oz)	canned straw mushrooms, drained and sliced
90 g (3 oz)	canned quail eggs, drained
1	spring onion (scallion), trimmed and shredded
2 slices	fresh ginger, shredded
2 tablespoons	frying oil

Seasoning A:

⅓ teaspoon	salt
½ teaspoon	m.s.g. (optional)
⅓ teaspoon	sugar
¼ cup (2 fl oz)	chicken stock

Seasoning B/Sauce:

2/3 cup	chicken stock
2 teaspoons	light soy sauce
1 teaspoon	rice wine or dry sherry
1 teaspoon	sesame oil (optional)
½ teaspoon	sugar
2 teaspoons	cornflour (cornstarch)

Squeeze the water from the mushrooms, remove the stems and cut the caps into quarters. Mix with the seasoning A ingredients and steam for 20 minutes. Drain.

Blanch the bamboo shoots in boiling water. Drain well and soak in the chicken stock with the sliced straw mushrooms and quail eggs.

Heat the frying oil in a wok and fry the spring onion and ginger for 1 minute, then add the pre-mixed seasoning B/sauce ingredients and bring to the boil. Add the drained vegetables and eggs and simmer until the sauce thickens.

Transfer to a warmed serving plate.

BRAISED 'SNOW' FUNGUS IN CLEAR SOUP

45 g (1½ oz)	dried 'snow' fungus, soaked
210 g (7oz)	fresh pea sprouts or young spinach leaves
	chicken stock
	cornflour (cornstarch)
2 tablespoons	rendered chicken fat (chicken grease)

Seasoning:

1¼ teaspoons	salt
1½ teaspoons	sugar
¼ teaspoon	m.s.g (optional)

Prepare the dried 'snow' fungus following the directions on page 393. Drain well. Leave the root section in place and arrange, roots upward, in a dish. Cover with stock and seasonings. Set on a rack in a steamer and steam for 15 minutes. Drain off the stock and reserve. Upturn the dish onto a serving plate but do not remove the dish.

Bring the retained liquid to the boil and add the pea sprouts. Simmer briefly, then drain. Again reserve the stock. Remove the dish from the 'snow' fungus and arrange the pea sprouts around the base of the mound.

Bring the stock to the boil, adjust the seasoning and add the chicken fat. Thicken with a solution of cornflour and cold water and pour over the fungus. Serve at once.

THREE KINDS OF MUSHROOMS

6	dried black mushrooms, soaked for 25 minutes
½	fresh lettuce, well washed
½ 315 g (10 oz) can	straw mushrooms, drained
½ 315 g (10 oz) can	champignons, drained
½ cup (4 fl oz)	frying oil

Seasoning/Sauce A:

½ cup (4 fl oz)	chicken stock
2 teaspoons	rice wine or dry sherry
1 tablespoon	softened lard or frying oil
½ teaspoon	salt
¼ teaspoon	m.s.g. (optional)
½ teaspoon	sugar
1½ tablespoons	oyster sauce
1 teaspoon	cornflour (cornstarch)

Seasoning/Sauce B:

¼ cup (2 fl oz)	chicken stock
1¼ tablespoons	light soy sauce
1 teaspoon	rice wine or dry sherry
⅓ teaspoon	salt
¼ teaspoon	ground black pepper
1 teaspoon	cornflour (cornstarch)
1 tablespoon	rendered chicken fat (chicken grease)

Seasoning/Sauce C:

¼ cup (2 fl oz)	chicken stock
⅓ teaspoon	salt
¼ teaspoon	m.s.g. (optional)
¼ teaspoon	sugar
¼ teaspoon	ground black pepper
1 teaspoon	cornflour (cornstarch)
1 tablespoon	evaporated milk

Drain the black mushrooms and squeeze out the water. Remove the stems and place the mushrooms in a dish with the seasoning/sauce A ingredients, except the oyster sauce and cornflour. Steam for 25 minutes.

Dip the lettuce into boiling lightly salted water with 1 tablespoon oil added and cook for 45 seconds. Remove, drain well and arrange on a large oval serving plate.

Heat one-third of the oil and stir-fry the straw mushrooms for 1 minute, then add the seasoning/sauce B ingredients, except the chicken fat and simmer until the sauce thickens. Add the chicken fat and stir thoroughly, then transfer to one side of the serving plate.

Heat another one-third of the oil and stir-fry the champignons for 30 seconds, then add the pre-mixed seasoning/sauce C ingredients, except the evaporated milk, and simmer until the sauce thickens. Stir in the evaporated milk and heat through briefly. Transfer to the other side of the serving plate.

Heat the remaining one-third of the oil and stir-fry the drained black mushrooms for 1 minute. Add ¼ cup of the reserved steaming liquid, stir in the cornflour and bring to the boil. Simmer until thickened, then add the oyster sauce. Arrange in the centre of the serving plate and serve.

ASSORTED VEGETABLES WITH BEANCURD SKIN

60 g (2 oz)	dried rolled beancurd skin
3 cups (24 fl oz)	deep-frying oil
3	dried gluten balls
30 g (1 oz)	canned bamboo shoots, drained and sliced
45 g (1½ oz)	dried lotus seeds, steamed to soften
6	dried black mushrooms, soaked for 25 minutes
20 g (¾ oz)	dried lily buds, soaked for 25 minutes
20 g (¾ oz)	dried 'wood ear' fungus, soaked for 25 minutes
125 g (4 oz)	young bok choy
1½ tablespoons	light soy sauce
1 teaspoon	sesame oil (optional)

Seasoning/Sauce:

1½ cups (12 fl oz)	chicken stock or water
1 teaspoon	salt
¾ teaspoon	m.s.g. (optional)

Fry the beancurd skin in smoking hot deep-frying oil until crisp and bubbly on the surface, about 20 seconds. Drain and cut into 5 cm (2 in) pieces, then soak with the gluten balls in cold water until softened.

Drain the soaked ingredients, remove the mushroom stems and cut the 'wood ears' into smaller pieces. Thoroughly wash the *bok choy* and cut each piece lengthways into quarters.

Pour off all but 3 tablespoons of the oil and stir-fry the ingredients together for 2 minutes, then add the Seasoning/Sauce ingredients and bring to the boil. Cover and simmer for 10 minutes, add the soy sauce and sesame oil, if used, and thicken the sauce with a paste of cornflour (cornstarch) and cold water. Serve.

STUFFED RED PEPPERS

Serve as an appetiser or main dish.

12	large red chilli peppers*
125 g (4 oz)	lean pork, finely chopped
45 g (1½ oz)	raw peeled shrimps, chopped cornflour (cornstarch)
1¼ cup (10 fl oz)	frying oil
1 tablespoon	fermented black beans, washed and chopped
1 tablespoon	finely chopped spring onion (scallion)
½ teaspoon	finely chopped fresh ginger
½ teaspoon	finely chopped garlic

Seasoning A:

⅓ teaspoon	salt
½ teaspoon	sugar
¼ teaspoon	ground black pepper
1 tablespoon	cornflour (cornstarch)

Seasoning B/Sauce:

⅓ cup	chicken stock or cold water
1 tablespoon	light soy sauce
¼ teaspoon	salt
½ teaspoon	m.s.g. (optional)
¼ teaspoon	sugar

Cut the chillies along one side and press open. Trim away the stem and remove the seed core and the inner white ribs. Mix the pork and shrimps with the seasoning A ingredients, working to a smooth paste. Lightly coat the inside of the chilli with cornflour and fill generously with the pork mixture. Dip the whole stuffed chillies into cornflour.

Heat the oil almost to smoking point and fry the chillies, filling side downwards, until golden, turning once. Remove and drain off all but 2½ tablespoons of the oil. Add the black beans, onion, ginger, and garlic and stir-fry on moderate heat for 1 minute, then pour in the pre-mixed seasoning B/sauce ingredients and bring to the boil. Reduce the heat to low. Return the chillies and simmer, covered, for about 5 minutes. Serve hot.

* Although hot red chilli peppers are used, they have a mild almost sweet taste when cooked in this way.

Egg Custard (recipe page 321) and Sweet Rice Balls in Red Bean Soup (recipe page 319).

SHARK'S FIN AND CRABMEAT SOUP

250 g (8 oz)	prepared shark's fin, about 60 g (2 oz) dry weight
⅓ cup	softened lard
3	spring onions (scallions), trimmed and sliced
3 slices	fresh ginger
185 g (6 oz)	fresh crabmeat
1 tablespoon	rice wine or dry sherry
5 cups (1¼ litres)	chicken stock
2 tablespoons	cornflour (cornstarch)
2	egg whites, well beaten
1 tablespoon	rendered chicken fat (chicken grease) (optional)

Seasoning:

1½ teaspoons	salt
¾ teaspoon	m.s.g. (optional)
1 teaspoon	sugar
¼ cup (2 fl oz)	light soy sauce
¼ teaspoon	white pepper

Prepare the shark's fin according to the instructions on page 00, allowing about 4 hours advance preparation. Drain well.

Sauté the spring onions and ginger in the lard for 2 minutes. Add the crabmeat and fry briefly, then sizzle the wine onto the sides of the wok and stir in. Add the shark's fin and fry for 1 minute, then add the chicken stock and seasoning ingredients and bring to the boil.

Simmer for 10 minutes, then remove from the heat and slowly drizzle in the beaten egg whites and leave to set into strands in the soup. Thicken with the cornflour mixed with an equal quantity of cold water and simmer until the soup becomes clear. Pour into a soup tureen. Serve with a small jug of Chinese red vinegar to be added to taste.

MUSHROOMS WITH CHICKEN WINGS IN SOUP

12	dried black mushrooms, soaked for 25 minutes
6	chicken wings, cut in halves
6 cups (1½ litres)	chicken stock
1 tablespoon	rendered chicken fat (chicken grease) or lard
1 teaspoon	m.s.g. (optional)
1½ tablespoons	cornflour (cornstarch)

Seasoning A:

½ teaspoon	salt
½ teaspoon	m.s.g. (optional)
1 teaspoon	sugar
1	spring onion (scallion), trimmed and sliced
1 slice	fresh ginger

Seasoning B:

½ teaspoon	salt
¼ teaspoon	m.s.g. (optional)
2 teaspoons	light soy sauce
2 teaspoons	rice wine or dry sherry
2	spring onions (scallions), trimmed and sliced
3 thick slices	fresh ginger
¼ teaspoon	ground black pepper

Drain the mushrooms and remove the stems. Place in a dish with the seasoning A ingredients and add 1 cup of the chicken stock. Steam for 30 minutes, then drain.

Wash the chicken wings, debone if preferred, and place in a dish with the seasoning B ingredients. Leave for 10 minutes, then sauté in the chicken fat or lard until lightly coloured. Pour in the remaining chicken stock and bring to the boil. Reduce the heat and simmer until the wings are tender, about 20 minutes.

Add the mushrooms and simmer a further 10 minutes, then stir in the m.s.g., if used, and thicken the soup with the cornflour mixed with an equal quantity of cold water. Stir until the soup clears, then pour into a soup tureen and serve hot.

WATERCRESS AND LIVER SOUP

185 g (6 oz)	fresh watercress
125 g (4 oz)	lamb or pork liver
4 cups (1 litre)	chicken stock

Seasoning:

1	spring onion (scallion), trimmed and shredded
2 slices	fresh ginger, shredded
¾ teaspoon	salt
¼ teaspoon	m.s.g. (optional)
1 tablespoon	light soy sauce
2 teaspoons	rice wine or dry sherry

Thoroughly wash the watercress and remove the stems. Cut the liver into very thin slices and blanch in boiling water for 20 seconds, drain and soak in cold water for 5 minutes.

Bring the chicken stock to the boil and add the seasoning ingredients. Simmer for 2 minutes, then add the sliced liver and simmer a further 2 minutes. Add the watercress, stir in and cook until just softened. Pour into a soup tureen.

SWEET CORN AND CHICKEN SOUP

1 500 g (1 lb) can	sweet corn kernels
90 g (3 oz)	coarsely minced chicken breast
4 cups (1 litre)	chicken stock
¼ cup	cornflour (cornstarch)

Seasoning:

1½ teaspoons	salt
¾ teaspoon	m.s.g. (optional)
1 tablespoon	light soy sauce

Drain the corn and crush lightly in a mortar or food processor. Pour into a saucepan and add the chicken, stock, and seasonings. Bring to the boil and simmer for 3 minutes, then add the cornflour mixed with an equal quantity of cold water and simmer until the soup thickens and turns clear. Pour into a soup tureen and serve.

SHRIMP BALL SOUP

125 g (4 oz)	raw peeled shrimps
30 g (1 oz)	pork fat
½ 315 g (10 oz) can	straw mushrooms, drained
4 cups (1 litre)	chicken stock
1¼ teaspoons	salt
¾ teaspoon	m.s.g. (optional)
1	spring onion (scallion), trimmed and sliced

Seasoning A:

1	egg white, beaten
¼ teaspoon	salt
¼ teaspoon	m.s.g. (optional)
2 teaspoons	ginger wine
1 tablespoon	cornflour (cornstarch)

Seasoning B:

½ teaspoon	salt
¼ teaspoon	m.s.g. (optional)
1 tablespoon	rice wine or dry sherry
1 teaspoon	sesame oil
½ cup (4 fl oz)	chicken stock

Finely mince (grind) the shrimps and pork fat and add the seasoning A ingredients. Mix into a smooth paste, then form into small balls and simmer in gently boiling, lightly salted water for 2 minutes. Remove on a slotted spoon and place in a dish of cold water.

Place the mushrooms and the seasoning B ingredients in a small saucepan and bring to the boil. Simmer for 2 minutes.

Bring the chicken stock to the boil, add the salt, m.s.g., if used, and spring onion and simmer briefly. Add the shrimp balls and drained mushrooms and simmer for 3 minutes, then pour into a soup tureen and serve.

WONTONS IN SOUP WITH MIXED MEAT AND VEGETABLES

18	uncooked wontons (see recipe page 376)
60 g (2 oz)	cooked chicken breast, shredded
60 g (2 oz)	cooked pork fillet or roast pork, shredded
6 stalks	fresh young bok choy*
1 medium	carrot, shredded
30 g (1 oz)	canned bamboo shoots, drained and shredded
1	small leek, shredded
4 cups (1 litre)	chicken stock
3 thick slices	fresh ginger, shredded
1½ teaspoons	salt
½ teaspoon	m.s.g. (optional)
	pinch of ground black pepper
½ teaspoon	sesame oil

Bring a large saucepan of salted water to the boil and add the wontons. Simmer until they rise to the surface, then cook for 2½ — 3 minutes more. Drain and place in six soup bowls.

Bring the stock to the boil and add the ginger, salt, m.s.g., if used, and pepper. Simmer briefly, then add the shredded meat and vegetables and simmer for 2½ — 3 minutes. Add the sesame oil and divide the soup among the bowls. Serve hot.

* Or use other fresh green vegetables.

SWEET RICE BALLS IN RED BEAN SOUP

1 cup	glutinous rice powder
¼ cup (2 fl oz)	boiling water
1 tablespoon	sugar
1 tablespoon	softened lard
1½ — 2 tablespoons	cold water
1 280 g (9 oz) can	sweet red bean paste
1 cup	sugar (or to taste)
4 cups	water

Place the rice powder in a mixing bowl and add the boiling water, sugar, and lard. Work with the handle of a wooden spoon until well mixed, then add cold water to make a smooth, fairly hard dough. Knead for 2 minutes, then roll out into a long sausage shape and cut into small pieces. Roll each piece into a ball.

Bring a large saucepan of water to the boil and add the rice balls. Simmer until they rise to the surface, about 3 minutes, then remove with a slotted spoon into a dish of cold water.

Mix the red bean paste with the sugar and water. Heat to boiling and reduce to a simmer. Add the rice balls and simmer for about 3 minutes, then serve hot.

GLAZED SWEET POTATO BALLS WITH SESAME SEEDS

500 g (1 lb)	sweet potato or yams
2	whole eggs, beaten
½ cup	cornflour (cornstarch)
5 cups (1¼ litres)	deep-frying oil
½ cup	toasted white sesame seeds
1½ cups	sugar

Peel the sweet potato and form into small balls using a melon scoop. Soak in cold water for 20 minutes, then dry thoroughly and coat very lightly with cornflour. Dip into beaten egg and coat again with cornflour. Heat the deep-frying oil to moderately hot and deep-fry the potato balls for 3 minutes. Remove and drain well.

Transfer about 2 tablespoons of the oil to another wok and add the sugar. Stir on moderate heat until the sugar melts and turns into a thick golden syrup. Remove from the heat.

Reheat the deep-frying oil and fry the potato balls for a second time until cooked through, about 2 minutes, then transfer to the syrup. Carefully turn the balls in the syrup until evenly coated.

Spread the sesame seeds on a piece of greaseproof paper. Add the glazed sweet potato balls and turn until thickly coated with the sesame. Transfer to an oiled serving plate and serve while still hot.

ALMOND JELLY WITH FRESH FRUIT

2/3 cup	boiling water
1⅓ tablespoons	unflavoured gelatine
1½ cups (12 fl oz)	lukewarm water or milk
⅓ cup	evaporated milk or fresh cream
2 teaspoons	almond essence
250 g (8 oz)	diced fresh fruit, chilled
⅓ cup	liquid from canned fruit or sugar syrup

Mix the boiling water and gelatine together and stir slowly until dissolved, then add the water or milk, evaporated milk or cream, and the almond essence and mix throughly.

Pour into a lightly oiled jelly mould and leave to set. Chill thoroughly.

Turn the jelly out onto a serving plate and surround with the diced fruit. Pour on the fruit or sugar syrup and serve.

ALMOND AND QUAIL EGG TEA

12	canned or fresh quail eggs
60 g (2 oz)	blanched almonds
1 teaspoon	bicarbonate of soda
1 tablespoon	Chinese black tea leaves
1 cup	sugar
1 10 cm (4 in)	cinnamon stick

Boil fresh quail eggs, if used, in water for about 4½ minutes until firm. Cool under running cold water and remove the shells. Drain canned eggs. Cover with cold water and set aside.

Place the almonds and bicarbonate of soda in a saucepan and add about 1½ cups of water. Bring to the boil and simmer until the almonds are tender, about 45 minutes. Drain well and rinse with clean cold water.

Brew half the tea with 1 cup boiling water. Place the remaining tea in a bowl and add one-quarter of the sugar and the drained eggs. Add boiling water to cover and place in a steamer.

Place the cinnamon stick in another bowl and set in the steamer also. Cover and steam over rapidly boiling water for 25 minutes.

Bring 2 cups of water to the boil and add the remaining sugar, stirring until dissolved.

Into 6 dessert bowls divide the almonds and place 2 drained eggs in each. Add a splash each of the tea and cinnamon water and top up with the sugar water. Serve hot.

This is an unusual blend of ingredients for a sweet dish, but the result is a cooling, refreshing dessert which can also be served chilled.

If preferred, substitute poached fruit or softened lotus seeds for the quail eggs.

EGG CUSTARD

6	whole eggs
3	egg whites
1½ cups (12 fl oz)	fresh milk
1½ tablespoons	clear honey or white sugar
2 teaspoons	cornflour (cornstarch)
¾ teaspoon	grated lemon rind

Beat the eggs well together, then add the milk, honey, and cornflour and beat to a smooth batter. Stir in the lemon rind, then pour the mixture into a greased ovenproof dish or six individual heatproof dessert dishes. Set on a rack in a steamer and steam over gently boiling water for about 15 minutes, or until just set. Serve immediately.

CHAPTER VII
Dishes for Special Occasions

SHARK'S FIN WITH SHREDDED MEAT IN RICH SOUP

The Chinese name for this dish translates as
'Happiness to Everyone.'

500 g (1 lb)	prepared shark's fin (see page 393), about 125 g (4 oz) dry weight
6	dried black mushrooms, soaked for 25 minutes
125 g (4 oz)	Chinese or cured (Smithfield) ham
125 g (4 oz)	pork fillet (tenderloin)
125 g (4 oz)	boneless chicken breast
125 (4 oz)	canned bamboo shoots, drained
2 tablespoons	finely chopped spring onion (scallion)
2 tablespoons	finely shredded fresh ginger
2 tablespoons	frying oil
7 cups (1¾ litres)	enriched stock
	fresh coriander

Seasoning A:

1	small egg white, beaten
1 tablespoon	ginger wine
¾	cornflour (cornstarch)

Seasoning B:

1 tablespoon	light soy sauce
1 teaspoon	rice wine or dry sherry
1 tablespoon	cold water
½ teaspoon	ground black pepper
¾ teaspoon	cornflour (cornstarch)

Seasoning C:

1¾ teaspoons	salt
1 teaspoon	sugar
2 tablespoons	dark soy sauce
1½ tablespoons	rice wine or dry sherry
¼ cup (2 fl oz)	cold water
⅓ cup	cornflour (cornstarch)
1½ teaspoons	sesame oil (optional)

Allow at least 4 hours advance preparation for the shark's fins. In the meantime, squeeze the water from the mushrooms and shred the caps. Finely shred the ham, pork, chicken, and bamboo shoots. Place the shredded chicken in a dish with the seasoning A ingredients, mix well and leave for 15 minutes. Mix the shredded pork with the seasoning B ingredients in another dish and leave for 10 minutes.

Heat the frying oil and sauté the chicken until whitened. Remove and add the pork. Sauté for about 1 minute, then remove. Add the remaining shredded ingredients and the spring onion and sauté for 1½ minutes, then remove. Pour in the enriched stock and bring to the boil.

Add the drained shark's fins and reduce the heat to simmer for 25 minutes, return the shredded ingredients and add the seasoning C ingredients. Simmer for about 10 minutes, then transfer to a soup tureen and garnish with the fresh coriander.

WHOLE STEAMED FISH

1 1 kg (2 lb)	whole fresh fish
5 cm (2 in) piece	fresh ginger
5	spring onions (scallions), trimmed
¼ cup (2 fl oz)	frying oil
⅓ cup	chicken stock
¼ cup (2 fl oz)	light soy sauce
¼ teaspoon	ground black pepper
1 teaspoon	sesame oil (optional)
	few sprigs of fresh coriander

Clean and scale the fish. Peel the ginger and cut into thin slices. Place several slices inside the fish and shred the remainder finely. Set the fish on a large plate, push two of the spring onions under it and shred the remainder.

Set the plate on a rack in a steamer and steam over rapidly boiling water for 18 — 20 minutes. Remove from the steamer and garnish with the shredded spring onions and ginger.

Heat the frying oil to smoking point and pour over the fish, then heat the remaining ingredients, except coriander, together and pour over the fish as well. Garnish with the coriander and serve at once.

BRAISED ABALONE IN OYSTER SAUCE

750 g (1½ lb)	fresh abalone*
2 teaspoons	salt
	cornflour (cornstarch)
250 g (½ lb)	fresh pork or ham skin
4 cups (1 litre)	enriched or chicken stock
3	spring onions (scallions), trimmed and sliced
5 cloves	garlic, sliced
⅓ cup	frying oil

Seasoning A:

2 tablespoons	rice wine or dry sherry
3	spring onions (scallions), cut in halves
4 thick slices	fresh ginger, bruised

Seasoning B:

⅓ cup	oyster sauce (or use ½ cup light soy sauce)
2 teaspoons	dark soy sauce
2 teaspoons	rice wine or dry sherry
¾ teaspoon	salt
2½ teaspoons	sugar

Rub the abalone with the salt and plenty of cornflour. Rinse well with cold water, then cover with fresh cold water and bring to the boil. Simmer for 20 minutes, then drain well.

Heat a saucepan and add the seasoning A ingredients and the abalone. Add enough water to cover the abalone and simmer, covered, for 3 hours. Top up with boiling water as the level drops. Discard the onion and ginger.

Warm a large casserole and rub with an oiled cloth. Cut the ham or pork skin in halves and place one piece in the bottom of the casserole. Arrange the abalone on this and add the seasoning B ingredients and the stock. Cover with the remaining pork or ham skin and put the lid tightly in place. Simmer for 1 hour on low heat. Discard the skin and keep the abalone warm.

Saute the sliced onion and garlic in the oil until lightly coloured and beginning to soften. Add to the casserole and heat through for 5 minutes. Thicken the sauce with a thin paste of cornflour (cornstarch) and cold water and serve.

If preferred, remove the abalone before thickening the sauce and slice each piece thinly then return to the sauce.

* Dried abalone may be used, about 440 g (14 oz). Soak in cold water overnight then simmer in plenty of lightly salted water for at least 6 hours, rinse thoroughly and use as above.

Canned abalone is unsuitable for this type of dish, as the result would be tough, rubbery meat and the loss of its natural flavour.

DRIED SCALLOPS BRAISED WITH GARLIC

250 g (8 oz)	dried scallops, soaked for 30 minutes
3 whole heads	fresh garlic
¼ cup (2 fl oz)	frying oil
90 g (3 oz)	fresh chicken fat (chicken grease) or ham skin
250 g (8 oz)	young bok choy
1 tablespoon	softened lard
2 teaspoons	rice wine or dry sherry
1½ teaspoons	cornflour (cornstarch)
1 tablespoon	oyster sauce

Seasoning:

1 teaspoon	salt
¾ teaspoon	sugar
1 cup (8 fl oz)	chicken stock

Drain the scallops and place in a dish with water to cover. Set in a steamer and steam over gently boiling water for 1½ hours.

Peel the garlic and sauté the whole cloves in the oil until softened, about 3 minutes. Remove the scallops from the steamer, discard the liquid and add the garlic and seasoning ingredients. Cover with sliced chicken fat or the ham skin and return to the steamer. Steam for a further 1½ hours.

Simmer the bok choy in lightly salted water until tender. Drain and stir in the lard. Arrange on a serving plate. Remove the scallops from the steamer again, drain the liquid into a wok and arrange the scallops and garlic over the vegetables. Discard the chicken fat or ham skin.

Bring the liquid to the boil, sizzle the wine onto the sides of the pan, then thicken the sauce with the cornflour mixed with a little cold water. Simmer for 1 minute, stir in the oyster sauce and pour over the dish. Serve at once.

KUNG HEI FAT CHOY

Seasonal Vegetables with Dried Oysters, Mushrooms and *Fa Ts'ai (Fat Choy)*

The title translates as 'Happy and Prosperous New Year.'

125 g (4 oz)	dried oysters,* or 250 g (8 oz) fresh shelled oysters
12	dried black mushrooms, soaked for 25 minutes
15 g (½ oz)	dried fa ts'ai, soaked for 25 minutes
250 g (8 oz)	fresh young bok choy, or other Chinese green vegetables
1	spring onion (scallion), trimmed and shredded
2 slices	fresh ginger, shredded
½ cup (4 fl oz)	softened lard or vegetable oil
1¼ teaspoons	cornflour (cornstarch)

Seasoning A:

½ teaspoon	salt
½ teaspoon	sugar
1 tablespoon	ginger wine (see page 387)
1 tablespoon	oyster sauce
¾ cup (6 fl oz)	chicken stock

Seasoning A (if using fresh oysters):

2 slices	fresh ginger, shredded
1	spring onion (scallion), trimmed and shredded
⅓ cup	chicken stock
½ teaspoon	salt

Seasoning B:

⅓ teaspoon	salt
1 teaspoon	sugar
2 teaspoons	light soy sauce
2 teaspoons	rice wine or dry sherry
¼ cup (2 fl oz)	chicken stock

Seasoning C:

¾ teaspoon	salt
1½ teaspoons	ginger wine
¼ cup (2 fl oz)	chicken stock

Seasoning D:

½ teaspoon	salt
¼ teaspoon	m.s.g. (optional)
½ teaspoon	sugar'
2 teaspoons	ginger wine
¼ cup (2 fl oz)	chicken stock

Drain the soaked oysters and wash thoroughly. Rinse fresh oysters, if used, in cold, lightly salted water and drain well.

Heat 1 tablespoon of the softened lard or frying oil in a wok and sauté the spring onion and ginger lightly. Add the dried oysters and seasoning A ingredients and simmer briefly, then transfer to a dish and set in a steamer to steam until the oysters are tender.

If using fresh oysters, omit the sautéd onion and ginger and place the oysters and the alternative seasoning A in a dish. Steam for 10 minutes, then remove from the heat and set aside.

While the oysters are cooking, steam the black mushrooms with the seasoning B ingredients in a separate dish for 30 minutes. Remove and drain. Cut off the stems.

Drain the fa ts'ai and sauté in 1 tablespoon of the softened lard or oil for 30 seconds on moderate heat. Add the seasoning C ingredients and simmer until softened, about 1½ minutes, then drain very thoroughly and spread over the centre of a serving plate.

Arrange the drained oysters over the fa ts'ai and surround with the drained mushrooms.

Heat the wok with the remaining oil and sauté the vegetables for 2 minutes, then add the seasoning D ingredients and cover the pan. Cook until the vegetables are tender, then drain and arrange around the edge of the dish.

Wipe out the wok and strain in the liquid in which the oysters were cooked. Add the cornflour mixed with a little cold water and simmer until the sauce thickens. Adjust the seasoning to taste and pour over the oysters. Serve at once.

* Soak dried oysters overnight.

Roast Suckling Pig (recipe page 328).

ROAST SUCKLING PIG

1 5 — 6 kg (10 — 12 lb)	suckling pig
¾ cup	malt sugar
⅓ cup	Chinese red vinegar
1 cup (8 fl oz)	boiling water

Seasoning:

1 tablespoon	salt
¼ cup	sugar
2 teaspoons	five spice powder
¼ cup (2 fl oz)	rice wine or dry sherry
¼ cup	sweet bean paste
¼ cup (2 fl oz)	sesame oil
½ cup (4 fl oz)	light soy sauce
¼ cup (2 fl oz)	sesame oil
3 tablespoons	finely chopped spring onion
3 tablespoons	finely chopped fresh ginger

Accompaniments:

24	'Mandarin' pancakes (see recipe, page 373)
1 cup	'duck' sauce (see page 385)
12	spring onions (scallions)

Pour boiling water over the pig and scrape with a sharp knife to remove any short hairs, then pour on several lots of boiling water to shrink the skin slightly. This will improve the quality of the crackling.

Slit the pig along its length underneath and insert one long metal rod the length of the body, or use the rod of an outdoor charcoal-heated rotisserie. Pass several small metal skewers across the body to prop it open.

Turn upside down on a board and wipe out the inside. Mix the seasoning ingredients together, and smear thickly and evenly over the inside. Leave for at least 2 hours.

Turn right side up and coat with the pre-mixed malt sugar, vinegar, and boiling water. Catch any drips in a tray placed under the pig and brush these again over the skin until all is used up. There should be no holes in the skin as these will allow fat to escape during cooking and spoil the crackling. Small holes may be held together with toothpicks or by stitching with a larding needle and strong thread.

Leave for 1½ — 2 hours for the skin to dry.

Prepare the pancakes and pour the sauce into several small dishes. Trim the spring onions and cut each in halves. Place in a dish.

Prepare a charcoal fire outdoors and leave until the coals are glowing red. Place the pig, skin-side down about 30 cm (12 in) above the coals and turn the pig from side to side so that the skin cooks evenly, for about 8 minutes. Lower the pig to about 15 cm (6 in) above the coals, making sure the coals are still glowing red, and cook the pig, moving it constantly from side to side to ensure even crisping of the skin.

After about 15 minutes, turn the pig over to cook the underside. Raise it a little higher and cook until the meat is firm and white. Test by inserting a skewer into the thigh. If no pink liquid runs off, the meat is ready. Remove to a carving board. The crisp skin is served as the first course.

Serve with half the pancakes, sauce, and spring onions. The crackling should be dipped into the sauce and several pieces placed on a pancake. Add a piece of spring onion and roll up the pancake to contain the filling. Dip into the sauce before eating.

To prepare the second course, cut the pig in halves lengthwise, cutting right through the head, and splay the two sections flat on a large serving platter. Slice off the juiciest pieces of meat and cut into bite-sized pieces. Rearrange on the carcass and serve with the remaining pancakes, spring onion, and sauce.

See the recipe, Three Courses of Roast Suckling Pig for use of the remaining meat (Page 290).

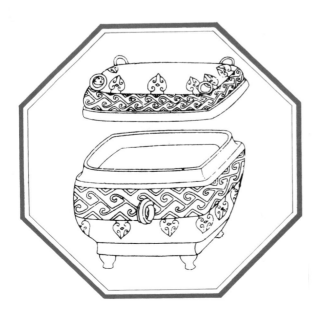

PEKING ROAST DUCK

1 2½ kg (5 lb)	plump duck
⅓ cup	malt sugar
½ cup (4 fl oz)	boiling water
18	'Mandarin' pancakes (see recipe, page 373)
1 cup	'duck' sauce (see page 385)
9	spring onions (scallions)

Clean the duck and wash well, then tie a string securely around the neck and pass it under the wings to hold them away from the body. Suspend over a drip tray and pour on several lots of boiling water, then pour more boiling water into the cavity. Leave to dry for a few minutes.

Mix the malt sugar and boiling water together. Pour it slowly and evenly over the duck, allowing some inside. Leave duck to hang over the drip tray in a well-ventilated place for at least 4 hours.

Preheat the oven to moderately hot 200°C (400°F). If the oven is a large one, place one rack on the highest setting, hang the duck on this with a metal hook and place a drip tray in the bottom. Otherwise lay the duck on a rack in a roasting pan and roast for about 1½ hours until the skin is a deep shiny red colour and the meat moist and tender. When the duck is done, increase the heat to very high for about 10 minutes to crisp the skin.

In the meantime, prepare the pancakes and keep warm. Or prepare in advance and reheat by steaming for about 7 minutes. Prepare the sauce and pour into several small dip dishes. Trim the spring onions, using only the white parts. Cut each into two pieces.

Arrange the pancakes and onions on two plates. Slice the crisp skin from the duck and spread on a serving plate. Keep the remainder of the duck warm. Serve the skin with one plate of the pancakes and onions and the sauce.

To eat, dip several pieces of skin in the sauce and place in the centre of a pancake. Add a piece of spring onion and roll up. Dip into the sauce again before eating.

Serve the choicest parts of the meat next, thinly sliced, with the remaining pancakes, sauce, and onions. Roll up in the same way.

Left-over meat and the carcass can be used for additional dishes and soup, refer to Three Courses of Peking Duck (page 52).

BEGGAR'S CHICKEN

1 1½ kg (3 lb)	chicken
12	dried black mushrooms, soaked for 25 minutes
185 g (6 oz)	salted mustard leaves, soaked for 25 minutes
125 g (4 oz)	fat pork
¼ cup (2 fl oz)	frying oil
4	fresh or dried lotus leaves*
1½ kg (3 lb)	pond mud**
	vegetable oil

Seasoning:

2 tablespoons	sugar
¼ teaspoon	ground black pepper
1 tablespoon	dark soy sauce
2 tablespoons	rice wine or dry sherry
2 teaspoons	sesame oil

Wash and dress the chicken. Drain the mushrooms, squeeze out excess water and remove the stems. Cut the caps into dice. Drain and shred the mustard leaves. Dice the fat pork and sauté in the oil until lightly coloured. Add the seasoning ingredients, the mushrooms, and salted vegetables and mix well.

Stuff into the chicken and close the opening with poultry pins. Blanch the lotus leaves in boiling water until softened. Drain and squeeze out the water. Brush the chicken thoroughly with vegetable oil, wrap in the leaves, pork fat, or greased paper and cover with a thick coating of the mud, clay, or dough. Seal completely.

Place on a baking sheet in a moderately hot oven 220°C (425°F) and bake for 1¾ — 2 hours.

To serve, break open the casing and discard. Place on a serving plate, and tear away the leaves or paper.

* Or use pork omentum (caul net/fat) or well-oiled greaseproof paper.

** Modelling clay, or use a flour and water dough.

329

'CHIN HUA' CHICKEN

The city of Chin Hua (Jinhua) in Chekiang (Zhejiang) has long been famed for its quality ham which is at its tastiest in this dish combined with poached spring chicken and fresh seasonal vegetables.

1 1¼ kg (2½ lb)	spring chicken
155 g (5 oz)	Chin Hua or cured (Smithfield) ham
315 g (10 oz)	young choy sum or broccoli
3 thin slices	fresh ginger
2	spring onions (scallions), cut in halves
2	star anise
1¼ teaspoons	salt
1 tablespoon	rice wine or dry sherry

Seasoning A:

¼ teaspoon	m.s.g. (optional)
2 teaspoons	rice wine or dry sherry
1 tablespoon	chicken stock
1 tablespoon	frying oil

Seasoning B/Sauce:

1 cup (8 fl oz)	chicken stock
2 tablespoons	frying oil
1 teaspoon	rice wine or dry sherry
½ teaspoon	sesame oil
½ teaspoon	sugar
1 teaspoon	cornflour (cornstarch)

Clean and dress the chicken. Rub with salt and wine inside and out and place the ginger, spring onions, and star anise inside the cavity. Put the chicken into a dish and set on a rack in a steamer. Steam over rapidly boiling water for about 40 minutes. The meat should be just firm and white with a touch of pink near the bones.

Remove and cut the breast and thigh meats into thin slices. Shred the remaining chicken and arrange in the centre of an oval serving dish.

Wash the ham, place in a dish and steam for 20 minutes with the seasoning A ingredients. Remove and cut into slices the same size as the chicken. Arrange alternate slices of chicken and ham over the shredded chicken.

Cook the choy sum or broccoli in boiling, slightly salted water with 1 tablespoon of oil and ½ teaspoon sugar for 3 — 4 minutes until just tender. Drain and place in rows over the chicken and ham, or arrange around the rim of the dish.

Heat the frying oil from the seasoning B/sauce ingredients in a wok to smoking point and add the remaining ingredients. Bring to the boil and simmer until thickened. Pour over the dish and serve at once.

STEAMED PIGEONS WITH WHITE FUNGUS

This dish represents Peace and Brotherhood.

4	young pigeons (about 1-1/8 kg / 2¼ lb dressed weight)
2 tablespoons	ginger wine (see page 387)
125 g (4 oz)	pork fillet (tenderloin)
45 g (1½ oz)	dried 'snow' fungus, soaked for 25 minutes
2 pieces	dried orange peel
3 thin slices	fresh ginger
6 cups (1½ litres)	chicken stock or cold water

Seasonings:

1¼ teaspoons	salt
1 teaspoon	sugar
1 tablespoon	rice wine or dry sherry
¼ teaspoon	ground black pepper

Wash the pigeons, drain well and wipe dry. Blanch in boiling, slightly salted water and rub with the ginger wine. Blanch the pork for 1 minute and drain well.

Drain the fungus and place in a saucepan with water to cover. Add the seasoning ingredients and simmer for 5 minutes.

Drain the liquid into another saucepan and add the chicken stock or cold water. Bring to the boil and add the orange peel and ginger. Simmer briefly, then add the pigeons and pork. Transfer to a deep dish. Cover the dish firmly with a lid or with a piece of greaseproof paper tied in place with string, or sealed with a flour and water paste.

Set the dish on a rack in a steamer and steam over gently boiling water for about 2 hours. Remove the lid or paper, add the white fungus and simmer a further 20 minutes. Check the seasonings, adjusting according to taste. Serve in the dish.

Steamed Pigeons with White Fungus (recipe this page).

PORK SHOULDER WITH *FA TS'AI*

Fa ts'ai is a kind of seaweed, black in colour and resembling human hair. Its name *fa ts'ai*, or *fat choy* in Cantonese, forms part of the New Year greeting and represents wealth and riches. Thus, to serve a dish containing this unusual but nutritionally rich ingredient is to extend the very best of good wishes to the recipient. Pork shoulder or pork knuckle with fa ts'ai is usually featured at Lunar New Year banquets.

1¼ kg (2½ lb)	pork shoulder
1 tablespoon	dark soy sauce
45 g (1½ oz)	fa ts'ai (fat choy)
6 cups (1½ litres)	deep-frying oil
1	fresh lettuce
	cornflour (cornstarch)

Seasoning:

1¾ teaspoons	salt
2 tablespoons	sugar
1 teaspoon	m.s.g. (optional)
3	star anise
4 cubes	fermented beancurd with the liquid, mashed
1½ cups (12 fl oz)	chicken stock or water

Cut the pork into large chunks without removing the skin. Place in a saucepan, cover with cold water and bring to the boil. Simmer for about 45 minutes, then remove and leave to dry. Rub with the dark soy sauce and leave for 15 minutes.

Soak the fa ts'ai in cold water until softened, then drain.

Heat the deep-frying oil to smoking point, reduce the heat slightly and fry the pork cubes until well browned, about 4 minutes. Remove and drain well, wipe with kitchen paper to remove excess oil and place in a casserole. Add the fa ts'ai and seasoning, bring to the boil, then cover and reduce the heat to low. Simmer until the meat is completely tender, about 45 minutes.

Separate the leaves of the fresh lettuce, wash well and drop into boiling water with 1 tablespoon frying oil and 1 teaspoon salt added. Simmer for 20 seconds, then drain well and arrange on a serving plate. Place the pork pieces on the lettuce.

Reheat the sauce and thicken with a paste of cornflour and cold water. Simmer briefly, then pour over the pork and serve with plain white rice.

MONGOLIAN BARBECUE

Serves 6 — 8.

250 g (8 oz)	lean lamb
250 g (8 oz)	beef fillet (tenderloin)
250 g (8 oz)	boneless chicken breast
315 g (10 oz)	raw peeled prawns (shrimps)
500 g (1 lb)	fresh bean sprouts
500 g (1 lb)	fresh Chinese cabbage or young lettuce
3	young leeks
1	large bunch of fresh coriander
4 squares	fresh soft beancurd
1	large green capsicum (bell pepper)
2	fresh red chilli peppers

Seasoning/Sauce:

6 cups (1½ litres)	chicken stock
¾ cup (6 fl oz)	light soy sauce
1¾ tablespoons	sesame oil
½ cup (4 fl oz)	rice wine or dry sherry
1½ tablespoons	sugar
1¼ teaspoons	m.s.g. (optional)
½ cup (4 fl oz)	vegetable oil

Special Equipment: A table-top hotplate, wooden chopsticks or fondue forks.

Partially freeze the lamb, beef, and chicken, then cut into paper-thin slices and arrange individually on plates. Thoroughly wash the prawns under cold water, rubbing with salt and cornflour (cornstarch) in the process. Devein with a toothpick (see page 00), cut each into several thin slices and arrange on a plate.

Wash the bean sprouts and drain thoroughly. Place on several plates. Wash the cabbage or lettuce, separate the leaves and cut the larger ones in halves. Thoroughly wash the leeks, then cut into 5 cm (2 in) pieces and shred finely lengthwise. Wash the coriander and remove the stems. Arrange the cabbage or lettuce, leeks, and coriander on separate plates.

Soak the beancurd in cold water for 10 minutes, then remove and drain well. Cut into thin slices and place on a plate. Trim away the stem, seed-core, and the inner white ribs from the capsicum and chilli peppers and arrange on a plate.

Mix the sauce ingredients together and pour into 6 — 8 individual small jugs or bowls. Pour additional vegetable oil into several small jugs.

Take all the ingredients and the sauces to the table. Heat the hotplate.

Dip the meat or vegetables into the sauce, then fry quickly on the well-oiled hot plate. Splash on a little of the sauce and some vegetable oil during cooking.

Mongolian Barbecue can be accompanied by Sesame Pocket Bread or Steamed Bread (see pages 372 and 370).

PORK KNUCKLES WITH GINGER AND SWEET RICE VINEGAR

After a baby is born to a Cantonese family, it is the custom that this dish be cooked for the confined mother to share with friends, family, and relatives during the first month. It is offered to all who visit the new mother and baby. The Chinese title translates as 'A Gift from the Stork.'

1½ kg (3 lb)	pork knuckles (trotters/shanks)
1 kg (2 lb)	fresh ginger
6	chicken eggs

Seasoning:

6 cups (1½ litres)	sweet rice vinegar
2 cups (16 fl oz)	Chinese brown vinegar
¼ cup	sugar
1 tablespoon	chicken stock powder (or 2 stock cubes)

Drop the knuckles into boiling water and simmer for 2 minutes. Remove and scrape off any hair, then cut into 5 cm (2 in) pieces. Return to the saucepan, cover with cold water and bring to the boil. Simmer for 35 minutes. Drain and rinse with cold water.

Peel the ginger and cut into pieces about 5 cm (2 in) long. Pour the vinegar into a large saucepan and bring to the boil. Add the remaining seasoning ingredients and mix well, then add the ginger and simmer for 25 minutes.

Add the knuckles and bring back to the boil, then reduce heat and simmer until the pork is completely tender.

Hard boil (hard cook) the eggs and cool under running cold water, then peel. Add to the dish. Remove from the heat and let stand for about 3 hours before reheating to serve.

Chicken can be used instead of pork to produce a dish which is said to be most beneficial to new mothers.

MONGOLIAN FIRE-POT

Serves 6 — 8.

250 g (8 oz)	beef fillet (tenderloin)
250 g (8 oz)	lean lamb or mutton
250 g (8 oz)	lean pork
250 g (8 oz)	venison steak (optional)
250 g (8 oz)	boneless duck or chicken breast
500 g (1 lb)	fresh young Chinese cabbage or bok choy
500 g (1 lb)	fresh spinach (collard green)
6 squares	soft beancurd
12	spring onions (scallions)
90 g (3 oz)	bean thread vermicelli, soaked
3 slices	fresh ginger, shredded

Sauce:

3 tablespoons	finely chopped spring onions (scallions)
2 tablespoons	finely chopped fresh ginger
1½ tablespoons	finely chopped garlic
2½ tablespoons	finely chopped fresh coriander
	light soy sauce
	rice wine or dry sherry
	sesame oil
	sesame paste
	sha chia jiang or hoisin sauce
	chilli sauce
	salt
	sugar
	m.s.g. (optional)

Special Equipment: A table-top charcoal 'fire-pot' or fondue pot, or a portable gas or electric ring and a saucepan, wooden chopsticks.

Partially freeze the beef, lamb or mutton, pork, venison, and duck or chicken, then cut into paper-thin slices and arrange individually on serving plates. Or prepare a plate with a selection of the meats for each diner.

Thoroughly wash the cabbage or bok choy and spinach, trim the stems and drain well, then arrange on serving plates. Soak the beancurd in cold water for 10 minutes. Drain and cut into cubes. Trim the spring onions and cut in halves. Drain the vermicelli. Place the beancurd, spring onions, and vermicelli on serving plates.

Place the sauce ingredients on the table to be mixed to individual taste. The sesame paste should be diluted with cold water until quite thin.

Heat the fire-pot and fill with boiling water. Add the sliced ginger and salt to taste. Use the wooden chopsticks to suspend slices of meat in the hot stock until cooked to individual taste, preferably rare. Dip into the sauce before eating.

When most of the meat has been cooked, add vegetables, beancurd, spring onions, and the vermicelli. Serve the remaining slivers of the meat in the rich stock with the other ingredients as a soup, adding sauce ingredients to taste.

Serve Sesame Pocket Bread (page 372) or deep-fried Steamed Bread (page 370) with the fire-pot.

'BUDDHA'S HAND'

(Pork-Filled Egg Pancake Rolls)

250 g (8 oz)	lean pork, finely minced (ground)
1 tablespoon	finely chopped spring onion (scallion)
1 teaspoon	grated fresh ginger
1	egg, well beaten
4 cups (1 litre)	deep-frying oil
	spiced salt or Chinese pepper-salt

Batter:

6	eggs, well beaten
2½ tablespoons	chicken stock
2¼ teaspoons	cornflour (cornstarch)
2 teaspoons	frying oil
	pinch of salt

Seasoning:

½ teaspoon	salt
¼ teaspoon	m.s.g. (optional)
¼ teaspoon	sugar
	pinch of white pepper
1 tablespoon	light soy sauce
2 teaspoons	rice wine or dry sherry
2 teaspoons	cold water
½ teaspoon	sesame oil (optional)
1 tablespoon	cornflour

Mix the pork with the spring onion, ginger, and seasoning ingredients and work to a smooth paste by throwing repeatedly against the inside of the mixing bowl. Refrigerate for 1 hour.

Make a smooth creamy mixture with the batter ingredients and beat for 2 minutes. Leave to sit for at least 15 minutes.

Heat a frying or omelette pan with a 30 cm (12 in) diameter. Rub with an oiled cloth. Pour in half the batter and tilt the pan so it forms into a thin pancake covering the complete base of the pan. Cook on moderate heat until bubbles appear on the surface and the underside is flecked with brown. Lift one corner then carefully turn. Cook the other side until firm and lightly coloured. Remove to a board to cool. Cook the remaining batter in the same way.

Divide the meat filling between the two pancakes spreading in a rectangular shape across the centre of each pancake leaving a border at the sides. Fold the sides over and brush with beaten egg. Fold over one flap and stick down with egg, then fold the remaining flap and stick onto the first fold with egg. Turn over.

Cut the two rolls in halves and cut five 'fingers' in each by slicing three-quarters of the way through the rolls four times, evenly spaced. Pull the rolls into crescent shapes so the 'fingers' fan out.

Heat the deep-frying oil to moderately hot and fry the 'Buddha's hands' until well coloured, turning once. Drain and serve on shredded lettuce with spiced salt and/or Chinese pepper-salt as dips (see recipes page 384).

MUTTON HOT-POT

1 kg (2 lb)	lean mutton (or kid), cubed
1	white turnip, peeled and cubed
90 g (3 oz)	canned water chestnuts, drained
5 cm (2 in) piece	fresh ginger, peeled and thickly sliced
1	leek, trimmed and cut into 2.5 cm (1 in) pieces
2 tablespoons	frying oil
6 cups (1½ litres)	chicken stock
1	fresh young lettuce
	fresh coriander or finely shredded lemon leaves
	fermented beancurd, mashed

Seasoning:

1 piece	dried orange peel, soaked and shredded
¼ teaspoon	salt
1 tablespoon	sugar
½ teaspoon	ground black pepper
2 tablespoons	soybean paste
3 cubes	fermented beancurd with the liquid, mashed
1 tablespoon	rice wine or dry sherry

Blanch the mutton or kid in boiling water for 2 minutes. Drain well. Heat the frying oil and stir-fry the turnip, water chestnuts, ginger, and leek for 2 minutes. Add the mutton and stir-fry until lightly coloured, then add the seasoning ingredients and cook with the meat and vegetables for 2 minutes, mixing well. Pour in the stock and bring to the boil.

Transfer to a casserole and simmer for 30 minutes. Pick out the turnip and discard. Cook for a further 30 minutes, then check the seasonings and serve in the casserole.

Serve the well-washed lettuce, leaves separated, on a plate to be added to the casserole at the table.

Serve fresh coriander or shredded lemon leaves and mashed fermented beancurd as accompaniments.

Sautéd Snake in Gravy (recipe page 336).

SAUTÉD SNAKE IN GRAVY

185 g (6 oz)	frozen cooked snake meat*
60 g (2 oz)	boneless chicken breast
60 g (2 oz)	prepared fish maw (see page 392)
60 g (2 oz)	canned bamboo shoots, drained
15 g (½ oz)	cooked ham
5 cm (2 in)	fresh ginger, peeled
6	dried black mushrooms, soaked for 25 minutes
1 piece	dried orange peel, soaked for 25 minutes
⅓ cup	frying oil
1 tablespoon	rice wine or dry sherry
6 cups (1½ litres)	chicken stock
1	spring onion (scallion), sliced
2 thick slices	fresh ginger
2	white chrysanthemums
2 — 3	lemon leaves
10 — 12 pieces	frozen wonton wrappers**
3 cups (24 fl oz)	deep-frying oil

Seasoning A:

¼ teaspoon	salt
¼ teaspoon	m.s.g. (optional)
½ teaspoon	cornflour (cornstarch)
	pinch of white pepper

Seasoning B:

1½ teaspoons	salt
¼ teaspoon	m.s.g. (optional)
	pinch of white pepper

Thaw the snake meat and shred finely. Shred the chicken and mix with the seasoning A ingredients, leaving for 10 minutes. Drain the prepared fish maw and cut into fine shreds. Shred the bamboo shoots, ham, and peeled ginger. Squeeze the water from the mushrooms, remove the stems and shred the caps finely. Drain and shred the orange peel.

Heat half of the frying oil in a wok and stir-fry the chicken until it turns white, then remove and drain. Add the remaining oil and fry the spring onion and ginger slices briefly, then add the wine and stock. Bring to the boil, then remove the onion and ginger and discard.

Add the shredded ingredients and the seasoning B ingredients and simmer for 2 — 3 minutes, then thicken with a paste of 1½ tablespoons cornflour and water. For a less distinct ginger flavour, blanch the shredded ginger in boiling water before adding to the dish.

Wash the chrysanthemums and remove the petals. Arrange on a serving plate with the very finely shredded lemon leaves. Cut the wonton wrappers into strips and deep-fry in the hot deep-frying oil until crisp. Serve the snake dish with the crisp pretzels, chrysanthemum, and lemon leaves to be added to individual taste.

* Available from specialist Chinese food stockists.

** The traditional accompanying pretzels for this dish are made of a dough comprising flour and mashed fermented beancurd. This is rolled out paper-thin and cut into small rectangular shapes before deep-frying.

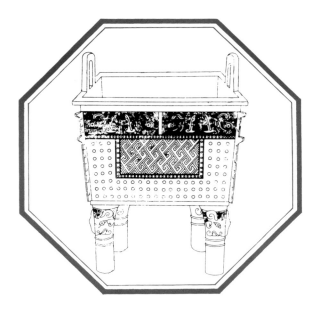

CRISP FRIED EGG ROLLS

These are traditionally served in Peking during the Lunar New Year festivities marking the beginning of the new year. As this also means the end of the winter months, they have come to be known as the popular 'Spring' Rolls.

Makes 12.

Batter:

4	large eggs, well beaten
1 tablespoon	flour
1 tablespoon	water
6 cups (1½ litres)	deep-frying oil
	Chinese pepper-salt

Filling:

250 g (8 oz)	lean pork, finely shredded
125 g (4 oz)	fresh bean sprouts
1	medium carrot, finely shredded
1 small stalk	fresh celery, finely shredded
12	garlic chives, sliced
2 tablespoons	softened lard or frying oil

Seasoning A:

½ teaspoon	salt
2 teaspoons	rice wine or dry sherry
1½ teaspoons	cornflour (cornstarch)

Seasoning B:

1½ teaspoons	salt
⅓ teaspoon	m.s.g. (optional)
1 tablespoon	sugar
¼ teaspoon	ground black pepper
1½ teaspoons	sesame oil

Sauce Dip:

2 tablespoons	tomato sauce
1 tablespoon	Worcestershire Sauce
2 tablespoons	light soy sauce
1 teaspoon	hot bean paste or chilli sauce
1½ teaspoons	finely chopped garlic
1 teaspoon	sugar

Mix the batter ingredients together thoroughly. Wipe out an omelette pan with an oiled cloth and heat to moderate. Pour in about 2 tablespoons of the batter. Lift the pan and swirl it slowly around so the mixture flows into a thin circle about 17.5 cm (7 in) in diameter. Cook until the sides lift from the pan, then carefully flip over and briefly cook the other side. The pancake should be firm, but not crisp. Remove to a piece of greaseproof paper. Cook the remaining pancakes, making 12. Stack between pieces of greaseproof paper. Leave to cool.

Mix the pork with the seasoning A ingredients and leave for 10 minutes. Blanch the bean sprouts, carrot, and celery separately. Drain well and set aside.

Heat the lard or frying oil to moderate and stir-fry the shredded pork until white and firm, about 1½ minutes. Add the seasoning B ingredients, the garlic chives, and blanched vegetables and stir-fry together for about 2 minutes. Remove and spread on a plate to cool.

Prepare Chinese pepper-salt, according to the directions on page 384, and pour into several small dishes to use as a dip, or prepare the sauce dip by mixing the ingredients together.

Place a portion of the filling in a sausage shape slightly off centre on each pancake. Fold over the closest edge, then fold in the two sides and roll up. Stick the flaps down with a paste made from flour and water.

Heat the deep-frying oil to moderately hot. Fry the rolls, several at a time, until golden and crisp. Remove and drain well. Arrange on a paper-lined serving plate, or on a bed of finely shredded lettuce and serve with the prepared dips.

NEW YEAR'S CAKE

Served as a snack during the Lunar New Year festivities. Its companion dish is the salty Turnip Cake on page 364.

5 cups	glutinous rice flour
1 2/3 cups	brown sugar
1 2/3 cups	boiling water

Special Equipment: A 20 cm (8 in) steaming basket lined with cellophane or greaseproof paper.

Sift the flour into a mixing bowl. Dissolve the sugar in the water and add to the flour, mixing in thoroughly. Pour into the prepared basket and cover.

Set on a rack in a steamer and steam over rapidly boiling water for about 2 hours. To test if the cake is cooked through, insert a chopstick into the centre. If it comes out dry, the cake is ready. Invert onto a plate and remove the paper. Refrigerate, well covered with plastic, for about 2 days before cutting into diamond-shaped pieces to serve.

Use brown sugar or a small amount of molasses to add colour.

LONG-LIFE BUNS

The peach is found in much traditional Chinese art and represents longevity. Here soft dough buns with mashed date filling are formed into peach shapes, tinted a delicate pink for serving at New Year and other auspicious occasions. They are also highly regarded as altar offerings.

Makes 24.

1 recipe	steamed bread dough (see page 370, Steamed Bread)
	rose pink food colouring

Filling:

700 g (1⅓ lb)	dates*
2½ tablespoons	sugar
2 tablespoons	softened lard

Prepare the dough and cover with a damp cloth. Put the dates into a saucepan with water to cover. Bring to the boil and simmer until softened, then transfer to a piece of clean cheesecloth and squeeze out as much water as possible.

Return to the saucepan and add the sugar and lard. Cook on low heat until the mixture is thick and fairly dry. Leave to cool, then form into 24 balls.

Roll the dough into a long sausage shape and cut into 24 pieces. Press each into a flat circle with the fingers and put a ball of filling on each. Pull the dough up around the filling to form a ball shape and pinch the edges together, pulling into a point. Press the back of a knife blade along the bun from base to point to create a peach shape and brush a touch of pink food colouring around the point.

For added authenticity, stamp out leaf shapes from left-over dough, brush with green food colouring and stick to the base of the peaches.

Stick a square of greaseproof paper under each bun and arrange the buns in two steaming baskets. Set on racks in a two-tiered steamer and steam over rapidly boiling water for 10 — 12 minutes. Lift the lid two or three times during cooking to prevent the buns bursting open. Keep the buns well separated in the basket as they expand during cooking. Serve hot.

* Or use sweet red bean paste (see page 389) or sweet lotus seed filling (page 368).

Crisp Fried Egg Rolls (recipe page 337).

SALTY 'JUNDZ'

Created for the Dragon Boat Festival, these bamboo leaf bundles of stuffed glutinous rice represent the rice grains thrown into the river to entice the fish away from the drowning heroine of the legend around which this festival has been created.

Makes 12.

3½ cups	raw long grain glutinous rice
2 tablespoons	dried shrimps, soaked for 1 hour
375 g (12 oz)	'five flowered' pork (belly/fresh bacon)
3 — 4	dried black mushrooms, soaked for 25 minutes
2	salted duck egg yolks (see recipe page 263)*
⅓ cup	frying oil
24	dried bamboo leaves, soaked

string

Seasoning A:

1 teaspoon	salt
½ teaspoon	m.s.g. (optional)
¼ teaspoon	sugar
¼ teaspoon	ground black pepper
1 teaspoon	rice wine or dry sherry
¼ cup (2 fl oz)	light soy sauce
2 tablespoons	finely chopped spring onion (scallion)

Seasoning B:

¾ teaspoon	salt
¾ teaspoon	m.s.g. (optional)
2 teaspoons	dark soy sauce

Soak the rice for 2 hours, then drain and change the water. Soak a further 30 minutes. Drain.

Drain the shrimps. Dice the pork. Drain the mushrooms, remove the stems and dice the caps. Chop the egg yolks and set aside.

Heat the oil in a wok and fry the shrimps, pork, and mushrooms for 1½ minutes. Add the seasoning A ingredients and heat through. Set aside.

Fry the rice, adding a little more oil if needed, for 2 minutes, then add the seasoning B ingredients and mix thoroughly.

Drain the bamboo leaves and wipe dry. Brush one side with frying oil. Place two leaves side by side and fold the two bottoms over together to form a triangular-shaped pouch. Add a portion of the rice, some chopped egg yolk, and the shrimp and pork mixture and top with more rice. Fold the leaves over the top and around the pouch to produce a plump triangular-shaped bundle. Wrap string securely around the bundle and set aside.

When all are done place side by side in a saucepan and cover with cold water. Bring to the boil, reduce heat and simmer for 1 hour. Drain well if the water has not been completely absorbed. Unwrap to serve.

* Omit or use hard-boiled (hard cooked) egg yolk.

MOON CAKES

Through the centuries, Chinese pastry cooks have vied for supremacy in the production of their special version of these sweet cakes. They are sold and consumed in untold numbers during the Moon Festival, and come with a variety of fillings from sweetened mashed lotus seeds, to sweet red bean paste, mashed salted egg yolks, nuts and sesame seeds, and come in pastry from sweet to salty. Bedecked with colourful food dye stamps, or artistic impressions made by special moon cake moulds, they are sold in gaily decorated presentation boxes and it would be unthinkable to arrive at a friend's house during this holiday without a gift box of the best moon cakes one could afford.

Makes 24.

As moon cake moulds are not readily available, this recipe for flaky pastry Moon Cakes with sweet red bean filling is more applicable here.

Pastry A:

2¼ cups	*flour*
⅓ cup	*softened lard or pastry shortening*
150 ml (5 fl oz)	*water*
2 teaspoons	*pinch of salt*

Pastry B:

1¼ cups	*flour*
⅓ cup	*softened lard or pastry shortening*

Filling:

2 cups	*sweet red bean paste (see recipe, page 389)* *red food colouring*

Sift the flour for pastry A into a mixing bowl and add the water and lard. Slowly work in, adding the sugar and salt. Knead until smooth.

Sift the flour for pastry B into another bowl and add the lard or shortening. Work in and knead until smooth. Roll the two portions of dough into sausage shapes and divide each into 24 parts.

Roll into balls and flatten each with the fingers, or gently with a rolling pin, making the pastry A circles larger than those of B. Place B pastry circles on top of the A circles. Fold four corners of the A over the B pastry to form a square and gently roll out into a rectangular shape. Fold the two ends in to the centre to form a square again, then lightly roll out into a circular shape, fairly thin.

When all the pastry cases are ready, divide the red bean paste into 24 portions and roll each into a ball, then flatten slightly. Place one piece in the centre of each circle of pastry and pull the edges together. Brush with a little water or beaten egg if the edges do not stick well.

Place on a greased and floured baking tray and brush on a design with the red food dye, using a small paint brush. Bake in a preheated moderate oven 200°C (375 — 400°F) for about 20 minutes. Remove and serve hot or cold.

CHAPTER VIII
Noodles and Rice-
Accompaniments

'GREAT GRAVY' NOODLES

500 g (1 lb)	fresh thick egg noodles, or about 250 g (8 oz) dried noodles
250 g (8 oz)	boneless chicken breast
6	large dried black mushrooms, soaked for 25 minutes
45 g (1½ oz)	dried 'wood ear' fungus, soaked for 25 minutes
45 g (1½ oz)	'golden needles' (dried lily flowers), soaked for 25 minutes
3	eggs, well beaten
1 teaspoon	cornflour (cornstarch)
¼ cup (2 fl oz)	frying oil
½ cup (4 fl oz)	sesame oil
1½ teaspoons	Chinese brown peppercorns

Seasoning A:

1 tablespoon	finely chopped spring onion (scallion)
1 teaspoon	grated fresh ginger
2 teaspoons	light soy sauce
1 teaspoon	sesame oil
1 teaspoon	cornflour (cornstarch)

Seasoning B/Sauce:

1¼ teaspoons	salt
1 tablespoon	dark soy sauce
7 cups (1¾ litres)	chicken stock
⅓ cup	cornflour (cornstarch)

Wash the fresh noodles or soak dried noodles in hot water to soften. Cut the chicken into fine shreds and place in a dish with the seasoning A ingredients, mix well and leave for 15 minutes.

Squeeze the water from the mushrooms, remove the stems and shred the caps. Drain the 'wood ears' and cut into small pieces. Drain the 'golden needles.' Mix the eggs and cornflour together and set aside.

Heat the frying oil and stir-fry the chicken briefly, then add the mushrooms, 'wood ears,' and 'golden needles' and stir-fry briefly. Add the pre-mixed seasoning B/sauce ingredients, except the cornflour, and bring to the boil. Simmer for 15 minutes.

In the meantime, drop the noodles into a large saucepan of boiling, salted water and simmer on moderate to low heat until the noodles are tender. Drain well and divide among large soup bowls.

Thicken the sauce with the cornflour mixed to a paste with an equal quantity of cold water and when boiling again, reduce the heat and slowly drizzle in the beaten egg. Leave to cook in the hot sauce, without stirring, for 45 seconds.

In another pan, heat the sesame oil to smoking point and add the peppercorns. Cook until the peppercorns turn black and the oil is very aromatic, then strain into the chicken sauce. Divide into the noodles and serve at once.

SHANGHAI NOODLES WITH BEAN SPROUTS AND BROWN SAUCE

500 g (1 lb)	fresh thick egg noodles (or use cooked spaghetti)
1½ teaspoons	salt
125 g (4 oz)	fresh bean sprouts
8	garlic chives
⅓ cup	frying oil
2 teaspoons	sesame oil

Seasoning/Sauce:

¾ cup (6 fl oz)	chicken stock
2 tablespoons	light soy sauce
1 tablespoon	dark soy or oyster sauce
1 teaspoon	rice wine or dry sherry
2 teaspoons	sesame oil (optional)
¼ teaspoon	crushed garlic
¾ teaspoon	salt
½ teaspoon	m.s.g. (optional)
¼ teaspoon	ground black pepper
1 teaspoon	cornflour (cornstarch)

Boil the fresh noodles in plenty of water with the salt added for 2 minutes. Drain cooked spaghetti, if used.

Remove the roots and pods of the bean sprouts. Shred the garlic chives.

Heat the frying oil in a large wok and add the bean sprouts and garlic chives. Stir-fry lightly, then add the seasoning/sauce ingredients and bring to the boil. Add the noodles and gently stir on moderate heat until the liquid is completely absorbed into the noodles. Serve hot.

RED-COOKED BEEF AND CARROTS ON NOODLES

625 g (1¼ lb)	rump steak or (top round) topside
2	spring onions (scallions), trimmed and sliced
3 thick slices	fresh ginger, shredded
1 teaspoon	chopped garlic
¼ cup (2 fl oz)	frying oil
8 cups (2 litres)	water
2	medium carrots, cubed
2 teaspoons	sesame oil (optional)
½ teaspoon	ground black pepper
2 tablespoons	finely chopped spring onion (scallion)
625 g (1¼ lb)	fresh thick egg noodles

Seasoning:

2 tablespoons	soybean paste
2 tablespoons	rice wine or dry sherry
½ cup (4 fl oz)	light soy sauce
2 teaspoons	dark soy sauce
1½ tablespoons	sugar
2	star anise

Cut the beef into bite-sized cubes. Blanch in boiling water and drain. Stir-fry the spring onions, ginger, and garlic in the frying oil for 1 minute. Push to one side of the pan and add the beef. Stir-fry until evenly coloured, then stir in the onions, ginger, and garlic and add the seasoning ingredients. Stir-fry together on moderate heat until well mixed, then add the water and bring to the boil.

Cover the pan, reduce the heat to low and simmer until the meat is tender, about 50 minutes. Add the cubed carrots and cook for a further 20 minutes. Stir in the sesame oil, if used, black pepper, and spring onion and keep warm.

Boil the noodles in plenty of lightly salted water until just tender. Drain and divide among 6 large soup bowls. Pour on the sauce and divide the meat and carrots evenly among the dishes. Serve at once.

FRIED EGG NOODLES WITH MEAT AND VEGETABLES

4 cakes (250 g/8 oz)	dried thin egg noodles
125 g (4 oz)	pork fillet (tenderloin)
125 g (4 oz)	boneless chicken breast
125 g (4 oz)	raw peeled shrimps
2	dried black mushrooms, soaked for 25 minutes
185 g (6 oz)	fresh bean sprouts
8	garlic chives
¾ cup (6 fl oz)	frying oil
2 tablespoons	light soy sauce

Seasoning A:

½ teaspoon	salt
½ teaspoon	sugar
1 teaspoon	rice wine or dry sherry
1 teaspoon	cornflour (cornstarch)

Seasoning B:

¼ teaspoon	salt
¼ teaspoon	m.s.g. (optional)
1½ teaspoons	ginger wine
1 teaspoon	cornflour (cornstarch)

Seasoning C/Sauce:

1¼ cups (10 fl oz)	chicken stock
1¼ teaspoons	salt
½ teaspoon	m.s.g. (optional)
¼ teaspoon	ground black pepper
1½ teaspoons	cornflour (cornstarch)

Soak the dried egg noodles in boiling water until softened enough to unravel, then drop into boiling water and cook for 1½ minutes. Drain well. Stir in 1 tablespoon of the frying oil and set aside.

Cut the pork and chicken into fine shreds and place in a dish with the seasoning A ingredients. Mix well and leave for 15 minutes. Devein the shrimps with a toothpick (see page 394) and rinse well. Mix with the seasoning B ingredients and leave for 10 minutes.

Squeeze the water from the mushrooms, remove the stems and shred the caps. Remove roots and pods from the bean sprouts and cut the garlic chives into 2 cm (¾ in) lengths.

Heat one-third of the oil in a wok and stir-fry the garlic chives for 30 seconds. Push to one side of the pan and add the pork and chicken. Stir-fry until white, about 1 minute, then move to the garlic chives and stir-fry the shrimp until pink and firm. Add the mushrooms and bean sprouts and stir-fry together until the sprouts soften, then sizzle the soy sauce onto the sides of the pan and stir in. Remove from the heat.

In another wok, heat the remaining frying oil to smoking point. Add the noodles and cook on one side, then lift the whole lot on a spatula and turn. Cook until the underside is lightly coloured and crisped on the edges.

Transfer to a serving plate. Return the other wok to the heat. Add the pre-mixed seasoning C/sauce ingredients and bring to the boil. Pour over the noodles and serve at once.

SHRIMPS AND SQUID WITH ASSORTED VEGETABLES ON SOFT EGG NOODLES

4 cakes (250 g / 8 oz)	dried thin egg noodles
250 g (8 oz)	raw peeled shrimps
185 g (6 oz)	cleaned fresh squid
1	small carrot, peeled and thinly sliced
30 g (1 oz)	canned bamboo shoots, drained and thinly sliced
3	canned champignons, drained and horizontally sliced
3	canned water chestnuts, drained and horizontally sliced
1/3 stick	fresh celery, diagonally sliced
2	spring onions (scallions), trimmed and sliced
3 slices	fresh ginger
1/2 teaspoon	crushed garlic (optional)
1/2 cup (4 fl oz)	frying oil
1 teaspoon	salt

Seasoning A:

1/2 teaspoon	salt
1/4 teaspoon	m.s.g. (optional)
1 1/2 teaspoons	ginger wine
1 teaspoon	cornflour (cornstarch)

Seasoning B/Sauce:

1 cup (8 fl oz)	chicken stock
2 tablespoons	light soy sauce
3/4 teaspoon	salt
1/2 teaspoon	sugar
1/4 teaspoon	ground black pepper
1 teaspoon	sesame oil (optional)
2 1/2 teaspoons	cornflour (cornstarch)

Soak the noodles in boiling water until softened enough to untangle. Devein the shrimps and rinse well. Place in a dish and add the seasoning A ingredients, mix well and leave for 10 minutes. Cut open the squid and score in a close criss-cross pattern on the inside, see page 397, then cut into 2.5 cm (1 in) squares. Blanch briefly in boiling water and drain well.

Blanch the carrot for 20 seconds and drain well. Stir-fry the vegetables in the frying oil, reserving 1 tablespoon, with the spring onions, ginger, and garlic until the vegetables have softened, about 2 minutes. Remove. Stir-fry the shrimps and squid until the shrimps are pink and firm and the squid white and curled up, about 1 minute. Return the vegetables and add the seasoning B/sauce ingredients and bring to the boil. Remove from the heat.

Bring a saucepan of water to the boil and reduce to a simmer. Add the noodles and salt and simmer until the noodles are tender. Drain well and stir in the remaining frying oil.

Reheat the seafood and vegetables, pour over the noodles and mix lightly, then transfer to a serving plate and serve at once.

'MIEN SIEN' NOODLES WITH ROAST PORK AND VEGETABLES

500 g (1 lb)	mien sien or thin egg noodles
500 g (1 lb)	roast pork (see page 291)
375 g (12 oz)	choy sum, or broccoli florets
6 cups (1 1/2 litres)	chicken stock
2 teaspoons	salt
1 tablespoon	rice wine or dry sherry
2 tablespoons	light soy sauce
2 thick slices	fresh ginger, finely shredded
2	spring onions (scallions), finely shredded

Bring a saucepan of water to the boil and add the noodles. Reduce to a simmer and cook until the noodles are softened, then drain well and divide among 6 — 8 large soup bowls.

Thinly slice the pork and cut into 5 cm (2 in) squares. Wash the vegetables, cutting the choy sum stems into 5 cm (2 in) pieces. Bring the chicken stock to the boil and add the salt and rice wine. Add the vegetables and simmer until tender, then add the soy sauce, the sliced pork, ginger and spring onions and simmer for 4 minutes. Remove the meat and vegetables and divide among the soup bowls, then pour on the soup. Serve hot.

Red-Cooked Beef and Carrots on Noodles (recipe page 345).

SEAFOOD NOODLE HOT-POT

500 g (1 lb)	flat noodles
6	large green prawns (shrimps) in the shell (about 375 g / 12 oz)
250 g (8 oz)	fresh squid
250 g (8 oz)	fresh sea scallops or fish fillets
250 g (8 oz)	fresh oysters without shells, or fresh clams
10 cups (2½ litres)	water
2 tablespoons	frying oil
3	garlic chives, sliced
3 slices	fresh ginger, shredded
375 g (12 oz)	Chinese (celery) cabbage or young bok choy

Seasoning:

¼ cup (2 fl oz)	light soy sauce
1 tablespoon	rice wine or dry sherry (optional)
2½ teaspoons	salt
1 teaspoon	m.s.g. (optional)
1½ teaspoons	sugar
½ teaspoon	ground black pepper
2 teaspoons	sesame oil

Soak the noodles until softened. Peel the central shell from the prawns, leaving the heads and tails joined to the bodies. Devein with a toothpick (see page 394) and rinse thoroughly. Skin and clean the squid, discarding the heads, tentacles, and fins. Cut the bodies open flat and score in a close criss-cross pattern on the inside, then cut into 4 cm (1 2/3 in) squares. Rinse well. Cut the scallops in halves diagonally or cut the fish into bite-sized pieces. Rinse the oysters or clams in cold water.

Bring the water to the boil and simmer the prawns until pink, then remove and set aside. Add the squid, scallops, and oysters and simmer very briefly. If using clams, simmer separately until the shells open, then drain and discard the top shells. Simmer fish, if used, until white and firm. Drain seafood well.

Add the garlic chives, ginger, and cabbage to the stock and simmer until the cabbage softens, then drain very thoroughly and transfer to a heated wok with the frying oil and stir-fry for 1 minute. Remove. Add the well-drained noodles and stir-fry briefly, then pour in the hot stock and simmer until the noodles are just tender.

Transfer to a casserole and add the seasoning and seafood. Bring to the boil and serve in the casserole.

HOT BEAN THREAD NOODLES WITH SHREDDED PORK

75 g (2½ oz)	bean thread vermicelli
75 g (2½ oz)	pork fillet (tenderloin)
1	large green capsicum (bell pepper)
1	medium onion
1 — 2	fresh red chilli peppers
30 g (1 oz)	dried 'wood ear' fungus, soaked for 25 minutes, or use 3 dried black mushrooms, soaked
2 slices	fresh ginger, shredded
1 teaspoon	finely chopped garlic
¼ cup (2 fl oz)	frying oil
	fresh coriander

Seasoning A:

¼ teaspoon	salt
¼ teaspoon	m.s.g. (optional)
1 teaspoon	rice wine or dry sherry
1 teaspoon	cornflour (cornstarch)

Seasoning B/Sauce:

1 cup (8 fl oz)	chicken stock
1 tablespoon	dark soy sauce
¾ teaspoon	white vinegar
1 teaspoon	sesame oil
½ teaspoon	salt
½ teaspoon	sugar
1 teaspoon	chilli oil (or to taste)

Soak the vermicelli in warm water until softened then cut into 5 cm (2 in) lengths. Finely shred the pork and place in a dish with the seasoning A ingredients, mix well and leave for 20 minutes.

Cut the pepper in halves, remove the seed core and stem and trim away the inner white ribs. Cut into narrow shreds. Peel the onion and cut into narrow wedges from stem to root, then trim away the root section to allow the pieces to separate. Cut the chillies into thin slices, discarding the seeds for a milder taste. Drain the 'wood ears' and chop finely.

Heat the frying oil in a wok and stir-fry the vegetables for 2 minutes. Push to one side of the pan and add the ginger and garlic. Stir-fry briefly, then add the shredded pork and stir-fry until white, about 45 seconds. Add the well-drained bean threads and stir-fry briefly.

Pour in the pre-mixed seasoning B/sauce ingredients and simmer until the liquid has been absorbed and the noodles are tender. Stir in plenty of chopped fresh coriander to taste, or use as a garnish. Serve.

RICE RIBBON NOODLES WITH BEEF AND BROCCOLI

500 g (1 lb)	fresh rice flour sheets*
250 g (8 oz)	beef steak (rump, fillet/tenderloin)
250 g (8 oz)	fresh broccoli, broken into small florets
2	spring onions (scallions), trimmed and sliced
⅓ cup	frying oil
1½ tablespoons	sweet bean paste or oyster sauce

Seasoning A:

½ teaspoon	salt
½ teaspoon	m.s.g. (optional)
1 teaspoon	light soy sauce
1 teaspoon	rice wine or dry sherry
1 tablespoon	frying oil
1 teaspoon	cornflour (cornstarch)

Seasoning B/Sauce:

1 cup (8 fl oz)	chicken stock
1½ tablespoons	sweet bean paste or oyster sauce
2 teaspoons	dark soy sauce
½ teaspoon	salt
½ teaspoon	m.s.g. (optional)
1 teaspoon	sugar (or to taste)
1 teaspoon	cornflour (cornstarch)

Cut the rice flour sheets into strips about 0.8 cm (⅓ in) wide. Drop into boiling salted water and cook for 1½ minutes. Drain well. Drizzle on 1 — 2 tablespoons frying oil and mix in lightly, then cover with cold water.

Very thinly slice the beef across the grain and cut into 4 cm (1 2/3 in) squares. Place in a dish and add the seasoning A ingredients. Leave for 20 minutes, turning once.

Blanch the broccoli and drain well. Stir-fry in the frying oil with the spring onions until beginning to soften, about 2 minutes. Push to one side of the pan and add the beef. Stir-fry on high heat until the meat changes colour. Add the bean paste or oyster sauce and stir until well mixed, then push to the side of the pan. Add the noodles, very well drained, and stir-fry until lightly crisped on the edges. Stir in the meat and vegetables and add the pre-mixed seasoning B/sauce ingredients. Bring to the boil and cook, stirring continually, until the noodles are evenly glazed with the sauce and the liquid almost absorbed. Transfer to a serving dish and serve at once.

* Sold fresh or frozen by specialist Chinese food stockists

COLD BEAN SHEET NOODLES WITH CHICKEN AND TWO SAUCES

5	bean sheets
250 g (8 oz)	boneless chicken breast
125 g (4 oz)	fresh bean sprouts
5	garlic chives, sliced
¾ stick	fresh celery

Sesame Sauce:

2 tablespoons	sesame paste
2 tablespoons	light soy sauce
1 teaspoon	sugar
1 teaspoon	sesame oil
½ teaspoon	m.s.g. (optional)
1 teaspoon	finely chopped spring onion (scallion)
1 teaspoon	grated fresh ginger
½ teaspoon	crushed garlic
2 tablespoons	cold water
1 teaspoon	lemon juice, or white vinegar to taste
2 tablespoons	frying oil

Hot Sauce:

1 tablespoon	chilli oil, or use commercial chilli sauce, or hot mustard thinned with a little sherry

Cut the bean sheets into narrow shreds and drop into a dish of boiling water. Leave for 1 minute, then drain well and arrange in a serving dish.

Poach or steam the chicken until just cooked, then tear into narrow slivers and set aside. Blanch the bean sprouts and garlic chives in boiling water until just softened. Place with the chicken.

Finely shred the celery and blanch for 1 minute in lightly salted boiling water. Place over the noodles and arrange the lightly tossed mixture of shredded chicken, bean sprouts, and garlic chives on top.

Mix the sesame sauce ingredients together and pour over the chicken. Serve the hot sauce separately to add at the table or to individual taste.

*Dried bean sheets should be soaked until soft before shredding.

Overleaf, left Lotus Rice (recipe page 357) and right, Shrimps and Squid with Assorted Vegetables on Soft Egg Noodles (recipe page 346)

RICE VERMICELLI IN SOUP WITH CRABMEAT AND EGG FLOWER

155 g (5 oz)	dried rice vermicelli
250 g (8 oz)	fresh crabmeat
3	egg whites, well beaten
90 g (3 oz)	fresh 'silver' sprouts, blanched
5 cups (1¼ litres)	chicken stock
1½ teaspoons	salt
¼ teaspoon	ground black pepper
⅓ teaspoon	m.s.g. (optional)
	light soy sauce
	sesame oil (optional)

Seasoning:

½ teaspoon	salt
½ teaspoon	m.s.g. (optional)
1 tablespoon	ginger wine (see page 387)

Soak the noodles in warm water until softened. Drain well and rinse in cold water. Place the crabmeat in a dish with seasoning A ingredients.

Bring the chicken stock to the boil and add the salt and pepper. Add the noodles and simmer until softened, approximately 3 minutes, but this depends on the brand of noodles used as they can vary considerably.

Add the crabmeat and simmer, gently stirring, until cooked through and beginning to flake. Slowly drizzle in the beaten egg whites and leave without stirring until the egg sets in white strands in the soup. Add the blanched 'silver' sprouts and the m.s.g., if used.

Season to taste with soy sauce and add a few drops of sesame oil, if used. Pour into a soup tureen and serve at once.

Rice vermicelli is often crisp fried to serve under a dressing of stir-fried meats, vegetables, and seafood. One of the most popular toppings with these deliciously light and crisp fried noodles is fried fresh milk with crabmeat (see page 78).

'SILVER PIN' NOODLES

315 g (10 oz)	'silver pin' noodles*
185 g (6 oz)	raw peeled shrimps
185 g (6 oz)	pork fillet (tenderloin)
185 g (6 oz)	'silver' sprouts
3	dried black mushrooms, soaked for 25 minutes
18	snow peas
1	egg, well beaten
⅓ cup	softened lard or frying oil

Seasoning:

½ teaspoon	salt
2 teaspoons	ginger wine (see page 387)
1 teaspoon	cornflour (cornstarch)

Seasoning B:

½ teaspoon	salt
½ teaspoon	light soy sauce
½ teaspoon	rice wine or dry sherry
½ teaspoon	cornflour (cornstarch)

Seasoning C/Sauce:

2 teaspoons	light soy sauce
2 teaspoons	rice wine or dry sherry
1 teaspoon	salt
1 teaspoon	sugar
¼ teaspoon	white pepper
¾ teaspoon	sesame oil

Prepare the noodles and cover with a damp cloth until needed. Devein the shrimps with a toothpick (see page 394), and wash well. Pat dry then mix with the seasoning A ingredients and leave for 10 minutes. Finely shred the pork and place in a dish with the seasoning B ingredients. Mix well and leave for 10 minutes.

Blanch the 'silver' sprouts for 5 seconds in boiling water and drain well. Squeeze the water from the mushrooms, remove the stems and shred the caps. String the peas and blanch for a few seconds in boiling water. Drain well.

Wipe out an omelette pan with an oiled cloth, heat to moderate and pour in the beaten egg. Tilt the pan so it sets in a thin covering over the entire bottom of the pan and cook on one side until firm, then turn and cook the other side. Remove, roll up and shred finely.

Heat the lard or frying oil to moderate and stir-fry the noodles for about 3 minutes. Remove. Add the pork with a little more oil if needed and stir-fry until it changes colour, then push to one side of the pan and add the shrimps. Stir-fry until pink, about 45 seconds. Remove and add the vegetables, stir-frying briefly.

Return the meat, shrimps, and noodles and add the seasoning C/sauce ingredients. Stir-fry for 1 minute, then stir in half the shredded egg. Transfer to a serving plate and garnish with the remaining egg. Serve.

* Made with leftover shrimp dumpling (har gow) dough (see page 360).

RICE SHEET ROLLS WITH SHREDDED MEAT AND VEGETABLE FILLING

Makes 18.

3	rice sheets
250 g (8 oz)	boneless chicken breast
75 g (2½ oz)	raw peeled shrimps
2	dried black mushrooms, soaked for 25 minutes
45 g (1½ oz)	canned bamboo shoots, drained
90 g (3 oz)	'silver' sprouts
12	garlic chives
5 slices	fresh ginger, finely shredded
2 tablespoons	frying oil
1 tablespoon	lightly toasted white sesame seeds

Seasoning A:

½ teaspoon	salt
2 teaspoons	rice wine or dry sherry
1 teaspoon	sugar
1 teaspoon	cornflour (cornstarch)

Seasoning B:

½ teaspoon	salt
1½ teaspoons	ginger wine (see page 387)
1 teaspoon	cornflour (cornstarch)

Seasoning C:

1 teaspoon	salt
½ teaspoon	m.s.g. (optional)
1 teaspoon	sugar
¼ teaspoon	ground black pepper
2 teaspoons	light soy sauce
2 teaspoons	rice wine or dry sherry
½ teaspoon	sesame oil
⅓ cup	chicken stock
1 tablespoon	cornflour (cornstarch)

Cover the rice sheets with a damp or oiled cloth until needed. Finely shred the chicken, mix with the seasoning A ingredients and leave for 10 minutes. Devein the shrimps with a toothpick (see page 394), rinse and wipe dry, then mix with the seasoning B ingredients and leave for 10 minutes.

Squeeze the water from the mushrooms, remove the stems and shred the caps. Shred the bamboo shoots. Blanch the sprouts in boiling water for 4 seconds, drain well. Cut the garlic chives in halves lengthwise, then cut into 4 cm (1 2/3 in) lengths.

Heat the frying oil in a wok and stir-fry the chicken and shrimps for 45 seconds. Push to one side of the pan and add the garlic chives. Stir-fry briefly, then add the vegetables and ginger. Stir-fry all the ingredients together, adding the pre-mixed seasoning C ingredients. Cook until the mixture is thick.

Spread the rice sheets on a board and cut each into 6 pieces. Place a line of the filling along the centre of each roll and roll up without tucking the ends in. Place the rolls with the fold underneath on an oiled plate. Set on a rack in a steamer and steam for 6 minutes over gently boiling water. Serve hot, garnished with the sesame seeds and with dips of light soy and chilli sauces.

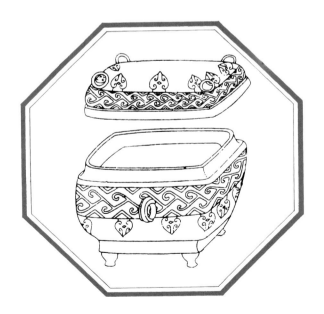

PLAIN WHITE RICE

The absorption method of cooking rice is the one most often used by Chinese, though the rice cooker which works on the same principle replaces a saucepan in most households.

It requires a fairly heavy-based saucepan with a very tight-fitting lid. The rice is placed in the saucepan dry, a specific amount of water added and the lid placed securely in position. When the water comes to the boil, the heat is turned down to the lowest point and the rice left to cook until the water is completely absorbed, leaving the rice dry, fluffy, and each grain separate, but sticky enough to cling together for easy eating with chopsticks.

Allow 90 g (3 oz / ½ cup) short grain rice per person and place in a saucepan. Add some salt, though most Chinese cooks prefer their rice unsalted, and water to cover the rice by 2 cm (¾ in). The rice should be smoothed flat in the saucepan to accurately gauge the water level. For more accurate measurement, use 2 cups rice and 3 cups water. (Two cups of raw short grain rice make 5 cups cooked rice.)

FRIED RICE

4 cups	cooked short grain white rice (see above)
60 g (2 oz)	raw peeled shrimps
½ teaspoon	salt
1½ teaspoons	cornflour (cornstarch)
1 teaspoon	ginger wine (see page 387)
2	eggs, well beaten
⅓ cup	softened lard or frying oil
60 g (2 oz)	roast pork or cooked ham, diced
60 g (2 oz)	cooked green peas
2 tablespoons	finely chopped spring onion (scallion)

Seasoning:

2 teaspoons	salt
½ teaspoon	sugar
¼ teaspoon	m.s.g. (optional)
1 tablespoon	light soy sauce
¾ teaspoon	dark soy sauce
¼ teaspoon	ground black pepper

There are several schools of thought about the method for producing perfect fried rice. One insists that the rice be at least one day old and refrigerated overnight so that each grain becomes slightly dry and all are separated. The other, that the rice should be freshly cooked and steaming hot.

Devein the shrimps with a toothpick (see page 394) and rub with the salt and cornflour, then rinse well. Wipe dry with kitchen paper, then rub with the ginger wine.

Heat a very little lard or oil in the wok and add the beaten eggs, tilting the pan so that the egg forms into a thin pancake over the entire bottom of the pan. Cook until lightly coloured and firm underneath, then turn and briefly cook the other side. Remove and leave to cool, then shred finely.

Reheat the wok and add the remaining oil. Stir-fry the shrimps, pork or ham, peas, and onion together for 2 minutes. Add the seasoning ingredients and fry briefly, then add the rice and stir-fry on moderate heat until each grain is coated with the seasonings, and the other ingredients evenly distributed.

Stir in half of the shredded egg and transfer to a serving plate. Garnish with the remaining egg and a few shreds of fresh red chilli pepper or sprigs of fresh coriander.

Hot Bean Thread Noodles with Shredded Pork (recipe page 348).

MULTI-COLOURED RICE

2 cups	raw short grain white rice
45 g (1½ oz)	dried shrimps, soaked for 1 hour
3	dried black mushrooms, soaked for 25 minutes
1	medium carrot
45 g (1½ oz)	canned bamboo shoots, drained
125 g (4 oz)	fresh or frozen peas
125 g (4 oz)	roast pork (see page 291), diced
3 tablespoons	finely chopped spring onion (scallion)
⅓ cup	frying oil
3 cups (24 fl oz)	water

Seasoning:

1½ teaspoons	light soy sauce
1¼ teaspoons	salt
1 teaspoon	m.s.g. (optional)
1 teaspoon	sugar
¼ teaspoon	ground black pepper
½ teaspoon	sesame oil

Thoroughly wash the rice and drain well. Drain the shrimps and cut the larger ones in halves. Squeeze the water from the mushrooms and dice the caps. Finely dice the carrot and bamboo shoots. Parboil the carrot and peas and drain well.

Heat the frying oil in a wok and stir-fry the diced pork and spring onion for 45 seconds. Add the shrimps, mushrooms, carrot, bamboo shoots, and peas and stir-fry for 2 minutes. Add the seasoning ingredients and the drained rice and water and mix thoroughly.

Bring to the boil, cover tightly and reduce the heat to very low. Cook until the rice is tender, about 15 minutes. Stir up lightly with a chopstick and serve.

CHICKEN AND RICE POT WITH CHINESE SAUSAGE

2 cups	raw short grain white rice
3 cups (24 fl oz)	chicken stock
185 g (6 oz)	boneless chicken
3	dried black mushrooms, soaked for 25 minutes
1	dried Chinese sausage, steamed for 10 minutes
2	spring onions (scallions), trimmed and sliced
2 slices	fresh ginger, shredded
1 tablespoon	frying oil

Seasoning:

1¼ teaspoons	salt
¼ teaspoon	m.s.g. (optional)
½ teaspoon	sugar
¼ teaspoon	white pepper
1 tablespoon	light soy sauce
1 teaspoon	sesame oil

Thoroughly wash the rice and pour into a saucepan with the chicken stock. Cut the chicken into bite-sized pieces and arrange over the rice. Bring to the boil, then reduce the heat to simmer until the rice is partially cooked and the water level has reduced to the top of the rice.

Squeeze the water from the mushrooms and remove the stems. Cut the caps into quarters. Cut the sausage into diagonal slices about 2 cm (¾ in) long. Stir-fry the mushrooms, sausage, spring onions, and ginger lightly in the oil, then place on top of the rice and add the pre-mixed seasoning ingredients.

Cover the pan and continue to cook on very low heat until the rice and chicken are both cooked. The rice should be dry and fluffy. Use chopsticks to stir the meat and seasonings evenly into the rice. Transfer to a deep covered dish and serve at once.

'LOTUS' RICE

1	fresh or dried lotus leaf
4 cups	cooked white rice (see page 354)
185 g (6 oz)	boneless chicken breast, diced
125 g (4 oz)	roast duck or pork, diced
125 g (4 oz)	raw peeled shrimps, or 2 tablespoons soaked dried shrimps
90 g (3 oz)	canned straw mushrooms or champignons, drained and diced, or used 4 dried black mushrooms, soaked and diced
2½ tablespoons	softened lard or frying oil
1½ tablespoons	finely chopped spring onion (scallion)
½ teaspoon	grated fresh ginger
1¾ teaspoons	salt
1 tablespoon	light soy sauce
2 teaspoons	sesame oil (optional)
¼ teaspoon	ground black pepper

Soak the dried lotus leaf or blanch the fresh leaf until softened, then squeeze out the water and brush the underside with oil. Cook the rice and set aside.

Stir-fry the chicken, duck or pork, shrimps, and mushrooms in the lard or oil for 2 minutes, then add the spring onion and ginger and cook briefly. Add the salt, soy sauce, sesame oil, if used, and the black pepper and mix in the rice. Stir thoroughly on moderate heat until evenly blended.

Place the lotus leaf in a wide bowl and pile the rice onto it. Fold in the sides to completely enclose the rice, then invert the parcel so the folds are underneath. Set the bowl on a rack in a steamer and steam over high heat for 15 — 20 minutes.

Serve hot with the top of the leaf parcel cut open to give access to the rice. If preferred, wrap the rice in smaller individual parcels.

This dish may also be made with steamed glutinous rice. It is a popular dish in dim sum restaurants and makes a delicious alternative to plain white rice at a dinner.

RICE CONGEE WITH SLICED FISH

3 cups	raw short grain white rice, soaked for 4 hours
8 cups (2 litres)	chicken stock or water
2 teaspoons	salt
½ teaspoon	m.s.g. (optional)
125 g (4 oz)	white fish fillets
2	spring onions (scallions), trimmed and thinly sliced
45 g (1½ oz)	Szechuan (Sichuan) preserved vegetables or salted mustard root, soaked for 25 minutes
	white pepper
	crisp-fried Chinese crullers (see page 374), or fried bread croutons
	fresh coriander or parsley

Drain the rice and transfer to a large saucepan. Add the chicken stock or water and the salt. Bring to the boil, then reduce to a simmer and cook until the rice is reduced to a starchy soup.

Stir in the m.s.g., if used. Very thinly slice the fish and place several pieces of fish and spring onion in each of 6 — 8 soup bowls. Drain the preserved vegetables or mustard root and shred finely. Stir into the rice and heat to boiling.

Pour over the fish and season with white pepper. Garnish with thinly sliced deep-fried crullers or bread croutons and sprigs of fresh coriander or parsley.

Reheating improves the flavour of congee. Serve as a breakfast or snack food with a variety of additives in place of the fish and pickled vegetables. Try thinly sliced liver, fish balls, roast pork, sliced chicken, pork fillet, or beef.

In Fukien (Fujian), thin rice congee is served in place of steamed white rice or noodles as the accompaniment to most meals.

CHAPTER IX
Dim Sum, Bread and Cold Platters~Appetisers

SHRIMP DUMPLINGS (HAR GOW)

Makes 24.

Pastry:

1 cup	gluten-free wheat flour (tang fun/cheng mien)
150 ml (5 fl oz)	boiling water
2 teaspoons	cornflour (cornstarch)
¾ teaspoon	softened lard

Filling:

155 g (5 oz)	raw peeled shrimps
45 g (1½ oz)	pork fat
45 g (1½ oz)	canned bamboo shoots

Seasoning:

2/3 teaspoon	salt
½ teaspoon	m.s.g. (optional)
½ teaspoon	sugar
1¼ teaspoons	cornflour (cornstarch)
	pinch of white pepper
¼ teaspoon	sesame oil

Special equipment: A special blunt cleaver for pastry making, or a large spatula.

Prepare the filling first. Finely chop the shrimps, pork fat, and bamboo shoots and mix thoroughly with the seasoning ingredients. Refrigerate for 1 hour.

Sift the gluten-free flour into a mixing bowl and add the cornflour. Bring the water to boil in a saucepan, covered so none is lost in evaporation as the amount of water is critical to success. Add the flour to the water and quickly stir in with the handle of a wooden spoon, then cover and leave for about 5 minutes so the heat softens the flour completely.

Remove from the saucepan, add the lard and knead until smooth and shiny. Roll into a long sausage shape and leave to cool a little, covered with a damp cloth. Divide into 24 equal parts.

On a clean, dry board place one piece of pastry. Flatten slightly with the fingers, then use the greased pastry cleaver to smear the pastry across the board in a circular motion resulting in a thin clear round wrapper. Carefully lift from the board on the spatula and place a spoonful of the filling in the centre. Fold over and pinch-pleat the edges together. (Place the filling on the side of the pastry that faced the board, as the upper side will be too greasy to allow the edges to stick together.)

An easier method is to pinch-pleat one side so the pastry is formed into a cup shape, add the filling, then press the smooth edge onto the pleated edge and pinch firmly together.

Steam the pastries in a lightly greased steaming basket for 4 — 5 minutes. Serve hot with dips of hot mustard and light soy sauce.

Use any leftover pastry to make 'Silver Pin' Noodles. Break off small pieces of the dough and place on an oiled board. Rub the palm of the hand back and forth across the dough until pieces about the same size as a bean sprout are obtained, about 5 cm (2 in) long.

Stir-fry in frying oil and use in the same way as egg noodles.

PORK DUMPLINGS (SIEW MAI)

Makes 18.

18	wonton wrappers (see recipe, page 376)*
125 g (4 oz)	lean pork
45 g (1½ oz)	pork fat
125 g (4 oz)	raw peeled shrimps
2	dried black mushrooms, soaked for 25 minutes

Seasoning:

1	small egg white, beaten
½ teaspoon	salt
½ teaspoon	m.s.g. (optional)
1 teaspoon	sugar
1 teaspoon	light soy sauce
½ teaspoon	dark soy sauce
¼ teaspoon	sesame oil
2 teaspoons	cornflour (cornstarch)

Finely dice the pork, pork fat, and shrimps and mix with the seasoning ingredients. Squeeze the water from the mushrooms, remove the stems and cut the caps into fine dice. Add to the pork mixture, mixing well.

Cut the freshly made or frozen wonton wrappers into 7.5 cm (3 in) circles. Hold the point of the thumb and forefinger of the left hand together and place a wonton wrapper over the circle it makes. Place a spoonful of the filling on the wrapper and push the whole thing through the circle made by the thumb and finger. This will result in the pastry forming into an open-topped cup shape around the filling. Flatten the bottom and stand in a lightly greased steaming basket.

When all are done, steam over rapidly boiling water for about 10 minutes. Serve hot in the steaming basket with dips of chilli sauce, hot mustard, and light soy sauce.

* Or use frozen wonton wrappers, thawed under a damp cloth.

PORK WONTONS

Makes 36.

36	fresh or frozen wonton wrappers (see recipe page 376)
250 g (8 oz)	pork fillet (tenderloin)
125 g (4 oz)	raw peeled shrimps
45 g (1½ oz)	pork fat
60 g (2 oz)	canned water chestnuts, drained
1	spring onion (scallion), finely chopped
1 tablespoon	finely chopped fresh coriander
6 cups (1½ litres)	deep-frying oil

Seasoning:

1½ teaspoons	salt
¼ teaspoon	white pepper
2 teaspoons	sugar
2 teaspoons	light soy sauce
2 teaspoons	cornflour (cornstarch)

Prepare the wonton wrappers and cover with a damp cloth until needed. If using frozen wrappers, remove from the freezer about 3 hours before using.

Mince (grind) the pork fillet, shrimps, and pork fat together and add finely diced water chestnuts, spring onion, fresh coriander, and the seasonings. Mix thoroughly and chill for 1 hour.

Place a spoonful of the mixture in each wonton wrapper. Pull the edges up around the filling forcing it into a ball shape just slightly off-centre. Brush the three corners closest to the filling with water and press them together. Fold over the filling and pinch onto the base of the final corner, completely sealing in the filling. Fold the final corner up and outwards in a petal shape. The resultant wonton is the classic goldfish shape.

A simpler shape is to gather the four corners together, then run the fingers from the tips down to the filling. Pinch together above the filling, then flare the corners outwards.

Heat the deep oil to moderately hot and add several wontons. Fry to a light golden brown, about 2 minutes. Drain. Repeat.

Serve with dips of light soy sauce, chilli sauce, or sweet and sour sauce (see recipe, page 385).

Use unfried wontons in soup and soup-noodle dishes. They may be frozen before cooking and require only a brief thawing before deep-frying or using in soup.

STEAMED CHICKEN TURNOVERS

Makes 24.

Pastry:

1 recipe	har gow pastry, see previous page

Filling:

90 g (3 oz)	boneless chicken breast
30 g (1 oz)	pork fat
75 g (2½ oz)	raw peeled shrimps
30 g (1 oz)	canned bamboo shoots, drained and finely diced
30 g (1 oz)	parboiled carrot, finely diced
1	dried black mushroom, soaked for 25 minutes
1½ teaspoons	finely chopped fresh coriander
1 clove	garlic
2 tablespoons	frying oil

Seasoning:

½ teaspoon	salt
½ teaspoon	m.s.g. (optional)
1 teaspoon	sugar
1 teaspoon	light soy sauce
¼ teaspoon	sesame oil
2 tablespoons	water
1 teaspoon	cornflour (cornstarch)
	pinch of white pepper

Special Equipment: A blunt bladed pastry cleaver or large spatula.

Finely dice the chicken, pork fat, and shrimps. Heat the frying oil and sauté the garlic for 30 seconds, then discard. Add the chicken, fat and shrimps and stir-fry for 30 seconds, then add the bamboo shoots and carrots and stir-fry briefly.

Squeeze the water from the mushroom, remove the stem and cut into small dice. Add the mushroom and coriander to the filling and add the seasoning ingredients. Stir-fry a further 45 seconds, then spread on a plate to cool.

Make the pastry and divide into 24 equal parts. Cover with a cloth while each piece is being prepared. Using the greased blunt pastry cleaver on a clean board, spread the pastry in a circular motion into a thin round shape and scrape up from the board. Place a portion of filling on the ungreasy side and fold over. Pinch the edges together.

Place the turnovers in a greased steaming basket and steam over rapidly boiling water for 3 minutes. They should not overlap in the steamer so it will be necessary to cook in two or three lots.

Serve hot with chilli or light soy sauce dips.

STEAMED ROAST PORK BUNS (CHA SIEW POW)

Makes 12.

Dough:

2¼ cups	flour
⅓ cup	sugar
1 tablespoon	baking powder
1 tablespoon	softened lard
⅓ cup	lukewarm water

Filling:

155 g (5 oz)	roast pork (see recipe page 291)
2	spring onions (scallions), trimmed and diced
1 tablespoon	frying oil
⅓ cup	water

Seasoning:

½ teaspoon	salt
2 teaspoons	light soy sauce
1 teaspoon	dark soy sauce
2 teaspoons	oyster sauce
1 tablespoon	sugar
1 tablespoon	cornflour (cornstarch)

Sift the flour into a mixing bowl and add the sugar, baking powder, and lard. Pour in the water and knead until smooth and soft. Cover with a damp cloth and leave for 30 minutes.

Sauté the spring onions and roast pork in the oil for 45 seconds. Add the water and seasoning ingredients and simmer until the sauce thickens. Spread onto a plate to cool.

Roll the dough into a long sausage shape and cut into 12 portions. Roll each into a ball and flatten with the fingers. Place a portion of the filling in the centre of each and ease the dough up around the filling, pinching firmly together underneath. Brush with a little water and stick a square of plain paper under each bun.

Set in a steaming basket and steam over rapidly boiling water for 10 minutes. Serve hot in the basket.

SPRING ROLLS

Makes 12.

12	fresh or frozen spring roll wrappers (see recipe page 374)
45 g (1½ oz)	boneless chicken breast, shredded
45 g (1½ oz)	raw peeled shrimps, halved lengthwise
30 g (1 oz)	pork fat, finely diced
1 10 cm (4 in) piece	fresh celery, shredded
30 g (1 oz)	fresh bean sprouts
2	dried black mushrooms, soaked for 25 minutes
30 g (1 oz)	canned bamboo shoots, drained and shredded
8 cups (2 litres)	deep-frying oil

Seasoning:

¾ teaspoon	salt
2 teaspoons	sugar
1 teaspoon	light soy sauce
¾ teaspoon	dark soy sauce
	pinch of ground black pepper
¼ teaspoon	chilli oil (optional)
¼ teaspoon	sesame oil
2 teaspoons	cornflour (cornstarch)

Prepare the spring roll wrappers and cover with a damp cloth until needed. Season the chicken, shrimps, and pork fat with a dash of ginger wine and soy sauce and leave for 10 minutes.

Heat 1 tablespoon of the oil in a wok and stir-fry the shredded celery and bean sprouts until softened, about 1½ minutes. Remove from the heat. Squeeze the water from the mushrooms and remove the stems. Shred the caps and stir-fry lightly, then mix the vegetables with the chicken, shrimps and pork fat and add the seasonings. Mix thoroughly.

The filling may be stir-fried with the seasoning at this point. The flavour is better if the filling is uncooked before deep-frying, but if the rolls are to be kept for some time the filling should be cooked first. If freezing or storing for more than a few hours, omit the bean sprouts and substitute shredded carrot, water chestnut, or additional bamboo shoots.

Place a portion of filling diagonally across the centre of each wrapper. Fold over the lower flap, then the two sides and roll up. Stick the final end down with a little water.

Deep-fry in moderate oil for about 8 minutes. If the filling has been cooked, deep-fry at a slightly higher temperature for about 2 minutes.

Serve hot on a bed of shredded lettuce with dips of light soy sauce and chilli sauce.

TARO PASTRIES

Makes 24.

Filling:

125 g (4 oz)	pork fillet (tenderloin)
60 g (2 oz)	raw peeled shrimps
3	dried black mushrooms, soaked for 25 minutes
1 teaspoon	rice wine or dry sherry
2 tablespoons	frying oil
6 cups (1½ litres)	deep-frying oil

Seasoning:

1 teaspoon	salt
½ teaspoon	m.s.g. (optional)
1 teaspoon	sugar
¼ teaspoon	ground black pepper
1 tablespoon	light soy sauce
1 teaspoon	sesame oil (optional)
1 tablespoon	cornflour (cornstarch)

Pastry:

500 g (1 lb)	peeled taro, yam, or sweet potato
⅓ cup	softened lard or ghee
½ teaspoon	salt
1¼ tablespoons	sugar
3 — 4 tablespoons	cornflour (cornstarch), or potato flour

Mince or finely chop the pork, shrimps, and mushroom caps. Stir-fry in 2 tablespoons of oil until the pork changes colour, then sizzle the wine onto the sides of the pan, stir in and add the seasoning ingredients, except the cornflour. Stir-fry briefly, then mix the cornflour with ¼ cup cold water and pour in. Simmer until the mixture is smooth and creamy. Spread on a plate to cool.

Boil the taro, yam, or sweet potato until soft, then drain very thoroughly. Mash to a smooth paste, adding the lard, salt, and sugar. Add the cornflour and knead until the mixture is completely smooth and pliable. Yam and sweet potato are more moist than taro and may require additional cornflour or potato flour to achieve the right consistency.

Divide the dough into 24 pieces and roll each into a ball. Flatten with the fingers into a circle about 7.5 cm (3 in) in diameter. Place a spoonful of the filling in the centre of each pastry and fold in halves. Pinch the edges firmly together, then carefully roll into a cigar shape.

Heat the deep-frying oil to moderate and fry the taro pastries, several at a time, until golden brown and crumbly on the surface, about 1 minute, then increase the heat for a further 30 seconds. Remove, drain well, and serve at once.

They can be reheated, if necessary, by frying in fairly hot oil for 45 seconds.

TURNIP CAKE

500 g (1 lb)	raw long grain white rice
825 g (1¾ lb)	sweet white turnips or giant white (icicle) radishes
2 teaspoons	salt
½ teaspoon	ground black pepper
45 g (1½ oz)	streaky bacon, diced
3	spring onions (scallions), trimmed and diced
2 tablespoons	dried shrimps, soaked for 1 hour
¼ cup (2 fl oz)	frying oil

Soak the rice overnight in plenty of cold water. Drain and transfer to a food processor or heavy-duty blender. Add a very little water and grind to a smooth paste.

Peel the turnips or radish and grate. Add to the rice paste with the salt and pepper. Heat the oil and sauté the bacon and spring onion briefly, then add the drained shrimps and sauté for 30 seconds. Stir into the rice and turnip paste and mix well.

Pour the mixture into a well-greased 25 cm (10 in) baking tin with the bottom lined with a piece of greased greaseproof paper. Smooth the top and set on a rack in a steamer. Steam, tightly covered, over gently boiling water for about 1 hour, or until the cake is firm. Test by inserting a chopstick. If it comes away clean the cake is done.

Leave to cool, then remove from the tin and cut into slices. Serve hot or cold. If preferred, the slices can be shallow-fried or cooked on a lightly oiled hotplate until crisp on the surface.

Serve with dips of chilli sauce and light soy sauce.

STEAMED BEANCURD SKIN ROLLS IN OYSTER SAUCE

Makes 12.

12 pieces	beancurd skin, each about 12 cm (5 in) square
90 g (3 oz)	lean pork, shredded
60 g (2 oz)	raw peeled shrimps
2	dried black mushrooms, soaked for 25 minutes
60 g (2 oz)	fresh bean sprouts
45 g (1½ oz)	canned bamboo shoots, drained and shredded
6 cups (1½ litres)	deep-frying oil

Seasoning A:

⅓ teaspoon	salt
¼ teaspoon	sugar
1 teaspoon	light soy sauce
1 teaspoon	vegetable or seame oil
2½ teaspoons	cornflour (cornstarch)

Seasoning B:

¼ teaspoon	salt
¼ teaspoon	m.s.g. (optional)
1 teaspoon	rice wine or dry sherry
1¼ teaspoons	cornflour (cornstarch)

Sauce:

¾ cup (6 fl oz)	water
1 teaspoon	light soy sauce
½ teaspoon	dark soy sauce
2½ teaspoons	oyster sauce
½ teaspoon	salt
½ teaspoon	m.s.g. (optional)
1 teaspoon	sugar
¼ teaspoon	ground black pepper
1½ — 2 teaspoons	cornflour (cornstarch)

Wipe the beancurd skins with a damp cloth, cover and leave until needed. Place the shredded pork in a dish and add the seasoning A ingredients, mix in and leave for 15 minutes. Place the shrimps in another dish and add the seasoning B ingredients, mix in and leave for 10 minutes.

Mix the pork, shrimps, mushrooms, and bamboo shoots together. Heat 1 tablespoon of the frying oil and stir-fry the bean sprouts for 1 minute, then add the mixed meat and vegetables. Stir-fry briefly, then remove to a plate to cool.

Divide the mixture between the wrappers and brush all around the edge with a mixture of plain flour and water. Fold one corner over the filling, then fold in two sides and roll up. Stick down the final flap with more flour and water paste if needed.

Heat the deep-frying oil to smoking point and deep-fry the rolls for 2 — 3 minutes. Drain well. Prepare to this stage in advance and keep in the refrigerator.

Pour the pre-mixed sauce ingredients into a wok and bring to the boil. Simmer for 2 minutes. Place the rolls in a dish, pour on the sauce and set on a rack in a steamer. Steam over rapidly boiling water for about 25 minutes.

Serve in the dish.

MARBLED TEA EGGS

12	chicken eggs
1¾ tablespoons	salt
½ cup	black tea leaves
3	star anise
2 sticks	cinnamon bark
8 cups (2 litres)	water

Place the eggs in a saucepan of cold water and bring slowly to the boil. Simmer for 10 minutes, then drain. Gently tap the eggs together until each shell is thoroughly crazed with small cracks. Place in a saucepan with the remaining ingredients and bring to the boil. Simmer on very low heat for 1 hour. Remove and cool under running cold water. Peel and cut in halves. Arrange on a serving platter with slices of fresh young ginger lightly pickled in sweetened white vinegar.

The eggs can be kept for 2 — 3 days in the refrigerator.

STEAMED BEEF MEATBALLS ON WATERCRESS

250 g (8 oz)	lean beef
¾ teaspoon	bicarbonate of soda (optional)
30 g (1 oz)	pork fat
2 teaspoons	finely chopped fresh coriander*
250 g (8 oz)	fresh watercress leaves

Seasoning:

½ teaspoon	salt
½ teaspoon	m.s.g. (optional)
2 teaspoons	sugar
¼ teaspoon	ground black pepper
1 tablespoon	light soy sauce
½ teaspoon	sesame oil (optional)
¼ cup (2 fl oz)	vegetable oil
¼ cup (2 fl oz)	water
2 tablespoons	cornflour (cornstarch)

Pulverise the beef in a food processor or mince (grind) very finely. Add the bicarbonate of soda, if used, and ¼ cup of cold water and mix in thoroughly. Cover with plastic wrap and refrigerate for 4 hours.

Place the pork fat in a saucepan or wok and add ½ cup of water. Simmer, covered, until the fat is transparent, then remove and cut into very small dice. Mix with the beef, adding the coriander and seasonings. Work until thoroughly blended and smooth. Gather the meat into the hand and throw repeatedly against the side of the mixing bowl. Or place in the food processor and mix with the dough blending blade for 1 minute. Return to the refrigerator for at least 1 hour.

Place the watercress in a dish. Form the meat into 12 balls and place on the watercress. Set the dish on a rack in a steamer and steam over rapidly boiling water for about 8 minutes. Serve hot.
* Or use a small piece of dried orange peel, soaked to soften and finely chopped.

CLEAR-AS-GLASS COOKIES

Makes 12.

125 g (4 oz)	gluten-free flour (tang fun/cheng mien)
1 cup (8 fl oz)	boiling water
¼ cup	sugar
1 teaspoon	cornflour (cornstarch)
½ teaspoon	lard
90 g (3 oz)	sweet red bean paste*

Special Equipment: A wooden mould with engraved decoration. The number of cakes will depend on the size of the mould.

Boil the water and sugar together in a saucepan, simmering until the sugar is dissolved. Pour in the flour and add the cornflour. Stir quickly with the handle of a wooden spoon, then cover and leave for about 5 minutes.

Remove to a board, add the lard and knead until smooth and shiny. Roll into a sausage shape and divide into 12 pieces. If the mould is about 5 cm (2 in) in diameter it will make about 12. Adjust accordingly.

Flatten each portion. Form the filling into balls and place one on each piece of pastry. Fold in the edges and pinch together, sealing closely. Dust the mould with the same flour or a little cornflour or glutinous rice flour. Do not use plain wheat flour as it will show in white spots on the cooked cakes.

Place the cookies one by one in the mould with the joined part upmost. Press gently and flatten with the palm of the hand. Slap the mould sharply on the edge of the table to release the cookie. Place, decorated surface upwards, in a greased steaming basket and steam over rapidly boiling water for about 5 minutes. Glaze by brushing lightly with vegetable oil. Serve hot or cold.
* Or use sweet lotus seed paste, see recipe following (steamed buns with lotus seed filling), or a mixture of crunchy peanut paste and sugar.

Walnut Crisps (recipe page 368) and above *Steamed Sponge Cake (recipe page 369).*

WALNUT CRISPS

Makes 12.

1 cup	*flour*
¼ cup	*castor sugar*
¼ cup (2 fl oz)	*melted lard*
	pinch of bicarbonate of soda
	(optional)
¼ teaspoon	*baking powder*
½	*egg, beaten*
12	*blanched walnuts*

Sift the flour into a mixing bowl. Add the sugar, three-quarters of the melted lard, the bicarbonate of soda, if used, and the baking powder. Add the beaten egg and work slowly into a firm, fairly dry dough. Add the remaining lard if the dough is crumbly.

Divide into 12 portions, roll each into a ball and press flat with the fingers. Place on a greased baking tray and press one walnut in the centre of each biscuit. Brush with the beaten egg to glaze.

Bake on the centre rack in a moderately hot oven (220°C/425°F) for 20 — 25 minutes. Cool on a cake rack before serving.

STEAMED BUNS WITH LOTUS SEED FILLING

1½ cups	*flour*
2 teaspoons	*baking powder*
	pinch of salt
¼ cup	*sugar*
1 tablespoon	*melted lard*
¼ cup (2 fl oz)	*warm water*
90 g (3 oz)	*lotus seed paste**
1 — 2	*salted egg yolks (see recipe, page 363)*

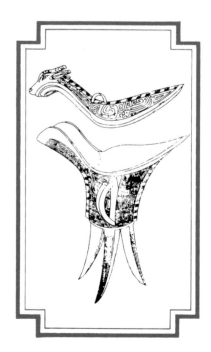

Sift the flour and baking powder into a mixing bowl and add the salt and sugar. Stir in the lard and water slowly and mix with a knife to a smooth soft dough. Cover with a damp cloth and leave for at least 30 minutes. Remove to a lightly floured board and knead lightly.

Divide into 6 pieces and press into rounds with the fingers. Divide the lotus seed paste into 6 pieces also and roll into small balls. Push a finger into each ball and insert a piece of egg yolk, then re-form the ball around it.

Place a ball of lotus paste in the centre of each piece of dough and pull the dough up around it, pinching the edges together. Brush the joined part with water and stick a piece of plain paper over it.

Place the buns in a steaming basket and steam over rapidly boiling water for 12 — 15 minutes. Lift the lid several times during cooking to prevent the buns from bursting open.
* Soak 125 g (4 oz) dried lotus seeds in cold water for 2 — 3 hours, then drain and rinse well. Place in a saucepan with 1 cup of sugar and add plenty of water. Bring to the boil and simmer until the lotus seeds are completely tender and the liquid absorbed or evaporated, then mash to a smooth paste with a fork, working in a little vegetable oil to give a smooth shiny texture. Store leftover paste in the refrigerator. It will keep for several weeks.

Substitute ingredients include sweet red bean paste (see page 389), or a mixture of even quantities of sesame or peanut paste and sugar.

STEAMED SPONGE CAKE

1¼ cups	flour
60 g (2 oz)	butter
½ cup	sugar
2	eggs
2 tablespoons	cream
¼ cup (2 fl oz)	melted lard
½ teaspoon	bicarbonate of soda
¼ teaspoon	molasses (optional)

Special Equipment: One 18 cm (7 in) cake tin thoroughly perforated with holes and lined with perforated greased paper.

Sift the flour into a mixing bowl. Cream the butter and sugar together and add the eggs and cream. Work into the flour, then add the lard and soda mixed with a little cold water. Stir in the molasses, if used, to add colour. Mix well, then leave for about 30 minutes. The batter should be of dropping consistency, soft and moist.

Line the base of the tin, then thickly grease the sides. Pour the batter into the tin and set on a rack in a steamer. Steam over rapidly boiling water for about 35 minutes until well expanded, firm and dry. Test by inserting a chopstick in the centre, it should come out clean and dry.

Turn out onto a wire rack and remove the paper. Cut into large pieces and serve hot. This is particularly excellent served with a dressing of hot clear honey.

'LAUGHING MOUTHS'

Makes 12.

1 cup	flour
1¼ teaspoons	baking powder
2 tablespoons	castor sugar
¼ cup (2 fl oz)	water
1 teaspoon	softened lard
2 tablespoons	white sesame seeds
5 cups (1¼ litres)	deep-frying oil

Sift the flour and baking powder into a mixing bowl and add the sugar and lard. Work in lightly, then gradually add the water to make a soft dough. Knead gently until smooth.

Roll the dough into a sausage shape and divide into 12 pieces. Roll each into a ball. Brush each ball with water and coat with the sesame seeds. Roll between the hands to press the seeds firmly into place.

Heat the deep-frying oil to moderate and fry the balls, several at a time, until golden and well expanded, about 8 minutes. If the balls do not rise to the surface within the first 3 — 4 seconds of cooking, the oil is not hot enough.

For extra tasty 'laughing mouths,' roll the dough around a small ball of sweet lotus seed or red bean paste and proceed as above. Serve hot or cold.

SWEET WALNUTS

125 g (4 oz)	walnuts
1 cup (8 fl oz)	water
¼ cup (2 fl oz)	sugar
¼ cup (2 fl oz)	clear honey
5 cups (1¼ litres)	deep-frying oil

Bring the walnuts to the boil with water to cover and cook for 1 minute, then drain and peel off the brown skin. Return to the saucepan with the remaining ingredients except oil and bring to the boil again. Simmer on reduced heat for 10 minutes. Drain and leave to cool and dry.

Heat the deep-frying oil to moderate. Fry the nuts in a basket until well coloured, about 8 minutes. Remove and drain well. Leave to cool, then serve.

STEAMED BREAD

Makes 6 loaves.

3 cups	flour
1½ tablespoons	sugar
1 3/8 cups	warm water
2 teaspoons	dry yeast (granulated)
1 tablespoon	softened lard or pastry shortening

Sift the flour into a mixing bowl. Dissolve the sugar in the water, then add the yeast and stir until dissolved. Leave for about 10 minutes until the yeast begins to activate and form a foam on the water, then add the softened lard or shortening to the flour and slowly work in the yeast mixture. Knead into a soft ball and remove to a floured board. Knead gently until smooth and elastic. Place in a bowl and cover with a damp cloth. Leave to rise for at least 3 hours in a warm place. It should more than double in bulk.

Use to form any of the following bread shapes and steam until cooked through and dry to the touch, about 18 minutes for loaves, 12 minutes for individual buns.

Steamed Bread Loaves. Divide the dough into 6 equal parts and form into oval shaped loaves. Pull the sides and ends under the roll so that the top is smooth and rounded. Stick a piece of plain paper underneath and steam for 15 — 18 minutes until dry and springy to the touch. Lift the lid of the steamer once or twice during cooking to allow excess steam to escape. This prevents the tops of the loaves from bursting open.

Serve the rolls straight from the steamer, or deep-fry until the surface is golden brown and serve hot.

Yin-sz-juan (Silver Thread Loaves). Divide the dough into two parts and roll one half out flat, then cut into 5 or 6 pieces. Roll the other half out flat and brush generously with a mixture of vegetable and sesame oil. Fold into a long rectangle, brushing each fold with more oil. Cut across the rectangle, cutting the dough into narrow shreds. Divide the shreds into equal portions to fit the squares. Hold each bundle of strips firmly at each end and gently pull until about 10 cm (4 in) long. Place on a square and fold in the two sides, then tuck the ends underneath, making a rectangular-shaped loaf. Press a piece of plain paper under each roll and place them all in a steaming basket. Steam over high heat for at least 15 minutes, lifting the lid of the steamer once or twice during cooking to allow excess steam to escape.

Lwo-sz-juan (Snail Breads). Shred the whole of the dough as explained above, brushing generously with vegetable and sesame oil. Divide into 24 groups, and stretch fairly long. Wrap each group separately around a finger to produce little curled bundles. Steam for about 12 minutes.

These breads can also be made with the simpler baking powder activated dough of the following recipe.

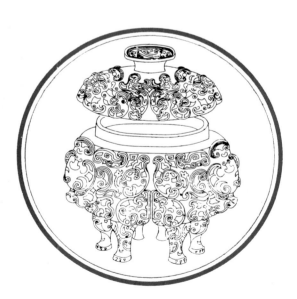

370

Clear-As-Glass Cookies (recipe page 366) and above Steamed Buns with Lotus Seed Filling (recipe page 368).

STEAMED FLOWER-SHAPED BUNS

Makes 24.

3 cups	*flour*
1 tablespoon	*baking powder*
1½ tablespoons	*sugar*
1 tablespoon	*softened lard or pastry shortening*
7/8 cup (7 fl oz)	*lukewarm water*

Sift the flour and baking powder into a mixing bowl. Add the softened lard or shortening and sugar, then mix in the water. Form into a ball and remove to a lightly floured board. Knead gently until smooth and elastic. Wrap in a warm cloth and leave for 20 minutes.

Roll out into a long sausage shape and divide into 24 pieces. Flatten each with the fingers and fold in the centre, pressing lightly on the fold. Decorate with a series of indentations along the edges, made with the back of a kitchen knife.

Place on perforated greaseproof paper in a steamer, arrange the bread on top and steam over rapidly boiling water for about 12 minutes. Serve with any crisp-fried dish, particularly whole chickens or ducks.

If preparing as an accompaniment to Honey-glazed Ham. (see page 210), make twice the size so that the sliced meat can be inserted into the bun, hamburger fashion.

Steamed Flower Shaped Buns can also be made with the yeast-activated dough of the previous recipe for Steamed Bread.

SESAME POCKET BREAD

Makes 18.

½ cup	*oil*
7 cups	*flour*
1½ cups	*boiling water*
½ cup	*cold water*
1 tablespoon	*salt*
¼ cup	*white sesame seeds*
5 cups (1¼ litres)	*deep-frying oil*

Heat the oil in a frying pan and add about 1 cup of the flour. Cook on low heat until the mixture is smooth and golden, stirring constantly. The mixture will appear too dry at first, but gradually the oil will soften the flour to produce a smooth oily paste. Remove from the heat and leave to cool.

Sift the remaining flour, reserving about 1½ tablespoons, into a mixing bowl. Pour the boiling water in and quickly work into the flour using the handle of a wooden spoon to stir. Add the cold water and work a little more, then transfer to a lightly oiled board and knead until smooth and elastic, about 7 minutes. Roll the dough into a long sausage shape and divide into 18 pieces. Cover with a damp cloth while preparing the bread to prevent drying out.

Roll each piece out separately into a square shape roughly 15 × 15 cm (6 × 6 in). Spread on a coating of the flour and oil paste, season generously with salt and sprinkle lightly with the reserved flour. Fold in two sides to just overlap in the centre, pinch the two ends so the filling is contained, then fold these in to just overlap in the centre. Use a rolling pin to gently roll in the direction of the folds into a rectangular shape. Dip the smooth side into sesame seeds, pressing on lightly. If necessary, brush the top with a little water so the seeds will stick.

Place on an oiled and floured baking tray and bake in a preheated hot oven 200°C (400°F) for 5 minutes on each side. The breads will puff up during cooking and when removed from the oven they may flatten again.

Cut the breads in halves. Serve hot as an edible pouch for shredded meat dishes (see page 67 Shredded Pork in Sesame Pouches).

The rolls may be frozen, uncooked, and baked after a brief thawing period.

'MANDARIN' PANCAKES

Makes 18.

1½ cups	flour
½ cup	boiling water
	sesame oil

Sift the flour into a mixing bowl and pour in the water. Work with the handle of a wooden spoon until the dough is completely amalgamated. When cool enough to handle, knead briskly for 10 minutes. Cover with a damp cloth and leave in a warm place for 15 minutes.

Roll the dough into a long sausage shape and divide into 18 pieces. Cover roll with a damp cloth while working each piece. Press two pieces into small round cakes and brush one side of each with sesame oil. Press the two oiled surfaces together, then roll out together until paper-thin.

When all are rolled out, heat a heavy frying pan or hot plate and rub with an oiled cloth, cook the pancakes on moderate heat until brown flecks appear on the underside. Turn and cook the other side, then peel apart and fold the two pancakes into triangular shapes. Wrap in a cloth until ready to serve.

The pancakes can be stored in plastic bags in the refrigerator or freezer until needed. To reheat spread on a plate and set on a rack in a steamer. Steam for 6 — 8 minutes. Serve at once.

SPRING ONION PASTRIES

Makes 6.

3½ cups	flour
1 cup	boiling water
2 — 3 tablespoons	cold water
1 tablespoon	vegetable oil
1 tablespoon	sesame oil
6	spring onions (scallions), trimmed and finely chopped
1 tablespoon	salt
1½ cups (12 fl oz)	frying oil

Sift the flour into a mixing bowl. Pour the boiling water into the centre and quickly mix in, using the handle of a wooden spoon. Add the cold water to produce a fairly hard dough. Begin by adding only 2 tablespoons of the cold water. Leave for 10 minutes, then remove to a floured board and knead until smooth and easy to work. Add extra cold water at this point if needed.

Roll out to about 1 cm (1/5 in) thickness and cut into 6 rectangles or divide into 6 pieces and roll out individually. Brush the top of each piece with a mixture of vegetable and sesame oil, scatter on the spring onions and add a generous amount of salt.

Fold over one of the longer edges and roll the dough up into a long roll, then twist the roll into a spiral and place on the board so the spiral faces upwards. Flatten gently with a rolling pin into a round pastry about 7.5 cm (3 in) in diameter.

Heat the frying oil in a wok or frying pan and fry the pastries slowly, two or three at a time with the pan covered. Turn once and shake the pan frequently to encourage the pastries to puff out a little. Cooking time is about 5 minutes.

Remove from the oil, drain and wrap in a cloth or foil until ready to serve. Cut into quarters and serve on a warmed plate.

Serve as a snack or an accompaniment to Northern dishes.

CRISP-FRIED CHINESE CRULLERS

Makes 24.

4 cups	flour
1½ teaspoons	salt
30 g (1 oz)	fresh yeast
2 teaspoons	sugar
1¼ cups	lukewarm water
6 cups (1½ litres)	deep-frying oil

Sift the flour and salt into a mixing bowl. Mix the yeast with the sugar and 1 — 2 tablespoons of the water. Leave for 2 minutes, then make a well in the centre of the flour, pour in the yeast and carefully work into the flour, adding the remaining water slowly.

When all the liquid has been added, gather the dough into one ball and knead gently for 2 minutes. Cover with a damp cloth and leave in a warm place to rise for 2 hours. Turn onto a lightly floured board and knead gently for 5 — 6 minutes.

Pull out into a long strip about 10 cm (4 in) wide. Cut across the strip into 24 pieces, then roll and stretch each piece into a long strip.

Heat the deep-frying oil to smoking point, then reduce the heat to moderate. Deep-fry several at a time until crisp and puffy, about 3 minutes. Serve hot.

These Crullers are usually served as an accompaniment to breakfast or snack dishes such as Rice Congee (see page 357). In the North they are stuffed into Sesame Pocket Bread to form a substantial snack. Sliced Crullers lend an interesting taste and texture to stir-fried dishes.

SPRING ROLL WRAPPERS

Makes 24.

4 cups	flour
1 teaspoon	salt
2 cups	water

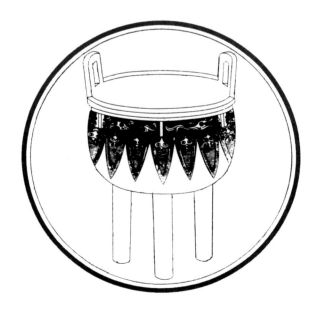

Special Equipment: A heavy flat iron griddle or frying pan.

Sift the flour and salt into a mixing bowl and gradually add the water, mixing thoroughly. Work through the fingers for about 5 minutes until the mixture is smooth and elastic. Cover with a thin layer of water to keep from drying out and leave for 1 hour to allow the gluten in the flour to soften. Work again with the fingers after pouring off the water. The dough should be very soft and sticky.

Heat the griddle and wipe over with a damp cloth, then rub vigorously with an oiled cloth. The surface should be smooth but not oily. Heat to moderate.

To make the spring roll wrappers, take a large handful of the dough and wipe it in a circular motion around the pan so that a thin layer of the dough adheres to the pan. When the edges begin to curl up, remove to a cooling rack. Wipe the pan again with the cloth.

Continue until the wrappers are all made. They should be dry, but not so crisp that they will crack. If necessary, cook very briefly on the other side before removing from the heat. Use for Spring Rolls, page 362, with a variety of meat or vegetable fillings.

Spring roll wrappers can be kept in the refrigerator for several days, sealed in a plastic bag, and they freeze well. Thaw slowly before use and separate carefully. Discard those that are torn or cracked.

Keep under a cloth until ready to use as they dry out and crack on exposure to the air.

'Exotic Tasting' Chicken (recipe page 376).

WONTON WRAPPERS

The first recipe gives professional results if the ingredients are obtainable, otherwise use the following recipe using plain flour.

Recipe 1:
Makes 30.

125 g (4 oz)	high gluten flour (gun mien fun)
¼ cup (2 fl oz)	mixture of beaten egg and water

Recipe 2:
Makes 24.

1½ cups	flour
⅓ cup	water
½ teaspoon	lard

Sift the flour into a basin and add the egg and water mixture. Knead firmly until smooth, then leave covered with plastic wrap for 4 hours. The gluten will soften in this time, giving the dough a softer more elastic quality.

To roll out, dust a large surface with cornflour (cornstarch) or glutinous rice flour. Do not use flour as this will mix in with the dough, making it too dry. Use a very large rolling pin and roll into a fairly large square, then dust with cornflour or glutinous rice flour and fold two or three times then roll thinner. Unfold and add more glutinous rice flour or cornflour and refold. Continue to fold and roll, dusting with more cornflour each time until the dough is completely thin. It should be almost transparent. Cut into squares or rounds for use.

To store in the refrigerator or freezer, ensure that each piece is thoroughly dusted with cornflour or glutinous rice flour. Stack together and wrap in plastic.

Sift the flour into a bowl and add a pinch of salt. Bring the water to the boil and pour into the flour. Stir quickly with the handle of a wooden spoon, add the lard and remove to a floured board.

Knead for about 5 minutes until smooth and pliable. Wipe over a large board and dust lightly with flour. Roll the dough out paper-thin. Cut into 24 even-sized squares.

'EXOTIC TASTING' CHICKEN

1 1⅓ kg (2 2/3 lb)	chicken
2 teaspoons	sesame oil
½ cup	white sesame seeds

Sauce:

2 tablespoons	finely chopped spring onion (scallion)
2 tablespoons	light soy sauce
2 tablespoons	sesame paste (or smooth peanut paste/butter)
1 tablespoon	cold water
1 teaspoon	white vinegar
½ teaspoon	chilli oil (or to taste)
½ teaspoon	ground black pepper
½ teaspoon	m.s.g. (optional)
2 teaspoons	sugar
½ teaspoon	finely chopped garlic (optional)
	salt to taste

Clean and dress the chicken and place in a saucepan of cold water. Bring to the boil and simmer for 5 minutes, then remove the pot from the heat and cover with warm towels. Leave for 1¼ hours, then remove the chicken and drain well. Brush with sesame oil and set aside.

Toast the sesame seeds in a dry pan until they begin to pop, then transfer to a mortar and grind to a coarse powder. Leave to cool.

Mix the sauce ingredients together, adjusting the taste, as preferred.

Debone the chicken and tear the meat into shreds. Pile onto a serving plate. For a more substantial dish, arrange the chicken over a bed of shredded cucumber, carrot, and celery.

Pour on the sauce and sprinkle on the crushed sesame seeds. Serve.

COLD SLICED PORK WITH GARLIC SAUCE

1½ kg (3 lb)	pork foreloin (loin)
2 whole heads	garlic
¾ cup (6 fl oz)	light soy sauce
⅓ cup	sesame oil
2 teaspoons	white vinegar
1 teaspoon	sugar

Wash the pork and scrape the skin with a sharp knife to remove any small hairs. Place in a large saucepan and cover with boiling water. Return to the boil, then reduce the heat and simmer until the pork is completely tender, 1½ — 1¾ hours. Add more boiling water as the level drops to ensure the meat is always covered. Remove from the stock and drain well. Leave to cool, then chill thoroughly before cutting into wafer-thin slices.

Arrange the meat attractively on a wide plate.

Very finely chop the garlic and mix with the remaining ingredients. Pour into several small dishes and serve as dips with the pork.

For extra piquancy, add 1 — 2 teaspoons finely chopped fresh red chilli pepper to the sauce.

CHINESE HAM

1 kg (2 lb)	pork leg (fresh ham)
1½ teaspoons	saltpetre
2 tablespoons	table salt
1 teaspoon	Chinese brown peppercorns, coarsely ground
3	spring onions (scallions), cut in halves
3 thick slices	fresh ginger
1 tablespoon	rice wine or dry sherry

Wash the pork and wipe dry. Rub the saltpetre into the skin and meat evenly. Heat the table salt and ground peppercorns in a dry pan until fragrant, then rub into the meat also. Wrap in plastic and store in the refrigerator for at least 48 hours, preferably 3 full days.

Rinse well, then place in a saucepan and add water to cover. Add the spring onions, ginger, and wine and bring to the boil. Simmer for about 1 hour until the pork is just tender. Remove and drain well.

Place in a dish and cover with a cloth. Weight heavily and return to the refrigerator for 5 — 6 hours.

Cut into wafer-thin slices to serve.

A delicious accompanying sauce can be made with 1 tablespoon each of light soy sauce and white vinegar, 2 teaspoons sugar and 2 — 3 teaspoons each of finely chopped spring onion and ginger.

COLD SLICED SPICY BEEF

1¼ kg (2½ lb)	silverside (brisket)
8 cups (2 litres)	water
2/3 cup	rice wine or dry sherry
2 tablespoons	salt
½ cup	sugar
3	spice bags (see page 386)
3 cups (24 fl oz)	light soy sauce

Wash the beef and drain. Bring the water to the boil in a large saucepan and add the remaining ingredients, except the soy sauce. Add the whole piece of beef and return to the boil. Simmer for 10 minutes, skimming occasionally, then add the soy sauce and reduce the heat to very low.

Cover tightly and simmer until the beef is completely tender, about 1¾ hours. Drain well. Place in a dish and weight slightly. Chill before cutting into wafer-thin slices.

To serve, arrange the sliced meat attractively on a wide platter and pour on a small amount of the sauce.

JELLIED MUTTON

625 g (1¼ lb)	lean mutton or lamb
185 g (6 oz)	
piece	pork rind (skin) or use 1 envelope (10 g / ⅓ oz) unflavoured gelatine
4	large spring onions (scallions), cut in halves
3 thick slices	fresh ginger
1	spice bag (see page 386)
⅓ cup	light soy sauce
2 tablespoons	rice wine or dry sherry
½ teaspoon	salt
2 teaspoons	sugar
	few drops of red food colouring (optional)
2 tablespoons	finely chopped fresh coriander
7 — 8 cups	
(1¾ — 2 litres)	chicken stock

Place the whole piece of mutton or lamb in a saucepan and place the pork skin on top. Add water to cover and bring to the boil. Simmer for 15 minutes. Drain, then cut the mutton and skin into chunks and add the chicken stock, the spring onions, ginger, and spice bag and bring to the boil. Simmer for about 1 hour, then remove the pork rind and cut into very small pieces. Discard the spice bag, onions, and ginger.

Add the soy sauce, wine, salt, and sugar to the saucepan and add red food colouring, if used. Continue to cook for a further 10 minutes, then remove the meat and cut into small cubes. Return to the pan with the diced pork rind and simmer until the liquid has reduced to about 1 cup.

If using gelatine, dissolve in ½ cup (4 fl oz) of warm water and add at this point. Heat gently for 10 minutes.

Remove the pan from the heat, stir in the coriander and pour the lot into a greased cake tin. Flatten the top and leave to cool, then refrigerate until set.

Remove from the tin and cut into slices. Arrange on a serving plate and serve with dips of light soy sauce, spiced salt, or hoisin sauce and finely shredded young ginger.

COLD MARINATED SEA SCALLOPS

Serve as an appetiser.

280 g (9 oz)	fresh sea scallops without the shell and coral
½ teaspoon	m.s.g. (optional)
¼ teaspoon	bicarbonate of soda
2 tablespoons	ginger wine (see page 387)
3 cups (24 fl oz)	water
2	spring onions (scallions), trimmed and sliced
4 thick slices	fresh ginger
5 cm (2 in)	
piece	fresh ginger, finely shredded
4	spring onions (scallions), trimmed and finely shredded
1 — 2	fresh red chilli peppers, finely shredded

Sauce:

2 tablespoons	cold water
1½ tablespoons	light soy sauce
1 teaspoon	dark soy sauce
2 teaspoons	sesame oil
2½ teaspoons	sugar
1 teaspoon	white vinegar

Very thinly slice the scallops and rub with the m.s.g., if used, and the bicarbonate of soda. Leave for 20 minutes, then rinse thoroughly, wipe dry and place in a dish with the ginger wine. Leave for 25 minutes.

Bring the water to the boil and add the sliced spring onions and ginger. Simmer for 2 minutes, then add the scallops and cook for about 12 seconds. Lift out and drain well.

Arrange the shredded spring onions, ginger, and chilli peppers on a serving plate. Place the scallops in a dish and cover with the pre-mixed sauce ingredients. Marinate for 1 minute, then strain the sauce into another bowl. Arrange the scallops over the prepared vegetables and serve with the sauce as a dip.

Phoenix Cold Meat Combination (recipe page 381).

SALTED JELLYFISH SALAD

125 g (4 oz)	salted jellyfish*
1	small cucumber
½	giant white (icicle) radish

Sauce:

1½ tablespoons	light soy sauce
1½ teaspoons	white vinegar
1½ teaspoons	sesame oil
¾ teaspoon	salt
1 teaspoon	sugar
¼ teaspoon	ground black pepper
1½ teaspoons	finely chopped garlic (optional)

Rinse salted jellyfish in cold water shred finely, then cover with warm water and bring almost to the boil. Drain and cover again with cold water. Leave for about 1 hour. If the water is allowed to boil, the jellyfish will become tough and stringy.

Peel and shred the cucumber and radish and arrange on a serving plate. Pile the jellyfish on top. Mix the sauce ingredients together and pour over the salad. Toss lightly before serving.

* Salted jellyfish is available in specialist Chinese food stockists and is usually stored in brine. If only the dried product is available, this will need to be soaked for at least 6 hours, then rinsed well and simmered gently for 20 minutes to soften. It should remain quite crunchy.

ROAST SUCKLING PIG APPETISER

500 g (1 lb)	Roast Suckling Pig (crackling and meat) (recipe page 328)
125 g (4 oz)	Jellied Chicken (recipe page 46)
155 g (5 oz)	Honey-Basted Roast Duck (recipe page 259)
125 g (4 oz)	Cold Spicy Peking Pork (recipe page 66)
⅓ recipe	salted jellyfish (see above) or page 392
3 slices	canned or fresh pineapple parsley sliced cucumber, carrot, or white radish

Cut the suckling pig through the crackling into strips. Thinly slice the chicken, duck, and pork. Prepare the jellyfish and pile in the centre of a large round plate. Arrange the suckling pig in a sunburst pattern on top of the jellyfish. Place sprigs of parsley or overlapping thin slices of cucumber, white radish, or carrot around the suckling pig, to decorate.

Arrange the other meats in overlapping rows around the plate. Cut the pineapple slices in halves horizontally and cut each piece in two. Place in a scalloped design around the edge of the dish and set a small bunch of parsley in the centre of each.

Serve with dips of 'duck' sauce (see page 385), plum, or hoisin sauce, and light soy sauce.

PLUM BLOSSOM COLD PLATTER

½	Poached Soy Sauce Chicken (recipe page 249)
155 g (5 oz)	Slow Cooked Corned Pork (recipe page 136)
155 g (5 oz)	Cold Sliced Spicy Beef (recipe page 377)
155 g (5 oz)	Jellied Mutton (recipe page 378)
½ recipe	Salted Jellyfish (see page 392)
155 g (5 oz)	Smoked Vegetarian Duck (recipe page 82)
3	Spiced Pigeon Eggs (recipe page 79)
1	tomato or white onion
2	small cucumbers parsley

Cut the meat into very thin slices, then into bite-sized pieces. Prepare the jellyfish. It should be finely shredded. Thinly slice the vegetarian duck.

Cut the tomato into a flower shape, or, if using the onion, shred into a chrysanthemum shape and dye yellow or pink with food colour mixed with water.

Pile the shredded jellyfish in the centre of a large round plate and make a depression in the centre. Set the tomato or onion in this and garnish with parsley.

Cut the pigeon eggs in halves in a zig-zag design and set aside. Very thinly slice the cucumbers and place in an overlapping row around the edge of the plate.

Arrange the meat in layered groups on the plate, each group to resemble a rounded flower petal (plum blossom). Place half an egg between each lot of meat and garnish with small sprigs of parsley.

Serve with dips of Ginger and Spring Onion Sauce (see page 384), hot mustard, and chilli sauce and light soy sauce.

PHOENIX COLD MEAT COMBINATION

½	Crisp Skin Chicken (recipe page 248)
155 g (5 oz)	Cold Sliced Pork (recipe page 377)
155 g (5 oz)	Red-Braised Five Spice Beef (recipe page 71)
½ recipe	Duck Livers with Hot Pepper Sauce (recipe page 262)
125 g (4 oz)	Boneless Rack of Lamb (recipe page 142)
½ 500 g (1 lb) can	abalone
½ recipe	salted jellyfish (previous recipe)
¼ recipe	Salted Duck Egg (see page 263) or use a hard boiled (hard cooked) chicken egg
8	dried black mushrooms, soaked for 25 minutes
125 g (4 oz)	canned pickled cabbage
2	medium cucumbers, or use canned asparagus
2	medium carrots, or use canned asparagus
1	small tomato, or use a cooked chicken head
⅓	giant white (icicle) radish
½	large cucumber

Seasoning A:

½ cup (4 fl oz)	chicken stock
1 teaspoon	light soy sauce
1 teaspoon	rice wine or dry sherry
1 teaspoon	sugar
⅓ teaspoon	salt
¼ teaspoon	m.s.g. (optional)
¼ teaspoon	sesame oil

Seasoning B: (optional)

2 tablespoons	white vinegar
¼ cup (2 fl oz)	hot water
2 teaspoons	sesame oil
1 teaspoon	salt
1 tablespoon	sugar

Prepare the meats and chill thoroughly. Cut the chicken into narrow sticks, leaving the skin on. Cut the pork, beef, and lamb into thin slices, and the duck livers into narrow strips. Very thinly slice the abalone. The jellyfish should be finely shredded.

Place the mushrooms in a dish with the seasoning A ingredients and set on a rack in a steamer. Steam for 30 minutes, then drain, remove the stems and cut into thin slices.

Finely shred the pickled cabbage and set aside. Cut the medium cucumbers and carrots into thin slices then into matchstick strips, or use a feather design vegetable cutter to stamp out feather shapes. If using the asparagus in place of the cucumbers and carrots, cut the spears in halves lengthwise and soak in cold chicken stock until needed. Marinate cucumber and carrot in the seasoning B, if used.

Cut a slice from the tomato, if used and set to one side of a large plate. Cut the slice into a pointed shape to resemble the beak and set in front of the carrot (phoenix head). If using the chicken head, set on a thick slice of tomato, with the face pointing upwards and outwards to the rim of the plate.

Very thinly slice the radish and large cucumber and cut the slices in halves.

Place the chicken leg and wing bones in a long shape from the tomato or chicken head and cover it with the sticks of chicken to form the phoenix neck. Pile the shredded pickled cabbage in the centre as the body. Arrange overlapping half slices of cucumber and radish in separate rows as the neck feathers.

Use the sliced meat, mushrooms (reserving several pieces) and abalone to form the wings, working away from the body in two directions to form two large curved wings. Cover the pickled vegetables with the strips of spiced liver.

Use the carrot and cucumber 'feathers' or matchstick strips to form a long flowing tail shape, or use the halved asparagus spears. Cut the reserved mushroom pieces into small diamond or oval shapes and use to decorate the tail.

Place the shredded jellyfish in a round shape to one side of the phoenix and place the half egg, yolk upwards, in the centre. Garnish the dish with parsley.

Serve with dips of Vinegar and Garlic Dip (see page 384), plum, or hoisin sauce and light soy sauce.

CHAPTER X
Sauces, Spices and Seasonings

CHINESE PEPPER-SALT/ONION-PEPPER-SALT

1½ tablespoons	Chinese brown peppercorns
4 tablespoons	table salt

Dry-fry the peppercorns in a wok over low to moderate heat until aromatic, about 3 minutes, stirring constantly. Remove to a mortar or spice grinder and grind to a fine powder. Return to the wok with the salt and dry-fry together, turning the mixture constantly with a wok spatula until thoroughly mixed and aromatic. Do not allow the salt to colour. Leave to cool, then store in an airtight jar.

Add finely chopped spring onion to the pepper-salt in quantities to taste for use where onion-pepper-salt is required.

SPICED SALT

4 tablespoons	table salt
1½-2 teaspoons	five spice powder

Dry-fry the salt in a wok over low to moderate heat until well warmed through. Stir constantly to avoid burning. Remove from the heat and stir in the five spice powder. Leave to cool, then store in an airtight jar.

VINEGAR AND GINGER DIP/VINEGAR AND GARLIC DIP

4 tablespoons	Chinese red vinegar*
2 tablespoons	finely shredded fresh ginger (or garlic)

Mix the vinegar and ginger or garlic at least 30 minutes before use. Serve in small dishes as a dip. This is particularly good with seafood.

For a hot vinegar and garlic dip, add 2 tablespoons light soy sauce, a dash each of sugar and m.s.g., and 1-1½ teaspoons of chilli oil.

*If Chinese red vinegar is unobtainable, use white vinegar. White vinegar should also be used if the sauce is to accompany meat or poultry.

GINGER AND SPRING ONION SAUCE

2 tablespoons	fine shredded fresh ginger
3 tablespoons	finely shredded spring onion (scallion)
½ cup (4 fl oz)	vegetable oil
1½ teaspoons	salt

Heat the vegetable oil to moderate and add the ginger, spring onion, and salt. Warm through and remove from the heat. Serve with poached, steamed, or crisp deep-fried poultry.

SWEET AND SOUR SAUCE

1 tablespoon	frying oil
1 tablespoon	finely chopped Chinese pickles
1 tablespoon	finely chopped fresh ginger
½ teaspoon	crushed garlic (optional)
½ cup (4 fl oz)	chicken stock
⅓ cup	sugar
⅓ cup	white vinegar
¼ teaspoon	salt
1 tablespoon	liquid from Chinese pickles
2½ teaspoons	cornflour (cornstarch)

Mix all the ingredients in a saucepan and bring to the boil. Simmer for about 3 minutes. As a dip for pork meatballs or fresh fish, add ¼ cup (2 fl oz) tomato sauce (ketchup) as well.

SWEETENED SOY SAUCE

2 tablespoons	dark soy sauce
2 tablespoons	sugar
1¼ tablespoons	malt sugar
2 teaspoons	sesame oil

Mix all the ingredients together, stirring until the sugar has completely dissolved. Excellent with fish, prawn, and crab meatballs.

'DUCK' SAUCE

The classic accompaniment to Peking roast duck, roast suckling pig, and most crisp-fried poultry.

2 tablespoons	sesame oil
½ cup	sweet bean paste
½ cup	sugar
½ cup (4 oz)	water

Heat the sesame oil in a wok and add the remaining ingredients, mixing thoroughly. Simmer, stirring, until the sauce thickens, about 2 minutes. Store in an airtight jar. Keeps for several weeks.

CHILLI OIL

½ cup	vegetable oil
2½ tablespoons	dried chilli flakes

Heat the vegetable oil to smoking hot, then reduce the heat and allow to cool for a while. Add the chilli flakes, stir and leave for 2 to 3 days, then strain into a jar for storage. Keeps indefinitely without refrigeration.

FIVE SPICE POWDER/SPICE BAGS

A finely ground aromatic powder now readily available under the well known spice brands, as well as popular Chinese brandnames.

To make an acceptable substitute, combine 20 brown peppercorns, ¾ teaspoon fennel seeds, 1 5 cm (2 in) piece of cinnamon bark, 1 whole star anise, and 6 whole cloves. Grind to a very fine powder and store in a screwtop jar.

The same spices in whole form and tied in a small piece of clean muslin or cheese-cloth constitute the Spice Bag referred to in many recipes. The above quantities of whole spices make 1 spice bag. Like the five spice powder, this can now be purchased in prepared form and is usually labelled Mixed Spice in Chinese food stockists. Not to be confused with the Western type of Mixed Spice used for pickling.

RICE CAKES

When rice is cooked by the absorption method, see page 00, there is usually a thick crust of rice around the bottom and sides of the saucepan. This can be lifted off, dried in a warm oven, and used as rice cakes.

Alternatively, cook 2½ cups of short grain white rice by the same method and transfer to an oiled baking tray, pressing it firmly into place. Set in a warm oven to slowly cook until lightly coloured, then increase the heat for 10 minutes to cook to a light golden colour. Remove and cool.

Break or cut into squares and deep-fry immediately before use.

Use where recipes call for crisp rice cakes. This amount of rice yields about 20 4 cm (1 2/3 in) squares, sufficient for 2 recipes. When cool, store in an airtight jar.

SPICED RICE POWDER

1½ cups	raw long grain white rice
3	whole star anise*

Toast the rice with the star anise in a dry wok until the rice turns a rich golden brown. Cool slightly, then grind to a coarse powder. Keeps indefinitely in an airtight jar.
* Some cooks prefer using 1 tablespoon Chinese brown peppercorns, while others choose a mixture of the two.

ONION AND GINGER INFUSION

3	spring onions (scallions), finely chopped
5 thick slices	fresh ginger, finely chopped
½ cup (4 fl oz)	boiling water

Mix the ingredients together and cool rapidly. Store in the refrigerator until ready to use. This keeps for up to a week. To avoid fermentation, strain the liquid into a screw-top jar after 24 hours.

SWEET FERMENTED RICE/WINE LEES

These two recipes give good results and require one week's advance preparation. The finished product can be stored for some time in the refrigerator in a sealed jar. Remove the lid from time to time to release excess gases created by the fermentation.

| 2 kg (4 lb) | raw glutinous rice |
| 3 packages | beer yeast* (about 30 g / 1 oz) |

Soak the rice for 6 hours, drain and cover with water again. Set on a rack in a steamer and steam over gently boiling water until tender. Remove and rinse thoroughly in plenty of warm water. Leave the rice fairly wet. Dissolve the yeast in ½ cup of warm water and pour into the rice. Mix in well and make a depression in the centre. Wrap warmly in towels and leave in a warm place. After about 36 hours, the fermentation will begin, producing a quantity of clear liquid in the depression. Transfer rice and liquid to a preserve jar or any jar which can be tightly sealed, and leave for at least 1 week.
* Granulated dried yeast used for home-brewed beer.

Alternatively soak and steam 1½ kg (3 lb) raw long grain glutinous rice and rinse with warm water. Crumble 2 wine balls (wine cubes)* and mix with 1½ tablespoons of flour. Stir into the rice and make a depression in the centre. Wrap warmly in towels and store in a warm place for 36 hours. Transfer to a sealed jar and refrigerate.
* Wine cubes or wine balls are a kind of compressed distiller's yeast available from specialist Chinese food and drug suppliers.

Japanese light yellow miso paste, a fermentation of soybeans, wine, and spices, makes a good substitute for wine lees, but should be diluted to a thin paste with cold water and a dash of rice wine or sherry.

GINGER WINE/GINGER JUICE

| ¼ cup (2 fl oz) | rice wine or dry sherry |
| 2 tablespoons | grated fresh ginger |

Mix the wine and ginger and refrigerate. This keeps for many weeks.

Place grated fresh ginger in a piece of fine cheesecloth or muslin and squeeze tightly to extract ginger juice. Alternatively, infuse ginger in a small amount of boiling water and squeeze to extract this diluted form of ginger juice. Commercial brands of ginger wine can be substituted.

RENDERED CHICKEN FAT (CHICKEN GREASE)

Trim the white fat from a dressed chicken. (There is usually a larger accumulation of fat near the breast of a force-fed chicken than on those raised on a free-range system.) Place the fat in a wok and add ¼ cup (2 fl oz) water. Cook on moderate heat until there is a considerable amount of liquid fat in the pan, the water has evaporated and the piece of fat has reduced to a crisp brown lump. Remove and discard.

Store rendered chicken fat in the refrigerator. Soften to room temperature for easier measuring.

SUGAR COLOURING

Recipe 1:

500 g (1 lb)	sugar
2½ cups (20 fl oz)	water

Heat the sugar in a dry pan until it melts, then continue to cook, stirring frequently, until it boils and turns a rich dark brown. Quickly remove from the heat and pour in the water. Stir until it stops bubbling and is thoroughly combined. To stop the cooking quickly, hold the bottom of the saucepan in a dish of cold water. Cover the hand holding the pan while adding the cold water to avoid burns.

Recipe 2:

Boil 500 g (1 lb) of sugar and 3 cups (24 fl oz) of water together until the sugar turns dark brown. Cool before using.

Sugar colouring keeps for weeks without refrigeration.

CHICKEN STOCK

2	chicken carcasses and giblets
1	leek
4 slices	fresh ginger
8 cups (2 litres)	water
1½ teaspoons	salt

Wash the chicken bones and giblets well. Sauté the leek in oil until lightly coloured. Place the bones, giblets, leek, and ginger in a saucepan and add the water and salt. Simmer for 1¼ hours, skimming off excess fat frequently. Strain into a storage jar.

For convenience, freeze small lots of stock in sealed plastic bags. Label clearly with quantities to avoid confusion when using. Frozen stock may be added in solid form to braised dishes or soups. However, it should be completely thawed for quick-cooked dishes such as sautés and stir-fries.

ENRICHED STOCK

Proceed as for Chicken Stock, but add 1 pork knuckle (hock) or a ham bone and 1 duck carcass or duck giblets. The cooking time should be increased to about 1¾ hours. Enriched stock will have a white creamy appearance.

For additional flavour, add 500 g (1 lb) chicken meat on the bone.

SOY-PRESERVED GINGER/CUCUMBER

These are available under certain specialty brandnames. The ginger or cucumber is peeled and pickled in a mixture of brine, soy sauce, and spices, resulting in a very salty, dark brown, dry pickle which keeps indefinitely.

If unobtainable, use salted mustard root, or any of the spiced preserved vegetables currently on the market. A substitute can be made by infusing the cucumber or ginger in salted vinegar, adding plenty of dark soy sauce. Leave for at least 4 hours.

SWEET RED BEAN PASTE

2 cups   red beans*
2 tablespoons   lard
     sugar to taste

Rinse the beans and cover with water. Bring to the boil and simmer until softened, adding additional water as necessary. Drain very well and mash to a smooth paste. Work in the lard and plenty of sugar. Usually the mixture is very sweet.

The sweet red bean paste required for these recipes should be firm and dry. If too wet, place in a piece of cheesecloth and squeeze to remove as much water as possible. Add cornflour (cornstarch) to bind.

Red bean paste is available in cans, but is too wet for recipes where it is to be rolled into balls. It can be thickened by heating and adding cornflour paste or a little water chestnut, rice, or potato flour.
* A small red bean similar in appearance to mung beans. Or use kidney beans.

BEANCURD

Canned, frozen, or dehydrated forms of beancurd have still to be perfected. As yet, the soft gelatinous texture of soft beancurd has defied packaging. However some specialist Chinese food suppliers now have stocks of fresh soft beancurd, while the dried beancurd products, beancurd skin, dried beancurd cakes, and rolled beancurd skin sticks, are usually readily available.

750 g (1½ lb)   soybeans
1½ tablespoons   gypsum or plaster of Paris powder
1 cup (8 fl oz)   water

Rinse the soybeans in cold water and place in a large pot. Cover with about 12 cups of cold water and leave overnight. Rinse with cold water then grind to a smooth paste in a food processor or heavy duty blender. About 10 cups of water should be added while blending to keep the paste quite thin.

Strain the liquid through a cheesecloth and squeeze tightly. Bring the liquid to the boil and simmer for about 10 minutes. The cooking process removes the raw taste of the bean water. Mix the gypsum or plaster of Paris powder with the 1 cup of water and pour into the bean water. Stir well then pour into a muslin- or cheesecloth-lined mould, preferably a scrubbed wooden box about ½ meter square. When the liquid has set into a soft jelly, cover with another piece of soft cloth and weight heavily. Leave for about 35 minutes to compress into a soft cake.

Cut into squares about 6.5 cm (2½ in) square. To make dry beancurd, weight heavily for a further 20 minutes.

CHAPTER XI
Preparation and Cooking Techniques

A guide to the preparation of ingredients, the use of the Chinese cleaver, cooking processes and terms, and kitchen layout.

Seafood plays an important role in the Chinese diet. To ensure that most products are available all year round, the art of sun-drying to preserve a vast variety of fish and shellfish was long ago mastered.

Abalone, the large oysters fished off the China coast, *conpoy* (a close rela-

light soy sauce but with a marked fish flavour.

Additionally, several kinds of mushrooms and fungi are gathered from fields and woods for sun-drying. A variety of seaweeds, in particular the curly hair-like *fa ts'ai* (black moss), and the paper-thin discs of compressed laver are also sold in dried form.

Another highly regarded dried food is Birds' Nests, the best of which come from island caves off the coast of Fukien (Fujian) and Thailand.

boil. Simmer for 3 — 4 hours, then remove and rinse in cold water. Scrub with a soft brush to clean, then return to the saucepan and cover with hot water again. Simmer until tender with a dash of rice wine and several slices of spring onion (scallion) and ginger.

Remove from the water, pull out any small bones and discard, then trim off the ragged edges. Soak in cold water until ready to use. May be frozen at this stage, ready for later use.

FISH MAW: This gelatinous white membrane, removed from the stomachs of certain very large fish, is sold in dried form in large sheets resembling cream-coloured polyurethane foam. To prepare, soak in warm water for at least 6 hours, weighted if necessary to keep it under the water. Drain and rinse well. Trim off any yellow membrane. Heat a saucepan of water and add 1 tablespoon of white vinegar. Cut the fish maw into the required pieces as indicated in the recipe and cook for 1 - 2 minutes. Drain well. Soak in cold water until ready to use, then drain and squeeze out the water before using.

JELLYFISH, SALTED: Soak dried jellyfish in cold water for several hours. It is sometimes sold already soaked, making this step unnecessary. Drain and shred. Place in a dish with 1 tablespoon of rice wine (dry sherry) and several slices of spring onion (scallion) and ginger. Cover with warm water and leave for 10 minutes, then drain well and use.

Do not use hot or boiling water on the jellyfish as it will shrink and toughen. The texture should be tender, yet crunchy.

Preparation of ingredients in the kitchen of the Pine and Crane restaurant, Souchow (Suzhou), China.

tion to the sea scallop), sea cucumber (sea slug), squid, jellyfish, shrimps, and the more esoteric shark's fin, shark's skin, fish maw, and fish lips are preserved by sun-drying, and in this form last indefinitely provided they are kept dry.

Salting, usually in combination with sun-drying and sometimes also combined with a fermentation process, is a technique also valued for preservation of seafoods. In particular, shrimps are ground raw and thoroughly salted before sun-drying and fermentation in large underground tanks to provide a pungent, salty seasoning (shrimp sauce). Fish, salted before sun-drying, have a similar strong, fishy and salty flavour, and are used both as an ingredient or a tasty additive. A by-product of this is the aromatic Fish Sauce, a clear seasoning liquid not dissimilar to

PREPARATION OF DRIED INGREDIENTS

ABALONE: Soak dried abalone for 6 hours in cold water. Drain and scrub with a soft brush, then cover with boiling water. Simmer for 4 hours, then rinse in cold water. Trim off the ruffled edges.

Abalone may be sliced from top to bottom to give small oval-shaped pieces, or sliced 'horizontally' (flat slicing, see Preparation Techniques below). Whole abalone may be scored (see below) in a criss-cross pattern to aid in tenderising and to allow the seasonings to penetrate.

FISH LIPS: The mouth section of certain types of very large fish is sun-dried into hard sheets. To prepare, place in a saucepan of hot water and bring to the

SCALLOPS, DRIED (CONPOY): These should be soaked for at least 25 minutes in cold water, then steamed or very slowly simmered in water or chicken stock with rice wine (sherry), spring onion (scallion), and ginger to season. When tender, remove the very thin skin surrounding the scallop and break into shreds by rubbing between the forefinger and thumb.

SEA CUCUMBER: Choose the darkest coloured ones. Soak in cold water until softened, then drain and cut open. Remove the stomach and pull away the surrounding yellow membrane. Wash well. Return to the saucepan and add 1 tablespoon of rice wine (dry sherry) and several pieces of spring onion (scallion) and ginger. Cover with chicken, enriched stock or water, and simmer for several hours until completely tender.

If using in a slow-cooked or braised dish, precook for only about 1 hour, then complete the cooking in the dish. Thirty (30) g (1 oz) of dried sea cucumber gives approximately 90 g (3 oz) when prepared.

OYSTERS: Soak in cold water for at least 6 hours, then drain and clean by brushing gently with a soft brush. Return to the saucepan and cover with cold water. Add a dash of rice wine (sherry) and several slices of spring onion (scallion) and ginger and simmer until softened. Drain and rinse with cold water. Do not overcook if the oysters are to be added to a dish that requires more than 5 — 7 minutes cooking.

SHARK'S FIN: Place whole shark's fins in a saucepan with water to cover and bring to the boil. Simmer for 1½ — 2 hours, then remove form the heat and leave to cool in the water. Rinse and cover with fresh water. Refrigerate overnight at this stage if possible. Reheat to boiling, then reduce to a simmer and cook for 1 hour, then leave to cool again. Repeat if the shark's fins are still not completely tender, or add to the dish and continue cooking until done. Pick out any small pieces of skin.

Shark's fin 'needles,' the thread-like strands of processed shark's fin which are more expensive, are used in soups or dishes where only a moderate amount of shark's fin is needed. They do not require such long cooking or soaking. They should be soaked for several hours in cold water, then brought to the boil and simmered for 2 — 3 hours. Add to the dish and complete the cooking.

When buying shark's fins in whole form, select the lighter coloured ones that appear relatively free from skin and grit, or they will require thorough cleaning after soaking. 'Needles' are sold in packs usually weighing 30 g (1 oz), and when prepared they will weigh approximately 125 g (4 oz).

SHARK'S SKIN: This is prepared in the same way as whole shark's fin. When softened, the large sheets should be cut into narrow shreds or bite-sized squares before use. Wash shark's skin

thoroughly and rinse well. Place shark's skin in a pot of boiling water and simmer until slightly tender. Remove and soak in warm water, scrub well and rinse several times. Place scrubbed shark's skin in a pot of freshly boiling water, simmer until tender. Remove, trim and soak in cold water. To store: cured shark's skin can be kept in a refrigerator, soaked in water, for 2 — 3 days, with the water changed daily, or freeze.

SQUID: Dried squid is sold in two forms, whole or flattened into sheets by passing through a roller. The latter are mostly used as a snack food, being first roasted over a charcoal fire.

Soak whole dried squid in cold water for 2 hours, then bring to the boil and simmer for 1 hour. Transfer to another saucepan and cover with fresh cold water and add a large pinch of bicarbonate of soda. Boil slowly until softened, then rinse thoroughly. The stock from the first boiling can be used as a base for seafood soups.

PREPARATION OF OTHER DRIED FOODS

BIRDS' NESTS: Soak in boiling water, covered, until the water cools. Drain and cover again with boiling water and again leave until the water cools. Drain. If the nests are to be used in a seasoned dish, pour 1 tablespoon of clear vegetable oil over them and cover with boiling water. The oil traps any fragments of grit or feather for easy removal by rinsing. Otherwise, pick out the impurities with tweezers.

Sprinkle a large pinch of bicarbonate of soda over the nests and cover again with boiling water. Leave for a few minutes, then drain and rinse well in cold water. From this stage, birds' nests require only minimal cooking.

FUNGUS, 'SNOW'(WHITE): Soak in warm water until it swells, then rinse well in several lots of cold water. Cut away the small hard root section and return to warm water. Bring to the boil and add a dash of bicarbonate of soda. Stir quickly and immediately remove from the heat. Pour in a little cold water to stop the cooking and leave for about 5 minutes. Drain and rinse thoroughly. Soak in cold water until ready to use.

FUNGUS, 'WOOD EAR' (BROWN):

Soak until softened. Remove the small tough root section and cut the 'wood ears' into bite-sized pieces, shreds, or strips as indicated in the recipe. Soak in cold water until needed.

FA TS'AI (*FAT CHOY*/BLACK MOSS): Soak in cold water until soft enough to untangle the curly mass. Squeeze out the water, then rinse very thoroughly in cold running water until it runs clear. Cover with cold water and bring to the boil. Drain and cover again with cold water. Soak until needed, then drain and squeeze out as much water as possible.

Prepared fresh ingredients are attractively displayed in this Hong Kong noodle shop.

BLACK MUSHROOMS: Soak for at least 25 minutes in cold water. Remove, squeeze out the water and cut off the stems as close to the caps as possible. Return to cold water until ready to use.

The best flavour is acquired by steaming the mushrooms in chicken stock or water with a dash of rice wine (dry sherry), sugar, and salt until plump and tender. The liquid can be retained for adding to the dish or to soups or stews.

USEFUL HINTS ON THE PREPARATION OF FRESH INGREDIENTS

GINGER: Choose firm, smooth-skinned ginger and remove the skin with a potato peeler. Trim off the buds and cut the pieces diagonally into thick or thin slices as required. To SHRED ginger, stack several thin slices together and cut along the length into very fine strands. To CHOP, first shred, then turn the bundle of shreds and cut across into minute dice, or place on a chopping board and chop energetically

393

with a cleaver until reduced to a pulpy mass.

Ginger can be GRATED with a cheese grater or in a food processor using large pieces of peeled ginger. Grate on as small a setting as possible to give very small pulpy shreds with plenty of juice. Work over a plate to save the juice. BRUISE ginger slices by batting with the end of a rolling pin or cleaver handle. This crushes the cells to release the juice. See also page 387 for details of preparing GINGER JUICE, GINGER WINE, and ONION AND GINGER INFUSION.

ONIONS: Some confusion has arisen over this vegetable. In Australia, the tall green tubular-stemmed SPRING ONIONS may also be known as SHALLOTS or ESCHALLOTS, while in America they are SCALLIONS.

To add further to the confusion, SCALLIONS can also refer to the small red-skinned onions which grow in clove-clusters resembling oversized red garlics. We have used the term SPRING ONIONS with SCALLIONS in parentheses throughout this book.

White onions, therefore, refer to the large common onion with white peel. Brown or Spanish onions can also be used. Leeks have a milder flavour and are an excellent substitute for either spring or white onions in most recipes.

GARLIC CHIVES resemble young spring onions (scallions), having paler green stems and a very short white base. They have a mild onion flavour with a hint of fresh garlic. If unavailable, substitute shredded leek.

For a majority of these recipes, spring onions (scallions) should be TRIMMED by cutting just above the roots and removing roots and any limp outer leaves. Discard the topmost parts of the green stems and use only the firmly packed white lower section with a short length of the more tightly packed part of the green section. Trimmings are useful to add flavour to soups. SLICE the onions diagonally into 2 cm (¾ in) lengths. Larger spring onions (scallions) can be cut in halves lengthwise to facilitate fast cooking, then cut into short lengths. CHOP by shredding lengthwise, then cutting across into very small pieces, or chop with the cleaver as indicated above (Ginger). DICE spring onions (scallions) by cutting straight across the

stems, or diagonally if preferred, into very small pieces.

To cut white onions Chinese style, peel, then cut in halves from top (stem) to bottom (root). Trim away the root section using a V-shaped cut, then slice from top to bottom into wedges of required size. Separate each segment into individual slices for faster cooking.

CHICKENS: To DEBONE (BONE) a whole chicken, place the bird on its back on a chopping board and use a short sharp knife to work around the entire rib cage up to the backbone. When the wing and thigh bones are reached, cut through the middle joint so that the lower part of the wing and leg bones remain intact. Continue up to the backbone and remove the whole carcass in one piece. The retention of the lower wing and leg bones aids in the reshaping of the chicken when stuffed.

To SKIN a whole chicken, work in a similar way as for deboning, but this time separate the meat from the skin. Use a small sharp knife and the fingers to cut and gently pull away the skin, taking care not to pierce through the skin. Small kitchen scissors can be invaluable for snipping through tough connective tissue. Again, leave the lower bones of the wings and legs in place to aid in restructuring the bird later. DUCKS are deboned (boned) and skinned in the same way.

Whole chickens (or other poultry) are often cut for serving by slicing straight through the bones. The cleaver is best for this as it has the sharpness as well as the size and weight for cutting through even the largest thigh bones with ease.

To CUT A CHICKEN FOR SERVING, place the chicken on a chopping board, breast upwards, and cut straight through the breast bone along its length. Open flat and cut through the backbone, then turn the two parts upwards. Cut off the head and neck, remove the wing tips, then remove the wings by cutting through the upper joint. Slice off the thighs whole. Trim off the knuckles by chopping straight through the bone below the drumstick meat (or leave in place, if preferred) and cut the drumstick into two pieces, or leave whole. Remove the thigh bone, then cut the thigh meat into thick diagonal fingers. Cut the wings in halves at the central joint, or leave whole.

Remove the breast meat in a piece from each side and cut into thick

diagonal slices. Then cut straight through the bones of the meaty back section, cutting into bite-sized squares. Use the point of the cleaver to lift out the breast bone meat and cut or tear this into slivers.

When cutting through the larger bones, chop down with the cleaver, then hit the top of the cleaver firmly and sharply with the base of the left hand to force it through (see also page 396, Chopping, below).

To ARRANGE A CHICKEN FOR SERVING, set the head at the edge of an oval plate facing outwards over the rim. Place the neck and thigh bones in a row away from the head. Arrange any unevenly cut pieces of meat and the slices from the back on both sides of the row of bones, then place the sliced breast meat crosswise in a shape resembling the whole chicken.

Set the two wings on either side of the body, and cross the drumsticks at the end with the 'parson's nose' between the legs. Finish by arranging the sliced thigh pieces along the length of the body on both sides.

PRAWNS (SHRIMPS): In many of these recipes, it is recommended that the heads be left on as they lend their own rich flavour and a bright red-pink colour to the dish. They can, of course, be removed if preferred. Tail sections are generally left on only for aesthetic reasons and may be similarly discarded if preferred.

If the tail section is to be left intact, this includes the last joint of the shell covering the body, though it can be trimmed shorter using a pair of small kitchen scissors. The sharp 'horn' in the centre should be pulled or snipped off. To DEVEIN using a toothpick, as mentioned in many recipes, hold the prawn (shrimp) in the left hand with the back curving upwards. Push the toothpick (or use the point of a fork) into the centre top of the prawn (shrimp) back and gently ease upwards. It should hook out the dark gritty vein and it can then be eased out from the full length of the prawn (shrimp).

Alternatively, cut along the back with a sharp knife and pull out the exposed vein. Cutting deeply in this way gives prawn (shrimp) cutlets (butterflies).

Rinse fresh prawns (shrimps) in their shells in plenty of cold water. Peeled prawns (shrimps) can be washed under cold running water, using a little salt and cornflour (cornstarch) to gently rub while rinsing. This helps to whiten the meat and eliminate the fishy smell.

Fresh prawns (shrimps) are easily peeled as the shells slide off with a minimum of effort. If cooking in the shells, however, cut along the underside between the two rows of legs with a short, sharp knife either before or after cooking. The whole shell can then be lifted off without cutting the meat. The term 'green' used in this book refers to fresh uncooked prawns (shrimps).

FISH: In certain baked, poached, and steamed dishes using a whole fish, it is recommended that the scales be left on. This is to retain the natural juices and oils in the fish. When the dish is cooked, the scales with skin attached can be lifted off cleanly.

A fish is SCORED both for aesthetic and technical reasons. A pattern of diagonal or criss-cross scoring along the sides of the fish improves the appearance of the finished dish and additionally aids in fast cooking and the thorough permeation of the seasonings.

To score diagonally, use a sharp knife to cut across the body from top fins to the lower opening, cutting at an angle to the head and deep enough to just touch the bones. Four or five scores across an average-sized fish is usually sufficient. Criss-cross scoring requires an additional row of cuts from the opposing angle to result in a diamond-shaped pattern across the fish.

To SQUIRREL a fish, cut off the two fillets and place on a board, meat upwards. Score in a close criss-cross pattern, holding the knife at a slight angle and cutting right through to the skin without piercing it. Brush a finger along the cut area from tail to head to make the 'points' stand up. This gives an attractive appearance to the finished dish and allows the meat to cook very quickly.

To DEBONE (BONE) a fish, cut open along the underside, then work the point of a short sharp knife along the backbone, gently easing the meat away on both sides. Cut through the bone at both ends using scissors or a knife and lift out the backbone in one piece.

EEL: Best bought live, if possible, dropped into a pot of boiling water, and left for a few minutes. Skin by securing the head to a strong support such as the edge of a table, cut around the head, then use a pair of pincers to strip away the skin in one piece.

Fillets may be obtained by securing the eel in the same way and using a sharp knife to cut three or four strips from the length of the eel, leaving the backbone attached to the head.

The skin may be left on. Rub with plenty of salt to remove the slimy residue, then rinse thoroughly. Steaks may be cut crosswise through the bone and pressed out flat.

TURTLE: Place the live turtle on a board, upside down, and cut off the head. Lift and drain the blood. Place the whole turtle in a large saucepan of boiling water and leave for 2 minutes, then remove and use a knife to scrape off the skin. Remove the shell and cut open the under side to remove the stomach. Cut the meat into strips and simmer in boiling water for several minutes. Drain well.

Cook according to the recipe, removing all small bones when the meat is tender.

MEATBALLS: Very finely mince (grind) the meat, see below (Mincing With Two Cleavers), or pulverise in a food processor using the chopping blade. Transfer to a mixing bowl and add the seasoning ingredients. Squeeze the mixture through the fingers until sticky, then gather into one lump. Lift from the bowl and throw back against the inside of the bowl repeatedly until the mixture is thoroughly softened, about 3 minutes. Chill until firm. Use for beef, pork, and chicken balls. Squid can also be prepared in this way for seafood balls. To make smooth-textured fish or prawn (shrimp) balls, smash the meat until pulverised, using the cleaver blade held flat in parallel with the cutting board, or pulverise in a food processor. Add the seasoning ingredients and binding agents and beat in one direction only with a wooden spoon or a pair of cooking chopsticks until the mixture is smooth and thick.

To form meat or seafood balls, have a saucepan of water gently simmering or a pan of deep-frying oil heated to just below smoking point. Gather up a large portion of the paste in the left hand and squeeze out an amount between the curled forefinger and thumb. Scoop it off with a spoon and drop into the oil or water. Cook the balls until they rise to the surface, then drain and transfer to a dish of cold water until ready to use.

COOKING OIL: The term 'frying oil' is used in most recipes for sautéed or stir-fried dishes. This refers to vegetable oil that has been used at least once before, probably for deep-frying. It has a richer taste than the bland, almost raw flavour of new vegetable oil and should be used in preference to new oil.

Cantonese cooks prefer the strong, slightly nutty flavour of peanut (groundnut) oil for their cooking. It is a matter of individual taste whether this or one of the lighter tasting pure vegetable oils is used.

LARD (rendered pork fat) is also used in many stir-fried and sautéed dishes as an alternative cooking oil. It gives a much richer taste and should be avoided by the diet-conscious. It is also used in sweets, bread and pastry making,

Chopping.

and in cakes for the rich taste and the smooth texture it gives to dough and pastries. In fact, lard (and very occasionally rendered chicken fat) replaces butter or other forms of shortening in all Chinese cooking.

RENDERED CHICKEN FAT (CHICKEN GREASE) is occasionally used as a cooking oil, but more usually to add a rich taste and shine to sauces and finished dishes (see also page 413).

Oil for DEEP-FRYING can be kept clean by straining through a special filter or a paper coffee filter after each use. A few slices of peeled raw potato dropped into the oil after use, but while still hot, helps absorb impurities.

Choose a good quality oil and keep one lot for cooking fish and seafoods and another for meats. New cooking

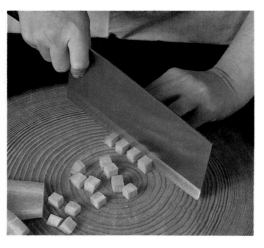

oil should be used for deep-frying ingredients used in sweets, cakes, or puddings.

Chinese cooks often splash a quantity of piping hot frying oil over a finished dish to add flavour and shine. This does not result in a greasy tasting dish, but it can be too oily for some tastes and may be omitted.

SESAME OIL is only occasionally used for cooking, being of a strong distinct flavour. It is used frequently to add taste and aroma to marinades and sauces. It may be omitted unless specifically indicated.

With the exception of lard and rendered chicken fat, animal fats are not used in Chinese cooking.

THICKENING: Most stir-fried and sautéd dishes require a clear, viscous sauce which is best obtained by the addition of a paste of starch and cold water. Cornflour (cornstarch) is the most commonly used starch, though a powder of green mung beans is preferred by some Chinese cooks as it results in a thicker sauce and is therefore more economical.

Ordinary wheat flour will not give similar results and should not be used as an alternative. The sauce will invariably turn lumpy and will not acquire the desired clear, syrupy appearance.

A CORNFLOUR SOLUTION or PASTE as required in these recipes should be a mixture of approximately equal amounts of cornflour (cornstarch) and cold water. Never use hot or boiling water as this will cause the flour to partially cook, resulting in a thin lumpy sauce.

In dishes with a large quantity of sauce, such as stewed or braised dishes, the sauce may be reduced first by boiling in an open pan, then thickened with a cornflour paste.

As a general rule, use 1 tablespoon of cornflour mixed with 1 tablespoon of cold water to thicken 1 cup (8 fl oz) of sauce.

PREPARATION TECHNIQUES AND THE USE OF THE CHINESE CLEAVER.

CHOPPING: The term is applied to any technique involving straight-through cutting of food. Place the item on a cutting board and use a straight, sharp downwards motion with the cleaver, holding the blade parallel with the surface of the board.

To chop through bones, hit down with the blade, then bat the top of the blade with the base of the left hand to force it through the bone. See also Preparation of Chicken and Ginger for specific application to these ingredients.

DICING/CUBING: Cutting into very small cubes (dice) or slightly larger cubes (approximately 2 cm / ¾ in). The ingredient should be first cut into slices the thickness of the required dice or cube, then into sticks. Turn crosswise and cut the sticks into cubes or dice, maintaining even-sized pieces.

MINCING (GRINDING) WITH TWO CLEAVERS: To obtain a pulverized paste of meat, seafood, or vegetables, place the item on a cutting board and take a sharp cleaver in each hand. Chop with alternate hands in a fast rhythm until the item is spread out and partially chopped. Scrape into a pile again and continue chopping and reshaping the pile until the item is completely pulverised. Draw out any tendons or pieces of skin or hard tissue and discard.

Soft seafoods like fish and prawns can be pulverised by placing on a board and batting with the flat side of the cleaver until reduced to a pulp.

SLICING: When applied to meats for

Chinese cooking, the meat should be cut across the grain, unless otherwise specified. This severs the tough connective tissue making the meat more tender. To obtain the wafer-thin or paper-thin slices often required, freeze the meat until the piece is quite firm and use a very sharp knife or cleaver to pare off slices so thin they are almost transparent.

When cutting, hold the item firmly with the left hand, with the forefinger of the left hand raised at the central joint and pressed against the cleaver. This acts as a guide for thickness and prevents slips which might result in an accidental cut.

STRIPS AND SHREDS: Stack the slices of meat or vegetables, two or three slices at a time, and cut along the longest part into strips of required width. Strips may vary from 1 cm (1/5 in) to 2.5 cm (1 in). Narrower strips would be called shreds or 'matchsticks.'

HORIZONTAL SLICING (FLAT SLICING): The cleaver is ideally suited to this task. It is applied to round flat-shaped foods such as whole abalone, champignons, water chestnuts, and kidneys, which are required to be sliced while maintaining the natural shape.

Place the ingredient on a board and press the fingers of the left hand firmly

Mincing (Grinding).

Stripping and Shredding.

on top, holding the ingredient securely in position. Using the cleaver held flat and parallel with the board, cut through the item under the fingers. Remove each slice when cut to avoid slips.

DIAGONAL SLICING/ROLL CUTTING: Vegetables with long thin shapes such as celery and carrots, radishes, and spring onions are usually cut on the diagonal to expose a greater cut surface to the heat during cooking and also to improve the appearance. Generally, diagonal slices will be around 1.25 cm (½ in) between cuts, resulting in pieces about 3.75 cm (1½ in) long from end to end.

When larger pieces of vegetable are required, these may be ROLL-CUT by first cutting one diagonal slice, then rolling the vegetable one-quarter turn and cutting at the same angle as the first cut. This gives pleasing shapes as well as exposing a maximum of cut surface area for faster cooking and better penetration of seasonings.

GRINDING: When applied to spices and small, hard ingredients such as nuts, rice, and beans, this is done in a mortar or in a spice or coffee grinder. Unless otherwise specified, the items should be ground to a fine powder.

In some recipes, ingredients are ground with water to produce a smooth paste. This should be done in a food processor, using the chopping blade or a blender on the setting for grind or purée. Add enough water to prevent the machine from clogging, or the amount suggested in the recipe, and grind until the mixture is smooth and lump-free.

SCORING (CRISS-CROSS): Certain smooth-surfaced ingredients are scored to facilitate fast cooking and to give aesthetic appeal. Kidneys, squid, and thickly sliced liver are usually scored with a close criss-cross pattern which results in a diamond-shaped design on the surface.

Cut about 0.3 cm (1/8 in) deep and at a slight angle and work closely so that the diamonds are no more than ½ cm (1/5 in) wide.

A GUIDE TO COOKING PROCESSES AND TERMS.

STIR-FRYING: Used to describe a process in which small slivers of food are quickly cooked in a small amount of cooking oil. Cooking is usually done over intensely high heat to seal in the natural flavours and to retain the natural colour and texture of the food. The wok was created for just such a cooking process with sufficient depth to allow for a lot of movement of the contents as they are constantly stirred and turned during cooking to prevent burning and to distribute the seasonings thoroughly.

The wok is first heated, then the oil (usually vegetable oil which has been previously used, see Cooking Oil, above) is swirled around the inside of the pan so that it runs slowly over the whole surface and accumulates in the bottom. The wok is heated to 'smoking point,' i.e. when a faint blue smoky haze appears above the oil and when a drop of water added to the oil will immediately splutter and evaporate. The prepared ingredients are added at this stage, energetically tossed around with the wok spatula, then the seasonings are added and the ingredients again tossed until all are well coated with the seasonings and the cooking oil. Seasoning such as soy sauce and rice wine (or sherry) are usually swirled onto the sides of the wok rather than straight onto the ingredients. This allows them to sizzle and partially evaporate, releasing their full flavour before reaching the food. Lastly, the sauce ingredients are added together with the thickening agent, well mixed with cold water or stock, and the contents of the wok continue to be stirred until the sauce thickens and acquires a clear, viscous quality (see thickening, above).

All components required to produce a good stir-fried dish should be assembled before cooking begins, with the ingredients completely prepared. There is no time once cooking commences to search for an additional condiment, or fumble for the wok spatula. Have the wok, spatula, a sturdy oven glove or thick cloth, the prepared ingredients, seasonings, cooking oil, and sauce ingredients assembled close to the cooker before beginning. And commence cooking only when diners are seated at the table in readiness. The success of a stir-fried dish lies in its being brought straight from the wok to the table.

Sautéd foods are cooked at a very slightly lower temperature than stir-fried foods, but a similar technique of constant stirring and moving is also employed, though in a less vigorous fashion. Sautéing often applies to more friable ingredients, or those which have a tendency to burn on higher heats, such as fish or soft beancurd.

Shallow Frying implies food cooked in a shallow level of oil, usually vegetable oil but occasionally lard. There should be sufficient oil in frying that such composite foods as meatballs

and fritters can float free of the surface of the pan. Soft-textured foods like soft beancurd, the pot-sticker types of dumplings, and crispy breads such as 'spring onion pastries' require merely a well-oiled pan.

Dry-Frying is employed to parch certain ingredients, thereby toasting them lightly without subjecting them to oil which would spoil their texture. This is best done in a cast-iron wok or frying pan/skillet over moderate heat.

DEEP-FRYING: Cooking in oil with the food completely immersed. Vegetable or peanut oil (see Cooking Oil, above) and occasionally lard is used, and it should be heated to moderate, around 160°C (325°F) for most seafoods, and to 190°C (375°F) for meats, poultry, and vegetables or foods coated in batter. Smoking hot

Scoring.

oil, at around 200°C (400°F) is required for 'instant' cooking of such ingredients as crisp-fried rice vermicelli, prawn crackers, or crisp rice cakes. Deep-fried foods should be well drained after cooking, preferably in a drainer lined with absorbent paper. For best results, particularly with batter or crumb-coated foods, fry once on moderate heat, allow to cool completely in a drainer, then re-fry on a higher temperature immediately before serving. This is particularly useful for foods which require preparation in advance. Leave the second frying until ready to serve.

Deep-frying is employed at varying stages in Chinese cooking. Certain foods, particularly whole cuts of meat or whole poultry, are deep-fried prior to steaming or simmering. This adds colour to the surface and extra flavour

to the finished dish. As these meats are usually marinated before frying they have a tendency to spatter when they enter the hot oil. Care should be taken to protect the arms and hands from flying droplets of hot oil. If meat is to be deep-fried as the final stage of the cooking process, ensure that the surface is thoroughly dry and that there is no residue of liquid inside the meat or bird before frying.

Many of these recipes require that the prepared and marinated main ingredient be deep-fried as the initial cooking step, prior to stir-frying. This is desirable to perfect the dish as it prevents the shreds, slices, or strips of food from sticking together during cooking. It is, however, quite impractical in the home kitchen. Stir-frying is just as successful without the preliminary deep-frying with the following considerations. Use less, or omit entirely, the egg white and/or cornflour (cornstarch) in the marinade as this will cause the food to stick to the pan and usually results in a thick deposit of particles in the bottom of the pan which spoils both the appearance and taste of the dish. Add a little (extra) oil to the marinade to prevent the meat from sticking together, and use slightly more oil for stir-frying than is recommended. Additionally, ensure that the meat is cooked before the other ingredients, except possibly spring onions and ginger, and remove when cooked. Return to the dish when the seasonings and sauce ingredients are added.

When deep-frying whole poultry, use wooden cooking chopsticks or the handles of two wooden spoons to gently turn the bird, thus ensuring that the skin does not tear.

STEAMING: The Chinese invented steam cooking many hundreds of years ago and continue to praise it as the purest method of cooking.

Intense moist heat keeps the ingredients succulent and bright in colour, leaving the natural taste unimpaired, and there is no contact with anything which could impart its own flavour, save the added seasonings. Steaming is used in many Chinese recipes, either as the only cooking process or as one stage in the cooking of a dish which may also be deep-fried. Many ingredients, additionally, are steamed prior to use to soften them and release their full flavours. This particularly applies to the many dried ingredients used in Chinese cooking.

Steaming is done in a container set on a rack within a large pot or wok which is tightly covered to prevent the steam from escaping. Wet ingredients, or foods with added stock or sauce are steamed in dishes, on plates, or in bowls, while dry foods such as buns can be placed directly onto the greased slatted bamboo bases of tiered bamboo steaming baskets. See Chinese Cooking Utensils, Condiments and Methods, Chapter XI, for detailed notes on setting up a steamer. Steaming is done 'over high heat' or over 'rapidly boiling water,' which dictates that the water producing the steam should be kept at a constant bubbling boil. As the water will evaporate over a period of time, the level should be frequently topped up with boiling water. Keep the lid of the steamer firmly in place during cooking to avoid heat loss. Dishes or whole foods inside a steamer should be positioned well above the water level and should not be covered unless specified in the recipe. Slow steaming is required for certain foods. The water in the steamer should be maintained at a gentle simmer.

SMOKING: Smoking over fragrant smokefuel such as tea leaves, pine needles, fragrant wood shavings, sugar, or dried orange peel lends a rich colour and flavour to certain foods, in particular fish and poultry. The smokefuel ingredients are placed in the bottom of a heavy iron wok or old cooking pot which has a well-fitting lid and set over heat until the fuel begins to smoke. The heat is then reduced and a rack set in position over the fuel, high enough to allow a free flow of smoke around the ingredients. Smoking can be done in the oven. Place the smokefuel ingredients in a baking dish and set in the bottom of a hot oven. When the fuel begins to smoke, decrease the heat slightly and place the ingredients on a rack over the fuel. Close the oven and smoke for the required time. Wipe out the oven with a damp cloth when the operation is completed.

Smoked food is usually steamed or deep-fried, or a combination of both, either before or after the smoking.

POACHING: This involves very gentle cooking of an ingredient, usually a whole cut of meat or a whole bird or fish. The ingredient is covered with seasoned water or stock which is then brought to a gentle simmer. Fish are usually poached in a fish kettle, an oval-shaped deep saucepan with a removable perforated base which can be lifted out with the fragile fish in one piece after cooking. In certain cases, the pan will be removed from the heat source after a very short cooking time, merely a few minutes. The pan is then covered with a thick, warm cloth or towel and the ingredients left to gently poach in the warm liquid until cooked. This particularly applies to chicken, and the result is tender, succulent pinky-white meat of delicate flavour. Poaching can also describe a technique of cooking whole cuts of meat of whole poultry or fish by immersion in warm oil. Gentle heat is applied, sufficient to cook without the ingredient becoming greasy, but low enough that the meat does not change colour. Oil-poached foods should be very well drained before further cooking, or before serving.

SLOW-SIMMERING: This differs little from poaching. The liquid is never brought quite to the boil, however, the heat being decreased as soon as the first bubbles break the surface. The food is very slowly and gently cooked in the stock or sauce until completely tender. Slow-simmering, also known as clear-simmering, results in moist and tender ingredients in a completely clear stock. It is important to keep the pan tightly closed during cooking, and not to stir the contents.

SIMMER-STEWING: This refers to the process of slowly cooking an ingredient in well-seasoned liquid so that the ingredient absorbs both the colour and flavour of the seasonings applied. The liquid may be served as the sauce, straight from the pan, or it may be thickened and poured over the ingredient on the serving plate. In certain cases, the cooking liquid is retained for use with other dishes.

RED-BRAISING/RED-STEWING: A term generally applied to the cooking of ingredients, particularly large cuts of meat or whole poultry, which have been deep or shallow-fried for colour and extra flavour, and are then slowly cooked in a well-flavoured sauce of which the principle ingredients are soy sauce and sugar. The meat acquires a rich red-brown colour. Also known as red-cooking.

KITCHEN LAYOUT

As so much Chinese cooking requires fast work at the wok, it is vital that the kitchen be well laid out in order to avoid the kind of confusion which might spoil a dish.

The preparation section should be separate from the cooking area and have one or two cutting boards, the knives and cleavers and the various preparation utensils on hand, plus a supply of small plates and dishes to

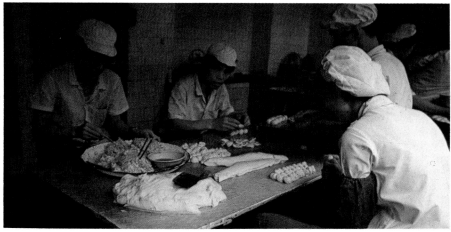

In a Chinese kitchen, food is usually prepared away from the cooking area, then placed in dishes and containers at a handy distance from the cook.

contain the prepared ingredients.

Position the wok cooker as close to the sink as possible as it will have to be carried to the sink for washing between each use. Have the cooking utensils — spatula, ladle, strainers, chopsticks, wooden spoons, etc. — close by and the seasoning ingredients, thickeners, and cooking oils readily available.

Certain brands of soy sauce are marketed in small bottles with shaker/pourer nozzles. These make it clean and easy to measure the sauce and to swirl it around the sides of the wok, as is required in so many recipes.

Use them also for cooking wine and oil. Experience soon becomes a better judge than a measuring spoon for these ingredients. There are also small sauce jugs available, resembling tiny teapots with long spouts. These are excellent for dispensing all liquid seasonings and cooking oils.

Keep salt, pepper, m.s.g., and other frequently used dry ingredients in squat containers with tight-fitting lids. These can be lined up close to the work area and make it easier for spoon measuring than if they are retained in their original packaging.

Make sure there is a pair of sturdy oven gloves or a thick cloth readily on hand for holding and lifting the wok as the handles can become very hot during cooking.

CHAPTER XII
A Word on Wines and Spirits

12×21.=252.↓

According to the ancient legend, wine was first discovered in China by a careless cook: having set some rice to soak in water in a covered crock one day, he promptly forgot about it. Several days later, he noticed the crock and uncovered it: a powerful aroma overwhelmed him. Curious, he dipped his ladle into the murky liquid and tasted it. He found the flavour palatable and the after-effects quite pleasant. So he dipped and drank again. Pretty soon, all the cooks and helpers in the kitchen were gathered about the crock, dipping their ladles deeply, talking and laughing merrily. No doubt the master of the house went hungry that evening.

Since earliest antiquity, wine has formed an integral part of Chinese culinary culture. The earliest of all ancient artifacts unearthed in China are ceremonial bronze drinking vessels dating from the Shang dynasty (ca. 1500 B.C.). Indeed, excessive indulgence in wine has often been cited as a major reason for the fall of the house of Shang. Along with drinking vessels, the Shang artifacts include similar bronze vessels for food: from the very beginning, eating and drinking, food and wine, have been as intimately associated as *yin and yang*, and one rarely appeared on the table without the other.

Even Confucius, that paragon of moderation, viewed drinking with great tolerance, and he usually enjoyed wine with his meals. His meticulous eating habits, which included set limits for every type of food, have been described in Chapter I. But when it came to wine, the Sage's guideline was liberal: 'There is no limit to wine-drinking, as long as one does not become disorderly.'

Of course, not everyone followed Confucius' 'Golden Mean,' most notably China's famous 'Drunken Dragons,' scholars and poets renowned for having the 'capacity of the ocean' when it came down to drinking. Chinese poets have praised the delights of wine almost as much as they have women, and any poet worth his verse was expected to be able to down 'a hundred cups at a sitting.' A common Chinese adage states, 'When drinking among intimate friends, even 1,000 cups are not enough.' China's most famous 'Drunken Dragon' was the colourful T'ang poet Li Bo, who is said to have died in a lotus pool when, reaching drunkenly from a boat to embrace the image of the moon in the water, he fell overboard and drowned. Li Bo and other poets who shared his love of drinking regarded wine as the key to the sublime. He left us this couplet to prove it:

The rapture of drinking and wine's dizzy joy,
No sober man deserves to enjoy!

Food and wine go hand in hand in Chinese culinary culture. The Chinese rarely drink alone, and they never drink on an empty stomach. While banquets are considered incomplete without an accompanying alcoholic beverage or two, drinking is equally incomplete without a few *jiu-cai* ('wine-foods') to line the stomach. Whenever a few friends go out to have a few drinks together in China, they always order a few side-dishes such as dried meats and beancurd, cold poultry, salted nuts, pickled vegetables, and so forth. In addition to lining and protecting the stomach, *jiu-cai* also increase the appetite for and appreciation of the wine itself.

A wide variety of fermented wines and distilled spirits have been produced in China for millenia, and most of these traditional beverages are still on the market today. Fermented wines, such as the rice-wine discovered by the

402

careless cook, have been imbibed in China since pre-historic times. They were fermented from grains, mostly rice, millet, or sorghum. Later, these fermented grain-wines were further enhanced and flavoured with fragrant herbal additives such as fagara pepper, realgar, artemisia, cassia blossom, pomegranate blossom, and others. During the T'ang dynasty, fermented grape-wines were introduced from the western frontier regions, and they enjoyed immense popularity in China. Vines were imported and transplanted in northern China, which today still produces a variety of good grape-wines.

Traditional methods of aging and bottling Chinese wines are still much in evidence in this Hong Kong wine shop. (p.401, left and above)

During the Sung era, the art of distilling spirits from fermented grain-mash was introduced and quickly adopted in China. A wide range of potent spirits soon appeared in the wine-shops and restaurants throughout the empire. Among the most renowned Chinese spirits are the various forms of 'white lightning:' *mao-tai, bai-ga'r*, and *gaoliang*. Made from *gaoliang* (sorghum), these spirits are distilled over and over until they approach 150 proof or more in strength. At banquets, they are generally used only for toasting. Chinese herbalists also use them to make potent tonic potions: tonic herbs, reptiles, poisonous snakes, deer-horn, etc. are steeped in 150 proof spirits for a year or more to extract their potent elements. The resulting brew is taken as a tonic medicinal drink, especially during the winter.

Today, the most suitable and the most popular beverage with Chinese food is chilled beer. All over China and the Far East, people drink beer with Chinese food more than any other beverage, and beer consumption has grown by leaps and bounds in recent decades. This may seem ironic, since beer is a Western beverage, but throughout their history the Chinese have adapted useful foreign innovations to their own culinary culture. Beer turns out to fit Chinese culinary requirements like a glove, which accounts for its immense popularity today.

The first breweries were established in China during the early decades of this century by Germans. The Chinese have well maintained these facilities and kept the quality of their beers up to original European standards. Everyone in China drinks beer today, and the most popular nationally distributed brand is Qing-Dao lager. In addition to Qing-Dao, every province and every major city of China produce their own local brews under colourful Chinese labels, and these are consistently good. Peking (Beijing) offers 'Great Wall Beer' and an excellent dark porter; in Shanghai you can swig 'Swan Lager;' Kweilin (Guilin) brews an excellent 'Guilin Beer;' in Hangchow (Hangzhou) you'll enjoy 'West Lake Beer' with your West Lake Sour Fish; and in every other city you'll find a refreshing local brew waiting. In Hong Kong, Singapore, and Tokyo, excellent local brews as well as the full gamut of international brands are available. In Taipei (Taibei), the award-winning 'Taiwan Beer' is the national brew, and it is consumed by the sybaritic populace of the island in incredible quantities.

What's so great about beer with Chinese food? One of the main functions of beverages at Chinese banquets is to clean the palate and throat of residual oils and lingering flavours, thereby clearing the way for better culinary appreciation of the subtle points of each different dish and each successive bite. The carbonation in beer fulfulls this function ideally, effectively cleaning the mouth with each swig. Brewed purely from grains, beer is also an indirect form of *fan*, and both its flavour and pharmacological nature are perfectly suited to the flavours and natures of Chinese *cai*. Beer promotes digestion, helping the stomach to deal with the many different types of food ingested during the course of a typical Chinese meal. And chilled beer is probably the world's most effective thirst-quencher. Many spicy Chinese dishes leave the palate thirsty for cool liquid refreshment, and you can resort to beer often during the course of a meal without risking excess intoxication, as you do with more traditional Chinese beverages. At formal banquets, beer is usually provided along with a potent spirit used for toasting. If you use beer to toast, however, be sure to use small (four to six ounce) tumblers because most Chinese toasts demand that you *gan-bei*! or 'bottoms up!'

The most traditional Chinese banquet beverage is *Shaoxing* wine, a famous rice-derived wine of Chekiang (Zhejiang) province. It is served piping hot in small liqueur glasses and is often flavoured with preserved plums or slices of fresh lemon. It has the same advantages of beer: it is made from grain, so its flavour and nature suit the requirements of Chinese cuisine. Served hot, it effectively cleanses the palate of residual oils and tastes, as does beer's carbonation. Since it is less than 40 proof, *Shaoxing* wine may also be drunk in copious quantities without risking excessive intoxication. Mr. James Wei, Taipei's (Taibei's) master gourmet and consummate banqueteer, insists that hot *Shaoxing* is the only appropriate beverage to drink at Chinese banquets. His advice, which cites the authority of the Sage himself, is instructive and convincing:

You must drink Shaoxing at blood temperature. When cold, reject. Drink with full heart and open throat. Remember that over-indulgence brings neither headache nor thirst in the morning. Remember, also, that while Confucius, a diner of moderation, argued that the meat a man ate should not be enough to make his breath smell of meat rather than rice, he imposed no limit on wine consumption, so long as the diner 'did not become disorderly.'

Besides beer and *Shaoxing*, there are many other traditional Chinese liquors which commonly appear on banquet tables in China and elsewhere in the Orient. The most famous is the fiery *mao-tai*, which Zhou Enlai used to toast Richard Nixon during his visit to Peking (Beijing). *Da-zhu, bai-ga'r*, and *gaoliang*, similar in strength and taste, are also common toasting drinks. Beginners are advised to approach these with caution at banquets. None are likely choices for home consumption in the West.

The aromatic Chinese wines are far better choices for Western palates. Kweilin's (Guilin's) 'Cassia Blossom Wine' (*gui-hua-jiu*) tastes like a light, fragrant vermouth. Nanking's (Nanjing's) viscous 'Sealed Jug Wine' (feng-gang-jiu) is vaguely reminiscent of a good German dessert wine on the palate, although it is made of rice. There are wines made from fruits, wines flavoured with honey and herbs, medicinal wines, and many others. All told, China's far-flung provinces probably produce as varied an array of alcoholic beverages as all of Europe. The best are available the world over, wherever Chinese products are sold.

It remains an issue of continuing debate among Western connoisseurs of Chinese food whether fine Western grape wines go well with Chinese food. In our opinion, they do not. The delicate bouquets of fine French and California wines are lost among the strong flavours and powerful aromas of Chinese food. Nor are they strong enough to effectively clear the palate with each sip, an important function of wine at Chinese banquets. However, should you prefer drinking Western grape wines with Chinese food, the best choices are rosé and other sparkling wines. Their carbonation helps clear the palate and throat, which, in addition to facilitating better appreciation of the food, also permits the subtle flavours of the wine to come through.

One of the most popular banquet beverages among wealthy gourmets in Hong Kong, Singapore, and Taipei (Taibei) is good French cognac. This is an excellent choice, both for toasting and for taste. Cognac is far smoother and more pleasant tasting than any of the traditional Chinese spirits used for toasting, and it is not as strong. Unlike French wine, however, cognac is strong enough to effectively cleanse the palate and throat. Distilled from grape wine, cognac possesses the fragrant bouquet of wine in concentrated form, which enables it to penetrate the strong flavours of Chinese food and be savoured by the palate. Though cognac is a fairly strong drink, taken on a stomach full of good Chinese food, it does not intoxicate as readily as when drunk by itself. At Chinese meals, cognac should be served in small, one ounce liqueur glasses, which may be 'bottomed-up' for toasts without excessive intake.

Other Western spirits may also be served in this manner with Chinese food. Scotch, bourbon, vodka, and gin are acceptable substitutes for Chinese spirits. They should be served 'straight' in liqueur glasses, or with a little water and ice in small tumblers.

Iced drinks, especially sweet colas, should be avoided with Chinese food — as with all food. The concentrated sweeteners and artificial flavours used to manufacture such beverages

clog the palate and numb its sensitivity to subtle fresh flavours. Ice-cold liquids of any kind numb the palate and sinuses. They also freeze the ducts which secrete digestive juices into the stomach, effectively delaying digestion and absorption of ingested food for several hours. Nothing could be worse for the aesthetic appreciation and harmonious digestion of gourmet food than ice-cold, artificially flavoured drinks.

For teetotalers, hot tea is indeed the best banquet beverage. Hot tea clears the palate and throat better than any other drink, and many Chinese gourmets always keep a cup of fragrant hot tea steaming next to their beer and toasting glasses. Tea also facilitates the harmonious blending of foods in the stomach and promotes digestion.

Toasting is the customary method of drinking at Chinese banquets. Rarely is one permitted to raise a glass to his lips alone. Usually the host starts the ball rolling at the beginning of the banquet by proposing a toast to his guests and to the occasion of the banquet. Thereafter, toasting continues throughout the meal, and anyone may propose a toast to anything. Rapturous toasts are often proposed to a particularly good dish or a clever comment, to a good friend who missed the banquet, to the host and the chef, and to anything else that comes to mind. The toasts tend to wax more eloquent as the meal progresses. It is considered impolite not to respond to a toast which is directed at you, but those who sincerely wish to avoid liquor may substitute tea, or even water, in a symbolic gesture.

In China, drinking is an extension of eating and is pursued in the same spirit of robust enjoyment and gourmet refinement. Wines and spirits permit more complete aesthetic enjoyment of good food and facilitate its digestion and absorption in the system. Even the Bible suggests that man 'take a little wine for the stomach's sake.' Furthermore, wines and spirits elevate, in comfortable increments, the mood of each guest and of the banquet in general, greatly enhancing the spirit of communal camaraderie which is so vital to Chinese eating habits. By the end of a Chinese banquet, everyone at the table should feel the cherished 'rapture of drinking and wine's dizzy joy,' which the 'Drunken Dragon' Li Bo insisted was the exclusive domain of wine-tipplers.

The variety of China's traditional wines and spirits is almost as great as the variety of foods. In China there's a drink for every occasion and season: warming wines for winter, cooling ones for summer; strong herbal wines for potency, potent straight spirits for toasting at banquets; like Yin and Yang, food and drink in China are always combined for maximum balance and harmony.

GLOSSARY

ABALONE:
A mollusc, the hard outer shell of which is removed to obtain its firm textured meat. Sold canned in water, dried or fresh. Canned abalone requires minimal cooking and is suited to cold or sautéd dishes. The dried type requires lengthy soaking and slow-simmering to soften and is used in braised dishes, while the fresh fish, if obtainable, can be used for all types of dishes, but also requires lengthy cooking to tenderise.

ANISE, STAR:
See star anise.

BAMBOO SHOOTS:
Rapid sprouting edible shoots from certain bamboo plants. The tough outer leaves must be removed before cooking the internal 'point.' Available fresh in some Chinese food stores, but most commonly sold canned in water. Avoid bamboo shoots canned in soy sauce or with spices, unless specifically required for a recipe.

Winter Bamboo Shoots: More slender and long and have a delicate, though slightly sap-like taste. Also sold canned in water.

Canned bamboo shoots can be kept for several weeks after opening if transferred to a clean jar, covered with cold water and refrigerated. Change the water daily.

BEANCURD:
A soft jelly-like, cream-coloured food made by adding a setting agent to a thin liquid of ground boiled soybeans and water.

SOFT BEANCURD is the first setting of this liquid, produced by weighting lightly. It is usually sold in square pieces about 7.5 cm (2½ in) in size and 3.5 cm (1⅓ in) deep.

Soft beancurd can be purchased in cans, packed in water, but the consistency is harder and the flavour stronger than the fresh kind, making it suitable only for braised dishes or soups.

Powdered preparations are available, but few give more than reasonably satisfactory results. Refer to page 389 for instructions on making fresh soft beancurd. Store beancurd for several days in the refrigerator covered with cold water and plastic wrap. Change the water daily.

Dry Beancurd: Made by pressing soft beancurd with heavier weights for an extra 30 minutes or so. Shredded dry beancurd is used in sautéd and braised dishes and in salads.

Fried Beancurd Cubes are obtained by deep-frying cubes of dry beancurd until the surface is crisp and golden and the inside practically dried up. They store well in an airtight jar.

Fermented Beancurd: Otherwise known as Chinese cheese for its resemblance in taste to a strong blue-vein cow's milk cheese. Cubes of dry beancurd are cured in a mixture of Chinese wine, salt, and chopped fresh chillies to produce a red-coloured, very salty and pungent ingredient used as a seasoning and condiment. It is usually mashed and mixed with a little of its liquid before use.

Dried Beancurd Skins: The residue from beancurd milk forms into a thick yellow coloured semi-transparent sheet which is dried and used as an edible food wrapping and an ingredient in vegetarian and braised dishes. Specialist shops stock the very large round skins typical of Shanghai beancurd makers, these being large enough to make wrappers for about 12 rolls. Packaged dried beancurd is slightly more fragile and comes in smaller pieces which usually result in more wastage than the larger kind. Beancurd skins should be gently dabbed with a fairly damp cloth until soft enough to fold, before use. Packaged dried beancurd skins may need to be soaked until soft enough to handle.

Rolled Beancurd Skins: The same product as above, but before drying the sheets are pleated to produce wrinkled-looking sticks. Used in vegetarian dishes, braised dishes, and soups as a main ingredient. They are usually deep-fried before use, which makes them turn crisp and bubbly.

BEAN PASTES/DRIED BEAN SEASONINGS: A variety of useful strong-tasting seasoning pastes and sauces are made using fermented soybeans as the prime ingredient. Bean pastes can be stored for months in screw-top jars and do not require refrigeration except in very hot climates.

Soybean Paste: A thick, dark brown and salty seasoning paste made with the addition of flour, salt, and water. Used frequently in Cantonese cooking and also in Northern and Western cooking, it gives a rich salty taste. Substitute dark soy sauce or oyster sauce.

Sweet Bean Paste: Soybeans fermented with salt, sugar, and seasonings produce this rich and salty sweet sauce which is useful in marinades, as a seasoning and as a delicious dip for roasted meats. The following sauce (hoisin sauce) is a commercially labelled product having similar qualities as sweet bean paste, for which it makes an acceptable substitute.

Hoisin Sauce: Sold in cans, jars, and bottles. Hoisin sauce follows a basic traditional recipe, but varies considerably in taste and thickness from brand to brand. Use as a substitute for sweet bean paste, above, or as a dip in place of 'duck' sauce on page 385.

It will keep for several months without refrigeration.

Hot Bean Paste: Fermented mashed soybeans, salt, spices, garlic, and chillies are used to make this black, thick seasoning paste which adds strong and piquant flavour to many types of dishes. There are many variations on the mixture and its consistency, being from very hot and pasty, to almost whole beans with whole or sliced garlic and chilli pieces in a thin salty sauce. All give similar results.

Hot Black Bean Sauce: Similar to the above, with a well-balanced combination of whole black beans, mashed chillies and garlic in a rich-tasting sauce. Substitute any of the hot bean paste varieties or use fermented black beans and chopped red chilli peppers.

Yellow Bean Sauce: A salty sauce of fermented whole yellow soybeans. Soybean paste or Japanese yellow miso, see below, are good substitutes.

Fermented Black Beans: Soft, dried, salted, black beans used as a flavouring. May be labelled as salted or preserved black beans. Keep indefinitely in a screw top jar. Should be washed and dried before use.

Red Bean Paste, Sweet: Not a seasoning but a sweet-tasting paste used for stuffings in cakes and buns and as a sweet soup. See red bean paste, sweet, following.

BEAN SHEETS:
See noodles.

BEAN SPROUTS:
Sprouted mung or soybeans resulting in a crisp fresh-flavoured vegetable used in much Chinese cooking. Sold fresh or canned in water, the latter having lost much of its particular taste and crispness in the canning process. Fresh sprouts can be kept for at least a week in a sealed plastic bag or box. They can be sprouted at home using the kits supplied at health food or organic gardening centres.

Mung sprouts have a more delicate taste and are smaller in size than the soy sprouts which have large yellow pods.

'Silver' Sprouts:
Mung sprouts with roots and seed pods removed. They have a clear, silvery appearance when cooked.

BITTER MELON:
A nobbled cucumber-like vegetable with soft flesh, a central seed core, and strong bitter taste. Best used in braised dishes and often stuffed. Sold fresh or canned in water.

BIRDS' NESTS:
The edible nest made by a specie of swift or swallow which nest in caves off the coast of Southern China and Thailand. The dangerous methods employed in gathering the nests from the ceilings of these enormous caves makes them one of the most expensive of the Chinese ingredients. They are highly regarded equally by Chinese gourmets for their delicate taste and soft gelatinous, but very

slightly crunchy texture, and by those who believe in their purifying, tonifying qualities.

BOK CHOY:
See Chinese vegetables.

BROWN SUGAR:
See sugar, brown (sticks).

BROWN (BLACK) VINEGAR:
See vinegar.

CASHEW NUTS:
The raw, unsalted nuts should be used for Chinese cooking, and are generally deep-fried until golden and crisp before use. If unobtainable, use salted roasted nuts and blanch in boiling water before using. Substitute almonds.

CANDY, ROCK (SUGAR):
Crystal-like cubes of compressed white sugar, used in braised dishes to give a rich shine to meat and sauce. It requires time to dissolve and is best lightly crushed before use. Substitute white granulated sugar.

Use rock candy sugar in those dishes, particularly sweets, which require a very clear syrup or stock.

CARAMELIZED SUGAR:
Made by melting white sugar in a small amount of very hot vegetable oil until the mixture turns into a sticky golden syrup. Often used as the base of sweet and sour dishes, and as a glaze for fruit and vegetables (see candied apples, page 90).

CHENG MIEN:
See flour.

CHESTNUTS, WATER:
See water chestnuts.

CHICKEN STOCK:
Used in many Chinese dishes and sauces. See recipe, page 388, or use a crumbled chicken stock cube or chicken stock powder mixed with water and adjust the amount of salt accordingly.

CHICKEN FAT (CHICKEN GREASE), RENDERED:
A rich fat obtained by cooking pieces of fresh chicken fat (see page 387). Used more for flavouring and to give a shine to sauces than as a cooking medium.

CHILLI OIL:
A very hot flavouring oil made by infusing chilli flakes in cooking oil (see page 395). If unavailable, use commercial chilli sauce.

CHILLI PEPPERS, HOT RED:
Fresh red chilli peppers, a thin, long red (or green when unripe) fruit of the capsicum (bell pepper) family. The seeds should be removed for a milder taste.

Chillies are dried and crushed to obtain chilli flakes, and are preserved in a vinegar and salt solution for storage and to make the PICKLED RED CHILLIES, common in Western Chinese dishes.

CHINESE BROWN PEPPERCORNS:
Also known as Szechuan (Sichuan) peppercorns, flower pepper, fagara or xanthoxylum. They bear little resemblance to black peppercorns, being small berry-like seeds in a red-brown skin and with a mildly anise flavoured taste. Brown peppercorns keep indefinitely in a screwtop jar in dry conditions. They are at their best if lightly toasted in a dry frying pan before use. Used in combination with table or kosher salt to produce CHINESE PEPPER-SALT (see recipe page 384).

CHINESE (CELERY) CABBAGE:
See Chinese vegetables.

CHINESE HAM:
A top quality ham produced primarily in Yunnan province and in Chekiang (Zhejiang) where *chin hau* ham is the most highly regarded. Processed by salting and smoking, the ham has an almost black skin which should be removed before use.

Smithfield or very good quality salt-cured and smoked ham can be substituted.

CHINESE PICKLES:
Sweet-tasting mixtures of ginger, onions, gourds, and peppers preserved in a sweet syrup. They may be marketed as *chow chow* or mixed pickles. Keep indefinitely in a screw-top jar without refrigeration.

CHINESE SAUSAGE:
Dried thin sausages made with pork, pork fat, pork liver, and preservatives. Sold by most Chinese food stockists and available in some delicatessens. Should be steamed to soften, before use. They keep indefinitely in dry conditions. Substitute sticks of Chinese or cured ham or Spanish 'chorizo' sausages.

CHINESE VEGETABLES:
An extensive range of leafy green vegetables are grown in China. Increasingly, they are becoming available in the West from the larger Chinese food suppliers, particularly in areas with sizeable Chinese populations.

Bok Choy or *Pau Ts'ai*: Dark green leaves on crisp milk-white stems. The whole vegetable may be used, or the outer leaves removed and the inner tightly packed heart used in recipes requiring vegetable hearts. A crisp-textured, mild-tasting vegetable. May be known as Chinese (or Chinese white) cabbage.

Broccoli, Chinese: Unlike the Western type of broccoli, of which the large flowering head is the only part that is eaten, Chinese broccoli is picked while quite young and the dark green leaves and thick round green stems cooked in the same way as choy sum following, which it closely resembles.

Choy Sum: This vegetable has thick round green stems, sparsely leafed and with small yellow flowered heads. The taste is very slightly bitter. The stems may be peeled and cooked as a vegetable by themselves, though usually the whole stalk, cut into two or three pieces, is used.

Chinese (Celery) Cabbage: Actually the pale yellow, tightly packed Tientsin (Tianjin) cabbage, which has a light but distinct taste. If unobtainable, use white cabbage or *bok choy*.

Kale: Dark green, small-leafed vegetable not unlike spinach, which can be substituted.

Mustard: A cabbage-like plant with thick pale green stems and large green leaves. It has a slightly pungent, almost bitter taste. Used fresh, but more commonly as a preserved vegetable or pickle, see preserved vegetables.

Pea Sprouts/Leaves: Small bright green leaves from a sweet pea plant. Very delicate flavour. Substitute young spinach leaves.

Water Spinach: Deep green pointed leaves on long white tubular stems are very mild in taste. Young spinach could be substituted.

CHOY SUM:
See above, Chinese vegetables.

CHRYSANTHEMUM:
The petals, preferably white, of fresh chrysanthemum flowers are used as a delicately flavoured ingredient and as a garnish for game dishes, in particular dishes made with snake meat.

The leaves and buds of a different type of chrysanthemum, though one quite similar to that cultivated domestically, are used as a fresh-flavoured vegetable. Substitute spinach leaves.

CINNAMON:
The bark and flowers of the cassia, or cinnamon tree, are used frequently as an aromatic spice in Chinese cooking. Smaller quantities of powdered or stick cinnamon, or a cinnamon stick infused in boiling water, can be used as a subsititute.

CORIANDER, FRESH:
Otherwise known as Chinese parsley. The leafy young coriander plant is actually a type of flat-leafed parsley closely related to the 'cilantro' used in Mexican cooking, which is an excellent substitute.

Coriander can be grown in a domestic herb bed and even sprouted on damp cotton wool in the kitchen. It goes to seed quickly so should be used when the plants reach about 15 cm (6 in). To store fresh coriander, wash well and shake out excess water. Place in a sealed plastic box and refrigerate for up to 6 days.

CORN, SWEET YOUNG:
See sweet corn.

CORNFLOUR (CORNSTARCH):
See flour.

DATES, BLACK:
Used in mashed form as a filling for cakes and pastries, and as a substitute for Chinese red dates, see below.

DATES, CHINESE RED:
Small, wrinkled, dried red fruit with a strong date-plum taste. Used in braised dishes and in sweets. Substitute black dates or Japanese dried plums, 'umeboshi.'

DRY BEANCURD:
See beancurd.

'DUCK SAUCE':
A blend of sweet bean paste, sugar, and sesame oil used as a dip for Peking duck and many other crisp roasted meats. See recipe page 385, or substitute sweet bean paste, hoisin sauce or plum sauce.

ENRICHED STOCK:
Often called 'superior stock' for its rich flavour. Basically chicken bone stock with additives of ham hock, pork, and duck bones to give a strong, rich flavour and a cream-white colour (see recipe page 388).

As a substitute, use chicken stock with additional crumbled chicken stock cube or chicken powder, or a slice of ham or streaky bacon.

FA TS'AI (FAT CHOY, Cantonese):
A dark greenish-brown dried seaweed resembling human hair, and sometimes known as hair vegetable or black moss. No substitute. Used in dishes served at Chinese New Year because of its similar connotation of prosperity as the New Year greeting, *Kung Hei Fat Choy.*

FERMENTED BEANCURD:
See beancurd.

FERMENTED BLACK BEANS:
See bean pastes/dried bean seasonings.

FERMENTED SWEET RICE:
Cooked glutinous rice with a yeast additive, resulting in fermentation. Both the rice and the liquor are used in dishes of Northern and Eastern origin. See details for making sweet rice fermentation, page 187. See also rice, following.

FISH LIPS:
The dried mouth sections of certain types of very large fish. Used as an ingredient in seafood dishes. Has a soft almost gelatinous texture and a mild though distinct fishy taste. See page 392 for directions on the preparation of fish lips.

FISH MAW:
A light and bubbly textured tissue removed from the stomachs of very large fish. Sold dried in large sheets resembling polyurethane foam. Should be soaked to soften and remove the fishy smell before use. If unavailable, substitute gluten balls or rolled beancurd sticks, agar agar strips, or salted jellyfish.

FISH, SALTED:
Salt-cured and sun-dried fish used as a flavouring agent and occasionally as a main ingredient. Should be soaked in vegetable oil until softened, then deep-fried. Brill fish is said to have the best flavour. It has a strong, pungent flavour and aroma when cooked. Keeps indefinitely in dry conditions. Substitute dried shrimps.

'FIVE FLOWERED' PORK:
Belly pork (fresh bacon), the cut from the lower part of the stomach beneath the rib cage. So named because of its five alternating layers of meat and fat.

FIVE SPICE POWDER:
A blend of five aromatic spices used as a seasoning and condiment. Chinese brown peppercorns, cinnamon bark, clove, fennel, and star anise are the components.

Available commercially in both Western and Chinese spice ranges. Keeps indefinitely in an airtight jar (see also page 386).

FLOURS:

Cornflour (Cornstarch): Finely milled maize flour used as a thickener for sauces in preference to ordinary flour as it blends in easily and results in a transparent, viscous sauce.

Also used in batters and for coating fried foods. Water chestnut flour (see below) gives a crisper and finer textured batter.

Some cooks prefer mung bean flour for thickening as it produces thicker sauces.

Cheng Mien (Tang Fun): Gluten-free flour used in Chinese pastry making. It turns almost transparent when mixed with boiling water and makes unique clear wrappers for dumplings. Also used to make 'silver pin' noodles (see page 352).

If unobtainable, use potato starch (flour).

Flour: When mentioned in all recipes in this book, flour refers to plain or all purpose non-leavened wheat flour.

Glutinous Rice Powder (Flour): A fine white flour made from ground glutinous rice. Used in making cakes and puddings and as a binding agent. Substitute plain flour.

Potato Flour: Finely ground dried potato. Very starchy. Use as a thickener and for pastry making. Substitute taro flour, below.

Rice Flour: Finely ground rice. Used in sweets and cake making.

Spiced Rice Powder: See SPICED RICE POWDER and also page 386.

Taro Flour: Finely ground dried taro root. Excellent as a thickener and binding agent and in pastry making.

Water Chestnut Powder (Flour): Ground dried water chestnuts. Used in

sweets making and as a coating or in batters for deep-fried foods. Substitute cornflour (cornstarch).

FUNGUS, WHITE (SNOW):
Pale cream-coloured crinkly lichin used as an ingredient in meat, vegetarian, and sweet dishes. For directions on the preparation of dried white fungus, see page 393. Keeps well in dry conditions.

Brown ('Wood Ear'): A dark brown ear-shaped lichin said to have high nutritional content. Used to impart its particular musty taste and crunchy texture to many meat dishes, particularly in Northern cooking. Also very important as an ingredient in vegetarian cooking.

Soak to soften, then cut into small pieces before use. Keeps well in dry conditions.

GARLIC CHIVES:
Pale green shoots resembling chives, but with a mild though distinct garlic flavour. Often grown under cover to reduce the colour to the lightest yellow green and keep the flavour very mild. Used when milder tastes than those imparted by spring onions (scallions) and garlic are required in a dish.

To store, seal in a plastic bag or box and refrigerate for up to a week.

GINGER, FRESH:
The root of the rhizome ginger, with a crinkling greyish-yellow skin and fibrous flesh. Older ginger is stronger in taste than YOUNG GINGER which has a pale cream, smooth skin and pink buds.

Fresh ginger should be peeled before use and may be preserved by infusing in rice wine or dry sherry to produce GINGER WINE (see page 387), or it may be grated and the juice extracted to produce GINGER JUICE (see also page 387).

Powdered and dried root ginger are not suitable substitutes, having a quite different flavour. Fresh ginger is now readily available but, if necessary, substitute sweet or salt-pickled ginger which can be bought at both Chinese and Japanese food stockists.

GINGER AND ONION INFUSION:
A mildly flavoured seasoning liquid made by infusing grated ginger and chopped spring onions (scallions) in hot water (see page 386). Substitute ginger juice in smaller amounts.

GINGKO NUTS:
Small oval shaped white nuts, sold dried or in cans packed in water. May also be labelled 'White Nuts'. A fresh crisp nutty flavour which is useful in stuffings, braised dishes and soups. If unavailable, substitute lotus seeds, see below.

GLUTEN BALLS (mien jin pau):
Round light balls made from wheat gluten and water. Used primarily as an

ingredient in vegetarian dishes. If unavailable, omit or use fried rolled beancurd skins. Deep-fry before use.

GLUTINOUS RICE:
See rice.

GLUTINOUS RICE POWDER (FLOUR):
See flours.

GOLDEN MUSHROOMS:
See mushrooms.

GOLDEN NEEDLES (DRIED LILY FLOWERS):
The flower buds of the tiger lily. Used to impart a rich, slightly musky flavour to stewed and vegetarian dishes. Sold dried and should be soaked before use. If unobtainable, omit from the dish.

GUEI HWA:
Cassia flower wine.

HAM, CHINESE:
See Chinese ham.

HOISIN SAUCE:
See bean pastes/dried bean seasonings.

HOT BLACK BEAN SAUCE:
See bean pastes/dried bean seasonings.

HOT BEAN PASTE:
See bean pastes/dried bean seasonings.

JELLYFISH, SALTED:
A gelatinous oceanic 'fish' with a flat saucer-shaped body and a proliferation of long tentacles. The body is salted, dried, and sold in flat squares, or it may be shredded before drying. For the preparation of dried salted jellyfish, see page 392.

KALE:
See Chinese vegetables.

LARD:
Rendered pork fat. A rich-tasting white fat used as a cooking medium, particularly for stir-fried dishes and in sweets and pastry making (see cooking oil, page 395).

LAVER:
Dark greenish black, paper-thin sheets of a compressed form of mossy seaweed. Used as an ingredient mainly in soups. Available from Chinese and Japanese food suppliers ('nori' in Japanese). Should be lightly toasted over a naked flame before use to make crisp. Store in an airtight container. Keeps well in dry conditions. *Fa ts'ai (fat choy)*, see above, could be used as an alternative.

LILY FLOWERS, DRIED:
See golden needles.

LOTUS LEAVES:
Sold in dried form for use as a food wrapper. Fresh leaves, if available can also be used after blanching to clean and soften.

LOTUS ROOT:
An elongated tubular root growth of the lotus plant, characterised by a series of even-shaped round holes running the length of the root. Usually cut in cross-section to produce an attractive flower shaped slice. The flesh is crisp and bland tasting. Used as a vegetable and in certain sweet dishes.

Occasionally sold fresh, and usually available canned in water. Also available dried and must be soaked to soften before use. The fresh root must be thoroughly washed, peeled and boiled until tender.

LOTUS SEEDS:
The hard oval-shaped seeds found in the flat-faced fleshy centres of lotus blossoms. Used as an ingredient in soups, stews, and sweets and also mashed to make a sweet paste, see below. Sold in dried, canned, or fresh form. The dried nuts must be soaked to soften before use. The nuts have a bitter tasting central core which should be removed.

LOTUS SEED PASTE:
A sweet, thick, almost dry paste made with mashed cooked lotus seeds, sugar, and vegetable oil or lard. Used as a sweet filling for buns and pastries (see recipe page 368, steamed buns with lotus seed filling).

MALT SUGAR (MALTOSE):
A thick, very sticky molasses-like substance extracted from wheat. Used to glaze roast meats, notably Peking duck. If unobtainable, use treacle, golden syrup, or undiluted clear honey or light corn syrup as alternatives.

MISO PASTE:
A Japanese product made by combining fermented soybeans with salt and seasonings. Sold in varying grades from dark red-brown to a pale yellow coloured paste. The latter makes an excellent substitute for yellow bean sauce (see page 406). Also use as an alternative to wine lees (see page 387), which is not easily obtainable. Dark miso paste is a suitable alternative to soybean paste, see above, as its preparation is similarly based on soy sauce.

M.S.G. (MONOSODIUM GLUTAMATE):
Also known variously as taste powder, gourmet powder, or *ve tsin*. A crystalline flavouring agent which heightens the natural flavours of meat and vegetables and acts as a tenderiser on meats. Used prodigously in Chinese cooking, but may be omitted without undue alteration to the taste of a dish. Many doctors today discourage its use.

MUSHROOMS:
There are a number of different mushrooms used in Chinese cooking. Most common are the large DRIED

BLACK MUSHROOMS which are readily available, though costly. The best have thick caps of a darkish brown colouring with pale cream-coloured undersides. They must be soaked to soften before use, and have the stems removed.

Champignons: Canned button mushrooms.

Golden Mushrooms are small capped golden-coloured mushrooms with characteristic long thin stems. Sold canned in water. Substitute champignons. Available from Chinese or Japanese food stockists.

Peking Mushrooms are very large, creamy yellow-coloured mushrooms with long edible stems. Sold dried or canned in water, they have a good mushroom flavour and aroma and are excellent in braised dishes and stir-fried. Can be used as a substitute for dried black mushrooms or straw mushrooms, below.

Straw Mushrooms: Globe-shaped mushrooms with a greyish-black outer skin and a cream-coloured layered interior. Usually available canned in water. To store, cover with cold water and change the water daily. Fresh straw mushrooms do not keep for more than a few days in the refrigerator.

MUSTARD GREENS (LEAVES), SALTED:
See preserved vegetables.

MUSTARD ROOT, SALTED:
See preserved vegetables.

MUSTARD GREENS:
See Chinese vegetables.

NOODLES:
A variety of fresh and dried noodles are used in Chinese cooking, and in certain areas, noodles replace rice as the staple and the accompaniment to meat and vegetable dishes. They are invaluable as snack and breakfast foods and are also used in some sweet dishes. Most noodles are extruded strands of pastes made from water mixed with wheat flour, powdered beans, or powdered rice. In some, eggs are added to provide extra flavour and nourishment. Seafood flavourings are sometimes added to those noodles which will be used in soup noodle dishes.

Egg Noodles, Thin: Long narrow strands of wheat flour and egg paste. Sold dried in 'cakes' or curled strands.

Egg Noodles, Thick: Spaghetti-like thick wheat flour and egg noodles, often sold fresh and also available dried, or 'oiled.' May also be called Shanghai noodles. Fresh noodles keep for at least one week in a sealed plastic bag in the refrigerator.

Flat Noodles: Wheat flour and egg paste processed into thin flat sheets, then shredded into strands about 1 cm (⅓ in) wide. Dried and sold in bundles.

Mien Sien Noodles: Very thin, white-coloured wheat flour and water noodles. Sold dried and occasionally fresh, usually used in soup-based dishes. May be known as thin Shanghai noodles. Substitute rice vermicelli or thin egg noodles.

Rice Vermicelli: Thin extruded rice flour paste noodles. Sold in bundles in dried form. When deep-fried, they expand into a cloud of light-as-air crisp white noodles. Used also in stir-fried dishes and soups. Also known as rice sticks.

Rice Sheets: Rice flour and water paste compressed into flat sheets and steamed. Sold fresh in rolls and used as a wrapper for diced meats and vegetables. Also cut into strips about 1.25 cm (½ in) wide to make RICE RIBBON NOODLES.

Bean Thread Vermicelli: 'Glass' noodles. Extruded semi-transparent mung bean flour noodles. Used mostly in soups and stews where they turn transparent and almost gelatinous in texture. Deep-fried they expand and become light and crisp in the same way as rice vermicelli, which can be substituted. Soak before use, except when deep-frying.

Bean Sheets: Made from a paste of mung bean flour and water, they are rolled into thin sheets and dried to use as an ingredient in soups, stews, and vegetarian dishes. Substitute bean thread vermicelli.

Beancurd Noodles: Extruded paste of ground dried soybeans. A pale yellow colour and slightly thinner than thick egg noodles with the characteristic beancurd smell. Usually sold in dried form, in tangled bundles. Other beancurd 'noodles' are made from shredded dried beancurd skins.

'Silver Pin' Noodles: Hand-made short noodles made with *Cheng Mien* flour (see page 352).

OILS, COOKING:
Peanut oil, pure vegetable oil, and lard are the most common cooking mediums (see page 395 for additional information).

OMENTUM, PORK, CAUL FAT/NET:
A large lace-like sheet of fat which can be purchased from Chinese or Continental food suppliers. Sold by weight, it keeps for 2 - 3 days in the refrigerator and can be frozen. Used to wrap foods before cooking and particularly to form rolls of minced (ground) meats. It holds the foods together while frying, but eventually melts to nothing unless coated with batter or flour, when it forms a crisp crust. Also used to add oil and to seal in moisture in whole poultry or fish. Suggestions are given with the individual recipes for alternatives, if unobtainable.

ONIONS:
See page 394.

ONION AND GINGER INFUSION:
A flavouring solution made with fresh ginger and spring onions (see page 386).

ONION-PEPPER-SALT:
A seasoning combining chopped spring onions (scallions), table salt, and Chinese brown peppercorns (see page 384).

ORANGE PEEL, DRIED:
Actually the sun-dried peel of tangerines or mandarins. Imparts a delicate citrus flavour to stewed dishes and soups, and is used finely chopped in stuffings and meatballs. To prepare, peel the fruit and scrape away the white pith inside. Place in a tray and leave in the sun or in a warm oven until thoroughly dried. Store in an airtight jar. Keeps well in dry conditions.

A 'piece' as required in these recipes is approximately one-quarter of an average-sized peel.

OYSTERS, DRIED:
Sun-dried and lightly salt-cured oysters. Must be soaked overnight and thoroughly rinsed before use. Fresh oysters removed from the shells may be used in most recipes.

OYSTER SAUCE:
A dark brown, viscous, and salty sauce used both as a flavouring and condiment. For the latter, the more expensive brands are recommended for their superior flavour and less salty taste.

PEA SPROUTS:
See Chinese vegetables.

PEPPER-SALT, CHINESE:
A seasoning and condiment made from a mixture of table salt and ground Chinese brown peppercorns (see page 384). Keeps well in dry conditions.

PICKLED VEGETABLES:
See preserved vegetables.

PICKLED RED CHILLI PEPPERS:
Fresh red chilli peppers preserved in a vinegar and brine solution. Used to add hot taste and flavour to dishes from the West of China. Substitute dried or fresh red chilli peppers.

PICKLES, CHINESE SWEET:
See Chinese pickles.

PIGEON EGGS:
See quail eggs.

PINE SEEDS (NUTS):
Small, cream-coloured seeds with a layered construction, usually available in dried form from Middle Eastern food stockists. May also be known as pine kernels and in some Chinese reference books as olive seeds/beans. If unobtainable, use chopped raw cashew nuts.

PLUM SAUCE:
A commercial preparation of mashed

plums and seasonings. Used as a sauce dip for roast meats and occasionally as a seasoning in stir-fried dishes. Readily available in jars and small cans. Substitute hoisin sauce.

PRAWN CRACKERS:
Compressed slivers of shrimp and flour paste. When deep-fried, they expand into large, almost transparent crisps. Used as a tasty edible garnish for roasted and deep-fried poultry. Sold as 'krupuk' or 'kroepuk' in Malaysian/Chinese food stores.

PRESERVED VEGETABLES:
Certain salt-cured vegetables are used to add their pungent, salty flavour to Chinese cooking. Preserved mustard is the most common and comes in two forms, the salty MUSTARD GREENS (LEAVES) and the thick stem/root section which needs to be shredded or diced before use and is known as MUSTARD ROOT. Pickled in brine and packaged in large pottery containers, this preserved vegetable keeps indefinitely. Store in an airtight jar. Refrigerate in hot climates.

Szechuan (Sichuan) Pickle: Sold in jars or small cans, Szechuan (Sichuan) pickles are made from salt and chilli-pickled cabbage or mustard and have a strong, salty and hot flavour. Often served as an accompaniment to Northern or Western Chinese meals.

Pickled Cabbage: Whole young *bok choy* or mustard plants pickled in brine and packed into 500 g (1 lb) cans. Readily available. Transfer to a screw-top jar for storage.

Preserved Vegetables: Soy sauce and salt-cured dried vegetables such as shredded mustard or gourd. Has a strong, vaguely fermented flavour and is used mainly in soups and stewed dishes as the taste is strong and somewhat unrefined. Sold by weight in plastic bags. May also be know as spiced vegetables.

Soy-Preserved Ginger/Cucumber: Thinly sliced young ginger or cucumber preserved with soy sauce, salt, and spices. Strong in taste and dark brown-black in colour. Substitute other soy sauce-preserved vegetables or use pickled ginger or cabbage and additional soy sauce to balance the recipe, or omit completely.

QUAIL EGGS/PIGEON EGGS:
Quail eggs, hard boiled (hard cooked) and packed in water, are readily available in canned form. Pigeon eggs are harder to obtain and slightly larger in size. Substitute the smallest size of chicken eggs available, as the taste differs only minimally.

RADISH, GIANT WHITE (ICICLE):
May be called long turnip or 'daikon' (Japanese). A white-skinned, crisp-textured radish with a sharp taste which

turns sweet when cooked. Substitute sweet white turnips.

RED BEAN PASTE, SWEET:
A thick, sweet mixture made by boiling kidney beans or a smaller variety of dried red beans with sugar until reduced to a paste, then lard or oil is added and the mixture further cooked until fairly dry and thick. Used as a filling for cakes and sweet buns and in a variety of desserts (see page 389).

RED DATES, DRIED:
See dates, dried red.

RED FERMENTED RICE:
See wine lees.

RED VINEGAR:
See vinegar.

RICE:

Short Grain White: Most commonly used in Chinese cooking (see also page 354).

Long Grain: Used occasionally in rice dishes and for stuffings and sweets.

Glutinous: Comes in short and long grain varieties. A cloudy white appearance in comparison to ordinary rice which has a pearly white. It cooks to a sticky thick mass, hence the common name 'sticky rice.' Most often used for sweets and cake-making and used to make spiced rice powder, below. Also used in the manufacture of Chinese wines.

Red Fermented Rice: See wine lees.

Sweet Fermented Rice: Cooked glutinous rice treated with beer (brewers') yeast to produce a fermentation with a strong brewed flavour. Used as a flavouring agent in many Northern Chinese dishes, particularly with seafood and served as a sweet with sugar syrup and fresh fruit (see page 387).

Spiced Rice (Powder): See spiced rice powder.

Rice Paper, Edible: More commonly made with potato flour. Paper-thin sheets of compressed and dried paste, used as an edible food wrapping. Readily available and keeps well in dry conditions.

Rice Sheets: See noodles.
Rice Wine: See wines.

ROCK CANDY (SUGAR):
See Candy, Rock (Sugar).

ROSE DEW WINE:
See wines.

SALT-FISH:
See Fish, Salted.

SALTED MUSTARD ROOT/GREEN (LEAVES):
See preserved vegetables.

SALTED YELLOW BEAN SAUCE:
See bean pastes/dried bean seasonings.

SALTPETRE:
A crystalline substance used as a meat preservative. Also known as potassium nitrate or niter.

SEA CUCUMBER, DRIED:
Also known as SEA SLUGS. Brown to black sea creatures with soft, almost gelatinous fresh and tubular nobbled bodies resembling cucumbers. Sizes vary from 5 cm (2 in) to about 30 cm (12 in). Sold dried and will keep indefinitely in dry conditions (see page 392 for preparation details).

SESAME OIL:
A brownish, strong-flavoured cooking and seasoning oil extracted from sesame seeds. Readily available and keeps well without refrigeration. Sold in bottles and cans of varying sizes. Strong in taste. May be omitted.

SESAME PASTE:
Sold in both Chinese and Middle Eastern food stores. A yellow thick paste made from ground white sesame seeds. Known in the Middle East as 'tahini.' The Chinese variety is stronger in taste and more suitable for these recipes. Smooth peanut butter (paste) is a reasonable substitute. Keeps for several months in the refrigerator.

SESAME SEEDS:
Small flat oval-shaped seeds which come in white and black colours. Both have a similar flavour and are used as an ingredient in sweets, as a garnish, and as a coating for fried foods. Should be lightly toasted in a dry pan before use, except when being fried. Store in an airtight jar. Keep indefinitely in dry conditions.

SCALLOPS, DRIED:
May be called 'CONPOY' in Chinese stores. Round golden-brown discs cut from a type of elongated round sea scallop. Sun-dried and strong flavoured. One of the most expensive of the Chinese dried ingredients and used in small quantities mainly as a flavouring agent.

Must be soaked and steamed or simmered to soften. Substitute dried shrimps, or omit if unobtainable.

SHA CHIA JIANG:
A sweet and salty sauce used as a condiment and seasoning. Made from a mixture of ground peanuts, spices, garlic and dried shrimps. The nearest equivalent is commercially prepared satay sauce, or use sweet bean paste or hoisin sauce.

SHARK'S FIN:
Edible gelatinous thread-like strands called 'needles' from the fins of sharks. Also sold in whole form for cooking in braised dishes. Choose those that are palest cream in colour and free of specks of skin or tissue. Dried shark's fin keeps indefinitely in dry conditions. Expensive.

Substitute 'silver pin' noodles or bean thread vermicelli, or use these to supplement shark's fin in soups, for economy (see page 393 for preparation of dried shark's fin).

SHARK'S SKIN:
The thick greyish, dried skin from a shark. Sold in sheets. For method of preparation of dried shark's skin, see page 393. Substitute fish maw, page 392.

SHRIMP EGGS, DRIED:
Minute granular red shrimp or prawn eggs, sold dried. Used to add flavour to sauces, stuffings, soups, and noodles. Use ground dried shrimps as a substitute.

SHRIMP SAUCE, CHINESE:
A pale pink, strong flavoured, and salty seasoning paste and condiment. Made from salted, sun-dried ground raw shrimps. The paste is cured, then stored in large underground tanks to ferment. If unobtainable, use anchovy essence or paste.

SHRIMPS, DRIED:
Small peeled shrimps, sun-dried and with a strong shellfish flavour. Used to add taste to stuffings and a variety of dishes. Soak before use. Store indefinitely in an airtight container.

'SILVER PIN' NOODLES:
See noodles.

'SILVER SPROUTS':
See bean sprouts.

'SNOW' FUNGUS:
See fungus.

SOYBEAN PASTE:
See bean pastes/dried bean seasonings.

SOY SAUCE:
There are two main kinds of soy sauce. LIGHT SOY SAUCE is used to add flavour to stir-fried dishes, sauces, and stocks, and as a dip, particularly with fried or roasted meats.
DARK SOY SAUCE is stronger and saltier in taste and colour and is used primarily to add colour and a salty taste. When labelling is not clear, dark soy sauce can be identified by its thicker consistency. Sometimes labelled 'mushroom' soy.

Choose the best quality soy sauce available as the less expensive types or those manufactured in Western countries often have a metallic 'manufactured' taste due principally to insufficient maturation in the fermentation tanks.

Soy sauce keeps almost indefinitely without refrigeration.

SOY-PRESERVED GINGER/CUCUMBER:
See preserved vegetables.

SNOW PEAS:
Also known as mange tout and sugar peas. Flat, bright green pea pods containing very small green peas.

Intended to be eaten whole so should be picked early. Remove the short stem and string before use.

A trellis-grown vegetable, they are easily cultivated domestically and are usually available in better market gardens throughout the year.

SPICE BAG:
A small cloth bag containing five aromatic spices used to impart flavour to stewed dishes. Sold as mixed spice (see also page 386).

SPICED SALT:
Table salt flavoured with five spice powder (see page 384).

SPICED RICE POWDER:
Long grain rice dry-fried with star anise or Chinese brown peppercorns until the rice is golden brown, then ground to a coarse powder (see page 386). Used as a seasoning in steamed dishes.

SPRING ONIONS:
Long-stemmed mild tasting onions, known also as scallions and shallots (see page 394).

SPRING ROLL WRAPPERS:
Paper-thin near-transparent sheets used as edible food wrappers. Can be purchased in frozen form in packs of 20 — 30, and in several sizes. Must be slowly thawed before use and carefully separated. Keep covered with a cloth during use as they dry and crack when exposed to the air (see page 374 for preparation of spring roll wrappers).

SQUID, FRESH:
The tubular fish known also as the cuttlefish or calamari. Only the white-fleshed boneless body section is used, this being first skinned and scored to tenderise (see page 397).

STAR ANISE:
An eight-pointed star-shaped spice with a strong aniseed flavour. Substitute aniseed or fennel, if unavailable. Sold in plastic bags by weight. Store in an airtight jar. Keeps well in dry conditions.

SPARE RIBS:
Some confusion has arisen over this term. In Australia, it applies to thick fingers of 'five flowered' pork on the rind with a few segments of the lower rib bones left intact. American spare ribs have been classified in this book as the actual pork rib after meat has been trimmed away, leaving just a scant covering of meat on the bones.

SUGAR CANDY:
See candy, rock (sugar).

SUGAR, BROWN (STICKS):
Compressed sticks of layered dark and light brown sugar sold in packs of ten. Each stick weighs approximately 45 g (1 ½ oz). Substitute soft brown or raw sugar.

SUGAR, WHITE:
Where sugar is required in a recipe, use granulated white sugar unless otherwise specified.

SUGAR COLOURING:
A dark-brown liquid made from sugar and water and used to add a rich brown colour to sauces and stews. Does not add sweetness to a dish, so do not substitute sugar (see page 388 for details on preparing sugar colouring).

SWEET BEAN PASTE:
See bean pastes/dried bean seasonings

SWEET CORN, YOUNG:
Small whole cobs of young corn sold canned in water. Readily available.

SWEET FERMENTED RICE:
See rice (fermented sweet rice) and also page 387.

SWEET RED BEAN PASTE:
See red bean paste, sweet.

SWEET VINEGAR:
See vinegar, below.

SZECHUAN (SICHUAN) PICKLED (PRESERVED) VEGETABLES:
See preserved vegetables.

VINEGAR:

White: Distilled white vinegar used as an acidulant and to add its sharp sour taste to many sauces, particularly sweet and sour dishes. Use a good quality distilled white vinegar.
Chinese Red: A bright amber-red coloured vinegar distilled from rice and used both in cooking and as a dip, particularly for seafoods. It has a mild, slightly sweet taste. Substitute white vinegar, to taste.
Brown (Black): An almost black-coloured rice vinegar used as a flavouring and condiment. Readily available. Its flavour is mild and soft. Substitute smaller amounts of white vinegar.
Sweet: A pungent tasting, though quite sweet, dark vinegar with limited use in Chinese cooking. Readily available in bottles.

VERMICELLI, BEAN THREAD:
See noodles.

VERMICELLI, RICE:
See noodles.

WATER CHESTNUTS:
Dark brown-skinned bulbs from a type of water plant. The flesh is crisp, white, and with a slightly sweet taste. Sold canned in water and occasionally fresh. Peel fresh-water chestnuts before use. The canned type will keep for several weeks in the refrigerator if covered with fresh water which is changed daily.

In many parts of China, fresh-water chestnuts are threaded onto thin bamboo skewers, soaked in lightly salted water and sold at street-side stalls as a refreshing snack.

WATER CHESTNUT POWDER (FLOUR):
See flours.

WATER SPINACH:
See Chinese vegetables.

WINE, CHINESE:
The yellow coloured rice wine, *Shao Hsing*, is most favoured for Chinese cooking. Dry sherry is a suitable substitute and readibly available, though Japanese 'sake' is even more similar in taste, being also a rice fermentation. Where a sweet rice wine is required, Japanese 'mirin' is the best substitute, though sweet sherry gives good results.

Rose Dew Wine: A strong-flavoured, rose essence liquor. Substitute brandy.

WINE LEES:
A paste-like sour mash of red rice and wine. Very difficult to obtain. Japanese light yellow 'miso' can be used as a substitute. Also known as red fermented rice.

WINE CUBE (WINE BALL):
A type of compressed beer (brewers') yeast used to produce a fermentation, usually of rice (see page 387, fermented sweet rice).

WINTER BAMBOO SHOOTS:
See bamboo shoots.

WINTER MELON:
A large, light-green skinned melon with bland-tasting crisp flesh. Used as a vegetable. Available canned in water. Substitute choko, cucumber, corghette (zucchini), or squash.

'WOOD EAR' FUNGUS:
See fungus.

WONTON WRAPPERS:
Thin pastries made from a high-gluten flour and egg paste. Sold fresh or frozen, and must be slowly thawed before use. Keep moist under a damp cloth during use as they dry and crack easily. If unobtainable, see the recipes on page 376.

YELLOW BEAN SAUCE, SALTED:
See bean pastes/dried bean seasonings.

YUNNAN HAM:
See Chinese Ham.

GUIDE TO RECIPES

RECIPE PREPARATION

This listing is intended as a quick reference to recipes which can be prepared with relative ease, or to those which require varying degrees of time and skill.

Following this listing is a complete list of recipes in their order of appearance in the book.

A. Simple one-step dishes such as stir-fried, poached and stewed dishes and easy to prepare sweets, using common Chinese ingredients and seasonings.

B. Dishes requiring more than one cooking process or more lengthy or complicated preparation, including dishes requiring some less common ingredients, or seasoning ingredients which must be made up at home.

415

INDEX

418

421

MEASUREMENT CHARTS

Equivalent Values for Masses		
Avoirdupois		**Metric**
½ oz	is the equivalent of	15 g
1 oz	is the equivalent of	30 g
2 oz	is the equivalent of	60 g
3 oz	is the equivalent of	90 g
4 oz (¼ lb)	is the equivalent of	125 g
5 oz	is the equivalent of	155 g
6 oz	is the equivalent of	185 g
7 oz	is the equivalent of	220 g
8 oz (½ lb)	is the equivalent of	250 g
9 oz	is the equivalent of	280 g
10 oz	is the equivalent of	315 g
11 oz	is the equivalent of	345 g
12 oz (¾ lb)	is the equivalent of	375 g
13 oz	is the equivalent of	410 g
14 oz	is the equivalent of	440 g
15 oz	is the equivalent of	470 g
16 oz (1 lb)	is the equivalent of	500 g (0.5 kg)
24 oz (1½ lb)	is the equivalent of	750 g
32 oz (2 lb)	is the equivalent of	1000 g (1 kg)
3 lb	is the equivalent of	1500 g (1.5 kg)
4 lb	is the equivalent of	2000 g (2 kg)

Equivalent Values for Liquid and Cup Measurements				
Imperial			**Metric**	
Liquid Measures	Cup Measures		Cup Measures	Liquid Measures
1 fl oz		is the equivalent of		30 ml*
2 fl oz	¼ cup	is the equivalent of	¼ cup	
	⅓ cup	is the equivalent of	⅓ cup	
3 fl oz		is the equivalent of		100 ml
4 fl oz	½ cup	is the equivalent of	½ cup	
5 fl oz (¼ pint)		is the equivalent of		150 ml
	⅔ cup	is the equivalent of	⅔ cup	
6 fl oz	¾ cup	is the equivalent of	¾ cup	
8 fl oz	1 cup	is the equivalent of	1 cup	250 ml
10 fl oz (½ pint)	1¼ cups	is the equivalent of	1¼ cups	
12 fl oz	1½ cups	is the equivalent of	1½ cups	
14 fl oz	1¾ cups	is the equivalent of	1¾ cups	500 ml
16 fl oz	2 cups	is the equivalent of	2 cups	
20 fl oz (1 pint)	2½ cups	is the equivalent of	2½ cups	

*30 ml is 1 standard tablespoon plus 2 standard teaspoons

Metric Cup and Spoon Sizes	
Cup	**Spoon**
1 cup = 250 ml	1 tablespoon = 20 ml
½ cup = 125 ml	1 teaspoon = 5 ml
⅓ cup = 83.3 ml	½ teaspoon = 2.5 ml
¼ cup = 62.5 ml	¼ teaspoon = 1.25 ml

ATLAS OF ANCIENT EGYPT

Editor Graham Speake
Art editor Andrew Lawson
Map editor John-David Yule
Design Bernard Higton
Production Clive Sparling
Index Scott Glover

 AN EQUINOX BOOK

Published by Phaidon Press Ltd,
Littlegate House, St Ebbe's Street,
Oxford 1980; reprinted 1983, 1984,
1985

Planned and produced by
Equinox (Oxford) Ltd, Littlegate
House, St Ebbe's Street, Oxford,
England, OX1 1SQ

British Library Cataloguing in
Publication Data
Baines, John
    Atlas of ancient Egypt.
    1. Egypt—Civilization—Dictionaries
    I. Title   II. Málek, Jaromír
    932'.003   DT61
    ISBN 0–7148–1958–1

Origination by Art Color Offset,
Rome, Italy; Chapman Brothers, Oxford;
M.B.A. Ltd, Chalfont St Peter, Bucks
Filmset by Keyspools Ltd,
Golborne, Lancs
Printed in Spain by Heraclio
Fournier SA, Vitoria

Frontispiece Ornamental titulary
of Ramesses VI (1151–1143), on
the pillars of a hall in his tomb
(No. 9) in the Valley of the Kings.
Adapted from the illustration in
Ippolito Rosellini, *I monumenti
dell'Egitto e della Nubia*, Vol. I:
Monumenti storici (Pisa, 1832).

ATLAS OF
ANCIENT
EGYPT

by John Baines
and Jaromír Málek

Phaidon · Oxford

CONTENTS

Part One – The Cultural Setting

Part Two – A Journey down the Nile

Part Three – Aspects of Egyptian Society

List of Maps

CHRONOLOGICAL TABLE

Dates marked * are absolute. All others are subject to margins of error. A full king list appears on pp. 36–37.

	BC 6500	4500	4000	3500	3000	2500
EGYPT	Late Paleolithic	Badarian (Nile valley) Merimda (delta) Faiyum	Naqada I (Nile valley)	Naqada II (Nile valley) Ma'adi el-'Omari (Memphite area)	**Foundation of the Egyptian state** (late Naqada II) **c.3050** **Early Dynastic Period 2920–2575** 1st Dynasty 2920–2770 2nd Dynasty 2770–2649 3rd Dynasty 2649–2575	**Old Kingdom 2575–2134** 4th Dynasty 2575–2465 5th Dynasty 2465–2323 6th Dynasty 2323–2150 **1st Intermediate Period 2134–2040** 9th–10th Dynasties (Herakleopolis) 2134–2040 11th Dynasty (Thebes) 2134–2040

Painted terracotta figure of a dancing woman. Naqada I Period.

The Step Pyramid of Djoser at Saqqara. c.2630.

Painting of geese from the tomb of Itet at Maidum. c.2560.

	BC 6500	4500	4000	3500	3000	2500
LOWER NUBIA/ UPPER NUBIA	Late Paleolithic	Neolithic Abkan Post-Shamarkian Khartum Variant		Early A Group	Classic A Group Terminal A Group Little settled population	C Group *Kerma culture*
SYRIA/ PALESTINE	*Neolithic Jericho 8500*			Urban society: Habuba el-Kebira	Early Bronze Age *Egyptian contact with Palestine* Ebla	Egyptian contact with Byblos Destruction of Ebla Middle Bronze Age
MESOPOTAMIA/ IRAN	*Neolithic 6500* *Neolithic 6000* Late Neolithic *Neolithic 'Ubaid 5000* Irrigation farming 5500			Urban society: Uruk Invention of writing *Proto-Elamite expansion (literacy)*	Jamdat Nasr Early Dynastic Period	Sargonid Dynasty 3rd Dynasty of Ur
ANATOLIA	Neolithic Catal Hüyük 6500					
AEGEAN	Neolithic 6500				Early Bronze Age	Middle Bronze Age

8

2000	1500	1000	500	AD

Middle Kingdom 2040–1640
11th Dynasty (all Egypt)
2040–1991
12th Dynasty *1991–1783
13th Dynasty 1783–after 1640
**2nd Intermediate Period
1640–1532**
15th Dynasty (Hyksos)
1640–1532
17th Dynasty (Thebes)
1640–1550

New Kingdom 1550–1070
18th Dynasty 1550–1307
ʿAmarna Period 1352–1333
19th Dynasty 1307–1196
20th Dynasty 1196–1070
**3rd Intermediate Period
1070–712**
21st Dynasty 1070–945

22nd Dynasty 945–712
23rd Dynasty c.828–712
24th Dynasty 724–712
25th Dynasty (Nubia
and Theban area)
770–712
Late Period 712–332
25th Dynasty (Nubia and
all Egypt) 712–657
26th Dynasty *664–*525

27th Dynasty (Persian)
*525–*404
28th Dynasty *404–*399
29th Dynasty *399–*380
30th Dynasty *380–*343
2nd Persian Period
*343–*332
**Greco-Roman Period
*332–*395 AD**
Macedonian Dynasty
*332–*304
Ptolemaic Dynasty *304–*30 BC

Roman
emperors
*30 BC–395 AD
**Byzantine
Period
*395–*640**

ad of Maʿya, relief in
e Theban tomb of Raʿmose
o. 55. c.1360.

Inlaid gold funerary
mask of
Tutʿankhamun.
c.1325.

Detail of facade of the Great
Temple of Abu Simbel. c.1270.

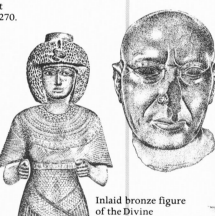

Inlaid bronze figure
of the Divine
Adoratrice
Karomama. c.850.

The "Berlin Green
Head," from a
private statue of
schist. c.75 BC (?).

Facade of the temple of
Hathor at Dendara.
Construction dedicated
17 November 34 AD (the
decoration is later).

Egyptian occupation
Kerma state
Kerma conquest
Pan-grave culture

Egyptian conquest
(Upper and Lower)

Depopulation

Egyptian
withdrawal

*Rise of Napata-Meroë
(the later 25th Dynasty)*
25th Dynasty
*Napata-Meroë state
—4th century* AD

Meroïtic-
Egyptian
condominium
in Dodekaschoinos
Meroïtic writing

Meroïtic
settlement
*Fall of
Meroë*
X Group

Egyptian contact
with Byblos

Hittite
incursions

Late Bronze Age:
city states
Egyptian occupation
c.1530–1200
Mitanni 1520–1330
Hittite domination
Neo-Hittite states
Joshua and Judges

*United Israelite
monarchy
Kingdoms of
Israel and Judah*
Assyrian
expansion
Babylonian captivity
Jews in Egypt

Persian rule
Revolt of
Satraps
Alexander
the Great
Seleucid Empire
Ptolemies

*Roman
Empire*

*Byzantine
Empire*

1st Dynasty of Babylon
Old Elamite Kingdom
Fall of Babylon
(1595 or 1531)
Kassite Dynasty

Independence of
Assur c.1380
Elamite expansion
2nd Dynasty
of Isin

Assyrian
Empire

Fall of Nineveh
Neo-Babylonian
Empire
Medes

Persian conquest
Alexander
the Great
Seleucid Empire
*Parthian
Dynasty*

Parthian
Dynasty
*Sasanid
Dynasty*

Hittite Old Kingdom

Hittite Empire
Fall of Hittite
Empire

Urartu
SW Anatolian
states
Gyges of Lydia

Persian rule
Alexander
the Great
Seleucid Empire
Ptolemies

Roman
Empire

Byzantine
Empire

Late
Bronze Age

Linear B
Cretan destruction
Mycenaean
destruction
Sub-Mycenaean

Protogeometric
Geometric
Orientalizing
Period
Greeks in Egypt
Archaic Period

Classical Period
Wars with Persia;
aid to Egypt
Alexander
the Great *336–*323
Macedon
Seleucid Empire
Ptolemies

Roman
Empire

Byzantine
Empire

INTRODUCTION

The monuments – pyramids, temples and tombs, statues and stelae – represent the most valuable source for our knowledge of ancient Egypt. A study of Egyptian monuments, either those still at various sites all over Egypt, or those in their new locations in museums and collections, is a happy meeting-ground of specialists and non-specialists. No special knowledge is required in order to be impressed by the grandeur and technical accomplishment of the Great Pyramid at Giza, to be enchanted by paintings in the Ramessid private tombs at Deir el-Medina, or be left dumbfounded by the opulence and – rather erratic – taste shown in the objects from the tomb of Tut'ankhamun in the Valley of the Kings, and now in the Cairo Museum. Nonetheless, knowledge may add to our appreciation and enjoyment.

So the aim of this book is easily defined: to provide a systematic survey of the most important sites with ancient Egyptian monuments, an assessment of their historical and cultural importance and a brief description of their salient features, based on the most up-to-date Egyptological knowledge. Further chapters and special features deal with general aspects of Egyptian civilization. These enable the reader quickly to find his bearings in the initially bewildering mass of names of places, kings and gods, and at the same time help him to understand the broader issues in the development of Egyptian society, and provide a background to the fluctuating fortunes of Egyptian towns and temples.

Geographically, the basic limits of the book are set by the frontiers of Egypt along the Nile, at the first cataract of the Nile and at the sea; the main exception is Egypt's traditional imperial extension of Lower Nubia. The maps present much of the book's content topographically, and supplement the information in the text at many points. Those in Parts One and Three are organized by theme and period. In Part Two the maps for each section present a detailed, large-scale view of the successive stages of our journey, including both ancient and modern features.

The period covered by the native Egyptian dynasties of kings (with the brief interruptions of foreign rule), about 2920 BC to 332 BC, provides the temporal setting. But some knowledge of the Predynastic Period is essential for understanding the earliest stages of Egyptian dynastic history, while for centuries the culture of the Greco-Roman Period remained largely Egyptian; these two phases, sometimes treated as separate units, are referred to and discussed where appropriate.

In writing this book we have envisaged our "typical reader" as anybody interested in ancient Egypt. We hope we have succeeded in eliminating the technical Egyptological jargon of our everyday work. The book is arranged in such a way that there is no need to read it straight through for its individual sections to remain comprehensible. There is a firm geographical framework, and the sites are discussed proceeding from south to north. The ancient Egyptians themselves used this scheme, and began their systematic lists at Elephantine (Aswan). Many modern books are arranged from north to south, which was the approach experienced by a traveler of the last century who arrived by boat at Alexandria, went from there to Cairo and, provided he was adventurous and prepared to accept some discomfort, further south. We have decided instead to follow the Egyptians, so that we can see the country as far as possible from their own viewpoint. The reader is, of course, free to begin his personal journey wherever he wishes. One of our aims has been to help those intending to visit Egypt by pointing out sites of interest to them and "briefing" them in advance. Those who have already seen that fascinating country might like to refresh their memory, and perhaps broaden their understanding of it, while those who simply like reading about civilizations of long ago may enjoy a new approach to one of the greatest. We hope that students in related disciplines will find this book useful when seeking reliable information about ancient Egypt.

Last, and most important, we hope that we shall communicate to our readers some of the enjoyment that brought us to the subject in the first place.

Part One is largely the work of John Baines and Part Two of Jaromír Málek; Part Three has been shared between us. We are particularly grateful to Helen Whitehouse for contributing "Egypt in Western Art," in which she is a leading expert. We should also like to thank Revel Coles, John Rea and John Tait for help with topics in their special fields.

PART ONE
THE CULTURAL SETTING

THE GEOGRAPHY OF ANCIENT EGYPT

Ancient Egypt was exceptional in its setting and unique in its continuity. The setting is the extreme case among several cultural and physical oases which were the great states of antiquity. It is almost impossible for us to recapture a feeling for this situation, with its mixture of geographical and human elements, just as we find it difficult to comprehend the time-span involved, half as long again as the Christian era. The position of the designer of the first pyramid, who created the earliest stone building on its scale in the world and lived in the only large, united state of the time, can never be recaptured. Any understanding of ancient Egypt must include an awareness of these and other enormous differences between antiquity and our own times. Yet mankind is the same everywhere, and much of our detailed knowledge of other civilizations will include material as ordinary as anything in our own lives. When approaching an alien civilization we need knowledge about both the ordinary and the exotic. Both are affected by the constraints of the environment. One exploits it in a routine fashion, the other more creatively; neither is independent of it.

In its geographical context Egypt is part of the larger area of northeastern Africa, and within this wider region its proximity to the heartlands of agricultural development in western Asia was initially of great significance. Dynastic Egypt was largely self-contained at most periods, but this was only because its economy was very heavily agricultural; for many important raw materials and for the requirements of high civilization foreign trade or travel into the desert was necessary, so that the perspective of the wider region is essential for understanding Egyptian culture. The same is true of the population of the country, which probably came from all the surrounding areas, and was always racially heterogeneous.

The boundaries of ancient Egypt

A definition of the boundaries of Egypt in antiquity – a theme of which the ancient texts are very fond and which reflects the Egyptian obsession with demarcations in general – is not simple. The basic areas of the country, the Nile valley, the delta and the Faiyum, were supplemented by parts of the surrounding regions over which the Egyptians exerted particular rights, such as those of mining. The southern frontier, traditionally at the first cataract of the Nile just south of Aswan, moved further south in some periods; in the New Kingdom, texts sometimes use words for Egypt to refer also to parts of Nubia, which were then incorporated into the state. Apart from these extensions of Egyptian territory, the line of oases that runs from Siwa in the north to el-Kharga in the south, approximately parallel to the Nile and about 200 kilometers west of it, was settled and governed by Egyptians during most of the Dynastic Period, reaching the peak of its prosperity in Roman times.

The main areas of Egypt form a river oasis in the desert. As such, the country was isolated from its neighbors to a greater extent than the other major states of antiquity, and its exceptional stability was due in large measure to this isolation, a striking indication of which is the complete absence of mention of Egypt in texts of the third millennium BC from Mesopotamia and Syria. Egypt was a magnet for settlers, but not for a concerted invasion, until perhaps the 13th century BC, and immigrants were always absorbed quickly into the population. But while much of Egyptian history is internal history, this is less true of the broader, imperfectly known changes of prehistory. Although the oasis of Egypt was fully formed by the end of the third millennium, it is necessary to relate this stage of climatic evolution to the more extensive alterations in earlier periods.

In the millennia after the end of the last Ice Age (about 10,000 BC) the Nile valley was one of the areas that attracted population from the Sahara and much of North Africa. During the Pleistocene era the valley was for much of the time impassable swamp, and river levels were very much higher than now. As the Sahara dried out at the end of this phase, it became progressively more inhospitable to the nomadic bands which had originally spread over much of its area. From as early as 15,000 BC there is a concentration of Paleolithic sites on the desert plateau on the edge of the valley, and one detail of the cultures may indicate that they were already feeling the effects of shortages and population pressure. Some of the flint blades from sites in both Egypt and Nubia show traces of use for gathering grasses, most probably wild grasses that could yield cereal grains. This is perhaps the earliest indication of cereal consumption known in the world, rivaled only by the site of Hayonim Terrace in Palestine. It is not evidence for a settled, agricultural life, but rather for an intensified use of resources by a still nomadic population.

This isolated instance of "progress" in Egypt seems not to have had any long-term influence. In the years from about 10,000 to 5000 BC there was a continuation of late and epi-Paleolithic modes of life, and there is no clear continuity between remains of this period and of the succeeding cultures. These are normally termed "Predynastic" by Egyptologists, and are Neolithic (with some use of metal), agricultural and settled; some stimuli in their development probably came from western Asia. They date from perhaps 4500 BC to the beginning of the Dynastic Period. The Egyptian setting of the Predynastic Period offered opportunities for exploitation not fundamentally different from those found at the beginning of the 19th century AD. The analogy is important, because most settlement has always been within the Nile valley and the delta, not on the desert edges (all areas not reached by the inundation are desert, or at best desert savanna, unless irrigated). It is likely that the

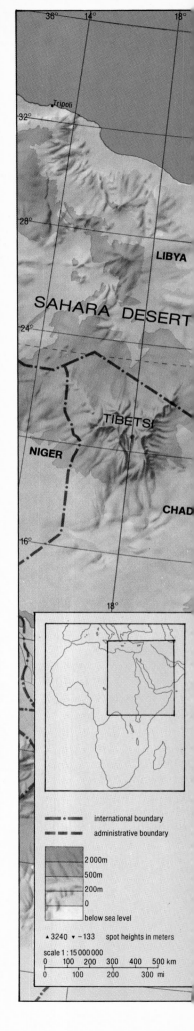

international boundary

administrative boundary

2 000m
500m
200m
0
below sea level

▲ 3240 ▼ −133 spot heights in meters

scale 1 : 15 000 000
0   100 200 300 400 500 km
0   100   200   300 mi

GREECE

Crete

Cyrenaica

MEDITERRANEAN SEA

TAURUS MOUNTAINS
TURKEY

CYPRUS

SYRIA

LEBANON
Qurnet el-Sawda 3083

•Damascus

ISRAEL

Jerusalem•
Dead
Sea

JORDAN

IRAN

ZAGROS MOUNTAINS

Euphrates
Mesopotamia

Tigris

Baghdad

IRAQ

KUWAIT

PERSIAN
GULF

32°

28°

Alexandria

LIBYAN
PLATEAU

QATTARA
DEPRESSION
-133

Siwa Oasis

Cairo

FAIYUM

Bahariya Oasis

Farafra Oasis

LIBYAN
DESERT

WESTERN
DESERT

Asyut•

Dakhla Oasis

el-Kharga Oasis

Kufra Oasis

EGYPT

GILF
KEBIR
PLATEAU

Kurkur Oasis
Dunqul Oasis

°UWEINAT

Salima Oasis

GEBEL
ABYAD
PLATEAU

Suez Canal

SINAI

Gebel Musa
(Mt Sinai)
2285

Mt Catherine 2634

EASTERN
DESERT

Nile

Gulf of Suez

RED SEA HILLS

Jordan

Gulf of 'Aqaba

NAFUD

SAUDI ARABIA

BAHRAIN

QATAR

U.A.E.

24°

Aswan
1st Cataract

Lake Nasser

Wadi Halfa
2nd Cataract

Tropic of Cancer

•Riyadh

ARABIAN PENINSULA

Dal Cataract

NUBIAN DESERT

3rd Cataract

4th Cataract

5th Cataract

BAYUDA
DESERT

6th Cataract

SUDAN

Darfur

el-Fasher

Jebel Marra 3088

Kordofan

Port Sudan

RED SEA

Mecca•

RUB° AL-KHALI

20°

YEMEN DEMOCRATIC
REPUBLIC

HADRAMAWT

16°

Atbara

Khartum

BUTANA

Sennar

White Nile

SAHEL

Massawa

Axum

Eritrea

Ras Dashan 4620

Hadur
Shu°ayb
3760

San°a

YEMEN ARAB
REPUBLIC

Bab el Mandeb

Aden

GULF OF ADEN

12°

DJIBOUTI
Djibouti

Blue Nile

Lake Tana

ETHIOPIAN
HIGHLANDS

Punt?

CENTRAL
AFRICAN
EMPIRE

Bahr el- Ghazal

Malakal

Sudd

Jonglei Canal
(under construction)

Sobat

Bahr el-Jebel

ETHIOPIA

Addis Ababa•

Batu 4307

SOMALIA

OGADEN

8°

4°

Juba

ZAIRE

Albert Nile

UGANDA

Lake Turkana
(Lake Rudolf)

KENYA

Juba

Mogadishu•

INDIAN OCEAN

0°

26°   30°   34°   38°   42°   46°   50°

22°   26°   38°   46°   50°

13

precise location of settlements has not changed much, as there is the advantage in building on an earlier site that any accumulation of debris will raise a village above the valley floor and the danger of high floods. Both because earlier sites will be buried under modern ones and because 3 or more meters of silt have been deposited over the whole valley since 3000 BC, the archaeological record of settlement within the inundated and cultivated area is almost nil. Much of Egyptian archaeology is therefore very hypothetical.

The Nile valley of the Predynastic and later periods was a focal point in northern Africa for the development of agriculture and, later, urban society (agriculture is found at an earlier date further west along the Mediterranean coast). The whole region from the confluence of the Blue and White Niles to the delta may originally have been culturally similar, but the differences became marked by the beginning of the 1st Dynasty in Egypt proper. The concentration of population from various sources brought innovation from different directions, with the main stimulus perhaps coming from the Near East. It is a striking feature of native Egyptian culture at all periods that it is not technically innovative. Possibly the very prodigality of the land and its water has not encouraged invention.

In these formative periods contact between Egypt and neighboring areas was easier than it is now, as the desiccation of the Sahara was not yet complete, and the desert to the west, and especially the east, of the Nile valley supported a wider variety of flora and fauna and perhaps a larger nomadic population than now. Even for the inhabitants of the Nile valley these regions had some significance. During the later fourth and third millennia the desert became progressively more arid, a development that may be significant for the formation of the Egyptian state. The political collapse at the end of this climatic phase (c. 2150 BC) may have been triggered off by low inundations, which could be a symptom of a dry phase over the whole of northern Africa, rather like the drought in the Sahel in the early 1970s, another time of low floods.

Climate and geography played an important part in these developments. It is not possible to say that they determined their direction, for different results can be imagined, but they did rule out a continuation of previous subsistence patterns. The Nile and its flooding were dominant factors in the organization of the newly formed Egyptian state.

The Nile valley

Rainfall in the Nile valley is negligible, and it is no more than 100–200 millimeters per year in the delta; without the Nile, agriculture would be impossible in Egypt, except perhaps on the Mediterranean coast. It is a more regular and predictable source of water than any other of the world's great rivers whose valleys are used for irrigation farming. In antiquity its annual inundation between July and October covered most of the land in the Nile valley and the delta, and with careful management the water deposited was adequate to produce a crop. The pattern of the inundation can no longer be seen in operation, because the river has been checked by a whole series of dams and sluices built since 1830. These provide regulation of water levels from Sennar on the Blue Nile to the apex of the delta

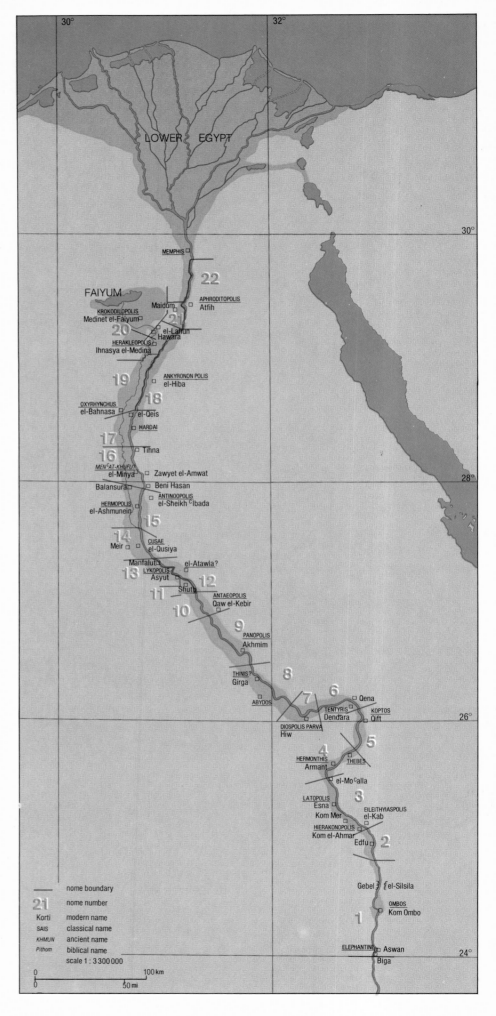

Left: The nomes of Upper Egypt
The nomes were the administrative divisions of Egypt, whose origins go back to the Early Dynastic Period. The 22 nomes of Upper Egypt were fixed by the 5th Dynasty, and their lengths along the river are recorded in the kiosk of Senwosret I at Karnak. The divisions on this map are based on the interpretation of these measurements, and are not valid for all periods. For Lower Egypt, the definitive number of 20 nomes was not established until the Greco-Roman Period. The Faiyum and the oases were not part of the scheme.

The total number of 42 had a symbolic value: there were 42 judges of the dead, and the early Christian writer, Clement of Alexandria (2nd century AD), states that the Egyptians had 42 sacred books.

Names underlined are those of ancient nome capitals. Where more than one is given, the capital shifted or the nome division changed at some period; where none is given, the capital is uncertain.

Right: The nomes of Lower Egypt
This arrangement of the 20 nomes of the Greco-Roman Period is based on lists in the temples of Edfu and Dendara. Many nome boundaries run along waterways whose reconstructed position is tentative. The names of known nome capitals are underlined.

Nomes had ensigns, which were worn on the heads of rows of nome personifications that decorate the base areas of temples. The ensigns of Upper and Lower Egypt are:

Upper Egypt

Lower Egypt

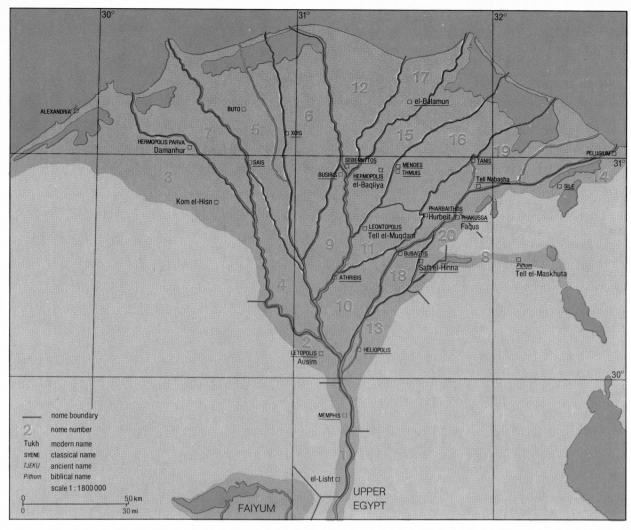

Key: nome boundary; nome number; Tukh modern name; SYENE classical name; TJEKU ancient name; Pithom biblical name. scale 1:1 800 000

north of Cairo, and will be joined by the Jonglei canal on the White Nile in southern Sudan, between the Bahr el-Jebel and the Sobat river. Instead of observing modern conditions we must rely on earlier sources, from pharaonic documents to the *Description de l'Égypte* produced by Napoleon's expedition, and the writings of 19th-century irrigation engineers. In order to establish the precise area cultivated at any time in the past it is necessary to make detailed local studies. An estimate for early periods is shown in the map on p. 31.

The waters of the Nile come from the Blue Nile, which rises in the Ethiopian highlands, and the White Nile, which divides into a bewildering variety of smaller rivers in southern Sudan and reaches as far as Lake Victoria in central Africa. The White Nile is fed by the rains of the tropical belt, and provides a relatively constant supply through-

out the year, mediated by the Sudd, which absorbs much of the water in the rainy season. The Blue Nile and the 'Atbara, which flows into the Nile some way north of Khartum, bring vast quantities of water from the Ethiopian summer monsoon, and provide almost all the water in the river from July to October (earlier in Sudan itself). This period corresponds to the time of the rains on the savanna in central Sudan. In Egypt the water in the river was at its lowest point from April to June. In July the level rose, and the flood normally began in August, covering most of the valley floor approximately from mid-August to late September, washing the salts out of the soil and depositing a layer of silt, which built up at the rate of several centimeters per century. After the water level fell, the main crops were sown in October and November, ripening from January to April according to variety. In antiquity

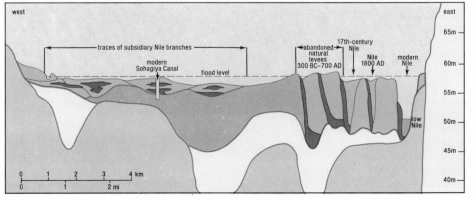

Generalized cross section through the Nile valley between Sohag and Asyut (after Butzer). In historical times the main river has migrated eastward leaving traces of its earlier raised banks. The vertical scale is greatly exaggerated.

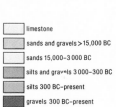

limestone
sands and gravels >15,000 BC
sands 15,000–3 000 BC
silts and gravels 3 000–300 BC
silts 300 BC–present
gravels 300 BC–present

agriculture was possible over much of the Nile valley and in large parts of the delta, the chief exceptions being tracts of swamp.

The valley and delta together form an area of about 34,000 square kilometers (1949–50 figures). Over long periods the valley area has varied considerably, but there has been no fundamental change in the last 5,000 years. The accumulation of silt and the management of water by man have, however, led to a gradual increase in useful land as the swamps that used to lie at the desert edge have been reclaimed for cultivation and flat stretches of desert have been incorporated in the flood plain. The profile of the valley and the detailed pattern of the flooding are relevant to this process. The water in the channel itself tended to erode the bed, and the deposition of silt during the flood raised the level of the land nearest the river, where the flow was strongest. So the profile of the valley is convex, and land near the river was drier and more readily settled than that further away. The flood was not a general overflowing of the bank, but ran through overflow channels on to the lower-lying land behind the banks. The flood crest ran more or less in parallel on the main area of the plain and in the river.

Agriculture involved controlling this flow pattern as far as possible. The areas of the plain were leveled to some extent, and formed into a series of basins of considerable size that "terraced" the land for irrigation in stages both down river and away from the banks (each terrace was only imperceptibly lower than the last, as the drop in river level from Aswan to the sea is no more than 85 meters). Because of the large size of the irrigated units a certain degree of central organization must have been needed for efficient exploitation of the land. Effective units would have been as large as the ancient provinces or nomes, of which there were just over 20 from the first cataract to south of Memphis. In the Dynastic Period the irrigated area in the valley increased gradually, with occasional setbacks, especially around 2100 BC, partly through improved technology (most imported), and partly through the reclamation of low-lying and swampy land. In early periods the areas of swamp provided a refuge for wild life that was hunted by the rich, and were the source of papyrus, which was made into a writing material and used for making mats, boats and utensils. These resources were replaced by those of intensive agriculture, and papyrus died out in the Middle Ages.

The main crops were cereals, emmer (*Triticum dicoccum*) for bread, and barley for beer (wheat was introduced in the Greco-Roman Period). In addition to these there were pulses, like lentils and chickpeas; vegetables – lettuces, onions and garlic; fruit, especially dates; an uncertain amount of fodder crops for animals, which were important for hides as well as meat; and plants grown for oil, such as sesame. Little is known about herbs, spices and seasonings. Honey was the chief sweetener, and bee keeping must have been an important activity. Meat was a luxury. Herds were probably grazed on swampy, marginal land, especially in the delta. The most prestigious meat was beef, but mutton, pork and goat were probably also eaten, as was the flesh of various species of antelope. Fowl was the food of the rich. Pigeon, which is very common in Egypt today, was eaten, probably the birds being raised in

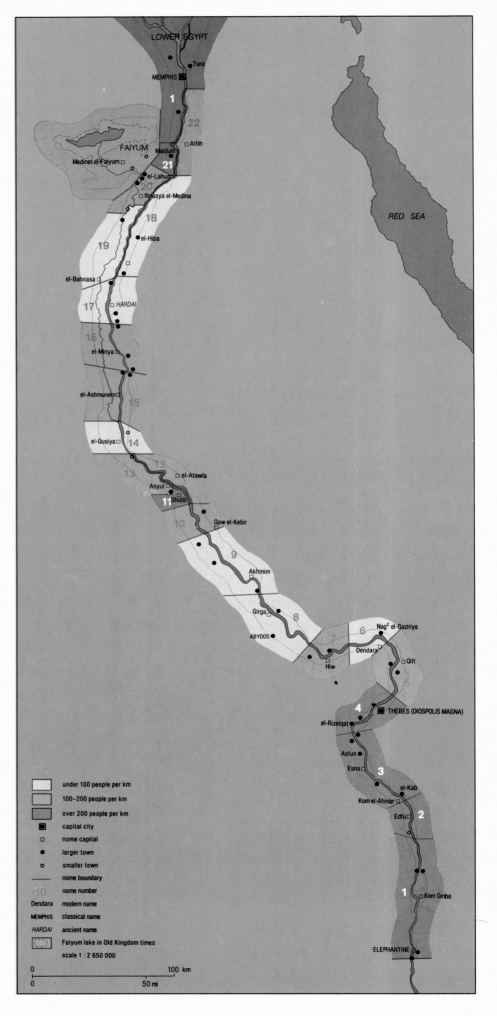

Population density in the Nile valley
Estimated population densities in the nomes of the Nile valley in dynastic times (after Butzer). The densities are higher in narrow parts of the valley and near the capital, probably because these areas were fully settled at an earlier date, and may have been easier to exploit. The evidence does, however, favor them, since sites are preserved more easily where the desert is closer to the river; the result may therefore be a little exaggerated. The population of the delta, where there is no basis for a detailed estimate, probably overtook that of the valley in the New Kingdom.

Large settlements are indicated according to approximate size, giving a rough supplementary guide; all are attested from Dynastic sources. Villages are not shown.

dovecotes, as were ducks, geese and various game birds. Chickens were not known before the New Kingdom, and probably became common only in the Greco-Roman Period. Grapes were grown chiefly in the western delta and in the oases, and made into wine, which was a luxury product; red wines are well attested, and white ones are known from Greek sources. The normal alcoholic drink was a coarse barley beer, which was made in the home; pomegranate and date wines are also known. Finally, two very important plant crops were papyrus and flax, which was used for almost all clothing and for sails and ropes (and possibly linseed oil), and also exported. The date palm was an additional important source of fiber.

The delta
The delta presents a generally similar picture to the Nile valley, but must have been a more difficult

challenge for reclamation for agriculture. Even now large areas remain unsuitable for cultivation, but some of these may be swamps and lagoons created by later incursion of the sea. Because of the conditions, land reclamation was probably significant for the development of the area at all times. This was true already by the 4th Dynasty, when the delta is prominent in the lists of estates in Memphite tombs. Through its agricultural strength it dominated Egyptian political and economic life to an increasing extent from about 1400 BC on. The amount of land available in the delta was double that in the Nile valley, and the delta was closer to the Near East, contacts with which played an increasing part in later Egyptian history.

The delta was created by an interplay between the sea, in periods of high sea levels in earlier geological ages, and the mud deposited by the Nile. The areas suitable for permanent settlement were

Early photograph of a Nile boat with a cargo of water pots. Because of the ease of river transport, cheap and bulky objects are sent great distances and probably always have been. These pots are made near Qena, where there are suitable clays for porous jars that keep water cool by evaporation.

Old photograph of a pair of *shaduf*s – weight arms with buckets – being used to lift water for irrigation (the women in the foreground are collecting it for domestic purposes). The *shaduf*, which was introduced in the New Kingdom, could lift water as much as 3 meters, or more when used in tandem, as here, but it is so labor-intensive that its value is limited to garden crops or to topping up the water level of inundated areas.

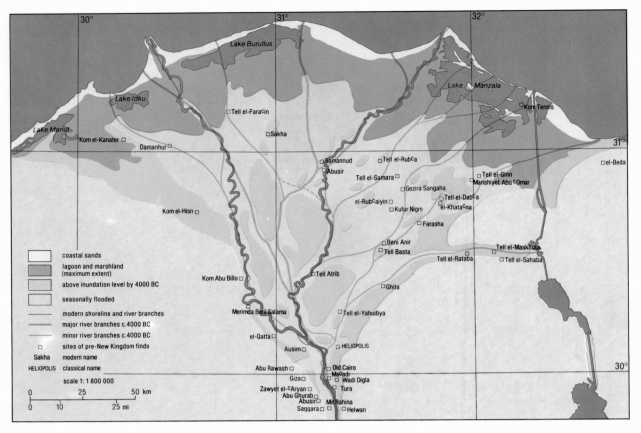

Map legend:
- coastal sands
- lagoon and marshland (maximum extent)
- above inundation level by 4000 BC
- seasonally flooded
- modern shoreline and river branches
- major river branches c.4000 BC
- minor river branches c.4000 BC
- □ sites of pre-New Kingdom finds
- Sakha modern name
- HELIOPOLIS classical name

scale 1:1 800 000

0   25   50 km
0   10   25 mi

Map labels: Lake Burullus, Lake Idku, Lake Mariut, Lake Manzala, Kom Tennis, Tell el-Faraᶜin, Sakha, Kom el-Kanater, Damanhur, el-Beda, Samannud, Tell el-Rubᶜa, Abusir, Tell el-Ginn, Manshiyet Abu ᶜOmar, Tell el-Samara, Gezira Sangaha, Tell el-Dabᶜa, el-Rubᶜaiyin, Kufur Nigm, el-Khataᶜna, Kom el-Hisn, Farasha, Beni Anir, Tell Basta, Tell el-Maskhuta, Tell el-Rataba, Tell el-Sahaba, Kom Abu Billo, Tell Atrib, Ghita, Merimda Beni-Salama, Tell el-Yahudiya, el-Qatta, Ausim, HELIOPOLIS, Abu Rawash, Old Cairo, Maᶜadi, Wadi Digla, Giza, Tura, Zawyet el-ᶜAryan, Abu Ghurab, Abusir, Mit Rahina, Saqqara, Helwan

Delta topography
The topography of the delta reconstructed for c.4000 BC (after Butzer), and compared with the modern situation.

The northern delta was formerly lagoon and swamp, and was gradually coated with layers of Nile mud, slowly increasing the area of land that was only seasonally flooded. The northernmost margin may, however, have been more attractive for early settlement than this might imply; there are early sites in the northeast and a nome around Lake Burullus. As is suggested by submerged sites on the coastline, this area may later have warped downwards in relation to the southern delta, roughly on the axis of the Wadi Tumilat.

The general development of the river branches – probably much influenced by man – has been to reduce their number and to shift the main discharge westward.

Areas above inundation by 4000 BC are composed of sand and mud, and are often known by the Arabic word *gezira*, "island." Their edges are particularly favorable for settlement. The sites shown have produced significant pre-New Kingdom finds. A number of further place names are known from texts, but these are omitted.

sandy ridges between the Nile branches and other water channels. Some of these were probably occupied from the beginning of the Predynastic Period; the general pattern of expansion was probably northwards. The land around the ridges could be used for crops or, if wetter, for grazing, and the swamps, like those in the Nile valley, contained wild life, fish and papyrus. Because of the different characters of the two main regions, their agricultural uses will have been substantially different, and there is evidence for trade between them. No large cities of the earlier periods have been found in the delta. This apparent lack of centers of population may be due in part to the relative proximity of Memphis, south of the delta apex, but it may also be illusory, as ancient sites in the delta are far less accessible even than those in the Nile valley. It is not surprising that the archaeological material from the delta is only a small fraction of that from Upper Egypt, and does not reflect the area's true importance.

The Faiyum
The third sizable area of ancient settlement was the Faiyum. This is a lakeside oasis west of the Nile valley and south of Memphis, which is fed by the Bahr Yusuf, a branch of the Nile that diverges westward north of Asyut and terminates in the Birket Qarun or Lake Moeris of antiquity. The lake has dwindled gradually from its Neolithic extent, which was little less than that of the entire Faiyum. The lake was already a focus for settlement in the late Paleolithic (about 7000 BC) and Neolithic periods, and is also attested for the Old Kingdom. The earlier cultures were of hunters and gatherers, but by the Old Kingdom agriculture had no doubt been introduced. Intensive exploitation of the area depended on lowering the water level in the lake to reclaim land, and using the water that would

otherwise have filled it to irrigate both above and below the natural lake level. Major works were undertaken by 12th-Dynasty kings, who must, to judge by the siting of some of their monuments, have reduced the lake considerably and won back about 450 square kilometers for cultivation. Later the Ptolemies made it into one of the most prosperous and heavily populated parts of the country, with about 1,200 square kilometers of agricultural land; much of the area irrigated then is now desert. A different form of irrigation is required in the Faiyum from the rest of Egypt, relying on large amounts of labor rather than any very advanced techniques. In the lower-lying areas it will have been possible to produce two crops per year, and this may have been true of most of the region in the Ptolemaic Period.

An area analogous to the Faiyum but very much less significant is the Wadi el-Natrun, a natural oasis close to the delta, northwest of Cairo and south of Alexandria. The word "Natrun" in its name refers to the salt lakes there. These were the chief ancient source of natron, which was used for cleaning, ritual purposes including mummification, and the manufacture of Egyptian faience and of glass. The oasis is poor in agricultural resources; in the Byzantine Period it became a refuge for Christian ascetics.

The western desert
The remaining areas to be discussed were more peripheral to Egypt, and could be held only when there was a strong government.

The oases of the western desert produced some valuable crops like grapes and the best dates, and were also important as links in trade with more remote areas. From north to south four main oases were governed by Egypt: Bahariya, Farafra, el-Dakhla and el-Kharga (east of el-Dakhla), of which the last two were by far the most significant. In addition, the more remote westerly oasis of Siwa was incorporated into Egypt in the Late Period; it acquired world renown through the abortive mission of Cambyses to it in 525 BC (it has recently been reported that remains of Cambyses' army have been found in the desert) and Alexander the Great's subsequent consultation of the oracle there. There are also smaller oases west of the Nile and further south, Kurkur, Dunqul and Salima, which are staging posts on long-distance caravan routes, but have not produced any ancient remains.

There is Middle and New Kingdom evidence for people fleeing from justice or from persecution to el-Kharga and el-Dakhla oases, while in the 21st Dynasty political exiles were banished there. In this respect the area was one facet of the Egyptian Siberia, the other being forced labor in appalling conditions, with great loss of life, in the mines of the eastern desert.

The entire area west of the Nile valley was called Libya in antiquity. The coastal region west of Alexandria as far as Cyrenaica probably contained the majority of the Libyan population, and was less inhospitable than it now seems. Almost all the Egyptian evidence from here dates to the reign of Ramesses II, who built forts along the coast as far as Zawyet Umm el-Rakham, 340 kilometers west of Alexandria, and to the Greco-Roman Period, when the Ptolemies built in both Greek and Egyptian style at Tolmeita in Cyrenaica, about 1,000 kilometers from Alexandria.

For most of Egyptian history the oases were an Egyptian outpost against the Libyans, who tried to infiltrate at many periods. In the reigns of Merenre' and Pepy II the expedition leader Harkhuf made several journeys to Yam, a country probably in the region of modern Kerma and Dongola south of the third cataract of the Nile. On one occasion he took the "desert road," leaving the Nile valley near Abydos and no doubt passing through el-Dakhla. When he arrived he found that the ruler of Yam had gone to "smite the ruler of the Libyan land to the western corner of the sky" – a discovery probably related to the western route used for this expedition. This detail shows that "Libya" for Egyptians extended 1,500 kilometers or so south from the sea. Remains from the Fezzan, probably dating to around the time of Christ, show the possibilities of settlement in southern Libya in antiquity, while the 'Uweinat area was settled in the third millennium BC. In early periods the Libyans were culturally similar to the Egyptians and may have spoken a dialect of the same language, but contacts during the Dynastic Period were mostly hostile.

From the western oases a trail now called the Darb el-Arba'in ("40-day track") leads to el-Fasher, the capital of Darfur province in western Sudan. Harkhuf used the first part of this, but it is possible that its entire length was opened up to trade in antiquity. Harkhuf traveled with donkeys, but effective exploitation of such routes may have depended on the camel, apparently introduced to Egypt in the 6th–5th centuries BC.

The eastern desert

To the east of Egypt were a number of important sources of minerals. The northernmost is Sinai, which supplied turquoise, mined by the Egyptians from the 3rd Dynasty to the end of the New King-

dom, but not later (finds dating to the beginning of the Dynastic Period have recently been reported from the area). The main sites with Egyptian remains are in western Sinai at Wadi Maghara and Serabit el-Khadim, and there was at times semi-permanent Egyptian settlement there. Sinai is also a source of copper, and copper mines contemporary with the Egyptian 18th–20th Dynasties have been excavated at Timna near Eilat. These were probably worked by the local population under Egyptian control; there is no evidence that the Egyptians

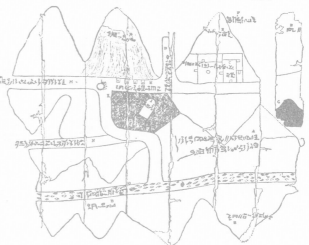

themselves mined copper anywhere in Sinai. It is possible that, as with Egyptian trade in grain with the Near East, the Egyptians did mine copper but did not consider the activity prestigious enough to record. Otherwise they may have employed local labor, as at Timna, or traded with the local population for copper, or acquired most of their supplies from elsewhere.

The eastern desert of Egypt yielded a number of building and semiprecious stones, and was the route to the Red Sea. Some quarries were near the Nile valley, like Gebel Ahmar for quartzite and Hatnub for Egyptian alabaster, but others, especially the sources of graywacke (a hard, blackish stone) in the Wadi Hammamat and the gold mines, most of which are south of the latitude of Koptos, required large-scale expeditions. They could not have been exploited without Egyptian domination of, or collaboration with, the local nomadic population. The Egyptians also needed control in order to use the three main routes to the Red Sea. These run by way of the Wadi Gasus to Safaga, the Wadi Hammamat to Quseir, and the Wadi 'Abbad to Berenike; there is also a minor route from about 80 kilometers south of Cairo to the Gulf of Suez, attested from the reign of Ramesses II. The earliest evidence for their use is from the end of the Predynastic Period (Wadi el-Qash, leading from Koptos to Berenike); this may relate to Red Sea trade or to mining. The northerly routes are attested for all the main periods of Egyptian history, and the southernmost from the New Kingdom on.

At the termination of the Wadi Gasus was a temple of the 12th Dynasty, and in 1976 remains from the nearby Egyptian port of the same date were discovered. There is renewed evidence in the 25th and 26th Dynasties (700–525 BC), and the pattern probably continued in the Persian Period (6th–5th century BC), when there were links with Iran around the Arabian coast. The Roman Period is

The only ancient Egyptian map. A fragment of a sketch map that probably shows the central area of the Wadi Hammamat, where there are graywacke quarries and gold mines. Further fragments (not shown) give a long track with few topographical details. The hieratic captions describe man-made and natural features, and the whole is related to the extraction of a half-worked statue that was taken to the Theban West Bank in year 6, perhaps of Ramesses IV. Turin, Museo Egizio.

represented at the sites of Quseir and Berenike, which were ports for trade with East Africa and India. Although we have no evidence that the Egyptians had contacts so far afield, such ports were probably used for trade with the semimythical land of Punt, which is mentioned in texts from the Old Kingdom on. The location of Punt is not firmly established, and the country had a number of idealized associations for the Egyptians, but it is most likely to have been in the region of modern Eritrea or Somalia, where finds of the Hellenistic and Roman Periods have recently been reported. The articles obtained from Punt were all exotic or luxury goods, the most important being incense. Whether the Punt trade was the only reason for navigation on the Red Sea, apart from access to some areas of Sinai, is quite uncertain. There is a report of Egyptian 18th-Dynasty beads found on the coast south of the river Juba near the Equator; but this does not mean that the Egyptians themselves penetrated this far.

Nubia

The political boundary of Egypt at the first cataract was probably established in the late Predynastic or Early Dynastic Period, replacing an earlier natural frontier at Gebel el-Silsila, where the limestone hills to either side of the Nile give way to sandstone, which is the basic element in the rock as far south as the Butana in central Sudan. At Gebel el-Silsila the sandstone comes down to the river on either side, and the site was the Egyptians' main quarry for building stone from the New Kingdom on. Limestone has allowed the Nile to carve a relatively broad floodplain, whereas the useful area of land beside the sandstone reaches is very small.

South of Gebel el-Silsila was the first Egyptian nome or province, whose main towns were Aswan and Kom Ombo. Its early separate status was recorded in its name "Nubia." Between the first and second cataracts lay Lower Nubia, which was always the prime target for incorporation into Egypt. Early Dynastic rock inscriptions and reliefs in the second cataract area show Egyptian interest in it at that date. In the 4th and 5th Dynasties there was almost no settled population in Lower Nubia. An Egyptian settlement at Buhen north of the second cataract implies hegemony, if not rule. In the 6th Dynasty the Egyptians yielded to local inhabitants, but control was regained in the 11th Dynasty and again at the end of the 17th. The 18th-Dynasty kings extended Egyptian rule as far as Kurgus, south of the caravan route across the desert from Korosko to Abu Hamed. This acquisition of territory was very important for later history, as an Egyptian-influenced culture became established at Napata, the capital of Upper Nubia, and eventually produced the 25th Egyptian Dynasty and the kingdom of Napata-Meroë, which survived into the 4th century AD.

Lower Nubia seems to have been regarded almost as being Egyptian by right, and was significant for access to raw materials, principally hard stones and gold, in the desert to either side of the Nile. At an early period it was used as a source of wood, but it can never have been agriculturally important, as the cultivable area is no more than a narrow strip on either side of the river. It was also, however, the route through which came many of the African products prized by the Egyptians. These included spices, ivory, ebony, ostrich feathers and certain species of baboon; pygmies were also traded occasionally, and figured in the stereotyped landscape of the Nile in Classical antiquity. It is not known what the Egyptians paid in return for all this, and virtually no archaeological evidence for ancient trade with Egypt has so far been found in sub-Saharan Africa. The ultimate provenance of many of the goods is unknown – pygmies probably never spread north of the Nile–Congo divide, while some other commodities must have come from the rain forest – and they may have passed through a number of intermediaries before reaching Egypt. It is difficult for us to evaluate the importance of these products for the Egyptians, which was often religious, but they were made into a focus for prestige comparable to precious stones today.

Palestine and Syria

The last major area that needs to be mentioned here is the coastal region of Palestine and Syria. Contacts between Egypt and the Near East are attested already in the Predynastic Period, and the name of Naʿrmer, the latest Predynastic king, has been found at Tel Gat and Tel ʿArad in Palestine. Trade in lapis lazuli, whose main ancient source was Badakshan in Afghanistan, was flourishing at that time, and Egypt may already have been importing metal from Asia. Connections between Egypt and Byblos in the Lebanon are attested in the Old Kingdom, and the funerary boat of Khufu, the builder of the Great Pyramid, was made of Lebanese cedar. There are few trees in Egypt, and their wood is of poor quality, so that good timber always had to be imported from the Near East. The Middle Kingdom saw an intensification of these links, while in the New Kingdom Egyptian kings conquered large parts of the area and held them for more than two centuries, exploiting subject peoples and trading with neighbors. During resurgences of Egyptian power in the 22nd and 26th Dynasties parts of Palestine were again conquered, and the pattern was repeated in the Ptolemaic Period. The possession of part of Syria-Palestine was a natural goal for a strong regime in Egypt, but its achievement was far more difficult than in Nubia.

Many advances in Egyptian material culture came from the Near East. In return for these "invisible" imports and for wood, copper, possibly tin, silver, precious stones, wine and oil, the Egyptians could offer four main resources: gold, food surpluses, linen and, particularly in later periods, papyrus. Trade in gold and the bartering of African goods imported into Egypt are well known, but exports of food and other non-prestige products can be proved only in exceptional cases. They leave little mark in the archaeological record and are almost never mentioned in texts, the best-known textual allusion being a gift of grain by Merneptah to the Hittites during a famine, which is not trade. But Egyptian agriculture was far more secure and productive than any in the Near East, and just as Rome's granary in imperial times was Egypt, so may the Near East's have been in earlier periods. Grain was very important in Late Period foreign policy.

A number of areas more remote from Egypt played a part in Egyptian history at different times, among them Mesopotamia, Hittite Anatolia, Crete and Cyprus; these cannot be surveyed here.

Below Granite outcrop near Aswan with quarry marks. The rows of tooth-like indentations are where slots were cut before inserting wooden wedges. The wedges were wetted and swelled to split the stone. The scorings on some surfaces were probably made with iron tools, and thus date after c. 700 BC.

Bottom Landscape in the southern part of the eastern desert. Although this area is somewhat less arid than the western desert, the organization of expeditions to mine or collect minerals in it must have posed formidable problems. Even so, exploration was very thorough; few significant mineral deposits have been found that were not exploited in antiquity.

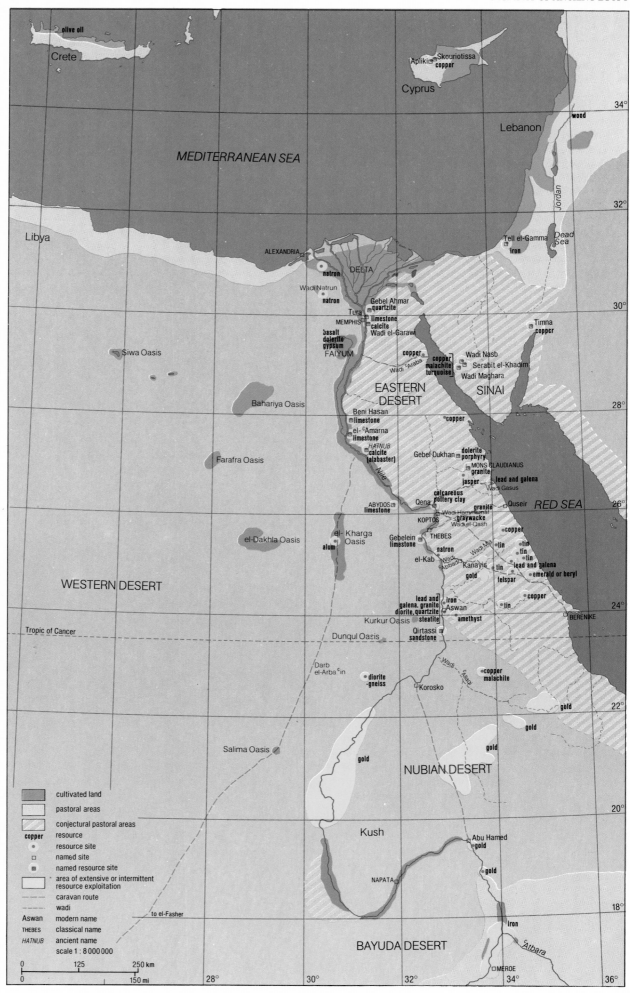

Natural resources of ancient Egypt

The sites indicated are places where there are ancient workings of the minerals named. It is often impossible to date these workings precisely, but several are exclusively Greco-Roman, such as the sources of emerald or beryl, porphyry and the granite of Mons Claudianus.

Further semiprecious stones and minerals are found scattered over the eastern desert: agate; breccia; calcite (for 140 km north of Asyut); carnelian; chalcedony; felspar; garnet; iron; jasper; rock crystal (quartz); serpentine.

Gypsum is found west of the Nile for 100 km south from Cairo, and flint is widespread on either side of the valley, especially from Luxor to el-Kab. The hills near the Nile are composed of limestone as far south as Gebel el-Silsila; only quarries of good-quality building stone are marked.

Commodities imported from further afield included incense and myrrh from Punt (northern Somalia?) and Yemen (?), obsidian from southern Ethiopia, silver from Syria and lapis lazuli from Badakshan in northeastern Afghanistan. Most of these were luxury products; the normal Egyptian lived as a subsistence farmer and had little economic contact with the outside world.

The area under cultivation fluctuated, while the land available for grazing varied with long-term climatic changes.

Map labels:

olive oil, Crete, Cyprus, Aplikia, Skouriotissa copper, Lebanon, wood, MEDITERRANEAN SEA, Jordan, Libya, Dead Sea, Tell el-Gamma, iron, ALEXANDRIA, natron, DELTA, Wadi Natrun, natron, Gebel Ahmar quartzite, Tura, limestone, MEMPHIS, calcite, Wadi el-Garawi, basalt, dolerite, gypsum, FAIYUM, copper, copper malachite turquoise, Wadi Nasb, Serabit el-Khadim, Wadi Maghara, Timna copper, Siwa Oasis, EASTERN DESERT, SINAI, Bahariya Oasis, copper, Beni Hasan, limestone, el-Amarna limestone, HATNUB calcite (alabaster), Gebel Dukhan, dolerite porphyry, MONS CLAUDIANUS granite, jasper, lead and galena, Farafra Oasis, Nile, calcareous pottery clay, Wadi Gasus, ABYDOS limestone, Qena, granite, Quseir, RED SEA, KOPTOS, graywacke, Wadi el-Qash, el-Dakhla Oasis, el-Kharga Oasis, alum, Gebelein limestone, THEBES, copper, tin, tin, tin, natron, Wadi Mia, tin, lead and galena, WESTERN DESERT, el-Kab, Wadi Abbad, Kanayis, tin, felspar, emerald or beryl, gold, copper, lead and galena, granite diorite, quartzite, iron, Aswan, steatite, amethyst, tin, Kurkur Oasis, BERENIKE, Tropic of Cancer, Dunqul Oasis, Qirtassi sandstone, Darb el-Arba'in, diorite, Wadi Gabal, copper malachite, diorite -gneiss, Korosko, gold, gold, Salima Oasis, gold, NUBIAN DESERT, gold, to el-Fasher, Kush, Abu Hamed gold, gold, NAPATA, iron, BAYUDA DESERT, Atbara, MEROE

Legend:

- cultivated land
- pastoral areas
- conjectural pastoral areas
- **copper** resource
- resource site
- named site
- named resource site
- area of extensive or intermittent resource exploitation
- caravan route
- wadi
- Aswan modern name
- THEBES classical name
- HATNUB ancient name

scale 1 : 8 000 000

0 — 125 — 250 km
0 — 150 mi

THE STUDY OF ANCIENT EGYPT

Egypt has been of almost continual interest to Europeans, and has been written about by authors from the Greek Hekataios of Miletos in the 6th century BC (whose book is lost) to today. When ancient Egyptian civilization became extinct in the later Roman Period it could no longer be an object of contemporary study, but it continued to be remembered throughout the Middle Ages for its monuments, most notably the pyramids. A number of medieval pilgrims to the Holy Land visited Egypt, mostly to see the sites associated with Christ's stay there, and even the pyramids were believed to relate to the biblical story, being the "granaries of Joseph."

The first stages

Interest in antiquity and knowledge of it revived in the Renaissance, and among the first Classical texts to be brought to light in the 15th century was the *Hieroglyphica* of Horapollo, a work of the 4th century AD, which purports to be Egyptian in origin and gives symbolic explanations of the meaning of a number of signs in the hieroglyphic script, and the Hermetic Corpus, a set of philosophical tracts of the early centuries AD, which were probably written in Egypt and contain genuine Egyptian ideas interspersed with Neoplatonist and other material. Texts of the latter type tended to support the assumption, which goes back to early Greek philosophers, that Egypt was the fount of wisdom. The same is true of the *Hieroglyphica*, which was held to describe a method of encapsulating profound truths in pictorial signs.

In the 16th century antiquarians studied more than before the physical remains of antiquity, and in Rome, the chief center of their researches, they were immediately confronted with Egyptian objects, most of which had been imported for the popular Isis cult in the early empire. These are found in early publications of antiquities, and formed, with the obelisks that are still such a striking element in the Roman scene, a nucleus for study that was mostly recognized as being Egyptian, and interpreted with the aid of writings about Egypt by Classical authors. Illustrators of the time had no conception of the differences in character between their own methods of representation and those of ancient Egypt, so that many of their reproductions resemble the originals only very remotely.

The late 16th and early 17th centuries were the time of the first visits to Egypt in search of antiquities. Pietro della Valle (1586–1652) traveled all over the eastern Mediterranean, staying in the east from 1614 to 1626, and brought Egyptian mummies and important Coptic manuscripts back with him to Italy. The manuscripts were in the latest form of the Egyptian language, written in Greek letters, and this language was regularly learned by priests in the Coptic Church in Egypt, where it is used for liturgical purposes to this day. They could therefore be studied by those who knew Arabic, the

Block statue of the Chief Lector-Priest Petamenope: engraving in G. Herwart von Hohenburg, *Thesaurus Hieroglyphicorum* (1620), the earlist published collection of hieroglyphic inscriptions. Herwart shows the same object as two different ones, using two 16th-century manuscript sources. From Rome (?), originally from Thebes; c.650 BC. Paris, Musée du Louvre.

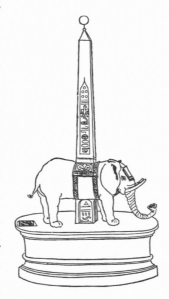

Obelisk and elephant: illustration of a mausoleum from Francesco Colonna, *Hypnerotomachia Polifili* (Venice, 1499). The "hieroglyphic" inscription is mostly after a Roman temple frieze that was believed to contain Egyptian hieroglyphs.

Map of ancient Egypt by Abraham Ortelius, Amsterdam, 1595. The motto reads "Rich in natural resources, Egypt places all her trust in the Nile, and so has no need of either foreign trade or the rain of heaven" (Lucan, *Civil War* 8. 446–47). As on many other pre-1800 maps, north is placed on the right in order to give a "landscape" of the Nile. The map is a remarkable achievement, showing most towns and nomes in their correct relative positions, including

Thebes 125 years before its site was identified on the ground. The information is almost all from Classical sources, the only ones then available for ancient Egypt, so that, for example, the Classical river mouths are shown. Note the list of unidentified places. The topography is not based on a survey and is very inaccurate. London, British Library.

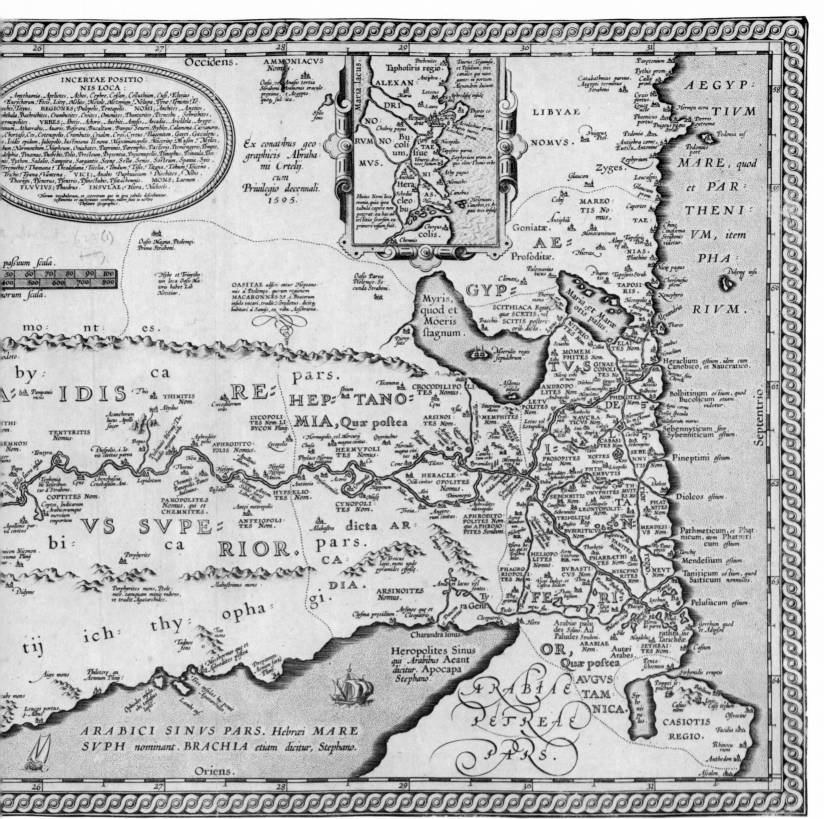

language in which the primers of Coptic were written. Two centuries later Coptic was to form the basis of the decipherment of the hieroglyphic script. It was also the initial study of the great polymath Athanasius Kircher (1602–80), who wrote numerous works about ancient Egypt, and was one of the first to attempt a decipherment.

A fascinating byway in the development of European knowledge of Egypt is revealed by a manuscript recording the visit of an anonymous Venetian in 1589, who traveled through Upper Egypt and Lower Nubia as far south as el-Derr. The author says he "did not travel for any useful purpose, but only to see so many superb edifices, churches, statues, colossi, obelisks and columns." But "even though I went a great distance, none of the buildings I saw was worthy of admiration, except for one, which is called Ochsur [Luxor, within which he includes Karnak] by the Moors." His judgment was to be fashionable about 250 years later, when Luxor became a center of tourism, and here he shows himself especially prophetic. Of

23

Karnak he says: "Judge whether this tremendous building is superior to the seven wonders of the world. One of them still exists, one of the pyramids of the pharaohs; in comparison with this construction it is a small thing. I am not sending anyone who wishes to see the monument to the end of the world; it is only ten days' journey from Cairo, and one can go there quite cheaply." This amazing work was not published until the 20th century, and seems to have had no influence on other writers.

In the next century the most nearly comparable text, known from secondary publications, is a narrative of the visit of two Capuchin friars to Luxor and Esna in 1668 where, they say, "in the memory of man no Frenchman had ever been." Like their predecessor, they were pressed for time, but they succeeded in crossing to the west bank at Thebes and seeing the Valley of the Kings, the prime tourist attraction that had eluded the Venetian.

Travelers and archaeologists

Explorations like those just mentioned cannot be termed archaeological. The word can, however, be used for the work of John Greaves (1602–52), an English astronomer who published his *Pyramidographia, or a Discourse of the Pyramids in Aegypt* in 1646. Greaves visited Giza on two occasions in 1638–39, measured and examined the pyramids thoroughly, and made a critical analysis of ancient writings about them; he also went to Saqqara. The resulting work was more penetrating than any other of its time on ancient Egypt; a notable feature is the citation of medieval Arabic sources. Essentially Greaves followed the example of humanist scholarship of the Renaissance, but his application of the methods to Egypt was scarcely imitated by others.

From the later 17th century the number of travelers to Egypt increased gradually, and their writings started to incorporate usable drawings of the monuments. The most significant advance in knowledge was made by the Jesuit Claude Sicard (1677–1726), who was commissioned by the French regent to investigate ancient monuments in Egypt. Only some of his letters on the subject are now preserved. He visited Upper Egypt four times, and was the first modern traveler to identify the site of Thebes, and to ascribe correctly the colossi of Memnon and the Valley of the Kings – all on the basis of Classical descriptions. His most important successor was the Dane Frederik Ludwig Norden (1708–42), who visited Egypt in 1737–38, and whose posthumously published volume of travels, magnificently illustrated with his own drawings, appeared in various editions from 1751 to the end of the 18th century.

The increase in the numbers of visitors to Egypt went together with an improvement in the treatment of Egyptian matters – and of antiquity and exotic cultures as a whole – in the more famous works of the 18th century, of which the most important are the multi-volume compilations of Bernard de Montfaucon (published in 1719–24) and the Baron de Caylus (1752–64). Both give a surprising amount of space to Egyptian objects, while also assigning to Egypt much that came from elsewhere. Considerable collections of antiquities already existed, and some, like the small group that belonged to Archbishop Laud in the 1630s, even included forgeries.

Far left Part of the titulary of Domitian on the Piazza Navona obelisk in Rome; engraving from Athanasius Kircher, *Obeliscus Pamphilius* (Rome, 1650). The small numbers refer to allegorical explanations of the signs in the text of the book.

Left Bronze statuette of Ha'py, the inundation, dedicated by Pahap, son of Ptahirdis; engraving from B. de Montfaucon, *L'Antiquité expliquée et représentée en figures. Supplément* (Paris, 1724). The figure was then in Montpellier, but has not been seen since, so that the record is valuable.

Below Group of small objects from the collection of Archbishop William Laud (1573–1645), which were given to Oxford University in 1635. The two figures on the left are genuine, but those on the lower right are forgeries. No. 32 may imitate an "Isis-knot" amulet; D is a *shawabty* of Roman or Renaissance date. Oxford, Ashmolean Museum.

Bottom View of rock-cut shrines and inscriptions at Gebel el-Silsila, from F. L. Norden, *Voyage d'Égypte et de Nubie* (Copenhagen, 1755).

Vue des Chapelles taillées dans le roc près de la Pierre de la Chaine à Tshibel Egselsele.

Travelers to Egypt and Sudan before 1800

The towns and sites marked are prominent in the records of travelers before Napoleon's expedition of 1798. Some of their names and the dates of their visits are given in bold type.

Also shown are:
+ Egyptian sites visited principally for their Christian associations.
——— the conventional itinerary of medieval pilgrims to the Holy Land who also went to Sinai and Egypt
——— the route of Felix Fabri through Sinai in 1483
——— a caravan route to the Red Sea on the 15th-century map *Egyptus novelo*
◇ sites visited by the anonymous Italian of 1589
——— the itinerary followed by a group of Franciscans (including Theodor Krump), French Jesuits, and the doctor Poncet towards the Funj capital Sennar and Gondar in Ethiopia in 1698–1710
——— the route by which the Scot, James Bruce, returned to Aswan from Gondar in 1771–72.

Inset Excerpts from the books of less important travelers, published on their return to Europe. There are more than 200 accounts of travelers whose journeys included Egypt between 1400 and 1700.

Top Christoph Fürer von Haimendorf, aged 69, dated 1610; from *Itinerarium Aegypti, Arabiae, Syriae, aliumque regionum orientalium* (Nuremberg, 1610).

Center Jean de Thevenot (1633–67), frontispiece of *Voyages de M. de Thevenot en Europe, Asie & Afrique* (Amsterdam, 1727; originally Paris, 1665). The inscription says "Friend, you may know the author from this portrait;/you could not find a traveler more perfect."

Bottom Obelisk of Senwosret I at Heliopolis; the hieroglyphs are legible but quite un-Egyptian, and the landscape is European. From Gemelli Careri, *Voyage du tour du monde* (Paris, 1729), who implies that the obelisk was at Alexandria.

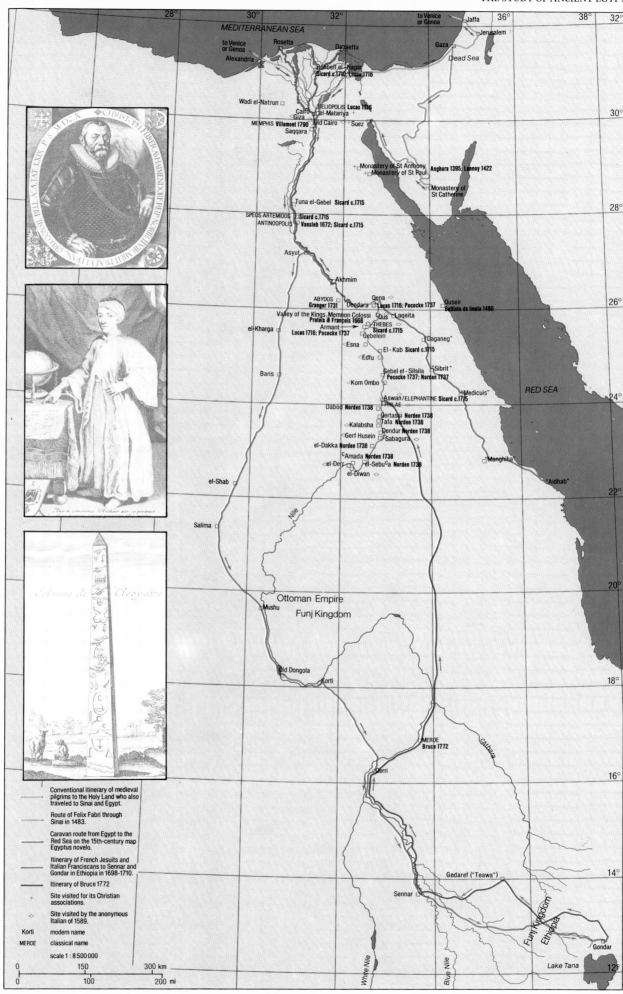

Decipherment of the hieroglyphic script

Throughout the 18th century the hieroglyphic script continued to be studied, although little progress was made towards a decipherment. Both the antiquarian and the linguistic interest in Egypt culminated in Georg Zoëga (1755–1809), whose two major works, a treatise on obelisks, which includes a section on the hieroglyphic script, and a catalog of Coptic manuscripts in the Vatican collections, are of lasting value. The date of the work on obelisks, 1797, is symbolic as the culmination of Egyptian studies before Napoleon's expedition in 1798. Although the script could, and no doubt would, have been deciphered without the discovery of bilingual inscriptions, Egyptology as we know it is a product of the expedition, the unearthing of the Rosetta stone, the associated surge of enthusiasm for Egypt, and of gradual changes in the intellectual climate of western Europe.

The campaign was accompanied by a team of scholars who were to study and record all aspects of Egypt, ancient and modern. The Rosetta stone soon passed into English hands, but the team produced a fundamental multi-volume work, the *Description de l'Égypte*, first published in 1809–30. This was the last, and much the most important, such work produced before the decipherment of the script by Jean François Champollion le Jeune (1790–1832) in 1822–24, which is the beginning of Egyptology as a separate subject. Champollion and Ippolito Rosellini (1800–43), an Italian from Pisa, mounted a joint expedition to record monuments in Egypt in the 1820s, but by that time they were latecomers in the field. In the previous 20 years numerous travelers had visited Egyptian and Lower Nubian sites and had rifled them for antiquities, written books about them, or both. Prominent among them were the consuls Anastasi, d'Athanasi, Drovetti and Salt, the Italian strong man Belzoni, the French sculptor Rifaud, and the Swiss travelers Gau and Burckhardt. The collections gathered by some of these men formed the nuclei of the Egyptian

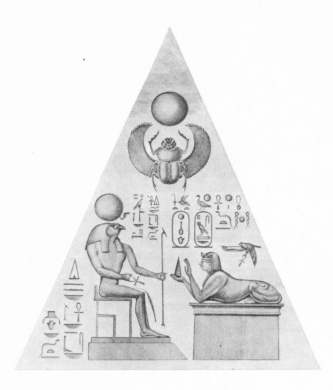

sections of the British Museum, the Louvre in Paris, the Rijksmuseum van Oudheden in Leiden and the Museo Egizio in Turin (there was no Egyptian Museum in Cairo until the late 1850s). In the first half of the 19th century digging in Egypt was primarily for objects. The recovery of information, as opposed to objects, came a very poor second.

Before his death in 1832 Champollion had already made great progress in understanding the Egyptian language and in reconstructing Egyptian history and civilization, but this work had little impact, both because of delays in publication and because of its strictly academic nature. By 1840 the first generation of Egyptologists was already dead, and the subject retained a precarious existence in France, with Vicomte Emmanuel de Rougé (1811–

Above Frontispiece of F. L. Norden, *Voyage d'Égypte et de Nubie* (Copenhagen, 1755). The central allegory shows: Fame; Ancient Egypt displaying her treasures; a lion with the arms of ancient kings of Denmark; and the Nile. There is also a Classical figure of Isis, and Egyptian monuments and other motifs.

Left Pyramidion of the obelisk of Psammetichus II by the Palazzo di Montecitorio in Rome; from G. Zoëga, *De origine et usu obeliscorum* (Rome, 1797). The copy is accurate and legible, but its style is un-Egyptian.

72), in Holland with Conrad Leemans (1809–93), and especially in Prussia with Carl Richard Lepsius (1810–84). Lepsius's 12-volume *Denkmaeler aus Aegypten und Aethiopien* (1849–59), the result of an expedition up the Nile as far as Meroë in 1842–45, is the earliest reliable publication of a large selection of monuments, and is still of fundamental importance. The English pioneer Wilkinson is treated in detail below on pages 106–07.

The growth of Egyptology
In the middle of the century Lepsius, his younger contemporary Heinrich Brugsch (1827–94) and a handful of other scholars continued to advance the subject, while work in Egypt was placed on a permanent footing by Auguste Mariette (1821–81), a Frenchman who was originally sent to acquire Coptic manuscripts for the Louvre in 1850. Mariette entered the service of the Khedive Saïd in 1858, excavated a large number of sites before and after that date, and founded the Egyptian Museum and Antiquities Service. The aims of the latter were to preserve and record the monuments, to excavate, and to administer the museum. Until the Egyptian Revolution of 1952 its directors were European, the most famous of them being Mariette's successor Gaston Maspero (1846–1916).

The aims of scientific excavation in Egypt were first stated in 1862 by the Scot Alexander Rhind (1833–63), but they were not realized on any scale until the work of W. M. F. Petrie (1853–1942). Petrie first went to Egypt in 1880 to make measurements of the Great Pyramid for pyramidological purposes. He later excavated at sites all over Egypt, publishing a volume almost every year on the results of the preceding winter. Among his excavations were some spectacular discoveries, but his work was far more important in providing a framework of information about the different areas and periods, often resulting from a reworking of sites that had already been excavated summarily by others. During his own lifetime Petrie's standards were overtaken, notably by the American G. A. Reisner (1867–1942), but Reisner published little of his results, thereby lessening their value.

From about 1880 to 1914 there was a great deal of archaeological work in Egypt, and sites in Nubia came into prominence with the building and subsequent raising of the first Aswan dam (1902 and 1907). The end of the 19th century also saw major advances in the understanding of Egyptian language and chronology, made in Berlin by Adolf Erman (1854–1937) and Eduard Meyer (1855–1930) respectively, and the discovery of remains of all historical periods, and of Predynastic times from Naqada I on. Egyptological work since then has developed knowledge greatly in all areas, but in few of them has it changed the outlines fundamentally. In comparison, the 19th century was a time of continuous change. Up till about 1870 most Egyptological knowledge related to the latest stages of the civilization, while there was no proper division of the physical remains or of the language into periods. As this changed, interest tended to focus on the earlier, more "classical" phases of both.

Excavation in the 20th century
Excavation in this century has been dominated by a few spectacular discoveries and by the salvage campaigns in Nubia occasioned by the second raising of the first Aswan dam and the construction of the High Dam. There has been no systematic survey, but increasing numbers of sites have nonetheless been explored. Complementary to excavation, and at least as important, is the recording and publication of standing monuments, which first reached adequate standards around 1900. This does not have the glamor of excavation, and has seldom attracted the same public interest or support.

Foremost in the attention it has received has been

Palestinian temple of the Middle Bronze Age at Tell el-Dab'a in the delta, excavated by an Austrian mission in the late 1960s. Techniques of European archaeology have been used. The site is dug in 10-meter squares, with grid sections left as a check on stratification.

exploration in the Valley of the Kings at Thebes. The first find of royalty was the discovery in the 1870s by the 'Abd el-Rasul family of Qurna of the pit containing the mummies of a majority of the New Kingdom kings. They had been removed from their original tombs early in the 21st Dynasty and reburied in the area of Deir el-Bahri for greater security. Like so many of the most important discoveries, this was the result of the search by local inhabitants for marketable antiquities, not of systematic excavation. While Egyptologists rightly deplore the loss of valuable information that goes with these discoveries, many of them would never have been made by orthodox expeditions.

In 1898 the tomb of Amenophis II was discovered by Victor Loret (1859–1946) in the Valley of the Kings, and proved to contain the mummies of most of the kings missing from the earlier find. Work on the valley continued almost without interruption until 1932. The most methodical of these examinations was by Howard Carter (1874–1939), mostly working for the Earl of Carnarvon. Carter's main discovery was, of course, the tomb of Tut'ankhamun, which he found in 1922 and worked on almost continuously for ten years. Although other largely intact royal burials have been found in the Near East, it is the richest single find of the sort, and contained many unique objects.

Several other royal burials or cemeteries have been excavated in Egypt in this century. Reisner's discovery of the tomb of Hetepheres at Giza in 1925 is the only major find of jewelry and furniture of the Old Kingdom; the recovery of the forms of the objects, whose wood was completely decayed, was a triumph of painstaking recording. In the 1940s Pierre Montet (1885–1966) excavated a set of intact tombs of the 21st- and 22nd-Dynasty kings and royal family at Tanis, which provide rare examples of art in precious materials from a period that has left few significant remains.

The most important excavated settlement sites, el-'Amarna and Deir el-Medina, have both been the objects of different expeditions and numerous campaigns. After the clandestine discovery of the el-'Amarna cuneiform tablets in the 1880s Urbain Bouriant (1849–1903) worked there, and produced a volume with the memorable title *Two Days' Excavation at Tell el Amarna*. He was followed by Petrie (1891–92), whose brief stay produced much of value, but was overshadowed by a German expedition in 1913–14 under Ludwig Borchardt (1863–1938), during which the house of the sculptor Thutmose was found. This contained the world-famous bust of Nefertiti, and a number of other masterpieces. In the 1920s and 1930s there were several seasons of British excavation, which contributed both to the history of the later 18th Dynasty and to the understanding of the short-lived capital; work has recently resumed on the site. Deir el-Medina was a source of finds throughout the 19th century, and was excavated by an Italian expedition at the turn of the century and a German one under Georg Möller (1876–1921) in 1911 and 1913. In 1917 the Institut Français d'Archéologie Orientale in Cairo began excavations at the site which have continued, with interruptions, up till now, and have almost completely uncovered the workmen's village and adjacent necropolis.

It is fitting to mention here the activities of the

Egyptian Antiquities Service and of Egyptian Egyptologists. After the foundation of the Service under Mariette the first Egyptian official in it was Ahmed Kamal (1849–1932), who worked in the Cairo Museum and excavated at a number of sites. From the beginning of this century an increasing proportion of the staff of the Service was Egyptian, and Egyptians taught Egyptology at Cairo University. Since 1952 both sectors have been completely Egyptian. The Service has excavated more than any other body, and much of the material in the Cairo Museum, as well as in Alexandria, Minya, Mallawi, Luxor and Aswan, comes from its excavations. The most striking Egyptian discoveries are probably those at Tuna el-Gebel, where an animal necropolis and a Greco-Egyptian city of the dead have been excavated, and the pioneer work of Ahmed Fakhry (1905–73) in the oases of the western desert.

Surveys and publications

There have been exhaustive surveys of Nubia as far as the Dal cataract, and in archaeological terms Lower Nubia is now perhaps the most studied area in the world. Only the fortress site of Qasr Ibrim remains above water, and this is still being excavated. The expansion in Nubian studies, and the wide spread of finds from the Paleolithic to the 19th century AD, have led to the creation of a virtually separate field of study.

The recording of complete monuments in Egypt was initiated by Maxence de Rochemonteix (1849–91) and Johannes Dümichen (1833–94), but neither lived to complete his work. In the years after their deaths the Egypt Exploration Fund (later Society) began an "Archaeological Survey of Egypt," which was to record standing monuments, while Jacques de Morgan (1857–1924) started a *Catalogue des monuments*, which published the temple of Kom Ombo in its entirety. Both these projects were too ambitiously conceived, but the Archaeological Survey initiated the work of N. de G. Davies (1865–

Group of foreign captives – a Libyan, a man from Punt (?), an Asiatic and another Libyan – on a relief from the causeway of the mortuary complex of Sahure' at Abusir. The superbly accurate drawing is from L. Borchardt, *Das Grabdenkmal des Königs Śa3ḥu-Re'*, Vol. II (Leipzig, 1913).

Relief of Ramesses III in battle against the ''sea peoples''; in his temple at Medinet Habu, north exterior wall. From *Medinet Habu*, the definitive publication by the Oriental Institute of the University of Chicago.

1941), the greatest copyist of Egyptian tombs. He published more than 25 volumes on tombs alone, almost always presenting a complete record of the decoration in them, and his wife Nina and others made colored reproductions of selected scenes. There have not been complete publications of monuments in color photographs until recently, and even these are not fully satisfactory; really effective presentation of the unique and fast-vanishing legacy of color on Egyptian monuments has yet to be achieved.

The most important epigraphic venture to follow Davies was the foundation of Chicago House, a field station of the Oriental Institute of the University of Chicago at Luxor, in 1924. The Oriental Institute itself was the creation of James H. Breasted (1865–1935), who was effectively the founder of American Egyptology, and a major scholar in his own right. For Chicago House he gained the support of John D. Rockefeller. The Chicago expedition has produced the only exhaustive record of a large Egyptian temple in facsimile (*Medinet Habu*, 1930–70) and a number of other volumes. Another work that set comparable standards, also funded by Rockefeller, was the publication of the inner parts of the temple of Sethos I at Abydos by A. M. Calverley (1896–1959) and M. F. Broome. After a lull the flow of publications has increased recently.

Egyptology outside Egypt

Indispensable though it is, activity in Egypt is a small part of the total work of Egyptologists, and there is often surprisingly little contact between the field and the study. It is far more difficult to select names from the list of mainly armchair Egyptologists than it is for fieldworkers, but it is necessary in order to provide a balance.

The first objective of Egyptologists has always been to understand the language. Early in this century F. Ll. Griffith (1862–1934) and Wilhelm Spiegelberg (1870–1930) advanced enormously the knowledge of demotic, the cursive script and

language of the Late and Greco-Roman Periods, while Adolf Erman continued to make discoveries in the earlier phases of Egyptian. In 1927 Sir Alan Gardiner (1879–1963) produced a grammar of Middle Egyptian which incorporated discoveries of his own and of Battiscombe Gunn (1883–1950), and has yet to be superseded. In 1944 H. J. Polotsky, the grand old man of Egyptology today, published a revolutionary study of some aspects of Egyptian and Coptic grammar, and over the last 30 years he has transformed our understanding of much of the language of all periods. The day when all our difficulties with Egyptian will have been solved is, however, nowhere in sight. Similarly, the 11-volume dictionary edited by Adolf Erman and Hermann Grapow (1885–1967), which was published between 1926 and 1953, marked a great advance on the pioneer work of Heinrich Brugsch, but is still the beginning rather than the end of the study of the meaning of Egyptian words.

For his work away from the monuments the Egyptologist needs publications of the monuments, more detailed studies on texts – hieroglyphic and hieratic and demotic – and numerous other types of aid. In these areas Kurt Sethe (1869–1934) was perhaps the leading scholar. He started as a grammarian, but later made contributions in almost all areas of the subject, and was the most prolific of all editors of texts, whose work will remain indispensable for generations. Sir Alan Gardiner was the most important editor of papyrus texts, who set new standards in the treatment of the papyri themselves and in their presentation. His collaborator Jaroslav Černý (1898–1970) was the outstanding worker on the ostraca and other cursive documents from Deir el-Medina in particular.

As examples of more general Egyptological studies it is worth singling out, more or less arbitrarily, the work of two writers who have changed whole areas of the subject; further important names may be found in the bibliography. Heinrich Schäfer (1868–1957) published the fundamental work on Egyptian art, which analyzes how the Egyptians depict objects and figures in the natural world (see pp. 60–61). Gerhard Fecht has similarly transformed our way of looking at the organization of Egyptian texts. He has shown that the majority of them are written in a kind of meter; it seems that writing was more normally in ''verse'' than in ''prose,'' so that in order to compose texts it was necessary to become a versifier, if not a poet. Both these scholars have illuminated areas that are very alien to modern eyes, and both have demonstrated features that are a prerequisite to a true comprehension of the ancient sources. Everywhere in Egyptology what has been done is a prelude to what might be done.

Today Egyptology is a conventional academic discipline, whose study is centered on universities, museums and national archaeological institutes; there are more than 20 countries where the subject is represented. The 300 or so Egyptologists cover fields such as language, literature, history, religion, art, which for the modern world would be separate. This has advantages in forcing one to maintain a general perspective, but drawbacks for detailed work or for major projects like dictionaries. Sadly, original work in Egyptology has become an almost exclusively academic pursuit.

THE HISTORICAL BACKGROUND

Predynastic Egypt

The culture of northern Africa was very uniform as late as the end of the last Ice Age (c. 10,000 BC), and the gradual formation of Egypt was a separation from this background, much affected by changes in climate. The most striking features of this process are the rapid acceleration of change in the centuries before the beginning of the Dynastic Period, and the lack of resemblance between the Egyptian state of the 4th Dynasty and its Predynastic antecedents, perhaps half a millennium earlier. Egyptian culture did not then become static, but there was never again such a surge of growth, and there is a continuity discernible from the Old Kingdom to the Roman Period, which cannot be found between Predynastic and Dynastic Egypt.

The earlier Predynastic cultures were not uniform over the country, and the two main areas cannot easily be related in their development. In the Nile valley the earliest Neolithic, settled, food-producing cultures are the Tasian and the Badarian (named for the sites at which they were first identified, as are those mentioned below), which may not in fact be separate (c. 4500 BC). These are confined to an area south of Asyut, and consist mainly of modest cemetery sites, probably near settlements that are now lost. In the Faiyum, cultures of an approximately similar date are known from the shore of the lake at its level of the time, but there is little evidence that these people were farmers; they may have lived largely by hunting and gathering. On the delta margins the large site of Merimda may be older than Badari, and there was probably also settlement of the central delta at that time. Several further Neolithic cultures are known from the second cataract area.

Naqada I (sometimes called Amratian) is, like its predecessors, a local, small-scale village culture, which shows little sign of social stratification. It is, however, known from a rather wider area, and is a prelude to the more expansive phase of Naqada II (or Gerzean); it shows no trace of foreign influence.

Naqada II forms the turning point in the development of Predynastic Egypt. It is the first culture to have contacts with other countries, while it spread over the entire Nile valley north of Gebel el-Silsila and into the delta. There is also social stratification and a development of significant population centers, notably Hierakonpolis (Kom el-Ahmar), Koptos (Qift), Naqada and Abydos. It is, on the other hand, the last period during which there was some cultural uniformity extending south of the first cataract. The Nubian cultures of this period, which are found as far south as Khartum, are not sharply distinct from those of Egypt. There was probably exchange over the whole area, and no central political authority. The cultural demarcation with the Nubian A group, which becomes noticeable south of Gebel el-Silsila in Naqada II, probably accompanies the beginnings of state organization in Egypt and the definition of a political frontier. This process leads into the Early Dynastic Period, in which Egypt is united, within boundaries comparable to those of later periods, under a single ruler. There is no sharp cultural break between Naqada II and the Early Dynastic Period, even though the transformation over the centuries is almost total.

During Naqada II some motifs in art and items of technology demonstrate cultural contact with Mesopotamia. Egyptian writing may have been invented in response to stimulus from Mesopotamia, but the systems of the two countries are not closely similar. The most likely method of

Predynastic and Early Dynastic Egypt
Egyptian-type sites are marked in black and numbered according to cultures attested:
1 from Tasian/Badarian
2 from Naqada I
3 from Naqada II
4 Lower Egyptian and delta cultures (contemporary with Badarian to mid-Naqada II, but not uniform)
5 Faiyum Predynastic culture
6 late Naqada II and Early Dynastic
Categories 1–5 are listed much more comprehensively than category 6. Many Predynastic sites ceased to be used in the Early Dynastic Period, probably because their inhabitants no longer exploited the desert margins so much, and moved further into the valley.

Rock drawings of very varying dates are common in all areas of the desert, many of them probably carved by nomads. Most often they are close to tracks; in Lower Nubia they are also frequent near the Nile. Their style continues to be un-Egyptian in the Dynastic Period. The hard stones of the eastern desert were used by the valley dwellers throughout the Predynastic and Early Dynastic Periods.

The precise political status of the capital cities marked, with the exceptions of Abydos and Memphis, is unknown.

Nubian-type sites are marked in brown. Those of the A group are distinguished as:
• from early A group (contemporary with late Naqada I and early Naqada II)
○ Classic and Terminal A group (contemporary with late Naqada II and 1st Dynasty respectively)
Nubian-type sites of the second cataract area include:
△ Khartum Variant, c.4500–3500 BC
▽ Post-Shamarkian, c.3500 BC
◇ Abkan, c.4000–3200 BC and overlapping with Classic A group. Favorable conditions and extensive surveys have led to the identification of numerous sites of all these types, which are much better known than their Egyptian counterparts.

Far right: The second cataract area in Predynastic times

Left Objects from tombs of the Naqada I period. Left: mud statuette of a woman with her right hand under her left breast, with exaggerated thighs and legs. Center: fine black-topped red-ware pot with an incised design of uncertain meaning. Right: elaborately worked flint knife, probably a ceremonial object. Oxford, Ashmolean Museum.

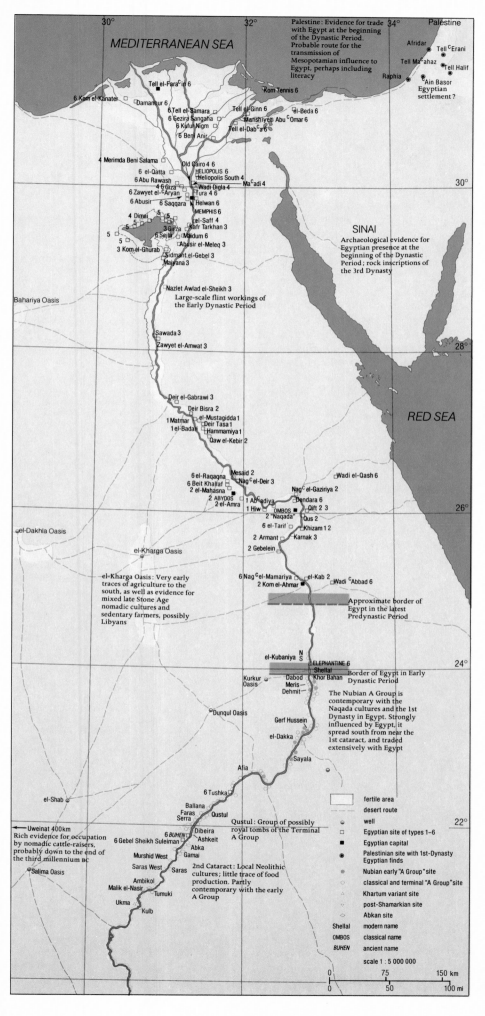

cultural transmission between the countries is trade, which was already far-flung. Evidence for trade between Egypt and Sinai and southern Palestine in the Early Dynastic Period has been found, but it is an open question whether this trade was accompanied by immigrants or by invasions. It is possible for a small nomadic group to conquer a large sedentary one; a takeover of this sort in late Naqada II cannot be ruled out, and would have left virtually no archaeological trace.

Our later written sources suggest that there were rulers of all Egypt before the beginning of the 1st Dynasty, and that they succeeded earlier dynasties of rulers of the two lands of Upper and Lower Egypt. But the idea of two Predynastic kingdoms may be a projection of the pervasive dualism of Egyptian ideology, not a record of a true historical situation. More probably there was a gradual unification of a previously uncentralized society, reflected in the cultural uniformity of the country in later Naqada II, and in objects bearing early versions of the later royal emblem of the *serekh*. This is a brick facade whose developed form is the king's Horus name, consisting of a hawk surmounting a *serekh* with a space for a name. Motifs of this sort have been found in Upper Egypt, in the area around Memphis and in the delta. The appearance of the motif is roughly contemporary with a cemetery at Abydos, near the later tombs of the 1st-Dynasty kings, which may contain Predynastic royal tombs. If so, there were rulers in later Naqada II, centered on Abydos, who controlled most of the country.

The monumental slate palettes and mace heads of the latest Predynastic kings, especially Na'rmer, are similar in type to later royal reliefs, and appear to record victories over places in the delta and in Libya, and agricultural and ritual events. At later periods, however, most scenes of this sort convey no precise historical information; these reliefs are significant rather in showing that the king's role was defined and given a visual formulation by this early date. The historical events in question were probably earlier in date.

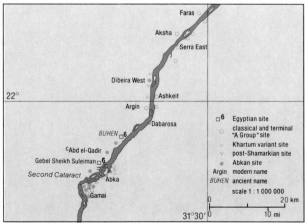

Early Dynastic Period

Two main changes appear to mark the beginning of the 1st Dynasty: a spread in the use of writing, and the founding of Memphis, which may have been the political capital from that time on. There may also have been a change of ruling family, as is suggested by differences in the naming of the kings. Writing was used notably for year names, which recorded a salient event for each year for dating purposes. Lists of these year names later formed the first annals.

The 1st Dynasty begins with the legendary Menes, whose name is known from later Egyptian king lists and from Classical sources. In their own time these kings were mostly known by their Horus names, the official royal element in the titulary, and not by their birth names, which are those used in the lists. As a result both the identification and the existence of Menes are disputed, but he is most probably the same as King ʿAha, to whose reign dates the earliest tomb at Saqqara. The two main centers of power at this time were Abydos and Memphis, while Hierakonpolis, a very old site, also has substantial Early Dynastic remains. The two guardian deities of the Egyptian king, Nekhbet and Wadjit, belong to Hierakonpolis and to Buto (Tell el-Faraʿin) in the delta, and it is probable that Buto too was important from an early period. The duration of the 1st Dynasty is estimated at about 150 years. Large cemeteries of the period, with rich burials, have been found in many parts of the country, including the delta; the finest of these date to the long reign of Den. Their spread implies that there was less centralization of wealth than in the central Old Kingdom, when provincial cemeteries of importance disappear.

Little direct evidence of Egyptian relations with the Near East or with Libya is preserved for the 1st Dynasty, but this may be due to chance. In Nubia a graffito of roughly this period has been found in the second cataract area, and shows a king triumphing over enemies, indicating that the Egyptians did not simply come to trade.

The kings were buried at Abydos in a cemetery set well back in the desert, while areas near the cultivation appear to have been marked out for the royal mortuary cult, and may have contained ceremonial buildings of flimsy materials which were renewed as the need arose. The royal tombs themselves were modest in size, and were thoroughly ransacked in later periods, but what little remains from them is of superb workmanship.

While the kings and their court were buried at Abydos, a group of high officials had imposing mud-brick tombs of a different design on the edge of the desert escarpment at north Saqqara (similar tombs have also been found at other sites). There were probably no more than one or two of these officials at one time, since the number of tombs is only slightly greater than that of the kings, with more tombs dating to the reigns of the longer-lived kings. The contents of some of the storage chambers in the superstructures of these tombs have been preserved, and include a remarkable array of objects in copper and, most striking of all, huge quantities of stone vessels in a wide variety of materials and shapes. The genre of stone vessels originated in Predynastic times, and they were the principal luxury product of the country until the 3rd Dynasty.

At the beginning of the 2nd Dynasty the royal necropolis moved to Saqqara. After the third king of the dynasty, Ninetjer, the record is very uncertain; there were probably rival claimants to the throne, and later traditions include names from both sides. The first king of the dynasty whose name has been found at Abydos is Peribsen, the only king in Egyptian history to bear the title Seth instead of Horus. Peribsen apparently altered his name from a

Horus name, Sekhemib. Horus and Seth are the two warring gods of Egyptian myth, who struggle to gain the inheritance of the land – but this myth could have been formulated after the 2nd Dynasty – and the change in title might refer to a belief in the triumph of Seth, or to a difference in local loyalties, among other possibilities. Peribsen's actions seem to have provoked opposition from a king Khaʿsekhem, of whom objects are known only from Hierakonpolis in the south. The next king, Khaʿsekhemwy, was probably the same person as Khaʿsekhem; his name has been found over the whole country on objects that presumably date from after Peribsen's death. The name Khaʿsekhem alludes to a "power" (*sekhem*), which means Horus, while Khaʿsekhemwy refers to two "powers" – Horus and Seth – and is surmounted by figures of both gods. It is accompanied by a sentence, "the two lords are at rest in him." The whole is therefore an announcement that the struggle is over. Khaʿsekhemwy's reign looks forward to the 3rd Dynasty. His queen, Nimaʿathapi, is associated with its first two kings, and architecture of his time shows great advances.

The first king of the 3rd Dynasty, Zanakht (2649–2630), is a shadowy figure who was probably the same as a king Nebka. His successor, Djoser (2630–2611), is known above all as the builder of the Step Pyramid at Saqqara, the oldest stone building of its size in the world. In addition to this, fragments of a shrine from Heliopolis of his reign show a fully developed Egyptian style and iconography. The Step Pyramid is in many ways a tentative structure, and shows many changes of plan, but it is evidence of astonishing technical mastery and economic power.

The time of Djoser was later looked back upon as a golden age of achievement and wisdom. The name of Imhotep, the probable architect of the Step Pyramid – he held the titles of a master sculptor among others – came to be especially venerated, and in the Greco-Roman Period he was a popular deity, associated particularly with healing. His name is also found as a graffito on a stretch of the enclosure wall of the pyramid of Djoser's successor, which was buried almost at once in a modification of the original plan. Perhaps he was a hero among the workmen of his own time.

Djoser's buildings stood out from the group of massive mud-brick mastabas of his reign at north Saqqara; not until the next dynasty did other men have stone tombs. But the perfection of relief work extended beyond the royal monument, and the wooden reliefs from the contemporary tomb of Hezyreʿ are among the finest ancient sculpture in the material. Although they were made for a private person, they may be from a royal workshop.

The still more grandiose monument of Djoser's successor Sekhemkhet (2611–2603) scarcely progressed beyond ground level, and his reign is followed by an obscure period. This interlude before the 4th Dynasty is an illustration of how the rulers predominate in the record and hence in our view of the history. Where the king and his organization were strong the country's resources could be harnessed in a most impressive way, probably through corvée labor. When he was weak the normal subsistence pattern continued without harming the economic fabric of the country, but without dedicating its potential to the same enduring end.

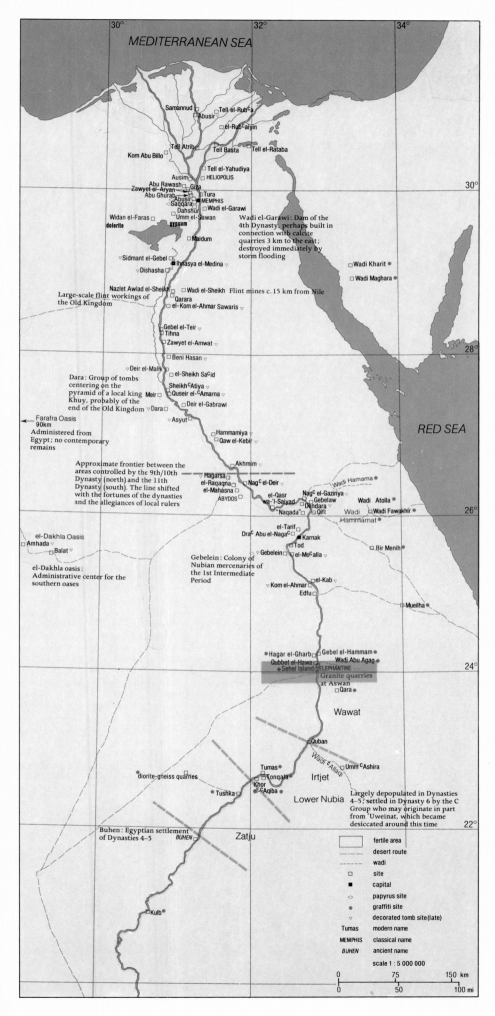

By the end of the Early Dynastic Period Egypt had acquired its classical southern frontier at the first cataract, while its script, administration and technical and artistic capabilities had evolved virtually into their classic forms. There had been a progressive centralization of power which cannot be seen in the record, except in the decline of provincial cemeteries. This was the precondition for the exploits of the 4th-Dynasty rulers.

Old Kingdom

The 4th Dynasty is the time of the great pyramids, but it would be wrong to allow our view of it to be dominated by their massive durability. No less than any other, it is a period of change and of political conflict.

Snofru (2575–2551), the first ruler of the dynasty, built the two pyramids at Dahshur and completed – or possibly built – the Maidum pyramid. This building program is as vast as those of his successors, and implies the same level of efficiency in the economy and in organization. In addition to the pyramids there are mastabas of his reign at Maidum and Saqqara. The reliefs and paintings in these contain the earliest examples of the repertory of subjects found in later Old Kingdom tombs (mid-4th-Dynasty tombs are largely undecorated).

Some details of the administration of the time are known, especially from the inscriptions in the tomb of Metjen from Saqqara. Widely separated estates were given to high officials, possibly in order to discourage the creation of baronial areas. Metjen's estates were mostly in the delta, perhaps on previously uncultivated land. Unlike the very highest officials of the time, Metjen was not a member of the royal family, which dominates our other records.

During the reign of Snofru there was a major campaign or campaigns to Nubia, which is recorded in the fragmentary royal annals (the Palermo Stone) and may be linked with rock inscriptions in Nubia itself. This led to the foundation of an Egyptian settlement at Buhen, which lasted for centuries and was probably used as a base for mining expeditions and for trade. Between the 1st and 4th Dynasties Egyptian activities, perhaps combined with a worsening of the climate, seem to have eliminated the settled Nubian A group, which is followed by a gap before the arrival of the C group about 2250 BC.

A major factor in 4th- and 5th-Dynasty history is solar religion. The true pyramid is most probably a solar symbol, so that Snofru himself was a solar innovator. But the compounding of royal names with the sun god Re' and the use of the royal epithet "Son of Re'" are not found until the reign of Ra'djedef (the name of Re'neb of the 2nd Dynasty is probably irrelevant in this respect). It seems that the influence and importance of the sun god grew continuously until the mid-5th Dynasty, and that the different political factions were united in their adherence to Re'.

Of the remaining rulers of the 4th Dynasty Khufu (2551–2528) and Khephren (2520–2494) stand out through their buildings; Menkaure' (2490–2472) comes a considerable way behind. The placing of their monuments in a close group at Giza may show factional solidarity, while the pyramid of Ra'djedef (2528–2520) at Abu Rawash, the excavation for a pyramid at Zawyet el-'Aryan (whose builder's name is uncertain) and the tomb of Shepseskaf (2472–2467) at south Saqqara perhaps belonged to more ephemeral rival factions. The centralization of rule and the authority of the two main kings can be read off the rigidly ordered groups of tombs around the pyramids. This concentration of power is not, however, the cause of power, since Snofru was as strong as his successors, but did not use the same methods. It may be no coincidence that he later had a good reputation and was deified, whereas Khufu and Khephren were said in folklore to be tyrants.

In addition to buildings, the 4th Dynasty produced much of the finest sculpture of the Old Kingdom, and the scanty surviving reliefs, inscriptions and tomb furniture are of the same quality. In terms of material culture it is the high point of the period, but of its intellectual culture and daily life we know almost nothing.

Shepseskaf built himself a massive mastaba instead of a pyramid, and this almost unique departure may be reflected in the practice of the 5th-Dynasty kings. The first of these, Userkaf (2465–2458), built a small pyramid at Saqqara, east of the Step Pyramid, and a sun temple near Abusir, the idea for which was copied by five of his successors. The temples were separate institutions from the pyramids, but were closely associated with the kings who built them, and probably had a mortuary significance for them.

The architectural continuity which may be posited between the two dynasties has a parallel in the ruling families. In both respects Shepseskaf forms the turning point as much as Userkaf. Khentkaus, the mother of Userkaf and Sahure' (2458–2446), was a member of the 4th-Dynasty royal family. The father of the kings is unknown, but he may have been from another branch of the same very large group. Despite this continuity, the internal policies of the 5th Dynasty were very different from those of the 4th. The reduction in the size of pyramids was not accompanied by a compensating increase in other construction, and the change must reflect either economic decline or an increase in the consumption of things that leave no trace. While there is clear evidence of decline in the late 6th Dynasty, the level of activity in the two preceding centuries was roughly constant. There is no simple explanation for this pattern, and we should perhaps ask instead what provoked the departure from convention in the extraordinary phase of building in the 4th Dynasty.

In the 5th Dynasty private tombs are no longer regimented into rows or confined on a single site, and the amount of decoration in them increases continually. This is evidence for greater freedom of expression – within close limits – for the elite, but not necessarily for any increase in their wealth. A further significant change is the location of some tombs in the provinces towards the end of the dynasty. The provincial administrators, originally central appointees, turned slowly into local ruling families. By the end of the Old Kingdom there are large provincial cemeteries, and this development marks a loosening of royal power. It is seen rather earlier in the holders of high office, who are no longer members of the royal family, although they may marry into it. An administration based on autocracy and kinship gives way to something like a fixed bureaucracy.

The latest royal name found at the Egyptian settlement of Buhen is that of Neuserre' (2416–2392), and Egypt probably lost control of Nubia soon after. Some generations later there are records of trading expeditions to the south from Egypt, which presumably replaced the permanent depot.

The last kings of the 5th Dynasty did not build sun temples, which implies a lessening in the importance of solar religion. Wenis (2356–2323) appears to be a transitional figure, heralding the 6th Dynasty. His pyramid complex, with its remarkably small pyramid, is of great interest both for the reliefs on its causeway and for the texts on the walls of the internal chambers. The texts had probably been used for earlier kings, so that they do not necessarily point to a change in belief. The practice of inscribing them is continuous from Wenis to the 8th Dynasty, but the selection in the different pyramids varies greatly.

We know more of the political history of the 6th Dynasty than we do for earlier periods, but it is still a random selection of information; much of what we regard as typical of it could have happened at other times too. This applies particularly to military campaigns, like those to the east of Egypt recorded by the high official Weni. The location of the area attacked is uncertain – immediately east of the delta or in southern Palestine – and the nature of the enemy is not clear. But even if the import of these campaigns is unknown, their existence is certain. Campaigns recorded in royal mortuary reliefs have no simple relationship with fact. A campaign to Libya shown in the complex of Sahure' (2458–2446)

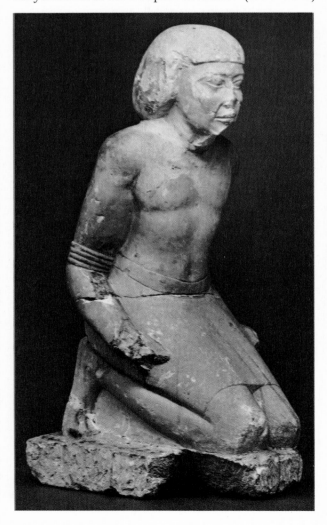

Statue of an Asiatic (?) captive, perhaps from the mortuary complex of Djedkare' Izezi at Saqqara. There were large numbers of these statues depicting various different nationalities, in 5th- and 6th-Dynasty complexes, but the sites have been so ransacked that we do not know how they were arranged. They are the counterpart of relief scenes of the defeat of enemies. New York, Metropolitan Museum of Art.

Roughly worked funerary stela of the Nubian Senu, from el-Rizeiqat near Gebelein. The texts state that the owner and his son, who is shown directly under him, are Nubian; both wear a distinctive, sporran-like garment. They were probably mercenaries. Height 37 cm. First Intermediate Period. Boston, Museum of Fine Arts.

is repeated by Neuserre' (2416–2392), Pepy I (2289–2255), Pepy II (2246–2152) and finally Taharqa (690–664); this is a ritual event, which probably corresponds with a real campaign earlier than the reign of Sahure', but with no other specific happening.

Occasional archaeological evidence highlights our ignorance of Egyptian relations with the Near East. Pieces of 5th-Dynasty goldwork have appeared in Anatolia, and stone vases of Khephren and Pepy I have recently been excavated at Tell Mardikh in Syria, the capital of the important state of Ebla that fell around 2250 BC. We can only guess at the degree of contact implied by these finds. As in the Middle Kingdom, the main channel of communication must have been Byblos, where a number of Old Kingdom objects have been found.

The inscriptions of the expedition leaders in their tombs at Aswan give much information about trade to the south in the 6th Dynasty, some of it through the oases of el-Kharga and el-Dakhla. Among other events, they show the settling of the C group in Lower Nubia, first in three princedoms, and later in a single political unit, with which Egypt's relations gradually deteriorated.

This deterioration is probably an aspect of Egypt's declining power during the immense reign of Pepy II (2246–2152, of which the latter part is not attested from contemporary sources). The decline can be seen in private tombs in the Memphite area, whose decoration is much more modest than hitherto, and sometimes all underground, perhaps for reasons of security. But even though we can point to details of this sort, nothing prepares for the eclipse of royal power and the poverty that come after Pepy II. The numerous kings of the next 20 years (late 6th and 7th–8th Dynasties) were nominally accepted in the whole country, but there was no real central control. Provincial officials had become hereditary holders of their posts, and treated their nomes virtually as their property, whose interests they defended, often by force, against their neighbors. Famine was common and

may be the key to understanding the period, since it has been suggested that the political collapse was due primarily to a series of disastrous low inundations. This would explain why there is relatively little indication of decline before the catastrophe, but the human elements of a line of weak kings and failing administration should also be taken into account. The reality of disaster is confirmed by an analysis of death rates in cemeteries, which show a marked increase at this time.

First Intermediate Period and the 11th-Dynasty reunification

The 1st Intermediate Period (2134–2040) is the time during which Egypt was divided, being ruled by the 9th/10th Dynasty from Herakleopolis (Ihnasya el-Medina) and another from Thebes (the 11th); at its beginning the Herakleopolitans may have had control of the whole country for some years. The new dynasties were started by nomarchs who proclaimed themselves kings, and were able to gain acceptance among their neighbors. At first the change to dual sovereignty probably made little difference to the running of the country, since the dynasties were too weak to exert much influence on local politics. Their power gradually increased, however, and there were frequent clashes at the border, which was mostly north of Abydos. The presence of considerable numbers of Nubian mercenaries in Upper Egypt is an indication of how violent the times were. Despite general poverty, there are relatively large numbers of modest, and frequently crude, monuments of the period, made for lower strata of society than hitherto.

The Herakleopolitan Dynasty suffered frequent changes of ruler, and produced no outstanding kings. The most important king of the more stable Theban Dynasty was the fourth, Nebhepetre' Mentuhotpe (called I or II by different writers, 2061–2010), who defeated the northern dynasty and reunited the country. Mentuhotpe began with a programmatic Horus name, "Who gives heart to the Two Lands," which was replaced first by "Divine of the White Crown" (the crown of Upper Egypt) and later by "Uniter of the Two Lands." These changes may correspond to stages in the reunification, the second indicating that he had united all of Upper Egypt and the third – a traditional epithet which was given a new iconographic formulation by Mentuhotpe – that he had accomplished the conquest of the whole country. His reign also includes activity in Lower Nubia (possibly building on campaigns of his predecessors), and the construction of a novel and impressive mortuary complex at Deir el-Bahri, from which reliefs and sculpture have been recovered. The artistic style is a refined version of 1st Intermediate Period work rather than a resumption of Old Kingdom traditions, and emphasizes, as does the Theban location of the complex, the local base of the king's power. Mentuhotpe was held in later periods to be one of the founders of Egypt; part of this prestige may go back to his own self-glorification, for he was shown in relief in a form more nearly divine than that of most Egyptian kings. This was probably intended also to enhance the status of the kingship at an important juncture; it continued under his successor.

Kings of Egypt

The list on these pages contains the names and *approximate* dates of most of the important kings of Egypt, with the names of queens regnant designated Q.

A king's full titulary consisted of five main elements, of which the first three were given in their order of origin. These are (1) Horus, (2) Two Ladies, (3) Golden Horus, all of which are epithets that seem to refer to aspects of the king's being as a manifestation of a deity. The fourth, the first cartouche name, is prefaced by two words for king, which came to be identified with the two halves of the country, and usually contains a statement about the sun god Re' in relation to the king. The fifth, the second cartouche, is normally the king's own birth name, and is preceded by the designation "Son of Re'."

Since the pronunciation of names is often unknown, Greek forms, from the history of Manetho (3rd century BC), are used for many kings. In the list the birth name is normally given first, followed by the first cartouche, which is always in *italics*. The kings of the 20th Dynasty used Ramesses as a dynastic name in their second cartouches, and Ptolemaic kings were similarly called Ptolemy.

Overlapping dates within dynasties indicate coregencies. Where two or more dynasties overlap they were mostly accepted in different parts of the country.

Dates that are known with precision are marked *.

The dates are computed from ancient lists, especially the Turin royal papyrus, and various other sources, including a few pieces of astronomical evidence. The margin of error rises from about a decade in the New Kingdom and 3rd Intermediate Period to as much as 150 years for the beginning of the 1st Dynasty. Most 12th-Dynasty dates are fixed precisely, and 18th- and 19th-Dynasty ones must fit one of three astronomically determined alternatives; here a combination of the middle and lowest ones is used. All dates from 664 BC are precise. All native rulers mentioned in Part Two are included in the list.

Above A typical full titulary. "Horus: Mighty bull, perfect of glorious appearances; Two Ladies: Enduring of kingship like Atum [the aging sun god]; Golden Horus: Strong of arm, oppressor of the Nine Bows [traditional enemies]; *Nisut* and *bity* [terms for king]: Menkheprure' [Re' is enduring of manifestations]; Son of Re': Tuthmosis [IV], greatly appearing one; beloved of Amon-Re', giver of [or: given] life like Re'."

Right Typical hieroglyphic writings of selected kings' names; those in the first line are Horus names. Most of the rest are pairs of throne names, by which the kings' contemporaries knew them, and birth names, by which we now know them.

LATE PREDYNASTIC c.3000
Zekhen; Na'rmer

EARLY DYNASTIC PERIOD 2920–2575

1st Dynasty 2920–2770
Menes (= 'Aha?); Djer; Wadj; Den; 'Adjib; Semerkhet; Qa'a

2nd Dynasty 2770–2649
Hetepsekhemwy; Re'neb; Ninetjer; Peribsen; Kha'sekhem(wy)

3rd Dynasty 2649–2575
Zanakht (= Nebka?) 2649–2630
Djoser (Netjerykhet) 2630–2611
Sekhemkhet 2611–2603
Kha'ba 2603–2599
Huni(?) 2599–2575

OLD KINGDOM 2575–2134

4th Dynasty 2575–2465
Snofru 2575–2551
Khufu (Cheops) 2551–2528
Ra'djedef 2528–2520
Khephren (Ra'kha'ef) 2520–2494
Menkaure' 2490–2472
(Mycerinus)
Shepseskaf 2472–2467

5th Dynasty 2465–2323
Userkaf 2465–2458
Sahure' 2458–2446
Neferirkare' Kakai 2446–2426
Shepseskare' Ini 2426–2419
Ra'neferef 2419–2416
Neuserre' Izi 2416–2392
Menkauhor 2396–2388
Djedkare' Izezi 2388–2356
Wenis 2356–2323

6th Dynasty 2323–2150
Teti 2323–2291
Pepy I (*Meryre'*) 2289–2255
Merenre' Nemtyemzaf 2255–2246
Pepy II (*Neferkare'*) 2246–2152

7th/8th Dynasty 2150–2134
Numerous ephemeral kings, including Neferkare'

1st INTERMEDIATE PERIOD 2134–2040

9th/10th Dynasty 2134–2040
(Herakleopolitan)
Several kings called Khety; Merykare'; Ity

11th Dynasty (Theban)
2134–2040
Inyotef I (Sehertawy) 2134–2118
Inyotef II (Wah'ankh) 2118–2069
Inyotef III 2069–2061
(Nakhtnebtepnufer)
Nebhepetre' 2061–2010
Mentuhotpe

MIDDLE KINGDOM 2040–1640

11th Dynasty 2040–1991
(all Egypt)
Nebhepetre' 2061–2010
Mentuhotpe
S'ankhkare' 2010–1998
Mentuhotpe
Nebtawyre' 1998–1991
Mentuhotpe

12th Dynasty 2465–2323
Amenemhet I *1991–1962
(*Sehetepibre'*)
Senwosret I *1971–1926
(*Kheperkare'*)
Amenemhet II *1929–1892
(*Nubkaure'*)
Senwosret II *1897–1878
(*Kha'kheperre'*)
Senwosret III *1878–1841?
(*Kha'kaure'*)
Amenemhet III 1844–1797
(*Nima'atre'*)
Amenemhet IV 1799–1787
(*Ma'akherure'*)
Nefrusobk 1787–1783
(*Sebekkare'*) Q

13th Dynasty 1783–after 1640
About 70 kings. Better-known ones are listed; the numbers are their positions in the complete list
Wegaf (*Khutawyre'*) 1 1783–1779
Amenemhet V (*Sekhemkare'*) 4
Harnedjheriotef (*Hetepibre'*) 9
Amenyqemau 11b
Sebekhotpe I c.1750
(*Kha'ankhre'*) 12
Hor (*Awibre'*) 14; Amenemhet VII (*Sedjefakare'*) 15; Sebekhotpe II (*Sekhemre'-khutawy*) 16;
Khendjer (*Userkare'*) 17
Sebekhotpe III c.1745
(*Sekhemre'-swadjtawy*) 21
Neferhotep I c.1741–1730
(*Kha'sekhemre'*) 22
Sebekhotpe IV c.1730–1720
(*Kha'neferre'*) 24
Sebekhotpe V c.1720–1715
(*Kha'hotepre'*) 25
Aya c.1704–1690
(*Merneferre'*) 27
Mentuemzaf (*Djed'ankhre'*) 32c;
Dedumose II (*Djedneferre'*) 37;
Neferhotep III (*Sekhemre'-s'ankhtawy*) 41a

14th Dynasty
A group of minor kings who were probably all contemporary with the 13th or 15th Dynasty

2nd INTERMEDIATE PERIOD 1640–1532

15th Dynasty (Hyksos)
Salitis; Sheshi;
Khian (*Swoserenre'*)
Apophis c.1585–1542
(*Awoserre'* and others)
Khamudi c.1542–1532

16th Dynasty
Minor Hyksos rulers, contemporary with the 15th Dynasty

17th Dynasty 1640–1550
Numerous Theban kings; numbers give positions in the complete list
Inyotef V c.1640–1635
(*Nubkheprure'*) 1
Sebekzamf I (*Sekhemre'-wadjkha'u*) 3; Nebireyeraw (*Swadjenre'*) 6; Sebekamzaf II (*Sekhemre'-shedtawy*) 10; Ta'o (or Djehuti'o) I (*Senakhtenre'*) 13;
Ta'o (or Djehuti'o) II (*Seqenenre'*) 14
Kamose c.1555–1550
(*Wadjkheperre'*) 15

NEW KINGDOM 1550–1070

18th Dynasty 1550–1307
'Ahmose (*Nebpehtire'*) 1550–1525
Amenophis I 1525–1504
(*Djeserkare'*)
Tuthmosis I 1504–1492
(*'Akheperkare'*)
Tuthmosis II 1492–1479
(*'Akheperenre'*)
Tuthmosis III 1479–1425
(*Menkheperre'*)
Hatshepsut 1473–1458
(*Ma'atkare'*) Q
Amenophis II 1427–1401
(*'Akheprure'*)
Tuthmosis IV 1401–1391
(*Menkheprure'*)
Amenophis III 1391–1353
(*Nebma'atre'*)
Amenophis IV/Akhenaten
(*Neferkheprure' wa'enre'*)
1353–1335
Smenkhkare' 1335–1333
(*'Ankhkheprure'*) (= Nefertiti Q?)
Tut'ankhamun 1333–1323
(*Nebkheprure'*)
Aya 1323–1319
(*Kheperkheprure'*)
Haremhab 1319–1307
(*Djeserkheprure'*)

19th Dynasty 1307–1196
Ramesses I 1307–1306
(*Menpehtire'*)
Sethos I 1306–1290
(*Menma'atre'*)
Ramesses II 1290–1224
(*Userma'atre' setepenre'*)
Merneptah 1224–1214
(*Baenre' hotephirma'at*)
Sethos II 1214–1204
(*Userkheprure' setepenre'*)
Amenmesse (*Menmire'*), usurper during reign of Sethos II
Siptah 1204–1198
(*Akhenre' setepenre'*)
Twosre 1198–1196
(*Sitre' meritamun*) Q

20th Dynasty 1196–1070
Sethnakhte 1196–1194
(*Userkha'ure' meryamun*)
Ramesses III 1194–1163
(*Userma'atre' meryamun*)
Ramesses IV 1163–1156
(*Heqama'atre' setepenamun*)
Ramesses V 1156–1151
(*Userma'atre' sekheperenre'*)
Ramesses VI 1151–1143
(*Nebma'atre' meryamun*)
Ramesses VII 1143–1136
(*Userma'atre' setepenre' meryamun*)
Ramesses VIII 1136–1131
(*Userma'atre' akhenamun*)
Ramesses IX 1131–1112
(*Neferkare' setepenre'*)
Ramesses X 1112–1100
(*Kheperma'atre' setepenre'*)
Ramesses XI 1100–1070
(*Menma'atre' setepenptah*)

3rd INTERMEDIATE PERIOD 1070–712

21st Dynasty 1070–945
Smendes 1070–1044
(*Hedjkheperre' setepenre'*)

Row 1: Na°rmer | °Aha | Den | Peribsen | Kha°sekhemwy | Djoser | Snofru

Row 2: Khufu | Sahure° | Wenis | Pepy II | Mentuhotpe | Amenemhet I

Row 3: Senwosret I | Senwosret III | Neferhotep I | Apophis | Ta°o

Row 4: °Ahmose | Tuthmosis III | Hatshepsut | Amenophis III | Akhenaten (Amenophis IV)

Row 5: Sethos I | Ramesses II | Ramesses III | Ramesses IX | Psusennes I

Row 6: Shoshenq I | Piye | Taharqa | Psammetichus I | Amasis

Row 7: Darius | Nectanebo II | Ptolemy I Soter | Ptolemy IV Philopator | Ptolemy XII Auletes

Row 8: Cleopatra VII Philopator | Augustus | Domitian | Trajan | Septimius Severus

Amenemnisu (*Neferkare'*)	1044–1040
Psusennes I (*'Akheperre' setepenamun*)	1040–992
Amenemope (*Userma'atre' setepenamun*)	993–984
Osorkon I (*'Akheperre' setepenre'*)	984–978
Siamun (*Netjerkheperre' setepenamun*)	978–959
Psusennes II (*Titkheprure' setepenre'*)	959–945

22nd Dynasty   **945–712**

Shoshenq I (*Hedjkheperre' setepenre'*)	945–924
Osorkon II (*Sekhemkheperre' setepenre'*)	924–909
Takelot I (*Userma'atre' setepenamun*)	909–
Shoshenq II (*Heqakheperre' setepenre'*)	–883
Osorkon III (*Userma'atre' setepenamun*)	883–855
Takelot II (*Hedjkheperre' setepenre'*)	860–835
Shoshenq III (*Userma'atre' setepenre'/amun*)	835–783
Pami (*Userma'atre' setepenre'/amun*)	783–773
Shoshenq V (*'Akheperre'*)	773–735
Osorkon V (*'Akheperre' setepenamun*)	735–712

23rd Dynasty   **c.828–712**

Various contemporary lines of kings recognized in Thebes, Hermopolis, Herakleopolis, Leontopolis and Tanis; precise arrangement and order are still disputed

Pedubaste I	828–803
Osorkon IV	777–749
Peftjau'awybast (*Neferkare'*)	740–725

24th Dynasty (Sais)   **724–712**

(Tefnakhte (*Shepsesre'* ?)	724–717
Bocchoris (*Wahkare'*)	717–712

25th Dynasty   **770–712**
(Nubia and Theban area)

Kashta (*Nima'atre'*)	770–750
Piye (*Userma'atre'* and others)	750–712

LATE PERIOD   **712–332**

25th Dynasty   **712–657**
(Nubia and all Egypt)

Shabaka (*Neferkare'*)	712–698
Shebitku (*Djedkaure'*)	698–690
Taharqa (*Khure' nefertem*)	690–664
Tantamani (*Bakare'*)	664–657
(possibly later in Nubia)	

26th Dynasty   ***664–525**

(Necho I	*672–664)
Psammetichus I (*Wahibre'*)	*664–610
Necho II (*Wehemibre'*)	*610–595
Psammetichus II (*Neferibre'*)	*595–589
Apries (*Ha'a'ibre'*)	*589–570
Amasis (*Khnemibre'*)	*570–526
Psammetichus III (*'Ankhkaenre'*)	*526–525

27th Dynasty   ***525–404**
(Persian)

Cambyses	*525–522
Darius I	*521–486
Xerxes I	*486–466
Artaxerxes I	*465–424
Darius II	*424–404

28th Dynasty   ***404–399**

Amyrtaios	*404–399

29th Dynasty   ***399–380**

Nepherites I (*Baenre' merynetjeru*)	*399–393
Psammuthis (*Userre' setepenptah*)	*393
Hakoris (*Khnemma'atre'*)	*393–380
Nepherites II	*380

30th Dynasty   ***380–343**

Nectanebo I (*Kheperkare'*)	*380–362
Teos (*Irma'atenre'*)	*365–360
Nectanebo II (*Senedjemibre' setepenanhur*)	*360–343

2nd Persian Period   ***343–332**

Artaxerxes III Ochus	*343–338
Arses	*338–336
Darius III Codoman	*335–332

Period interrupted by a native ruler Khababash (*Senentanen setepenptah*)

GRECO-ROMAN PERIOD
  *332 BC–395 AD

Macedonian Dynasty   ***332–304**

Alexander III the Great	*332–323
Philip Arrhidaeus	*323–316
Alexander IV	*316–304

Ptolemaic Dynasty   ***304–330**

Ptolemy I Soter I	*304–284
Ptolemy II Philadelphus	*285–246
Ptolemy III Euergetes I	*246–221
Ptolemy IV Philopator	*221–205
Ptolemy V Epiphanes	*205–180
Ptolemy VI Philometor	*180–164, *163–145
Ptolemy VIII Euergetes II (Physkon)	*170–163, *145–116
Ptolemy VII Neos Philopator	*145
Cleopatra III Q and Ptolemy IX Soter II (Lathyros)	*116–107
Cleopatra III Q and Ptolemy X Alexander I	*107–88
Ptolemy IX Soter II	*88–81
Cleopatra Berenice Q	*81–80
Ptolemy XI Alexander II	*80
Ptolemy XII Neos Dionysos (Auletes)	*80–58, *55–51
Berenice IV Q	*58–55
Cleopatra VII Q	***51–30**
Ptolemy XIII	*51–47
Ptolemy XIV	*47–44
Ptolemy XV Caesarion	*44–30

There were further coregencies with queens called Arsinoe, Berenice and Cleopatra, who had no independent reigns. Native usurpers: Harwennofre (205–199), 'Ankhwennofre (199–186), Harsiese (131)

Roman emperors *30 BC–395 AD
(names found in hieroglyphic and demotic texts, down to the tetrarchy)

Augustus	*30 BC–14 AD
Tiberius	*14–37
Gaius (Caligula)	*37–41
Claudius	*41–54
Nero	*54–68
Galba	*68–69
Otho	*69
Vespasian	*69–79
Titus	*79–81
Domitian	*81–96
Nerva	*96–98
Trajan	*98–117
Hadrian	*117–138
Antoninus Pius	*138–161
Marcus Aurelius	*161–180
Lucius Verus	*161–169
Commodus	*180–192
Septimius Severus	*193–211
Caracalla	*198–217
Geta	*209–212
Macrinus	*217–218
Diadumenianus	*218
Severus Alexander	*222–235
Gordian III	*238–244
Philip	*244–249
Decius	*249–251
Gallus and Volusianus	*251–253
Valerian	*253–260
Gallienus	*253–268
Macrianus and Quietus	*260–261
Aurelian	*270–275
Probus	*276–282
Diocletian	*284–305
Maximian	*286–305
Galerius	*293–311

Gallery of Kings

The image of an Egyptian king is more a statement of an ideal than a portrait. Of those shown, only Amenophis IV and Ptolemy IV depart from the norm, one highly stylized, the other influenced by Hellenistic portraiture.

Faces may depict general qualities. Some early figures convey an impressive strength, which becomes greatly refined. Neferhotep I follows the 12th-Dynasty tradition of the "suffering king." The later heads are mostly rather blander.

Kings normally wear a crown, uraeus (cobra on the forehead) and false beard. The most important of the many crowns are the tall white crown, the primary symbol of kingship in early periods, associated with *nisut* (the normal word for king) and with Upper Egypt; and the squat blue crown – blue is the most prestigious color – from the 18th Dynasty on. Further crowns on these figures are the *nemes* head-cloth, typical of the Middle Kingdom; a flat cap; and a skull cap. Merenre' is youthful and bareheaded.

Palette of Na'rmer, late Predynastic (c.2950). Schist.

1st-Dynasty king, c.2850. Ivory.

Kha'sekhem, 2nd Dynasty (c.2670). Limestone.

3rd-Dynasty king, c.2600. Pink granite.

Shepseskaf, 2472–2467 (?). Diorite.

Merenre' Nemtyemzaf, c.2255. Copper.

Neferhotep I, c.1741–1730. Black basalt.

Amenophis IV (Akhenaten), c.1350. Sandstone.

Tut'ankhamun, 1333–1323. Wood and gesso.

Ramesses II, 1290–1224. Black granite.

Sethos I, 1305–1290. Black basalt.

King of the 3rd Intermediate Period, c.1000–800. Quartzite.

Amasis, 570–526 (?). Quartzite.

Ptolemy IV Philopator, 221–205 (?). Schist.

39

Middle Kingdom

The last two kings of the 11th Dynasty retained Thebes as the capital. The second, Nebtawyre' Mentuhotpe, is ignored by later lists, probably being seen as an illegitimate ruler. During their reigns there was building activity in much of the country. Quarries were opened up, most notably in the Wadi Hammamat, and the Red Sea route was revived. All this indicates that Egypt was strong, but the political order did not last. The vizier under Nebtawyre' Mentuhotpe, Amenemhet, was also the first king of the 12th Dynasty, but the mode of transfer of power to him is unknown; he came from a prominent family in Elephantine.

The most important political act of Amenemhet I (1991–1962) was to move the royal residence from Thebes to near Memphis, where he founded a city called Itjtawy, "[Amenemhet is] seizer of the Two Lands." The site itself was probably an administrative area, including the pyramids of Amenemhet I and Senwosret I, while the main city remained at Memphis. The capital was both an innovation and a return to Old Kingdom traditions, which were also taken up in art.

In foreign policy Amenemhet I built on the work of Nebhepetre' Mentuhotpe in Nubia, and in several campaigns in the last years of his reign, in which he did not take part himself, conquered the whole area as far as the second cataract. The leader of these campaigns was Senwosret I (1971–1926), and the ten-year overlap between their reigns was another innovation, setting the institutional pattern for coregencies. Senwosret I was the more active partner for the joint years. Amenemhet I was apparently murdered while his son was on a campaign to Libya, but, perhaps because of the coregency, there was no resulting disorder.

During the reigns of Amenemhet I and Senwosret I there was much building in Egypt, and the great series of forts in Lower Nubia was begun. At the same time a number of important works of literature were written, and the material and intellectual achievements of the dynasty made it classical in later Egyptian and in modern eyes. An instance of this is the relief carving of the chapel of Senwosret I at Karnak, which served as a model for early 18th-Dynasty artists. But despite these achievements of its first rulers, far more archaeological material is preserved for the reigns of Senwosret III (1878–1841), Amenemhet III (1844–1797), and later, than there is for the years 2000–1900 BC.

The 12th-Dynasty king with the most lasting reputation was Senwosret III. He is noted especially for his Nubian campaigns, in which the frontier was moved south to Semna, at the southern end of the second cataract, for the establishment of new forts and for the extension of others. In later times he was worshiped there as a god, and the temple of Tuthmosis III at Semna is dedicated to him and to Dedwen, a local deity. The main purpose of this military activity may have been to counter the increasing influence of the Kerma rulers to the south. During his reign there was also a campaign to Palestine, which was apparently not intended to conquer the area, but which came at the beginning of a period of considerable Egyptian influence there. The region was then seminomadic, and did not become settled until the end of the 12th Dynasty. Senwosret III worked with a sizable standing army, whose organization has only recently begun to be understood.

Senwosret III made important reforms in the administration of Egypt, which seem to have completed the removal of power from provincial governors. The country was organized into four "regions," each of which corresponded to roughly half the Nile valley or the delta. From documents of the late 12th and 13th Dynasties, principally from el-Lahun, we gain an impression of a pervasive bureaucratic organization, which came to run the country under its own momentum.

Within Egypt the most striking visible legacy of Senwosret III is his royal sculpture, which breaks earlier conventions in showing an aging, careworn face, perhaps symbolizing the burdens of kingship, as depicted in the literature of the period. The same style was used in statues of his successor Amenemhet III, whose long reign was apparently peaceful. Amenemhet III was deified later in the Faiyum, where he built one of his two pyramids and a number of other monuments, and where he may have begun a land reclamation scheme. His predecessors had, however, also taken an interest in the area, and he may have reaped the glory of a long enterprise.

In the reigns of Amenemhet IV (1799–1787) and Queen Nefrusobk (1787–1783) there was no loss of prosperity in the country, but the presence of a woman on the throne indicates that the ruling family was dying out. There is a complete continuity in the archaeological record between the 12th and 13th Dynasties, even though the nature of

Right: Egypt in the Middle Kingdom and Second Intermediate Period
● Sites with finds of the Palestinian Middle Bronze culture of the 18th–17th century BC.
▽ Selected sites of the "pan-grave" culture of the Second Intermediate Period. These people were nomads of the eastern desert, many of them mercenaries in the service of various rulers. Pottery similar to theirs has been found in the Red Sea hills and at Kassala in southeastern Sudan. By the New Kingdom they were completely assimilated in Egypt, giving their name, *Medjay*, to the police force.

Far right: The second cataract forts of the Middle Kingdom
The cataract area is a largely unnavigable stretch of rapids 30 km long. The chain of 12th-Dynasty frontier forts was the largest surviving ancient group in the world until it was submerged in Lake Nasser. The northern forts were begun under Senwosret I; Semna and Kumma were added by Senwosret III.

Below Reliefs in the chapel of Senwosret I at Karnak, reconstructed from blocks found in the 3rd pylon. The scene shows Atum leading the king before Amon-Re' Kamutef. The elaborate, refined style inspired artists of the early 18th Dynasty.

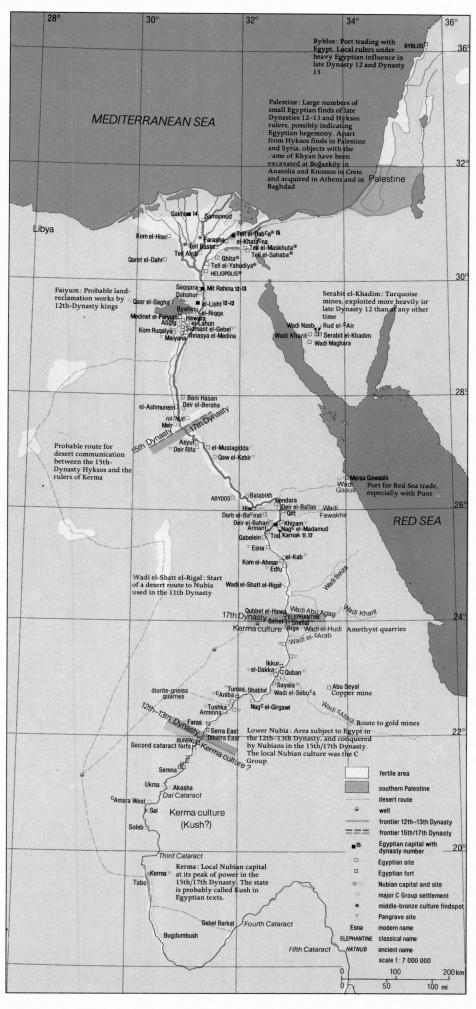

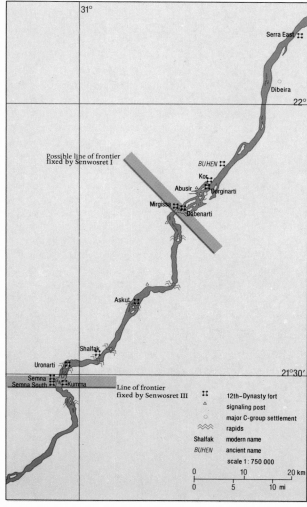

the kingship seems to have changed considerably.

In about 150 years some 70 kings of the 13th Dynasty came and went. While at times there were no doubt rival claimants to the throne, this was not the rule. The country seems to have remained stable, even though there was no official means of replacing kings in rapid succession, but the kings themselves must have been of relatively little account. The most important people in the country seem instead to have been the viziers, the highest officials, of whom a family is known that spanned a large part of the 18th century. Official titles of all ranks proliferated at this time, quite possibly because of an increase in the size of the bureaucracy, a phenomenon with parallels elsewhere in the world in periods of slow decline.

As late as 1720 Egypt appears to have lost little power or prestige at home or abroad. If we use the number of private monuments as a measure, there seems even to have been an increase in prosperity in the country, and a leveling of wealth, since there are few royal monuments. There were many immigrants from Palestine, apparently peaceful arrivals, who were absorbed into the lowest levels of Egyptian society, but at least one of whom, Khendjer, became king of Egypt. They probably came as a result of shifts of population in the Near East after 1800, and were forerunners of the movement that was to bring foreign rule in the 2nd Intermediate Period. In the later 13th Dynasty the eastern delta was heavily settled by Asiatics, including areas that had been completely Egyptian in the 12th Dynasty, such as that around

Qantir, which became the Hyksos and later the Ramessid capital of Egypt. Egypt retained control of Lower Nubia, probably until near the end of the 13th Dynasty, but the local army contingents became increasingly independent, and settled as permanent inhabitants, some of whom stayed behind after the area was overrun from the south at the beginning of the 15th/17th Dynasties.

Second Intermediate Period

Around 1640 the position of the 13th Dynasty was usurped by a foreign group conventionally called the Hyksos, a Greek form derived from an Egyptian phrase meaning "ruler of foreign lands"; the method of takeover is uncertain. The Hyksos, the 15th Egyptian Dynasty, seem to have been recognized as the chief line of kings in the whole country, but they tolerated other contenders. The 13th Dynasty may have continued in existence, as may also the 14th, a line of rulers in the northwestern delta (whose existence has been doubted).

There was also a parallel group of Hyksos rulers known as the 16th Dynasty, a term which may simply cover other Asiatic rulers who proclaimed themselves king, wherever they may have been. The most important of these dynasties was the 17th, a line of native Egyptians who ruled from Thebes, holding the Nile valley from the first cataract north as far as Cusae (el-Qusiya). In the south Lower Nubia was conquered by the Nubian rulers of Kerma. There were therefore three main divisions of the area that had been held by the 12th–13th Dynasties. For almost a century there appears to have been peace among them.

The names of 15th-Dynasty kings have been found on small objects from widely separated sites in the Near East, showing that they had diplomatic or trading relations over a very large area. Contact abroad brought with it a number of primarily technical innovations which were to be important in later periods. Some of the novelties probably came with Asiatic immigrants, while other specifically military ones may have been acquired during campaigns, in some cases in the early 18th Dynasty. Until this time Egypt had been technologically backward in comparison with the Near East; during the New Kingdom the two were roughly on a par. Among the new techniques were bronzeworking, which replaced the importation of ready-alloyed bronze and the use of arsenic copper; an improved potter's wheel and the vertical loom; hump-backed cattle (zebu) and new vegetable and fruit crops; the horse and chariot, composite bows, and new shapes of scimitar and other weapons. On a different plane new musical instruments came into fashion, and 18th-Dynasty dances are different from those of earlier periods.

With Seqenenre' Ta'o II of the 17th Dynasty the Thebans began their struggle to expel the Hyksos. The first episode of the battle is known only from a New Kingdom story, the "Quarrel of Apophis [the Hyksos king] and Seqenenre'," but Seqenenre''s mummy shows that he died violently, possibly in battle. Two stelae of his successor Kamose describe extensive skirmishes between Thebes and the Hyksos, who were allied with the Nubian kings. Kamose nearly reached Avaris, the Hyksos capital, and campaigned as far south as Buhen, but we hear nothing of him after his third year.

New Kingdom

Kamose's successor 'Ahmose (1550–1525) finally drove out the Hyksos rulers around 1532 – many years after Kamose's attempts. The course of the expulsion is recorded very briefly by 'Ahmose, son of Ebana, a soldier from el-Kab. After his victory 'Ahmose continued his thrust into Palestine, where the Hyksos may have had allies or some measure of control, and campaigned there for some years. In Nubia he fought as far south as the island of Sai, near the third cataract, while he also apparently had to deal with a rebellion in Egypt. His reign has left a number of inscriptions from different parts of the country, including one showing family piety to his grandmother in Abydos; there is a notable emphasis on the women of the royal family at this time.

'Ahmose left behind him a unified state with a much-improved economy. It stretched from south of the second cataract to somewhere in Palestine, and was the chief power in the Near East of the time. His son Amenophis I (1525–1504) may have extended Egyptian influence still further south; nothing is known of Asian affairs during his reign. In the late 18th–20th Dynasties Amenophis and his mother 'Ahmose-Nofretari were revered by the inhabitants of Deir el-Medina, possibly because he had founded the institutional complex to which they belonged, which built the royal tombs. The first burial in the Valley of the Kings and the foundation of the village itself appear, however, to date to the next reign.

Tuthmosis I (1504–1492) was a relative by marriage of his predecessor, who had probably left no male heir. His military exploits were the most extraordinary of any Egyptian king. In the first years of his reign he reached the Euphrates in the north and Kurgus, upstream of the fourth cataract of the Nile, in the south. These feats define the limits of territory ever conquered by Egypt, but may not have been such a leap forward as they seem. In Syria-Palestine there may have been preparatory battles in the previous reigns, and it seems that the Egyptians laid claim to the area when there was no other major power there. During the reign of Amenophis I the kingdom of Mitanni, Egypt's chief rival for a century, was formed in northern Syria, and this was Tuthmosis I's adversary on the Euphrates.

The petty states of Syria and Palestine that formed the Egyptian "empire" were bound to the Egyptian king by oaths of allegiance and paid him tribute, but remained self-governing and pursued their own local political ends. Egyptian presence was maintained by relatively small army detachments and a few high officials. Nubia, however, was treated as a colonial land and administered directly by Egyptians under a viceroy who was responsible to the Egyptian king. Both areas included territories that formed part of the endowment of Egyptian institutions such as temples, but the harsher terms of the Nubian system seem to have contributed to widespread depopulation in the 19th–20th

Right: Egypt in the New Kingdom and Third Intermediate Period
The political divisions shown are those of the Third Intermediate Period, when the area including el-Hiba and stretching south to Aswan was ruled by the high priests in Thebes, who were only nominally subject to the northern kings of Dynasties 21–23. North of el-Hiba the kings of Dynasties 21–22 ruled directly, their territory being later subdivided into virtually autonomous areas (see map p. 47).

Left Two name scarabs and a cowroid of the Second Intermediate period. These are typical of the time, and our main source for its history and administration.
a The Eldest King's Son Ipeq, who is known from more than 40 scarabs; 15th Dynasty.
b The Ruler of Foreign Countries ("Hyksos") Khian, 4th ruler of the 15th Dynasty.
c Cowroid of King Nikare', an obscure ruler, perhaps of the 16th Dynasty. Steatite. Maximum height 17·5 mm. Frazer – von Bissing Collection, University of Basel.

Below Dagger handle of the reign of Nebkhopeshre' Apophis (probably the same as 'Awoserre') of the 15th Dynasty. The man hunting antelopes is the "servant of his lord [Apophis], Nahman" (a Semitic name). From Saqqara. Length of handle 11·4 cm. Cairo, Egyptian Museum.

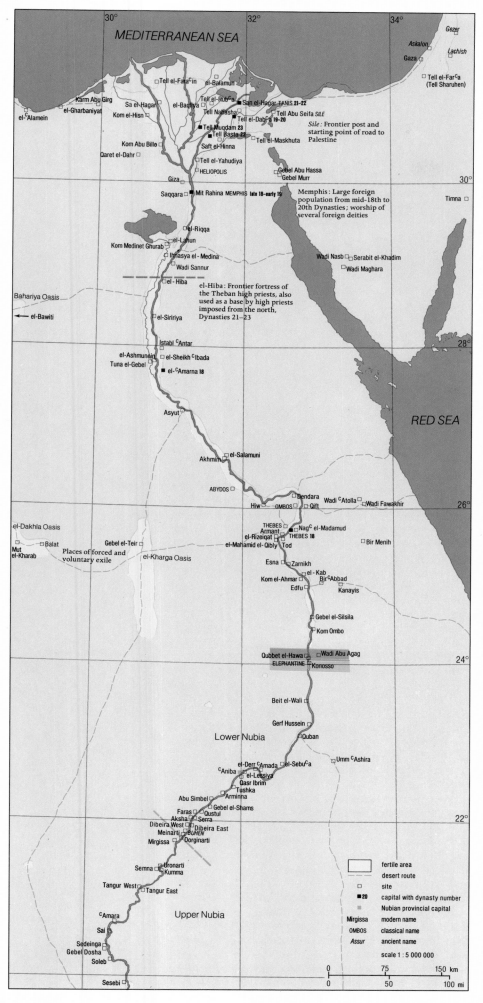

Sile: Frontier post and starting point of road to Palestine

Memphis: Large foreign population from mid-18th to 20th Dynasties; worship of several foreign deities

el-Hiba: Frontier fortress of the Theban high priests, also used as a base by high priests imposed from the north, Dynasties 21–23

Places of forced and voluntary exile

	fertile area
	desert route
□	site
■20	capital with dynasty number
	Nubian provincial capital
Mirgissa	modern name
OMBOS	classical name
Assur	ancient name

scale 1 : 5 000 000

0   75   150 km
0   50   100 mi

Dynasties. Both in the Near East and in Nubia a prime motive for Egyptian presence was to secure the routes for long-distance trade and access to raw materials; defense was probably a secondary consideration. Trade and Nubian gold produced much of the country's wealth and power in international relations.

Within Egypt the corollary of the continued wars of expansion was an enlarged standing army. In effect there were two new forces in the internal politics of the country, the priesthood and the army. These became ever more important in later Egyptian history, but even in the 18th Dynasty the role of religion may be seen in royal donations to the temples – particularly that of Amun at Karnak – in gratitude for success in war, and in the oracular choice of some kings by gods. On the military side a number of the most important men of the period were former army officers, and the army itself was drafted for constructional work.

Tuthmosis II (1492–1479), whose reign has left little trace, was succeeded by his young son by a minor wife, Tuthmosis III (1479–1425), for whom Hatshepsut, Tuthmosis II's widow, acted initially as regent. During the first 20 years of Tuthmosis III's reign there was little military activity, and Egypt seems to have lost ground considerably in Asia. In Tuthmosis III's seventh year Hatshepsut proclaimed herself female "king" (there was no place in Egyptian ideology for a queen regnant), and ruled as the dominant partner and personality in a coregency with her nephew until her death around his year 22. Tuthmosis III clearly acquiesced in the situation to some extent, since for much of the time he was old enough to have organized resistance to his aunt if he had wished.

Under Hatshepsut there flourished one of Egypt's few great commoners, Senenmut, who was tutor and steward to her daughter. About 20 statues of Senenmut have been recovered from sites in the Theban area, and he was uniquely privileged in having himself depicted among the reliefs in the temple of Deir el-Bahri. His charge, Nefrure', who is also very prominent in the record, may have been intended to be the future coregent or wife of Tuthmosis III, but died shortly after he assumed sole rule.

There is no record of campaigns to Asia under Hatshepsut. A curious inscription in the temple of Speos Artemidos near Beni Hasan details her hatred for the Hyksos, stating that she restored good order – a strange assertion two generations after their expulsion. It is as if her rejection of the Hyksos, who had not previously come in for such vilification, justified her not following her predecessors' policy in Asia. At her death Tuthmosis III launched a long series of Near Eastern campaigns, in which he began by reconquering territory in Palestine that had recently fallen away from allegiance to Egypt. In the next 20 years the Egyptians fought mainly in Syria, where the Mitanni resisted successfully, and Tuthmosis had to renounce his furthest points of expansion on the Euphrates. This conflict was to last for another generation. Tuthmosis III also campaigned in Nubia late in his reign, and established the provincial capital of Napata near the fourth cataract.

Tuthmosis III built at many sites, and important private tombs date to his reign. All this activity is a

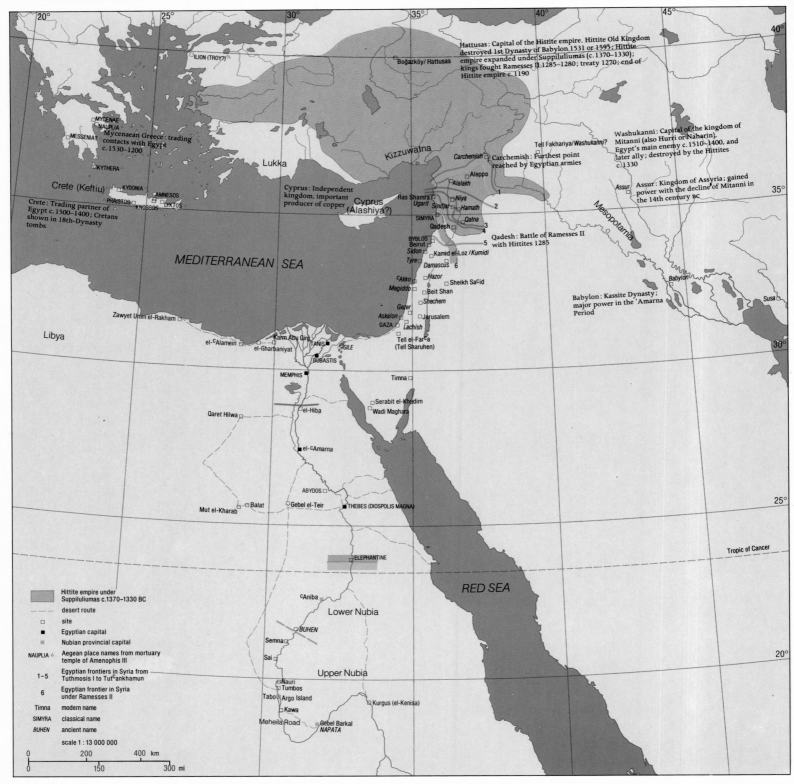

Hattusas: Capital of the Hittite empire. Hittite Old Kingdom destroyed 1st Dynasty of Babylon 1531 or 1595; Hittite empire expanded under Suppiluliumas (c. 1370–1330); kings fought Ramesses II 1285–1280; treaty 1270; end of Hittite empire c. 1190

Washukanni: Capital of the kingdom of Mitanni (also Hurri or Naharin), Egypt's main enemy c. 1510–1400, and later ally; destroyed by the Hittites c. 1330

Carchemish: Furthest point reached by Egyptian armies

Assur: Kingdom of Assyria; gained power with the decline of Mitanni in the 14th century BC

Cyprus: Independent kingdom, important producer of copper

Qadesh: Battle of Ramesses II with Hittites 1285

Crete: Trading partner of Egypt c. 1500–1400; Cretans shown in 18th-Dynasty tombs

Mycenaean Greece: trading contacts with Egypt c. 1530–1200

Babylon: Kassite Dynasty; major power in the 'Amarna Period

Hittite empire under Suppiluliumas c.1370–1330 BC

- - - - desert route

□ site

■ Egyptian capital

■ Nubian provincial capital

NAUPLIA △ Aegean place names from mortuary temple of Amenophis III

1–5 Egyptian frontiers in Syria from Tuthmosis I to Tut'ankhamun

6 Egyptian frontier in Syria under Ramesses II

Timna modern name

SIMYRA classical name

BUHEN ancient name

scale 1 : 13 000 000

sign of the economic benefits of expansion. Late in his reign he turned against the memory of Hatshepsut, ordering that her images in relief be erased and replaced with figures of himself and his two predecessors, and that statues of her be smashed. This change of heart may have been due as much to the internal politics of the time when it was done as to actions of Hatshepsut herself.

In his last years Tuthmosis III took his son Amenophis II (1427–1401) as his coregent. Amenophis fought campaigns both before and after his father's death, and, like other kings, was faced with the problem that petty rulers owed allegiance to and had respect for a king rather than for Egypt in general. New kings often needed to assert their authority afresh. His military exploits were parades of strength as far as Syria – he presented himself as a formidable athlete – not campaigns of strategic significance. The parades had a message for foreign powers; at the end of the campaign of year 9 Amenophis received presentations of gifts (the normal mode of diplomatic contact) from the three major powers of the time, the Hittites, Mitanni and Babylon. The Hittites and Babylon were emerging from a period of relative weakness, while Mitanni was at the peak of its power.

Both abroad and at home the reigns of Tuthmosis IV (1401–1391) and Amenophis III (1391–1353) form

Egypt and the Near East (c.1530–1190 BC)
The successive frontiers of Egyptian possessions in Syria-Palestine, from north to south and in chronological order, are (after Helck):

———— the limit of Egyptian expansion under Tuthmosis I

———— late in the reign of Tuthmosis III

———— year 7 of Amenophis II

———— under Tuthmosis IV

———— under Tut'ankhamun

- - - - under Ramesses II

△ places in the Aegean area identified in a list from the mortuary temple of Amenophis III

a single phase. Egypt lost more ground to Mitanni under Tuthmosis IV, but the two powers made a peace before his death and sealed it with the marriage of a Mitanni princess as a minor wife of Tuthmosis IV. The one-way traffic in women shows either that Egypt was acknowledged to be the superior power or simply that, in the words of Amenophis III to the king of Babylon, "since antiquity, a daughter of the king of Egypt has not been given to anybody." In his turn Amenophis III married more than one Mitanni princess.

Peace brought with it a further upsurge in the country's wealth. For the number and size of buildings erected the reign of Amenophis III can be compared only with the much longer one of Ramesses II, while royal and private sculpture was produced on a greater scale than at any other time. Much of this work is of a very high quality. New approaches were exploited in the planning of the whole Theban area (and probably Memphis), with processional ways lined with sphinxes linking the main temples. An enormous artificial lake on the west bank, the Birket Habu, acted as the focus of a new quarter that included a royal palace at el-Malqata and the king's massive mortuary temple. In a significant ideological shift, the king deified himself in his own lifetime. The most important private individual of the reign, Amenhotpe son of Hapu, was a retired military official who directed much of the building work and was honored with a mortuary temple of his own. In later periods he was deified, his reputation in death building on his status in life.

Amenophis IV (1353–1335) became crown prince after the death of a prince Thutmose. He started his reign by giving himself the title of high priest of the sun god, a role which was traditional for Egyptian kings but was not incorporated into their titulary. He then formulated a new dogmatic name for the sun god, "Reʿ-Harakhty who rejoices on the horizon in his name of Shu [or 'light'] which is the sun disk [Aten]." This was soon incorporated into a pair of cartouches, giving the god the character of a king, and a new representation of the god was devised, which shows a disk with rays ending in hands that hold out the hieroglyph for "life" to the king and queen. The development of this cult, which left almost no place for any of the traditional deities except the sun god, became, with self-glorification, the king's main purpose in life. His chief wife, Nefertiti, played an almost equally prominent role in the changes. There was a vast building program at Karnak in the first six years of the reign, in addition to structures in a number of other towns. All were decorated with reliefs in a radically new artistic style and iconography. One of the Karnak shrines contained a series of colossal royal statues, of which perhaps a quarter were of the queen; pictures of temple decoration at el-ʿAmarna from later in the reign show equal numbers of colossi of king and queen.

Probably in his fifth year of reign Amenophis IV changed his name to Akhenaten ("beneficial to the disk") and began a new capital on a virgin site at el-ʿAmarna. The remains of the city were very thoroughly dismantled in the following period, but have nevertheless produced much valuable evidence. Akhenaten's great sun hymn was inscribed in the tomb of his chief official, Aya, and other

reliefs and small objects demonstrate the development of his religion. Around year 9 the god's dogmatic name was changed to the more purist "Reʿ, horizon ruler, who rejoices on the horizon in his name of Reʿ the father, who has returned as the sun disk," but after this there was little further development, and the number of monuments from the latest years of the reign is small. Probably at the time of the introduction of the second dogmatic name Akhenaten closed temples for other gods throughout the country, and had the word Amun, and occasionally "gods" in the plural, hacked out wherever they occurred – a vast undertaking, which must have had military support. There was probably little popular enthusiasm for these changes.

Akhenaten had six daughters but no sons by Nefertiti; his second successor Tutʿankhamun was probably the son of a secondary wife, Kiya, whose memory was persecuted late in the reign. At about the same time as this a coregent appeared on the monuments who seems to have been Nefertiti, using her second name Nefernefruaten with additional elements and wearing the attributes of kingship – like Hatshepsut earlier in the dynasty. The titulary of Nefernefruaten changed rapidly; in the final version Smenkhkareʿ displaced the original name – a stage which may correspond to a brief reign by the former Nefertiti after Akhenaten's death. Tutʿankhaten, later Tutʿankhamun, a boy of about seven, then succeeded (1333–1323). Early in his reign the new religion was abandoned, although its complete exclusion and persecution date rather later, and Memphis, which had long been the chief city, became the capital.

While Tutʿankhamun was king, power was in the hands of Aya and the general Haremhab. Tutʿankhamun's inscriptions record the restoration

Above Cuneiform letter from Tushratta of Mitanni to Amenophis III. At the bottom of the tablet is an Egyptian hieratic filing note of year 36 of Amenophis, in ink. The letter accompanied a statue of Ishtar of Nineveh that was sent to Egypt as a healing deity. The statue had been in Egypt once before in the time of Tushratta's predecessor Suttarna II. From el-ʿAmarna. London, British Museum.

Above Cartouches of the sun god of Amenophis IV/Akhenaten. The left pair is the early form and the right the late form; translations in the text.

Right Squatting statue of Amenhotpe, son of Hapu, shown as a corpulent, elderly man (he lived more than 80 years); found by the 7th pylon at Karnak. The statue was later venerated, and its nose was recut in antiquity. Height 1·42 m. Reign of Amenophis III. Cairo, Egyptian Museum.

of the temples, but no details of foreign policy; Egyptian possessions in the Near East were in disarray after the campaigns of the Hittite king Suppiluliumas. Aya (1323–1319) occupied the throne briefly, and was succeeded by Haremhab (1319–1307), who is normally placed in the 18th Dynasty, but was considered by Egyptians of the next century to be the first king of their era, which we call the 19th Dynasty.

Haremhab dismantled the temples of Amenophis IV at Karnak and built there extensively himself. He also annexed most of Tut'ankhamun's inscriptions, perhaps from a feeling that they recorded his own exploits. His second successor, Sethos I (1305–1290), carried his restoration work to fruition, repairing countless monuments, persecuting the memory of Akhenaten, and removing his name and those of his three successors from the official record. He also built extensively himself. In the Near East he fought several campaigns, succeeding, during a period of Hittite weakness, in regaining temporarily some Egyptian possessions in Syria. The main records of the campaigns are impressive battle reliefs of a new, more realistic type.

Late in his reign Sethos I associated his son Ramesses II (1290–1224) with him on the throne. The new king inherited his father's problems in Syria. After a success in year 4 he confronted the Hittite army for the first time in year 5 in an indecisive battle at Qadesh, which Ramesses presented as a great victory and recorded in many temple reliefs. After further engagements in the next few years there was a truce, followed by a formal treaty in year 21. The text of this is preserved in Egyptian in temple reliefs of Ramesses II, and in Akkadian on cuneiform tablets from the Hittite capital Boğazköy (ancient Hattusas). Peace continued for more than 50 years, confirmed by marriages between Ramesses II and Hittite princesses.

Ramesses II built more buildings and had more colossal statues than any other Egyptian king, also having his name carved or reliefs cut on many older monuments. Like Amenophis III, he was deified in his own lifetime, and by his projection of his personality he made the name Ramesses synonymous with kingship for centuries. But the official building program was not accompanied by as many works for private individuals as that of Amenophis III. Many projects date to early in his reign, while the later buildings show a fall-off in craftsmanship. It seems that there was considerable economic decline in his later years.

One of the most important undertakings of Ramesses II was the removal of the capital to a new site in the delta called Pi-Ri'amsese ("Domain of Ramesses"), probably at modern el-Khata'na and Qantir. The royal family came from this area, but the main reason for the move was probably that the international and economic center of the country had shifted into the delta proper. This change is one reason why we know less of the history of the Late Period than we do of the New Kingdom.

Ramesses II survived many of his enormous family, and was succeeded by his 13th son Merneptah (1224–1214). Early in his reign Merneptah was confronted with Libyan aggression, which had already been resisted by Sethos I and had led to Ramesses II's construction of forts westwards along the Mediterranean coast. A battle was fought in the western delta against invading Libyans and "sea peoples" – a group of tribes with names that suggest Mediterranean origin. The invaders had intended to settle, and brought their wives and children with them. The battle went against them, however, and some fled, while others were forcibly settled as prisoners of war.

After the death of Merneptah there was a period of dynastic struggles which ended in the brief sole rule of a queen, Twosre (1198–1196), the widow of the short-lived Sethos II (1214–1204). During this time the true power in the land seems to have been a high official, Bay, perhaps of Syrian origin, who may be mentioned under an alias in a later document that presents such a person as the evil genius of the period.

The first king of the 20th Dynasty, Sethnakhte (1196–1194), refers in an inscription to a period of civil war which lasted into the second and last year of his own reign, and ended with his defeat of the rebels. He implies that disorder was widespread in the country before his arrival, but there were officials who lived from the reign of Merneptah into that of Ramesses III, so the violence was probably limited to court and military circles. Ramesses III (1194–1163) inherited a stable internal situation, and exploited it in a number of building works, but was severely pressed from the north by two attempted Libyan invasions and by a renewed attack of the "sea peoples" that came in the gap between them. All of these were defeated, and Egypt also retained control of Sinai and southern Palestine.

Ramesses III's titulary was almost identical to that of Ramesses II, and his mortuary complex at Medinet Habu was modeled closely on Ramesses II's Ramesseum. He and the other 20th-Dynasty kings were unusually conservative in their presentation of themselves, as if they did not have the confidence to be self-sufficient. But whereas the achievements of Ramesses III were considerable, this is not true of his successors. In 90 years there were eight more kings called Ramesses, a name they adopted in addition to their birth names on becoming king. All were apparently descended from Ramesses III, but the throne was the center of much rivalry, beginning with the death of Ramesses III himself, before which there was a conspiracy among his wives to place one of his sons on the throne. Abroad Egypt lost control of Palestine during the dynasty, while Nubia fell away at its end. Its only major monuments after the reign of Ramesses III are the royal tombs and the temple of Khons at Karnak, which was not completed until the Ptolemaic Period.

It is possible to reconstruct much of the administration of the country in the 19th and especially the 20th Dynasty from papyrus documents and ostraca. The most important long-term change was that a high proportion of land passed to temples, in particular that of Amun at Karnak. State and temple were interlocked in the management of the country, but the temple of Amun eventually acquired virtual control of Upper Egypt. The major priestly offices became hereditary, and thus largely independent of the king, so that the high priests formed a dynasty that came to rival him. Another significant practice was the settling of prisoners of

Egypt in the late Third Intermediate Period
This map shows the political divisions of Egypt about the time of the campaign of Piye (c.730).

■ cities ruled by a king, with dynasty number if appropriate

• cities listed with their rulers in the victory stela of Piye; several further cities cannot be located. Compare Assurbanipal's list marked on map p. 49.

The frontiers of the areas ruled by Hermopolis and Herakleopolis are very hypothetical.

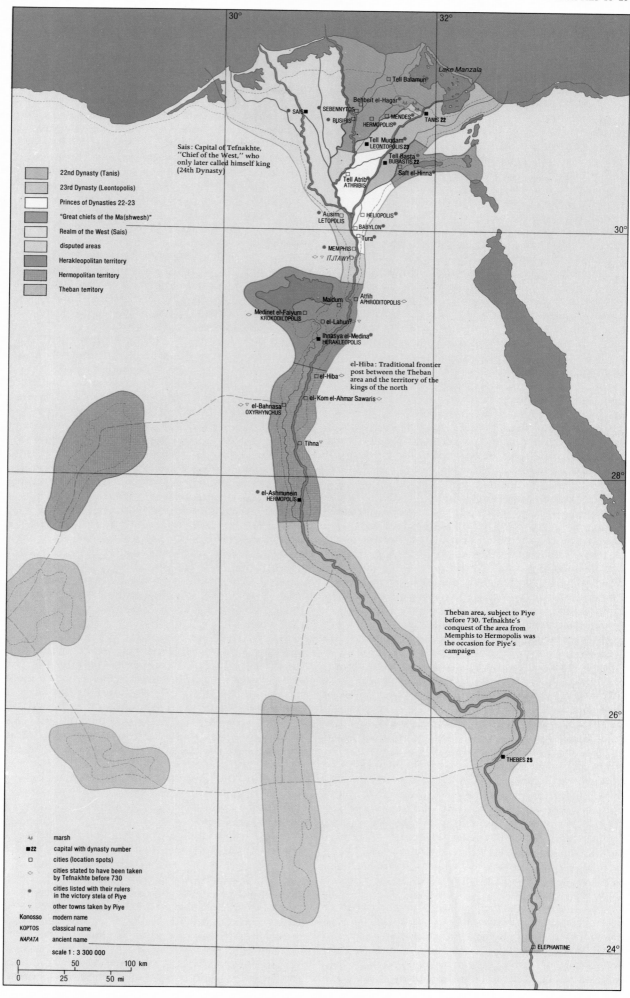

	22nd Dynasty (Tanis)
	23rd Dynasty (Leontopolis)
	Princes of Dynasties 22-23
	"Great chiefs of the Ma(shwesh)"
	Realm of the West (Sais)
	disputed areas
	Herakleopolitan territory
	Hermopolitan territory
	Theban territory

Sais: Capital of Tefnakhte, "Chief of the West," who only later called himself king (24th Dynasty)

el-Hiba: Traditional frontier post between the Theban area and the territory of the kings of the north

Theban area, subject to Piye before 730. Tefnakhte's conquest of the area from Memphis to Hermopolis was the occasion for Piye's campaign

Teli Balamun
Behbeit el-Hagâr
SAIS
SEBENNYTOS
MENDES
HERMOPOLIS
TANIS 22
BUSIRIS
Tell Muqdam
LEONTOPOLIS 23
Tell Basta
BUBASTIS 22
Tell Atrib
ATHRIBIS
Saft el-Hinna
Lake Manzala
Ausim
LETOPOLIS
HELIOPOLIS
BABYLON
Tura
MEMPHIS
ITJTAWY
Maidum
Atfih
APHRODITOPOLIS
Medinet el-Faiyum
KROKODILOPOLIS
el-Lahun?
Ihnasya el-Medina
HERAKLEOPOLIS
el-Hiba
el-Bahnasa
OXYRHYNCHUS
el-Kom el-Ahmar Sawaris
Tihna
el-Ashmunein
HERMOPOLIS
THEBES 25
ELEPHANTINE

⚬	marsh
■22	capital with dynasty number
□	cities (location spots)
◇	cities stated to have been taken by Tefnakhte before 730
•	cities listed with their rulers in the victory stela of Piye
▽	other towns taken by Piye
Konosso	modern name
KOPTOS	classical name
NAPATA	ancient name

scale 1 : 3 300 000

0   50   100 km
0   25   50 mi

war in military colonies. The Libyans were the most important of these groups. Although they were soon completely Egyptian, they kept a separate identity, marked by the tribal name Meshwesh (often abbreviated to Ma), and in time became the main political force in the country.

While these elements were splitting Egypt into a loose-knit, almost feudal society, the movements of peoples in the Near East at the beginning of the dynasty introduced the Iron Age there, but not in Egypt. The entire eastern Mediterranean entered a twilight period, from which Egypt suffered less than other countries, but the Near East emerged technologically more advanced, and Egypt lost its preeminent position for good.

In the reign of Ramesses XI (1100–1070) the viceroy of Nubia, Panehsy, fought a battle for the Theban area which he ultimately lost, retiring to 'Aniba in Lower Nubia, where he was buried. After his intervention the previous line of high priests disappeared from office, and a military man called Herihor replaced them in Ramesses' year 19. Priest and officer made a powerful combination, and Herihor enhanced his status beyond that of any of his predecessors, having himself portrayed as king and using an alternative dating system, which probably alludes to the presence of two "kings" in the country. After only five years he died. His successor Pi'ankh also predeceased Ramesses XI, but by then the virtual partition of the country was established, although later high priests only occasionally claimed the titles of king. The pattern had been set for the next period.

Third Intermediate Period

Ramesses XI was succeeded by Smendes (1070–1044), the first king of the 21st Dynasty, and Pi'ankh by Pinudjem I. The kings ruled from Tanis in the northeastern delta, controlling the country north of el-Hiba. They may have been collateral descendants of the 20th-Dynasty royal family. Their capital city had not previously been an important center, and its monuments were mostly transferred from other sites in the delta. It was close to the Ramessid capital, and the move to it may have been dictated by the silting-up of waterways.

The Nile valley from el-Hiba to Aswan was controlled by the Theban high priests, who acknowledged the Tanite kings, dated by their regnal years, and married into their family, but were effectively rulers of a separate state. The Thebans harked back to their military origins, and it is clear from the names of many of them that the "Libyan" element among them was strong. The Libyans were also active in the north of the country – their chief area of settlement – and Osorkon I (984–978), the obscure fifth king of the Tanite Dynasty, was a member of their group. The last king, Psusennes II (959–945), was probably also high priest of Amun, uniting the two realms in his person, but not turning them into a single unit.

Shoshenq I (945–924), the first king of the 22nd Dynasty, belonged to a "Libyan" family from Bubastis (Tell Basta) that had been prominent for at least a generation before he gained power. He took advantage of the simultaneous extinction of the line of high priests to install his son in Thebes, thus attempting to centralize Egypt once again. This precedent was followed by some of his successors.

But, although there was never a fully independent ruler of Thebes, the area was not integrated into the country for another 300 years.

Shoshenq I fought a campaign in Palestine, which is recorded in reliefs at Karnak, where he began extensive building works. In Asia he may have followed an initiative of Siamun (978–959), but his undertaking was more ambitious. He also revived relations with Byblos, Egypt's traditional trading partner on the Phoenician coast, which were maintained for several generations. The basis for Shoshenq I's activities was an increase in prosperity which can be seen in renewed building activity early in the dynasty.

After nearly a century of peace the 22nd Dynasty from the reign of Takelot II (860–835) was a period of conflict and decline. The first major cause of unrest was the appointment of Takelot's son and heir, Osorkon, as high priest of Amun, an office which he combined with military functions. Osorkon was rejected by the Thebans, and a long civil war followed, which he recorded in an enormous inscription at Karnak.

Beginning with the reign of Shoshenq III (835–783), who apparently usurped the throne which had been destined for his brother, the high priest Osorkon, the kingship became split between different claimants. The first rival was Pedubaste I (828–803) of the 23rd Dynasty, who was recognized alongside Shoshenq III. From this time on the way was open for any minor potentate to call himself king, and to be accepted wherever this suited the local population. By the end of the 8th century there were therefore numerous kings in the country, with the 22nd–25th Dynasties all ruling simultaneously, quite apart from other kings who are ignored by the official list. In about 770 an important force joined the melee. A Nubian king Kashta (770–750), whose capital was at Gebel Barkal, was accepted as a ruler in Upper Egypt as far north as Thebes, and marks the arrival of the 25th Dynasty in Egypt.

While the kingship weakened, so also did the high priesthood of Amun. Osorkon IV of the 23rd Dynasty (777–749) installed his daughter Shepen-wepet in an old office with the title of "divine adoratrice of Amun" in Thebes. From this time on the adoratrice, who could not marry, and passed on her office by "adoption," was a member of the royal family and the chief religious figure in the Theban area. For later periods we know that the real power lay with nominally subordinate male officials, but in the case of Shepenwepet this is not clear. The 23rd-Dynasty control of the office was short-lived. Shepenwepet soon adopted Amenirdis I, a sister of Kashta, who had presumably been forced on her by the more powerful Nubians. The instigator of this was Kashta's brother and successor Piye (formerly read Pi'ankhi, 750–712).

In the later 8th century the most important factions in Egypt were the ancestors of the 24th Dynasty, who were local rulers in Sais in the western delta, and the 25th Dynasty. Around 730 they came into conflict, perhaps because of the expansion of Saite influence into the Nile valley, which was the traditional Theban preserve, and therefore part of the area to which the 25th Dynasty were the chief claimants. Piye set out from Napata on a campaign through Egypt as far as Memphis to claim submission from local rulers,

Egypt in the Late Period, with the state of Napata-Meroë (712 BC-4th century AD)
Egyptian sites are marked in black.
○ cities whose "kings" are listed in Assurbanipal's annals (several further Assyrian names cannot be identified in Egypt). Compare those of the campaign of Piye on map p. 47.
● sites where texts in Aramaic, the official language of the Persian empire, have been found; these include papyri, ostraca and rock graffiti. The route of the Nubian campaign sent by Psammetichus II in 591 BC is conjectural; its soldiers left Greek and Carian graffiti at Buhen and Abu Simbel, and probably at Gebel el-Silsila.
The canal from the Nile to the Red Sea appears on this map. This was begun by Necho II, completed by Darius I, who set up stelae c.490 at locations marked ▲ , and later restored by Ptolemy II Philadelphus, Trajan and Hadrian, and Amr ibn el-'Asi, the Muslim conqueror of Egypt. Its length from Tell el-Maskhuta to Suez was about 85 km.
Sites of the Napata-Meroë state are marked in brown.

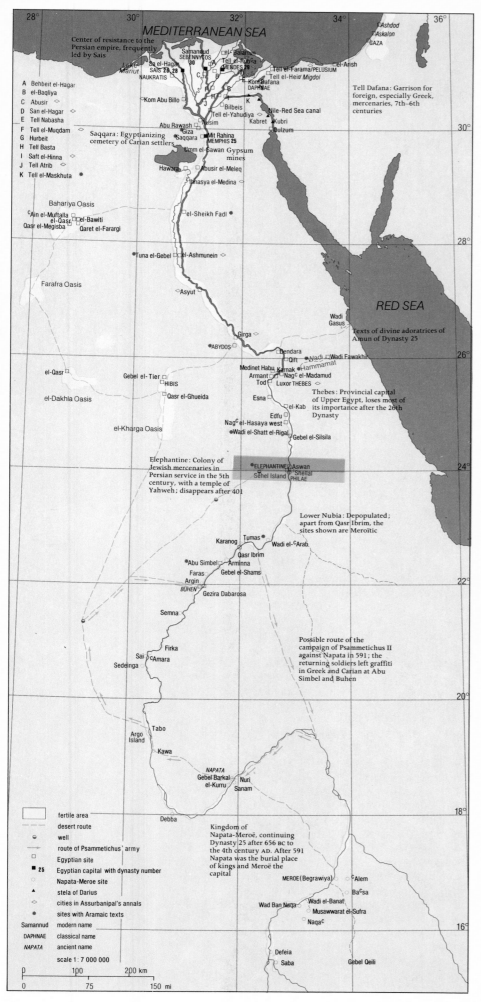

A Behbeit el-Hagar
B el-Baqliya
C Abusir
D San el-Hagar
E Tell Nabasha
F Tell el-Muqdam
G Hurbeit
H Tell Basta
I Saft el-Hinna
J Tell Atrib
K Tell el-Maskhuta

MEDITERRANEAN SEA

Center of resistance to the Persian empire, frequently led by Sais

Saqqara: Egyptianizing cemetery of Carian settlers

Umm el-Sawan Gypsum mines

Tell Dafana: Garrison for foreign, especially Greek, mercenaries, 7th–6th centuries

Bahariya Oasis

Farafra Oasis

RED SEA

Wadi Gasus

Texts of divine adoratrices of Amun of Dynasty 25

el-Dakhla Oasis

el-Kharga Oasis

Thebes: Provincial capital of Upper Egypt, loses most of its importance after the 26th Dynasty

Elephantine: Colony of Jewish mercenaries in Persian service in the 5th century, with a temple of Yahweh; disappears after 401

Lower Nubia: Depopulated; apart from Qasr Ibrim, the sites shown are Meroïtic

Possible route of the campaign of Psammetichus II against Napata in 591; the returning soldiers left graffiti in Greek and Carian at Abu Simbel and Buhen

fertile area
desert route
well
route of Psammetichus' army
Egyptian site
Egyptian capital with dynasty number
Napata-Meroe site
stela of Darius
cities in Assurbanipal's annals
sites with Aramaic texts
Samannud modern name
DAPHNAE classical name
NAPATA ancient name
scale 1 : 7 000 000

Kingdom of Napata-Meroë, continuing Dynasty 25 after 656 BC to the 4th century AD. After 591 Napata was the burial place of kings and Meroë the capital

in particular Tefnakhte of Sais. The episode was recorded on an enormous stela set up in the temple of Amun at Napata, which is of outstanding interest both for its text and for its relief showing four kings, whose names are written in cartouches, doing obeisance to Piye. Tefnakhte (who did not call himself king) was in theory forced to submit, but he did not come to Piye in person. The affair had little immediate impact, since Piye was content to establish his claim, and returned to Napata without making himself the sole king of Egypt. In his inscription he is presented as being more Egyptian than the Egyptians, while the campaign is almost a holy mission to right the evils of the land. Napata was an old center of the worship of Amun, so that this may be true, but Piye could have been providing a religious justification for a political act.

Late Period

Shabaka (712–698) marks the beginning of the Late Period in Egypt. In his first year of reign the conflict between Napata and Sais was renewed, and the 24th-Dynasty King Bocchoris (717–712) was killed in battle between the two powers. Shabaka's action finally disposed of all the other kings in the country. From his reign on the Nubians took a far greater interest in Egypt as a whole, making Memphis their capital, and residing in Egypt for some of the time. The elimination of other kings did not, however, alter the political structure much, since local rulers remained largely independent, and were indeed called "kings" in the Assyrian records of the invasion of Egypt 40 years later. Nonetheless, the economic gains from the change were considerable. The half-century of Nubian rule produced as many monuments in Upper Egypt as the previous two and saw a notable artistic revival, which looked to earlier periods for its inspiration.

Under Shebitku (698–690) and Taharqa (690–664) economic improvement continued. Taharqa left monuments over much of Egypt and Nubia, where his name has been found at the later capital of Meroë. Several inscriptions recount the beneficial effects of a high inundation in his year 6, which is also documented by records of water levels on the quay at Karnak. There may have been a general increase in inundation levels at the time, which would have contributed to prosperity.

In Thebes Shebitku's sister Shepenwepet II was adopted by Amenirdis I, and members of the Nubian royal family held high offices in the cult. Under Taharqa Shepenwepet II adopted Amenirdis II. The real power in the area lay, however, with one or two local families. The most important person in Thebes was Montemhet, the fourth priest of Amun and "prince of the city," who was the effective ruler of much of Upper Egypt, and survived well into the 26th Dynasty. His tomb, statues and inscriptions are the first great private monuments of the Late Period, on a grander scale than New Kingdom tombs and displaying much learning and technical accomplishment.

The unified Egyptian and Nubian state was a major power, whose only rival in the Near East was Assyria, which had been expanding since the 9th century. The furthest southwestern extension of the Assyrian empire was Palestine, whose small states were constantly attempting to throw off Assyrian rule, and looked to Egypt for assistance.

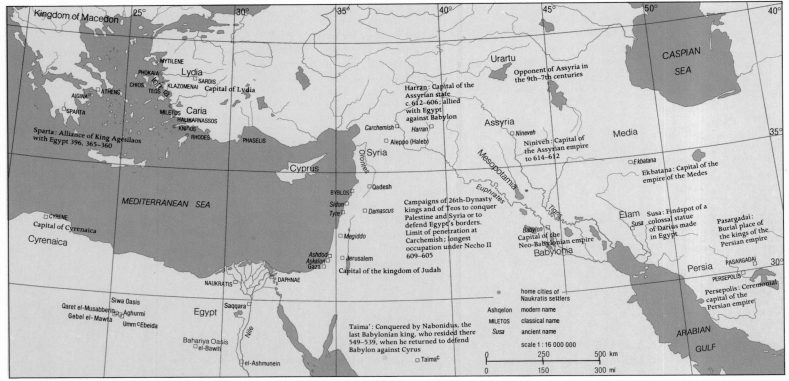

Initially the Nubian kings did not respond to these approaches, but in 701 an Egyptian force fought the Assyrian King Sennacherib (704–681) in Palestine on the side of the kings of Judah. The engagement was inconclusive, and for 30 years the two main powers kept a buffer of small states between each other.

The Assyrian King Esarhaddon (681–669) attempted to conquer Egypt in 674, but was defeated at the frontier post of Sile. A renewed attack in 671 was successful; Memphis was taken and the whole country forced to pay tribute. Taharqa fled south, but returned within two years to retake Memphis. Esarhaddon died on the way to Egypt for a counterattack, and the next campaign was sent by his son Assurbanipal (669–627) in about 667. Assurbanipal used the ruler of Sais, Necho I (672–664), who now styled himself king, and his son Psamtik (later Psammetichus I) as his chief allies in reestablishing Assyrian rule. In 664 Tantamani (664–657 in Egypt, possibly later in Nubia) succeeded Taharqa and immediately mounted a campaign through Egypt as far as the delta (in his account of this he does not even mention the Assyrians). The main opponent of the Nubians was Necho I, who appears to have died in the fighting. The remaining local rulers accepted Tantamani fairly readily.

Sometime between 663 and 657 Assurbanipal led a campaign of reprisal in person, and plundered the whole country, while Tantamani fled to Nubia. This was the last phase of the Assyrian occupation; Assurbanipal had to combat a rebellion in Babylon, and Psammetichus I (664–610) was able to make himself independent from him before 653. These events mark the end of Egypt's isolation in the world; it was involved with all the empires of antiquity.

Between 664 and 657 Psammetichus I eliminated all the local rulers in Lower Egypt, and in 656 he had his daughter Nitocris adopted by Shepenwepet II as the next divine adoratrice in Thebes, bypassing

Amenirdis II. Until the previous year dating in Thebes had been by Tantamani's years of reign.

Psammetichus I's campaigns of unification were of significance in another way. He was the first king to employ Greek and Carian mercenaries, setting the pattern for 300 years. By the 4th century all the major powers used Greek troops, who were a prerequisite for engaging in international conflict, and often determined its course. Some of them settled in Egypt, building up a nucleus of foreigners in the country who played a disproportionate part in history because of their specialization in trade and warfare. The Greeks also influence our view of the history of this time, because native Egyptian sources are sparser than Classical ones.

In the Late Period the Egyptian economy was less self-sufficient than before, since the most important metal, iron, was imported, apparently from the Near East rather than Nubia. Egypt had exports to offer in return – notably grain and papyrus – but, unlike Greece and Anatolia, did not have coinage, and was forced back on more cumbersome systems of exchange.

The reunification of Egypt and the imposition of a central administration in place of local rulers brought a continuation of the 25th-Dynasty increase in prosperity, culminating in the later 26th Dynasty, but relatively little of this wealth can now be seen, because it was concentrated in the delta. The chief exception is the small group of grandiose private tombs of the later 7th century in Thebes. The artistic revival also continued, and there is an archaizing flavor in the use of some titles and religious texts, but in most respects this is a superficial phenomenon. The kings of the period may have wished to bypass the importance of temples in the country's politics and reach back towards earlier, more secular periods, but in this they failed.

There were two main features of 26th-Dynasty policy in the Near East: maintenance of a balance of power by supporting the rivals of whichever power

Right Figures of an Egyptian and a Persian, from the base of a statue of Darius I found at Susa. The base has 24 figures representing provinces of the Persian empire. They kneel with their hands raised in adoration of the king; their names are written in ovals beneath. The statue was made in Egypt, but the figures were carved according to a foreign model. The statue as a whole seems to be an attempt at an international style for the whole empire. Tehran, Museum Iran Bastan.

was dominant, and attempts to repeat New Kingdom conquests in Palestine and Syria. Thus Psammetichus I supported Lydia and later Babylon against Assyria until the Assyrian decline after 620, when he changed his allegiance to Assyria; in the 6th century Egypt continued to support the enemies of Babylon until Persia had become the main power. Necho II (610–595), Psammetichus II (595–589) and Apries (589–570) built on the work of Psammetichus I and moved into attack. Necho II, possibly following an initiative of Psammetichus, campaigned in Syria from 610 to 605, but was forced to withdraw. In 601 he repulsed an attack by the Babylonian King Nebuchadnezzar II (604–562) on Egypt. He also fitted out Egyptian fleets with triremes in both the Mediterranean and the Red Sea, attempting at the same time to link the Nile and the Red Sea with a canal. In the 5th century this sea route was to become of international importance. There is evidence for a later persecution of Necho's memory, which may account for the small number of monuments with his name.

Psammetichus II made a single campaign to Asia, with no apparent long-term effects. His most significant political act, however, was a major campaign to Nubia in 591, which brought an end to 60 years' peaceful relations. The invading army, which included Egyptians, Greeks and Carians, apparently reached Napata, but no conquest seems to have been intended. On the return journey the foreign soldiers left graffiti at Buhen and Abu Simbel in Lower Nubia, from which the course of the campaign has been reconstructed. After 591 the memory of the 25th-Dynasty kings was persecuted in Egypt.

In 595 the divine adoratrice of Amun, Nitocris, who must have been in her seventies, adopted Psammetichus II's daughter 'Ankhnesneferibre' as her successor. 'Ankhnesneferibre' took office in 586, and was still alive in 525. Thus only two women acted as the representatives of the royal family in Thebes for 130 years.

Like his predecessors, Apries supported the Palestinian states against Babylon. The Babylonian captivity of the Jews occurred during his reign, and many Jews fled to Egypt. From the next century we have records of a Jewish colony in Elephantine. Some of those in the rest of the country may have been ancestors of the Jewish population of Alexandria.

In 570 Apries supported a local Libyan ruler in Cyrene against Greek colonists. An all-Egyptian army was sent, which was defeated and then mutinied. Apries sent a general, Amasis, to quell the revolt, but Amasis joined it, declared himself king (570–526), and drove Apries into exile. In 567 Apries returned with a Babylonian invading force sent by Nebuchadnezzar II, but was defeated and killed. Amasis then buried him with royal honors and recorded the whole episode on a stela, in terms that disguise his seizure of power.

From the point of view of the Greeks, who are our sources, Amasis' most notable policy was his treatment of the Greeks, whose trading activities were confined to the delta town of Naukratis, while foreign soldiers were kept in garrisons in Memphis only. The Greeks felt that the special status of Naukratis was a favor to them, yet the policy reduced the possibilities of friction between Egyptians and Greeks by restricting contact of any sort. Amasis was also remembered as a drinker and a philanderer; both Herodotus and later Egyptian sources tell stories to illustrate these characteristics.

The end of Amasis' reign was overshadowed by the growing power of Persia, but it was his short-lived successor Psammetichus III (526–525) who had to face the Persian invasion, which was immediately successful. Cambyses (525–522), the first ruler of the 27th Dynasty, was also the first outsider, whose main interest was not Egypt, to become king of Egypt. He undertook campaigns through Egypt to Nubia and to the western oasis of Siwa, but both failed. His rule was later resented bitterly, partly because of an attempt to reduce the incomes of the politically influential temples. Darius I (521–486) followed a more conciliatory line, commissioning temple buildings, including the temple of Hibis in el-Kharga oasis, the only substantially complete temple that remains from the period 1100–300. The importance of the oases at this time may be connected with the momentous Persian introduction of the camel. In a similar vein Darius completed Necho II's Nile–Red Sea canal, adorning it with monumental stelae in a mixture of Egyptian and Near Eastern style. Until it silted up, the canal provided a direct sea link between Persia and Egypt. The mixed style, which was first used in statues of Darius, proclaimed the cosmopolitan character of Darius' empire.

The reign of Darius was prosperous, but Persian rule was tolerated in Egypt only so long as there was no real chance of escaping from it. The Persian defeat at the battle of Marathon in 490 signaled the beginning of 80 years of Egyptian resistance, in which Egyptian rebels traded grain with Greek states in return for military aid. The western delta was the center of resistance; Persian rule was more easily maintained in the Nile valley, which could be reached by the Red Sea route. Foreign troops were also used by the Persians, in whose employ was the Jewish frontier garrison at Elephantine. A number of papyri in Aramaic, the administrative language of the Persian empire, have been found there and at other sites. There are scarcely any Egyptian documents or monuments from the period 480–400. This reflects insecurity, hatred of the Persians, and the impoverishment of the country.

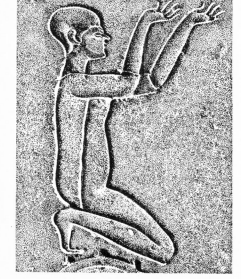

In 404 Amyrtaios of Sais freed the delta from Persian rule, and by 400 the entire country was in his hands. Like some earlier rebels against the Persians he styled himself king, but unlike them he became part of the official listing as the sole ruler of the 28th Dynasty. In 399 Nepherites I of Mendes (399–393) usurped the throne, founding the 29th Dynasty. He and Psammuthis (393) and Hakoris (393–380) built at numerous sites and warded off a Persian attack in 385–383. In these battles the Egyptians relied on Greek mercenaries. The 4th-century generations of them had no intention of settling in Egypt, and their loyalty was variable – as proved fatal more than once.

Nectanebo I (380–362), a general from Sebennytos in the delta, usurped the throne from Nepherites II (380) and founded the 30th Dynasty. In his inscriptions he was quite frank about his non-royal origins. He began a period of great prosperity, in which there was building all over the country, and artistic traditions of the 26th Dynasty were taken up again and developed. In 373 a Persian invasion was defeated, and in the 360s Nectanebo I joined a defensive alliance of Persian provinces. His successor Teos (365–360 with a coregency) moved into the offensive in Palestine, but was betrayed by a rebellion in Egypt, in which a cousin, Nectanebo II (360–343), was placed on the throne, and by the defection of his Spartan ally to the new king.

Nectanebo II withstood an invasion attempt by the Persian Artaxerxes III Ochus in 350, but the attack of 343 was successful. The ten-year Second Persian Period (also called the 31st Dynasty) was itself interrupted for about two years by a native king Khababash, whose memory lived on for many years; he appears to have controlled all of Lower Egypt. Renewed Persian rule was oppressive and predisposed the country towards almost any alternative.

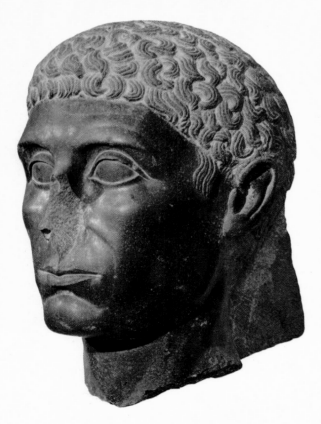

Greco-Egyptian terracotta statuettes. *Left*: the Egyptian god Bes holding a knife and a Roman shield. *Above*: a high relief of Herakles-Harpokrates (Horus the Child) holding a cornucopia and seated on a phoenix. The whole genre of terracotta is Greek rather than Egyptian; but while the former is close to Egyptian style, the latter is almost wholly Classical. Roman Period. Cairo, Egyptian Musuem.

Greco-Roman Period

In 332 Alexander the Great took possession of Egypt without a struggle. During his brief stay the plan was made to build Alexandria, and he sacrificed to the Egyptian gods, and consulted the oracle of Ammon (probably not the Egyptian Amun) in the oasis of Siwa. At his death Ptolemy, son of Lagus, succeeded in acquiring Egypt as his satrapy, and buried his king in Memphis (the body was later moved to Alexandria). In late 305 or early 304 he followed the lead of other satraps and made himself the independent king of Egypt.

For the next 250 years Egypt was ruled by Greeks, but as a separate country with its own interests to pursue, even if they were not always those of the native population. Ptolemaic rule was oppressive in some ways – possibly no more than its native forerunners – and provoked nationalistic uprisings, but, unlike its predecessor and successor, it was centered on Egypt. An indication of this is that the Ptolemies sought to enlarge Egyptian possessions in a traditional way, by annexing Palestine and later moving a short distance into Lower Nubia, where there was some sort of condominium with the Meroïtic state. In addition, Cyrene, Cyprus (already held briefly by Amasis), parts of Anatolia and some Aegean islands came under Ptolemaic control for a time.

The reigns of the first three Ptolemies were a period of development for Egypt, in which the country was brought into the Hellenistic world in terms of agriculture, commerce and, for the Greek population, education. The most important agricultural innovation was the widespread introduction of two crops per year. Many economic changes were managed by state monopolies; it is uncertain whether the Ptolemies followed earlier Egyptian kings in this. There was also a policy of settling foreign soldiers on crown land, which they

Left Over-life-size diorite head of an Egyptian of the 1st century BC, from Mit Rahina (Memphis). This commanding piece continues the traditions of Late Period portraiture; only the rendering of the hair shows Greek influence. Brooklyn Museum.

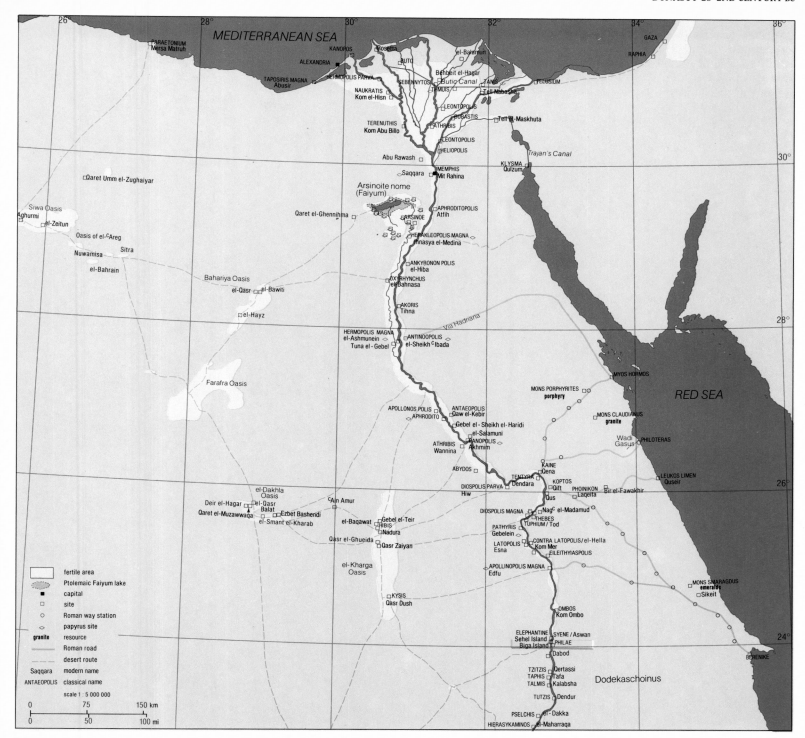

MEDITERRANEAN SEA

PARAETONIUM
Mersa Matruh

GAZA

RAPHIA

KANOPOS
Rosetta
BUTO
el-Balamun

ALEXANDRIA
TAPOSIRIS MAGNA
Abusir
HERMOPOLIS PARVA
Behbeit el-Hagar
Butic Canal
TANIS
PELUSIUM

NAUKRATIS
Kom el-Hisn
SEBENNYTOS
THMUIS
Tell Nabasha

LEONTOPOLIS

TERENUTHIS
Kom Abu Billo
ATHRIBIS
BUBASTIS
Tell el-Maskhuta

LEONTOPOLIS
HELIOPOLIS
Trajan's Canal

Abu Rawash
KLYSMA
Qulzum

MEMPHIS
Saqqara Mit Rahina

Qaret Umm el-Zughaiyar

Arsinoite nome
(Faiyum)

Siwa Oasis
Aghurmi
el-Zeitun

Qaret el-Ghennihma
ARSINOE
APHRODITOPOLIS
Atfih

Oasis of el-cAreg
Nuwamisa
Sitra
el-Bahrain

HERAKLEOPOLIS MAGNA
Ihnasya el-Medina

Baharia Oasis
el-Qasr el-Bawiti

ANKYRONON POLIS
el-Hiba

el-Hayz

OXYRHYNCHUS
el-Bahnasa

AKORIS
Tihna

Via Hadriana

Farafra Oasis

HERMOPOLIS MAGNA
el-Ashmunein
ANTINOOPOLIS
Tuna el-Gebel el-Sheikh cIbada

RED SEA

MYOS HORMOS

MONS PORPHYRITES
porphyry

APOLLONOS POLIS
APHRODITO
ANTAEOPOLIS
Qaw el-Kebir
MONS CLAUDIANUS
granite

Gebel el-Sheikh el-Haridi
el-Salamuni
PANOPOLIS
Akhmim
Wadi
Gasus
PHILOTERAS

ATHRIBIS
Wannina

ABYDOS

LEUKOS LIMEN
Quseir

el-Dakhla
Oasis
Deir el-Hagar el-Qasr
Qaret el-Muzawwaqa Balat
Ezbet Bashendi
el-Smant el-Kharab
cAin Amur

DIOSPOLIS PARVA
Hiw
KAINE
Oena
TENTYRA
Dendara
KOPTOS
Qift
PHOINIKON
Laqeita
Bir el-Fawakhir

el-Baqawat
Gebel el-Teir
HIBIS
Nadura
Qasr el-Ghueida
Qasr Zaiyan
DIOSPOLIS MAGNA
Nagc el-Madamud
THEBES
TUPHIUM / Tod
PATHYRIS
Gebelein
LATOPOLIS CONTRA LATOPOLIS/el-Hella
Esna Kom Mer
EILEITHYIASPOLIS

el-Kharga
Oasis

APOLLINOPOLIS MAGNA
Edfu

MONS SMARAGDUS
emerald
Sikeit

KYSIS
Qasr Dush

OMBOS
Kom Ombo

ELEPHANTINE SYENE / Aswan
Sehel Island PHILAE
Biga Island
Dabod

BERENIKE

TZITZIS Qertassi
TAPHIS Tafa
TALMIS Kalabsha
Dodekaschoinus

TUTZIS Dendur

PSELCHIS el-Dakka
HIERASYKAMINOS el-Maharraqa

fertile area
Ptolemaic Faiyum lake
■ capital
□ site
○ Roman way station
◇ papyrus site
granite resource
—— Roman road
- - - desert route
Saqqara modern name
ANTAEOPOLIS classical name
scale 1 : 5 000 000

0 — 75 — 150 km
0 — 50 — 100 mi

Above: Egypt in the Greco-Roman Period
◇ important finds of Greek papyri and ostraca
○ Roman way-stations, sited at regular intervals along roads in the eastern desert; these normally had a well. The roads led to four Red Sea ports, which traded with East Africa and India throughout the period.

Right: The Faiyum in the Greco-Roman Period
Land reclamation from Lake Moeris and desert irrigation made the Faiyum (the Arsinoite nome) into the most prosperous area of Greek agricultural settlement.
◇ important finds of Greek papyri. Many of the sites are now in the desert, where papyrus is easily preserved.

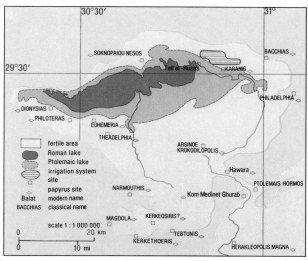

30°30' 31°

29°30'

SOKNOPAIOU NESOS
BACCHIAS

Tell el-Ruses
KARANIS

DIONYSIAS
PHILOTERAS
PHILADELPHIA

EUHEMERIA
THEADELPHIA

ARSINOE
KROKODILOPOLIS

Hawara

NARMOUTHIS
PTOLEMAIS HORMOS

Kom Medinet Ghurab

fertile area
Roman lake
Ptolemaic lake
irrigation system
site
papyrus site
Balat modern name
BACCHIAS classical name
scale 1 : 1 000 000

MAGDOLA
KERKEOSIRIS?

TEBTUNIS
KERKETHOERIS

HERAKLEOPOLIS MAGNA

0 — 20 km
0 — 10 mi

cultivated in return for a liability for military service. Greek settlements grew up in many areas, especially where, as in the Faiyum, there were land reclamation schemes. Although contact between native and Greek was limited, this new activity, and the increase in the area of cultivated land, generated wealth for the country as a whole. The chief development was, however, foreign: the building of Alexandria, which became the leading city in the Greek world. In later parlance Alexandria was "adjoining," not "in" Egypt. By acting as a magnet for the country's wealth and as the kings' chief concern it restricted expansion in other areas, especially because of its location in the extreme northwest.

The 2nd century was a time of decline in the economy and of political strife. Within the ruling family there were conspiracies, while native revolts

53

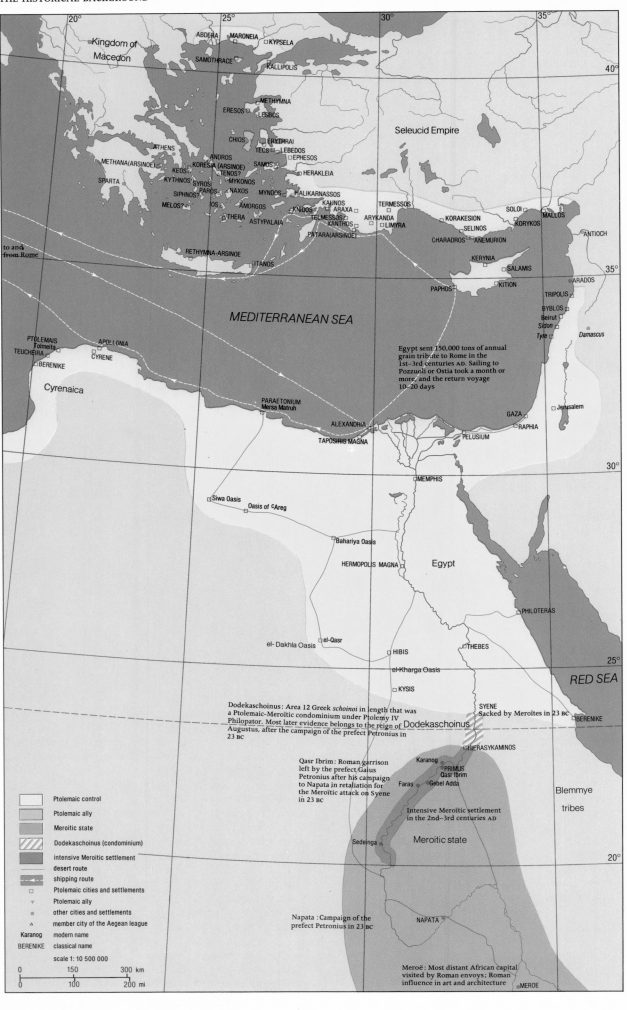

20° 25° 30° 35°

ABDERA MARONEIA
KYPSELA
Kingdom of SAMOTHRACE
Macedon KALLIPOLIS

40°

METHYMNA
ERESOS LESBOS

Seleucic Empire

CHIOS ERYTHRAI
ATHENS TEOS EPHESOS
METHANA(ARSINOE) ANDROS KORESIA (ARSINOE) SAMOS
KEOS TENOS? HERAKLEIA
KYTHNOS? SYROS? MYKONOS
SPARTA SIPHNOS? PAROS NAXOS MYNDOS HALIKARNASSOS
MELOS? IOS AMORGOS KAUNOS TERMESSOS
THERA KNIDOS ARAXA ARYKANDA SOLOI MALLOS
ASTYPALAIA TELMESSOS? LIMYRA KORAKESION KORYKOS
XANTHOS SELINOS ANTIOCH
to and RETHYMNA-ARSINOE PATARA(ARSINOE) CHARADROS ANEMURION
from Rome ITANOS KERYNIA 35°
SALAMIS ARADOS
PAPHOS KITION TRIPOLIS

MEDITERRANEAN SEA BYBLOS
Beirut
Sidon Damascus
Tyre

PTOLEMAIS APOLLONIA
Tolmeita CYRENE
TEUCHEIRA Egypt sent 150,000 tons of annual
BERENIKE grain tribute to Rome in the
1st–3rd centuries AD. Sailing to
Cyrenaica Pozzuoli or Ostia took a month or
more, and the return voyage
10–20 days GAZA
PARAETONIUM Jerusalem
Mersa Matruh RAPHIA
ALEXANDRIA
TAPOSIRIS MAGNA PELUSIUM

30°
MEMPHIS

Siwa Oasis
Oasis of ᶜAreg

Bahariya Oasis
HERMOPOLIS MAGNA **Egypt**

PHILOTERAS

el- Dakhla Oasis el-Qasr
HIBIS THEBES 25°
el-Kharga Oasis **RED SEA**
KYSIS

Dodekaschoinus: Area 12 Greek *schoinoi* in length that was SYENE
a Ptolemaic-Meroïtic condominium under Ptolemy IV Sacked by Meroïtes in 23 BC BERENIKE
Philopator. Most later evidence belongs to the reign of Dodekaschoinus
Augustus, after the campaign of the prefect Petronius in
23 BC HIERASYKAMINOS

Qasr Ibrim: Roman garrison Karanog
left by the prefect Gaius PRIMUS
Petronius after his campaign Qasr Ibrim
to Napata in retaliation for Faras Gebel Adda
the Meroïtic attack on Syene **Blemmye**
in 23 BC
Intensive Meroïtic settlement **tribes**
in the 2nd–3rd centuries AD
Meroitic state
Sedeinga 20°

Napata : Campaign of the
prefect Petronius in 23 BC NAPATA

Meroë : Most distant African capital
visited by Roman envoys; Roman
influence in art and architecture MEROE

Legend:
- Ptolemaic control
- Ptolemaic ally
- Meroitic state
- Dodekaschoinus (condominium)
- intensive Meroitic settlement
- desert route
- shipping route
- □ Ptolemaic cities and settlements
- ▾ Ptolemaic ally
- ● other cities and settlements
- △ member city of the Aegean league
- Karanog modern name
- BERENIKE classical name

scale 1: 10 500 000

0 150 300 km
0 100 200 mi

**Egypt and the east
Mediterranean in the Greco-
Roman Period**
In the 3rd century BC the
principal powers in the Near East
were the kingdom of Macedon,
the Seleucid empire and the
Ptolemaic kingdom. This map
shows the approximate
maximum extent of Ptolemaic
possessions in the reigns of
Ptolemy III Euergetes I and IV
Philopator. Almost all were lost
before 30 BC, when the entire
Mediterranean area shown was
incorporated in the Roman
empire.
□ cities through which the
Ptolemies exercised control. The
kingdom was one of cities, not
regions; the edge of the colored
area indicates the approximate
limit of their control, but is not a
political frontier.
△ names of islands belonging
to the Aegean league of the 3rd
century BC; probable members
are queried. This league was
formed under Ptolemaic
influence. Chios, an independent
state, was a Ptolemaic ally.

Right Pair of over-life-size statues of Ptolemy II Philadelphus and his queen Arsinoe II Philadelphus, who holds a necklace counterpoise in her left hand. The style and iconography are wholly Egyptian; even the "smile" occurs in native works. Found in 1710; from the imperial pavilion in the Gardens of Sallust on the Monte Pincio in Rome, where they were set up under Domitian or Hadrian; originally from Heliopolis. Highly polished pink granite. Rome, Città del Vaticano, Museo Gregoriano Egizio.

Below Coffin of Artemidorus with portrait, from Hawara in the Faiyum. The coffin goes back to Late Period models. Top register: Anubis embalms the mummy; center: Horus and Thoth protect an emblem of Osiris; bottom: the resurrecting Osiris with Isis hovering over him in the form of a kite. The portrait is one of many hundreds, very few of which are still with their coffins. They are the only substantial legacy of Classical painted portraiture. 2nd century AD. London, British Museum.

in Upper Egypt were common from the reign of Ptolemy IV Philopator (221–205); the most serious was put down as late as 85. Egypt lost most of its foreign dependencies, and was even conquered by Antiochus IV Epiphanes of Syria, who proclaimed himself king for a short time in 168. In the 1st century the weakness of government continued, working in some ways to the native population's advantage. But the overshadowing force of Rome doomed Egyptian independence.

The Ptolemies and the Roman emperors appeared on the native monuments as traditional Egyptian kings, and the earlier ones set up inscriptions in Egyptian with accounts of such of their deeds as were intended to benefit the native population. Public announcements that were for all were set up in three scripts, hieroglyphic Egyptian, demotic Egyptian and Greek. The most famous of these is the decree preserved on the Rosetta stone, which was promulgated in 196 by Ptolemy V Epiphanes (205–180).

Throughout the dynasty traditional Egyptian temples were built. It seems that the temple lands, which produced the everyday income of temples, were more or less unchanged from earlier periods, so that the additional resources for building programs probably came from the kings. The benefactions for building temples were not greatly affected by the ebb and flow of the economy, but may have been a consistent royal policy aimed at attracting native support – and, perhaps, pleasing the native gods. Within the temples, however, the king who performed the traditional cult was a completely artificial figure. In times of confusion images of kings continued to be carved in temple reliefs but the cartouches for their names were left blank.

There was a rich development of traditional private sculpture in the period, showing the continuing vitality and wealth of the native elite, even though their sphere of action was curtailed, as is reflected in the tone of pietism and resignation in temple and private inscriptions. Only in the 1st century is there clear evidence in their monuments of receptiveness to Greek influence. The Greek population was itself influenced by Egyptian religion, in increasing measure as the Greco-Roman Period progressed.

The Ptolemaic Period saw the greatest development of animal worship in Egyptian religion. The cults attracted both Egyptians and Greeks, and created mortuary towns for the mummification of animals, pilgrimage and oracular consultations.

Under Roman rule (after 30 BC) there was an initial increase in prosperity. But the improved administration was aimed at securing wealth for Rome, not at developing Egypt for its own sake, and by the later 1st century AD problems of excessive taxation and official coercion were serious. Some emperors, most notably Hadrian (117–138 AD), showed a special regard for Egypt, but there was never any fundamental change in policies to the benefit of the local Greek population, let alone the Egyptian. Unlike other provinces of the empire, Egypt was not granted any degree of local autonomy, but was administered by a prefect under the jurisdiction of the emperor.

In terms of Egypt's later fame the Greco-Roman Period was very important. Egyptian cults spread into the Mediterranean world under the Ptolemies, but their greatest popularity was in early imperial times, when native Egyptian priests, as well as many Egyptian objects, came to Rome, while the cults traveled to much of the empire. Prominent among them was that of Sarapis, a Greco-Egyptian god created as a deliberate hybrid at the beginning of the Ptolemaic Dynasty. Egypt was also the exotic land *par excellence*, whose landscape was shown in a fanciful form in Roman paintings and mosaics.

Native-style temples were built in Egypt in the Roman Period, and the native religion continued to function. Very few new structures were erected after the 1st century AD, perhaps because of the general impoverishment of the country, but the decoration of existing ones continued, even keeping up with the struggles for the imperial throne in the names used in cartouches. The latest inscription in hieroglyphs dates to 394 AD, while Egyptian demotic documents and literary texts are common as late as the 3rd century.

The force that eventually destroyed traditional Egyptian culture and led to the mutilation of the monuments was not Roman rule but Christianity, whose success was due in large measure to its not being Roman. Native Egypt may, however, have contributed also to Christianity: the role of the Virgin Mary and the iconography of Virgin and Child resemble strikingly the myth and representation of Isis and the infant Horus. The notional end of ancient Egyptian history in 395 AD is the date of the final separation of the Roman Empire, by then strongly Christian, into east (Byzantine) and west; Egypt belonged with the east.

ART AND ARCHITECTURE

Egyptian representational art forms – sculpture in the round, relief and painting – acquired a distinctive character around the beginning of the Dynastic Period. At the same time the level of work in decorative and functional art forms, such as painted pattern work, stone vase manufacture, ivory carving, furniture making and metalwork, was very high, while architecture evolved rapidly from then on, continuing to develop with the mastery of new materials and the introduction of new forms. From the beginning, works of art in a wide range of genres are the most important single legacy from ancient Egypt, and one that is remarkably homogeneous. Changes in art through the different periods reflect changes in society and throw light on them, although art seeks its inspiration more in other art than in the world. Egyptian art is superficially approachable, but at another level very alien from western art.

Very few Egyptian works were produced as "art for art's sake." They all had a function, either as everyday objects or, more commonly among those preserved, in a religious or funerary context. It has sometimes been said that they should not be called "art," but there is no necessary contradiction between an object's artistic character and its function. One might say that the artistic quality of an object is the aesthetic element that is additional to its functional character. The status of Egyptian art as "art" in the minds of Egyptians was different in degree from that of western art for western viewers, but there is no fundamental difference in kind. Indeed, Egyptian and western genres resemble each other strikingly. In Egypt as in western society art was an important focus of prestige.

Relief and painting

Relief achieves its effect through modeling, light and shade, while painting works with line and color, but the techniques of representation in both are basically the same; both were also colored. Relief can be raised or sunk. In raised relief the surface surrounding the figures is removed to the

depth of perhaps 5 millimeters, so that they stand out against it; in sunk relief the outlines of the figures are incised in the surface, which is then left, and the figures are modeled within it. Raised relief was generally used indoors, and sunk relief, which shows up better in the sun, out of doors. There were, however, variations in fashion in different periods; sunk relief was also cheaper. Major religious buildings and the better private tombs were decorated in relief. Painting was used in private tombs where poor rock made relief impossible, or in order to save expense, or where the work was not permanent and the surface to be covered was not suitable for relief, as in mud-brick private houses and royal palaces. Although painting was second best, there are many magnificent works in paint, whose techniques encouraged artists to work more freely than in relief.

A third, very rare type is representation in inlay. A small group of 4th-Dynasty tomb scenes at Maidum was made of colored paste set in the stone, while in later times glass and colored stones were used in the same way, chiefly on small objects, and to supply details in elaborate reliefs, a method typical of the 'Amarna Period.

In Egypt writing and representation are very closely linked. The hieroglyphic signs are themselves pictures, whose conventions, apart from the linguistic and ornamental ones that govern their juxtaposition, are not very different from those of representation. Conversely, most pictures contain hieroglyphic texts, which may comment on the scene, supplying non-pictorial information, or may completely dominate the visual component, as they do in some temple reliefs. In tomb reliefs the main figure is a greatly magnified hieroglyph, replacing a sign that is omitted from the text caption, which supplies the person's name. Figure and text are mutually dependent.

Methods of representation

In contrast with western art and with the optical devices of photography and motion pictures, Egyptian representation is not based on either of the two main principles of perspective, the use of foreshortening and the adoption of a single, unified viewpoint for an entire picture. Instead, figures are rather like diagrams of what they show, whose aim is to convey information. The picture surface is mostly treated as a neutral element, not as an illusionistic space; spatial features are commonest in small groups of figures. These characteristics are universal in the world; perspective became the norm of representation only very slowly, and its adoption seems almost everywhere to have been the result of direct or indirect Greek influence.

In order to understand Egyptian "diagrams" it is necessary to become familiar with their conventions, rather as we do when we learn to read a map. In theory the conventions could be as arbitrary as in a map, but in fact they are not, and

Right Schist statue of Amenopemhat kneeling to present an emblem of Hathor to Ptah. The momentarily flexed calf muscle is clearly visible (the forearm is also tensed); a comparable treatment occurs already in the Old Kingdom. c.630 BC. Height 64 cm. New York, Metropolitan Museum of Art.

Above Statue of Metjetjy, carved from a single block of wood. The medium is exploited in a subtle composition that departs from conventional standing types. Note the detail of the right hand holding the kilt. Height 61·5 cm. Reign of Wenis, from Saqqara. Brooklyn Museum.

Left Inlay relief from the tomb of Itet at Maidum. Most of the inlay is restored, but the man's kilt and right leg retain substantial areas of the original paste. Early 4th Dynasty. Oxford, Ashmolean Museum.

Below Raised and sunk relief, after Schäfer. A Stages in carving raised relief. B Stages in carving sunk relief. C Sunk relief with beveled incisions. D Raised relief with two thicknesses and with one thickness.

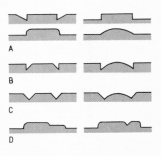

their very resemblance to perspective images often seduces the modern viewer into reading whole works in perspective. Among non-perspective representational systems the Egyptian is one of the closest to the visual image. It allows objective and mathematically precise depiction, as in the human figure, and it is relatively simple to transmit and to understand, unlike the highly elaborate conventions of early Chinese or Central American art. There must be further reasons for this visual character, which have not so far been identified. It has been suggested that the Egyptians' belief in the recreative force of representation was its origin, but the strength of this belief has probably been exaggerated, and in its extreme form such an idea would imply that they were more literal-minded than is easily credible. On a different plane, the conventions of artistic representation are, as we shall see, a repository of Egyptian values.

The Egyptians typically depicted an object by means of an assembly of its most characteristic aspects, which was contained within an outline that itself conveyed much of the necessary information. The various aspects were shown without foreshortening, which means that rectilinear forms were rendered precisely. In such a scheme the front and side of a box, for example, might well be next to each other. With objects with curved surfaces the method is more paradoxical, and very occasional foreshortenings are found, although they are not significant for the system as a whole (in true perspective, too, such objects cause the greatest difficulty). There are many further conventions that stem from the basic principles. Thus a part of an object that would not be visible in reality may be shown in a "false transparency," or the contents of something may be shown above it. The number of parts shown and the choice of them depend on the information that is to be conveyed rather than on visual considerations.

The representation of single objects is best exemplified by the human form, which is an elaborate composite. The description here is of the standing figure at rest; there are many possible variations of pose and of detail. The basic type faces to the right. The head is a profile, into which a half-mouth is set, which may be less than half the width of a mouth in full view. A full-view eye and eyebrow are placed within the profile. The shoulders are shown at their full width, but on the forward side of the body the line from armpit to waist is a profile which includes the nipple. The expanse of the chest may show details of clothing, most commonly necklaces and the shoulder straps of dresses, but, except in occasional figures that are turning or in other unusual poses, does not depict any specific part of the body. The line from the back armpit to the waist appears similarly to be no more than a connecting line. The waist is in profile, as are the legs and feet. The navel is placed near the front line of the waist, which often bulges slightly at that point (it could not be shown in the profile). The rendering of the feet is an instance of how the form is an assembly rather than a view. Until the mid-18th Dynasty, and often after that, both feet were shown from the inside, with a single toe and the arches indicated. Since arches cannot otherwise be shown without indication of depth, the whole foot leaves the ground to form them. This feature

acquires a life of its own, and the second foot may be seen through the gap of the arch, so that the drawing convention has been interpreted visually. This is one of countless self-generating elaborations of the system.

In the Egyptian language color, skin and nature are related words. A colorless figure would not be complete, and the intentional absence of color is rare. The color is as diagrammatic as the figures to which it is applied. Since they do not render views, light and shade are irrelevant. The color is uniform over the whole figure. It may be a single tone or a texture or pattern, such as are used for wood grain or for the skins of some animals. The basic repertory of colors is small: black, white, red, yellow, blue, green. From the 18th Dynasty on the range becomes wider, but is still simple and clear. Colors are not mixed, and there are few transitions from one to another. Despite the ubiquitousness of color, it is dominated by line, and is never the only means of conveying information. Outlines are picked out in contrasting colors, chiefly black.

There are two main approaches to composing scenes and whole walls: arranging the elements on a neutral surface, or using the surface as a depicted flat area, as we do in maps. The former is almost universal, the latter being used only for specialized purposes and during particular periods.

The basis of articulation according to the first approach is the register. The figures stand on horizontal lines called base lines, which may represent the ground but more often do not, and are spaced at intervals up the wall. Thematically related scenes may be next to one another in a single register, may be read in sequences up or down a wall, or may follow both principles. Two different versions of the same set of scenes – for example, a sequence from plowing to reaping – may be organized in opposite fashion, showing that the position on the wall does not in itself convey information.

Examples of the alternative, "map" method of composition are plans of houses and areas of desert. In either case the outline that defines the map – which seldom shows a specific location – may also serve as a base line for figures depicted in registers. Very occasionally a group of figures in a "map" composition is rendered in a set of vertical layers which coincides strikingly with images of recession in the optical field. This is, however, virtually the only feature that tends towards the assumption of a unifying viewpoint, as in perspective. Such an assumption is contradicted by other features.

A vital characteristic of all Egyptian representation is the treatment of scale, which forms, with iconography, the main means of ideological expression. Within a figure the parts are shown in their natural proportions, and this is often true also of whole scenes, but entire compositions are organized by scale around their chief figures. The larger the figure, the more important it is. In private tombs a single figure of the owner is often the height of the entire relief area of a wall, as many as six registers, whose scenes he is "viewing" as he faces them. He may also be several times the size of figures of his wife and children, who have their arms around his calves. The king towers similarly above his subjects. In New Kingdom battle reliefs an enormous figure of the king and his chariot may

Detail of hunting scene in the tomb of Qenamun at Thebes (No. 93). The speckled picture surface shows the desert, and is both ground and background. Blank areas adapt to the animals' forms and make lairs for some; the outlines are base lines and perhaps paths. Reign of Amenophis II.

False transparency. The man is dipping a ladle into a cooking cauldron. Ladle and contents are visible inside the cauldron, but could not be seen in reality. Tomb of Ramesses III.

Contents above an object. A man lifts the lid of a jewel box; within is another box in the form of two royal cartouches, which is shown on the rim. Theban Tomb 181. Reign of Amenophis III.

Internal elaboration of the system. The arches of the feet are shown as a curve above the base line. The dogs' paws are visible through the non-existent "hole." 12th-Dynasty stela. Berlin (East) Museum.

occupy almost half the area, the rest being filled with Egyptian soldiers, defeated enemies, and an enemy fort on a hilltop, containing tiny people whom the king reaches out to grasp. The internal visual logic and the ideological message win over verisimilitude. The main reliefs in which there are few variations in scale are in temples, where only the king and deities are normally shown, all being of comparable rank within the context. Scaling may also be adjusted for reasons of style. Thus offering bearers of all periods often lead minute animals that overlap their legs in an arrangement that economizes on space and produces a neat grouping. At the opposite extreme, 4th-century bearers sometimes carry strangely colossal geese around their shoulders; here the reason seems to be stylistic exuberance.

A further ideological feature of Egyptian art is not representational, but is almost as fundamental as if it were. In most preserved works there is a pervasive idealization; things are shown as they should be, not as they are. The idealization is, however, as selective as the treatment of scale. Major figures are in ideal form, mostly shown in youthful maturity, while the women are all young and slim. They are normally at rest. Subordinate figures, on the other hand, may be depicted as wrinkled, balding and deformed, and they may argue and fight. Details of this sort are commonest in the finest Old Kingdom tombs, where they may be added partly in order to give interest and individuality to the scenes. They are absent from temple reliefs, which show a timeless, abstract world.

Sculpture in the round

The obvious stylistic similarity between sculpture in the round and relief and painting is based in part on techniques that are common to both. There may be more fundamental reasons for the rigid axes of sculpture, since the characteristic is nearly as widely distributed in the world as non-perspective representation in two dimensions, but it is not clear what they are. Whatever the answer to this wider question may be, the continuity and parallels in development between the two forms are remarkable.

Almost all major statues show a figure that looks straight ahead in a line at right angles to the plane of the shoulders, and whose limbs are constrained within the same planes. Mostly it stands at rest or is seated, and is not engaged in any activity. The organic interplay of the parts of the body is scarcely indicated, so that statues resemble the two-dimensional "diagram" in being an assembly of discrete parts. The analogy suggests that this may be a basic feature of representation, not an element of style. Part of the similarity between the genres is due to sculpture's dependence on drawings in a modified version of normal Egyptian two-dimensional representation.

The chief exceptions to rigid geometry are heads that look up, perhaps in order to see the sun, or down, in scribe statues, to look at a papyrus unrolled across the lap. Kneeling figures sometimes have flexed calf muscles, presumably showing that their pose is a momentary gesture of deference. Details of this sort, and slight indications of the organic coherence of the body, are restricted to the

finest works, in which the normal rigidity is taken for granted and softened, probably for aesthetic reasons. There are also some small works, principally in wood and of the later 18th Dynasty, that depart from the rules in showing turns and contrapposto, and retaining no more than traces of the normal defining sets of axes. These are important in showing that the strict forms were not the only ones the Egyptians had at their disposal.

Techniques in painting, relief and sculpture

In two and in three dimensions the basis of the artist's work was the preparatory drawing. Squared grids or sets of guide lines were used in order to ensure accurate representation. For the human body the grids were founded, until the 26th Dynasty, on a square the size of the fist of the figure being drawn, which is related proportionally to all the other parts of the body. In theory the grid had to be redrawn for each figure of a different size, but in practice the less important ones may often have been drawn freehand. The preliminary drawings were inscribed within the grids, and were then turned into the finished product in a multi-stage process of correction and elaboration. Artists evidently worked in groups, and were probably specialized in the tasks they performed.

Paintings were produced by this process, using a prepared background of stone or mud plaster with a fine gypsum plaster wash. Reliefs were carved and then painted. This involved the initial drawing, carving, and then fresh drawings which served as the basis for painting.

Works of sculpture started as squared blocks, the main sides of which served as surfaces for grids and drawings. The stone was then removed, with the drawing acting as a guide. As work progressed the drawings were renewed again and again; there are almost completely finished works that have the line

Boxwood statuette of a servant girl carrying an unguent jar. The equilibrium of a body carrying a weight is well rendered; the figure is almost free from the axial constraints of most Egyptian sculpture. Height 15 cm. Reign of Amenophis III. Durham, Gulbenkian Museum of Oriental Art.

Block statue of Petemihos. The sloping line of the arms balances the raised head. Gray granite. From Tell el-Muqdam. Height 46·3 cm. Brooklyn Museum.

Conventions of Representation

Egyptian representation is rooted in Egyptian culture. Unlike perspective, it is not based on scientific laws, but it does respect a "lowest common denominator" of ease of recognition. Where what is shown is familiar to us, we have little difficulty in understanding it, although it is easy to be misled. Where the object or scene is unfamiliar, it may be impossible to identify it, or we may fail to apply a rule that explains a puzzling feature. On this page different methods of representation are illustrated, all of them operating within the basic rules.

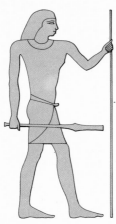 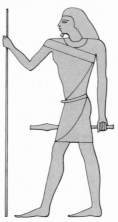   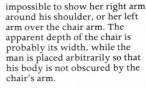 

Orientation

Figures are designed to face right, and the relationship between right and left is symbolically important. Where a figure faces left, it sometimes retains the "correct" hands for the insignia it holds. Here the staff is held by a left hand, on what looks like a right arm, and the scepter is in a right hand. Probably because of the visual incongruity of this, there are several different solutions to this problem in left-facing figures.

Oxen with artificially deformed horns illustrate the same point. Their left horns are bent down, but where the ox faces left, the bent horn is the apparent "right" one. The effect is so natural that it is very easy to misunderstand the detail.

Assembly of parts: depiction of turns and occasional views

Statues of women show that they wore dresses whose shoulder straps covered their breasts.

In relief such figures show a bare breast, because the forward line of the body is a chest profile at this point. The shoulder straps are within the torso.

When a figure is turning, the normal scheme may be modified. Occasional nude figures show both breasts from the front and on the profile. These are often musicians, whose bodily attractions were important. Very rare figures in complex groups are shown full face, but they too are composites.

In the freest pictures, such as this sketch of a woman blowing into an oven, figures can be in almost pure profile (except for the eye). The indication of breath is an unusual detail. A broken hieratic text states that her "head is towards the chamber (opening?)," and she is "blowing into the oven."

Some statues of lions have crossed paws, with the head at 90° to the body. In a painting, the lion appears to face straight ahead; there is no means of deducing the form of the statue from the painting.

Relationship of parts; materials

Furniture is particularly difficult to depict clearly, because it is both three-dimensional and rectilinear.

This early painting shows two-legged couches whose surfaces slope to the ground. They are in a side profile both with and without indication of the surface, which ceases to be right-angled. There seem to be two couches, but these may be two pictures of the same one.

When two people sit on a chair, their ranking is shown. The man is ahead of the woman, who is on his left, inferior side. But in this position it is impossible to show her right arm around his shoulder, or her left arm over the chair arm. The apparent depth of the chair is probably its width, while the man is placed arbitrarily so that his body is not obscured by the chair's arm.

The material of which an object is made may be indicated in unexpected ways. This man's shelter is made of fresh reed matting (painted green) and his chair is on a mat. The thickness of the "walls" is enough to show that they are of matting; in reality they would have been no more than 2 cm thick.

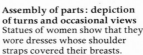

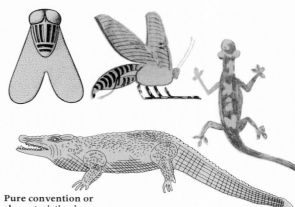

Pure convention or characteristic views

In some cases arbitrary rules help to distinguish similar forms. Crocodiles are always in a side profile, while lizards are shown from above. This takes into account the size of the creatures, and hence the angle from which they are normally seen. But with flies and bees the difference is simply a convention.

The production of a relief

Reliefs and paintings depended heavily on preliminary drawings, which were prepared according to guidelines, or from the Middle Kingdom within squared grids. Grids were also drawn over existing works to facilitate copying.

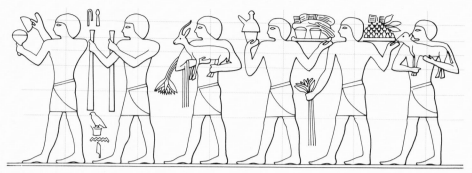

In the early scheme six horizontal guidelines intersected with the vertical median lines of the body to define its proportions. The horizontal lines were often continued through long processions of figures. For the human figure both the guidelines and the grids worked according to the canon of proportion, which was closely related to normal Egyptian measures of length. When these changed in the Late Period, the canon was modified too. Existing lines are shown in red, conjectural ones in yellow.

The earlier grid is based on 18 squares from the ground to the hair line (the part above is variable in size according to the type of headdress worn). Although it relates only to figures at one scale at a time, it sometimes covers the whole area that is to be filled with a scene; the design may then have been enlarged mechanically from a smaller draft. Occasionally the grid is subdivided.

The later grid has 21 squares up to a new, lower measuring point at the eyes. Differences in proportions between the two systems are infinitesimal.

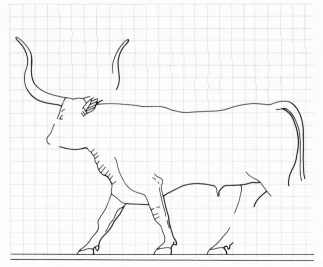

Grids were also used for animals. In this example the squares are preserved above the ox, but the figure itself has been modeled in the stone, removing the original surface and the drawing.

of the vertical axis marked down the middle of the face. As in relief, the final stages involved smoothing the surface, obliterating tool marks and applying paint.

The technical difficulty of sculpture varied greatly with the different materials, but the Egyptians mastered with the simplest tools even the hardest substances available to them. Unstinting labor was the chief component of success, but cannot account by itself for the artistry and sophistication of its products.

All the basic techniques had been acquired by the beginning of the Dynastic Period, so that artistic development was chiefly in the elaboration of representational forms and in iconography and composition. The main equipment consisted of copper (later bronze) saws, drills and chisels, all used with wet sand as the abrasive that did most of the actual cutting, and hammers of very hard stone. The latter could have various forms; one example from the Great Pyramid is about the size and shape of a tennis ball. For wooden sculpture the tools and techniques were those of carpentry. Iron tools appeared around 650.

For large works of sculpture technical problems turned into ones of engineering. The first stages of work on a colossal statue had more in common with quarrying than with art. Such statues were probably transported in a state of near completion, in order to make them as light as possible, and finished off at their destination. Moving them involved specially constructed roads and ships, and extensive earthworks for the final siting.

Architecture

Religious buildings form the vast majority of surviving works of architecture. Virtually all of them were symbolic as well as narrowly functional. The precise nature of the symbolism in mortuary buildings — pyramids, mastabas and rock-cut tombs — is not well established, but with temples the matter is relatively clear. The principles are, however, probably similar for both types: they recreate the cosmos or part of it. This cosmos is an ideal one, purified and set apart from the everyday world, and its relationship with the latter is one of analogy, not of direct representation. Its aim is to make the inhabitant of the temple (or tomb) partake symbolically in the process of creation itself or in the cosmic cycles, in particular that of the sun.

This symbolism is expressed in the siting and design of temples and in the decoration of the walls and ceilings. All of this is most easily observed in the temples of the Greco-Roman Period, which are probably little different in meaning from their New Kingdom forerunners. The structure is set apart from the outside world by a massive mud-brick enclosure wall, which may mimic the watery state of the cosmos at creation. Within this is the main pylon or entrance wall, decorated on the outside with scenes of the king slaughtering enemies; these ensure magically that disorder should not enter the temple behind. The pylon is the largest element in the temple; viewed in section, it encloses the area behind it within its height. At the same time its two massifs with the gap between them resemble the hieroglyph for "horizon" ☉. The theoretical orientation of most temples is east–west (since this is based on the Nile and not on the cardinal points

Tomb Stelae

The tomb stela (gravestone) and the coffin with the mummy were the most important elements of Egyptian tombs (as opposed to simple graves).

The stela usually identified the deceased by his name and titles (the Egyptians said that it "made his name live"), and showed him seated at a table laden with offerings or receiving offerings from members of his family. On later stelae, the deceased was represented in the company of gods. This was the ideal state of affairs which everyone wished for his *ka*; the stela therefore helped to perpetuate it eternally. In early periods a list or representations of the provisions the *ka* needed for its existence was an important element of the stela. The *hotep-di-nesu* formula, which was a constant feature, ensured that these commodities were forthcoming: "A boon which the king gives to Osiris, so that he may give invocation-offerings of bread, beer, oxen, fowl, alabaster, clothing, and all things good and pure on which a god lives, to the *ka* of the deceased." The ancient formula shows how the provisioning of the tomb was thought to have been done: the king presented offerings to Osiris, the ruler of the underworld, and it was through him that the *ka* of the deceased received its share. Visitors and passers-by were asked to recite the formula and thus make the wish contained in it come true.

Unlike the burial chamber, the tomb stela was usually publicly accessible. It was the focus of the funerary cult of the deceased, and offerings were brought and placed on offering-tables in front of it on prescribed days.

Royal stelae of the 1st Dynasty (*right*) are known from Abydos. Two of them, round topped, symmetrically designed and free standing, were set up against one of the faces of the mastaba (*below*). They contained only the name of the king.

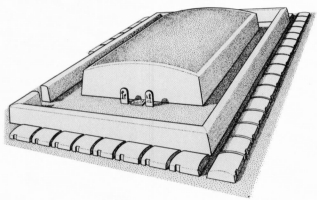

The false door (*left*) was the typical stela of the Old Kingdom, which developed from the earlier "palace facade" and its niche stela. While the stela can still be recognized in the false door's panel, the "palace facade" was transformed into a complex system of jambs and lintels designed along the lines of real doorways (*below*). This dummy "door" connected the world of the living with the world of the dead, and the *ka* was believed to pass freely through it. The false door was usually made of stone, less often of wood, and formed part of the western wall of the tomb chapel.

Provincial stelae of the 1st Inter-mediate Period (*left*) gave up the elaborate design of the false door in favor of flat rectangular forms and simple decoration, as if looking back to the tradition of niche stelae. Their representations were often crude and the writing of their inscriptions poor, but these features enable us to ascribe stelae to specific areas of Egypt with remarkable accuracy.

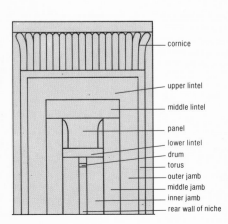

- cornice
- upper lintel
- middle lintel
- panel
- lower lintel
- drum
- torus
- outer jamb
- middle jamb
- inner jamb
- rear wall of niche

Stelae of the Middle Kingdom (*left and right*) developed from those of the 1st Intermediate Period, and can be either rectangular or round topped. They varied enormously in their subject matter and texts, but many criteria have been established by which they can be dated (e.g. the type of the *hotep-di-nesu* formula) and ascribed to a particular necropolis (e.g. the selection of the deities invoked).

Brick-built superstructures of private tombs of the first three dynasties had a "palace facade," an elaborate design of recesses (niches) (*above*). In the rear wall of one of these, near the south-eastern corner of the mastaba, was a stone or wooden *niche stela* (*left*). The "palace facade" was occasionally used in the chapel inside the mastaba; the number of niche stelae was then increased.

Slab stelae (*above*) were characteristic of the earliest mastabas with stone super-structures built at Giza during the 4th Dynasty. Positioned in the eastern face of the mastabas, they were, like the tombs themselves, presented by the king, and made by the best craftsmen.

Despite the enormous variety in form and decoration, designers employed simple constructional procedures. These, rather than mysterious "systems," are responsible for the interplay of proportions, as shown here on a *Late Period stela*.

Apart from some new forms, the most striking feature of *New Kingdom stelae* (*above*) was the appearance of gods (in particular Osiris) in their main scenes.

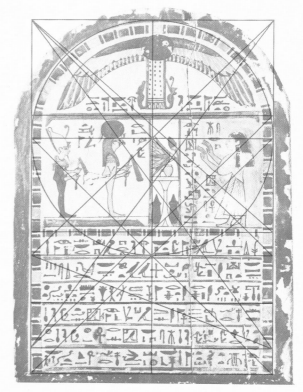

there is in fact considerable variation), so that the sun "rises" in the pylon gateway, sending its rays into the sanctuary, which is placed directly in the axis, and runs its course through the temple.

The most imposing part of the main temple is the hypostyle or columned hall, which conveniently summarizes the decorative scheme of the whole. The column capitals show aquatic plants, and the lowest register of the walls has similar plants in relief; symbolically the hall is the marsh of creation. The architraves and ceiling have reliefs of the sky, so that the decoration encompasses the whole world. What is shown on the walls is the activity of this world. Instead of marsh, the lowest register may contain offering bearers who do duty for the king in bringing the produce of the land to provide for the temple. Neither is part of the more abstract main scheme, which consists of several registers of scenes, arranged like a checkerboard, showing the king, who faces in towards the sanctuary, making offerings to and performing rituals for the god. The god, who takes up residence in the temple, faces outwards; the deities shown in the reliefs are a wider range than that worshiped in any one temple. Many scenes show rituals performed in the temple, but others have a less specific meaning. In terms of the temple, the give and take between king and god is the focus of the world's activities. Most of the reliefs in the temple are of the same character.

The inner areas have a raised floor level and lower ceiling than the hypostyle hall. They are therefore contained within the protection of the outer area, and are more sacred. There are a number of relatively small rooms around the sanctuary, whose outside wall mimics the outside of a temple, forming a structure within a structure. The sanctuary represents the mound of creation, and relates to the marsh of the hypostyle hall; in passing towards the sanctuary a procession goes through the stages of creation.

Techniques

Egyptian stone working produced rock-cut structures with techniques akin to those of quarrying, solid mounds – the pyramids – and more conventional free-standing structures. Here work on the latter is described.

We know very little of how the planning and surveying of sites was done; most reconstructions of the processes are almost entirely speculative. However it was achieved, there was enormous expertise in maintaining an accurate plan and elevation for a large pyramid, or in constructing the sloping walls of a pylon.

The foundations of Egyptian buildings were often surprisingly meager, consisting of a trench filled with sand and topped with a few courses of rough stonework (the sand may even have had a symbolic as much as a functional purpose). Only in the Greco-Roman Period were there regularly massive foundations of proper masonry, much of it constructed from earlier buildings demolished to make way for the new ones.

In masonry mortar was used very sparingly. The technique was to lay a course of blocks, level it along the top, coat the surface with a thin layer of mortar whose prime purpose was to act as a lubricant, and slide the next course into position. The under surfaces and probably the rising joints of the blocks were dressed before they were used. Each block was fitted individually to the next, since the rising joints were not always vertical, or at right angles to the surface. A single block could even form an internal corner, and the levels of the horizontal courses might be maintained only for a short distance. Wooden cramps were often set into the horizontal joints behind the surface in order to provide extra rigidity or to prevent slippage while the mortar was setting. The main purpose of the complex jointing techniques was probably to minimize waste and to use the largest practicable size of block. The edges of the blocks were cut to size when they were mounted, but the main surface was left rough.

The Egyptians probably worked without mechanical lifting devices; the basic method of raising weights was to bury the wall that was being built behind a rubble ramp. This was added to continually until the walls reached their full height. The stones were then dressed smooth, either from the ramps as they were dismantled, or from wooden scaffolding, which was probably used at a later stage for carving the relief decoration. The various stages of work on a building often proceeded at once, so that stonemasons, draftsmen, plasterers, relief carvers and painters could all be employed together. Something of this can be seen in the private tombs at el-'Amarna and in the tomb of Haremhab (1319–1307) in the Valley of the Kings. Since few Egyptian tombs or temples were ever completely finished, the resulting confusion may have seemed the natural state of affairs.

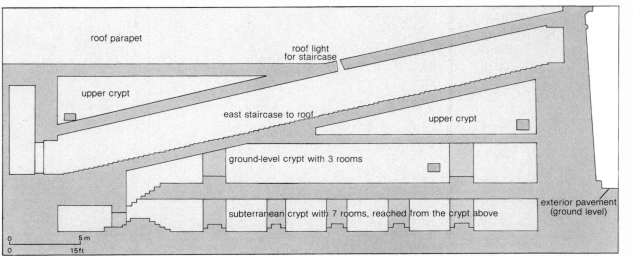

roof parapet

roof light for staircase

upper crypt

east staircase to roof

upper crypt

ground-level crypt with 3 rooms

subterranean crypt with 7 rooms, reached from the crypt above

exterior pavement (ground level)

0   5 m
0   15 ft

Temple of Dendara, section of east wall. The massive wall accommodates suites of rooms, called crypts, and a staircase within its thickness. The lowest set of crypts is below ground, contained within foundations about 10 meters deep. The roof area is similarly lavish; above the ceiling line on the left the outside wall forms a parapet 8·5 meters high. The blue squares in the ground-level and upper crypts are access holes from within the temple. Those in the upper crypts are 4 meters above ground level. All were concealed within the decoration of the rooms that contained them. 1st century BC.

PART TWO

A JOURNEY DOWN THE NILE

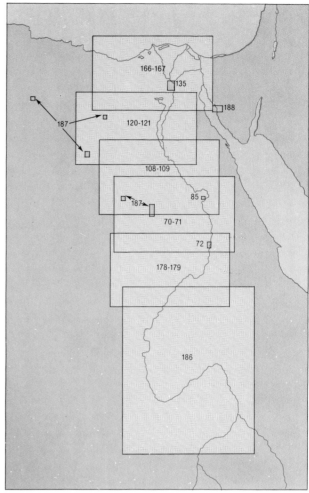

The land of Egypt has been likened to a lotus, with the heavy flower of the delta on the very long and thin stalk of the Nile valley, and the bud of the Faiyum nestling close to it. The surrounding areas, with the exception of the chain of oases running parallel to the river on the west, were arid and inhospitable, and thus unsuitable for settled habitation.

Two cities played key roles in Egyptian history until the scene shifted northwards during the 19th Dynasty: Memphis, close to the apex of the delta, and Thebes, its counterbalance in the south. These provide two of the points at which we break our imaginary boat journey down the Nile through ancient Egypt. The first Nile cataract in the south is our logical point of departure.

Nubia, the oases and Sinai, though never described as parts of Egypt, were colonized, in the case of the first two, and frequented, in the case of the third, to such an extent that their inclusion is essential. Going upstream into Nubia is, however, a different proposition from sailing gently down the Nile, and a donkey must replace our boat for the journeys into the oases and Sinai.

Boats on the Nile

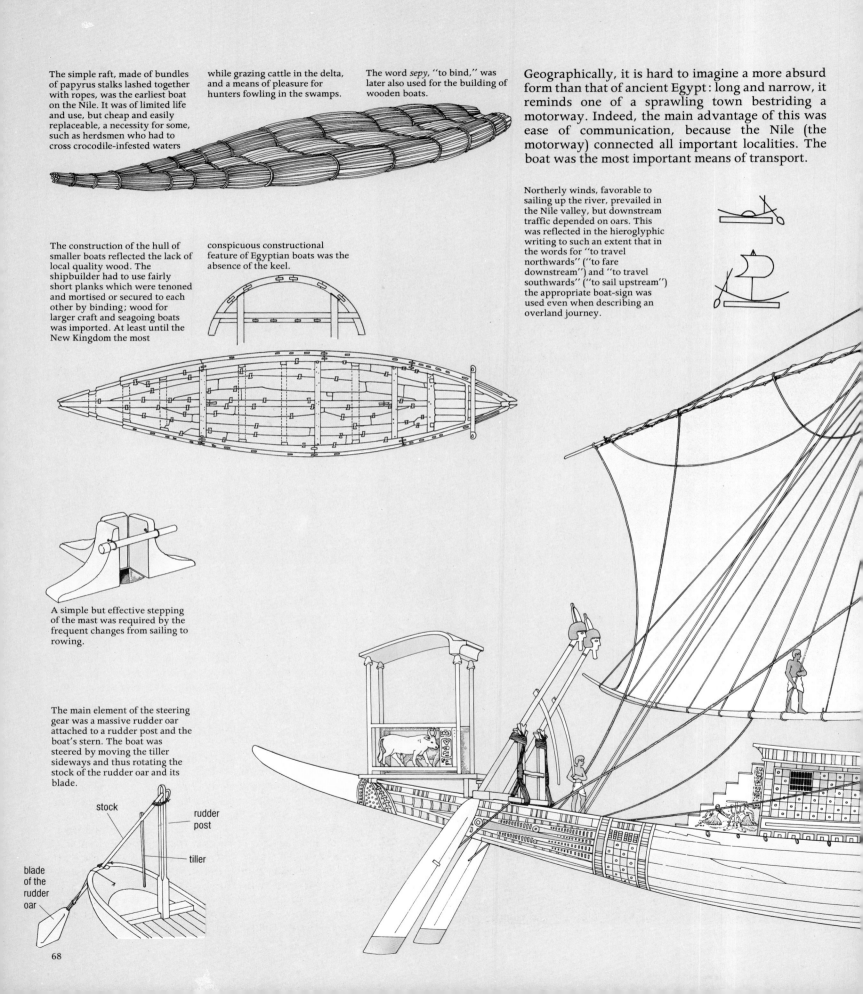

The simple raft, made of bundles of papyrus stalks lashed together with ropes, was the earliest boat on the Nile. It was of limited life and use, but cheap and easily replaceable, a necessity for some, such as herdsmen who had to cross crocodile-infested waters while grazing cattle in the delta, and a means of pleasure for hunters fowling in the swamps.

The word *sepy*, "to bind," was later also used for the building of wooden boats.

Geographically, it is hard to imagine a more absurd form than that of ancient Egypt: long and narrow, it reminds one of a sprawling town bestriding a motorway. Indeed, the main advantage of this was ease of communication, because the Nile (the motorway) connected all important localities. The boat was the most important means of transport.

The construction of the hull of smaller boats reflected the lack of local quality wood. The shipbuilder had to use fairly short planks which were tenoned and mortised or secured to each other by binding; wood for larger craft and seagoing boats was imported. At least until the New Kingdom the most conspicuous constructional feature of Egyptian boats was the absence of the keel.

Northerly winds, favorable to sailing up the river, prevailed in the Nile valley, but downstream traffic depended on oars. This was reflected in the hieroglyphic writing to such an extent that in the words for "to travel northwards" ("to fare downstream") and "to travel southwards" ("to sail upstream") the appropriate boat-sign was used even when describing an overland journey.

A simple but effective stepping of the mast was required by the frequent changes from sailing to rowing.

The main element of the steering gear was a massive rudder oar attached to a rudder post and the boat's stern. The boat was steered by moving the tiller sideways and thus rotating the stock of the rudder oar and its blade.

stock

rudder post

tiller

blade of the rudder oar

Our knowledge of ancient Egyptian shipping derives from representational evidence (reliefs and paintings), model boats found in tombs, and isolated discoveries of buried funerary boats (at Giza and Dahshur). Textual sources are scarce and not very informative. Ancient Egyptian Nile boats varied greatly according to their purpose (traveling boats, cargo boats, ceremonial barks etc.), but a fairly reliable guide to their dating is provided by (1) the appearance of the hull, (2) the method of steering, (3) the type of the mast and sail, (4) the vessel's paddles or oars, (5) the disposition of the deckhouses, and (6) unusual features.

Predynastic Period: (1) sometimes, though not always, sharply upturned prow and stern (even large Nile craft were made mostly of papyrus or similar material); (2) one or more large steering oars; (3) rectangular sail; (4) and (5) paddles in two groups (interrupted by central deckhouse); (6) prow decoration of tree branches (?); standard close to deckhouse.
Old Kingdom: (1) "classical" Egyptian hull shape (wood now the main building material), often with animal-head prow; (2) several large steering oars, but from 6th Dynasty special steering gear; (3) usually bipod mast; probably trapezoidal sail, usually more tall than wide; (4) from 5th

Dynasty oars.
Middle Kingdom: (1) higher stern; (2) steering gear operated by a helmsman standing between the massive rudder post and the usually single large rudder oar; (3) single mast, lowered and supported on a forked stanchion when sailing downstream; (5) deckhouse forward of the rudder post.
New Kingdom (large range of specialized types): (2) steering gear with usually two rudder oars, operated by a helmsman standing in front of the rudder post; (3) sail more wide than tall; (5) castles forward and aft, with centrally placed deckhouse.
Late Period: (1) tendency towards a higher stern.

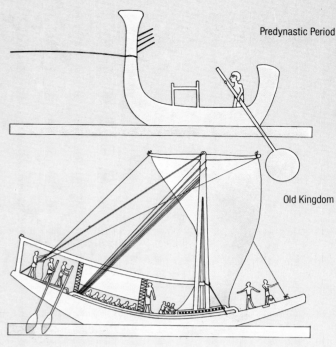

Predynastic Period

Old Kingdom

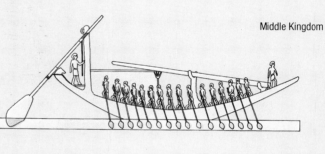

Middle Kingdom

Late Period

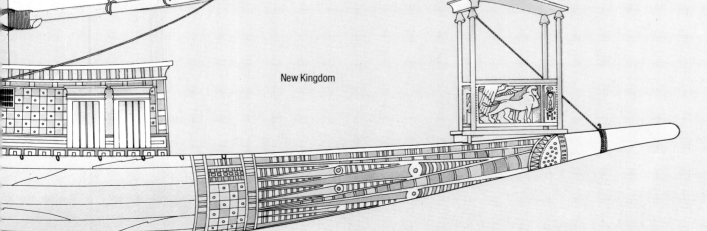

New Kingdom

69

SOUTHERN UPPER EGYPT

Because the Egyptians oriented towards the south, Aswan was the "first" town in the country north of the actual frontier at Biga island.

The southernmost part of the country falls into the natural divisions of the 1st Upper Egyptian nome, from Biga to north of Gebel el-Silsila, and the 2nd–4th nomes as far as Thebes. The two are roughly equal in length along the river, but the former belongs to the sandstone belt of Nubia, and is forbidding, infertile country, dominated by the desert and rich in minerals. To this day its character is strongly Nubian.

Kom el-Ahmar was one of the earliest urban centers, but declined in importance during the historical period. Probably because of the dominant position of Thebes, the districts to the south were included in the Viceroy of Nubia's territory during the New Kingdom. In this stretch of the river the

valley is relatively narrow, and could not support as large a population as the Theban area. There are, however, desert routes for trade and mining expeditions to east and west that were significant at most periods.

As befits its early importance, there are numerous Predynastic and Early Dynastic sites in Southern Upper Egypt. The best-represented later periods are the late Old Kingdom and 1st Intermediate Period, early New Kingdom and Greco-Roman Period. These were all times when government was not very strongly centralized, so that an outlying area could benefit. Apart from the magnificent landscape, best seen from the river, the most impressive monuments are now probably the chapels and shrines of Gebel el-Silsila, with their reminder of the importance of the inundation for Egypt, and the major Greco-Roman temples, Philae, Kom Ombo, Edfu and Esna.

Top left Elephantine island from the east bank of the river. In the foreground are restored Roman walls near the Nilometer.

Above left Kiosk of Trajan at Philae, with foundations of a small chapel in the foreground; photographed in 1964 before the building of the High Dam.

Top right Colossal gray granite hawk at the entrance to the hypostyle hall of the temple of Edfu; probably Ptolemaic.

Above right Tomb complex of Pepynakht and others at Qubbet el-Hawa, north of Aswan; late 6th Dynasty. The entrance court, columns and stairways are cut in the sandstone cliff.

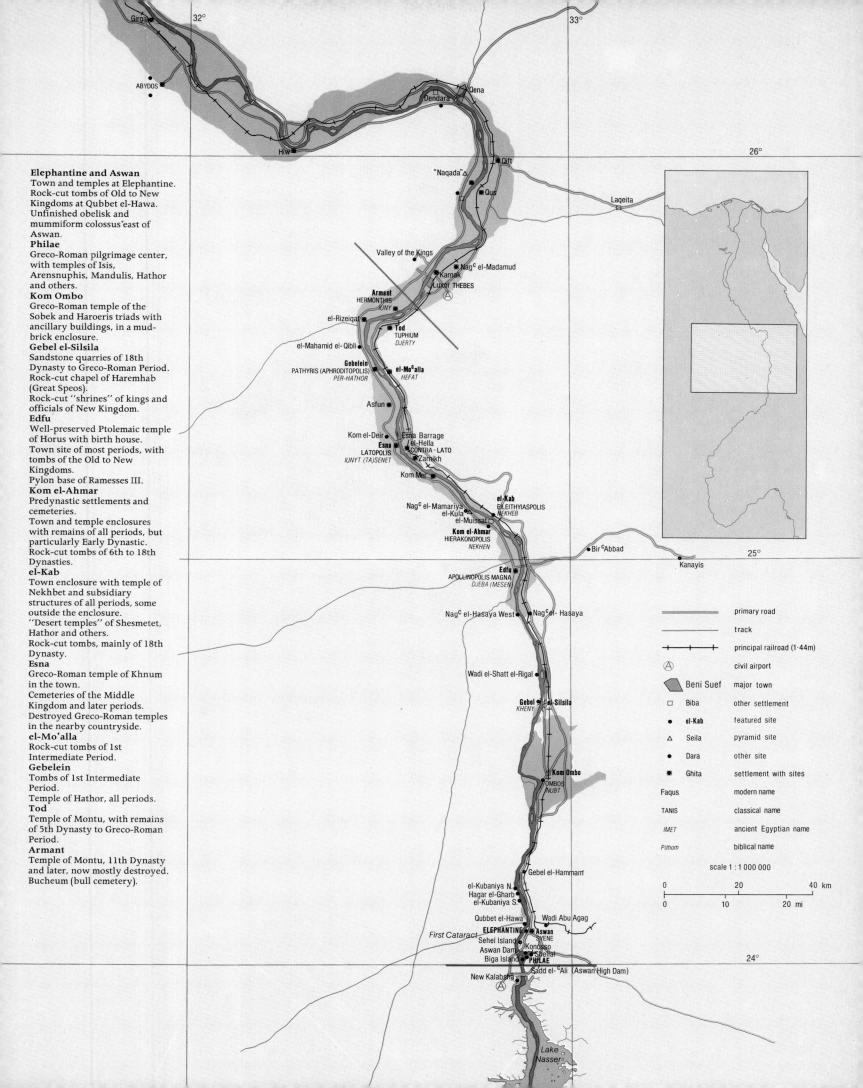

Elephantine and Aswan
Town and temples at Elephantine.
Rock-cut tombs of Old to New
Kingdoms at Qubbet el-Hawa.
Unfinished obelisk and
mummiform colossus east of
Aswan.

Philae
Greco-Roman pilgrimage center,
with temples of Isis,
Arensnuphis, Mandulis, Hathor
and others.

Kom Ombo
Greco-Roman temple of the
Sobek and Haroeris triads with
ancillary buildings, in a mud-
brick enclosure.

Gebel el-Silsila
Sandstone quarries of 18th
Dynasty to Greco-Roman Period.
Rock-cut chapel of Haremhab
(Great Speos).
Rock-cut "shrines" of kings and
officials of New Kingdom.

Edfu
Well-preserved Ptolemaic temple
of Horus with birth house.
Town site of most periods, with
tombs of the Old to New
Kingdoms.
Pylon base of Ramesses III.

Kom el-Ahmar
Predynastic settlements and
cemeteries.
Town and temple enclosures
with remains of all periods, but
particularly Early Dynastic.
Rock-cut tombs of 6th to 18th
Dynasties.

el-Kab
Town enclosure with temple of
Nekhbet and subsidiary
structures of all periods, some
outside the enclosure.
"Desert temples" of Shesmetet,
Hathor and others.
Rock-cut tombs, mainly of 18th
Dynasty.

Esna
Greco-Roman temple of Khnum
in the town.
Cemeteries of the Middle
Kingdom and later periods.
Destroyed Greco-Roman temples
in the nearby countryside.

el-Mo'alla
Rock-cut tombs of 1st
Intermediate Period.

Gebelein
Tombs of 1st Intermediate
Period.
Temple of Hathor, all periods.

Tod
Temple of Montu, with remains
of 5th Dynasty to Greco-Roman
Period.

Armant
Temple of Montu, 11th Dynasty
and later, now mostly destroyed.
Bucheum (bull cemetery).

Girga

ABYDOS

32°

Qena

Dendara

Hiw

33°

26°

"Naqada"△

Qift

Qus

Laqeita

Valley of the Kings

Nag^c el-Madamud

Karnak
Luxor THEBES

Armant
HERMONTHIS
IUNY

el-Rizeiqat

Tod
TUPHIUM
DJERTY

el-Mahamid el-Qibli

Gebelein
PATHYRIS (APHRODITOPOLIS)
PER-HATHOR

el-Mo^calla
HEFAT

Asfun

Kom el-Deir

Esna Barrage
el-Hella
Esna CONTRA - LATO
LATOPOLIS
IUNYT (TA)SENET Zarnikh

Kom Mer

el-Kab
Nag^c el- Mamariya   EILEITHYIASPOLIS
el-Kula△   *NEKHEB*
el-Muissat

Kom el-Ahmar
HIERAKONOPOLIS
NEKHEN

Bir ^cAbbad

25°

Kanayis

Edfu
APOLLINOPOLIS MAGNA
DJEBA (MESEN)

Nag^c el-Hasaya West   Nag^c el- Hasaya

Wadi el-Shatt el-Rigal

Gebel el-Silsila
KHENY

Kom Ombo
OMBOS
NUBT

Gebel el-Hammam

el-Kubaniya N.
Hagar el-Gharb
el-Kubaniya S.

Qubbet el-Hawa   Wadi Abu Agag

First Cataract **ELEPHANTINE** ■Aswan
SYENE
Sehel Island   Konosso
Aswan Dam   Shellal
Biga Island   **PHILAE**

Sadd el-^cAli (Aswan High Dam)

New Kalabsha

*Lake
Nasser*

24°

primary road

track

principal railroad (1·44m)

(A) civil airport

Beni Suef   major town

□ Biba   other settlement

● el-Kab   featured site

△ Seila   pyramid site

● Dara   other site

Ghita   settlement with sites

Faqus   modern name

TANIS   classical name

IMET   ancient Egyptian name

Pithom   biblical name

scale 1 : 1 000 000

0   20   40 km

0   10   20 mi

Elephantine and Aswan

Elephantine was the capital of the 1st Upper Egyptian nome, which was probably annexed to Egypt at the beginning of the Dynastic Period. The site is strategically important because of the natural barrier of the first cataract immediately to the south,

and because of the large number of nearby mineral deposits, but it is in an almost barren area, and the town may always have relied on food brought from further north. It made its living as a garrison and by trade. The common meaning of the ancient Egyptian word *swenet* from which the name Aswan was derived is "trade."

The main town and temple area were at the southern end of Elephantine island. This was inhabited almost continuously from the Early Dynastic Period. So far little can be said of the town, which is now the subject of a long-term excavation

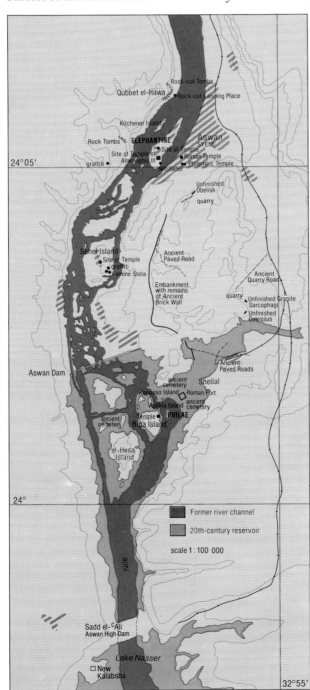

Above left Remains of the sacred area on Elephantine island, looking northwest, with the modern village in the background. The stone walls that are visible date to many different periods (the standing gateway is restored).

Left Mummiform colossus abandoned in the granite quarries east of Aswan; possibly 19th Dynasty. The rock outcrops are characteristic of the cataract area, while the boulder by the statue shows clear marks of quarrying. The figure itself has been much eroded, and its face polished by generations of visitors.

Above Decorated pillar in the tomb of Setka at Qubbet el-Hawa; late 6th Dynasty. This is perhaps the finest of the Old Kingdom relief work at Aswan. The figure of the deceased has the leopard skin, full kilt and cropped hairstyle of an elderly priest; he is described as the "Count, Overseer of the Phyles [groups of priests] of Upper Egypt." Setka confronts visitors to the tomb; just visible on the left face of the pillar are registers of animals and offering figures moving towards him.

program. The expedition has found an important deposit of Early Dynastic votive figurines, similar to those from Kom el-Ahmar (Hierakonpolis), showing indirectly that there was already a temple at that time. From the late Old Kingdom has come unique wooden relief paneling, which clad the entrance to a memorial chapel for one of the notables of the 6th Dynasty, whose tombs are across the river. A monument of rather similar character was the shrine of Heqaib, a 6th-Dynasty official who was deified after his death and remained the subject of a local cult into the Middle Kingdom. From most later periods down to the Roman come fragments of relief from the temples of Khnum, Satis and Anukis, the local triad of deities, but there are no complete structures, and few elements *in situ*. A small colonnaded temple of Amenophis III was, however, virtually complete as late as 1820, as was a building

of Tuthmosis III. In the area of a temple of Alexander IV burials of sacred rams of Khnum have been excavated, dating to the Greco-Roman Period. The mummies were given elaborate gilt cartonnage headpieces, some of which are now in the nearby museum, and were placed in stone sarcophagi that have been left where they were found. The best-known monument now visible on the island is the Nilometer, a staircase with cubit markings beside it for measuring the height of the river, on the east. The inundation levels recorded on it are of the Roman Period.

On the west bank north of the town, at Qubbet el-Hawa, "windy dome" in Arabic, are the rock-cut tombs of the Old Kingdom expedition leaders, Middle Kingdom nomarchs and some New Kingdom officials. The 6th-Dynasty tombs, some of which form linked family complexes, contain important biographical texts, but the decoration is sparse and provincial. The 12th-Dynasty tomb of the elder Sarenput is much more impressive both in architecture and in decoration, although it too has reliefs only in a few areas.

The granite rocks of the cataract south of Elephantine have quarrying marks in many places, and the quarry area also extends some 6 km east of the town center. The most striking remains are an abandoned obelisk and an almost complete mummiform colossus. The obelisk developed faults, but it is not clear why the colossus was never moved. Both in the river and on land there are numerous ancient graffiti, either commemorating quarrying expeditions or having a more general purpose. The greatest single body of them is on the island of Sehel, 3 km south of Elephantine.

Aswan town contains few visible remains, probably because they have been continuously built over. The two tiny Greco-Roman Period temples probably formed only a small proportion of the original sacred area.

Philae

In its grandiose setting in the first cataract, the lush island of Philae was the most romantic tourist attraction in 19th-century Egypt, but with the raising of the first Aswan dam it became submerged for most of each year. Now, as a result of the building of the High Dam, the temples have been dismantled and reerected on the nearby island of Agilkia.

The earliest monuments on the site are of the reign of Nectanebo I, but blocks discovered in foundations take the island's history back to the reign of Taharqa. Philae is the site of the latest hieroglyphic inscription (394 AD) and still later demotic graffiti (the latest of 452 AD).

The Egyptians gave an etymology to the name of

Philae, "island of the time [of Reʿ]," which implies that the site recreated the primeval world when the sun god ruled on earth. On the neighboring island of Biga was the Abaton or "pure mound," one of many tombs of Osiris in the country. This was approached by way of the small temple of Biga, which faces Philae. The temple of Isis was the architectural climax of Philae, so that the most important pair of

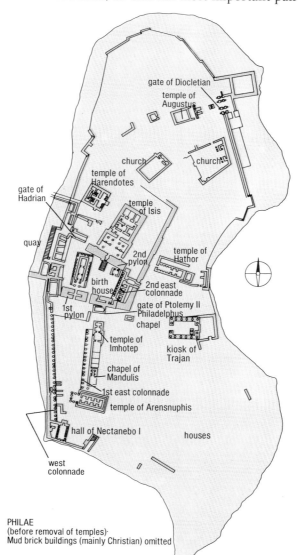

PHILAE
(before removal of temples)
Mud brick buildings (mainly Christian) omitted

Top The temple area at Philae, seen from nearby Biga; watercolor by David Roberts (published 1846). The temple of Biga, partly converted into a church, is visible in the foreground. The rear wall of the west colonnade forms the edge of Philae; to the left it continues into a landing stage and the entrance to the gate of Hadrian. Behind can be seen (right to left): the 1st east colonnade; kiosk of Trajan; 1st pylon; birth house and 2nd east colonnade; 2nd pylon and temple of Isis. There are remains of modern houses on the roof of the Isis temple (removed in the 19th century).

Above Sistrum figure of the reign of Ptolemy VI Philometor in the entrance to the main hall of the temple of Hathor at Philae. The motif, often a column capital, comprises a Hathor head on the sign for gold (the metal of Hathor), flanked by a pair of uraei, with a naos shape above (the actual sistrum).

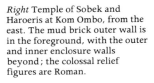

Below Gate of Hadrian at Philae:
relief of Isis (cow-headed)
pouring milk over the sacred
grove of trees on Biga, with the
resurrected "soul" of Osiris
above. Behind is the rocky
"landscape" of Biga with a figure
of the inundation in the cave
from which it emerges, and a
hawk and a vulture above.

Right Temple of Sobek and
Haroeris at Kom Ombo, from the
east. The mud brick outer wall is
in the foreground, with the outer
and inner enclosure walls
beyond; the colossal relief
figures are Roman.

who went south into Nubia spreading devastation,
and had to be pacified by Thoth before she would
return. The columns of the temple's entrance
courtyard contain figures of musicians, including
the god Bes, who held performances in order to
placate the goddess.

At the northern end of the island were a temple of
Augustus and a gate known as the "Gate of
Diocletian" (284–305 AD). Between these and the
temple of Isis were two churches; from the mid-4th
century AD these coexisted with the pagan cults,
which were finally suppressed under the Byzantine
Emperor Justinian (527–565 AD). The hypostyle hall
of the temple of Isis was turned into a church, and,
as on many other sites, the flesh areas of all accessible figures of kings and gods in the temple were
defaced.

deities of the period had an island each. Isis was
much the more popular, and had devotees to north
and south. In the Ptolemaic Period there was a short
condominium between Egypt and the Meroïtic
kings. This has left traces in the decoration of the
temple of Arensnuphis, which was done in the
names of Ptolemy IV Philopator and of the Meroïtic
Arqamani (c. 220–200 BC); there are also Meroïtic
graffiti dating from the 3rd century BC to the 3rd
century AD. Nonetheless, the buildings are completely Egyptian, and were presumably built with
Egyptian resources.

The southeast portions of the island probably
contained dwelling quarters. Pilgrims landed near
the hall of Nectanebo I on the south, and proceeded
into the open space bounded by the monumental
west colonnade and first east colonnade. These are
probably later structures added to round off the
group of buildings; they may be inspired by the
planning of public spaces in the Classical world. The
decoration of the west colonnade is mainly of
Roman date.

On the east were temples dedicated to the Nubian
gods Arensnuphis and Mandulis, and a temple of
Imhotep, the deified official of the reign of Djoser,
who is also mentioned in a Ptolemaic rock stela on
the island of Sehel to the north. In the gap north of
the first east colonnade is a gate of Ptolemy II
Philadelphus, leading to a small chapel and to the
much later kiosk of Trajan by the eastern shore of
the island.

The first part of the temple of Isis is composed of
isolated elements. Behind the first pylon a
courtyard is formed by the birth house, which is
unconventionally placed parallel with the temple
axis, and the second east colonnade with a set of
rooms leading off it. The decoration of these areas is
late Ptolemaic and early Roman. The main temple
behind, whose earliest decoration dates to Ptolemy
II Philadelphus, contains an abbreviated version of
the full pylon, court and hypostyle hall, and is on a
smaller scale than the other great temples of the
period. On the roof are chapels dedicated to Osiris.

The most notable of the remaining temples is that
of Hathor, who was here the angry goddess of myth,

Kom Ombo

Kom Ombo stands on a promontory at a bend in the
Nile, at the northern end of the largest area of
agricultural land south of Gebel el-Silsila. Because of
improved agricultural techniques it was prominent
in the Ptolemaic Period, to which almost all the
monuments date. An 18th-Dynasty gateway was,
however, seen by Champollion in the southern
enclosure wall, and scattered New Kingdom blocks
have been found on the site. Part of the temple
forecourt has been eroded by the river, while the

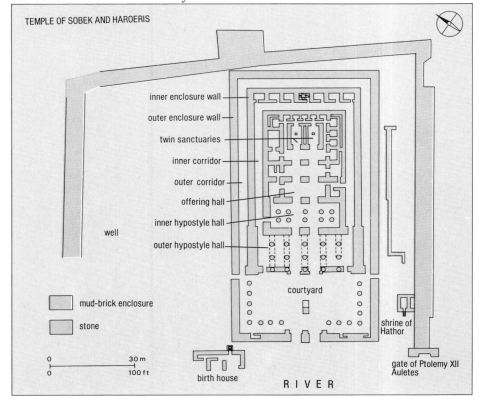

TEMPLE OF SOBEK AND HAROERIS

inner enclosure wall
outer enclosure wall
twin sanctuaries
inner corridor
outer corridor
offering hall
inner hypostyle hall
outer hypostyle hall
well

mud-brick enclosure
stone

courtyard

shrine of
Hathor

0   30 m
0   100 ft

birth house

gate of Ptolemy XII
Auletes

RIVER

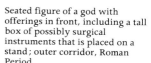

Well-preserved colored detail of the king on a column in the forecourt; reign of Tiberius. The crown relates the king to Onuris-Shu; the sign behind him symbolizes protection.

area behind the enclosure is little explored, so that further early evidence may have been swept away or lie buried.

The earliest king named in the temple is Ptolemy VI Philometor; most of the decoration was completed by Ptolemy XII Auletes. In the early Roman Period the courtyard was decorated and the outer corridor added. The temple is dedicated to two triads of deities: Sobek, Hathor and Khons; and Haroeris (Horus the elder), Tasenetnofret (the good sister) and Panebtawy (the lord of the two lands). The last two have artificial names, which express the function of the goddess in such a group as a companion, and of the young god to be kingly. Sobek and his triad are the primary deities, as is shown by his occupying the southern part, because south is prior to north in Egyptian ordering schemes.

The birth house, nearest to the river, has lost its western half. It abuts closely on the pylon of the main temple, perhaps because space was short already in antiquity (the rear of the temple is similarly cramped against the enclosure wall). The pylon has a double gateway, which is the first sign of a complex plan, in which there is an axis for each main gateway and an unusually large number of intermediate rooms, culminating in two sanctuaries. From the first hypostyle hall runs a corridor which

encloses the entire inner part of the temple and has within its width a number of small chambers at the back. This is enclosed in its turn by a second wall and corridor, which take in the courtyard. Thus the double axis goes together with other dual features. Some of the reliefs in the inner corridor and its small rooms are unfinished, giving valuable insight into artists' methods in this period. On the inner face of the outer corridor there are some unique and bizarre scenes, and a representation of a set of instruments that have traditionally been assumed to be those of a surgeon.

A figure of Haroeris in the first hypostyle hall revives an ancient technique of relief embellishment: it has a hole instead of an eye; this must have been inlaid in order to give special opulence and liveliness to the figure of the god.

The small Roman shrine of Hathor to the south of the courtyard is now used to store the mummies of sacred crocodiles from a nearby necropolis. The well north of the temple is complex and, because of the elevation of the temple, very deep. Like other wells in temple enclosures, it allowed pure water, in theory from the primeval waters themselves, to be drawn within the sacred area, avoiding pollution from the outside world.

Gebel el-Silsila

Some 65 km north of Aswan, at Gebel el-Silsila, steep sandstone cliffs narrow the stream and present a natural barrier to river traffic. The ancient Egyptian name of the place, *Kheny* (or *Khenu*), which has been translated as "The Place of Rowing," seems to reflect this fact. Local quarries, particularly those on the east bank, were exploited from the 18th Dynasty until the Greco-Roman Period.

On the west bank is the Great Speos (rock-cut chapel) of Haremhab. The seven deities to whom the chapel was dedicated were represented as seated statues in the niche at the back of the sanctuary, with the local crocodile god Sobek and King

Haremhab himself among them. Numerous rock-cut "shrines" (chambers), functioning as cenotaphs, were made south of the Speos by kings (Sethos I, Ramesses II, Merneptah) as well as high officials, particularly those of the 18th Dynasty.

The rock faces on both sides of the river abound in rock stelae and graffiti.

Edfu

The site of Edfu, near the river and raised above the broad valley around, is an ideal position for settlement, since it is safe from the inundation but not isolated near the desert. The Ptolemaic temple was part of a larger area extending to the east and south under the modern town, which must have balanced the extensive remains to the west. The western side has an inner and outer enclosure wall, which date to the Old Kingdom. A later wall runs outside the outer one, and may be of the 1st Intermediate Period. Within the walls and on top of them are remains of the Old Kingdom and Greco-Roman town site. The later wall overlaps an area of late Old Kingdom and 1st Intermediate Period tombs, which extends further to the west. These include quite large mastabas, and there are also scattered finds of stelae, statues and offering tables from the 2nd Intermediate Period and New Kingdom.

Only the base of the pylon of a temple of Ramesses III is preserved. It is oriented, conventionally, towards the Nile, and must have been part of a much smaller structure than its successor. The later temple alludes to this forerunner by aligning a gateway in its first court with that between the two massifs of the earlier pylon. It forms a complex with a small gateway to the south and, just south of the gate, the birth house, at right angles to the main temple. The temple is the most completely preserved in Egypt, and its form is archetypal. The building inscriptions, written in horizontal bands in the outer areas, give numerous details of construction. Building began in 237 (Ptolemy III Euergetes I). The inner part was finished in 212 (Ptolemy IV Philopator) and decorated by 142 (Ptolemy VIII Euergetes II). The outer hypostyle was built separately, being completed in 124 (Ptolemy VIII Euergetes II). Decoration of this and of the other outer parts was finished in 57. Mostly work continued regardless of the political situation, but it was suspended for more than 20 years during disturbances in Upper Egypt under Ptolemy IV and Ptolemy V Epiphanes.

The unusual orientation of the temple towards the south may be due to the nature of the site. Behind the pylon the courtyard, the only large one preserved, has columns with paired capitals of distinctive forms, as in other buildings of the

period, which give variety to otherwise uniform shapes. Gates lead behind the temple into an area bounded by the stone enclosure wall, which is a continuation of the outer wall of the courtyard. The scenes and inscriptions here and on the outer face of the enclosure wall include a list of donations of land to the temple, probably transferred from a demotic original, a narrative of its mythical foundation, and a grandiose set of reliefs with a "dramatic" text of a ritual in which Horus defeated his enemy Seth.

A striking feature of the inner part of the temple is the subtle exploitation of light – or of darkness. Some rooms are completely dark, while elsewhere the light comes from the openings between the columns of the hypostyle hall and from apertures in the roof or at the angle between the roof and a wall. The general progress is from light to dark, with the sanctuary receiving illumination only from the axis. The effect of all this must have been incomparably richer when the reliefs retained their original colors.

The monolithic naos of highly polished syenite in the sanctuary will have contained a wooden shrine with the cult image of the god – probably about 60

Top Aerial view from the north, taken in 1932. Both the temple's domination of the site and much of the town mound can be clearly seen. The monumental reliefs on the outside walls convey their message even at this distance.

Above Set of column capitals in the forecourt. Two are composite forms, one with multiple papyrus umbels (?) and the other the shape of a single umbel with stem decoration. The palm frond capital is an ancient type with solar associations, but is also aquatic, since date palms often grow by pools. The architraves contain solar scenes.

Right View east across the hypostyle hall at Edfu. The height and close spacing of the columns restrict the feeling of space; the result reflects the room's marsh or thicket symbolism. The columns have plant forms at the bottom, and several bands of emblematic motifs above and below central offering scenes.

cm high and made of wood, overlaid with gold and semiprecious stones – inside it. It is the oldest object in the temple, dating to Nectanebo II.

The outer areas of the birth house are much ruined, but the sanctuary and ambulatory are well preserved. In the south ambulatory the reliefs are sheltered from the prevailing north wind. Some of them preserve their color, giving an idea of the effect over large areas of the tones used in this period.

Like the other late temples, Edfu was emptied of its furniture and equipment when it fell out of use. We are fortunate, therefore, to have the pair of colossal statues of hawks flanking the entrance and a single one by the door into the hypostyle hall. A group of over-lifesize statues of naked boys – probably the young god Ihy or Harsomtus – that is now lying in the courtyard must also have formed part of the monumental decoration of the temple, relieving its present austere appearance.

Kom el-Ahmar

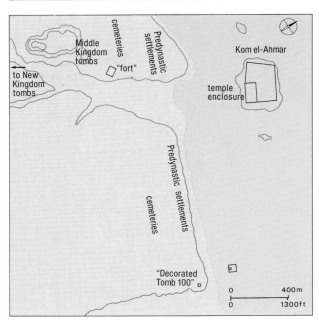

Kom el-Ahmar ("The Red Mound"), ancient *Nekhen*, lies a little over 1 km southwest of the village of el-Muissat, on the west bank of the Nile. *Nekhen* played an important part in Egyptian mythology: together with *Nekheb* (el-Kab) on the opposite bank, it represented the Upper Egyptian counterpart of the twin towns *Pe* and *Dep* (modern Tell el-Fara'in) in the delta. The jackal-headed figures known as "The Souls of *Nekhen*" might be personifications of the early rulers of *Nekhen*. The chief god of the town was a falcon with two tall plumes on its head (*Nekheny*, "The Nekhenite"), assimilated very early with Horus ("Horus the Nekhenite"), and the town's Greek name,

Hierakonpolis, acknowledged this fact. *Nekhen* was the early center of the 3rd Upper Egyptian nome. During the New Kingdom it was replaced in this role by el-Kab, and belonged to the territory administered by the viceroy of Kush.

Extensive remains of Predynastic settlements and cemeteries are discernible for some 3 km along the edge of the desert to the south and southwest of el-Muissat, and are particularly dense east of the wadi opposite which Kom el-Ahmar is situated. A brick-built structure of uncertain purpose ("The Fort"), probably Early Dynastic, stands some 500 m into the wadi. The famous "Decorated Tomb 100" was found in the easternmost part of the settlement/cemetery area at the end of the last century, but is now lost. This brick-built underground tomb of a modest size (4·5 by 2 by 1·5 m) had its west wall decorated with a remarkable painting showing boats, animals and men. It probably belonged to one of the local chiefs of the late Predynastic Period, and is important as an indicator of the growing social stratification of Egyptian society, as well as a document showing the conventions and motifs of Egyptian art in process of formation.

At the beginning of the 1st Dynasty the irregularly shaped town enclosure known as Kom el-Ahmar replaced the earlier settlement on the edge of the desert. In its south corner, occupying about

Above Small ivory and faience votive statuettes of the Early Dynastic Period, from the "Main Deposit" of the temple at Kom el-Ahmar. Oxford, Ashmolean Museum.

Left Seated lion, pottery with a shiny red slip, probably of the 3rd Dynasty. Several features of this sculpture are unusual, in particular the schematic treatment of the ears and the mane falling down on the chest of the animal like a bib in imitation of a headcloth. Height: 42·5 cm. Found in the temple. Oxford, Ashmolean Museum.

Limestone ceremonial mace head of king "Scorpion" (from the sign of a scorpion near the face of the king), perhaps identical with Naʿrmer. The main scene of the relief decoration shows a temple-founding ceremony with the king digging the first trench. Height: 25 cm. From the "Main Deposit." Oxford, Ashmolean Museum.

one sixth of the total area, was the temple complex. This was partially uncovered during the principal excavations at Hierakonpolis carried out in 1897–99. The excavators, J. E. Quibell and F. W. Green, faced great technical difficulties, for which Egyptian archaeology was not yet properly equipped. In its earliest form the brick-built temple apparently contained a mound of sand revetted with stones, perhaps the prototype of the hieroglyphic sign ⊚ with which the name of *Nekhen* was written. King Naʿrmer was the main benefactor, together with Khaʿsekhem/Khaʿsekhemwy. At some later point, many of the votive objects which had been presented to the temple were brought together and deposited in a cache (the so-called "Main Deposit"). It is not clear when and why this took place: it could have been caused by a rebuilding of the temple or by the uncertainty of the times. Many

of the objects in the "Main Deposit" (palettes, mace heads, stone vessels, carved ivory figures, etc.) date to the two Early Dynastic kings already mentioned, though a later date has been proposed for some uninscribed pieces. Monuments of practically all later periods have been found in the temple, but they are not very numerous or spectacular. Only those of the 6th Dynasty form an exception (two large copper statues representing Pepy I and Merenreʿ, a granite stela showing a king Pepy in the company of Horus and Hathor, a statue base of Pepy II, possibly also the head of a gold falcon image); there may have been alterations to the structure at that time.

Decorated and inscribed rock-cut tombs ranging from the 6th to the 18th Dynasties have been found in the wadi of the "Fort" and its subsidiary branches.

el-Kab

The earliest traces of man's activities in the area of el-Kab go back to about 6000 BC: the so-called Kabian is a microlithic industry which predates the known Neolithic cultures of Upper Egypt. Ancient *Nekheb*, on the east bank of the Nile, and *Nekhen* (Kom el-Ahmar), on the opposite side of the river, were very important settlements in the Predynastic and Early Dynastic Periods. This was reflected in the elevation of Nekhbet, the vulture goddess of *Nekheb*, to the status of the tutelary goddess of Egyptian kings (together with the cobra goddess Wadjit of Lower Egypt). Nekhbet was regarded as the Upper Egyptian goddess *par excellence*. Also known as "The White One of Nekhen," she was one of the deities who assisted at royal and divine births, and so was equated with the Greek Eileithyia

in the Greco-Roman Period, when the town was called Eileithyiaspolis. At least from the beginning of the 18th Dynasty *Nekheb* served as the capital of the 3rd Upper Egyptian nome, though it later relinquished this role in favor of Esna.

The view of el-Kab's town enclosure, measuring about 550 by 550 m and surrounded by massive brick-built walls, is most impressive. The enclosure contains the main temple of Nekhbet with several subsidiary structures, including a birth house, as well as smaller temples, a sacred lake and some early cemeteries.

It is likely that modest temple structures were erected at el-Kab as early as the Early Dynastic Period. This is suggested by the presence of a granite block bearing the name of Kha'sekhemwy. During the Middle Kingdom Nebhepetre' Mentuhotpe, Sebekhotpe III (*sed*-festival chapel) and Neferhotep III (Sekhemre'-s'ankhtawy) paid attention to the site. Major building activities in the temple of Nekhbet started in the 18th Dynasty. Almost all the kings of the period contributed in smaller or larger measure, but Tuthmosis III and Amenophis II seem to have been the most prominent among them. After the interlude of the 'Amarna Period the Ramessids continued to honor Nekhbet by adding to her temple. Taharqa of the 25th Dynasty, Psammetichus I of the 26th Dynasty and Darius I of the 27th Dynasty are also attested, but the shape in which the now much-dilapidated temple presented itself to archaeologists was mainly due to the kings of the 29th and 30th Dynasties (Hakoris and Nectanebo I and II).

Left One of the desert temples at el-Kab, the Ptolemaic rock-cut sanctuary of the goddess Shesmetet, seen from the south.

"At a Place called *Caab* . . . we discover'd something that look'd like a Piece of Antiquity . . . we came to the Remains of an antient Temple, consisting of Six Pillars in Two Rows, with their Roofs intire. A little to the North of these are the fragments of many other broken Pillars, and considerable other Ruins, and curiously wrought with Hieroglyphics, &c." (C. Perry, *A View of the Levant*, 1743, p. 361, describing the columns of the hypostyle hall of Hakoris in the temple of Nekhbet).

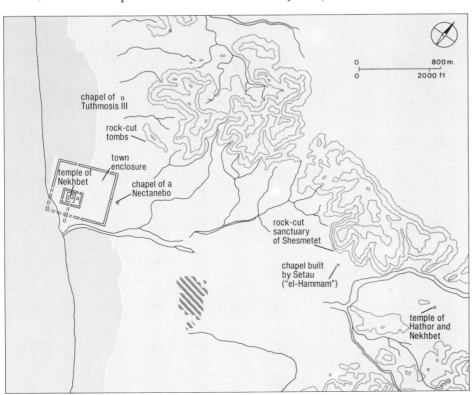

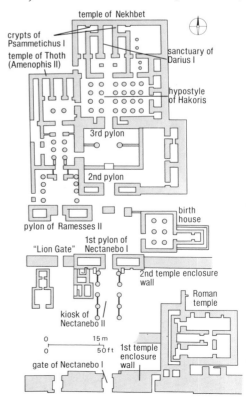

Temple of Khnum at Kom el-Deir, northwest of Esna, now destroyed; engraving made by Napoleon's expedition of 1798–1800.

There are rock-cut tombs, mainly of the first half of the 18th Dynasty, but also of the Middle Kingdom and the Ramessid Period, some 400 m north of the town enclosure. Two of them, those of 'Ahmose Pennekhbet (No. 2) and of 'Ahmose, son of Ebana (No. 5), are renowned for their biographical texts. The capture of the Hyksos capital Avaris, the siege of Sharuhen in Palestine by King 'Ahmose, and Syrian and Nubian campaigns of the kings of the early 18th Dynasty are among the historical events mentioned in them. Another tomb, of the mayor of *Nekheb*, Pahery, is remarkable for its reliefs. There is a decorated tomb which probably dates to Ptolemy III Euergetes I northwest of the others, nearer the river.

Esna

Esna, ancient Egyptian *Iunyt* or *(Ta)senet*, was called in Greek Latopolis, after the *Lates* fish, which was held sacred there and buried in a cemetery west of the town. In the same area there are human burials of the Middle Kingdom to Late Period.

The temple of Esna is about 200 m from the river, in the middle of the modern town. Because of the accumulation of occupation debris and silt, it is now about 9 m below street level. The ceremonial way, which probably linked the quay with the temple, has disappeared. The quay has cartouches of Marcus Aurelius, and is still in use. Texts in the temple relate it to four others in the area, three to the north and one on the east bank, all of which have now disappeared completely, although parts of them were still visible in the 19th century. Recently another temple of the same period has been excavated at Kom Mer, 12 km to the south.

The temple is dedicated to Khnum with several other deities, of whom the most prominent are Neith and Heka, whose name means "magical power," and who is here a child deity. As it stands, it consists only of a completely preserved hypostyle hall, whose west wall formed the beginning of the inner temple. This wall is earlier than the rest, with reliefs of Ptolemy VI Philometor and VIII Euergetes II. The rest of the hypostyle is the latest major temple preserved, and is decorated inside and out with reliefs from the 1st to 3rd centuries AD. Some scenes, notably that of gods and the king netting birds, are most imposing.

The most significant feature of the decoration is the series of texts written on the columns. These give a full and rich picture of some of the festivals of the sacred year at Esna, which is set out in schematic form in a calendar, also inscribed on a column. There is in addition a remarkable pair of cryptographic hymns to Khnum, one written almost entirely with hieroglyphs of rams, and one written with crocodiles.

Facade of the temple of Khnum at Esna; 1st century AD. The side doorways into the hypostyle hall have important mythological texts, and were the normal entrances for priests.

Two chapels, now destroyed, used to stand outside the enclosure. The first, about 750 m northwest of it, was built by Tuthmosis III; the other, outside the northeast enclosure wall, was the work of one of the Nectanebos. Some 2·2 km northeast of the enclosure, at the entrance to Wadi Hellal, there is the first of the so-called "desert temples," the partly free-standing and partly rock-cut sanctuary of the goddess Shesmetet (Smithis). It was built chiefly by Ptolemy VIII Euergetes II and Ptolemy IX Soter II. About 70 m southeast of it is the well-preserved chapel (known as "el-Hammam") built by the viceroy of Kush Setau during the reign of Ramesses II, and restored under the Ptolemies. It was probably dedicated to Re'-Harakhty, Hathor, Amun, Nekhbet and Ramesses II himself. Further away, about 3·4 km from the town enclosure, Tuthmosis IV and Amenophis III built a temple for Hathor "Mistress of the Entrance to the Valley" and Nekhbet.

el-Mo'alla

Two rock-cut decorated tombs of the beginning of the 1st Intermediate Period, belonging to 'Ankhtifi and Sebekhotpe, are the most important monuments at el-Mo'alla (probably to be equated with ancient Egyptian *Hefat*). Apart from its unconventional paintings, the tomb of 'Ankhtifi contains interesting biographical texts which describe the situation in the southern nomes following the end of the Old Kingdom.

Gebelein

The name of the locality means the same in Arabic as in ancient Egyptian: "The Two Hills." It derives from the most conspicuous landmark visible on the west bank of the Nile at the point where the 3rd and 4th Upper Egyptian nomes meet.

Tombs, mainly of the 1st Intermediate Period, were found on the west hill, while a temple of Hathor (hence the Greek name of the locality, Pathyris, from *Per-Hathor*, "The Domain of Hathor," or Aphroditopolis) stood on the east hill. The temple seems to have existed as early as the 3rd Dynasty, and reliefs, stelae or inscriptions dating to Nebhepetre' Mentuhotpe, several kings of the 13th (Djedneferre' Dedumose II, Djed'ankhre' Mentuemzaf and Sekhemre'-s'ankhtawy Neferhotep III) and 15th (Khian and 'Awoserre' Apophis) Dynasties

Far left top Tomb of 'Ankhtifi at el-Mo'alla: the deceased spearing fish from a papyrus boat. The figures of his wife and daughters standing behind him were destroyed by tomb robbers in recent years. Painting. 1st Intermediate Period.

Above and far left below Tomb of Iti at Gebelein. Three kneeling nude youths, perhaps engaged in gymnastics, and a scene of transport and storing grain in granaries. Painting. 1st Intermediate Period. Turin, Museo Egizio.

Left The Ptolemaic temple at Tod.

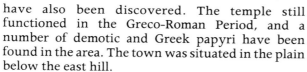

Black granite statue of the herald Sebekemsauf, the brother-in-law of one of the kings of the 2nd Intermediate Period. The sculpture, seen by John Gardner Wilkinson at Armant in the first half of the last century, is now in the Kunsthistorisches Museum in Vienna, but its base with the feet (on this photograph a cast) is in the National Museum of Ireland in Dublin. Height: 1·50 m.

have also been discovered. The temple still functioned in the Greco-Roman Period, and a number of demotic and Greek papyri have been found in the area. The town was situated in the plain below the east hill.

Tod

Apparently already in the reign of Userkaf of the 5th Dynasty there stood a brick-built chapel at ancient Egyptian *Djerty* (Tuphium of the Greco-Roman Period), on the east bank of the Nile. Major building activities connected with the local cult of the god Montu started in the Middle Kingdom, during the reigns of Nebhepetre' Mentuhotpe, S'ankhkare' Mentuhotpe and Senwosret I, but their temples are now destroyed. In the New Kingdom, Tuthmosis III erected a shrine, still partly preserved, for the bark of Montu, and Amenophis II, Sethos I, Amenmesse and Ramesses III and IV carried out some restoration work in it. Ptolemy VIII Euergetes II added his temple with a sacred lake in front of the temple of Senwosret I, and a Roman Period kiosk was located nearby.

Armant

Ancient *Iuny*, on the west bank of the Nile in the 4th Upper Egyptian nome, was one of the most important places of worship of the war god Montu, and until the beginning of the 18th Dynasty the capital of the whole nome, including Thebes. The modern name Armant derives from *Iunu-Montu*, Coptic *Ermont*, Greek Hermonthis.

A temple dedicated to Montu existed at Armant as early as the 11th Dynasty, the rulers of which perhaps originated there, and Nebhepetre' Mentuhotpe is the earliest builder known with certainty. Important additions were made during the 12th Dynasty and the New Kingdom, of which the remains of the pylon of Tuthmosis III are the only part still visible. The temple was destroyed some time during the Late Period, and its history can be traced only through reused or isolated blocks. In the reign of Nectanebo II a new temple was probably started, and the work was continued by the Ptolemies. The most important contribution to the appearance of the site was made by Cleopatra VII Philopator and Ptolemy XV Caesarion, who built a birth house with a lake. The building still existed in the first half of the last century, but is now completely destroyed. Two gates, one of them erected by Antoninus Pius, have also been found. The Bucheum (from ancient Egyptian *bekh*), the burial place of the sacred Buchis bulls of Armant, is located on the desert edge north of Armant. The earliest burial dates to Nectanebo II, and the Bucheum was in use for some 650 years, until the reign of Diocletian. The burial place of the "Mother of Buchis" cows has also been located. There are extensive cemeteries of all dates in the neighborhood of Armant.

THEBES

Ancient Egyptian *Waset* was called Thebai by the Greeks, but we are at a loss when searching for a reason for this. It has been suggested that the pronunciation of the Egyptian names *Ta-ipet* (*Ipet-resyt* was the Luxor temple) or *Djeme* (Medinet Habu) sounded similar to that of their Boeotian city, but the argument lacks conviction.

Waset was in the 4th Upper Egyptian nome, deep in the south. Its geographical position contributed greatly to the town's importance in history: it was close to Nubia and the eastern desert with their valuable mineral resources and trade routes, and distant from the restricting power centers in the north. Theban local rulers of the earlier part of Egyptian history pursued active expansionist policies, particularly during the 1st and 2nd Intermediate Periods; in the latter this was disguised as an Egyptian reaction against foreign invaders (the Hyksos). Monuments earlier than the end of the Old Kingdom are scarce, and *Waset* was little more than a provincial town. Its rise to prominence occurred during the 11th Dynasty; although the capital was moved to Itjtawy at the beginning of the 12th Dynasty, Thebes with its god Amun was established as the administrative center

of southern Upper Egypt. The peak came during the 18th Dynasty when the town acted as the capital of the country. Its temples were the most important and the wealthiest in the land, and the tombs prepared for the elite among its inhabitants on the west bank were the most luxurious Egypt ever saw. Even when in the later 18th Dynasty and during the Ramessid Period the residence and the center of royal activities moved to the north (el-'Amarna, Memphis and Pi-Ri'amsese), Theban temples continued to flourish, monarchs were still buried in the Valley of the Kings and the town retained some importance in the administrative life of the country. During the 3rd Intermediate Period Thebes, with the High Priest of Amun at its head, formed a counterbalance to the realm of the 21st- and 22nd-Dynasty kings, who ruled from Tanis in the delta. Theban influence ended only in the Late Period.

The main, and probably the earliest, part of the town and the principal temples were on the east bank. Across the river, on the west bank, was the necropolis with tombs and mortuary temples, but also the west part of the town; Amenophis III had his palace at el-Malqata, and in the Ramessid Period Thebes itself centered north of it, at Medinet Habu.

"The Pyramids, the Catacombs, and some other Things to be seen in Lower Egypt, are look'd upon as great Wonders; and are justly held in Preference to whatever the rest of the World can boast of. But if these challenge the Pre-eminence to all the extra Egyptian World, on the one hand, they must yield the Glory of Superiority to the many ancient Temples, &c. of Saaide [Upper Egypt] on the other" (C. Perry, *A View of the Levant*, 1743, Preface).

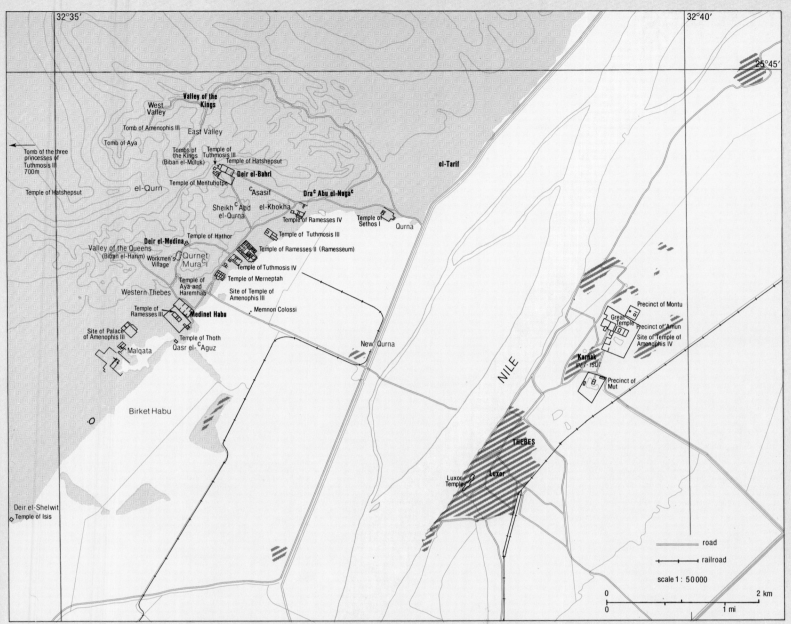

32°35'   32°40'

25°45'

West
Valley

Valley of the Kings

Tomb of Amenophis III

East Valley

Tomb of Aya

el-Tarif

Tomb of the three
princesses of
Tuthmosis III
700m

Tombs of
the Kings
(Biban el-Muluk)

Temple of
Tuthmosis III

Temple of Hatshepsut

Deir el-Bahri

Temple of Hatshepsut

el-Qurn

Temple of Mentuhotpe

ᶜAsasif

Draᶜ Abu el-Nagaᶜ

Sheikh ᶜAbd
el-Qurna

el-Khokha

Temple of Ramesses IV

Temple of
Sethos I

Qurna

Temple of Tuthmosis III

Deir el-Medina

Temple of Hathor

Temple of Ramesses II (Ramesseum)

Valley of the Queens
(Biban el-Harim)

Workmen's
Village

Qurnet
Muraᶜi

Temple of Tuthmosis IV

Temple of Merneptah

Western Thebes

Temple of
Aya and
Haremhab

Site of Temple of
Amenophis III

Precinct of Montu

Great
Temple

Temple of
Ramesses III

Medinet Habu

Memnon Colossi

Precinct of Amun

Site of Temple of
Amenophis IV

Site of Palace
of Amenophis III

Temple of Thoth

New Qurna

Karnak
IPET-ISUT

Malqata

Qasr el-ᶜAguz

Precinct of Mut

NILE

Birket Habu

THEBES

Luxor

Luxor
Temple

Deir el-Shelwit

Temple of Isis

road

railroad

scale 1 : 50 000

0   2 km

0   1 mi

Luxor
Temple of Amun, chiefly of
Amenophis III, Ramesses II and
Alexander the Great.
Karnak
Precincts of Amun, Montu and
Mut, with temple of Khons and
numerous smaller temples and
chapels, 12th Dynasty to Greco-
Roman Period.
The West Bank: Temples
Deir el-Bahri: mortuary temples
of Nebhepetreᶜ Mentuhotpe and
Hatshepsut, and temple of Amun
by Tuthmosis III.
Ramesseum: mortuary temple of
Ramesses II.
Medinet Habu: temple of Amun
of the 18th Dynasty and later,
and mortuary temple of Ramesses
III.
Other mortuary temples,
particularly those of Sethos I at
Qurna and Amenophis III with
"Memnon Colossi."

Royal Tombs
el-Tarif: 11th Dynasty.
Draᶜ Abu el-Nagaᶜ: 17th Dynasty.
Valley of the Kings: 18th to 20th
Dynasties, including tomb of
Tutᶜankhamun.
Deir el-Medina: workmen's
village.
Private Tombs
Tombs dating from the 6th
Dynasty to Greco-Roman Period.

Luxor

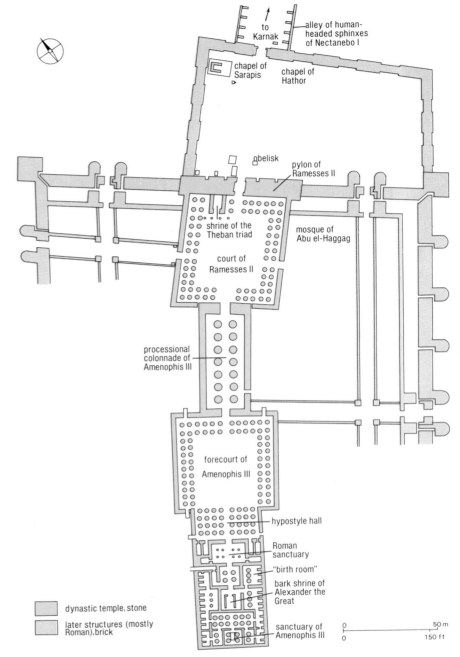

Textual and archaeological evidence indicates that a sanctuary stood on the site of the Luxor temple or in its vicinity at the beginning of the 18th Dynasty, or even earlier, but the temple we see today was built essentially by two kings, Amenophis III (the inner part) and Ramesses II (the outer part). Several other rulers contributed to its relief decoration and inscriptions, added minor structures or made alterations, chiefly Tut'ankhamun, Haremhab and Alexander the Great. An earlier shrine of the Theban triad was incorporated into the court of Ramesses II. The overall length of the temple between the pylon and the rear wall is nearly 260 m.

The temple was dedicated to Amun (Amenemope) who at Luxor took the form of the ithyphallic Min. It was closely connected with the Great Temple of Amun at Karnak, and once a year, during the second and third months of the inundation season, a long religious festival was held at Luxor during which the image of Amun of Karnak visited his *Ipet-resyt*, "Southern *Ipet*," as the temple was called.

At the end of the reign of the Roman Emperor Diocletian, just after 300 AD, the first of the antechambers in the inner part of the temple was converted into a sanctuary of the imperial cult serving the local military garrison and town. The standards and insignia of the legion were kept there. It was decorated with exquisite paintings which were still visible in the 19th century but are now almost completely lost. A small mosque of Abu el-Haggag was built in the court of Ramesses II in the Ayyubid Period (13th century AD), and still stands there.

An *alley of human-headed sphinxes of Nectanebo I* linked Karnak, some 3 km to the north, with Luxor, and brought the visitor to a *brick-built enclosure wall*. Several later structures stood in the forecourt which preceded the temple itself, including a colonnade of Shabaka (later dismantled) and chapels of Hathor, built by Taharqa, and of Sarapis, built by Hadrian. The burned brick walls visible to the east and west of the temple are remains of the late Roman town, contemporary with the imperial sanctuary.

The temple is fronted by a *pylon of Ramesses II*, with reliefs and texts on its outside relating the

Far left The colonnade of Amenophis III from southwest, with the pylon of Ramesses II visible behind, and the mosque of Abu el-Haggag on the right.

Left The pylon from the north, with the remains of standing colossal statues of Ramesses II outside the side doorway to the court, and the massive papyriform columns of the processional colonnade of Amenophis III on the right.

Right The pylon in 1838, shortly after the removal of the northern obelisk, as seen by the Scottish artist David Roberts (1796–1864). The colossal seated statues of Ramesses II outside the pylon were still half-buried in debris.

Far right top Columns of the hypostyle hall, with capitals in the form of unopened papyrus umbels, and abaci and architraves with names and texts of Amenophis III.

Above and far right bottom Paintings on the walls of the Roman *sacellum*: section of the east wall, and part of the representations left of the apse (a semicircular recess created by conversion of the doorway between the 1st and 2nd antechamber of the older temple). Recorded by Sir John Gardner Wilkinson in or before 1856 (earlier than the date quoted in specialized studies). Now almost completely lost.

Overleaf Detail of a granite statue, probably of Amenophis III, with an added cartouche of Merneptah. From Luxor. "A goodly office is that of king: as it has no son or brother who would make its monuments endure, it is one who looks after the other; a man does things for his predecessor hoping that what he has done will be taken care of by another who will come after him" (Papyrus Leningrad 1116 A recto, 116–18).

story of the famous battle against the Hittites at Qadesh in Syria in 1285 BC. Two red granite obelisks originally stood in front of the pylon but only one, approximately 25 m high, remains now: the other was removed to the Place de la Concorde in Paris in 1835–36. Several colossal statues of Ramesses II, two of them seated, flank the entrance. The central gateway of the pylon was partly decorated by Shabaka.

The *peristyle court of Ramesses II* which opens behind the pylon has 74 papyrus columns with scenes of the king before various deities. The columns are arranged in a double row around its sides, and are interrupted by a shrine consisting of three chapels (or bark stations) of Amun (center), Mut (left) and Khons (right), built by Hatshepsut and Tuthmosis III and redecorated by Ramesses II. It was the existence of this shrine which probably caused the considerable deviation of the axis of the buildings of Ramesses II from that of the earlier temple of Amenophis III. Colossal standing statues of the king are placed in the gaps between the front row of columns at the south end of the court.

The entrance to the *processional colonnade of Amenophis III*, with seven columns on either side, has two seated colossi of Ramesses II with Queen Nefertari by his right leg on the north side, while two seated double statues of Amun and Mut are on the south side. The walls behind the columns were decorated by Tut'ankhamun and Haremhab with reliefs depicting the Festival of Opet: those on the west wall show a procession of barks from Karnak to Luxor, while the eastern wall shows their homeward journey.

A *peristyle forecourt of Amenophis III* is fused with the *hypostyle hall*, which is the first room in the inner, originally roofed, part of the temple. This leads to a series of *four antechambers* with subsidiary rooms. The so-called "Birth Room," east of the second antechamber, is decorated with reliefs showing the symbolic "divine birth" of Amenophis III resulting from the union of his mother Mutemwia and the god Amun. Alexander the Great built a bark shrine in the third of the antechambers. The *sanctuary of Amenophis III* is the last room on the central axis of the temple.

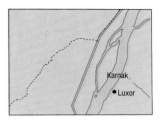

Karnak

The name Karnak, from that of a modern village nearby (el-Karnak), is used to describe a vast conglomeration of ruined temples, chapels and other buildings of various dates, measuring some 1·5 by at least 0·8 km. This was ancient Egyptian *Ipet-isut*, "The Most Select of Places," the main place of worship of the Theban triad with the god Amun at its head, and also the home of various "guest" deities. No site in Egypt makes a more overwhelming and lasting impression than this apparent chaos of walls, obelisks, columns, statues, stelae and decorated blocks. After the Theban kings and the god Amun came to prominence at the beginning of the Middle Kingdom, and particularly from the beginning of the 18th Dynasty, when the capital of Egypt was firmly established in Thebes, the temples of Karnak were built, enlarged, pulled down, added to and restored for more than 2,000 years. The temple of Amun was ideologically and economically the most important temple establishment in the whole of Egypt.

The site can conveniently be divided into three groups, which are defined geographically by the remains of brick-built walls enclosing the temple precincts. The largest and most important is the central enclosure, the temple of Amun proper. It is also the best preserved. The northern enclosure belongs to Montu, the original local god of the Theban area, while the enclosure of Mut lies to the south and is connected with Amun's precinct by an alley of ram-headed sphinxes. An avenue bordered by sphinxes linked Karnak with the Luxor temple, and canals connected the temples of Amun and Montu with the Nile.

The precinct of Amun
The trapezoidal central enclosure contains the Great Temple of Amun, built along two axes (east–west and north–south), a number of smaller temples and chapels and a sacred lake. East of the enclosure stood a now completely destroyed temple of Amenophis IV (Akhenaten), built on a huge scale, as well as two minor Ptolemaic structures, now also destroyed. Remains of some of the earliest buildings at Karnak, dating to Senwosret I, were discovered still *in situ* in the east part of the Great Temple, in the so-called Central Court behind Pylon VI.

The layout of the Great Temple can be described as consisting of a series of pylons of various dates, with courts or halls between them, leading to the main sanctuary. The earliest are Pylons IV and V, built by Tuthmosis I; from then on the temple was enlarged by building in a westerly and in a southerly direction.

Pylon I is preceded by a quay (probably reconstructed in its present form during the 25th Dynasty), and an avenue of ram-headed sphinxes

protecting the king, most of which bear the name of the high priest of Amun, Pinudjem I of the 21st Dynasty. South of the avenue there are several smaller structures, including a bark shrine of Psammuthis and Hakoris, and parapets of the 25th–26th Dynasties with texts connected with the ceremony of refilling the jars of the Theban triad. The date of the pylon itself is not quite certain: it is probably of the 30th Dynasty. The forecourt which opens behind it contains a triple bark shrine of Sethos I consisting of three contiguous chapels dedicated to Amun, Mut and Khons. In the center of the forecourt there are remains of a kiosk of unusual construction of Taharqa, with one of its columns standing. A small temple (bark station) of Ramesses III faces into the forecourt from the south.

Pylon II, probably a work of Haremhab, who reused a large number of earlier blocks to build it, is preceded by colossal statues of Ramesses II,

Top Ram-headed sphinxes ("criosphinxes") outside Pylon I. The ram was the sacred animal of Amun; the motif of an animal, bird or serpent "protecting" a king or even a private individual was common in Egyptian two- and three-dimensional sculpture.

Above left Headless statue of Sethos II kneeling with an offering table, now restored and set up north of the 4th column on the north side of the central aisle of the hypostyle hall.

Above The rear part of the Great Temple of Amun from the east.

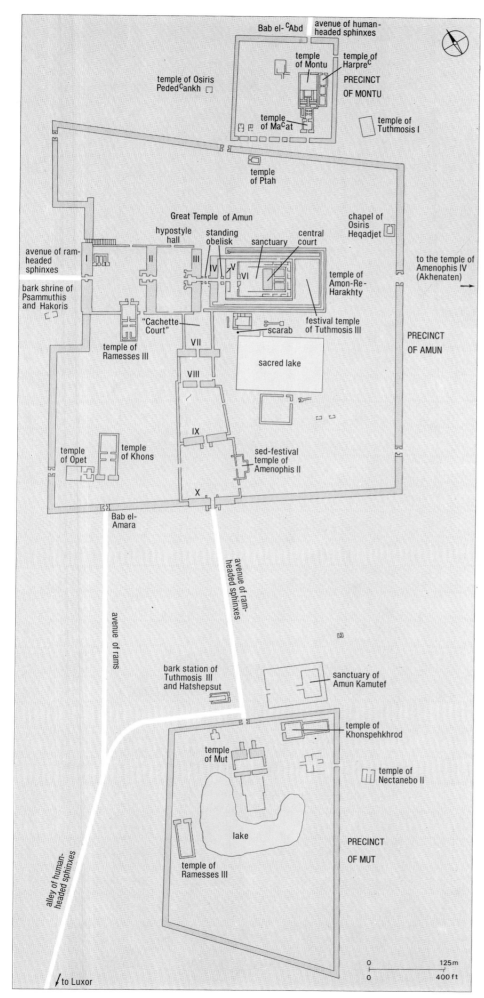

The small temple of Ramesses III between Pylons I and II: Osirid pillars on the west side of the court seen from the temple entrance. Reliefs on the sides of the pillars show the king before various gods.

including one (on the north) showing him with Princess Bent'anta. Behind the pylon, the now lost roof of the hypostyle hall, the most impressive part of the whole temple complex, was borne by 134 papyrus columns, of which the 12 in the central aisle are larger and have capitals of a different type. The relief decoration of the hypostyle hall is the work of Sethos I and Ramesses II. The exterior walls depict military campaigns of these kings in Palestine and Syria, including Ramesses II's battle at Qadesh.

Pylon III was built by Amenophis III, but the porch in front of it was decorated by Sethos I and Ramesses II. Numerous blocks from earlier buildings were found reused in the pylon: a *sed*-festival shrine of Senwosret I (the "White Chapel," now reerected to the north of the hypostyle hall), shrines of Amenophis I and II, Hatshepsut (the "Red Chapel," so called for its material, red quartzite) and Tuthmosis IV, and a pillared portico of the same king. The four obelisks which stood behind the pylon were erected by Tuthmosis I and III to mark the entrance to the original temple; only one obelisk of Tuthmosis I is still standing.

Between *Pylons IV and V*, both of Tuthmosis I, there is the earliest part of the temple still preserved, with 14 papyrus columns, originally gilded, and two obelisks of Hatshepsut (one standing, one fallen).

Pylon VI and the court which precedes it were built by Tuthmosis III. Behind them is a vestibule with two magnificent granite pillars with the emblems of Upper and Lower Egypt, both still standing. The bark shrine (sanctuary) dates to Philip Arrhidaeus and stands on the site of an earlier shrine built by Tuthmosis III.

Behind the Central Court is the Festival Temple of Tuthmosis III. One room in the temple is known as the "Botanical Garden," because of its representations of exotic plants, birds and animals.

Another four pylons were added along a new axis which extended the Great Temple of Amun in a southerly direction. The court north of Pylon VII is known as the "Cachette Court": it was here that a deposit of thousands of statues which originally stood in the temple was found at the beginning of this century. Remains of earlier buildings were also

found in this court, including pillars of Senwosret I and several chapels of Amenophis I. *Pylons VII and VIII* were built by Tuthmosis III, and the court between them contains his bark station.

Pylons IX and X are due to Haremhab. Many "talatat," blocks from buildings of Amenophis IV (Akhenaten), mostly dating before his move to el-'Amarna, were found reused in these pylons. A *sed*-festival temple of Amenophis II stands in the court between them.

Near the northwest corner of the temple's sacred lake there is a colossal statue of the sacred scarab beetle, dating to Amenophis III.

The temple of Khons stands in the southwest corner of the enclosure. Its propylon (a gate in the enclosure wall), built by Ptolemy III Euergetes I and known as the Bab el-'Amara, is approached from the south by an avenue of rams protecting Amenophis III. The pylon was decorated by Pinudjem I, the forecourt by Herihor, and the inner part by various Ramessids (at least part of the temple was built by Ramesses III); there is also some Ptolemaic relief work.

The temple of the hippopotamus goddess Opet, close to the last, was chiefly built by Ptolemy VIII Euergetes II. The decoration was completed by several later rulers, including Augustus. There is a symbolic "Crypt of Osiris" below the sanctuary at the back of the temple.

Nearly 20 other small chapels and temples are within the precinct of Amun, including a temple of Ptah built by Tuthmosis III, Shabaka, the Ptolemies and Tiberius (north of the Great Temple, close to the enclosure wall), and a chapel of Osiris Heqadjet "Ruler of Time" of Osorkon IV and Shebitku (northeast of the Great Temple, close to the enclosure wall).

The precinct of Montu
The square-shaped northern enclosure is the smallest of the three precincts. It contains the main temple of Montu, several smaller structures (particularly the temples of Harpre' and Ma'at) and a sacred lake. In 1970 an early temple of Montu, built by Tuthmosis I, was found outside the east enclosure wall.

The temple of Montu is fronted by a quay and an avenue of human-headed sphinxes which approaches the temple from the north. The propylon, known as Bab el-'Abd, was built by Ptolemy III Euergetes I and IV Philopator, and the temple by Amenophis III, but later kings, particularly Taharqa, carried out some modifications of the original plan.

The precinct of Mut
The southern enclosure contains the temple of Mut, surrounded by a crescent-shaped lake, and subsidiary structures, particularly the temple of Khonspekhrod, originally of the 18th Dynasty, and a temple of Ramesses III.

The temple of Mut was built by Amenophis III, but here too the propylon in the enclosure wall is Ptolemaic (Ptolemy II Philadelphus and III Euergetes I), and there are later additions to the temple by Taharqa and Nectanebo I among others. Amenophis III dedicated hundreds of black granite statues of the lioness goddess Sakhmet to the temple. Some of these can still be seen at Karnak.

Far left Ramesses II returning home from an expedition to Palestine, driving before him the captured "chiefs of Retjenu": bottom register on the south outside wall of the hypostyle hall, close to Pylon II.

Right A princess, perhaps Bent'anta, standing between the feet of a colossal statue of her father Ramesses II (with added cartouches of Ramesses VI and the High Priest of Amun Pinudjem I of the 21st Dynasty). Restored and reerected before Pylon II of the Great Temple of Amun, on the north side of the entrance.

Below Countless private individuals had statues of themselves set up in the temples of Karnak. The main function of these sculptures was similar to that of votive stelae: to perpetuate the donor's presence in the temple in order for him to benefit from being by the side of the god.

Left The Chief Steward Senenmut, a contemporary of Hatshepsut, in his role of the tutor of the princess Nefrure'. Black granite. Height: 53 cm. Chicago, Field Museum of Natural History.

Below The Third Prophet of Montu, Pakhelkhons, kneels with a naos containing a statuette of Osiris. Black granite. Height: 42 cm. 3rd Intermediate Period. Baltimore (Md.), Walters Art Gallery.

"The Northernmost, said to be the statue of *Memnon*, is cover'd with a great Number of *Greek* and *Latin* Inscriptions; being so many testimonies of Persons who pretend to have heard it utter a Sound at Sun-rise" (C. Perry, *A View of the Levant*, 1743, p. 348).

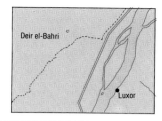

The West Bank

The temples

Across the Nile from the temples of Karnak and Luxor, the remains of temples occupy a stretch of some $7\frac{1}{2}$ km. Most of these were royal mortuary temples of the New Kingdom, and their main function was to maintain the cult of the deceased kings buried in their tombs cut in the cliffs further to the west, though gods also were worshiped there, particularly Amun and Re'-Harakhty. The most important of these temples are those of Deir el-Bahri, the Ramesseum and Medinet Habu. The mortuary temple of Sethos I stands at Qurna, while only huge seated statues, the "Memnon Colossi," and other fragmentary sculptures now mark the site of the temple of Amenophis III. Several of the temples on the west bank were not mortuary, such as the temples of Hathor (Deir el-Medina), Thoth (Qasr el-'Aguz) and Isis (Deir el-Shelwit), all of the Greco-Roman Period.

Deir el-Bahri

Deir el-Bahri, the place traditionally connected with the local cult of the cow goddess Hathor, almost directly opposite Karnak, was chosen by Nebhepetre' Mentuhotpe of the 11th Dynasty and Queen Hatshepsut of the 18th Dynasty for the site of their mortuary temples (in the case of Mentuhotpe the temple was directly connected with the burial, while Hatshepsut had two tombs prepared for her, one in a remote valley behind, the Wadi Sikket Taqet Zaid, the other in the Valley of the Kings). Shortly after the completion of Hatshepsut's temple, Tuthmosis III built a temple complex for the god Amun (*Djeser-akhet*) and a chapel for Hathor between the two earlier structures, and a kiosk (*Djeser-menu*) in the court of Mentuhotpe's temple.

The mortuary temple of Nebhepetre' Mentuhotpe (Akh-isut). Although the basic idea must have already been present in the minds of the

95

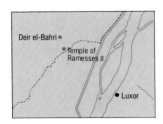

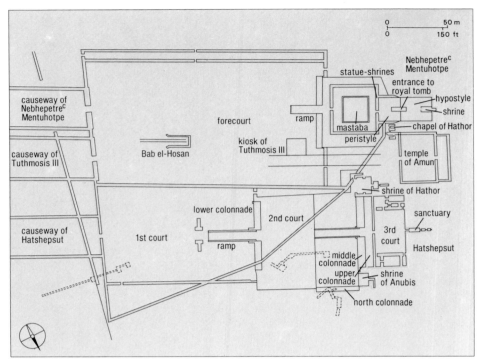

architects of the pyramid complexes of the Old Kingdom, a design which consciously placed different parts of a temple on terraces of varying height was not attempted in Egypt until Nebhepetre' Mentuhotpe built his temple at Deir el-Bahri. Another new element introduced there, the colonnade (portico) at the back of the terrace, may have derived from the appearance of the *saff*-tombs of the earlier kings of the 11th Dynasty.

The front, free-standing, part of the temple is approached by a 46-m-wide causeway from the now lost valley temple, and consists of a forecourt, enclosed by walls on its three sides, and a terrace with a now much-ruined mastaba-shaped structure, probably associated with the cult of the sun god. In the east part of the forecourt is the opening known as "Bab el-Hosan," which is connected by a long underground passage with a probably symbolic royal tomb, left unfinished. The west part of the forecourt originally contained a grove of tamarisk and sycamore trees on either side of an ascending ramp leading on to the terrace. Behind the colonnade at the west end of the forecourt and another on the terrace, were reliefs showing boat processions, foreign campaigns, hunting scenes etc.; of these a large number of small fragments are preserved in various museums. The mastaba, which was the dominant feature of the temple, is surrounded by a pillared ambulatory on all sides. In its west wall there are six statue-shrines (and, further west, tombs) of royal ladies of the reign of Nebhepetre' (from the north: Myt, 'Ashayt, Zadeh, Kawit, Kemsyt and Henhenet).

The inner part of the temple, cut into the cliff, consists of peristyle and hypostyle courts east and west of the entrance to an underground passage which after some 150 m leads to the tomb proper. Little of the royal burial and funerary equipment was found. The rock-cut shrine at the back of the inner part of the building was the main cult place of the deceased king in the temple.

The mortuary temple of Hatshepsut (*Djeser-djeseru*). The temple is a partly rock-cut and partly free-standing terraced structure. Its builders took up and developed the remarkable architectural ideas of its 550-year-old predecessor to the north of

which it stands. Even now, in its incompletely preserved state, the temple conveys a unique harmony between man's creation and the natural environment. The effect of its original appearance, with trees, flowerbeds and numerous sphinxes and statues, must have been even more overwhelming. The temple was built between years 7 and 22 of the reign of Hatshepsut and Tuthmosis III, and a number of high officials of the state were involved in its construction, including the influential "Chief Steward of Amun" Senenmut.

The valley temple of the complex is attested by its foundation deposits, but the building itself has disappeared, at least partly as a result of the proximity of the later temple of Ramesses IV. The monumental causeway, some 37 m wide, lined by sphinxes and provided with a bark chapel, led on to a series of three courts at different levels, approached by ramps and separated by colonnades (porticoes) protecting the now famous reliefs. These show huge barges specially constructed to bring obelisks from Aswan for the temple of Amun at Karnak (the lower colonnade), scenes of the divine birth and coronation of Hatshepsut (the north half

Top left Soldiers taking part in a boat procession: relief on the north wall of the hypostyle hall of the shrine of Hathor, in the south part of Hatshepsut's temple.

Above The temples at Deir el-Bahri from the cliff to the north.

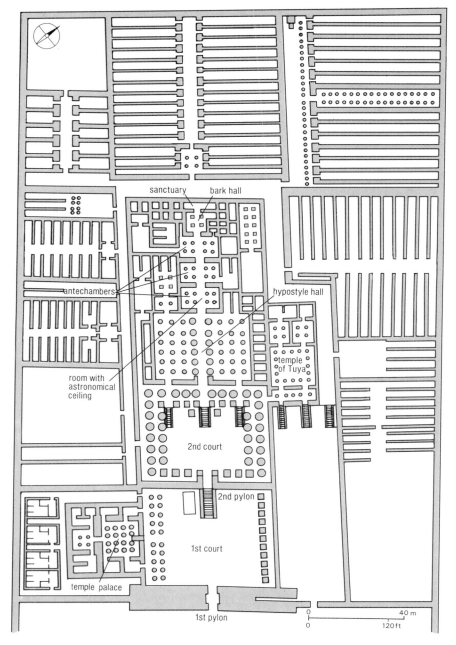

Top right The hypostyle hall of the Ramesseum from the southwest.

Above right The east wall of the hypostyle hall of the Ramesseum, south of the entrance, bottom register: detail of relief showing the assault on the fort of Dapur, "the town which His Majesty sacked in the land of Amor," in year 8 of the reign of Ramesses II. The exact location of this northern Syrian town, perhaps in the region of Aleppo, is not known.

of the middle colonnade) and a trade expedition by sea to the exotic African land of Punt (the south half of the middle colonnade). The upper colonnade, formed by Osirid pillars flanked by colossal statues of the queen, preceded the upper court. Vaulted rooms on the north and south sides of this court were dedicated to Hatshepsut and her father Tuthmosis I, and the gods Re'-Harakhty and Amun. Theirs were the main cults maintained in the temple. A series of niches at the back (the west side) of the hall contained statues of the queen, and an entrance in the same wall led to the sanctuary proper. The innermost room of the present sanctuary was cut by Ptolemy VIII Euergetes II; otherwise, the temple's architecture is remarkably free from later interference. Special shrines of Anubis and Hathor were approached from the second court.

The mortuary temple of Ramesses II (*Khnemtwaset*) or Ramesseum

The mortuary complex of Ramesses II, somewhat misleadingly described by Diodorus as "the tomb of Osymandyas" (from Userma'atre', part of the praenomen of Ramesses II), nowadays known as the Ramesseum, consists of the temple proper and the surrounding brick-built magazines and other buildings (the tomb of Ramesses II is in the Valley of the Kings).

The interior disposition of the stone-built temple is fairly orthodox, though somewhat more elaborate than usual: two courts, a hypostyle hall, a series of antechambers and subsidiary rooms, the bark hall and the sanctuary. The temple's overall plan is, unusually, a parallelogram rather than a rectangle. This was probably caused by retaining the orientation of an earlier small temple, dedicated to Tuya, the mother of Ramesses II, while making the pylons face the temple of Luxor on the east bank. Tuya's temple is north of the hypostyle hall of the Ramesseum.

The 1st and 2nd pylons of the Ramesseum are decorated with reliefs depicting, among other things, the battle of Qadesh (also known from Karnak, Luxor, Abydos and Abu Simbel). Two granite colossi of Ramesses II originally stood before a platform preceding the hypostyle hall: the upper part of the southern statue is now in the British Museum, but the head of the companion piece can still be seen in the Ramesseum. The first room behind the hypostyle hall has an astronomical ceiling and might have served as the temple's library. The usual temple palace stood south of the first court.

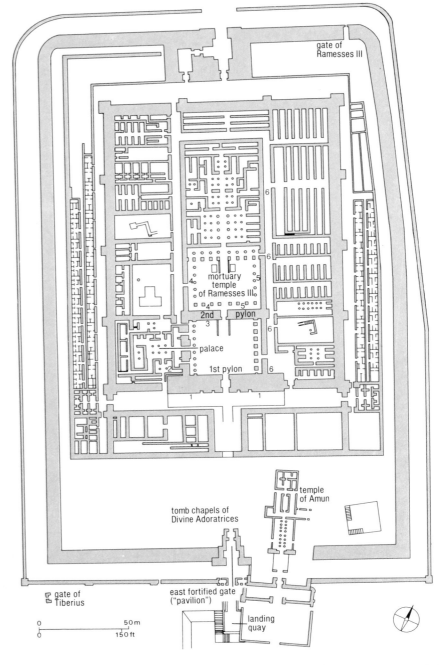

1 Ramesses III smiting captives
2 Ramesses III hunting
3 Ramesses III presents captives to Amun and Mut
4 festival of Sokar and Libyan war
5 festivals of Min and Amun
6 campaigns against the Libyans, Asiatics and the "sea peoples"

Medinet Habu

Situated opposite Luxor, ancient Egyptian *Tjamet* (or *Djamet*), Coptic *Djeme* (or *Djemi*), was one of the earliest places in the Theban area to be associated closely with Amun. Hatshepsut and Tuthmosis III built a temple for him there. Next to it, Ramesses III erected his mortuary temple, and enclosed both structures within massive brick-built walls. There were magazines, workshops, administrative buildings and dwellings of priests and officials within its enclosure walls. Medinet Habu became the focus of the administrative and economic life of the whole of Thebes, and performed this role for the next several hundred years. Even tombs and tomb chapels started being built there, in particular those of the Divine Adoratrices of the 25th and 26th Dynasties. The site continued to be inhabited well into the Middle Ages (9th century AD).

The temple of Amun (*Djeser-iset*). The original temple, built by Hatshepsut and Tuthmosis III, underwent many alterations and enlargements in the course of the following 1,500 years, mainly during Dynasties 20 (Ramesses III), 25 (Shabaka and Taharqa), 26, 29 (Hakoris), 30 (Nectanebo I) and the Greco-Roman Period (Ptolemy VIII Euergetes II, X Alexander I and Antoninus Pius). These considerably extended its plan by adding a columned hall, two pylons, and a court at the front.

The mortuary temple of Ramesses III (*Khnemt-neheh*). The temple used to be connected with the Nile by a canal, a feature of some importance since boat processions played an important part in religious festivals, and a landing quay was built outside the enclosure. The entrance to the temple enclosure was through one of the two fortified gates in the east and west; only the former, sometimes called the "Pavilion," now remains.

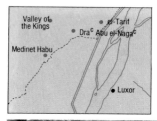

Above The kneeling Ramesses III being crowned and receiving a symbolic *sed*-festival emblem from the Theban triad: the enthroned Amon-Re' accompanied by Khons and Mut (behind the king, not shown on the photograph). East part of the south wall of the 1st hypostyle hall, temple of Ramesses III at Medinet Habu, lower register.

Above right The Valley of the Kings.

Left The temple of Ramesses III: from the right, the 1st pylon, the wall of the 1st court with three doorways and a "window of appearances" connecting the court with the palace south of it, the 2nd pylon, and the south wall of the 2nd court and the inner part of the temple.

The temple itself is of orthodox design, and resembles closely the mortuary temple of Ramesses II (the Ramesseum), which it probably consciously imitates. South of the 1st court stood the brick-built palace, now badly damaged, which was used by the king during religious festivals held at Medinet Habu. Two building phases of the structure have been recognized. The palace's interior walls were originally decorated with exquisite faience tiles, similar to those known from contemporary palaces in the delta (Tell el-Yahudiya and Qantir). The "window of appearances" connected the palace with the temple.

Some of the reliefs at Medinet Habu are not only artistically but also historically important, because they record historical events of the reign of Ramesses III:

1st pylon: On the outside, the king is shown smiting foreign captives in front of Amun and Re'-Harakhty in symbolic scenes of triumph. The subjugated foreign lands and towns are represented by their names inscribed in rings that have human heads. Hunting scenes are on the short outside west face of the south massif.

2nd pylon: On the outside (east face) of the south massif, the king presents captives to Amun and Mut. On the inside, and also on the south and north walls of the 2nd court, are representations of the festivals of Sokar and Min.

The exterior of the temple: Campaigns against the Libyans, Asiatics and the "sea peoples" are shown on the north wall.

There are more strictly religious scenes on the walls of the rooms of the inner part of the temple.

Royal tombs

el-Tarif

The ambitious rulers of the early Theban 11th Dynasty, vying with the northern Herakleopolitan (9th/10th) Dynasty for supremacy over Egypt, built their tombs at el-Tarif, in river terms the northernmost part of the Theban necropolis. Although the tombs are comparable in type to contemporary provincial tombs elsewhere, their majestic size and truly monumental architecture connect them with the mortuary temple and tomb of the king who finally gained control over the whole of Egypt, Nebhepetre' Mentuhotpe, at Deir el-Bahri.

The tombs consist of an open excavation running into the rock which forms a huge court (as much as 300 m long and 60 m wide). At the back of the court a series of door-like openings creates the impression of a pillared facade. This gave the tombs the name *saff*-tombs (from *saff*, "row" in Arabic). The fairly modest burial chamber and other rooms are cut in the rock behind the facade, and a brick-built valley temple completes the complex. Little of the decoration of the tombs is preserved.

Three *saff*-tombs are known:
Inyotef I (Horus Sehertawy): Saff el-Dawaba
Inyotef II (Horus Wah'ankh): Saff el-Kisasiya
Inyotef III (Horus Nakhtnebtepnufer): Saff el-Baqar.

Dra' Abu el-Naga'

Theban rulers of the 17th Dynasty and their families were buried in modest tombs at Dra' Abu el-Naga', between el-Tarif and Deir el-Bahri. The relative position of these tombs and their ownership are known from a papyrus recording an inspection of them in about 1080 BC (the Abbott Papyrus). A number of inscribed objects, including the so-called *rishi*-coffins, decorated weapons and jewelry, were found during excavations conducted by Mariette before 1860. The architecture of the tombs, which may have had small brick-built pyramids, is little known.

The Valley of the Kings ("Biban el-Muluk")

After the defeat of the Hyksos the Theban rulers of the 18th Dynasty began to build themselves tombs in a style befitting kings of all Egypt. The tomb of Amenophis I was probably at Dra' Abu el-Naga'. Its position is not known for certain, but the esteem in which the king was held by the community of specialized workmen engaged in making royal tombs suggests that his was the earliest tomb of the new type. Tuthmosis I was the first to have his tomb cut in the cliffs of a desolate valley behind Deir el-Bahri, now known as the Valley of the Kings. The area is dominated by the peak of el-Qurn ("the horn"), and the valley consists of two main branches, the East Valley, with most of the tombs, and the West Valley, with the tombs of Amenophis

III and Aya. The total number of tombs is 62 (tomb No. 62 is that of Tut'ankhamun, discovered last), but some of them are not royal tombs, while the ownership of others is still disputed. The tombs were separated from the corresponding mortuary temples, which were built at the edge of cultivation. The motivation for separating temple and tomb was not just security: there were also religious and architectural reasons.

The plan of the royal tombs of the 18th to 20th Dynasties (the last is the tomb of Ramesses XI) in the Valley of the Kings consists of a long inclined rock-cut corridor with one or more halls (sometimes pillared), terminating in the burial chamber. In the earlier tombs the corridor turns right or left, usually at a right angle, after some distance, but from the end of the 18th Dynasty it was straight. Its length could be considerable: Haremhab's is 105 m long, Siptah's 88 m and Ramesses VI's 83 m. The decoration of the tombs is almost exclusively religious. There are numerous scenes of the king in the presence of gods, but the most striking elements are the texts and accompanying illustrations of various religious compositions ("books"), such as the Book of *Amduat* ("that which is in the netherworld"), of Gates, of Caverns, the Litany of Re', and others. Early examples of these texts were made in such a way as to create the impression of huge funerary papyri unrolled on the tomb walls. From the end of the 18th Dynasty the decoration was carved in relief.

It is not easy to imagine the original wealth and beauty of the contents of these royal sepulchers. The only one which has been found largely intact and which provides a tantalizing glimpse of what is lost, that of Tut'ankhamun, may well not be typical.

The workmen's village at Deir el-Medina
The everyday life of the community of workmen ("Servants in the Place of Truth") employed in the

construction of royal tombs in the Valley of the Kings can be reconstructed in considerable detail from ostraca, papyri and other evidence. The ruins of the walled settlement (some 70 houses), in which workmen and their families lived from the reign of Tuthmosis I, can be seen in a small valley behind the hill of Qurnet Mura'i, at Deir el-Medina. The workmen's own tombs and the chapels of their local gods are nearby.

The "gang" of workmen, numbering some 60 men or more, was divided into two "sides," each with a foreman, his deputy, and one or more scribes. Their superior was the vizier, who occasionally came, or sent one of the royal "butlers," to visit the site and inspect the progress of work. The workmen's wages were paid in goods, mainly grain, received at the end of each month. Other commodities, such as fish and vegetables, and occasionally meat, wine, salt etc., were also supplied. It was symptomatic of the period that during the 20th Dynasty there were times when the rations were overdue, and on several occasions the workmen resorted to demonstrations. The earliest recorded "industrial action" took place in the 29th year of Ramesses III. The workmen normally stayed at the site of the tomb in the Valley of the Kings during the working "week" of 10 days, returning to the village for rest days or for religious festivals which were also holidays.

Valley of the Kings.
Above left Tomb of Haremhab (No. 57): the king offers jars of wine to the hawk-headed Harsiese, "great god, king of the gods, lord of heaven," and stands in adoration before Hathor, "the chieftainess of Thebes, lady of all gods, mistress of heaven" (painted relief on east wall of the room preceding the sarcophagus chamber).

Above Tomb of Tuthmosis III (No. 34): scenes and texts of the 3rd "hour" (division) of the Book of *Amduat* (wall painting in the oval-shaped sarcophagus chamber).

Left Workmen's village at Deir el-Medina.

Tut'ankhamun: The Real Untold Story

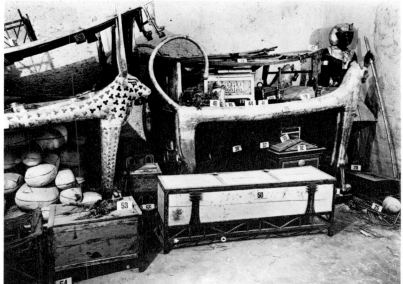

"At last have made wonderful discovery in Valley; a magnificent tomb with seals intact; re-covered same for your arrival; congratulations" (Cable sent by Carter to Lord Carnarvon on the morning of 6 November 1922).

The tomb of Tut'ankhamun (No. 62 in the Valley of the Kings) was discovered in 1922 by the English Egyptologist Howard Carter, whose work was financed by the Earl of Carnarvon. It is the only royal tomb of the New Kingdom found largely intact, and will probably stay unique in this respect for ever. Although it is the most widely publicized discovery made in Egypt in this century, and despite all the public interest generated by the traveling exhibitions all over the world, the majority of Tut'ankhamun's treasures have not yet been properly evaluated by Egyptologists, so that this exceptional find has not yet made its full contribution to our knowledge of ancient Egypt. Tut'ankhamun's objects are kept in the Egyptian Museum in Cairo; the detailed notes taken by Carter and his collaborators during the years of painstaking clearing of the tomb are in the Griffith Institute in Oxford.

Some of the objects found in the tomb:
Connected with the mummy
four wooden shrines
quartzite sarcophagus
outer and middle wooden coffins
inner gold coffin
gold mask and trappings
gold diadem
gold dagger
canopic canopy
canopic chest
Funerary equipment
statuettes of the king
dismantled chariots
couches and beds
headrests
throne of gilded wood (*right*)
chairs and stools
boxes
vases and lamps
bows, bow cases and shields
sticks, whips and scepters
garments
writing palettes
gaming boards
jewelry
fans
musical instruments
model boats
shrines of wood and gold
statuettes of gods
shawabtis

Far left Tomb of the Vizier Ra'mose at Sheikh 'Abd el-Qurna (No. 55), of the early part of the reign of Amenophis IV. Relief.

Left Coffin base-board of Soter, early 2nd century AD, with a representation of the goddess Nut surrounded by signs of the zodiac. From a communal tomb at Sheikh 'Abd el-Qurna. London, British Museum.

Below Tomb of the God's Father Amenemone at Qurnet Mura'i (No. 277), of the early 19th Dynasty: episode from the funeral of the deceased. Painting.

Private tombs

The larger and more important Theban tombs are concentrated in several areas on the west bank. Starting from the river north, these are: Dra' Abu el-Naga', Deir el-Bahri, el-Khokha, 'Asasif, Sheikh 'Abd el-Qurna, Deir el-Medina and Qurnet Mura'i. Altogether 409 tombs received official numbers of the Egyptian Antiquities Service, but another five have been added recently. The tombs' dates range from the 6th Dynasty to the Greco-Roman Period, but the majority are of the New Kingdom. There are many further tombs, some large and decorated, others little more than simple graves. Perhaps the most important of these are in the Valley of the Queens, south of Deir el-Medina, and in smaller valleys nearby, including the "Tomb of Three Princesses" of the reign of Tuthmosis III in Wadi Qubbanet el-Qirud ("Valley of the Tombs of the Monkeys") with a treasure of gold and silver vessels, now in the Metropolitan Museum in New York.

As one would expect, many of the lesser tombs and burials at el-Tarif and Dra' Abu el-Naga', not included in the official series of Theban tombs, are contemporary with the royal tombs of the 11th and 17th Dynasties, but the latter area in particular continued to be used well into the Late Period. The same applies to the cemeteries of 'Asasif and el-Khokha around the causeways leading to the temples of the 11th and 18th Dynasties at Deir el-Bahri, and to Deir el-Bahri itself.

A number of important caches with group burials have been found. In 1891 E. Grébaut and G. Daressy found a large cache of coffins of "Priests of Amun" of the 3rd Intermediate Period at Deir el-Bahri. It was the second find of this type; already in 1858 Mariette had found a cache of coffins of "Priests of Montu." The most spectacular of these secret hideaways was that found in tomb No. 320, in the first of the valleys south of Deir el-Bahri, in 1881. It contained coffins and mummies of the most renowned Egyptian kings of the 17th to 20th Dynasties, assembled there for security during the 21st Dynasty.

Some of the tombs at Sheikh 'Abd el-Qurna, south of Deir el-Bahri, belonged to the family of the

Below Tomb of Amenemone at Qurnet Mura'i (No. 277), of the early 19th Dynasty: two anthropoid coffins of the deceased set up outside the tomb entrance during the funeral. Painting.

Right Tomb of the Servant in the Place of Truth Pashed at Deir el-Medina (No. 3), of the reign of Sethos I: the painted burial chamber.

celebrated commoner Senenmut of the reign of Hatshepsut. A tomb of the 3rd Intermediate Period (known as the "Prince of Wales Tomb"), with some 30 coffins (though this cache was probably at least partly set up in modern times, and the coffins brought from elsewhere), and another with 14 coffins, dating to the reign of Hadrian, were also found.

As the name suggests, the Valley of the Queens ("Biban el-Harim") contains tombs of queens and other members of the royal family, particularly those of Ramessid princes.

Most of the larger Theban tombs were rock-cut, and few of them had any free-standing super-structure. Their plans vary greatly; the following are only very general characteristics.

Late Old Kingdom. One or two rooms of an irregular shape, sometimes with pillars. Sloping shafts lead to one or more burial chambers.

Middle Kingdom. The rear wall of an open forecourt forms the facade of the tomb. A long corridor is followed by a chapel connected with the burial chamber by a sloping passage.

New Kingdom. An open forecourt, often with stelae, precedes the facade with a row of pottery "funerary cones" above the doorway. A transverse ("broad") hall, sometimes with stelae on the narrow walls, is followed by a "long" hall on the central axis of the tomb. The sanctuary has a statue niche or a false door. All inner rooms can have pillars. The shaft of the burial chamber is usually cut in the forecourt.

Ramessid tombs at Deir el-Medina combine a completely, or partly, free-standing superstructure (pylon, open court, portico and vaulted chapel with statue niche and brick-built pyramid above) with rock-cut chambers approached by a shaft.

Late Period. Some of these tombs are enormous and their plans very complex. Brick-built pylons and open courts precede a series of underground rooms, usually with pillars, leading to the burial chamber.

Painting is the usual method of decoration of Theban tombs, but relief is not uncommon. The subject matter includes both scenes of everyday life and religious themes, which predominate from the Ramessid Period on.

J.G.Wilkinson at Thebes

Modern Egyptologists stand on the shoulders of the scholars who, often under incredibly hard conditions, pioneered the discipline in the first half of the last century. It was a period during which Egyptology was assembling its basic corpus of material for study, a time of intensive recording and copying of Egyptian inscriptions, reliefs and paintings. Some of the works published at that time remain indispensable for a good Egyptological library even now, 150 years later.

John Gardner Wilkinson came to Egypt as a young man of 24 in 1821, a year before Champollion rediscovered the principles of the Egyptian script. For the next 12 years he stayed there continuously, and there was hardly an ancient Egyptian site which the skillful and compulsive copyist did not visit and record in his notebooks. His interest was almost an obsession: no inscription, however small or incomplete, was too insignificant for him. He was one of the first who mastered the conventions of Egyptian representation to such an extent that he was able to produce completely faithful copies. Thanks to this, his papers, now kept in the Griffith Institute in Oxford, contain a wealth of information on the most varied aspects of ancient Egypt. Wilkinson published the theoretical results of his work in a number of books, but not all of his copies; those which appeared in books were often badly disfigured by inadequate reproduction. His most important work was entitled *Manners and Customs of the Ancient Egyptians, including their private life, government, laws, arts, manufactures, religion, agriculture, and early history, derived from a comparison of the paintings, sculptures, and monuments still existing, with the accounts of ancient authors.* It was published in three volumes in 1837, and remained the best general treatment of ancient Egypt for almost 50 years. It brought to its author a

knighthood in 1839, and made him the first British Egyptologist of distinction.

Many a difficult problem has been solved by consulting Wilkinson's copies, because they show monuments as they were between 1821 and 1856 (the date of his last visit to Egypt). His work in Theban private tombs is a case in point: many of the scenes copied by Wilkinson have since been damaged or even completely destroyed, while others, including entire tombs, still await publication or are now inaccessible.

Top Craftsmen at work: relief from Theban Tomb 36 of the Chief Steward of the Divine Adoratrice, Ibi, of the reign of Psammetichus I (the scene partly imitates a relief of the 6th Dynasty at Deir el-Gabrawi). The following crafts are represented (from left): 1st register from top, leather workers making sandals, makers of stone vessels, shawabtis and canopic jars, metal workers; 2nd register, chariot makers, sculptors, joiners and makers of stone vessels; 3rd register, joiners, sculptors, jewelers; 4th register, metal workers, men carrying a wooden plank, boat builders; 5th register, boat builders and scribes. Now badly damaged.

Center left Two bearded men plucking geese: painting in Theban Tomb 88 of the Standard-Bearer of the Lord of the Two Lands, Pehsukher Tjenenu, dated to Tuthmosis III or Amenophis II. The scene takes place in a hut, and the birds

already dealt with are hung from its rafters. There are three other dead geese on the ground. Now damaged, the figure of the man on the left completely lost.

Bottom left Two scribes and an overseer, from a scene of the counting of cattle: painting in Theban Tomb 76 of the Fan-Bearer on the Right of the King Tjenuna, of the reign of Tuthmosis IV. The men are squatting in the typical posture of Egyptian scribes, with their feet tucked under their thighs, holding an unrolled papyrus (writing tables were not used in ancient Egypt). Containers for papyri are placed nearby. Now badly damaged.

Center right The Vizier Paser and his wife, followed by relatives, assist at the purification of offerings by censing and libation: relief in Theban Tomb 106 of Paser, Vizier of Sethos I and Ramesses II. The tomb has not yet been fully published, and

the scene is now almost completely destroyed.

Bottom right A Nubian dancing-girl accompanied by female and male musicians playing the lyre, double flute and harp: painting from Theban Tomb 113 of the Priest, Keeper of Secrets of the Domain of Amun, Keynebu, dated to the reign of Ramesses VIII. This Nubian dance, perhaps called *keskes*, is shown on several other monuments. Apart from the Nubian girl, the participants are Keynebu's sons and daughters; this may indicate the popularity of the dance in the Ramessid Period. Now completely destroyed.

NORTHERN UPPER EGYPT

Northern Upper Egypt extends between Thebes and Asyut. It was the heart of ancient Egypt, the cradle and forge of her earliest dynasties, the hinterland which remained Egyptian in times of crisis and from which, with Thebes at the head, attempts for new political unity were launched. Economically, control of access to the gold and minerals of the eastern desert was always of paramount importance, while politically Thebes in the south dictated the course of events from the 11th Dynasty.

Naqada, Qift and Abydos dominated the scene in the Predynastic and Early Dynastic Periods, with Dendara gaining in importance during the Old Kingdom. Abydos became something of a religious center for the whole country in the Middle Kingdom. The rise of Thebes stifled its northerly neighbors in the New Kingdom, though Abydos held its position, and Qift continued to be favored by royal building activities. The temple of Dendara is easily the most impressive structure of late antiquity in the area.

Left The name of this basalt statuette in the Ashmolean Museum in Oxford, the "MacGregor man," derives from the Revd. William MacGregor, from whom it was acquired at Sotheby's in 1922. The well-known collector had bought it, together with a group of ivory figurines, from a dealer. All the objects were claimed to have been found at Naqada, a site which produced large numbers of Predynastic and Early Dynastic artefacts. Most books on Egyptian art start with this magnificent piece, although recently its authenticity has been questioned on stylistic grounds. Height: 39 cm. Predynastic Period.

Far left Typical landscape of limestone cliffs west of the Nile near Nag' Hammadi, with a very narrow flat strip by the river. A geologist can read the history of the ice ages off the layering and terracing of the cliffs.

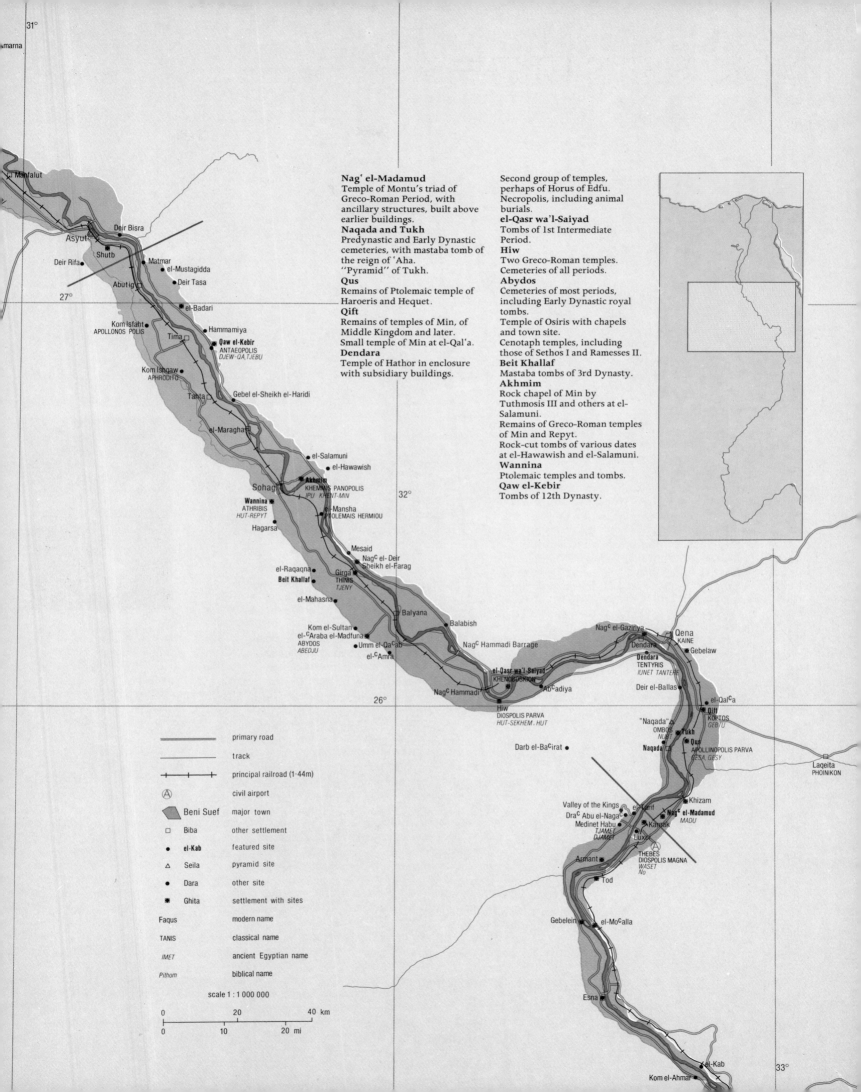

Nag' el-Madamud
Temple of Montu's triad of
Greco-Roman Period, with
ancillary structures, built above
earlier buildings.

Naqada and Tukh
Predynastic and Early Dynastic
cemeteries, with mastaba tomb of
the reign of 'Aha.
"Pyramid" of Tukh.

Qus
Remains of Ptolemaic temple of
Haroeris and Hequet.

Qift
Remains of temples of Min, of
Middle Kingdom and later.
Small temple of Min at el-Qal'a.

Dendara
Temple of Hathor in enclosure
with subsidiary buildings.

Second group of temples,
perhaps of Horus of Edfu.
Necropolis, including animal
burials.

el-Qasr wa'l-Saiyad
Tombs of 1st Intermediate
Period.

Hiw
Two Greco-Roman temples.
Cemeteries of all periods.

Abydos
Cemeteries of most periods,
including Early Dynastic royal
tombs.
Temple of Osiris with chapels
and town site.
Cenotaph temples, including
those of Sethos I and Ramesses II.

Beit Khallaf
Mastaba tombs of 3rd Dynasty.

Akhmim
Rock chapel of Min by
Tuthmosis III and others at el-
Salamuni.
Remains of Greco-Roman temples
of Min and Repyt.
Rock-cut tombs of various dates
at el-Hawawish and el-Salamuni.

Wannina
Ptolemaic temples and tombs.

Qaw el-Kebir
Tombs of 12th Dynasty.

31°

amarna

Manfalut

Deir Bisra

Asyut

Shutb

Deir Rifa

Matmar

el-Mustagidda

Abutig

Deir Tasa

27°

el-Badari

Kom Isfaht
APOLLONOS POLIS

Hammamiya

Tima

Qaw el-Kebir
ANTAEOPOLIS
DJEW-QA,TJEBU

Kom Ishqaw
APHRODITO

Tahta

Gebel el-Sheikh el-Haridi

el-Maragha

el-Salamuni

el-Hawawish

Akhmim
KHEMMIS PANOPOLIS
IPU KHENT-MIN

Sohag

Wannina
ATHRIBIS
HUT-REPYT

el-Mansha
PTOLEMAIS HERMIOU

32°

Hagarsa

Mesaid

Nagᶜ el-Deir
Sheikh el-Farag

el-Raqaqna

Girga
THINIS
TJENY

Beit Khallaf

el-Mahasna

Balyana

Kom el-Sultan
el-ᶜAraba el-Madfuna
ABYDOS
ABEDJU

Balabish

Nagᶜ el-Gaziriya

Qena
KAINE

Umm el-Qaᶜab

Nagᶜ Hammadi Barrage

Dendara

Gebelaw

el-ᶜAmra

Dendara
TENTYRIS
IUNET TANTERE

El-Qasr wa'l-Saiyad
KHENOBOSKION

Abᶜadiya

Deir el-Ballas

26°

Nagᶜ Hammadi

el-Qalᶜa

Hiw
DIOSPOLIS PARVA
HUT-SEKHEM . HUT

Qift
KOPTOS
GEBTU

"Naqada"
OMBOS
NUB

Tukh

Darb el-Baᶜirat

Qus
APOLLINOPOLIS PARVA
GESA. GESY

Naqada

Laqeita
PHOINIKON

Valley of the Kings

el-Tarif

Khizam

Draᶜ Abu el-Naga

Nagᶜ el-Madamud
MADU

Medinet Habu
TJAMET
DJAMET

Karnak

Luxor

THEBES
DIOSPOLIS MAGNA
WASET
No

Armant

Tod

Gebelein

el-Moᶜalla

Esna

el-Kab

Kom el-Ahmar

33°

---

	primary road
	track
	principal railroad (1·44m)
Ⓐ	civil airport
Beni Suef	major town
□ Biba	other settlement
• **el-Kab**	featured site
△ Seila	pyramid site
• Dara	other site
⊛ Ghita	settlement with sites
Faqus	modern name
TANIS	classical name
IMET	ancient Egyptian name
Pithom	biblical name

scale 1 : 1 000 000

0   20   40 km

0   10   20 mi

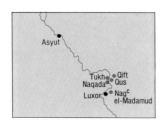

Below left Remains of the outer hypostyle hall of Ptolemy VIII Euergetes II in the temple of Montu at Nag' el-Madamud, seen from the northwest.

Below Lintel of Senwosret III from Nag' el-Madamud: double scene, with the king offering white bread (left) and cake (right) to Montu "Lord of Thebes." Paris, Musée du Louvre.

Nag' el-Madamud

In addition to Karnak, Tod and Armant, ancient Egyptian *Madu*, about 8 km northeast of Luxor, was an important place of worship of the falcon-headed god Montu in the Theban area.

The early temple at Madamud, now destroyed, dated to the Middle Kingdom (perhaps Nebhepetre' Mentuhotpe, mainly Senwosret III), but may have stood on the site of an earlier shrine. Kings of the late Middle Kingdom and the 2nd Intermediate Period continued to build there, particularly Amenemhet VII (Sedjefakare'), Sebekhotpe II (Sekhemre'-khutawy) and Sebekhotpe III (Sekhemre'-swadjtawy) of the 13th Dynasty, and Sebekemzaf I (Sekhemre'-wadjkha'u) of the 17th Dynasty, but none of their buildings has survived. There are also a few scattered monuments of the New Kingdom and the Late Period which indicate that the site was not forsaken at that time.

The temple of Montu, Ra'ttawy and Harpokrates, which is still partly standing, is of the Greco-Roman Period. It was built above the earlier structures, and a number of rulers contributed to its final appearance. A quay and remains of an avenue of sphinxes precede a gate in the brick-built enclosure wall of Tiberius. The facade of the temple itself is formed by three kiosks of Ptolemy XII Auletes, and from there one proceeds through the court of Antoninus Pius. From the outer hypostyle hall of Ptolemy VIII Euergetes II the temple is conventional in plan. Immediately behind is a second temple, dedicated to the sacred bull of Montu. Some of its rooms probably served to accommodate the animal itself. The exterior walls of the temples were decorated by Domitian and Trajan.

There was a sacred lake south of the temple of Montu, and a foundation deposit and blocks show that an early Ptolemaic temple (Ptolemy II Philadelphus, III Euergetes I, and IV Philopator) once stood in the southwest corner of the enclosure.

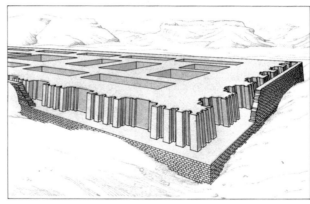

Naqada and Tukh

Archaeologists often use the names of important sites as descriptive terms for whole archaeological cultures. The last two Egyptian Predynastic cultures are usually called Naqada I and II, after the cemeteries excavated by W. M. Flinders Petrie in 1895. In this case the term is something of a misnomer: although Naqada is the largest modern settlement in the area, the cemeteries are in fact about 7 km north of it, between Tukh and el-Ballas.

About 3 km northwest of the village of Naqada, on the edge of the desert, an Early Dynastic mastaba tomb was found by J. de Morgan in 1897. It was a large (54 by 27 m) brick-built structure with a "palace facade" on all sides. Ivory tablets, vase fragments and clay sealings bearing the names of King 'Aha as well as Neithotpe, perhaps his wife and subsequently a queen regnant, were found. The tomb was most probably built for a local administrator of the beginning of the 1st Dynasty. The nearby cemeteries have also produced a number of stelae of the end of the Old Kingdom and the 1st Intermediate Period. The necropolis belonged to the town of Qus, on the east bank of the Nile.

The size of the cemeteries and settlement sites excavated by Petrie ("Naqada") shows that ancient

Above left Reconstruction of the Early Dynastic mastaba found by J. de Morgan at Naqada. The structure was surrounded by an enclosure wall some 1·1 m thick. In the center of the core of the mastaba were five rooms for the burial and equipment, surrounded by a further 16 compartments filled with gravel and sand.

Above Decorated pot of the Naqada I culture. Oxford, Ashmolean Museum.

Senwosret I, holding a *hep* (a ritual object of unknown origin) and an oar, performs a ceremonial *sed*-festival run before the god Min: limestone relief from the earlier structures below the Northern Temple at Qift. London, Petrie Collection (University College).

important town in the early part of Egyptian history. This was probably because at that time it served as the point of departure for expeditions to Wadi Hammamat quarries and the Red Sea. Nowadays only two pylons of the Ptolemaic temple of Haroeris and Heqet remain.

Qift

The town of *Gebtu* (Coptic *Kebto* or *Keft*, Greek Koptos [not connected with the word "Coptic"]), modern Qift, was the capital of the 5th Upper Egyptian nome. The town's prominence was due to its geographical position: it was here (or at Qus, a little to the south) that trading expeditions heading for the Red Sea coast and many mining expeditions into the eastern desert left the Nile valley. *Gebtu* soon became the most important religious center of the area, and its local god Min was also regarded as the god of the desert region to the east. Isis and Horus became prominent deities connected with Qift, particularly during the Greco-Roman Period; one of the reasons for this was a reinterpretation of the two falcons of the nome standard as Horus and Min. As one would expect, monuments discovered at Qift span the whole of Egyptian history, though only temple structures of the Late and Greco-Roman Periods were found *in situ*.

Remains of three temple groups surrounded by an enclosure wall were located during the excavations of W. M. Flinders Petrie (1893–94) and R. Weill and A. J. Reinach (1910–11).

The largely undecorated Northern Temple of Min and Isis, which still stands, was the work of an official called Sennuu on behalf of Ptolemy II Philadelphus, with some later additions of Ptolemy IV Philopator, Caligula and Nero (particularly the three pylons). The temple stands on the site of earlier structures of Amenemhet I, Senwosret I and Tuthmosis III, the last ruler being attested by a large number of foundation deposits. Remains of a chapel of Osiris erected by Amasis were found south of the 3rd pylon of the Northern Temple.

The site of the Middle Temple also had a long history: blocks of Senwosret I and a gate of Tuthmosis III with additions made by Osorkon (probably II) were found, and also a set of stelae ("Koptos Decrees"), dating to the 6th and 7th Dynasties, with copies of royal decrees concerning the temple and its personnel. The Middle Temple itself was built by Ptolemy II Philadelphus, with minor additions by Caligula, Claudius and Trajan.

Gates of Nectanebo II, Caligula and Claudius, and a chapel of Cleopatra VII Philopator and Ptolemy XV Caesarion were found at the site of the Southern Temple.

Claudius built a small temple (approximately 24 by 16 m) dedicated to Min, Isis and Horus northeast of Qift, at el-Qal'a.

Nubt (Greek Ombos), usually connected with modern Tukh, some 4 km to the southeast, must have been a very important town in the later Predynastic Period. The name probably derives from ancient Egyptian *nub*, "gold," on account of the proximity of gold mines in the eastern desert accessible from the Wadi Hammamat, and this could also explain the town's rise to prominence. The local god was Seth (*Nubty*, "The Ombite"), later regarded as the Upper Egyptian god *par excellence*. So far only a New Kingdom temple dedicated to him has been located. Various kings of the 18th Dynasty (Tuthmosis I and III, Amenophis II) and several Ramessids contributed to it.

A somewhat puzzling monument is the "pyramid" of Tukh. It is built of undressed stone, and its date and even its identification as a pyramid remain in doubt.

Above Red granite colossal head of a Roman emperor, probably Caracalla, found at the 2nd pylon of the Northern Temple of Min and Isis at Qift. Height: 51 cm. Philadelphia (Pa.), Pennsylvania University Museum.

Below Qus at the time of Napoleon's expedition to Egypt: the west pylon of the temple of Haroeris and Heqet and the modern town.

Qus

Judging by its cemeteries, Qus, northwest of Naqada, ancient Egyptian *Gesa* or *Gesy* (Apollinopolis Parva of the Greco-Roman Period), on the opposite bank of the Nile, must have been an

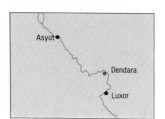

Below Dendara: central area of the main temple enclosure.

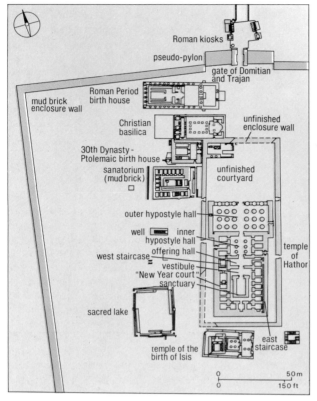

Above Temple of Hathor from the southwest, with reliefs of Ptolemy XV Caesarion and Cleopatra VII Philopator. The mutilated colossal sistrum originally had a wooden canopy. The characteristic lion gargoyles remove rain water from the roof.

Left Gateway of the Roman Period east of the main enclosure. This and a few remaining wall bases formed part of a complex perhaps dedicated to Horus of Edfu.

Dendara

Dendara, ancient Egyptian *Iunet* or *Tantere*, Greek Tentyris, was the capital of the 6th nome of Upper Egypt, and a town of some importance, but since antiquity the center of population in the area has moved to Qena on the east bank. The temple complex now stands isolated on the desert edge.

The necropolis of Dendara included tombs of the Early Dynastic Period, but its most important phase was the end of the Old Kingdom and the 1st Intermediate Period. The provinces were virtually autonomous at that time and, although Dendara was not the most important of the factions of Upper Egypt, its notables built a number of mastabas of some size, only one of which has any decoration apart from stelae and false doors. On the western side of the site are brick-vaulted catacombs of animal burials, primarily of birds and dogs, while cow burials have been found at various points in the necropolis – one of Hathor's forms being as a cow.

A small chapel of Nebhepetre' Mentuhotpe has been recovered from the site and is now reerected in the Cairo Museum. The building, which also has inscriptions of Merneptah, was more for the cult of the king than for the goddess, and was probably ancillary to the main temple of the time.

The temple complex is oriented, as usual, towards the Nile, which here flows east–west, so that the temple faces north, although this was symbolically "east" for the Egyptians. In this description the points of the compass are used.

The monumental gateway of Domitian and Trajan is set in the massive mud-brick enclosure wall, and leads to an open area with the Roman Period birth house on the west. This is the latest preserved temple of its type; it was the ritual location where Hathor gave birth to the young Ihy, who stands for the youthful phase of creator gods in general. The temple was built when the earlier structure, begun by Nectanebo I and decorated early in the Ptolemaic Period, was cut through by the foundations of the first court of the main temple of Hathor (which was never completed). Both birth houses are now accessible; they differ considerably in plan and in decoration.

Immediately south of the earlier birth house is a mud-brick "sanatorium," where visitors could bathe in the sacred waters or "incubate" – spend the night in the hope of having a healing dream of the goddess.

The main temple is the grandest and most elaborately decorated of its period; the massive foundations probably contain many of the blocks of the earlier structure it replaced. Fragments of earlier periods have been found on the site, but no buildings; Pepy I and Tuthmosis III in particular were remembered in the temple inscriptions.

The rear part of the temple was built first, probably at the end of the 2nd century BC. The earliest king named is Ptolemy XII Auletes, but mostly the cartouches are blank, probably because of the struggles in the royal family in the 1st century BC. The outer hypostyle hall was decorated between

Left The Roman hypostyle hall. The pale north light effectively brings out the relief surfaces, on some of which the white background is preserved.

Below Birth house, reign of Trajan: elaborately detailed relief of the king offering to Hathor, who is suckling the young Ihy, with a second Ihy behind.

the reigns of Augustus and Nero, and has a dedicatory inscription in Greek of 35 AD.

The temple follows the classic plan. The columns of the two hypostyle halls and the "new year court" have capitals in the form of a sistrum, a musical instrument sacred to Hathor. Their use evokes the image of Hathor as a cow appearing between the plants in the marsh of creation. There was also a relief of a sistrum at the center of the south outside wall, which was gilded, both to show its importance and to evoke Hathor, the "gold of the gods." All sistrum figures were severely mutilated in the early Christian Period.

Within the temple the most unusual parts are the decorated "crypts." These are suites of rooms on three stories, set in the thickness of the outside wall. Their main use was for storing cult equipment, archives and magical emblems for the temple's protection. Their decoration conforms to the temple's axis, and the most important reliefs, among which sistra are again prominent, were on the axis itself. Also within the thickness of the wall are the staircases, which lead up to and return from the roof. On the roof is a kiosk, in which the ritual of the goddess's union with the sun disk was performed. There is also a pair of shrines of Osiris, from one of which came the famous Dendara zodiac, now in the Louvre in Paris. Dendara was one of Osiris' many tombs, and the shrines, which have no direct link with Hathor, were used to celebrate his resurrection. His death may have been reenacted in the sacred lake to the west of the temple.

Immediately south of the Hathor temple is the temple of the birth of Isis, decorated under Augustus, and using foundation blocks from a destroyed Ptolemaic building. The east gateway of the enclosure, also Roman in date, leads to this temple, which is unique in having a dual orientation, in which the outer rooms face east and the inner ones north towards the temple of Hathor. The central scene of Isis' birth has been mutilated.

East of the temple lay part of the town, with a temple of Horus of Edfu in its midst. This may be the same as some temple remains of the Roman Period about 500 m from the main enclosure.

The triads of deities worshiped at Edfu and at Dendara were very similar, consisting of Horus, Hathor (or Isis) and Ihy or Harsomtus. Hathor of Dendara and Horus of Edfu met at a sacred marriage ceremony, when she made a progress to the south.

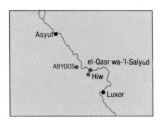

el-Qasr wa-'l-Saiyad

The rock-cut tombs near the modern village el-Qasr wa-'l-Saiyad, northeast of Hiw, on the right bank of the Nile in the 7th Upper Egyptian nome, date to the beginning of the 1st Intermediate Period. Only two of them, of the "Great Overlords of the Nome" Idu Seneni and Tjauti, deserve special attention because of their preserved relief decoration.

Hiw

During the reign of Senwosret I, a royal estate named "Kheperkare' [Senwosret I] the Justified is Mighty" was founded on the west bank of the Nile in the 7th Upper Egyptian nome. The locality soon became more important than the original nome capital, and its long-winded name started being abbreviated to *Hut-sekhem* or *Hut*. *Hut-sekhem* was reinterpreted as "The Mansion of the Sistrum," an allusion to the local goddess Bat worshiped in the form of a sistrum-shaped object with human head and bovine ears and horns. However, already during the New Kingdom the goddess Bat was completely assimilated to Hathor of the neighboring Dendara. In the Greco-Roman Period Hiw was known as Diospolis Mikra or Diospolis Parva. The Coptic version of the name, *Ho* (or *Hou*), led to the name by which the place is known nowadays.

Despite the fact that they are mentioned in Egyptian texts (e.g. Papyrus Harris I, recording a temple donation in the reign of Ramesses III), no pharaonic temples have yet been discovered at Hiw. The only two existing structures date to the Greco-Roman Period: one was probably built by Ptolemy VI Philometor, the other by Nerva and Hadrian.

About 1·5 km south of the temples, there used to be a Ptolemaic tomb of a certain Harsiese Dionysius. It is now destroyed but, fortunately, some of the early Egyptologists (Wilkinson, Nestor l'Hôte,

Burton, Hay and others) recorded its texts and relief decoration in the first half of the last century.

East of the town, there are extensive cemeteries of all periods, and burials of sacred animals (dogs, ibises and falcons) of the Greco-Roman Period.

Abydos

Ancient Egyptian *Abedju* (Coptic *Ebot* or *Abot*) was the most important burial ground in the land at the beginning of the Early Dynastic Period, and has produced traces of settlement going back to the Predynastic Naqada I Period. The political importance of the town of Abydos and its relationship with the nome capital *Tjeny* (perhaps modern Girga) is less clear.

The temple of the local necropolis god Khentamentiu ("Foremost of the Westerners," i.e. ruler of the dead) was an important religious center in the first dynasties. During the 5th and 6th Dynasties the god became identified with the originally Lower Egyptian Osiris, and in the Middle Kingdom Abydos was the chief popular religious center of Egypt. The "mysteries of Osiris," during which there was a ritual enactment of the death and resurrection of the god, attracted pilgrims from all over Egypt. Many people wished to share in the ceremonies in the afterlife, as a token of sharing in Osiris' resurrection, and they built small brick cenotaphs and set up stelae in the area between the temple of Osiris and the cemeteries. The cemeteries themselves, which extend for about 1·5 km southwest of Kom el-Sultan as far as the temple of Sethos I, are far more extensive than other local burial grounds. In the Middle Kingdom kings began to build cenotaphs at Abydos, and in the 19th Dynasty this culminated in the temples of Sethos I and Ramesses II. Later Period private tombs at Abydos commonly had brick-built pyramids with a stone pyramidion (capstone).

Burials of dogs or jackals, ibises and falcons, dating to the Late and Greco-Roman Periods, have also been found.

Left Fragments of furniture from the Early Dynastic royal tombs at Abydos. Left: piece of schist of unknown use, carved with extraordinary accuracy and skill. Right: leg of a bed, in the form of a bull's hind leg, with tenon for insertion in the frame and holes for leather lashings; ivory. Oxford, Ashmolean Museum.

Bottom left Baying hippopotamus made of pottery, from an early Naqada II grave at Hiw. Animal sculpture of the Predynastic and Early Dynastic Periods is often superior in quality to human figures of the time. Oxford, Ashmolean Museum.

Below Clapper in the form of a forearm (a common musical instrument), made of bone and inscribed for the Female Servant of the Goddess Heqet, Sithathor. 2nd Intermediate Period. From Hiw. London, British Museum.

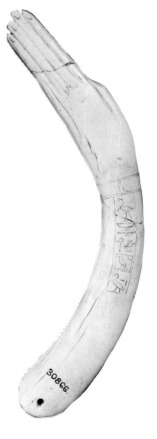

Temple of Sethos I, relief in the king's chapel showing the Iunmutef priest or deity before the mummified king, who is seated on a throne on top of the hieroglyph for "festival." The text is an elaborate version of a censing formula.

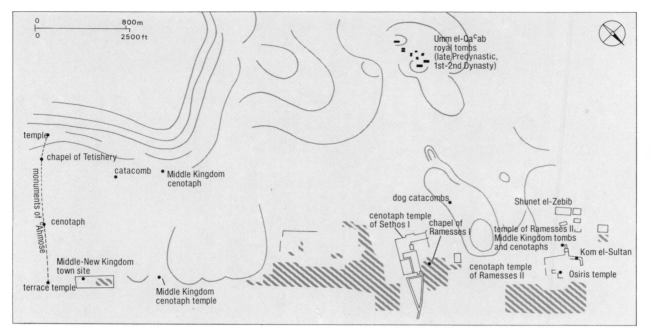

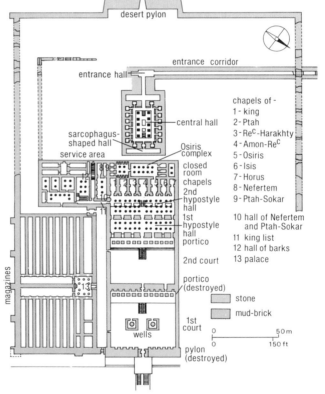

Far left Temple of Ramesses II from northwest. Most of the structure is preserved up to about 2 meters. In the foreground is the inner suite of rooms with mortuary scenes; beyond are the two hypostyle halls, with square pillars instead of columns, and the portico. Outside the modern entrance was a further court with a side chapel, and a pylon.

Structural supports are in sandstone, which can span considerable widths, but the relief surfaces are in limestone; the two gateways are of gray granite. Similar composite techniques are found in the temple of Sethos I.

The early royal tombs

In 1895–96 É. Amélineau excavated a series of tombs containing objects with the names of Early Dynastic kings at Umm el-Qaʿab ("Mother of Pots" – so called for the large amount of pottery found in the area). After Amélineau's somewhat unsatisfactory campaigns, W. M. Flinders Petrie reworked the site in 1900–01. Monuments of all the kings of the 1st Dynasty and two of the 2nd Dynasty (Peribsen and Khaʿsekhemwy) were discovered. The superstructures of the tombs had been lost, and only brick-lined pits with rows of subsidiary burials remained. The finds included magnificent stone name stelae of the kings, and small objects such as clay sealings, ivory and ebony labels, parts of stone vessels and fragmentary furniture. The tomb of Djer was later regarded as the tomb of Osiris himself, and was surrounded by votive pottery of the 18th Dynasty and later.

The cemetery went back beyond the beginning of the 1st Dynasty, and may also have been the burial place of the latest Predynastic kings.

There are further Early Dynastic remains near the cultivation, in the area of the temple of Osiris. These consist of cemeteries surrounding bare areas which may have had temporary buildings erected on them for the mortuary ceremonies of particular kings. The Shunet el-Zebib, a massive mud-brick enclosure a little way into the desert, is thought to be a monumental version of one of these areas, possibly the ancestor of the step pyramid enclosure at

Saqqara. A Coptic monastery to the north also seems to be built on foundations of huge Early Dynastic walls.

The town and temple of Osiris

The center of the ancient walled town is the mound called Kom el-Sultan. The most important feature of the town must have been the temple, at first of Khentamentiu and from the 12th Dynasty of Osiris. The temple was built in brick, with only a few elements, such as door jambs and lintels, in stone. This accounts in part for its almost complete destruction. The earliest objects found are of the beginning of the 1st Dynasty: a vase fragment of

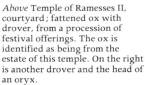

Above Temple of Ramesses II, courtyard; fattened ox with drover, from a procession of festival offerings. The ox is identified as being from the estate of this temple. On the right is another drover and the head of an oryx.

Above right Temple of Ramesses II, 1st hypostyle hall, north wall. Personification of Dendara, from a series carrying food offerings and libations. The figure's fatness symbolizes abundance, and its blue flesh and green wig are part of a patterning scheme, also symbolic. The text identifies him with the king: "Ramesses has come, bringing food offerings" (the right band relates to the next figure). Above is part of a scene with priests carrying a divine bark in procession.

King 'Aha, and a number of small stone and faience figures of men, animals and reptiles. Starting with Khufu of the 4th Dynasty (an ivory statuette, the only preserved likeness of him), almost all kings of the Old Kingdom down to Pepy II are attested among the finds. In the Middle Kingdom Nebhepetre' Mentuhotpe probably added a small shrine to the existing temple, and from then on many kings are attested down to the 17th Dynasty. In the 18th Dynasty Amenophis I, Tuthmosis III and Amenophis III did rebuilding work, and all the major Ramessids are represented, Ramesses II by a complete temple nearby, while in the Late Period Apries, Amasis and Nectanebo I feature prominently. The temple probably continued to function well into the Greco-Roman Period. The site of Kom el-Sultan is enclosed by massive mud-brick walls of the 30th Dynasty.

Royal cenotaph temples

The cenotaph temples are secondary mortuary temples of their builders, serving regular deities and the cult of the deceased king as Osiris. Senwosret III is the first king who is known to have built one, some 3 km south of Kom el-Sultan. All the other identifiable buildings in the same area seem to be connected with 'Ahmose, including one he built for his grandmother Tetisheri. Several temples of the 18th Dynasty are known from texts but have not been located.

The temple of Sethos I (the "Memnonium" of Strabo) has a highly unusual L-shaped plan, but its internal arrangements are a variation of the norm. It has two pylons (the outer one almost completely lost) with two courts and pillared porticoes, followed by two hypostyle halls and seven chapels side by side. Moving from the south, the chapels were dedicated to Sethos I, Ptah, Re'-Harakhty, Amon-Re', Osiris, Isis and Horus. The Osiris chapel leads into an area devoted to the Osiris cult, running the whole width of the temple, and including two halls and two sets of three chapels for Osiris, Isis and Horus. Its strangest feature is a room with two pillars that was designed to be completely inaccessible. The southern extension of the temple contains rooms for the cult of the Memphite gods Nefertem and Ptah-Sokar and a gallery in which is a magnificent relief of Sethos I and Ramesses II lassoing a bull and, on the other side, one of Egypt's few king lists, here serving the cult of the royal ancestors. The gallery leads to a set of storerooms. In front of this extension is a brick-built palace with storerooms that was probably used when the king visited during festivals.

The reliefs in the inner parts of the temple, which were completed by Sethos I, are exceptionally fine. The outer areas, including the first hypostyle hall, were completed by Ramesses II, in some instances overlaying the work of his father.

Behind the temple of Sethos I and on the same axis is the cenotaph proper. Both in its plan and in its decoration (mainly executed by Merneptah) it resembles a royal tomb. It is approached from the north through a long, sloping corridor. The main rooms are a hall imitating an island and another resembling a sarcophagus, with an astronomical ceiling. The massive granite architraves roofed only part of the island hall, the center remaining open. It was meant as a recreation of the primeval waters — the island being surrounded by the ground water — with in their midst the solid primeval mound on which barley was probably germinated to symbolize the resurrection of Osiris.

Ramesses II built himself a smaller temple northwest of his father's. This is noteworthy for the excellent color preservation on its reliefs, which may be seen in full sunlight. The plan is very similar to that of the temple of Medinet Habu.

Beit Khallaf

Five large brick-built mastabas (the dimensions of K.1 are 85 by 45 m) with clay sealings bearing the names of Zanakht and Netjerykhet (Djoser) were found near the village of Beit Khallaf, some 20 km northwest of Abydos. The tombs were probably made for administrators of the Thinite area of the early 3rd Dynasty.

Akhmim

Akhmim (ancient Egyptian *Ipu* or *Khent-min*, Coptic *Khmin* or *Shmin*, hence Greek Khemmis and the modern name), on the east bank of the Nile, was once the flourishing center of the important 9th Upper Egyptian nome. Very little of its past glory remains nowadays: nothing is left of the town, the temples were almost completely dismantled and their material reused in nearby villages in the Middle Ages, and the extensive cemeteries of ancient Akhmim have never been systematically explored.

Northeast of Akhmim, at el-Salamuni, there is a rock chapel dedicated to the local god Min. Min was equated with Pan by the Greeks, so that another name given to the town in Classical antiquity was Panopolis. The chapel was probably cut by Tuthmosis III. During the reign of Aya it was decorated by the "First Prophet of Min," Nakhtmin. The reliefs show Aya and his wife Teye before local gods, and some 1,000 years later representations of Ptolemy II Philadelphus, depicted in a similar fashion, were added by his contemporary, the "Chief Priest of Min" Harma'kheru.

Far left Offering table of Harsiese from Akhmim, with fecundity figures bearing trays with gifts, and the owner and his *ba* (represented as a human-headed bird) receiving libation from a tree goddess. Granite. About 56 by 53 cm. Ptolemaic Period. London, British Museum.

Left Lid of the outer anthropoid coffin of Espamai, a priest at Akhmim in the 26th or 27th Dynasty. The Pyramid Texts on the lid were compiled some 2,000 years earlier. Wood. Height: 2·10 m. West Berlin Museum.

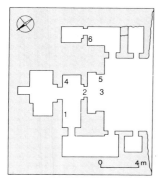

1 two registers: *Ptolemy II
Philadelphus before Min
and other deities*

2 above doorway: *Aya
and Queen Teye before Min
and other deities*

3 above doorway: *Aya and
Queen Teye before Min and Hathor,
and before Horus and Mehyt*

4 *Tuthmosis III before Min*

5 *Tuthmosis III before Amon-Re*

6 *Tuthmosis III
before deities*

Above Rock-cut chapel of Min
near Akhmim.

Right Limestone sarcophagus lid
of the Prophet Shepen-min, the
son of Heprenpu and Tashent-
min, probably of the Ptolemaic
Period. Theophoric names (those
containing names of deities) are
good evidence of the probable
provenance of the monument: in
this case the names of the owner
and his mother relate them to the
local god Min. Height: 1·80 m.
Copenhagen, Ny Carlsberg
Glyptotek.

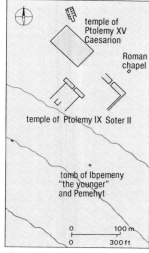

Above Wannina.

Far right Head of a statue of Ibu,
probably a contemporary of
Senwosret III, from his tomb at
Qaw el-Kebir. Painted limestone.
Height: 25 cm. Turin, Museo
Egizio.

Wannina

Wannina, some 10 km southwest of Akhmim, is the
site of a temple (ancient *Hut-Repyt*, hence Greek
Athribis) built for the goddess Triphis (Repyt) in the
reign of Ptolemy XV Caesarion. South of it, there
was an earlier temple of Ptolemy IX Soter II. One of
the tombs nearby, belonging to the brothers
Ibpemeny "the younger" and Pemehyt of the late
2nd century AD, has two zodiacs on its ceiling.

Qaw el-Kebir

Several large terraced funerary complexes built by
officials of the 10th Upper Egyptian nome in the
area of the modern village Qaw el-Kebir (ancient
Tjebu, later *Djew-qa*, Antaiopolis of the Greco-
Roman Period) during the 12th Dynasty represent
the peak of private funerary architecture of the
Middle Kingdom. A causeway approached a series
of courts and halls, partly cut in the rock, from the
valley. The innermost room of the chapel was
connected by a shaft with the burial chamber.

Cemeteries of other dates have been found in the
vicinity. A Ptolemaic temple (probably of Ptolemy
IV Philopator, enlarged and restored under Ptolemy
VI Philometor and Marcus Aurelius) which stood
near the river was destroyed in the first half of the
last century.

The two temples which once stood west of the
modern town of Akhmim were built for Min (Pan)
and the goddess Repyt (Triphis), regarded as his
companion. Both apparently dated from the Greco-
Roman Period; although some earlier blocks were
also found, it is not clear whether they belonged
to these temples or whether they were reused.

Several groups of rock-cut tombs of various dates
are known in the area, at el-Hawawish, northeast of
Akhmim, and at el-Salamuni, some 3 km further
north. The ceilings of the tombs of the Greco-Roman
Period at el-Salamuni are decorated with painted
circular zodiacs. Some of the tombs at el-Hawawish
were made for officials of the Panopolite nome
during the late Old Kingdom and the early Middle
Kingdom.

A large number of monuments, in particular
stelae and coffins, which are known from various
museum collections, can be ascribed to Akhmim,
although it is not possible to establish the exact
circumstances of their discovery.

MIDDLE EGYPT

The term Middle Egypt describes the area between Asyut and Memphis, therefore, somewhat confusingly, the northern part of Upper Egypt of the traditional terminology; both limits are geographically well defined and historically significant. Asyut became the southernmost area of the Herakleopolitan kingdom during the 1st Intermediate Period. The boundary between the southern and northern administrative regions remained in its vicinity until the end of the New Kingdom.

The area is characterized by the provincial tombs of the late Old Kingdom and the 1st Intermediate Period cut in the cliffs on the edge of the desert plateau. Ihnasya el-Medina was the residence of the Herakleopolitans, while in the 12th Dynasty the capital was further north, at Itjtawy, somewhere near el-Lisht. During the Middle Kingdom the Faiyum gained in importance, never to lose it. el-ʿAmarna became the royal residence for a few years in the 18th Dynasty. During the 3rd Intermediate and Late Periods Middle Egypt was the meeting ground of the delta and the south. In late antiquity it prospered and traded extensively with the oases: although smaller and less spectacular than their southern contemporaries, many temples testify to the renewed vitality of Middle Egyptian towns.

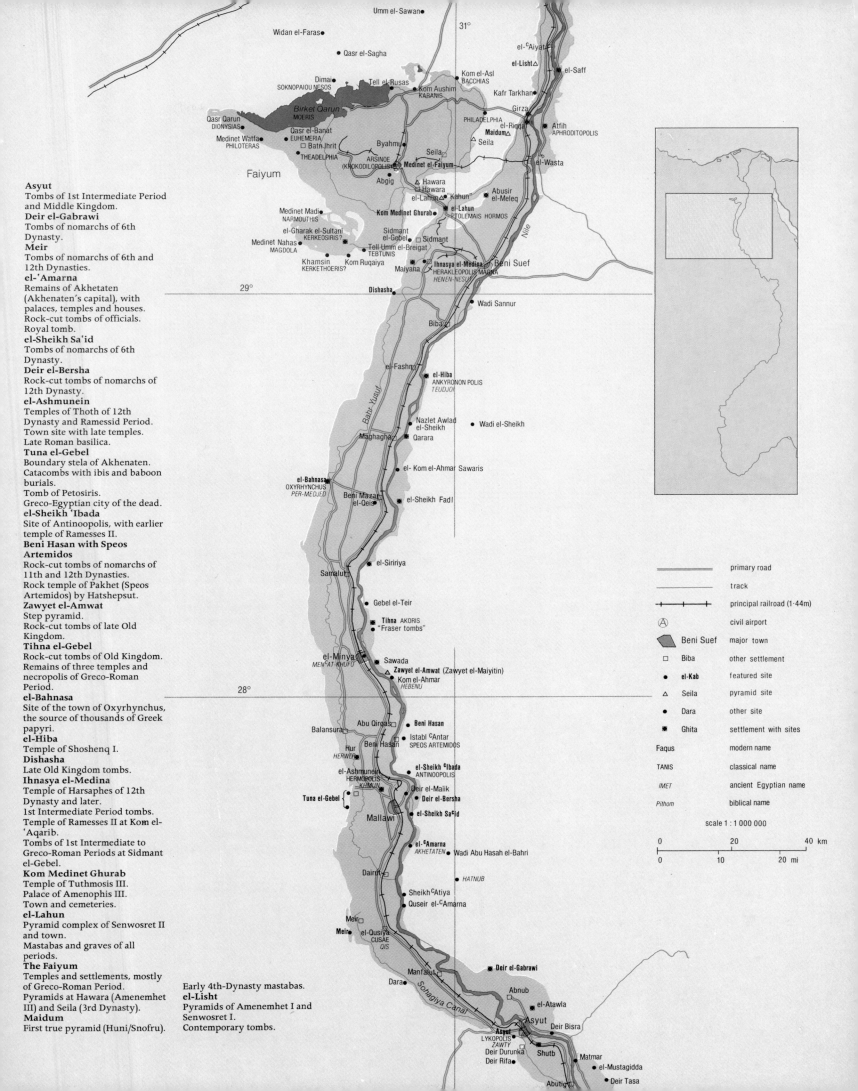

Asyut
Tombs of 1st Intermediate Period and Middle Kingdom.
Deir el-Gabrawi
Tombs of nomarchs of 6th Dynasty.
Meir
Tombs of nomarchs of 6th and 12th Dynasties.
el-'Amarna
Remains of Akhetaten (Akhenaten's capital), with palaces, temples and houses.
Rock-cut tombs of officials.
Royal tomb.
el-Sheikh Sa'id
Tombs of nomarchs of 6th Dynasty.
Deir el-Bersha
Rock-cut tombs of nomarchs of 12th Dynasty.
el-Ashmunein
Temples of Thoth of 12th Dynasty and Ramessid Period.
Town site with late temples.
Late Roman basilica.
Tuna el-Gebel
Boundary stela of Akhenaten.
Catacombs with ibis and baboon burials.
Tomb of Petosiris.
Greco-Egyptian city of the dead.
el-Sheikh 'Ibada
Site of Antinoopolis, with earlier temple of Ramesses II.
Beni Hasan with Speos Artemidos
Rock-cut tombs of nomarchs of 11th and 12th Dynasties.
Rock temple of Pakhet (Speos Artemidos) by Hatshepsut.
Zawyet el-Amwat
Step pyramid.
Rock-cut tombs of late Old Kingdom.
Tihna el-Gebel
Rock-cut tombs of Old Kingdom.
Remains of three temples and necropolis of Greco-Roman Period.
el-Bahnasa
Site of the town of Oxyrhynchus, the source of thousands of Greek papyri.
el-Hiba
Temple of Shoshenq I.
Dishasha
Late Old Kingdom tombs.
Ihnasya el-Medina
Temple of Harsaphes of 12th Dynasty and later.
1st Intermediate Period tombs.
Temple of Ramesses II at Kom el-'Aqarib.
Tombs of 1st Intermediate to Greco-Roman Periods at Sidmant el-Gebel.
Kom Medinet Ghurab
Temple of Tuthmosis III.
Palace of Amenophis III.
Town and cemeteries.
el-Lahun
Pyramid complex of Senwosret II and town.
Mastabas and graves of all periods.
The Faiyum
Temples and settlements, mostly of Greco-Roman Period.
Pyramids at Hawara (Amenemhet III) and Seila (3rd Dynasty).
Maidum
First true pyramid (Huni/Snofru).

Early 4th-Dynasty mastabas.
el-Lisht
Pyramids of Amenemhet I and Senwosret I.
Contemporary tombs.

Faiyum

	primary road
	track
	principal railroad (1·44m)
Ⓐ	civil airport
Beni Suef	major town
□ Biba	other settlement
● el-Kab	featured site
△ Seila	pyramid site
● Dara	other site
⊛ Ghita	settlement with sites
Faqus	modern name
TANIS	classical name
IMET	ancient Egyptian name
Pithom	biblical name

scale 1 : 1 000 000

0   20   40 km

0   10   20 mi

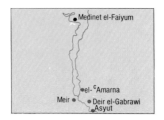

Group of 40 model soldiers armed with spears and shields, from the tomb of Mesehti at Asyut, probably 12th Dynasty. Painted wood. Length: 1·93 m. Cairo, Egyptian Museum.

Asyut

Asyut (ancient Egyptian *Zawty*) was the capital of the 13th nome of Upper Egypt. Its place in Egyptian history was ensured by its strategic position at a point where the Libyan desert encroaches on the cultivated land and narrows the Nile valley, and where the Darb el-Arba'in caravan route departs for el-Kharga oasis and further south.

Although the town of Asyut and its shrines (particularly the temple of the local wolf god Wepwawet) are often mentioned in Egyptian texts, the actual remains so far discovered are almost exclusively connected with Asyut necropolis, west of the modern town. The most important tombs date to Dynasties 9/10 and 12, but two Ramessid tombs have also been found (those of Siese and Amenhotpe).

During the 1st Intermediate Period, the "Great Overlords of the Lycopolite Nome," Khety I, Itefibi and Khety II, were staunch supporters of the Herakleopolitan kings, and the nome formed the southernmost limit of the Herakleopolitan dominion. Biographical texts from Asyut provide valuable information on the history of the conflict with "the southern nomes" (i.e. the 11th Dynasty). The ultimate victory of Thebes adversely affected the status of Djefaiha'py I–III, the nome officials of the 12th Dynasty, but their tombs retained the high artistic standards of the earlier period.

Deir el-Gabrawi

During the 6th Dynasty, the powerful nomarchs of the 12th Upper Egyptian nome were buried in two groups of rock-cut tombs near the modern village of Deir el-Gabrawi. Some of these local rulers also held the title of the "Great Overlord of the Abydene Nome," and so controlled a large area extending from the 8th nome (Abydos) in the south as far north as the 12th (or 13th) nome.

It is remarkable that some of the scenes in the tomb of one of them, Ibi, were copied about 1,600 years later, during the reign of Psammetichus I, in the Theban tomb (No. 36) of a man of the same name.

Meir

There is nothing at el-Qusiya, on the west bank of the Nile, to suggest that this is the site of ancient *Qis* (Cusae), once the center of the 14th Upper Egyptian nome. Some 7 km west of el-Qusiya is the village of

Meir, which gave its name to several groups of tombs further west, in a low slope leading on to the desert plateau.

The most important of these rock-cut tombs belong to the men who were in charge of the nome during the 6th and 12th Dynasties. It is of the greatest interest that for both these periods the sequence of tombs is unbroken as the hereditary office passed from one man to his son or younger brother.

The decoration was, as a rule, executed in relief. Some astonishingly lively scenes were created by

"William," the blue faience hippopotamus decorated with aquatic plants, in the Metropolitan Museum of Art in New York. It was found at Meir in tomb B.3 of Senbi, dating to Senwosret I – Amenemhet II. Height: 11·5 cm.

the craftsmen of the 12th Dynasty, e.g. the desert-hunt scene in tomb B.1 of Senbi, dating to Amenemhet I. In the latest of the tombs, that of Wekh-hotpe (C.1), the walls were only painted.

In the past, Meir suffered much from illicit digging. The most prominent among the archaeologists who worked there in the first half of this century was Aylward M. Blackman.

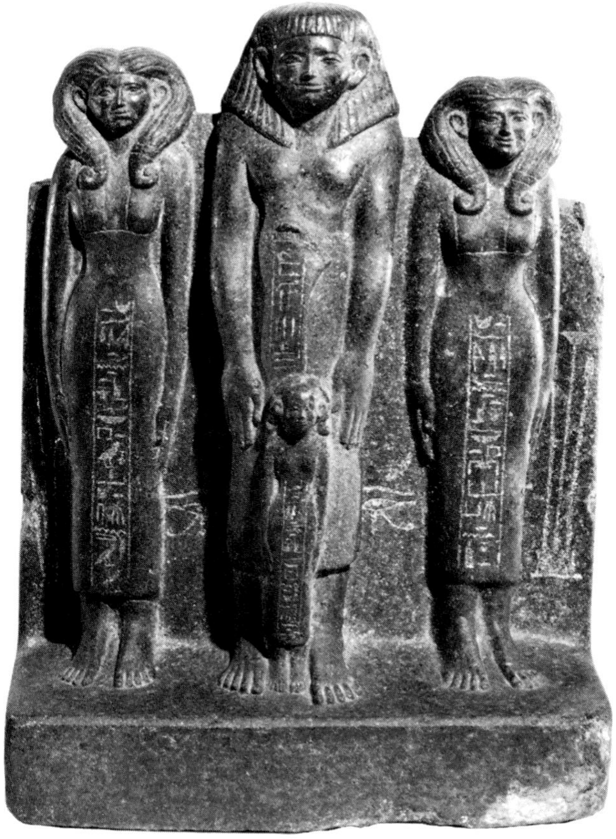

Left Wekh-hotpe (the owner of tomb C.1 at Meir) with his two wives Khnemhotpe and Nebkau, and a small daughter. Granite. Height: 37 cm. Reign of Senwosret II or III. Boston (Mass.), Museum of Fine Arts.

el-ʿAmarna

el-ʿAmarna (also Tell el-ʿAmarna), ancient Egyptian Akhetaten ("The Horizon of the Sun Disk"), was the short-lived capital of Egypt, the royal residence during much of the reign of King Akhenaten, and the center of the new state religion introduced at that time. It is one of the very few Egyptian towns which it has been possible to excavate to any significant extent. Its layout and architecture are fairly well known because the site was abandoned some 15 years after it had been founded, and the town thus escaped the destruction which would have resulted from continuous habitation. King Akhenaten built it on virgin soil, not tarnished by an earlier presence of people and their gods, but the exact reasons for his choice of the large bay on the east bank of the Nile, north of the massif of Gebel

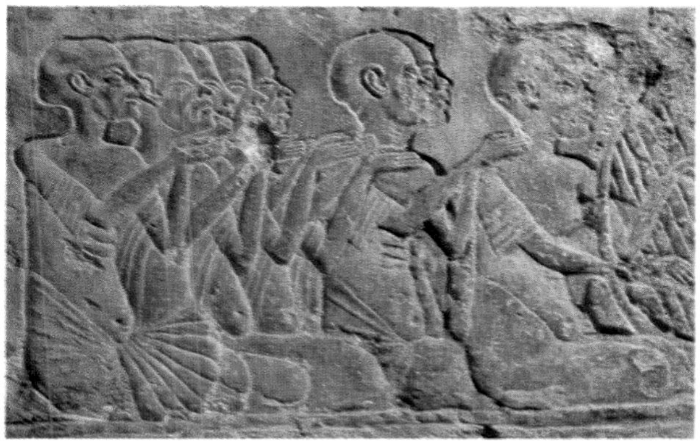

Below left Blind singers, one of the smaller groups below a large scene of Akhenaten and family offering to the Aten. Tomb of Meryreʿ I (No. 4) at el-ʿAmarna, south wall of the pillared hall, east side.

Abu Feda, are not known. Recently it has been suggested that the appearance of the landscape, resembling a large "horizon" hieroglyph might have been one of them.

The boundaries of Akhetaten were marked by a chain of stelae surrounding the area on both banks of the river. On the west bank, the northernmost of these (Stela A) is at Tuna el-Gebel, while on the east bank Akhetaten extended close to the tombs of el-Sheikh Saʿid (Stela X).

Although it has produced a number of famous works of art, for the visitor el-ʿAmarna is disappointing because there are hardly any buildings standing. The spoliation started soon after the town was abandoned, with the removal of stone to building sites nearby, notably to el-Ashmunein.

Except for the side facing the river, the plain of

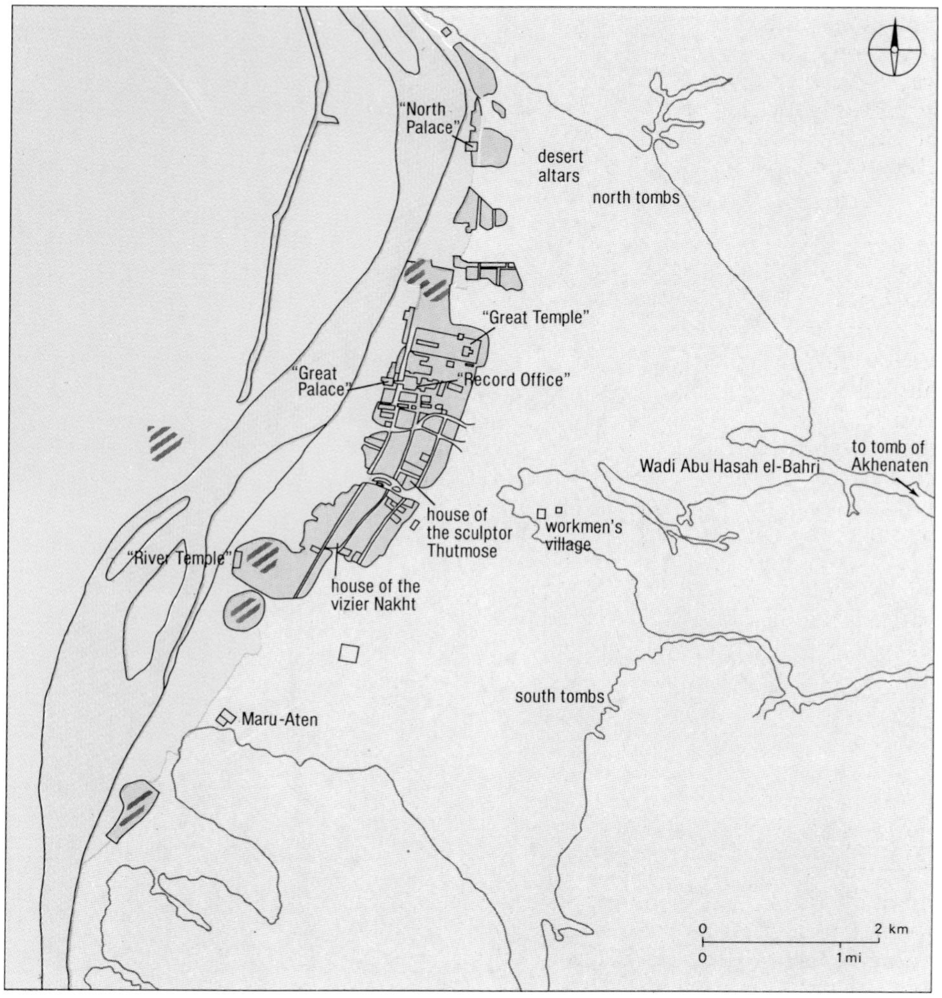

el-ʿAmarna is entirely enclosed by rock cliffs, occasionally broken by wadis. The bay is some 10 km long and about 5 km deep, but the town itself occupies only the area closest to the river. Its most important central part contained the *Per-Aten-em-Akhetaten* ("The Temple of the Aten in Akhetaten"), known as "The Great Temple," and the official state building, "The Great Palace." The main features of the latter were (1) the "State Apartments," formed by a series of courts and columned halls and built of stone, (2) the "Harim," with adjacent servants' quarters, and (3) the so-called "Coronation Hall." Akhenaten's private residence was across the road from "The Great Palace" and was connected with it by a bridge. Close to it was the "Record Office," which in 1887 produced the cuneiform diplomatic correspondence (ʿAmarna Letters) exchanged between Amenophis III, Akhenaten and Tutʿankhamun, and rulers and vassals of Palestine, Syria, Mesopotamia and Asia Minor. This conglomeration of official buildings

was surrounded by private houses, workshops, sculptors' studios etc., on the north and south sides. The names of the owners of many of the houses are known from inscribed architectural elements found during their excavation (the sculptor Thutmose, the vizier Nakht and others).

Near the southern extremity of the ʿAmarna bay there was the *Maru-Aten*, a group of buildings which also included a lake, a kiosk on an island and flower beds, and was adorned with painted pavements. At the north end of the bay there stood the "North Palace" and perhaps yet another royal residence. However, the exact purpose of some of el-ʿAmarna's buildings is still a matter of conjecture.

ʿAmarna officials had their tombs cut in the cliffs encircling the plain. Thebes and Saqqara apart, el-ʿAmarna is the only site which can be described as a New Kingdom necropolis of importance. The tombs form two large groups, and their plan is similar to that of the Theban tombs of the 18th Dynasty: (1) an outer court, (2) and (3) a long hall and a broad hall,

Left Painted limestone bust of Nefertiti wearing her characteristic crown with the uraeus. It was found with many other pieces in the studio of the sculptor Thutmose during the German excavations at el-ʿAmarna in 1912. Height: 48 cm. West Berlin Museum.

Above Painting from the king's private residence, showing two small daughters of Akhenaten, Neferneferuaten-tasherit and Neferneferure'. This is part of a much larger composition which included the whole royal family (the heel of a foot of the seated Nefertiti is next to the head of the princess on the right). Oxford, Ashmolean Museum.

Left Fragment of a red quartzite female statue, probably of Nefertiti. This is one of the most sensitive studies of the female body from the 'Amarna Period, belonging to the same class as the similarly incomplete sculptures of princesses in the Petrie Collection at University College in London and the Ashmolean Museum in Oxford. Height: 29 cm. Paris, Musée du Louvre.

Below "Talatat," the typical building blocks of Akhenaten: the king's hand holding an olive branch, and attendants kissing the ground in obeisance. New York, Schimmel collection.

both sometimes with columns, (4) a statue niche. The decoration was in sunk relief. The date is betrayed by the novel subject-matter and the unusual artistic conventions of 'Amarna art. How many of these tombs were actually put to use is not clear; some of their owners had other tombs made elsewhere, either before the move to el-'Amarna or afterwards. Tomb No. 25 of the south group was prepared for Aya, who later became the penultimate king of the 18th Dynasty and was buried in a tomb in the Valley of the Kings at Thebes (No. 23).

For his own family tomb Akhenaten chose a ravine about 6 km from the mouth of the large Wadi Abu Hasah el-Bahri, which it joins.

el-Sheikh Sa'id

The tombs of the men governing the Hare nome (15th Upper Egyptian nome) during the 6th Dynasty were cut in the steep cliffs named after a Muslim saint buried in the area. Their importance is greatly enhanced by the absence of contemporary evidence from el-Ashmunein, the capital of the nome.

Deir el-Bersha

Almost opposite the town of Mallawi, on the east bank of the Nile, a valley called the Wadi el-Nakhla breaks through the cliffs and runs in a southeasterly direction. Apart from limestone quarries of various periods it contains a number of rock-cut tombs. Some of them belong to the nomarchs of the 15th Upper Egyptian nome and date to the 12th Dynasty, though several are probably a little earlier. The name Deir el-Bersha, by which the site is known, is from that of the village west of the wadi.

The most spectacular of the tombs was made for the "Great Overlord of the Hare nome" called Djehutihotpe, who lived during the reigns of Amenemhet II, Senwosret II and Senwosret III. The chapel consists of a deep portico of two columns with palm capitals, and the inner room with a niche at the back. The decoration is executed in very low relief, at places only in paint. The west wall of the inner room bears the famous scene of the transport of a colossal statue from the alabaster quarries at Hatnub.

The tombs were excavated by expeditions of the Egypt Exploration Fund (P. E. Newberry and others) between 1891 and 1893, and the combined mission of the Harvard University and the Boston Museum of Fine Arts in 1915 (G. A. Reisner and others).

el-Ashmunein

el-Ashmunein, ancient Egyptian *Khmun* ("8-town"), named for the group of eight deities (ogdoad) who represented the world before creation, was called in Greek Hermopolis after Hermes (= Egyptian Thoth). It was the capital of the 15th Upper Egyptian nome and the main cult center of Thoth, the god of healing and of wisdom, and the patron of scribes. No early remains have been found there, but this is probably the result of chance destruction.

The site is in a broad and rich area of the Nile valley. It is now very badly ruined, with small parts of temples standing above the general rubble. Only the Roman Period *agora* with its early Christian basilica is at all well preserved, giving evidence of the great prosperity of the town in late antiquity.

A native Egyptian monument that was still

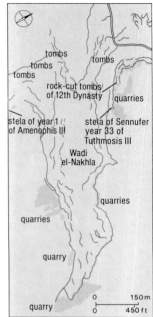

Above Wadi el-Nakhla.

Below Scene in the tomb of Djehutihotpe at Deir el-Bersha (copied by John Gardner Wilkinson before 1856).

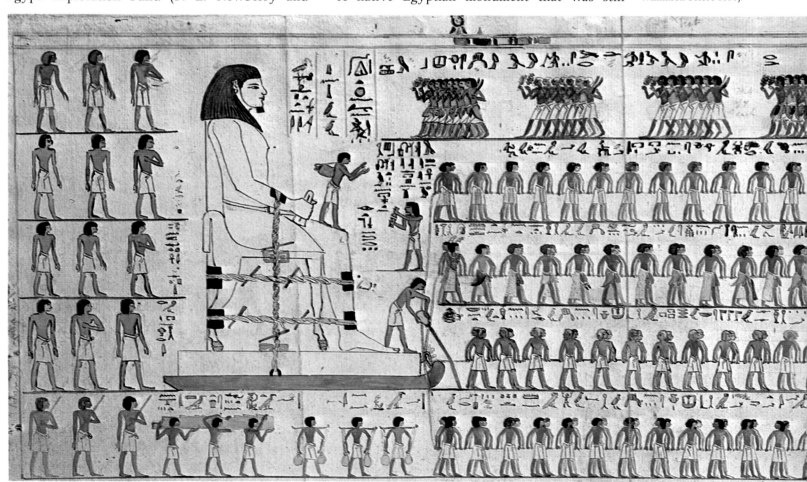

Below Granite columns of the late Roman basilica at el-Ashmunein, the only surviving large building of its kind in Egypt.

standing in 1820 consisted of two rows of columns from the hypostyle hall of the temple of Thoth, dating to Alexander the Great and Philip Arrhidaeus. About 200 m south of this temple was an earlier pylon of Ramesses II, in whose foundations more than 1,500 blocks from dismantled temples of Akhenaten at el-'Amarna were found by a German expedition under Günther Roeder between 1929 and 1939. Other monuments of the Dynastic Period that can now be seen are the entrance to a temple of Amenemhet II and the first pylon of a 19th-Dynasty temple of Amun with reliefs of Sethos II. All these buildings were in a central sacred area of the town, surrounded by a massive mud-brick enclosure of the 30th Dynasty.

The prosperity of the Greco-Roman Period was due to agriculture and to the prestige of Thoth, who was worshiped as Hermes Trismegistos ("thrice-great Hermes") by Greek and Egyptian alike, and had the Hermetic Corpus of mystical writings ascribed to him. Hermopolis and Tuna el-Gebel became centers of pilgrimage for Greeks and Egyptians.

Tuna el-Gebel

The site of Tuna el-Gebel is scattered for about 3 km along the desert 7 km west of el-Ashmunein. A boundary stela of Akhenaten, the earliest monument, is one of the most accessible of a series of such stelae. A group of six, of which this is the northwestern (stela A), is named in the text as marking the limits of el-'Amarna with its agricultural hinterland. The monument consists of a rock-cut "shrine" a little way up the escarpment, with the stela, with its much-eroded text, to one side. The top of the stela has a relief of the royal couple adoring the solar disk. Beside it are two pair statues of the king and queen, also rock-cut, whose arms are in different gestures, probably of adoration and of offering; the pairs are accompanied by much smaller figures of princesses.

To the south is the late necropolis of el-Ashmunein. The earliest objects found here are Aramaic papyri of the 5th century BC. These administrative documents of the Persian occupation were in a jar in the catacombs of ibis and baboon burials that are the largest feature of the site, and included a baboon sarcophagus dated to the Persian King Darius I. Most of the material in the catacombs was Greco-Roman in date, and a selection of pottery, bronze statuettes and mummies is now shown in the museum in the nearby town of Mallawi. Ibis and baboon are the two chief sacred animals of Thoth, the god of el-Ashmunein.

The site also contains the almost unique tomb of the family of Petosiris, which dates to the reign of Philip Arrhidaeus. It is in the form of a temple, with

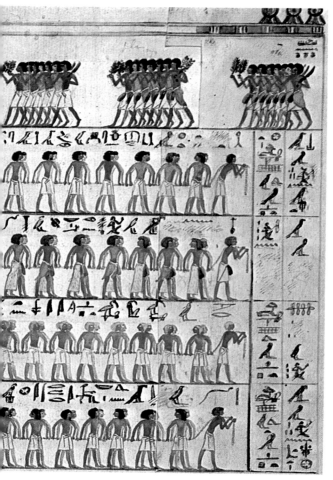

Above Ramessid calcite statuette of a priest with leopard-skin garment and a baboon squatting around his neck. The man probably dedicated a baboon in the temple of Thoth at el-Ashmunein. Oxford, Ashmolean Museum.

an entrance portico and a cult chapel behind (the burials are in underground chambers). In the portico there are scenes of daily life and of offering bearers in a mixed Egyptian-Greek style. The chapel contains traditional religious scenes and important texts, including an extensive description of works in the temples of Hermopolis.

South of the tomb of Petosiris is a large Greek city of the dead of the first centuries AD, with tombs and mortuary houses decorated in a complex mixture of Greek and Egyptian styles. Both the galleries and the city of the dead were excavated by the Egyptian Egyptologist Sami Gabra between the two world wars.

el-Sheikh 'Ibada

This is the site of the ancient Antinoopolis, founded by Emperor Hadrian in 130 AD to commemorate his favorite Antinous who had drowned here. Among the earlier monuments the largest is the temple of Ramesses II, dedicated to the gods of el-Ashmunein and Heliopolis.

Beni Hasan with Speos Artemidos

Beni Hasan, some 23 km south of el-Minya, on the east bank of the Nile, is the most important and informative Middle Kingdom provincial necropolis between Asyut and Memphis. It contains 39 large rock-cut tombs, at least eight of them belonging to the "Great Overlords of the Oryx nome" (the 16th nome of Upper Egypt) of the end of the 11th and the early 12th Dynasties.

The biographical text in the tomb (No. 2) of the last of the holders of the title, Amenemhet, is dated "Year 43, month 2 of the inundation season, day 15" of the reign of Senwosret I. Although the tombs of his two successors, Khnumhotpe II (No. 13) and Khnumhotpe III (No. 3), do not show an appreciable diminution of material resources, the centralization that was gradually achieved by the early kings of the 12th Dynasty ultimately broke the string of the families of nomarchs in the whole of Middle Egypt, and large rock-cut tombs ceased to be built. The plan of the latest among the tombs consists of (1) an outer court with a portico formed by two pillars, (2) a rectangular main room with four polygonal pillars and (3) a statue niche. The decoration, now rapidly deteriorating, is painted throughout, and military activities, such as siege scenes, figure very prominently. Below these tombs there are others, more modest, some of which go back to the 6th Dynasty.

South of Beni Hasan is Speos Artemidos (locally known as Istabl 'Antar), a rock temple dedicated to the local lioness goddess Pakhet, built by Queen Hatshepsut. The architrave bears a long dedicatory text with the famous denunciation of the Hyksos.

Zawyet el-Amwat

The most important features at this site are a step pyramid, perhaps of the 3rd Dynasty, and a necropolis of rock-cut tombs, mainly of the end of the Old Kingdom, which belonged to ancient *Hebenu* (modern Kom el-Ahmar), the early capital of the 16th Upper Egyptian nome.

Tihna el-Gebel

The rock-cut tombs ("Fraser Tombs") at Tihna date to the Old Kingdom. About 2 km north of them, close to the modern village, there are remains of the ancient town Akoris and three small temples and a necropolis of the Greco-Roman Period.

Left Greco-Egyptian painting in mortuary "house" 21 at Tuna el-Gebel, c. 2nd century AD. Apart from the decorative panel at the bottom, the motifs are Egyptian, and the hieroglyphs are intelligible. Above: Horus and Thoth pour libations over the deceased, shown in Greek style; to the right is her "shadow," shown as a symbolically black, emaciated corpse. Below: adoring figures of the "Mistress of the West," Atum and two further deities face into an opening.

Right Gold statuette of the god Harsaphes, with an inscription on the lower side of its base naming Neferkare' Peftjau'awybast, the local king at Herakleopolis contemporary with Piye of the 25th Dynasty. Height: about 6 cm. From the hypostyle hall of the temple at Ihnasya el-Medina. Boston (Mass.), Museum of Fine Arts.

Section of the step pyramid at Zawyet el-Amwat.

The detective side of Egyptology: a keen eye, retentive memory and sense of detail can often help to identify errant monuments. The tomb relief on the right, now in the collection of the Museo Arqueológico Nacional in Madrid, was found during the excavation of a 1st Intermediate Period cemetery south of the temple of Harsaphes at Ihnasya el-Medina in 1968. The fragment on the left was, in disguise, on the New York art market already in 1964, incorrectly dated and with a misleading indication of its provenance.

Above Wooden statue of the Lector-Priest Meryre'-haishtef as a naked youth. This type of wooden statue is characteristic of the end of the Old Kingdom, and similar pieces are known from Memphite as well as provincial cemeteries. Height: 51 cm. 6th Dynasty. From Sidmant el-Gebel. London, British Museum.

el-Bahnasa

Little is known about *Per-medjed* (Coptic *Pemdje*), the capital of the 19th Upper Egyptian nome, from the Dynastic Period. Although it played an interesting part in Egyptian mythology, its pharaonic remains are unknown.

The town came to prominence during the Greco-Roman Period when it was called Oxyrhynchus, after the local cult of the *Mormyrus* fish. Its rubbish heaps have produced many thousands of Greek papyri (Grenfell and Hunt, 1896–1907), equaled in numbers only by those found in the towns of the Faiyum.

el-Hiba

This is a town site (ancient Egyptian *Teudjoi*) with a much-destroyed temple built by Shoshenq I. It was the northern limit of the Thebaid during the 21st–25th Dynasties.

Dishasha

Dishasha is known for its late Old Kingdom tombs, including some belonging to the chief officials of the 20th Upper Egyptian nome. The rock-cut tomb of Inti contains a rare scene of the siege of a fortified town.

Ihnasya el-Medina

About 15 km west of Beni Suef, on the right bank of the Bahr Yusuf, is the modern village of Ihnasya el-Medina. The village derives its name from ancient Egyptian *Henen-nesut* (Coptic *Hnes*), the capital of the 20th Upper Egyptian nome, which was situated nearby, probably mainly west of it. As the chief god of the ancient town was the ram-headed Harsaphes (Egyptian Herishef, literally "He who is on his Lake"), later identified with Greek Herakles, it acquired the Classical name Herakleopolis Magna.

The remains of the temple of Harsaphes lie southwest of the village, and have been excavated by E. Naville (1891–92), W. M. Flinders Petrie (1904) and in recent years by a Spanish expedition (J. López). The earliest monuments date to the 12th Dynasty. During the 18th Dynasty the temple was enlarged, but the major rebuilding program was due to Ramesses II. The temple continued to be used during the 3rd Intermediate and Late Periods.

The most prominent part Herakleopolis ever played in Egyptian history was during the 1st Intermediate Period when it was the seat of the rulers of the 9th/10th (Herakleopolitan) Dynasty. No temples of this or earlier periods have yet been located, but tombs of contemporary officials have been found some 300 m south of the temple.

Southeast of the temple of Harsaphes, at Kom el-'Aqarib, there was another temple built by Ramesses II. Sidmant el-Gebel, about 7 km to the west, was probably the main necropolis serving the town, with graves and rock-cut tombs ranging from the 1st Intermediate to the Greco-Roman Periods.

Kom Medinet Ghurab

At the south side of the entrance to the Faiyum, on the edge of the desert some 3 km southwest of el-Lahun, there are scanty remains of two temples and adjacent town quarters and cemeteries. The larger of the temples was built by Tuthmosis III, and the settlement thrived during the second half of the 18th and in the 19th Dynasty. A number of objects found there represent or are connected with Amenophis III and Queen Teye, and one of the buildings is often described as a palace of his reign.

el-Lahun

The pyramid of el-Lahun, some 3 km north of the modern town of this name, was built by Senwosret II. It is on the right side of the opening through which the Bahr Yusuf enters the Faiyum, opposite Kom Medinet Ghurab, and overlooks the area to which the kings of the 12th Dynasty devoted much attention. Its builders used a natural knoll of rock for siting the pyramid, and employed the well-established Middle Kingdom method of core construction. This was based on stone retaining walls radiating from the center, and the filling of chambers formed between them with mud bricks.

The stone outer casing produced an effect comparable to that of pyramids completely built of stone, but nowadays, with the revetment gone, the structure is little more than a large mound of earth. The entrance to the interior of the pyramid was through two shafts near the south face; this is very unusual (normally the entrance is in the north face) and presented W. M. Flinders Petrie, the excavator, with considerable problems.

Beautiful Middle Kingdom jewelry, comparable to that discovered at Dahshur, was found south of the pyramid, in the shaft tomb of Princess Sithathoriunet.

There are mastabas and graves dating to practically all periods of Egyptian history in the neighborhood of the pyramid.

The valley temple lies about 1 km to the east, near the line of cultivation. Close to it is the walled settlement of el-Lahun (also known as Kahun), excavated by Petrie. Most of the town was planned and laid out at the same time, with streets and houses arranged in neat geometrical rows. At least three town quarters, separated by walls, can be distinguished: (1) the "acropolis," perhaps intended for the king himself, (2) the eastern quarter, with large mansions (about 40 by 60 m) centered around a court and consisting of as many as 70 or 80 rooms, (3) the western quarter of smaller uniform dwellings (about 10 by 10 m) with 4 to 12 rooms. The town housed priests and officials connected with the pyramid; although it is unique to date, it must have been one of many built near pyramid complexes. The town is famous because of the hundreds of hieratic papyri ("Kahun Papyri") found there. These contained texts of varying nature, such as literary, mathematical, medical and veterinary works, and also legal and temple documents, accounts, letters etc.

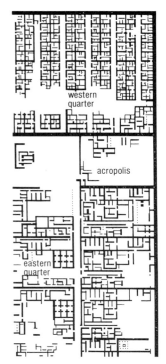

Above Plan of the northern part of the town of el-Lahun.

Left Head of a queen, probably Teye, the wife of Amenophis III, from Kom Medinet Ghurab. The shrewd and world-weary expression of the queen makes this head perhaps the most individually conceived female portrait known from ancient Egypt. Yewwood, glass, gesso, cloth etc. Height: 9·5 cm. West Berlin Museum.

Below The pyramid of Senwosret II at el-Lahun.

Top right The temple at Qasr el-Sagha.

Far right Black granite colossal statue of a king (almost certainly Amenemhet III) dressed as a priest, wearing an unusual heavy wig, and carrying two hawk-headed standards (long staves sacred to the local god). Height: 1 m. 12th Dynasty. From Mit Faris in the Faiyum. Cairo, Egyptian Museum.

The following are the most important places of interest in the Faiyum:

Kom Aushim (Karanis)
A temple of the Greco-Roman Period dedicated to the local gods Petesuchos and Pnepheros.

Dimai (Soknopaiou Nesos)
A Ptolemaic temple of Soknopaios (a form of the crocodile god Sobek).

Qasr el-Sagha
An unfinished Middle Kingdom temple.

Qasr Qarun (Dionysias)
A late Ptolemaic temple.

Batn Ihrit (Theadelphia)
A Ptolemaic temple of Pnepheros.

Byahmu
The masonry-built bases of a pair of colossal seated statues of Amenemhet III.

Medinet el-Faiyum, also el-Medina (Krokodilopolis or Arsinoe)
A 12th-Dynasty temple of Sobek, rebuilt or enlarged in later times.

Abgig
A large freestanding stela (previously called "obelisk") of Senwosret I, now removed to Medinet el-Faiyum.

Hawara
The pyramid of Amenemhet III (another pyramid of the same king stands at Dahshur). A large mortuary temple (known as "The Labyrinth" to Classical authors), formerly to be seen south of the pyramid.
Cemeteries of rock-cut tombs and graves (Middle Kingdom and Late and Greco-Roman Periods).

Seila
A small step pyramid, dated with some hesitation to the 3rd Dynasty.

Medinet Madi (Narmouthis)
A temple complex of the serpent goddess Renenutet (Termuthis), initially built by Amenemhet III and IV, with Ptolemaic additions.

Tell Umm el-Breigat (Tebtunis)
Ptolemaic temple and town.

Kom Ruqaiya
Rock-cut tombs, probably of the 12th Dynasty.

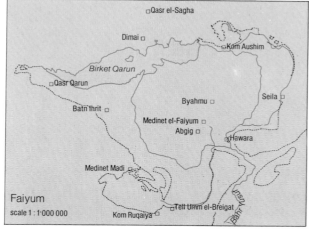

Faiyum
scale 1 : 1'000 000

[Map labels: Qasr el-Sagha, Dimai, Birket Qarun, Kom Aushim, Qasr Qarun, Batn Ihrit, Byahmu, Seila, Medinet el-Faiyum, Abgig, Hawara, Medinet Madi, Tell Umm el-Breigat, Kom Ruqaiya, Bahr Yusuf]

The Faiyum

Although usually described as an oasis, the Faiyum is connected with the Nile by a river arm known as the Bahr Yusuf (Arabic: "The River of Joseph"). The Faiyum (ancient Egyptian *She-resy*, "The Southern Lake," later divided into *She-resy* and *Mer-wer*, "The Great Lake," Greek Moeris) is a large, extremely fertile depression some 65 km from east to west, with a lake (modern Birket Qarun, Lake Moeris of Classical writers) in its northwestern part. Nowadays the lake only occupies about one fifth of the Faiyum and is some 44 m below sea level, but in the past it was much larger, teeming with wild life, and with abundant vegetation on its shores. Crocodiles must have been very common in the region, hence the role of the species as the chief deity of the area (Sobek, Greek Suchos). The name

Faiyum derives from that of the lake, Coptic *Peiom*.

Two periods in Egyptian history were of great significance for the area. When during the 12th Dynasty the capital of Egypt was moved to el-Lisht, measures were taken to enhance the economic importance of the nearby Faiyum, probably by reducing the inflow of water into the lake and reclaiming land. The majority of temples and settlements uncovered so far date to the Greco-Roman Period, when the area once again became the focus of royal attention. The lake was artificially reduced to win further arable land, and new settlers, particularly Greco-Macedonian veterans, were introduced there by Ptolemy II Philadelphus. Thousands of Egyptian (demotic) and Greek papyri have been found in Faiyum town sites of this period.

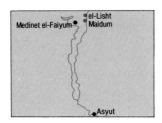

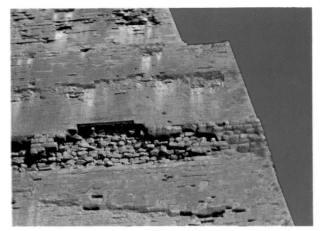

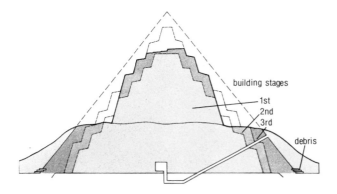

building stages

1st
2nd
3rd

debris

Maidum

The unmistakable view of Maidum is one showing a huge tower-shaped structure appearing above a hill formed by stone debris. These are the remains of the first true pyramid ever attempted in Egypt, and the earliest-known developed pyramid complex (together with the "Bent Pyramid" at Dahshur).

Experiments with the design of the pyramid are the cause of its present appearance. The monument started as a seven-stepped pyramid, but was subsequently altered into an eight-stepped structure; finally the steps were filled and an outer casing was applied to complete its conversion into a proper pyramidal form. The king for whom the pyramid was begun was probably Huni, the last ruler of the 3rd Dynasty, but since New Kingdom graffiti tell us that the Egyptians themselves later connected it with Huni's successor Snofru, the latter may have been responsible for its completion. However, the smooth dressing of the walls which were originally intended to be exposed as outer faces of the step pyramid (some can still be seen on the pyramid) did not provide sufficient bonding for later fill leaning against them. Furthermore, the outer casing did not rest on sound

Top left External masonry of the buttress walls and the less carefully built interior.

Above Aerial view of the pyramid from the east, showing the causeway, the mortuary temple, and the vast amount of material now surrounding the remains of the pyramid core following the partial collapse of the structure.

Above left Section of the pyramid looking west.

Left Statues of the Greatest of the Seers (i.e. High Priest) of Heliopolis and King's Son of his Body (of Snofru) Re'hotpe and his wife Nofret. Limestone with remarkably well-preserved original coloring. Height: 1·20 and 1·18 m. Cairo, Egyptian Museum.

foundations, and the method employed in laying its blocks was not well chosen. As a result of these constructional deficiencies the bases of the four outer buttress walls gave way and the walls slid down and collapsed, creating the tower that we see today. The date at which this happened is still hotly disputed; attempts have been made to connect this "building disaster" with the change of the angle of the "Bent Pyramid" at Dahshur, but the presence of an extensive contemporary necropolis speaks against such an early date. Bar the discovery of some unexpected textual or pictorial evidence elsewhere, only further excavations in the immediate vicinity of the pyramid can provide a satisfactory solution to this problem.

Cemeteries of large brick-built mastabas of the beginning of the 4th Dynasty lie to the north and east of the pyramid. The best-known among them are the twin mastabas of Reʻhotpe and his wife Nofret, and of Nefermaʻat and his wife Itet.

Although the site has not been by any means systematically explored, a number of excavators have worked at it. The most distinguished of them were A. Mariette, W. M. Flinders Petrie and Alan Rowe.

el-Lisht

Early in his reign, King Amenemhet I of the 12th Dynasty moved the administrative capital of Egypt and the royal residence from Thebes to Itjtawy, a newly founded walled town somewhere between the Faiyum and Memphis. Paradoxical though it may seem, nothing has yet been found of the town itself, and its exact location is still unknown. It is, however, certain that the pyramid field of el-Lisht was its main necropolis, and so Itjtawy probably spread in the cultivated area to the east of it. The town retained its importance for at least 300 years, only to relinquish it to the Hyksos center Avaris in the northeastern delta and to Thebes during the 2nd Intermediate Period.

The main features of el-Lisht are the two dilapidated pyramids of Amenemhet I and his son Senwosret I, some 1·5 km apart, surrounded by smaller pyramids and mastabas of members of the royal family and officials and cemeteries of ordinary graves. The proximity of the Memphite necropolis provided Amenemhet I with a source of conveniently prepared building material, and as a result a large number of decorated blocks originating in earlier royal temples have been recovered from the core of the pyramid by archaeologists.

The most interesting among the 12th-Dynasty mastabas near the north pyramid of Amenemhet I belong to the Vizier Inyotefoqer, the Chief Steward Nakht, the Overseer of Sealers Rehuerdjersen and the Mistress of the House Senebtisy, while close to the south pyramid of Senwosret I there are the tombs of the High Priest of Heliopolis Imhotep, the Steward Sehetepibreʻ-ʻankh, the High Priest of Memphis Senwosret-ʻankh and others. The monuments of el-Lisht have been explored by the expeditions of the Institut Français d'Archéologie Orientale (1894–95) and the Metropolitan Museum of Art in New York (1906–34).

Below Limestone relief of archers: one of the many Memphite blocks of the Old Kingdom reused at el-Lisht by Amenemhet I. Most of these reliefs come from royal monuments and are of superb quality. New York, Metropolitan Museum of Art.

Below right The goddess Seshat records foreign captives and booty: limestone relief of the 12th Dynasty which continues an Old Kingdom tradition of similar scenes in royal temples. From the mortuary temple of Senwosret I at el-Lisht. New York, Metropolitan Museum of Art.

MEMPHIS

The city of Memphis, which has now disappeared almost completely, was the administrative and religious center of the 1st Lower Egyptian nome. It was the royal residence and capital of Egypt during the Early Dynastic Period and the Old Kingdom, and many later kings maintained a palace there. The city's temples were among the most important in the land. Memphis always remained one of the most populous and renowned places of Egypt and, indeed, of the whole ancient world, inhabited by a truly cosmopolitan community. Its harbor and local workshops played an important part in Egypt's foreign trade.

A reflection of the size and importance of Memphis is the stretch, more than 30 km long, covered by its cemeteries, on the edge of the desert on the west bank of the Nile. These together form the Memphite necropolis: (1) Dahshur, (2) Saqqara, (3) Abusir, (4) Zawyet el-'Aryan, (5) Giza, (6) Abu Rawash. Administratively, Giza and Abu Rawash were already in the 2nd nome of Lower Egypt.

The names by which the various parts of the Memphite necropolis are now known derive from the names of modern villages nearby. Egyptians themselves had no special term for the whole necropolis, but a number of ancient Egyptian place names which used to be applied to its various parts are known, such as *Rasetau* (probably southern Giza). The most conspicuous features of the necropolis, the royal pyramids, sometimes lent their names to the adjacent quarters of the city which had grown out of the original "pyramid towns" of priests and pyramid officials. One of these terms, the name of the pyramid of Pepy I at Saqqara, *Mennufer*, Coptic *Menfe*, and Memphis in its Grecized form, was adopted as early as the 18th Dynasty to describe the whole city.

The town itself, or whatever may remain of its palaces, temples and houses, is to be sought in the cultivated area to the east of the necropolis, buried under the deposits of silt left behind by Nile inundations, and covered by modern settlements, fields and vegetation. So far only small parts have been revealed at Mit Rahina and at Saqqara (east of the pyramid of Teti). The position of the city, or at least of its center, probably did not remain stable throughout Egyptian history, new thriving areas gaining in importance to the detriment of others whose popularity had waned. This must have been one reason for the very long expanse covered by the city's cemeteries, though undoubtedly there were others, such as the search for suitable sites for the large-scale projects of building pyramids. Our modern concept of the city of Memphis and of its shadowy counterpart, the Memphite necropolis, is therefore very artificial, because neither of them ever existed completely at any one time.

Classical sources as well as archaeological discoveries show that Memphis became one of the most important administrative centers of the country at the very beginning of Egyptian history, after 2920

BC. Herodotus says that it was Menes, the traditional first king of Egypt, who raised a dike to protect the city from the inundations of the Nile. According to Manetho the successor of Menes, called Athothis, was the builder of the earliest of the palaces of Memphis. The oldest name of the district was *Ineb-hedj*, "The White Wall," possibly reflecting the appearance of its fortified residence to which it could also be applied. Perhaps the most apt was the term which appeared in the Middle Kingdom, 'Ankh-tawy, "That which Binds the Two Lands," stressing the strategic position of the town at the tip of the economically important delta, between Lower and Upper Egypt of the traditional terminology. This, indeed, was probably the reason why the rulers of the 1st Dynasty chose the area for the site of the capital.

One of the most familiar faces of Memphis: the calcite sphinx at Mit Rahina.

Only Thebes in the south was comparable in religious, political and economic importance to Memphis, yet our knowledge of the remains of this truly national shrine of Egypt is infinitely smaller. For foreigners Memphis represented Egypt. According to some scholars, the name of one of its New Kingdom temples and of the neighboring quarters of the city, *Hikuptah* ("The Temple of the *ka* of Ptah"), gave rise to the name of the whole country, Greek Aigyptos, and our Egypt. This is also the etymology of the word "Coptic."

The city of Memphis did not survive the gradual eclipse of ancient Egyptian civilization in the early centuries of our era. Economically, it suffered even earlier from the growth of Alexandria. Its religious importance was lost when Theodosius I (379–95 AD) decreed that Christianity should be the religion of the whole of the Roman Empire. The final *coup de grâce* was delivered in 641 AD, when the Muslim conqueror 'Amr ibn el-'Asi founded a new capital of Egypt, el-Fustat, on the east bank of the Nile at the south end of modern Cairo.

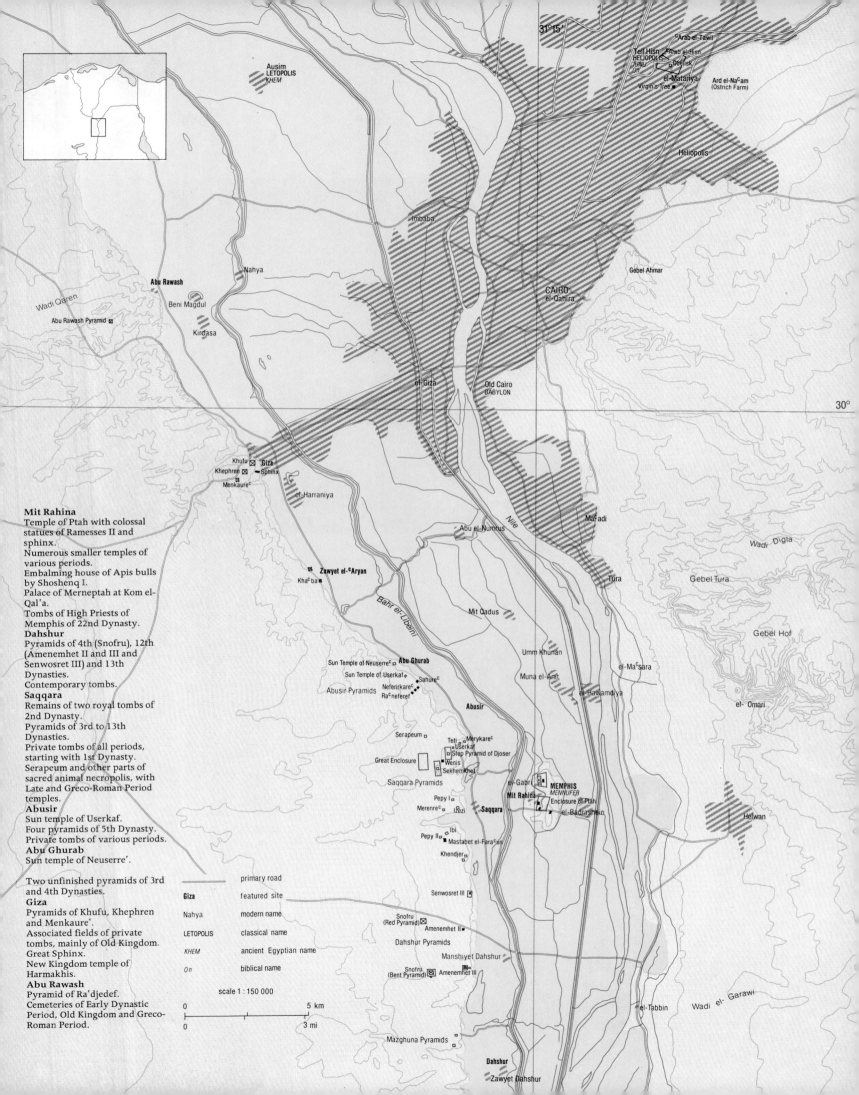

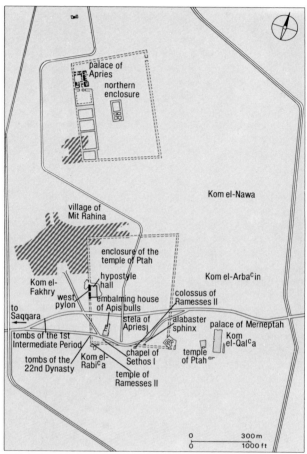

Mit Rahina

Extensive remains of ancient Memphis can be seen in a picturesque setting of palm groves close to the modern village of Mit Rahina.

The most important of the still discernible structures is the enclosure of the temple of Ptah, with colossal statues of Ramesses II and a large alabaster sphinx of approximately the same date. Ptah was the chief Memphite god, and in Classical antiquity was identified with Hephaistos and Vulcan. Only a small west section of the temple complex, once one of the largest in Egypt, has been systematically excavated (mainly by W. M. Flinders Petrie between 1908 and 1913), due to technical difficulties and the proximity of the village. The west pylon, leading into the columned hypostyle hall, was built by Ramesses II, but elsewhere in the enclosure isolated earlier elements were found (a lintel of Amenemhet III, blocks of Amenophis III etc.), suggesting the presence of older structures in the vicinity. Apart from the west pylon with the hypostyle hall, Ramesses II also built the gates on the north and south sides of the enclosure and had, in characteristic fashion, colossal statues of himself placed outside the gates. Yet another, smaller,

temple was built just outside the southwest corner of the enclosure during his reign. Later kings continued constructing within the enclosure. Thus Shoshenq I added an embalming house of Apis bulls, and Shabaka and Amasis erected smaller chapels there.

Foundation deposits discovered west of the Ptah enclosure indicate the position of an earlier temple, built by Tuthmosis IV and enlarged by other rulers of the 18th Dynasty.

An enclosure of the Late Period is visible north of the precinct of Ptah. The names of Psammetichus II and Apries of the 26th Dynasty, and of Teos of the 30th Dynasty, have been found there.

A number of mounds formed by continuous habitation are situated to the south and east of the Ptah enclosure. The most important among them are Kom el-Rabi'a, with the temple of Hathor built by Ramesses II, and Kom el-Qal'a, with a smaller temple dedicated to Ptah and a palace of Merneptah. The last was excavated by C. S. Fisher and the expedition of the University Museum in Philadelphia (Pa.) some 50 years ago, but still awaits publication.

There are few tombs at Mit Rahina. The most important among them date to the 1st Intermediate Period or early Middle Kingdom, at Kom el-Fakhry, and to the 22nd Dynasty (tombs of the High Priests of Memphis called Shoshenq, Tjekerti, Peteese and Harsiese), close to the southwest corner of the Ptah enclosure.

Fallen granite colossus of Ramesses II wearing the white crown, found near the south gate of the enclosure of the temple of Ptah, some 30 m from the famous huge statue of the same king made of limestone. The original colors of the colossus are still partly preserved. Fragments of a companion piece were also discovered, as well as lower parts of smaller seated colossi.

Dahshur

The pyramid field of Dahshur forms the southern-most extension of the Memphite necropolis. The site is some 3·5 km long, and the pyramid variously called "Bent," "Blunted," "Rhomboidal" or "False," the only one of its shape in Egypt, is the most conspicuous landmark on the horizon of Dahshur.

For royal tombs, the change from the 3rd to the 4th Dynasty is signaled by the transition from step pyramid to true pyramid. This radical move was initiated and completed during the reigns of the last king of the 3rd Dynasty, Huni, and the first king of the new dynasty, Snofru. The pyramids in which the process can be observed are at Maidum and Dahshur. The southern pyramid at Dahshur was the earliest to be planned as a true pyramid from its inception. However, when the structure reached more than half of its intended height, the slope of its outer faces was sharply reduced (from 54°27'44" to 43°22'), thus creating the characteristic "bent" silhouette, and the method of laying the casing and packing blocks was improved. This change of design was probably caused by constructional flaws which had appeared either in the structure itself or in its contemporary at Maidum. The Bent Pyramid is unique in having two separate entrances, one in its northern face and another in the western face. Large areas of the pyramid have retained their original smooth exterior casing. South of the pyramid there is the usual subsidiary ritual pyramid. The valley temple is situated about 700 m northeast of the pyramid, and has provided a series of remarkable reliefs, some of them showing processions of female figures personifying Snofru's estates in Upper and Lower Egypt.

Snofru, apparently, was not content with one pyramid at Dahshur but had another, the so-called "Red" or "Pink Pyramid" (from the color of the reddish limestone used to build it) erected some 2 km to the north. The reason for this has not been established, but the fact that the incline of the faces of the later pyramid was from the very beginning that of the upper part of the Bent Pyramid may be significant. The dimensions of the base of this pyramid (220 by 220 m) are surpassed only by those of the Great Pyramid of Khufu at Giza.

The remaining pyramids at Dahshur, at some distance from each other and not forming any group, are smaller structures of the 12th Dynasty, of Amenemhet II (the so-called "White Pyramid"), Senwosret III and Amenemhet III (the so-called "Black Pyramid"). The last two are brick built. A remarkable discovery of at least six wooden boats was made near the pyramid of Senwosret III, comparable to the find of a dismantled boat of Khufu at Giza. Near the pyramid of Amenemhet III there is the tomb of an ephemeral king Awibre' Hor, and a small pyramidal structure of Amenyqemau, both of the 13th Dynasty.

Following the usual pattern, the pyramids are accompanied by tombs of members of the royal family, officials and priests. Near the pyramids of Amenemhet II and Senwosret III, but still within the pyramid enclosure walls, there are the mastabas of princesses (Iti, Khnemt, Itiwert and Sitmerhut, all daughters of Amenemhet II, and Ment and Sent-senebtisi, daughters of Senwosret III) and queens. These tombs contained some superb examples of Middle Kingdom jewelry (bracelets, pectorals, collars, necklaces etc.), now in the Cairo Museum.

Among the archaeologists who have excavated at Dahshur, two names are prominent: J. de Morgan, to whom we owe our knowledge of the Middle Kingdom pyramids and tombs (1894–95), and Ahmed Fakhry, who explored the Bent Pyramid (1951–55). In recent years, excavations at Dahshur have been resumed by the German Archaeological Institute.

The "Bent Pyramid" and the "Red Pyramid" of Dahshur seen behind the landmarks of south Saqqara, the "Mastabet el-Fara'un" and the pyramid of Pepy II, and showing how artificial the dividing line between Saqqara and Dahshur is.

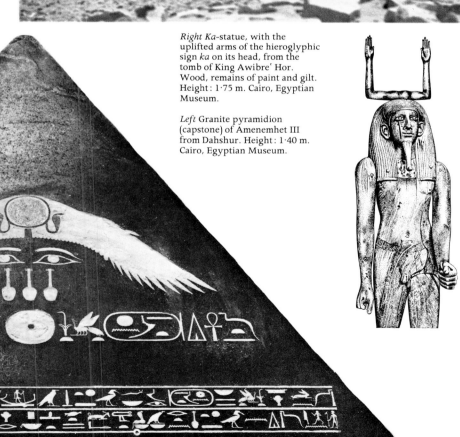

Right Ka-statue, with the uplifted arms of the hieroglyphic sign *ka* on its head, from the tomb of King Awibre' Hor. Wood, remains of paint and gilt. Height: 1·75 m. Cairo, Egyptian Museum.

Left Granite pyramidion (capstone) of Amenemhet III from Dahshur. Height: 1·40 m. Cairo, Egyptian Museum.

The Pyramids: Types and Construction

Between 2630 and 1640 BC, Egyptian kings built for themselves tombs in the form of pyramids. Architectural as well as religious considerations played a part in the pyramid's introduction and development; although united by their purpose, pyramids differ in their form, size, interior design and other details. There are two basic types: the step pyramid and the true pyramid.

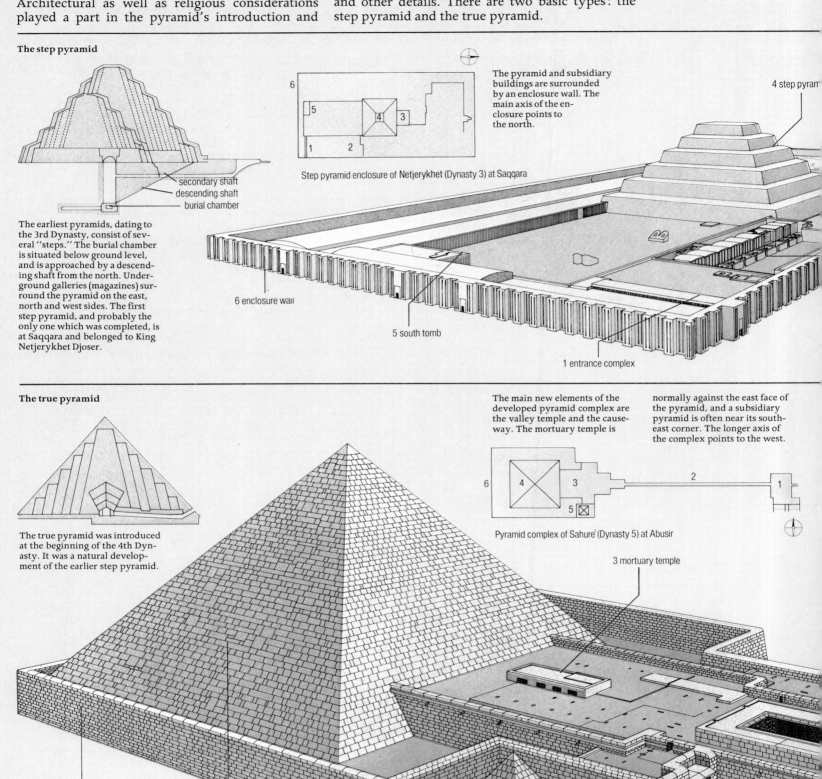

The step pyramid

The pyramid and subsidiary buildings are surrounded by an enclosure wall. The main axis of the enclosure points to the north.

Step pyramid enclosure of Netjerykhet (Dynasty 3) at Saqqara

secondary shaft
descending shaft
burial chamber

The earliest pyramids, dating to the 3rd Dynasty, consist of several "steps." The burial chamber is situated below ground level, and is approached by a descending shaft from the north. Underground galleries (magazines) surround the pyramid on the east, north and west sides. The first step pyramid, and probably the only one which was completed, is at Saqqara and belonged to King Netjerykhet Djoser.

4 step pyramid

6 enclosure wall

5 south tomb

1 entrance complex

The true pyramid

The main new elements of the developed pyramid complex are the valley temple and the causeway. The mortuary temple is normally against the east face of the pyramid, and a subsidiary pyramid is often near its southeast corner. The longer axis of the complex points to the west.

Pyramid complex of Sahure (Dynasty 5) at Abusir

The true pyramid was introduced at the beginning of the 4th Dynasty. It was a natural development of the earlier step pyramid.

3 mortuary temple

6 enclosure wall

4 pyramid

5 subsidiary pyramid

Internal construction

In most true pyramids, the structure consists of a series of buttress walls (coatings of masonry) surrounding the central core. The buttress walls decrease in height from the center outwards; in other words, there is a step pyramid within most true pyramids. This clever internal arrangement

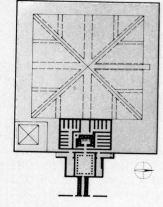

added stability to the structure but evolved historically, together with the pyramid itself. Packing blocks were used to fill the "steps" formed by the faces of the outermost buttress walls, and casing blocks (often of better-quality Tura limestone) completed the transformation into a true pyramid.

A different method of construction was employed in the pyramids of the 12th and 13th Dynasties. The main reason for its introduction was economy: it was suitable for relatively modest structures in inferior materials. Solid stone walls ran from the center of the pyramid, while shorter cross walls created a series of internal chambers filled with stone blocks, rubble or mud bricks. The whole structure then received the usual outer casing. Although quite effective in the short term, this could not compare with the earlier constructional methods, and all pyramids built in this way are now very dilapidated.

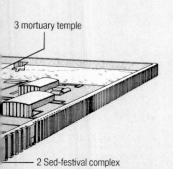

3 mortuary temple

2 Sed-festival complex

The subsidiary buildings, in particular the south tomb and the mortuary temple, ensured the deceased king's well-being in his new existence, and served to maintain his cult. Djoser's *sed*-festival complex is a special feature not attested elsewhere.

The funerary monument of Sahure' at Abusir is a good example of the pyramid complex. The landing stages of the valley temple show that it could be approached by boat. The ascending causeway connects it with the mortuary temple. This consists of the outer part, with an entrance passage and a columned court, and the inner part, with five niches for statues, magazines to the north and south, and a sanctuary. In most pyramids the interior is reached by a descending passage starting in the north face. The roof of the burial chamber is formed by the largest and heaviest blocks in the whole structure.

Building ramps

A major problem facing the pyramid builders was how to lift the heavy stone blocks to the required height. The only method proved to have been used by the ancient Egyptians is based on ramps. These were inclined planes, built of mud brick and rubble, along which the blocks were dragged on sledges (wheeled transport was not used in the

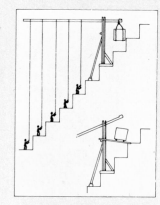

pyramid age). As the pyramid grew in height, the length of the ramp and the width of its base were increased in order to maintain a constant gradient (about 1 to 10) and to prevent the ramp from collapsing. Several ramps approaching the pyramid from different sides were probably used.

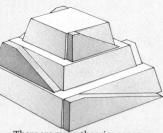

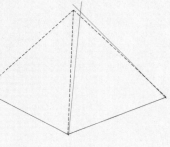

There are many theories concerning the actual arrangement of building ramps. Assuming that the "step pyramid within the pyramid" was built first, the ramps could have run from one step to another rather than approaching the pyramid face at right angles.

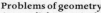

Other methods of lifting

The size of the ramps and the volume of material required to build them have prompted alternative suggestions as to how the problem of raising the building blocks was solved. One, proposed by L. Croon, uses the principle of the *shaduf*. The Egyptians knew the *shaduf* for raising water, but there is no evidence that they used a similar device for lifting weights.

Problems of geometry

A very slight error in the angle of incline of a pyramid would have resulted in a substantial misalignment of the edges at the apex. The principles of pyramid construction are familiar, but the exact procedure and practices remain unknown.

This is the main objection to this and similar ideas.

Models of "rockers," wooden cradle-like appliances, are known, and it has been thought that these were used to lift stone blocks. The rocker, with the stone placed on it, would have been raised by positioning wedges below its sides and rocking it up onto them. Stones might have been handled this way at some stage, but as a main lifting method this does not seem adequate.

Some of the pyramid measurements show an accurate use of π (e.g. height of Khufu's pyramid = $\dfrac{\text{perimeter of the base}}{2\pi}$). The mathematical knowledge of the Egyptians was not sufficient to arrive at this by calculation, but it could have been produced "accidentally," for example through measuring distances by counting revolutions of a drum.

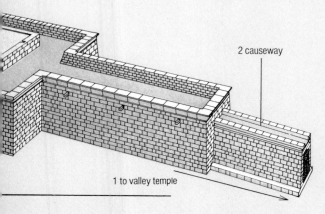

2 causeway

1 to valley temple

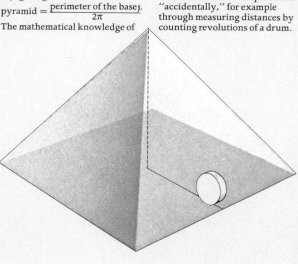

The Pyramids: Checklist

This list contains all the royal pyramids known from Egypt to date. The pyramids tend to form pyramid fields which are referred to by the names of the modern villages situated nearby. There are various reasons for these groupings but, broadly speaking, the Old Kingdom pyramids were concentrated near Memphis while those of the Middle Kingdom were built close to Itjtawy (near modern el-Lisht), the capital of the land at that time. At the beginning of the 4th Dynasty the pyramids, together with the buildings associated with them, started being named. During the 12th Dynasty each part of the pyramid complex probably had a name of its own.

△ true pyramid

⊓ step pyramid

△ bent pyramid

⊔ sarcophagus-shaped pyramid

Each entry in the table lists the following information (if available): king's name and dynasty; ancient name of pyramid in hieroglyphs and English; modern name; dimensions (α = angle of incline); associated pyramids (△).

Abu Rawash

△ Ra'djedef/Dyn 4
"The Pyramid which is the *Sehedu*-star"
104·5m sq; α = 60°
Subsidiary △
Unfinished; remains of granite casing

Giza

△ Khufu/Dyn 4
"The Pyramid which is the Place of Sunrise and Sunset"
Modern name: "The Great Pyramid" or "The First Pyramid of Giza"
230m sq; α = 51°50′35″; original ht 146m
Subsidiary △; queens △ △ △
5 boat pits, one containing a dismantled wooden boat, one as yet unopened

△ Khephren/Dyn 4
"The Great Pyramid"
Modern name: "The Second Pyramid of Giza"
214·5m sq; α = 53°7′48″; ht 143·5m
Subsidiary △
Lowest course of casing in granite; remains of original limestone casing near summit; 5 boat pits

△ Menkaure'/Dyn 4
"The Divine Pyramid"
Modern name: "The Third Pyramid of Giza"
105m sq; α = 51°20′25″; original ht 65·5m
queens △ △ △
Pyramid refurnished during Dyn 26; bottom 16 courses of casing in granite

Zawyet el-'Aryan

△ Owner unknown (probably the successor of Khephren)
Name unknown
Modern name: "The Unfinished Pyramid"
209m sq
Only the underground part begun; sarcophagus of unusual form found embedded in floor of burial chamber

⊓ Probably Kha'ba/Dyn 3
Modern name: "The Layer Pyramid" or "el-Medowwara"
78·5m sq
Ownership inferred from inscribed alabaster vessels found nearby; unfinished

Abusir

△ Sahure'/Dyn 5
"The Pyramid where the *Ba*-spirit rises"
78·5m sq; α = 50°11′40″; original ht 47m
Subsidiary △

△ Neuserre'/Dyn 5
"The Pyramid which is Established of Places"
81m sq; α = 51°50′35″; original ht 51·5m
Subsidiary △
Valley Temple and part of causeway originally built for Neferirkare' and usurped

△ Neferirkare'/Dyn 5
"The Pyramid of the *Ba*-spirit"
105m sq; α = 53°7′48″; original ht 70m
Valley Temple and causeway unfinished at time of king's death and later usurped by Neuserre'

△ Probably Ra'neferef/Dyn 5
"The Pyramid which is Divine of the *Ba*-spirits"
65m sq
Hardly begun; name of Pyramid known from titles of priests connected with it but identification, though logical, is not supported by any evidence

Saqqara

△ Teti/Dyn 6
"The Pyramid which is Enduring of Places"
78·5m sq; α = 53°7′48″; original ht 52·5m
Subsidiary △; queens △ (Iput I), △ (Khuit)
Pyramid Texts

△ Probably Merykare'/Dyn 9 or 10
"The Pyramid which is Flourishing of Places"
Estimated 50m sq

⊓ Pepy I/Dyn 6
"The Established and

No evidence for ownership except for titles of priests buried nearby; not yet excavated

△ Userkaf/Dyn 5
"The Pyramid which is Pure of Places"
Modern name: "el-Haram el-Makharbish"
73·5m sq; α = 53°7′48″; original ht 49m
Subsidiary △
Mortuary Temple placed, unusually, south of Pyramid

⊓ Netjerykhet (Djoser)/Dyn 3
Modern name: "The Step Pyramid" or "el-Haram el-Mudarrag"
140 × 118m; ht 60m
Begun as a mastaba tomb; plan modified 6 times; final form of superstructure a pyramid in 6 steps, the earliest pyramid built in Egypt

△ Wenis/Dyn 5
"The Pyramid which is Beautiful of Places"
57·5m sq; α = 56° 18′ 35″; original ht 43m
Subsidiary △
Pyramid Texts
Causeway decorated by series of remarkable reliefs; 2 boat pits

⊓ Sekhemkhet/Dyn 3
Modern name: "The Buried Pyramid"
120m sq
Unfinished; raised to ht of only c.7m; sealed but empty sarcophagus found in burial chamber

⊓ (probably) Owner unknown, perhaps a king of Dyn 3
Modern name: "The Great Enclosure"
Outlines of enclosure walls only; not yet excavated; perhaps only begun, but on a grandiose scale; possibly not a pyramid at all or not of Dyn 3

△ Pepy I/Dyn 6
"The Established and

Beautiful Pyramid"
78·5m sq; α = 53°7′48″; original ht 52·5m
Pyramid Texts
Pyramid lent its name to city of Memphis

△ Izezi/Dyn 5
"The Beautiful Pyramid"
Modern name: "el-Shawwaf"
78·5m sq; α = 53°7′48″; original ht 52·5m
queen △

△ Merenre'/Dyn 6
"The Shining and Beautiful Pyramid"
78·5m sq; α = 53°7′48″; original ht 52·5m
Pyramid Texts

△ Ibi/Dyn 8
Name unknown
31·5m sq; α = ?; original ht ?
Pyramid too damaged to provide accurate measurements; Mortuary Temple only brick-built; apparently no Valley Temple or causeway; Pyramid Texts

△ Pepy II/Dyn 6
"The Established and Living Pyramid"
78·5m sq; α = 53°7′48″; original ht 52·5m
Subsidiary △; queens △ (Neit), △ (Iput II), △ (Wedjebten); Pyramid Texts

⊔ Shepseskaf/Dyn 4
"The Purified Pyramid"
100 × 72m
Not really a pyramid but a sarcophagus-shaped structure though even the Egyptians sometimes used to write its name with the sign showing a pyramid

△ Khendjer/Dyn 13
Name unknown
52·5m sq; α = 55°; original ht 37m
queen (?) △
Mainly brick-built

△ Owner unknown/Dyn 13
Name unknown
80m sq; α = ?; original ht ?
Too damaged to provide accurate measurements; mainly brick-built; at present only c. 3m high

Dahshur

△ Senwosret III/Dyn 12
Name not certain
105m sq; α = 56°18′35″; original ht 78·5m
Brick-built; 6 wooden boats buried near Pyramid

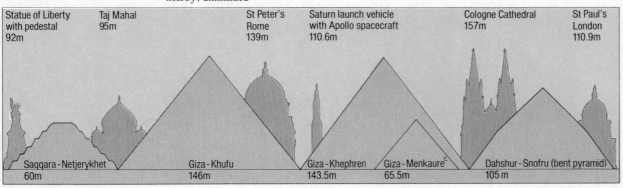

| Statue of Liberty with pedestal 92m | Taj Mahal 95m | | St Peter's Rome 139m | Saturn launch vehicle with Apollo spacecraft 110.6m | | Cologne Cathedral 157m | St Paul's London 110.9m |

| Saqqara - Netjerykhet 60m | | Giza - Khufu 146m | | Giza - Khephren 143.5m | Giza - Menkaure' 65.5m | Dahshur - Snofru (bent pyramid) 105 m | |

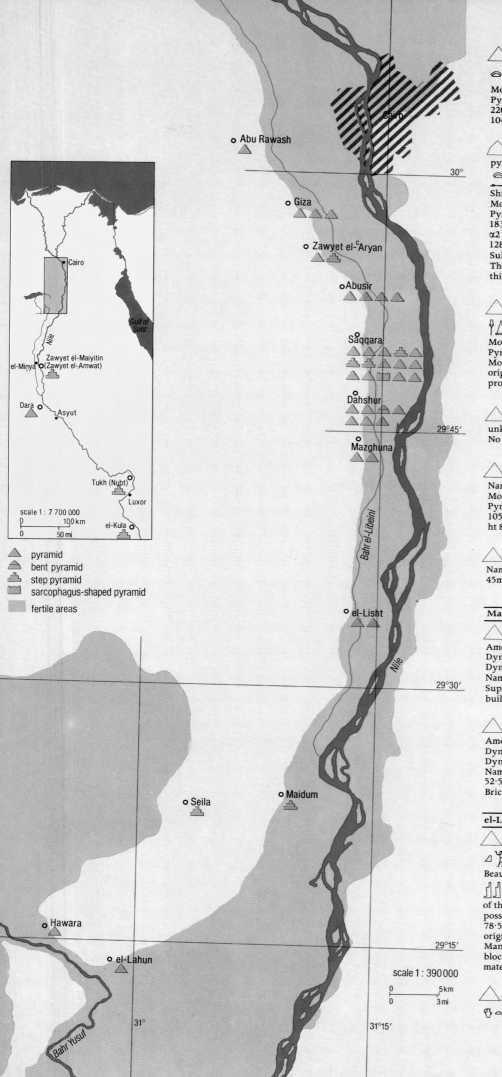

Abu Rawash

Cairo

30°

Giza

Zawyet el-ᶜAryan

Abusir

Saqqara

Dahshur

29°45'

Mazghuna

Bahr el-Libeini

29°30'

el-Lisht

Nile

Seila

Maidum

scale 1 : 390 000

0 — 5 km
0 — 3 mi

29°15'

Hawara

31°

el-Lahun

Bahr Yusuf

31°15'

Inset map:

Cairo

Nile

Gulf of Suez

el-Minya

Zawyet el-Maiyitin (Zawyet el-Amwat)

Dara Asyut

Tukh (Nubt)

Luxor

el-Kula

scale 1 : 7 700 000

0 — 100 km
0 — 50 mi

Legend key:

△ pyramid
⟁ bent pyramid
⬟ step pyramid
▱ sarcophagus-shaped pyramid
▨ fertile areas

Right-hand column text:

△ Snofru/Dyn 4

◠△ "The Shining Pyramid"
Modern names: "The Red Pyramid," etc
220m sq; α = 43°22'; original ht 104m

△ Snofru (another pyramid)/Dyn 4

◠△ "The Southern Shining Pyramid"
Modern names: "The Bent Pyramid," etc
183·5m sq; α1 = 54° 27' 44'';
α2 = 43° 22'; intended ht 128·5m; original ht 105m
Subsidiary △
The only Egyptian pyramid of this form

△ Amenemhet II/Dyn 12

"The Mighty Pyramid"
Modern name: "The White Pyramid"
More than 50m sq; α = ?;
original ht ? Too damaged to provide accurate measurements

△ Owner unknown, date unknown
No data available

△ Amenemhet III/Dyn 12
Name not certain
Modern name: "The Black Pyramid"
105m sq; α = 57°15'50''; original ht 81·5m; brick-built

△ Amenyqemau/Dyn 13
Name unknown
45m sq; unfinished

Mazghuna

△ Owner unknown, perhaps Amenemhet IV or Nefrusobk of Dyn 12, or more likely a king of Dyn 13
Name unknown
Superstructure, probably stone-built, now completely lost

△ Owner unknown, perhaps Amenemhet IV or Nefrusobk of Dyn 12, or more likely a king of Dyn 13
Name unknown
52·5m sq; α = ?; original ht ?
Brick-built

el-Lisht

△ Amenemhet I/Dyn 12

"The High and Beautiful Pyramid" or
"The Pyramid of the Places of Arising," and possibly others
78·5m sq; α = 54°27'44'';
original ht 55m
Many decorated Old Kingdom blocks reused as building material in the core

△ Senwosret I/Dyn 12

"The Pyramid

which is Favored of Places" or
"The Pyramid which overlooks the Two Lands"
105m sq; α = 49°23'55''; original ht 61m
Subsidiary △; queens and princesses △ △ △ △ △ △ △ △

Maidum

▱ altered to △ Probably Huni/Dyn 3
147m sq; α = 51°50'35''; original ht 93·5m
Subsidiary △
Perhaps completed by Snofru

Seila

⬟ Owner unknown (most probably not a royal pyramid), thought to be of Dyn 3
26m sq
Never properly investigated

Hawara

△ Amenemhet III/Dyn 12
100m sq; α = 48°45'; original ht 58m
Name not certain
Brick-built

el-Lahun

△ Senwosret II/Dyn 12

◠△ "The Shining Pyramid," and probably others
106m sq; α = 42°35'; original ht 48m
queen △

Zawyet el-Maiyitin (or Zawyet el-Amwat)

⬟ Owner unknown (most probably not a royal pyramid), thought to be of Dyn 3
18m sq

Dara

△ Probably Khui/Dyns 7–10
Name unknown
130m sq
Brick-built; present ht only 4m

Tukh (Nubt)

⬟ Owner unknown (most probably not a royal pyramid), thought to be of Dyn 3
18m sq

el-Kula

⬟ Owner unknown (most probably not a royal pyramid), thought to be of Dyn 3
18m sq

Location unknown

△ Menkauhor/Dyn 5
Undoubtedly at Saqqara

"The Pyramid which is Divine of Places"

△ Neferkareᶜ/Dyns 7 or 8
Almost certainly at Saqqara

"The Enduring and Living Pyramid"

△ Ity/Dyns 7/10

"The Pyramid of the Ba-spirits"

Saqqara

Saqqara is the most attractive and the most interesting site in Lower Egypt, though it must be stressed that the infinitely lesser chances of preservation of monuments in the delta distort any attempt at a fair comparison. It is the most important link in the chain of cemeteries belonging to the ancient city of Memphis, and covers an area over 6 km long, measuring more than 1·5 km at its widest.

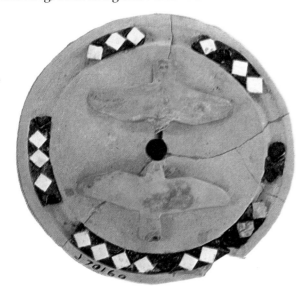

Before the pyramids (Dynasties 1 and 2)
The earliest royal name which the archaeologists have so far met at Saqqara is that of Na'rmer, whom some Egyptologists equate with Menes, the legendary founder of Memphis. It is engraved on a porphyry bowl which, together with thousands of other complete and fragmentary vessels of magnificent craftsmanship, was discovered in one of the subterranean magazines under the Step Pyramid of Djoser. The earliest mastaba tomb at Saqqara is only a little later, dating to the reign of King 'Aha (Menes according to another school of thought, probably Na'rmer's successor).

Mastaba tombs of the 1st Dynasty form an almost continuous line along the eastern edge of the large plateau north of the Step Pyramid of Djoser, above the modern village of Abusir. Their superstructures, built of sun-dried bricks and provided with a paneled "palace facade," were of considerable size: tomb S 3504, for example, of the reign of King Wadj, measured 56·45 by 25·45 m. Chambers for funerary equipment were situated in the core of the mastaba, while the substructure contained a centrally placed burial chamber and subsidiary rooms. The most important of these mastabas were excavated by W. B. Emery between 1936 and 1956. It was believed that at least some of them were royal tombs, mainly because of their size, but now most

scholars consider them to be the tombs of high officials resident at Memphis.

At the end of the 1st Dynasty the "palace-facade" paneling on the outside of the mastaba was reduced to two niches in the east face, of which that near the southeast corner was the more important and became the focus of the mortuary cult of the deceased. The generally smaller private mastabas of the 2nd Dynasty continued to be built in an apparently haphazard way in the area west of the large tombs of the 1st Dynasty. A large complex of underground rock-cut chambers has also been located under the east side of the pyramid of Wenis, and another about 140 m east of it. Nothing has been preserved of their brick-built superstructures, but the names on some clay sealings, originally used to seal jars and other articles of burial equipment, suggest that these galleries were made during the reigns of two early kings of the 2nd Dynasty, Re'neb and Ninetjer. When this fact is connected with the finding of a stela of Re'neb, probably reused in a modern village nearby (though the exact circumstances of the discovery are not clear), it seems likely that the galleries were once royal tombs, and that Egyptian kings were first buried at Saqqara as early as the beginning of the 2nd Dynasty.

The pyramid builders (Dynasties 3–13)

The pyramids. Altogether 15 royal pyramids, treated here in chronological order, are known from Saqqara. Most of them have now lost their original, strictly geometrical, forms and are reduced to artificial hills. Incredible though it may seem, it is almost certain that other pyramids are still to be discovered (for example that of Menkauhor).
(1) The Step Pyramid of Netjerykhet Djoser was built some time after 2630 BC. It was the first pyramid in Egyptian history, and the earliest stone structure of its size in the world. The pioneering character of the project is shown by the hesitation about its form, probably largely influenced by the new building material. Altogether six different plans were adopted in the course of the construction: the monument was started as a large mastaba tomb, thus following the well-established Saqqara tradition, but ended up as a pyramid of six steps. The design of the Step Pyramid was traditionally credited to Imuthes (in Egyptian: Imhotep), described by Manetho some 2,400 years later as "the inventor of the art of building with hewn stone." During the excavation of the entrance complex of the Step Pyramid in 1925–26 the name of Imhotep was, indeed, found inscribed on the pedestal of a statue of Netjerykhet, and so provided fascinating contemporary evidence for the correctness of Manetho's statement.

The complex of buildings near the southeast corner of the pyramid represents a stone replica of the chapels and pavilions built for the celebration of the *sed* festival. The festival was held to mark the

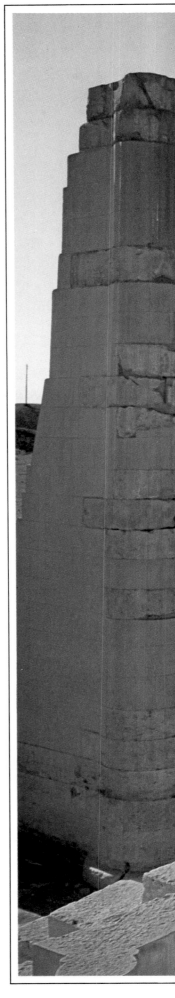

1	Netjerykhet Djoser	6	Izezi	11	Pepy II
2	Sekhemkhet	7	Wenis	12	Ibi
3	"Great Enclosure"	8	Teti	13	Merykare[C](?)
4	Shepseskaf	9	Pepy I	14	Khendjer
5	Userkaf	10	Merenre[C]	15	unknown king of 13th Dynasty

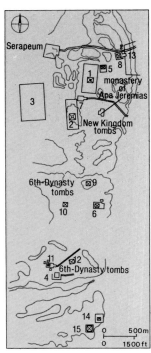

beginning of a new phase in the reign of the king, and the presence of these buildings in lasting stone guaranteed that Djoser would not be unprepared for the many celebrations of the *sed* festival he hoped to enjoy in his life after death. A closed room (*serdab*) near the northeast corner of the pyramid contained his seated statue, the earliest large stone royal statue known from Egypt.

For more than 50 years the Step Pyramid has been connected with the name of the French Egyptologist Jean-Philippe Lauer. At present his remarkable work is concentrated on the chapels in the *sed*-festival court; no visitor to Saqqara should miss a chance to see these unique examples of the earliest Egyptian stone architecture restored to their original beauty.

(2) King Sekhemkhet intended to build an even larger step structure southwest of that of his predecessor, but the pyramid remained unfinished and gradually disappeared under the sand. It was only in 1950 that it was discovered by the Egyptian Egyptologist M. Zakaria Goneim, who aptly called it "The Buried Pyramid."

(3) Aerial photographs show the outlines of a huge enclosed area (known as the "Great Enclosure" to Egyptologists), as yet unexcavated, west of the

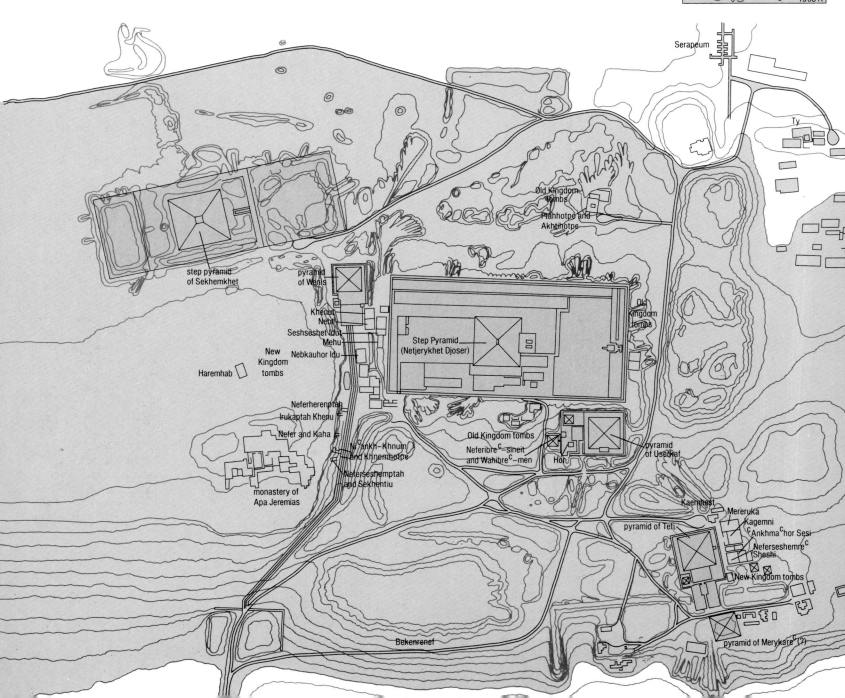

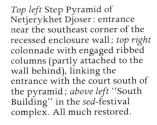

Top left Step Pyramid of
Netjerykhet Djoser: entrance
near the southeast corner of the
recessed enclosure wall; *top right*
colonnade with engaged ribbed
columns (partly attached to the
wall behind), linking the
entrance with the court south of
the pyramid; *above left* "South
Building" in the *sed*-festival
complex. All much restored.

Above Upper part of the
limestone seated statue of Djoser
found in the *serdab*. The king is
clad in a ceremonial robe, and
wears an unusual headdress. The
pose, with the right arm bent and
the hand clenched against the
chest, is typically archaic. Most
of the paint, yellow for the skin
and black for the hair and beard,
has been lost; the mutilation of
the face is the result of the
gouging out of the inlaid eyes.
Height: 1·40 m. Cairo, Egyptian
Museum.

Above right Pyramid complex of
Wenis: two boat pits, some 39 m
long, by the south side of the
causeway, about 180 m east of
the pyramd.

enclosure of Sekhemkhet. There may be another
building of the same type immediately west of the
Step Pyramid of Djoser. These could be monuments
of the 3rd Dynasty, but only future excavations can
settle the problems of their dating and ownership.

(4) The burial complex of Shepseskaf, one of the last
kings of the 4th Dynasty, is not a pyramid but a
structure resembling a huge sarcophagus. It is
known as "Mastabet el-Fara'un." The only parallel
is the Giza tomb of Khentkaus, the mother of the
early kings of the 5th Dynasty.

(5) Userkaf, the first king of the 5th Dynasty, built
his pyramid near the northeast corner of Djoser's
enclosure, but his successors abandoned Saqqara
for Abusir, further north. It is likely that the return
to Saqqara was initiated by Menkauhor, but his
pyramid has not yet been located.

(6) The pyramid of Menkauhor's successor, Izezi,
was built in the southern part of Saqqara.

(7) The pyramid of Wenis, the last king of the 5th
Dynasty, stands near the southwest corner of the
step pyramid enclosure of Djoser. The walls of the
interior of this pyramid are inscribed with the
Pyramid Texts, a collection of spells designed to
help the deceased king in the netherworld, which
may have been used during the burial ceremony.
The pyramid of Wenis was the first to contain the
Pyramid Texts, which subsequently became a
standard feature of Old Kingdom pyramids.

On the south face of the pyramid there is a
hieroglyphic inscription of Kha'emwese, one of the
sons of Ramesses II. It records restoration work
carried out by the prince, who was known for his
interest in ancient monuments. Kha'emwese was
connected with the Memphite region in his function

Hetepka
temple of
Nectanebo II
the "Iseum"
(gallery of "Mother
of the Apis" cows)

galleries of ibises,
falcons and baboons

Hezyre^c

Hemaka

tombs of the 2nd
and 3rd Dynasties

tombs of the 1st Dynasty

3504

0   300 m
0   1000 ft

Left The causeway of Wenis, with the remains of the mortuary temple and the pyramid.

Below Wooden panel showing the Chief of Dentists and Physicians Hezyre' of the 3rd Dynasty. Originally in a niche in his tomb. Cairo, Egyptian Museum.

as the High Priest of Ptah.

The causeway, linking the mortuary temple against the east face of the pyramid with the valley temple, was decorated with reliefs. These depict, among other scenes, boats transporting granite columns and architraves from the granite quarries near Aswan to the building site of Wenis' pyramid. The journey, we are told, took seven days.

(8) The pyramid of Teti, the founder of the 6th Dynasty, is the northernmost royal pyramid of Saqqara. The other rulers of the dynasty, Pepy I (9), Merenre' (10) and Pepy II (11), followed Izezi's example and moved to the southern part of Saqqara. Since 1965, the interior passages and rooms of the pyramids of the 6th Dynasty have been systematically cleared, and the Pyramid Texts inscribed on their walls copied and studied by Jean Leclant and Jean-Philippe Lauer.

(12) The small brick-built pyramid of the little-known King Ibi of the 8th Dynasty is in the same area.

(13) The as yet unexcavated remains of the pyramid discernible to the east of the pyramid of Teti, at north Saqqara, might belong to King Merykare', one of the two reasonably well-known kings of the Herakleopolitan Period (9th/10th Dynasty). This assumption is based on the fact that the part of Memphis adjacent to the pyramid complex of Teti was very popular at that time: the area is densely covered by contemporary tombs, some of them belonging to priests of Merykare', and the city quarter is mentioned (as *Djed-isut*, from the name of Teti's pyramid) in the ancient Egyptian literary composition known as the "Instruction for Mery-kare'."

(14) and (15) The two southernmost Saqqara pyramids belong to kings of the 13th Dynasty and, characteristically for the period, are built of sun-dried bricks. The owner of one of these pyramids was Khendjer, while the other remains anonymous.

Private tombs. The largest conglomeration of private tombs, contemporary with the pyramids, occupies the area north of the Step Pyramid of Djoser, and is a natural outgrowth of the earlier cemeteries of Dynasties 1 and 2. Many of these tombs, mainly of Dynasties 3–5, were partly excavated more than a century ago under the direction of the French archaeologist Auguste Mariette. Archaeological techniques and practices used during the excavation were those of the period. Before long the tombs were sanded up again and are now inaccessible.

All Old Kingdom pyramids are surrounded by cemeteries of private tombs. Those which were situated south of the Step Pyramid were in the way when the pyramid of Wenis was begun, with the result that some of them were literally covered by Wenis' causeway, and so avoided the destruction and plundering of later times (the much later tomb of King Tut'ankhamun in the Valley of the Kings at Thebes escaped looting for similar reasons). Some of these were partly rock-cut, a less usual occurrence at Saqqara where the rock is not very suitable for this form of tomb. Tombs of the late Old Kingdom and of the 1st Intermediate Period, which have been found north and east of the pyramid of Teti and around the pyramid of Pepy II, are also of exceptional interest, mainly on account of their relief decoration or their unusual architectural features.

The series of private tombs at Saqqara is uninterrupted for at least the first ten Egyptian dynasties (2920–2040 BC), and possibly even longer. The cult niche in the east face of the mastaba of the 1st and 2nd Dynasties was withdrawn into the body

Right Sheikh el-Beled, "the headman of the village," was the name given to this statue by the local workmen who discovered it in 1860. It is made of wood (the arms were carved as separate pieces and joined to the body) and was originally covered with plaster coating and painted, with the eyes inlaid. The feet and lower parts of the legs and the stick are modern. The statue is uninscribed, but the tomb in which it was found belonged to the Chief Lector-Priest Ka'aper of the early 5th Dynasty. It is an apparently realistic portrait of a corpulent aging man, and one of the finest of its type. Height: 1·10 m. Cairo, Egyptian Museum.

Far right Reliefs from Old Kingdom tombs. From the top: fowl-yard, with men force-feeding geese and cranes (from an unknown tomb of the 5th Dynasty, in East Berlin Museum); group of butchers felling an ox (Mereruka, reign of Teti); members of the household approaching the deceased with offerings for his tomb, partly unfinished (Akhtihotpe, end of the 5th Dynasty); cattle crossing a canal, with a hippopotamus and fish (Kagemni, reign of Teti); shrine with a statue of the deceased dragged on a sled to the tomb (Hetepka, late 5th or early 6th Dynasty).

of the mastaba during the 3rd or early 4th Dynasty, probably in order to protect its decorated parts more effectively against the elements. It was connected with the outside by means of a passage, thus creating the classical Saqqara cruciform chapel. This, the simplest tomb chapel, developed further during the 5th and 6th Dynasties through the addition of more rooms. These finally filled practically the whole body of the mastaba, originally a solid mass of mud brick or stone, and provided large areas suitable for relief decoration. The most famous Saqqara mastabas of the Old Kingdom are of this type, for example the mastaba of Ty with a portico, a pillared court and another four rooms, and the family tomb of Mereruka.

The New Kingdom

Private tombs. Only one important burial of the period immediately preceding the rise of the 18th Dynasty has so far been found at Saqqara. In view of the politically and socially unsettled situation in the country at that time, this is not altogether surprising. Much more puzzling, however, is the absence of tombs which could be dated to the early and middle 18th Dynasty, i.e. before the reign of Amenophis III. Several texts record hunting and other activities of Egyptian princes in the Giza area, the inference being that Memphis was at least a temporary abode for some members of the royal family, probably including the king himself, and therefore required an establishment to accommodate them and staff to maintain it. Furthermore, it is hard to conceive that there would not be a substantial number of administrative personnel in the Memphite area, and Memphite temples must have been served by a permanent priesthood. Unless the tombs of these people were not at Saqqara – a somewhat unlikely proposition – we must assume that they have not yet been discovered. The most promising area in which to look for them is the escarpment on the east edge of the necropolis, particularly between the pyramid of Teti and the northern tip of the plateau north of it. The tombs were probably rock-cut; this would conform to what we know about provincial tombs of the 18th Dynasty elsewhere (e.g. el-Kab), and would explain the almost total absence of isolated relief fragments. So far only a few rock-cut tombs of the New Kingdom, among them one belonging to a vizier called 'Aperia, have been found at Saqqara.

The large stone-built (as opposed to rock-cut) tomb of the New Kingdom appeared at Saqqara in the reign of Amenophis III, but the majority of those known so far are somewhat later. When Tut'ankhamun abandoned el-'Amarna, the royal residence was moved to Memphis rather than to Thebes. Memphis, and Saqqara as its most important cemetery, retained this position until the reign of Ramesses II, when the center of activities shifted to the northeastern delta. The finest Saqqara tombs

of the New Kingdom therefore date between the reigns of Tut'ankhamun and Ramesses II; they cover some 100 years, and present a fairly uniform group. The best craftsmen and artists in the land accompanied the court and took part in their preparation. The high artistic standard of relief work at Saqqara during this period was not achieved again in private monuments of the New Kingdom. Unfortunately, very few of these Saqqara tombs have been excavated under controlled conditions. They were fairly close to the surface, sometimes overlaying tombs of the Old Kingdom, and so they became an easy prey for collectors of antiquities of the last century, for whom the situation was made even easier by the proximity of Saqqara to Cairo. It was quite simple to dismantle the tombs, which were lined with stone blocks, and remove the decorated reliefs. New Kingdom tombs, as known at present, are concentrated in two areas of Saqqara: (1) in the vicinity of the pyramid complex of Teti; (2) in the area south of the causeway of Wenis, defined by the ruins of the Coptic monastery of Apa Jeremias to the east and the pyramid enclosure of Sekhemkhet to the west.

Opposite above The Overseer of Craftsmen Amenemone, followed by his wife Tahesyt and sons, offers papyrus and lotus flowers to Sakhmet, the lioness-headed Memphite goddess. End of the 18th Dynasty. Cairo, Egyptian Museum.

Opposite below Hoisting the mast of a sailing boat on the Nile, on the east wall, and (*above*) part of the west wall, with a series of false doors of various members of the family, in the tomb chapel of the Director of Singers, Nufer. Mid- to late 5th Dynasty.

Center left The Inspector of Hairdressers, Hetepka, represented on the jambs and the rear wall of the niche of his false door. Late 5th or early 6th Dynasty.

Left Painted limestone statue of a scribe reading from a papyrus, his eyes fixed on his listener. A roll of papyrus is placed on the flat surface formed by his kilt stretched over his knees, and while his left hand presses the beginning of the papyrus roll against it, his right hand is ready to unroll it as required. The papyrus still bears traces of a text in ink, but the statue itself is uninscribed and the exact circumstances of its discovery are not known, so that the owner remains anonymous. This type of sculpture was introduced in the 4th Dynasty and remained popular. Height: 49 cm. 5th Dynasty. Cairo, Egyptian Museum.

The Memphite tomb of Haremhab, east wall of the 2nd columned court. A group of courtiers dressed in long pleated costumes billowing at the front, fashionable at the end of the 18th Dynasty, and sporting long walking sticks with ornamental knobs, take part in a social occasion. Their individual tastes are shown by the different types of wig they wear. The event is a review of African and Asiatic captives brought from military campaigns abroad by the "General of the Generals" Haremhab. The captives are dragged into his presence unwillingly and subjected to various indignities by Egyptian soldiers escorting them. The scene is surprisingly unconventional, and the harsh treatment meted out to the foreigners contrasts markedly with the effeminate finery of the courtiers. The relief is very fine, with beautifully modeled details such as the hands of the men, and is in many respects a continuation of the best ʿAmarna tradition. Some of the relief fragments which have been known for a long time could now be directly fitted on to this wall (a block with black captives in the Museo Civico in Bologna, and another which used to be in the Zizinia collection in Alexandria).

A spectacular discovery, and one which settled an Egyptological dispute of long standing, was made a few years ago by the Anglo-Dutch expedition of the Egypt Exploration Society and the National Museum of Antiquities, Leiden, led by G. T. Martin. Since the first half of the last century, many national museums, in particular those of Berlin, Bologna, Leiden, Leningrad, London and Vienna, have proudly displayed reliefs and stelae from the tomb of the Great Commander of the Army, Haremhab. Haremhab was the military power behind the throne in the post-ʿAmarna period,

during the reigns of Tutʿankhamun and Aya, and himself became king at the close of the 18th Dynasty. His royal tomb is in the Valley of the Kings at Thebes (No. 57), but the monuments in museums must have come from an earlier tomb which he had built for himself before ascending the throne. The position of the tomb from which the monuments came was nowhere precisely recorded, and even the area of Egypt in which it was situated was not certain. Both Thebes and Memphis were initially considered until the Belgian Egyptologist Jean Capart advanced strong arguments in favor of a

Those allowed to enter the underground parts of the animal necropolis during an animal funeral used to leave behind small votive stelae as tokens of their piety. Nowadays only their emplacements are sometimes left.

Memphite location in 1921. However, it was not until 54 years later, in January 1975, that he was proved right, and the position of the tomb was established with certainty.

The main features of the plan of the typical Saqqara tomb chapel of the New Kingdom were an open court, sometimes with columns on one or more of its sides, and the cult room situated at the back of the mastaba. The main element of the cult room was a stela, usually placed on the central east–west axis of the tomb, while there were often further stelae and statues in other parts of the mastaba. A small pyramid was usually built above the cult room. The mouth of the shaft leading to the underground burial chamber opened into the court.

The tombs of Apis bulls. The cult of the Apis bull was closely connected with that of the chief Memphite god Ptah. From the reign of Amenophis III onwards the tombs of the mummified Apis bulls are known from the Serapeum at Saqqara.

The Late and Greco-Roman Periods

Private tombs. During the 26th Dynasty the designers of Egyptian tombs apparently achieved what they had vainly attempted for the previous two millennia: they designed an almost completely safe tomb. In many Saqqara tombs of this period a vaulted burial chamber was built at the bottom of a very large and deep shaft which was subsequently filled with sand. Somewhat paradoxically, removing the enormous mass of this unstable material from the shaft presented the tomb robbers with much greater technical difficulties than cutting through or around the stone blocking of the shafts of the earlier periods. The other type of tomb known from this period is the more conventional rock-cut tomb.

The majority of the tombs of the Late and Greco-Roman Periods are near the Step Pyramid enclosure: (1) to the north, approximately along the avenue of sphinxes leading to the Serapeum: mainly 30th Dynasty and Greco-Roman; (2) to the east, particularly shaft tombs in the area of the pyramid of Userkaf, with rock-cut tombs further east, in the face of the cliff: mainly 26th Dynasty; (3) to the west: mainly Greco-Roman; (4) to the south, and close to the pyramid of Wenis: mainly 26th and 27th Dynasties, but also a large Ptolemaic tomb.

The Serapeum and other parts of the sacred animal necropolis. The Apis bulls were by far the most important cult animals buried at Saqqara. Already during the New Kingdom Ramesses II abandoned the earlier isolated tombs and started an underground gallery (the so-called Lesser Vaults) in which the mummified bodies of Apis bulls were deposited in large niches on either side. As there was only one of these animals at a time, an Apis bull burial occurred about once every 14 years. The

gallery of Ramesses II ultimately reached a length of 68 m. A second gallery (the so-called Greater Vaults), cut at right angles to the earlier one, was inaugurated during the 26th Dynasty, and the first Apis bull laid to rest there died in year 52 of Psammetichus I. This gallery, of a total length of 198 m, remained in use until the Greco-Roman Period.

A complex of chapels and smaller temples grew up in the neighborhood of the catacombs of Apis bulls, together forming the Serapeum (from *Usir-Hapy*, i.e. the deceased Apis bull, Greek Osorapis, later identified with the artificially introduced god Sarapis of the Ptolemies). Nectanebo I and II of the 30th Dynasty were the two most distinguished contributors, the former probably also setting up the alley of human-headed sphinxes that approached the Serapeum from the city of Memphis, in the east, below the Saqqara plateau. It is said that in 1850 one of these sphinxes, which was visible above the sand, gave Auguste Mariette the idea that the Serapeum mentioned by Classical authors should be sought at Saqqara. New unpublished evidence indicates that the English antiquarian A. C. Harris came to the same conclusion several years earlier.

At the eastern end of the alley of sphinxes, immediately adjoining the city of Memphis, there were temples, among them the famous Anubieion and the Asklepieion, most of which were built by the Ptolemies. In the vicinity were cemeteries of mummified jackals and cats.

The excavations conducted since 1964 by the Egypt Exploration Society near the northwestern edge of the Saqqara necropolis have revealed galleries of the mummified "Mother of the Apis" cows, falcons, ibises and baboons.

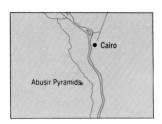

Below Abusir from the northeast: the pyramid of Sahure' in the foreground, followed by those of Neuserre' and Neferirkare', with the remains of Ra'neferef's structure at the back. This aerial view was taken before the excavations of the Czechoslovak Institute of Egyptology (still in progress).

Right Cultivation extends close to the valley temples, though there are still the long ascending causeways to climb before one reaches the pyramids. That of Sahure' measures about 230 m, but the unfinished causeway of Neferirkare' was planned to be almost twice as long.

Abusir

The sun temple

The northernmost monument at Abusir, halfway between Abu Ghurab and the Abusir pyramids and isolated from all other buildings, is the sun temple built by King Userkaf. This is the earliest preserved sun temple in Egypt, so its simplicity and lack of relief decoration come as no surprise; but Userkaf's reign of only seven years did not allow him to complete the temple. Some Egyptian texts write its name with a hieroglyphic sign showing only an obelisk base surrounded by an enclosure wall. This seems to indicate that the obelisk itself was a later feature, and the excavation and architectural study of the temple undertaken by H. Ricke and G. Haeny between 1954 and 1957 indeed show this to be the case. Altogether four building phases of the upper part of the temple can be discerned, the first three of them dating to the 5th Dynasty.

Some uncertainty remains attached to the lower part of the monument, the so-called valley temple. A suggestion has been made (by S. Schott and H. Ricke) that this structure was connected with the cult of the goddess Neith, who originated in the delta but became very popular in the Memphite area during the Old Kingdom. Her common Memphite epithets were ''North-of-the-Wall'' (presumably indicating that her sanctuary in this region was situated north of the town wall of the capital Memphis) and ''Opener-of-the-Ways'' (a reference to her bellicose character, a ''path-finder''). Her temple has not yet been positively located. Absence of any inscriptional evidence from Abusir referring to Neith, however, demands that the problem be approached with caution.

The pyramids

The founder of the 5th Dynasty, Userkaf, built his pyramid at Saqqara, but four of the next five kings moved to Abusir (the pyramid of Shepseskare' has not yet been located).

The pyramid complex of Sahure' was a magnificent structure both in size and in its decoration. Its plan can serve as a typical example of Egyptian royal funerary architecture of the 5th Dynasty. The basic building material throughout its temples was local limestone, with finer limestone from the quarries at Tura (ferried across the river from the east bank) employed for reliefs, red granite from Aswan used for columns, door jambs and lintels, and black basalt for pavements. The pyramid also was built of local limestone, with Tura limestone reserved for its outer casing and the lining of passages, and granite used for some of its interior elements. The quality of the core masonry was very poor; it was originally concealed behind the outer casing, and this saved labor. As a result, however, the structure is now little more than a huge pile of rubble.

Although most of the limestone relief decoration and inscriptions from the temples were turned into lime by industrious entrepreneurs of later times (only a little more than one hundredth of the original 10,000 square m of decoration has been preserved), the fragmentary scenes are spectacular in their subject matter as well as their technical accomplishment. It is true that the decoration of none of the earlier pyramid temples has been preserved to any significant degree, so that comparative material is lacking, but all the same it is certain that the architects and artists employed in building the pyramid complex of Sahure' were faced with entirely new problems. Their solutions set the standard for many generations to come.

The theme of the reliefs is the king himself, his

King Userkaf or the goddess Neith? An almost perfectly preserved head of a graywacke statue wearing the Egyptian red crown, found near the sun temple. This type of headdress was worn by the king, but also by the goddess Neith; the former seems a more likely identification. Cairo, Egyptian Museum.

worldly activities and achievements as well as scenes characterizing his position in relation to the gods. Perhaps the most remarkable are the large wall compositions showing Sahure' shooting desert animals with a bow and arrows and Egyptian seagoing boats returning from an Asiatic expedition. The technique of the scenes is the best "low" raised relief (painted, as was always the practice) in which figures and texts project only a few millimeters above the surface of the stone.

The pyramid complexes of Neferirkare' and Neuserre' have suffered even more than that of their predecessor. Neferirkare' designed his funerary complex on a larger scale than Sahure', but did not succeed in completing it; indeed, its unfinished lower part was later appropriated by Neuserre', who diverted the causeway to his own pyramid temple. There is no tangible evidence which would identify the remains of the fourth pyramid, which is generally regarded as belonging to Ra'neferef. Nevertheless, the name of Ra'neferef's pyramid is mentioned in Egyptian texts and the identification, though not certain, is very probably correct.

The exploration of the pyramids at Abusir was carried out by L. Borchardt at the beginning of this century.

The mastaba tombs

Among the private tombs at Abusir by far the most important is the family mastaba of Ptahshepses, the vizier (the highest state official) and son-in-law of Neuserre'. It is one of the largest private tombs of the Old Kingdom, so much so that in the first half of the 19th century C. R. Lepsius numbered it as his nineteenth Egyptian pyramid. The mastaba has recently been excavated by the Czechoslovak Institute of Egyptology.

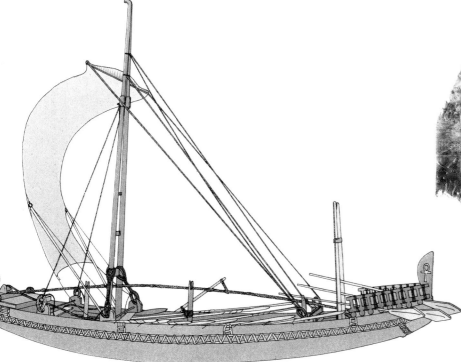

Although the mortuary temple of Sahure' produced the earliest pictorial record of Egyptian seagoing boats, their sophisticated features point to a long period of maritime activities before that (their appearance is shown here in a reconstruction). In particular, in the absence of a keel, Egyptian boats had to rely on a hogging truss (a cable connecting the prow and the stern of the vessel) for longitudinal rigidity. Old Kingdom representations of seagoing boats are rare: in addition to these only reliefs from the causeway of Wenis and another reused at el-Lisht are known. East Berlin Museum.

Abu Ghurab

The rulers of the 5th Dynasty, with the exception of the last two, expressed their preference for the Heliopolitan sun god Re' by building special temples designed for his worship. The names of altogether six of these temples are known from Egyptian texts but the remains of only two have so far been located by archaeologists.

The sun temple built by King Neuserre' at Abu Ghurab is a splendid example of this type of building, and one unlikely to be surpassed even if the four as yet unaccounted for are found in the future. In its general features it owes much to the typical pyramid complex of the same period. Its main axis is east–west and it consists of:
(1) the valley temple (close to a canal, so that it could be approached by boat)

(2) the causeway (linking the valley temple with the upper part of the complex)
(3) the upper temple.

The dominant feature of the upper temple was a large open court with an altar and a masonry-built (not monolithic) obelisk, the symbol of the sun god. A corridor around the temple and the chapel south of the obelisk were decorated with scenes showing the king taking part in the ceremonies of the *sed* festival. Much more unusual were, however, scenes in the ''Room of the Seasons.'' The creative influence the sun god exerted on nature was expressed there by scenes characteristic of the Egyptian countryside in the *akhet* season (the inundation) and in the *shemu* season (the harvest). Reliefs of this type are very unusual in the royal monuments of the Old Kingdom, and are only partly paralleled by much less extensive representations in the pyramid complexes of the same king at Abusir and of Wenis at Saqqara.

Left Open court of the upper temple at Abu Ghurab from the east, with the obelisk base and the altar, and (*right*) the latter seen from the west. The unusually shaped alabaster altar consists of four *hetep* signs, each representing a simple offering mat with a loaf of bread placed on it; its diameter is some 6 m. The large calcite basins in the southeastern corner of the court belong to the slaughterhouse in the north, and may have served to catch the blood of sacrificed animals.

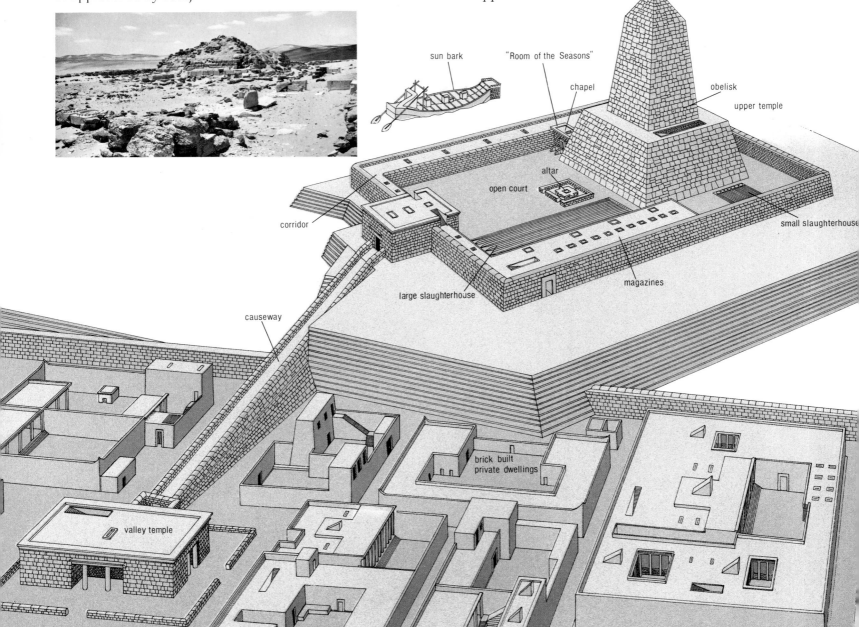

South of the upper temple was a brick-built imitation of the bark of the sun god (about 30 m long).

The temple, known to early travelers as the "Pyramid of Reegah," was uncovered by the German archaeologists Ludwig Borchardt, Heinrich Schäfer and F. W. von Bissing in 1898–1901, and its relief fragments were scattered among many museums and collections, mainly in Germany. Many of them perished during World War II. Drawings of those from the "Room of the Seasons" were published only recently, but their evaluation, nearly 80 years after their discovery, has not yet been completed.

Zawyet el-'Aryan

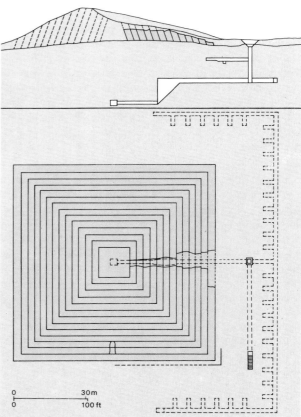

Plan and section of the "Layer Pyramid."

Below Egyptian countryside in summer (*shemu*), on a relief from the west wall of the "Room of the Seasons" at Abu Ghurab: mullet in water, and two registers of animals, some of them giving birth, including addax (upper register, 5th from left), oryx (upper register, 4th from left, also below), gazelle, with an ostrich (upper register); the hounds on the left of the lower register belong with the figure of a hunter, of which only a basket for carrying young captured animals which was slung over the shoulder remains. East Berlin Museum.

Neither of the two pyramids at Zawyet el-'Aryan was completed. The earlier one, the "Layer Pyramid," which was started as a step pyramid, is attributed to King Kha'ba of the 3rd Dynasty, while the other, the "Unfinished Pyramid," is dated to the 4th Dynasty by its more advanced architectural features.

One of the tombs near the pyramid of Kha'ba contained clay sealings and a pottery fragment with the name of the late Predynastic ruler Na'rmer.

Giza

The three Giza pyramids of the 4th Dynasty start looming on the horizon as soon as one has passed through the Cairo suburb which lent them its name and proceeds in a southwesterly direction along Shari'a al-Ahram (Avenue of the Pyramids). The history of the site, however, goes back much further, at least to the reign of King Ninetjer of the 2nd Dynasty, whose name occurs on some jar sealings found in a tomb in the southern part of the site. An even earlier tomb of the reign of King Wadj of the 1st Dynasty was located to the south of the area usually described as the Giza necropolis.

The present appearance of the site is the result of the natural configuration of the terrain combined with man's activities, in particular the quarrying of the local, fossil-rich limestone which was used as a building material for the pyramids and mastabas, and the leveling of the site by dumping builders' refuse. The most pronounced effects of the quarrying activities can be seen to the southeast of the pyramids of Khephren and Menkaure'.

The site falls naturally into two well-defined groups situated on higher ground and separated by a broad wadi. The first and much the larger and more important unit consists of the pyramids and the surrounding fields of private mastabas. The valley temples belonging to the pyramids, and the Great Sphinx with the adjacent temples, are situated below this elevated plateau. The smaller and less important group, containing only private tombs, is on a ridge to the southeast.

The systematic study of the site started in the first half of the 19th century. Among the early explorers the most prominent were Giovanni Battista Caviglia, Giovanni Battista Belzoni, R. W. Howard Vyse and J. S. Perring. C. R. Lepsius and the Prussian Expedition worked there in the early 1840s. Auguste Mariette and W. M. Flinders Petrie were active at the site in the second half of the last and at the beginning of this century. George Andrew Reisner, Hermann Junker and Selim Hassan, however, contributed more than anybody else to our knowledge of Giza. Although probably more systematically excavated than any other Egyptian site, its exploration cannot even now be regarded as completed.

The pyramid complex of Khufu

Khufu's pyramid, usually called the "Great Pyramid," must be one of the most famous monuments in the world. Its majestic size and perfection of construction have made it the focus of attention of visitors to the Memphite area since time immemorial. The pyramid was almost certainly robbed of its original contents during the period of political instability and social unrest which followed the collapse of the central royal power after

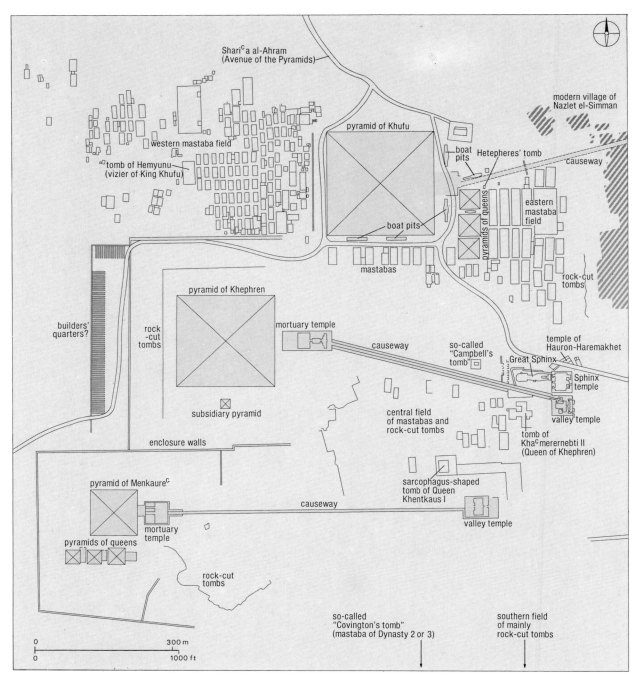

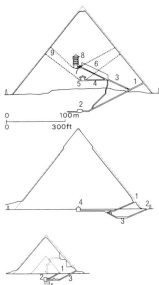

Above Sections of the pyramids looking west:
Khufu: 1 descending passage, 2 burial chamber of the 1st plan, 3 ascending passage, 4 level passage, 5 burial chamber of the 2nd plan ("Queen's Chamber"), 6 great gallery, 7 burial chamber of the 3rd plan ("King's Chamber"), 8 weight-relieving rooms, 9 "air shafts" (perhaps of religious significance).
Khephren: 1 upper entrance, 2 lower entrance, 3 burial chamber of the 1st plan, 4 burial chamber of the 2nd plan.
Menkaure': I abandoned descending passage of the 1st plan, 2 burial chamber of the 1st plan, 3 descending passage, 4 burial chamber of the 3rd plan.

the end of the Old Kingdom but definite evidence is lacking. Reuse of Khufu's decorated blocks started at el-Lisht during the reign of Amenemhet I. Modern explorers found the Great Pyramid empty, with only the massive granite sarcophagus in the burial chamber of the 3rd construction plan indicating its original purpose.

During the Middle Ages the outer limestone casing of the pyramid was completely stripped off, with the result that many buildings of old Giza and Cairo probably owe their stone material to the Great Pyramid. Today it is, apart from the small pyramids of Khufu's queens, the only element of the original pyramid complex which remains spectacularly obvious and, despite all spoliation, seems little affected. The valley temple is buried somewhere under the houses of the modern village of Nazlet el-Simman, and there is little chance of recovering it in the foreseeable future. The causeway, discernible on old maps of the site and still visible in the last century, also disappeared when the modern village

started growing. Only a patch of a basalt pavement against the east face of the pyramid shows the position of the pyramid temple. Khufu may not have succeeded in his plan to provide a safe place where his body might rest eternally, but he seems to have been completely successful in building an almost indestructible monument.

The interior of the Great Pyramid (see section) shows that the initial plan underwent at least two alterations in the process of the construction. The modern visitor enters the pyramid by an opening forced by Caliph Ma'amun's men in the 9th century AD, which is situated below and somewhat west of the original entrance. The descending passage leads to the burial chamber of the 1st plan below ground level. Before this could have been completed, the design was enlarged and altered in favor of the burial chamber of the 2nd plan, which is placed in the mass of the pyramid and approached by the ascending and level passages. Yet another change of the plan caused even this to be abandoned, and the

Right "There is no way to ruin it, but by beginning at the top. It rests upon a basis too firm to be attacked on that part; and whoever would undertake it, would find as much difficulty, as there was to raise it" (F. L. Norden, *Travels in Egypt and Nubia*, i, 1757, p. 72).

ascending passage was extended by the great gallery to reach the burial chamber of the 3rd plan. The great gallery, with its high corbeled ceiling, is easily the most impressive part of the whole interior. One of its purposes was probably to provide space for storing the granite blocks which were slid down the ascending passage after the funeral to seal it permanently. The frequent changes of plan are not so difficult to understand when one realizes that the architects were faced with the impossible task of being expected to have the complex ready to receive the burial when the king's death occurred, yet not being able to predict this "completion date" with any certainty.

Even nowadays building the Great Pyramid would present considerable technological and managerial problems. The project must have been more or less completed by the end of Khufu's 23-year reign, and that meant that every year 100,000 large blocks (i.e. about 285 a day), each weighing on average $2\frac{1}{2}$ tons, must have been quarried, dressed, brought to the building site and set in place. As the building progressed, the height to which it was necessary to lift the blocks increased, while at the same time the working platform at the top of the pyramid was rapidly decreasing in size. Once the project was "off the ground," transport of material was almost certainly exclusively effected by human force, because restricted space prevented the use of draft animals. Even such simple devices as the pulley or wheeled carriages were yet to be invented, and the problems connected with moving and lifting of heavy stone blocks must have been enormous. At least as many people as those actually dealing with the stone blocks must have been engaged in auxiliary works such as construction of inclined ramps along which the blocks were dragged, maintenance of tools, provision of food and water etc. Because of the uncertainty about the methods the Egyptians actually used, any estimate of the size of the labor force must remain a mere guess.

The sheer size of the task, the accuracy with which the structure was designed and built, the fact that no burial is on record as having ever been found in the Great Pyramid, and the seemingly absurd idea that the object of all this exercise would have been to provide a tomb for one individual, have worried scholars as well as amateurs for a long time. The interest does not seem to be abating even now but, unfortunately, not all "students" of the Great Pyramid adhere to strict scholarly methods; the esoteric approach to the pyramid is normally called "pyramidology." It would, however, be futile to maintain that Egyptologists have solved all problems connected with this or other pyramids.

A remarkable discovery was made in the early 1950s. A rectangular pit close to the south face of the pyramid of Khufu was found to contain parts of a dismantled wooden boat. In the airtight surroundings they remained almost perfectly preserved, and

Left The great gallery of Khufu's pyramid, as seen by the artists accompanying Napoleon's expedition. "You advance on with crouching. For though it is twenty-two feet in height, and has a raised way on each side, it is, however, so steep and slippery, that if you happen to fail of the holes, made for facilitating the ascent, you slide backwards, and return, in spite of yourself, quite to the resting place" (F. L. Norden, *Travels in Egypt and Nubia*, i, 1757, p. 79). Nowadays the "advance" is much easier.

Right One enters the valley temple of Khephren through one of the two doorways in its eastern facade: short passages lead into a transverse antechamber connected by another short passage with main T-shaped pillared hall.

Below When C. R. Lepsius and his team visited Giza in 1842–43, Khufu's causeway was still clearly visible. According to Herodotus the causeway was "all of stone polished and carven with figures"; although some decorated blocks have been found, his statement has not yet been fully confirmed.

the vessel, which is over 40 m long and has a displacement of about 40 tons, has now been reassembled, though it is not yet accessible to visitors. The location of another pit, almost certainly containing another boat, is known, but the pit is still to be opened. The boats were perhaps used to convey the body of the deceased king to the place of purification and embalmment and finally to the valley temple.

The pyramid complex of Khephren

Khufu's son and successor Ra'djedef started constructing his own pyramid at Abu Rawash, north of Giza, but the next king, Khephren, another son of Khufu, built his funerary complex beside his father's. Although it was designed on a more modest scale, a slight increase in the incline of the faces of the pyramid produced the effect of a structure comparable in size to the Great Pyramid. The pyramid (usually known as the "Second Pyramid") retains some of its original smooth outer casing near its summit, perhaps due to a change in the method of positioning the blocks.

The valley temple of Khephren's complex, next to the Great Sphinx, is a soberly designed building which, in the absence of almost any decoration, relies on the effect produced by the polished granite casing of the walls of its rooms and its calcite floors. A pit in one of the rooms contained a set of diorite-gneiss and graywacke sculptures of Khephren,

Left Khephren and Horus, the majesty of the pharaoh and his proximity to gods: an abstract concept expressed in stone. This type of sculpture was probably already introduced in the reign of Khufu, and certainly more than one piece was made for Khephren's temples. Epigones exist, but they all fade into nothingness in comparison. Diorite-gneiss. Height: 1·68 m. Cairo, Egyptian Museum.

Top right Menkaure' with Hathor "Lady of the Sycamore in all her Places (of worship)" and a personification of the 7th Upper Egyptian nome. Graywacke. Height: 96 cm. From the valley temple of Menkaure'. Cairo, Egyptian Museum.

Center right Restored columned portico of the family tomb of Seshemnefer, near the southeast corner of the pyramid of Khufu. Two seated statues and six small obelisks originally flanked the approach. End of the 5th or early 6th Dynasty.

Bottom right The dwarf Seneb with his wife Sentyotes and a small son and daughter. Painted limestone. Height: 33 cm. Mid-6th Dynasty or a little later. From Seneb's tomb west of the pyramid of Khufu. Cairo, Egyptian Museum.

Below "Reserve head" of an unknown lady. Limestone. Height: 25 cm. Reign of Khufu. From the tomb of Kanefer, west of the pyramid of Khufu. Berkeley (Ca.), Robert H. Lowie Museum of Anthropology.

deposited there in a later period, among them probably the most famous Egyptian statue, which shows the king seated with a hawk perched on the back of the throne.

The pyramid complex of Menkaure'

The pyramid complex of Menkaure', another king of the 4th Dynasty, is somewhat dwarfed by its two Giza companions. Although hastily finished in mud brick, its valley temple produced a superb collection of royal statues. Some of these were triads (groups of three figures) and showed the king accompanied by the Memphite goddess Hathor and personifications of nomes (provinces) of Egypt. There was also a standing double statue of the king and one of his wives, the earliest of this type in Egyptian sculpture.

The pyramid (known as the "Third Pyramid") was refurnished, probably during the 26th Dynasty when the cult of the kings buried at Giza was revived. The basalt sarcophagus found in the burial chamber was, unfortunately, lost at sea while being shipped to England so that its date cannot be verified, but remains of a wooden coffin, purporting to be that of Menkaure', were certainly put in the pyramid some 1,800 years later. An inscription discovered in 1968 on the remains of the casing near the entrance of the pyramid probably refers to this remarkable ancient effort of restoration.

Private tombs

Close to each pyramid complex there are fields of tombs of officials and priests. This proximity is explained by the fact that many of these tombs were presented by the king himself, built by royal craftsmen, and benefited from the redistribution of offerings brought to the nearby pyramid complexes. A large number of people buried in these tombs were connected with the Giza necropolis by priestly functions in their lifetime.

The most extensive mastaba fields are to the west, south and east of the pyramid of Khufu. The nuclei of the west and east fields, contemporary with the Great Pyramid, consist of stone-built mastabas of a uniform size and arranged in regular rows. These fields continued to be used through the rest of the Old Kingdom, with smaller tombs often being added in between the larger mastabas. The quarries to the southeast of the pyramids of Khephren and Menkaure', with their artificially created rock faces, provided ideal conditions for rock-cut tombs, the earliest of this type in Egypt.

A typical mastaba, such as was built at Giza in the reign of Khufu, had a stone-built superstructure with a rectangular plan and slightly sloping faces. A shaft sunk through this superstructure and cut in the rock substratum terminated in a simple burial chamber. This shaft was permanently sealed after the burial had been deposited in the chamber. The original cult chapel consisted of one or two brick-built rooms against the east face of the

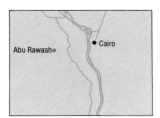

The Great Sphinx before the removal of the sand covering its body: a photograph taken before 1875.

mastaba. The main element of this primitive chapel was an inscribed slab stela with a representation of the deceased seated at a table and with a list of offerings. Offerings were brought for the *ka* (spirit) of the deceased before this stela on prescribed days. There were no other decorated elements in the tomb.

The mastabas at Giza were the earliest private stone-built tombs in Egypt, and so it is not surprising that the original simple design underwent a rapid development. The greatest changes occurred in the chapel. In some of the mastabas an interior chapel was introduced, i.e. the offering room and subsidiary rooms were contained in the core of the mastaba itself, while others continued to be built with an exterior chapel. The slab stela was replaced by a false door, and the walls of the chapel began to be lined with fine limestone and decorated with reliefs.

The chief royal wives were the only persons apart from the king himself who were granted the privilege of being buried in small pyramids, situated close to the main pyramidal structure. However, the tomb of Queen Hetepheres, the wife of Snofru and the mother of Khufu, which was found to the east of the Great Pyramid in 1925, lacked a superstructure of any kind and, indeed, the most important object in the tomb, the queen's mummy, was missing. The whole tomb gave the impression of being a rather hasty reburial, and one can only speculate as to whether the original tomb, perhaps near one of Snofru's pyramids at Dahshur, could have been plundered and the mummy of the queen destroyed.

The Great Sphinx
The concept of the sphinx, a creature with a human head and a lion's body, is not known from Egypt before the reign of Ra'djedef, Khephren's immediate predecessor. The perfection with which these two incongruous elements were blended on a huge scale in the Great Sphinx is admirable, but the idea behind this creation is still rather obscure. The temple in front of it bears some resemblance to the later sun temples built by the kings of the 5th Dynasty at Abu Ghurab and Abusir, but there is no evidence for the religious significance of the Great Sphinx during the Old Kingdom. It was only some 1,000 years later that the colossal statue started being identified with the god Harmakhis ("Horus on the Horizon").

The sand which tends to cover the Sphinx has had to be cleared several times. Probably the earliest clearance was undertaken by King Tuthmosis IV, who left a record of it on the so-called "Dream Stela" erected between its forepaws.

Giza after the end of the Old Kingdom
With the end of the Old Kingdom the heyday of Giza's glory was over, and for the next 600 years nothing of significance took place there. It was only

Left Sethos I embraced by a goddess, perhaps Isis, on the doorway to the outer hall of the temple of Harmakhis.

Below Lid of the basalt anthropoid sarcophagus of Ptahhotpe, a contemporary of Darius I. From "Campbell's Tomb," close to Khephren's causeway. Oxford, Ashmolean Museum.

in the New Kingdom that the site profited from the renewed importance of Memphis (Mit Rahina). King Amenophis II of the 18th Dynasty built a small brick temple for Harmakhis northeast of the Great Sphinx, and Sethos I later enlarged it. The site became a place of pilgrimage, and several kings and many private individuals dedicated their votive stelae there.

During the 21st Dynasty the chapel of the southern of the queens' pyramids in the Khufu complex was reconstructed into a temple of Isis "Mistress-of-the-Pyramid." The temple was enlarged during the 26th Dynasty, and the refurnishing of the burial in the Third Pyramid might have been due to the priests of this temple. Several large isolated tombs of this period are scattered along the causeway of Khephren, and doorways leading to the plundered remains of others can be seen in the rock face west of the Great Sphinx.

Abu Rawash

The site, which took its name from the village of Abu Rawash situated to the east, served as the necropolis for an important administrative center as early as the very beginning of Egyptian history. Excavations have revealed objects inscribed with the names of two kings of the 1st Dynasty, 'Aha and Den.

King Ra'djedef, who chose the commanding plateau of Abu Rawash for the site of his pyramid complex, did not therefore move on to virgin ground. The pyramid is the northernmost in the Memphite necropolis, and remains of building material visible at the site indicate that it was planned to be at least partly cased with red granite. The causeway, about 1,500 m long, approaches the pyramid and its temple from the northeast instead of from the customary east, but this was determined by the character of the terrain rather than any religious considerations. Because Ra'djedef reigned

for only eight years, his funerary monument hardly got beyond the initial stages of its construction. Its most important parts have been excavated, but the burial chamber has not been reached in modern times.

Despite its incompleteness the pyramid complex gave us some excellent examples of royal sculpture of the first half of the 4th Dynasty, though even these are sadly fragmentary. The statues are made of the hard red quartzite of Gebel Ahmar (east of modern Cairo). Apart from providing us with the probably somewhat idealized features of the king, one of them is an attractive seated statue with a small figure of Ra'djedef's queen Khentetka shown kneeling holding the leg of her husband. Although eagerly taken up by makers of private statues, this type was not repeated in royal sculpture.

The site of Abu Rawash never regained its short-lived importance under Ra'djedef. However, one of the several late structures at Wadi Qaren, north of the pyramid, yielded the upper part of a beautiful statuette of Queen Arsinoe II, the sister and wife of Ptolemy II Philadelphus.

Above When discovered during the excavations of the Institut Français d'Archéologie Orientale by F. Bisson de la Roque in 1922–23, this alabaster head of Arsinoe II still possessed an equally attractive torso, now lost. Present height: 12·2 cm. New York, Metropolitan Museum of Art.

Right Quartzite head of King Ra'djedef wearing the royal *nemes* headcloth with the uraeus: the best-preserved of many fragments of at least 20 statues, originally painted. Found by E. Chassinat in 1900–01. Height: 28 cm. Paris, Musée du Louvre.

LOWER EGYPT–THE DELTA

Top Silver coffin of Psusennes I, from San el-Hagar. Cairo, Egyptian Museum.

Center Granite naos of Amasis at Tell el-Rub'a.

Bottom Remains of the temples at San el-Hagar.

The delta's most ancient history is still buried deep under the silt and little known, but no one doubts the antiquity of its towns or its economic importance from the very earliest times.

The eastern delta was the sensitive shoulder which Egypt rubbed with Asia. At the end of the Middle Kingdom it was overrun by Asiatics; later it became the Egyptian base for campaigns to Asia.

When the royal residence was moved to Pi-Ri'amsese in the 19th Dynasty, the delta took over the leadership from the rest of Egypt. Several of its towns saw their rulers at the helm of Egypt during the 3rd Intermediate and Late Periods. Its proximity to the political and economic centers of the ancient world favored the delta's development under the Ptolemies and the Romans.

Ausim
Scattered Late Period monuments.
Kom Abu Billo
Early Ptolemaic temple of Hathor.
Necropolis with burials from 6th
Dynasty to early centuries AD.
Kom el-Hisn
Temple of Sakhmet-Hathor of
Middle Kingdom and later.
Cemeteries of Middle and New
Kingdoms.
Naukratis
Greek trading town, with
temples of Greek gods, as well as
Amun and Thoth.
Alexandria
Ptolemaic and Roman temple of
Sarapis (Serapeum).
Catacombs with sculpture and
relief decoration, including Kom
el-Shuqafa.
Many fragmentary Classical
remains.
Abusir (Taposiris Magna)
Unfinished Ptolemaic temple.
Animal necropolis.
Sa el-Hagar
Few visible remains of temple of
Neith, but many objects in
museums.
Tell el-Fara'in
Three mounds, two with town
remains, one with temple
enclosure.
Behbeit el-Hagar
Temple of Isis of Late and
Ptolemaic Periods.
Tell Atrib
Temple of Amasis.
Town, temples and necropolis of
Greco-Roman Period.
Tomb of Queen Takhut.
Tell el-Muqdam
Remains of temple of Mihos.
Tomb of Queen Kamama.
Samannud
Remains of temple of Onuris-
Shu, of Late and Greco-Roman
Periods.
el-Baqliya
Town and temple of Thoth at
Tell el-Naqus.
Necropolis with cemetery of
ibises at Tell el-Zereiki.
Other remains at Tell el-Rub'a.
Tell el-Rub'a and Tell el-Timai
Late Old Kingdom mastabas,
temple of Amasis and cemetery
of rams at Tell el-Rub'a.
Greco-Roman Period structures
at Tell el-Timai.

Heliopolis
Temple of Re' and ancillary
structures of all periods at Tell
Hisn, with obelisk of
Senwosret I.
Tombs of High Priests of
Heliopolis of 6th Dynasty and
others of Late Period.
Ramessid tombs of Mnevis bulls
at 'Arab el-Tawil.
Tell el-Yahudiya
Earthwork enclosure of late
Middle Kingdom or 2nd
Intermediate Period, containing
temple and palace of Ramesses II.
Remains of temple and town of
Onias.
Cemeteries of Middle Kingdom
and later.
Tell Basta
Temple of Bastet by Osorkon II
and others.
Smaller temples of 6th, 12th,
18th and 22nd Dynasties and
Greco-Roman Period.
Cemeteries of animals, especially
cats.
Saft el-Hinna
Temple enclosure of Sopd.
el-Khata'na and Qantir
Mounds indicating settlements of
Middle Kingdom, 2nd
Intermediate and Ramessid
Periods.
Remains of 12th-Dynasty chapel
at Tell el-Qirqafa.
Temple of Seth at Tell el-Dab'a
(Avaris?).
Middle Kingdom town and
temple at Ezbet Rushdi el-
Saghira.
Palace of 19th and 20th Dynasties
at Qantir (Pi-Ri'amsese?).
Remains of colossus of Ramesses
II at Tell Abu el-Shafi'a.
Tell Nabasha
Enclosure with Ramessid temple
of Wadjit and temple by Amasis.
Remains of Greco-Roman town.
Cemetery of Late Period.
San el-Hagar
Enclosure with temple of Amun
by Psusennes I and others, with
ancillary buildings.
Precinct of Mut, built by
Siamun, Apries and Ptolemy IV
Philopator.
Six royal tombs of 21st and 22nd
Dynasties.
Tell el-Maskhuta
Temple enclosure.

MEDITERRANEAN SEA

	primary road
	track
	principal railroad (1·44m)
Ⓐ	civil airport
	major town
Beni Suef	
□ Biba	other settlement
● el-Kab	featured site
△ Seila	pyramid site
▽ Kubri	stela site
● Dara	other site
▣ Ghita	settlement with sites
Faqus	modern name
TANIS	classical name
IMET	ancient Egyptian name
Pithom	biblical name

scale 1 : 1 000 000

0 ——— 20 ——— 40 km

0 ——— 10 ——— 20 mi

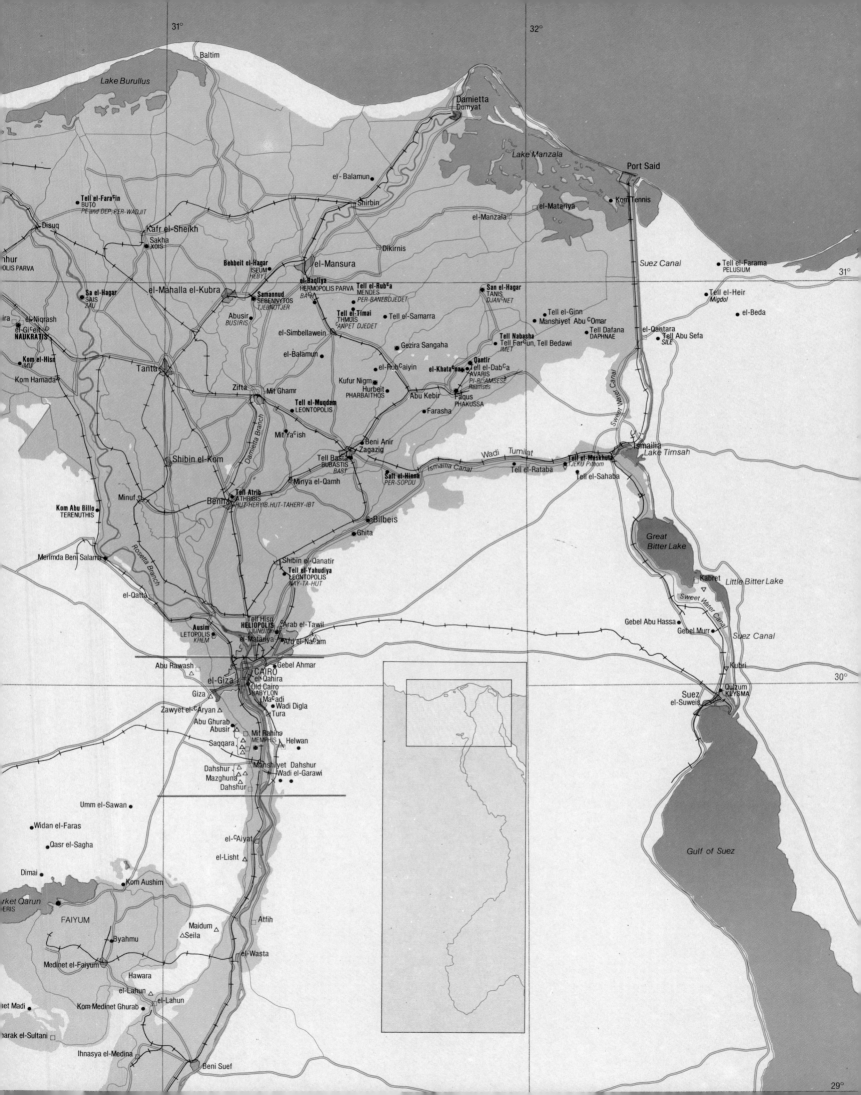

Ausim

Ancient Egyptian *Khem* (Greek Letopolis), some 13 km northwest of modern Cairo, was the capital of the 2nd Lower Egyptian nome. The nome and its falcon god Khenty-irty (a form of Horus, also referred to as Khenty-Khem, ''The Foremost One of *Khem*'') are mentioned in Egyptian texts as early as the 4th Dynasty, but so far only a few late monuments, bearing the names of Necho II, Psammetichus II, Hakoris and Nectanebo I, have been found at the site.

Kom Abu Billo

At the point where the route leading from Wadi Natrun approaches the Rosetta branch of the Nile, there lies the town of Tarrana (from Coptic *Terenouti* and classical Terenuthis). The name derives from that of the serpent goddess Renenutet (Termuthis) who was probably worshiped in the area. The remains of the temple and the necropolis have been found nearby, at the mound of Kom Abu Billo.

The temple of Kom Abu Billo, dedicated to Hathor ''Mistress of Mefket'' (ancient Tarrana, but *mefket* also means turquoise), was located by F. Ll. Griffith in 1887–88. It was not possible to establish its complete plan, but blocks decorated with exquisite low raised relief showed it to be one of the few surviving works of Ptolemy I Soter, completed by Ptolemy II Philadelphus. Burials of cattle in the vicinity are probably connected with the cult of Hathor.

The large necropolis of Kom Abu Billo contains burials ranging from the 6th Dynasty to the 4th century AD. A number of New Kingdom pottery sarcophagi (called ''slipper coffins''), with their lids modeled to imitate often very grotesque faces, have been found. The site is particularly well known for a special type of tomb stela dating to the first four centuries AD (called ''Terenuthis stelae''). The deceased, represented in un-Egyptian style, is usually standing with upraised arms or reclining on a couch, with a short text in demotic or Greek below.

Kom el-Hisn

A large mound, measuring some 500 m across, called Kom el-Hisn, covers the remains of the ancient town of *Imu*. From the New Kingdom onwards this was the capital of the 3rd Lower Egyptian nome,

replacing the earlier *Hut-ihyt*, which has not yet been located.

The most important feature at Kom el-Hisn is the rectangular outline of a temple enclosure (about 115 by 64 m). Statues of Amenemhet III and Ramesses II found there identify the temple as belonging to Sakhmet-Hathor. Hathor was the traditional goddess of the area.

The tomb of the ''Overseer of Prophets'' Khesuwer of the Middle Kingdom was found southwest of the temple enclosure.

Extensive cemeteries (at least 700 graves) of the Middle and New Kingdoms have been excavated in the vicinity. Many of the Middle Kingdom burials of men contained weapons (battle-axes, spears and daggers).

Naukratis

A mound near the villages el-Gi'eif, el-Nibeira and el-Niqrash (the last perhaps preserving the ancient name), in the 5th (Saite) nome of Lower Egypt, is the site of the Greek trading post Naukratis. The Greeks (initially Milesians) settled in the area some time during the 26th Dynasty, and under Amasis the town was granted a monopoly of Greek trade.

Naukratis contained several temples of Greek

Above Early Ptolemaic reliefs from Kom Abu Billo: Hathor, in Bolton Museum and Art Gallery, and Ptolemy I Soter, in Oxford, Ashmolean Museum.

Below Basalt royal head, probably of Amenemhet III, found in the tomb of Khesuwer at Kom el-Hisn, though originally from the temple nearby. The identification rests on the discovery of another sculpture of Amenemhet III in the temple. Height: 35 cm. Cairo, Egyptian Museum.

Right Alexandria. The necropolis areas are quite well preserved, being away from the center and mostly cut in the rock underground. The city center, however, has been constantly rebuilt, and land reclaimed from the sea.

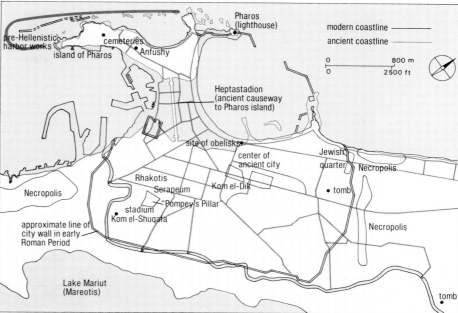

Below Excavated area of Naukratis.

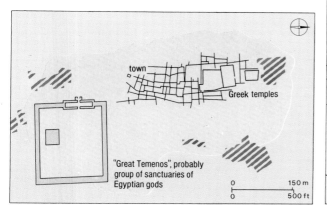

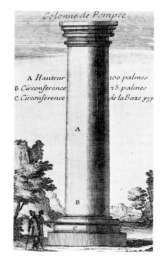

Above Engraving of "Pompey's pillar" in the Serapeum at Alexandria (reign of Diocletian), from Gemelli Careri, *Voyage du tour du monde*, i, Paris, 1729, p. 36. All the picture – evidently the engraver's free invention – records is dimensions; form and proportions are different from those of the original, and the scene is a landscape of European inspiration, not part of a Near Eastern city.

Right Painted tomb near Kom el-Shuqafa in Alexandria, c. 2nd century AD. The ornamentation is Classical, but the main scene is Egyptian-inspired, showing a winged disk above the mummy on a bier, with two mourning figures and two kites; both these pairs derive from Isis and Nephthys.

gods but also an Egyptian temple, dedicated probably to Amun and Thoth, in its southern part. Hardly anything of these monuments can be seen nowadays.

Alexandria

In the Egyptian language Alexandria was called Raqote, a name that was used by Ptolemy I Soter in a text inscribed before he was proclaimed king in 305, and was taken over from an Egyptian settlement on the site. Apart from Raqote, pre-Ptolemaic sea walls that have been found under water north and west of the island of Pharos are of quite uncertain date. A quarter of the city continued to be called Rhakotis by the Greek population. It was one of those where native Egyptians lived, and contained monuments in an Egyptian style. A second native quarter was a walled settlement on Pharos, near which are Egyptianizing tombs of the late Ptolemaic Period. Among the lower classes there was widespread intermarriage between Greeks and Egyptians, but otherwise Alexandria was a Greek city of very mixed population, whose most important non-Greek element was the Jewish community. As the chief city and port of the Hellenistic world it did, however, play a vital part in the dissemination of Egyptian lore in Classical antiquity.

The Serapeum, the most important temple of the Greco-Egyptian god Sarapis, was in the quarter of Rhakotis. Bilingual plaques date its foundation to the reign of Ptolemy III Euergetes I. The present remains, including the famous "Pompey's pillar" of the reign of Diocletian, date mainly to the first centuries AD, but incorporate a considerable amount of pharaonic Egyptian material, most notably sphinxes and other large sculpture, whose function will have been to set the scene. Objects like these, and numerous smaller pieces, were also exported, no doubt through Alexandria, to be used in Roman temples of Sarapis and Isis, or in the grounds of Hadrian's villa at Tivoli and Diocletian's palace at Split. The monuments in which they were placed were not in an Egyptian style.

Near the Serapeum is the catacomb of Kom el-Shuqafa. It dates to the 1st–2nd century AD, and contains a remarkable complex of burial areas with Egyptianizing scenes and motifs. Chambers near ground level have retained some painted decoration, while only sculpture and relief remain in the deeper parts. Unlike the tomb of Petosiris at Tuna el-Gebel, which has Grecizing scenes by Egyptian artists, the catacomb has Egyptian motifs in a simplified Classical style. For the Isis cult such work was influential in the Roman world at large, starting by running parallel with the use of genuine Egyptian objects and ending by assuming greater importance. The style was probably Alexandrian in origin.

Abusir

About 45 km west of Alexandria is Abusir, ancient Taposiris Magna, an important town in the Ptolemaic Period, which has an unfinished temple in native Egyptian style. The enclosure is in limestone instead of the traditional mud brick, but uses mud-brick building techniques. The east side of the enclosure wall is in the form of an entrance pylon. The temple is uninscribed, and so cannot be dated precisely. Nearby was a large animal necropolis, which is a further indication of the town's significance as a native center.

The Chief of Physicians Psammetik-seneb kneeling with a naos of Neith: basalt statue originally set up in the temple of the goddess at Sa el-Hagar. Heavily restored, probably in the 18th century. Height: 63 cm. 26th Dynasty. Vatican, Museo Gregoriano Egizio.

Sa el-Hagar

Sais (ancient Egyptian *Zau*) and its goddess Neith are known from the very beginning of Egyptian history. The town was the capital of the 5th Lower Egyptian nome, which until the 12th Dynasty also incorporated the area south of it, later the 4th nome. Politically, Sais came to prominence only towards the end of the 8th century BC when its ambitious local princes Tefnakhte and Bocchoris (24th Dynasty) clashed with the rulers of the 25th (Nubian) Dynasty. During the 26th Dynasty it was the capital of the country, with temples, royal palaces and tombs of the kings of the Saite Dynasty. Some idea about its topography can be gleaned from the remarks of Herodotus, who wrote in the middle of the 5th century BC.

Despite the city's famous past, no monuments except some isolated stone blocks are visible in the area nowadays. Even at the end of the last century it was still possible to trace remains of a huge rectangular enclosure (some 800 by 700 m, according to the plan published by G. Foucart in 1898) north of the village of Sa el-Hagar, on the right bank of the Rosetta branch of the Nile. Fifty years earlier, in the middle of the last century, the artists of Lepsius's expedition recorded a view of the sizable remains of the walls. The relatively recent but very quick disappearance of the enclosure was due to the activities of the *sabbakhin* who look for old mud-brick structures as a source of cheap fertilizer. Stone blocks had already been removed to be used as building material in the Middle Ages. It has been possible to locate some of them in various towns and villages along the Rosetta branch.

There is a substantial number of monuments, such as statues, stelae, sarcophagi etc., in museums whose texts show them to come from Sais. The great majority of them date to the 26th Dynasty, and none so far is earlier than the 3rd Intermediate Period.

Sa el-Hagar has been little explored by archaeologists, and the few small excavations have not been very successful.

Tell el-Fara'in

Tell el-Fara'in ("The Mound of the Pharaohs"), in the 6th Lower Egyptian nome, is the site of Buto (from ancient Egyptian *Per-Wadjit*, "The Domain of Wadjit," Coptic *Pouto*). The town was held to have consisted of two parts, called *Pe* and *Dep*, and was the home of the cobra goddess Wadjit, the tutelary goddess of Lower Egypt. In this it was paralleled by Upper Egyptian *Nekheb* (el-Kab) and *Nekhen* (Kom el-Ahmar) and the vulture goddess Nekhbet. "The

Souls of Pe," falcon-headed figures connected with Buto, may have represented the early local rulers ("Lower Egyptian kings") of the area.

The site of Tell el-Fara'in consists of three mounds, two with town remains and one with a temple enclosure. This corresponds to the expected layout of Buto, but the results of excavations carried out so far do not suggest that the town's size was commensurate with its ideological importance throughout Egyptian history. Apart from one Early Dynastic cylinder seal there are a few objects of the ubiquitous Ramesses II and a donation stela of year 38 of Shoshenq V; the rest are Late Period pieces of little significance.

Above Offering-bearers from the tomb of Harhotpe at Tell el-Fara'in, probably of the 30th Dynasty. Cairo, Egyptian Museum.

Below The ruins of Sa el-Hagar as seen by the artists of Lepsius's expedition in 1842.

Below A typical temple statue: Djeho, son of Neb'ankh and Hetepher, kneeling with a naos containing a statuette of Osiris. Hard black stone. Height: 54 cm. Ptolemaic. No recorded provenance, but according to its inscriptions certainly from Tell Atrib. Lisbon, Fundação Calouste Gulbenkian.

Early Ptolemaic granite relief from the temple of Isis at Behbeit el-Hagar, showing the king censing before a god with hawk's head and lunar disk, perhaps Khons, with parts of further scenes on either side. Richmond (Va.), Museum of Fine Arts.

classical image of Egypt. When temples to Isis were built, especially in Rome in the early empire, they were often adorned with them. Monuments of the Nectanebos and of Isis appear to have been particularly favored, and a block from this temple was found in the chief Isis temple in Rome.

Behbeit el-Hagar

Behbeit el-Hagar is the site of one of the most important temples of Isis in Egypt. It is near Samannud (ancient Sebennytos), the home town of the kings of the 30th Dynasty, who were reputed to have a special devotion to Isis. It is likely that the foundation dates to that period, or that a large temple was built on the site of an unimportant predecessor.

The temple is like many Late Period monuments in being built in hard stone, in this case granite, but it is the only remaining example of a structure of this size that uses only hard stone. The ruins occupy an area 80 by 55 m, and are set in an enclosure of which two sides can still be distinguished. The temple itself, however, has collapsed completely, either through quarrying activities or after an earthquake, and its plan has not been recovered; all that is visible is a disorderly mass of relief blocks and some architectural elements. The reliefs are very fine work of Nectanebo I–II and of Ptolemy II Philadelphus and III Euergetes I, much more delicate than that of the Greco-Roman temples of Upper Egypt. Reliefs in this style and material played an important part in formulating the

Tell Atrib

Tell Atrib, north of the town of Benha on the right bank of the Damietta branch of the Nile, derives its name from ancient Egyptian *Hut-hery-ib* (or *Hut-ta-hery-ibt*), Coptic *Athrebi* and Greek Athribis. It was the capital of the 10th Lower Egyptian nome, and the name *Kem-wer* ("The Great Black One," i.e. bull) could equally be applied to the local god, the nome and its capital. In the Dynastic Period the crocodile (or falcon) god Khentekhtai became the most prominent local deity.

Egyptian texts show that the history of Tell Atrib goes back at least to the beginning of the 4th Dynasty, but the remains of the earliest temple found there are dated by foundation deposits to the reign of Amasis. A town, temples and necropolis of the Greco-Roman Period have also been located. The topography of the little-excavated Tell Atrib still presents difficulties. Isolated monuments of various dates are known from, or have been ascribed to, Tell Atrib on the basis of their inscriptions, though none of them is earlier than the 12th Dynasty. As with all delta sites, caution is required when dealing with objects which might have been brought from elsewhere and reused. Many monuments have been found by the *sabbakhin* whose activities have seriously affected the site: in 1924 a large cache (some 50 kg) of silver treasure consisting of ingots, amulets, rings, earrings etc., dating to the 25th–30th Dynasties, was discovered by them. Other monuments have been uncovered accidentally by peasants or workmen, e.g. the tombs of Queen Takhut (wife of Psammetichus II), of a woman called Tadubaste, and Pefteu'awyamun Tjaiemhorimu of the Late Period, all in the north part of the tell.

Uninscribed statue of the 12th Dynasty from Tell Atrib. Granite. Height: 63·5 cm. London, British Museum.

Tell el-Muqdam

Some of the most extensive man-made mounds of earth in the Egyptian delta are on the right bank of the Damietta branch of the Nile, about 10 km southeast of Mit Ghamr, at Tell el-Muqdam. This is the site of ancient Leontopolis, an important town in the 11th Lower Egyptian nome and its capital during the Ptolemaic Period. There are indications that Tell el-Muqdam was the seat of a line of kings of

the 23rd Dynasty and perhaps their burial place, but so far only the tomb of Queen Kamama, the mother of Osorkon IV, has been found.

The temple of the local lion god Mihos (Greek Miysis), situated in the east part of the ruins, suffered the fate of many similar buildings in the delta: most of its stone blocks have been removed and reused, leaving even the date of the structure uncertain. Another tell in the neighborhood, Mit Ya'ish, has produced material of the 22nd Dynasty (a stela of Osorkon III) and of the Ptolemaic Period.

Some monuments (particularly statues) of earlier dates have been found usurped by later rulers and probably removed from their original places. At Tell el-Muqdam this certainly applies to the statue of a 14th- (or 13th-) Dynasty king Nehesy, usurped by Merneptah, and possibly to others, particularly some of Senwosret III. The number of monuments found in controlled excavations is small, but the original provenance of others (from the reign of Ramesses II or earlier) can be established from their inscriptions and other indications. Many objects, particularly statuettes of lions in bronze and other materials, which used to be in D. M. Fouquet's private collection, dispersed in 1922, derived from Tell el-Muqdam.

the remains of the temple of the local god Onuris-Shu. The granite blocks bear the names of Nectanebo II, Alexander IV, Philip Arrhidaeus and Ptolemy II Philadelphus. Some earlier monuments are said to have come from Samannud or its neighborhood, including an Old Kingdom false door of a certain Sesni, an altar of Amenemhet I, a statue dated to Psammetichus I, a fragment of a shrine of Nepherites (probably I) and sculpture of the reign of Nectanebo I. No blocks or other architectural elements of buildings earlier than the 30th Dynasty have been reported.

Samannud

Ancient *Tjebnutjer* (Coptic *Djebenoute* or *Djemnouti*, Greek Sebennytos), now on the left bank of the Damietta branch of the Nile, was the capital of the 12th Lower Egyptian nome and a town of some importance towards the end of the pharaonic period: according to Manetho, himself a native of Sebennytos, the kings of the 30th Dynasty came from there.

A large mound west of the modern town marks

el-Baqliya

South of the modern village el-Baqliya, three low mounds, rising only a few meters above the cultivated land, mark the site of the ancient *Ba'h* (Hermopolis Parva of the Greco-Roman Period), the capital of the 15th Lower Egyptian nome.

Tell el-Naqus probably covers the town and the temple of the local god Thoth. Outlines of an enclosure measuring some 350 by 384 m are visible,

Above Bronze inlay of the animal sacred to the god Mihos, originally probably part of a piece of temple furniture; early Ptolemaic, from Tell el-Muqdam. Height: 14·7 cm. Formerly in the Fouquet collection, now in the Brooklyn Museum (N.Y.).

Below left Procession of personifications bringing symbolic offerings to the god Onuris-Shu on behalf of Nectanebo II. Granite relief from the temple at Samannud. Baltimore (Md.), Walters Art Gallery.

Below Nekht-harhebi, whose "good name" was Nekht-harmenkhib, a contemporary of Psammetichus II, is known from his six statues from various delta sites, and his sarcophagus found at Sa el-Hagar. This sandstone kneeling statue, 1·48 m high, probably comes from el-Baqliya. Paris, Musée du Louvre.

Mastaba tombs and houses uncovered by the expedition of the Institute of Fine Arts of New York University at Tell el-Rub'a in 1977.

The Manager of the Estate Tetu, son of Nekhti: the *hotep-di-nesu* formula running down the front of his long kilt invokes Atum ''Lord of Heliopolis'' and so indicates the provenance of the statuette. Granite. Height: 27 cm. West Berlin Museum.

but few remains can be seen inside. There are some granite blocks lying outside the enclosure, including a large bell-shaped capital of a papyrus column which probably gave the tell its name (''The Mound of the Bell'').

The necropolis belonging to the town, including a cemetery of ibises, was probably situated at Tell el-Zereiki.

Tell el-Rub'a covers further, as yet unidentified, remains: a quartzite monolithic naos (shrine) dedicated to Thoth by Apries was found there, as well as the torso of a granite statue of Nectanebo I.

Blocks of Psammetichus I and Nectanebo I and a fragment of a basalt sarcophagus of a certain 'Ahmose of the 26th Dynasty have been found in the area of el-Baqliya. In recent years another statue of Nectanebo I was discovered, and in 1970 a granite block statue of a scribe called Nehesy, a contemporary of Ramesses II. The latter is so far the earliest monument known from the little-excavated el-Baqliya.

Tell el-Rub'a and Tell el-Timai

Two mounds several hundred meters apart, northwest of the modern town of el-Simbellawein, in the central delta, were in turn the site of the capital of the 16th Lower Egyptian nome: the northern Tell el-Rub'a (ancient Egyptian *Per-banebdjedet*, ''The Domain of the Ram Lord of *Djedet*,'' Greek Mendes) was in the Greco-Roman Period replaced in this role by the southern Tell el-Timai (Greek Thmuis). The earlier names of Tell el-Rub'a were '*Anpet* and *Djedet*. Originally, the fish goddess Hatmehyt was the local deity, but in the Dynastic Period the most prominent local cult was that of the Ram (*Ba*) of Mendes (*Djedet*). A cemetery of sacred rams with large sarcophagi, in which the animals were buried, can be seen in the northwest corner of the enclosure of Tell el-Rub'a.

The nome is mentioned in Egyptian texts as early as the 4th Dynasty, and the earliest monuments found at Tell el-Rub'a are mastaba tombs of the late Old Kingdom. A number of isolated monuments of the Ramessid kings, in particular Ramesses II, Merneptah and Ramesses III, suggest that there is a temple structure of that date, but none has yet been found. The earliest known temple, attested by its foundation deposits, was built by Amasis. A red granite monolithic naos, nearly 8 m high, dedicated by the same king, dominates the scene, but apart from the incompletely preserved enclosure walls nothing is left of the temple itself, and no fragments of temple reliefs have been found in the area. In the Late Period Tell el-Rub'a reached the peak of its glory, and, as the kings of the 29th Dynasty are said to have originated from there, it might even have functioned as the royal residence and capital.

Tell el-Timai, much spoiled by the *sabbakhin*, contains remains of brick-built structures of the Greco-Roman Period.

Heliopolis

Ancient Egyptian *Iunu* (Coptic and biblical *On*), the capital of the 13th Lower Egyptian nome, is at and around Tell Hisn, northwest of the modern el-Matariya (effectively a Cairo suburb, north of Misr el-Gedida). The temples of the sun god Re', Re'-Atum or Re'-Harakhty, at Heliopolis were among the most important and influential religious institutions in the land, economically and, still more, ideologically. The Heliopolitan doctrine with the god creator Atum and the sun god Re' (hence the Greek name of the town, from *helios* = sun) at its center played a very prominent part in the shaping of Egyptian religious and political history. The *benu* bird (phoenix) and the Mnevis bull were worshiped as manifestations of the god, and Hathor ''Mistress of Hetpet'' and Ius'as were the female deities connected with Heliopolis.

Despite the town's importance, no spectacular monuments can be seen in the area nowadays, except a still-standing obelisk of Senwosret I. Because Cairo is so near, most of the stone was removed from the temples and reused a long time ago, while the fact that the area is cultivated or built over hinders archaeological work. The main temple and probably also the town at Tell Hisn were surrounded by massive brick-built double walls. The enclosed area has been estimated to measure some 1,100 by 475 m, but the architectural history of the site and its precise topography are not clear. Isolated monuments (statues, reliefs, obelisks, offering tables etc.) dating between the 3rd Dynasty (Djoser) and the Ptolemaic Period have been found in abundance, and excavations, particularly those carried out in recent years and still in progress,

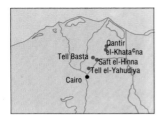

have revealed a number of buildings described as temples built by various New Kingdom kings: Amenophis III (restored by Ramesses II), Sethos I, Ramesses II and IX, Merneptah. It remains to be seen whether these buildings are temples in their own right attached to the great temple of Reʿ (at least ten of which are known to have existed at Heliopolis during the New Kingdom), or whether they are parts of the temple of Reʿ itself.

Tombs of the high priests of Heliopolis during the 6th Dynasty have been located some 550 m southeast of the obelisk of Senwosret I, near the southeast corner of the enclosure. Proceeding in the same general direction, at el-Matariya, about 950 m from the obelisk, there were tombs of the Late Period, while at a distance of some 3 km, at Ard el-Naʿam ("The Ostrich Farm"), objects indicating the presence of further tombs of the Ramessid and Late Periods have been found.

Tombs of Mnevis bulls, mainly of the Ramessid Period, have been discovered about 1·3 km northeast of the obelisk, at ʿArab el-Tawil.

Tell el-Yahudiya

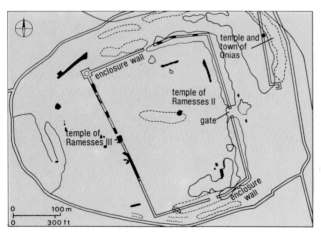

Tell el-Yahudiya ("The Mound of the Jews"), ancient Egyptian *Nay-ta-hut*, Greek Leontopolis, lies some 2 km southeast of the village of Shibin el-Qanatir, within the ancient 13th (Heliopolitan) nome of Lower Egypt.

The most conspicuous, as well as the most puzzling, feature of the site is the remains of a rectangular earthwork enclosure, the so-called "Hyksos Camp," measuring some 515 by 490 m. It is usually interpreted as fortifications and dated to the late Middle Kingdom or the 2nd Intermediate Period. No good Egyptian parallels for such massive defensive enclosure walls, plastered over and sloping ("glacis") on the outside and almost vertical inside, can be found, and so the builders of the enclosure have been sought outside Egypt, the immigrants from northwest Asia during the Hyksos

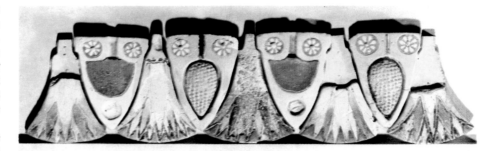

Period being the obvious choice. There is, however, a strong possibility that the structure is of a religious rather than military character.

Inside the enclosure, in its northeastern part, colossal statues of Ramesses II were found, which suggest that this was the site of a temple of that date. In its western part there stood a temple of Ramesses III, and faience tiles decorated with rosettes, *rekhyt* birds symbolic of the king's subjects, cartouches and foreign captives, probably originating in the temple palace and now in various museum collections, come from there.

Outside the enclosure, near its northeastern corner, are remains of a temple and town which the exiled Jewish priest Onias was given permission to build by Ptolemy VI Philometor. The settlement flourished for more than 200 years until the temple was closed by Vespasian in 71 AD.

Cemeteries of various dates, starting with the Middle Kingdom, extend to the east of the enclosure.

Above Obelisk of Senwosret I at Heliopolis. Granite. Height: about 20 m.

Tell Basta

Tell Basta, southeast of Zaqaziq, is the site of the ancient *Bast* (classical Bubastis, from *Per-Bastet*, "The Domain of Bastet"), the town of the lioness goddess Bastet (Bubastis), and the capital of the 18th Lower Egyptian nome during the Late Period. The town gained prominence very early in Egyptian history, at least partly because of its strategically important location controlling the routes from Memphis to Sinai (Wadi Tumilat) and to Asia.

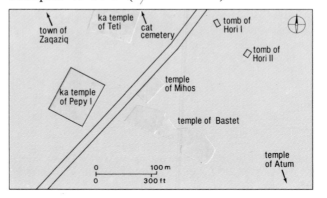

Right Bronze statuette of a cat, the sacred animal of Bastet of Bubastis (Tell Basta). Probably Late Period. Oxford, Ashmolean Museum.

Above Silver jug with a goat handle of gold, from a 19th-Dynasty hoard of gold and silver vessels and jewelry found at Tell Basta in 1906. Height: 16·8 cm; weight: 602 g. Cairo, Egyptian Museum.

Far right Bronze bust of a king, probably from Qantir. It is usually thought to show Ramesses II, but a much later date seems more likely. Height: 36 cm. Hildesheim, Roemer-Pelizaeus-Museum.

Below The form and finish brought to perfection, not diminished even by the present fragmentary state of the sculpture: Nectanebo I from Saft el-Hinna. Granite. Height: 67 cm. London, British Museum.

Politically, the peak of the town's influence was reached during the 22nd Dynasty, the kings of which came from Bubastis. The decline of Bubastis occurred in the first centuries AD.

The main temple, dedicated to Bastet, was excavated by E. Naville between 1887 and 1889. It was not possible to establish the plan of the edifice, some 200 or 300 m long, beyond its basic division into the entrance hall of Osorkon II, the *sed*-festival hall and the hypostyle hall of Osorkon III, and the hall of Nectanebo II. In the middle of the 5th century BC Herodotus described the temple as standing on an island, with two water channels running on its sides, and being on a much lower level than the city in the middle of which it was located. The excavation confirmed the correctness of both of these statements, though the channels would have been more appropriately described as the two arms of the sacred lake. Blocks of various dates, including some bearing the names of kings of the 4th Dynasty, were found reused in the temple.

Among the other buildings discovered at Tell Basta, there are the *ka* temples of Teti (a structure measuring some 108 by 50 m, about 250 m northwest of the temple of Bastet) and Pepy I, the *sed*-festival chapels of Amenemhet III and Amenophis III, a temple of Atum built by Osorkon II, a temple of Mihos (the lion god regarded as the son of Bastet) dedicated by Osorkon III, and a temple of the Roman Period.

Several burials of important officials have been found at Tell Basta, among them the vizier Iuti of the 19th Dynasty and two viceroys of Kush called Hori, who were father and son, of the end of the 19th and the 20th Dynasties. Some Old Kingdom monuments indicating the presence of tombs of this date were found recently. Extensive cemeteries of sacred animals, particularly cats (associated with Bastet from the 3rd Intermediate Period onwards) have also been located.

Saft el-Hinna

The village of Saft el-Hinna, east of Zaqaziq, stands on the site of ancient *Per-Sopdu* ("The Domain of Sopd"), the earlier capital of the 20th nome of Lower Egypt. In 1885 E. Naville partly uncovered the brick-built enclosure walls of the local temple, measuring some 75 (or more) by 40 m, as well as a number of uninscribed basalt blocks.

Few inscribed monuments have been found at Saft el-Hinna: statue fragments of Ramesses II are among the earliest, but the remains of a granite naos dedicated to Sopd by Nectanebo I are the most impressive.

The district of el-Khata'na and Qantir

el-Khata'na and Qantir are villages some 6 and 9 km respectively north of Faqus, in the northeastern delta. A number of sandy mounds in the area show signs of settlements of the Middle Kingdom and the 2nd Intermediate Period, and of the Ramessid Period. Avaris, the Hyksos center during the 2nd Intermediate Period, and Pi-Ri'amsese, the delta residence of the Ramessids and Raamses of the Exodus, are probably to be located somewhere here (Avaris perhaps in the south, at Tell el-Dab'a, and Pi-Ri'amsese probably in the north, near Qantir).

The southernmost site of importance, near el-Khata'na, is Tell el-Qirqafa, where remains of the

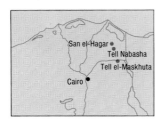

granite gate of a columned chapel of Amenemhet I and Senwosret III were found.

At Tell el-Dabʿa, east of the last, statues of Queen Nefrusobk and King Harnedjheriotef (Hetepibreʿ) were among the finds of the late 12th and 13th Dynasties. In the 2nd Intermediate Period Tell el-Dabʿa witnessed a large influx of foreign migrants from Asia, contemporary with the rise of the 15th (Hyksos) Dynasty. An apparent hiatus during the 18th Dynasty was followed by building activities under Haremhab and the Ramessids. These included a large temple structure (180 by 140 m), probably dedicated to Seth.

A Middle Kingdom town and a temple built by Amenemhet I were found at Ezbet Rushdi el-Saghira, north of Tell el-Dabʿa.

In the 1920s a number of decorated glazed tiles were reported to have been discovered in the vicinity of Qantir. Subsequent excavations confirmed that the tiles, bearing floral designs, fish, ducks, plants etc., had come from a palace of the 19th and 20th Dynasties. Some of them were inscribed with the names of Sethos I and Ramesses II. Importantly, contemporary stelae, statues, blocks from doorways and other monuments were also found.

At Tell Abu el-Shafiʿa, north of Qantir, there is the base of a seated colossus of Ramesses II, perhaps indicating the position of a temple.

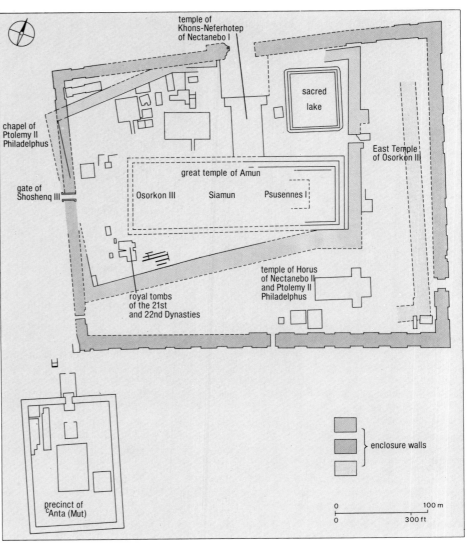

Tell Nabasha

A large mound, some 1·5 km across, in the northeastern delta, is the site of ancient Egyptian *Imet*. During the New Kingdom this was the capital of the district which was later divided into the 18th (capital: Bubastis) and 19th (capital: Tanis) Lower Egyptian nomes. The modern names of the locality are Tell Nabasha, Tell Farʿun or Tell Bedawi.

The outlines of the brick-built temple enclosure of the goddess Wadjit, measuring some 215 by 205 m, are still discernible. The enclosure originally contained at least two temples. The larger one (about 65 by 30 m), approached from the east, was probably built under the Ramessids (Ramesses II and others are attested). Although Middle Kingdom sphinxes usurped by later kings were found, it is likely that these had been brought from elsewhere. The smaller temple (about 30 by 15 m), near the northeast corner of the earlier temple and with its longer axis pointing to the north, is dated to Amasis by its foundation deposits. Reused Middle Kingdom monuments were also discovered here.

Remains of a town of the Greco-Roman Period were located southeast of the temple enclosure, and a cemetery, mostly of the Late Period, lies in the plain further to the east.

San el-Hagar

Situated in the northeastern part of the Nile delta, ancient *Djaʿnet* (Greek Tanis, modern San el-Hagar) was the residence and the burial place of the kings of the 21st and 22nd Dynasties. In the Late Period it became the capital of the 19th Lower Egyptian nome. In the present state of our archaeological knowledge of the delta it is easily the most impressive ancient site there, and one of the largest. The problems which one encounters when trying to interpret the monuments of Tanis in order to trace its history epitomize the difficulties connected with all the delta sites. The most prominent excavators at San el-Hagar have been A. Mariette in the second half of the last century, W. M. Flinders Petrie (1883–86) and P. Montet (1929–51).

The salient feature of San el-Hagar is a large brick-built rectangular enclosure measuring about 430 by 370 m. The enclosure walls were, amazingly, some 15 m thick and probably about 10 m high. Inside this precinct there is another, inner enclosure, with stamped bricks dating it to Psusennes I, which contains the great temple of Amun. Nowadays the temple is a mass of inscribed and decorated blocks, columns, obelisks and statues of various dates, some of them even bearing the names of rulers of the Old and Middle Kingdoms (Khufu, Khephren, Teti, Pepy I and II, Senwosret I).

Above San el-Hagar.

Below Seated colossus of Ramesses II, from Tell Nabasha. Granite. Height: 2·02 m. Boston (Mass.), Museum of Fine Arts.

Brutality personified? Not many Egyptian statues give a more powerful and awe-inspiring effect than this sphinx with its mane closely enveloping the face. Originally a work of the 12th Dynasty (probably of Amenemhet III), it was subsequently "usurped" by kings who added their names on it: Ramesses II, Merneptah and Psusennes I. The sphinx had been moved several times before it was set up at San el-Hagar by the last-named king. Granite. Length: 2·25 m. Cairo, Egyptian Museum.

blocks from several of these buildings, in particular a temple and a *sed*-festival chapel of Shoshenq V and a temple of Psammetichus I, were later reused by Nectanebo I when he built the sacred lake and a temple of Khons-Neferhotep nearby. Outside the enclosure, near the approach to the great temple, there stood a chapel of Ptolemy II Philadelphus.

The kings who built between the walls of the inner and outer enclosures were Osorkon III ("The East Temple") and Nectanebo II with Ptolemy II Philadelphus (temple of Horus). Outside the outer enclosure, near its southwest corner, there was a precinct of 'Anta (Mut), built mainly by Siamun and Apries, and rebuilt by Ptolemy IV Philopator.

In 1939 P. Montet found a group of royal tombs of the 21st and 22nd Dynasties inside the inner enclosure, near the southwest corner of the great temple. The habit of building tombs within temple precincts was characteristic of the 3rd Intermediate Period, and was probably dictated by the unstable conditions of the country. In all six tombs were found at San el-Hagar, belonging to Psusennes I, Amenemope, Osorkon III and Shoshenq III, with the two remaining tombs being anonymous. There probably were no superstructures or, at least, none were found. The underground parts, in most cases consisting of several rooms, were built of limestone (many of the blocks were reused material of an earlier date), granite or mud brick, and were entered through a shaft. The walls of the tombs of Psusennes I, Osorkon III and Shoshenq III were decorated with reliefs and inscriptions. Some of the tombs contained several burials, with sarcophagi often made of granite and usurped. Two additional royal burials were found: the sarcophagus used by Takelot II was discovered in one of the rooms of the tomb of Osorkon III, while the silver falcon-headed coffin of Shoshenq II was placed in the tomb of Psusennes I. The sarcophagus and coffin of Amenemope were discovered in the tomb of Psusennes I. Silver coffins and gold mummy masks and jewelry, such as pectorals, bracelets and collars, are the most spectacular finds. Apart from the tomb of Tut'ankhamun of the 18th Dynasty, the royal tombs of San el-Hagar are the only ones that have been discovered essentially intact.

However, the majority of the inscribed monuments are connected with Ramesses II, and this led P. Montet, the greatest expert on Tanis monuments, to believe that this was the site of the ancient Pi-Ri'amsese, the delta capital of the Ramessids. Nevertheless, none of the buildings so far excavated can be shown convincingly to have been built before the reign of Psusennes I of the 21st Dynasty, and the inescapable conclusion, therefore, is that all the Ramessid and earlier monuments must have been brought from other places. Some were reused as building material (a near-universal Egyptian practice; in the delta stone monuments often traveled considerable distances), while others were used to adorn the newly built temples.

Psusennes I is attested with certainty by foundation deposits in the sanctuary in the easternmost part of the great temple. Later Siamun contributed by building in the same general area, possibly adding a pylon and a court (the second from the outside), while Osorkon III (again, known by his foundation deposits) of the 22nd Dynasty completed the plan of the temple by adding another pylon and a court (the first from the outside). Finally Shoshenq III built a gate in the enclosure wall through which one approaches the first pylon. The only later name certainly connected with the great temple at San el-Hagar is that of Nectanebo I, who probably carried out some restoration work there.

Apart from the great temple there were other, smaller structures within the inner enclosure. The

Tell el-Maskhuta

In 1883 E. Naville excavated a large brick-built enclosure (some 210 by 210 m) with a badly damaged temple at Tell el-Maskhuta, in Wadi Tumilat (in the Late Period a canal through this wadi enabled ships to sail from the Nile into the Red Sea). Most scholars, though not all, identify Tell el-Maskhuta with ancient Egyptian *Tjeku* and Pithom (probably from *Per-Atum*, "The Domain of Atum") of the Exodus, and the capital of the 8th Lower Egyptian nome.

NUBIA

Nubia, the area south of the 1st cataract, was from the earliest times regarded as belonging to Egypt by right. Apart from forming a buffer zone at the southern frontier, it was a region through which exotic African goods reached Egypt, and an important source of gold, minerals and wood, but also of valued recruits for the Egyptian army and police force.

The crude Old Kingdom methods of exploitation consisted of raids aiming at bringing back captives and cattle. In the Middle Kingdom the area under direct military control, exercised through a series of strategically placed fortresses, extended to the 2nd cataract. During the New Kingdom the Egyptians went beyond the 4th cataract; in Lower Nubia many rock-cut temples were built, dating chiefly to the reign of Ramesses II. In the Late Period Nubia produced a royal dynasty, the 25th of Egypt, but after an unsuccessful encounter with the Assyrians its Napatan rulers withdrew to the 4th cataract, ceased to take an active interest in Egyptian affairs, and developed their own, Meroïtic, culture. A number of temples were built in the northern part of Lower Nubia during the condominium of the two cultures in the Ptolemaic and early Roman Periods.

In the 1960s many Nubian temples were removed to new locations in an act of international cooperation unprecedented in the history of archaeology.

Above The Roman Period temple of Sarapis at el-Maharraqa, painted by the French architect Hector Horeau in 1838. The temple was removed to the vicinity of el-Sebu'a in 1965–66.

Left The temple of Ramesses II at el-Sebu'a, as it used to be before the creation of the Lake Nasser: (*above*) one of the sphinxes in the outer court.

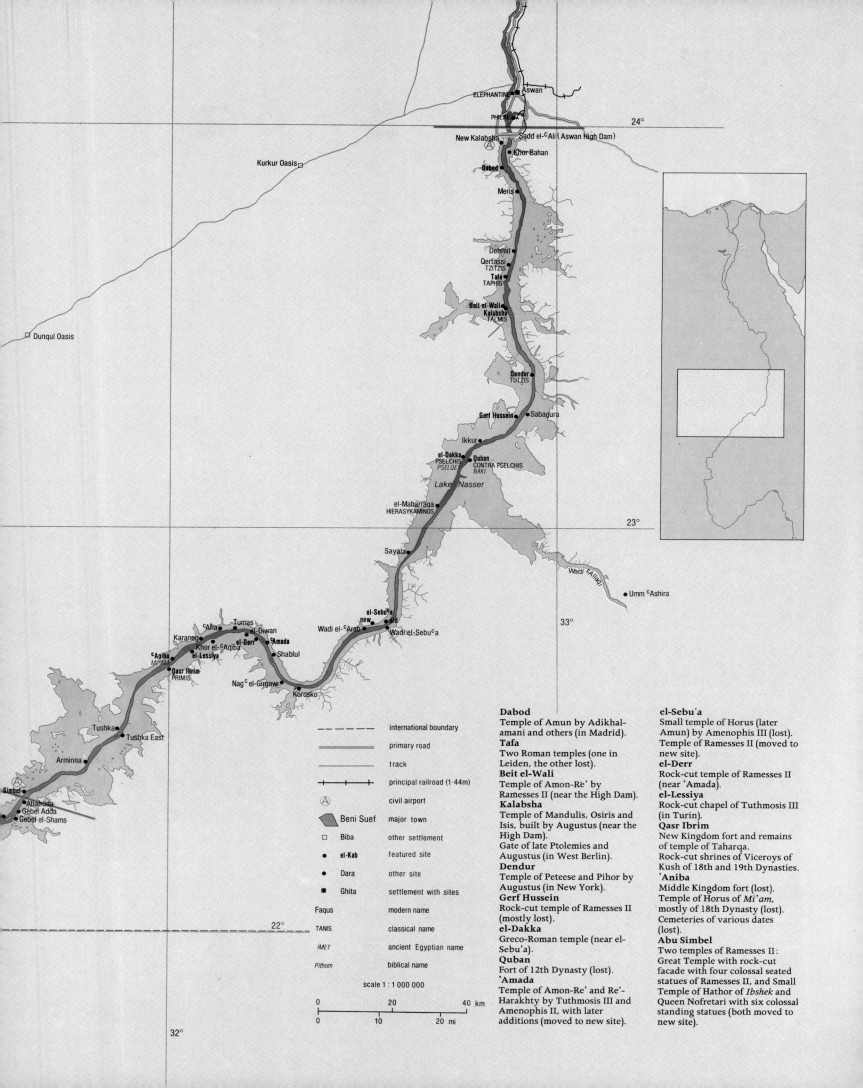

ELEPHANTINE ⊛ Aswan

24°

PHILAE

New Kalabsha ─── Sadd el-ᶜAli (Aswan High Dam)
● Khor Bahan

Dabod

Meris

Kurkur Oasis ☐

Dehmit
Qertassi
TZITZIS
Tafa
TAPHIS

Beit el-Wali
Kalabsha
TALMIS

Dunqul Oasis ☐

Dendur
TUTZIS

Gerf Hussein ● Sabagura

Ikkur
el-Dakka ● Quban
PSELCHIS CONTRA PSELCHIS
PSELQET BAKI

Lake Nasser

el-Maharraqa
HIERASYKAMINOS

23°

Sayala

Wadi ᶜAllaqi

● Umm ᶜAshira

33°

el-Sebuᶜa
Tumas new old
ᶜAfia el-Diwan
Karanog Khor el-ᶜAqiba ᶜAmada   Wadi el-ᶜArab
ᶜAqiba el-Derr Shablul   Wadi el-Sebuᶜa
el-Lessiya
ᶜAniba
MiᶜAM
Qasr Ibrim
PRIMIS
Nag ᶜel-Girgawi
Korosko

Tushka

Tushka East

Arminna

Simbel
Abahuda
Gebel Adda
Gebel el-Shams

22°

32°

─ ─ ─ ─   international boundary

━━━━━   primary road

─────   track

┼─┼─┼   principal railroad (1·44m)

Ⓐ   civil airport

▰ Beni Suef   major town

☐ Biba   other settlement

● el-Kab   featured site

• Dara   other site

▣ Ghita   settlement with sites

Faqus   modern name

TANIS   classical name

IMET   ancient Egyptian name

Pithom   biblical name

scale 1 : 1 000 000

0   20   40 km

0   10   20 mi

Dabod
Temple of Amun by Adikhal-
amani and others (in Madrid).
Tafa
Two Roman temples (one in
Leiden, the other lost).
Beit el-Wali
Temple of Amon-Rēᶜ by
Ramesses II (near the High Dam).
Kalabsha
Temple of Mandulis, Osiris and
Isis, built by Augustus (near the
High Dam).
Gate of late Ptolemies and
Augustus (in West Berlin).
Dendur
Temple of Peteese and Pihor by
Augustus (in New York).
Gerf Hussein
Rock-cut temple of Ramesses II
(mostly lost).
el-Dakka
Greco-Roman temple (near el-
Sebuᶜa).
Quban
Fort of 12th Dynasty (lost).
ᶜAmada
Temple of Amon-Reᶜ and Reᶜ-
Harakhty by Tuthmosis III and
Amenophis II, with later
additions (moved to new site).

el-Sebuᶜa
Small temple of Horus (later
Amun) by Amenophis III (lost).
Temple of Ramesses II (moved to
new site).
el-Derr
Rock-cut temple of Ramesses II
(near ᶜAmada).
el-Lessiya
Rock-cut chapel of Tuthmosis III
(in Turin).
Qasr Ibrim
New Kingdom fort and remains
of temple of Taharqa.
Rock-cut shrines of Viceroys of
Kush of 18th and 19th Dynasties.
ᶜAniba
Middle Kingdom fort (lost).
Temple of Horus of *Miᶜam*,
mostly of 18th Dynasty (lost).
Cemeteries of various dates
(lost).
Abu Simbel
Two temples of Ramesses II:
Great Temple with rock-cut
facade with four colossal seated
statues of Ramesses II, and Small
Temple of Hathor of *Ibshek* and
Queen Nofretari with six colossal
standing statues (both moved to
new site).

1	Dabod
2	Tafa
3	Beit el-Wali
4	Kalabsha
5	Dendur
6	Gerf Hussein
7	el-Dakka
8	Quban

Dabod

The early temple of Dabod was built and decorated by the Meroïtic ruler Adikhalamani, probably in the first half of the 3rd century BC, and was dedicated to Amun. In the Greco-Roman Period several Ptolemies (VI Philometor, VIII Euergetes II and XII Auletes) enlarged it and rededicated it to Isis. The decoration of the vestibule dates to the Emperors Augustus and Tiberius. Old views show a series of three pylons in front of the temple, but only two were to be seen in this century.

In the years 1960–61 the temple was dismantled and in 1968 presented to Spain; since 1970 it has adorned one of the parks of Madrid.

Tafa

Two temples of Roman date used to stand at Tafa. The so-called "North Temple," with no relief decoration, was dismantled in 1960 and given to the Rijksmuseum van Oudheden in Leiden. The "South Temple" was lost as early as the end of the last century.

There were two sanctuaries of Isis of the same date in the area, one of them overlooking the dangerous "minor" cataract of Bab el-Kalabsha.

Beit el-Wali

The small rock-cut temple of Beit el-Wali, on the west bank of the Nile, was built by Ramesses II and dedicated to Amon-Re' and other gods. Originally fronted by a brick-built pylon, its simple plan consists of an entrance hall (at one time roofed with a brick-built vault), a columned hall and the sanctuary. The temple has now been moved to a new site (New Kalabsha) close to the new Aswan dam.

Kalabsha

The largest free-standing temple of Egyptian Nubia, measuring some 74 m from the pylon to the rear wall and about 33 m wide, was built at Kalabsha (ancient Talmis) in the reign of Augustus, and was dedicated to the Nubian god Mandulis, accompanied by Osiris and Isis. In front of the pylon there is a quay and a terrace, and to reach the sanctuary one proceeds through a forecourt, a hypostyle hall and two vestibules. Only the three inner rooms are fully decorated with reliefs. The walls of the temple precinct also enclose a birth house (in the southwest corner), and a chapel built probably by Ptolemy IX Soter II (in the northeast corner).

Since the beginning of this century the temple was under water for most of the year. In 1962–63 it was dismantled and its 13,000 blocks transferred to the vicinity of the new Aswan dam (New Kalabsha), where it was rebuilt. During the dismantling operation reused blocks from a gate built by the late Ptolemies and Augustus were found. The gate, 7·35 m high, has now been reerected in the Ägyptisches Museum in West Berlin.

Dendur

In order to save it from the waters of Lake Nasser, the temple of Dendur was dismantled in 1963 and a few years later presented by the Egyptian government to the United States and shipped to New York. Its 642 blocks have now been reassembled at the Metropolitan Museum of Art where (since

The temple of Kalabsha in 1839; watercolor painting by Hector Horeau.

September 1978) the temple forms the Sackler wing of the museum.

Augustus built the small temple (the main building measures about 13·5 by 7 m) for two local "saints," Peteese and Pihor, sons of Quper. The exact reason for their deification at Dendur is not clear; perhaps they drowned at that spot. The original place of their worship was a rock chamber behind the temple, which may have dated back to the 26th Dynasty. The temple, fronted by a terrace, has a simple plan: a pylon and the main building some 10 m behind it. The latter consists of a columned pronaos, a vestibule and the sanctuary. The reliefs in the temple show Augustus before various deities, among them the two deified brothers and the Nubian gods Arensnuphis and Mandulis.

35 and 50 of Ramesses II. The gods to whom it was dedicated were represented by four seated statues in the niche at the back of the sanctuary: Ptah, the deified Ramesses II, Ptah-tanen with a hawk above his head, and Hathor.

The temple, on the west bank of the Nile, was partly free-standing and partly cut in the rock, and its plan was remarkably similar to that of the great temple of Abu Simbel. Unfortunately, most of it fell victim to the progress of modern civilization, and disappeared under the newly created Lake Nasser.

Gerf Hussein

"The Temple of Ri'amsese-meryamun [Ramesses II] in the Domain of Ptah" at Gerf Hussein was built by the viceroy of Kush, Setau, sometime between years

el-Dakka

Several rulers contributed to the building and decoration of the temple of el-Dakka (ancient Egyptian *Pselqet*, classical Pselchis), notably Ptolemy IV Philopator, Ptolemy VIII Euergetes II, the Meroïtic King Arqamani of the turn of the 3rd century BC, and the Roman emperors Augustus and Tiberius.

Between 1962 and 1968 the temple was dismantled and removed to a new site near el-Sebu'a. During the work a number of reused blocks were found. These come from an earlier temple built by Hatshepsut and Tuthmosis III for Horus of *Baki* (Quban), probably on the opposite side of the river.

Quban

The fort of Quban (ancient Egyptian *Baki*, classical Contra Pselchis) was built at the beginning of the 12th Dynasty, probably by Senwosret I, but may have had a precursor in the Old Kingdom. During the New Kingdom Quban was the most important settlement in Nubia north of 'Aniba, controlling access to the gold mines of Wadi 'Allaqi. Several ruined temple structures have been reported from the area.

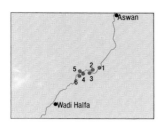

1 el-Sebu{`}a
2 {`}Amada
3 el-Derr
4 el-Lessiya
5 {`}Aniba
6 Qasr Ibrim

'Amada

The temple of 'Amada was originally built by Tuthmosis III and Amenophis II, and was dedicated to the gods Amon-Re' and Re'-Harakhty. A hypostyle hall was later added by Tuthmosis IV. Various kings of the 19th Dynasty, in particular Sethos I and Ramesses II, carried out minor restorations and added to the temple's decoration.

There are two important historical inscriptions in the 'Amada temple. The earlier of them, dated to year 3 of Amenophis II, is on a round-topped stela on the rear (eastern) wall of the sanctuary. The text describes a victorious military campaign into Asia: "His Majesty returned in joy to his father Amun after he had slain with his own mace the seven chiefs in the district of *Takhesy*, who were then hung upside down from the prow of the boat of His Majesty." The other text, on a stela engraved on the left (northern) thickness of the entrance doorway, concerns the defeat of an invasion of Egypt from Libya in year 4 of Merneptah.

Between December 1964 and February 1975 the temple was moved to a new position, some 65 m higher and 2·5 km away from its original site. Part of the temple, weighing about 900 tons, was transported to its new setting in one piece.

el-Sebu'a

el-Sebu'a, on the west bank of the Nile, was the site of two temples of the New Kingdom.

The earlier temple was built by Amenophis III. In its first stage it consisted of a rock-cut sanctuary (about 3 by 2 m) fronted by a brick-built pylon, a court and a hall, partly decorated with wall paintings. Originally the temple seems to have been dedicated to one of the local Nubian forms of Horus, but his representations were altered to Amun at some later point. During the 'Amarna persecution of images of Amun the decoration suffered, but Ramesses II restored it and also extended the temple by building in front of the pylon of the original plan.

The large temple of el-Sebu'a, known as "The Temple of Ri'amsese-meryamun [Ramesses II] in the Domain of Amun," was built about 150 m northeast of the temple of Amenophis III; monuments and representations of the viceroy of Kush, Setau, indicate that this was between regnal years 35 and 50 of Ramesses II. The temple is partly free-standing and partly rock-cut.

Proceeding along its central axis, one passes through a series of three pylons and courts to reach the hypostyle hall (later converted into a Coptic church) where the rock-cut part of the temple starts.

The antechamber opens into two side rooms, two side chapels and the sanctuary itself. The statues in the niche of the sanctuary are destroyed, but there is little doubt that they represented Amon-Re', Re'-Harakhty and Ramesses II himself.

During the UNESCO campaign to save the monuments of Nubia the temple was removed to a new site, some 4 km to the west.

el-Derr

The only Nubian rock-cut temple built by Ramesses II on the right bank of the Nile used to stand at el-Derr. The position was probably due to the fact that the river on its approach to the Korosko bend flows in an ''unnatural'' southeasterly direction. In 1964 the temple was dismantled and removed to a new site near 'Amada.

''The Temple of Ri'amsese-meryamun [Ramesses II] in the Domain of Re''' was built in the second half of the king's reign, and in plan and decoration resembles the Great Temple of Abu Simbel (minus the colossal seated statues against the facade). After cleaning, the temple's relief decoration is unusually bright and vivid, contrasting strongly with the more subdued color tones to which we are used from elsewhere. The chief deities worshiped in the temple had seated statues in the sanctuary niche: Re'-Harakhty, Ramesses II himself, Amon-Re' and Ptah.

el-Lessiya

At el-Lessiya, on the right bank of the Nile, a small chapel was cut in the reign of Tuthmosis III. The plan consists of a single room (5·5 by 3 m) with a niche (2 by 3 m), and the relief decoration shows the king before various deities, including the Nubian god Dedwen and the deified Senwosret III. The niche originally contained statues of Tuthmosis III between Horus of *Mi'am* ('Aniba) and Satis, but these were damaged during the 'Amarna Period, and Ramesses II had them restored to represent himself between Amon-Re' and Horus of *Mi'am*.

The chapel was presented to Italy in 1966 and is now in the Museo Egizio in Turin.

Qasr Ibrim

The central of the three sandstone massifs which used to loom south of the village of Ibrim (the name probably derives from the classical Primis), on the east bank of the Nile, was the most important one. On its top, the fort of Qasr Ibrim (''The Castle of Ibrim'') no doubt stood on pharaonic foundations, as suggested by a number of reused or isolated monuments dating to the New Kingdom (the earliest is a stela of year 8 of Amenophis I) and a temple structure of Taharqa (with a painting showing the king offering to a god). Parts of the fortress were constructed during the short stay of the Roman garrison under the prefect Gaius Petronius in the reign of Augustus, and from then on Qasr Ibrim remained occupied until the beginning of the last century.

Rock-cut shrines (chapels) dedicated to the reigning king and various gods were made by viceroys of Kush of the 18th and 19th Dynasties at the bottom of the cliff. During the salvage operation carried out while the new Aswan dam was being built, their reliefs were cut away and removed to the vicinity of el-Sebu'a.

The large rock stela of Sethos I and the contemporary viceroy of Kush, Amenemope, which used to be south of the fort, has been transferred to the neighborhood of the reconstructed Kalabsha temple at Aswan.

'Aniba

'Aniba, ancient *Mi'am*, was prominent in the New Kingdom, when it served as the administrative center of *Wawat* (Lower Nubia, between the 1st and 2nd cataracts).

The town contained a fort, probably of Middle Kingdom origin, and the temple of Horus of *Mi'am*. The temple may go back to the beginning of the 12th Dynasty (Senwosret I), but most of the evidence dates to the 18th Dynasty (Tuthmosis III and later kings).

There were cemeteries of various dates in the vicinity, including tombs of the New Kingdom. One of these, the rock-cut tomb of Penniut, the deputy of *Wawat* under Ramesses VI, has now been removed to a new site near 'Amada.

Abu Simbel

Of the seven temples in Nubia built by Ramesses II (Beit el-Wali, Gerf Hussein, el-Sebu'a, el-Derr, two at Abu Simbel, and Aksha), the rock temples at Abu Simbel (Ibsambul), on the west bank of the Nile, are the most impressive.

The Great Temple was first reported by J. L. Burckhardt in 1813 and opened by G. B. Belzoni in 1817. As a result of the widely publicized dismantling and removal operation it has become one of the best-known monuments of Egypt. Its ancient name was simply "The Temple of Ri'amsese-meryamun [Ramesses II]," and it was probably built early in the reign of the king.

A gateway leads into a forecourt and on to a terrace. There the visitor is confronted by the temple's rock-cut facade, some 30 m high and 35 m wide, with four colossal seated statues of Ramesses II (about 21 m high), accompanied by smaller standing statues of relatives by his legs. These are as follows:

1st southern colossus: Queen Nofretari by the king's left leg, the king's mother (and the wife of Sethos I) Muttuya by his right leg, and Prince Amenhirkhopshef in front.

2nd southern colossus (in the same order as for the previous statue): Princesses Bent'anta, Nebettawy and one unnamed, probably Esenofre.

1st northern colossus: Queen Nofretari by the king's right leg, Princess Beketmut by his left leg and Prince Ri'amsese in front.

2nd northern colossus: Princess Merytamun, Queen Muttuya and Princess Nofretari.

A niche above the temple entrance contains a symbolic sculptural group representing a cryptographic writing of the praenomen of Ramesses II, Userma'atre': the falcon-headed god Re' has by his right leg the hieroglyph showing the head and neck of an animal which is read as user while the goddess by his left leg stands for ma'at. At the top of the temple facade is a row of statues of baboons in adoring attitudes whose cries were held to welcome the rising sun.

The temple was built in such a way that twice a year, when the rising sun appeared above the horizon on the east bank of the Nile, its rays penetrated the temple entrance, shot through the great hall with eight pillars in the form of colossal statues of the king, the second pillared hall, the vestibule and the sanctuary, and rested on the four statues in the niche at the back, which they illuminated fully. The statues represented the three most important state gods of the Ramessid Period: the Memphite Ptah (first on the left), the Theban Amon-Re' (second) and the Heliopolitan Re'-Harakhty (fourth). The third figure from the left was the king himself.

The Great Temple of Abu Simbel bears witness to the deification of Ramesses II during his lifetime, including scenes showing the king performing rites before the sacred bark of his deified self (on the north wall of the second pillared hall, and on the north wall of the sanctuary). The reliefs in the great hall show scenes of historical or symbolic character: on the long north wall the battle of Qadesh in Syria, and on the south wall the Syrian, Libyan and Nubian wars.

The Small Temple of Abu Simbel, contemporary with the Great Temple, was dedicated to Hathor of Ibshek and Queen Nofretari. The facade is formed by six colossal standing statues (about 10 m high) cut in the rock. Four of them represent the king and two the queen, each being flanked by princes and princesses. In its plan the Small Temple is an abbreviated version of the Great Temple: a hall with Hathor pillars, a vestibule with side rooms, and the sanctuary. The niche at the back contains a statue of a Hathor cow protecting the king.

Between 1964 and 1968 both temples were removed to their new location, about 210 m further away from the river and 65 m higher, at the cost of some 40 million US dollars.

Left The gods of the Great Temple in the niche of the sanctuary.

Right The much more romantic Abu Simbel of the first half of the last century (David Roberts, November 1838).

Below right The "Abu Simbel Salvage Operation" was one of the results of the appeal of UNESCO to all its member states to help to rescue the monuments of Nubia threatened by the building of the new dam at Aswan. The protection of the temples at Abu Simbel, cut in the living rock, presented considerable technical and financial difficulties. Several projects were considered; that which was finally chosen consisted in dismantling the temple facades and the walls of their rooms by cutting them into large blocks, removing these, and rebuilding the temples inside concrete dome-shaped structures in a simulated environment. A cofferdam had to be built while the dismantling operation was in progress because of the already rising water of Lake Nasser. The whole huge Lego game was successfully completed, and the resited temples were reopened officially on 22 September 1968.

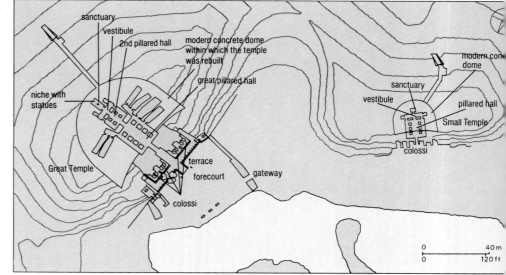

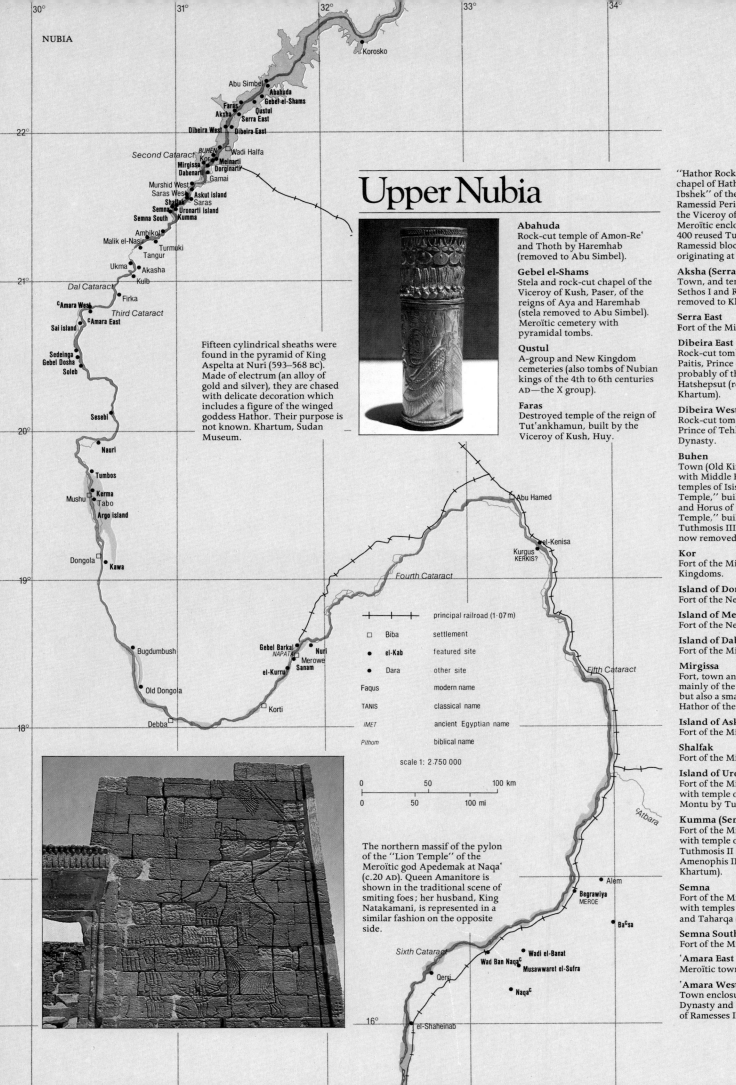

NUBIA

30° 31° 32° 33° 34°

Korosko

Abu Simbel
Abahuda
Gebel el-Shams
Faras
Aksha
Qustul
Serra East
Dibeira West
Dibeira East

Second Cataract BUHEN ☐ Wadi Halfa
Kor
Meinarti
Mirgissa Dorginarti
Dabenarti
Gamai
Murshid West
Saras West Askut island
Shalfak Saras
Semna Uronarti island
Semna South Kumma
Ambikol
Malik el-Nasir
Turmuki
Tangur
Ukma Akasha
Kulb
Dal Cataract
Firka
ᶜAmara West
Third Cataract
ᶜAmara East
Sai island
Sedeinga
Gebel Dosha
Soleb

Sesebi

Nauri

Tumbos
Kerma
Mushu ☐ Tabo
Argo island

Dongola ☐ Kawa

Bugdumbush

Abu Hamed

el-Kenisa

Kurgus
KERKIS?

Fourth Cataract

Gebel Barkal Nuri
NAPATA
Merowe
el-Kurru Sanam

Old Dongola

Debba ☐ Korti

Fifth Cataract

Upper Nubia

Abahuda
Rock-cut temple of Amon-Reʻ and Thoth by Haremhab (removed to Abu Simbel).

Gebel el-Shams
Stela and rock-cut chapel of the Viceroy of Kush, Paser, of the reigns of Aya and Haremhab (stela removed to Abu Simbel). Meroïtic cemetery with pyramidal tombs.

Qustul
A-group and New Kingdom cemeteries (also tombs of Nubian kings of the 4th to 6th centuries AD—the X group).

Faras
Destroyed temple of the reign of Tutʻankhamun, built by the Viceroy of Kush, Huy.

Fifteen cylindrical sheaths were found in the pyramid of King Aspelta at Nuri (593–568 BC). Made of electrum (an alloy of gold and silver), they are chased with delicate decoration which includes a figure of the winged goddess Hathor. Their purpose is not known. Khartum, Sudan Museum.

"Hathor Rock," with rock-cut chapel of Hathor "Lady of Ibshek" of the 18th Dynasty and Ramessid Period, and a niche of the Viceroy of Kush, Setau. Meroïtic enclosure with nearly 400 reused Tuthmosid and Ramessid blocks, probably originating at Buhen.

Aksha (Serra West)
Town, and temple and chapels of Sethos I and Ramesses II (temple removed to Khartum).

Serra East
Fort of the Middle Kingdom.

Dibeira East
Rock-cut tomb of Djehutihotpe Paitis, Prince of Tehkheti, probably of the reign of Hatshepsut (removed to Khartum).

Dibeira West
Rock-cut tomb of Amenemhet, Prince of Tehkheti, of the 18th Dynasty.

Buhen
Town (Old Kingdom and later), with Middle Kingdom fort and temples of Isis and Min ("North Temple," built by Amenophis II) and Horus of Buhen ("South Temple," built by Hatshepsut, Tuthmosis III and Taharqa), both now removed to Khartum.

Kor
Fort of the Middle and New Kingdoms.

Island of Dorginarti
Fort of the New Kingdom.

Island of Meinarti
Fort of the New Kingdom.

Island of Dabenarti
Fort of the Middle Kingdom.

Mirgissa
Fort, town and cemeteries, mainly of the Middle Kingdom, but also a small sanctuary of Hathor of the New Kingdom.

Island of Askut
Fort of the Middle Kingdom.

Shalfak
Fort of the Middle Kingdom.

Island of Uronarti
Fort of the Middle Kingdom, with temple of Dedwen and Montu by Tuthmosis III.

Kumma (Semna East)
Fort of the Middle Kingdom, with temple of Khnum built by Tuthmosis II and III and Amenophis II (removed to Khartum).

Semna
Fort of the Middle Kingdom, with temples of Tuthmosis III and Taharqa (in Khartum).

Semna South
Fort of the Middle Kingdom.

ʻAmara East
Meroïtic town and temple.

ʻAmara West
Town enclosure of the 19th Dynasty and later, with temple of Ramesses II.

principal railroad (1·07m)
☐ Biba settlement
● el-Kab featured site
● Dara other site
Faqus modern name
TANIS classical name
IMET ancient Egyptian name
Pithom biblical name

scale 1: 2 750 000

0 50 100 km

0 50 100 mi

The northern massif of the pylon of the "Lion Temple" of the Meroïtic god Apedemak at Naqaʼ (c.20 AD). Queen Amanitore is shown in the traditional scene of smiting foes; her husband, King Natakamani, is represented in a similar fashion on the opposite side.

ʻAtbara

Alem
Begrawiya
MEROE
Baᶜsa

Sixth Cataract
Wadi el-Banat
Wad Ban Naqaᶜ
Musawwaret el-Sufra
Qerri
Naqaᶜ

el-Shaheinab

22°
21°
20°
19°
18°
16°

Island of Sai
Town and fort with temple, 18th Dynasty and Meroïtic.

Sedeinga
Temple of Amenophis III. Meroïtic cemeteries.

Gebel Dosha
Rock-cut chapel of Tuthmosis III.

Soleb
Temple of Amenophis III. Cemetery of the New Kingdom.

Sesebi
New Kingdom town with temples of the Aten and the Theban triad, built by Akhenaten and Sethos I.

Nauri
Rock-cut stela of year 4 of Sethos I.

Tumbos
Stelae of Tuthmosis I and others, including the Viceroy of Kush, Setau, of the reign of Ramesses II.

Kerma
Settlement of the 2nd Intermediate Period, and cemetery with tumuli with reused Egyptian objects, including statues, stelae, and stone vessels. Colossal mudbrick tower (*deffufa*).

Island of Argo
Temple at Tabo, of the 25th Dynasty (Taharqa, reusing New Kingdom blocks) and Meroïtic.

Kawa
Temples of Amun, built mainly by Tut'ankhamun, Taharqa and Napatan and Meroïtic kings.

el-Kurru
Pyramid field, including burials of kings of the 25th Dynasty.

Sanam
Palace, storerooms and cemeteries of the 25th Dynasty, with temple of Amon-Re' built by Taharqa.

Gebel Barkal
Meroïtic pyramid field. A number of temples and chapels dedicated to Amon-Re', built by kings of the New Kingdom, Piye and Taharqa, and Napatan and Meroïtic kings.

Nuri
Pyramid field, including burial of Taharqa and those of various Napatan and Meroïtic kings.

Meroë (Begrawiya)
Temples and pyramid fields of the Meroïtic Period.

Ba'sa
Meroïtic temple.

Wadi el-Banat
Destroyed Meroïtic temple.

Wadi Ban Naqa'
Destroyed Meroïtic temple.

Musawwarat el-Sufra
Meroïtic temples.

Naqa'
Meroïtic temples.

The Oases

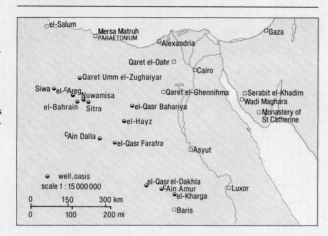

The western oases consist of a series of wind-eroded depressions in the Libyan desert, where there are natural springs, and wells are bored more than 100 meters below ground. There is enough water for agriculture, but wells are scattered and may fail. The population (75,000 in 1966) is spread over wide areas, with barren tracts between settlements.

The oases have been inhabited since Paleolithic times, and el-Kharga, the largest, has produced traces of very early agriculture, but their importance was due more to their location than to their produce. The local economy's fortunes fluctuated with those of Egypt proper, and for the Roman Period there is ample evidence for trade with the Nile valley.

Our knowledge of the area's early history is still rudimentary. For the Old–New Kingdoms the four southern oases are mentioned in Egyptian texts, and there have been some finds, chiefly in el-Dakhla. They were probably all administered by Egypt during these periods. From the 3rd Intermediate Period remains are more frequent, and prosperity increased until the Roman Period, when some Greeks settled. Siwa was colonized in the 26th Dynasty, and remained in Egyptian control; its population, now Berber-speaking, was probably always more Libyan than Egyptian.

In late Roman times there was widespread depopulation. The oasis economy has never recovered fully, so that the naturally good conditions for preserving sites are enhanced.

Below left el-Dakhla oasis, the village of el-Smant el-Kharab. In antiquity lakes were more prominent in the oases than they are now. Preservation is so good that it can be difficult to distinguish a Roman farmhouse from a recently abandoned one.

el-Kharga
'Ain Amur Temple and settlement of the Roman Period.
Hibis Well-preserved temple of Amun, Darius, Nectanebo II and Ptolemaic.
Qasr el-Ghueida Temple of Amun, Mut and Khons, 25th Dynasty – Ptolemaic.
Gebel el-Teir Rock inscriptions, 26th Dynasty – Ptolemaic.
Nadura Temple of the Roman Period.
Qasr Zaiyan Ptolemaic and Roman temple.
Qasr Dush Temple of Sarapis and Isis, Roman.

el-Dakhla
Many Old Kingdom settlements and cemeteries.
Balat Town site; mastabas of the 6th Dynasty and 1st Intermediate Period; temple of Mut, New Kingdom; tombs of the 3rd Intermediate and Roman Periods.
Amhada Tombs of the 1st Intermediate Period.
Mut Destroyed temple; objects of the 3rd Intermediate Period.
el-Qasr Temple of Thoth, Greco-Roman; necropolis.
Deir el-Hagar Temple, 1st century AD.
Qaret el-Muzawwaqa Decorated tombs of the Roman Period.
el-Smant el-Kharab Roman town site with small temple (ruined).

Farafra
No native Egyptian remains, but evidence for Roman occupation.

Bahariya
Monuments near *el-Qasr* and *el-Bawiti*:
Tomb of Amenhotpe Huy (18th–19th Dynasty).
Chapels and tombs of the reigns of Apries and Amasis and of the Greco-Roman Period.
Temple of Alexander the Great.
Destroyed Roman "triumphal arch."
el-Hayz Small center of the Roman Period.

Siwa
Aghurmi 26th Dynasty and Ptolemaic temple, assumed to be where Alexander the Great consulted the oracle of Ammon.
Umm el-'Ebeida Temple of Nectanebo II.
Gebel el-Mawta Necropolis, 26th Dynasty and Greco-Roman, including some decorated tombs. Cemeteries and small, undecorated temples at a number of further sites.

Small oases with ancient remains: *Qaret Umm el-Zughaiyar, el-'Areg, Nuwamisa, el-Bahrain, Sitra.*

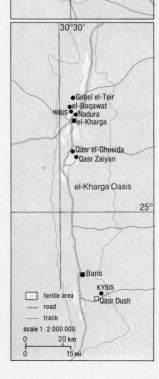

Sinai

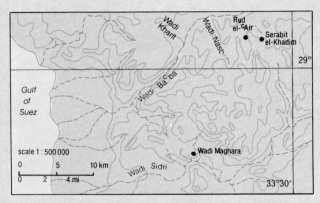

Right Head of a statuette of Teye, the chief consort of Amenophis III, identified by a cartouche bearing her name on the headdress. Green steatite. Height 6·5 cm. Found at Serabit el-Khadim. Cairo, Egyptian Museum.

Below left A relief of King Sekhemkhet, rediscovered at Wadi Maghara in 1973. It is almost identical with another, some 35 m to the south. The two reliefs are among the earliest Egyptian inscriptions at Sinai.

Below A recently taken view of the temple of Hathor at Serabit el-Khadim, showing some of the stelae that are still standing.

The Egyptians were attracted by the mineral deposits of the valleys of southwestern Sinai as early as the 3rd Dynasty. The objective of the expeditions regularly sent out to work the mines during the Old to New Kingdoms was to bring back turquoise and to acquire copper; the copper workings over much of Sinai are mostly not associated with Egyptian finds. Egyptian activities in Sinai ceased at the end of the New Kingdom.

There were several routes which these expeditions could follow, and the choice probably varied with the period: the long overland journey around the Gulf of Suez or the combined land/sea/land travel which in its first stage involved crossing the eastern desert, and perhaps also the Nile/sea/land route through the Wadi Tumilat canal.

The mines of the Wadi Maghara were the first to be exploited, with the earliest rock inscriptions and reliefs dating to Zanakht, Netjerykhet (Djoser) and Sekhemkhet. The last Old Kingdom expedition was that of Pepy II in the "year of the 2nd census" (around his 3rd year); although some Middle and New Kingdom rulers are attested (Amenemhet III and IV, Hatshepsut and Tuthmosis III, perhaps

Ramesses II), the site did not regain its former significance.

The most important site of Egyptian activities in Sinai is Serabit el-Khadim with its temple of Hathor. The temple's earliest part, the rock-cut "Cave of Hathor" preceded by a court and a portico, goes back to the beginning of the 12th Dynasty. In the New Kingdom, a shrine for Sopd, the god of the eastern desert, was built to the south, and the temple of Hathor was much enlarged (mainly by Hatshepsut and Tuthmosis III). Thoth was also worshiped locally, together with several deified kings of the past, notably Snofru. Ramesses VI is the last ruler whose name has been encountered. A new Middle Kingdom rock text has recently been found at Rud el-ʿAir, some 1·5 km west of the Serabit el-Khadim temple. Several others have been known from there for some time.

A rock text of Sahureʿ and a large stela of Senwosret I date the third important center of turquoise mining, which was located recently in the Wadi Kharit. Nearby, in the Wadi Nasb, were found a rock stela of year 20 of Amenemhet III and Middle Kingdom and Ramessid texts.

PART THREE
ASPECTS OF EGYPTIAN SOCIETY

EVERYDAY LIFE

Agricultural scenes in Theban tomb No. 1 at Deir el-Medina, belonging to Sennedjem, of the reign of Sethos I. The setting is the mythical Fields of Ialu, where Sennedjem, accompanied by his wife Iyneferti, is shown reaping grain, plowing with a pair of dappled cattle, and harvesting flax. Only the heads of grain were cut off with a short-handled wooden sickle, whose serrated blade was formed of sharp flakes of flint; the remaining much-valued straw was pulled up later. Many examples of sickles and whips of the types used by Sennedjem have been preserved.

There is no one method of studying the everyday life of the ancient Egyptians, but a mosaic of different approaches which draw on various sources. Tomb reliefs and paintings provide a wealth of material; although only members of the top stratum of society were buried in large decorated tombs, subsidiary scenes afford glimpses of the life of ordinary people. These are supplemented by tomb models and objects of daily use which often form part of funerary equipment; less common are those found in excavations of settlements. Literary and administrative texts on papyri and ostraca are invaluable because they provide details not available from elsewhere.

Farms and Vineyards

For sowing, the ground was prepared by plowing, usually done with oxen, or hoeing. The seed was then scattered and cattle, sheep or goats were used to tread it in.

The monotony of the reapers' work was relieved by a flute player. After cutting, the ears of grain were collected into baskets and either carried or transported on donkeys to threshing floors. The threshing was done by cattle, sheep or goats which were driven over the ears and trod the grain out. The chaff was separated laboriously by winnowing and sifting. The grain was then deposited in granaries.

Scenes of watering grapevines and picking and crushing grapes are often shown. The crushing was done by men treading grapes in a vat, often to the accompaniment of the rhythmical beating of resonant sticks, and the must was later strained by twisting in a sack. Hieratic labels on wine jars found in excavations give us names of many vineyards and vintners as well as the vintage of the wines they originally contained.

Plowing, Middle Kingdom.

Reaping grain, 5th Dynasty.

Granary, Middle Kingdom.

Winnowing and carrying ears of grain to granary, 18th Dynasty.

Threshing with cattle, 18th Dynasty.

Picking grapes, 18th Dynasty.

Herds and Herdsmen

Scenes from the life of herdsmen include cows being mounted by bulls, calving, suckling calves or being milked; bulls fighting, cattle being fed, and goats browsing on trees or bushes. Inspections of cattle, goats, donkeys, sheep and fowl by the owner of the estate, during which they were counted and their numbers were recorded, were a regular occurrence. Herdsmen may be shown cooking and eating, skinning a goat hung from a tree, or making mats, apparently their favorite pastime. The prestige of stock rearing was reflected in the number of officials bearing titles connected with it.

Inspection of cattle, 18th Dynasty.

Herdsman with goats, 19th Dynasty.

Hunter with dogs, 5th Dynasty.

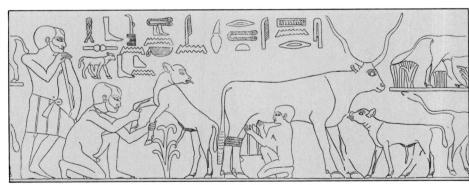

Milking, 5th Dynasty.

Cow calving, 5th Dynasty.

Hunting and Fishing

The contribution of the hunting of desert animals to the Egyptian economy was limited, and the activity soon became the sport of the rich.

Marsh scenes with people fishing, fowling, harvesting papyrus and making papyrus rafts are usually closely associated with cattle-breeding activities. The final stage of seining (or netting) fish by fishermen is often shown, as are several other methods, in particular catching fish in baskets and by means of small hand-held clap-nets. Spearing fish and angling, both usually done from a small papyrus raft, must have been regarded as enjoyable relaxations. Hippopotamus hunting was probably a necessary task rather than a sport.

Seining fish, 5th Dynasty.

Fishhook, 18th/19th Dynasties. Angling, 6th Dynasty.

Fishing with clap-net and angling, 6th Dynasty.

Fishing with clap-net and hippopotamus hunt, 6th Dynasty.

Hippopotamus hunt, 5th Dynasty.

Trades and Crafts

Important stages in the manufacture of objects by craftsmen are shown with surprising technical knowledge in tomb reliefs and paintings: a goldworker is weighing gold; joiners are adding final touches to wooden *djed*-signs (symbolizing endurance) for a shrine; boat-builders have nearly completed the hull of a large wooden boat; men with blowpipes are busy smelting metal. Other craftsmen often represented include sculptors (the making of statues was as much a craft as an art), carpenters, leather-workers, potters, makers of stone vessels, rope-makers and brick-makers. Many models as well as real tools of craftsmen have been found.

Goldsmith, joiners, jewelers and engravers, 18th Dynasty.

Model tools, 18th Dynasty.

Boat-builders, 5th Dynasty.

Metalworkers, 5th Dynasty.

Because of their role in ensuring that the tomb was provided with meat offerings, scenes and models of butchers were among the commonest.

There were many different qualities and shapes of bread and cakes. The grinding of grain was common to all, but different methods of baking were employed. Sometimes the dough was poured into preheated earthenware pots and gently baked without direct fire.

Egyptian beer was brewed by fermenting part-baked bread; brewers standing in vats treading pieces of bread or leaning over a large vessel straining the mash are a common theme in statuettes, models and reliefs.

Butchers, 18th Dynasty.

Butchers, bakers and brewers, Middle Kingdom.

Brewer, cook and woman grinding grain, First Intermediate Period.

Preheating pots for baking bread, 5th Dynasty.

Granaries with grain, 5th Dynasty.

Brewing, Middle Kingdom.

Domestic Life

A number of musical instruments were known from the earliest times, and many of them have been found in excavations. The flute, double clarinet, double oboe and trumpet were the commonest wind instruments; stringed instruments included various types of harp, lute and lyre, and the tambourine and drum were the normal membranophones. On another level, sistra and clappers were used as percussion instruments in rituals.

Occasional finds of model houses usefully complement information gathered from excavations of settlements. Our knowledge of ancient Egyptian domestic architecture is still very incomplete, particularly for the Early Dynastic Period and Old Kingdom, in comparison with what we know about the architecture of temples and tombs.

Details of the day-to-day running of ancient Egyptian households remain obscure, and only exceptionally are we able to penetrate beyond the rather general and very selective information provided by tombs. An attempt to reconstruct an ordinary day, month or year in the life of an ancient Egyptian family would still involve much guessing, a telling indicator of the difficulties Egyptologists face.

Female musicians and dancers, 18th Dynasty.

Model house, Middle Kingdom.

Offering bearers, Middle Kingdom.

Reed brush, 18th Dynasty.

Basketwork and matting, Middle Kingdom.

Sandals, 18th Dynasty or Greco-Roman Period.

"Place myrrh upon your head, and clothe yourself in fine linen," exhorts the "Song of the Harper." Rich Egyptians appreciated beautiful objects of daily use, in particular toilet articles, such as combs, ointment spoons (often in the form of a musician, a servant carrying a large jar on his shoulders, or a swimming girl), kohl-containers (for eye makeup), vases, and mirrors (made of polished copper or bronze, usually circular, with a decorative handle). They liked to surround themselves with elegant furniture (chairs, stools, beds, chests and boxes) and valued fine clothes, wigs and jewelry. They also enjoyed good food, drink, music, singing and dancing (they do not seem to have participated actively in dances, but rather watched dancing displays).

Representations of banquets are very common, particularly in Theban tombs of the New Kingdom. One of the features of these merry-making scenes is the cone of a scented greasy substance (the "myrrh" of the "Song of the Harper") placed on the wig of each reveler; as the party progressed, these slowly melted and gave off a pleasant aroma.

Ancient Egyptian children played much the same games and amused themselves in similar ways to Egyptian children of today. A number of simple toys have been found, though wooden horses on wheels are not known before the Greco-Roman Period.

Detail of banquet scene, 18th Dynasty.

Mirror, New Kingdom.

Toy horse, Greco-Roman Period.

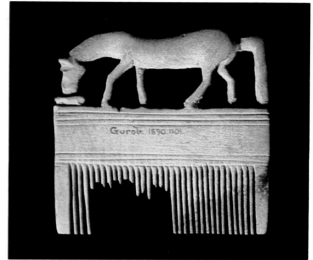

Comb, 19th Dynasty.

Toilet spoon, 18th Dynasty.

Folding stool, 18th Dynasty.

SCRIBES AND WRITING

The invention of writing around 3000 BC defines the beginning of Egyptian history more than any other single change. Similarly, literacy set the chief cultures of the ancient Near East apart from their contemporaries, opening up new possibilities in social organization and in the transmission, and occasionally criticism, of growing bodies of received knowledge. But the script was complex, and literacy was confined to a small elite. Not until the spread of alphabetic scripts was anything like the full potential of writing for society exploited.

It seems that there was no separate, illiterate class of nobility, as a landed aristocracy might be. All high-ranking people had scribal careers in official-dom, army or priesthood; kings too were literate. Among administrative titles the highest do not allude to writing, but we know from representations that such people were scribes; they had surpassed the level of achievement at which writing was the main occupation, not bypassed it. In all spheres writing formed the basis of official organization.

A scribe was trained in his first job by another scribe, and the children of important people could enter office very young – perhaps about the age of 12. After his training, or in its later stages, the scribe would rise gradually through the administrative hierarchy. Basic literacy was probably acquired before he started a job. At Deir el-Medina, the only school for which we have evidence, the initial training seems to have been copying passages from a cursive hieroglyphic text called the "Book of Kemyt." From there the scribe progressed to classic works of literature and, after moving to a job, to contemporary miscellanies of model letters, satirical compositions, poems and panegyrics, which may have been set as daily exercises by pupil-masters. A surprising number of these have been preserved, which suggests that they may ultimately have been put in their owners' tombs.

There are two noteworthy features of this training. First, it was mainly in cursive writing, which was from the beginning the commonest form. Further instruction was probably needed for proficiency in the monumental hieroglyphic script, which was therefore comprehensible to rather fewer people; in the Late Period the two forms diverged sharply. Second, although the Egyptians dissolved their language into a syllabary and had an "alphabetical" order into which lists were some-times arranged, learning was by copying sentences or words, not by starting from individual signs. Writing was perceived in groups of signs, and there was little stimulus to minute analysis of the script.

Apart from administration, letters etc., the cursive script was used for non-essential purposes, the most interesting of which, from our point of view, was transmitting works of literature. Literary texts are preserved both from schools and from other sources. They include narrative fiction, instruction and "philosophical" texts, cult and

Top Granite scribe statue of the Chief Lector-Priest Petamenope, c. 650 BC. The figure is in the traditional cross-legged writing pose, with a papyrus spread between the knees. The statue form is a conscious revival of an Old Kingdom model by one of the richest men of the Late Period. Quartzite, height 75 cm. From Karnak. Cairo, Egyptian Museum.

Above Typical scribe's palette with a long slot for reed pens (the original ones are preserved) in addition to depressions with cakes of ink. Middle Kingdom. Wood. From Beni Hasan. Oxford, Ashmolean Museum.

The scribe's basic tools make up the hieroglyph on the left, which shows a palette with depressions for cakes of red and black pigment mixed with gum, a water pot or bag, and a reed pen or papyrus smoother, all tied together. Ink was made by adding water to the cake of pigment. The scribe painted rather than wrote, with his hand held above the surface. Because of the right-to-left direction of writing, originally in vertical columns, he would have smudged his text if he let his hand rest. In hieratic he could write about a dozen signs before recharging his pen.

religious hymns, love poetry, royal inscriptions and miscellaneous texts used secondarily as literature, and various genres we would not consider literary: medical and mathematical texts, rituals, and some mortuary books. The chief center of production was the "house of life," a scriptorium attached to temples, which evidently made copies of the entire range of traditional writings, not only of belles-lettres. The tradition continued almost without a break into the 3rd century AD, although few texts survived the transition from hieratic to demotic. Some literary works became generally familiar and were alluded to in later texts, playing on a lettered culture common to writer and reader.

Above Specimen of literary hieratic of the 12th Dynasty with transcription into hieroglyphs. Translation: "The vizier Ptahhotpe says: Sovereign, my lord, decrepitude has come, old age has descended, feebleness has arrived, dotage has returned; one is lying in a second childhood all the time. Eyes are feeble, ears deaf, and the tired heart fails. The mouth is silent and cannot speak." Pap. Prisse 4.2–4. Paris, Bibliothèque Nationale.

Below Extract from a statement of the misfortunes of Peteese's family, perhaps submitted to a high financial official in the reign of Darius I. The text and transcription between the lines read from right to left, but the individual words of the transcription read from left to right. Translation: "The master of harbors dispatched a military officer, saying: 'Arrest anybody Peteese (an ancestor of the author)/tells you to arrest.' The officer came to Teudjoi (el-Hiba), and Peteese had the two priests arrested. He went north with them to the royal palace./In Pharaoh's presence Peteese recounted everything they had done. Pharaoh passed sentence on the two priests." From el-Hiba. Manchester, John Rylands Library, Pap. 9.

p3-dj-jst jw ntj nb rmt n jmhtj m-sm dd mr-ms' w' jw "-n-mr p' dj

pr-" pr'p'r jrmw hdjf 2 w'b p' n mhw p'-dj-jst dj t'jw-d'j r jw mr-ms' p' n-jmw mhw mj nk dd r

2 s(?) w'b p' n hp jrw pr-" dj pr-" m-b'h jjrw nb md p'-dj-jst dd

There are several forms of the script. Hieroglyphic was used for monumental and ornamental inscriptions, cursive hieroglyphs for religious texts and the "Book of Kemyt," and hieratic, the normal cursive, for everyday purposes. In the 3rd Intermediate Period some monumental inscriptions were written in hieratic, which was also the point of departure for abnormal hieratic, used in the Theban area in the 9th–7th centuries, and for demotic, the cursive of the north after 700 and of all Egypt by 600. Hieratic can always be transcribed into hieroglyphs, although the result is not the same as a text originally composed in hieroglyphic, but demotic is self-sufficient, referring at most to hieratic. Cursive hieroglyphs died out in the first millennium BC, while hieratic was used for religious texts until the end; demotic was used for business, literature and occasional inscriptions on stone.

The spoken language developed continuously, but written forms changed only fitfully, and were linked to the script form used to write them. Between the Old and Middle Kingdoms, the period of Old and Middle Egyptian, the change was more or less consistent with the script, but speech and writing had diverged greatly by the 18th Dynasty. Late Egyptian, the spoken language of the New Kingdom, was used for hieratic documents of the 19th–20th Dynasties, while hieroglyphic texts were still written in a loose form of Middle Egyptian; hieratic forms began to differ between Middle Egyptian religious texts and Late Egyptian business documents. Demotic, roughly the spoken language of the 7th–6th centuries BC, supplanted Late Egyptian, but Middle Egyptian remained the formal, monumental language until the end of Egyptian civilization. In the 2nd century AD Egyptian magical texts began to be written in Greek letters, and from the 4th century this developed into Coptic, the language of Christian Egypt, which gradually gave way to Arabic after 640 AD.

Egyptian is a member of the Afro-Asiatic language family, which includes Semitic and groups in Africa ranging from Berber in the northwest to Chadic (around Lake Chad) and Kushitic and Omotic in southern Sudan and Ethiopia. It resembles Semitic most closely, but nonetheless forms a branch of its own. In word formation and phonetics the two have much in common, including tricon-sonantal roots and the consonants '('ayin), q and ḥ, but Egyptian's structure is as far from Semitic's as modern English is from Latin.

Right Ink hieroglyphs and vignette from the Book of the Dead papyrus of the lady Anhai, 19th Dynasty. The red groups of signs (rubrics) mark the beginnings of sections. The text is corrupt and untranslatable, but derives from a formula for appearing in the form of Ptah and another for eating, drinking and taking up a throne in the next world. London, British Museum.

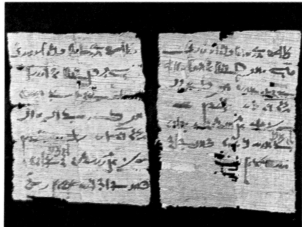

Left A pair of demotic questions to the oracle of Sobek and Isis at Soknopaiou Nesos (Dimai) in the Faiyum; 149 or 138 BC. The two tiny slips of papyrus (7·5 × 5·5 cm) were placed before the god, and in some way the relevant one was chosen and removed. The texts are almost identical; the first reads: "Plea of the servant Teshnufe (son of) Ma're', who says/before his master Sobek lord of Pay, great god,/and Isis, perfect of throne. If my/soundest course is to plow/the bank of the lake this year,/year 33,/and I should not sow, let this slip/be brought out to me." The second has the corresponding negative provision "if it is not my soundest course . . . ," and omits the reference to sowing, which is not applicable.

199

Inscription on a naos of Tuthmosis IV, recording the king's discovery of a stone. The lines of text and transcription give a step-by-step analysis of the Egyptian and its translation into English.
(a) Copy of the hieroglyphs, written from left to right for convenience. Signs enclosed by

[ ] are restored.
(b) Sign-by-sign transcription, divided into words, with indication of taxograms and orthograms above the line.
(+) marks a phonogram complement, which is not to be read separately. Logograms are written in CAPITALS; there is no sharp distinction between a

single phonogram writing a whole world and a logogram. *nsjt* is a complex historical writing that has to be read as a group.
(c) Conventional Egyptologist's transcription, giving the linguistic structure of the text.
(d) Word-for-word indication of the meaning of the Egyptian.
(e) English translation.

All the forms of the script use signs in two overlapping categories: phonograms (phonetic signs) and semograms (conveying meaning). The phonograms form a syllabary, but one in which the vowels are not specified. Because they write consonants + any vowel or no vowel, the information they convey is only consonants. Transcriptions are into consonantal skeletons. The examples of different types of sign are drawn from the text illustrated *right*. In theory there are vast numbers of possible writings of any word, but in practice words have standard writings, mostly of phonograms with semograms at the end. These are read as groups, not broken down into their components – as is true also of reading an alphabetic script. Standard writings make the script easily legible, and are particularly important in hieratic and demotic, with their simplified sign forms.

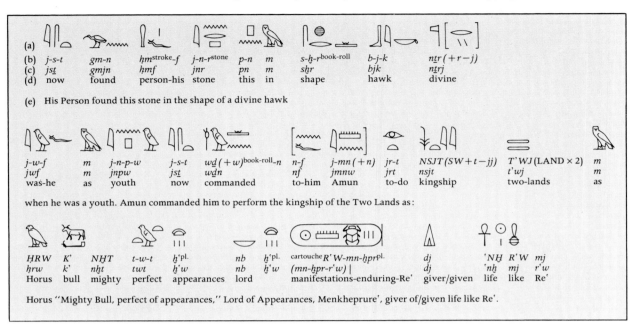

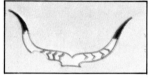

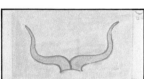

Representational aspects
Most hieroglyphs are pictures; they may evolve with the artistic styles of different periods. This group shows a pair of cattle horns and a clump of papyrus, both in versions of the Old and of the Middle Kingdom, and a reed mat.

Derivation of values

- *s*   from *sw* "length of cloth"
- *t*   from *tj* "loaf of bread"
- *gm* from *gmt* "black ibis"
- *r*   from *r'* "mouth"
- *p*   from *pj* "mat"
- *jr* from *jrt* "eye"
- *h'* from *h'j* "appear (the sun over the horizon)"

A sign's consonantal reading is mostly determined by what it represents, but one sign may have several values, and may function both as a phonogram and as a semogram. ,
a seated man, may read *rmt* "human being," *zj* "man" or *rhw* "companion," or may be a taxogram, as in *hm-ntr* "priest."

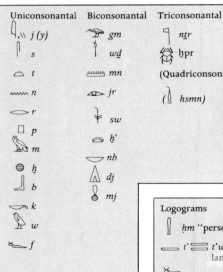

Uniconsonantal	Biconsonantal	Triconsonantal
j (y)	*gm*	*ntr*
s	*wd*	*hpr*
t	*mn*	(Quadriconsonantal)
n	*jr*	(*hsmn*)
r	*sw*	
p	*h'*	
m	*nb*	
h	*dj*	
b	*mj*	
k		
w		
f		

Above Signs can write one to four consonants. Uniconsonantal signs are common, but a set of them is not an alphabet, because in theory it writes vowels with the consonants, and it has no special position among phonograms as a whole.

Right There are two types of semogram: logograms, which write complete words, and signs that are placed after the phonograms in a word. The most important of these are taxograms, or determinatives, which indicate the class or area of meaning to which a word belongs. Strokes, or orthograms, show that a preceding sign is a logogram; sets of two or three strokes write the dual or the plural.

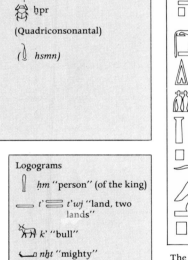

Logograms

hm "person" (of the king)

t' wj "land, two lands"

k' "bull"

nht "mighty"

r'w "Re"

'nh "life"

Taxograms

stone

book-roll: abstraction, word

cartouche; surrounds royal names

Orthograms

| logogram indicator

||| plural indicator

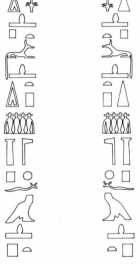

The writing of the signs in a text fixes the direction of reading. Signs facing right – the normal direction – show that the text reads from right to left. Columns or lines may be used. Here an identical text has been written once from right to left and once from left to right. Offering formula on a false door in the mastaba of Kahayf. Late 6th Dynasty. Giza.

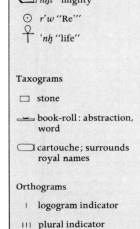

Ornamental caption to a hunting scene in the tomb of Amenemhet at Thebes (no. 82, reign of Tuthmosis III). Words containing the name of Amun have been erased, probably during the ʿAmarna Period. The text reads: ''Crossing the valleys, treading the hills, taking pleasure, shooting the game of the desert, by the one beloved of his lord, steward of the vizier, scribe accountant of the grain of [Amun, Amenemhet], justified.''

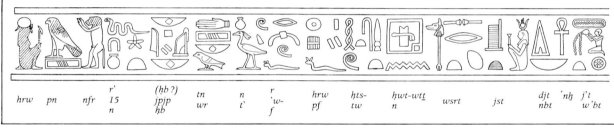

hrw	pn	nfr	r' 15 n	(ḥb ?) jpjp ḥb	tn wr	n t'	r w- f	hrw pf	ḥts- tw	ḥwt-wtt n	wsrt	jst	djt nbt	ʿnḥ	jʿt w ʿbt

Above Outline hieroglyphs in a caption in the tomb of Pere' at Thebes (no. 139, reign of Tuthmosis IV). The text reads: ''Going north to the district of Poqer [Abydos]; seeing Wennofre [Osiris] at the festival.'' The sign  *m* has been replaced by ⊂⊃, also *m*, in order to make a better grouping. Both versions are now visible. a sign is changed in form: ⊂⊃ (human mouth), *r*, becomes ⊋. The result of all this is that a single value may be written by many different signs: all *m* (from a total of more than 25), and one sign can have many values: , *š s ḫ ḥ n m jnr*.

Cryptography

The use of the script's principles in a deliberately misleading way is called cryptography. This is found at all periods, chiefly as a challenge to persuade the reader to read a standard formula. During the Late and Greco-Roman Periods, however, the hieroglyphic script was elaborated from a repertoire of a few hundred signs to one of several thousand, using every possible method for devising new signs and combinations, and not observing the former economy of means. At this stage hieroglyphs had lost their connection with the everyday script. They could be read only by a tiny elite, mainly of priests, who wished to cultivate complexity almost for its own sake.

Above Facsimile of an ornamental inscription of the reign of Tiberius in the birth house at Philae. Translation: ''This good day, the 2nd of Epiphi [month name]: This festival, the great festival of the entire land; that day when the birth house was completed for the mighty one, Isis, giver of life, mistress of the Abaton [see page 73].'' The transcription follows the grouping of the signs. The writing, especially of the first few words, uses numerous non-traditional sign-values. Examples of early and late values are:

p; early *bjk*

n; early *š*

t'; early *ʿḫ*

t; early *d*

Some signs do not occur in early periods: *nfr*. In other cases

A letter of the 11th Dynasty (2002 BC) that never reached its destination. The papyrus is folded into a packet (8 × 4 cm) and sealed, with the addressee's name above the seal. The text reads: ''The overseer of Lower Egypt, Re'nofre.'' From Deir el-Bahri. New York, Metropolitan Museum of Art.

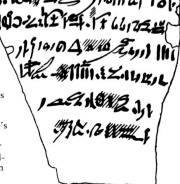

Ostraca were used for writing drafts of texts or as cheap substitutes for papyrus. In this example an illiterate man asks another to write a pledge for him in respect of a debt; the ostracon was probably kept by the creditor until the matter was settled. At this date – between Ramesses III and IX – the tunic was equivalent in value to 1–3 sacks of grain.

Translation: ''Year 5, month 3 of *peret* (approx. winter), day 22. What the guardian of the estate Penrenenutet said: 'By Amun and the ruler, if I enter a(nother) week without having given this tunic to Harmin, it (my debt) will be doubled to my debit.' Done (i.e. written) by the foreman of the gang Nekhemmut.'' From Deir el-Medina. London, Petrie Collection (University College).

THE ARMY

The earliest battle in the history of mankind whose course can be reconstructed in detail took place near the city of Qadesh on the river Orontes in 1285 BC. The combatants were Ramesses II and the Hittite king Muwatallis, and at stake was the control of Syria. In the end, both armies suffered heavily, but neither was annihilated. Ramesses II gained a moral victory, but the encounter was indecisive.

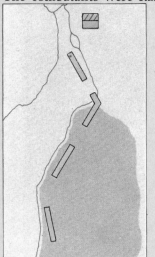

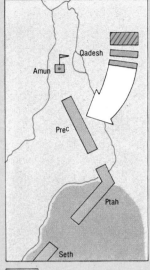

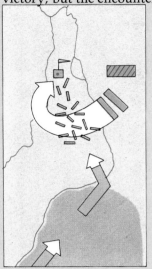

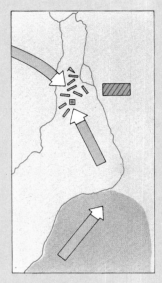

▭	Egyptian infantry and chariotry, total 20,000 men
•	Ramesses II
⚑	Egyptian camp

▭	Hittite chariotry, 3,500 chariots with 10,500 men
▨	Hittite infantry, 8,000 men

1. The Egyptian army consisted of four divisions, with a smaller unit operating independently. Through false information planted on them, the Egyptians were misled into believing that the Hittite host had retreated. The Egyptian divisions advanced northwards along the Orontes, unaware that the Hittites lay concealed beyond Qadesh.

2. The Egyptian van, the division of Amun led by the king himself, reached the rendezvous point northwest of the city and set up camp. When the division of Pre', suspecting no danger, approached, its right flank was subjected to a devastating charge of Hittite chariotry.

3. The division of Pre', caught by surprise, was broken and scattered. Survivors of the Hittite ambush were fleeing northwards in the direction of the Egyptian camp, with Hittite chariots in pursuit. The division of Ptah was still emerging from the Robaui forest south of the town of Shabtuna and crossing on to the west bank of the river, and was too far away to render any assistance to the attacked unit.

4. The camp was overrun and the division of Amun suffered heavy losses. The king and his guard desperately tried to fight their way to meet the approaching division of Ptah. Muwatallis committed his chariot reserve in order to bring the battle to a quick conclusion.

5. By his gallant, though forced, action the Egyptian king gained enough time: the special task force appeared at last, and with the division of Ptah now reaching the scene, crushed the Hittite chariotry. Muwatallis' infantry remained inactive beyond the river.

One of the advantages Egypt derived from her unique geographical position was relative safety. Nomadic tribes in the deserts on either side of the Nile valley soon ceased to pose a serious threat to the highly organized and much more powerful Egyptian civilization; only during periods of instability were they a force to be reckoned with. Colonial expansion in the 12th Dynasty led to intensive campaigning and building of fortresses in Nubia, but it was not until the 18th Dynasty that the Egyptians encountered real opposition, when they entered the military arena of the Near East by contending for Syria and Palestine.

The word *mesha'*, "army," originally described both military forces and peaceful expeditions sent to quarry minerals: "task force" would be the most fitting translation. During the Old Kingdom, when an emergency arose, a body of men was mustered to back the small specialized permanent units. The situation changed in the 1st Intermediate Period: instability brought about the creation of private armies of nomarchs and the use of non-Egyptian mercenary troops. The Middle Kingdom already knew well-organized standing military units, supplemented when needed by local militia. The force consisted mainly of infantry, with boat personnel integrated into it. The 2nd Intermediate Period and the 18th Dynasty saw an unprecedented advance in the development of weapons, military organization (the appearance of chariotry, organization of infantry into companies of some 250 men led by a standard-bearer), strategy and tactics. The standing army and professional army officers began to play an important part in internal politics. In the Late Period, foreign mercenaries formed the core.

Ancient Egyptian weapons of various types are known from contemporary representations and models as well as archaeological finds.

The bow, the most important long-range weapon, was used at all times, either the archaic compound horn-bow consisting of two antelope horns joined by a wooden central piece, or the wooden, slightly double-convex, "self" bow. During the 2nd Intermediate Period the composite bow was introduced from Asia. It was made of laminated strips of various materials, and had a much-improved range and power. When strung, the bow acquired a characteristic triangular shape. *The quiver* was in use from the Old Kingdom onwards.

The spear was employed throughout Egyptian history.

The mace with a stone mace-head of varying form, the most powerful weapon of close combat in the Predynastic Period, was in historic times replaced by *the battle-ax* with a copper ax-head. Some of the early semicircular ax-heads differed little from contemporary tools of craftsmen, but already during the Old Kingdom a specialized shallow type appeared. This, and the scalloped ax-head, were characteristic of the weapons of the Middle Kingdom. In the 2nd Intermediate Period a new type with a narrow ax-blade and therefore much-improved power of penetration appeared, probably an indigenous development. *The scimitar* (sickle sword), an Asiatic weapon used in the same way as the Egyptian battle-ax (as a cutting or piercing rather than thrusting weapon), is also met in the New Kingdom.

Cudgels, *clubs* and *throwing-sticks* of various types remained in use as side arms at all times. *The dagger* was used in the same way.

Personal protection was afforded by *the shield*, already attested during the late Predynastic Period. Light *body armor* was known from the New Kingdom but its use remained limited.

The two-wheeled horse-drawn *chariot*, introduced to Egypt in the 2nd Intermediate Period, was a light vehicle, made of wood with some leather and metal elements. It was manned by two soldiers: the charioteer, and the chariot-warrior armed with a bow and spear and carrying a shield. The chariot's main contribution to the art of warfare was mobility and the element of surprise connected with it: in the attack, the chariots approached at full speed and the chariot-warriors delivered their arrows while passing the massed enemy ranks. The chariot was not armored in any way and therefore was not suitable for a direct attack. Once the enemy lines were broken, the chariotry was ideally suited for pursuing and harassing the scattered foot soldiers. Judging from the appearance of special titles, the chariotry formed a separate arm of the Egyptian army from the reign of Amenophis III.

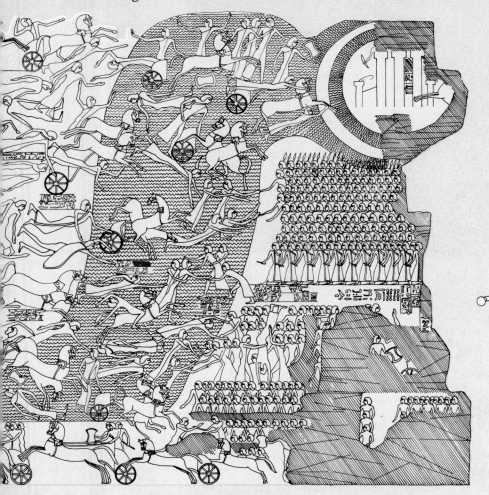

WOMEN IN SOCIETY

The position of women in Egypt is neatly summarized in their roles in early tomb decoration. At the top of the hierarchy is the wife, or sometimes the mother, of the tomb owner, who is simply but elegantly dressed, and sits at leisure with her husband at a table of offerings, in a statue group or on a false door. She sometimes accompanies her husband when he watches scenes of work, but is more often shown when offerings are presented to the couple; this distinction may show that she is normally expected to stay at home. At the other extreme are scenes or statuettes of servant girls and of women engaged in menial tasks, making bread and beer, spinning and weaving. These too are sedentary activities, probably conducted in the domestic quarters of a house or estate. The female flesh color, yellow, indicates among other things less exposure to the sun than the male red, and therefore a more enclosed existence – as it does on successful male bureaucrats.

It may have been unsafe for women to venture out. Ramesses III is made to say in a posthumous text, ''I enabled the woman of Egypt to go her way, her journeys being extended where she wanted, without any other person assaulting her on the road'' – which implies that this was not always the case.

In early tombs women are absent from the most important work shown and from the most pleasurable diversions, but do not have to engage in the roughest tasks. Men, for example, make wine, which is more strenuous than brewing. Apart from scenes of musicians and of very athletic girls' dances, the role of women in early periods seems very decorous, although this may be because we cannot interpret our sources fully. In the New Kingdom women become much more prominent, their clothing more elaborate, and the erotic content of scenes in which they appear more definite – if still heavily coded. The Late Period mostly returns to earlier decorum.

Women did not hold any important titles, except some priestly ones, and apart from a few members of

Women in different roles and artistic media
Far left bottom The corpulent Ka'aper embraces his slender wife. His body depicts wise and prosperous age, hers the blander feminine ideal. Embraces are very rarely shown. The small musical scenes and the monkey have erotic overtones. In his mastaba at Saqqara. Early 5th Dynasty.

Left Wooden statue of a servant carrying offerings, unusual for its large size (c.110 cm) and for the coloring of the garments. The type derives from Old Kingdom reliefs of bearers bringing the produce of estates. c.2020 BC. From Theban Tomb 280 of Meketre'. New York, Metropolitan Museum of Art.

Below left Sketch of a woman performing an acrobatic dance on a 19th-Dynasty limestone ostracon from Deir el-Medina. Width 16·8 cm. Turin, Museo Egizio.

the royal family and queens regnant they had little political power. Their commonest title, "mistress of the house," is a term of respect, and may mean little more than "Mrs." Almost all were illiterate, and therefore barred from the bureaucracy – to which they are in any case unlikely to have aspired – and from the major intellectual areas of culture. Symptomatic of this is the fact that age and wisdom were qualities respected in men, who were represented as corpulent elder statesmen, but not in women. Even a man's mother is indistinguishable from his wife in tomb depictions; both are youthful figures. The way women are shown is, of course, part of men's definition of them, and displays a public, ideal state of affairs. In reality women's influence may not have been so circumscribed, and they may have been far more varied in their roles than our evidence would suggest.

Family structures, for example, appear severely simplified. The norms of tomb and stela decoration leave no room for the widow or widower, the divorcee, homosexuals, or deviations from monogamy – yet all of these are known to have occurred. A story recounts an affair between a king and a military officer, and there are homosexual episodes in the myth of Horus and Seth. There was a limited amount of polygyny in the Old and Middle Kingdoms, and the king could have many wives, although only one – in addition to his mother, if she was still alive – bore the title "great royal wife."

Above Black granite statue group of Tuthmosis IV and his mother Ti'a. Kings shown with their mothers may not yet have had a chief wife, but this is unlikely here, because Tuthmosis had three in ten years. Height 110 cm. From Karnak. Cairo, Egyptian Museum.

Right Mereruka's wife plays the harp to him on a bed. Beneath are pots and chests containing "the best of the treasures of gold, all sorts of oil, and clothing." These are probably all for the adornment of the couple in their amorous encounters. In his tomb at Saqqara. Reign of Teti.

Left Miy, a lady of the court of Amenophis III, ebony statuette from a tomb near the royal harem complex at Kom Medinet Ghurab; one of a group of similar works. Height 15·6 cm. Brooklyn Museum.

Marriage

Egyptians were mostly monogamous. Inheritance passed from father to children, but followed no very rigid pattern, and family property was defined by a marriage settlement – documentation of which is not known before the 3rd Intermediate Period – and by deeds of transfer made either between the living or as wills. In all of this the woman's role was important, though not equal to that of her husband. She brought a proportion of the property into the marriage, which was in theory a new household, not an extension of parental home, and had some rights over it in a divorce. She could also make a will and leave her property as she wished, although the extent of this freedom is not known. It is most striking that we have no evidence either for marriage ceremonies of any sort or for judicial processes in divorce. Even so, the legal status of a couple living together was different from that of a married pair. There is even a case where a man is accused for having intercourse with a woman who is living with another man but not married to him, something which might seem unlikely to constitute an offence. Despite these relatively free institutions, a woman's adultery was, at least in theory, a serious offence. Apart from gradations of this sort, mortality and the frequency of divorce led to complicated situations with regard to property and inheritance. Life expectancy was probably around 20, so that it was not unusual for a man or a woman

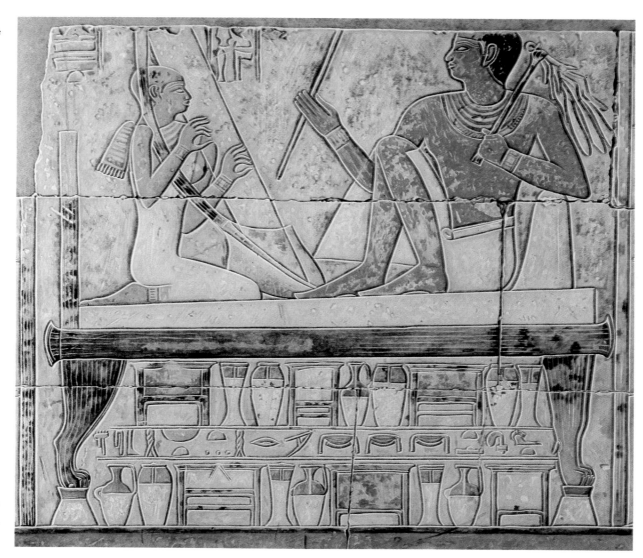

to be widowed several times. A Middle Kingdom deed illustrates the complexity of inheritance. A man retires and hands over his office to his son while disinheriting the son's mother and leaving his remaining property to his children (who may not yet be born) by another woman; it seems that neither woman is his wife.

Very little is known of the social background to marriage. It was possible to marry quite close blood relatives, including on occasion half-siblings, but the precise definition of permitted and prohibited partners is not known. In the royal family there was some brother–sister marriage, but this practice may be in intentional contrast with that of ordinary people. In Greco-Roman Egypt such marriages are well attested among the Greek population. Our chief difficulty in understanding the framework lies in Egyptian kinship terms, of which there were very few. A single word could mean brother, mother's brother or brother's son (and no doubt more besides); others will have had similarly extended meanings. This means that reconstructed genealogies can seldom be verified.

The age of either partner at marriage is unknown. Some family trees show that men on occasion had children well before they were 20, but the clearest cases are in the royal family, which may be untypical here too. At first marriage women were no doubt younger than their husbands, but this may not have been true of subsequent marriages.

Sexuality and fertility

Men, who produced our evidence, will have been concerned to enhance women's sexuality for their own ends – which were religious as well as pleasurable – but not to promote it as an independent and subversive force. Their attitude to it was ambivalent. In stories the evil seductress is a common motif, and love poetry of the New Kingdom is often written in the words of the ardent woman, in this case without the same moralistic overtones. Although the stories have religious elements, both these sources give a secular view of the matter. In religious terms, however, sexuality was important because of its relationship with creation, and, by association, with rebirth in the hereafter. It was also significant for the character of certain deities – Hathor among goddesses and Min among gods. In a funerary context the covert erotic references in tomb scenes could have two purposes: to ensure rebirth through potency in the next life, or to enable the deceased to lead an enjoyable existence. Scenes with an erotic content include ones of hunting in the marshes, where the deceased is accompanied by his wife, who is somewhat implausibly dressed in her most elaborate costume, wears a heavy wig and carries two symbols of Hathor. Heavy wigs, especially when associated with nudity, could be erotic signals. In a New Kingdom story the evil wife accuses her husband's brother of attempting to seduce her by reporting him as saying, "Come, let us spend an hour lying. Put on your wig."

Motifs like this are rarer in earlier periods, the best example being a scene in the 6th-Dynasty tomb of Mereruka at Saqqara, where the owner and his wife sit facing each other on a bed and she plays the harp to him. Such a scene was intended partly to ensure an erotic ambiance for him in the next life. A spell or a female statuette placed in a tomb could

Right Hunting in the marshes. Nebamun and his wife and daughter are on a papyrus boat, all elaborately dressed. The duck on the front of the boat has erotic associations, as do the wife's wig and the counterpoise and sistrum she holds in her left hand. Nevertheless, the text refers simply to "having pleasure, seeing good things, trapping birds as a work of Sekhet [the marsh goddess] . . ." Reign of Tuthmosis IV. London, British Museum.

Below Copulating couple. One of a number of positions of intercourse shown in a humorous obscene papyrus of the late New Kingdom. As in one other scene, the woman appears to be indifferent to the man. Turin, Museo Egizio.

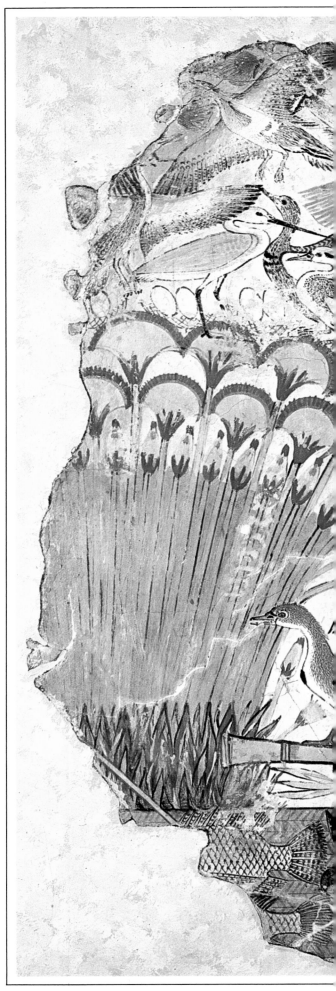

have a similar purpose, but was less conjugal in its reference. A Middle Kingdom spell in the Coffin Texts has the simple beginning, "Copulating by a man in the necropolis." On a mythological plane the same concerns are seen in the Book of the Dead, where Osiris complains to the creator god Atum that after the end of the world "There will be no [sexual] gratification there," to which Atum replies, "I have given transfiguration in place of water, air and gratification" – here held to be the three preconditions of life – "and peace of heart in place of bread and beer."

There is only one obscene document of any size, which dates to the late New Kingdom. This is a set of drawings with brief captions on a papyrus, which shows a variety of sexual encounters between a fat, priapic man (or perhaps men) and a woman (or women) who is dressed in a wig, necklace, armlets, bracelets and a belt. The papyrus also contains humorous sketches of animals in human roles – a well-known motif – suggesting that the obscene part may be humorous too. From about the same time there is a case of prudery, where paintings of nude dancing girls and lightly clothed women in an 18th-Dynasty tomb were covered in drapery by a later owner. On Late Period dwelling sites obscene objects, mostly statuettes of men with enormous penises, are often found. These did exist earlier, but are mostly lost because of the scarcity of settlement material. They were probably charms intended to increase men's potency.

If potency was a man's worry, where the death rate was so high fertility was inevitably important to women – as well as to men. In all but the wealthiest families children would be vital to contribute their labor, particularly in agriculture, and on another plane to carry on the family line, whose most obvious feature was the common practice of giving a son the name of his grandfather. Gynecological texts are known, including prescriptions for reproductive disorders, birth prognoses, contraception and abortion, but it is unlikely that any of these, except perhaps those for abortion, were very effective. From shrines of Hathor as well as dwelling sites and tombs we have numerous clay figurines of women whose forms emphasize the genitals. The most likely explanation of these is that they were offered by women for their own fertility. It is noteworthy that they do not conform to the norms of Egyptian representation. They may come from a different class of the population from most representational works, or have been considered to be outside the canon for some other reason. Until modern times the gift of such offerings was probably as effective a way of helping to produce a child as visiting a doctor.

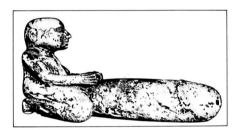

Far left Limestone statuette of a squatting man with an enormous erect penis; probably a fertility or potency charm. Late New Kingdom, from Deir el-Medina. Turin, Museo Egizio.

Left Decorated spoon, perhaps a ritual ointment container, in the form of a swimming girl holding out a duck. The girl has an elaborate wig, heavy earrings and a necklace, but is clothed only in a belt with a diagonal strap on the back. The motif of a girl presenting an animal to her lover in order to attract him is known from love poetry. Wood and bone. 18th Dynasty. Length c. 30 cm. Paris, Musée du Louvre.

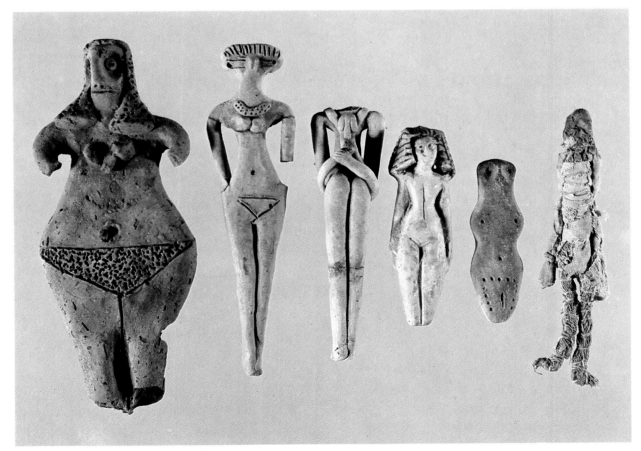

Left Fertility statuettes of naked women in clay and faience, with a "doll" of reed and linen. The forms of all except the faience figure (3rd from right) emphasize the genitals. The 4th figure from the right (photographed from the back) holds a child, and has an "Isis-knot" amulet, which is associated with life and sexual fertility, hanging around its neck. Middle-New Kingdom. Height 15–20 cm. London, Petrie Collection (University College).

RELIGION

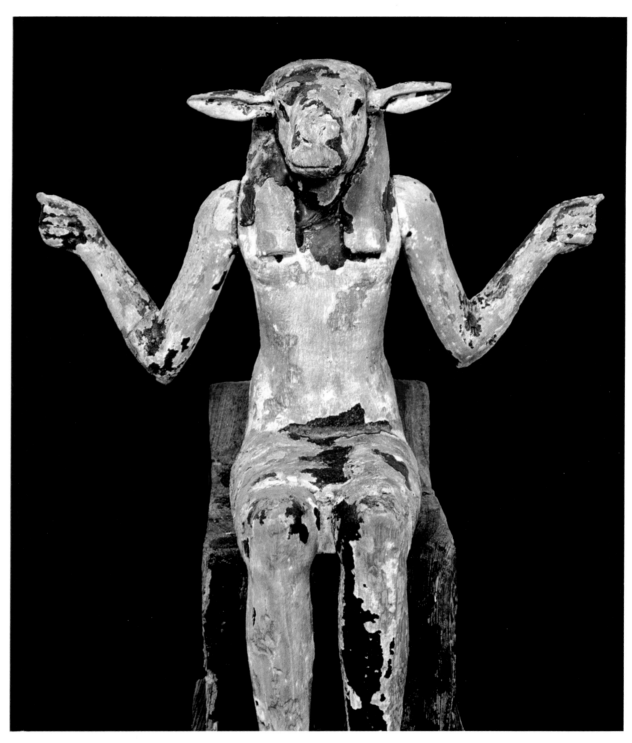

Wooden figure of a ram-headed demon, probably originally holding a pair of snakes. Like a number of mortuary objects, it was covered in black resin. One of a group from the Valley of the Kings that have parallels in New Kingdom underworld books and mythological papyri; this type was not found in the tomb of Tut'ankhamun. Height 45·7 cm. London, British Museum.

Egyptian culture was pervaded by religion, and the official version of Egyptian history was a religious one. In later periods the economy itself was organized around the temples – which does not necessarily mean that it became more religious, since temples were probably not very different from other landlords. However this may be, it is clear that the pattern of secularization, which we tend to take for granted in the development of societies, was absent. The central institution of the kingship ended by losing its charisma, but in other respects society became if anything more religious. Religion in Egypt divides sharply into the official, state aspect, about which we know a great deal, the mortuary sphere, which is also well represented, and the everyday practices of most of the population, which were largely separate from the official cult, and are very poorly known.

hence to humanity. The almost commercial nature of the relationship is expressed quite plainly in offering formulae in the lowest register of temple decoration (see p. 64), which say "The king has come to you [the deity], bringing offerings which he has given to you, so that you may give to him all lands [or a similar gift]." The same point is made in the main areas of relief, but more discreetly. The contract between deity and mankind does not exclude other facets from the relationship, any more than a marriage contract does. The king expresses his adoration and veneration of the deity, and celebrates the deity's qualities. The deity responds with love for the king and delight in his presence. The Egyptian language has an enormous vocabulary to express these basic ideas, some of whose key elements work in unexpected ways. Man or the king cannot "love" a god, but only "respect," "adore" or "thank" him. Qualities attributed to kings or deities are often what we would consider reactions to them, so that "fear" means the capacity to arouse fear, and "love" that to inspire love. The relationships between the participants are very hierarchical, and the lower party to any grouping is an active provider of humble benefits, but a passive recipient of higher ones.

The aim of the cult is the aim of history: to maintain and enhance the established order of the world. The chief temples were dedicated to local deities, who were mostly held within their areas to be the creators, and to encompass the important aspects of the divine world. The cult was carried out by a hierarchy of priests. It did not concern the mass of the population, except for part-time priests, who served one month in four, and people who worked on temple lands. Only priests could enter the temple. The god left the temple for various festivals during which he could be approached by normal people, notably for oracular consultations, but even then the cult image was kept hidden in a shrine that was carried on a symbolic bark, so that the god was known to be present, but not seen.

Outside these festivals, the official cult was irrelevant to the private individual. It is impossible to know his attitude to it, whether he viewed it as essential but not concerning him, or as a meaningless extravagance. There are one or two passages

Left Entrance to room 31 in the temple of Ramesses III at Medinet Habu. The king holds a mace and scepter, symbols of his divine and ritual role, and says "Everybody who enters the shrine, purify four times."

Above Tubular case of gold made to contain a rolled strip of papyrus with a decree by Khons for the protection of the owner, who would wear it around his neck. The text says "Speech by Khons in Thebes, Neferhotep. He made good protection [of] Shaq, deceased." One of three similar cases. 22nd Dynasty. Height 5·2 cm. Cambridge, Fitzwilliam Museum.

The king and history

In the official view society consisted of the gods, the king and mankind. But mankind is absent from most official pictorial records, which represent history and religion as the interplay of gods and the king. Part of the reason for this is a set of rules governing the compatibility of different types of figure in representation and the contexts in which they may occur; in early periods these do not permit a private individual and a god to be shown together, and they never allow normal people to be shown in temples. But in addition the king acts as a mediator – in some respects the only one – between god and man. He represents man to the gods and the gods to man. He is also the living exemplar of the creator god on earth – an idea which is defined by a terminology of great richness and complexity – and reenacts the creator god's role of setting order in place of disorder. History is a ritual in the cosmos, of which this reenactment is a principal theme.

The king is responsible for the well-being of the people, and takes their cares on himself like the "good shepherd" of the Old Testament – a formulation known from Egypt too. Kings also sought to enhance their status before the people, by identifying with gods or, in some instances, by deifying themselves, so that they could even be shown in their normal guise offering to their divine alter egos, as is attested for Amenophis III and Ramesses II. Finally, kings could be deified after death, more on the model of deified private individuals than as if they were true gods. So the king did not have a simple status as god or man. By virtue of his office he was a being apart, and his role differed according to the context in which he acted.

Official and private religion

The official religion consisted of cult and festivals in the main temples, and of the process of history in the way just mentioned. The cult was founded on reciprocity. The king (in theory, but in practice the priests) provided for the gods and cared for their cult images. In return, the gods took up residence in the images and showed their favor to the king and

Left Relief of Amenophis III offering to his deified self, in the temple of Soleb in Upper Nubia. The presentation is that of any normal temple relief. The deified king, "Nebma'atre' [Amenophis' praenomen], great god," has a lunar headdress and divine scepter, but wears the royal uraeus, headcloth and false beard.

Above Group of faience amulets from a single mummy. Above: *wedjat* eye, scarab and winged scarab pectoral, all symbols of rebirth. Below: mummiform Duamutef and Qebehsenuf, Sons of Horus; Isis and Nephthys, who mourn for Osiris; ram-headed god, probably Amun; two *djeds* and papyrus stem, symbolizing duration and freshness. From Abydos. 30th Dynasty. Width of winged scarab 8·7 cm. Oxford, Ashmolean Museum.

Below Group of animal mummies: elaborately wrapped ibis (with a figure of Thoth), cat and snake; fish in a box. Late or Greco-Roman Period. Oxford, Ashmolean Museum.

in texts that question the value of offerings, but these must be seen against the background of the general assumption that they were necessary. Whatever his attitude was, for his own religious needs he turned elsewhere. Apart from the main temples there were many local shrines to lesser deities, or to different forms of the main ones, throughout the country, rather as in European cities cathedrals coexist with smaller churches. Normal people went to these shrines, where they prayed, placed offerings or deposited oracular questions. There were also centers of pilgrimage, such as Abydos, which had its heyday in the Middle Kingdom, and Saqqara, where the animal necropolis acted as a focus in the Late and Ptolemaic periods. If we are to believe letter formulae, people would visit shrines – or possibly pray in their homes – every day in order to intercede for the welfare of the absent correspondent. Such formulae are not necessarily good evidence, but certain details suggest that there is a core of genuine practice in these ones.

Religious activities of this sort are paralleled by a host of other practices, many of which shade off into the magical. Among types of religious objects one may cite, almost at random, amulets, including divine decrees safeguarding their bearers, busts of ancestors in houses, and numerous special objects and modes of dress surrounding childbirth. From texts we know of magical cures for illness, love charms, calendars of lucky and unlucky days, the avoidance of the evil eye, divination through dreams and various rarer practices, letters written to dead relatives who were thought to hold a grudge against the living, and much else besides. Despite the multifarious forms of religious observance and

the hundreds of different deities, some important events in life were rather surprisingly secular. We have no evidence for rituals performed on the newborn child, only of ones aimed at easing the birth and removing pollution from the mother after it. Similarly, phases of life like the circumcision of boys, apparently just before puberty, or marriage, do not seem to have been ritualized.

One area of popular and official religious life that impressed foreigners in antiquity was animal worship. There had always been animals kept as sacred to particular deities – or possibly worshiped as deities in their own right – and buried ceremonially. In the Late Period these practices proliferated enormously. The species associated with the main deity of an area was often held sacred there, and either a single member of it or all members were mummified and buried. To pay for an animal's burial was a "good deed." In Memphis, whose population was no doubt very mixed, many species were buried. The most famous is the Apis bull, sacred to Ptah, which was buried in one catacomb (the Serapeum) and its mother in a second, while ibises, dogs or jackals, cats, baboons, ichneumons and rams are all attested in varying numbers. Other species, including several types of fish, snakes and crocodiles, are known from other parts of the country. A whole town sprang up in the desert at north Saqqara to cater for these needs, and ibises were farmed on an almost industrial scale, before being probably hastened to their death. These practices, whose precise understanding eludes us still, were common to all classes of society. Their public character and the decline of private tombs at the time may be related to a weakening of the belief in individual life after death.

The Egyptian Pantheon
Local Gods

It is impossible to arrange Egyptian deities into neat categories; any attempt to do so involves simplification. There are two main reasons for this: the complexity of Egyptian religious ideas and the long period over which they developed. The religious practices of ordinary people differed considerably from the official religion of the large temples.

In addition to their representations and hieroglyphic forms of their names, the following lists provide three types of information: 1. the main iconographic features by which the deity can be recognized; 2. the character and function of the deity, its relationship with other gods etc.; 3. its main places of worship.

Many of the gods and goddesses can be described as local deities because from the earliest times they were closely connected with a particular locality. Nonetheless, numerous apparently local deities are found over much of the country from early times. The gods shared the fate of their home towns, and while some of them were ultimately promoted to be Egyptian "state gods" (e.g. the Memphite Ptah, the Theban Amon-Re', and the Heliopolitan Re'-Harakhty) whose cult spread over the whole of Egypt, others fell into obscurity and oblivion and were replaced by, or more often assimilated with, the more

vigorous gods of other localities. The latter could be done in two different ways: by adopting another god's attributes (e.g. Osiris took some of his iconographic characteristics from the god 'Andjety) or by the creation of a composite deity (e.g. Ptah-Sokar-Osiris), a process known as syncretism. Because of their connection with the resident god, various "guest deities" were worshiped in local temples.

Re'(Re'-Harakhty) Sun-disk on head, hawk-headed (Re'-Harakhty)/sun god, identified with Harakhty and the primeval creator god Atum as Re'-Harakhty-Atum; often linked with other gods (Amon-Re' etc.)/Heliopolis; as a state god of the New Kingdom worshiped at many other places.

Bastet Lioness-headed or cat-headed/war goddess; closely connected with Mut and Sakhmet/Tell Basta.

Neith Red crown or two crossed arrows and shield on her head (also held in hands)/goddess of war and hunting; closely connected with Sobek; guardian deity/Sa el-Hagar, also Memphis, the Faiyum and Esna.

Thoth Ibis-headed, often with moon crescent/god of writing and counting; baboon another sacred animal/el-Ashmunein and el-Baqliya.

Harsaphes Ram-headed or ram/gained importance during the 1st Intermediate Period when Herakleopolis was Egypt's northern capital; closely connected with Re', Osiris, and Amun/Ihnasya el-Medina.

Hathor Sun-disk, cow's horns, also cow-headed, cow, "Hathor-pillar" or sistrum etc./goddess of women, also sky goddess, tree goddess (Thebes)/Heliopolis, Memphis, Atfih, el-Qusiya, Dendara, Thebes, Gebelein, Abu Simbel, Sinai (Serabit el-Khadim).

Montu Often hawk-headed, sun-disk and two plumes/war god; connected with the Buchis bull of Armant/Armant, but also Karnak, Tod, Nag' el-Madamud.

Khons ,Mut and Amun (Amon-Re') Khons: child's side-lock of hair, sometimes with moon crescent, often mummiform; Mut: vulture headdress or crowns (white or double), also lioness-headed; Amun (head of the triad): two plumes, sometimes ithyphallic/Mut a war goddess; Amun's female counterpart Amaunet/Theban triad (Karnak, Luxor), but Amun also important at el-Ashmunein; as a state god of the New Kingdom Amon-Re' worshiped at many other places (Tanis, Memphis, the oases).

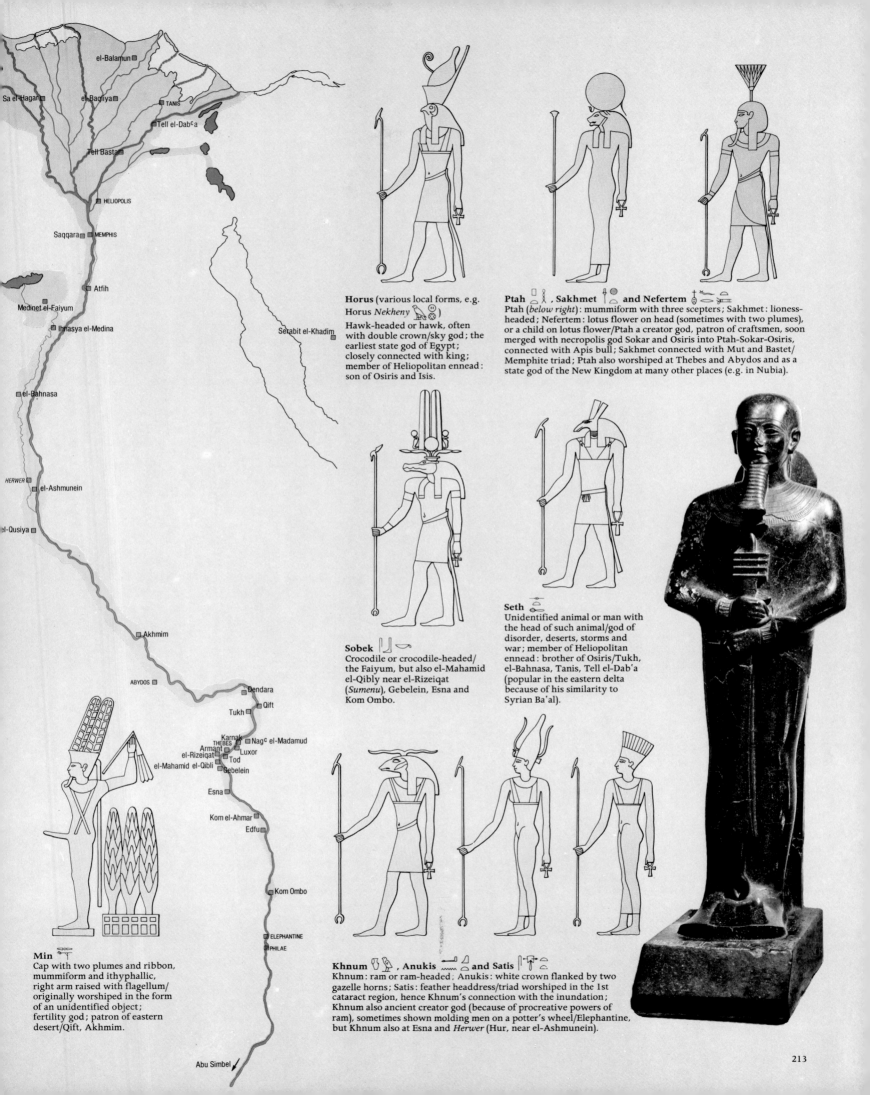

Horus (various local forms, e.g. Horus *Nekheny*)
Hawk-headed or hawk, often with double crown/sky god; the earliest state god of Egypt; closely connected with king; member of Heliopolitan ennead: son of Osiris and Isis.

Ptah , **Sakhmet** **and Nefertem**
Ptah (*below right*): mummiform with three scepters; Sakhmet: lioness-headed; Nefertem: lotus flower on head (sometimes with two plumes), or a child on lotus flower/Ptah a creator god, patron of craftsmen, soon merged with necropolis god Sokar and Osiris into Ptah-Sokar-Osiris, connected with Apis bull; Sakhmet connected with Mut and Bastet/ Memphite triad; Ptah also worshiped at Thebes and Abydos and as a state god of the New Kingdom at many other places (e.g. in Nubia).

Sobek
Crocodile or crocodile-headed/ the Faiyum, but also el-Mahamid el-Qibly near el-Rizeiqat (*Sumenu*), Gebelein, Esna and Kom Ombo.

Seth
Unidentified animal or man with the head of such animal/god of disorder, deserts, storms and war; member of Heliopolitan ennead: brother of Osiris/Tukh, el-Bahnasa, Tanis, Tell el-Dab'a (popular in the eastern delta because of his similarity to Syrian Ba'al).

Min
Cap with two plumes and ribbon, mummiform and ithyphallic, right arm raised with flagellum/ originally worshiped in the form of an unidentified object; fertility god; patron of eastern desert/Qift, Akhmim.

Khnum , **Anukis** **and Satis**
Khnum: ram or ram-headed; Anukis: white crown flanked by two gazelle horns; Satis: feather headdress/triad worshiped in the 1st cataract region, hence Khnum's connection with the inundation; Khnum also ancient creator god (because of procreative powers of ram), sometimes shown molding men on a potter's wheel/Elephantine, but Khnum also at Esna and *Herwer* (Hur, near el-Ashmunein).

213

Universal Gods etc.

Some Egyptian gods were "universal" in the sense that there was no particular place with which they were connected; this, however, did not prevent them from becoming members of local theological systems (e.g. Isis belonged to the Heliopolitan ennead) and having temples built for them (Isis was the chief deity worshiped at Philae). Conversely, some of the "universal gods" probably started as local deities (e.g. Anubis).

Isis 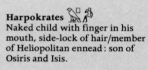 **and Harpokrates**
Woman, often hieroglyph of her name on her head/member of Heliopolitan ennead: wife of Osiris; guardian and magician.

Harpokrates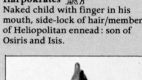
Naked child with finger in his mouth, side-lock of hair/member of Heliopolitan ennead: son of Osiris and Isis.

Below **Apis**
Bull with markings on hide and sun-disk between horns, or bull-headed/connected with Ptah; burial place at Saqqara.

Above **Geb and Nut**, **Shu**
Members of Heliopolitan ennead; deities of earth (Geb), air and light (Shu) and sky (Nut).

Osiris
Mummiform, scepter and flagellum white crown with plumes and horns/dying god of vegetation; ruler of netherworld.

Anubis
Recumbent dog ("jackal") or dog-headed, black/necropolis god; connected with mummification.

Bes
Dwarf with mask-like face, often crown of feathers and lion's mane/family god; protector of pregnant women.

Imhotep
Deified official of Djoser; patron of scribes; healer, sage and magician; regarded as son of Ptah and a woman Khredu'ankh.

Nephthys
Woman with hieroglyphs of her name on her head/member of Heliopolitan ennead: sister of Isis; guardian deity.

Taweret
Composite of hippopotamus and woman, with lion's paws and crocodile's tail/protectress of pregnant women.

The priesthood

Before the New Kingdom there was no large, full-time priesthood. The growth of temples in the 18th Dynasty, accompanied by other religious changes, saw the rise of the priesthood as a class, a rise that continued with few checks into the Late Period. The basic needs of the cult could be satisfied by an officiant, a ritual specialist or lector priest, who might be the same person as the officiant, and the part-time priests who saw to the practical and less sacred functions. But at Karnak, for example, there were first to fourth priests of Amun at the head of a huge staff, which wielded considerable power. There was a constant tendency, which accorded with a basic Egyptian principle, for son to follow father in his priestly office. This was opposed by another tenet, that the king should freely appoint the best man for the job. By the end of the New Kingdom the former was triumphant, and Egyptian society was developing towards a rigid condition somewhat like that described by Herodotus in the 5th century BC, in which there was a division into various occupational types almost similar to castes. The analogy is reinforced by the restrictions priests had to observe in their diet, mode of dress, shaving, and sexual continence when they were in service – but perhaps not at other times.

The priests received income from the temples and often held sinecures at several of them. Offerings were laid before the god and, "after he had satisfied himself with them," reverted first to minor shrines and then to the priests, who consumed their less spiritual residues. The offerings themselves must, however, have been only a small proportion of the temples' income, so that much – also notionally offerings – was devoted directly to paying staff and to barter for particular products the temple lacked. Temples also had workshops and schools attached to them, which functioned in a broader context as well as supplying the needs of the institution to which they belonged.

Professional priests and bureaucrats, including those in the army, were the two basic categories of literate people. The bureaucracy seems to have lost its independence and importance in politics in the course of the Ramessid Period, being replaced by the army and the priesthood (often one and the same). Thus priests became the repository of intellectual culture. Legitimate or "white" magic had been the traditional preserve of lector priests, but in the Late Period priests assumed a wider cultural importance. Greek visitors speak frequently of them, and they influenced events, chiefly by mobilizing opinion against cuts in their revenues, at vital points in history, notably after the death of Cambyses (522) and in the reign of Teos (360). The culture of Greco-Roman Period temples was a priestly culture, of which one notable feature is the devaluation of the king's role: in earlier periods priests came before the god as deputies of the king, but now the king approached by virtue of his being a priest. The stereotype of an Egyptian society dominated by priests is not valid for earlier periods, but has some accuracy for later times.

Gods and myths

Egyptian polytheism clothes man's response to the world in a highly complex form. The gods themselves are more prominent in it than are myths

about them; myth was not so striking a feature of the religion as, for example, in ancient Greece. Some gods are defined by myth, others by geographical location and by organization into groups. Most also have a basic association with an aspect of the world, such as Re' with the sun, Ptah with crafts, Hathor with women etc., but this does not exhaust their characteristics. In particular contexts many gods may exhibit the same features, while any god can take on virtually all the characteristics of divinity for a particular worshiper.

There are scarcely any complete native versions of Egyptian myths, and for some we have to rely on Classical authors. The form of most Egyptian religious texts excludes narrative, and it has been doubted whether there were any large-scale texts that recounted entire myths. We have versions of episodes in the conflict between Horus and Seth for the inheritance of Osiris from the Middle Kingdom, the late New Kingdom and the 4th century, but the text is not the same in any two of them, and the episodes vary. The versions have in common a rather secular tone and an unflattering portrayal of the gods. They belong as much with fiction as with religious texts, although there are mythical narratives that are comparable in tone which are embedded in religious and especially magical compositions.

Creation myths give primacy to the sun god Re', who may also be called Re'-Harakhty or (Re'-)Atum. The most widespread one has the creator appearing from the watery chaos on a mound, the first solid matter, and creating a pair of deities, Shu and Tefenet, by masturbation or by spitting. Shu and Tefenet in their turn produced Geb and Nut, the earth and the sky, whose children were Osiris, Isis, Seth and Nephthys. This group of nine deities formed the ennead of Heliopolis; other centers had similar groups. Osiris and Isis are the main actors in

Right Bronze hawk's head finial, made to be attached to a staff or piece of temple furniture by the inverted T-shape projection at the back. The flange at the top probably supported a crown in a different material. Late Period. Height 12·1 cm. London, British, Museum.

the best-known Egyptian myth, which concerns Seth's murder of Osiris, Isis' conception of Horus on Osiris' dead body, and Horus' eventual defeat of Seth. This was recorded in Greek by Plutarch in the 1st century AD; most of his basic narrative appears to be authentically Egyptian.

Perhaps more typically Egyptian than these myths are ideas about the solar cycle. These use a small repertory of basic motifs, which is varied endlessly. It would be wrong to seek complete consistency in the variations; the constant meaning is the cycle itself. The sun god is born anew each morning, crosses the sky in the solar bark (boats being the normal mode of transport), ages, dies – which is never stated explicitly – and travels through the underworld during the night in a cycle of regeneration. Whereas in the creation myth the sky goddess Nut is the granddaughter of the sun god, for the purposes of the cycle she is his mother, into whose mouth he enters at night, and from whom he is born in the morning. At the rebirth she may also be Hathor, who is otherwise called the daughter of Re'. Possibly in allusion to these ideas creator gods, notably Amon-Re', may be called "bull of his mother." These motifs are mythical situations rather than complete myths, since they are not combined to form narratives. They may, however, generate myths, and we know two complete ones, the "Destruction of Mankind" and "Isis and Re'," that take as their starting point the old age of the sun god, which is one of the basic features of the cosmographic cycle, and elaborate it in terms of bodily decay and of its consequences for the god's kingship at the end of the primeval age on earth.

The solar cycle gave rise to a host of linked conceptions, the most striking of which surround the crucial moment of sunrise. In his travels through the night the god is accompanied in his boat by a group of deities, most of whom are personifications of aspects of his being, with names like "magical power" and "perception"; at one point in its journey the boat is towed by a team of jackals. Both the personnel and the furniture of the boat vary in different "books," as the mixed pictorial and textual compositions about the underworld are known. When the sun god emerges from the night the whole of creation rejoices, and he may be greeted by gods and goddesses, the king, the "eastern souls," personifications of categories of humanity, and baboons that screech acclamation. It is noteworthy that, as in temples, normal humanity is excluded from the scene. All these elements seem almost to be responses to questions such as: "What are the changing aspects of the sun god's being in the night?" or "How is his appearance at dawn heralded?" The answers are more tableaux than myths.

The organization of gods into local sets is comparable in its variety and seeming arbitrariness. The commonest grouping is the triad, consisting of two "adult" deities and one youthful one. The triads are, however, only selections, and other deities may have a loose connection with the group or may interchange with members of it. Thus the Theban triad consists of Amon-Re', Mut and Khons, the deities of the three main temples at Karnak. It has the form of a family group, but Mut is not the wife of Amon-Re', nor is Khons their son. Rather,

Below One version of the sun god's journey through the night. The boat is towed by jackals and uraei with human heads. Seth spears Apopis; behind Re'-

Harakhty are mummiform figures of Horus and Thoth. Papyrus of Hirweben, 21st Dynasty. Cairo, Egyptian Museum.

Above The setting sun. Center: the hieroglyph for "west" surmounted by a sun disk and placed in the desert. Top: two winged Horus eyes protect the sun. Below: adoring figures of: "subjects"; groups of deities; baboons; Isis and Nephthys; the deceased's *ba*, shown as a hawk with human head and arms. Papyrus of Anhai. 19th Dynasty. London, British Museum.

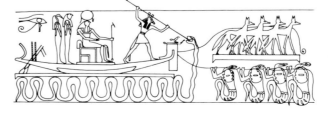

Right Bronze statuette of Wadjit with lioness's head and a uraeus above. The uraeus is the normal animal of Wadjit, while the lioness embodies her ferocious aspect in myth. Height 45 cm. Reign of Apries. Probably from Tell el-Fara'in. Bologna, Museo Civico.

Below Bronze statuette of Atum. The creator god of Heliopolis is shown in a form modified from the much commoner one for Osiris. The face is that of the aged, setting-sun god. Bronzes were dedicated in temples by private worshipers. This one has a dedication by Peteese son of Harwedja. Height 23·5 cm. Oxford, Ashmolean Museum.

Faience "pilgrim" flask with a scene of Bes with plumed headdress, wings and pendent breasts, holding a pair of *wedjat* eyes; between his face and arms are two signs of life. There are floral motifs above, below and in the corners, and sun disks (?) on either side. Height of figure 5·6 cm. Early 19th Dynasty (?). From el-Riqqa. Oxford, Ashmolean Museum.

Sakhmet, Nefertem and Sokar (the god of the necropolis), were similarly varied in their association: the first three form a triad, while Sokar is frequently identified with Ptah. Hathor and Neith, whose cults were important in Memphis, are excluded from the main group. At Heliopolis the sun god, whose cult was split into separate ones of Re' and Atum, stood most naturally by himself, but acquired two female companions, Ius'as and Hathor-Nebethetepet, who are in essence personifications of the sexual aspect of the solar creation myths.

A further important means of associating deities is called syncretism. A deity acquires a multiple name, mostly by taking on the name and character of a more important one. Amon-Re' is thus Amun in his aspect of Re', and this can be expanded to form Amon-Re'-Atum, Amun as Re' *and* Atum, the aged aspect of the sun god. Re' is by far the commonest name in such groupings; this reflects the sun god's universality and his importance in early periods. In a slightly different case, at Abydos Osiris is identified, as Osiris-Khentamentiu, with a local god whose cult may have been the original one in the area. Such associations never submerge completely the identities of the deities whose names are linked.

The gods mentioned so far may be called major deities. Almost all had a cult and an area in which they were sovereign. Some cosmic deities, such as Geb, had no local cult. But there are also minor deities found only in restricted contexts. The best known of these are probably Bes and Taweret, who are "household" figures associated particularly with childbirth. Both have monstrous composite forms of a sort not found among major deities, Bes as a dwarf with an outsize mask-like face, and Taweret as a mixture of hippopotamus and crocodile, with pendent, apparently human, breasts and a huge belly. In addition, there are enormous numbers of demons, attested from magical and underworld texts, who have very diverse names and often grotesque forms. Most of them seem to be restricted to one or two contexts each – a particular text, or one hour of the night. The chief exception is Apopis, a gigantic snake, who is the sun god's enemy as he passes through the crucial phases of his cycle, and must be defeated by Seth, who spears him from the prow of the solar boat.

The world of the dead

The underworld that has been mentioned is one particular version of the realm of the dead, known mainly from New Kingdom royal tombs; as in all areas of Egyptian religion, there are many alternatives. Conceptions of the afterlife of the king, who was held to join the gods in death, were initially different from those for the rest of humanity, although they came to be diffused among more and more people. Whatever one's destiny, it was by no means assured. The afterlife was full of dangers, which were mostly to be surmounted by magical means.

The starting point for all these ideas was the tomb. The Egyptians' unparalleled expenditure of the resources of the rich on burial was evidently intended in part to enhance the tomb owner's prestige while he was alive, but this is a sideline to the ultimate purpose. The deceased might continue to exist in and around the tomb, or he could travel

three local deities with different origins are associated using a family model, whose lack of realism is clear from the fact that there is only one "child." The importance of the number three and a principle of economy may together account for this simplification. Amaunet, a female Amun, is another Theban deity, who is sometimes found in place of Mut, while Montu, probably the original god of the Theban nome, had his own temple complex immediately to the north of the main enclosure at Karnak. At Memphis the four chief deities, Ptah,

through the afterworld. His aim was to identify with gods, in particular Osiris, or to join, as a transfigured spirit, in the solar cycle, as a member of the "boat of millions." The boat is never shown with its vast complement, possibly because human beings were excluded from the type of picture in which it occurs. Both these latter destinies seem to have been restricted originally to the king, and Old Kingdom private texts refer instead to "walking on the perfect ways of the west [the realm of the dead]."

Between death and incorporation in the divine world came judgment, a theme that is less prominent for kings than for the rest of humanity. The judgment is shown very often, in tombs, on papyri, coffins and shrouds. Its central motif is the weighing of the deceased's heart in a balance against Ma'at, the Egyptian conception of right order, which is mostly shown as a hieroglyph, either an ostrich feather or a figure of the personification Ma'at, a goddess with the feather inserted in a band

around her wig. Thoth, the scribe god of wisdom and justice, performs the weighing before Osiris, who presides over a judgment hall with 42 judges. If the heart and Ma'at are in equilibrium the test is successful, and the deceased is presented to Osiris in triumph. The judgment is of conformity to Ma'at, that is, correct conduct in life. Everybody naturally wished to avoid it, and the deceased had ready a declaration of innocence from all manner of sins. Both the declaration and the illustration of a successful outcome were magical ways around the judgment, just as funerary literature and other provisions in the tomb were magical aids to success in the hereafter.

Judgment scenes show a female hybrid monster called "Eater" or "Eater of the Dead." Her role was to consume those who failed the test, and a Roman Period example shows this happening. For Egyptians departure from this life was a first stage, and the second death, which brought complete annihilation, was what had to be avoided. Here,

Scene of weighing the deceased's heart in the Book of the Dead papyrus of Hunefer. On the left Anubis leads Hunefer in. A second figure of Anubis checks the balance while Thoth records the result and the "Eater" stands at the ready. Horus then presents Hunefer to Osiris, whose throne is placed on the "Lake of Natron," out of which a lotus emerges with the four "Sons of Horus" on it; behind are Isis and Nephthys.

In the small register above Hunefer adores a group of deities consisting of the Heliopolitan ennead without Seth, but with Utterance, Perception and the Southern, Northern and Western Ways (presumably in the hereafter) added. 19th Dynasty. London, British Museum.

however, the categories they used become strange to western eyes. The annihilation did not remove the victims entirely, but the "dead" – that is, second dead – are shown being punished in the lower registers of the underworld books. They entered another mode of existence, which was a threat to the ordered world, and had to be combated.

Scenes on tomb walls were part of the provision for life after death, but in many cases their relevance to survival is not clear and their superficial content secular. In addition to them, the burial contained material possessions in great variety, including (in early periods) enormous quantities of food, statues which could be inhabited by the "soul" of the deceased – as a cult statue was by a god – and the mummy itself, elaborately wrapped, protected with numerous amulets, placed in a coffin or nest of coffins, and magically brought to life in a ritual called the "opening of the mouth." Many of the possessions in the tombs repeated the motif of rebirth in symbolic form; the idea was expressed in

an enormous variety of ways. Some objects provided for particular needs in the hereafter. As many as 400 *shawabty* figures, perhaps the commonest of all Egyptian antiquities, accompanied burials. These were substitute figurines of the deceased, one of whose functions was to act as workers, who were to answer a possible call for corvée duty which involved carrying sand. This conception is obscure; it does not appear to be part of a coherent body of belief, but to be an isolated idea.

The accent in mortuary beliefs changed, but few disappeared. Instead, objects corresponding to a number of different conceptions were used in tombs. No overall consistency need be sought in them, except insofar as they relate to the hope for rebirth and continued life after death. The most extensive and varied provision preserved is that for Tut'ankhamun, but his funerary equipment was, no doubt, modest in comparison with that for Amenophis III or Ramesses II.

Burial Customs

Mummification

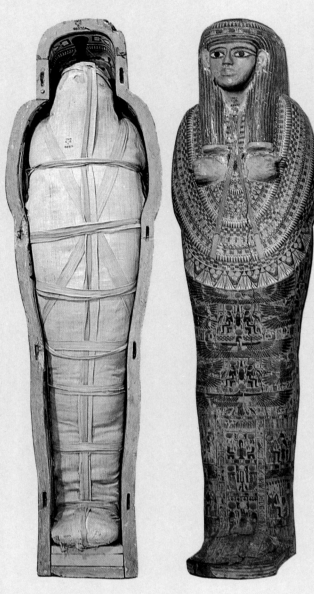

Mummification is a method of preserving artificially the bodies of deceased people and animals. Ancient Egyptian civilization is not the only one in the world to have practiced this custom, but Egyptian mummies are the best known and often, to the chagrin of professional Egyptologists, tend to be regarded as the embodiment of ancient Egypt itself and the main object of interest for those who study it. Mummies can contribute to our knowledge in various ways, in particular by providing information on such subjects as illnesses and conditions of ancient Egyptians, their diet etc. In the case of royal mummies, we can add to our understanding of Egyptian chronology by helping to establish the age of a king at the time of his death; family relationships can also be discovered from examination of mummies.

Development

Like many other practices, mummification was introduced as a result of man's interaction with his natural environment. It was an attempt to preserve an element of it by artificial means when his own action started threatening it.

For most of the Predynastic Period burials were very simple. Bodies were placed in shallow graves dug on the edge of the desert and covered with sand. In the dry atmosphere the contact with hot sand produced dehydration (desiccation) very quickly, often before the tissues decomposed, so that bodies were sometimes preserved by entirely natural means. This did not escape attention because such "mummies" were from time to time accidentally uncovered, and a belief developed that the preservation of the body was essential for man's continued existence after death. When at the end of the Predynastic Period some of the graves turned into larger tombs and coffins were introduced, these natural conditions were altered, in particular the contact with sand. It became necessary to look for methods which would achieve by artificial means what nature had previously accomplished unaided, and thus the custom of mummification was introduced. Its history is one of a continuous struggle between two approaches to the problem. The first aimed at a genuine preservation of the body, while the other, more formalistic, concentrated on the mummy's wrappings and packing. The peak of the craft of mummification was reached at the end of the New Kingdom and in the period immediately following; from then on, there was a sharp decline, as if in recognition of the impossibility of the task, and the formalistic approach prevailed.

Procedure

Mummification was carried out in workshops attached to the necropolis; these also supplied most of the funerary equipment. Methods varied according to the period and the wealth of the deceased's family. Although there is no detailed ancient Egyptian description of the procedure, its steps can be reconstructed from the examination of mummies.

The method described here was used at the end of the New Kingdom and during the 3rd Intermediate Period; it took some 70 days, and its most important part was dehydration of the body by burying it in natron, a naturally occurring dehydrating agent (a mixture of carbonate, bicarbonate, chloride and sulphate of sodium):

1. Extraction of the brain.
2. Removal of the viscera

through an incision made in the left flank.
3. Sterilization of the body cavities and the viscera.
4. Treatment of the viscera: removal of their contents, dehydration by natron, drying, anointing, and application of molten resin.
5. Temporary packing of the body with natron and fragrant resins.
6. Covering the body with natron for some 40 days.
7. Removal of the temporary packing materials.
8. Subcutaneous packing of the limbs with sand, clay etc.
9. Packing the body cavities with resin-soaked linen and bags of fragrant materials, such as myrrh and cinnamon, but also sawdust etc.
10. Anointing the body with unguents.
11. Treatment of the body surfaces with molten resin.
12. Bandaging and inclusion of amulets, jewelry etc.

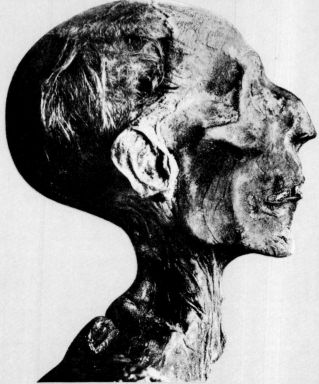

Royal mummies

Egyptologists have the unparalleled advantage of being face to face with the protagonists of their subject. The cache of royal mummies, discovered at Deir el-Bahri in 1881, contained the bodies of some of the most important rulers of the New Kingdom, including Sethos I (*above*) and Ramesses II (*below*).

Canopic Jars

The term canopic jars was devised by early Egyptologists, who mistakenly associated them with Kanopos, the pilot of Menelaos of the Trojan war. He was said to have died tragically and been buried at Kanopos (Egyptian *Per-gwati*, present Abu Qir) in the northwestern delta, and was worshiped there in the form of a jar.

The jars were usually made of calcite ("alabaster"), but also of limestone, pottery or faience, and contained the viscera removed from the cavities of the body during mummification. They were placed in the burial chamber of the tomb, close to the coffin. Simple lids became human-headed in the Middle Kingdom, and from the Ramessid Period they began to be made in the form of the heads of the four Sons of Horus. Texts on the jars placed each one under the protection of a goddess. Although reliable evidence is scarce, jars probably contained particular organs.

	head	goddess	contents
Imset	man	Isis	liver
Ha'py	baboon	Nephthys	lungs
Duamutef	jackal	Neith	stomach
Qebehsenuf	hawk	Selkis	intestines

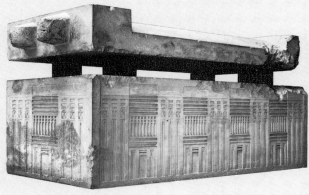

Coffins and Sarcophagi

Most of our material for the study of ancient Egypt derives from tombs. Coffins and sarcophagi are thus among the commonest antiquities, though this somewhat somber aspect of Egyptology is brightened by their often very attractive appearance. Dating into broader periods presents no problems, but only exceptionally have a more detailed typology and chronology been worked out.

The terms *coffin* and *sarcophagus* are used by some as though they were interchangeable; here they denote chests made of wood and stone (limestone, granite, basalt etc.) respectively, regardless of shape. Each consists of the lid and the lower part ("case"). Coffins were often placed inside a sarcophagus, and we find whole sets of them (inner and outer, or 1st, 2nd and 3rd), though sometimes only a *mummy board* (another "lid") was placed on top of the mummy. A third type of material, particularly common during the 3rd Intermediate and Greco-Roman

Periods, was *cartonnage* (the term is also conveniently used in the same way as "coffin" or "sarcophagus"). This was made by successive application of linen (papyrus in the Greco-Roman Period), glue and gesso around a "model mummy," and painting it with bright watercolors.

Coffins and sarcophagi are of two basic forms: *rectangular* and *anthropoid* ("mummiform"), but only the latter is known in cartonnage. Anthropoid coffins appeared in the Middle Kingdom as a natural extension of the earlier mummy-masks covering the upper part of the mummy.

Decoration varies according to date. Some of the coffins of the Early Dynastic Period have a "palace facade," as do sarcophagi of the Old Kingdom. In the 1st Intermediate Period and the Middle Kingdom the interior of the Herakleopolitan type of rectangular coffin was often inscribed with the Coffin Texts, and there were also representations of various items of funerary equipment and an offering-list. Anthropoid *rishi*-coffins (named for the decoration imitating feathered wings) are characteristic of the 17th Dynasty, while white coffins with bands suggesting mummy bandages were common in the 18th Dynasty. For the rest of the New Kingdom and later the tendency was to increase the amount of decoration by adding small scenes with various deities and texts. Rectangular coffins and sarcophagi became rare, and were only partly revived towards the end of the Late Period. The perfection of workmanship and finish of anthropoid sarcophagi of the Late Period are justly famous. They were made of a dark hard stone, usually basalt, but there were also imitations in wood. The decoration and inscriptions on coffins and sarcophagi of the Late and Greco-Roman Periods drew their inspiration from religious texts and their vignettes,

including the Book of the Dead, the Pyramid Texts and underworld books. The outside of the lid was often inscribed with Chapter 72 of the Book of the Dead, the "spell for going forth by day and penetrating the netherworld."

Funerary Statuettes

From the end of the Middle Kingdom one or more funerary statuettes (the Egyptian terms vary between *shabty, shawabty* and *ushebty*) formed an important part of the funerary equipment. In the 18th Dynasty the statuettes started to combine, in a somewhat incongruous fashion, a likeness of the mummified body of the deceased with agricultural or other implements. This was a reflection of the two main ideas connected with these objects: a body substitute and a worker who acted as the deceased's deputy when he was called upon to perform various corvée tasks in the netherworld. The formula inscribed on the statuettes (Chapter 6 of the Book of the Dead) contained appropriate instructions, but reflected a similar ambiguity concerning the statuette's identity. An increase in the number of funerary statuettes can be detected in the Ramessid Period; in the Late Period there were often several hundreds of them in the tomb of one person.

The following are some of the more important clues to the dating of funerary statuettes:
made of dark hard stone probably Middle Kingdom or 25th Dynasty, certainly not later than 26th Dynasty;
made of wood if very crude, end of 17th and early 18th Dynasties; at any rate not later than New Kingdom;
tools mid-18th Dynasty or later (statuettes without tools also continued to be made);
baskets held at front, 18th Dynasty; on the back, 19th Dynasty and later;
polychrome (red, blue/green, yellow, black) decoration on white background end of 18th Dynasty or Ramessid Period;
flat back and/or head fillet 3rd Intermediate Period;
small pedestal and back pillar mid-26th Dynasty and later.

221

EGYPT IN WESTERN ART

Although Egyptian culture had influenced various peoples around the Mediterranean since the second millennium, the Romans were the first to show interest in Egyptian objects for their very Egyptian-ness – an interest colored, as later, by the Greek view of Egypt as the repository of esoteric wisdom, and manifested in a superficial imitation of Egyptian art without comprehension of its basic character.

The appeal of things Egyptian was linked to the worship of the Alexandrian deities Isis and Sarapis, whose cults were established at Rome by the late Republic (1st century BC). The conquest of Egypt in 30 BC opened the way for the importation of antiquities to serve as public monuments, to adorn houses and gardens, or to decorate the temples of the Egyptian gods, like this baboon in gray granite, one of a pair from the Iseum Campense, Rome. Roman taste favored the exotic rather than the intrinsically Egyptian. With the creation of

The monuments exported to Rome and her empire constituted the west's only visual source of Egyptian art until the 18th century. Some remained visible throughout the Dark Ages, like the lions and sphinxes copied in 13th-century Roman sculpture. This one is from the Duomo at Città Castellana. The reemergence of others, and the discovery of Classical texts which included accounts of Egypt, aroused the interest of the humanists of the Renaissance.

Egyptianizing pieces, like this double-headed herm made for the Nilotic garden, or Canopus, of Hadrian's villa at Tivoli, the bizarre aspect became more pronounced. By the mid-4th century, Rome boasted numerous obelisks, two pyramids and a variety of sculpture.

By Classical authors they were told that hieroglyphs embodied abstract concepts in a symbolic, universally intelligible form. Leon Battista Alberti's (1404–72) device symbolizing divine omniscience (*above*) is an early example of the application of this idea.

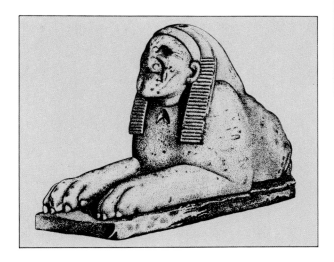

The allegorical use of "hieroglyphs" flourished, perfected in the work of Dürer and trivialized in the 16th-century literature devoted to emblems. The major technical feat of the century was the reerection of the Vatican obelisk in front of St Peter's in 1586, illustrated here by Domenico Fontana; the resurrection of others followed, and the obelisk entered the repertory of European architecture, where it

soon shed its specifically Egyptian character. More important was the serious interest in Egypt which the event excited; in the following century the hieroglyphs were subjected to fresh examination and the first scholarly publications of Egyptian antiquities appeared, culminating in the great encyclopedic works of the 18th century, where Egyptian objects figured beside Classical. From such sources, and from the first

well-illustrated travelers' accounts published around the mid-century, came the inspiration for Egyptianizing works like Dinglinger's gem-studded Apis Altar (1731) or the exuberant decor created for the Caffè Inglese, Rome (1760), by Piranesi. His championship of the majestic Egyptian style was echoed in the work of French and British architects towards the close of the century.

the decorative arts sometimes entailed no more than a playfully ornamental use of motifs, as in Wedgwood's "hieroglyphic" tea service of about 1810 (*bottom*).

Other designs represent a more straightforward imitation of the form of Egyptian objects, as in Holman Hunt's chairs of 1855, the furniture produced later by Liberty, or the occasional pieces of silver plate based on the shape of ancient vessels, like the claret jug below. The decipherment of hieroglyphs, the growth of Egyptology as a scholarly discipline and the formation of large collections of antiquities in the museums of Europe and America ensured a continuing popular interest in Egypt; from time to time the fashion for Egyptianizing designs received fresh impetus from events like

Alongside this new appreciation of Egypt, the mystic tradition continued. The field of *arcana* already prospected by the Rosicrucians was exploited by Freemasonry, and the brotherhood's newly adopted Egyptian rites supplied Schikaneder, librettist of Mozart (himself a Freemason), with some of the ideas expressed in *The Magic Flute*. This frontispiece to the 1791 edition is full of occult gloom.

The French invasion of Egypt seven years later brought with it scholars as well as soldiers, outstanding among them Vivant Denon; his medal cabinet was designed after the picture of a pylon in his own book on Egypt which, together with the expedition's official publication, the *Description de l'Égypte*, provided a wealth of illustrations.

The detailed drawings of the great Egyptian temples, in particular the Greco-Roman with their exaggerated cornices and ornate column capitals, served as models for architecture of a more soberly imitative kind than that advocated by Piranesi. The Egyptian style was considered

appropriate for the massive, the monumental and the funereal. In Europe and America courthouses, jails, factories, railway stations, bridges, churches and, especially, cemeteries, like this one at Alberobello, south Italy, received Egyptian treatment.

the opening of the Egyptian Court in the Crystal Palace in 1854. This much-admired extravaganza, replete with replicas of the most famous monuments of Egypt, is probably the inspiration behind the later Egyptian garden at Biddulph Grange (*top right*) with its stone sphinxes and topiary pyramid, a trim Victorian descendant of Hadrian's Canopus, Angelo Querini's Egyptian garden at the Villa Altichiero in 18th-century Padua, and Canina's charming Egyptian Portico in the Borghese Gardens, Rome (1827).

The discovery of Tut'ankhamun's tomb in 1922 generated a new wave of Egyptianizing trivia in the decorative arts, but the monumental building style has been employed in this century only in the fantasy architecture of the cinema; the pharaonic splendors of Grauman's Egyptian Theater, Hollywood (1922), are reflected in some less grandiose creations in England, like the 1930 Carlton in Islington (*above*).

Appreciation of modern art has helped towards an understanding of the different representational principles of the ancient Egyptians, and their sculpture in particular has influenced contemporary artists. David Hockney's 1978 sets for *The Magic Flute* (*below*) present a starker vision of Egypt than Schinkel's elaborate compositions for the 1815 production, but a sense of majestic spaciousness is common to both.

The elegant designs of Napoleon's interior decorators, Percier and Fontaine, were the forerunners in the fashion for *Égyptiennerie* on the continent

during the three decades following the French campaign, paralleled by the work of Thomas Hope (1807) and others in England. The Egyptian style in

MUSEUMS WITH EGYPTIAN COLLECTIONS

Although collections of ancient Egyptian antiquities, consisting of curiosities and tourist mementos, had been formed earlier, it was mainly in the first half of the 19th century that museums which displayed Egyptian objects for the delectation and edification of the general public came into existence. Nowadays over 500 of these, scattered over five continents, hold Egyptian objects of importance, and in thousands of others ancient Egypt is represented to some degree. Trained Egyptologists are on the staff of many of these establishments, and museums have also become important centers for the research and study of ancient Egypt. "Excavation" in museum storerooms and basements in order to make available the treasures kept there both to the specialist and to the layman is one of the most urgent tasks of the discipline.

Australia
Melbourne
National Gallery of Victoria
Sydney
Australian Museum
Nicholson Museum of Antiquities

Austria
Vienna
Kunsthistorisches Museum

Belgium
Antwerp
Museum Vleeshuis
Brussels
Musées Royaux d'Art et d'Histoire
Liège
Musée Curtius
Mariemont
Musée de Mariemont

Brazil
Rio de Janeiro
Museu Nacional

Canada
Montreal
McGill University, Ethnological Museum
Museum of Fine Arts
Toronto
Royal Ontario Museum

Cuba
Havana
Museo Nacional

Czechoslovakia
Prague
Náprstkovo Muzeum

Denmark
Copenhagen
Nationalmuseet
Ny Carlsberg Glyptotek
Thorwaldsen Museum

East Germany
Berlin
Staatliche Museen, Ägyptisches Museum
Staatliche Museen, Papyrussammlung
Dresden
Albertinum
Leipzig
Ägyptisches Museum

Egypt
Alexandria
Greco-Roman Museum
Aswan
Museum on the island of Elephantine
Cairo
Egyptian Museum
Luxor
Luxor Museum
Mallawi
Mallawi Museum
Minya
Minya Museum

Limestone tomb stela of Wadj, from the king's tomb at Abydos. Paris, Louvre, E.11007.

Musée Rodin
Strasbourg
Institut d'Egyptologie
Toulouse
Musée Georges Labit

Greece
Athens
National Museum

Hungary
Budapest
Szépmüvészeti Múzeum

Ireland
Dublin
National Museum of Ireland

Italy
Bologna
Museo Civico
Florence
Museo Archeologico
Mantua
Museo del Palazzo Ducale
Milan
Museo Archeologico
Naples
Museo Nazionale
Parma
Museo Nazionale di Antichità
Palermo
Museo Nazionale
Rome
Museo Barracco
Museo Capitolino
Museo Nazionale Romano delle Terme Diocleziane

France
Avignon
Musée Calvet
Grenoble
Musée de Peinture et de Sculpture
Limoges
Musée Municipal
Lyons
Musée des Beaux-Arts
Musée Guimet
Marseilles
Musée d'Archéologie
Nantes
Musée des Arts Décoratifs
Orléans
Musée Historique et d'Archéologie de l'Orléanais
Paris
Bibliothèque Nationale
Louvre
Musée du Petit Palais

Limestone relief showing a blind harpist, from the Saqqara tomb of the Royal Butler Patenemhab of the end of the 18th Dynasty. Leiden, Inv. AMT.1–35.

Rovigo
Museo dell'Accademia dei Concordi
Trieste
Civico Museo di Storia ed Arte
Turin
Museo Egizio
Vatican
Museo Gregoriano Egizio
Venice
Museo Archeologico del Palazzo Reale di Venezia

Relief with Negro captives, from the Saqqara tomb of Haremhab, probably of the reign of Tut'ankhamun. Bologna, 1887(1869).

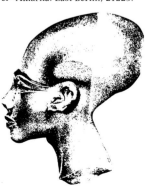

Brown quartzite head of a princess, from the so-called sculptor's studio of Thutmose at el-'Amarna. East Berlin, 21223.

Diorite-gneiss statue of seated Khephren, with Horus-falcon perched on the back of the throne, from Giza. Cairo, CG 14.

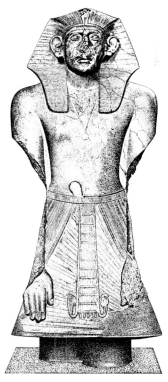

Granite statue of Senwosret III, from Deir el-Bahri. London, British Museum, 684.

Japan
Kyoto
University Archaeological Museum

Mexico
Mexico City
Museo Nacional de Antropologia

Netherlands
Amsterdam
Allard Pierson Museum
Leiden
Rijksmuseum van Oudheden
Otterlo
Rijksmuseum Kröller-Müller

Poland
Kraków
Muzeum Narodowe
Warsaw
Muzeum Narodowe

Portugal
Lisbon
Fundação Calouste Gulbenkian

Spain
Madrid
Museo Arqueológico Nacional

Sudan
Khartum
Sudan Museum

Sweden
Linköping
Östergöttlands Museum
Lund
Kulturhistoriska Museet
Stockholm
Medelhavsmuseet
Uppsala
Victoriamuseum

Wall painting of two daughters of Queen Nefertiti, from a palace at el-'Amarna. Oxford, Ashmolean, 1893. 1–41(267).

Switzerland
Basel
Museum für Völkerkunde
Geneva
Musée d'Art et d'Histoire
Lausanne
Musée Cantonal d'Archéologie et d'Histoire
Musée Cantonal des Beaux-Arts
Neuchâtel
Musée d'Ethnographie
Riggisberg
Abegg-Stiftung

United Kingdom
Bristol
City Museum
Cambridge
Fitzwilliam Museum
Dundee
Museum and Art Gallery
Durham
Gulbenkian Museum of Oriental Art and Archaeology
Edinburgh
Royal Scottish Museum

Glasgow
Art Gallery and Museum
Burrell Collection
Hunterian Museum
Leicester
Museums and Art Gallery
Liverpool
Merseyside County Museums
School of Archaeology and Oriental Studies
London
British Museum
Horniman Museum
Petrie Collection (University College)
Victoria and Albert Museum
Manchester
University Museum
Norwich
Castle Museum
Oxford
Ashmolean Museum
Pitt Rivers Museum

United States of America
Baltimore (Md.)
Walters Art Gallery
Berkeley (Ca.)
Robert H. Lowie Museum of Anthropology
Boston (Mass.)
Museum of Fine Arts
Brooklyn (N.Y.)
Brooklyn Museum
Cambridge (Mass.)
Fogg Art Museum, Harvard University
Semitic Museum, Harvard University
Chicago (Ill.)
Field Museum of Natural History
Oriental Institute Museum

Below Colossal diorite head of Amenophis III. Brooklyn, 59.19.

Left Blue faience sphinx of Amenophis III. New York, M.M.A. 1972.125.

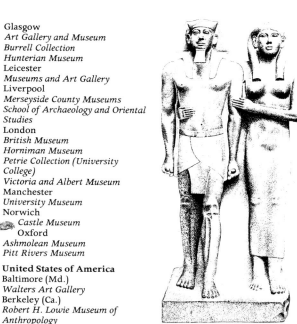

Graywacke pair-statue of Menkaure' and Queen Kha' merernebty II, from the king's valley temple at Giza. Boston, 11.1738.

Cincinnati (Ohio)
Art Museum
Cleveland (Ohio)
Museum of Art
Denver (Col.)
Art Museum
Detroit (Mich.)
Detroit Institute of Arts
Kansas City (Miss.)
William Rockhill Nelson Gallery of Art
Los Angeles (Ca.)
County Museum of Art
Minneapolis (Minn.)
Institute of Arts Museum
New Haven (Conn.)
Yale University Art Gallery
New York
Metropolitan Museum of Art
Palo Alto (Ca.)
Stanford University Museum
Philadelphia (Pa.)
Pennsylvania University Museum
Pittsburgh (Pa.)
Museum of Art, Carnegie Institute
Princeton (N.J.)
University Art Museum
Providence (R.I.)
Rhode Island School of Design
Richmond (Va.)
Museum of Fine Arts
St Louis (Miss.)
Art Museum
San Diego (Ca.)
Museum of Man
San Francisco (Ca.)
M. H. De Young Memorial Museum
San José (Ca.)
Rosicrucian Museum
Seattle (Wash.)
Art Museum
Toledo (Ohio)
Museum of Art
Washington D.C.
Smithsonian Institution
Worcester (Mass.)
Art Museum

U.S.S.R.
Leningrad
State Hermitage Museum
Moscow
State Pushkin Museum of Fine Arts

West Germany
Berlin
Staatliche Museen Preussischer Kulturbesitz, Ägyptisches Museum
Essen
Folkwang Museum
Frankfurt-am-Main
Liebieghaus
Hamburg
Museum für Kunst und Gewerbe
Museum für Völkerkunde
Hanover
Kestner-Museum
Heidelberg
Ägyptologisches Institut der Universität
Hildesheim
Roemer-Pelizaeus-Museum
Karlsruhe
Badisches Landesmuseum
Munich
Staatliche Sammlung Ägyptischer Kunst
Tübingen
Ägyptologisches Institut der Universität
Würzburg
Martin von Wagner Museum der Universität

Yugoslavia
Zagreb
Archeološki Muzej

Painted limestone head of Queen Nefertiti, from the so-called sculptor's studio of Thutmose at el-'Amarna. West Berlin, 21300.

GLOSSARY

Wherever possible in this book we have avoided using specialized terms. A certain number, for which there was not sufficent space in the text for an explanation, are treated in this Glossary, and supplementary information is given, especially for administrative and priestly titles. Any terms that are not covered can be found easily in appropriate works listed in the Bibliography. Cross-references within the Glossary are underlined.

abacus Rectangular block placed on top of a column capital in order to support the architrave.

ambulatory Roofed colonnaded walkway, often running around the outside of small New Kingdom temples and bark stations, and of Greco-Roman birth houses.

architrave Horizontal stone beam between columns, or between a column and a wall, which supports a ceiling.

ba One of many Egyptian words for aspects of the personality, often translated "soul." The ba is associated with divinity and with power; gods have many bas. It also describes the ability to take on different manifestations, which are themselves bas, as the Apis bull is of Ptah. The ba of the deceased is able to move freely in the underworld and return to earth. See also ka.

Badarian From el-Badari, the type site of the earliest certainly identified Neolithic culture of the Nile valley (c. 4500 BC).

bark shrine Deities were carried in model barks when they went out from temples in procession at festivals; larger divine barks were used on the river. The model barks were kept in shrines in the temples; those at Karnak and Luxor are sizable structures.

birth house Special type of small temple (also called mammisi), attached to the main temples of the Late and Greco-Roman Periods. These were where the god of the main temple was born, or, if the main temple was dedicated to a goddess, where she bore her child. The birth scenes derive from earlier cycles depicting the birth of kings.

Book of the Dead A collection of spells mostly written on papyrus and placed with the mummy in a burial, attested from the New Kingdom to the Greco-Roman Period. The texts continue the tradition of the Pyramid Texts and Coffin Texts. The choice of spells, of which about 200 are known, some very long, varies from copy to copy.

cartouche Circle with a horizontal bar at the bottom, elongated into an oval within which kings' names are written from the 4th Dynasty on. Detailed examples show that the sign represents a knot of rope, looped so that it is never-ending; it thus symbolizes cyclical return, probably with solar reference. Kings had two cartouche names, the first a statement about the god Re' (praenomen) and the second their birth name.

cataract Stretch of rapids interrupting the flow of the Nile, caused by areas of granite interspersed in the Nubian sandstone belt. There are six numbered and several minor cataracts between Aswan and Khartum. All are hazards to navigation. The 2nd Cataract, the most formidable, was impassable except during the annual inundation. Cataracts 1–4 and the Dal Cataract were political frontiers at different times.

cavetto cornice Crowning element of walls, doorways, flat-topped stelae and false doors, consisting of a semicircular forward flaring, with a scalloped decoration, often with a winged disk in its middle; probably derived from reed or other plant architectural forms. It was much imitated outside Egypt.

cenotaph Symbolic tombs or mortuary cult places additional to the owner's burial place. The south tomb of the Step Pyramid of Djoser is a cenotaph, as are probably the subsidiary pyramids of the 4th–6th Dynasties. At Abydos cenotaph chapels for private individuals are characteristic of the Middle Kingdom, and there are royal cenotaph temples of the Middle and New Kingdoms. Other sites with cenotaphs are Gebel el-Silsila and Qasr Ibrim.

Chief Steward New Kingdom and Late Period title of the administrator of an estate of the temple of a god, the king or his mortuary temple, of a member of the royal family (e.g. a Divine Adoratrice) or even a private individual. Because of the economic importance of the function, Chief Stewards were very influential, e.g. Senenmut, who combined the offices of Chief Steward of Amun, of Queen Hatshepsut and of Princess Nefrure'; or Amenhotpe Huy, the brother of the vizier Ra'mose, who was Chief Steward of Memphis in the reign of Amenophis III.

Coffin Texts Texts written inside coffins of the Middle Kingdom that are intended to aid the deceased in his passage to the hereafter. The texts continue and develop the tradition of the Pyramid Texts, but are used by private individuals. More than 1,000 spells are known.

colossus Over-lifesize statue, usually of a king, but also of private individuals and gods; typically set up outside the gates or pylons of temples, and often receiving some sort of cult or acting as intermediaries between men and gods.

contrapposto The depiction in sculpture in the round of the organic adjustment of the human body to asymmetrical poses; very rare in Egyptian art.

count Conventional translation of a ranking title of the Old and Middle Kingdoms. As with many titles, the word lost its original meaning, and modern translations are therefore conventional rather than precise. In the New Kingdom the same title was used for a local administrative function and is better rendered "mayor."

cuneiform The Mesopotamian script, written with a stylus on clay tablets, with characteristic wedge-shaped (cuneiform) strokes. The script wrote many different languages, the most widespread being Akkadian, which was the diplomatic language of the late second millennium BC. Cuneiform texts have been found in Egypt at el-'Amarna, and on various objects of the Persian Period. In the Near East cuneiform tablets from Egypt have been found at Boğazköy in Anatolia and Kamid el-Loz in Syria.

cursive Rapid, handwritten forms of the script, chiefly hieratic and demotic. Cursive hieroglyphs are special simplified sign forms, similar to hieratic, written in ink and used for religious texts and for the initial training of scribes; the form died out in the first millennium BC.

demotic From Greek "popular," a further elaboration of hieratic, developed in northern Egypt in the 7th century BC; the normal everyday script of the Late and Greco-Roman Periods. Latest dated text 452 AD.

Divine Adoratrice Chief priestess of Amun in Thebes, an office known from the New Kingdom–Late Period. The priestess was celibate. In the 23rd–26th Dynasties princesses held it, notionally "adopting" their successors, and acting as important vehicles of political control.

ennead Group of 9 deities. Enneads are associated with several major cult centers. The number 9 embodies a plurality (3) of pluralities (3, i.e. 3 × 3), and so stands for large numbers in general; hence some enneads have more than 9 members. The best-known, the great ennead of Heliopolis, embodies two myths within its composition. It consists of Re'-Atum, Shu, Tefenet, Geb, Nut, Osiris, Isis, Seth and Nephthys.

Fan-Bearer on the Right of the King Court title, probably purely honorific or ranking, of high officials of the New Kingdom. The right was the prestigious side.

fecundity figure Type of offering bearer shown at the base of temple walls bringing offerings into the temple; mostly personifications of geographical areas, the inundation, or abstract concepts. The male figures have heavy pendulous breasts and bulging stomachs, their fatness symbolizing the abundance they bring with them.

funerary cones Pottery cones found mostly in Theban tombs of the Middle Kingdom to Late Period, with a flat circular or rectangular base bearing an impression of a stamp with the titles and name of the tomb owner. The cones, some 30 cm long, were originally inserted in the brick-built tomb facade or tomb pyramid to form horizontal rows.

God's Father Common priestly title of the New Kingdom and later, usually further extended by the name of a god (e.g. God's Father of Amun). God's Fathers mostly ranked above ordinary wa' eb-priests ("the pure ones") but below "prophets."

Herald Middle and New Kingdom title borne by an official whose function was probably to report to the king and make his commands known, both at court and, for example, on the battlefield.

hieratic From Greek "sacred," the normal form of the script, mostly written on papyrus or ostraca, and used throughout Egyptian history. In later periods hieratic was restricted to religious texts, hence its name. Hieratic signs lost the pictorial character of hieroglyphs, and are often joined together.

hieroglyph Sign in the Egyptian script, from Greek "sacred carving"; used only for the monumental form of the script, in which most signs are identifiable pictures, and no signs are joined together.

High Priest Conventional translation of the title of the head of the local priesthood. The Egyptian forms of the most important among them were as follows:
Amun (Thebes): "The First Prophet of Amun"
Ptah (Memphis): "Greatest of the Directors of Craftsmen"
Re' (Heliopolis): "Greatest of the Seers"
Thoth (el-Ashmunein): "Greatest of the Five."

Horus name The first name in a king's titulary, normally written inside a serekh, and consisting of an epithet that identifies the king as a manifestation of an aspect of Horus.

hypostyle hall Term for columned halls, from the Greek for "bearing pillars." The halls are the outermost, and grandest, parts of the main structures of temples, frequently added after the rest, and exhibit an elaborate symbolism. Many temples have two hypostyle halls.

ichneumon A small rodent that kills snakes and destroys crocodile eggs, akin to the Indian mongoose. The ichneumon and the shrewmouse formed a pair of animals associated with the sun god. Ichneumons in particular were often buried in the Late and Greco-Roman Periods; many bronze statuettes of them are known.

ithyphallic With erect penis (from the Greek). Various gods were shown in this form, such as Min, Amun (especially at Luxor) and the revitalized Osiris.

ka Obscure conception of an aspect of the personality, perhaps associated originally with sexual fertility. The ka was born as a "double" of the living person, but came into its own in the afterlife, when it received mortuary offerings and ensured the deceased's survival. See also ba.

kiosk Small, open temple structure used as a way station for statues of gods during festivals when they left their main temples, or in the sed festival.

Lector Priest Priest (literally "One who bears the ritual book") whose function was to declaim the ritual texts in funerary and temple cult. He wore a distinctive broad white sash diagonally across the chest. "Chief Lector Priest" was a higher rank.

logogram Sign in the script that writes an entire word, often with the addition of a stroke and/or the feminine ending -t.

mastaba Arabic word for bench, used as the term for free-standing tombs of the Early Dynastic Period and Old Kingdom (and some later ones). The basic form of a mastaba's superstructure is a rectangle with flat roof and vertical (mud-brick) or slightly inclined (stone) walls.

Mistress of the House Housewife, title given to married ladies from the Middle Kingdom onwards.

naos Shrine in which divine statues were kept, especially in temple sanctuaries. A small wooden naos was normally placed inside a monolithic one in hard stone; the latter are typical of the Late Period, and sometimes elaborately decorated. Also used as a term for temple sanctuary.

necropolis Greek word for cemetery. "Necropolis" normally describes large and important burial areas that were in use for long periods, "cemetery" smaller and more homogeneous sites; cemeteries may also be subdivisions of a necropolis.

Nilometer Staircase descending into the Nile and marked with levels above low water; used for measuring, and in some cases recording, inundation levels. The most famous are on Elephantine island and on Roda island in Cairo.

nomarch The chief official of a nome. In the late Old Kingdom–early Middle Kingdom nomarchs became local, hereditary rulers, who governed their nomes more or less independently of the central authority; the kings of the 11th Dynasty began in this way. During the 12th Dynasty the office ceased to have political importance.

nome Administrative province of Egypt, from Greek *nomos*; the ancient Egyptian term was *sepat*. The nome system seems to have been elaborated in the Early Dynastic Period, but did not reach final form until the Ptolemies. During some periods of highly centralized administration (e.g. late Middle Kingdom) the nomes had little real importance.

obelisk Monolithic tapering shaft, mostly of pink granite, with a pyramidion at the top; from a Greek word for a spit. Obelisks are solar symbols, probably similar in meaning to pyramids, and associated with an ancient stone called *benben* in Heliopolis. They were set up in pairs outside the entrances to some Old Kingdom tombs, and outside temples; a single obelisk in east Karnak was the object of a cult.

ogdoad Term describing the group of 8 deities (four male-female pairs) associated with Hermopolis, who symbolize the state of the world before creation. The group's composition varies, but its primeval form is: Nun and Naunet, the primeval waters; Huh and Hauhet, endless space; Kuk and Kauket, darkness; Amun and Amaunet, what is hidden.

orthogram Sign in the script whose function is to elucidate the function of another sign or to write a dual or plural.

Osirid pillar Pillar, mostly in an open court or portico, with a colossal statue of a king forming its front part; unlike caryatids in Classical architecture, the statues are not weight-bearing elements. Most are mummiform, but not all; the connection with Osiris is doubtful.

ostracon Flake of limestone or potsherd used for writing (from the Greek for potsherd); also fragment from an inscribed jar (e.g. a wine jar inscribed with the details of a vintage). Ostraca are known from all periods, but 19th- and 20th-Dynasty examples are commonest (up to 20,000 have been found). Most texts are in hieratic or demotic, but there are also cursive hieroglyphic texts and numerous pictures, including drafts of hieroglyphic inscriptions.

Overseer of Sealers Typical administrative title of the 12th Dynasty borne by a high official of the Treasury. The "Overseer of Sealers" was responsible to the head of the Treasury ("The Overseer of the Seal") and his deputies. The term derives from the fact that most containers of produce and goods were sealed when entering or leaving the Treasury magazines. Clay impressions of seals are common finds.

papyrus The chief Egyptian writing material, and an important export. The earliest papyrus (blank) dates to the 1st Dynasty, the latest to the Islamic Period, when the plant died out in Egypt. Sheets were made by cutting the pith of the plant into strips laid in rows horizontally and vertically, which were then beaten together, activating the plant's natural starch to form an adhesive. Separate sheets were gummed together to form rolls. The better surface of a papyrus (the normal recto) had the fibers running horizontally, but letters were normally begun on strips inscribed across the fibers.

peristyle court Court with a roof around the sides supported by rows of columns (from Greek *peristylon*) and an open space in the center.

phonogram Sign in the script that records a sound. Only consonants are precisely recorded, and phonograms may write 1–4 consonants.

praenomen A king's first cartouche name, which he adopted on his accession; also called "throne name." It consists of a statement about the god Re', later with additional epithets, e.g. Menkheprure' (Tuthmosis IV)

"Re' is enduring of manifestations."

pronaos Room in front of the sanctuary (naos) of a temple, whose exact location varies with the design of individual temples; sometimes used as a term for hypostyle hall.

Prophet Priestly title (literally "God's Servant"), ranking above wa'eb-priests and God's Fathers, usually extended by the name of a god (e.g. "Prophet of Montu"). The head of the local priesthood, particularly in the provinces, was often called "Overseer of Prophets." The high priest of Amun at Thebes was "The First Prophet of Amun"; below him were the Second, Third and Fourth Prophets.

propylon Gateway that stands in front of a pylon.

pylon Monumental entrance wall of a temple, from the Greek for gate; consists of a pair of massifs with an opening between, mostly elaborated into a doorway. All the wall faces are inclined; the corners are completed with a torus molding and the top with torus and cavetto cornice. Pylons are the largest and least essential parts of a temple, mostly built last. Some temples have series of them (e.g. 10 at Karnak, on two axes).

pyramidion Capstone of a pyramid or top of an obelisk. The pyramidion was decorated and became a symbolic object in its own right, being used also as the most striking feature of the small brick pyramids of private tombs of the New Kingdom (Deir el-Medina, Saqqara) and Late Period (Abydos).

Pyramid Texts Texts on the walls of the internal rooms of pyramids of the end of the 5th and 6th–8th Dynasties, later used by private individuals for most of Egyptian history. Some texts may relate to the king's burial ceremonies, but others are concerned with temple ritual and many other matters.

ranking title Title that indicates status but does not go with any specific function; very important in the Old and to a lesser extent the Middle Kingdom. The typical sequence of titles, in ascending order, is "Royal Acquaintance," "Sole Companion," "Count," "Hereditary Prince."

reserve heads Old Kingdom tomb sculptures in the round, aiming at a realistic representation of the head of the deceased (hence the alternate term "portrait heads"), and acting as its substitute. Some 30 have been found, mainly at Giza.

revetment Cladding of a wall surface or bastion; may be ornamental, e.g. stone covering mud brick, or structural, and intended to give stability to a core of rubble.

sabbakhin Arabic word for diggers of *sabbakh*, nitrogenous earth from ancient sites used as fertilizer; *sabbakh* may be mud brick or remains of organic refuse. *Sabbakhin* are among the chief agents of destruction of ancient sites.

saff tomb Arabic word for row, describing rock-cut tombs of the early 11th Dynasty that consist of a row of openings – or colonnade – in the hillside.

sea peoples Invaders of Egypt in the late 19th and early 20th Dynasties, probably associated with a wave of destruction on Near Eastern sites and more remotely with the fall of Mycenaean Greece and the Hittite empire. Their precise identity and origin are much disputed by scholars.

sed festival Ritual of royal regeneration, almost always celebrated after 30 years of a king's reign, and thereafter at three-yearly intervals, but very occasionally performed earlier; features prominently in the decoration of royal mortuary temples, reflecting the king's wish to rule long in the next world.

semogram Sign in the script that conveys meaning, not sound. Subcategories are logograms, taxograms and orthograms. Also called ideograms.

serekh Image of a brick facade to a palace or enclosure, with a rectangular space above; the facade is in the style of the beginning of the Early Dynastic Period. A falcon (the sign for Horus) perches on the top horizontal of the rectangle, which encloses a king's Horus name.

sistrum Musical instrument – a kind of rattle – sacred to Hathor. Two types are common: (a) a naos shape above a Hathor head, with ornamental loops on the sides (the rattle was inside the box of the naos); (b) a simple loop with loose cross bars of metal above a smaller Hathor head; both had long handles. (a) was used from the New Kingdom on as a type of column capital, making play with the association between the rustle of aquatic plants and the joyful sound of the sistrum (plant and sistrum forms are occasionally combined). At Dendara the sistrum (mostly type (a)) was an important sacred object.

Standard Bearer of the Lord of the Two Lands Military title of the New Kingdom, borne by an officer of the infantry, chariotry, or one attached to a ship, who was in charge of a company of some 250 men. Companies of the Egyptian army had distinguishing "standards."

stela Slab of stone or sometimes wood with texts, reliefs or paintings. Commemorative or votive stelae are placed in temples; tomb stelae function within the decoration of a tomb.

talatat Arabic word for three (handbreadths), describing the length of the typical small stone building blocks of temples of Amenophis IV/Akhenaten. They are found reused at a number of sites (some 30,000 at Karnak), and are decorated with scenes in the 'Amarna style. Some complete walls have been reassembled from scattered blocks.

Tasian From Deir Tasa, a Predynastic site in Upper Egypt; name of a Predynastic culture that may not be distinct from Badarian.

taxogram Sign in the script that is placed after the phonograms in the writing of a word, and indicates the class or area of meaning to which it belongs.

torus molding Semicircular or cylindrical band forming the edge of a stela or the corner of a stone wall. Detailed examples are decorated with a pattern that suggests lashings around a pole or reed bundle, almost certainly indicating that the form derives from architecture in flimsy materials.

tree goddess A goddess associated with a sacred tree and represented as a tree with arms or a woman emerging from a tree. Hathor, Isis and Nut are found as tree goddesses, all in the context of mortuary cult.

underworld books Mixed pictorial and textual compositions inscribed in New Kingdom royal tombs that describe the passage of the sun god through the underworld and the sky; taken over by private individuals in the Late Period.

uraeus The most characteristic symbol of kingship, a rearing cobra worn on the king's forehead or crown. The cobra is associated with the goddess Wadjit or with the sun, whose "eye" it is held to be. It is an agent of destruction and protection of the king, spitting out fire.

Viceroy of Kush Administrator of Nubia during the New Kingdom, at first called "King's Son," from the mid-18th Dynasty "King's Son of Kush." Despite the form of the title, its holder was not a real son of the king. The area governed by the viceroy extended as far north as Kom el-Ahmar (Hierakonpolis). His two deputies, one for Lower Nubia (Wawat), the other for Upper Nubia (Kush), resided at 'Aniba and 'Amara respectively.

vizier The highest official in the administration, whose post is found already in the Early Dynastic Period. In the New Kingdom there were two viziers, at Memphis and Thebes; from this period on, the most important individuals were often not viziers, and the office was less important in the Late Period. There are texts that describe the installation of a vizier and detail his functions.

winged disk A sun disk with an outspread pair of wings attached. The earliest possible example of the motif is of the 1st Dynasty. It is associated with Horus of Behdet (Edfu), and symbolizes the sun, especially in architecture on ceilings, cornices and stelae. It was often copied outside Egypt.

zodiac The Babylonian and Greek signs of the zodiac were introduced into Egypt in the Greco-Roman Period, "translated" into Egyptian representational forms, and used in the decoration of astronomical ceilings of tombs and temples, and on coffin lids.

LIST OF ILLUSTRATIONS

All linework by Marion Cox, Abingdon. All maps by Lovell Johns, Oxford. Abbreviations: Ash. = Ashmolean Museum, Oxford; BL = British Library, London; BM = British Museum, London; DAI = Deutsches Archäologisches Institut, Cairo; EM = Egyptian Museum, Cairo; GI = Griffith Institute, Ashmolean Museum, Oxford; JF = John Fuller, Cambridge; LJ = Lovell Johns, Oxford; Louvre = Musée du Louvre, Paris; ME = Museo Egizio, Turin; Met. = Metropolitan Museum of Art, New York; MH = Michael Holford, Loughton; OI = Oxford Illustrators, Oxford; RW = Roger Wood, London; WF = Werner Forman, London.

Ramesseum: Relief – assault on Dapur: A. A. M. van der Heyden, Amsterdam.
98. Medinet Habu: Plan: LJ (after Hölscher).
Medinet Habu: Temple of Ramesses III: Hirmer Verlag, Munich.
99. Medinet Habu: Ramesses III being crowned: Rosalind Hall, London.
Valley of Kings: J. Baines, Oxford.
100. Valley of Kings: Relief – king offering to Harsiese: Rosalind Hall, London.
Valley of Kings: Painting in tomb of Tuthmosis III: Rosalind Hall, London.
Workmen's village at Deir el-Medina: Rosalind Hall, London.
101. Objects from Tut'ankhamun's tomb: (all now in EM): top – GI; bottom – John Hillelson Agency, London.
102. Thebes: Tomb of Ra'mose: A. A. M. van der Heyden, Amsterdam.
103. Thebes: Coffin base board: BM 6705 (Photo: MH).
Thebes: Tomb of Amenemone: A.-P. Zivie, Paris.
104. Thebes: Tomb of Amenemone: A.-P. Zivie, Paris.
105. Thebes: Tomb of Pashed: John Hillelson Agency, London.
106–07. J. G. Wilkinson at Thebes: GI (Photos: Elsevier).
108. Nile near Dendara: J. Ruffle, Birmingham.
Landscape near Nag' Hammadi: J. Baines, Oxford.
Naqada and Tukh: Basalt statuette: Ash. 1922.70.
110. Nag' el-Madamud: Outer hypostyle hall of Ptolemy VIII: A.-P. Zivie, Paris.
Nag' el-Madamud: Lintel of Senwosret III: Louvre, E.13983.
Naqada: Reconstruction of mastaba: D. Barnard, London (after de Morgan).
Naqada: Decorated pot: Ash. 1895.482 (Photo: Elsevier).
111. Qift: Relief – Senwosret I before Min: University College, London, 14786.
Qift: Red granite head of Roman emperor: Reproduced by permission of the University Art Museum, University of Pennsylvania, E.976.
Qus: Site at time of Napoleon's expedition to Egypt: Expedition Française.
112. Dendara: Plan: LJ (after Daumas).
Dendara: Temple of Hathor: Hirmer Verlag, Munich.
Dendara: Gateway of SE complex: J. Baines, Oxford.
113. Dendara: Outer hypostyle hall: A. A. M. van der Heyden, Amsterdam.
Dendara: Birth house relief: Rosalind Hall, London.
114. Hiw: Pottery hippopotamus: Ash., E.3267.
Hiw: Bone clapper of Sithathor: BM 30866.
Abydos: Fragments of furniture: Ash. E.3255, E.1283 (Photo: Elsevier).
115. Abydos: Relief: A. M. Calverley. The Temple of King Sethos at Abydos, 3, London and Chicago, Ill., 1938, pl. 37.
116. Abydos: Map: OI (after Kemp).
Abydos: Temple of Ramesses II: J. Baines, Oxford.
Abydos: Plan of temple of Sethos I: OI (after Kemp, and Porter and Moss).
117. Abydos: Relief – fattened ox: J. Baines, Oxford.
Abydos: Personification of Dendara: J. Baines, Oxford.
118. Akhmim: Offering table of Harsiese: BM 1227.
Akhmim: Coffin of Espamai: Ägyptisches Museum, W. Berlin, 12/66 (Photo: Bildarchiv Preussischer Kulturbesitz).
119. Akhmim: Plan: LJ (after Lepsius).
Akhmim: Sarcophagus lid of Shepen-min: Ny Carlsberg Glyptothek, Copenhagen, AE.I.N. 923.
Wannina: Plan: LJ (after Petrie).
Qaw el-Kebir: Head of statue of Ibu: ME, Suppl. 4411 (Photo: H. W. Müller, Munich).
120. Beni Hasan: Model boat: Ash., E.2301 (Photo: Elsevier).
Beni Hasan: Landscape: RW.
The Faiyum: landscape: A. A. M. van der Heyden, Amsterdam.
122. Asyut: Model soldiers: EM, CG 258 (Photo RW).
Meir: Faience hippopotamus: Met. 17.9.1.
123. Meir: Wekh-hotpe with wives and daughter: Courtesy Museum of Fine Arts, Boston, 1973.87.
el-'Amarna: Tomb of Meryre' I: WF.
el-'Amarna: Plan: LJ (after W. S. Smith).
124. el'Amarna: Nefertiti: Ägyptisches Museum, W. Berlin, 21300 (Photo: Hirmer Verlag, Munich).
el-'Amarna: Akhenaten's daughters: Ash. 1893.1–41 (Photo: MH).
125. el-'Amarna: Fragmentary female statue: Louvre, E.25409.
el-'Amarna: Talatat – king's hand: Schimmel Collection (Photo: WF).
el-'Amarna: Talatat – attendants in homage: Schimmel Collection (Photo: WF).
126. Deir el-Bersha: Map of Wadi el-Nakhla: LJ (after Griffith and Newberry).
Deir el-Bersha: Tomb of Djehutihotpe, painting by J. G. Wilkinson: GI (Photo: Elsevier).
127. el-Ashmunein: Basilica: A. A. M. van der Heyden,

Amsterdam.
el-Ashmunein: Statuette with baboon: Ash. 1961.536 (Photo: Elsevier).
128. Tuna el-Gebel: Greco-Egyptian painting: S. Gabra and E. Drioton, Peintures à fresques et scènes peintes à Hermoupolis-Ouest, Cairo, 1954, pl. 25.
Zawyet el-Amwat: Section of step pyramid: OI (after Lauer).
129. Ihnasya el-Medina: Statuette of Harsaphes: Courtesy of Museum of Fine Arts, Boston, 06.2408.
Ihnasya el-Medina: Relief – ox heads: JF (after Parke Bernet Galleries Sale Catalogue, 29–30 April 1964).
Ihnasya el-Medina: Relief – cattle: Museo Arqueológico, Madrid.
Ihnasya el-Medina: Statue of Meryre'-haishtef: BM 55722.
130. Kom Medinet Ghurab: Head of Queen Teye: Ägyptisches Museum, W. Berlin, 21834 (photo: Bildarchiv Preussischer Kulturbesitz).
el-Lahun: Plan: OI (after Petrie).
el-Lahun: Pyramid of Senwosret II: Rosalind Hall, London.
131. The Faiyum: Temple at Qasr el-Sagha: D. Johannes, Cairo.
The Faiyum: Statue of King Amenemhet III: EM, CG 395 (photo: WF).
132. Maidum: Masonry of buttress walls: A. A. M. van der Heyden, Amsterdam.
Maidum: Aerial view: Institute of Archaeology, University of London (photo: RAF, copyright reserved).
Maidum: Section of pyramid: D. Barnard, London (after Mendelssohn).
Maidum: Statues of Re'hotpe and Nofret: EM, CG 3,4 (photo: RW).
133. el-Lisht: Relief – archers: Met. 22.123 (Drawing: JF).
el-Lisht: Relief – goddess Seshat: Brooklyn Museum, Brooklyn, N.Y., Charles Edwin Wilbour Fund, 52.129.
134. Giza: Pyramids at sunset: WF.
Mit Rahina sphinx: A. A. M. van der Heyden, Amsterdam.
136. Mit Rahina: Plan: LJ (after Anthes).
Mit Rahina: Colossus of Ramesses II: A. A. M. van der Heyden, Amsterdam.
137. Dahshur: Pyramids: Rosalind Hall, London.
Dahshur: Pyramidion of Amenemhet III: EM, JE 35745 (Photo: Phaidon Press).
Dahshur: Ka-statue: EM, CG 259 (Drawing: JF).
138–39. Pyramids: D. Barnard, London (after Borchardt, Fakhry, Lauer and Mendelssohn).
140. Diagram showing relative heights of pyramids: D. Barnard, London.
142. Saqqara: Gaming disks: EM, JE 70160 (photo: RW).
143. Saqqara: Step Pyramid of Netjerykhet Djoser: RW.
144. Saqqara: Location map: LJ (after Porter and Moss).
Saqqara: Plan: LJ (after Lauer).
145. Top left and right – Saqqara: Step Pyramid of Netjerykhet Djoser: A. A. M. van der Heyden, Amsterdam.
Bottom left – Saqqara: Step Pyramid of Netjerykhet Djoser: J. Baines, Oxford.
Saqqara: Upper part statue of Djoser: EM, JE 49158 (Photo: RW).
Saqqara: Wenis boat pits: B. D. Anson, Cheltenham.
146. Saqqara: Causeway and mortuary temple of Wenis: A. A. M. van der Heyden, Amsterdam.
Saqqara: Hezyre': EM, CG 1426 (Photo: Hirmer Verlag, Munich).
147. Saqqara: Statue of corpulent aging man: EM, CG 34 (Photo: RW).
Saqqara: Relief – men force-feeding geese and cranes: Staatliche Museen, E. Berlin, 14642 (Photo: WF).
Saqqara: Butcher felling ox: Colorific! London.
Saqqara: Relief – offering to deceased: Rosalind Hall, London.
Saqqara: Relief – cattle crossing canal: Rosalind Hall, London.
Saqqara: Relief – shrine with statue of deceased: RW.
148. Saqqara: Relief – offering to Sakhmet: EM, Temp. No. 5.7.24.15 (Photo: RW).
Saqqara: Tomb of Nufer – hoisting mast on boat: DAI.
149. Saqqara: Tomb of Nufer – false doors: Daily Telegraph Colour Library, London.
Saqqara: Tomb of Hetepka – false door: RW.
Saqqara: Statue of scribe: EM, CG 78 (Photo: RW).
150. Saqqara: Tomb of Haremhab – courtiers: Egypt Exploration Society, London.
Saqqara: Tomb of Haremhab – captive: Egypt Exploration Society, London.
Saqqara: Tomb of Haremhab – detail of captives: Egypt Exploration Society, London.
Saqqara: Tomb of Haremhab – 2nd court: Egypt Exploration Society, London.
151. Saqqara: Serapeum: RW.
152. Abusir: Aerial view: Institute of Archaeology,

University of London (Photo: RAF, copyright reserved).
Abusir: King Userkaf or goddess Neith: EM, JE 90220 (Photo: Hirmer Verlag, Munich).
153. Abusir: Pyramids: A. A. M. van der Heyden, Amsterdam.
Abusir: Reconstruction of seagoing boat: D. Barnard, London (after Faulkner).
Abusir: Relief – seagoing boats: Staatliche Museen, E. Berlin, 21833.
154. Abu Ghurab: Obelisk base: Hirmer Verlag, Munich.
Abu Ghurab: Reconstruction of temple: D. Barnard, London (after von Bissing).
Abu Ghurab: Altar: D. Johannes, Cairo.
Abu Ghurab: Relief – Egyptian countryside: Staatliche Museen, E. Berlin, 20036.
155. Zawyet el-'Aryan: Plan and section of "Layer Pyramid": OI (after Reisner).
156–57. Giza: Pyramids: A. A. M. van der Heyden, Amsterdam.
158. Giza: Plan: LJ (after Reisner).
Giza: Diagram of pyramids: OI (after Edwards).
159. Giza: Masonry of Great Pyramid: A. A. M. van der Heyden, Amsterdam.
160. Giza: Great gallery of Great Pyramid: Description de l'Égypte, 5, Paris, 1823, pl. 13 (right).
161. Giza: Valley temple of Khephren: J. Baines, Oxford.
Giza: Khufu's causeway: C. R. Lepsius, Denkmäler aus Ägypten und Äthiopien, 1, Berlin, 1849, pl. 20.
162. Giza: Statue of Khephren and Horus: EM, CG 14 (Photo: John Hillelson Agency, London).
163. Giza: Reserve head: Robert H. Lowie Museum of Anthropology, Berkeley, Ca., 6.19767 (Photo from: H. F. Lutz, Egyptian Statues and Statuettes in the Museum of Anthropology of the University of California, Leipzig, 1930, pl. 38a).
Giza: Menkaure', Hathor and nome: EM, JE 46499 (Photo: Hirmer Verlag, Munich).
Giza: Tomb portico with seated statues: J. Baines, Oxford.
Giza: Statue of dwarf Seneb and family: EM, JE 51280 (Photo: RW).
164. Giza: The Great Sphinx: GI (Photo: Elsevier).
Giza: Relief – Sethos I embraced by goddess: RW.
Giza: Sarcophagus of Ptahhotpe: Ash. 1947.295.
165. Abu Rawash: Head of Arsinoe II: Met. 38.10.
Abu Rawash: Head of King Ra'djedef: Louvre, E.12626.
166. San el-Hagar: Silver coffin of Psusennes I: EM, JE 85912 (Photo: RW).
Tell el-Rub'a: Naos of Amasis: Mendes Expedition, Institute of Fine Arts, New York University.
Remains of San el-Hagar temples: A.-P. Zivie, Paris.
168. Kom Abu Billo: Relief – Hathor: Bolton Museum and Art Gallery, Lancs., 14.89.
Kom Abu Billo: Relief – Ptolemy I Soter: Ash. 1889.182.
Kom el-Hisn: Royal head: EM, JE 42995 (Photo: Bildarchiv Foto Marburg, Marburg).
169. Naukratis: Plan: LJ (after Petrie).
Alexandria: Plan: OI (after Fraser and Brunner-Traut).
Alexandria: "Pompey's Pillar": Careri, op. cit. I, facing p.37.
Alexandria: Painted tomb near Kom el-Shuqafa: J. Baines, Oxford.
170. Tell el-Fara'in: Relief – tomb of Harhotpe, offering bearers: EM, JE 46591 (Photo: H. W. Müller, Munich).
Sa el-Hagar: Statue of Psammetik-seneb kneeling: Museo Gregoriano Egizio, Vatican, 166 (Photo: Alinari, Florence).
Ruins of Sa el-Hagar in 1842: Lepsius, op. cit. I, pl. 56 (lower).
171. Tell Atrib: Statue of Djeho kneeling with naos: Fundação Calouste Gulbenkian, Lisbon, 403.
Behbeit el-Hagar: Relief – king censing before god: Museum of Fine Arts, Richmond, Va., 63.45.
Statue from Tell Atrib: BM 1237.
172. Tell el-Muqdam: Bronze inlay of lion: Brooklyn Museum, Brooklyn, N.Y., Charles Edwin Wilbour Fund, 55.177.
Sammanud: Relief – offering bearers: Walters Art Gallery, Baltimore, Md., 22.119.
el-Baqliya: Kneeling statue of Nekht-harhebi: Louvre, A 94 (Photo: Alinari, Florence).
173. Tell el-Rub'a: Mastaba tombs and houses: Mendes Expedition, Institute of Fine Arts, New York University.
Heliopolis: Statue of Tetu: Ägyptisches Museum, W. Berlin, 8432 (Photo: Bildarchiv Preussischer Kulturbesitz).
174. Tell el-Yahudiya: Plan: OI (after du Mesnil du Buisson and Wright).
Tell el-Yahudiya: Faience tiles: Brooklyn Museum, Brooklyn, N.Y., Charles Edwin Wilbour Fund, 55.182.
Heliopolis: Obelisk of Senwosret I: D. Johannes, Cairo.
Tell Basta: Plan: OI (after Habachi).
175. Tell Basta: Gold jug: EM, CG 53262.
Tell Basta: Bronze statuette of cat: Ash., Fortnum B.2 (Photo: Elsevier).

BIBLIOGRAPHY

Much of the work of Egyptologists is published in specialist journals, of which a dozen are devoted exclusively to the subject. These are listed in the *Lexikon der Ägyptologie* (see below). The presentation in this book is often based on material in journals, and may differ from that in other books. This applies especially to "The Historical Setting."

*Has been translated into other languages.

General and Reference Works
British Museum, *An Introduction to Ancient Egypt.* London 1979.
F. Daumas, *La Civilisation de l'Égypte pharaonique.* Paris 1965.
A. Erman and H. Ranke, *Ägypten and ägyptisches Leben im Altertum.* 2nd ed. Tübingen 1923.*
W. C. Hayes, *The Scepter of Egypt,* i–ii. New York 1953, Cambridge (Mass.) 1959.
W. Helck and E. Otto, *Kleines Wörterbuch der Ägyptologie.* 2nd ed. Wiesbaden 1970.
W. Helck *et al.* (eds.), *Lexikon der Ägyptologie* (6 vols. planned). Wiesbaden 1972–.
E. Hornung, *Einführung in die Ägyptologie.* Darmstadt 1967.
H. Kees, *Ägypten.* Munich 1933.
S. Moscati (ed.), *L'alba della civiltà,* i–iii. Turin 1976.
C. F. Nims, *Thebes of the Pharaohs.* London 1965.
E. Otto, *Wesen und Wandel der ägyptischen Kultur.* Berlin etc. 1969.
G. Posener *et al., Dictionnaire de la civilisation égyptienne.* Paris 1959.*
J. A. Wilson, *The Burden of Egypt/The Culture of Ancient Egypt.* Chicago (Ill.) 1951.*

Part One: The Cultural Setting
The geography of ancient Egypt
W. Y. Adams, *Nubia: Corridor to Africa.* London 1977.
K. W. Butzer, *Early Hydraulic Civilization in Egypt.* Chicago (Ill.) and London 1976.
H. Kees, *Das alte Ägypten, eine kleine Landeskunde.* 2nd ed. Berlin 1958.*
A. Lucas and J. R. Harris, *Ancient Egyptian Materials and Industries.* 4th ed. London 1962.
P. Montet, *Géographie de l'Égypte ancienne,* i–ii. Paris 1957–61.
B. Trigger, *Nubia under the Pharaohs.* London 1976.

The study of ancient Egypt
W. R. Dawson and E. P. Uphill, *Who was who in Egyptology.* 2nd ed. London 1972.
L. Greener, *The Discovery of Egypt.* London 1966.
Works of travellers to Egypt are also available; many are collected in "Voyageurs occidentaux en Égypte," Cairo 1970–.

The historical setting
E. Bevan, *A History of Egypt under the Ptolemaic Dynasty.* London 1927.
J. H. Breasted, *A History of Egypt.* 2nd ed. New York 1909.*
Cambridge Ancient History, i–iv. 3rd ed. Cambridge 1970–.
A. H. Gardiner, *Egypt of the Pharaohs.* Oxford 1961.*
W. Helck, *Geschichte des alten Ägypten.* Leiden and Cologne 1968.
E. Hornung, *Grundzüge der ägyptischen Geschichte.* 2nd ed. Darmstadt 1978.
F. K. Kienitz, *Die politische Geschichte Ägyptens vom 7. bis zum 4. Jahrhundert vor der Zeitwende.* Berlin 1953.
K. A. Kitchen, *The Third Intermediate Period in Egypt (1100–650 B.C.).* Warminster 1973.
J. G. Milne, *A History of Egypt under Roman Rule.* 3rd ed. London 1924.

Principles of art and architecture
A. Badawy, *A History of Egyptian Architecture,* i–iii. Giza 1954, Berkeley (Cal.) 1966–68.
S. Clarke and R. Engelbach, *Ancient Egyptian Masonry.* London 1930.
J.-L. de Cenival, *Égypte. Époque pharaonique.* Fribourg 1964.*
E. Iversen, *Canon and Proportions in Egyptian Art.* 2nd ed. Warminster 1975.

K. Lange and M. Hirmer, *Ägypten.* 4th ed. Munich 1967.*
H. Schäfer, *Von ägyptischer Kunst.* 4th ed. Wiesbaden 1963.*
W. S. Smith, *The Art and Architecture of Ancient Egypt.* Harmondsworth 1958.
—— *A History of Egyptian Sculpture and Painting in the Old Kingdom.* 2nd ed. London and Boston (Mass.) 1949.
C. Vandersleyen *et al., Das alte Ägypten.* Berlin 1975.

Stelae
J. Vandier, *Manuel d'archéologie égyptienne,* ii(1). Paris 1954.

Part Two: A Journey down the Nile
For most sites we have faced the almost impossible task of limiting the selection of publications to one or two items. We have chosen those which give the best idea of the present state of knowledge of the area in question, either by presenting general information or by illustrating a particular feature. Complete bibliographical data are given by B. Porter and R. L. B. Moss, *Topographical Bibliography of Ancient Egyptian Hieroglyphical Texts, Reliefs, and Paintings,* i–vii, i² (Oxford 1927–), quoted here as PM. Regular reports on current archaeological work in Egypt and Nubia are published by J. Leclant in *Orientalia* (since 1950).

Elephantine and Aswan (PM v.221–44)
E. Bresciani and S. Pernigotti, *Assuan. Il tempio tolemaico di Isi. I blocchi decorati e iscritti.* Pisa 1978.
E. Edel, *Die Felsengräber der Qubbet el-Hawa bei Assuan,* i–. Wiesbaden 1967–.

Philae (PM vi.203–56)
H. Junker and E. Winter, *Philä,* i–. Vienna 1958–.
H. G. Lyons, *A Report on the Island and Temples of Philae.* [London 1897].
S. Sauneron and H. Stierlin, *Die letzten Tempel Ägyptens. Edfu und Philae.* Zürich 1978.*

Kom Ombo (PM v.179–203)
J. de Morgan *et al., Kom Ombos,* i–ii. Vienna 1909.

Gebel el-Silsila (PM v.208–18, 220–21)
R. A. Caminos and T. G. H. James, *Gebel es-Silsilah,* i–. London 1963–.

Edfu (PM v.200–05; vi.119–77)
M. de Rochemonteix and É. Chassinat, *Le Temple d'Edfou,* i–xiv. Paris 1892, Cairo 1918–.

Kom el-Ahmar (PM v.191–200)
B. Adams, *Ancient Hierakonpolis,* with *Supplement.* Warminster 1974.
W. A. Fairservis, Jr. *et al.,* "Preliminary Report on the First Two Seasons at Hierakonpolis," *Journal of the American Research Center in Egypt,* ix (1971–72), 7–68.
J. E. Quibell (vol.ii with F. W. Green), *Hierakonpolis,* i–ii. London 1900, 1902.

el-Kab (PM v.171–91)
P. Derchain, *Elkab,* i. *Les Monuments religieux à l'entrée de l'Ouady Hellal.* Brussels 1971.
Fouilles de el Kab, i–iii. Brussels, 1940–54.

Esna (PM v.165–67; vi.110–19)
D. Downes, *The Excavations at Esna 1905–1906.* Warminster 1974.
S. Sauneron, *Esna,* i–. Cairo 1959–.

el-Moʻalla (PM v.170)
J. Vandier, *Moʻalla, la tombe d'Ankhtifi et la tombe de Sébekhotep.* Cairo 1950.

Gebelein (PM v.162–64)

Tod (PM v.167–69)
F. Bisson de la Roque, *Tôd (1934 à 1936).* Cairo 1937.

Armant (PM v.151–61)
R. Mond and O. H. Myers, *Temples of Armant. A Preliminary Survey.* London 1940.
—— *The Bucheum,* i–iii. London 1934.

Luxor (PM ii.²301–39)
H. Brunner, *Die südlichen Räume des Tempels von Luxor.* Mainz 1977.
A. Gayet, *Le Temple de Louxor.* Cairo 1894.

Karnak (PM ii.²1–301)
P. Barguet, *Le Temple d'Amon-Rê à Karnak. Essai d'exégèse.* Cairo 1962.

Reliefs and Inscriptions at Karnak, i–, by the Epigraphic Survey. Chicago (Ill.) 1936–.

The West Bank (PM i² and ii.²339–537)
H. Carter and A. C. Mace, *The Tomb of Tut.ankh.amen,* i–iii. London etc. 1923–33.
E. Hornung and F. Teichmann, *Das Grab des Haremhab im Tal der Könige.* Bern 1971.
Medinet Habu, i–viii, by the Epigraphic Survey. Chicago (Ill.) 1930–70.
E. Naville, *The Temple of Deir el Bahari,* Introductory Memoir and i–vi. London 1894–1908.
J. Osing, *Der Tempel Sethos' I. in Gurna. Die Reliefs und Inschriften,* i–. Mainz 1977–.
G. Thausing and H. Goedicke, *Nofretari. Eine Dokumentation der Wandgemälde ihres Grabes.* Graz 1971.

Nagʻ el-Madamud (PM v.137–50)
F. Bisson de la Roque, J. J. Clère *et al., Rapport sur les fouilles de Medamoud (1925–32).* Cairo 1926–36.

Naqada and Tukh (PM v.117–19)
J. de Morgan, *Recherches sur les origines de l'Égypte,* ii, 147–202. Paris 1897.

Qus (PM v.135–6)

Qift (PM v.123–34)
W. M. F. Petrie, *Koptos.* London 1896.

Dendara (PM v.109–16; vi.41–110)
É. Chassinat and F. Daumas, *Le Temple de Dendara,* i–. Cairo 1934–.
F. Daumas, *Dendara et le temple d'Hathor.* Cairo 1969.
A. Mariette, *Denderah,* i–iv. Paris 1870–73.

el-Qasr wa-ʼ l-Saiyad (PM v.119–22)

Hiw (PM v.107–09)
W. M. F. Petrie, *Diospolis Parva: the Cemeteries of Abadiyeh and Hu, 1898–9.* London 1901.

Abydos (PM v.39–105; vi. 1–41)
A. M. Calverley *et al., The Temple of King Sethos I at Abydos,* i–. London and Chicago (Ill.) 1933–.
A. Mariette, *Abydos,* i–ii, Paris 1869–80.
W. M. F. Petrie, *The Royal Tombs of the First Dynasty/Earliest Dynasties.* London 1900–01.

Beit Khallaf (PM v.37)
J. Garstang, *Mahâsna and Bêt Khallâf.* London 1903.

Akhmim (PM v.17–26)

Wannina (PM v.31–34)
W. M. F. Petrie, *Athribis.* London 1908.

Qaw el-Kebir (PM v.9–16)
H. Steckeweh, *Die Fürstengräber von Qaw.* Leipzig 1936.

Asyut (PM iv.259–70)
F. L. Griffith, *The Inscriptions of Siut and Der Rifeh.* London 1889.

Deir el-Gabrawi (PM iv.242–46)
N. de G. Davies, *The Rock Tombs of Deir el Gebrawi,* i–ii. London 1902.

Meir (PM iv.247–58)
A. M. Blackman, *The Rock Tombs of Meir,* i–vi. London 1914–53.

el-ʻAmarna (PM iv.192–237)
N. de G. Davies, *The Rock Tombs of El Amarna,* i–vi. London 1903–08.
G. T. Martin, *The Royal Tomb at el-ʻAmarna,* i–. London 1974–.
T. E. Peet, C. L. Woolley, J. D. S. Pendlebury *et al., The City of Akhenaten,* i–iii. London 1923, 1933, 1951

el-Sheikh Saʻid (PM iv.187–92)
N. de G. Davies, *The Rock Tombs of Sheikh Saïd.* London 1901.

Deir el-Bersha (PM iv.177–87)
P. E. Newberry and F. L. Griffith, *El Bersheh,* i–ii. London 1892.

el-Ashmunein (PM iv.165–69)
G. Roeder, *Hermopolis 1929–1939.* Hildesheim 1959.

Tuna el-Gebel (PM iv.169–75)
S.Gabra and E. Drioton, *Peintures à fresques et scènes peintes à Hermoupolis ouest (Touna el-Gebel).* Cairo 1954.
G. Lefebvre, *Le Tombeau de Petosiris,* i–iii. Cairo 1923–24.

el-Sheikh 'Ibada (PM iv.175–77)
*Antinoe (1965–1968). Missione archeologica in Egitto dell'
Università di Roma.* Rome 1974.

Beni Hasan with Speos Artemidos (PM iv.140–65)
P. E. Newberry, F. L. Griffith *et al.*, *Beni Hasan*, i–iv.
London 1893–1900.

Zawyet el-Amwat (PM iv.134–39)
A. Varille, *La Tombe de Ni-Ankh-Pepi à Zâouyet el-
Mayetîn.* Cairo 1938.

Tihna el-Gebel (PM iv.127–33)
R. Holthoer and R. Ahlqvist, "The 'Roman Temple' at
Tehna el-Gebel, *Studia Orientalia*, xliii.7 (1974).

el-Bahnasa (PM iv.124)
W. M. F. Petrie, *Tombs of the Courtiers and Oxyrhynkhos.*
London 1925.
The Oxyrhynchus Papyri, i–. London 1898–.

el-Hiba (PM iv. 124–25)
H. Ranke, *Koptische Friedhöfe bei Karâra und der
Amontempel Scheschonks I bei el Hibe.* Berlin and Leipzig
1926.

Dishasha (PM iv.121–23)
W. M. F. Petrie, *Deshasheh 1897.* London 1898.

Ihnasya el-Medina (PM iv.118–21)
E. Naville, *Ahnas el Medineh (Heracleopolis Magna).*
London 1894.
W. M. F. Petrie, *Ehnasya 1904.* London 1905.

Kom Medinet Ghurab (PM iv.112–15)
L. Borchardt, *Der Porträtkopf der Königin Teje.* Leipzig
1911.

el-Lahun (PM iv.107–12)
W. M. F. Petrie, *Kahun, Gurob, and Hawara.* London
1890.
—— *Illahun, Kahun and Gurob 1889–90.* London 1891.

The Faiyum (PM iv.96–104)
E. Bresciani, *Rapporto preliminare delle campagne di scavo
1966 e 1967.* Milan and Varese 1968.
A. Vogliano, *Rapporto degli scavi … Madînet Mâḍi*, i–ii.
Milan 1936–37.

Maidum (PM iv.89–96)
W. M. F. Petrie, *Medum.* London 1892.

el-Lisht (PM iv.77–85)
H. Goedicke, *Re-used Blocks from the Pyramid of
Amenemhet I at Lisht.* New York 1971.

Mit Rahina (PM iii.217–27)
R. Anthes *et al.*, *Mit Rahineh 1955 and 1956.* Philadelphia
(Pa.) 1959 and 1965.
W. M. F. Petrie *et al.*, *Memphis*, i–v. London 1909–13.

Dahshur (PM iii.228–40)
J. de Morgan, *Fouilles à Dahchour*, i–ii. Vienna
1895–1903.
A. Fakhry, *The Monuments of Sneferu at Dahshur*, i–ii.
Cairo 1959–61.

Saqqara (PM iii.83–215 and iii.²393–776)
P. Duell *et al.*, *The Mastaba of Mereruka*, i–ii. Chicago
(Ill.) 1938.
M. Z. Goneim, *Horus Sekhem-khet. The Unfinished Step
Pyramid at Saqqara*, i: Cairo 1957.
J.-P. Lauer, *Saqqara. The Royal Cemetery of Memphis.*
London 1976.★
Le Tombeau de Ti, i–iii (i by L. Epron and F. Daumas, ii
and iii by H. Wild). Cairo 1939–66.
A. M. Moussa and H. Altenmüller, *Das Grab des
Nianchchnum und Chnumhotep.* Mainz 1977.

Abusir (PM iii.²324–50)
L. Borchardt, *Das Grabdenkmal des Königs Śa3ḫu-rēˊ*, i–ii.
Leipzig 1910–13.
H. Ricke *et al.*, *Das Sonnenheiligtum des Königs Userkaf*,
i–ii. Cairo 1965, Wiesbaden 1969.

Abu Ghurab (PM iii.²314–24)
E. Edel and S. Wenig, *Die Jahreszeitenreliefs aus dem
Sonnenheiligtum des Königs Ne-user-Re.* Berlin 1974.

Zawyet el-'Aryan (PM iii.²312–14)
D. Dunham, *Zawiyet el-Aryan. The Cemeteries Adjacent to
the Layer Pyramid.* Boston (Mass.) 1978.

Giza (PM iii.²10–312)
D. Dunham and W. K. Simpson, *The Mastaba of Queen
Mersyankh III.* Boston (Mass.) 1974.
H. Junker, *Gîza*, i–xii. Vienna and Leipzig 1929–55.
G. A. Reisner, *Mycerinus. The Temples of the Third*

Pyramid at Giza. Cambridge (Mass.) 1931.
—— *A History of the Giza Necropolis*, i–ii. Cambridge
(Mass.) 1942–55.
W. K. Simpson, *The Mastabas of Kawab, Khafkhufu I and
II.* Boston (Mass.) 1978.
C. M. Zivie, *Giza au deuxième millénaire.* Cairo 1976.

Abu Rawash (PM iii.²1–10)
F. Bisson de la Roque, *Rapport sur les fouilles d'Abou-
Roasch (1922–1923) and (1924).* Cairo 1924–25.

Ausim (PM iv.68)

Kom Abu Billo (PM iv.67–68)

Kom el-Hisn (PM iv.51–52)

Naukratis (PM iv.50)
D. G. Hogarth, H. L. Lorimer and C. C. Edgar, "Naukratis,
1903,"*Journal of Hellenic Studies*, xxv (1905), 105–36.

Alexandria (PM iv.2–6)
A. Adriani, *Repertorio d'arte dell'Egitto greco-romano*,
series C, i–ii. Palermo 1966.
P. M. Fraser, *Ptolemaic Alexandria*, i–iii. Oxford 1972.

Sa el-Hagar (PM iv.46–49)
R. el-Sayed, *Documents relatifs à Saïs et ses divinités.* Cairo
1975.

Tell el-Fara'in (PM iv.45)

Behbeit el-Hagar (PM iv.40–42)

Tell Atrib (PM iv.65–67)
P. Vernus, *Athribis.* Cairo 1978.

Tell el-Muqdam (PM iv.37–39)
E. Naville, *Ahnas el Medineh (Heracleopolis Magna).*
London 1894, 27–31.

Samannud (PM iv.43–44)
G. Steindorff, "Reliefs from the Temples of Sebennytos
and Iseion in American Collections," *Journal of the
Walters Art Gallery*, vii–viii (1944–45), 38–59.

el–Baqliya (PM iv.39–40)
A.-P. Zivie, *Hermopolis et le nome de l'Ibis.* Cairo 1975.

Tell el-Rub'a and Tell el-Timai (PM iv.35–37)
H. De Meulenaere and P. MacKay, *Mendes II.* Warminster
1976.

Heliopolis (PM iv.59–65)
W. M. F. Petrie and E. Mackay, *Heliopolis, Kafr Ammar
and Shurafa.* London 1915.
H. Ricke, "Eine Inventartafel aus Heliopolis im Turiner
Museum," *Zeitschrift für ägyptische Sprache und
Altertumskunde*, lxxi (1935), 111–33.

Tell el-Yahudiya (PM iv.56–58)
E. Naville, *The Mound of the Jew and the City of Onias.*
London 1890.
G. R. H. Wright, "Tell el-Yehūdīyah and the Glacis,"
Zeitschrift des Deutschen Palästina-Vereins, lxxxiv (1968),
1–17.

Tell Basta (PM iv.27–35)
Labib Habachi, *Tell Basta.* Cairo 1957.

Saft el-Hinna (PM iv.10–11)
E. Naville, *The Shrine of Saft el Henneh and the Land of
Goshen 1885.* London 1887.

District of el-Khata'na and Qantir (PM iv.9–10)
M. Bietak, *Tell el-Dab'a II.* Vienna 1975.

Tell Nabasha (PM iv.7–9)
W. M. F. Petrie, *Tanis II, Nebesheh (Am) and Defenneh
(Tahpanhes).* London 1888.

San el-Hagar (PM iv.13–26)
P. Montet, *La Nécropole royale de Tanis*, i–iii. Paris
1947–60.
—— *Les Énigmes de Tanis.* Paris 1952.

Tell el-Maskhuta (PM iv.53–55)
E. Naville, *The Store City of Pithom and the Route of the
Exodus.* London 1903.

el-Dakka (PM vii.40–50)
G. Roeder and W. Ruppel, *Der Tempel von Dakke*, i–iii.
Cairo 1913–30.

Quban (PM vii.82–83)

'Amada (PM vii.65–73)
H. Gauthier, *Le Temple d'Amada.* Cairo 1913–26.

el-Sebu'a (PM vii.53–64)
H. Gauthier, *Le Temple de Ouadi es-Sebouâ.* Cairo 1912.

el-Derr (PM vii.84–89)
A. M. Blackman, *The Temple of Derr.* Cairo 1913.

el-Lessiya (PM vii.90–91)
S.Curto, *Il tempio di Ellesija.* Turin 1970.

Qasr Ibrim (PM vii.92–94)
R. A. Caminos, *The Shrines and Rock-inscriptions of Ibrim.*
London 1968.

Dabod (PM vii.1–5)
M. Almagro, *El templo de Debod.* Madrid 1971.

Tafa (PM vii.8–9)
H. D. Schneider, *Taffeh. Rond de wederopbouw van een
Nubische tempel.* The Hague 1979.

Beit el-Wali (PM vii. 21–27)
H. Ricke, G. R. Hughes and E. F. Wente, *The Beit el-Wali
Temple of Ramesses II.* Chicago (Ill.) 1967.

Kalabsha (PM vii.10–21)
K. G. Siegler, *Kalabsha. Architektur und Baugeschichte des
Tempels.* Berlin 1970.

Dendur (PM vii.27–33)
C. Aldred, "The Temple of Dendur," *Metropolitan
Museum of Art Bulletin*, xxxvi (1) (Summer 1978).

Gerf Hussein (PM vii.33–37)

'Aniba (PM vii.75–81)
G. Steindorff, *Aniba*, i–ii. Glückstadt etc. 1935–37.

Abu Simbel (PM vii.95–109)
C. Desroches-Noblecourt and C. Kuentz, *Le Petit Temple
d'Abou Simbel*, i–ii. Cairo 1968.
W. MacQuitty, *Abu Simbel.* London 1965.

Sinai
A. H. Gardiner, T. E. Peet and J. Černý, *The Inscriptions
of Sinai*, i–ii. London 1952–55.

Boats
B. Landström, *Ships of the Pharaohs. 4000 Years of
Egyptian Shipbuilding.* London 1970.
M. Z. Nour *et al.*, *The Cheops Boats*, i. Cairo 1960.

Pyramids
I. E. S. Edwards, *The Pyramids of Egypt.* London. Various
editions.★
A. Fakhry, *The Pyramids.* Chicago (Ill.) and London 1969.
J.-P. Lauer, *Le Mystère des pyramides.* Paris 1974.

Part Three: Aspects of Egyptian Society
Women in society
P. W. Pestman, *Marriage and Matrimonial Property in
Ancient Egypt.* Leiden 1961.
S. Wenig, *Die Frau im alten Ägypten.* Leipzig 1967.

Scribes and writing
There are grammars of different stages of the language
by: J. B. Callender; J. Černý and S. I. Groll; E. Edel; A. H.
Gardiner; H. Junker; G. Lefebvre; F. Lexa; W.
Spiegelberg; and dictionaries by: W. Erichsen; A. Erman
and H. Grapow; R. O. Faulkner. The terminology used in
the description of the script is that of W. Schenkel.

The army
A. R. Schulman, *Military Rank, Title, and Organization in
the Egyptian New Kingdom.* Berlin 1964.
W. Wolf, *Die Bewaffnung des altägyptischen Heeres.*
Leipzig 1926.
Y. Yadin, *The Art of Warfare in Biblical Lands in the Light
of Archaeological Discovery.* London 1963.

Religion
H. Frankfort, *Ancient Egyptian Religion.* New York 1948.★
E. Hornung, *Der Eine und die Vielen.* Darmstadt 1971.
S. Morenz, *Ägyptische Religion.* Stuttgart 1960.★
E. Otto, *Osiris und Amun. Kult und heilige Stätten.* Munich
1966.★

Burial customs
J.-F. and L. Aubert, *Statuettes égyptiennes, chaouabtis,
ouchebtis.* Paris 1974.
M.-L. Buhl, *The Late Egyptian Anthropoid Stone
Sarcophagi.* Copenhagen 1959.
W. R. Dawson and P. H. K. Gray, *Mummies and Human
Remains.* London 1968.
A. M. Donadoni Roveri, *I sarcofagi egizi dalle origini alla
fine dell'Antico Regno.* Rome 1969.
J. Hamilton-Paterson and C. Andrews, *Mummies: Death
and Life in Ancient Egypt.* London 1978.
H. Schneider, *Shabtis*, i–iii. Leiden 1977.

GAZETTEER

INDEX

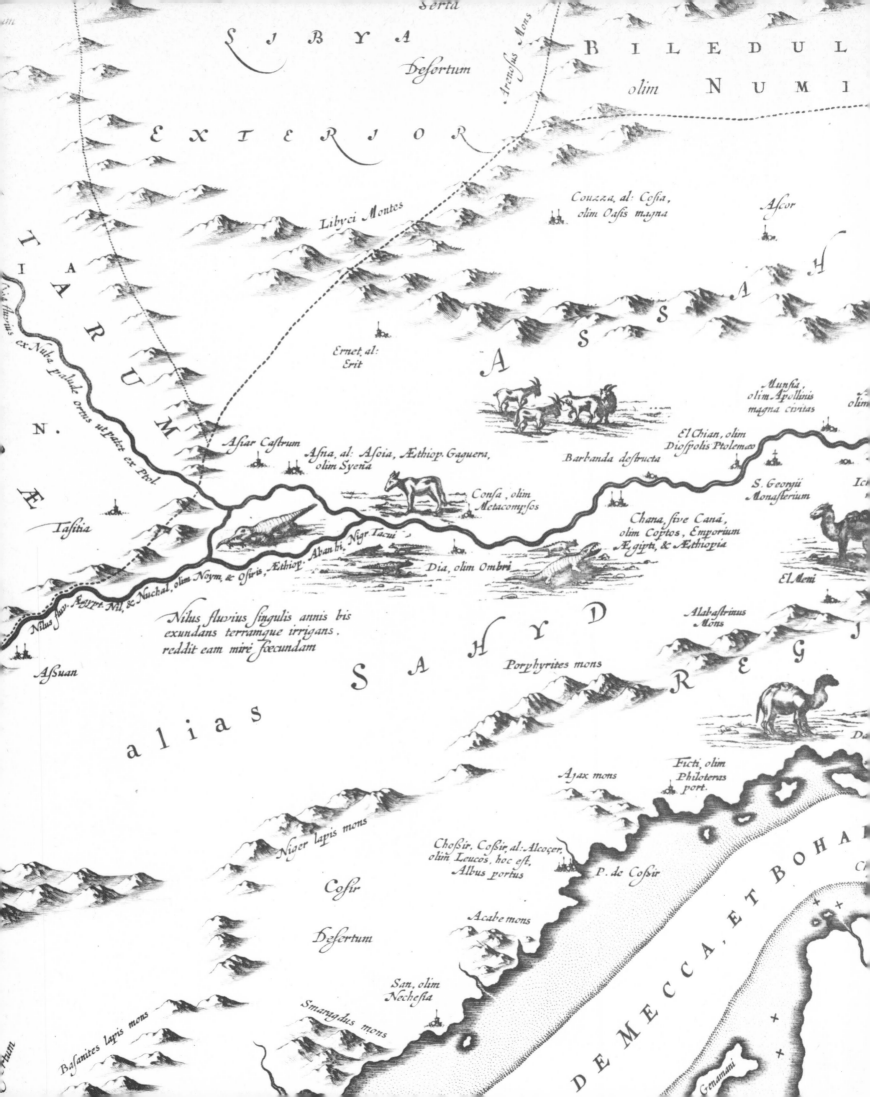

S I B Y A

Serta

B I L E D U L

Desertum

olim NUMI

Arenosus Mons

E X T E R J O R

I A R U M

N.

Libyci Montes

Couzza, al: Cosia,
olim Oasis magna

Ascor

A
S
S
A
H

Via fluvius ex Nubia Palude ortus ut patet ex Ptol.

Ernet, al:
Erit

Munsa,
olim Apollinis
magna civitas

olim

Assar Castrum

Assa, al: Asoia, Æthiop. Gaguera,
olim Syena

Barbanda destructa

El Chian, olim
Diospolis Ptolemæo

Æ

Tasitia

Consa, olim
Metacompsos

S. Georgii
Monasterium

Ich

Nilus fluv. Ægypt. Nil, & Nuchal, olim Noym, & Osiris, Æthiop. Aban hi, Nigr. Tacui

Chana, sive Caná,
olim Coptos, Emporium
Ægipti, & Æthiopia

Dia, olim Ombri

El Meni

Nilus fluvius singulis annis bis
exundans terramque irrigans,
reddit eam miri fœcundam

S A H Y D

Alabastrinus
Mons

R
E
G
J

Assuan

Porphyrites mons

alias

Ajax mons

Ficti, olim
Philoteras
port.

Da

Niger lapis mons

Chossir, Cossir, al: Alcoçer,
olim Leucos, hoc est,
Albus portus

P. de Cossir

Ch

Cossir

D E M E C C A , E T B O H A I

Acabe mons

Desertum

San, olim
Nechesia

Smaragdus mons

Basanites lapis mons

Gensami